# Handbook of Research on Supply Chain Resiliency, Efficiency, and Visibility in the Post-Pandemic Era

Yanamandra Ramakrishna
*Skyline University College, UAE*

A volume in the Advances in Logistics, Operations, and Management Science (ALOMS) Book Series

Published in the United States of America by
 IGI Global
 Business Science Reference (an imprint of IGI Global)
 701 E. Chocolate Avenue
 Hershey PA, USA 17033
 Tel: 717-533-8845
 Fax:  717-533-8661
 E-mail: cust@igi-global.com
 Web site: http://www.igi-global.com

Copyright © 2022 by IGI Global.  All rights reserved. No part of this publication may be reproduced, stored or distributed in any form or by any means, electronic or mechanical, including photocopying, without written permission from the publisher. Product or company names used in this set are for identification purposes only. Inclusion of the names of the products or companies does not indicate a claim of ownership by IGI Global of the trademark or registered trademark.

Library of Congress Cataloging-in-Publication Data

Names: Ramakrishna, Yanamandra, 1966- editor.
Title: Handbook of research on supply chain resiliency, efficiency, and
 visibility in the post- pandemic era / Yanamandra Ramakrishna, editor.
Description: Hershey, PA : Business Science Reference, [2022] | Includes
 bibliographical references and index. | Summary: "This book explores
 diverse strategies for achieving capabilities related to supply chain
 resilience and to expand the existing body of knowledge in this area to
 help develop models, frameworks, and theoretical concepts related to
 supply chain resilience to enhance efficiency and improve the visibility
 of supply chain"-- Provided by publisher.
Identifiers: LCCN 2021035413 (print) | LCCN 2021035414 (ebook) | ISBN
 9781799895060 (hardcover) | ISBN 9781799895084 (ebook)
Subjects: LCSH: Business logistics. | Strategic planning. | COVID-19
 (Disease)--Economic aspects.
Classification: LCC HD38.5 .H355746 2022  (print) | LCC HD38.5  (ebook) |
 DDC 658.5--dc23
LC record available at https://lccn.loc.gov/2021035413
LC ebook record available at https://lccn.loc.gov/2021035414

This book is published in the IGI Global book series Advances in Logistics, Operations, and Management Science (ALOMS) (ISSN: 2327-350X; eISSN: 2327-3518)

British Cataloguing in Publication Data
A Cataloguing in Publication record for this book is available from the British Library.

All work contributed to this book is new, previously-unpublished material. The views expressed in this book are those of the authors, but not necessarily of the publisher.

For electronic access to this publication, please contact: eresources@igi-global.com.

# Advances in Logistics, Operations, and Management Science (ALOMS) Book Series

John Wang
Montclair State University, USA

ISSN:2327-350X
EISSN:2327-3518

## Mission

Operations research and management science continue to influence business processes, administration, and management information systems, particularly in covering the application methods for decision-making processes. New case studies and applications on management science, operations management, social sciences, and other behavioral sciences have been incorporated into business and organizations real-world objectives.

The **Advances in Logistics, Operations, and Management Science** (ALOMS) Book Series provides a collection of reference publications on the current trends, applications, theories, and practices in the management science field. Providing relevant and current research, this series and its individual publications would be useful for academics, researchers, scholars, and practitioners interested in improving decision making models and business functions.

## Coverage

- Operations Management
- Information Management
- Finance
- Services management
- Networks
- Production Management
- Decision analysis and decision support
- Computing and information technologies
- Organizational Behavior
- Risk Management

IGI Global is currently accepting manuscripts for publication within this series. To submit a proposal for a volume in this series, please contact our Acquisition Editors at Acquisitions@igi-global.com or visit: http://www.igi-global.com/publish/.

The Advances in Logistics, Operations, and Management Science (ALOMS) Book Series (ISSN 2327-350X) is published by IGI Global, 701 E. Chocolate Avenue, Hershey, PA 17033-1240, USA, www.igi-global.com. This series is composed of titles available for purchase individually; each title is edited to be contextually exclusive from any other title within the series. For pricing and ordering information please visit http://www.igi-global.com/book-series/advances-logistics-operations-management-science/37170. Postmaster: Send all address changes to above address. © © 2022 IGI Global. All rights, including translation in other languages reserved by the publisher. No part of this series may be reproduced or used in any form or by any means – graphics, electronic, or mechanical, including photocopying, recording, taping, or information and retrieval systems – without written permission from the publisher, except for non commercial, educational use, including classroom teaching purposes. The views expressed in this series are those of the authors, but not necessarily of IGI Global.

## Titles in this Series

*For a list of additional titles in this series, please visit: http://www.igi-global.com/book-series/advances-logistics-operations-management-science/37170*

*Empowering Sustainable Industrial 4.0 Systems With Machine Intelligence*
Muneer Ahmad (University of Malaya, Malaysia) and Noor Zaman (Taylor's University, Malaysia)
Business Science Reference • © 2022 • 315pp • H/C (ISBN: 9781799892014) • US $225.00

*Interdisciplinary and Practical Approaches to Managerial Education and Training*
Luísa Cagica Carvalho (Polytechnic Institute of Setúbal, Portugal & CEFAGE, University of Évora, Portugal) Nuno Teixeira (Polytechnic Institute of Setúbal, Portugal) and Pedro Pardal (Polytechnic Institute of Setúbal, Portugal)
Business Science Reference • © 2022 • 353pp • H/C (ISBN: 9781799882398) • US $195.00

*Handbook of Research on the Future of the Maritime Industry*
Nihan Senbursa (University of Ordu, Turkey)
Business Science Reference • © 2022 • 465pp • H/C (ISBN: 9781799890393) • US $395.00

*Handbook of Research on Museum Management in the Digital Era*
Francesco Bifulco (University of Naples Federico II, Italy) and Marco Tregua (University of Naples Federico II, Italy)
Information Science Reference • © 2022 • 412pp • H/C (ISBN: 9781799896562) • US $245.00

*Management Strategies for Sustainability, New Knowledge Innovation, and Personalized Products and Services*
Mirjana Pejic-Bach (University of Zagreb, Croatia) and Çağlar Doğru (Ufuk University, Turkey)
Business Science Reference • © 2022 • 365pp • H/C (ISBN: 9781799877936) • US $215.00

*Cases on Supply Chain Management and Lessons Learned From COVID-19*
Ana Paula Lopes (Polytechnic of Porto, Portugal)
Business Science Reference • © 2022 • 238pp • H/C (ISBN: 9781799891406) • US $225.00

*Key Factors and Use Cases of Servant Leadership Driving Organizational Performance*
Maria Pressentin (International School of Management, France)
Business Science Reference • © 2022 • 368pp • H/C (ISBN: 9781799888208) • US $215.00

*Handbook of Research on Innovative Management Using AI in Industry 5.0*
Vikas Garg (Amity University, Greater Noida, India) and Richa Goel (Amity University, Noida, India)
Business Science Reference • © 2022 • 351pp • H/C (ISBN: 9781799884972) • US $295.00

701 East Chocolate Avenue, Hershey, PA 17033, USA
Tel: 717-533-8845 x100 • Fax: 717-533-8661
E-Mail: cust@igi-global.com • www.igi-global.com

# EDITORIAL ADVISORY BOARD

Naseem Abidi, *School of Business, Skyline University College, Sharjah, UAE*

G. V. R. K. Acharyulu, *School of Management Studies, University of Hyderabad, India*

Asit Bandyopadhayay, *Harrison College of Business and Computing, Southeast Missouri State University, USA*

Neeta Baporikar, *Namibia University of Science and Technology, Namibia*

Ashish Dwivedi, *Hull University Business School, University of Hull, UK*

Md. Mamun Habib, *School of Business and Entrepreneurship, Independent University, Bangladesh (IUB), Dhaka, Bangladesh*

Gangaraju Vanteddu, *Department of Marketing, Harrison College of Business and Computing, Southeast Missouri State University, USA*

# List of Contributors

**Agha, Kakul** / *Skyline University College, UAE* ........................................................... 226

**Attarwala, Abbasi** / *Kohinoor Business School, India* .................................................. 115

**Bandyopadhayay, Asit** / *Southeast Missouri State University, USA* ............................... 316

**Baral, Manish Mohan** / *Department of Operations, GITAM School of Business, GITAM (Deemed), Visakhapatnam, India* ..................................................................................... 242

**Chittipaka, Venkataiah** / *School of Management Studies, Indira Gandhi National Open University, New Delhi, India* ......................................................................................... 242

**Das, Rashmi Prava** / *CV Raman Global University, Odisha, India* ................................ 335

**Dhingra, Deepika** / *Bennett University, Greater Noida, India* ...................................... 467

**El Bhilat, El Mehdi** / *Mohammed V University, Rabat, Morocco* .................................. 505

**Fritz, Morgane M. C.** / *Excelia Business School, France* ............................................ 402

**Gupta, Rahul** / *Amity University, Noida, India* ........................................................... 443

**Gurrala, Kavitha Reddy** / *ESM Program, American University of Sharjah, UAE* ........... 18

**Habib, Md Mamun** / *Independent University, Bangladesh* ............................................. 81

**Hamidi, Lalla Saadia** / *Mohammed V University, Rabat, Morocco* ............................... 505

**Hanes, Emanuela** / *Independent Researcher, Austria* .................................................. 195

**Higuera, María Fernanda** / *Autonomous University of Sinaloa, Mexico* ....................... 100

**Iyer, Shankar Subramanian** / *S.P. Jain School of Global Management, Dubai, UAE* ..... 267

**Jinugu, Anjaneyulu** / *Universitat Oberta de Catalunya, Spain* ..................................... 295

**Jinugu, Vishnu Teja** / *Kasturba Medical College, Mangalore, India* ............................. 295

**Karthik, Sai Prasanna** / *Chaitanya Bharathi Institute of Technology, Hyderabad, India* .... 158

**Krishnamurthi, Subramani** / *Vignana Jyothi Institute of Management, Hyderabad, India* ........... 378

**Liu, Ziqi** / *Independent Researcher, Suzhou, China* ..................................................... 195

**Madhavi Lalitha V. V.** / *Qatar University, Qatar* ........................................................ 295

**Mohammed, Aezeden** / *UNITECH, Papua New Guinea* ............................................... 335

**Mohanty, Sagyan Sagarika** / *Vignana Jyothi Institute of Management, Hyderabad, India* ........... 378

**Muduli, Kamalakanta** / *Papua New Guinea University of Technology, Papua New Guinea* ......... 335

**Mukherjee, Subhodeep** / *Department of Operations, GITAM School of Business, GITAM (Deemed), Visakhapatnam, India* ..................................................................................... 242

**Mulukutla, Srirama K.** / *Cistech Inc., USA* .................................................................. 1

**Pal, Surya Kant** / *Department of Mathematics, School of Basic Sciences and Research, Sharda University, Greater Noida, India* .................................................................................. 242

**Patnaik, Priyadarsini** / *Birla Global University, Odisha, India* ...................................... 352

**Praveenraj, David W.** / *Bannari Amman Institute of Technology, Erode, India* .............. 378

**Ramakrishna, Yanamandra** / *Skyline University College, UAE* ..................................... 61

**Ramasamy, Adimuthu** / *The Papua New Guinea University of Technology, Papua New Guinea* .. 335
**Rath, Kali Charan** / *GIET University, Odisha, India* ....... 335
**Raut, Sachin Kumar** / *University of Agder, Norway & Fortune Institute of International Business, India* ....... 136
**Sakpal, Subodh** / *Oriental Institute of Management, Mumbai University, India* ....... 136
**Saleheen, Ferdoush** / *Universiti Utara Malaysia, Malaysia* ....... 81
**Sangaraju, Sowmya** / *Volkswagen of America, USA* ....... 61
**Santhanam, Balasbramaniam** / *Kohinoor Business School, India* ....... 115
**Sathyavani, Lakshmi** / *TriHealth, USA* ....... 158
**Sekhar, Satya Venkata** / *GITAM Visakhapatnam, India* ....... 488
**Selvaraj, Franklin John** / *Vignana Jyothi Institute of Management, Hyderabad, India* ....... 378
**Sinha, Gyanesh Kumar** / *Bennett University, Greater Noida, India* ....... 467
**Soni, Rashmi** / *KJ Somaiya Institute of Management, Mumbai, India* ....... 136
**Srivastava, Babita** / *William Paterson University, USA* ....... 423
**Tiwari, Saurabh** / *University of Petroleum and Energy Studies, Dehradun, India* ....... 40
**Tripathi, Rajesh** / *University of Petroleum and Energy Studies, India* ....... 175
**Vanteddu, Gangaraju** / *Southeast Missouri State University, USA* ....... 316
**Vargas-Hernández, José G.** / *Instituto Tecnológico Mario Molina, Unidad Académica Zapopan, Mexico* ....... 100
**Veluthakkal, Jayashree** / *Vignana Jyothi Institute of Management, Hyderabad, India* ....... 378
**Vivek, Sai Krishna** / *Philips Innovation Campus, India* ....... 1, 158
**Wanganoo, Leena** / *University of Petroleum and Energy Studies, India* ....... 175
**Yanamandra, Ramakrishna** / *Skyline University College, UAE* ....... 175
**Yu, Poshan** / *Soochow University, China & Krirk University, Thailand* ....... 195

# Table of Contents

**Foreword** ...................................................................................................................... xxiii

**Preface** ......................................................................................................................... xxv

### Section 1
### Supply Chain Resiliency

**Chapter 1**
Achieving Supply Chain Resilience Through Smart Supply Chain Practices Leading to Circular
Economy ............................................................................................................................ 1
*Srirama K. Mulukutla, Cistech Inc., USA*
*Sai Krishna Vivek, Philips Innovation Campus, India*

**Chapter 2**
Proactive Change Management to Enhance Supply Chain Resilience ................................. 18
*Kavitha Reddy Gurrala, ESM Program, American University of Sharjah, UAE*

**Chapter 3**
Supply Chain Innovation in the Era of Industry 4.0 .......................................................... 40
*Saurabh Tiwari, University of Petroleum and Energy Studies, Dehradun, India*

**Chapter 4**
Supply Chain Planning to Achieve Resilience Capabilities................................................ 61
*Sowmya Sangaraju, Volkswagen of America, USA*
*Yanamandra Ramakrishna, Skyline University College, UAE*

**Chapter 5**
Supply Chain Practice Towards Resilience: A Study on the Bangladeshi Manufacturing Industry
During COVID-19 .............................................................................................................. 81
*Ferdoush Saleheen, Universiti Utara Malaysia, Malaysia*
*Md Mamun Habib, Independent University, Bangladesh*

**Chapter 6**

Supply Chain Resilience as a Productive Relocation Strategy for Multinational Companies ........... 100
> *José G. Vargas-Hernández, Instituto Tecnológico Mario Molina, Unidad Académica Zapopan, Mexico*
> *María Fernanda Higuera, Autonomous University of Sinaloa, Mexico*

**Chapter 7**

Supply Chain Resilience in Service Organizations: A Case Study of Kohinoor Hospital, Kurla, Mumbai .......................................................................................................................................... 115
> *Abbasi Attarwala, Kohinoor Business School, India*
> *Balasbramaniam Santhanam, Kohinoor Business School, India*

**Chapter 8**

Understanding the Service Quality Dimensions and Achieving Resilience in Service Retail ........... 136
> *Sachin Kumar Raut, University of Agder, Norway & Fortune Institute of International Business, India*
> *Subodh Sakpal, Oriental Institute of Management, Mumbai University, India*
> *Rashmi Soni, KJ Somaiya Institute of Management, Mumbai, India*

**Section 2**
**Supply Chain Efficiency**

**Chapter 9**

Investigating the Influence of Supply Chain Practices on Healthcare Organizational Performance: An Integrated Framework ....................................................................................................................... 158
> *Lakshmi Sathyavani, TriHealth, USA*
> *Sai Krishna Vivek, Philips Innovation Campus, India*
> *Sai Prasanna Karthik, Chaitanya Bharathi Institute of Technology, Hyderabad, India*

**Chapter 10**

Revamping Reverse Logistics to Enhance Customer Satisfaction .................................................... 175
> *Leena Wanganoo, University of Petroleum and Energy Studies, India*
> *Rajesh Tripathi, University of Petroleum and Energy Studies, India*
> *Ramakrishna Yanamandra, Skyline University College, UAE*

**Chapter 11**

Supply Chain Resiliency, Efficiency, and Visibility in the Post-Pandemic Era in China: Case Studies of MeiTuan Waimai, and Ele.me ........................................................................................... 195
> *Poshan Yu, Soochow University, China & Krirk University, Thailand*
> *Ziqi Liu, Independent Researcher, Suzhou, China*
> *Emanuela Hanes, Independent Researcher, Austria*

**Chapter 12**

Training and Upgrading Skills of Employees Towards Building Resilience Among the Workforce . 226
> *Kakul Agha, Skyline University College, UAE*

**Section 3**
**Supply Chain Technologies for Visibility**

**Chapter 13**
A Structural Equation Modelling Approach to Develop a Resilient Supply Chain Strategy for the COVID-19 Disruptions ............................................................................................................... 242
> *Subhodeep Mukherjee, Department of Operations, GITAM School of Business, GITAM (Deemed), Visakhapatnam, India*
> *Manish Mohan Baral, Department of Operations, GITAM School of Business, GITAM (Deemed), Visakhapatnam, India*
> *Venkataiah Chittipaka, School of Management Studies, Indira Gandhi National Open University, New Delhi, India*
> *Surya Kant Pal, Department of Mathematics, School of Basic Sciences and Research, Sharda University, Greater Noida, India*

**Chapter 14**
Application of Digital Technologies: Integrated Blockchain With Emerging Technologies ............. 267
> *Shankar Subramanian Iyer, S.P. Jain School of Global Management, Dubai, UAE*

**Chapter 15**
Bigdata Intervention in the Healthcare Supply Chain: Future Directions ......................................... 295
> *Anjaneyulu Jinugu, Universitat Oberta de Catalunya, Spain*
> *Vishnu Teja Jinugu, Kasturba Medical College, Mangalore, India*
> *Madhavi Lalitha V. V., Qatar University, Qatar*

**Chapter 16**
Blockchain Technology Aptness for Improving Supply Chain Visibility, Resiliency, and Efficiency 316
> *Gangaraju Vanteddu, Southeast Missouri State University, USA*
> *Asit Bandyopadhayay, Southeast Missouri State University, USA*

**Chapter 17**
Disruptive Technology-Enabled Circular Economy for Improving the Sustainability of the Supply Chain: A Case of an Emerging Economy ........................................................................................... 335
> *Kali Charan Rath, GIET University, Odisha, India*
> *Kamalakanta Muduli, Papua New Guinea University of Technology, Papua New Guinea*
> *Rashmi Prava Das, CV Raman Global University, Odisha, India*
> *Adimuthu Ramasamy, The Papua New Guinea University of Technology, Papua New Guinea*
> *Aezeden Mohammed, UNITECH, Papua New Guinea*

**Chapter 18**
Supply Chain Building Blocks and Post-COVID-19 Recovery Measures With Artificial Intelligence ......................................................................................................................................... 352
> *Priyadarsini Patnaik, Birla Global University, Odisha, India*

**Chapter 19**
Supply Chain Techno-Umbrella for Supply Chain Resilience..........................................................378
*Jayashree Veluthakkal, Vignana Jyothi Institute of Management, Hyderabad, India*
*Subramani Krishnamurthi, Vignana Jyothi Institute of Management, Hyderabad, India*
*David W. Praveenraj, Bannari Amman Institute of Technology, Erode, India*
*Sagyan Sagarika Mohanty, Vignana Jyothi Institute of Management, Hyderabad, India*
*Franklin John Selvaraj, Vignana Jyothi Institute of Management, Hyderabad, India*

**Section 4**
**Ethical and Green Supply Chain Practices**

**Chapter 20**
Ethical Supply Chain Practices to Achieve Supply Chain Resilience .............................................402
*Morgane M. C. Fritz, Excelia Business School, France*

**Chapter 21**
Green Supply Chain Management Post-COVID-19 Pandemic ........................................................423
*Babita Srivastava, William Paterson University, USA*

**Chapter 22**
Sustainable Green Supply Chain Management Trends, Practices, and Performance .......................443
*Rahul Gupta, Amity University, Noida, India*

**Section 5**
**Supply Chain Risks and Disruptions**

**Chapter 23**
Managing Supply Chain Risk and Uncertainty in the Post-Pandemic Era: A Strategic Perspective.. 467
*Gyanesh Kumar Sinha, Bennett University, Greater Noida, India*
*Deepika Dhingra, Bennett University, Greater Noida, India*

**Chapter 24**
Pricing and Hedging of Weather and Freight Derivatives: Analysis of the Post-Pandemic Situation 488
*Satya Venkata Sekhar, GITAM Visakhapatnam, India*

**Chapter 25**
Supply Chain Risks in Transportation and Distribution .................................................................505
*El Mehdi El Bhilat, Mohammed V University, Rabat, Morocco*
*Lalla Saadia Hamidi, Mohammed V University, Rabat, Morocco*

**Compilation of References** .........................................................................................................532

**About the Contributors** .............................................................................................................613

**Index** .........................................................................................................................................623

# Detailed Table of Contents

Foreword .................................................................................................................................. xxiii

Preface ..................................................................................................................................... xxv

## Section 1
## Supply Chain Resiliency

**Chapter 1**
Achieving Supply Chain Resilience Through Smart Supply Chain Practices Leading to Circular
Economy ...................................................................................................................................... 1
> *Srirama K. Mulukutla, Cistech Inc., USA*
> *Sai Krishna Vivek, Philips Innovation Campus, India*

This chapter develops a framework by integrating digital technologies and supply chain practices to achieve supply chain resilience which in turn leads to circular economy. A systematic literature review methodology was adopted by analyzing the published literature in leading journals available in popular databases like Proquest, Ebsco, Web of Science, and Google Scholar. It is found that implementation of smart supply chain practices through digital technologies by redesigning the existing traditional supply chains will lead to achievement of resilience in supply chains, and in turn, it will also lead to achievement of circular economy. The traditional supply chain is mostly based on linear flow of materials, and it fails to address issues related to environmental aspects and reduction of waste in the system. Given this background, this chapter develops a framework by integrating digital technologies and supply chain practices to achieve supply chain resilience and in turn lead to circular economy.

**Chapter 2**
Proactive Change Management to Enhance Supply Chain Resilience ..................................... 18
> *Kavitha Reddy Gurrala, ESM Program, American University of Sharjah, UAE*

Modern supply chains (SC) are highly vulnerable to risks that evolve and cascade from internal or external disturbances. Additionally, resilience capabilities aid the SC to thrive against such challenges. Indeed, change management complements the resilience behaviour towards facing changes induced from SC disruptions and proactive change management strategies foster smooth transitions to facilitate faster recovery to steady-state conditions following future change events. Conversely, most SC employ a reactive approach to change management aiming at reducing the impact of disruptions already in place, consequently forcing the SC to instill, develop, and implement change capabilities in a chaotic fashion with reduced efficiency to infuse resilience capabilities for speedy and effective recovery from future disruptive events. Hence, an in-depth literature study is needed to leverage proactive change management processes for resilience enhancements within SC.

**Chapter 3**
Supply Chain Innovation in the Era of Industry 4.0 .......................................................................... 40
*Saurabh Tiwari, University of Petroleum and Energy Studies, Dehradun, India*

Industry 4.0, also known as the fourth industrial revolution, has had a profound impact on business, society, and the supply chain. In Industry 4.0, the supply chain will be digitalized, opening up new opportunities for competitive advantage through innovative supply chain designs, processes, and enabling technology. In any industry or supply chain function, changes can occur to enhance the creation of new value for stakeholders in the supply chain by changing processes, current practices within networks, technology, and processes (or a combination of all of these). This chapter finds how supply chain innovation is transformed in the era of Industry 4.0 using the digital transformation based on digital innovation along with developing a framework based on supply chain innovation (consisting of product, process, organizational, technological, and marketing innovation) and Industry 4.0 (digital transformation).

**Chapter 4**
Supply Chain Planning to Achieve Resilience Capabilities ............................................................... 61
*Sowmya Sangaraju, Volkswagen of America, USA*
*Yanamandra Ramakrishna, Skyline University College, UAE*

Supply chain resilience (SCR) has emerged as a buzz word during the COVID-19 pandemic situation. With the emerging digital technologies and methodologies, optimizing SCM has become the utmost priority for any organization to achieve the SCR capabilities. The pandemic has compelled organizations to rethink about their SC processes and perform risk analysis to achieve SC resilience. Regional diversification of vendors, proactive identification of potential risks, usage of digital technologies lead to increase in factors such as SC visibility, agility, and flexibility to develop SCR. This chapter develops a SC resilience model by linking the SC planning processes, strategies, and application of digital technologies to achieve capabilities of SCR by a business organization in a pandemic situation. The outcome of this research would be very useful to the industry practitioners and academic researchers in the SC area.

**Chapter 5**
Supply Chain Practice Towards Resilience: A Study on the Bangladeshi Manufacturing Industry During COVID-19 .............................................................................................................................. 81
*Ferdoush Saleheen, Universiti Utara Malaysia, Malaysia*
*Md Mamun Habib, Independent University, Bangladesh*

The global pandemic outbreak has been affecting an enormous impact on people's lives and societies. It is evident that crafting the supply chain procedures and results based upon cost-competitiveness are no longer adequate and businesses will be required to reconsider approaches that hold "risk-competitiveness" to warrant resilience moving forward. In this context, the Bangladesh supply chain industry is no exception. The supply chain practitioners have faced an unprecedented challenge from the supplier timely shipment failure to a long delay in the voyage, congestion at transshipment and at the customs, delay in the clearance procedure, and finally, difficulties in the distribution. This chapter justifies the current global disruption demands to revalidate the supply chain performance measurement (SCPM) of an organization, and the Bangladeshi supply chain needs to become more agile and adaptable to these acute crisis moments and should emphasize building effective response strategies.

## Chapter 6
Supply Chain Resilience as a Productive Relocation Strategy for Multinational Companies............ 100
*José G. Vargas-Hernández, Instituto Tecnológico Mario Molina, Unidad Académica*
*Zapopan, Mexico*
*María Fernanda Higuera, Autonomous University of Sinaloa, Mexico*

This chapter aims to critically analyze the implications that the national protectionist policies have on the global supply and value chains and the relocation of production. The analysis is based on the assumptions that the global economy is facing the possibility of decoupling of many trade connections, and this trend favors deglobalization processes that have long been promoted by populism, nationalism, and economic protectionism. It is concluded that global supply, production, and value chains, although being economically efficient, are no longer any more secure under national protectionist policies, and therefore, the relocation of production processes is mainly due to the increase in the level of income and wages of the developing countries that are the destination and which reduce the advantages to relocate.

## Chapter 7
Supply Chain Resilience in Service Organizations: A Case Study of Kohinoor Hospital, Kurla, Mumbai ..................................................................................................................................... 115
*Abbasi Attarwala, Kohinoor Business School, India*
*Balasbramaniam Santhanam, Kohinoor Business School, India*

Supply chain operations by means of manual systems are no longer economical. Though manufacturing sector organizations require supply chain systems in place to react to such events which will reduce the impact and quickly recover, the experience of service organizations, particularly hospitals and healthcare organizations, assumes crucial importance in the current context of the COVID pandemic. Kohinoor Hospital (KH) has become a leading multi-specialty tertiary care hospital since its commencement of services in January 2010. Data had been gathered for analysis from the primary sources/information provided by KH. The study of major crisis management like COVID-19 and resilience path is significant to formulate novel and innovative responses as part of competitive strategies to the hospitals and related to the healthcare sector. This study is highly relevant to researchers, industry practitioners/sector consultants, and policy makers in government.

## Chapter 8
Understanding the Service Quality Dimensions and Achieving Resilience in Service Retail ........... 136
*Sachin Kumar Raut, University of Agder, Norway & Fortune Institute of International*
*Business, India*
*Subodh Sakpal, Oriental Institute of Management, Mumbai University, India*
*Rashmi Soni, KJ Somaiya Institute of Management, Mumbai, India*

Innovation has increasingly supported the way businesses across the globe operate; however, this phenomenon often increases uncertainty around supply chain disruptions and management. The COVID-19 pandemic clearly reveals the lack of resilience in the supply chain domain, and the business failures show the impact of disruptions may have on a global network scale as individual supply chain connections and nodes fail. This cascading failure also has an impact on service quality dimensions of a business. Service quality advances have profoundly changed the way service organizations and consumers interact.

This impact can be observed across sectors and industries. Service quality has become a popular area of researchers and academic investigation and has become recognized as a key factor in differentiating service products and building competitive advantage. Any shortcoming of a lack in service quality is easily identified and is translated into negative reviews on social media through word-of-mouth and other channels.

### Section 2
### Supply Chain Efficiency

**Chapter 9**
Investigating the Influence of Supply Chain Practices on Healthcare Organizational Performance:
An Integrated Framework ........................................................................................................ 158
*Lakshmi Sathyavani, TriHealth, USA*
*Sai Krishna Vivek, Philips Innovation Campus, India*
*Sai Prasanna Karthik, Chaitanya Bharathi Institute of Technology, Hyderabad, India*

This chapter attempts to expand the knowledge in healthcare supply chain by analyzing the impact of implementation of supply chain practices on the overall performance of organizations in healthcare industry through a systematic literature review. The study also develops an integrated healthcare supply chain framework by linking digital technologies and supply chain practices. This framework will act as a tool and add value to organizations in healthcare industry by specifically providing them with supply chain strategies to achieve improved organizational performance with digital technologies as enablers. The framework will attract special significance in view of the prevailing COVID-19 pandemic situation in which the healthcare sector has played a very vital and major role. It will also be helpful in improving healthcare systems in all types of countries, which is the need of the hour. A systematic analysis of published literature is adopted as the methodology to conduct this research.

**Chapter 10**
Revamping Reverse Logistics to Enhance Customer Satisfaction ........................................... 175
*Leena Wanganoo, University of Petroleum and Energy Studies, India*
*Rajesh Tripathi, University of Petroleum and Energy Studies, India*
*Ramakrishna Yanamandra, Skyline University College, UAE*

The cross-border reverse logistics operations are different from forward logistics. They are complex and fragmented due to multiple intermediaries participating in the operation. The retailer goes through a re-export process to fulfil the customs documentation requirement in the reverse logistics process. A heavy paper process with low digitization, low transparency, and multiple entities is the trickiest barrier to optimizing the process and achieving customer satisfaction. Integration of technology with external organizations will aid in improving real-time visibility in the process. Blockchain and other emerging technologies have the potential to improve the reverse logistics process and contracts with intermediaries. The objective of this chapter is twofold. At first, the author reviewed the main barriers in the cross-border reverse logistics operation and later provided an insight on the potential of blockchain technology in the process.

**Chapter 11**
Supply Chain Resiliency, Efficiency, and Visibility in the Post-Pandemic Era in China: Case Studies of MeiTuan Waimai, and Ele.me ........................................................................................ 195
*Poshan Yu, Soochow University, China & Krirk University, Thailand*
*Ziqi Liu, Independent Researcher, Suzhou, China*
*Emanuela Hanes, Independent Researcher, Austria*

The sudden COVID-19 pandemic had a serious impact on the catering industry, and lockdown policies put a strain on the food supply chain. However, online food delivery (OFD) services have played an important role in the fight against the epidemic in the catering industry. In this chapter, the authors analyzed the development of keywords attributed to supply chains in the academic view by investigating the core selection of Web of Science and China National Knowledge Infrastructure, respectively, and drew keywords cluster graphs of Chinese catering supply chain by using CiteSpace. The contrastive analysis shows that more attention has been turned to supply chain resiliency, efficiency, and visibility in the post-pandemic era. Moreover, this chapter discusses whether and how Chinese OFD platforms contribute to the food supply chain. The results show that these OFD platforms, with domestic policy support, internet technologies, and the ecosystem advantages, have effectively enhanced supply chain resiliency, efficiency, and visibility.

**Chapter 12**
Training and Upgrading Skills of Employees Towards Building Resilience Among the Workforce . 226
*Kakul Agha, Skyline University College, UAE*

Organizations worldwide realize the value of creating and sustaining a resilient workforce as employees have been battered with physical, social, and psychological pressures due to the unexpected and challenging demands of pandemic. This chapter revolves around training, upskilling, and reskilling in organizations and establishes their relationship with building resilience in employees. It is significantly relevant and timely as work relationships and expectations have suddenly changed across sectors and industries. It is imperative to include scenarios gathered from the United Arab Emirates (UAE), hence a case study of EFS Facilities Services Group using primary and secondary data has been added. This case is a direct evidence of building resilience in workforce with the help of upskilling and reskilling. This chapter will inform of practices adopted for building resilience among workforce at a global level. Conclusions and recommendations inform about different interventions that organizations can adopt in order to build a resilient workforce.

**Section 3**
**Supply Chain Technologies for Visibility**

## Chapter 13

A Structural Equation Modelling Approach to Develop a Resilient Supply Chain Strategy for the COVID-19 Disruptions ................................................................................................................. 242

>   *Subhodeep Mukherjee, Department of Operations, GITAM School of Business, GITAM*
>       *(Deemed), Visakhapatnam, India*
>   *Manish Mohan Baral, Department of Operations, GITAM School of Business, GITAM*
>       *(Deemed), Visakhapatnam, India*
>   *Venkataiah Chittipaka, School of Management Studies, Indira Gandhi National Open*
>       *University, New Delhi, India*
>   *Surya Kant Pal, Department of Mathematics, School of Basic Sciences and Research, Sharda*
>       *University, Greater Noida, India*

Due to COVID-19, the supply chains were disrupted in many ways. This chapter aims to identify the strategies that can help the industries develop a resilient supply chain that can handle any kind of disruption. Five strategies are determined from the literature review. A questionnaire is being developed for survey-based research in four types of industries. The industries that are targeted are automobile industries, garment industries, steel industries, cement industries. For data analysis, exploratory factor analysis and structural equation modelling are used. In this research, an empirical investigation is carried out to present the research framework. All the proposed hypotheses are accepted, and the developed model satisfied all the parameters.

## Chapter 14

Application of Digital Technologies: Integrated Blockchain With Emerging Technologies ............. 267

>   *Shankar Subramanian Iyer, S.P. Jain School of Global Management, Dubai, UAE*

The application of digital technologies in supply chain and logistics is immense and the most important happening in the last decade. The advent of COVID-19 has forced changes in the supply chain and some cases disrupted it. In some cases, it has been a do-or-die situation as social distancing and passenger travel and essentials have affected most economies. China controlled about 40% of the global supply chain, and most countries were made to change and initiate alternative supply chains to reduce the risk. The purpose of this study is to study how the emerging technologies of blockchain, virtual reality, artificial intelligence, machine learning are the few additions to enhance the supply chain. The supply chain digitalization will lead to cost reduction, improved efficiency, data security, and storage of the information. The emerging technologies are poised to revolutionize the supply chain and logistics. The study uses qualitative approach to showcase the expert opinion of stakeholders on this topic and contribute to the scarce data available currently.

**Chapter 15**
Bigdata Intervention in the Healthcare Supply Chain: Future Directions ......................................... 295
    *Anjaneyulu Jinugu, Universitat Oberta de Catalunya, Spain*
    *Vishnu Teja Jinugu, Kasturba Medical College, Mangalore, India*
    *Madhavi Lalitha V. V., Qatar University, Qatar*

The buzz word "big data" has fueled the global healthcare supply chains (HCSCs) by providing capability to analyse bundles of data. On one hand, the intervention of big data technologies made the SCs more resilient, and on the other, it increased the digital divide between the high-end and low-end healthcare facilities. To bridge the gap within and between the healthcare entities and to advocate strategies or models that can not only strengthen the SCs in the times of COVID-19 pandemic but also strengthen the weakest links in the HCSCs, present research work is undertaken. A comprehensive analysis of the frameworks, models, and strategies is performed, and needed solutions and recommendations are furnished for future endeavours. Suitable managerial and theoretical implications coupled with research prospects are also advocated.

**Chapter 16**
Blockchain Technology Aptness for Improving Supply Chain Visibility, Resiliency, and Efficiency 316
    *Gangaraju Vanteddu, Southeast Missouri State University, USA*
    *Asit Bandyopadhayay, Southeast Missouri State University, USA*

Frequently recurring supply chain disruptions due to natural and manmade calamities are highlighting the importance of the supply chain ability to prevent, withstand, and overcome disruptions of all kinds. Blockchain technology (BCT), a key Industry 4.0 technology, with its inherent strength as an open-sourced distributed database with the immutability of transactions has the potential to transform traditional supply chain (SC) operations. In spite of the potential advantages of the BCT in the supply chain management (SCM) area, the adoption of this novel technology is still in its very early stages. This chapter per the authors proposes a quality function deployment (QFD)-based strategic decision support tool to determine the aptness of BCT adoption in a given SC context. In addition, the proposed tool also allows us to understand the maturity of BCT capabilities in addressing the key SC performance aspects. The application of the proposed tool is explained through a couple of illustrative examples.

**Chapter 17**
Disruptive Technology-Enabled Circular Economy for Improving the Sustainability of the Supply Chain: A Case of an Emerging Economy ....................................................................................... 335
    *Kali Charan Rath, GIET University, Odisha, India*
    *Kamalakanta Muduli, Papua New Guinea University of Technology, Papua New Guinea*
    *Rashmi Prava Das, CV Raman Global University, Odisha, India*
    *Adimuthu Ramasamy, The Papua New Guinea University of Technology, Papua New Guinea*
    *Aezeden Mohammed, UNITECH, Papua New Guinea*

Most industries are faced with the challenges of how the supply chain can be made sustainable with the assistance from digital technology and circular economy (CE). A survey has been carried out to review the involvement of disruptive technology (DT) and CE in certain sections of supply chain system and identify a clear path that need to be routed to best integrate sustainable practices in the industries to make supply chain more sustainable. Some of the major barrier factors identified are funding support, availability, and technological expertise or 'know how', and management and policy regulation to implement CE and DT in supply chain management (SCM) to make it more sustainable. It also showed some of the adjustments that need to be made especially in developing countries before introducing the practices of sustainable SCM. When scrutinizing the entire process of SCM and its members, it shows that a single component of SCM cannot implement CE in isolation; it requires collective effort from all members of the supply chain, which is facilitated by integration of DT.

**Chapter 18**
Supply Chain Building Blocks and Post-COVID-19 Recovery Measures With Artificial Intelligence................................................................................................................................ 352
    *Priyadarsini Patnaik, Birla Global University, Odisha, India*

Supply chain reach is vast and touches every aspect of business. As profitability of any business is directly impacted by its inventory, so any basic changes in operations would impact its performance. However, established supply chain paradigms are no longer valid as they are shaken up by VUCA economy, demographic change, sustainability, globalization, digitization, rise of ecommerce, political turmoil, social media, buying behaviour, and most importantly, by COVID-19. This COVID-19 pandemic crisis has taken over the world and brought additional challenges at an unprecedented scale. Since identifying and structuring the problem are the first steps towards effective SCM, so redesigning the distribution strategy is the need of the hour. Companies should innovate with data and new digital technologies to increase automation in their core process to forecast predictive analysis for greater customer experience and harness the disruption. In the context of disruption, this study explored how to utilize and optimize supply chain tools and models to make decisions during times of disruption.

**Chapter 19**
Supply Chain Techno-Umbrella for Supply Chain Resilience...................................................... 378
    *Jayashree Veluthakkal, Vignana Jyothi Institute of Management, Hyderabad, India*
    *Subramani Krishnamurthi, Vignana Jyothi Institute of Management, Hyderabad, India*
    *David W. Praveenraj, Bannari Amman Institute of Technology, Erode, India*
    *Sagyan Sagarika Mohanty, Vignana Jyothi Institute of Management, Hyderabad, India*
    *Franklin John Selvaraj, Vignana Jyothi Institute of Management, Hyderabad, India*

The pandemic has devastated the whole economy with losing many human lives as well. The hard-hit aspect of the pandemic was gathering the people in public and working together in any industry. It has resulted in a deviation of planning in the supply chain and its related services. Technology adoption has dramatically changed many organizations' revenue patterns with high income on technology adoption and low income on non-adoption. The timeline of technology adoption was also the biggest concern for many firms because of restrictions on the people's movement. The research has been done on technology usage in different supply chain functions and its effectiveness in business performance. The chapter contents displayed the possible outcomes of the technology and its importance of adoption. The supply chain techno-umbrella has been portrayed as a saver of the pandemic during the non-revenue time. The chapter also described the various available forms of technology in the decision-making of the supply chain processes.

**Section 4**
**Ethical and Green Supply Chain Practices**

**Chapter 20**
Ethical Supply Chain Practices to Achieve Supply Chain Resilience ............................................... 402
    *Morgane M. C. Fritz, Excelia Business School, France*

Following the COVID-19 pandemic, ethical supply chain practices have been in the focus of several supply chain stakeholders such as firms, suppliers, government, and consumers. The pandemic caused a disruption that forced supply chains to reorganise their activities and sometimes take unethical decisions to ensure the business survival or satisfy customers. In light of several scandals, stakeholders require to increase transparency in the supply chain and recent norms on sustainable procurement highlight the importance of sustainable procurement in this mission. The chapter revises all key concepts of business ethics, supply chain practices, and supply chain resilience to explore, through the COVID-19 pandemic, unethical supply chain practices and propose solutions and recommendations based on practitioners' and researchers' studies.

**Chapter 21**
Green Supply Chain Management Post-COVID-19 Pandemic ........................................................... 423
    *Babita Srivastava, William Paterson University, USA*

In this chapter, the author reviews the literature to understand the association between the adoption of green supply chain practices and abnormal returns during COVID-19 outbreak to test whether companies adopting green supply chain policies experienced lesser negative returns during the market collapse. In this chapter, the author discusses various drivers for establishing sustainability in supply chain following the COVID-19 pandemic and establishes an empirical relation between sustainability and effectiveness. The following topics are highlighted in this chapter: (1) introduction to green supply chain management, (2) environmental benefit of green supply chain management, (3) economic aspect of green supply chain management, (4) trend in supply chain management, (5) sustainable supply chain and COVID-19, (6) drivers of supply chain sustainability in context of COVID-19, and (7) green supply chain management policies.

**Chapter 22**
Sustainable Green Supply Chain Management Trends, Practices, and Performance......................... 443
    *Rahul Gupta, Amity University, Noida, India*

Innovative adoption of green supply chain management (GSCM) practices has witnessed a great surge in the last couple of decades. Its positive impact on the individual, society, and environment advocates the organization's commitment to progressively work with all stakeholders. Efforts are accelerated for identifying and understanding the opportunities to support green practices. Global warming and climate change have warned that scarce natural resources are not forever GSCM practices help to mitigate these hazards and ideologically enhance sustainability. Stake holders are committed to reuse, reduce, redesign, and recycle products in support of waste reduction and sustainable environmental protection. The sustainable supply chain is integrating sustainable environmental progressions into processes like selecting suppliers who ensure green manufacturing, buying green raw material, designing, assembling, and distribution with reverse logistics. Current research discusses sustainable green supply chain concepts, present and future trends, and performances.

**Section 5**
**Supply Chain Risks and Disruptions**

**Chapter 23**
Managing Supply Chain Risk and Uncertainty in the Post-Pandemic Era: A Strategic Perspective.. 467
*Gyanesh Kumar Sinha, Bennett University, Greater Noida, India*
*Deepika Dhingra, Bennett University, Greater Noida, India*

The pandemic due to COVID-19 has not only disrupted supply chains all around the world but has also tested the resilience and flexibility of supply chain leaders globally. With the virus still alive and several regions and economies in lockdown, disruption to supply chains continues to be severe. As economies restart, having an efficient supply chain will be critical to supplying goods and services quickly, safely, and securely. Business leaders are expected to respond and take immediate actions to sustain business operations to serve their customers, clients, and stakeholders that includes protecting and supporting their human resources. The chapter discusses the risk and uncertainties that have arisen due to pandemics. It also presents the framework for the supply chain post-COVID-19 scenario and proposes an action plan and the model that can build resiliency and improve efficiency and visibility across the supply chain. The action plan will facilitate communities to manage short-term crises and enable businesses to be customer-centric and help economies rebound.

**Chapter 24**
Pricing and Hedging of Weather and Freight Derivatives: Analysis of the Post-Pandemic Situation 488
*Satya Venkata Sekhar, GITAM Visakhapatnam, India*

It is known that the entire physical activity of business faced several hurdles due to lockdown implemented phase-wise. The COVID-19 pandemic period has shown its impact on various sectors across the globe. One should keep in mind that there are no obstacles to online activity irrespective of political, legal, and environmental factors. During the last couple of months, the pandemic situation raised the need to assess 'derivative' impacts, particularly weather and freight derivatives. All the business organizations face many problems in the shipment of their products and confusion about pricing. This chapter aims to appreciate issues and challenges relating to weather and freight derivatives' functioning in the present pandemic. The objectives are 1) to understand the genesis of weather and freight derivatives and empirical research in a global context and 2) to understand the impact of the pandemic situation on weather and freight derivatives.

**Chapter 25**
Supply Chain Risks in Transportation and Distribution ....................................................................... 505
*El Mehdi El Bhilat, Mohammed V University, Rabat, Morocco*
*Lalla Saadia Hamidi, Mohammed V University, Rabat, Morocco*

The coronavirus pandemic has massively disrupted supply chain performance at the global and local stage, and the concept of supply chain risk management and resilience has been pushed to the forefront. In order to overcome all these challenges and changes, it's time for businesses and supply chains to learn from the past and to develop new strategical and organizational dimensions and to be ready with alternative strategy which has not been widely discussed, 'risks mitigation in distribution', to ensure the delivery of final products to the end consumers. This chapter presents a review of literature that addresses supply chains risks, which are generated in transportation and distribution. In this regard, it's crucial to bring to light as well some measures and strategies that companies can implement to cope with the risks caused by some disruptions. These include the rising importance of safety, digitalization, and the need to revisit the meaning of efficiency in transportation and distribution management.

**Compilation of References** ....................................................................................................... 532

**About the Contributors** ............................................................................................................. 613

**Index** ............................................................................................................................................ 623

# Foreword

The COVID-19 pandemic has created large-scale disruption and triggered many changes in ways we live and do our socio-economic activities. Lockdowns, restriction on movement of people and goods, implementation of protocols, change in processes and operations resulted huge imbalance in supply and demand patterns. Initially the duration of pandemic was estimated to be of short-term, but with the emergence of new variants, the pandemic continued to extend further and there is no clear indication that it will end soon. In the past, supply chain met the enterprise and customer needs through beginning-to-end model, which was largely stable and was not affected by the global pandemic disruption. In these challenging times, organizations prepared themselves for uncertainties and disruptions by focusing on transforming their supply chains to make them smarter through the implementation of digital technologies to make them more agile and resilient.

This book titled *Handbook of Research on Supply Chain Resiliency, Efficiency, and Visibility in the Post-Pandemic Era* is the best, timely and great contribution to evolving concepts and practices of supply chain management, by my colleague, who possesses twenty five plus years of experience as a practitioner, researcher and academician. This contemporary, truly global book has twenty-five innovative research chapters by several authors, representing from twenty countries encompassing diverse concepts, theories and practices to make the supply chain more effective. The book is meticulously divided into five sections based on the current required interventions in the supply chain.

The first section of the book is titled as 'Supply Chain Resiliency' consisting of eight chapters. Innovative supply chain strategies and practices such as improved information sharing, proactive change management, innovative supply chain in Industry 4.0, integrated supply chain planning, relocation strategy, supply chain service quality, and improving velocity, visibility and reliability are extensively covered in these chapters. They provided the much-needed contribution during the pandemic situation.

Contributions related to strategies to achieve 'Supply Chain Efficiency' in various sectors such as healthcare, retail sector and reverse logistics formed part of second section of the book. Interesting conclusions of these chapters include strategies such as stakeholder management, sub-division of suppliers and localization in reverse logistics in retail sector and training and upskilling the supply chain employees. A detailed review of these chapters would provide the readers more insights on developing resilient supply chains in the post-pandemic era.

Whereas application of digital and smart technologies such as big data, supply chain analytics, automation and robotics, internet-of-things, block chain technologies and radio frequency identification are extensively analyzed in the third section on 'Supply Chain Technologies for Visibility' through seven chapters. Supply chain practitioners looking for enhancing visibility of their supply chains would be immensely benefitted by reading these contributions.

*Foreword*

Balancing profits and ethics in supply chains has always been an ambiguous situation for top managements, more so during the pandemic. Contributions in the fourth section on 'Ethical and Green Supply Chain Practices' of the book exactly highlighted this ambiguity and provided some of the best ethical practices to promote green supply chain. During the Covid-19 pandemic, ethical practices have gained the highest importance for achieving the abilities of resilience for sustainability.

Absence of a systematic risk management plan is considered as the major reason for impact of Covid-19 on the supply chains of business organizations. To address this issue, contributions in the last section on 'Supply Chain Risks and Disruptions' have recommended several innovative solutions to manage supply chain risks and disruptions by the business organizations in the post-pandemic era.

This book is an essential reading for all researchers, academicians, industry practitioners, students and regulatory agencies with a keen interest in understanding how to manage supply chains in fast changing, uncertain future to achieve resilience during the post-pandemic era.

I thank the editor for providing me an opportunity to write the foreword. I congratulate the editor for his efforts in publishing this useful book.

*Naseem Abidi*
*Skyline University College, Sharjah, UAE*

# Preface

The Covid-19 pandemic has severely disrupted the global supply chain and compelled the organizations to redesign their business strategies to prepare for supply chain resiliency, efficiency and visibility. Prolonged lockdowns, unpreparedness of managements, unpredictability and ambiguity in demand and supply resulted in reduction of profits for many organizations. Lack of risk management plan and absence of proactive initiatives to achieve the abilities of supply chain resilience are cited to be the major reasons for this severe impact. The pandemic has created an awareness among organizations to prepare their businesses for encountering severe disruptions in future. With multiple variants of Covid-19, the duration of pandemic became unpredictable. Therefore, it is too early to conclude that the threat of this pandemic has ended. Hence, this is the right time for researchers and practitioners of supply chain to identify the loopholes in the existing strategies and to focus on developing vibrant, resilient, and visible supply chains to manage the organizations efficiently during the post-pandemic era.

Given this background, this book titled *Handbook of Research on Supply Chain Resiliency, Efficiency, and Visibility in the Post-Pandemic Era* rightly fulfills the need of all stakeholders and provides a set of diverse solutions to achieve sustainability and resilience in future. The book consists of five sections with contributions from authors belonging to around twenty nations.

The first section focuses on "Supply Chain Resiliency" and consists of eight chapters. The first chapter starts the discussion with a chapter titled "Achieving Supply Chain Resilience Through Smart Supply Chain Practices Leading to Circular Economy." In this chapter, the authors discussed about contemporary smart supply chain practices, which can develop resilience and lead to circular economy by promoting recycling, reuse, and redesign.

The second chapter of this section is "Proactive Change Management to Enhance Supply Chain Resilience." The authors identified several change management strategies such as dynamic knowledge capabilities, advanced digital capabilities, and collaborative culture to achieve resilience in supply chains. These proactive strategies would improve the flexibility, visibility alignment, agility, and resilience of supply chains. The authors developed a resilience model as an outcome of this research.

The third chapter of this section, "Supply Chain Innovation in the Era of Industry 4.0," highlights the role of digital and smart supply chain in innovating the supply chains in Industry 4.0 era. In this era, aspects like coordination, integration and information sharing in supply chain will improve with the help of digital technologies.

The fourth chapter of this section, "Supply Chain Planning to Achieve Resilience Capabilities," explores the relationship between proactive supply chain planning and achievement of resilient capabilities. The research develops an integrated model to achieve capabilities of supply chain resilience through a systematic planning process. This process involves identification of risks, regional diversification of vendors, analysis of SC dependencies, performing a SWOT analysis, developing SC disruption mitigation strategies, and implementation of digital technologies. This type of planning is found to achieve visibility, flexibility, and agility in supply chain.

The fifth chapter, "Supply Chain Practice Towards Resilience: A Study on the Bangladeshi Manufacturing Industry During COVID-19," provides an overview of various SC practices in Bangladesh. The research used a questionnaire to collect primary data from manufacturing companies in different industry sectors to understand the impact of Covid-19. The chapter concludes through a comparative analysis of impact of pandemic in these diverse sectors. It recommends collaboration, velocity, visibility and reliability as abilities of achieving resilience.

The sixth chapter is titled "Supply Chain Resilience as a Productive Relocation Strategy for Multinational Companies." The authors find very interesting aspects like 'de-globalization' and 'protectionist economy' as strategies to achieve SCR in the post-pandemic era.

The seventh chapter is on "Supply Chain Resilience in Service Organizations: A Case Study of Kohinoor Hospital, Kurla, Mumbai." It illustrated the achievement of SCR with the success story of a leading hospital in India as a case study. The authors conducted focused interviews of employees at different hierarchical positions and collected primary data on SC initiatives by the hospital during the Covid-19 pandemic. The hospital managed its SC by maintaining SC processes related to blood bank, disposables, medical equipment, medicines, oxygen, protective equipment related to Covid-19 and integrated Patient Information Management Systems.

Moving from SCR in a specific hospital, Chapter 8 of the book focused on service quality dimensions in achieving SCR in retail sector. The chapter is titled "Understanding the Service Quality Dimensions and Achieving Resilience in Service Retail." The author developed a model by using Structural Equation Modelling to explain how the five dimensions of service quality influence the perceptions of the overall retail service quality and how these overall perceptions influence the customer's satisfaction level.

The second section of the book presented four chapters related to "Supply Chain Efficiency" aspect. It begins with Chapter 9, titled "Investigating the Influence of Supply Chain Practices on Healthcare Organizational Performance: An Integrated Framework." The authors of this chapter explored the best practices of supply chain, which influenced the performance of healthcare sector in general, and every healthcare organization in particular. An integrated framework depicting relationship and inter-dependence among various aspects like members of SCM, Supply Chain Practices (SCPs) in healthcare sector, and organizational performance measures was developed through systematic literature review. 'Diagnostic centers' was added as a new stakeholder and member of healthcare supply chain in this chapter based on the gaps in the existing models. The authors concluded that a collaborative implementation of SCPs through the application of 'technology enablers' would lead to the achievement of SCR in the post-pandemic era.

Chapter 10, with a title "Revamping Reverse Logistics to Enhance Customer Satisfaction," explored the practices of reverse logistics chain of supply chain for enhancing customer satisfaction and improving the abilities of SC resilience in retail sector. The author developed a model of reverse logistics by integrating the block chain technology to improve the efficiency.

Chapter 11 is a research based on case studies from China. The chapter is titled "Supply Chain Resiliency, Efficiency, and Visibility in the Post-Pandemic Era in China: Cases Study of MeiTuan Waimai and Ele.me." In this chapter, the authors analyzed the supply chain of catering industry, mainly focusing on mass consumption market, namely the online food delivery (OFD) industry, which provides food delivery services and related services primarily for household consumption. The research concluded that

xxvi

*Preface*

taking advantages of policy support, smart technologies and ecosystem resources, the Chinese Online Food Delivery platforms contributed to food supply chain resilience and enhanced efficiency and visibility on both the supply side and demand side.

Chapter 12, titled "Training and Upgrading Skills of Employees Towards Building Resilience Among the Workforce," focused on employees and workforce being adaptable and flexible to newness at work along with being agile and resilient for successful work experiences. It recommended training interventions, which includes strategies such as training, reskilling, upskilling and upgradation of skills in building resilience during difficult times, with a special focus on the impact of pandemic COVID19 on the workforce. The author validated the viewpoint by analyzing the success story of EFS Facilities Services Group (EFS) as a case study.

The next section of the book consists of chapters related to "Supply Chain Technologies for Visibility" in which there are seven chapters with interesting outcomes.

Chapter 13 of the book, "A Structural Equation Modelling Approach to Develop a Resilient Supply Chain Strategy for the COVID-19 Disruptions," aimed at identifying the strategies that can help the industries develop a resilient supply chain to handle any kind of disruption using an empirical approach. Data from four types of industries namely, automobile industries, garment industries, steel industries, cement industries was collected. Exploratory factor analysis and structural equation modelling are used.

Chapter 14 of the book highlighted the "Application of Digital Technologies-Integrated Blockchain With Emerging Technologies." It dealt with the role of digital technologies, especially the blockchain technology on SCM. Through focused interviews of experts in SCM and by performing a qualitative analysis, the author concluded that these emerging technologies are poised to revolutionize the way SCM will be managed in the post-pandemic era. This research also found that block chain technologies would improve SC operational performance by increasing the SC transparency, SC flexibility, information sharing, mutual coordination, and trust among SC members.

Chapter 15 is titled "Big Data Intervention in Healthcare Supply Chain-Future Directions." This chapter too focuses on digital technologies, especially the application Big Data in healthcare SC. The authors found that there is a scarcity of research in healthcare SC in terms of frameworks, models and innovative strategies. The research concluded that there is a need to develop new models to guide the practitioners of SC and make them aware of the need to redesign their existing traditional SC practices and make them more vibrant through digital technologies.

Continuing further, Chapter 16 explored the "Blockchain Technology Aptness for Improving the Supply Chain Visibility, Resiliency, and Efficiency." The authors investigated through literature review visibility, resiliency, and efficiency aspects of a supply chain and how Block Chain Technology (BCT) enables those aspects. The research developed a strategic tool which provides an idea in regards to the maturity of specific BCT capabilities in addressing a specific set of performance aspects as relevant to a given supply chain. The proposed Quality Function Deployment (QFD) based strategic tool through hypothetical examples facilitates the application of the tool to consider the adoption of BCT as a possible technology solution based on the perceived strength of association between the BCT capabilities, and the importance attached to the visibility, resiliency, and efficiency aspects of a given supply chain.

Chapter 17 is titled "Disruptive Technology-Enabled Circular Economy for Improving Sustainability of Supply Chain: A Case of an Emerging Economy." The authors found that a single component of SCM cannot implement Circular Economy (CE) in isolation and it requires a collective effort from all members of the supply chain, which is facilitated by the integration of Disruptive Technology (DT). The chapter concluded on how the CE-based Sustainable Supply Chain Management (SSCM) practices

xxvii

could deliver more socio-environmentally friendly products and processes through the integration of digital technologies.

Contributions towards digital technologies continued further through Chapter 18, titled "Supply Chain Building Blocks and Post-COVID-19 Recovery Measures With Artificial Intelligence." The study identified the critical barriers in SC and recommended some strategies on how to overcome them. The study also developed Artificial Intelligence (AI) enabled SC solution that can withstand the extreme disruptions caused by COVID-19.

Another contribution to SC technology and visibility area in this book is through Chapter 19, titled "Supply Chain Techno-Umbrella for Supply Chain Resilience." Application of technology enabled SC for SCR is illustrated through case studies of successful business organizations in this chapter. The authors opined that by managing key processes such as customer relationship management (CRM), customer service management (CSM), demand management (DM), order fulfilment (OF), manufacturing flow management (MFM), supplier relationship management (SRM), product development and commercialization, and return management (RM) the business organizations can improve their profitability. The chapter contributed a supply chain techno-umbrella model for tour ordering process.

The fourth section of the book consists of research contributions in "Ethical and Green Supply Chain for Achieving SCR." In this section, there are three chapters with interesting themes and outcomes. The first one among them is Chapter 20, titled "Ethical Supply Chain Practices to Achieve Supply Chain Resilience." The objectives of this chapter are mainly on ethical issues related to the Covid-19 pandemic, identification of ethical solutions to achieve SCR.

The next chapter in this section is on "Green Supply Chain Management: Post COVID-19 Pandemic." This is the twenty-first chapter of book. In this chapter, the author conducted a systematic literature review to understand the association between the adoption of green supply chain practices and abnormal returns during COVID-19 outbreak and tested whether companies adopting green supply chain policies experienced lesser negative returns during the market collapse. In addition, the author discussed various drivers for establishing sustainability in supply chain following the COVID-19 pandemic and established an empirical relation between sustainability and effectiveness. The chapter concluded that Green Supply Chain Management is one of the sustainability approaches that will positively affect not only the environment but also the firm's efficiency in terms of its resources, firms' profit margins, and reduction of carbon and other waste emissions.

Chapter 22 of the book is on "Sustainable Green Supply Chain Management Trends, Practices, and Performance." The author analyzed various dimensions of GSCM such as green design, green sourcing, green manufacturing, green marketing, green logistics, green warehousing, reverse logistics, customer's environmental concern, investment recovery, green training, and mitigating use of hazardous material.

Chapter 23 of the book is on "Managing Supply Chain Risk and Uncertainty in Post Pandemic Era: A Strategic Perspective." The chapter conducted an empirical approach through case studies to understand various types and sources of supply chain risks and uncertainties in post COVID-19 outbreak and the strategies adopted by global firms to meet the challenges associated with them. The chapter concluded by recommending the application of Multiple Criteria Decisions Making (MCDM), implementing digital technologies real-time information sharing and supply chain integration for mitigating supply chain risk and disruptions.

Chapter 24 of the book is on "Pricing and Hedging of Weather and Freight Derivatives: An Analysis of Post-Pandemic Situation." The chapter analyzed the impact of pandemic on logistics particularly with

*Preface*

special emphasis on weather and freight derivatives. The importance of temperature in pricing weather derivative and Baltic indices in derivatives has been discussed.

Chapter 25 of the book is on "Supply Chain Risks in Transportation and Distribution." This chapter researches and discusses the set of challenges and constraints confronted by the majority of companies in transportation and distribution systems during the pandemic era. The outcome of this research provided very interesting results and recommended strategies such as development of contingency plans, risk identification and implementation of risk management plans.

*Yanamandra Ramakrishna*
*Skyline University College, UAE*

# Section 1
# Supply Chain Resiliency

# Chapter 1
# Achieving Supply Chain Resilience Through Smart Supply Chain Practices Leading to Circular Economy

**Srirama K. Mulukutla**
*Cistech Inc., USA*

**Sai Krishna Vivek**
*Philips Innovation Campus, India*

## ABSTRACT

*This chapter develops a framework by integrating digital technologies and supply chain practices to achieve supply chain resilience which in turn leads to circular economy. A systematic literature review methodology was adopted by analyzing the published literature in leading journals available in popular databases like Proquest, Ebsco, Web of Science, and Google Scholar. It is found that implementation of smart supply chain practices through digital technologies by redesigning the existing traditional supply chains will lead to achievement of resilience in supply chains, and in turn, it will also lead to achievement of circular economy. The traditional supply chain is mostly based on linear flow of materials, and it fails to address issues related to environmental aspects and reduction of waste in the system. Given this background, this chapter develops a framework by integrating digital technologies and supply chain practices to achieve supply chain resilience and in turn lead to circular economy.*

## INTRODUCTION

The concept of supply chain management (SCM) has gained lot of importance in business organizations and research areas due to its ability to develop capabilities required to achieve optimization of costs, improved product availability and increased customer satisfaction. However, today SCM has been facing many challenges due to a variety of disruptions, both external and internal. Highly competitive global

DOI: 10.4018/978-1-7998-9506-0.ch001

Copyright © 2022, IGI Global. Copying or distributing in print or electronic forms without written permission of IGI Global is prohibited.

scenarios, lack of knowledge in SCM, absence of proactive risk management plans (Manhart et al., 2020), unpreparedness of organizations and lack of long-term approaches towards SCM are some of the major reasons for these disruptions (Nadeesha et al., 2019). The current Covid-19 pandemic situation has been one such unprecedented disruption for SCM. It is not uncommon for SCM to encounter disruptions. SCM has witnessed such disruptions previously too. Some of those disruptions are external in nature and some other are internal ones caused due to coordination and cooperation issues in the internal processes of business organizations. Many of these disruptions impact the supply chain operations severely and they give very less time to respond. Therefore, there is an urgent need to identify such disruptions, predict their possible impacts reasonably, develop a systematic risk management plan (Manhart et al., 2020) and create strategies to recover quickly. Economic recessions, health-related pandemic and epidemic situations, disruptions due to natural calamities and disruptions due to non-cooperation from other members of supply chain, geographic concentration of strategic suppliers in a single location are all some of the examples of external and internal disruptions posing challenges to the routine process flows of SCM (Ponomarov & Holcomb, 2009).

The concept of SCM has been evolving in the recent past to mitigate some of these disruptions with the help of technology and also by developing robust supply chain network (Park et al., 2021). However, there is a lot to be done in this area to successfully encounter the pandemic situations. Traditionally supply chains have been built on trust and mutual cooperation. But, the traditional supply chain suffers from many weaknesses resulting into excess production, excess storage of inventory and thus leading the entire system to produce more wastage. This wastage is also a result of excess buffer inventories, mismatch between supply and demand and lack of proper information sharing across the members of supply chain. This wastage directly and indirectly contributes to the global environmental problems being faced by the world, inspite of several efforts by nations to achieve the 'circular economy'(herein after referred as CE) concept. A clear cut strategy by the members of supply chains across the world and by the policies and actions of business organizations, it is possible to transform the traditional supply chain to 'smart supply chain' to achieve the CE by taking advantage of applications of digital technologies. This chapter explores the concepts of supply chain resilience, role of digital technologies in the transformation of traditional supply to smart supply chain to achieve the concept of CE. The chapter develops a framework towards achieving CE through supply chain resilience with the help of digital technologies. Considering the above discussion, the study proposes the following objectives.

- To expand the knowledge of Supply Chain Resilience (SCR)
- To examine the practices leading to SCR and Circular Economy (CE)
- To analyze the role of digital technologies in enabling Smart Supply Chain
- To develop a framework of SCR by integrating digital technologies

The remaining sections of this chapter will delve with the aspects related to the above objectives.

*Achieving Supply Chain Resilience*

## BACKGROUND

### Supply Chain Resilience and Circular Economy

There have been many disruptions in the activities of SCM in the history. Natural disasters like volcano disruptions, earthquakes, hurricanes, cyclones, tsunamis, severe floods and medical disruptions due to SARS in 2003, bird flu in 2005, swine flu in 2009 and the present Covid-19 pandemic situations have impacted severely in the previous past. Despite their best of efforts to face these disruptions, organizations are still not able to fully develop strategies to quickly counter the disruptions. This is due to the short-term policies of organizations and also due to lack of knowledge in designing strategies which can develop the abilities to achieve supply chain resilience and quickly recover from the negative impacts of disruptions. Covid-19 pandemic resulted in prolonged lockdowns, stoppage of flights among countries, hindrance to movement of cargo between the countries resulting in non-availability of products. All this resulted in increased research interest and focus among the research community to explore the strategies needed for developing abilities to achieve SCR (Henry and Ronald, 2018). Severity of disruption is sometimes so high that it can result into closure of organizations (Skipper and Hanna, 2009; Blackhurst et al., 2011). Therefore, it is essential to develop plans to manage supply chains to sustain from disruptions through SCR. Existing research focused on risk management plans to manage supply chains during disruptions (Lavastre et al., 2012; Pfohl, et al., 2010). However, severity of disruptions is going beyond the ability of strategies to manage them. This is compelling the organizations to focus on SCR (Bhamra et al., 2011; Mandal 2012).

This section highlights the concepts of SCR, definitions of SCR, strategies to achieve SCR, role of digital technologies to make traditional supply chain to smart supply chain and role of SCR and smart supply chain in achieving CE.

Many authors have opined that SCR has the ability to develop strategies to reduce the influence and impact of disruptions through supply chain redesign. This concept will focus on firms to quickly regain their original status after the disruption and minimizes the negative impact (Christopher and Peck, 2004; Knemeyer et al, 2009; Agigi et al., 2016). This concept refers to the proactive ability of an organization to get prepared for unpredictable and unanticipated disruptive event and enables it to regain its original position quickly (Juttner & Maklan 2011; Klibi & Martel 2012; Soni & Jain 2011).

In the wake of increased research interest in SCR, there has been an increase in the research contributions. Authors have focused on developing models and frameworks related to SCR (Christopher and Peck 2004; Peck 2003; Henry and Ronald, 2018). However, the approaches to achieve SCR are still not clear and this area remains to be nascent in terms of precisely concluding specific strategies and practices of supply chain (Knemeyer et al., 2009) and it requires further exploration (Wieland and Wallenburg, 2013; Hohenstein et al., 2015). Additionally, there is a necessity to study diverse aspects of supply chain contributing to SCR, leading to smart supply chains and in turn to CE in an integrated manner rather than studying them as a single entity (Hohenstien et al., 2015; Gorane and Ravikant 2016).

Many authors are of the opinion that SCM is a broad, diverse and cross-functional area. Practices, strategies and policies related to many other domains of business organizations influence SCM (Hariharan et al. 2019). Due to this, it is necessary that the strategies, policies and frameworks in SCM should be developed in an integrated manner rather than focusing on a single or specific perspective.

## Circular Economy

The concept of CE has been gaining importance due to the global issue of wastage resulting into environmental imbalance and damage. Technological growth, industrial revolution, and excess production in the existing traditional SCM has led to challenges to the humanity in terms of environmental pollution, biodegradation, deforestation, degeneration of natural resources of the plant, which resulted in social inequality (Deineko et al., 2019). The concept of circular economy enables the recycling of waste in a sustainable manner in which supply chain management plays a major role (De Souza, 2021; Lacy et al., 2020; Park et al., 2021). The unused and excess materials and items are re-used in the process of achieving circular economy instead of leaving them as wastage and ultimately damaging the environment (Daou et al., 2020; Kravchenko et al. 2020; Park et al., 2021).

It is also a way in which the production levels and utilization levels are aligned with each other to the maximum possible extent and thus it challenges the existing traditional models by moving towards a circular model (Rizos et al., 2016; Ivanov, 2020; Zaman et al, 2021).The circular economy focuses on sustaining the ecological balance by minimizing the mass consumption in the existing supply chain to responsible consumption (Weetman, 2017; Park et al., 2021). As supply chain management plays a major role in achieving the objectives of circular economy, it is also known as closed supply chain. The objectives of this closed supply chain are to minimize the waste in the supply chain processes by recycling the excess production or reusing the consumed production (Ellen MacArthur Foundation, 2019). This concept of circular economy has gained lot of momentum in the recent past due its ability to address the weaknesses in the existing traditional model (Deineko et al., 2019). Major reasons for weaknesses in the existing supply chainsare rapid growth of urban areas and lack of coordination and accurate information sharing among the stakeholders leading to the profit maximization concept and increasing the non-value added activities (Weetman, 2017). Due to these weaknesses, this existing model also contributes to the excess utilization and wastage of natural resources. Moreover, this model also focuses only on profit maximization and competition leading to excess production (WEF *et al.,* 2014). Another major drawback of this model is that it does not lead supply chain to achieve resilience.

The circular economy model can be achieved by focusing on two directions, forward and reverse of supply chain. Flow of products in the forward chain is closely monitored and the recovery and reuse of products is monitored in the reverse process (Wells & Seitz, 2005). This kind of monitoring leads to the in-supply chain and enables the system to achieve circular economy in which digital technologies play a major role (Mandal, 2012; Handfield, 2016; Govindan & Soleimani, 2017; Govindan et al., 2015; EMF-Ellen MacArthur Foundation, 2012).

Advancements in SCM related to other important aspects like reusability and recyclability of products, development of eco-friendly logistics and manufacturing systems, and usage of alternate environmentally friendly energy resources are yet to gain momentum (Angelis et al, 2018).These advancements in SCM will shift the focus of SCM from a traditional one to a futuristic, sustainable and the one leading towards achieving the objectives of what is known as circular economy (Genovese et al., 2017). Circular economy is an economic model which provides economic growth with a focus on green development to transform the present mass consumption to what is known as responsible consumption, in which supply chain management plays a major role (Weetman, 2017). The supply chain in circular economy is also known as 'closed supply chain'. This type of economy is supposed to reduce the waste, improve reuse and recyclability (Deineko et al., 2019). The circular economy has seen a significant increase in interest

*Achieving Supply Chain Resilience*

by the researchers and practitioners over the past few years and is continuing to gain steady momentum (EMF. 2019)

Traditional SCM is also considered as an approach based on the linear flow of materials and fails to include both environmental aspects and management of the end-of-life phase of products (Sarkis et al., 2011). Thus, the concepts of reverse supply chains, closed supply chain, green and sustainable supply chains have emerged which have the ability to deal with the accumulation of waste and provide an appropriate methodology to minimize the waste (Junjun Liu et al., 2018) and contribute towards circular economy (EMF, 2019).

The weaknesses of traditional supply chains without much focus on reuse and reduce of waste also contributed to the evolution of concept of circular economy (Deineko et al., 2019). Increasing urbanization, rising inequality and political upheaval are also some other reasons. The traditional supply chain in many business enterprises works on the principle of profit maximization, leakage of value, excessive usage of raw material, and finally selling the products in high volumes (Weetman, 2017). This leads to the wastage of many natural resources like water, energy, land and finally causes harm to the environment. The linear operating models in economy and supply chain management also face challenges like expansion of middle class consumers, regulatory restrictions, and unprecedented competition. These challenges have become a threat to the sustainability of linear models in economy and supply chain management (WEF *et al.,* 2014). Supply chain management has evolved from linear model to sustainable supply chain to green supply chain to presently the closed loop or circular supply chain (Ferreira et al., 2017; Weetman, 2017; Angelis et al., 2018).

Seven SC practices (SCPs) such as strategic supplier partnership, level and quality of information sharing, customer relationship management, internal lean practices, postponement, and total quality management are identified to be the major contributors for the achievement of smart supply chain and circular economy (Al-Shboul et al., 2017). The objectives of circular economy are considered as reduce, reuse, recover and redesign (Weetman, 2017). In addition to these SCPs, there are many other practices, which have the ability to lead to smart SC and CE.

These other practices are,

- diversified geographical sourcing,strategic supplier partnership (Ramakrishna 2018),
- information sharing and cooperative relationships (Wieland and Wallenburg 2013),
- sharing trusted transaction and tracking data (Ali et al. 2016; Min, 2019),
- firm innovation (Sima and Mahour, 2020),
- flexibility, redundancy, visibility (Skipper and Hanna, 2009; Scholten and Schilder 2015; Dubey et al. 2019),
- SC Ambidexterity (Thillairaja and Lawrence, 2019),
- achievement of agility and robustness through communication, cooperation and integration (Wieland and Wallenburg 2013),
- re-engineering, agility, collaboration, and development of SC risk management culture (Nadeesha et al., 2019) and SC responsiveness.

To achieve success through the implementation of SCPs, top management commitment and dynamic leadership is essential. A non-hierarchical organizational structure with minimum number of layers, employee autonomy, and a transparent reward system such as positive feedback, recognition and employee growth consists of dynamic leadership (Becky, 2015). Similarly, it is opined that SC leaders should combine their technical skills and cross-functional business knowledge with collaboration and communication skills to enable the transformation of traditional SC towards technology-based smart SC. Implementing a sweeping organizational cultural change and development of talent in SC are highly essential requirements of SC leadership (Kevin, 2018). Analysis of literature in SCM and SCR area indicate that there is a scarcity for such an integrated framework by using the digital technologies as enabler.

The present chapter addresses this gap. The chapter intends to fill the existing body of knowledge and address the issue of developing an integrated framework of SCR, smart SC to achieve CE through the mediating role of digital technologies as enablers.

## MAIN FOCUS OF THE CHAPTER

### Issues, Controversies and Problems

As discussed in the previous sections, the main focus of this chapter is to expand the knowledge of SCR by studying the existing practices of SCM and to identify and analyze the strategies leading to SCR. Also, the study attempts to critically review the traditional SCM, its philosophies, theories and the gaps in it which lead to the accumulation of wastage, excess production and the resulting environmental issues. The study then explores the SC and digital technologies practices leading to the development of capabilities required for transforming this existing traditional SCM towards a vibrant, dynamic, agile, flexible, resilient and sustainable 'smart supply chain'. The role of this smart supply chain is studies towards attaining the goals of a circular economy. At the same time, the ability of digital technologies in this transformation from 'traditional' to 'smart' supply chain is examined to develop an integrated framework.

The methodology adopted for this study is a Systematic Literature Review (SLR). Research studies published in leading Scopus indexed journals in popular databases like ProQuest and EBSCO have been considered for review. In the initial attempt to collect the articles, key words such as supply chain management, resilience, supply chain resilience, supply chain practices, supply chain strategies, digital technologies, smart supply chain and circular economy were used. During the first phase of screening, articles which dealt purely on SCM concepts were ignored as they do not match the objectives of this study. To collect more relevant articles, the key words were refined and the second phase of collection of articles resulted in some more appropriate articles. Key words such as 'circular economy', 'closed loop', 'sustainable supply chains', 'reverse logistics', 'green supply chain' were used in the second phase of collection of articles. All articles published during 2000 to 2021 have been considered for this study. Articles which mentioned only about digital technologies without applying them to SCR were also ignored. Finally, all the articles which dealt with SCM, SCR, digital technologies, smart supply chain and circular in an integrated manner were also considered. Based on this SLR, the present study developed an integrated framework as mentioned above.

The broad nature of SCM is initially discussed in this section to explore it further to the concept of SCR. Among many other definitions provided by several authors, the most popular definition of SCM given by Council of Supply Chain Management Professionals (CSCMP, 2020) is considered for the purpose of this study. CSCMP defines it as a process which encompasses the planning and management of all activities involved in sourcing and procurement, conversion, and all logistics management activities. Importantly, it also includes coordination and collaboration with channel partners, which can be sup-

*Achieving Supply Chain Resilience*

pliers, intermediaries, third party service providers, and customers. In essence, SCM integrates supply and demand management within and across companies (Scholten and Schilder, 2015).

The above definition clearly indicates that the concept of SCM is very broad by its scope and its activities percolate and depend on the activities in many other fields of an organization. This calls for a broader approach and focus by the organizations while dealing with decisions related to SCM. This broad scope of SCM has become much broader due to globalization, wide network of supply chain, presence of stakeholders of supply chain in various parts of the world and e-commerce and e-business platforms. SC managers need to understand its complex structure, diverse set of legal issues and policies of different countries, diverse buying habits of customers, diverse cultures, diverse geographical climates and regional restrictions. This complexity and diversity also requires the managers to understand, predict and manage the risks and disruptions involved in SCM and their influence on the overall business operations and outcomes (Li et al. 2017; Timothy et al. 2019). The influence of these risks and disruptions is more intense during pandemic situations like Covid-19 and also during many other external disruptions like earthquakes, sandstorms, volcano disruptions, hurricanes, and fire accidents, local strikes by workers, cyclones and tsunamis (Blackhurst et al. 2011; Manhart et al., 2020). Therefore, there is a need to conduct an in-depth research to study the strategies and practices of facing these disruptions on SCM and how to achieve SCR by developing a systematic risk management plan. However, an analysis of existing set of studies reveals that the number of studies conducted focusing on this area is very limited and there is a huge scope for future study.

## SOLUTIONS AND RECOMMENDATIONS

In order to address the problems, issues and challenges addressed in the previous sections, it is recommended that the existing traditional SCM should be redesigned to achieve what is known as 'smart supply chain' with the help of digital technologies to achieve SCR and to achieve the objectives of circular economy. Disruptions in supply chain activities and processes are also termed by many authors as supply chain risks. Therefore, before focusing on the solutions and recommendations, a brief overview of SC risks has been provided here.

SC risk is defined as the degree of impact on the outcomes of SC goals or objectives due to the disturbance or disruptions whether external or internal in the activities of SC (Speier et al. 2011). It is also defined as any kind of risk in the smooth flow of information, raw material, and product from the original suppliers to the delivery of final product (Christopher and Holweg, 2011). SC risk management is a process of identification, prediction, and management of all types of risks through a systematic, coordinated and process-oriented approach among the members of SC (Juttner and Maklan, 2011) to ensure profitability and continuity of supply chain and to achieve efficiency and effectiveness.This kind of process improves the agility of the chain (Wieland and Wallenburg, 2013) and enables business organizations to be ready to face the risks, react quickly in case of occurrence of risks and recover in a speedy manner with minimal or no damage to the existing system of SC (Ponomarov and Holcomb 2009). Majority of the organizations have incurred losses during the Covid-19 pandemic situation as they were not ready with such SC risk management plan.

As discussed in the previous sections, implementation of SCM, implementation of SC Practices using digital technologies to achieve smart supply chain has the potential ability to achieve circular economy. In order to explore more about digital technologies, this section focuses on various types of digital

*Achieving Supply Chain Resilience*

technologies and how they would able to transform traditional supply chains to smart supply chains and pave way for the achievement of objectives of circular economy in long run.

## Digital Technologies and Smart Supply Chain

Application of digital technologies is found to improve the efficiency of supply chains in all sectors and prepares the organizations to tackle the disruptions effectively. These technologies such as information and communications technology (ICT), big data analytics (Wang et al. 2016; Fosso et al 2017; Wamba et al. 2017; Papadopoulos et al., 2017; Gunasekaran et al., 2018; Lai et al, 2018), block chain technologies (Kshetri 2018; Litke et al., 2019; Min, 2019, Hasselgren et al. 2020),cloud computing, internet of things (IoT) (Chui et al., 2010), artificial intelligence (Ali et al. 2016; BCI, 2019; Min, 2019), and Digital Supply Chain Twin, 3D printing and robotics (Ivanov and Dolgui, 2020) have the ability to transform the traditional, linear supply chains to smarter and agile supply chains. They also increase the speed of flows in the supply chains and improve the product availability, customer satisfaction and reduce the overall costs. The supply chain managed through the usage of digital technologies and big data analytics (Papadopoulos et al., 2017; Gunasekaran et al., 2018; Lai et al., 2018), sometimes also known as supply chain analytics is going to transform the existing traditional and linear supply to 'smart supply chain'. In the digital era supply chain is known as 'Smart Supply Chain' (Jeble et al 2018). Wide variety of processes and functions of supply chain such as process and product design, SC network, sourcing and procurement, manufacturing, storing and warehousing, distribution and transportation, and finally the product availability at the point of sale generate huge amounts of data. With the help of these technological devices, which are inter-connected, collaboration and information sharing among the SC members is improved, visibility is increased, real-time response is developed and supply-demand gap is minimized and finally resilience is developed (Papadopoulos et al. 2017; Dubey et al. 2019; Min 2019).

They also have the ability to capture, store, analyze, and interpret large amounts of information to predict the risks and disruptions to a reasonably acceptable levels. This ability helps the organizations to plan and react quickly with minimum damage to their supply chain processes. Also, they develop the SCR abilities and contribute towards CE. Integrating big data analytics (BDA) in SCM processes enables the organizations to make effective decision-making and a possible reduction of costs (Arunachalam et al., 2017; Gunasekaran et al 2017; Winarsih et al 2020).

BDA also helps in the preparation of all types of schedules related to sourcing and production. It develops an organization's ability to share information quickly and accurately, helps in the preparation of risk mitigation strategies and paves way for redesigning linear supply chains towards smarter supply chains (Wamba et al. 2017). These abilities also contribute to the achievement of objectives to circular economy such as reusability, redesign and recover (Weetman, 2017; Deineko et al., 2019). Implementation of BDA improves preparedness of SC, develops alertness of SC and finally makes SC more agile. As a result of all these abilities, the SC managers will be able to accumulate, convert and reorganize resources to respond and adapt to changing business scenarios (Zhong et al., 2016).

The IoT is a network of hardware, software, devices, databases, objects, sensors, and systems, all working at the service of humanity. This technology is going to change the way supply chains are managed in future and the way business organizations execute their activities (McKinsey 2016). Many business organizations commenced implementation of these technologies as they understood their potential in developing capabilities related to SCR. By improving abilities like SC flexibility and agility, organizations can monitor real time information, track data related to many SC activities and processes (Timothy et al. 2019; Resilinc 2018).

One of the important and emerging technology among the supply chain related digital technologies is the application of block chain technology (Litke et al., 2019). It has become very popular due to its transparency and applicability for all types of industrial sectors in addition to financial sector (Tapscott and Tapscott, 2018, Kshetri, 2018). This technology also enables faster and accurate information sharing and data security, which are essential and highly significant requirements in supply chain processes (Khanfar et al. 2021). Inspite of its benefits, the implementation of block chain technology is yet to gain popularity among the businesses due to lack of awareness and skepticism. Top managements of several business organizations are not yet clear about which digital technologies would precisely enable the achievement of 'smart supply chains' leading to resilience and circular economy. Moreover, they face many challenges and issues in its implementation (Saberi et al. 2019). Internet of things (IOT) is another variety of digital technology used prominently in supply chains. Usage of IOT is found to be very useful in mitigating the disruptions in supply chain and increase the visibility, flexibility, collaboration and control to achieve SC resilience (Mandal, 2012; Al-Talib, 2020).

Based on the above discussions, an integrated framework is developed by linking supply chain practices (SCPs) and SCR to achieve the objectives of CE through digital technologies.

*Figure 1. An integrated framework of SCR and CE*
*(Source: Developed by the author)*

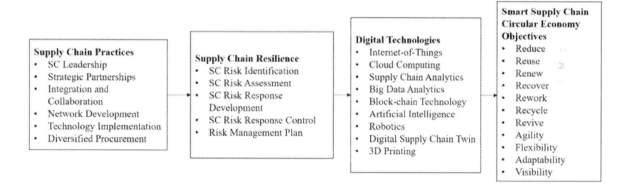

## DISCUSSION AND RESULTS

### Integrated Framework of SCR and CE

The above framework (Figure 1) is developed based on the discussions and analysis of published works in the previous sections. Major SCPs considered for the purpose of this framework are SC leadership, strategic partnerships, Integration and Collaboration, network development, technology implementation and diversified procurement. Implementation of these SCPs leads to the achievement of SCR.

Achievement of Supply Chain Resilience through the support of digital technologies leads to smart supply chain and circular economy. Organizations, which proactively implement the processes related to supply chain risk identification, assessment, risk response development, control and finally a well-structured risk management plan, will be able to achieve SCR. However, in the traditional supply chain processes, the usage and application of digital technologies were found to be limited. While the usage of these technologies, as discussed in the previous sections transforms the traditional SCM into a Smart SCM.

A business organization is said to be in the direction of achieving SCR when it has proactive processes to identify, assess, respond, control risks by developing a risk management plan. The shift from traditional supply chain to smart supply chain enables the organizations to achieve the objectives such as reduce, reuse, renew, recover, rework, recycle and revive. Achievement of these objectives through the implementation of supply chain practices with the support of digital technologies fills some of the most important gaps in the existing traditional supply chains. Most importantly, smart supply chain reduces the excess inventory and minimizes the waste in the entire supply chain system. This is achieved through accurate information sharing using the technology. Suppliers, manufacturers, distributors and retailers will be able to stock right levels of inventory and make right decisions related to re-orders of inventory. This improves the decision-making ability of all the stakeholders in supply chain and the entire system moves towards achieving a right balance between supply and demand. Moreover, information sharing also improves the supply chain coordination, integration and cooperation among the stakeholders. The major drawback of traditional supply chain is lack of these aspects, which leads to wastage and defeating the purpose and objectives of resilience and circular economy. Therefore, the role of digital technologies is highly significant in this process of supply chain to improve the information sharing and reduction of wastage.

Digital technologies such as BDA, block chain technologies, cloud computing, internet of things, artificial intelligence digital supply chain twin, 3D printing and robotics have the ability to transform the traditional, linear supply chains to smarter and agile supply chains.

The framework links SCPs and SCR through the implementation of digital technologies. This integration leads to the overall objectives of developing a smart supply chain and the achievement of objectives of circular economy.

## FUTURE RESEARCH DIRECTIONS AND IMPLICATIONS

The outcome of this research is significantly useful from two perspectives. The first one is from the industry and the second one is from the academic perspective. The above framework is highly useful to the practitioners of supply chain. On the other side, it opens up new vistas of research for academic researchers.

## CONCLUSION

Implementation of digital technologies is going to change the future of supply chain. It is going to bring sweeping changes in the manner supply chain processes are managed in future.

It is also concluded that the implementation of digital technologies in managing supply chains would reduce the overall cost of supply chain and increase its efficiency, flow, and speed and product availability.

## REFERENCES

Agigi, A., Niemann, W., & Kotzé, T. (2016). Supply chain design approaches for supply chain resilience: A qualitative study of South African fast-moving consumer goods grocery manufacturers. *Journal of Transport and Supply Chain Management*, *10*(1), a253. doi:10.4102/jtscm.v10i1.253

Al-Shboul, M. A. R., Barber, K. D., Jose, A. G., Kumar, V., & Abdi, M. R. (2017). The effect of supply chain management practices on supply chain and manufacturing firms' performance. *Journal of Manufacturing Technology Management*, *28*(5), 577–609. doi:10.1108/JMTM-11-2016-0154

Al-Talib, M., Melhem, W. Y., Anosike, A. I., Garza Reyes, J. A., Nadeem, S. P., & Kumar, A. (2020). Achieving resilience in the supply chain by applying IoT technology. *Procedia CIRP*, *91*(91), 752–757. doi:10.1016/j.procir.2020.02.231

Ali, M., Nelson, J. C., Shea, R., & Freedman, M. J. (2016). Blockstack: A Global Naming and Storage System Secured by Blockchains. *Proceedings of the 2016 USENIX Annual Technical Conference (USENIX ATC '16)*, 181–94.

Angelis, R. D., Howard, M., & Miemczyk, J. (2018). Supply chain management and the circular economy: Towards the circular supply chain. *Production Planning and Control*, *29*(6), 425–437. doi:10.1080/09537287.2018.1449244

Arunachalam, D., Kumar, N., & Kawalek, J. P. (2017). Understanding big data analytics capabilities in supply chain management: Unravelling the issues, challenges and implications for practice. *Transportation Research Part E, Logistics and Transportation Review*. Advance online publication. doi:10.1016/j.tre.2017.04.001

BCI. (2019). *Supply chain resilience report*. https://insider.zurich.co.uk/app/uploads/2019/11/BCISupplyChainResilienceReportOctober2019SingleLow1.pdf

Bhamra, R., Dani, S., & Burnard, K. (2011). Resilience: The concept, a literature review and future directions. *International Journal of Production Research*, *49*(18), 5375–5393. doi:10.1080/00207543.2011.563826

Blackhurst, J., Dunn, K. S., & Craighead, C. W. (2011). An empirically derived framework of global supply resiliency. *Journal of Business Logistics*, *32*(4), 374–391. doi:10.1111/j.0000-0000.2011.01032.x

Christopher, M., & Holweg, M. (2011). Supply Chain 2.0: Managing supply chains in the era of turbulence. *International Journal of Physical Distribution & Logistics Management*, *41*(1), 63–82. doi:10.1108/09600031111101439

Christopher, M., & Peck, H. (2004). Building the resilient supply chain. *International Journal of Logistics Management*, *15*(2), 1–13. doi:10.1108/09574090410700275

Chui, M., Loffler, M., & Roberts, R. (2010). The internet of things. *The McKinsey Quarterly*, *2*, 1–9.

CSCMP. (2020). *Council of Supply Chain Management Professionals*. www.cscmp.org

Daou, A., Mallat, C., Chammas, G., Cerantola, N., Kayed, S., & Saliba, N. A. (2020). The Ecocanvas as a business model canvas for a circular economy. *Journal of Cleaner Production, 258*, 120938. doi:10.1016/j.jclepro.2020.120938

De Souza, M., Pereira, G. M., de Sousa Jabbour, A. B. L., Jabbour, C. J. C., Trento, L. R., Borchardt, M., & Zvirtes, L. (2021). A digitally enabled circular economy for mitigating food waste: Understanding innovative marketing strategies in the context of an emerging economy. *Technological Forecasting and Social Change, 173*, 121062. doi:10.1016/j.techfore.2021.121062

Deineko, L., Tsyplitska, O., & Deineko, O. (2019). Opportunities and barriers of the Ukrainian industry transition to the circular economy. *Environment and Ecology, 10*(1), 79–92. doi:10.21511/ee.10(1).2019.06

Dubey, R., Gunasekaran, A., Childe, S. J., Wamba, F., Roubaud, S., & Foropon, C. (2019). Empirical investigation of data analytics capability and organizational flexibility as complements to supply chain resilience. *International Journal of Production Research, 59*(1), 110–128. doi:10.1080/00207543.2019.1582820

EMF (Ellen MacArthur Foundation) & McKinsey & Co. (2019). *Towards the Circular Economy: Economic and Business Rationale for an Accelerated Transition.* Accessed on 15[th]July 2021 from https://www.ellenmacarthurfoundation.org/business/reports

Ferreira, M. A., Jabbour, C. J. C., & Jabbour, A. B. L. S. (2017). Maturity levels of material cycles and waste management in a context of green supply chain management: An innovative framework and its application to Brazilian cases. *Journal of Material Cycles and Waste Management, 19*(1), 516–525. doi:10.100710163-015-0416-5

Fosso, W. S., Gunasekaran, A., Akter, S., Ren, S. J. F., Dubey, R., & Childe, S. J. (2017). Big data analytics and firm performance: Effects of dynamic capabilities. *Journal of Business Research, 70*, 356–365. doi:10.1016/j.jbusres.2016.08.009

Genovese, A., Acquaye, A. A., Figueroa, A., & Koh, S. L. (2017). Sustainable supply chain management and the transition towards a circular economy: Evidence and some applications. *Omega, 66*, 344–357. doi:10.1016/j.omega.2015.05.015

Gorane, S. J., & Kant, R. (2016). Supply chain practices: An implementation status in Indian manufacturing organizations. *Benchmarking, 23*(5), 1076–1110. doi:10.1108/BIJ-06-2014-0059

Govindan, K., & Soleimani, H. (2017). A review of reverse logistics and closed-loop supply chains: A journal of cleaner production focus. *Journal of Cleaner Production, 142*(Part 1), 371–384. doi:10.1016/j.jclepro.2016.03.126

Govindan, K., Soleimani, H. & Kannan, D. (2015).Reverse logistics and closed-loop supply chain:a comprehensive review to explore the future. *European Journal of OperationalResearch, 240*(3), 603-626. doi:10.1016/j.ejor.2014.07.012

Gunasekaran, A., Papadopoulos, T., Dubey, R., Wamba, S. F., Childe, S. J., Hazen, B., & Akter, S. (2017). Big data and predictive analytics for supply chain and organizational performance. *Journal of Business Research, 70*, 308–317. doi:10.1016/j.jbusres.2016.08.004

*Achieving Supply Chain Resilience*

Handfield, R. (2016). Preparing for the Era of the Digitally Transparent Supply Chain: A Call to Research in a New Kind of Journal. *Logistics, 1*(2), 2. Advance online publication. doi:10.3390/logistics1010002

Hariharan, G., Suresh, G. P., & Sagunthala, C. (2019). Critical Success Factors for the Implementation of Supply Chain Management in SMEs. *International Journal of Recent Technology and Engineering, 7*(5S3), 540-543.

Henry A, and Ronald S. M (2018). Supply chain resilience: a dynamic and multidimensional approach. *The International Journal of Logistics Management.* doi:10.1108/IJLM-04-2017-0093

Hohenstein, N.-O., Feisal, E., Hartmann, E., & Giunipero, L. (2015). Research on the phenomenon of supply chain resilience: A systematic review and parts for further investigation. *International Journal of Physical Distribution & Logistics Management, 45*(1/2), 90–117. doi:10.1108/IJPDLM-05-2013-0128

Ivanov, D. (2020). Viable supply chain model: Integrating agility, resilience and sustainability perspectives—lessons from and thinking beyond the COVID-19 pandemic. *Annals of Operations Research.* Advance online publication. doi:10.100710479-020-03640-6 PMID:32836614

Ivanov, D., & Dolgui, A. (2020). A digital supply chain twin for managing the disruption risks and resilience in the era of Industry 4.0. *Production Planning and Control*, 1–14. doi:10.1080/09537287.2020.1768450

Jeble, S., Dubey, R., Childe, S. J., Papadopoulos, T., Roubaud, D., & Prakash, A. (2018). Impact of big data and predictive analytics capability on supply chain sustainability. *International Journal of Logistics Management, 29*(2), 513–538. doi:10.1108/IJLM-05-2017-0134

Juttner, U., & Maklan, S. (2011). Supply chain resilience in the global financial crisis: An empirical study. *Supply Chain Management, 16*(4), 246–259. doi:10.1108/13598541111139062

Khanfar, A. A. A., Iranmanesh, M., Ghobakhloo, M., Senali, M. G., & Fathi, M. (2021). Applications of Block chain Technology in Sustainable Manufacturing and Supply Chain Management: A Systematic Review. *Sustainability, 13*(14), 7870. doi:10.3390u13147870

Klibi, W., & Martel, A. (2012). Modeling approaches for the design of resilient supply networks under disruptions. *International Journal of Production Economics, 135*(2), 882–898. doi:10.1016/j.ijpe.2011.10.028

Knemeyer, A. M., Zinn, W., & Eroglu, C. (2009). Proactive planning for catastrophic events in supply chains. *Journal of Operations Management, 27*(2), 141–153. doi:10.1016/j.jom.2008.06.002

Kravchenko, M., Pigosso, D. C., & McAloone, T. C. (2020). Circular economy enabled by additive manufacturing: Potential opportunities and key sustainability aspects. *DS 101: Proceedings of Nord-Design 2020*, 1-14. 10.35199/NORDDESIGN2020.4

Kshetri, N. (2018). Blockchain's roles in meeting key supply chain management objectives. *International Journal of Information Management, 39*, 80–89. doi:10.1016/j.ijinfomgt.2017.12.005

Lacy, P., Long, J., & Spindler, W. (2020). Disruptive Technologies. In The Circular Economy Handbook (pp. 43-71). Palgrave Macmillan. doi:10.1057/978-1-349-95968-6_3

Lai, Y., Sun, H., & Ren, J. (2018). Understanding the determinants of big data analytics (BDA) adoption in logistics and supply chain management: An empirical investigation. *International Journal of Logistics Management, 29*(2), 676–703. doi:10.1108/IJLM-06-2017-0153

Lavastre, O., Gunasekaran, A., & Spalanzani, A. (2012). Supply chain risk management in French companies. *Decision Support Systems, 52*(4), 828–838. doi:10.1016/j.dss.2011.11.017

Li, X., Wu, Q., Holsapple, C. W., & Goldsby, T. (2017). An empirical examination of firm financial performance along dimensions of supply chain resilience. *Management Research Review, 40*(3), 254–269. doi:10.1108/MRR-02-2016-0030

Litke, A., Anagnostopoulos, D., & Varvarigou, T. (2019). Blockchains for Supply Chain Management: Architectural Elements and Challenges towards a Global Scale Deployment. *Logistics, 3*(1), 5. doi:10.3390/logistics3010005

Liu, J., Feng, Y., Zhu, Q., & Sarkis, J. (2018). Green supply chain management and the circular Economy-Reviewing theory for advancement of both fields. *International Journal of Physical Distribution & Logistics Management, 48*(8), 794–817. doi:10.1108/IJPDLM-01-2017-0049

Mandal, S. (2012). An empirical investigation into supply chain resilience. *The IUP Journal of Supply Chain Management, 9*(4), 46–61.

Manhart, P., Summers, J. K., & Blackhurst, J. (2020). A Meta Analytic Review of Supply Chain Risk Management: Assessing Buffering and Bridging Strategies and Firm Performance. *The Journal of Supply Chain Management, 56*(3), 66–87. doi:10.1111/jscm.12219

McKinsey & Company. (2016). *Big Data and the Supply Chain: The big supply chain analytics landscape.* Author.

Min, H. (2019). Blockchain technology for enhancing supply chain resilience. *Business Horizons, 62*(1), 35–45. doi:10.1016/j.bushor.2018.08.012

Nadeesha, A., Haijun, W., & Duminda, K. (2019). Effect of supply-chain resilience on firm performance and competitive advantage - A study of the Sri Lankan apparel industry. *Business Process Management Journal, 25*(7), 1673–1695. doi:10.1108/BPMJ-09-2018-0241

O'Marah. (2018). Lessons in Excellence from Five Supply Chain Leaders, SCM world learning engine. *SCM World.* https://www.forbes.com/sites/kevinomarah/2018/05/30/lessons-in-excellence-from-five-supply-chain-leaders/#403559551545

Papadopoulos, T., Gunasekaran, A., Dubey, R., Altay, N., Childe, S. J., & Fosso-Wamba, S. (2017). The role of big data in explaining disaster resilience in supply chains for sustainability. *Journal of Cleaner Production, 142*, 1108–1118. doi:10.1016/j.jclepro.2016.03.059

Park, Y. W., Blackhurst, J., Paul, C., & Scheibe, K. P. (2021). An analysis of the ripple effect for disruptions occurring in circular flows of a supply chain network. *International Journal of Production Research*, 1–19. doi:10.1080/00207543.2021.1934745

Partida, B. (2019). Using Dynamic Leadership to Prepare for the Future. *Supply Chain Management Review.* https://www.scmr.com/article/using_dynamic_leadership_to_prepare_for_the_future

*Achieving Supply Chain Resilience*

Peck, H. (2003). *Creating resilient supply chains: A practical guide.* Centre for Logistics and Supply Chain Management. http://www.som.cranfield.ac.uk/som/dinamic-content/research/ lscm/download/57081_Report_AW.pdf

Pfohl, H., Köhler, H., & Thomas, D. (2010). State of the art in supply chain risk management research: Empirical and conceptual findings and a roadmap for the implementation in practice. *Logistics Research, 2*(1), 33–44. doi:10.100712159-010-0023-8

Ponomarov, S. Y., & Holcomb, M. C. (2009). Understanding the concept of supply chain resilience. *International Journal of Logistics, 20*(1), 124–143.

Ramakrishna, Y. (2018). Development of an integrated healthcare supply chain model. *Supply Chain Forum: An International Journal, 19*(2), 111-121. 10.1080/16258312.2018.1475823

Resilinc. (2018). *Event Watch AI – Monitoring Your Global Supply Chain Has Never Been So EASY.* Retrieved from https://www.resilinc.com/resilinc-eventwatch/)

Rizos, V., Tuokko, K., & Behrens, A. (2017). *The Circular Economy: A review of definitions, processes and impacts.* CEPS Papers, (12440).

Saberi, S., Kouhizadeh, M., Sarkis, J., & Shen, L. (2019). Blockchain technology and its relationships to sustainable supply chain management. *International Journal of Production Research, 57*(7), 2117–2135. doi:10.1080/00207543.2018.1533261

Sarkis, J., Zhu, Q., & Lai, K. H. (2011). An organizational theoretic review of green supply chain management literature. *International Journal of Production Economics, 130*(1), 1–15. doi:10.1016/j.ijpe.2010.11.010

Scholten, K., & Schilder, S. (2015). The role of collaboration in supply chain resilience. *Supply Chain Management, 20*(4), 471–484. doi:10.1108/SCM-11-2014-0386

Sima, S., & Mahour, M. P. (2020). Firm innovation and supply chain resilience: A dynamic capability perspective. *International Journal of Logistics Research and Application, 23*(3), 254–269. doi:10.108 0/13675567.2019.1683522

Skipper, J. B., & Hanna, J. B. (2009). Minimizing supply chain disruption risk through enhanced flexibility. *International Journal of Physical Distribution & Logistics Management, 39*(5), 404–427. doi:10.1108/09600030910973742

Soni, U., & Jain, V. (2011). Minimizing the vulnerabilities of supply chain: A new framework for enhancing the resilience. *Industrial Engineering and Engineering Management (IEEM), IEEE International Conference,* 933–939.

Speier, C., Judith, M., David, J. W., Closs, M., & Voss, D. (2011). Global supply chain design considerations: Mitigating product safety and security risks. *Journal of Operations Management, 29*(7-8), 721–736. doi:10.1016/j.jom.2011.06.003

Tapscott, D., & Tapscott, A. (2018). *Blockchain Revolution: How the Technology Behind Bitcoin and Other Cryptocurrencies Is Changing the World.* Penguin Random House.

Thillairaja, P., & Lawrence, A. (2019). The relationship between Supply Chain Resilience Elements and Organizational Performance: The Mediating Role of Supply Chain Ambidexterity. *Global Business and Management Research, 11*(1), 583–592.

Timothy, J. P., Keely, L. C., & Fiksel, J. (2019). The Evolution of Resilience in Supply Chain Management: A Retrospective on Ensuring Supply Chain Resilience. *Journal of Business Logistics, 40*(1), 56–65. doi:10.1111/jbl.12202

Wamba, S. F., Gunasekaran, A., Akter, S., Ren, S. J. F., Dubey, R., & Childe, S. J. (2017). Big data analytics and firm performance: Effects of dynamic capabilities. *Journal of Business Research, 70*(1), 356–365. doi:10.1016/j.jbusres.2016.08.009

Wang, G., Gunasekaran, A., Ngai, E. W., & Papadopoulos, T. (2016). Big data analytics in logistics and supply chain management: Certain investigations for research and applications. *International Journal of Production Economics, 176*(6), 98–110. doi:10.1016/j.ijpe.2016.03.014

Weetman, C. (2017). *A Supply Chain Revolution: How the Circular Economy Unlocks New Value.* KoganPage. https://www.koganpage.com/article/a-supply-chain-revolution-how-the-circular-economy-unlocks-new-value

WEF (World Economic Forum), EMF, & McKinsey & Company. (2014). *Towards the Circular Economy: Accelerating the scale-up across global supply chains.* Retrieved from https://ellenmacarthurfoundation.org/business/reports

Wells, P., & Seitz, M. (2005). Business Models and Closed-Loop SupplyChains: A Typology. *Supply Chain Management, 10*(4), 249–251. doi:10.1108/13598540510612712

Wieland, A., & Wallenburg, C. M. (2013). Dealing with supply chain risks: Linking risk management practices and strategies to performance. *International Journal of Physical Distribution & Logistics Management, 42*(10), 887–905. doi:10.1108/09600031211281411

Winarsih, I. M., & Fuad, K. (2021). Impact of Covid-19 on Digital Transformation and Sustainability in Small and Medium Enterprises (SMEs): A Conceptual Framework. In Complex, Intelligent and Software Intensive Systems. CISIS 2020. Advances in Intelligent Systems and Computing (vol. 1194). Springer. doi:10.1007/978-3-030-50454-0_48

Zaman, G., Radu, A. C., Răpan, I., & Berghea, F. (2021). New wave of disruptive technologies in the healthcare system. *Economic Computation and Economic Cybernetics Studies and Research, 55*(1).

Zhong, R. Y., Newman, S. T., Huang, G. Q., & Lan, S. (2016). Big data for supply chain management in the service and manufacturing sectors: Challenges, opportunities, and future perspectives. *Computers & Industrial Engineering, 101*(11), 572–591. doi:10.1016/j.cie.2016.07.013

## KEY TERMS AND DEFINITIONS

**Circular Economy:** An emerging model of economy, which focuses on a sustainable means of production and consumption in which existing materials retain their reusability value for as long as possible.

**Smart Supply Chain:** An opposite model of linear supply chain, which uses digital technologies. Supply chain analytics and big data to manage efficiently the supply chain processes towards sustainability and efficiency.

**Supply Chain Disruption:** It is an unexpected event, which can disrupt the entire supply chain process, flow and activities leading to disturbance in the business organization.

**Supply Chain Practice (SCP):** Any practice related to the management and implementation of supply chain in an organization, sector and industry, which enables product availability and provides value and satisfaction to the customer.

**Supply Chain Resilience:** The ability of an organization and an industry to regain quickly its previous business position after absorbing the supply chain disruption successfully.

**Supply Chain Risk:** It is any uncertain event, which has the ability to disrupt the supply chain activity of an organization

**Traditional/Linear Supply Chain:** An existing model of supply chain that emphasizes more on profit maximization, consumption and sales leading to wastage. This model doesn't focus on recyclability, reusability and renewal of products leading to sustainability and protection of environment.

# Chapter 2
# Proactive Change Management to Enhance Supply Chain Resilience

**Kavitha Reddy Gurrala**

https://orcid.org/0000-0001-7342-5817

*ESM Program, American University of Sharjah, UAE*

## ABSTRACT

*Modern supply chains (SC) are highly vulnerable to risks that evolve and cascade from internal or external disturbances. Additionally, resilience capabilities aid the SC to thrive against such challenges. Indeed, change management complements the resilience behaviour towards facing changes induced from SC disruptions and proactive change management strategies foster smooth transitions to facilitate faster recovery to steady-state conditions following future change events. Conversely, most SC employ a reactive approach to change management aiming at reducing the impact of disruptions already in place, consequently forcing the SC to instill, develop, and implement change capabilities in a chaotic fashion with reduced efficiency to infuse resilience capabilities for speedy and effective recovery from future disruptive events. Hence, an in-depth literature study is needed to leverage proactive change management processes for resilience enhancements within SC.*

## INTRODUCTION

A supply chain (SC) involves an intervened network of players including suppliers, producers, and distributors who aim at delivering the right products, in the right quantities, to the right locations at a right time in order to minimize the system-wide costs while meeting the service level requirements (Cutting-Decelle et al., 2007). Owing to globalization, raw material procurement, component assembly, product manufacturing, and distribution activities are spread across the globe. Thus, even minor disruptions arising from internal sources such as lack of integration, cultural differences, and infrastructure malfunctions or disruptions arising from external sources such as natural disasters, pandemic outbreaks, geo-political instabilities, regulatory changes, and currency fluctuations create a pronounced impact on

DOI: 10.4018/978-1-7998-9506-0.ch002

Copyright © 2022, IGI Global. Copying or distributing in print or electronic forms without written permission of IGI Global is prohibited.

the operational and financial standing of the supply chains due to the rippling/domino effects within the upstream or downstream counterparts.

However, to manage the increasing tendency of risks induced from internal and external disruptions, the supply chains need to develop capabilities towards providing and initiating innovative responses for their survival and continuity. Therefore, supply chains are in dire need to develop a capacity/capability termed as "resilience" that aids them to persist, adapt or transform to the changes imposed towards maintaining the basic identity/equilibrium of the systems in place (Ponomarov & Holcomb, 2009).

Further, resilience also defines the amount of change a supply chain can undergo while retaining the structural and functional controls in place (Barroso et al., 2015). On the other hand, change management provides the needful processes, tools, and techniques to manage the supply chain transitions efficiently. Thus, change management complements the resilience behaviour within the supply chains to bounce back from the adverse effects such as shocks and disruptions forced from the imposed changes and further to demonstrate capabilities essential for survival and continuity. Besides, process-oriented change management techniques stand fundamental towards enhancing resilience capabilities within the supply chains (Ates and Bititci, 2011). Nonetheless, such techniques are highly systematic and time-consuming.

Moreover, change management can be embraced through two different approaches, namely proactive and reactive approaches. A proactive approach is a planned and intentional process involving the alteration of existing systems to build resilience capabilities in anticipation of future disruptions. This approach not only facilitates avoidance of potential damages from future disruptions but also fosters capitalization on potential future opportunities. Further, it anticipates the needful changes and initiates response options in advance. On the other hand, a reactive approach tends to respond to changes imposed from a disruption already in place (Wong & Kwak, 2001). However, as the supply chains operate in an environment characterized by constant changes and uncertainties. It is highly desirable, that they accept the inevitability of change and develop advanced capabilities to adapt to new conditions and mandates.

Conversely, most of the supply chains across the globe opted for reactive measures towards survival within pandemic situations like Covid-19 sabotaging their normal functionality. Forcing them to develop and implement change capabilities in a turbulent fashion. Consequently, depriving the effectiveness of the change management processes to inculcate resilience capabilities towards speedy and efficient recovery from future disruptive events. In contrast, the adaptation of proactive change management strategies enabled Amazon, Amul, Terraboost, Uber Eats, etc., to not only survive against the devastating effects of the pandemic but also to develop capabilities for long-term resilience and growth. Besides, such strategies can also convene supply chains to perceive pandemic situations like Covid-19 as an opportunity to transform massive challenges into meaningful changes towards developing capabilities to resist future crisis/disruptions with similar dynamics, scope, and scale (Arora, 2020; Dereń & Skonieczny, 2021).

Based on the premises, the research study presents a structured and systematic review to comprehensively cover and investigate the available models, frameworks, and strategies relative to change management and resilient behaviour within supply chains.
Further, the broad objectives of this study include:

- Pinning down the key success factors and potential barriers towards managing and adapting changes for resilient capability enhancements.
- Providing a conceptual framework that employs proactive change management to foster resilient behaviour within supply chains.

## BACKGROUND AND LITERATURE REVIEW

### Supply Chain Environment and Resilient Behaviour

The supply chain environment represents an integrated system of organizations, activities, information, and resources laid out to procure, manufacture, and distribute products from source to sink, i.e., from supplier to an end consumer. Further, as the supply chains tend to globalize with intervened networks and activities crisscrossing the globe. They are subjected to additional challenges towards maintaining international relationships and combating man-made or natural disruptions across the world. Besides, they also tend to become highly complex and volatile at the same time.

Additionally, global chains encounter volatility not only from shifts in demand, but also from multiple other sources such as the increase in product varieties, longer lead times, soar market competitions, growing product complexities, reduced inventory levels, stringent government regulations, new technology introductions, shorter product life-cycles, and raw material price fluctuations (Christopher and Holweg, 2011).

Thus, the supply chains are highly vulnerable to disruptions from both internal issues related to physical resources, logistic controls, information systems, and intra-organization structures that are supply chain specific or individual organization-specific and external issues related to financial, market, legal, infrastructural, societal, and environmental concerns (Stone et al., 2015). Further, the disruptions are inevitable by nature arising from the multi-tiered global configurations, forcing the supply chains to face constant challenges towards exhibiting abilities to reflect sustained performance outcomes. Moreover, these disruptions are characterized by highly unplanned and unanticipated events that interrupt the flow of materials and products forcing the supply chains to face operational and financial risks and further tend to result in subsequent shocks within the related networks due to ripple effects (Ivanov & Dolgui, 2021).

Therefore, supply chains must enhance their resilience behaviour to cope up with the adversities and deviations from the planned normal status quo and bounce back to functionality demonstrating capabilities for continual growth and survival. Thus, supply chains need to develop the capabilities and abilities to return to their original state or move to a more desirable state upon confrontation with disruptions.

Besides, this is only possible when supply chains tend to anticipate the sources, likelihood, and the severity of the disruptions in advance and take pro-active measures to implement the needful changes to avoid the disruptions in the first place or at least reduce the detrimental effects of the disruptions (Barroso et al., 2010). Thus, proactive change management strategies not only help the supply chains to survive against the devastating effects of the disruptions but also help them to develop capabilities for long-term resilience and growth.

### Pro-Active Change Management

According to the ancient Greek philosopher Heraclitus of Ephesus (530-470 BC), "The only thing that is constant is change". Equally, the philosopher highlighted the inevitability of change and the importance of going with the flow and enjoying the ride characterized by peaks, troughs, pits, and swirls (Kirk, 1951). Thus, supply chains need to accept the inevitability of change and embrace the changes positively making space for new opportunities and further learn to thrive the disruptions through planned transitions.

The changes within supply chains can be classified as planned and unplanned. Wherein, the planned changes are characterized with premeditated, agent-facilitated interventions aimed at modifying the supply

*Proactive Change Management to Enhance Supply Chain Resilience*

chain functionality towards a more favourable state. Further, planned initiatives accept the inevitability of change and thus foster the development of systems capable of adapting to new conditions and mandates. In contrast, unplanned changes are initiatives undertaken towards making adjustments for changes within regulations, natural events/calamities, geopolitical events, etc., These changes are often initiated after the event occurrence, thus they are reactive by nature (Greer & Ford, 2009). However, most of the supply chains invoke changes to evolve in response to business dynamics in a reactive fashion aiming only for survival, although embracing pro-active strategies facilitate continuous optimization towards a holistic development.

Further, reactive change management practices are highly traditional in nature and only aid with recovering from disruptions or events that have already occurred. Whereas, pro-active change management practices are quite evolved and are broader in perspective, as they anticipate and plan for the needful changes in advance that might help avoid or at least reduce the negative impacts of the potential future threats/disruptions and might as well aid with capitalizing on potential future opportunities (Jackson & Ferris, 2015).

Likewise, the name pro-active change management also characterizes actions (active-doing something) before (pro) a disruption occurs, thus aiding the supply chains to be prepared for future events/disruptions through enhancement of resilient capabilities. Consequently, supply chains need to foster a positive attitude towards needful changes through anticipation and purposeful planning. Hence, planned changes help supply chains to avoid being victims of change. Instead, aid the supply chains to become co-creators of needful changes towards enhancing resilient behaviour.

Besides, changes can be planned and programmed in advance to adapt to new conditions and mandates. In this regard, Bullock and Batten (1985) developed a change management model for implementing planned/programmed changes. The model was based on the ideas derived from the project management domain. Further, the model included 4-phases towards the realization of the desired/planned changes. The phases towards transformation included "Exploration", "Planning", "Action", and "Integration". Wherein, the exploration phase is focused on answering the questions "why", "what" and "how" related to the change. Additionally, the planning phase is focused on a detailed diagnosis of the problems to determine the goals, objectives, and specific activities to be pursued for the transformation. The output of the planning phase includes a change plan that is thoroughly reviewed, accepted, and fully supported by all the stakeholders. Further, the action phase is focused on enacting the change plan, monitoring and evaluating the desired changes, communication of results, and initiation of needful adjustments and refinements to reach the planned targets. Finally, the integration phase is focused on stabilizing and embedding the implemented changes towards alignment with strategic goals and objectives through some degree of formalization, such as policies and procedures.

Similarly, Jeffery Hiatt, founder of Prosci developed a change model titled ADKAR (Hiatt, 2006). The model is highly perspective by nature, as it is result-oriented determining the essential elements for successful change implementation. Thus, it defines a road map for transformation in advance to drive action. Further, the model is built on five sequential building blocks to embrace the needful changes. The entire model is aimed at building trust to embed changes in a faster and steady fashion through setting clear milestones throughout the process. The building blocks include, "Awareness", "Desire", "Knowledge", "Ability" and "Reinforcement" to help prepare, manage and reinforce changes. Firstly, awareness relates to understanding the nature of the change, the need for the change, and further understanding the risks involved with ignoring the needful changes. The second step involves fostering the desire to change by listing out the benefits of change to all the stakeholders through effective leadership practices. The third step concentrates on providing the stakeholders the needed knowledge towards understanding how to pursue the needful changes. Consequently, the fourth step involves transforming the knowledge gained into capabilities and abilities to enact changes. Finally, reinforcement involves taking necessary steps to sustain the changes implemented. Additionally, the author also highlighted "Engagement", "Communication", "Culture", "Transparency", and "Complexity" as barriers for successful implementation of change projects.

In addition to the above models, that aid the supply chains to pursue changes in a planned/ proactive fashion. Olaf (2010) formulated a 4-C toolbox model for change management that lists out the important elements/drivers for implementing changes. The drivers/elements within the model include "Content", "Commitment", "Capabilities", and "Culture". Wherein, the content involves understanding the potential vulnerabilities within the supply chain through the identification of key sources of disruptions. It aids with understanding the underlying forces creating the symptoms. This involves an in-depth evaluation of supply chain performance and capabilities against goals and objectives defined for current and future survival. On the other hand, commitment relates to the willingness of the supply chain stakeholders to participate and embrace the needful changes towards reducing vulnerabilities and potential risks identified. Additionally, capabilities determine the supply chain competencies towards forecasting the needful changes and further the abilities to enact changes in a pro-active manner to perceive disruptions as opportunities for sustained growth. Further, culture lays out a strong foundation that fosters the implementation of the needful changes in a smooth and streamlined fashion.

Besides, Tajri & Chafi (2018) introduced a Supply Chain Operations Reference Model (SCOR Model) for implementing changes within the supply chains. According to the authors, the model divides the change implementation process into five phases. Wherein the first phase, concentrates on defining the supply chain processes, locating the problems, and further identifying opportunities for improvements within the processes. Subsequently, the second phase concentrates on identifying the root causes for the problems associated with the processes. Then, the third phase concentrates on examining and choosing the appropriate solution scenarios with abilities to resolve the identified problems at individual and holistic levels. Next, the fourth phase concentrates on documenting the target processes, technologies, organization structures considering the selected solution scenarios. Finally, the fifth phase concentrates on planning and initiating the change projects.

Additionally, Hoek et al. (2010) conducted a case study research to study the change implementations within three supply chains and defined capability and capacities as major constructs towards successfully implementing the planned changes. Similarly, Jindal (2013) emphasized the need for wholehearted support of all the stakeholders within the supply chains to facilitate the change implementation, as such changes don't happen in isolation and additionally impact the whole spectrum of the supply chain stakeholders. Moreover, the author indicated that culture stands out as the major determinant that facilitates wholehearted support of all the stakeholders within the supply chains. Further, the author also highlighted the importance of developing change systems to handle necessary adjustments relevant to the variations within the anticipated environmental parameters in order to derive the desired results from the change projects implemented.

However, the 2-C's "Capabilities" and "Culture" from the 4-C toolbox model stand out as dominant drivers towards embracing changes in a pro-active fashion. As they enable the supply chains to identify the key sources for disruptions and potential vulnerabilities (Content) and additionally facilitate trust enhancement between supply chain partners to work cohesively as a team through strategic long-term relationships (Commitment). Further, the capabilities and culture aid the supply chains to explore, plan,

*Proactive Change Management to Enhance Supply Chain Resilience*

act, and integrate towards successful implementation of the planned/programmed changes. Moreover, they also foster the supply chains to enhance the awareness, desire, knowledge, and abilities needed to prepare, manage and reinforce changes. Besides, they also promote engagement, communication, and transparency within the supply chains to help understand and manage the complexities.

Further, an in-depth diagnosis of the 2-C's "Capabilities" and "Culture" would help understand their significance, role, and importance towards positively embracing the changes as opportunities for balanced and healthy growth.

## Dynamic Knowledge Capabilities

Dynamic Knowledge Capabilities (DKC) result from the combination and reconfiguration of management processes developed over time through a learning routine allowing the supply chains to discern the environmental changes in order to adapt their activities in line with the needs recognized.

Further, DKC reflects the integration of expertise across the whole supply chain, built through the absorption of knowledge and best practices from the supply chain partners as a part of a continuous learning routine. Additionally, such capabilities are an outcome of the horizontal scanning activities that facilitate the identification of new trends and technological breakthroughs.

Besides, they are fostered through deliberate learning efforts, based on selection and retention of knowledge and new information over time. It also involves the knowledge from experiential learning. Additionally, the deliberate learning efforts help the supply chains to continuously transform the tangible and intangible assets towards remaining competent even within turbulent environments. Moreover, DKC is based on the principle of unlearning and relearning facilitating the old and outdated knowledge to be discarded, and fostering the acquisition and storage of new knowledge towards maximization of the innovation capabilities (Aslam et al., 2020a).

In addition, DKC drives effective usage of static capabilities towards the acquisition of knowledge through sensing, learning, integrating, and coordinating strategies and also facilitates the development and deployment of new reformed capabilities in line with the environmental requirements (Masteika & Čepinskis, 2015). Furthermore, DKC fosters capitalizing on past experiences to respond efficiently and effectively to future disturbances/turbulences.

Likewise, the DKC framework encompasses adaptive capability (ability to seize opportunities present within the environment), absorptive capability (ability to identify the value of new, external information towards assimilation/application and an ability to generate new knowledge and capabilities from the existing supply chain resources and capabilities), and innovative capability (ability to generate innovative outcomes) to aid the supply chains to constantly integrate, reconfigure, renew, and recreate its resources and capabilities towards upgrading and re-constructing its core capabilities in response to dynamic changes within the environments (Yao & Meurier, 2012).

Moreover, Sonar and Mankenzie (2018) developed dynamic models as an extension of the Wagner-Whitin dynamic lot-sizing model to convene proactive preparation for future disruptions. Consequently, the extended models facilitate the supply chains to enhance their dynamic capabilities towards the selection of an appropriate change strategy that minimizes the total cost of implementations.

Thus, the DKC fosters the supply chains to assess and anticipate the nature, magnitude, and impact of disruptive events in advance, so that system changes can be initiated in advance to efficiently respond to the disruptive events.

## Advanced Digital Capabilities

Advanced Digital Capabilities (ADC) are fostered through the implementation of data-driven, real-time monitoring and visibility systems within the supply chains, towards enhancing its transparency, and readiness. Besides, they are an amalgamation of information, computing, communication, and connectivity technologies facilitating change implementation in a pro-active fashion. Moreover, they are trans-functional by nature encompassing multiple supply chain functions enabling rich information exchange through digital platforms.

Further, they help transform data into real-time predictive insights to make informed decisions and also aid with the democratization of content convening subsequent sharing, re-mixing, re-distribution, and re-syndication of content in new and innovative formats. Additionally, the ADC are built through leveraging the digital competencies from the cloud, mobility, big data analytics, the internet of things (IoT), machine learning, robotics, and B2B networks, etc.,

Consequently, with the increased handiness and dependency on clod computing resources the supply chains are empowered with dynamic capabilities towards enhancing/reducing the infrastructure requirements promoting dynamic realignments of its supply chain partners, as the cloud-computing infrastructure enables the supply chains to access a shared pool of computing resources (Bharadwaj et al., 2013).

Likewise, Deloitte developed a digital capability model for supply networks based on the framework provided by Association for Supply Chain Management (ASCM). The model is structured around six capabilities, i.e., Synchronized Planning capabilities (SPC), Intelligent Supply capabilities (ISC), Smart Operations capabilities (SOC), Dynamic Fulfilment capabilities (DFC), Digital Development capabilities (DDC), and Connected Customer capabilities (CCC). Wherein, SPC fosters the integration of strategic goals, financial objectives, and tactical supply network plans into a connected, concurrent, and synchronized business plan facilitating the achievement of business strategies through the deployment of planning and operational levers across the whole chain. The ISC fosters the inclusion of automation and intelligence capabilities into the sourcing and procurement functions. The SOC fosters the adoption of digital and cognitive technologies within all aspects of production and operations across the supply chain. The DFC fosters the development of interconnected cross-enterprise systems through the application of leading practices, empowering technologies, and collaboration in order to enhance the customer experience. The DDC fosters the technology deployment towards the development of new product designs and models. Finally, the CCC fosters technology usage towards effective and integrated customer engagement. Further, the digital capability model serves as an important tool to help the supply chains articulate and build advanced digital capabilities in order to transform the linear networks within the supply chains into connected, intelligent, scalable, customizable, and active digital networks. In addition, the model strongly demonstrates the role of digital capabilities within the supply chains to leverage the digital threads in order to streamline process integrations between supply chain functional silos (Richard et al.,2020).

Similarly, Queiroz et al. (2021) developed a robust framework that integrates cutting-edge technologies i.e., Big data analytics, Blockchain, Artificial intelligence, Cloud computing, Cyber-physical systems, and the Internet of Things towards building ADC within the supply chains. The authors also highlighted that the cutting-edge technologies serve as enablers/building blocks towards the development and deployment of ADC within the supply chains.

Besides, such capabilities facilitate correct deployment of information processing and diffusion across the chain to thrive the disruptions through planned transitions (Nath, 2009).

## Collaborative Culture

Collaborative Culture (CC) relates to the transformation from efficient management of transactions between supply chain partners to enhanced relationship management towards promoting creativity and continuous improvements. Indeed, culture defines how an individual, firm, network of firms interacts with the outside world. Further, Kumar et al. (2016) developed a model to investigate collaborative culture and the role of relationship strengths within supply chains to highlight the idea of a shared culture that distinguishes collaboration from the traditional relationship constructs communication, integration, and cooperation. Besides, CC facilitates whole-hearted support from all the stakeholders within the supply chains to pursue the change implementations. Consequently, it determines the degree to which the partners intend to work as a team (trust), urge for relational continuity (commitment), facilitate joint decision making (digital synchronization), desire to share costs, risks, and benefits (incentive alignment), and acknowledge to share strategic and tactical data (information sharing).

Moreover, Han & Chu (2009) developed a framework titled CSCOR based on the SCOR model to enhance the collaborative culture within the supply chains. The framework encompasses a high-end strategic business model, a middle-end procedural model, and a low-end detailed model. Wherein the high-end model facilitates the planning of the five SC core processes. The middle-end model facilitates collaborations and interactions within the supply chain. Finally, the low-end model facilitates operational analysis and control. Moreover, the multi-leveled framework fosters integration between the partners to act as an extended enterprise with a mutual set of strategies/goals for survival.

As the supply chains are often bombarded with multi-faceted disruptions. A single entity within a supply chain stands incompetent towards facing the challenges imposed by itself. Hence, CC facilitates the supply chains to combat the challenges in cohesion. Further, alliances and partnerships between supply chain entities facilitate competency sharing towards the development of proactive change management/mitigation strategies to avoid or at least reduce the impact of future disruptions (Yunus, 2018).

Consequently, the knowledge capabilities, digital capabilities, and collaborative culture facilitate the supply chains to be prepared for future events/disruptions through anticipation and purposeful planning.

## POTENTIAL IMPACTS OF PRO-ACTIVE CHANGE MANAGEMENT AND FRAMEWORK FOR RESILIENCE ENHANCEMENT

Pro-active changes facilitated through "Dynamic Knowledge Capabilities", "Advanced Digital Capabilities" and "Collaborative Culture" enable the supply chains to orchestrate the needful transitions through pre-determined and well-planned strategies towards the realization of the desired goals and objectives. Additionally, they help the supply chains to think and act ahead to promote a sense of control over any future disruptions. Besides, such transitions help plan for the inevitable and thus enhance the momentum and commitment towards the needful changes. Likewise, the planned transitions enable continuous monitoring and measurement of change performance. Consequently, facilitate corrective action initiatives that leverage the capability and cultural assets towards sustaining and enhancing the supply chain performance. Moreover, they also foster Flexibility, Visibility, Alignment, Agility, and consequently Resilience enhancements within the supply chains.

## Flexibility Enhancements

Supply chain flexibility empowers the supply chain to utilize its resources efficiently and effectively towards responding to uncertainties and disruptions without additional costs, time, and performance losses. Further, a high degree of flexibility can be achieved through pro-actively re-designing and re-configuring the products, processes, and networks within the supply chain and through establishing long-term strategic relationships with the trading partners.

In this regard, Duclos et al. (2003) developed a conceptual model for flexibility highlighting multiple components of flexibility within a supply chain. According to the authors, supply chains can be termed as strategically flexible, only if they can exhibit operations systems flexibility, market flexibility, logistics flexibility, supply flexibility, and information systems flexibility. Nonetheless, transitions initiated through DKC, ADC, and CC foster strategic flexibility within the supply chains, as such capabilities and cultural assets facilitate operations-reconfigurations, product-reconfigurations, logistics-reconfigurations, supply chain/network-reconfigurations, and information system assets/architecture-reconfigurations to be undertaken in a planned and pro-active manner towards positively embracing the changes. As the operations-reconfigurations provide the supply chains with the ability to synchronize the supply chain assets and operations in line with the demand changes. Similarly, the product-reconfigurations provide the supply chains with the ability to design new products or modify existing products in line with the market trends. Likewise, the logistics-reconfigurations provide the supply chains with the ability to cost-effectively receive and deliver products accommodating the changes within supply and customer locations. Equally, the supply chain/network-reconfigurations provide the supply chains with the ability to reconfigure the supply chain to balance the demand and supply requirements. Finally, the information system assets/architecture-reconfigurations provide the supply chains with the ability to align information system architectures in line with the changing information needs.

In addition, Stevenson & Spring (2007) characterized flexibility as a multi-dimensional concept, wherein the importance of flexibility elements varies based on the environmental challenges imposed. Further, the authors also indicated that the flexibility characteristic serves as a contingent resource without the need for demonstration at all times. Nevertheless, the DKC, ADC, and CC also demonstrate multi-dimensionality in line with the flexibility requirements and dimensions. Further, the capability and cultural assets can be aligned to anticipate and facilitate planned transitions within flexibility elements on a needed basis to respond to uncertain environments in both short-term and long-term, enhancing the micro and macro flexibilities within the supply chains. Additionally, a high degree of flexibility within dynamic conditions can be achieved when the pro-active changes are facilitated through the correct deployment of information processing and diffusion across the chain.

Similarly, Kumar & Shankar (2007), emphasized the importance of flexibility configurations within the supply chain activities towards facing environmental turbulences/disruptions. According to the authors, the flexibility configurations include range and response. Nonetheless, the capability and cultural assets enhance the range flexibility i.e., the extent to which the operations within a supply chain can be changed in advance, and additionally enhance the response flexibility i.e., the ease with which the operations within a supply chain can be changed in advance.

Thus, the planned transitions foster dynamic flexibility within the supply chains to rapidly respond, adapt, survive, and thrive through the disruptions sprouting from internal or external sources.

## Visibility Enhancements

Supply chain visibility empowers the supply chain to assess the state of its resources and the functioning of its activities in real-time. This supply chain characteristic is highly important for survival considering the increasing vertical complexity (increase in the number of tiers), horizontal complexity (increase in the number of members within each tier), and spatial complexity (increasing geographic distances between supply chain partners) impeding the panoramic view of flows, activities, processes, and resources across the chain.

According to Messina et al. (2018), the degree of visibility refers to the types and properties of the information shared between the supply chain partners to convene decision coordination, promptness, and effectiveness. Wherein the types of information correlate to internal information and external information and the properties of information correlate to the quantity and quality i.e., timeliness & accuracy of the information respectively.

Nevertheless, DKC, ADC, and CC aid the supply chains to assess and anticipate disruptions in advance to initiate planned transitions but also provide advanced visibility into the potential outcomes of the planned changes to foster decision coordination, promptness, and effectiveness. Thus, increasing the degree of visibility in terms of the availability of the right quality/quantity of internal information, and external information. Wherein, the right quality/quantity of information refers to the precise, correct, and apt amount of real-time data to be shared between supply chain partners. Further, the internal information refers to the firm-level or supply chain level information gathered from internal information systems. Finally, external information refers to the information related to supply chain macro-environmental factors-Political, Economic, Social, Technological, Legal, and Environmental.

In addition, the capability and cultural assets foster advanced and enhanced visibility through facilitating factors such as traceability (ability to capture granular data), transparency (open, honest, and straightforward communication), collaboration (enhanced, long-term, strategic relationships towards holistic information discernibility), alignment (equal access to all kinds of information) and information sharing (at all levels- operational, tactical and strategic) between the supply chain partners. Moreover, they also reduce the hindrances towards visibility enhancement such as information asymmetry (privatization of certain strategic information), complexity (incompatible information systems), and reluctance towards information sharing towards convening successful real-time deployment of well-planned and simulated strategies (Lechaptois, 2020).

Similarly, trust between the supply chain partners and the quality of information used for collective decision-making were identified as determinant factors promoting visibility within a conceptual model developed by Nikookar et al. (2016). However, the advanced visibility of the planned outcomes promotes trust and the quality of information shared between the partners.

Likewise, Wei & Wang (2010) emphasized that supply chain visibility is enabled through four dynamic constructs i.e., visibility of sensing, visibility of learning, visibility of coordinating, and visibility of integrating. Nonetheless, such dynamic constructs are facilitated through DKC, ADC, and CC as they convene deployment of planned scenarios and simulated supply chain reconfigurations towards handling and coping up with the environmental challenges. Further, they also foster the visibility of sensing i.e., the dissemination of real-time external information towards quick recognition of changes within the supply chain environment, visibility of learning i.e., continuous learning and new knowledge/information acquisition from supply chain partners, visibility of coordination i.e., acquisition of complete information to promote decision coordination between supply chain partners, and visibility of integration i.e., acquisition of information to reach consensus on collaborative goals and build a collective identity.

Hence, planned transitions initiated through DKC, ADC, and CC foster advanced visibility into potential impacts and consequences of the changes induced. Consequently, promoting the deployment of the change strategies in a productive fashion.

## Alignment Enhancements

Supply chain alignment establishes the strongest fit between objectives, structures, strategies, and processes of different supply chain functions and partners for enhanced collective performance. In addition, supply chains constantly face volatile environments calling out for changes in plans and strategies to combat the adversities. Thus, alignment of the change strategies between supply chain partners through pro-active planning is essential towards successful real-time implementation of the needful changes.

Further, John (2017) developed a conceptual model that emphasized the importance of alignment between the supply chain's external environmental dynamics, the supply chain's strategic responses, and the supply chain's internal capabilities/resources to cope up with the adversities and deviations. Indeed, proactive changes coordinated through DKC, ADC, and CC enable the supply chain partners to sense and seize potential opportunities towards transforming the design and infrastructure in advance to achieve alignment with the new shifts induced. Further, they enable the supply chain partners to align their change strategies in the wake of the sensed opportunities (Aslam et al., 2020b).

In addition, Wong et al. (2012) conducted a systematic literature review and identified supply chain structures, relational behaviors between the supply chain partners, management support, information sharing, and performance assessment as the enablers for alignment within a supply chain. In this context, the alignment enablers can be successfully paved through planned transitions complimented with DKC, ADC, and CC. As, the DKC fosters supply chains to integrate, build and reconfigure new competencies towards alignment with the new requirements imposed. Likewise, the ADC enables alignment of the information i.e., data, plans, etc., and digital strategies between the supply chain partners. Finally, the CC promotes the alignment between objectives, structures, strategies, and processes confined to different functions and organizations within the supply chains to convene collective decision-making and proactive implementation of change strategies.

Moreover, CC serves as a backbone or strength behind operating as an extended and aligned enterprise, ADC acts as the power to induce alignment as it provides a mechanism for smooth alignment through information/data sharing, and DKC acts as an alignment facilitator through its sensing, seizing and transforming abilities. Besides, supply chains cannot act as functional silos when it comes to combating/facing disruptions, hence the capability and cultural assets facilitate collaboration and alignment within the supply chain functional silos and provide them with the needful competencies to combat multi-faceted supply chain disruptions.

Thus, planned transitions seeded through DKC, ADC, and CC foster dynamic alignment within the supply chains, facilitated through operations-reconfigurations, product-reconfigurations, logistics-reconfigurations, supply chain/network-reconfigurations, and information system assets/architecture-reconfigurations in line with the supply chain environmental dynamics.

## Agility Enhancements

Supply chain agility turns out to be one of the most fundamental characteristics of a supply chain that promotes its survival within a highly turbulent and increasingly competitive environment. It defines the overall alertness to internal or external disturbances and overall capabilities to deploy the available resources of all the supply chain partners in a collective fashion (Sangari et al., 2015). It serves as the main driver towards the supply chain's success and competitive advantage. It is slightly distinctive from flexibility, as it is centered on speed whereas flexibility is centered on elasticity. Further, it aids the supply chains to react and respond to adversities or disruptions in a cost-effective, resource-efficient, and competitive fashion. Besides, pro-active change management complements the agility behaviour within the supply chains, as the agility induces planned transitions for survival. Finally, agility is not an end in itself, as it serves as an imperative to foresee new challenges and opportunities from the pursued changes towards continuous growth and prosperity.

Christopher (2000) formulated a framework highlighting the essential characteristics i.e., Market sensitivity (ability to consolidate knowledge on volatile supply chain environments towards seizing opportunities for creating superior customer value), Collaborative Planning (interactive consensus building for collective decision making), Process Integration (collaborative working between the supply chain partners), and Virtual Integration (information-based integration) to promote agility within the supply chains. Similarly, Gligor (2013) and Al Humdan et al. (2020) indicated that agility is facilitated through "Alertness" (ability to quickly detect the opportunities/threats and needful changes), "Accessibility" (ability to quickly source and drill all the relevant data), "Decisiveness" (ability to quickly decide on collective solutions), "Swiftness" (ability to quickly implement the planned changes), and "Flexibility" (ability to quickly implement the needful re-configurations for planned strategy implementations) within the supply chains. According to the authors, these elements enhance both the cognitive and physical capabilities within a supply chain, as alertness, accessibility and decisiveness enhance the cognitive dimension of agility, and swiftness and flexibility enhance the physical dimension of agility. Indeed, DKC empowers the supply chains with the needful competencies to promote alertness, swiftness, and market sensitivity. Likewise, ADC facilitates accessibility and virtual integration within the supply chain partners and CC enhances the decisiveness and collaborative planning within the supply chains. Moreover, DKC, ADC, and CC together collectively enhance the dynamic flexibility and process integration within the supply chains. Thus creating a culture of agility for long-standing continual growth, and competitive advantage.

Further, the capability and cultural assets set the stage for agility enhancements enabling successful exploration of competitive bases such as speed, flexibility, innovativeness reactiveness, quality, and profitability through the deployment of reconfigurable resources and best practices identified from the supply chain knowledge assets towards the development of new innovative products and services in line with the volatile market requirements (Braunscheidel, 2005). Moreover, they also aid the supply chains to overcome essential barriers to agility such as lack of skills, tools, resources, consensus, and alignment between short-term and long-term plans/change strategies.

Hence, planned transitions cultivated through DKC, ADC, and CC fosters proactive agility within the supply chains facilitating the anticipation of hidden problems, challenges, and opportunities within the planned changes. Thus, providing the supply chains with new avenues for long-term survival, holistic growth, and competitive advantage by linking short-term agendas with long-term agendas.

## Resilience Enhancements

The concept of resilience has been defined differently within different domains, i.e., within the material science domain, it is defined as the ability of the material to absorb energy during elastic deformation and release of energy after unloading (Campbell, 2008). Within the ecological science domain, it is defined as an ability of an ecosystem to undergo disturbances without crossing a critical threshold and returning to its original equilibrium status. Additionally, resilience within the engineering domain is defined as the speed with which a system returns to equilibrium status after facing a disturbance (National Research Council, 2013). Moreover, resilience within an organizational system domain as per BS 6500 standard, is defined as the ability of an organization to anticipate, prepare for, respond and adapt to incremental changes and sudden disruptions to convene survival and prosperity. As the supply chains are extended organizations, the supply chain resilience (SCR) can be defined as an inherent capability enabling the supply chains to resist, avoid and recover from disruptions or deviations from the planned normal status quo and an ability that allows the supply chains to bounce back to a stable state demonstrating capabilities for survival and growth. Besides, SCR is a smart feature within the supply chains that allows the supply chains to face and combat continual disruptions. Moreover, it aids the supply chains to be prepared for unexpected risks. Further, it allows the supply chains to survive, adapt and grow in the face of turbulent environments seeding from internal or external disruptions.

Moreover, collective enhancements within flexibility, visibility, alignment, and agility facilitated through planned transitions enrooted with DKC, ADC, and CC enhance SCR. In this regard, a study pursued within the US multi-modal transportation networks showcased resilience enhancements through flexibility improvements (Ishfaq, 2012). Likewise, flexibility portrayed a prominent role in boosting financial performance through the promotion of enhanced resilience capabilities (Chunsheng et al., 2020).

Similarly, deployment of flexible business strategies in line with the levels of complexities faced fosters resilience enhancement within the supply chains, as such capabilities not only cater towards designing efficient responses to threats faced by the supply chains but also bolster resilience for survival and competitive advantage (Rajesh, 2020). Nevertheless, flexibility enhances resilience as it provides the supply chains with an ability to alter the plans in line with reality (Cascio, 2009).

Moreover, supply chains with ample agility are capable of sensing the environmental threats in a better fashion to facilitate risk responses through collaborative supplier networks, redundant resources, and through their collaborative infrastructures, thus enabling the supply chains to swiftly adapt to impulsive events through enhanced resilience (Aslam et al., 2020b). Besides, agility inducements within the supply chains not only aid the supply chains to survive within highly turbulent and increasingly competitive environments, but also promote resilience within the supply chains facilitating capabilities to successfully adapt to disruptions, to ensure continuity during distress, and to implement data-driven decisions within crises. Furthermore, agility was identified as a strategic tool for resilience enhancement through a 'top-down' strategic framework formulated for demonstrating a high degree of resilience within turbulent environments (Ismail et al., 2011). Finally, agility was discovered as a powerful means of achieving resilience within the SC, as it enables the creation of capable networks to rapidly respond to random events and consequently sustain within uncertain and fuzzy environments (Christopher & Peck, 2004).

In addition, visibility was presented as an essential tool towards enhancing SCR and agility within the SC, as it not only enables the SC to sense disruptions but also strongly influences disruption recovery (Nikookar et al., 2016). Indeed, visibility promotes decision-making, responsiveness, and supply chain performance, thus boosting robustness and resilience within the supply chains (Negri et al., 2021). Ad-

*Proactive Change Management to Enhance Supply Chain Resilience*

ditionally, it enables a capability to visualize from the downstream to the upstream of the supply chain, thus standing out as a vital element for event readiness and response generation (Jain et al., 2017).

As the supply chains are not single entities, alignment of resilience capabilities, i.e., flexibility, agility, and visibility between all of the SC entities is essential to respond, and thrive against challenges posed by turbulent environmental conditions (Scholten & Schilder, 2015). Nonetheless, the alignment of supply chain design principles and operational capabilities with the new reality stands out as a prominent driver towards fostering resilience capabilities within the supply chains (Katsaliaki et al., 2021). Further, alignment of capabilities within the four supply chain domains i.e., logistics, collaboration, sourcing, and knowledge management fosters readiness/responsiveness and consequently resilience within the supply chains (Umar et al., 2017).

Thus, the cohesion of flexibility, visibility, alignment, and agility capabilities within the supply chains promote resilience factors essential to prepare, respond, and recover successfully from unexpected events.

## SOLUTIONS AND RECOMMENDATIONS

The comprehensive analysis of the literature on the available models, frameworks, and strategies relative to change management and resilient behaviour within supply chains provided the requisite background to recommend an action plan for the supply chain fraternity to successfully face the challenges posed by turbulent environmental conditions. In this regard, few recommendations are proposed to effectively and efficiently leverage proactive change management processes for resilience enhancements within the supply chain.

- Firstly, all of the supply chain partners should work on integrating their expertise and on embracing continuous learning as a tool towards transforming the tangible and intangible assets into capabilities fostering survival and competitive strength within turbulent environments.
- Secondly, all of the supply chain entities should work towards embracing compatible digital capabilities and leverage the digital threads towards streamlining process integrations within supply chain functional silos through real-time data/information sharing, data analytics/predictions, and decision analysis/scenario planning.
- Thirdly, all of the supply chain members should embrace a collaborative culture to facilitate whole-hearted support for real-time collective strategy developments and successful/speedy implementations.
- Fourthly, the supply chain leaders should work cohesively utilizing the knowledge capabilities, digital capabilities, and collaborative culture to efficiently pursue proactive changes through anticipation and purposive planning.
- Finally, the conceptual framework proposed below can guide the supply chain fraternity to formulate proactive strategies towards combating and thriving supply chain disruptions.

## Conceptual Framework for Resilience Enhancement

The conceptual framework reflects on the antecedents for enhanced resilience within the supply chains. It is anchored based on the literature focusing on enablers for pro-active change management and then extended based on the literature concentrating on potential outputs realized from pro-active change management initiatives. Finally, the potential outputs were tied to resilience enhancement based on the literature directed on resilience enablers within the supply chains.

*Figure 1. Pro-active change management framework for supply chain resilience*

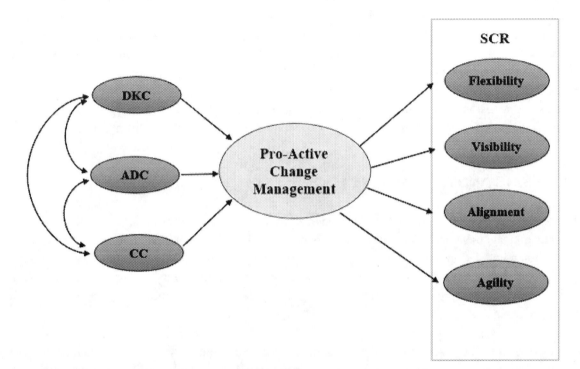

## CONCLUSIONS

In this study, a conceptual framework is proposed to leverage the success factors for managing and adapting changes towards promoting resilience capabilities within the supply chains. Moreover, the change management process complements the resilience behaviour towards pursuing constant and continuous changes to combat the ambiguity, chaos, uncertainty, and unpredictability of events within the supply chain environments. Thus, facilitating the deployment of pro-active strategies promoting a positive attitude towards needful changes through anticipation and purposeful planning.

Further, the framework helps to sum up the catalytic effect of proactive change management towards augmenting resilience capabilities within the supply chains, as it is formulated based on the literature premises highlighting Dynamic Knowledge Capabilities, Advanced Digital Capabilities, and Collaborative Culture as essential drivers towards deploying pro-active change management strategies within the supply chains. Additionally, the study reflects on supply chain research that emphasizes the role of capability and cultural assets in promoting dynamic flexibility, advanced visibility, dynamic alignment, and proactive agility within the supply chains. Thus, the developed framework embodies capability and cultural assets towards strengthening the supply chain's abilities to rapidly respond, adapt, survive, and thrive through disruptions. Likewise, to visualize the potential impacts and consequences of the changes induced. Similarly, to align the change strategies between the supply chain partners. Finally, to anticipate hidden problems, challenges, and opportunities within the planned changes. Besides, the framework also draws upon previous works articulating the importance of Flexibility, Visibility, Alignment, and Agility capabilities towards Supply Chain Resilience enhancement, i.e., enhancement of inherent capabilities to resist and recover from disruptions.

## IMPLICATIONS OF THE CONCEPTUAL FRAMEWORK

Owing to the vertical, horizontal, and spatial complexities within the modern-day supply chains, they are highly susceptible to multi-dimensional disruptions altering their basic ability and purpose of delivering value to the end customer market. Thus, the supply chain managers continuously face inevitable challenges and disruptions resulting from volatile business environments, inconsistent objectives, and adverse relationships among the supply chain partners. In this regard, the proposed framework acts as a directive aiding the supply chain managers and practitioners to leverage the inherent capabilities towards designing envisioned, planned, and collaborative strategic directions/action plans to combat turbulent environmental conditions and further to exhibit abilities to bounce back with sustained performance outcomes.

Besides, the relationships proposed within the framework can be deployed in a holistic and integrated fashion to formulate resilience strategies. Additionally, the framework facilitates a futuristic eye to needleful transitions through anticipation of hidden problems, challenges, and opportunities promoting capitalization on potential opportunities and successful navigation over inherent problems/challenges towards continuous growth, long-term survival, and competitive advantage. Likewise, the framework enables, end-to-end assessment, monitoring, and optimization towards the development of planned transitions for risk avoidance and mitigation. Further, as the framework enables advanced visualization of potential impacts and alignment of the change strategies, it can also embark on the reduction of cognitive dissonance towards successfully implementing the planned changes.

## LIMITATIONS AND SCOPE FOR FURTHER RESEARCH

The scope of the current study is only directed towards the development of a conceptual framework that leverages proactive change management strategies for resilience enhancements within the supply chains. Thus, providing the supply chain research fraternity an opportunity to empirically validate the relationships portrayed within the framework with real-time data using industrial interviews, surveys, and focus groups. Likewise, future research can be also directed towards pursuing longitudinal studies for collecting substantial pieces of evidence to validate the framework within different supply chain environments for the generalization of results. Further, additional studies are also needed to validate the alignment of the pro-active change management strategies designed and deployed employing the proposed framework with the strategies developed employing pre-established risk management frameworks.

Moreover, the current study only focuses on the essential drivers and outputs realized from the pro-active change management processes and claims to reduce cognitive dissonance towards successfully implementing the planned changes. Further, taking into consideration the complexities within the change management processes involving people and their behaviours. There lies a need to conduct additional research under the behavioural science perspective to learn how the transitions from the current state to a desired future state before event incitement are made possible through successful management of the people, stages, complexities, resistances, etc. underlying the planned changes.

## REFERENCES

Al Humdan, E., Shi, Y., Behnia, M., & Najmaei, A. (2020). Supply chain agility: A systematic review of definitions, enablers and performance implications. *International Journal of Physical Distribution & Logistics Management*, *50*(2), 287–312. doi:10.1108/IJPDLM-06-2019-0192

APICS. (2017). *Association for Supply Chain Management, Supply Chain Operations Reference Model*. Version: 12.

Arora, R. (2020). Which Companies did well during the Coronavirus Pandemic? *Forbes*. Available: https://www.forbes.com/sites/rohitarora/2020/06/30/which-companies-did-well-during-the-coronavirus-pandemic/?sh=4ec218447409

Aslam, H., Blome, C., Roscoe, S., & Azhar, T. H. (2020). Determining the antecedents of dynamic supply chain capabilities. *Supply Chain Management*, *25*(4), 427–442. doi:10.1108/SCM-02-2019-0074

Aslam, H., Khan, A. Q., Rashid, K., & Rehman, S. (2020). Achieving supply chain resilience: The role of supply chain ambidexterity and supply chain agility. *Journal of Manufacturing Technology Management*, *31*(6), 1185–1204. doi:10.1108/JMTM-07-2019-0263

Ates, A., & Bititci, U. (2011). Change process: A key enabler for building resilient SMEs. *International Journal of Production Research*, *49*(18), 5601–5618. doi:10.1080/00207543.2011.563825

Barroso, A. P., Machado, V. H., Barros, A. R., & Cruz Machado, V. (2010). Toward a resilient Supply Chain with supply disturbances. *IEEE International Conference on Industrial Engineering and Engineering Management*, 245-249, 10.1109/IEEM.2010.5674462

Barroso, A. P., Machado, V. H., Carvalho, H., & Cruz Machado, V. (2015). *Quantifying the Supply Chain Resilience, Applications of Contemporary Management Approaches in Supply Chains*. IntechOpen. . doi:10.5772/59580

Bharadwaj, A., El Sawy, O. A., Pavlou, P. A., & Venkatraman, N. (2013). Digital Business Strategy: Toward a Next Generation of Insights. *Management Information Systems Quarterly*, *37*(2), 471–482. doi:10.25300/MISQ/2013/37:2.3

Braunscheidel, M. J. (2005). *Antecedents of Supply Chain Agility: An Empirical Investigation* (PhD Thesis). School of Management University of Buffalo the State University of New York.

BSI. (2014). *BS 6500 Standard for Organizational Resilience*. Available: bsigroup.com/organizational-resilience.

Bullock, R. J., & Batten, D. (1985). It's just a phase we're going through: A review and synthesis of OD phase analysis. *Group & Organization Studies*, *10*(4), 383–412. doi:10.1177/105960118501000403

Campbell, F. C. (2008). *Elements of Metallurgy and Engineering Alloys.* ASM International Publication. doi:10.31399/asm.tb.emea.9781627082518

Cascio, J. (2009). Resilience. *Foreign Policy, 92.* Retrieved from https://www-proquest.com.aus.idm. oclc.org/magazines/resilience/docview/224032941/se-2?accountid=16946

Christopher, M. (2000). The agile supply chain competing in volatile markets. *Industrial Marketing Management, 29*(1), 37–44. doi:10.1016/S0019-8501(99)00110-8

Christopher, M., & Holweg, M. (2011). "Supply Chain 2.0": Managing supply chains in the era of turbulence. *International Journal of Physical Distribution & Logistics Management, 41*(1), 63–82. doi:10.1108/09600031111101439

Christopher, M., & Peck, H. (2004). Building the Resilient Supply Chain. *International Journal of Logistics Management, 15*(2), 1–14. doi:10.1108/09574090410700275

Chunsheng, L., Wong, C. W. Y., Yang, C.-C., Shang, K.-C., & Lirn, T. (2020). Value of supply chain resilience: Roles of culture, flexibility, and integration. *International Journal of Physical Distribution & Logistics Management, 50*(1), 80–100. doi:10.1108/IJPDLM-02-2019-0041

CSCMP. (2021). *CSCMP Supply Chain Management Definitions and Glossary.* Available at: https://cscmp.org/supply-chain-management-definitions

Cutting-Decelle, A. F., Young, B. I., Das, B. P., Case, K., Rahimifard, S., Anumba, C. J., & Bouchlaghem, D. M. (2007). A review of approaches to supply chain communications: From manufacturing to construction. *ITcon, 12*, 73–102.

Datta, P. (2017). Supply Network Resilience: A systematic literature review and future research. *International Journal of Logistics Management, 28*(4), 1387–1424. doi:10.1108/IJLM-03-2016-0064

Datta, P. P., Christopher, M., & Allen, P. (2007). Agent-based modelling of complex production/distribution systems to improve resilience. *International Journal of Logistics: Research and Applications., 10*(3), 187–203. doi:10.1080/13675560701467144

Dawson, P. M. (2006). Change management. In G. Ritzer (Ed.), *The Blackwell Encyclopedia of Sociology* (pp. 427–431). Blackwell Publishing.

Dereń, A. M., & Skonieczny, J. (2021). Proactive and Reactive Actions of the Organization during Covid-19 Pandemic Crisis. *European Research Studies Journal, 24*(2), 358–368.

Dolgui, A., Ivanov, D., & Sokolov, B. (2018). Ripple effect in the supply chain: An analysis and recent literature. *International Journal of Production Research, 56*(1-2), 414–430. doi:10.1080/00207543.2017.1387680

Duclos, L. K., Vokurka, R. J., & Lummus, R. R. (2003). A Conceptual Model for Supply Chain Flexibility. *Industrial Management & Data Systems, 103*(6), 446–456. doi:10.1108/02635570310480015

Gligor, D. M. (2013). *The Concept of Supply Chain Agility: Conceptualization, Antecedents, and the Impact on Firm Performance* (PhD diss.). University of Tennessee.

Greer, B. M., & Ford, M. W. (2009). Managing change in supply chains: A process comparison. *Journal of Business Logistics*, *30*(2), 47–63. doi:10.1002/j.2158-1592.2009.tb00111.x

Han, S., & Chan, C. (2009). Developing a Collaborative Supply Chain Reference Model: A case study in China. *International Journal of Electronic Customer Relationship Management*, *3*(1), 52–70. doi:10.1504/IJECRM.2009.024488

Hiatt, J. M. (2006). *ADKAR: A model for change in business, government, and our community*. Prosci Learning Center Publications.

Hoek, R., Johnson, M., Godsell, J., & Birtwistle, A. (2010). Changing chains: Three case studies of the change management needed to reconfigure European supply chains. *International Journal of Logistics Management*, *21*(2), 230–250. doi:10.1108/09574091011071933

Ibbs, C. W., Wong, C. K., & Kwak, Y. H. (2001). Project Change Management System. *Journal of Management Engineering*, *17*(3), 159–165. doi:10.1061/(ASCE)0742-597X(2001)17:3(159)

Ishfaq, R. (2012). Resilience through flexibility in transportation operations. *International Journal of Logistics Research and Applications.*, *15*(4), 215–229. doi:10.1080/13675567.2012.709835

Ismail, H. S., Poolton, J., & Sharifi, H. (2011). The role of agile strategic capabilities in achieving resilience in manufacturing-based small companies. *International Journal of Production Research*, *49*(18), 5469–5487. doi:10.1080/00207543.2011.563833

Ivanov, D., & Dolgui, A. (2021). OR-methods for coping with the ripple effect in supply chains during COVID-19 pandemic: Managerial insights and research implications. *International Journal of Production Economics*, *232*, 107921. Advance online publication. doi:10.1016/j.ijpe.2020.107921 PMID:32952301

Jackson, S., & Ferris, T. L. J. (2015). Proactive and Reactive Resilience: A Comparison of Perspectives. *Insight - International Council on Systems Engineering*, *18*(7).

Jain, V., Kumar, S., Soni, U., & Chandra, C. (2017). Supply chain resilience: Model development and empirical analysis. *International Journal of Production Research*, *55*(22), 6779–6800. doi:10.1080/00207543.2017.1349947

John, G. (2017). *Strategic supply chain alignment. Best practice in supply chain management*. CRC Press, Taylor & Francis Group.

Katsaliaki, K., Galetsi, P., & Kumar, S. (2021). Supply chain disruptions and resilience: A major review and future research agenda. *Annals of Operations Research*. Advance online publication. doi:10.100710479-020-03912-1 PMID:33437110

Kirk, G. S. (1951). Natural Change in Heraclitus. *Mind*, *60*(237), 35–42. doi:10.1093/mind/LX.237.35

Kumar, G., Banerjee, R. N., Meena, P. L., & Ganguly, K. (2016). Collaborative culture and relationship strength roles in collaborative relationships: A supply chain perspective. *Journal of Business and Industrial Marketing*, *31*(5), 587–599. doi:10.1108/JBIM-12-2014-0254

Kumar, P., & Shankar, R. (2007). Flexibility in global supply chain: a review of perspectives. In *Proceedings of GLOGIFT* 07. UP Technical University.

Lechaptois, L. (2020). *Framing supply chain visibility through a multi-field approach. Proceedings of the Hamburg International Conference of Logistics (HICL) – 29. Data science and innovation in supply chain management.*

Masteika, I., & Čepinskis, J. (2015). Dynamic Capabilities in Supply Chain Management. *Procedia: Social and Behavioral Sciences, 213*, 830–835. doi:10.1016/j.sbspro.2015.11.485

Messina, D., Barros, A. C., & Soares, A. L. (2018). *How much visibility has a company over its supply chain? A diagnostic metric to assess supply chain visibility.* In 22nd Cambridge International Manufacturing Symposium, University of Cambridge.

Nath, T. D. (2009). *Leveraging information technology in the supply chain for organizational transformation: a meta-analysis of the supply chain literature.* https://ro.ecu.edu.au/theses/159

National Research Council. (2013). *An Ecosystem Services Approach to Assessing the Impacts of the Deepwater Horizon Oil Spill in the Gulf of Mexico.* National Academies Press (US).

Negri, M., Cagno, E., Colicchia, C., & Sarkis, J. (2021). Integrating sustainability and resilience in the supply chain: A systematic literature review and a research agenda. *Business Strategy and the Environment, 30*(7), 2858–2886. Advance online publication. doi:10.1002/bse.2776

Nikookar, E., Nagalingam, S., Sosay, C. (2016). The role of visibility in supply chain resilience: A Resource-based approach. *Technology, Innovation & Supply Chain Management Competitive Session*, 1-19.

Olaf, P. (2010). *Change Management* (1st ed.). Bookboon Learning.

Oliver, R. (2001). *Managing Change – Definition und Phases in Change Processes.* Recklies Management Project GmbH. www.themanager.org

Ponomarov, S. Y., & Holcomb, M. C. (2009). Understanding the concept of supply chain resilience. *International Journal of Logistics Management, 20*(1), 124–143. doi:10.1108/09574090910954873

Queiroz, M. M., Pereira, S. C. F., Telles, R., & Machado, M. C. (2021). Industry 4.0 and digital supply chain capabilities A framework for understanding digitalisation challenges and opportunities. *Benchmarking, 28*(5), 1761–1782. doi:10.1108/BIJ-12-2018-0435

Rajesh, R. (2020). Flexible business strategies to enhance resilience in manufacturing supply chains: An empirical study. *Journal of Manufacturing Systems*, 1–17.

Richard, C., Deng, M., Kusters, J., & Carvell, K. (2020). *Deloitte's Digital Capabilities Model for Supply Networks | Introducing a new model for supply chain.* Deloitte Consulting LLP.

Sangari, M. S., Razmi, M., & Zolfagahari, S. (2015). Developing practical evaluation framework for identifying critical factors to achieve Supply Chain Agility. *Measurement., 62*, 205–214. doi:10.1016/j.measurement.2014.11.002

Scholten, K., & Schilder, S. (2015). The role of collaboration in supply chain resilience. *Supply Chain Management, 20*(4), 471–484. doi:10.1108/SCM-11-2014-0386

Sonar, A., & Mankenzie, C. A. (2018). In Y. Khojasteh (Ed.), *Supply Chain Disruptions Preparedness Measures Using a Dynamic Model* (pp. 123–137). Supply Chain Risk Management. Springer Nature Singapore Pte Ltd. doi:10.1007/978-981-10-4106-8_8

Stevenson, M., & Spring, M. (2007). Flexibility from a supply chain perspective: Definition and review. *International Journal of Operations & Production Management*, 27(7), 685–713. doi:10.1108/01443570710756956

Stone, J., Rahimifard, S., & Woolley, E. (2015). An overview of resilience factors in food supply chains. *11th Biennial Conference of the European Society for Ecological Economics*.

Tajri, H., & Chafi, A. (2018). Change management in supply chain: Supply chain urbanization method. *4th International Conference on Optimization and Applications (ICOA)*, 1-7. 10.1109/ICOA.2018.8370561

Umar, M., Wilson, M., & Hey, J. (2017). Food Network Resilience Against Natural Disasters: A Conceptual Framework. *SAGE Open*, 7(3). Advance online publication. doi:10.1177/2158244017717570

Wagner, H. M., & Whitin, T. (1958). Dynamic version of the economic lot size model. *Management Science*, 5(1), 89–96. doi:10.1287/mnsc.5.1.89

Wei, H. L., & Wang, E. T. G. (2010). The strategic value of supply chain visibility: Increasing the ability to reconfigure. *European Journal of Information Systems*, 19(2), 238–249. doi:10.1057/ejis.2010.10

WHO. (2021). *World Health Organization, Health Topics*. Available: https://www.who.int/health-topics/coronavirus#tab=tab_1

Wong, C., Skipworth, H., Godsell, J., & Achimugu, N. (2012). Towards a theory of supply chain alignment enablers: A systematic literature review. *Supply Chain Management*, 17(4), 419–437. doi:10.1108/13598541211246567

Yao, Y., & Meurier, B. (2012). *Understanding the supply chain resilience: a Dynamic Capabilities approach*. 9th International Logistics Research Meetings, Montreal, Canada.

Yunus, E. N. (2018). Leveraging supply chain collaboration in pursuing radical innovation. *International Journal of Innovation Science*, 10(3), 350–370. doi:10.1108/IJIS-05-2017-0039


## KEY TERMS AND DEFINITIONS

**Change:** Is the continuous adoption of strategies and structures to changing conditions (Oliver, 2001).

**COVID-19:** Is an infectious disease caused by a newly discovered coronavirus. It is declared as a pandemic by the World Health Organization (WHO), as it causes respiratory illness and spreads through droplets.

**Proactive Change:** Changes initiated ahead to avoid or manage future problems (Dawson, 2006).

**Reactive Change:** Changes initiated in response to unforeseen events within internal operations or external environmental conditions (Dawson, 2006).

**SCOR Model:** Supply Chain Operations Reference Model describes all of the business activities (plan, source, make, deliver, return, and enable) associated with satisfying the customer's demand. Further, the model is used to evaluate the supply chain performance and identify areas for improvement (APICS, 2017).

## APPENDIX

## Case Study: Amul India

The Gujarat Cooperative Milk Marketing Federation (GCMMF) is one of the largest dairy cooperative societies in India and markets its products under the brand name "Amul (Anand Milk Union Limited)". The supply chain of Amul has been formulated as a three-tiered structure from dairy cooperative societies at the village level, milk unions at the district level, and member unions at the state level. Thus, enabling the procurement of 3.3 million liters of milk daily from 16 million milk producers by 185903 district cooperatives across the country to be processed at 222 district cooperative milk unions and finally to be marketed by 28 state marketing federations.

The dairy industry in India faced severe repercussions from the Covid-19 pandemic, as there was a drastic fall in demand of about 20% for dairy products from the hospitality industry. However, Amul with its dynamic knowledge capabilities, advanced digital capabilities, and collaborative culture was able to foresee paradigm shifts in demand for dairy products. This fostered Amul to capitalize on the opportunities and thrive the disruptions through planned transitions.

Amul was able to foresee the shift in demand to home-cooked foods and packaged milk, due to the stringent Covid-19 safety protocols in place. Further, the knowledge capabilities enabled from previous leadership crisis management experiences, digital capabilities enabled from its strategic partnership with IBM for end-to-end visibility, and its cooperative culture with the milk farmers and milk unions aided Amul to introduce 33 new products to cater to home-cooking needs and procure 3.5 million litres of extra milk every single day to meet the increased demand for the packaged milk. Additionally, the capabilities enabled Amul to make planned transitions, i.e., pro-active changes towards efficiently using its factory resources through the elimination of idle capacities, towards outsourcing distribution activities to third-party vendors like Zomato, Swiggy, etc., towards utilizing government infrastructures like Indian railways for milk distribution to overcome truck shortages and finally towards utilizing idle production resources of competitive firms for meeting the increased demand requirements.

Such, proactive changes initiated by Amul, not only aided the firm to bounce back from the adverse effects of the pandemic, but also fostered the firm to demonstrate capabilities essential for survival, growth, and continuity. Hence, resilience enhancement through proactive change management aided Amul to perceive pandemic situations like Covid-19, as an opportunity to transform massive challenges into meaningful changes for survival, growth, and competitive advantage.

Amul. (2021). The Amul Model. Accessed on: Oct. 1, 2021. [Online]. Available: https://www.amul.com/m/about-us

ICMR India (2020). Unlocking in the Lockdown: Amul`s Surge during Testing Times. IBS Centre for Management Research. Accessed on: Oct. 1, 2021. [Online]. Available: https://icmrindia.org/casestudies/catalogue/Marketing/amul-surge-during-covid19-lockdown-excerpts.htm

# Chapter 3
# Supply Chain Innovation in the Era of Industry 4.0

**Saurabh Tiwari**

(iD) https://orcid.org/0000-0002-4278-0389

*University of Petroleum and Energy Studies, Dehradun, India*

## ABSTRACT

*Industry 4.0, also known as the fourth industrial revolution, has had a profound impact on business, society, and the supply chain. In Industry 4.0, the supply chain will be digitalized, opening up new opportunities for competitive advantage through innovative supply chain designs, processes, and enabling technology. In any industry or supply chain function, changes can occur to enhance the creation of new value for stakeholders in the supply chain by changing processes, current practices within networks, technology, and processes (or a combination of all of these). This chapter finds how supply chain innovation is transformed in the era of Industry 4.0 using the digital transformation based on digital innovation along with developing a framework based on supply chain innovation (consisting of product, process, organizational, technological, and marketing innovation) and Industry 4.0 (digital transformation).*

## INTRODUCTION

Industry 4.0, also known as the fourth industrial revolution, has had a profound impact on business, society, and the supply chain. In Industry 4.0, the supply chain will be digitalized, opening up new opportunities for competitive advantage through innovative supply chain designs, processes, and enabling technology. SCM stands for supply chain management and integrated logistics systems, with the objective of reducing the amount of inventory throughout the supply chain (Chong et al., 2011). SCM displays a crucial role in improving supply chain performance and fostering organisational performance (SCI). In response to social and technological changes, supply chain systems are constantly evolving (Zijm et al., 2019). To maximise the effectiveness of SC systems, businesses must ensure that they are running at peak efficiency (Azevedo, 2013). Economic progress in an organisation can be measured by its ability to create value from new ideas. It contributes significantly to the success and competitiveness of organisations, but it has also presented significant challenges (Gao et al., 2017; Wu & Tsai, 2018).

DOI: 10.4018/978-1-7998-9506-0.ch003

Copyright © 2022, IGI Global. Copying or distributing in print or electronic forms without written permission of IGI Global is prohibited.

*Supply Chain Innovation in the Era of Industry 4.0*

Companies in order to improve supply chain performance are investing in technological innovations which helps in effective information sharing among supply chain members and as well as to assist in the development of effective communication channels and collaboration mechanisms (Tiwari 2020). Supply chain innovation is becoming increasingly important for many businesses in the era of Industry 4.0. Supply chain integration made possible by Industry 4.0 reduces deployment time and costs while simultaneously fostering new ideas and faster response times (Tiwari 2020). Supply chain innovations improves operational productivity and service efficiency using new logistical and marketing procedures by combining advances in information and related technologies (Bello et al., 2004). One of the biggest challenges for organisations is the impact of advanced technological innovations, and Industry 4.0 helps to improve supply chain performance (Neely, 2005; Bititci et al., 2013; Bhagwat and Sharma, 2009). SCM and its impact on various supply chain processes have been discussed by Ben-Daya et al., (2019) on the impact of Industry 4.0 and the role of IOT. As a multifaceted process involving knowledge, organisation, technology, and market forces, and the innovation process has many facets. A company's supply chain operating model is transformed by implementing SC strategy and identifying key enablers that help it offer value to consumers (Stevens and Johnson 2016). The Fourth Industrial Revolution's conceptual and technological advances are hugely helpful in this effort (Kagermann et al. 2013). Innumerable research studies have confirmed the significance of ICT in supply chain management (Prajogo and Olhager 2012).

## BACKGROUND

Digital manufacturing will replace machine-dominated manufacturing as part of an emerging trend known as "Industry 4.0." (Oztemel and Gursev 2018). It is based on modern procedures becoming increasingly digital and computerised. When intelligent systems are integrated into manufacturing environments along with new methods of managing and controlling the production, the Industrial 4.0 scenario predicts new technologies and jobs, as well as an increase in human skill sets (Pacaux-Lemoine et al., 2017), and logistics processes will be altered (Ivanov et al., 2016). They will have a substantial influence on the manufacturing industry and the supply chains (Szozda 2017). With intelligent processes like Cyber-Physical Systems, alterations in production and failures that happen outside the industrial production chain can be addressed quickly (Haddara and Elragal 2015). Industry 4.0's success will be determined by the efficiency with which people, processes, equipment, and products are all integrated into one organisation (Gebhardt et al. 2015), this will lead to competitive advantages such as lower production costs and faster turnaround times, as well as improved product quality (Albers et al. 2016). Industry 4.0 takes a production-oriented operational stance. There is great potential for Industry 4.0 and its enabler technologies to take an enormous influence on logistics and supply chains (Macaulay et al. 2015). Industry 4.0 and advanced technological innovations, which help improve supply chain performance, have a substantial effect on organisations (Bititci et al. 2013). Process integration to a high degree is also essential for effective business performance (Tiwari 2020). Integrating the supply chain at all points in the business process and exchanging information effectively are essential (Chavez et al. 2017). Collaboration and integration allow for improved supply chain performance by increasing the chain's flexibility (Datta 2017). Big data, IoT, 3D printing and artificial intelligence are all part of Industry 4.0. (Yin et al. 2018). Autonomous systems which consists of smart products and machines and are part of self-operating and interconnected physical assets, will be part of Industry 4.0. New SC operating models enabled by these technologies can supplement or level substitute conventional methods (van Alstyne et al., 2016). Companies have long recognised supply chain performance that is innovative, and collaborative innovation activities have been found to improve supply chain performance in terms of innovation overall. I4.0 technologies will allow for greater virtualization of supply chain interactions, all organisations in a network stand to gain by being seamlessly connected and having actual access to product and production information (Brettel et al., 2014). Digitization in recent years promises radical changes in various industrial sectors as well as SC practices, comprising manufacturing and supply chain management (Kagermann 2015). A new (digital) approach to SCM is required because of the impact of the corresponding innovations (Büyüközkan and Göçer, 2018). The implementation of new technologies and innovations has had a substantial influence on supply chain evolution (MacCarthy et al. 2016). Digital transformation is accelerating across all aspects of supply chain management, including internal processes, products offered, communication channels, and many more. This study provides an existing definition on supply chain innovation and a framework from existing definition of supply chain innovation and Industry 4.0 along with certain gaps and directions for future research. The purpose of this paper is to contribute to the improvement of existing knowledge about the relationship between Industry 4.0 and Supply Chain Innovation and to provide a new perspective for further research. The following are two guiding research questions (RQs) that we've proposed in light of previous discussions:

RQ1. What is the current state of knowledge and understanding of Industry 4.0 and Supply Chain Innovation?

RQ2. What are the different types of innovation in the context of Industry 4.0 and Supply Chain innovation and to develop a framework?

This research has been broken down into six sections. As a starting point, we give an introduction and background overview of the subject and state a few key research questions. In the third section we present the main focus of the chapter which includes supply chain innovation and the various definition based on literature review method along with the theoretical framework on supply chain innovation and Industry 4.0 and the various variables and the types of innovation. In the fourth section, we present the solution and recommendation followed by conclusion. Finally, we present the future outlook.


## MAIN FOCUS OF THE CHAPTER

SCI is a procedure that can help organisations better manage SCM by interacting with suppliers, producers, distributors, and customers in a more integrated fashion (Lin 2007). Consequently, SCI cuts down on costs while also developing new operational techniques and a reliable supply chain to deal with the emergent variations in the business (Lee et al., 2011). New technologies can be used in supply chain innovations to improve organisational processes in new ways, dealing with environmental uncertainty and addressing customer demands (Lee et al., 2011). A "fairly continuous stream of innovations overtime" is the result of supply chain innovations being a relational phenomenon that is cultural and cross-organizational (Ojha et al., 2016). In the service sector, supply chain innovation can help to maintain a competitive advantage, promote sustainable development, and improve service quality (Isaksson et al., 2010). There are two ways to implement supply chain innovations according to Bello et al. (2004), which are increasing revenues and increasing joint profits through improved operational efficiency while reducing costs. Businesses in the service sector should put more emphasis on SCI in order to improve delivery services (Chapman et al., 2002). Companies benefit from improved supply chain performance and competitiveness as a result of supply chain innovation (Lee et al., 2011). The innovation management process and SC learning are

*Supply Chain Innovation in the Era of Industry 4.0*

two of a SCI's antecedents, according to Flint and Larsson (2007). Herzlinger (2006) identified three types of service sector innovation in the SCI process (customer-focused, technology-based, and integrated innovation). Participatory management has an impact on the supply chain's ability to innovate, as stated by Hui et al., (2015). Advances in technology are used to improve service effectiveness, raise revenue, improve operational efficiency, and maximise joint profits in the supply chain (Bello et al., 2004). With this definition and a resource-based perspective, supply chain innovations can be divided into three categories: logistics-focused, marketing-focused, and technology development-focused. In the context of logistics-related innovation, the term refers to the development of new and useful services for a specific target audience. Internal or external, this audience can benefit from innovations that increase operational efficiency or improve customer service (Flint et al., 2005; Grawe et al., 2009). In order to achieve supply chain logistics that a) provides firms with space and time, b) ensures that the quantity of goods needed at the right time and place, and c) reduce organisational slack, supply chain partners must collaborate closely, intensively, and in coordination (Chen and Paulraj, 2004). Sales management and order volume have a substantial outcome on supply chain performance as a result of innovations in the supply chain (Dubey et al., 2012). In order to succeed in the competitive industries, suppliers and manufacturers in SC must transform their businesses through innovation (Wong & Ngai, 2019). Modelling technologies permit managers in their companies to better accomplish data, resulting in rationality in the supply chain (Shapiro & Wagner 2009). Incorporating and distributing technological innovations as quickly as possible is the responsibility of the supply chains (Sabri et al., 2018). Supply chain models are available to SC-affiliated businesses to meet their regular innovative supply chain needs (Cai et al., 2009). SCI as defined by Arlbjørn et al. (2011) are the changes within the supply chain framework associated with supply chain network, technology, or business processes that are gradual or fundamental in nature. The management of materials, information, and coordination while taking economic, social, and environmental dimensions into account is referred to as a sustainable supply chain (SSC). Emerging companies outperform in terms of long-term supply chain performance (Nidumolu et al., 2015). Traditionally, the concept of SC has been rooted in sustainability. A supply chain performance evaluation can therefore help to increase supply chain transparency and innovation (Schaltegger & Burritt, 2014). Supply chain management has been shown to encourage organisations to innovate (Chong et al., 2011). Innovation is seen as critical to the supply chain because of the sustainability of current competitive business environments (Jellali & Benaissa, 2015). Another area where business processes are being rapidly affected by ICT is the information and communication industry. The ability and stimulus provided by technological innovation can help expand supply chain activities and processes. This is associated with the fact that technological innovation is the result of product innovation and business process innovation (process innovation). Innovation development, diffusion, and practical application can all serve as catalysts for the SCI process. Innovative thinking is crucial for long-term sustainability in business operations and in the supply chain (Klewitz and Hansen, 2014). Sustainable innovation uses new or modified processes and techniques, as well as methods, systems, and products, to reduce harm to society and the environment (Beise and Rennings, 2005). It has been proposed that innovation is fuelled by "sustaining" and "disruptive" technologies, respectively. New product and service overview, development of new models, and knowledge acquisition (education and training) are all considered to be parts of supply chain innovation. Collaboration across functions, international (global), cross-sector partnership and information gathering are a few examples of other activities (Moreira et al., 2018). When it comes to supply chain innovation, Eschenbacher et al. (2011) point to it as an excellent illustration of an inter-organizational and distributed process. An integrated change in the product, process, marketing, and/or organisation is recognized as Supply Chain. SCI is a term used to describe the collaborative process of developing new ideas and products. SCI benefits all parties involved in the supply chain because it addresses every facet of the process. Innovativeness is defined as a "multi-stage progression by which businesses transform their thoughts into innovative and value-added products and procedures." (Baregheh et al., 2009) also new technologies is seen as a chance to innovate and advance their businesses. Organizations are looking to their supply networks to improve processes, increase performance, and develop new business models. This has piqued the interest of a large number of supply chain experts (Kavin and Narasimhan, 2017).

Innovative marketing-related services are the result of customer research and new marketing-related services (Chen and Paulraj, 2004). Desbarats et al. (1999) claim that in its most basic form, marketing fulfils a primary strategic responsibility of the customer-supplier relationship.

A company's innovative activities include the development of new knowledge and skills that can aid in the creation of new products and services for customers (Lee et al., 2011). Innovations in the supply chain are often based on industry-wide and industry-driven innovations, such as information systems and new technologies that are mutually beneficial (Storer et al., 2014).

According to Desbarats et al. (1999), new products are introduced to the economy by professional teams from a variety of disciplines. While marketing and sales teams focus on customers, technical and creative teams focus on product specifications. Marketing, according to Chen and Paulraj (2004), is all about meeting customers' needs, which is the primary goal of any business. Archer et al. (2008) established that customers and suppliers of small and medium-sized businesses prioritise traditional product concerns (price, quality, support, and dependability) over supply chain process concerns that drive innovation (value engineering, e-business, value analysis, time to market, R&D, and procurement expertise).

On the basis of literature the various definitions on supply chain innovations are compiled in table 1.

*Supply Chain Innovation in the Era of Industry 4.0*

*Table 1. Supply chain innovation definitions*

| Author | Definition |
|---|---|
| Cohen and Levinthal (1990) | Process compliance is a method for effectively absorbing (recognising, evaluating, assimilation, and application) aspects of supply and demand-side competence from the absorptive capacity paradigm, which can aid in supply chain innovation. |
| Bello et al. (2004) | New logistical and marketing procedures are combined with information and related technology developments in supply chain innovations to increase operational effectiveness and improve service efficiency. |
| Coltman et al. (2010) | Innovative supply chains are necessary across all product and service categories to provide new services. |
| Arlbjørn et al. (2011) | It is defined as an improvement in the value creation for the stakeholder by altering the supply chain network, technology, or processes. |
| Lee et al., (2011) | Supply chain innovations are complex processes that use new technologies to transact with environmental uncertainty and answer to consumer requirements in novel ways. |
| Schoenherr and Swink (2012) | Innovation can flourish in companies that have a high level of process compliance. Employees are able to access and share information through established rules and systems as well as cross-functional relationships. |
| Munksgaard et al. (2014) | SCI conceptualization relies on future research examining how novel innovations are, as well as looking into more extreme examples of radical SCI. |
| Lee et al. (2014) | Distributors, manufacturers, customers, and suppliers can all work together to enhance supply chain management by leveraging SCI. |
| Storer et al. (2014) | In supply chain innovation, the use of industry-wide and industry-led innovations, such as information systems and new technologies, often leads to partnerships and collaborative relationships. |
| Ojha et al. (2016) | An effective supply chain innovation considered to a "fairly constant stream of innovations over time," which is a relational, cultural, and organisational phenomenon. |
| Jajja et al., (2017) | Supplier integration and collaboration are essential to achieving supply chain innovation goals. Supply chain innovations are less likely to occur if suppliers aren't interested in them. |
| Tebaldi et al., (2018) | A supply chain innovation is defined as a smooth transition from small to large-scale changes in a product, process, marketing, or company. Supply chain integrity (SCI) encompasses all of the product's suppliers, manufacturers, and distributors. |

On the basis of the above definitions on supply chain innovation, a framework was developed as shown in figure 1 which shows the involvement of Supply Chain Innovation & Industry 4.0

**Framework for Supply Chain Innovation and Industry 4.0**

Supply Chain Innovation (SCI) is recognized as an alteration in a product, process, marketing, technology, resource, and/or organisation that affects all aspects of the supply chain and enhances value for all shareholders. SCI has ties to everyone in the supply chain, from manufacturers to distributors to logistics providers. Products, processes, organisations, marketing, technology, and resource allocation are just a few examples of the many types of innovations listed in Table 1. (Tebaldi et al. 2018). The terms "technological innovations" refer to improvements in products and processes, whereas the terms "non-technological innovations" refer to alterations in organisations and marketing strategies. Among the five categories of technological innovation, we identified RFID tools as being at the top because of their radical newness. In resource allocation, innovation means redistributing resources in order to achieve new outcomes. Figure 1 shows how Supply Chain Innovation and Industry 4.0 are intertwined. There are numerous types of innovation concepts defined in Table 2. The compilation of various types of innovation as shown in shown table 2.

*Figure 1. Framework for supply chain innovation and industry 4.0*

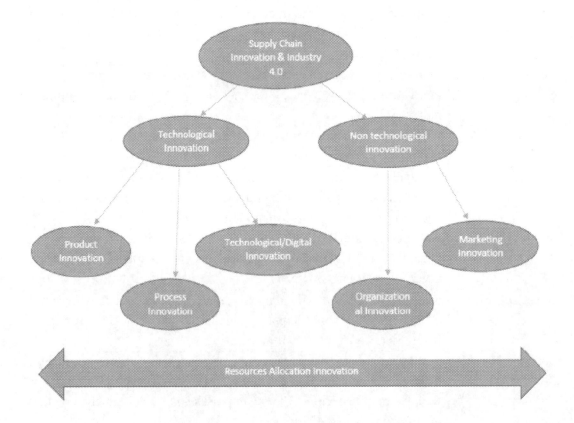

*Supply Chain Innovation in the Era of Industry 4.0*

*Table 2. Definitions of types of innovation*

| Innovation Types | Definition of Innovation | Author |
|---|---|---|
| Product Innovation | Product innovation is the creation of novel products, changes to current product designs, or the application of new techniques and methods in current manufacturing methods. | Bacchiega et al. (2011); Bocquet, (2011); Bigliardi & Dormio(2009); Wagner & Bode(2014); Ganotakis et al. (2013) |
| Process Innovation | Improvements to the production process' efficiency and effectiveness are at the heart of process innovation. Changing the way products and services are developed and delivered to customers is part of the process. | Higgins, (1995); Bigliardi & Dormio(2009; Wagner & Bode(2014); Ganotakis et al. (2013) |
| Technology/Digital innovation | Innovative digital technology as an innovation introduced and resulting in new forms of digital transformation or Almost anything modern that a company wishes to adopt and put into practise in command to increase productivity. | Yoo et al. (2010); Gao et al. (2017); Hazen et al. (2012) |
| Organizational Innovation | Organizational innovation signifies to the application of a novel organisational technique in a corporation's business approaches, such as workplace planning and similarly exterior relations or as a result of these organisational innovations, collaborations among various supply chain actors, primarily suppliers, allow for profit maximisation while also achieving high levels of eco-efficiency. | Higgins, (1995); Damanpour & Evan(1984); Bigliardi & Dormio(2009) |
| Marketing Innovation | To improve product design, placement, promotion, or pricing by implementing a new marketing strategy (marketing idea). | Wagner & Bode(2014); Ganotakis et al. (2013) |
| Resource Allocation innovation | Resource allocation (RA) refers to the process of allocating and utilising a system's resources. Because of the scarcity and high cost of resources, resource redistribution aids in the development of new ideas. | Malairajan et al. (2013); Perrin et al. (2017); Naspetti et al. (2017) |

## Digital Innovation

Digital innovations are a result of digital technologies that have been put into place and the properties of those technologies that have been combined. The introduction of the concept of digital innovation necessitates a fundamental shift in the way businesses are run. "Digital innovation" refers to incorporating digital technology into a previously unexplored product or service (Henfridsson et al., 2009). When it comes to business processes, culture and organisational aspects, digital transformation refers to the adoption of digital technologies in order to meet the needs of today's customers. "Digital business" refers to an entirely new way of thinking about and designing businesses in the digital age (Hinings et al., 2018; Pramanik et al., 2019). Innovating through the use of technology and creating new ways to transform the world through digital means (Yoo et al., 2010). The definition of digital innovation is similar to that of technological innovation, with the addition of the concept of new ICT products. A more narrow definition of "digital innovation" would be the implementation of an ICT product that is new or significantly improved over an existing one (solution). The use of information and communications technology (ICT) in business operations or external relations to implement new or significantly improved processes, marketing strategies or organisational methods can also be referred to as an innovation stimulated by technology. Thus, digital innovation can be defined as the creation (and subsequent changes) of new market offerings, business processes, and models as a result of the use of digital technology (Nowicka 2019). There is a strong connection between the development, diffusion, or assimilation of a new idea and digital technology and digital transformation (Nambisan et al. 2017). According to Lyytinen (2021), the ability to generate new ideas through digital technology is what drives digital innovation. Generativity and the platformization process are typical characteristics of digital innovation and its outcomes (Gawer 2021), which may be difficult to control at times (Leiponen et al., 2021). With the advent of digital technologies, a new supply chain business model has emerged, one that aims to deliver higher value than what is currently available (Nowicka 2019). Using digital technology's inherent generativity, Nambisan (2020) demonstrates how multinational corporations can now connect with global markets and resources while also pursuing innovation in new geographies. Hron et al. (2021) also warn that digital technology's generative nature may lead to innovation drift. Building digital supply chains (networks) can use them as a springboard for the next stage in their evolution. Managing supply chain processes and digital products and services are now part of the scope of supply chain digitalization in organisations that are undergoing these rapid transformations (Büyüközkan and Göçer, 2018). In order to reap the benefits of a digital supply chain, new approaches must be utilised, including digital transformation through the use of technology. Among the most important aspects of the digital transformation of companies is the digitization of all business processes that can be digitalized (Hagberg et al., 2016), the collection of massive volumes of data from various sources (Frank et al., 2019), and the creation of an efficient customer interface (Pramanik et al., 2019). A company's ability to adapt to new technologies is essential to its success in the digital transformation process (Frank et al., 2019). Suppliers and customers are involved in supply chain processes that are part of the digital supply chain (Büyüközkan and Göçer, 2018) as a collection of interconnected activities handled with new technologies. As a result of new approaches, such as digital transformation and technological innovations, the digital supply chain has the ability to generate competitive value and network effects (Büyüközkan and Göçer, 2018). Digital technologies, in general, their properties are the primary drivers of change in the modern economy. With digital technologies, information, processing, communication, and technology are all combined into one. Digital innovation is the application of digital technologies to the creation of novel products, processes,

*Supply Chain Innovation in the Era of Industry 4.0*

and business models for the market (the resulting changes). It's impossible to have a new idea without using digital technologies and the processes that go along with them (Nambisan et al., 2017). There are three aspects to digital innovation that can be defined by such a definition.

- Innovative new products, platforms, services, customer experiences and other methods of delivering value have emerged as a result of digital technologies, even if the effects (results) aren't necessarily digital.

  ○ In order to introduce new innovations, companies are turning to various digital tools and infrastructure (similar as the Internet of Things (IoT) and blockchain technology)
  ○ Digital innovations' effects can be disseminated, accepted, or personalized to meet particular needs, such as use on digital platforms.

The application of digital technologies to supply chain management is a novel approach. Supply chains are going through a digital transformation as a result of their implementation of these technologies. Transforming a company's business model to create new value using digital technologies is a key part of the supply chain's digital transformation. This will help supply chains become more efficient while also helping them meet their strategic objectives. The company's digital transformation strategy is what's driving the supply chain's digital transformation. Building the technology ecosystem infrastructure allows the company (as the digital chain leader) and supply chain to achieve strategic goals (Raab, Griffin-Cryan 2011).

## Digital Transformation Benefits

The availability of information is at the centre of supply chain digital transformation. To improve reliability, agility, and effectiveness, the right organisational design and governance across digital platforms can help. The risk of falling behind the competition will force organisations to move from traditional supply chains to digital supply chains, and the performance gap between these two will force organisations to adjust to new digital realities. A digital operational model that integrates digital capabilities across corporate governance, processes, data, performance management and information technology (IT). The major benefit of a digital transformation of processes are shown in figure 1, consists of

1. *Process automation-* It is defined as the complete execution and automate the process design of an end-to-end procedure, which helps the operation, without the necessity for re-keying or physical interference.
2. *Enhanced organization flexibility-* It helps the organization to take an appropriate decision needed to support specialization or minimize process costs based on the level and degree of centralization at a given different local labour costs and productivity levels across locations.
3. *Digital management of corporate assets-* The "digital finger prints" along-with the physical flows captured to create improved visibility of all corporate assets. With little extra cost, the utilization of a specific production line, truck or administrative function can be made visible.

*Figure 2. Benefits of digital transformation*

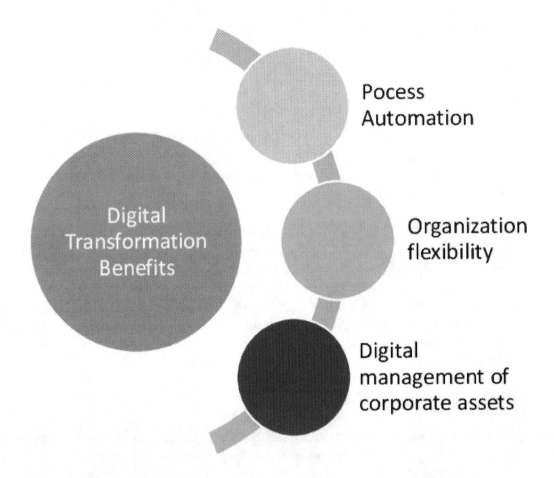

## SOLUTION AND RECOMMENDATIONS

This study explored the various research on supply chain innovation and Industry 4.0 using the available literature analysis. According to the results of the present study, the various variables/ dimension contributing to supply chain innovation and Industry 4.0 were discussed in two main areas (technological innovation and non-technical innovation). The two main dimensions were further divided in six variables (product innovation, process innovation, technological/digital innovation, organizational innovation, marketing innovation and resource allocation innovation). Resource allocation (RA) innovation refers to the process of allocating and utilising a system's resources, because of the scarcity and high cost of resources, resource redistribution aids in the development of new ideas. Managers, policymakers, and researchers are all aware of the importance of SCI in promoting competition and economic growth. Ideally, SCI could help the organization's operational effectiveness and performance while also reducing risk and expenses while also providing a competitive advantage. Business risks can be increased or decreased through supply chain innovation (Kwak et al., 2018). Improved service effectiveness, operational efficiency, revenue generation, as well as joint profit maximisation across the supply chain can

*Supply Chain Innovation in the Era of Industry 4.0*

be achieved through supply chain innovation (Bello et al., 2004). In order to improve competitiveness, supply chain design and redesign, product, process, and supply chain innovation, as well as a realignment of performance measures across the supply chain, more research is required (Melnyk et al. 2009). Innovation and its management have become increasingly important as a result of advancements in technology and knowledge, and managers must take this into account across the entire organisation. Industry 4.0's rapid adoption has heightened the need for supply chain innovation, which is a complex construct of great interest to many organisations. Digital technologies and their properties have changed the rules of competition in modern organisations. Innovations in supply chain management and performance can be spurred by the use of digital innovations. When digital supply chains are implemented, a large portion of operational (and tactical) activities can be automated. Digital technologies' progress is determined by the extent of their advantages – the values they provide – and the challenges they face in implementation. Consider that digital innovations that serve as a reference point for the development of digital supply chains drive the process of digital transformation of supply chains. Because of the rapid advancements in technology, as well as its inherent properties and effects when used in conjunction with one another, it is difficult to pin down exactly where this next stage in supply chain evolution will take place. The multi-fold benefits of digital transformation part of digital innovation helps the organization to automate the processes, better utilization of organization assets & provides better flexibility to the organization. There are many opportunities for future research

## CONCLUSION

This paper examined the effects of industrial digitalization on SCM in light of the current digital revolution and its business implications. Digital technology's characteristics alter a modern company's principles of competitiveness. Incorporating them into supply chain management improves results by encouraging the development of digital innovations. A substantial portion of operational as well as tactical accomplishments can be replaced by digital supply chains, which can be created when implementation results. The magnitude of the assistances – the values provided – and the obstacles to the application of digital technology determine their growth. The process of digital supply chain transformation is accelerated as a result of digital innovations that serve as a model for its development. The rapid changes in technologies, their properties, and how they interact as a result of their combination make it difficult to pin down, even though it helps move supply chains forward. Industry 4.0 that will unavoidably comprises of many innovative technologies like cloud computing, big data analytics, and advanced robotics. These include the Internet of Things, IoT, and IoT-enabled digital technologies. The Industry 4.0 paradigm is reshaping numerous sectors, including automotive, logistics, aerospace, defence and energy. The supply chain is undergoing significant transformation in light of the recent digital shift. Traditional supply chains, according to the findings of the study, must swiftly transform by adopting Industry 4.0 principles in order to remain relevant in quickly altering markets. Companies are looking for ways to embrace the new revolution beyond the supply chain's boundaries. Since businesses have promoted on-demand approaches, SC operating models' scalability and flexibility have grown traction in the conversation of digitalization's benefits beyond productivity improvement. Blockchain and robotics are widely used in supply chain operations, and businesses have begun to assimilate fundamentally different supply chain operational models by relying on platform economics and data analytics. Conventional businesses, on the other hand, appear to stick with their current business models while embracing new digital technologies to improve operational efficacy and productivity. Internal provision of services is preferable when differentiating involves the potential for additional value in the company's operational supply chain processes. Different digitalization strategies are available for these processes based on product, process, and organisational, marketing, and technological innovation. It's important to remember, however, that digital technologies are still considered a resource in supply chain management, and managers cite rise in implementation expenses and a shortage of experts as the key obstacles to implementing digital innovations.

## FUTURE DIRECTIONS

Digital supply chain innovation can help these specialists combine their knowledge of technology properties with the needs and strategic supply chain management priorities. This last argument seems to be very important, there are a lot of possibilities for future research because of the problems. In the first place, there are many different cases and dimensions of Industry 4.0 that can be looked at. This is because many different industries have started similar state-funded initiatives to make the industrial sector more digital. This would make it easier to look at existing businesses, how they use industry 4.0 enabled SCI, and how the size and type of business affect the effects of digitalization on businesses and their businesses. Second, numerous in-depth case studies could be used to delve deeper into the drivers, success factors, and challenges associated with industry 4.0-enabled SCI. This approach may assist us in comprehending how complementary technologies such as advanced manufacturing and the blockchain may contribute to the digital transformation of other technologies. Finally, business effects, such as increased productivity, could be looked at to figure out how much digital SC transformation would help the business.

## REFERENCES

Albers, A., Gladysz, B., Pinner, T., Butenko, V., & Stürmlinger, T. (2016). Procedure for defining the system of objectives in the initial phase of an industry 4.0 project focusing on intelligent quality control systems. *Procedia CIRP*, *52*, 262–267. doi:10.1016/j.procir.2016.07.067

Archer, N., Wang, S., & Kang, C. (2008). Barriers to the adoption of online supply chain solutions in small and medium enterprises. *Supply Chain Management*, *13*(1), 73–82. doi:10.1108/13598540810850337

Arlbjørn, J. S., de Haas, H., & Munksgaard, K. B. (2011). Exploring supply chain innovation. *Logistics Research*, *3*(1), 3–18. doi:10.100712159-010-0044-3

Azevedo, A. (Ed.). (2013). *Advances in sustainable and competitive manufacturing systems: 23rd international conference on flexible automation & intelligent manufacturing.* Springer Science & Business Media.

Bacchiega, E., Lambertini, L., & Mantovaini, A. (2011). Process and product innovation in a vertically differentiated industry. *International Game Theory Review*, *13*(02), 209–221. doi:10.1142/S0219198911002952

Baregheh, A., Rowley, J., & Sambrook, S. (2009). Towards a multidisciplinary definition of innovation. *Management Decision*, *47*(8), 1323–1339. doi:10.1108/00251740910984578

Beise, M., & Rennings, K. (2005). Lead markets and regulation: A framework for analyzing the international diffusion of environmental innovations. *Ecological Economics*, *52*(1), 5–17. doi:10.1016/j.ecolecon.2004.06.007

Belinski, R., Peixe, A. M., Frederico, G. F., & Garza-Reyes, J. A. (2020). Organizational learning and Industry 4.0: Findings from a systematic literature review and research agenda. *Benchmarking*, *27*(8), 2435–2457. doi:10.1108/BIJ-04-2020-0158

Bello, D. C., Lohtia, R., & Sangtani, V. (2004). An institutional analysis of supply chain innovations in global marketing channels. *Industrial Marketing Management*, *33*(1), 57–64. doi:10.1016/j.indmarman.2003.08.011

Ben-Daya, M., Hassini, E., & Bahroun, Z. (2019). Internet of things and supply chain management: A literature review. *International Journal of Production Research*, *57*(15-16), 4719–4742. doi:10.1080/00207543.2017.1402140

Bhagwat, R., & Sharma, M. K. (2009). An application of the integrated AHP-PGP model for performance measurement of supply chain management. *Production Planning and Control*, *20*(8), 678–690. doi:10.1080/09537280903069897

Bigliardi, B., & Dormio, A. I. (2009). An empirical investigation of innovation determinants in food machinery enterprises. *European Journal of Innovation Management*, *12*(2), 223–242. doi:10.1108/14601060910953988

Bititci, U. S., Firat, S. U. O., & Garengo, P. (2013). How to compare performances of firms operating in different sectors? *Production Planning and Control*, *24*(12), 1032–1049. doi:10.1080/09537287.2011.643829

Bocquet, R. (2011). Product and process innovations in subcontracting: Empirical evidence from the French "Sillon Alpin". *Industry and Innovation*, *18*(7), 649–668. doi:10.1080/13662716.2011.604471

Brettel, M., Bendig, D., Keller, M., Friederichsen, N., & Rosenberg, M. (2014). Effectuation in manufacturing: How entrepreneurial decision-making techniques can be used to deal with uncertainty in manufacturing. *Procedia CIRP*, *17*, 611–616. doi:10.1016/j.procir.2014.03.119

Büyüközkan, G., & Göçer, F. (2018). Digital Supply Chain: Literature review and a proposed framework for future research. *Computers in Industry*, *97*, 157–177. doi:10.1016/j.compind.2018.02.010

Cai, J., Liu, X., Xiao, Z., & Liu, J. (2009). Improving supply chain performance management: A systematic approach to analyzing iterative KPI accomplishment. *Decision Support Systems*, *46*(2), 512–521. doi:10.1016/j.dss.2008.09.004

Chapman, R. L., Soosay, C., & Kandampully, J. (2002). Innovation in logistic services and the new business model: A conceptual framework. *Managing Service Quality*, *12*(6), 358–371. doi:10.1108/09604520210451849

Chavez, R., Yu, W., Jacobs, M. A., & Feng, M. (2017). Data-driven supply chains, manufacturing capability and customer satisfaction. *Production Planning and Control*, 28(11-12), 906–918. doi:10.1080/09537287.2017.1336788

Chen, I. J., & Paulraj, A. (2004). Towards a theory of supply chain management: The constructs and measurements. *Journal of Operations Management*, 22(2), 119–150. doi:10.1016/j.jom.2003.12.007

Chong, A. Y., Chan, F. T., Ooi, K. B., & Sim, J. J. (2011). Can Malaysian firms improve organizational/innovation performance via SCM? *Industrial Management & Data Systems*, 111(3), 410–431. doi:10.1108/02635571111118288

Cohen, W. M., & Levinthal, D. A. (1990). Absorptive capacity: A new perspective on learning and innovation. *Administrative Science Quarterly*, 35(1), 128–152. doi:10.2307/2393553

Coltman, T., Gattorna, J., & Whiting, S. (2010). Realigning service operations strategy at DHL express. *Interfaces*, 40(3), 175–183. doi:10.1287/inte.1100.0491

Damanpour, F., & Evan, W. M. (1984). Organizational innovation and performance: The problem of" organizational lag. *Administrative Science Quarterly*, 29(3), 392–409. doi:10.2307/2393031

Datta, P. P. (2017). Enhancing competitive advantage by constructing supply chains to achieve superior performance. *Production Planning and Control*, 28(1), 57–74.

Desbarats, G. (1999). The innovation supply chain. *Supply Chain Management*, 4(1), 7–10. doi:10.1108/13598549910254708

Dubey, R., Singh, T., & Tiwari, S. (2012). Supply chain innovation is a key to superior firm performance an insight from Indian cement manufacturing. *International Journal of Innovation Science*, 4(4), 217–229. doi:10.1260/1757-2223.4.4.217

Eschenbächer, J., Seifert, M., & Thoben, K. D. (2011). Improving distributed innovation processes in virtual organisations through the evaluation of collaboration intensities. *Production Planning and Control*, 22(5-6), 473–487. doi:10.1080/09537287.2010.536620

Flint, D. J., & Larsson, E. (2007). Supply chain innovation. Handbook of Global Supply Chain Management, 49(4), 475–487.

Flint, D. J., Larsson, E., Gammelgaard, B., & Mentzer, J. T. (2005). Logistics innovation: A customer value-oriented social process. *Journal of Business Logistics*, 26(1), 113–147. doi:10.1002/j.2158-1592.2005.tb00196.x

Frank, A. G., Mendes, G. H., Ayala, N. F., & Ghezzi, A. (2019). Servitization and Industry 4.0 convergence in the digital transformation of product firms: A business model innovation perspective. *Technological Forecasting and Social Change*, 141, 341–351. doi:10.1016/j.techfore.2019.01.014

Ganotakis, P., Hsieh, W. L., & Love, J. H. (2013). Information systems, inter-functional collaboration and innovation in Taiwanese high-tech manufacturing firms. *Production Planning and Control*, 24(8-9), 837–850. doi:10.1080/09537287.2012.666876

Gao, D., Xu, Z., Ruan, Y. Z., & Lu, H. (2017). From a systematic literature review to integrated definition for sustainable supply chain innovation (SSCI). *Journal of Cleaner Production, 142*, 1518–1538. doi:10.1016/j.jclepro.2016.11.153

Gawer, A. (2021). Digital platforms and ecosystems: Remarks on the dominant organizational forms of the digital age. *Innovation*, 1–15. doi:10.1080/14479338.2021.1965888

Gebhardt, J., Grimm, A., & Neugebauer, L. M. (2015). Developments 4.0 Prospects on future requirements and impacts on work and vocational education. *Journal of Teacher Education, 3*(2), 117–133.

Grawe, S. J. (2009). Logistics innovation: A literature-based conceptual framework. *International Journal of Logistics Management, 20*(3), 360–377. doi:10.1108/09574090911002823

Haddara, M., & Elragal, A. (2015). The Readiness of ERP Systems for the Factory of the Future. *Procedia Computer Science, 64*, 721–728. doi:10.1016/j.procs.2015.08.598

Hagberg, J., Sundstrom, M., & Egels-Zandén, N. (2016). The digitalization of retailing: An exploratory framework. *International Journal of Retail & Distribution Management, 44*(7), 694–712. doi:10.1108/IJRDM-09-2015-0140

Hazen, B. T., Overstreet, R. E., & Cegielski, C. G. (2012). Supply chain innovation diffusion: Going beyond adoption. *International Journal of Logistics Management, 23*(1), 119–134. doi:10.1108/09574091211226957

Henfridsson, O., Yoo, Y., & Svahn, F. (2009). *Path creation in digital innovation: A multi-layered dialectics perspective.* Association for Information Systems.

Herzlinger, R. E. (2006). Why innovation in health care is so hard. *Harvard Business Review, 84*(5), 58. PMID:16649698

Higgins, J. M. (1995). *Innovate or evaporate: Test & improve your organization's IQ, its innovation quotient.* New Management Publishing Company.

Hinings, B., Gegenhuber, T., & Greenwood, R. (2018). Digital innovation and transformation: An institutional perspective. *Information and Organization, 28*(1), 52–61. doi:10.1016/j.infoandorg.2018.02.004

Hron, M., Obwegeser, N., & Müller, S. D. (2021). Innovation drift: The influence of digital artefacts on organizing for innovation. *Innovation*, 1–33. doi:10.1080/14479338.2021.1937185

Hui, Z., He-Cheng, W., & Min-Fei, Z. (2015). Partnership management, supply chain collaboration, and firm innovation performance: An empirical examination. *International Journal of Innovation Science, 7*(2), 127–138. doi:10.1260/1757-2223.7.2.127

Isaksson, R., Johansson, P., & Fischer, K. (2010). Detecting supply chain innovation potential for sustainable development. *Journal of Business Ethics, 97*(3), 425–442. doi:10.100710551-010-0516-z

Ivanov, D., Dolgui, A., Sokolov, B., Werner, F., & Ivanova, M. (2016). A dynamic model and an algorithm for short-term supply chain scheduling in the smart factory industry 4.0. *International Journal of Production Research, 54*(2), 386–402. doi:10.1080/00207543.2014.999958

Jajja, M. S. S., Kannan, V. R., Brah, S. A., & Hassan, S. Z. (2017). Linkages between firm innovation strategy, suppliers, product innovation, and business performance: Insights from resource dependence theory. *International Journal of Operations & Production Management, 37*(8), 1054–1075. doi:10.1108/IJOPM-09-2014-0424

Jellali, A., & Benaissa, M. (2015, May). Sustainable performance evaluation of the supply chain. In *2015 4th International Conference on Advanced Logistics and Transport (ICALT)* (pp. 151-156). IEEE. 10.1109/ICAdLT.2015.7136612

Kagermann, H. (2015). Change through digitization—Value creation in the age of Industry 4.0. In *Management of permanent change* (pp. 23–45). Springer Gabler. doi:10.1007/978-3-658-05014-6_2

Kagermann, H., Wahlster, W., & Helbig, J. (2013). *Recommendations for implementing the strategic initiative Industrie 4.0: Final report of the Industrie 4.0 Working Group*. Forschungsunion.

Kavin, L., & Narasimhan, R. (2017, July). An investigation of innovation processes: The role of clock speed. *Supply Chain Forum International Journal, 18*(3), 189–200.

Klewitz, J., & Hansen, E. G. (2014). Sustainability-oriented innovation of SMEs: A systematic review. *Journal of Cleaner Production, 65*, 57–75. doi:10.1016/j.jclepro.2013.07.017

Kwak, D. W., Seo, Y. J., & Mason, R. (2018). Investigating the relationship between supply chain innovation, risk management capabilities and competitive advantage in global supply chains. *International Journal of Operations & Production Management, 38*(1), 2–21. doi:10.1108/IJOPM-06-2015-0390

Lee, S. M., Lee, D., & Schniederjans, M. J. (2011). Supply chain innovation and organizational performance in the healthcare industry. *International Journal of Operations & Production Management, 31*(11), 1193–1214. doi:10.1108/01443571111178493

Lee, V. H., Ooi, K. B., Chong, A. Y. L., & Seow, C. (2014). Creating technological innovation via green supply chain management: An empirical analysis. *Expert Systems with Applications, 41*(16), 6983–6994. doi:10.1016/j.eswa.2014.05.022

Leiponen, A., Thomas, L. D., & Wang, Q. (2021). The dApp economy: A new platform for distributed innovation? *Innovation*, 1–19. doi:10.1080/14479338.2021.1965887

Lin, C. Y. (2007). Supply chain performance and the adoption of new logistics technologies for logistics service providers in Taiwan. *Journal of Statistics and Management Systems, 10*(4), 519–543. doi:10.1 080/09720510.2007.10701270

Lyytinen, K. (2021). Innovation logics in the digital era: A systemic review of the emerging digital innovation regime. *Innovation*, 1–22. doi:10.1080/14479338.2021.1938579

Macaulay, J., Buckalew, L., & Chung, G. (2015). Internet of things in logistics: A collaborative report by DHL and Cisco on implications and use cases for the logistics industry. DHL Trend Research and Cisco Consulting Services, 439-449.

MacCarthy, B. L., Blome, C., Olhager, J., Srai, J. S., & Zhao, X. (2016). Supply chain evolution–theory, concepts and science. *International Journal of Operations & Production Management, 36*(12), 1696–1718. doi:10.1108/IJOPM-02-2016-0080

Malairajan, R. A., Ganesh, K., Muhos, M., & Anbuudayasankar, S. P. (2013). Class of resource allocation problems in supply chain–a review. *International Journal of Business Innovation and Research, 7*(1), 113–139. doi:10.1504/IJBIR.2013.050559

Mandal, S. (2016). An empirical competence-capability model of supply chain innovation. *Verslas: teorija ir praktika, 17*(2), 138-149.

Martinez, V., Pavlov, A., & Bourne, M. (2010). Reviewing performance: An analysis of the structure and functions of performance management reviews. *Production Planning and Control, 21*(1), 70–83. doi:10.1080/09537280903317049

Melnyk, S. A., Lummus, R. R., Vokurka, R. J., Burns, L. J., & Sandor, J. (2009). Mapping the future of supply chain management: A Delphi study. *International Journal of Production Research, 47*(16), 4629–4653. doi:10.1080/00207540802014700

Moreira, A. C., Ferreira, L. M. D., & Zimmermann, R. A. (Eds.). (2018). *Innovation and supply chain management: Relationship, collaboration and strategies.* Springer. doi:10.1007/978-3-319-74304-2

Munksgaard, K. B., Stentoft, J., & Paulraj, A. (2014). Value-based supply chain innovation. *Operations Management Research, 7*(3-4), 50–62. doi:10.100712063-014-0092-y

Nambisan, S. (2020). Digital innovation and international business. *Innovation,* 1–10. doi:10.1080/14 479338.2020.1834861

Nambisan, S., Lyytinen, K., Majchrzak, A., & Song, M. (2017). Digital Innovation Management: Reinventing innovation management research in a digital world. *Management Information Systems Quarterly, 41*(1), 223–238. doi:10.25300/MISQ/2017/41:1.03

Naspetti, S., Mandolesi, S., Buysse, J., Latvala, T., Nicholas, P., Padel, S., Van Loo, E., & Zanoli, R. (2017). Determinants of the acceptance of sustainable production strategies among dairy farmers: Development and testing of a modified technology acceptance model. *Sustainability, 9*(10), 1805. doi:10.3390u9101805

Neely, A. (2005). The evolution of performance measurement research. *International Journal of Operations & Production Management, 25*(12), 1264–1277. doi:10.1108/01443570510633648

Nidumolu, R., Prahalad, C. K., & Rangaswami, M. R. (2015). Why sustainability is now the key driver of innovation. *IEEE Engineering Management Review, 43*(2), 85–91. doi:10.1109/EMR.2015.7123233

Nowicka, K. (2019). Digital innovation in the supply chain management. *Prace Naukowe Uniwersytetu Ekonomicznego we Wrocławiu, 63*(8), 202-214.

Ojha, D., Shockley, J., & Acharya, C. (2016). Supply chain organizational infrastructure for promoting entrepreneurial emphasis and innovativeness: The role of trust and learning. *International Journal of Production Economics, 179,* 212–227. doi:10.1016/j.ijpe.2016.06.011

Oztemel, E., & Gursev, S. (2020). Literature review of Industry 4.0 and related technologies. *Journal of Intelligent Manufacturing, 31*(1), 127–182. doi:10.100710845-018-1433-8

Pacaux-Lemoine, M. P., Trentesaux, D., Rey, G. Z., & Millot, P. (2017). Designing intelligent manufacturing systems through Human-Machine Cooperation principles: A human-centered approach. *Computers & Industrial Engineering, 111*, 581–595. doi:10.1016/j.cie.2017.05.014

Perrin, A., Wohlfahrt, J., Morandi, F., Østergård, H., Flatberg, T., De La Rua, C., Bjørkvoll, T., & Gabrielle, B. (2017). Integrated design and sustainable assessment of innovative biomass supply chains: A case-study on miscanthus in France. *Applied Energy, 204*, 66–77. doi:10.1016/j.apenergy.2017.06.093

Prajogo, D., & Olhager, J. (2012). The effect of supply chain information integration on logistics integration and firm performance. *International Journal of Production Economics, 135*(1), 514–522. doi:10.1016/j.ijpe.2011.09.001

Prajogo, D., & Olhager, J. (2012). Supply chain integration and performance: The effects of long-term relationships, information technology and sharing, and logistics integration. *International Journal of Production Economics, 135*(1), 514–522. doi:10.1016/j.ijpe.2011.09.001

Pramanik, H. S., Kirtania, M., & Pani, A. K. (2019). Essence of digital transformation—Manifestations at large financial institutions from North America. *Future Generation Computer Systems, 95*, 323–343. doi:10.1016/j.future.2018.12.003

Raab, M., & Griffin-Cryan, B. (2011). *Digital transformation of supply chains. Creating Value–When Digital Meets Physical*. Capgemini Consulting.

Sabri, Y., Micheli, G. J., & Nuur, C. (2018). Exploring the impact of innovation implementation on supply chain configuration. *Journal of Engineering and Technology Management, 49*, 60–75. doi:10.1016/j.jengtecman.2018.06.001

Schaltegger, S., & Burritt, R. (2014). Measuring and managing sustainability performance of supply chains. *Supply Chain Management, 19*(3). Advance online publication. doi:10.1108/SCM-02-2014-0083

Schoenherr, T., & Swink, M. (2012). Revisiting the arcs of integration: Cross-validations and extensions. *Journal of Operations Management, 30*(1-2), 99–115. doi:10.1016/j.jom.2011.09.001

Shapiro, J. F., & Wagner, S. N. (2009). Strategic inventory optimization. *Journal of Business Logistics, 30*(2), 161–173. doi:10.1002/j.2158-1592.2009.tb00117.x

Stevens, G. C., & Johnson, M. (2016). Integrating the Supply Chain . . . 25 Years on. *International Journal of Physical Distribution & Logistics Management, 46*(1), 19–42. doi:10.1108/IJPDLM-07-2015-0175

Storer, M., Hyland, P., Ferrer, M., Santa, R., & Griffiths, A. (2014). Strategic supply chain management factors influencing agribusiness innovation utilization. *International Journal of Logistics Management, 25*(3), 487–521. doi:10.1108/IJLM-02-2013-0026

Szozda, N. (2017). Industry 4.0 and its impact on the functioning of supply chains. *Logforum, 13*(4).

Tebaldi, L., Bigliardi, B., & Bottani, E. (2018). Sustainable supply chain and innovation: A review of the recent literature. *Sustainability, 10*(11), 3946. doi:10.3390u10113946

Tidd, J., & Bessant, J. R. (2020). *Managing innovation: integrating technological, market and organizational change*. John Wiley & Sons.

Tiwari, S. (2020). Supply chain integration and Industry 4.0: A systematic literature review. *Benchmarking*, *28*(3), 990–1030. doi:10.1108/BIJ-08-2020-0428

Van Alstyne, M. W., Parker, G. G., & Choudary, S. P. (2016). Pipelines, platforms, and the new rules of strategy. *Harvard Business Review*, *94*(4), 54–62.

Verny, J., Oulmakki, O., Cabo, X., & Roussel, D. (2020). Blockchain & supply chain: towards an innovative supply chain design. *Projectics/Proyectica/Projectique*, (2), 115-130.

Wagner, S. M., & Bode, C. (2014). Supplier relationship-specific investments and the role of safeguards for supplier innovation sharing. *Journal of Operations Management*, *32*(3), 65–78. doi:10.1016/j.jom.2013.11.001

Wang, C., & Hu, Q. (2020). Knowledge sharing in supply chain networks: Effects of collaborative innovation activities and capability on innovation performance. *Technovation*, *94*, 102010. doi:10.1016/j.technovation.2017.12.002

Wittenberg, C. (2016). Human-CPS Interaction-requirements and human-machine interaction methods for the Industry 4.0. *IFAC-PapersOnLine*, *49*(19), 420–425. doi:10.1016/j.ifacol.2016.10.602

Wong, D. T., & Ngai, E. W. (2019). Critical review of supply chain innovation research (1999–2016). *Industrial Marketing Management*, *82*, 158–187. doi:10.1016/j.indmarman.2019.01.017

Wu, Y. J., & Tsai, K. M. (2018). Making connections: Supply chain innovation research collaboration. *Transportation Research Part E, Logistics and Transportation Review*, *113*, 222–224. doi:10.1016/j.tre.2018.02.004

Yin, Y., Stecke, K. E., & Li, D. (2018). The evolution of production systems from Industry 2.0 through Industry 4.0. *International Journal of Production Research*, *56*(1-2), 848–861. doi:10.1080/00207543.2017.1403664

Yoo, Y., Henfridsson, O., & Lyytinen, K. (2010). Research commentary—the new organizing logic of digital innovation: An agenda for information systems research. *Information Systems Research*, *21*(4), 724–735. doi:10.1287/isre.1100.0322

Zijm, H., Klumpp, M., Heragu, S., & Regattieri, A. (2019). Operations, logistics and supply chain management: definitions and objectives. In *Operations, Logistics and Supply Chain Management* (pp. 27–42). Springer. doi:10.1007/978-3-319-92447-2_3

## KEY TERMS AND DEFINITIONS

**Digital Innovation:** Digital innovation is similar to that of technological innovation, with the addition of the concept of new ICT.

**Digital Transformation:** Digital transformation refers to the adoption of digital technologies in order to meet the needs of today's customers.

**Marketing Innovation:** It helps in designing, placement, promotion, or pricing by implementing a new marketing strategy.

**Organizational Innovation:** New and innovative way of managing and application of organizational technique collaborating supply chain actors.

**Process Innovation:** New way of developing and delivering product and services to customer.

**Resource Allocation:** It refers to the process of allocating and utilising a system's resources.

**Supply Chain Innovation:** It is recognized as an alteration in a product, process, marketing, technology, resource, and/or organisation that affects all aspects of the supply chain and enhances value for all shareholders.

# Chapter 4
# Supply Chain Planning to Achieve Resilience Capabilities

**Sowmya Sangaraju**
*Volkswagen of America, USA*

**Yanamandra Ramakrishna**
iD https://orcid.org/0000-0001-9101-6072
*Skyline University College, UAE*

## ABSTRACT

*Supply chain resilience (SCR) has emerged as a buzz word during the COVID-19 pandemic situation. With the emerging digital technologies and methodologies, optimizing SCM has become the utmost priority for any organization to achieve the SCR capabilities. The pandemic has compelled organizations to rethink about their SC processes and perform risk analysis to achieve SC resilience. Regional diversification of vendors, proactive identification of potential risks, usage of digital technologies lead to increase in factors such as SC visibility, agility, and flexibility to develop SCR. This chapter develops a SC resilience model by linking the SC planning processes, strategies, and application of digital technologies to achieve capabilities of SCR by a business organization in a pandemic situation. The outcome of this research would be very useful to the industry practitioners and academic researchers in the SC area.*

## INTRODUCTION

Supply Chain Management (SCM) has been a crucial part of every business organization since its emergence and it has evolved over the time. Recently, due to the COVID-19 pandemic, Supply Chain (SC) has experienced unprecedented and significant disruptions (Siagian et al., 2021). This unexpected and sudden development on a global scale created a major disruption in SC in both up-stream and down-stream activities (Handfield et al., 2020). This disruption also compelled the managements of organizations to develop alternate plans to mitigate disruptions and risks in SC due to the current pandemic situation (Black and Glaser-Segura, 2020). With the latest technologies and methodologies, optimizing SCM by identifying the risks and developing a plan has become the utmost priority for any organization.

DOI: 10.4018/978-1-7998-9506-0.ch004

Risk management is an important issue in supply chain management as uncertainty of the occurrence of an event in one function of supply chain brings undesirable chain effect for the supply chain network (Finch, 2004; Tummala and Schoenherr, 2011). Supply chain risk has been defined as an unplanned and unexpected incident that disrupts the flow of goods or services within the supply chain literature (Scholten et al., 2019). Assessment of risks and development of risk management plans has gained utmost importance for achieving sustainability and resilience in SC during this pandemic. These plans will enable the organizations sail smoothly the pandemic situation with minimum impact of risks and disruptions. These plans also enable the organizations to regain quickly their original positions by successfully countering the negative impact of pandemic (Das, 2018). Therefore, planning towards SC resilience is the need of the hour for business organizations. Organizations attempt to achieve this resilience through diversified approaches. The evolution and emergence of digital technologies made this process easier for those organizations, which have implemented them proactively to manage their supply chains. However, due to many issues and challenges most of the organizations are unable to take advantage out of these technologies to plan their SC processes by integrating the technologies (Das and Lashkari, 2015). Moreover, some of the organizations are confused about how this integration takes place at the SC planning stage. With this background, this chapter attempts to identify the role of SC planning in achieving the resilience and provides some feasible solutions towards resilience.

Based on the above discussion, the chapter intends to address the following objectives and research questions.

- How SC planning will lead to SC resilience especially during the pandemic?
- How identification of risks and risk management plan will help achieve resilience in pandemic?
- What are the existing models of SCR with integration of planning?
- How SC planning through digital technologies supports the achievement of SC resilience?

A Comprehensive Literature Review (CLR) approach (Onwuegbuzie and Freis, 2016) has been adopted as the methodology for achieving the above objectives of the chapter. Using a set of key words, articles published in Emerald, ScienceDirect, Scopus, Proquest, and ResearchGate between 2000 to 2021 were considered.

## BACKGROUND

SC planning to achieve resilience is dependent and linked to many factors such as risk assessment, SC dependencies, SC visibility, vendor localization and preparedness for facing disruptive situations (Hendricks and Singhal, 2005; Juttner and Maklan, 2011; Black and Glaser-Segura, 2020; Gaur and Gaiha, 2020). Through a literature review, these factors are mentioned briefly here.

Identification and assessment of all potential risks is the first of all factors to achieve the resilience. This step includes identification of all types of risks in addition to the financial risks. This kind of assessment provides the organizations with information about their status and their strengths and weaknesses in managing the risks. It also provides them a firsthand knowledge of weak and potential areas of vulnerability (Mandal, 2011).

The second important factor in the achievement of SC resilience is an analysis of 'dependencies' of organization on various stakeholders such as global suppliers, third party vendors, logistics providers, distributors, stock keeping units and regular and bulk customers (Juttner and Maklan, 2011). This analysis provides the organizations a clear picture of their dependencies and the alternative plan in case of disruptions for these dependencies. A proactive action plan can be developed by the organizations if the dependencies are analyzed well in advance. There are basically two types of dependencies for business organizations. These are internal and external. During the pandemic situations and disruptive situations, the internal dependencies can be managed with less difficulty than the external dependencies. The internal dependencies are generally manageable by employees at different hierarchical positions in the supply chain structure of an organization. The external dependencies are not directly in control of organization as they are related to external stakeholders. Any disruption in the operations of these external stakeholders would negatively impact the entire supply chain process.

The third factor is SC visibility. Given the wide nature and scope of SCM, it is a challenging task to make all the processes of SC visible (Mandal, 2011). However, implementation of digital technologies makes the process of SC more visible. By creating visibility, the organization can clearly know their strong and weak points. The fourth factor is vendor localization and diversification (Van Hoek, 2020). Organizations with local vendors have great advantage of reducing logistics cost and frequent vendor audits.

However, the organizations needs to make a trade-off between quality of supply and localization of vendors. Supplier and vendor training programs will help in improving the quality of supply from the local vendors. At the same time, the organizations can support the local vendors on improving their processes, systems and practices related to quality improvement programs. In addition to these factors, the organization should perform a honest SWOT (Strengths, Weaknesses, Opportunities and Threats) analysis of its current situation and assess its capabilities to achieve resilience in case of disruptions and risks. This kind of analysis also provides the organizations with an opportunity to analyze the existing market conditions to develop supply chain planning to achieve resilience. Therefore, the organizations can develop their supply chain plans by carefully analyzing the factors influencing supply chain resilience.

COVID'19 pandemic situation made organizations to realize that there are many weak areas in supply chain, which require their focus to develop the capabilities of resilience (Deloitte, 2020; Ivanov and Dolgui, 2020; Siagian et al., 2021). The pandemic was thought to be of temporary one in the initial period of its occurrence. However, with the emergence of many new and deadly variants, now the organizations have started realizing that they need to develop their supply chain plans for a longer and unpredictable duration. Therefore, it is highly essential for them to develop quickly their supply chain plans by incorporating the strategies to mitigate the risks and disruptions.

When companies perform risk analysis of their supply chains, they generally tend to look at company history, which would reduce the unseen and natural scenarios. Best example for this would be Toyota's Quake Proof supply chain (Amit Gautam, 2020). In March 2011, an earthquake in Japan, resulting in minimal supply of items to the assembly plant affected Toyota and it took lot of time for it to get back to their original position. During this process, the company decided to make a quakeproof plan and have stated about their strong plans to survive earthquake. They have developed a strategy known as RESCUE (Reinforce Supple Chain under Emergency) system with 60/20/20 supply model where if the main supplier fails to provide the supply, the immediate lower supplier will compensate the capacity. However, unfortunately, when they were hit again in April 2016, they were unable to recover back early as they mentioned. They still had issues reverting and other automobile companies reverted early to their original status. Therefore, it is important not to avoid the risks but to develop the ability to implement mitigation measures and get back immediately, and the ability to make their supply chain resilient enough to sustain any type of risk.

In a similar manner, many business organizations got impacted negatively in procuring the supply due to Covid19 and due to geographically concentrated suppliers, especially in China. In the era of digitalization, developing an appropriate implementation strategy for digital technologies to modernize their supply chains is the immediate need of the hour. Firms, which deployed these technologies, performed better in effective management of their supply chains than those who somehow either neglected their implementation or could not implement them in a right manner (Choi et al., 2020; Van Hoek, 2020). Similarly, emerging technologies such as blockchain in supply chain management is also found enable the business organizations with innumerable benefits. The objective blockchain in SCM is to allow a limited number of known parties to protect their business operations against malicious actors while supporting better performance (Gaur and Gaiha, 2020). It also develops visibility and transparency as blockchain has the ability to create place and ownership documentation instantaneously. It also creates immutable digital record of the inventory pipeline (Black and Glaser-Segura, 2020).

In the recent past, organizations have started giving more importance to SCM and focused their attention towards developing competitive strategies by redesigning their SCM activities (Deloitte, 2020). At the same time, increased complexity of these activities in the globalized era has also thrown many challenges and created new types of risks. In order to identify solutions to these challenges, organizations have been trying their best to improve their supply chains by focusing on innovation and new product development. Some of these new risks for instance are related to natural calamities like flooding, snow, hurricanes, earthquakes, storms etc. With increase in CO2 emission, the global warming has been increasing and there is an increase in these natural calamities in the recent past. Some of them have been occurring suddenly without giving any time to plan for the organizations. Thus, the risk management is not a onetime process but it is a continuous process with list of risks expanding with the addition of new risks. Being in multipolar economic system, there are new difficulties coming up out of blue.

Some of the existing practices of supply chain like Just-in-Time (JIT), Lean Management and Six Sigma have taken new modes of implementation, contributing to more visibility and transparency of processes in supply chain. Sudden emergence of Covid19 pandemic has once again compelled the organization to explore more innovation in these SC practices. The pandemic has resulted in closing of borders, restricted movement of goods and people, created panic for buying at all levels of supply chain, created imbalance between supply and demand for some products resulting in development of adhoc and short-term SC strategies by the managements. Overbuying and panic among customers and other channel members created sudden shortage of supply. Some of the organizations were unable to handle this sudden and unexpected change. Many authors and practitioners of supply chain attributed the reasons for this as shortage of raw materials due to imbalance in supply and demand, geographical concentration of vendors in affected regions of Covid19, lack of information sharing, lack of proper distribution channels and absence of proactive risk and disruption management plan (Siagian et al., 2021). These challenges also led to the closure of severely affected SMEs and some other medium sized organizations. All these happenings have once again reiterated the importance and need of developing a SC risk management plan, usage of digital technologies to achieve SC resilience. However, there is a shortage of literature including the empirical studies in this area with special focus on pandemic situation. Therefore, this chapter attempts to bridge this gap in the literature.

Given this background, the concept of SCR has been dealt here with a focus on its definition, existing literature works and models.

## SUPPLY CHAIN RESILIENCE (SCR)

Ponomarov and Holcomb (2009) considered supply chain resilience from a multifaceted approach encompassing environmental, societal, psychological, economic, and organizational dimensions. They define resilience as "the adaptive capability of the supply chain to prepare for unexpected events, respond to disruptions, and recover from them by maintaining continuity of operations at the desired level of connectedness and control over structure and function".

According to Sheffi (2005), resilience is when firms learn from disruptions and shift to a stronger position. Fiskel (2006) refers to resilience as the capacity for an organization to survive, adapt, and grow when faced with turbulent change. The company's ability to involve suppliers and customers

in dealing with disruption is called supply chain resilience (Shin and Park, 2019). Resilience has been used to offset increasing complexity in supply chain networks (Golicic et al., 2017), and by incorporation the more traditional concepts of risk management with resilience (Linkov and Florin, 2016). As stated by Pettit et al. (2019), "a firm's resilience is significantly affected by its customers' and suppliers' ability to anticipate and respond to disruptions". They advocate that organizations move beyond traditional enterprise risk management practices and learn to imbue a culture of resilience (Pettit et al., 2019). A company cannot control the disruption caused by a sudden environmental change and deep uncertainty poses a great challenge for supply chain managers when planning resilience strategies (Paul and Venkateswaran, 2020). A resilient company positively responds to maintaining its balance by paying attention to external changes (Mandal, 2020). Therefore, implementing SC plans to develop the ability to build a resilient SC is very important. Black and Glaser-Segura, (2020) proposed two areas to achieve resilience. These are SC strategies and demand management strategies. The resilience in SC is also enhanced due to the organizational innovation policies and quick adoption to unexpected and sudden disruptions in the external business environment (Zimmermann et al., 2016). Similarly, development of overall competencies of employees with special focus on SC related competencies improves the process of innovation, translates their ideas, and plans into real and implementable actions that impact SCR. A company's performance is also influenced by the efforts of management in encouraging product innovation which influences the SCR (Eltantawy, 2016).

The supply chain resilience is to make supply chain self-sufficient enough that it can withstand any kind of impact or disaster. The organizations have started taking steps towards it and making it sustainable enough. Consequences of SC risks and disruption on business organizations are classified in to four categories. These are sustainable consequence, need some time to recover, need very long time to recover and last category is 'couldn't withstand.

In any situation, only few companies reach the 'sustainable' stage and these are the companies which done their risk analysis in a rigorous way and would have considered all the possible outcomes. These companies also implemented innovative ways of producing the products to get the flexibility of choosing the right one for the situation. The main reasons for their sustainability may also be development of a systematic mitigation plan by their leadership.

Some companies might have a basic mitigation plan but lacked in implementing it due their inability to focus on required changes. Some companies would have taken more time for modifying their current mitigation plan to implement the modified one. While the other companies are not prepared with the mitigation plan but once the pandemic affected them suddenly, they realized the need but could not find a way out.

Some companies are not at all ready for any such out of blue impacts and they will not be able to withstand the pressure or the loss they incurred. These companies might have a plan but were not successful in implementing it. Another reason could be a wrong implementation of a proper mitigation plan. Therefore, for all the above cases, the common requirement is the preparation of of a plan and its implementation in a right away at a right time, for instance, the pandemic situation for SCM to be resilient. Of course, this depends on the workforce being flexible to change and the pace of adapting themselves to it makes a huge difference.

When the COVID pandemic hit the world, everyone thought it was for just few days and its temporary but it changed the whole dynamics of the company's functionalities and made everyone realize the importance of having the supply chain resilience. The following sections of the chapter elaborate the negative impact of pandemic in those companies, which lacked the ability to achieve supply chain resilience.

## Material Shortage

The raw material shortage was one of the major impact of this pandemic. It occurred in two ways. The first one was severe shortage of material for production purpose. This hampered the production of manufacturing companies significantly and created shortage of product availability in the market for many products (Siagian et al., 2021). This shortage was more prevalent for products related to immunity development and implementation of Covid19 protocol. Some of these products are sanitizers, facemasks, gloves, vaporizers etc. While second one was related to lack of demand for produced goods and services in some businesses. This situation was more prevalent in restaurants, movie theaters, exhibitions, sales in malls etc. In another extreme situation, business organizations faced with

Moreover, there was a panic buying for some products creating a total imbalance in supply and demand leading to confusion for planning by the business organizations. This temporary spike in demand disappeared after considerable period. Therefore, to face this kind of situations successfully, organizations should be proactive in their supply chain planning. There are two basic reasons for such a situation. The first one is dependency on very few international vendors (Van Hoek, 2020) and the second one is a wrong inventory policy. Due to the closure of borders during the pandemic, excess dependency on international vendors resulted in shortage of supply. Moreover, vendors could not meet their production schedules due to the prolonged lockdowns. All this tends to suggest that the organizations should have a sufficient buffer and safety stock levels or they need to diversify their procurement from alternative vendors from other countries. At the same time,

## Inventory Storage Charges for the Produced Products

The second major negative impact of Covid19 pandemic was lack sales and piling up of finished goods at various stages of supply chain. This is because there were prolonged lockdowns, restrictions on group gatherings, implementation of rigid protocols to control the virus. Many countries have implemented restrictions on vehicles transporting the cargo and free movement of people from one place to other place. For a long period, many malls and other large shopping establishments were closed for long period resulting to no sales and piling up of excess inventory of finished goods. As there was no other option, the business organizations discarded or recycled the unsold goods.

## Lack of Ways to Distribute the Finished Goods

The Covid19 pandemic has also posed many challenges for distribution of products due to the prolonged lockdowns. This created shortage for product availability in retail outlets. As an alternative, many companies provided opportunity for customers to order online either through their website or mobile application. Companies promoted digital marketing in order to sell their products and make them available to the customers. However, only some companies could take the advantage through digital marketing platforms and it was suitable for only some categories of products.

## Workforce Layoff

With unsold goods on one side and shortage of raw material supply on the other side, many companies were compelled to resort to downsizing their workforce at all levels to compensate the huge drop in profits. This led to the situation of workload imbalance and undue workload on the existing workforce. If the companies proactively implemented SCR in their human resources planning, this situation could be avoided largely. Overall reduction in income levels of workforce resulted in low levels of spending by the consumers leading to wrong projections of demand.

To summarize, the pandemic has created a major impact on the supply chains of companies and resulted in an heightened awareness about developing SCR capabilities.

## SOLUTIONS AND RECOMMENDATIONS

Though the research related to SC in the area of Covid19 pandemic is relatively low, some authors have contributed few models as solutions to the SC risks and disruptions. For instance, Black and Glaser-Segura, (2020) have developed a strategic mitigation model by identifying three stages of planning. They named them as i) Pre-Planning, ii) Pandemic Planning and iii) During Pandemic Planning. Leadership component is included in the pre-planning stage. Preparedness, digitalization and resilience are included in the pandemic planning stage. Pivoting is included in the 'during pandemic stage'. Similarly, Queiroz et al (2020) developed a framework with six factors such as adaptation, digitalization, preparedness, recovery, ripple effect and sustainability. In another effort to develop a model to make better decisions by the leaders of business organizations, Ivanov and Dolgui, (2020) proposed a prediction model for measuring the impact of a pandemic on supply chain network and manufacturing resilience. Models were developed on similar lines by covering aspects of supply chain resilience and SC network ability during disruptive situations like pandemic (Dolgui et al., 2020; Hosseini et al., 2019). Accenture (2020) developed a roadmap to navigate disruption. This model proposed an operational plan to effectively manage SC disruption by naming each aspect of this model as mobilize, sense, analyze and configure.

Taking cue from these models, the present chapter attempted to expand the knowledge in SCR area by developing an expanded model with the help of digital technologies.

## Digital Technologies and Supply Chain Resilience

Emergence of digital technologies has revolutionized the way supply chains are managed. Companies, which implemented these digital technologies proactively, have achieved significant reduction in the negative impact due to SC disruptions and risks such as pandemic. Researchers found that these technologies enabled the companies to recover quickly from the impact of disruption (Papadopoulos et al., 2017; Dubey et al., 2019; Papadopoulos et al 2020). Block chain technology, one of the most popular digital technology is found to improve the SC visibility, enable flexibility in sourcing, manufacturing and order fulfillment processes. The block chains have the ability to replace disparate invoicing, shipping and manufacturing systems through trusted information sharing and tracking data (Ali et al., 2016; Litke et al., 2019).

These technologies also have the ability to develop new competitive capabilities like visibility, real-time response and resilience in SCM. Distributed computing and cloud-based computing enable the achievement of transparency in supply chain, which in turn would improve the visibility of it (Brandon-Jones et al. 2014; Rob Handfield, 2016). Today's supply chains are becoming more complex, costly, risky and unpredictable with several disruptions. Therefore, usage of ICT, digital technologies, and big data analysis develops traditional supply chains into smarter supply chains and enable effective management of SCR (Butner, 2010).

Though managing SCR appears to be very simple at the planning stage, its implementation is a complex task and needs a systematic proactive approach by integrating all the stakeholders of the chain at all levels. There are many factors involved in this like the company leadership, priority, freedom for employee voice, workforce readiness for change, having right mitigation plan created, correct implementation of plans.

## DEVELOPMENT OF SCR MODEL

Based on the discussions until now, the present chapter developed the following model as shown in Figure-1. The model considers SC planning consists of SC Risk Assessment, Vendor Localization and regional diversification, SWOT analysis of SC, SC disruption mitigation plan and implementation of digital technologies to achieve the capabilities of SCR such as Visibility, Dependency, Flexibility and Agility.

*Figure 1. Supply chain resilience model in Covid-19 pandemic era*

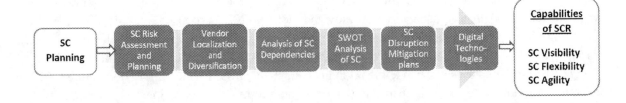

Subsequent sections of this chapter describe the above model.

## SC Risk Assessment and Planning

The model considers SC risk assessment as the first step in developing SC planning. Many authors have opined that identification, evaluation and assessment of SC risks and disruptions is basic requirement for developing any mitigation plan to prepare the organization towards SC resilience (Juttner and Maklan, 2011; Das, 2018; Siagian et al., 2021). Therefore, SC risk planning is vital and important component of SCR. An analysis of relationship between SC risk and SCR, improves the flexibility, visibility, velocity and collaboration capabilities of SC and hence it enables organizations to reduce the impact of vulnerability of SC to a disruptive event like Covid19 pandemic. This calls for a focused effort of organizations to develop and impart a risk management culture across its stakeholders and across all the internal processes (Mandal, 2012). Traditionally, organizations neglect the SC risks and disruptions by focusing at their rare occurrence and by analyzing the history of organizations. But, SC risks can impact negatively any type of organization irrespective of their success, size, market share and profit. Sometimes, these risks emerge within a very short span of time and severely damage the SC operations of the organizations. Covid19 pandemic is one such instance of sudden and severely damaging risk. Thus, it is essential to develop a SC risk assessment and plan by classifying risks into different categories such as operations, people, and process, external, legal, and compliance related risks (Fahimnia et al., 2019; Govindan et al., 2017; Xu et al., 2020).

## Vendor Localization and Diversification

The second aspect considered in this model is vendor localization and diversification. Organizations depend on many vendors for sourcing and procurement of their raw material. Covid19 pandemic has affected the sourcing and procurement channels severely resulting in shortage of raw material due to the geographical concentration of vendors in virus zones of the world. The importance of procurement in the supply chain can also be realized from the percentage of cost it takes in the industry (Maucher and Hofmann, 2011) which has increased tremendously during the pandemic. To mitigate the risk, Mahapatra et al. (2017) suggested combining contract and open market to obtain the optimum procurement under the uncertain market price.

To avoid work stoppage from a supplier disruption, a firm should increase resilience by determining where it should arrange for multiple suppliers from diverse geographical regions (Van Hoek, 2020) and the determination should be based on quantitative analysis. In addition, sourcing from firms in a variety of countries reduces exchange rate risks. If multiple suppliers are difficult to find in a limited production market, it would make sense to develop trust-based relationships that encourage cost-sharing and other relationship-building practices. There is some validity to the notion of having backup suppliers in case one supplier is not able to deliver products. This concept could also be extended to contract producers, shipping suppliers, and alternate distribution channels (Black and Glaser-Segura, 2020).

In addition to geographic diversification of vendors, localization also plays a major role during the pandemic period. A business organization should focus on identifying local vendors for sourcing and procuring their raw material during the pandemic period. These local vendors serve the purpose of contingency procurement during the pandemic period along with the global vendors. This localization also enables organizations to resolve some of their production issues during prolonged lockdown periods. Along with localization, development of alternate vendors, locally and globally will also reduce the impact during pandemics. These vendors should represent different tiers of supply chain. While developing these vendors, the organizations should implement the quality standards, conduct quality audits and support the vendors through vendor development programs on a continuous basis. Business organizations should also share right information to vendors to minimize the disruptions in the flow of raw material. Sharing of information enables the vendors to prepare themselves for meeting the exigency situations by developing proactive plans.

Thus, a multi thronged strategy of development of local vendors, sourcing from alternate vendors and depending on global vendors would minimize the impact of pandemic on raw material supply (Van Hoek, 2020).

## Analysis of SC Dependencies

The next step in the model deals with analysis of dependencies in supply chain. This analysis of SC dependencies provides the organizations a clear picture of their dependencies and the alternative plan in case of disruptions for these dependencies. Some of these dependencies can be addressed by the organizations through the previous step diversified procurement strategy. A risk mitigation plan cannot be complete without identifying the SC dependencies. These dependencies relate to global suppliers, third party vendors, logistics providers, distributors, stock keeping units and regular and bulk customers and other stakeholders (Juttner and Maklan, 2011).

There are two types of dependencies for business organizations. These are internal and external. Internal dependencies are the dependencies of supply chain within the company like production capacity, inventory capacity, and workforce efficiency etc. The internal dependencies can be managed with less difficulty than the external dependencies. During the pandemic and disruptive situations, the internal dependencies are generally manageable by employees at different hierarchical positions in the supply chain structure of an organization. External dependencies are dependent on external factors like vendor quality, politics, and natural events. The external dependencies are not directly in control of organization as they are related to external stakeholders. Any disruption in the operations of these external stakeholders would negatively impact the entire supply chain process. Loopholes or the weak links of the supply chain can be analyzed by rightly analyzing the dependencies of the supply chain.

## SWOT Analysis of SC

SWOT analysis is the basic analysis done by a business organization to identify and evaluate its strong areas, weak areas, upcoming opportunities and threats in the business. Generally, majority companies perform a SWOT analysis for their entire organization. The author recommends through this model that a regular SWOT analysis should be performed exclusively for the SC activities and its related departments. This kind of analysis exposes the gaps in the existing SC and opens up new areas and options for improving the processes related to SC. While doing this analysis, the organization can integrate it with the SC risk management plan, SC dependencies and sourcing and procurement strategies. SWOT analysis is expected to improve the ability of an organization to face a disruption successfully with minimum impact and damage. SC Resilience planning can be improved based on this analysis on a continuous basis.

## SC Disruption and Mitigation plan

At this stage, the business organization develops its own SC disruption and mitigation plan by considering the actions taken during the previous stages. This plan is based on its SC Risk Assessment Plan, Vendor related plan, analysis of SC dependencies and SWOT analysis of SC processes. This plan is also integrated with the overall business strategy of the organization to mitigate the risks at organizational level. The top management of the organization through a bottom-up strategy generally develops it by collecting opinions and feedbacks from employees at different hierarchical levels of SC. The bottom-up strategy will enable the top management to realize the SC gaps in the organization, which require immediate focus.

## Digital Technologies and Supply Chain Resilience

A detailed strategy to implement digital technologies and an integrated plan related to their implementation to mitigate and quickly recover from disruptions is the last aspect of the model (Papadopoulos et al., 2017; Dubey et al., 2019; Papadopoulos et al 2020). Technologies such as block chain have the ability to improve the SC visibility, enable flexibility in sourcing, manufacturing and order fulfillment processes. Technologies such as distributed computing and cloud-based computing enable the achievement of transparency in supply chain, which in turn would improve the visibility of it (Brandon-Jones et al. 2014; Rob Handfield, 2016). Today's SC should develop into Smart SC by using the technologies such as ICT, digital technologies, and big data analysis to achieve the abilities of SCR (Butner, 2010).

To transform global supply chains into more efficient, interconnected, dynamic, sustainable and resilient production and supply chain networks, companies need to relinquish the way of operating through the traditional linear (or sequential) supply chain approach and embrace a more open system thinking and holistic approach such as digital supply networks (DSN) (Kilpatrick and Barter, 2020). DSNs enable suppliers, manufacturers and customers to work together through a dynamic digital core powered by real-time data (Downing, 2019). This allows companies to effectively collaborate and connect with their supply chain network partners that in turn improves end-to-end visibility, agility, optimization and overall business competitiveness. Technological advancements and innovations, such as sensors and Internet of Things, artificial intelligence, 3D printing, autonomous robots and control systems, machine learning and blockchains are key enabling ingredients for building effective and high performing DSNs (Laaper and Mussomeli, 2017; McKenzie, 2020; van Hoek, 2020) as well as a key facilitator for sustainable supply chain performance (Acioli et al., 2021).

## CAPABILITIES OF SCR

A business organization is said to be SC resilient when it is able to develop capabilities SC such as SC Visibility, SC Flexibility and SC Agility. If the organization is able to develop an integrated SC plan as shown in the model in Fig 1, it can acquire the capabilities of SC.

Organizational resilience capability is a critical element that enables an organization to avoid or limit the impacts of an adverse event such as the COVID-19 pandemic (Juttner and Maklan, 2011; Xu et al., 2020), effectively respond to an uncertain situation and recover faster to perform its normal functions (Linnenluecke, 2017; Visser, 2020). As Pettit et al. (2019) asserted, "resilience is a mandatory characteristic of a supply chain in order to survive in the short-term, but also provides the ability to adapt to change and thrive in the long-term." Linnenluecke (2017) suggests building resilience involves substantial investment, planning capability, decisive leadership and a higher degree of readiness to effectively respond to uncertain crises. Organizations move beyond traditional enterprise risk management practices and learn to imbue a culture of resilience (Pettit, et al., 2019). A detailed discussion about the three capabilities is provided in this section.

## SC Visibility

Many researchers have attributed lack of SC visibility as one of the major reasons for negative impact of Covid19 pandemic on business organizations (Gereffi, 2020; Handfield et al., 2020; Zhu et al., 2020). Accordingly, proactive companies have realized that they need to have greater visibility and transparency across the end-to-end SC operations to achieve the capabilities of SC resilience (Alicke et al., 2020; Jan, 2020; McHopa et al., 2020; van Hoek, 2020). Companies also need to focus on building SC agility and resilience by incorporating novel disruptive technologies that could help them to improve their capability to manage risks and disruptions and improve SC visibility (Ibn-Mohammed et al., 2020; Kilpatrick and Barter, 2020; Kumar and Mishra, 2020; Sarkis, 2020).

Digitalization allows an organization manage in a better way the SC coordination by utilizing software such as ERPP and data to create visibility among SC members leading to SC Resilience. Ivanov and Dolgui (2019) recommend greater visibility and communication along the SC to reduce the ripples caused by uncertainty. The authors also suggest that visibility may be a better approach to manage uncertainty and developed SC resilience capabilities. Block chain technology enables the achievement SC resilience by adding transparency as this technology creates place and ownership documentation instantaneously. It creates an immutable digital record of the inventory pipeline (Gaur & Gaiha, 2020).

## SC Flexibility

The second important capability to develop SC resilience is incorporating flexibility in SC operations and processes. Black and Glaser-Segura (2020) suggest that organizations may need to be flexible in adapting their manufacturing facilities accommodate readily the manufacturing of other products or services (e.g., small-batch products vs mass production) due to changes in consumer preferences but also for risk mitigation. In some situations, it may also make sense to collaborate with competitors and suppliers for small amounts of capacity at a local or relatively close production facility. SC Flexibility leads to the achievement of SCR through the implementation of digital technologies.

## SC Agility

COVID-19 pandemic has severely affected the ability of global supply chains to absorb and respond to supply (shortage of inputs' supply to businesses and consumers owing to the closure of supplying factories) and demand shocks (increased variability in demand caused by panic buying and stockpiling) (Ivanov, 2020; Sharma et al., 2020).

Agility of the supply chain is one of the most important factors in achieving the company agility and can meet the strategic goals of the company in today's competitive world (Nasrollahi et al., 2016). Agility in the supply chain is the ability of a supply chain to respond quickly to market changes and

*Supply Chain Planning to Achieve Resilience Capabilities*

customer needs (Gligor et al., 2016). No company has all the necessary resources to put any opportunity on the market. Therefore, to gain a competitive edge in the global market, companies must work with suppliers and customers to uniform synced operations and achieve a level of agility beyond the reach of exclusive companies, which in general has been conveyed to the chain of agility (Abdi and Abumusa, 2017). SC agility is linked to the achievement of SCR. SC agility improves through the implementation of digital technologies.

The SCR, in general, is related to the achievement of two types of capacities. One, resilience capacity and the second, recovery capacity. The first is the SC capacity for avoidance and containment. By achieving SC agility, SC flexibility and SC visibility through a systematic implementation of digital technologies, business organizations can move towards the achievement of SCR capabilities and the resilience capacity. Recovery capacity is the ability of the company to recover to the original SC positions after going through the impact of disruption. Developing SCR abilities will enable the organization to develop their recovery time and capacity. The recovery capacity also depends on the workforce adaptability for change and leadership commitment towards improving situation.

Some organizations have shifted their focus on a temporary basis to sustain their businesses. For instance, General Motors have used their resources and capabilities to manufacture facemasks for frontline works during COVID situation. The company reacted with a rapid response project and 7 days later, they have designed and produced first sample on the new production line. In addition, they also obtained a contract from US Department of health and human services for Ventec Life systems V+ Pro critical ventilators for COVID-19 patients. They produced 30,000 ventilators. They have effectively used their resources to help the society by producing the emergency products and also sustained their business.

## FUTURE RESEARCH DIRECTIONS

The Covid-19 pandemic has severely disrupted the activities and processes of supply chains worldwide. Initially, it was thought that this pandemic situation would last for short term. But, with the emergence of one variant after another, the pandemic continued for more than two years since its emergence. Business organizations have been exploring various possibilities and options to stabilize their supply chains and achieve SCR through diversified strategies. The outcome of this chapter is one such solution for achieving the capabilities to develop SCR. The research is purely based on systematic literature review. Expanding it further by validating the framework developed in this research through an empirical study would be the topic for future study. Moreover, relationship between achievement of SCR capabilities and nature of business and nature of industry with reference to pandemic can also be studied in future.

The present research provides new vistas of opportunities for researchers to expand the framework of this chapter by including more number of SC variables and SC practices. Influence of geographical location of business organization on SCR capabilities can be explored further.

## CONCLUSION

The outcome of the present research revealed many interesting results. It is concluded that business organizations can achieve SCR capabilities if they develop SC risk management plan proactively by identifying all types of risks and by incorporating action plans and strategies to mitigate the risk. It is also found that the process of developing SCR capabilities depends largely on the organization's ability to achieve SC visibility, agility and flexibility through the implementation and utilization of digital technologies. These technologies are also found to help in the improvement of SC processes like information sharing, mutual coordination and demand forecasting among all the members of SC.

SC planning by incorporating strategies related to vendor localization and diversification, risk assessment and planning, analysis of SC dependencies, conduct of SWOT analysis of SC, SC disruption and mitigation plans leads the achievement of capabilities of SCR. Thus, this research concludes on the note that SC Planning in a proactive manner by incorporating the strategies mentioned in the framework through the implementation of digital technologies provides a way forward for business organizations to achieve SC resilience capabilities in a pandemic situation.

To conclude, the author recommends the following strategies to minimize the SC risks to achieve resilience.

1. Diversifying and localizing the suppliers – Sourcing and procuring from local vendors and vendors from other locations to avoid the raw material shortage subject to high quality, right price, right quantity and right time.
2. selecting vendors who have a good track record of supply to meet all the procurement standards,
3. Making substitute products locally – Organizations can focus on manufacturing substitute products locally. This will enable to mitigate risks due to non-availability or stoppage of supply from global suppliers due to prolonged lockdowns and other issues related to the pandemic situation. For instance, producing facemasks and sanitizers locally.
4. Minimization of waste by maintaining quality standards and putting place the quality processes to produce a better product,
5. implementation of digital technologies through a proper strategy to improve the information sharing, coordination, manage demand and order well to improve the overall distribution of product,
6. automation of SC processes leading to the reduction and optimization of work force.

## REFERENCES

Abdi, M. R., Edalat, F. D., & Abumusa, S. (2017). Lean and Agile Supply Chain Management: A Case of IT Distribution Industry in the Middle East. In Green and Lean Management (pp. 37-69). Springer International Publishing.

Accenture. (2020). *COVID-19: How we are helping to build supply-chain resilience.* https://www.accenture.com/us-en/blogs/blogs-careers/covid-19-how-were-helping-to-build-supply-chain-resilience

Acioli, C., Scavarda, A., & Reis, A. (2021). Applying industry 4.0 technologies in the COVID–19 sustainable chains. *International Journal of Productivity and Performance Management, 70*(5), 988–1016. doi:10.1108/IJPPM-03-2020-0137

Alaoui, S. (2020). *How who connects the links in the covid-19 supply chain.* United Nations Foundation. https://unfoundation.org/blog/post/how-who-connects-links-covid-19-supply-chain/?gclid=EAIaIQobC hMI44Tf7PWl8QIVFuTICh2uPAGbEAAYAiAAEgItvPD_BwE

Ali, M., Nelson, J. C., Shea, R., & Freedman, M. J. (2016). Blockstack: A Global Naming and Storage System Secured by Blockchains. *Proceedings of the 2016 USENIX Annual Technical Conference (USENIX ATC '16)*, 181–94.

Alicke, K., Azcue, X., & Barriball, E. (2020). *Supply-chain recovery in corona virus times – plan for now and the future*. Available at: www.mckinsey.com/_/media/McKinsey/Business%20Functions/Operations/Our%20Insights/Supply%20chain%20recovery%20in%20coronavirus%20times%20plan%20for%20now%20and%20the%20future/Supply-chain-recovery-in-coronavirus-times-plan-for-now-andthe-future.pdf

Aymen, S. (2021). The COVID-19 pandemic, social sustainability and global supply chain resilience: A review. *Corporate Governance*, *21*(6), 1142–1154.

Barriball, E., George, K., Marcos, I., & Radtke, P. (2020). Jump-starting resilient and reimagined operations. *McKinsey*. https://www.mckinsey.com/business-functions/operations/our-insights/jump-starting-resilient-and-reimagined-operations

Bhamra, R., Dani, S., & Burnard, K. (2011). Resilience: The concept, a literature review and future directions. *International Journal of Production Research*, *49*(18), 5375–5393. doi:10.1080/00207543.2011.563826

Black, S., & Glaser-Segura, D. (2020). Supply Chain Resilience in a Pandemic: The Need for Revised Contingency Planning. *Management Dynamics in the Knowledge Economy*, *8*(4), 325–343. doi:10.2478/mdke-2020-0021

Brandon-Jones, E., Squire, B., Autry, C. W., & Petersen, K. J. (2014). A contingent resource-based perspective of supply chain resilience and robustness. *The Journal of Supply Chain Management*, *50*(3), 55–73. doi:10.1111/jscm.12050

Butner, K. (2010). The smarter supply chain of the future. *Strategy and Leadership*, *38*(1), 22–31. doi:10.1108/10878571011009859

Choi, T. M., Guo, S., & Luo, S. (2020). When blockchain meets social-media: Will the result benefit social media analytics for supply chain operations management? *Transportation Research Part E, Logistics and Transportation Review*, *135*, 101860. doi:10.1016/j.tre.2020.101860

Das, K. (2018). Integrating resilience in a supply chain planning model. *International Journal of Quality & Reliability Management*, *35*(3), 570–595. doi:10.1108/IJQRM-08-2016-0136

Das, K., & Lashkari, R. S. (2015). Risk readiness and resiliency planning for a supply chain. *International Journal of Production Research*, *53*(22), 6752–6771. doi:10.1080/00207543.2015.1057624

Dolgui, A., Ivanov, D., & Rozhkov, M. (2020). Does the ripple effect influence the bullwhip effect? An integrated analysis of structural and operational dynamics in the supply chain. *International Journal of Production Research*, *58*(5), 1285–1301. doi:10.1080/00207543.2019.1627438

Dubey, R., Gunasekaran, A., Childe, S. J., Fosso Wamba, S., Roubaud, D., & Foropon, C. (2019). Empirical investigation of data analytics capability and organizational flexibility as complements to supply chain resilience. *International Journal of Production Research*. Advance online publication. doi:10.1016/j.ijpe.2019.01.023

Eltantawy, R. A. (2016). The role of supply management resilience in attaining ambidexterity: A dynamic capabilities approach. *Journal of Business and Industrial Marketing, 31*(1), 123–134. doi:10.1108/JBIM-05-2014-0091

Fahimnia, B., Pournader, M., Siemsen, E., Bendoly, E., & Wang, C. (2019). Behavioral operations and supply chain management-a review and literature mapping. *Decision Sciences, 50*(6), 1127–1183. doi:10.1111/deci.12369

Freeman, O. (2020). *Supply Chain Resilience is a Priority after COVID-19*. Supply Chain Digital. https://supplychaindigital.com/supply-chain-2/supply-chain-resilience-priority-after-covid-19

Gaur, V., & Gaiha, A. (2020). Building a Transparent Supply Chain Blockchain can enhance trust, efficiency, and speed. *Harvard Business Review, 98*(3), 94–103.

Gautam, A. (2020). Building Supply Chain Resilience for A Post-Covid-19 World, Forbes Technology Council. *Forbes*. https://www.forbes.com/sites/forbestechcouncil/2020/09/25/building-supply-chain-resilience-for-a-post-covid-19-world/?sh=7a7240305aea

Gereffi, G. (2020). What does the COVID-19 pandemic teach us about global value chains? The case of medical supplies. *Journal of International Business Policy, 3*(3), 287–301. doi:10.105742214-020-00062-w

Gligor, D. M., Holcomb, M. C., & Stank, T. P. (2013). A multidisciplinary approach to supply chain agility: Conceptualization and scale development. *Journal of Business Logistics, 34*(2), 94–108. doi:10.1111/jbl.12012

Golicic, S., Flint, D., & Signori, P. (2017). Building Business Sustainability through Resilience in the Wine Industry. *International Journal of Wine Business Research, 29*(1), 74–97. doi:10.1108/IJWBR-02-2016-0005

Govindan, K., Fattahi, M., & Keyvanshokooh, E. (2017). Supply chain network design under uncertainty: A comprehensive review and future research directions. *European Journal of Operational Research, 263*(1), 108–141. doi:10.1016/j.ejor.2017.04.009

Handfield, R. (2016). Preparing for the Era of the Digitally Transparent Supply Chain: A Call to Research in a New Kind of Journal. *Logistics, 1*(2). Advance online publication. doi:10.3390/logistics1010002

Handfield, R. B., Graham, G., & Burns, L. (2020). Corona virus, tariffs, trade wars and supply chain evolutionary design. *International Journal of Operations & Production Management, 40*(10), 1649–1660. doi:10.1108/IJOPM-03-2020-0171

Hendricks & Singhal. (2005). An Empirical Analysis of the Effect of Supply Chain Disruptions on Long-Run Stock Price Performance and Equity Risk of the Firm. *Production and Operations Management, 14*(1), 35–52.

Hosseini, S., Ivanov, D., & Dolgui, A. (2019). Review of quantitative methods for supply chain resilience analysis. *Transportation Research Part E, Logistics and Transportation Review*, *125*, 285–307. doi:10.1016/j.tre.2019.03.001

Ibn-Mohammed, T., Mustapha, K. B., Godsell, J. M., Adamu, Z., Babatunde, K. A., Akintade, D. D., Acquaye, A., Fujii, H., Ndiaye, M. M., Yamoah, F. A., & Koh, S. C. L. (2020). A critical review of the impacts of COVID-19 on the global economy and ecosystems and opportunities for circular economy strategies. *Resources, Conservation and Recycling*, *164*, 105169. Advance online publication. doi:10.1016/j.resconrec.2020.105169 PMID:32982059

Ivanov, D. (2020). Predicting the impacts of epidemic outbreaks on global supply chains: A simulation based analysis on the coronavirus outbreak (COVID-19/SARS-CoV-2) case. *Transportation Research Part E, Logistics and Transportation Review*, *136*, 101922. Advance online publication. doi:10.1016/j.tre.2020.101922 PMID:32288597

Ivanov, D., & Dolgui, A. (2020). A digital supply chain twin for managing the disruptions risks and resilience in the era of Industry 4.0. *Production Planning and Control*. Advance online publication. doi:10.1080/09537287.2020.1768450

Jan, O. (2020). *COVID-19 impacts on supply chains, sustainability and climate change*. Available at: www2.deloitte.com/global/en/blog/responsible-business-blog/2020/covid-19-impacts-on-supply-chainssustainability-and-climate-change.html

Juttner, U., & Maklan, S. (2011). Supply Chain Resilience in the Global Financial Crisis: An Empirical Study. *Supply Chain Management*, *14*(4), 246–259. doi:10.1108/13598541111139062

Kilpatrick, J., & Barter, L. (2020). *COVID-19: managing supply chain risk and disruption*. Available at: www2.deloitte.com/content/dam/Deloitte/ca/Documents/finance/Supply-Chain_POV_EN_FINAL-AODA.pdf

Kumar, R., & Mishra, R. (2020). COVID-19 Global Pandemic: Impact on Management of Supply Chain. *International Journal of Emerging Technology and Advanced Engineering*, *10*(4), 132–139. doi:10.46338/IJETAE0416

Laaper, S., & Mussomeli, A. (2017). Introducing the digital supply network. *The Wall Street Journal*. Available at: https://deloitte.wsj.com/cio/2017/04/24/introducing-the-digital-supply-network/

Linkov, I., & Florin, M. (Eds.). (2016). *IRGC Resource Guide on Resilience*. International Risk Governance Center. Retrieved December 2021 from https://www.irgc.org/riskgovernance/resilience/

Linnenluecke, M. K. (2017). Resilience in business and management research: A review of influential publications and a research agenda. *International Journal of Management Reviews*, *19*(1), 4–30. doi:10.1111/ijmr.12076

Litke, A., Anagnostopoulos, D., & Varvarigou, T. (2019). Blockchains for Supply Chain Management: Architectural Elements and Challenges towards a Global Scale Deployment. *Logistics*, *3*(1), 5. doi:10.3390/logistics3010005

Mahapatra, S., Levental, S., & Narasimhan, R. (2017). Market price uncertainty, risk aversion and procurement: Combining contracts and open market sourcing alternatives. *International Journal of Production Economics, 185*(3), 34–51. doi:10.1016/j.ijpe.2016.12.023

Mandal, S. (2020). Impact of supplier innovativeness, top management support and strategic sourcing on supply chain resilience. *International Journal of Productivity and Performance Management, 70*(7), 1561–1581. https://doi.org/10.1108/IJPPM-07-2019-0349

Maucher, D., & Hofmann, E. (2011). *Procurmenet trends in the automotive supplier industry*. Available at: www.kerkhoff-group.com/en/press/press-reports/press-details/news/

McHopa, A. D., William, J. M., & Kimaro, J. M. (2020). Global supply chains vulnerability and distortions amidst covid19 pandemic: Antecedents for building resilience in downstream logistics. *Journal of Co-Operative and Business Studies, 5*(2), 64–74.

McKenzie, B. (2020). *Beyond COVID-19: supply chain resilience holds key to recovery*. Available at: www.bakermckenzie.com/-/media/files/insight/publications/2020/04/covid19-global-economy.pdf

Nasrollahi, M., Fattahy Takhtgahi, A., & Sajjadinia, Z. (2016). The role of IT in supply chain agility and its impact on organizational performance. In *Second International Conference on Management, Innovation and Entrepreneurship Paradigms*. Shahid Beheshti University

Onwuegbuzie, A. J., & Freis, R. (2016). *Seven Steps to a Comprehensive Literature Review: A Multimodal and Cultural Approach*. Sage Publication.

Papadopoulos, Konstantinos, Baltas, & Balta. (2020). The use of digital technologies by small and medium enterprises during COVID-19: Implications for theory and practice. *International Journal of Information Management*. doi:10.1016/j.ijinfomgt.2020.102192

Papadopoulos, T., Gunasekaran, A., Dubey, R., Altay, N., Childe, S. J., & Fosso-Wamba, S. (2017). The role of big data in explaining disaster resilience in supply chains for sustainability. *Journal of Cleaner Production, 142*, 1108–1118. https://doi.org/10.1016/j.jclepro.2016.03.059

Paul, S., & Venkateswaran, J. (2020). Designing robust policies under deep uncertainty for mitigating epidemics. *Computers & Industrial Engineering, 140*, 106221. https://doi.org/10.1016/j.cie.2019.106221

Pettit, T. J., Croxton, K. L., & Fiksel, J. (2019). The evolution of resilience in supply chain management: A retrospective on ensuring supply chain resilience. *Journal of Business Logistics, 40*(1), 56–65. https://doi.org/10.1111/jbl.12202

Ponomarov, S. Y., & Holcomb, M. C. (2009). Understanding the concept of supply chain resilience. *International Journal of Logistics Management, 20*(1), 124–143. https://doi.org/10.1108/09574090910954873

Queiroz, M. M., Ivanov, D., Dolgui, A., & Wamba, S. F. (2020). Impacts of epidemic outbreaks on supply chains: mapping a research agenda amid the COVID-19 pandemic through a structured literature review. *Annals of Operations Research*, 1-38. doi:10.1007/s10479-020-03685-7

Report, D. (2020). *COVID-19: Managing supply chain risk and disruption Coronavirus highlights the need to transform traditional supply chain models*. https://www2.deloitte.com/global/en/pages/risk/cyber-strategic-risk/articles/covid-19-managing-supply-chain-risk-and-disruption.html

Report, D. (2020). *Building Supply Chain Resilience beyond COVID-19.* https://www2.deloitte.com/content/dam/Deloitte/ch/Documents/consumer-business/deloitte-ch-study-building-supply-chain-resilience-covid-19-2020.pdf

Scholten, K., Stevenson, M., & van Donk, D. P. (2019). Dealing with the unpredictable: Supply chain resilience. *International Journal of Operations & Production Management, 40*(1), 1–10.

Sharma, A., Adhikary, A., & Borah, S. B. (2020). Covid-19's impact on supply chain decisions: Strategic insights from NASDAQ100 firms using Twitter data. *Journal of Business Research, 117,* 443–449.

Sheffi, Y. (2005). *The Resilient Enterprise: Overcoming Vulnerability for Competitive Advantage.* MIT Press.

Shih, W. C. (2020). Is it time to rethink globalized supply chains? *MIT Sloan Management Review, 61*(4), 1–3.

Shin, N., & Park, S. (2019). Evidence-Based Resilience Management for Supply Chain Sustainability: An Interpretive Structural Modelling Approach. *Sustainability, 11,* 484.

Siagian, H., Tarigan, Z. J. H., & Jie, F. (2021). Supply Chain Integration Enables Resilience, Flexibility, and Innovation to Improve Business Performance in COVID-19 Era. *Sustainability, 13,* 4669. https://doi.org/10.3390/su13094669

Van Hoek, R. (2020). Research opportunities for a more resilient post-COVID-19 supply chain–closing the gap between research findings and industry practice. *International Journal of Operations & Production Management, 40*(4), 341–355.

Visser, W. (2020). Measuring future resilience: a multilevel index. *Corporate Governance,* 21(2), 252–267.

Xu, S., Zhang, X., Feng, L., & Yang, W. (2020). Disruption risks in supply chain management: A literature review based on bibliometric analysis. *International Journal of Production Research, 58*(11), 3508–3526. https://doi.org/10.1080/00207543.2020.1717011

Xu, Z., Elomri, A., Kerbache, L., & El Omri, A. (2020). Impacts of COVID-19 on global supply chains: Facts and perspectives. *IEEE Engineering Management Review, 48*(3), 153–166.

Zhu, G., Chou, M. C., & Tsai, C. W. (2020). Lessons learned from the COVID-19 pandemic exposing the shortcomings of current supply chain operations: A long-term prescriptive offering. *Sustainability, 12*(14), 1–19.

Zimmermann, R., Ferreira, L. M. D., & Moreira, A. C. (2016). The influence of supply chain on the innovation process: A systematic literature review. *Supply Chain Management, 21,* 289–304.

## KEY TERMS AND DEFINITIONS

**Supply Chain Planning:** A proactive activity to design and develop a strategic plan to coordinate all the activities and processes involved in supply chain by integrating across all the entities of supply chain

**Vendor Localization:** The activity of identifying, selecting and approving vendors from local area of the organization instead of a global vendor to enable smooth flow of supply inspite of disruptions.

**Vendor Diversification:** The activity of identifying, selecting and approving vendors from multiple regions to minimize the impact of disruptions from a single region.

**Supply Chain Disruption:** Any unpredictable event that can impact the flow and activities of supply chain generally in a negative manner

**Supply Chain Mitigation Plan:** A systematic and proactive plan detailing the strategies to minimize / mitigate the impact of disruption in supply chain

# Chapter 5
# Supply Chain Practice Towards Resilience:
## A Study on the Bangladeshi Manufacturing Industry During COVID-19

**Ferdoush Saleheen**
*Universiti Utara Malaysia, Malaysia*

**Md Mamun Habib**
https://orcid.org/0000-0002-3192-2636
*Independent University, Bangladesh*

## ABSTRACT

*The global pandemic outbreak has been affecting an enormous impact on people's lives and societies. It is evident that crafting the supply chain procedures and results based upon cost-competitiveness are no longer adequate and businesses will be required to reconsider approaches that hold "risk-competitiveness" to warrant resilience moving forward. In this context, the Bangladesh supply chain industry is no exception. The supply chain practitioners have faced an unprecedented challenge from the supplier timely shipment failure to a long delay in the voyage, congestion at transshipment and at the customs, delay in the clearance procedure, and finally, difficulties in the distribution. This chapter justifies the current global disruption demands to revalidate the supply chain performance measurement (SCPM) of an organization, and the Bangladeshi supply chain needs to become more agile and adaptable to these acute crisis moments and should emphasize building effective response strategies.*

## INTRODUCTION

The spread of the COVID 19, an absolute unprecedented incident is being experienced worldwide, is putting global supply chains into the focus of a mass community. Even before the pandemic, managing a seamless supply chain operations were highly challenging and stressful. For many years, corporations pursued to aggressively optimize cost through economies of scale, frequently by relocating productions

DOI: 10.4018/978-1-7998-9506-0.ch005

Copyright © 2022, IGI Global. Copying or distributing in print or electronic forms without written permission of IGI Global is prohibited.

facilities to lower-cost labor regions—opted at the expense of other critical supply chain attributes like flexibility and agility. This pandemic is distracting supply chains activities, with significant shortcomings for businesses, consumers and the overall global economy. Leaders are scrambling to respond to critical uncertainties to protect their employees, safeguard supply security, alleviate the financial collision, tackle reputational risks and steer market uncertainty. In the meantime, enterprises and governments have occupied in business continuity and resilient supply chain management planning exercises in recent years, outdated risk management undertakings have largely involved on responding to national events relating to a specific geography or sector. The recent global interruptions emphasize the urgency for a new paradigm to develop supply chain resilience (Theodossiou et al., 2020; Saleheen et al., 2019; McKibbin & Fernando, 2020; Bevilacqua et al., 2017; Carlsson-Szlezak et al., 2020).

## BACKGROUND

Without any dispute, all supply chain practitioners admit: between the pandemic, shortage of containers, prolonged winter, the blockage of the Suez Canal by a container ship, frequent logistics miseries, things have been extremely challenging for the professionals to grip the operations under control.

These disturbances have already led to the current global shortage of raw & packaging materials, petrochemicals, bulk chemicals, basic suppliers, emergency medical equipment. The consequences of these limitations on the supplies lead to production at a halt, price inflation, and production. The impact has been multiform and across all industries both backward and forward. The raw materials made from these are used for food packaging, medical supplies, household appliances (Theodossiou et al., 2020; Altay & Green, 2006; McKibbin & Fernando, 2020; Altay et al., 2018; Bevilacqua et al., 2017; Carlsson-Szlezak et al., 2020).

The summary of the critical challenges faced due to COVID 19 during and post pandemics are as follows:

- Global supply crisis at production site due to shortage of labor
- Container constraints to ship goods at buyers and customer premises
- Shortage of staff due to quarantines and medical safety and/or lower supply.
- Restrictions on transport and distribution operations to deliver goods or services.
- Under-staffed, under-supplied, and store closures. Lack of consumers.
- Unavailability of transport operation crews and lack of demand for certain goods
- Challenges to reach consumers for delivery restrictions.

The impacts are resulted due to the above challenges as follows:

- Production shortage, unfulfilled customer orders, and spike of inventory
- Uncertainty of raw material and other input arrivals for production.
- Slow shipments and inconsistent delivery.
- Frequent delivery schedule failure.
- Fewer products on the shelves, diminished ability to serve the customers.
- Delivery is inconsistent, a model for timing is faulty, and increased costs
- Avoid shipping, delayed delivery timeline, and more volatile demand patterns.

## Impacts on Global Readymade Garments

The COVID-19 catastrophe has wrinkled the garment sector for countries like Bangladesh, India, and major exporting countries upsetting millions of workers and factory owners in the supply chains and with "ripple effects" across a number of magnitudes. The majority of the garment supply chain occupations are dependent on foreign consumer demand from countries in the US, Canada, and Europe where highly stringent lockdown and sharp declines in retail sales were observed. The global garment trade got nearly stagnant in the first half of 2020 (Theodossiou et al., 2020; Altay & Green, 2006; McKibbin & Fernando, 2020; Altay et al., 2018; Bevilacqua et al., 2017; Carlsson-Szlezak et al., 2020).

Import from garment-producing countries to major buying countries also slumped significantly. Terminations of buyers' orders were common at the beginning of the disaster. Garment manufacturers also faced interruptions to their imported input supply. Hundreds of support factories got shut down, workers were laid off. Factories that have since resumed also observed a shortage in their workforce presence (Theodossiou et al., 2020; Altay & Green, 2006; McKibbin & Fernando, 2020; Altay et al., 2018; Bevilacqua et al., 2017; Carlsson-Szlezak et al., 2020).

## Impacts on Global Shipping and Transport Industry

Small and medium businesses (SMB) globally drive over 25 percent of the $18 trillion maritime trade and this sector has been approaching an overwhelming and widespread crisis since the commencement of the Covid-19 pandemic and the rising economic decline. The economic slump due to Covid-19 led to the dilemma of the sector. Be it the supply chain disruption, the unavailability of shipping containers to high freight costs over the last year, many elements have collectively increased the troubles of the SMBs across the globe. China is the major exporter in the world, with 16.1 percent of global exports. Global shipping trade will drop by 4.1% in 2020 due to the pandemic (Theodossiou et al., 2020; Altay & Green, 2006; McKibbin & Fernando, 2020; Altay et al., 2018; Bevilacqua et al., 2017; Carlsson-Szlezak et al., 2020).

## Impacts on Global Retail Industry

The price hike on shipping and transportations is harshly affecting renowned retail chains in the US which will plunge their profit margin. This will escalate enormous cost pressures to many businesses and, will put further inflationary pressure on transportation rates in 2021. The price of goods arriving from China has also increased by 0.3 percent. In general, prices of imported goods increased to 0.9 percent. With continuing pandemic-related postponements and closures, non-stop demand for ocean freight from Asia to the US, and a lack of capacity, ocean rates have been increased and transit times volatility (Theodossiou et al., 2020; Altay & Green, 2006; McKibbin & Fernando, 2020; Altay et al., 2018; Bevilacqua et al., 2017; Carlsson-Szlezak et al., 2020).

## Impacts on Global Transportation and Freight Cost for Carrying Goods

The requirement for empty shipping containers has been multifold during the pandemic when the consumption pattern globally is sharply uptrend which includes medical equipment, surgical items, sanitizing bulk chemicals, and many other products etc. With the upsurge of e-commerce business and the large part of these import demand are shipped through the containers. The freight charge of the containers is the ever highest along with the crisis of the empty containers. Presently, the freight to South America and Western Africa are above to the other major trade region.

By early 2021, shipping freight from China to South America had soared 443% compared with 63% on the route between Asia and North America's eastern coast. Another factor is that the lack of return cargo. South American and western African nations import more manufactured goods than they export, and it's costly for carriers to return empty boxes to China on long routes (Theodossiou et al., 2020; Altay & Green, 2006; McKibbin & Fernando, 2020; Altay et al., 2018; Bevilacqua et al., 2017; Carlsson-Szlezak et al., 2020).

## BASIC CONCEPTS OF SUPPLY CHAIN MANAGEMENT

During the global pandemic disruption, due to COVID-19 manufacturing organizations have perceived the urgency of effective SCM in the operations. Conversely, numerous organizations disregarded to generate enthralling performance and operational measures which are indispensable to warrant a commendable and coordinated SCM. To realize the solitary of globalization and SCM objective, which is to indulge customers rapidly and effectively than other competitors, SCM necessities to participate in the nonstop execution of developmental strategies (Garay-Rondero et al., 2019; Molina-Besch, 2016).

Along these lines, to see how SCM contends, it is significant to comprehend the general performance of SCM. SCM is an integrated method in business from the suppliers of raw material, factories, inventory and delivering to the customers that ensures right product at an accurate price, are in an appropriate size, and at a right place that delivers the optimum lot size through proper distribution channel (Saleheen et al., 2018a; Aleksandra et al., 2017; Elnouaman & Ismail, 2016).

*Figure 1. Flow of SCM*
*(Huda et al., 2014)*

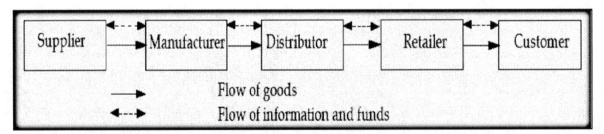

In a basic SCM conventionally entails suppliers, manufacturers, distributors, retailers, and customers. Every SCM prevails to satisfy customers' needs as well as to make the profit. Hence, the primary emphasis of all SCM is the customer (Elnouaman & Ismail, 2016; Saleheen et al., 2019) illustrated in figure 1.

*Supply Chain Practice Towards Resilience*

## Definition of Supply Chain Management

American Production and Inventory Control Society conceptualized the definition of Supply Chain Management (SCM) as the process of overseeing the flow from raw materials to the consumption of end products by consumers (Frederico et al., 2019; Septiani et al., 2016). This description implies that SCM is a system that synchronizes the entire functions and sub-functions of the internal and external entities of an organization.

In the same line, some other authors extended the importance of emphasizing the incorporation of the information system in the definition of SCM where the primary emphasis of all SCM is the customer (Elnouaman & Ismail, 2016; Saleheen et al., 2019; Agrawal et al., 2019).

In the same vein, SCM is defined practically as a chain that connects, manage and ensures the flow of products and services between manufacturers, suppliers, and customers. Furthermore, SCM is also responsible for the enhancement of competitive advantage by using an organization's operational capability, information, technology, and suppliers (Molina-Besch, 2016).

The definition of SCM implies that SCM operationally entails the management and overseeing the flow of products, information, and finance between and among the upstream and downstream levels of SCM. Organizations need a complete performance measurement framework to connect with their customers and competition (Verónica et al., 2017).

## Timeline of Supply Chain Management

*Figure 2. Timeline of SCM*
*(Saleheen et al., 2018)*

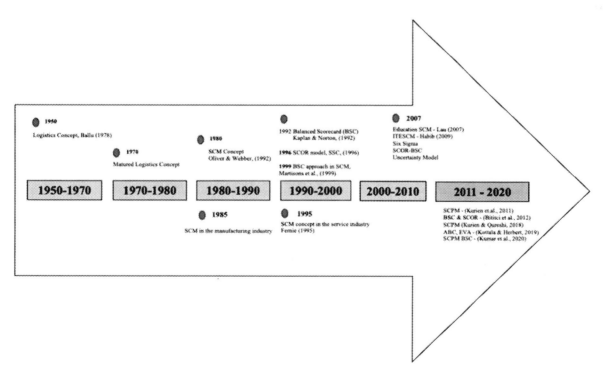

The concept of Supply Chain Management (SCM) has been evolved over past few decades illustrated in figure 2 and it is still adding value to the society and business. The term logistics was adopted as a general concept for the physical distribution of goods. Years before the adoption of logistics for strategic and managerial purposes are known as "dormant years" (Haraburda, 2016). The military-based orientation about logistics was reviewed during the "Transformation" era in the 1950s. This was when logistics was introduced as a term for transporting tangible goods (Ballou, 1992; 2007).

Alternatively, SCM was conceptualized by the logistics experts (O'Neall & Haraburda, 2017). The conceptualization of SCM was justified to approach and manage the supply chain (SC) with a unitary strategy. Hence, strategic decisions would be harmonized between the parties involved in the chain. This notion was considered unanimous among logistics and marketing theorists (Beamon, 1999). SCM is a central concept to the entire management theoretical realm. Hence, SCM eliminates across so many other management aspects (Gilling & Ulmer, 2016). Invariably, the importance of SCM has grown over time and continues to grow in a ponderous trend. Several researchers have examined the adoption of SCM in different industries (the primary emphasis of all SCM is the customer (Elnouaman & Ismail, 2016; Saleheen et al., 2019a).

Alternatively, SCM was conceptualized by the logistics experts (O'Neall & Haraburda, 2017). The conceptualization of SCM was justified to approach and manage the supply chain (SC) with a unitary strategy. Hence, strategic decisions would be harmonized between the parties involved in the chain. This notion was considered unanimous among logistics and marketing theorists (Beamon, 1999). SCM is a central concept to the entire management theoretical realm. Hence, SCM eliminates across so many other management aspects (Gilling & Ulmer, 2016). Invariably, the importance of SCM has grown over time and continues to grow in a ponderous trend. Several researchers have examined the adoption of SCM in different industries.

## SCM for the Manufacturing Industry

Manufacturers have been investigating innovative methods to attain competitive leverage in consequence of globalized competition. Practically, such methods can be referred to as SCM, which has been chosen as an enormous measure of consideration by the analysts and experts. SCM is reflected as an effective strategic approach to enhance competitive advantage in this modern era of intense global competition, and as such, SCM is gaining endless attention. Indeed, the effectiveness of SCM is impactful on the quality of product value, logistics and by extension on customer satisfaction and organizational profitability (Delic & Eyers, 2020).

Against this backdrop, manufacturing is the act of using different capabilities and approaches to add value to raw materials to satisfy certain demands. Manufacturing involves innovation, arts, and creativity to invent things that have not been created before.

Hence, manufacturers sometimes assume the position of suppliers and managers, managing resources and conveying their end products to end-users (Vanichchinchai, 2019).

Therefore, a strong and efficient relationship has to exist between manufacturers and consumers to ensure the commercial and practical achievement of manufacturers. Additionally, the core objectives of SCM is to ensure the quality, reduction of cost and time management in the cost of adding value to raw materials and conveying end products to end-users (Kottala & Herbert, 2019).

*Figure 3. The flow of SCM in the manufacturing industry*
(Chopra & Meindl, 2016)

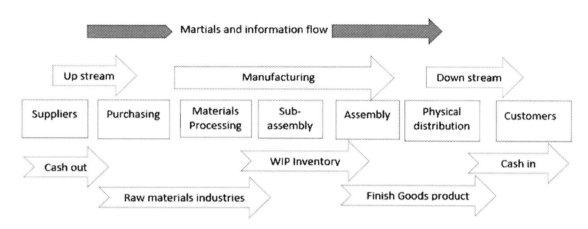

Illustrated in figure 3, in the process of manufacturing, which involves adding value to raw materials, turning raw materials to end products and meeting consumer demand, SCM functions both in upstream and downstream of manufacturing processes. The current intensified competition in the global market is posing some challenges to manufacturers. The myriad of challenges includes eliminating waste products, the innovation, and diffusion of new technologies, improvement of supplier-customer relations, complying with stringent regulations, adopting efficient inventory management and ultimately improving operational and performance effectiveness (Kottala & Herbert, 2019; Chopra & Meindl, 2016; Shamsuddoha, 2015).

## Supply Chain Drivers

*Figure 4. Supply Chain drivers*
(Chopra & Meindl, 2016)

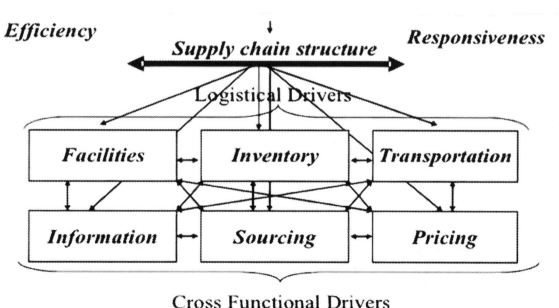

In order to bring a competitive position, a company needs to be strategically equipped to formulate its supply chain (SC) strategy either through responsiveness or efficiency, where six driving forces govern the competitive positions are - sourcing, facility, transportation, inventory, information, and pricing illustrated in figure 1.4. (Shamsuddoha, 2015).

## Sourcing

Four key methods are to be embraced in sourcing are - concentrate on corporate resources like Nike, and Dell kept an eye on, focus on subcontracting but expand the business like Nokia and Nortel followed, disruptive innovation where a company sets its prices comparatively lower in order to gain a market share and capture the customers and gradually increase the price as IKEA did, and strategic repositioning where companies provide business solutions of the problems of customers instead of offering services only related to the final products like IBM did (Singh & Misra, 2020; Ye et al., 2018; Monczka et al., 2016).

## Facilities

It makes major decisions on product, process and customer market coupled to each facility as well as the location of a facility are to be evaluated in an SC strategy planning. When determining a place, several aspects are to be considered, such as quality, speed, dependability, flexibility, and cost (Swierczek, 2019).

## Inventory

Inventory plays a crucial role in order to determine the performance of a company as most companies carry inventory in one way or another. Monczka et al. (2016) categorize that there are three types of inventory are raw material, work in progress, and finished goods inventory. Inventory holding cost is also an important factor for an organization in order to improve its operational efficiency and increase profitability.

Safety inventory also plays a significant role to support the customer during uncertainties and unforeseen situations when the demand fluctuates (Ye et al., 2018; Wang et al., 2016; World Bank, 2016a; Saleheen et al., 2014a).

## Transportation

It plays a significant role in the operation to reach its products to its customers where cost is relatively important to measure and determine the SC strategy. Faster transportation will increase the responsiveness but increase the cost; slower transport operations will lower the transport cost, but it increases the efficiency in the cost-benefit analysis.

## Information

E-commerce is a modern concept to share information effectively and timely among its SC network. Singh and Misra (2020) revealed that there are numerous challenges faced by a supplier or a customer in structuring themselves within an SC software.

Monczka et al. (2016) reviewed that if the information is not accurate, then decision- makers would be left to work with false or hoax measurement (Chopra & Meindl, 2016).

## Pricing

Researchers identified two approaches of pricing strategy, standard linear pricing approach, and strategy matrix pricing approach. The standard linear approach includes five steps to determine the correct price. Pricing based on business objective, policy-based pricing, develop a list price, discounts, and adjustments and final pricing (Singh & Misra, 2020).

## SCM Macro Process Flow

*Figure 5. SCM macro process*
*(Chopra & Meindl, 2015)*

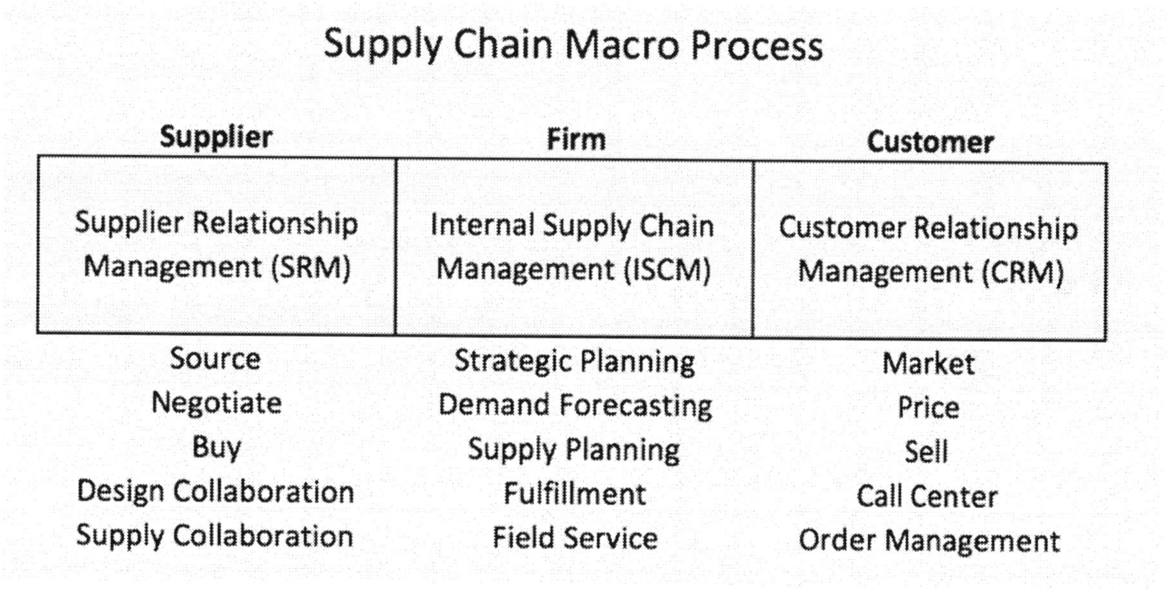

### Supply Chain Macro Process

| Supplier | Firm | Customer |
|---|---|---|
| Supplier Relationship Management (SRM) | Internal Supply Chain Management (ISCM) | Customer Relationship Management (CRM) |
| Source | Strategic Planning | Market |
| Negotiate | Demand Forecasting | Price |
| Buy | Supply Planning | Sell |
| Design Collaboration | Fulfillment | Call Center |
| Supply Collaboration | Field Service | Order Management |

The SCM macro process can be classified into three core components - upstream, internal process and downstream (Chopra & Meindl, 2015). Supplier Relationship Management (SRM) emphases the interaction with suppliers' supplier, supplier and the organization, and it deals with sourcing, negotiation with the supplier, purchase management, design collaboration, and supply collaboration illustrated in figure 5. Internal Supply Chain Management (ISCM) concentrates on the internal operations, production, planning at the strategic level, material requirement planning, supply planning, and order fulfilment, etc. are brought into the considerations. And finally, Customer Relationship Management (CRM) focuses on the market, call center operations and order management which are mostly the interaction between the enterprise and its customers (Chopra & Meindl, 2015).

## Supply Chain Risk Management

To handle supply chain resilience, an organization needs to address four types of comprehensive risk assessment which are as follows:

### Global Risk

In global risk management, an organization needs to critically address how the organization can be affected in its supply chain operations both upstream and downstream due to macro-economic factors, or some environmental issues such as natural calamity, pandemic, earthquake, airplane crashes, accident of ships in the ocean loaded with goods, etc. Also, there could be many factors such as political, economic, technological, government, legal, ethical business, and terrorist activities, etc.

This analysis and will help the organization to address its potential weakness and way forward when things go wrong (Altay & Green, 2006).

There should have always been an alternate plan when external factors in many cases are out of control. Considering the fact, SCM professionals need to address all these issues as these will play a vital role in their smooth operations and ensuring the availability of goods and services.

### Enterprise Risk

Enterprise risk mostly considers risk associated with in the industry nationally or regionally on within itself how an organization can be affected. The organization considers aspects from industry analysis, entry barriers, investment risk, technological risk planning to the payment process, security program, theft, sabotage, and counterfeit, etc. to measure its potential vulnerability and prepare accordingly.

### Human Capital and Management Risk

In this category, the risk assessment is focused associated with the critical resource issues related to human resources, brain drain, knowledge transfer, capacity building, and succession planning, etc.

### Supplier and Shipping Risk

The management also wants to assess a depth understanding of supply risk associated with international contracts, force majeure, failure to supply goods and services due to pandemic and global shipping crisis, and how the organization should react. The assessment goes further from supplier terms and conditions, credit extensions, port of destinations, port of loading, transshipments, free shipping time, penalty clauses, voyage lead time, the penalty in case of congestion during transshipment, lead time for reordering, availability of service spare parts, and raw materials in the nearest region to reduce the lead time, etc.

## Supply Chain Disruption Management

To handle global disruptions and prepare for resilient supply chain operations, an organization should ensure the following:

*Supply Chain Practice Towards Resilience*

## Collaboration (CL)

The idea of collaboration has been recognized in the upstream and downstream supply chain as CPFR which stands for collaborative planning forecasting and replenishment, in earlier times organizations were following vendor managed inventory (VMI) and continuous replenishment programs (CRP) as a form of collaboration illustrated in figure 6 (Panahifar et al., 2018; Nagashima et al., 2015). Collaboration is a broad and encompassing term, and in the perspective of the supply chain, further clarification is essential due to an over-reliance on technology, and failure to differentiate between whom to collaborate with (Panahifar et al., 2018; Salam, 2017; Saleheen et al., 2014).

*Figure 6. The scope of collaboration*
*(Barratt, 2004)*

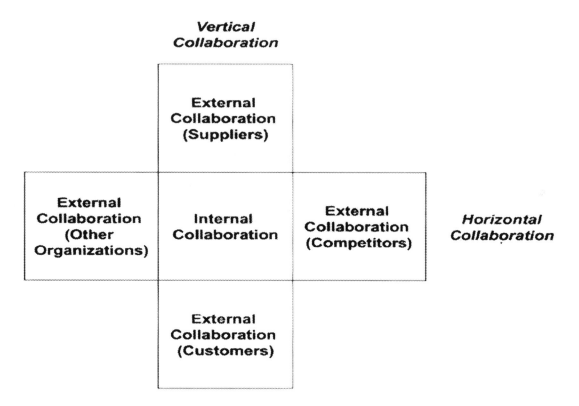

Collaboration in figure 6 is divided into horizontal and vertical, where vertical collaboration deals with customers, internally (across functions) with suppliers, and horizontal collaboration deals with competitors internally and with non-competitors such as sharing manufacturing capacity. The researcher highlighted some missing links such as common vision, shared resources, and joint goals that embrace a collaborative approach in its nature in practice (Salam, 2017; Nagashima et al., 2015).

*Figure 7. The scope of vertical collaboration*
*(Barratt, 2004)*

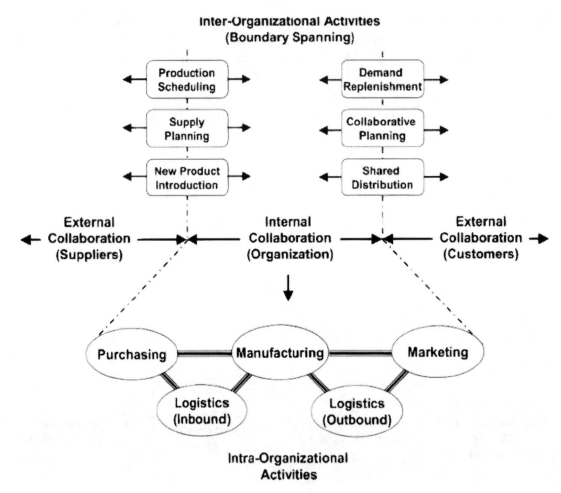

Internally, collaboration is not only building rapport amongst supply chain-related functions but also necessities to comprise marketing-commercial and R&D activities (Salam, 2017).

*Figure 8. Levels of inter-intra organizational integration*
*(Barratt, 2004)*

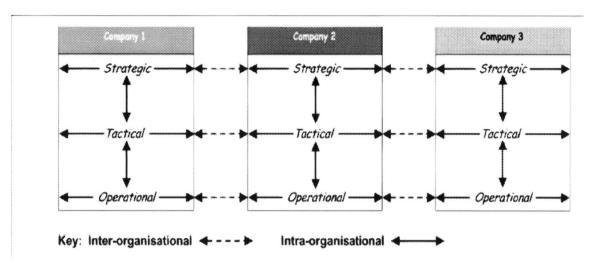

One of the constituents of collaboration is a collaborative culture that consists of an exchange of information, openness, communication, mutuality, and trust, etc. A collaborative culture is to accept, share, nourish information, and trust is extremely important (Narasimhan et al., 2015; Salam, 2017).

## Velocity (VC)

Due to market dynamics, demand fluctuations and technological innovations, the vocabulary of competitiveness has developed abruptly where it is influenced by the ability to reduce cycle time, lead time, total supply chain cost (TSCC), improving customer service level, and product quality. The ultimate rivalry for a supply chain is to warrant a balanced composition of efficiency and responsiveness towards its products and services, where a firm has been directed to design its supply chain more efficient considering its TSCC, supply chain cycle time, and time to market (Taghipour et al., 2015).

On the contrary, the responsive supply chain is critical to producing a competitive edge for an organization during new product development, products with a shorter life cycle to gain market competitiveness. Hence, it is inevitable to embrace responsiveness in the supply chain while blueprinting effective supply chain system design and operations, deliver a variety of products, reduce lead time, ensuring high volume flexibility at the manufacturing end, spanning network infrastructure, and inventory control (Taghipour et al., 2015).The following endeavors bring greater responsiveness in the supply chain are production time reduction by line balancing, setup time, idle time reduction & automation, and supplier engagement in product development, consider bullwhip effect both in the upstream and downstream supply chain to manage disruptions and invest in either finished products or raw materials safety stocks, reduction of time to market through improved transportation and supply chain cycle time, and focus on SC reliability, supplier performance assessment and risk assessment (Kurien & Qureshi, 2018; Taghipour et al., 2015).

### Visibility (VS)

Supply chain transparency, visibility, and information sharing between the supply chain partners is a prerequisite where the availability of authentic data can increase the supply chain visibility. In a rapidly changing and competitive business environment, an organization views its supply chain and its network as a critical determinant of efficiency and effectiveness where short product lifecycle and rapid market fluctuations trigger a higher level of bullwhip-effect in operation. Organizations have recognized collaboration as an apparatus to attain a greater level of efficiency and enhanced business performance. Accurate information sharing among its supplier network increases the visibility that is desirable to secure the benefits within the supply network, and members need timely access, appropriate and precise information (Shamsuddoha, 2015; Sundram et al., 2018; Maghsoudi & Pazirandeh, 2016).

### Reliability (RL)

To ensure reliability in the supply chain, a dependable association between the partners and mutual conviction in each other's abilities and undertakings is essential. An increase in assurance and conviction between the associates and conceiving trustworthiness from them enhances sustainable success in the supply chain. Three-level operational evaluation metrics are supported by the SCOR model such as level one, level two, and level three. The level one metric assesses the management, level two and level three comprise more precise and comprehensive principles with regards to the classifications and fundamentals of the methods.

The level one metric is logically distributed into five functioning standards asset, reliability, responsiveness, cost, and flexibility. To create a fruitful bond in SC, evaluating the reliability of the link is critical. The SCOR model, devised by the Supply Chain Council (SCC) is analyzed and configured the SCM in a comprehensive manner (Garay-Rondero et al., 2019; Chen, 2018).

## FUTURE RESEARCH AND RECOMMENDATIONS

To manage supply chain disruption, and ensure resilient supply chain operations, manufacturing companies have been studying innovative methods to attain competitive leverage where integrated SCM is reflected as an effective strategic approach to enhance competitive advantage in this modern era of intense global competition. Business dynamic forces have been transformed that put the arm on the legislative requirements to measure the performance for the manufacturing industry where companies have been witnessing to unlock the tools that can assess the supply chain performance measurement (SCPM) commendable (Kurien & Qureshi, 2018). Ideally, the performance measurement of an integrated SCM should consider quantitative as well as qualitative approach and have the capacity to apply existing different measuring tools such as the BSC model, the SCOR model, and different OR techniques such as through Analytical Hierarchy Process (AHP) or Structural Equation Modeling (SEM) technique etc. (Kumar et al., 2020).

## CONCLUSION

Managing risk and resilient supply chain in a borderless economy are getting exponentially challenging due to uncertainties in demand and supply to shorter product lifecycles to outsourcing, and many other issues. In reality, business is harshly influenced by multifold factors such as financial unpredictability, merger & acquisition, the innovation of technologies, e-business, shorter time-to-market, natural disasters, pandemic, terrorist activities, accidents in the shipping lines, etc. that pushes organizations to embrace a smarter way of doing business.

Due to internal & external interruption, and exponential vulnerability - risk management has become significant for SCM operations. Several factors fuel the risks in the supply chain. Macro factors like globalization, open internet access, and e-commerce provide opportunities for diversification of supply and trigger an intricate SC vulnerability (Chen, 2018; Panova & Hilletofth, 2018; Kurniawan et al., 2017). The urgency on efficiency and operating cost optimization motivated firms towards lean manufacturing, low-cost sourcing, just-in-time inventory, reduced product lifecycle, centralized distribution centers, and supplier rationalization. All these new supply chain management (SCM) concepts allowed the firms towards optimization on cost, time, investments, and service. Few series of threats recently evolved into the supply chain cycle - natural catastrophe, demand shocks, systemic vulnerability such as oil dependence and information fragmentation, cyber risk, rising insurance, trade finance costs, and the SC authorities are to investigate a new mitigation process. The researcher highlights that nowadays, the majority of the large corporations have the highest priority on the resilient issues in its end to end operations (Panova & Hilletofth, 2018; Chen, 2018).

## REFERENCES

Agrawal, P., Narain, R., & Ullah, I. (2019). Analysis of barriers in implementation of digital transformation of supply chain using interpretive structural modelling approach. *Journal of Modelling in Management*, *15*(1), 297–317. doi:10.1108/JM2-03-2019-0066

Aleksandra, C., Anna, B., & Halemba, H. (2017). Lean supply chain management. *World Scientific News*, 177–183.

Altay, N., & Green, W. G. III. (2006). OR/MS research in disaster operations management. *European Journal of Operational Research*, *175*(1), 475–493. doi:10.1016/j.ejor.2005.05.016

Altay, N., Gunasekaran, A., Dubey, R., & Childe, S. J. (2018). Agility and Resilience as Antecedents of Supply Chain Performance Under Moderating Effects of Organizational Culture Within the Humanitarian Setting: A Dynamic Capability View. *Production Planning and Control*, *29*(14), 1158–1174. doi:10.1080/09537287.2018.1542174

Araz, O. M., Choi, T.-M., Olson, D., & Salman, F. S. (2020). Data Analytics for Operational Risk Management. *Decision Sciences*.

Ballou, R. H. (1992). *Business Logistics Management* (3rd ed.). Prentice Hall.

Ballou, R. H. (2007). The evaluation and future of logistics and supply chain management. *European Business Review*, *19*(4), 332–348. doi:10.1108/09555340710760152

Barratt, M. (2004). Understanding the meaning of collaboration in the Supply chain. An International Journal. *Emerald Group Publishing Limited*, 9(1), 30–42. doi:10.1108/13598540410517566

Basole, R. C., & Bellamy, M. A. (2014). Supply Network Structure, Visibility, and Risk Diffusion: A Computational Approach. *Decision Sciences*, 45(4), 1–49. doi:10.1111/deci.12099

Beamon, B. M. (1999). Measuring Supply Chain Performance. *International Journal of Operations & Production Management*, 19(3), 275–292. doi:10.1108/01443579910249714

Bevilacqua, M., Ciarapica, F. E., & Marcucci, G. (2017). Supply Chain Resilience Triangle: The Study and Development of a Framework. *World Academy of Science, Engineering and Technology, International Journal of Social, Behavioral, Educational, Economic, Business and Industrial Engineering*, 11(8), 2046–2053.

Carlsson-Szlezak, P., Reeves, M., & Swartz, P. (2020). What Coronavirus Could Mean for the Global Economy. *Harvard Business Review*. https://hbr.org/2020/03/what-coronavirus-could-mean-for-the-global-economy

Chen, H. (2018). Supply chain risk's impact on corporate financial performance. *International Journal of Operations & Production Management*, 38(3), 713–731. doi:10.1108/IJOPM-02-2016-0060

Chopra, S., & Meindl, P. (2015). *Supply chain management: Strategy, Planning, and Operation* (4th ed.). Pearson Education.

Chopra, S., & Meindl, P. (2016). *Supply chain management: Strategy, planning, and operation* (6th ed.). Pearson.

Delic, M., & Eyers, D. R. (2020). The effect of additive manufacturing adoption on supply chain flexibility and performance: An empirical analysis from the automotive industry. *International Journal (Toronto, Ont.)*.

DuHadway, S., Carnovale, S., & Hazen, B. (2019). Understanding risk management for intentional supply chain disruptions: Risk detection, risk mitigation, and risk recovery. *Annals of Operations Research*, 283(1–2), 179–198. doi:10.100710479-017-2452-0

Elnouaman, S., & Ismail. K. (2016). The Relationship between IT and Supply chain management Performance: A Systematic Review and Future Research. *American Journal of Industrial and Business Management*, 480-495.

Erdogan, O., Tata, K., Karahasan, B.C., & Sengoz, M.H. (2013). Dynamics of the co-movement between stock and maritime markets. *Int. Rev. Econ. Financ., 25*, 282–290. doi:10.1016/j.iref.2012.07.007

Frederico, G., Garza-Reyes, J., Anosike, A., & Kumar, V. (2019). Supply Chain 4.0: Concepts, maturity and research agenda. *Supply Chain Management*, 25(2), 262–282. doi:10.1108/SCM-09-2018-0339

Garay-Rondero, C., Martinez-Flores, J., Smith, N., Caballero Morales, S., & Aldrette-Malacara, A. (2019). Digital supply chain model in Industry 4.0. *Journal of Manufacturing Technology Management*. doi:10.1108/JMTM-08-2018-0280

Gilling, R.-I., & Ulmer, J.-M. (2016). *Major Challenges in Supply Chain Management*. Academic Press.

Haraburda, S. S. (2016). Transforming military support processes from logistics to supply chain management. *Army Sustainment, 48*(2), 12–15. Retrieved from https://www.alu.army.mil/alog/2016/MarApr16/PDF/162197.pdf

Huda, A.K.M. N., Pathik, B.B., & Mohib, A.A. (2014). A Case Study Approach for Developing Supply Chain Management Models. *International Journal of Business and Economics Research, 3*(6), 6-14. doi:10.11648/j.ijber.s.2014030601.12

Kottala, S., & Herbert, K. (2019). An empirical investigation of supply Chain operations reference model practices and supply chain performance: Evidence from manufacturing sector. *International Journal of Productivity and Performance Management.* doi:10.1108/IJPPM-09-2018-0337

Kumar, A., Singh, R., & Modgil, S. (2020). Exploring the relationship between ICT, SCM practices and organizational performance in agri-food supply chain. *Benchmarking: An International Journal.* . doi:10.1108/BIJ-11-2019-0500

Kurien, G. P., & Qureshi, M. N. (2018). House of sustainable waste management: An implementation framework. *International Journal of Sustainable Manufacturing, 4*(1), 79–96. doi:10.1504/IJSM.2018.099583

Kurien, G. P., & Qureshi, M. N. (2018). House of sustainable waste management: An implementation framework. *International Journal of Sustainable Manufacturing., 4*(1), 79–96. doi:10.1504/IJSM.2018.099583

Kurniawan, R., Zailani, S., Iranmanesh, M., & Rajagopal, P. (2017). The effects of vulnerability mitigation strategies on supply chain effectiveness: Risk culture as moderator. *Supply Chain Management, 22*(1), 1–15. doi:10.1108/SCM-12-2015-0482

Maghsoudi, A., & Pazirandeh, A. (2016). Visibility, resource sharing and performance in supply chain relationships: Insights from humanitarian practitioners. *Supply Chain Management, 21*(1), 125–139. doi:10.1108/SCM-03-2015-0102

McKibbin, W., & Fernando, R. (2020). *The Global Macroeconomic Impacts of COVID-19: Seven Scenarios.* CAMA Working paper, The Australian National University.

Molina-Besch, K. (2016). Prioritization guidelines for green food packaging development. *British Food Journal, 2016*(118), 2512–2533. doi:10.1108/BFJ-12-2015-0462

Molina-Besch, K. (2016). Prioritization guidelines for green food packaging development. *British Food Journal, 2016*(118), 2512–2533. doi:10.1108/BFJ-12-2015-0462

Monczka, R. M., Handfield, R. B., Giunipero, L. C., & Patterson, J. L. (2016). *Purchasing and Supply chain management* (6th ed.). Cengage.

Nagashima, M., Wehrle, F., Kerbache, L., & Lassagne, M. (2015). Impacts of adaptive collaboration on demand forecasting accuracy of different product categories throughout the product life cycle. *Supply Chain Management, 20*(4), 415–433. doi:10.1108/SCM-03-2014-0088

Narayanan, S., Narasimhan, R., & Schoenherr, T. (2015). Assessing the contingent effects of collaboration on agility performance in buyer–supplier relationships. *Journal of Operations Management, 33*(1), 140–154. doi:10.1016/j.jom.2014.11.004

O'Neall, C. E., & Haraburda, S. S. (2017). *Balanced scorecards for supply Chain management*. Academic Press.

Panahifar, F., Byrne, P., Salam, M., & Heavey, C. (2018). Supply chain Collaboration and firm's performance: The critical role of information sharing and trust. *Journal of Enterprise Information Management*.

Panova, Y., & Hilletofth, P. (2018). Managing supply chain risks and delays in construction project. *Industrial Management & Data Systems*, *118*(7), 1413–1431. doi:10.1108/IMDS-09-2017-0422

Salam, M. (2017). The mediating role of supply chain collaboration on the relationship between technology, trust and operational performance: An empirical investigation. *Benchmarking*, *24*(2), 298–317. doi:10.1108/BIJ-07-2015-0075

Saleheen, F., Habib, M. M., & Hanafi, Z. (2018a). Supply Chain Performance Measurement Model: A Literature Review. *International Journal of Supply Chain Management*, *7*(3).

Saleheen, F., Habib, M. M., & Hanafi, Z. (2018b). An Empirical Study on Supply Chain Management Performance Measurement through AHP. *International Journal of Supply Chain Management*, *7*(6).

Saleheen, F., Habib, M. M., & Hanafi, Z. (2019). An Implementation of Balanced Scorecard on Supply Chain Performance Measurement in Manufacturing Industry. *Proceedings from 2nd International Conference on Business and Management (ICBM)*.

Saleheen, F., Habib, M. M., & Hanafi, Z. (2019a). A study on multi-dimensional supply Chain performance measurement (SCPM) models in manufacturing industries and way forward. *Proceedings from 2nd International Conference on Business and Management (ICBM)*.

Saleheen, F., Habib, M. M., & Pathik, B., & Hanafi, Z. (2014). Demand and Supply Planning in Retail Operations. *International Journal of Business and Economics Research*, *3*(6), 51-56. doi:10.11648/j.ijber.s.2014030601.18

Saleheen, F., Miraz, H. M. M. M., & Hanafi, Z. (2014). Challenges of Warehouse Operations: A Case Study in Retail Supermarket. *International Journal of Supply Chain Management*, *3*(4).

Septiani, W., Marimin, M., Herdiyeni, Y., & Haditjaroko, L. (2016). Method and Approach Mapping for Agri-Food Supply Chain Risk Management: A Literature Review. *International Journal of Supply Chain Management*, *5*, 51–64.

Shamsuddoha, M. (2015). Integrated Supply Chain Model for Sustainable Manufacturing: A System Dynamics Approach. *Sustaining Competitive Advantage Via Business Intelligence, Knowledge Management, and System*.

Singh, A., & Misra, S. (2020). Ordering drivers of green supply chain management practices in Indian construction industry: An impact assessment framework. *International Journal of Quality & Reliability Management*. doi:10.1108/IJQRM-03-2019-0076

Singh, A., & Misra, S. (2020). Ordering drivers of green supply chain management practices in Indian construction industry: An impact assessment framework. *International Journal of Quality & Reliability Management*. doi:10.1108/IJQRM-03-2019-0076

Sundram, V., Bahrin, A., Abdul Munir, Z., & Zolait, A. (2018). The effect of supply chain information management and information system infrastructure: The mediating role of supply chain integration towards manufacturing performance in Malaysia. *Journal of Enterprise Information Management, 31*(5), 751–770. doi:10.1108/JEIM-06-2017-0084

Swierczek, A. (2019). The effects of brokered network governance on relational embeddedness in the triadic supply chains: Is there a room for the "Coleman rent"? *Supply Chain Management: An International Journal.* doi:10.1108/SCM-04-2019-0170

Taghipour, M., Taghipour, M., Khodarezaei, M., & Farid, F. (2015). Supply Chain Performance Evaluation in the IT Industry. *IJRRAS, 23*(2). Retrieved from www.arpapress.com/Volumes/Vol23Issue2/IJRRAS_23_2_07.pdf

TheodossiouP.TsouknidisD. A.SavvaC. S. 2020. Freight rates in downside and upsidemarkets: pricing of own and spillover risks from other shipping segments. *J. R. Stat.Soc. Ser. A.* doi:10.2139/ssrn.3514142

Verónica, L., Federico, C., Maria C., & Thomas, J. (2017). Collaboration for Sustainability in the Food Supply chain management: A Multi-Stage Study in Italy. *Sustainability MDPI, 11*(5), 407–414.

Wang, B., Childerhouse, P., Kang, Y., Huo, B., & Mathrani, S. (2016). Enablers of supply chain integration: Interpersonal and interorganizational relationship perspectives. *Industrial Management & Data Systems, 116*(4), 838–855. doi:10.1108/IMDS-09-2015-0403

World Bank. (2016a). *Logistics performance index.* Retrieved from: https://lpi.worldbank.org/report

Ye, Y., Lau, K., & Teo, L. (2018). Drivers and barriers of omni-channel retailing in China: A case study of the fashion and apparel industry. *International Journal of Retail & Distribution Management, 46*(7), 657-689.

# Chapter 6
# Supply Chain Resilience as a Productive Relocation Strategy for Multinational Companies

**José G. Vargas-Hernández**
https://orcid.org/0000-0003-0938-4197
*Instituto Tecnológico Mario Molina, Unidad Académica Zapopan, Mexico*

**María Fernanda Higuera**
https://orcid.org/0000-0001-8285-1076
*Autonomous University of Sinaloa, Mexico*

## ABSTRACT

*This chapter aims to critically analyze the implications that the national protectionist policies have on the global supply and value chains and the relocation of production. The analysis is based on the assumptions that the global economy is facing the possibility of decoupling of many trade connections, and this trend favors deglobalization processes that have long been promoted by populism, nationalism, and economic protectionism. It is concluded that global supply, production, and value chains, although being economically efficient, are no longer any more secure under national protectionist policies, and therefore, the relocation of production processes is mainly due to the increase in the level of income and wages of the developing countries that are the destination and which reduce the advantages to relocate.*

## INTRODUCTION

The process of economic globalization is undergoing one of the greatest difficulties in recent decades, showing a contraction of international trade flows of 17.7% in May 2020 compared to the same month in 2019, according to the ECLAC (2020). These contractions in trade flows have been further aggravated by the poor responses that governments and companies have given to the health contingency. Examples of the difficulties that globalization has gone through are the third largest recession in the United States in 1885, after the Great Depression of 1929 and the Great Depression of 1873 and the 2009 recession

DOI: 10.4018/978-1-7998-9506-0.ch006

Copyright © 2022, IGI Global. Copying or distributing in print or electronic forms without written permission of IGI Global is prohibited.

*Supply Chain Resilience*

arising from the collapse of the US housing market that as a result, several companies and banks had to be rescued by central governments around the world.

It is believed that Supply Chains (SC) were the main transmission channel for the effects of COVID-19 on world trade, since the measures adopted by countries (the closure of non-essential activities and national borders) meant that exports supply for industries were suspended. Hence, commercial corporations and companies are forced to rethink their CS and logistics, to understand market forces and reposition themselves competitively in the global market.

This analysis shows that periods of expansion of free trade alternate with others in which protectionist measures and the relocation of production form part of a process called deglobalization and is characterized by a reduction in export growth that is offset by an increased consumption of the domestic market to defend national interests. It means she deglobalization process is based on the promotion of protectionist measures and is characterized by flows of exports, investments, migratory movements, and technological innovation that are reduced or diminished, reflected in political and economic decisions to target domestic demand with tariff measures, restrictions and limitations on cross-border investment and foreign labor (Shavshukov and Zhuravleva, 2020).

The current environment of economic, social, political and health instability has intensified the increase in the economic costs of transaction and coordination of the subsidiaries of multinational companies located in other international host territories, making relocation processes unfeasible, for which they have initiated processes of repression or deglobalization to return their production to the countries of origin. This situation has meant a stagnation, and in some cases a setback in the business strategy to deepen the processes of globalization of companies (Meyer and Peng, 2016).

The level of economic integration in the processes of globalization is very advanced, an example of this is the case of China, when production is paralyzed in some provinces, the supply of inputs to companies in other provinces and nations has been affected, "the measures adopted by China in January (the temporary closure of Hubei province and national borders) meant that exports of inputs for industries such as automobiles, electronics, pharmaceuticals and medical supplies were suspended (ECLAC, 2020, p.3). Situation of vulnerability that has motivated deglobalization as a response that makes relocation more profitable with the repatriation of factories (Zhu, Chou, and Tsai, 2020).

First, this article makes a critical analysis of national protectionist policies and their implications for achieving supply chain resilience (SCR) and how these two factors determine the production relocation strategy. Finally, a discussion of these issues is offered.

## BACKGROUND: PROTECTIONISM AND ITS EFFECTS ON THE SUPPLY CHAIN

Protectionism has returned, but we will have to think if we really want to ignore the fruits of globalization and opt for the reasoned "deglobalization" that it called for and that now seems inevitable (Sapir, 2016). The term deglobalization was coined by Sapir (2011) in his work "La démondialisation", to refer to the protectionism of countries that have a similar level of development, based on the understanding that globalization in its commercial and financial dimensions has not allowed economic growth to be achieved.

The deglobalization process is characterized by the recovery of the sovereignty of nations (due to the reduction of interdependence) and a decreasing trend in the share of exports in the country's gross domestic product (due to the implementation of policies automatic and protectionist measures to reduce economic and trade relations).

In other words, deglobalization is understood as the reverse process of globalization that is manifested by the protectionist and regulatory economic and commercial policies of national states, as well as the commercial wars that are carried out between the great economic and commercial powers, with the aim of protect domestic production, domestic markets increase tariff barriers with the intensification of trade wars between western and eastern markets. What the health crisis has done is accelerate the process.

James defines the protectionist policy of a country as the increase in restrictions on the free flow of trade, finance, and people, reinforcing its national borders and oriented towards deglobalization processes (2018), that threaten the internationalization of companies, because of production stoppages, shortages of raw materials and finished products, delayed shipments, and shortages. An example of this is the impact of the COVID-19 pandemic, which caused subsequent interruptions, including the closure of production facilities, distribution bottlenecks that posed considerable risks for the supply chain (SC). It is urgent to point out that nationalist and populist protectionist policies may or may not be functional, depending on their correct design and implementation.

The concern about the effects is because the implications are quite unique for CS, since unlike singular geographically focused disasters, a health crisis such as the one we are experiencing is not limited to a particular region or weather. Thus, "the different components of a supply chain are affected at the same time, and markets can be paralyzed within overlapping time windows"(Nayler and Subramanian, 2021, p.9).

Some of the phenomena that disappointed the scope of the globalized economy is that its scope has been uneven. "Significant trade barriers remain in key sectors of export interest to developing countries, such as agriculture and textiles and clothing, and trade remedy measures (anti-dumping, countervailing and safeguard measures, often targeting developing countries), in many cases replacing previous actions. duty"(Trebilcock, 2005, p.237). In addition to the extreme right that has channeled discontent to promote protectionist measures. What makes necessary a greater presence of the State in the face of the challenges of economic growth, economic and social equality, inclusion, environmental sustainability, protection of biodiversity and conservation of the environment, among others.

The abandonment of global economic integration is an option for national states framed in a Keynesian scheme through the implementation of trade protectionist measures and the maintenance of democracy. Rodrik (2000) and Steinberg (2005) They assure that this policy has favored the economic growth of some developed countries after they will embrace economic globalization. It is worth mentioning that they opted for this measure because, because they remained with the borders closed to trade.

An example of the above, but from governance is the Slow Food movement founded by Carlo Petrini and a group of activists in 1980, with the aim of protect the consumption of local products, cultures, traditions, and gastronomic customs perceived as healthier and safer (Petrini, 2001). The movement also seeks to raise awareness about food consumption decisions and their origin.

However, despite the pros of protectionism, during the real estate crisis that arose in 2009, the leaders of the most advanced economies (Norway, Australia, Switzerland, the Netherlands, the United States, Germany, etc.) chose to avoid the trend of protectionist economic nationalism. This is since States and international institutions preferred to recover those functions that were taken from them, thus assuming responsibilities to protect national economies and societies. In the same sense, in 2017 China integrated market socialism, a mechanism of economic integration, generator of wealth and multilateral cooperation, while the United States preferred to promote trade protectionism (Liu, Dunford, and Gao, 2018). In short, protectionist trade policies used as an instrument for multilateral and bilateral negotiations do not always result in benefits for the country that promotes them, as has recently been shown in the case

*Supply Chain Resilience*

of the United States, which has encountered strong resistance from the tendency of the processes of economic globalization.

On the other hand, the unilateral discourses practiced by some powers seek to control the world agenda of globalization processes through neo-protectionist mechanisms under a world economy that revolves around multipolarity. Meanwhile, geoeconomics and geopolitical analyzes show a transition from the leadership of the global economy to China and the United States takes a more protectionist stance that drastically affects the economies that are most dependent on global trade (developing economies).

The health crisis caused by the pandemic has accelerated the protectionist tendencies and populist and nationalist policies of nations and has caused tensions and trade wars in the face of the fall in international trade flows and foreign direct investment. And although the health crisis has accelerated and deepened this trend of economic deglobalization through protectionist actions, reduction of multilateral treaties, etc., with legible economic consequences, but uncertain and unpredictable (Didea and Ilie, 2020).

Even so, this economic slowdown that is being talked about started long before the pandemic. Well, before the COVID-19 pandemic, the world economy faced challenges such as trade wars characterized by unfair tariff practices. In the case of the United States, it seeks to eliminate the trade deficit by implementing protectionist and nationalist fiscal policies and has launched a trade war against its trading partners, but above all with China, its main competitor.

As a result of protectionist tensions in the global market, a trade war has been sparked that constitutes a rethinking in the opposite direction to commercial progress. This situation that it presents itself unilaterally resists the continuous opening of international markets and economies to position itself as a closed economy, erodes economic, commercial, and political relations with its partners. In other words, the country that was the greatest promoter of the processes of economic globalization is now the greatest opponent to the deepening of economic, commercial, and financial relations.

In addition, these actions had repercussions worldwide, because by drastically reducing world trade and China being the largest producer of medical supplies (Qin, 2020), several countries were left unprotected in the face of the needs posed by the health crisis. Consequently, countless countries want to maintain their own and local economic activities through protectionism. In line with this, multinational companies plan to repatriate their production process. So, national markets and economies are now less dependent on international markets and rely on the regulations of national economies to protect themselves. Thus, the deglobalization of economic integration processes shifts the center of gravity from the market to the local sustainable market through a commercial policy and the use of fiscal, tariff and quota mechanisms to protect national production from transnational companies (IMCO, 2020).

However, according to Findlay and O'Rourke (2008), deglobalization processes have repercussions that damage economies that promote protectionist economic policies, since the uniformity and standardization of trade regulations threaten regional and local development where asymmetry is normal for self-protection. Therefore, the protectionist attempt of an economy has a negative impact on national companies in such a way that the protectionist measures taken unilaterally by a country damage the competitiveness of its companies and therefore its own economy. So, it is the same multinational companies that promote the relocation of production, distribution, and consumption processes. And although some choose to relocate the production of goods and services within their borders or integrated regions,

Once again from the trenches of the companies, the SCs of the same were formed and maintained with little attention to resilience, since prior to the pandemic keeping costs, low was essential, and that meant establishing where the inputs were cheapest (when the location was what governed prices), labor was cheaper, technology and know-how were available, or there were incentives from local govern-

103

ments. Currently, supply chains are functional, but, in most cases, subject to certain restrictions such as shipping, bureaucracy, costs. So, the best option is to bet on the SCR, since it will allow it to meet the challenges arising from the pandemic, as well as understand the market forces and the competitive positioning of the company.

## MAIN FOCUS: SUPPLY CHAIN, RESILIENCE (SCR) AND PRODUCTIVE RELOCATION FOR MULTINATIONAL COMPANIES

The entire world economic structure is reeling from the health crisis of the pandemic, the Nation-state governments and corporations are assessing the global marketplace as a growing source of disruption to supply, production and logistics chains, as well as a source of risk and competitive disadvantage. Likewise, local governments are withdrawing from global policies of economic integration and are increasing protectionist policies for the repatriation of manufactured goods. (Abdal and Ferreira 2021). However, other national economies have already developed capacities to become resilient, recover, restructure, and improve the new institutional governance that emerges from the pandemic.

Trade liberalization, the economy, financial and trade liberalization, innovations in information and communication technologies facilitated the special and operational expansion of transnational and multinational companies that, in turn, contributed to altering the exchange of flows of resources and supply chain (SC) between companies to a global redistribution. In the words of Kano, Tsang, and Yeung (2020) the process of economic globalization it accelerated the flow of goods through global supply chains and global trade.

The development of ICTs and the emergence of the Internet accelerated the processes of globalization with world communication in real time, financial digitization, and the logistical development of SCs, accelerated the scope of a global economy. Regarding this, the countries belonging to the BRICS (Brazil, Russia, India, China, and South Africa) have become the agents of changes in global competitiveness (Barykin, Kapustina, Korchagina, Sergeev, Yadykin, Abdimomynova, Stepanova, 2021).

The SCs of companies in a global economy scenario are distributed all over the world. Multinational and transnational corporations have established networks of SCRs, subcontractors, and logistics throughout the world. Thus, the global network-based economy is made up of chains developed by a large group of shadow companies that are connected to carry out economic activities across country borders and make the concept of distance and borders nationals does not make sense.

In a competitive global market, the costs of all CS, production and consumption spread throughout the world should be the lowest (Bello, 2013). However, globalization based on economies of scale and scope due to the location of production where it is most efficient has ended, while the concern is about the fragility of supply chain diversification, because its processes depend on each other. others to add value.

The global chains of production and distribution show the fragility of the high dependence on the processes of economic globalization to provide products and inputs to the economies that require them to continue with their manufacturing processes. This failure in global production chains has exposed the weaknesses of national security and national industry, arguments that support protectionist positions, such as measures to guarantee supply in national markets. The national security policy acquires greater force by pressing for reversals in global production chains encouraged by supply decisions in local markets.

Beginning in the 1990s, global production and SCs grew steadily. Since 2007, with the outbreak of the economic and financial crisis, the indicators of the globalization processes show a tendency towards

*Supply Chain Resilience*

a decrease in global production and supply chains, due to a drop in demand from international markets and not so much to structural changes. Since the financial crisis of 2008-2009, world trade has failed to keep up with world GDP, due to the rise of protectionist policies (WTO, 2021). Global economic, financial, health and contingency crises such as natural disasters have a domino effect that has a greater impact on global production and value chains (FAO, 2021), for example, the case of the tsunami in Japan in 2011 that affected global automobile production chains.

These stagnation in the processes of economic globalization have negative effects for the world economy due to the relocation of the production chain, although the reorientation may have some positive effects for certain national territories where some phases of this production chain can be carried out taking advantage of the low costs labor. Reversing or slowing down the processes of economic globalization will entail changes in the practices and activities of multinational and transnational companies

In 2019 there is a high fragmentation of global supply chains, which deepens with the health crisis of 2020. The breaks in global supply chains produce a dislocation of production that produces in response the withdrawal of companies based abroad by the Coronavirus that has paralyzed the growth of global trade, which contributes more than 60% of the world's gross domestic product (Ellyat, 2021). This situation has been called deglobalization, aggravated by the health crisis, which has made interconnections difficult for commercial practices between different countries.

The current health crisis scenario has affected the complex global supply and value chains of intermediate goods, without being able to stop their fragmentation. This has shown that global supply chains are too vulnerable and complicated for companies to immediately redesign and redirect, which has accelerated deglobalization processes.

The critical situation of the health crisis has forced to reduce the space of global logistics and supply chains to replace them with shorter chains, in such a way that the locations for the supply of raw materials and the production of inputs or parts of a product they should be shorter than the places where the final product is assembled (Shih, 2020).The health crisis has highlighted the limitations of global logistics and supply chains in sectors such as electronics, automotive, aeronautics, medical equipment, pharmaceuticals, the textile industry, etc. In short, the health crisis has broken global production chains.

Well, the inability of globalization processes to find a way out of SC relocation, as well as the inability of the national industry in many countries to produce the required medical supplies, has complicated the economic scenario. Likewise, the health crisis has exposed the dysfunctionality of global and multinational supply chains, leaving excessively dependent companies vulnerable (Baldwin and di Mauro, 2020), thus affected the global production chains of countries prone to international trade, although it is contradictory that this depends on corporate companies that originally relocated their production processes.

That is why many nation-states have accelerated deglobalization processes by strengthening the production of inputs and operations in local spaces. These processes imply having greater controls over commercial, financial, migratory, travel flows, etc., which generates setbacks in global supply and production chains. Thus, multinational corporations moved their production operations to places where costs were lower, achieving supply through long global supply chains, which were suddenly interrupted during the Covid-19 health crisis, with serious threats of paralyze the production of certain essential products such as ago-food.

In short, deglobalization processes attempt to decouple local production from global supply chains to redirect production towards the domestic market, supported by movements in favor of self-sufficiency and food sovereignty based on national industrial and agricultural production. In the words of Boiral, Brotherton, Rivaud and Guillaumie (2021) countries have had to rethink their supply chains and the value of strategic productive activities, such as food production. For this reason, strategic productive industries are a priority for national development, which is why they are maintained and strengthened with actions such as the development of local, flexible, and fast production chains of value chains.

Thus, globalization undergoes profound changes and will not be as we knew it before in the modes of production, distribution, and consumption and in the global chains of production, supply, and value. Rather, the dynamics of contemporary globalization processes have registered a strong interruption that questions the entire international economic system, disrupts global supply and value chains, as well as a slowdown in all economic sectors.

The continuity of the processes of economic globalization requires leadership in mitigating the negative impacts on production and supply chains in the global economy by locating in places where costs are lower. Through the change of priorities in the productive systems of distribution and consumption, through the relocation of supply chains (Ibn-Mohammed, Mustapha, Godsell, Adamu, Babatunde, Akintade, Acquaye, Fujii, Ndiaye, Yamoah, Koh, 2021). As a result of this situation, he economic efficiencies of globalization processes are being highly questioned with the dysfunctionality of global supply chains leading to more protectionist economic and fiscal policies.

Deglobalization is a period of slowdown and decline in international economic, trade, financial and people flows intensified by the coronavirus that has caused companies to rethink the risks of global supply chains that are produced in remote locations. The economic phenomenon of the deglobalization of the world economy is a period marked by a drop in trade and financial flows, intensified by the coronavirus pandemic that has caused a rethinking of the risks of the global supply chain that come from geographically remote places. The interruption of the supply chains of local companies' dependent on a global system generates economic losses.

With the disruption of global production and supply chains, and due to perceived risks, production and consumption turn to alternative sources of inputs, goods, and services from local suppliers, shifting the cost of acquisition to the background. In the words of Witt (2019) the deglobalization that was previously talked about, it involves considering the strategic policies that affect the political sustainability of multinational companies, the dynamic organizations of value chain specializations, and the national context in which decisions about strategies, structures, and behaviors are made. Therefore, the breakdown of global supply chains is interpreted as having direct consequences on the profitability of many of these multinational companies.

The main causes that have given rise to the processes of deglobalization, the slowdown in the growth of the global economy, the retreat of global supply and value chains and the increase in protectionism of local economies in the face of multilateral processes, to reduce concerns about external dependence on essential supplies (Abdal and Ferreira, 2021).The regression of the global logistics supply and value chains enter regression processes for different reasons, such as protectionism, salary increases and the level of income reduce the advantages of the countries that were the destination of the relocations. If production is less offshored, flows in global supply and value chains are reduced, along with the investments that accompany them.

The interruption of global supply chains and therefore of value is a consequence of trade wars initiated by countries with deficiencies in commercial and financial exchanges The Sino-US trade war is the historical event to promote the trend of deglobalization with the disruption of the global supply chain and the decline of global trade flows in value and volume.

Trade wars added to the risks of the coronavirus have led to the blockage of global supply chains and international supplies. They have been shortening their global supply and value chains for several

*Supply Chain Resilience*

years, due to trade wars, due to the relocation of their plants, production processes and the manufacture of their own components that came from distant places and due to the diversification of the origin of inputs. and products Companies around the world are rethinking their internationalization decisions as a reaction to the dependence on global supply chains that distribute the production of products with the relocation of their plants and production processes (Nandi, Sarkis, Hervani, Helms, 2021). This situation has highlighted the vulnerability of companies due to their excessive dependence on these chains.

Deglobalization manifests itself in changes in production systems based on the places where production is most efficient, which generates many logistical imbalances in supply and value chains in commercial connections, as is the case in the United States, where the intensity of globalization shows such vulnerabilities where the creation of alternative supply chains has been necessary. Globalization is transforming to be different from what it was before the health crisis and modes of production and distribution may be transformed due to changes in global value, supply and SCR. Global SCs are more complex in the production, distribution and consumption of products that have had to be interrupted or reduced due to the lack of supply of essential components.

From the reduction of global value and supply value chains, companies are moving away from conventional just-in-time production systems towards safer SC, as such reductions negatively affect the flow of trade, finance, investment and of people. And although the DEs that structure the networks that currently continue to include strategic activities of the SCs, production, management and distribution on a global scale are organized and interconnected in real time in a sophisticated information and communication system, deglobalization processes continue to put pressure on global production, supply, and value chains to change in organizational forms subject to local decisions.

Regarding logistics, multinational companies are already reconsidering their processes of transportation of goods, considering socio-ecosystem concerns to try to shorten geographical distances and links in their global supply chains through the use and development of new technologies that reduce production costs and risks, increase quality, and respond more quickly to market demand. Multinational companies reconfigure global value chains to strengthen themselves against shocks.

In accordance with the previously described Paul and Dhir (2021) point out that business organizations are evaluating the location of global supply chains, with the aim of relocating their production to another place, which is a globalization trend of natural rotation and facilities. And as national economies are linked in globalization through supply chains to achieve manufacturing and better prices in international trade, the flow of international trade activities retracts as global supply and relationships are reconfigured. supply chains, prioritizing production over economic efficiency.

That is, the international trade replicates its operations while reconfiguring SCR, sacrificing economic efficiencies in exchange for greater security in the supply of its inputs. Thus, international trade territorially withdraws from national trade through the reconfiguration of its production and supply chains, which leads importers to raise tariff barriers.

Regarding the issue, populist and nationalist nation-states have taken up this message, supported by political parties and social organizations to promote actions of deglobalization of the economy that try to dismantle globalization through withdrawals from global value chains, repatriation of investments and strategic relocation of companies.

Relocating global SCs implies the reorganization of production, distribution, and marketing activities, while at the same time making it necessary to reinforce government public policies, especially in sectors considered to be of national security. In addition to that, returning the plants to the country of origin may be more expensive, but, in the current conditions of interrupted global CS, it is more productive and competitive due to savings in logistics risks, transportation, tariffs, etc. The reduction dependence on the provision of supplies from other geographically distant places through global chains of manufactured inputs has led to relocation or relocation trends, characterized by relocating production sites not only near markets, but also in those places where the conditions are conducive to developing innovations, design, logistics, distribution, marketing, among others.

Another reason why global supply and value chains have been losing importance is localized and automated production, due to advances in technology, innovations in automation, robotization, artificial intelligence, internet of things, etc., which tend to replace the more routine and cheaper workforce.

The trend of deglobalization turned into regional trade agreements allows economies to fully integrate and take advantage of regional and local value chains. From the crisis that economic globalization is going through, companies with supply chains that are less global, more regional, and therefore shorter in terms of assembly or marketing lines will emerge stronger, not necessarily from lower-cost suppliers and with minimal inventory levels, confirming deglobalization. Global SC disruptions forced individuals and businesses to look for alternative local or regional sources of supply, even if they were more expensive.

Less advanced economies have seen their global value chains shrink with premature deindustrialization processes, slower economic growth, a commodity boom that has given rise to the Dutch disease phenomenon, non-redistributive and regressive tax reforms with rising tax levels. poverty and income. inequality. Therefore, the countries are going backwards in their globalization advances and trying to avoid the continuity of outsourced productive chains to maintain strategic productive activities at the internal level or as regionally as possible, with more agile and faster local value chains.

The blockade of global supply chains represents the opportunity for Mexico to be the beneficiary due to its proximity to the North American market, as has been the case in the automotive, electronics and aeronautical sectors. Without the inputs produced in Mexico by these industrial sectors, the manufacture of finished products is interrupted. Deglobalization and the T-MEC favor the rapid integration of the electrical, automotive, medical equipment, aeronautical, pharmaceutical, aeronautical, etc. industry sectors. to the supply chains of North American companies. The complementation between the T-MEC member countries facilitates regional integration processes and solves the problem of logistics and supply chains.

Risk assessment focuses on disturbances in production processes mainly due to SC of inputs that come from geographically distant places, or other phenomena such as natural disasters, wars, etc. One of the risks that deglobalization runs stems from geopolitical and geoeconomics uncertainty and its impact on investments with repercussions on the production levels of global supply chains, exports, and market volatility. Companies have reacted to the perception of risks through a strategy of geographic diversification of supply and production sources that can affect global trade by relocating production in the country itself.

The inability of globalization processes to find a way out of the relocation of production and supply chains, as well as the inability of the national industry in many countries to produce the required medical supplies, has complicated the economic scenario.


## SOLUTIONS AND RECOMMENDATIONS

In a free market system under the invisible hand, companies continue to track the location of their production, distribution and consumption systems through offshoring decisions that mean profits and profitability. In the same scenario, tensions and trade wars accelerated deglobalization processes under

*Supply Chain Resilience*

the premise of relocating production and the supply of resources from sources as close as possible, which confirms the trend towards open regionalism.

Hence, economic, and financial deglobalization processes are considered as proposals for local economies to reorient themselves in short circuits towards production for local consumption, avoiding the relocation of companies that generate competition because they seek places where labor costs are lower. lower, the production and ecological standards are lower. restrictive etc. On the other hand, foreign direct investment movements facilitate the relocation of production systems in global factories, taking advantage of the advantages offered by other national economies in cheap labor, more direct transport systems, privatization of public companies, etc. (Grunwald and Flann, 1985).

The relocation of production processes is mainly due to the increase in the level of income and salaries of the developing countries that are destinations, and that reduce the advantages for the relocation of production. Discontent over the growing impoverishment of the working middle classes in the most developed countries, the precariousness of employment and labor benefits, and the loss of employment, due to the relocation and flight of companies to places where labor costs are lower, supposes advantages for the relocation process since the production, distribution and consumption systems have been reduced due to the increase in income and living standards of workers in the destination countries of these relocations.

There are several reasons that are making the processes of economic globalization dysfunctional for the growth and development of some countries, such as the loss of their political and economic sovereignty, the increase in unemployment due to the relocation of production and the increase in systems automation and robotization, which also reduces relocations.

Companies have reacted to the perception of risks through a strategy of geographic diversification of supply and production sources that can affect global trade by relocating production in the country itself. Extraterritoriality when characterizing economic globalization by the ability of transnational companies to relocate production with geographical fragmentation (Palomares, 2006). In this way, there is this trend of regional proximity of production, pointing to a relocation of production processes in countries that belong to the same economic region. Thus, the processes of regionalization of production constitute a trend in proximity to consumer markets that ensures the supply of resources, goods, and services in places to consumer markets to respond quickly and flexibly to demand through customization or personalization of the product.

With globalization, companies become more dependent on the places from where the supplies and products necessary for production are provided, so now national states are offering incentives to their companies to resume operations that they had relocated to other countries. The continuity of the processes of economic globalization currently marks a break in the rupture of international economic relations that, although they try to relocate production, compete for the attraction of talent, technology, and more advanced productive capacity.

Offshoring as a strategy of deglobalization processes has the immediate consequences of increasing labor costs due to differences between nations, but also due to the health crisis, with a tendency to reduce economic inequality. Like the health crisis, robotization accelerates relocation, it should be noted that in these times of pandemic it has been of great help by reducing risks or eliminating face-to-face contacts. On the other hand, the increase and consolidation of teleworking and electronic commerce are also trending that favor relocation.

Thus, pandemics in general have shown the risks of the globalized economy under the logic of relocating production to take advantage of lower costs that are then marketed in other regions of the world without establishing the relevant health controls.

## FUTURE RESEARCH

Deglobalization processes and their implications on global supply chains remain a topic for future research, which can be presented in scenarios of their future development. A first scenario is that of gentle changes that do not modify the structures of international institutions, but rather focus on regulating distortions to free trade, as well as the conditions imposed on developing countries. The deconstruction of globalization processes, known as deglobalization, must be for a better reconstruction that truly integrates humanity through economic, political, and social change, and does not disintegrate. This change requires weakening the hegemony of the system of globalizing institutional powers, delegitimizing its ideology and its rules.

On the implications of digital technologies on supply chain values, international governance needs the potential transformation of information and communication technologies for BIG-DATA research and analysis. The integration of the process of economic globalization requires the use of digital technologies for the function of world government through the functions of institutionalization, market, and global redistribution. The design and implementation of economic policies to promote the positive effects of the digital and political dimensions and eliminate the negative ones of the processes of economic globalization, improve global governance and economic integration.

Another important issue to study in the future is the relocation of companies to local production and consumption sites based on protectionist regulations, recovery of customs duties on imported goods and services, control of capital transfers, and levies on financial transactions.

Another issue to consider for future research is the current deglobalization processes that show a clear subordination of emerging and less developed countries to powerful international financial interests, international organizations, and multinational companies. The construction of alternative integration processes requires national initiatives under a scheme different from that of financial and transnational capitalist capitalism, not only at the economic and commercial level, which is based on self-organization and self-management to satisfy social needs. These alternative processes of deglobalization have multiple economic, social, environmental, political, sociocultural, gender, etc. dimensions. For the deglobalization alternatives to deepen their changes, they must acquire the character of anti-capitalism.

An analysis should be made of the difficulties in completely reversing the processes of economic globalization, after the necessary adjustments that have slowed down progress in overcoming the health crisis and the crisis of neoliberal financial capitalism. The construction of alternative integration processes requires national initiatives under a scheme different from that of financial and transnational capitalist capitalism, not only at the economic and commercial level, which is based on self-organization and self-management to satisfy social needs. These alternative processes of deglobalization have multiple economic, social, environmental, political, sociocultural, gender, etc. dimensions.

*Supply Chain Resilience*

## CONCLUSION

The post-pandemic world economy tends to be less globalized, as national governments and populations reject it to protect their national economies. The processes of economic globalization are deepening instead of a gradual process of deglobalization, under the argument of the principle of sovereignty with economic policies and measures that show a tendency towards nationalist, protectionist, and populist retreat. The actions of national states and international organizations that promote globalization processes such as regional integration treaties for free trade tend to weaken the sovereignty of states. This is somewhat paradoxical in its contradictory processes due to its origin of globalized localisms that have contributed to strengthening hierarchies and inequalities both between nations and between individuals, the creation of victims who lack the protection of the State subject to their localities or forced to abandon them.

The world order that has prevailed since the Second World War has been considered under the conception of linear processes of irreversible economic globalization and has undergone structural changes in the last ten years that require a reconfiguration. This reconfiguration has been called the deglobalization stage and corresponds to a regression of the global integration processes in the form of retractions in world trade and international financial investments through nationalist, populist, and protectionist policies.

The trade protectionism movement as a withdrawal from the processes of economic globalization with the renegotiation of trade agreements and trade wars was initiated by the United States. The trade war declared by the United States against China tries to weaken its strategic position in economic growth, cooperation, trade, finance, etc. The phenomenon of deglobalization is a popular political cause motivated by protectionist and reindustrializing economic forces.

National states face great challenges to guarantee the protection of the minimum well-being of citizens. Another consequence of the reversal of the global integration of production processes is the increase in costs and therefore in consumer prices, which translates into a drop in welfare. From an ethical perspective, deglobalization processes should prioritize values over interests, cooperative relationships over competition, and community well-being over efficiency. From this same perspective, real economic thought strengthens the values of social solidarity, justice, equity, and community to subordinate market action.

Local economies must exercise fiscal and economic policy mechanisms to protect their own production, distribution, and consumption systems, as well as their socio-ecosystems, from the subsidized importation of large transnational companies that establish subsidized and artificial prices. A viable alternative as a sample is the emergence of large egocentric spaces that are constituted as poles of economic, political, social, cultural, and civilizational power.

The new nationalist and protectionist sentiments that drive the decisions of the n countries have a high impact on migrant workers who seek better economic conditions and greater well-being for their families. National states can prevent the flight of endogenous technological talent to other economies by creating institutional and instrumental frameworks for the establishment and protection of competitive advantages through reindustrialization processes.

## REFERENCES

Abdal, A., & Ferreira, D. M. (2021). Deglobalization, Globalization, and the Pandemic: Current Impasses of the Capitalist World-Economy. *Journal of World-systems Research*, *27*(1), 202–230. doi:10.5195/jwsr.2021.1028

Baldwin, R., & di Mauro, B. W. (Eds.). (2020). *Economics in the time of COVID-19*. CEPR Press.

Barykin, S. E., Kapustina, I. V., Korchagina, E. V., Sergeev, S. M., Yadykin, V. K., Abdimomynova, A., & Stepanova, D. (2021). Digital Logistics Platforms in the BRICS Countries: Comparative Analysis and Development Prospects. *Sustainability*, *13*(20), 11228. doi:10.3390u132011228

Bello, W. (2013). *Capitalism's Last Stand? Deglobalization in the Age of Austerity*. Zed Books. doi:10.5040/9781350218895

Boiral, O., Brotherton, M.-C., Rivaud, L., & Guillaumie, L. (2021). Organizations' Management of the COVID-19 Pandemic: A Scoping Review of Business Articles. *Sustainability*, *2021*(13), 3993. doi:10.3390u13073993

Didea, L., & Ilie, D. M (2020). The State of Emergency and the Economic Repercussions. A New "Avalanche" of Insolvencies *J.L. & Admin. Sci.*, *89*(13).

Economic Commission for Latin America and the Caribbean. (2020). *Special Report COVID-19: The Effects of the coronavirus disease (COVID-19) pandemic on international trade and logistics*. United Nations. https://repositorio.cepal.org/bitstream/handle/11362/45878/1/S2000496_en.pdf

Ellyat, H. (2021). *Supply chain chaos is already hitting global growth. And it's about to get worse*. CNBC.

FAO. (2021). *The impact of disasters and crisis on agriculture and food security*. Food and Agriculture Organization of United Nations.

Findlay, R., & O'Rourke, K. (2008). *Power and Plenty: Trade, War, and the World Economy in the Second Millennium*. Princeton University Press.

Grunwald, J., & Flamm, K. (1985). *The global factory: Foreign assembly in international trade*. Brookings Institution.

Ibn-Mohammed, T., Mustapha, K.B.; Godsell, J., Adamu, Z., Babatunde, K.A., Akintade, D. D., Acquaye, A., Fujii, H., Ndiaye, M.M., Yamoah, F.A., & Koh, S.C.L. (2021). *A critical analysis of the impacts of COVID-19 on the global economy and ecosystems and opportunities for circular economy strategies*. doi:10.1016/j.resconrec.2020.105169

IMCO. (2020). *Deglobalization. Implications for investors*. Oxford Economics.

James, H. (2018). Deglobalization: The Rise of Disembedded Unilateralism. *Annual Review of Financial Economics*, *10*(1), 219–237. doi:10.1146/annurev-financial-110217-022625

Kano, L., Tsang, E. W. K., & Yeung, H. (2020). Wc. (2020). Global value chains: A review of the multidisciplinary literature. *Journal of International Business Studies*, *51*(4), 577–622. doi:10.105741267-020-00304-2

Liu, W., Dunford, M., & Gao, B. A. (2018). Discursive construction of the Belt and Road Initiative: From neo-liberal to inclusive globalization. *Journal of Geographical Sciences*, *28*(9), 1199–1214. doi:10.100711442-018-1520-y

Meyer, K., & Peng, M. (2016). Theoretical foundations of emerging economy business research. *Journal of International Business Studies*, *47*(1), 3–22. doi:10.1057/jibs.2015.34

Nandi, S., Sarkis, J., Hervani, A. A., Helms, M. M. (2021). Redesigning Supply Chains using Blockchain-Enabled Circular Economy and COVID-19 Experiences. *Sustainable Production and Consumption.* . doi:10.1016/j.spc.2020.10.019

Nayler, J., & Subramanian, L. (2021). *Covid-19 Health Supply Chain Impact-Preliminary Evidence from Africa.* Pamela Steele Associates Ltd. https://www.pamsteele.co.uk/wp-content/uploads/2021/03/Covid19_Impact-on-health-supply-chain.pdf

Palomares, G. (2006). *Relaciones internacionales en el siglo XXI.* Tecnos.

Paul, J., & Dhir, S. (Eds.). (2021). *Globalization, Deglobalization, and New Paradigms in Business.* Palgrave Macmillan. doi:10.1007/978-3-030-81584-4

Petrini, C. (2001). *Slow food, the case for taste.* Columbia University Press.

Qin, J. Y. (2020). *WTO Reform: Multilateral Control over Unilateral Retaliation – Lessons from the US-China Trade War.* Wayne State University Law School Research Paper No. 2020-73, Available at https://ssrn.com/abstract=3654510 doi:10.2139/ssrn.3654510

Rodrik, D. (2000). How far will international economic integration go? *Journal of Economics.*

Sapir, J. (2011). *La demondialisation.* Seuil.

Sapir, J. (2016). Jacques Sapir: Donald Trump, président de la démondialisation? *Le Figaro.* Available on web: https://www.lefigaro.fr/vox/monde/2016/11/10/31002-20161110ARTFIG00233-jacques-sapir-donald-trump-president-de-la-demondialisation.php

Shavshukov, V. M., & Zhuravleva, N. A. (2020). Global Economy: New Risks and Leadership Problems. *Int. J. Financial Stud.*, *8*(1), 7. doi:10.3390/ijfs8010007

Shih, W. C. (2020). Global supply chain in a post-pandemic world. *Harvard Business Review*, (September-October), 2020.

Steinberg, F. (2005). *Cooperación y Conflicto en el Sistema Comercial Multilateral: La Organización Mundial de Comercio como Institución de Gobernanza Económica Global.* Tesis Doctoral presentada en el Departamento de Análisis Económico: Teoría Económica e Historia Económica de la Facultada de Ciencias Económicas y Empresariales de la Universidad Autónoma de Madrid, España.

Trebilcock, M. J. (2005). Criticizing the Critics of Economic Globalization. *Journal of International Law and International Relations, 1*, 213-238. Available at SSRN:https://ssrn.com/abstract=1214142

Witt, M. A. (2019). De-globalization: Theories, predictions, and opportunities for international business research. *Journal of International Business Studies*, *50*(7), 1053–1077. doi:10.105741267-019-00219-7

WTO. (2021). *World trade report 2021. Economic resilience and trade.* World Trade Organization.

Zhu, G., Chou, M. C., & Tsai, C. W. (2020). Lessons Learned from the COVID-19 Pandemic Exposing the Shortcomings of Current Supply Chain Operations: A Long-Term Prescriptive Offering. *Sustainability*, *2020*(12), 5858. doi:10.3390u12145858

## KEY TERMS AND DEFINITIONS

**Deglobalization:** The slowdown or reverse of globalization. A political project opposed to neoliberal globalization. In the first definition, the term describes how global flows of trade, investment and migration can decrease.

**Global Supply Chain:** It is the set of activities, facilities and means of distribution throughout the world necessary to carry out the entire process of selling a product. This is, from the search for raw materials, their subsequent transformation and even manufacturing, transport, and delivery to the final consumer anywhere in the world.

**Production Line:** It is a system formed by people and companies related to each other, by a succession of productive operations.

**Production Relocation:** the international displacement of a productive structure.

**Protectionism:** It is a commercial policy established by a government that aims to protect the national industry against foreign competition with the application of tariffs or any other type of import restriction.

**Value Chains:** It is a theoretical model that graphs and allows to describe the activities of an organization to generate value to the final customer and to the same.

# Chapter 7
# Supply Chain Resilience in Service Organizations:
## A Case Study of Kohinoor Hospital, Kurla, Mumbai

**Abbasi Attarwala**
*Kohinoor Business School, India*

**Balasbramaniam Santhanam**
*Kohinoor Business School, India*

## ABSTRACT

*Supply chain operations by means of manual systems are no longer economical. Though manufacturing sector organizations require supply chain systems in place to react to such events which will reduce the impact and quickly recover, the experience of service organizations, particularly hospitals and healthcare organizations, assumes crucial importance in the current context of the COVID pandemic. Kohinoor Hospital (KH) has become a leading multi-specialty tertiary care hospital since its commencement of services in January 2010. Data had been gathered for analysis from the primary sources/information provided by KH. The study of major crisis management like COVID-19 and resilience path is significant to formulate novel and innovative responses as part of competitive strategies to the hospitals and related to the healthcare sector. This study is highly relevant to researchers, industry practitioners/sector consultants, and policy makers in government.*

## INTRODUCTION

The Healthcare sector consisting of hospitals of multispecialty and tertiary, Clinical and radiological/pathological laboratories and pharmacies are one of the dominant and growing service organizations. Hospitals directly impact on the health of the patient's needs that require adequate medical supplies in accordance with their care and treatment. Supply chain management (SCM) in hospitals /healthcare sector is more complex as compared to other industries. Normally, smaller care facilities which are attached

DOI: 10.4018/978-1-7998-9506-0.ch007

Copyright © 2022, IGI Global. Copying or distributing in print or electronic forms without written permission of IGI Global is prohibited.

to a hospital system purchase their supplies through a group organization, contract with two or three large distributors. These large distributors, in turn, purchase from wholesalers or may contract directly with manufacturers to produce what is needed. Supplies, most of which are manufactured overseas, are then shipped to distributors' regional hubs and delivered periodically to individual health care facilities. Its facilities maintain supply levels sufficient for several days to a week of continuous operation. When a disaster or accident stresses local hospitals, supplies usually can be shifted between hospitals or regions to make up for local shortages. Widespread factory lockdowns, intense demand surges for essential goods have occurred on account of Covid 19 which resulted in shifting consumer behaviour. These challenged global value chain flows and posed significant questions about near- to medium-term supply chain resilience in hospitals/ health care organizations. With the recurrence of Covid 19 and other variants among all the classes of people, the sharp rise of various costs of materials, men, methods, machines with maintaining standards had become common and resulted in severe crisis for the intensive treatment in the hospitals. While traditionally global operating within the Government regulatory framework of healthcare institutions have created value chains have been designed around optimizing for cost-competitiveness, this pandemic further underlines the need for hospitals to orient the design the facilities and operations towards creating a supply chain resilient system. Supply chain management focuses on capacity building and response by the critical segments within the health care organizations to meet the vulnerabilities/challenges which have arisen in the recent period since April 2020. Under this scenario, our research study examines the supply chain effectiveness and resilience for hospitals on the basis of an illustration of Kohinoor Hospital located in Kurla , Greater Mumbai metropolitan area.

## BACKGROUND

During the Nineteen Forties, factories/workshops with large manufacturing/ assembly line facilities had relied on supply chains which were based on theories or relatively old methods. Because each individual business has its own needs, a generic supply chain solution could not be adopted. With this kind of varied SCM, business organizations and its logistics partner were able to determine the most effective methods and theories. In some instances, the methods applied which can favourably affect the related industries at the same time. However, not every method or theory is going to have a positive effect on their specific industry or business. The essentials of the major SCM methods in manufacturing industries are presented in the Table 1

*Supply Chain Resilience in Service Organizations*

*Table 1. The essentials of the major SCM methods in manufacturing sector*

| S.no. | Title of SCM Method /Main authors | Brief description /Assessment |
|---|---|---|
| (i) | Transaction Cost Analysis (TCA)/Aric Rindfleisch, Jan .B.Heide | This analysis is generally performed over a given period of operations. Given the needs, TCA could effectively determine the appropriate prices of materials /supplies. By considering the past data, TCA has enabled fair prices at which to purchase and sell goods. TCA as a method based on financial models, diligently evaluated the prices at which goods can be leveraged and sold to the varied buyers Materials managers can then apply such information to make better decisions for stocking in their warehouses. |
| (ii) | Channel Coordination/ CA Ingene, ME Parry | SCM in many businesses are managed by Logistics and supply chain enterprises. As a consequence, efforts are made by individual channels for coordination and to reduce overall costs. Channel coordination enables this practice effectively. |
| (iii) | Network Perspective(NP)/Borgatti Stephen, Lopez –Kidwell | In some organizations, the third-party logistics provider (3PL) work with businesses other than its own. Such a practice of SCM can leverage money and costs for all industries. This is accomplished through network perspective (NP). Alternatively, a common supply chain weaves together through their businesses. |
| (iv) | Materials Logistics Management (MLM)/Donald J Bowersox, Philip L Carter, Robert M.Monczka | MLM agencies operate for the planning, sourcing, stocking, production, and distribution of physical materials. A 3PL should ensure that a business firm receives the materials on time which can produce the final product. These agencies can use the aggregate demand to reduce the costs. |
| (v) | Material Requirements Planning (MRP)/ Orlicky | 1. MRP organizations help in identifying the lowest possible material inventory level without affecting production. This reduces warehousing costs and prevents businesses from over-purchasing materials. Further<br>2. Independent demand and Dependent demand for raw materials and accessories would be included in MRP. |
| (vi) | Theory of Constraints(TOC) Eliyahu M. Goldratt | TOC help in identifying the limits in production potential / supplies potential and bottlenecks. Quite often, 3PL partners would be able to implement the best practices in TOC. |
| (vii) | Total Quality Management (TQM) /Edwards Deming, Armand V. Feigenbaum, Kaoru Ishikawa, and Joseph M. Juran | TQM focuses on streamlining the entire supply chain. TQM also helps in training employees and ensuring customer satisfaction. This method is found to be more comprehensive than TOC. |
| (viii) | Customer Relationship Management(CRM)/ Francis A.Buttle, Stan Maklan | Generally 3PL partner directly impacts its customer relations. 3PLs can compile and analyse data to find customer trends based on buying history and other available information. CRM works best for both the customer and the customer's customers . |
| (ix) | Requirements Chain Management (RCM) Kozlenkova, Irina V.; Hult, G. Tomas M.; Lund, Donald J.; Mena, Jeannette A.; Kekec, Pinar | RCM is a 3PL's way of adjusting a firm's supply chain model to fit the needs and expectations. This is done through discussion between the businesses and the 3PL to determine how these needs and expectations are met. |

## Assessment of SCM Models for Manufacturing Industries

Since the late 1980s, Supply chains were defined as the network that contributes to the inbound and outbound of products and services within the value chain, and thus have gained importance from the theorists in organisations (Miles & Snow, 2007, p. 459). It was assumed that the introduction of the term 'network' was meant to widen the concept of supply chain management to gain more knowledge about resource potential and increase the effectiveness of partnerships (Lamming, Johnsen, Zheng, & Harland,

2000, p. 676). This was due to the fact that, the literature and certain empirical investigations discovered that organisations were generally embedded in more than one supply chain with several customers and different suppliers (Mills, et al., 2004, p. 1014). From that time on, the concept of 'supply networks' was researched in two different ways which influenced the development of the whole concept, described by Lamming, Johnsen, Zheng & Harland (2000). In their research they state that a descriptive study on industrial networks was conducted by the researchers of the Industrial Marketing and Purchasing Group (IMP), who created models in order to enhance a better consensus of business markets in relation with connections between buyers and suppliers and the interconnectivity of organisations in networks. Next to that another study, which belongs to the more prescriptive studies on the management of supply chains, was according to Lamming et al. (2000), investigated in the sector of strategic management, operations management and logistics (Lamming, et al., 2000, p. 675). Researchers have been primarily concerned with the grasp of what makes an organisation effective, and which processes are required for this. However, the understanding of achieving effectiveness though the exchange and interaction with other parties of the supply chain was recognized throughout the past decades (Håkansson & Snehota, 1989, p. 188). Companies are faced with a highly competitive environment through which they are forced to continuously improve quality and reduce lead times (Aksoy & Öztürk, 2011, p. 6351). Therefore, the purchasing departments aim to establish long-term partnerships with suppliers, and make effective use of the supply base by using fewer but reliable suppliers (Ho, Xu, & Dey, 2010, p. 16). Nevertheless, as Miles & Snow (2007) claim in their article, the emergence of the multi-firm network organization opened a whole new arena for strategic choice and many organizations became much stronger competitors by linking with specialist providers in an integrated supply chain (Miles & Snow, 2007, p. 460). These inter-actions involve various parties, be they manufacturers, distributors, retailers, as well as consumers. Due to the fact that this includes a large number of decision-makers, coupled with several decision-making criteria, managers are challenged to serve the demand of the partners, but also be careful to reach own goals (Nagurney, Cruz, Dong, & Zhang, 2005, p. 120). Further the large number of decision-makers might result in a failure of coordination and with this also a failure of achievement (Salancik, 1995, p. 346). While attempting assessment of various models of SCM as discussed above, we have the chance to apply strategies which best fit to a certain situation in the market. As the methods and theories apply to supply chain of the businesses, the production process will become more complex. Further, supply chains can be made more efficient or customer-friendly with the right approach. Some methods and theories don't apply to all businesses. Given the presence of complex nature of supply chains, the right combination of methods and theories could change over time and help to meet the needs of stakeholders that can grow and reach the scale that supports its business optimally. With the onset of 1990s, there has been an increasing focus on SCM and their role within the strategy of the firm. Effective SCM arises when the management of supply chain assets, products, data and money flow to optimize the overall profitability and improve consumer responsiveness. A successful supply chain is one that shares data between various stakeholders- suppliers, manufacturers, custom departments, Logistics Service Provider (LSP) and retailers. COVID-19 has also increased costs for all kinds of companies. From guaranteeing the safety of their operations and employees to reacting to increased pressure from retailers on service levels, the pandemic has often necessitated costly adjustments.

## SCM in Hospitals and Healthcare Organizations

All over the Globe, the SCM in hospital involve the flow of many different product types and the participation of several stakeholders. Based on their functions, stakeholders in the healthcare supply chain can be divided into three major groups: producers, purchasers, and providers. The logistics in Healthcare constitute medical and surgical supplies, devices, and other products as required by healthcare professionals enables physicians /surgeons, nurses, and administrative staff to reach the timely and best treatment and positive results to its customers . As every subsystem work independently, aligning all subsystems together becomes difficult. The resilience in SCM among hospitals /healthcare enterprises seeks to identify the weak areas to reach targeted health outcome and increases investments in patient health. The advantages of efficient Supply Chain in Healthcare are improved processes, efficient utilization of resources, satisfied employees, effective treatment and satisfied patients. An effective SCM ensures proper linkage of hospitals department, operations, and revenue cycle. The Top Management of the hospital would lend directions and support in setting the pace to the entire organization. (Figure 1)

*Figure 1. SCM framework in Hospitals*
*Source: IIM Lucknow Working Papers*

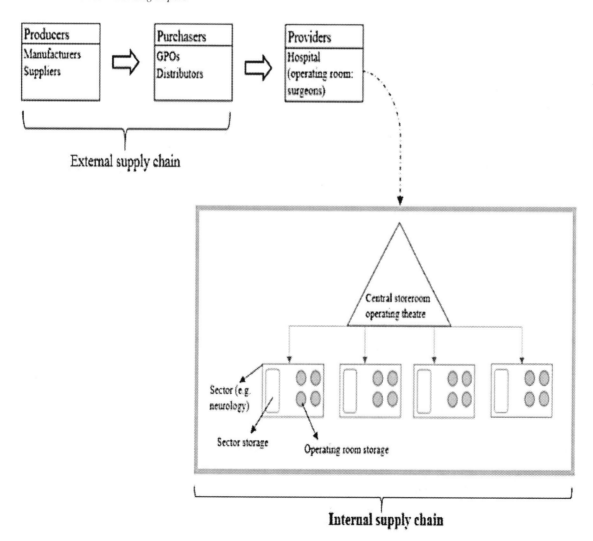

SCM is a sensitive function in hospitals as compared to other organizations as it has direct impact on the health of the people who require adequate medical supplies in accordance with the patient's needs. In healthcare, supply chain management is a new and improved way of managing the medical supplies. It is a set of methods to integrate suppliers and hospital services efficiently by optimising the utilization of resources and achieve total quality management by an efficient model on Structure of SCM in Hospitals (Figure 2). Recent trend setters of SCM in hospitals include Asset Flexibility, Internet of things, Big Data, Radio Frequency Identification (RFID), supply chain solutions and E-commerce. Generally in the hospitals, manpower strength comprising physicians/surgeons, nurses, ward staff are brought together to treat the sick patient efficiently at a reasonable and affordable cost in the shortest time, to best fulfil the patient's satisfaction.

*Figure 2. Structure of SCM in hospitals*
*Source: Jenna Koo, July 30, 2020*

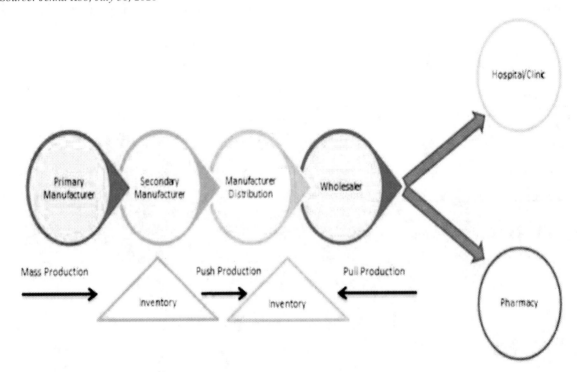

## MAIN FOCUS OF THE CHAPTER

### Issues, Controversies, and Challenges in the Healthcare Supply Chain

Supply chain management can be described as a stressful task in the hospitals. Issues, controversies and challenges in the healthcare supply chain deal with problems and circumstances of dilemma faced by hospitals /healthcare organizations in the context of typical disease /epidemic spread in the location / area of service adjoining it. These experiences would be can be identified in many hospitals /health care organizations and therefore can be considered generic across the world.

1. Network Configuration: Network Configuration in hospitals deals with the warehouse's location, production level of goods, etc. It also deals with overall reduction in transportation and inventory costs.
2. Supply Contracts: Supply Contracts deal with maintaining the optimal relationships between the suppliers and hospitals by signing. Price, discounts, lead time, quality, etc of the medicines, and other materials are elaborated in supply contracts.
3. Distribution of supplies: Decisions regarding the storage of supplies or direct delivery at the point of use are also made in the hospitals.
4. Integration and Partnering: Collaborative Planning, Forecasting and Replenishment (CPFR) are often resorted by hospitals with their suppliers and manufacturers of medical supplies.
5. Customer Value: Customer Value can be determined by the ability to deliver best quality service to the patients. Price charged to the patients and perceived value by the customers is measured in terms of services offered to them.

Benefits of SCM in healthcare are:

1. Streamlined workflow
2. Control over inventory
3. Improved synergy between finance and material department
4. Improvement in vendor management
5. Empowered procurement staff
6. Improvement in sourcing, pricing, contract management, inventory management, etc.

With the suitable SCM system in place, hospitals aim to reduce administrative duties and paper work significantly. By incorporating this, the hospital's staff can focus more on valuable and strategic tasks results in overall improve quality of care.

Generally, hospitals build capacities in terms of beds, operation theatres and support facilities to sustain long term customer loyalty and win new customers. This is dependent on its ability to ensure customer satisfaction from start to finish. The hospitals of all sizes have seen this clearly even during an unprecedented nationwide lockdown in the economy. Almost overnight, hospitals had to reassess, innovate and transform their customer service function to be available and effective for their customers in the best way possible to meet the challenges of the pandemic. Given this criticality, leading hospitals have focused on combining proactive approaches / reactive solutions while providing treatment to patients, who have considerably helped in improve their performance. Figure 3 elaborates the necessity of establishing a clinically integrated Supply chain Value Flow Chart.

*Figure 3. Chain value flow chart*
Source: Gartner Healthcare

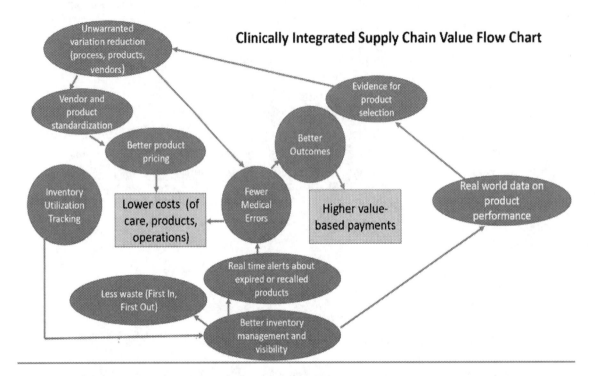

However the necessity and effective installation of SCM would vary with size, specialities and related supporting treatment facilities, administrative network required for hospitals. While factories manufacturing durable goods, consumer goods have realized the necessity of internally establishing a value driven efficient SCM long time since Nineteen 70s, hospitals /healthcare organizations have relied on external factors and vendors towards creating and maintaining the SCM. Capital has been a major constraint for the hospitals mainly in the private sector, though the public hospitals utilized their huge budgets funded by government at the state / national levels. SCM in private sector hospitals would attempt to optimize some aspects like patients' health care, health care delivery model controlling medical care cost.

Productivity at micro level in a hospital has to be examined in terms of parameters such as specializations, labour, surgical equipment, and other assets. This kind of assessment becomes very important since a hospital's standing in the competitive market place is determined by physician's productivity and the community needs to which he serves. Covid 19 has posed criticalities in measurement of parameters for performance, which has not been faced in the recent years.

## Challenges: Covid 19 and Supply Chain Resilience for Hospitals

The Covid-19 pandemic has laid bare the challenges of a supply chain optimized for efficiency. In a world in which large-scale disasters and disruptions are likely to become more common, finding ways to build resilience into the supply chain system has become essential. With the viability and customer satisfaction as the basic objectives of operating a hospital, the preparedness to a large crisis like Covid 19 among the various classes of hospitals can be classified as follows:

*Supply Chain Resilience in Service Organizations*

1.  Some hospitals acted prior to the crisis: Big hospitals with multispecialty and tertiary specialities created large access to capital and government support. If government support could not be garnered, these hospitals sought tie ups with large industries to service their employees and their families.
2.  Some hospitals sought tie ups with large pharmaceutical companies and surgical equipment / radiological and pathological diagnostic laboratories. Under the Covid 19 and the recurrent variants, these hospitals needed constant link up with Siemens, General Electric and other large surgical equipment manufacturers for their changing requirements of surgical equipment / radiological and pathological diagnostic laboratories.
3.  Big Hospitals created 'scenario planning groups 'which could cater to future /newer capacities or specialities or additional revenue potentials with lower operating costs
4.  Strong performers refined their core functions and improved their organizational capabilities which could result into reducing the expenses on staff and maintenance. These hospitals organized training sessions on additional functions /newer specialities and other potentials
5.  New acquisitions / mergers with wider capabilities: Big hospitals sought supportive tie ups with smaller hospitals with basic specialities and enlarge their service and revenue capabilities.
6.  Hospitals in metro /urban locations sought service arrangements with hospitals /NGOs in rural / tribal geographies
7.  Despite these advances in supply chain theory, traditional approaches to formulating and validating supply chain strategy in hospitals have not been consistently successful. This is largely because they have not paid enough attention to the connections and combinations among key drivers throughout the value chain, nor to their alignment with an industry's competitive framework and with each organization's unique value proposal. As the unrelenting COVID-19 pandemic rolls on with variants, the future scenario seems very uncertain and outcomes are not definite. Hospitals are trying hard to catch up with cascades of capital risk, among other challenges which will both reduce losses and save costs. While big hospitals can manage the crisis pretty well, medium sized or small hospitals find it difficult to meet problems in critical situations like Covid 19. Private Sector in Healthcare facilities is responding aggressively to meet the healthcare demands in times of pandemic. Public health care facilities which are managed by Union Government / State Government / Municipalities have limitations in such times. As our case study of Kohinoor Hospital belongs to medium size hospital, this case study would offer many useful insights to hospital managers particularly in emerging markets including India. These experiences may offer value based guidance for managing the impact of the corona virus pandemic on the well-being of their operations in hospitals located in Mumbai.

## Mumbai Metropolitan Area – A Brief Demographic Profile

Mumbai Metropolitan Area was declared as Independent District with effect from 1st October, 1990, as a result of the bifurcation of the Greater Mumbai into two revenue districts namely, Mumbai City and Mumbai Suburban. The jurisdiction of Mumbai Suburban District is from Bandra to Dahisar, from Kurla (Chuna Bhatti) to Mulund and from Kurla and upto Trombay Creek. Greater Mumbai serves as the core city of the Mumbai Metropolitan Region, which is among the ten most populated urban agglomerations in the world. It has been considered as the country's financial capital, and its main driver of growth. Geographically, Greater Mumbai is severely constrained and occupies a land area of only 458.28 sq km.

Mumbai city is India's commercial capital. It is situated in the Western state of Maharashtra. It is also the most populous metropolis of 22 million. It' s 51.91% of the total population live in the Eastern Suburbs resides in slums as compared to 42.69% of the total population in the Western Suburbs and 27.88% in the Island City. Ward S in the Eastern Suburbs has the highest proportion of slums with 72.32% of its population residing in slums. Kurla and neighbourhood suburbs including Vidyavihar, Ghatkopar have been chosen because it accommodates the highest slum population in numeric terms 537,900, among all 24 Wards and our case organization Kohinoor Hospital is located in the suburban area of Kurla .

## Kohinoor Hospital- A Profile

Kohinoor Hospital (KH) was established in January 2010 as a private limited company. Since then, it has become a leading multi-speciality tertiary care hospital. KH has adopted its "Vision and Mission" based on defined value propositions and attaining competitive advantage over the long-term outlook. Vision

*"Delivering self-sustaining tertiary healthcare in a compassionate environment that delights every Patient and his family"*

Mission

*"To operate 400 self-sustained tertiary care beds by 2022"*

KH has empanelled over 220 specialists/surgeons / medical professionals to provide a comprehensive care to the patients from all classes of the community mainly from the suburban areas of Mumbai such as Kurla, Ghatkopar, Vikhroli, Andheri etc. The medical professional's team of KH are renowned for the prowess in the fields of Orthopaedics, Ophthalmology, Diabetology, Dentistry, Bariatrics along with significant expertise in other super specialities like Cardiology and Cardiac Surgery, Oncology and Onco –Surgery, Neurology and Neuro surgery etc., In terms of infrastructure, KH has installed state of the art facilities which compare with other leading multi-speciality hospitals in Mumbai and India.

The details of the scope of services, specialities and facilities are presented in the Table 2.

*Supply Chain Resilience in Service Organizations*

*Table 2. Scope of services at KH*

| | | |
|---|---|---|
| **1)Clinical Services**<br>✓ Accident and Emergency Services<br>✓ Outpatient Services<br>✓ Inpatient Services<br>✓ Critical Care Medicine<br>**2) Diagnostic Services**<br>✓ Lab Medicine (Biochemistry, Haematology, Microbiology, Histopathology & Cytology)<br>✓ TMT, ECG, 2D Echo<br>✓ Radiology & Imaging (X ray, CT, MRI, USG, OPG, Mammography)<br>**3) Allied / Support Services**<br>✓ Physiotherapy<br>✓ Pharmacy & Stores<br>✓ Dietetics & Nutrition<br>✓ Central Sterile Supply Department<br>**4) Non-Medical Services**<br>✓ Administration<br>✓ Facility management (including F&B, Linen and Housekeeping services)<br>✓ Engineering and maintenance<br>✓ Security Services<br>✓ Human Resources<br>✓ Information Technology<br>✓ Medical Records<br>✓ Sales & Marketing<br>✓ Finance & Accounts<br>✓ Purchase & Stores | <u>**Specialties:**</u><br>✓ Anaesthesia<br>✓ Bariatric & Metabolic Surgery<br>✓ Cardiology (including Cathlab)<br>✓ Dental<br>✓ Dermatology<br>✓ Endocrinology<br>✓ ENT – Medical & Surgical<br>✓ Gastroenterology<br>✓ General Medicine<br>✓ Obstetrics & Gynaecology (incl. High risk Obstetrics)<br>✓ Orthopaedics<br>✓ Nephrology (including Dialysis)<br>✓ Neurology<br>✓ Ophthalmology<br>✓ Oncology<br>✓ Paediatrics<br>✓ Pulmonology<br>Surgical Specialties<br>✓ Cardiac Surgery<br>✓ General Surgery<br>✓ Minimal Access Surgery<br>✓ Neuro Surgery<br>✓ Onco Surgery<br>✓ Orthopaedic Surgery<br>✓ Paediatric surgery<br>✓ Urology | <u>**Facilities:**</u><br>✓ 175 bedded (123 operation/surgery related Multispecialty Hospital<br>✓ 16 outpatient clinics<br>✓ 4 well equipped operation theatres<br>✓ 27 bedded ICU<br>✓ Well-equipped 06 bedded Neonatal Intensive Care Unit<br>✓ 04 bedded Paediatric Intensive Care Unit<br>✓ 06 bedded dialysis unit<br>✓ Well-designed LDRP suite<br>✓ 06 bedded Emergency Care Unit<br>✓ Cardiac catheterisation lab<br>✓ Blood bank and Pathology lab<br>✓ Round-the-clock Radiology & Imaging with CT /MRI scan<br>✓ Cardiac Diagnostics, 2D Echo/ Stress Test, Colour Doppler, PFT<br>✓ 24 hours Pharmacy<br>✓ Well-equipped Physiotherapy Department |

Based on the above, a SWOC analysis has been made in Table 3 to facilitate the detailed study of KH in a competitive advantage approach.

*Table 3. SWOC analysis*

| Strengths | Weaknesses |
|---|---|
| • Consultant Engagement (Well –known consultants empanelled with KH)<br>• NABH Accredited Hospital (National Accreditation Board for Hospitals & Healthcare Providers - accreditation signifies quality conscious hospital)<br>• LEEDs Platinum recognition (Leadership in Energy and Environmental Design) standards met by KH for building construction, low energy consumption and energy costs.<br>• Brand Presence (KH belongs to Kohinoor Group which has an established brand presence)<br>• Corporate tie-ups (over 40+ corporate to boost hospital business)<br>• TPA tie-ups (over 45 + TPA's to ensure speedy assessment of claims & regularity in income)<br>• Young workforce<br>• State of the art Infrastructure | • Location and Visibility<br>• High Operation & treatment Cost<br>• Underutilized capacity<br>• Lack of Consultant support in few rare specialities |
| **Opportunities** | **Challenges** |
| • Only corporate tertiary care multispecialty hospital with strong critical care –in a radius of 5 km - Wider market prospect<br>• TPA based business approaches<br>• Brand establishment and branching out to different locations<br>• Operationalizing 5th Floor | • Emergence of Corporate Hospitals in the vicinity<br>• Changing Government Policies (e.g: Stent & Implant MRP re-pricing policy etc.)<br>• Newer treatment options which are expensive to the patients. |

Following Facilities make KH the Best Quality Hospital in the vicinity of Kurla, Ghatkopar, Vikhroli, Mulund and Andheri as adjudged by leading dailies including Times of India, Hindustan Times, Indian Express and the general public:

- 24 Hour Cardiac Ambulance
- 24 Hour Radiology and Imaging with CT/MRI Scan (Computed Tomography / Magnetic Resonance Imaging)
- I.C.C.U. (Intensive Coronary Care Unit
- N.I.C. U. /P.I.C.U.
- Cardiac Diagnostics
- 2D Echo with Colour Doppler /Stress Test /TMT (Treadmill Test)
- Blood Bank and Pathology Lab
- Microbiology Lab
- Picture Archiving and Communication System (PACS) for Speedy Diagnosis
- 24 Hour Pharmacy
- Ultrasonography & Colour Doppler
- Dialysis Unit
- State-of-the-art Operation Theatres with Laminar Air Flow, Hepa Filter & HVAC system (Heating, ventilation, and air conditioning)
- Custom-designed LDRP Suite (Labour, Delivery, Recovery and Postpartum)
- PFT (Pulmonary Function Tests)
- Catheterization Lab
- 3,300 Investigations - From Routine Checks to Special Tests
- OPG (Orthopantomogram)
- Sound Proof Audiometry Room
- Sleep Study Lab

## Objectives of the Study

1. To examine the rationale of key measures/efforts regarding SCM undertaken by KH on account of COVID 19 pandemic infection
2. To elaborate strategic processes as part of Supply Chain Resilience (SCR) responses necessary to manage crises and demonstrate competence and capacity building in times of crisis at KH which belongs to service sector

## Research Methodology

The research design adopted to test the proposed research propositions was exploratory. The mixed method of data collection had been applied to address the need of collecting and analysing the data. A detailed questionnaire had been administered to KH to elicit the responses and exercises to meet the rise in SCM during the COVID 19 infection and meet patient load. This intensive kind of services coupled with providing the best possible treatment assuring maximum patient satisfaction became a challenging period in KH. As a part of the research study, a number of interviews / meetings with key executives,

*Supply Chain Resilience in Service Organizations*

Medical and healthcare personnel and administrative employees have been conducted by the research team of KBS. Digitization and other measures which have been offered by KH as part of supply chain responses/solutions to the health care services and coping with crisis management on account of the COVID Pandemic have been elaborated.

## SOLUTIONS: NATURE OF THE SCM AND MEASURES TAKEN BY KOHINOOR HOSPITAL

Description of the COVID -19 Pandemic: COVID 19 belongs to lethal beta type belonging to a related group of viruses known as "coronaviruses" leading to severe infections in the respiratory tract of human beings (Fan et al 2019, Sivakumar 2020, Yang & Wang 2020). Many human coronaviruses have been discovered such as SARS- CoV, HCoV, NL 63, HK U1, MERS-CoV and SARS –CoV-2), causing COVID 19 disease (Suv et al 2016, Zhu et al 2020). The name 'Corona' viruses was derived from Latin meaning crown the name corresponds to their unique morphology due to the presence of viral spike proteins. In December 2019, COVID 19 emerged for the first time in China and has quickly transmitted across the world. Recently World Health Organization (WHO) declared COVID -19 as Pandemic outbreak in the world (Angel –Kormann et al 2020).

The coronavirus disease 2019 (COVID-19) challenged the health system leaders throughout the world. When many public health facilities and private hospitals are struggling to meet the surging patient load with health care system and employees stretched beyond its capacity, KH has geared up to tackle the rise in patient load and provide the best possible service and care and assuring maximum patient satisfaction during this challenging period. Key measures undertaken by KH on account of COVID 19 pandemic infection are discussed below:

### Oxygen

A huge demand for oxygen has become indicative of its importance in Covid-19 management in KH which provides multi-specialty healthcare treatment to its patients. A significant proportion of Covid-19 patients need oxygen support, when shortness of breath progresses to a more acute condition. Most patients with Covid-19 have a respiratory tract infection, and in the most severe cases their symptoms can include shortness of breath. In a small proportion of such cases, this can progress to a more severe and systemic disease characterised by Acute Respiratory Distress Syndrome (ARDS). Data with the National Clinical Registry for Covid-19 shows a new emerging trend of second wave. Shortness of breath is the most common clinical feature among symptomatic hospitalised patients at 47.5%, compared to 41.7% during the first wave. Simultaneously, other symptoms have dropped significantly compared to the first wave: dry cough (5.6% vs 1.5%); loss of smell (7.7% vs 2.2%); fatigue (24.2% vs 11.5%); sore throat (16% vs 7.5%); muscle ache (14.8% versus 6.3%). All these data indicate huge requirement of oxygen during the treatment of Covid among the patients admitted in large hospitals such as KH. By way of solution to the challenges described above, KH had organised its supplies of oxygen both internally within the hospital and networked with oxygen tanks available in the neighbourhood to meet the regular and emergency requirements to be dealt with in the context of Pandemic and its patient load.

## Medicines

Medicines play a vital role for treatment of patients. KH ensures timely availability of medicines at lowest possible purchasing cost. It is difficult to predict exact demand for medicines. Hence, it is important to capture accurate data on consumption of medicines, to get a trend of same. At KH, general storekeepers manage the supply chain, but they are not well aware of SCM principles, and hence at times, it ends up in either High Demand, Low availability or Reverse as Low Demand but High Availability for some of the medicines, leading to increased shelf life, and hence risk of expiry of medicines in pharmacy, KH has learnt the effective SCM because of high demand from patients suffering from Covid. Our Research has estimated that 40 per cent of patient's die annually just because of preventable medical errors, and poor safety cultures. KH had collected huge data of requirements of medicines and as a solution lies in the healthcare supply chain which plays a crucial role in maintaining the valuable life and flow of business in the times of pandemic during the last 15 months of April 2020 – June 2021. Better supply chain in healthcare leads to better quality of care and supports patient safety. KH has linked the patient safety and all other processes in proper format i.e. manage the expired medicines by automating the medicine/ product tracking and identifying, accordingly taking actions so that staff and patient are confident about treatment done. Streamline all time consuming supply chain processes to reduce the medicines finding times, human errors, redundant processes. The entire data sheet captured by doctors/physicians would be electronically captured using RFID technology eliminating redundancy and human errors. All the processes of treatment at KH follow supply chain transparency to gain patient satisfaction and considering human life the most important especially in Covid times.

## Blood Bank Supply Chain

The management of Blood supply is the critical issue for healthcare especially in times of Corona Treatment. The goal of KH is to dynamically manage the blood supply chain. As per our study, the supply of Donor blood is irregular, KH has taken care of following points: (a) Locations selected for blood collections, (b) Depending on the transfusion services commodity required should be stored, (c) Number of regional blood bank, (d) How supply and demand should be coordinated to meet the purpose, (e) Transportation of blood on demand, (f) Delivery system be closely connected to meet the run time requirement . Blood banks of KH have been kept open 24*7 for any emergencies in treatment of patients. It has maintained contact with blood banks in near-by hospitals also. Supply chain resilience has been integrated in the KH facilities which are segregated as COVID and non- COVID area to prevent transmission. Separate entry and exit routes have been created for this purpose. In this way cross contamination is restricted. The entry point for KH staff is also separate and the employees have access to separate staircase and lifts located at various points of KH premises:

- COVID- 19 Emergency Department
- NON COVID Emergency Department

## Personal Protective Equipment

Another major challenge at KH is ensuring adequacy of Personal Protective Equipment (PPE) Suits for the physicians /surgeons / other staff caring for the COVID-19 Patients as part of the treatment. KH

*Supply Chain Resilience in Service Organizations*

provides superior quality of PPE kits to its staff. In addition KH have provided the staff with scuba type glasses with PPE to prevent fogging. This equipment is treated as essential part of the treatment expenses /costs to the patients. Along with the patients the hospital, employees have also been adequately cared by KH during the pandemic. KH have very low employee infection rate. Mediclaim insurance facility is also provided to the employees and the infected employees are treated at KH itself. Employees are given healthy meal and adequate rest to function optimally on duty. KH have also taken many supportive measures to ensure workplace safety within the hospital facilities.

## Sanitizers and Other Cleansing Agents

KH requires huge quantity of sanitizers /other cleansing agents which are necessary as part of the treatment to Covid /other variants. As a solution, KH has allocated separate area where the employees enter which are continuously sanitized before they move in to their respective departments. Each department is sterilized with UV (ultra violet) light daily. Their employees have been provided proper uniforms, scrubs, aprons, PPE suits, N95 masks etc.

## Digitalization Challenge

Digitalization challenges as part of SCM are extensive on account of COVID 19. KH strives hard to create a milestone in aggregating, harmonizing, and enriching data to get a 360-degree view of a member or patient is more crucial, yet more difficult, than ever in the process of treatment due to COVID in implementing the changes in the healthcare services to the patients as customers. KH has recognized the importance of IT in supply chain systems and it has continuously succeeded in its attempts to promote the adoption of an integrated health-information systems. Regardless of its immediate impact, these data driven decision programs helped create an important and powerful infrastructure that certainly will be useful in meeting crisis like COVID 19 pandemic. Digitalization of healthcare information is opening up new possibilities for healthcare providers and patients/corporate payers to enhance the quality of care, improve healthcare outcomes, and reduce costs during COVID 19. Dealing with the sheer volume and diversity of standalone, proprietary healthcare systems and heterogeneous data is a significant hurdle to achieving healthcare business objectives. KH ranks among the leading hospitals in Mumbai which have revitalised their SCR responses following the outbreak of COVID-19. A '24x7 'digital app is provided by KH to all patients to access a range of Outpatient Department (OPD) services and other facilities. KH has set a trend in leveraging digitization which have been offered as part of supply chain system in the health care services and coping with crisis management on account of the Pandemic.

## Customer Satisfaction and Quality Management

Another challenge is ensuring Customer satisfaction and Quality Management in KH. KH has recognized that SCM effectively ties up customer satisfaction (patients –OPD/in the wards) with quality management. This is achieved by the comprehensive health care to the best degree in ethical practices and integrity of the medical profession and dignity of the customers along with the quality improvement in services provided in KH. Certain parameters are described in Table 4 with a view to integrate quality management and customer satisfaction in KH

*Table 4. Quality management and customer satisfaction in KH*

| S.No | Customer Satisfaction | Quality Management |
|---|---|---|
| (i) | Availability of Specialists | Delivery of Quality Medical /Health care |
| (ii) | Clarity of Information | Qualified & approachable employees (medical &administrative /accounts) |
| (iii) | Excellence in OPD Appointment process | Technology in facilities /services |
| (iv) | Promptness in services | Convenience in consulting hours (OPD/in the wards) |
| (v) | Cost affordability in Treatment | Excellence in trauma/emergency care |

With grading the degree of customer satisfaction and quality management facilities at KH in 'likert' scale which ranges between the low to the high, it is hoped that the parameters under study would enable the KH to reach the excellence in overall care to customers in a crisis management of COVID19.

The survey of respondents was undertaken to reflect the parameters in terms of customer satisfaction and quality management. The count of the sample was maintained at 450 respondents for each parameter under consideration. (Figure 4)

*Figure 4. Customer satisfaction*
Source: Primary Data

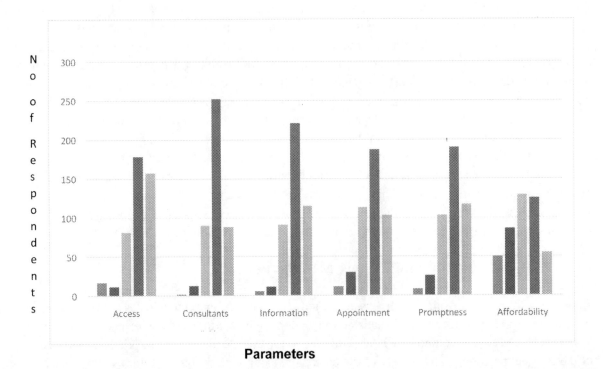

Legend

- Strongly disagree: Blue
- Disagree: Red
- Neutral: Green
- Agree: Purple
- Strongly Agree: Sky blue

Factors such as Access, Consultants Availability, Information, Appointment Process, Promptness and Affordability have been found favourable in attaining Customer Satisfaction.

## Customer Satisfaction

The onset of the COVID-19 Pandemic has left a perennial impact on interactions across the globe. Humans, known to thrive on constant communications and interactions, have been compelled to limit their in-person contact with others. Despite these limitations, customer service remains as important as ever and a top influencer in consumers' decisions. In fact, this is critical now more than ever. KH as an organization has recognized that Quality Management is essential to retain customer loyalty in the long term and win new customers continuously (Figure 5). KH has further realized that during an unprecedented nationwide lockdown these essential aspects of customer need fulfilment cannot be compromised. Almost overnight, KH as service sector organization had to reassess, innovate and transform their customer service function to be available and effective for their customers in the best way possible.

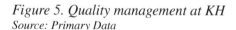

*Figure 5. Quality management at KH*
Source: Primary Data

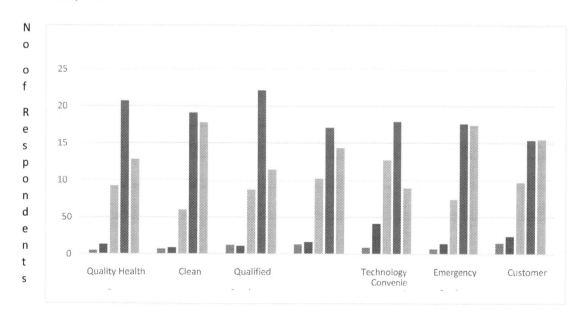

Legend

- Strongly Disagree: Blue
- Disagree: Red
- Neutral: Green
- Agree: Purple
- Strongly Agree: Sky blue

Parameters in terms of customer satisfaction and quality management have been integrated in MR planning and implementation and it is considered as an innovation building up a resilient SCM in KH. KH has continuously used the best possible technology and changed the treatment processes to leverage their technology and adopted other cost-saving measures in preparation for possible crisis in treatment

## Supply chain Management Models in Process

The relevant responsiveness-oriented supply chain models are preferred by KH when customer demand is highly unpredictable. These models are subject to overlap in various areas, and they should be designed by the supply chain manager so as to fit the unique supply chain for its healthcare diversity activities.

Supply chain modelling is a conscious attempt to bring order into supply chains' complexity to achieve certain business objectives. It deals with questions such as:

- Diverse nature of healthcare activities
- Market identification (patients from various areas of MMR described earlier)
- Operation theatres, air-conditioning plants, oxygen tanks, blood banks etc.
- Finding the best suppliers and alternative dealers
- Supplier locations
- Inventory and transport management
- Sending the patients to their homes after treatment at KH

KH has realized that supply chain's ultimate goal must be to offer satisfactory customer service because a satisfied customer is most likely to be loyal to its 'Kohinoor' brand. To achieve this, it's service system would not only need the right supply chain model but also someone to manage it effectively and efficiently.

- KH model must be fit for the required treatments and robust.
- KH should fit the internal visibility needed to identify and rectify problems when required.
- Its SCM must be continually evaluated and interrogated to discover the best solution for every key decision.

KH has recognised that Supply chain modelling provides with the tools needed to manage services to the patients /allied activities to:

- Control inventory
- Reduce costs

*Supply Chain Resilience in Service Organizations*

- Increase efficiency
- Meet customer demand
- Respond to demand
- All successful operations must recognize that as its business grows, their technological investments, supply chain strategies, and decision-making models must also evolve to incorporate future growth of activities at KH.

## Revenue and Competitive Price Structure in KH

Hospitals across India have been hit by the covid-19 pandemic, and the lower revenues at KH are no surprise. The April –June 2020 quarter was affected by a fall in outpatient and inpatient volumes across regions. Inpatient volumes declined 45% year-on-year (y-o-y), while outpatient volumes took a harder hit, tumbling 76% y-o-y. That led to average occupancies in hospitals declining to as much as 36% on an average from about 61% a year ago. As a result, standalone hospital revenues declined 22% y-o-y and it became a key challenge to its survival .

By way of financial solution, KH did well to pull up its budgets on the cost front and curtailed operating losses much better than healthcare sector expectations. While evolving a price structure during critical times like Corona Pandemic, KH has been guided by what other hospitals are charging than its own cost structure. The pricing policy of KH could be said to be market oriented. It is not essential the price structure has to be identical with other hospitals in the neighbourhood. It can be observed that KH's pricing policy is dynamic and competition oriented in responding to the rates charged by competitors rather than to reflect changes in its own cost structure. Further, the pricing of services rendered by doctors/surgeons at KH can be said to be personalized. KH has been following a pricing policy in charging its services rendered by their doctors/surgeons rationalized with the sophistication and the kind of skills / equipment required in critical times like Corona. KH has maintained its level of service and facilities with a competitive benchmarking pattern and in a manner of reputation and good will building with patients.

KH's pharmacy has been a silver lining amid the pandemic-hit quarter. The segment's 21% y-o-y revenue growth is pretty good and helped cushion the fall in overall revenues. Pharmacy department's operating profits also expanded due to the greater contribution of private-label sales.

Since space in the hospital at wards occupied by the patients is important limiting factor at KH, it has been following a deliberate policy of sending the specialists/ nurses to the patients' homes during these critical times like Covid. The charges of specialists/ nurses sent by KH to the homes of the patients would be based according to specialization criteria and financial viability of them.

## Limitations of the Study

A case study of KH is presented here with a view to demonstrate effective SCM and its strategies in live model with COVID-19 for a typical multispecialty hospital located in urban area of MMR. Resources, time and cost of the study are also considered as constraints of the research study here.

## CONCLUSION AND DIRECTIONS FOR FUTURE RESEARCH

- KH as a responsive healthcare organization strives to stay relevant by improving customer satisfaction, reducing costs, delivering better outcomes for patients, and building a modern sustainable enterprise. Its efforts have been considered meritorious by Municipal Corporation of Greater Mumbai (MCGM) as qualifying for "Swasthya Sabka" award among the competing hospitals in MMR.
- KH strives best to clinically integrate its patient services with SCM which has become more critical than ever. KH attempts to look at total cost of care, not just the price of the product or the cost of that particular hospitalization, but across the entire episodes of the treatment to the patients in the current healthcare environment.
- KH has designed a Management Information System which enables its Top Management / Administration to guide and conduct its services in critical times like Covid in a demonstrative manner to other hospitals in Mumbai.
  a. The pandemic has tested KH to the limit. By investing in supply-chain resilience now, KH has recognised that it has an opportunity to build critical agility into their supply chains, which will help to withstand not only the current crisis but also those to come.
- Traditionally a formulation of effective SCM strategies right from the commencement of the purchase of various factors /materials needed for Product Life Cycle of health care service sector organizations is followed in KH. As part of future directions for research, a cautious approach is desirable before arriving at replicative model for hospitals taking into consideration number of beds, Operation Theatres, Intensive Care Units, medical /surgical specialities, doctors / specialists, nurses /ward staff, administrative personnel and an overseeing Top Management / Executive Supervisory personnel.

## ACKNOWLEDGMENT

Authors express their gratitude and deep satisfaction to Shri Atul Modak FCA, Vice President, Dr. Nikhait Shaikh and other senior personnel for their efforts in providing the data enabling discussions regarding the study on KH in critical times like COVID 19. Confidentiality in providing data is recognised for reasons of competition and operational realities.

## REFERENCES

Aksoy, A., & Öztürk, N. (2011). Supplier selection and performance evaluation in just-in-time production environments. *Expert Systems with Applications, 38*(5), 6351–6359. doi:10.1016/j.eswa.2010.11.104

Angel-Korman, A., Brosh, T., Glick, K., & Leib, A. (2020). COVID-19, the kidney and hypertension. *Harefuah, 159*, 231–234. PMID:32307955

Borgatti, S., & Lopez–Kidwell, V. (2011). *Network Theory, Sage Handbook of Social Network Analysis.* Sage Publications.

*Supply Chain Resilience in Service Organizations*

Bowersox, D.J., Carter, P.L., & Monczka, R.L. (1985). Material Logistics Management. *International Journal of Physical Distribution& Materials Management, 15*(5), 27-35.

Buttle, F., & Maklan, S. (2019). *Customer Relationship Management: Concepts and Technologies.* Routledge. doi:10.4324/9781351016551

Deming, E. (1992). *Total Quality Management.* Defense Technical Information Centre.

Goldratt, E. H. (1997). *The Critical Chain.* Gower Book.

Government of India. (2020). *Measures undertaken To Ensure Safety of Health Workers drafted for Covid 19 Services.* Author.

Håkansson, H., & Snehota, I. (1989). No business is an island: The network concept of business strategy. *Scandinavian Journal of Management, 5*(3), 187–200. doi:10.1016/0956-5221(89)90026-2

Ingene, C. A., & Parry, M. E. (1995). Coordination and Manufacturer Profit Maximization. *Journal of Retailing, 71*(2), 129–151. doi:10.1016/0022-4359(95)90004-7

Kozlenkova, I. V., Hult, G., Tomas, M., Lund, D. J., Mena, J. A., & Kekec, P. (2015). The Role of Marketing Channels in Supply Chain Management. *Journal of Retailing, 91*(4), 586–609.

Lamming, R., Johnsen, T., Zheng, J., & Harland, C. (2000). An initial classification of supply networks. *International Journal of Operations & Production Management, 20*(6), 675–691. doi:10.1108/01443570010321667

Mills, J., Schmitz, J., & Frizelle, G. (2004). A strategic review of "supply networks". *International Journal of Operations & Production Management, 24*(10), 1012–1036. doi:10.1108/01443570410558058

Rindfleisch, A., & Heide, J.B. (1997). Transaction Cost Analysis: Past, Present and Future Applications. *Journal of Marketing, 61*(4).

## KEY TERMS AND DEFINITIONS

**Competitive Advantage:** The phenomena of competitive advantage have been added in the modern marketing approaches developed by Philip Kotler. It has been aimed to provide businesses the opportunity to increase their competitiveness in terms of the market performance in terms of its sales and its product presence in the marketplace.

**E-Commerce:** Electronic commerce is the buying and selling of goods and services, or the transmitting of funds over an electronic network, primarily the internet. These business transactions occur either as business-to-business (B2B), business-to-consumer (B2C), consumer-to-consumer or consumer-to-business.

**Likert Scale:** A one-dimensional scale that researchers use to collect respondents' attitudes and opinions.

**Radio Frequency Identification Technology (RFID):** A business tool used in Supply Chain Management. RFID is a growing technology that enables close cooperation of the supply chain partners by real-time information visibility.

**Stakeholder in Hospital:** Manufacturers, purchasers, distributors, and providers.

# Chapter 8
# Understanding the Service Quality Dimensions and Achieving Resilience in Service Retail

**Sachin Kumar Raut**

https://orcid.org/0000-0002-3808-1278

*University of Agder, Norway & Fortune Institute of International Business, India*

**Subodh Sakpal**

*Oriental Institute of Management, Mumbai University, India*

**Rashmi Soni**

*KJ Somaiya Institute of Management, Mumbai, India*

## ABSTRACT

*Innovation has increasingly supported the way businesses across the globe operate; however, this phenomenon often increases uncertainty around supply chain disruptions and management. The COVID-19 pandemic clearly reveals the lack of resilience in the supply chain domain, and the business failures show the impact of disruptions may have on a global network scale as individual supply chain connections and nodes fail. This cascading failure also has an impact on service quality dimensions of a business. Service quality advances have profoundly changed the way service organizations and consumers interact. This impact can be observed across sectors and industries. Service quality has become a popular area of researchers and academic investigation and has become recognized as a key factor in differentiating service products and building competitive advantage. Any shortcoming of a lack in service quality is easily identified and is translated into negative reviews on social media through word-of-mouth and other channels.*

DOI: 10.4018/978-1-7998-9506-0.ch008

*Understanding the Service Quality Dimensions*

## INTRODUCTION

The past decade of global economic integration through business and trade has seen a steady yet blooming march of progression (Kobrin, 2015; Canh, Schinckus and Dinh Thanh, 2021). From traditional brick and mortar structure to e-commerce, from container ships to supercomputers and from human resource to artificial intelligence- all have contributed to a web of businesses and trade so complex and detailed that it has taken roots to mark a new science (Yun et al., 2019; Betz et al., 2019; Bulturbayeyich and Jurayeyich, 2020). Supply chain management and logistics is a vital part of the business process, which, when managed effectively, can result in lowering a company's overall costs and boost profitability (Doktoralina and Apollo, 2019; Guo, Cheng and Liu, 2020).

The retail sector, in this perspective, has been quite mature in adopting supply chain management and logistics to emerge out as a strategic, competitive, growth-oriented and sustainable domain in business globally (Ketchen and Craighead, 2020). Retail or retailing provides a systematic response of the firms for the increasing uncertainty and complexity for the V-U-C-A environment (Bennis and Nanus 1987); therefore, such intricacy has pushed the adaptation of retail firms for a more holistic approach for the process management. In a recent piece of evidence, supply chains have proved that it isn't just a research theme for academicians and practitioners. The Covid- 19 pandemic is playing out in brutal ways. On a global level, economies, governments and authorities have failed in providing urgent medical goods and essential items. However, the system of supplying has continued to function remarkably well despite the most challenging times. There has been a new appreciation for the Indian supply chain management and logistics sector, particularly online retail stores such as, 'e.g., Grofers', food aggregator, 'e.g., Swiggy and Zomato', logistics 'e.g., India Post and Blue Dart', energy 'e.g., BSES', transportation, 'e.g., the Delhi transport corporation and Air India', health care 'e.g., AIIMS and National Institute of Virology' and other industries responsible for sustaining life during shutdowns.

Building service retail resilience has become ever important post the outbreak of the global COVID-19 pandemic. Several scholars and practitioners have shown increased interest in investigating retail service resilience. They have highlighted a call for enhanced management of the supply chain, which should deal with severe situations caused by the global pandemic (Jacobsen, 2020; Kumar and Managi, 2020). Nevertheless, despite the ripple effect spreading worldwide while most businesses shut down or struggled to operate, some companies are thriving in the pandemic. For example, an Indian online app-based aggregator Swiggy has touched a market valuation of nearly 5$billion. Here the question arises, why that is some businesses can sustain themselves and why the others fail. Therefore, black swan events, such as the recent pandemic, has brought with it short- and long-term implications and reasonable risk assessments which may result into paramount importance for businesses to establish sustainable response and develop mitigation strategies for such future events (Kochan and Nowicki, 2019; Nakamura and Managi, 2020). Thus, it is a timely motivation for the present study to investigate service retail resilience in this uncertain situation, by addressing two main research questions (RQs): (1) To identify Service Quality Dimensions that generate resilience and loyalty (2) To study the impact of retail service quality on resilience and loyalty during COVID-19 pandemic. In answering these RQs, we draw upon the retail perspective and Service Quality dimensions to guide the research methodology. Our contribution is twofold: first, we advance the literature on Global Retail and Supply Chain Management in the post-COVID-19 outbreak landscape. Second, we provide empirical validation on how retail service supply chains respond to the impact of COVID-19. We believe that this would guide practitioners, policy-makers, and other decision-makers in developing effective response strategies during and post-pandemic situations. Next, the authors discuss relevant constructs and highlight the research methodology to evaluate the survey administered in this study. In the last phase authors present the discussion and managerial implications of the findings. Finally, the authors give the conclusion and limitations of the research and some suggestions and plan to develop future research areas.

## BACKGROUND

### Global Retail and Supply Chain Under COVID-19 Outbreak

The COVID-19 pandemic has been regarded as one of the most severe disruptors of retail and supply chains in recent history (Ivanov and Dolgui, 2020). Further, it's effect is likely to weaken many businesses and supply chains in the world. In an attempt to curb the spread of the deadly virus, most governments across the globe is implementing lockdowns, containment measures and border closures as a last resort to contain the virus (Ivanov and Dolgui, 2020). Implementing such measures has severely impacted the global retail service operations (Ivanov and Dolgui, 2020). According to a PWC (2020) report, 87 per cent of cross-industry companies in the United States and Mexico are very concerned about the disastrous impact of the global COVID-19 outbreak.

Similarly, the global supply chain has begun responding to the US-China tensions, and COVID-19 may further accelerate the pace of this response. These immediate supply chain disruptions are bound to have a ripple effect on both complementary and supplementary industries and sectors, further declining the aggregate demand globally. While the extent and cost of this pandemic outbreak are still unrecognized, we are ascertaining the vulnerability and complexity of the supply chains that would affect global trade.

### Importance of the Retail Sector in the Global Supply Chains

Retail is the process of selling consumer goods or services to customers through multiple distribution channels to earn a profit (Gilbert 1999; Caro et al., 2020). An increasing number of retailers seek to reach broader markets by selling through multiple channels, including bricks and mortar and online retailing (Adivar et al., 2019). Retail shops occur in various types and contexts – from strip shopping centres in residential streets to large, indoor shopping malls (Medrano and Olarte-Pascual, 2016). To attract customers modern retailers typically make a variety of strategic level decisions including the multi channels and omni- channels presence, market segmentation, product mix, customer service, the store's overall market positioning, retail environment, marketing mix and promotional mix (Rahman and Kuzminov 2019; Hinsch et al. 2020). The increased competition in the global retail perspective puts pressure on retailers to make the products available at all times. Therefore, customer service is becoming the most critical factor for the retailers to acquire and compete to become a market leader, Factors such as convenience and comfort are getting considered by the customers; therefore, to maintain the performance of the product, supplementary efforts are employed by retailers in the form of 'customer service'.

### Resilience in Service Retail

Resilience in the Service retail sector refers to the service retailer's ability to absorb and mitigate changes and regain the initial performance level after an unexpected disturbance in the business environment

*Understanding the Service Quality Dimensions*

(Hendry et al., 2019). Much work in the past service retail resilience literature has focused on developing responses or mitigation strategies (Chowdhury and Quaddus, 2016; Ivanov et al., 2017; Graveline and Gremont, 2017; Hosseini et al., 2019). Authors such as Hosseini et al. (2019) have highlighted five evaluation metrics related to resilience enhancement, vulnerability, uncertainty, economic and recovery time. Further, Simchi-Levi et al. (2015) and Ivanov et al. (2017) have used recovery time to evaluate the impact of disruption in the supply chain management. Similarly, authors such as Schmitt and Singh (2012), Torabi et al. (2015) and Ojha et al. (2018) have used evaluation metrics that are directly related to Service Retail Resilience and have used it to measure service performance and supplier's capacity. While few authors have adopted an indirect quantification model to measure retail service resilience, for example, Jabbarzadeh et al. (2018) have the inventory levels with a supplier as a resilience strategy to overcome a disruptive performance. Yagi et al. (2020) evaluated supply chain vulnerability by utilizing a multi-input mitigation strategy. In comparison, Hosseini et al. (2020) evaluated resilience by measuring supplier segregation by considering geographically aggregate suppliers.

## MAIN FOCUS OF THE CHAPTER

## Service Quality

The topic of service quality has been quite popular in the service marketing literature. Operations and other Management scholars have shown keen interest to understand and identify service quality in the past three decades. Coined initially and developed by Parasuraman et al. (1988), the concept of service quality has been primarily employed to understand and compare the varying excellence in service encounters between customers and service providers. The term "quality" carries a different meaning from person to person. This is why defining "quality" is often the first step in most "quality improvement" journeys. A common understanding and vision of what is meant by "quality" can help the organization to focus its "quality improvement" efforts. Thus, defining "quality" is not only crucial from a semantic point of view but, more importantly, it is required to direct employees' efforts towards a particular common cause. The shared vision of quality is arguably more critical in-service organizations (Ghobadian et al 1994). The topic of service quality has its unique ability to cover several points. While Bitner (1990), defines service quality "as the customer's overall impression of the relative inferiority/superiority of a service provider and its services". Groonross (1990) on the other hand defines service quality as "what the customer received and process quality as how the service is delivered".

In this manner, while the first definition emphasises the attitude which includes process quality and outcome quality the second definition is more oriented towards credence quality. Scholars in the service research dimension have shown keen interest to study the issues of measurement. As a result, SERVQUAL has been designed as a multi-dimensional research instrument, to measure service quality by capturing consumer's perceptions and expectations along with the five dimensions of service quality (Parasuraman et al. 1994). Research on SERVQUAL has become quite widespread in services research literature, and represents a breakthrough in the measurement methods used for service quality research (Brown et al. 1993). Following its introduction several authors have attempted to refute and replicate its original structure and concepts in the past (Cronin and Taylor 1992; Teas 1993). Further, it has become the dominant measuring scale utilized in service quality and other cultural contexts. The diagnostic value

139

of the measurement instrument is supported by the model of service quality which forms the conceptual framework for the development of both questionnaire and instruments scales.

## Dimensions of Service Quality

Evaluation of service quality becomes difficult due to three significant inherences in service, inseparability, heterogeneity and intangibility (Berry and Parasuraman 1991). However, Parasuraman et al. (1985) proposed a framework consisting of ten dimensions or determinants of service quality: reliability, tangible considerations, credibility, responsiveness, security, communication, courtesy, competence, access, and knowing/ understanding the customers. These ten dimensions and their descriptions served as the basic structure of the service-quality domain from which items were derived for the SERVQUAL scale. The ten determinants are related to specific economic and socio-cultural factors. While the determinants of access and reliability are attributed to conventional economic development aspects such as levels of affluence, education, technology, competition and communications. The responsiveness determinant is linked to socio- cultures influences concerning the value of time. All the other remaining determinates are associated with socio-cultural factors (Maslow 1970; Hofstede 1980).

## Reliability

Parasuraman et al. (1985; 1988; 1994) found that reliability means organizations perform a service correctly the first time. Moreover, it shows that organizations strive to fulfil promises and pay attention to the results. Reliability has been classed as the first dimension of the SERVQUAL service quality model. Lam (2002) ranked reliability as first in the dimensions of the service quality model.

## Assurance

Assurance has been defined as employees' courtesy and knowledge, and their capacity to transfer confidence and trust to customers. Assurance means keeping customers informed and listening to them, regardless of their educational level, age, and nationality. It states that assurance indicates the employees' attitudes and their behaviour, and the staff's ability to provide friendly, confidential, courteous, and competent services (Parasuraman et al. 1994). Assurance is ranked first according to (Gronroos 1988) while (Parasuraman et al. 1994) rated it in fourth place.

## Tangibles

Parasuraman et al. (1985; 1988; 1994) identify tangibles as physical facilities (equipment, personnel and materials). It is the physical image of the service that customers will use to assess quality. Tangibles are associated with the physical facilities, tools and machines used to provide the service, and representations of the services, such as kiosks, variety of apparel, cost and efficiency of transactions i.e., billing. Several privileges are included in tangibles such as; colour of the store, employee uniform, variety of brands, discounts, changing rooms, opening hours and speed and efficiency of billing. (Parasuraman et al. 1994) stated that tangibles have the same importance as empathy.

## Empathy

In the services setting, empathy is a core determinant and is crucial for a mutual relationship between customer and service providers (Kenny and Albright 1987; Ahearne et al. 2007). It has been conceptualized as the service provider's ability to understand the thoughts and feelings of his consumer's (McBane 1995). The concept of empathy emerged from the social psychology discipline (Gump and Kulik 1997) and suggests that employees with a high level of empathy are more effective in addressing consumer's needs and desires (Homburg et al. 2009). In the service setting, this is especially important considering the greater amount of consumer – service provider interactions. Additionally, research suggests that when service employees are committed to their work and have a strong customer orientation, consumer loyalty and customer satisfaction increase towards the service provider (Markovic et al. 2018).

## Responsiveness

Parasuraman et al. (1985; 1988; 1994) highlighted that the responsiveness of willing employees involves telling customers exactly when things will be done, giving them undivided attention, promoting services, and responding per their requests. Responsiveness was ranked as the third dimension in SERVQUAL 1994.

Figure 1 shows a model representing the effects of service quality dimensions on customer satisfaction using the modified SERQUAL model.

*Figure 1. The service quality dimensions of resilience*
*Source: Author(s) own analysis, (2021)*

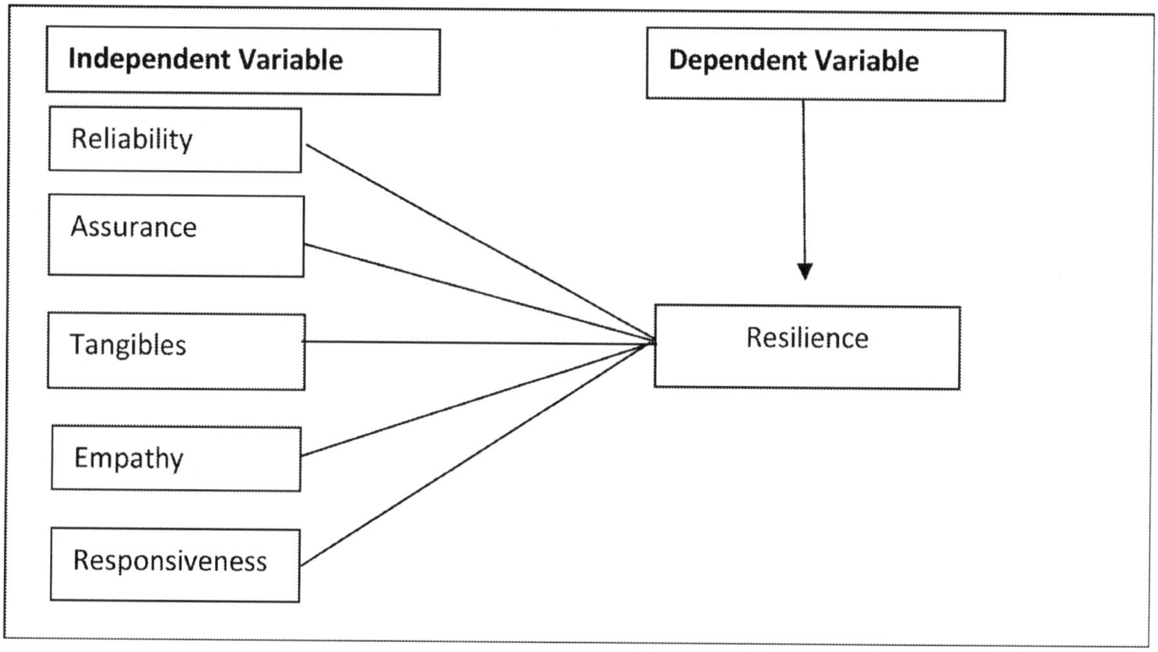

### Independent Variable

Service quality includes several dimensions that influence resilience. The model shows the improved service quality model with the following dimensions: tangibles, responsiveness, empathy, reliability and assurance (Parasuraman et al. 1985, 1988, 1994). The questionnaire for the service quality model was constructed for the independent variables with the number of questions as follows: 6 for tangibility, 4 for responsiveness, 4 for assurance, 5 for empathy and 6 for reliability. The number of questions selected was determined based on their importance in the literature.

### Dependent Variable

It is challenging to measure resilience without knowing what has to be measured precisely. This is because the resilience concept is defined variably in literature (Levine, 2014). Resilience has often been described as a positive adaptive capacity of individuals experiencing adverse conditions (Kantur and Say, 2015). Similarly, authors Hamel and Valikangas (2003) have defined business resilience as reinventing business ideas, and approaches as situations change dynamically. Sheffi and Rice (2005) have demonstrated that flexibility is a core pillar of business resilience.

## Data Collection

Books, annual reports, journals, and the Internet were the secondary research sources used to obtain the information needed to design the model and the analysis. As a primary source, the survey was used to collect the relevant data to study the impact of service quality on resilience in an Apparel retail store in the Mumbai region. The method of collecting data was done using traditional paper questionnaires, and an online Google Survey tailored to the convenience of the respondents. Store employees also assisted in the distribution and collection of questionnaires. The questionnaire consisted of three parts; the covering letter, questions related to demographic data, and a section that measured independent and dependent variables. A five-point Likert scale was applied for the variables, with responses as follows: Strongly agree = 5, agree = 4, neutral = 3, disagree = 2 and strongly disagree = 1.

## Methodology of Statistical Analysis

In the demographic analysis of data, we present the distribution of respondents by gender, age, occupational, educational and other aspects and then carry out statistical analysis of research questions. In doing so, we primarily consider the distribution of variables to assess the possibilities for further analysis. We then demonstrate the reliability of the scales selected from the literature, primarily by using the Cronbach-alpha indicator, including a series of questions that measure the overall resilience. Considering that the purpose of our research is mainly the effect of the selected five dimensions on overall resilience. We first examine whether the scales of the five dimensions are individually correlated with the target variable, as the items that do not correlate with the target variable are not essential and are unnecessary for us. We then analyse the internal structure of the five scales selected for the independent variables. It follows our assumption that the target variable is not included in this analysis.

## Validity and Reliability

Validity and reliability are among the most important criteria to assess the credibility of research outcomes and findings (Collis and Hussey 2013). Validity and reliability should be reflected in the measurements and variables of the research, in particular, and in the findings in general. They also apply to how these variables were chosen. (Saunders et al., 2009) pointed out that the measurements should be reliable and precise so that if another researcher uses the same instruments or measures, that researcher should obtain the same results.

*Table 1. Reliability of data*

| Customer Satisfaction & SERVQUAL dimension | Mean |
|---|---|
| Item Means | 3.622 |
| Item Variances | 0.019 |
| Inter-Item Covariance | 0.737 |
| Inter-Item Correlations | 0.555 |

Source: Authors Own

Inter-item correlation should exceed 0.30 for the data to be reliable. The item statistics present the current study statistic, where the Inter-item correlation is 0.577 for expected SERVQUAL dimensions.

## Service Quality Statements

Each question is bucketed into each dimension and has been used for the modelling.

*Understanding the Service Quality Dimensions*

*Table 2. Service quality statements used to create ServQual model*

| Question Number | Statements | Dimension |
|---|---|---|
| E1 | The retail store has a modern-looking equipment's and fixtures | *Tangibles* |
| E2 | The physical facilities like display shelves, counters etc. at this retail store are visually attractive | *Tangibles* |
| E3 | Materials associated with this retail store service (such as shopping bags, carry bags etc.) are visually appealing | *Tangibles* |
| E4 | The retail store has clean, attractive, and convenient physical facilities (restrooms, fitting rooms) | *Tangibles* |
| E5 | The layout of the retail store makes it easy for customers to find what they need | *Tangibles* |
| E6 | The store layout (arrangement) in this retail store makes it easy for customers to move around in this store | *Tangibles* |
| E7 | When the retail store promises to do something (such as repair, alterations) by a certain time, it will do so. | *Reliability* |
| E8 | The retail store provides its services at the time it promises to do so | *Reliability* |
| E9 | The retail store performs the service right at the first time | *Reliability* |
| E10 | The retail store has merchandise (stock) available when the customers want it | *Reliability* |
| E11 | The retail store insists on error – free sales transactions (relating to Billings, returns etc.) | *Reliability* |
| E12 | The employee in this retail store has enough knowledge to answer the customers' queries | *Responsiveness* |
| E13 | The behaviour of employees in this retail store instils confidence in customers mind with respect to transactions | *Responsiveness* |
| E14 | Customers feel safe with their transactions in this retail store | *Responsiveness* |
| E15 | Employees in this retail store give prompt service to customers | *Responsiveness* |
| E16 | Employees in this retail store tell customers exactly when services will be performed | *Reliability* |
| E17 | Employees in this retail store are never too busy to respond to customers' requests | *Assurance* |
| E18 | The retail store gives customers individual attention | *Assurance* |
| E19 | Employees in this retail store are consistently courteous with customers | *Assurance* |
| E20 | Employees in this retail store treat customers courteously on the telephone | *Assurance* |
| E21 | The retail store handles returns and exchanges at customers' flexibility | *Empathy* |
| E22 | The employees of this retail store are able to handle customer complaints directly and immediately in most cases | *Empathy* |
| E23 | When a customer has a problem, this retail store shows a sincere interest in solving it | *Empathy* |
| E24 | The retail store offers high quality merchandise | *Empathy* |
| E25 | The retail store provides plenty of convenient parking for customers | *Empathy* |

Source: Authors Own

Service Quality Statements are taken from the research paper: A Measure of Service Quality for Retail Stores: Scale Development and Validation written by Dabholkar et al. (1996).

*Understanding the Service Quality Dimensions*

## Reliability of the Variable (Cronbach's alpha)

Reliability has been examined for the items, like the table shown below, which includes the original 25 items, which become 21 after rotation; the new subscale score of the Cronbach's alpha value is 0.959. The new subscales of tangibles and reliability were originally made up of 6 items; but two from tangibles and reliability respectively have been deleted (E5, E6 and E7) because of cross-loading. The final Cronbach's alpha for tangibles is 0.958 and for reliability is 0.951. The subscale of responsiveness, assurance and empathy initially consisted of four, four and five items respectively; no items have been deleted, and the final Cronbach's alpha value is 0.951, 0950 and 0.955 respectively. Higher values of alpha are more desirable. As a rule of thumb, some professionals require a reliability of 0.70 or higher with 0.60 as the lowest acceptable threshold (obtained on from substantial sample) before they will use an instrument.

*Table 3. Reliability of the variable using Cronbach's Alpha*

| Variables | Original Number of Items | Items after Deletion | Cronbach's Alpha |
|---|---|---|---|
| *Tangibles* | 6 | 4 | 0.958 |
| *Reliability* | 6 | 4 | 0.951 |
| *Responsiveness* | 4 | 4 | 0.9514 |
| *Assurance* | 4 | 4 | 0.950 |
| *Empathy* | 5 | 5 | 0.955 |
| **Total/Overall Cronbach's alpha** | **25** | **21** | **0.959** |

Source: Authors Own

## Item-total Statistics

*Table 4. CFA loading of customer satisfaction dimensions*

| Question Number | Customer Satisfaction | Dimensions | CFA Loading | Cronbach's Alpha if Item Deleted |
|---|---|---|---|---|
| E1 | CS_1 | Tangibles | 0.517 | 0.969 |
| E2 | CS_2 | Tangibles | 0.848 | 0.966 |
| E3 | CS_3 | Tangibles | 0.796 | 0.967 |
| E4 | CS_4 | Tangibles | 0.756 | 0.967 |
| E9 | CS_9 | Reliability | 0.798 | 0.966 |
| E10 | CS_10 | Reliability | 0.791 | 0.966 |
| E11 | CS_11 | Reliability | 0.783 | 0.966 |
| E12 | CS_12 | Responsiveness | 0.777 | 0.966 |
| E13 | CS_13 | Responsiveness | 0.756 | 0.967 |
| E14 | CS_14 | Responsiveness | 0.823 | 0.966 |
| E15 | CS_15 | Responsiveness | 0.774 | 0.967 |
| E16 | CS_16 | Reliability | 0.828 | 0.966 |
| E17 | CS_17 | Assurance | 0.767 | 0.966 |
| E18 | CS_18 | Assurance | 0.806 | 0.966 |
| E19 | CS_19 | Assurance | 0.739 | 0.967 |
| E20 | CS_20 | Assurance | 0.802 | 0.966 |
| E21 | CS_21 | Empathy | 0.792 | 0.966 |
| E22 | CS_22 | Empathy | 0.785 | 0.966 |
| E23 | CS_23 | Empathy | 0.791 | 0.966 |
| E24 | CS_24 | Empathy | 0.817 | 0.966 |
| E25 | CS_25 | Empathy | 0.688 | 0.967 |

Source: Authors Own

All values of Cronbach Alpha are greater than 0.700, there is no necessity of deletion of any further question from the proposed model. (If value Cronbach Alpha is less than 0.700 then that question is to be deleted and again run the model for remaining question) which we have done for Q5, Q6, Q7 and Q8. Above model also confirm that there are four questions belongs to 'Tangible', four questions for 'Reliability', four questions for 'Responsiveness', four questions for 'Assurance' and five questions for 'Empathy'. The CFA loadings are indicated in the above table and suggest that all the items taken for scale construction qualify to develop the scale. This is due to the fact the CFA loadings are greater than 0.50 for all the items. Moreover, as all the dimensions have Cronbach's Alpha greater than 0.7, this establishes the reliability of all the items included under service quality dimension model.

*Understanding the Service Quality Dimensions*

## Structural Equation Modelling

*Figure 2. Structural equation modelling*

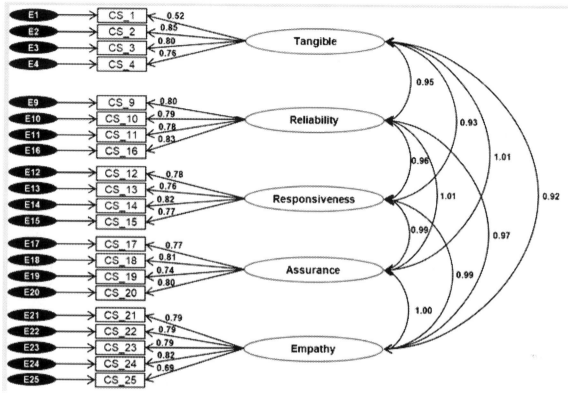

## Goodness of Fit

The goodness of fit of a statistical model describes how well it fits a set of observations. Measures of goodness of fit typically summarize the discrepancy between observed and expected values under the model in question.

*Table 5. Validity of the model using goodness of fit test*

| Goodness of Fit Statistics | Observed values | Fit Values |
|---|---|---|
| *Chi Square Value (CMIN)* <br> *Degree of Freedom (Df)* <br> *Chi Square / Df (CMIN/Df)* | *423.905* <br> *199* <br> *2.130* | 2 to 5 |
| Goodness of Fit Index (GFI) | 0.869 | >= 0.9 |
| Root Mean Square Error of Approximation (RMSEA) | 0.068 | < 0.08 |
| Adjusted Good of Fit Index (AGFI) | 0.917 | >= 0.9 |
| Normed Fit Index (NFI) | 0.910 | >= 0.9 |
| Comparative Fit Index (CFI) | 0.960 | >= 0.9 |

Source: Authors Own

To analyse, the validity CFA approach (AMOS 26) has been used. Results of the analysis and fit values are as follows:

6.3.1 *CMIN*: The chi-square for the model is also called the discrepancy function, likelihood ratio chi-square, or chi-square goodness of fit. In AMOS, the chi-square value is called CMIN. Required value is in the range of 2.0 to 5.0. Result of the model under the study is 0.246. Therefore, model value is satisfied.

## Goodness of Fit Index (GFI)

Required value for goodness of fit is greater than or equal to 0.900. GFI value for model under the study is 0.869. Since the GIF value is very close to 0.9, conclusion is model is moderately good to fit.

## Root Mean Square Error of Approximation (RMSEA)

A parsimony-adjusted index. Values closer to 0 represent a good fit. Minimum required value is below 0.08. Calculated value is 0.068. It is less than 0.08; hence RMSEA is accepted and fit for the model.

## Adjusted Good of Fit Index (AGFI)

AGFI is the proportion of variance accounted for by the estimated population covariance. Analogous to R2. AGFI favours parsimony. Required value is more than or equal to 0.90. Calculated value is 0.91. This indicates that AGFI value is accepted and fit for the model.

## Normed Fit Index (NFI)

An NFI of 0.95 indicates the model of interest improves the fit by 95% relative to the null model. NNFI is preferable for smaller samples. Sometimes the NFI is called the Tucker Lewis index (TLI). Model to be moderately fit required value is greater than or equal to 0.90. Calculated value is 0.91. This indicates that NFI value is accepted and fit for the model.

## Comparative Fit Index (CFI)

It is a revised form of NFI. It is not very sensitive to sample size. It compares the fit of a target model to the fit of an independent, or null, model. Required value is greater than or equal to 0.90. Since actual value of CFI is 0.96, therefore, it is fit for the model.

*Understanding the Service Quality Dimensions*

*Table 6. Summary of results from scale purification stage (actual table given by Parasuraman et al., 1985)*

| Dimension | Label | Reliability Coefficients (Alpha) | Number of Items | Factor Loading of Items on Dimensions to which they belong [a] |
|---|---|---|---|---|
| Tangibles | D1 | 0.72 | 4 | 63 75 62 47 |
| Reliability | D2 | 0.83 | 4 | 56 73 71 47 |
| Responsiveness | D3 | 0.84 | 5 | 60 73 59 76 66 |
| Communication Credibility Security Competence Courtesy | D4 | 0.79 | 4 | 35 53 66 56 |
| | D5 | 0.85 | 7 | 41 62 47 50 75 52 54 |
| Understanding/Knowing Customers' | D6 | 0.85 | 4 | 80 76 62 77 |
| Access | D7 | 0.78 | 5 | 47 50 75 52 71 |
| Reliability of Linear Combination (Total-Scale Reliability) | | 0.94 | | [a]Numbers are the magnitude of factor loadings multiplied by 100. The loadings of items on dimensions to which they did not belong were all less than 0.3. The percentage of variance extracted by the seven factors was 61.7% |

Source: Authors Own

## SOLUTIONS AND RECOMMENDATIONS

Based on the work of Parasuraman et al. (1988), Singh & Pandya (1991) and Smith (1999), this research presented a model to explain how the five dimensions of retail service quality influence perceptions of the overall retail service quality, and how these overall perceptions of retail service quality influence customer's satisfaction level. All hypotheses were confirmed albeit with Q5, Q6, Q7 and Q8 which have CFA loading less than 0.4 and hence are omitted from the model. Our results suggest that retail service quality is significant among respondents of Mumbai region. SERVQUAL model tested for respondents of Mumbai region is fit; and is accepted for all five variables and for corresponding group of questions. Respondents of age group 18-29 years old are considered for the study. Model of 21 questions with five service quality variables are considered. These five variables are Tangible, Reliability, Responsive, Assurance and Empathy. Now based on the model Q1 to Q4 fit with Tangibles, Q9-Q11 and Q16 fit with Reliability, Q12 to Q15 fit with Responsiveness, Q17 to Q20 fit with Assurance and Q21 to Q25 fit with Empathy. These dimensions directly affect retail service quality perceptions, which influences the retail outlet's overall resilience level. This exploration of those service quality dimensions that lead to overall retail service quality and its effect on overall satisfaction is a novel contribution to the literature.

*Table 7. Final 5 dimensions of SERVQUAL model*

| Reliability | Ability to perform the promised service dependably and accurately |
|---|---|
| Assurance | Knowledge and courtesy of employees and their ability to inspire trust and confidence |
| Tangibles | Physical facilities, equipment, and appearance of personnel |
| Empathy | Caring, individualized attention the firm provides its customers |
| Responsiveness | Willingness to help customers' and provide prompt service |

Source: Authors Own

# FUTURE RESEARCH DIRECTIONS

## Theoretical Research Opportunities

The past research has mainly adopted a positively influenced epistemological landscape (Radomir et al., 2012; Patten, 2017). It has further been concentrated primarily on qualitative methods conducted in the traditional service quality setting. Thus, the focus has been on putting the service quality dimensions objectively for quality measurement. Therefore, in the present article, the results are several generic service quality models generalisable across the retail stores setting in Mumbai Region (Parasuraman et al., 1988; Wolfinbarger and Gilly, 2003). While the focus of extant literature has investigated chiefly the service quality dimensions, as the antecedents of consumer's service quality perception (Parasuraman et al., 1985; Loiacono et al., 2002), the present article has been successful in generating a more dynamic representation of service quality dimension in the retailing perspective. The research findings suggest several implications for retail services management. This includes the need for managers to acknowledge that developing an integrated system is vital to understand the resilience phenomenon.

## Managerial Research Opportunities

Digital technologies have taken an essential long-term role in response to COVID-19 activities (Kumar and Managi, 2020). Manufacturing and Supply Chain technologies are trending towards automation and data exchange systems as in Industry 4.0. Businesses using Industry 4.0 technologies- cyber-physical systems (CPS), cloud computing, Internet of Things (IoT), and cognitive computing that can complement human decision making with technological backing can help in the decentralized decision-making

*Understanding the Service Quality Dimensions*

process. Other collaborative technologies such as blockchain technology allow for information sharing transparently, reasonably quickly, accurately and widely (Van Hoek, 2019). Understanding the supply chain capabilities and capacities is critical for building reliance in service quality. This crisis provides evidence that localized systems are more likely to be robust and resilient than global supply chains (Nandi, et al., 2021; Handfield et al., 2020). Localization is also essential to environmental supply chain sustainability (Holmstrom and Gutowski, 2017). Local production can mean rapid response to local needs, but with low energy and resources consumption. For example, in the COVID-19 pandemic, many 'hot-spots emerged. Ensuring critical equipment and materials through more agile production and rapid delivery logistics to hot spots can equate to saving more lives or slowing the spread of positive cases—a social sustainability concern. Flexible manufacturing system technologies such as additive manufacturing and robotics can localize production capabilities.

## Public Policy

In terms of providing services to the citizens of a nation, the government of a nation can also be considered a service institution. The government of any country has a far-reaching responsibility towards its citizens and the community. Almost every government agency, whether in India or in any country, provide public service through a one-stop integrated service. The low-quality public service provided by a department presents a poor image of the government within the public and the society. Similarly, it also affects trust in the government. And thus, public service quality has become one of the critical variables to study. This research article formulates the factors that influence public trust in a structural model. In the model, trust is directly and indirectly affected by Assurance, Empathy, Responsiveness, and Reliability.

## CONCLUSION

Our previous institutions and worldviews have changed. The current global environment is unprecedented. This pandemic – with its remaining uncertainties – and responses will be topics of discussion for the foreseeable future. The crisis and recovery period provides us with opportunities to observe and study how institutional changes can result in strategic and operational supply chain transformations. Our goal with this study was to understand service quality dimensions and achieving resilience in service retail. We extend and develop the literature and operationalize service quality dimensions relating to resilience in the pandemic landscape. Although the limitations and fragility of global supply chain resilience occurred early in the pandemic, they also highlighted potential transition opportunities and evolution towards sustainability. For example, the COVID-19 crisis teaches climate shock events (Nandi et al., 2021). It is not clear if we will return to our old ways after the panic and the crisis. After this black swan event subsides, will it be the accountants and financiers who decide how our supply chains operate; will the sustainability flame dim? We need to examine and study our world carefully; what we learn now and implement later can have beneficial or detrimental results for decades and generations. Only looking inwardly to our discipline will be short-sighted; we need to join forces with natural scientists, social scientists, industry, government and civil society to address these issues jointly. This crisis requires transdisciplinary interactions. Overall, as operations and supply chain researchers, we should not shirk our duties to contribute to recovery and a better – sustainable – world.

## REFERENCES

Adivar, B., Hüseyinoğlu, I. Ö. Y., & Christopher, M. (2019). A quantitative performance management framework for assessing omnichannel retail supply chains. *Journal of Retailing and Consumer Services, 48*(1), 257–269. doi:10.1016/j.jretconser.2019.02.024

Ahearne, M., Jelinek, R., & Jones, E. (2007). Examining the effect of salesperson service behavior in a competitive context. *Journal of the Academy of Marketing Science, 35*(4), 603–616. doi:10.100711747-006-0013-1

Bennis, W. G., & Nanus, B. (1985). *Leaders: Strategies for taking charge.* Harper & Row.

Berry, L. L., & Parasuraman, A. (1991). *Marketing services: Competing through quality.* Free Press.

Betz, U. A., Betz, F., Kim, R., Monks, B., & Phillips, F. (2019). Surveying the future of science, technology and business–A 35 year perspective. *Technological Forecasting and Social Change, 144*(1), 137–147. doi:10.1016/j.techfore.2019.04.005

Bitner, M. J. (1990). Evaluating service encounters; the effects of physical surroundings and employee responses. *Journal of Marketing, 54*(1), 69–82. doi:10.1177/002224299005400206

Brown, T. J., Churchill. G., & Peter, J. (1993). Research note: Improving the measurement of service quality. *Journal of Retailing, 69*(1), 127-139.

Bulturbayevich, M. B., & Jurayevich, M. B. (2020). The impact of the digital economy on economic growth. *International Journal of Business, Law, and Education, 1*(1), 4–7.

Canh, P. N., Schinckus, C., & Dinh Thanh, S. (2021). What are the drivers of shadow economy? A further evidence of economic integration and institutional quality. *The Journal of International Trade & Economic Development, 30*(1), 47–67. doi:10.1080/09638199.2020.1799428

Caro, F., Kök, A. G., & Martínez-de-Albéniz, V. (2020). The future of retail operations. *Manufacturing & Service Operations Management, 22*(1), 47–58. doi:10.1287/msom.2019.0824

Chowdhury, M. M., & Quaddus, M. (2016). Supply chain readiness, response and recovery for resilience. *Supply Chain Management, 21*(6), 709–731. doi:10.1108/SCM-12-2015-0463

Collis, J., & Hussey, R. (2013). Business research: A practical guide for undergraduate and postgraduate students. Palgrave Macmillan.

Cronin, J. J. Jr, & Taylor, S. A. (1992). Measuring service quality: A reexamination and extension. *Journal of Marketing, 56*(3), 55–68. doi:10.1177/002224299205600304

Dabholkar, P. A., Thorpe, D. I., & Rentz, J. O. (1996). A measure of service quality for retail stores: Scale development and validation. *Journal of the Academy of Marketing Science, 24*(1), 3–11. doi:10.1007/BF02893933

Doktoralina, C., & Apollo, A. (2019). The contribution of strategic management accounting in supply chain outcomes and logistic firm profitability. *Uncertain Supply Chain Management, 7*(2), 145–156. doi:10.5267/j.uscm.2018.10.010

*Understanding the Service Quality Dimensions*

Ghobadian, A., Speller, S., & Jones, M. (1994). Service quality. *International Journal of Quality & Reliability Management*, *11*(9), 43–66. doi:10.1108/02656719410074297 PMID:10134643

Gilbert, D. (1999). *Retail marketing management*. Financial Times Management.

Graveline, N., & Gremont, M. (2017). Measuring and understanding the microeconomic resilience of businesses to lifeline service interruptions due to natural disasters. *International Journal of Disaster Risk Reduction*, *24*, 526–538. doi:10.1016/j.ijdrr.2017.05.012

Gronroos, C. (1988). Service quality: The six criteria of good perceived service. *Review of Business*, *9*(3), 10–21.

Groonroos, C. (1990). *Service Management and Marketing*. Lexington Books.

Gump, B. B., & Kulik, J. A. (1997). Stress, affiliation, and emotional contagion. *Journal of Personality and Social Psychology*, *72*(2), 305–321. doi:10.1037/0022-3514.72.2.305 PMID:9107002

Guo, X., Cheng, L., & Liu, J. (2020). Green supply chain contracts with eco-labels issued by the sales platform: Profitability and environmental implications. *International Journal of Production Research*, *58*(5), 1485–1504. doi:10.1080/00207543.2019.1658911

Hamel, G., & Valikangas, L. (2003). The quest for resilience. *Harvard Business Review*, *81*, 52–65. PMID:12964393

Handfield, R. B., Graham, G., & Burns, L. (2020). Corona virus, tariffs, trade wars and supply chain evolutionary design. *International Journal of Operations & Production Management*, *40*(10), 1649–1660. doi:10.1108/IJOPM-03-2020-0171

Hendry, L. C., Stevenson, M., MacBryde, J., Ball, P., Sayed, M., & Liu, L. (2019). Local food supply chain resilience to constitutional change: The Brexit effect. *International Journal of Operations & Production Management*, *39*(3), 429–453. doi:10.1108/IJOPM-03-2018-0184

Hinsch, C., Felix, R., & Rauschnabel, P. A. (2020). Nostalgia beats the wow-effect: Inspiration, awe and meaningful associations in augmented reality marketing. *Journal of Retailing and Consumer Services*, *53*(1), 1–11. doi:10.1016/j.jretconser.2019.101987

Hofstede, G. H. (1980). *Organization Dynamics*. AMACOM.

Holmström, J., & Gutowski, T. (2017). Additive manufacturing in operations and supply chain management: No sustainability benefit or virtuous knock-on opportunities? *Journal of Industrial Ecology*, *21*(1), 21–24. doi:10.1111/jiec.12580

Homburg, C., Wieseke, J., & Bornemann, T. (2009). Implementing the marketing concept at the employee-customer interface: The role of customer need knowledge. *Journal of Marketing*, *73*(4), 64–81.

Hosseini, S., Ivanov, D., & Dolgui, A. (2019). Review of quantitative methods for supply chain resilience analysis. *Transportation Research Part E, Logistics and Transportation Review*, *125*, 285–307. doi:10.1016/j.tre.2019.03.001

Hosseini, S., Ivanov, D., & Dolgui, A. (2020). Ripple effect modelling of supplier disruption: Integrated Markov chain and dynamic Bayesian network approach. *International Journal of Production Research, 58*(11), 3284–3303. doi:10.1080/00207543.2019.1661538

Ivanov, D., & Dolgui, A. (2020). Viability of intertwined supply networks: Extending the supply chain resilience angles towards survivability. A position paper motivated by COVID-19 outbreak. *International Journal of Production Research, 58*(10), 2904–2915. doi:10.1080/00207543.2020.1750727

Ivanov, D., Dolgui, A., Sokolov, B., & Ivanova, M. (2017). Literature review on disruption recovery in the supply chain. *International Journal of Production Research, 55*(20), 6158–6174. doi:10.1080/002 07543.2017.1330572

Jabbarzadeh, A., Fahimnia, B., & Sabouhi, F. (2018). Resilient and sustainable supply chain design: Sustainability analysis under disruption risks. *International Journal of Production Research, 56*(17), 5945–5968. doi:10.1080/00207543.2018.1461950

Jacobsen, K. H. (2020). Will COVID-19 generate global preparedness? *Lancet, 395*(10229), 1013–1014. doi:10.1016/S0140-6736(20)30559-6 PMID:32199074

Kantur, D., & Say, A. I. (2015). Measuring organizational resilience: A scale development. *Journal of Business Economics and Finance, 4*(3), 2146–7943.

Kenny, D. A., & Albright, L. (1987). Accuracy in interpersonal perception: A social relations analysis. *Psychological Bulletin, 102*(3), 390–407. doi:10.1037/0033-2909.102.3.390 PMID:3317468

Ketchen, D. J. Jr, & Craighead, C. W. (2020). Research at the intersection of entrepreneurship, supply chain management, and strategic management: Opportunities highlighted by COVID-19. *Journal of Management, 46*(8), 1330–1341. doi:10.1177/0149206320945028

Kobrin, S. J. (2015). Is a global nonmarket strategy possible? Economic integration in a multipolar world order. *Journal of World Business, 50*(2), 262–272. doi:10.1016/j.jwb.2014.10.003

Kochan, C. G., & Nowicki, D. R. (2019). Supply chain resilience: A systematic literature review and typological framework. *International Journal of Physical Distribution & Logistics Management, 48*(8), 842–865. doi:10.1108/IJPDLM-02-2017-0099

Kumar, S., & Managi, S. (2020). Does stringency of lockdown affect air quality? Evidence from Indian cities. *Economics of Disasters and Climate Change, 4*(3), 481–502. doi:10.100741885-020-00072-1 PMID:32838121

Lam, T. K. P. (2002). Making sense of SERVQUAL's dimensions to the Chinese customers in Macau. *Journal of Market Focused Management, 5*(10), 43–58. doi:10.1023/A:1012575412058

Levine, S. (2014). *Assessing resilience: why quantification misses the point.* Humanitarian Policy Group, Overseas Development Institute. Retrieved from https://www.odi.org/sites/odi. org.uk/files/odi-assets/ publications- opinion-files/9049.pdf

Loiacono, E., Watson, R., & Goodhue, D. (2002). WEBQUAL: A measure of Website quality. *Marketing Educators' Conference. Marketing Theory and Applications, 13*(1), 432–437.

Markovic, S., Iglesias, O., Singh, J. J., & Sierra, V. (2018). How does the perceived ethicality of corporate services brands influence loyalty and positive word-of-mouth? Analyzing the roles of empathy, affective commitment, and perceived quality. *Journal of Business Ethics*, *148*(4), 721–740. doi:10.100710551-015-2985-6

Maslow, A. H. (1970). *Motivation and personality* (2nd ed.). Harper & Row.

McBane, D. A. (1995). Empathy and the salesperson: A multidimensional perspective. *Psychology and Marketing*, *12*(4), 349–370. doi:10.1002/mar.4220120409

Medrano, N., & Olarte-Pascual, C. (2016). An empirical approach to marketing innovation in small and medium retailers: an application to the Spanish sector. *Contemporary Economics*, *10*(3), 205-216.

Nakamura, H., & Managi, S. (2020). Airport risk of importation and exportation of the COVID-19 pandemic. *Transport Policy*, *96*, 40–47. doi:10.1016/j.tranpol.2020.06.018 PMID:32834679

Nandi, S., Sarkis, J., Hervani, A. A., & Helms, M. M. (2021). Redesigning supply chains using blockchain-enabled circular economy and COVID-19 experiences. *Sustainable Production and Consumption*, *27*, 10–22. doi:10.1016/j.spc.2020.10.019 PMID:33102671

Ojha, R., Ghadge, A., Tiwari, M. K., & Bititci, U. S. (2018). Bayesian network modelling for supply chain risk propagation. *International Journal of Production Research*, *56*(17), 5795–5819. doi:10.1080/00207543.2018.1467059

Parasuraman, A., Zeithaml, V. A., & Berry, L. L. (1985). A conceptual model of service quality and its implications for future research. *Journal of Marketing*, *49*(1), 41–50. doi:10.1177/002224298504900403

Parasuraman, A., Zeithaml, V. A., & Berry, L. L. (1988). SERVQUAL: A multiple-item scale for measuring consumer perceptions of service quality. *Journal of Retailing*, *64*(1), 12–40.

Parasuraman, A., Zeithaml, V. A., & Berry, L. L. (1994). Reassessment of expectations as a comparison standard in measuring service quality: Implications for further research. *Journal of Marketing*, *58*(1), 111–124. doi:10.1177/002224299405800109

Patten, E. (2017). *Conceptualizing service quality in multichannel fashion retailing* (Doctoral dissertation). University of Gloucestershire.

Radomir, L., Plaias, I., & Nistor, V. C. (2012). Review of the Service Quality Concept-Past, Present and Perspectives. In *Proceedings of the International Conference Marketing-from Information to Decision* (p. 404). Babes Bolyai University.

Rahman, M. M., & Kuzminov, A. N. (2019). Marketing Mix as A Source Of Increasing The Efficiency Of Marketing Activity. Modern Problems of Scientific Activity. Perspectives for Implementing Innovative Solutions, 66-68.

Saunders, M., Lewis, P., & Thornhill, A. (2009). *Research Methods for Business Students* (5th ed.). Pearson Education.

Schmitt, A. J., & Singh, M. (2012). A quantitative analysis of disruption risk in a multi-echelon supply chain. *International Journal of Production Economics*, *139*(1), 22–32. doi:10.1016/j.ijpe.2012.01.004

Sheffi, Y., & Rice, J. B. (2005). A supply chain view of the resilient enterprise. *MIT Sloan Management Review, 47*(1), 41–48.

Simchi-Levi, D., Schmidt, W., Wei, Y., Zhang, P. Y., Combs, K., Ge, Y., Gusikhin, O., Sanders, M., & Zhang, D. (2015). Identifying risks and mitigating disruptions in the automotive supply chain. *Interfaces, 45*(5), 375–390. doi:10.1287/inte.2015.0804

Singh, J., & Pandya, S. (1991). Exploring the effects of consumers' dissatisfaction level on complaint behaviours. *European Journal of Marketing, 25*(9), 7–21. doi:10.1108/EUM0000000000621

Teas, R. K. (1993). Expectations, performance evaluation, and consumers' perceptions of quality. *Journal of Marketing, 57*(4), 18–34.

Torabi, S. A., Baghersad, M., & Mansouri, S. A. (2015). Resilient supplier selection and order allocation under operational and disruption risks. *Transportation Research Part E, Logistics and Transportation Review, 79*, 22–48. doi:10.1016/j.tre.2015.03.005

Van Hoek, R. (2019). Exploring blockchain implementation in the supply chain: Learning from pioneers and RFID research. *International Journal of Operations & Production Management, 39*(6/7/8), 829-859.

White, C., & Yu, Y. T. (2005). Satisfaction emotions and consumer behavioral intentions. *Journal of Services Marketing, 19*(6), 411–420. doi:10.1108/08876040510620184

Wolfinbarger, M., & Gilly, M. C. (2003). eTailQ: Dimensionalizing, measuring and predicting etail quality. *Journal of Retailing, 79*(3), 183–198. doi:10.1016/S0022-4359(03)00034-4

Yagi, M., Kagawa, S., Managi, S., Fujii, H., & Guan, D. (2020). Supply constraint from earthquakes in Japan in input–output analysis. *Risk Analysis, 40*(9), 1811–1830. doi:10.1111/risa.13525 PMID:32506698

Yun, J. J., Won, D., Park, K., Jeong, E., & Zhao, X. (2019). The role of a business model in market growth: The difference between the converted industry and the emerging industry. *Technological Forecasting and Social Change, 146*, 534–562. doi:10.1016/j.techfore.2019.04.024

# Section 2
# Supply Chain Efficiency

# Chapter 9
# Investigating the Influence of Supply Chain Practices on Healthcare Organizational Performance:
## An Integrated Framework

**Lakshmi Sathyavani**
*TriHealth, USA*

**Sai Krishna Vivek**
*Philips Innovation Campus, India*

**Sai Prasanna Karthik**
*Chaitanya Bharathi Institute of Technology, Hyderabad, India*

## ABSTRACT

*This chapter attempts to expand the knowledge in healthcare supply chain by analyzing the impact of implementation of supply chain practices on the overall performance of organizations in healthcare industry through a systematic literature review. The study also develops an integrated healthcare supply chain framework by linking digital technologies and supply chain practices. This framework will act as a tool and add value to organizations in healthcare industry by specifically providing them with supply chain strategies to achieve improved organizational performance with digital technologies as enablers. The framework will attract special significance in view of the prevailing COVID-19 pandemic situation in which the healthcare sector has played a very vital and major role. It will also be helpful in improving healthcare systems in all types of countries, which is the need of the hour. A systematic analysis of published literature is adopted as the methodology to conduct this research.*

DOI: 10.4018/978-1-7998-9506-0.ch009

Copyright © 2022, IGI Global. Copying or distributing in print or electronic forms without written permission of IGI Global is prohibited.

*Investigating the Influence of Supply Chain Practices*

## INTRODUCTION

The Covid-19 pandemic situation has severely impacted many sectors in the world. The healthcare sector too got influence due to this pandemic. But, at the same time, it is one of the sectors which contributed to the economies of every country and supported the infected people. Healthcare sector employees and all the other stakeholders related to this sector have been providing their services at different levels during this pandemic with utmost commitment levels. Supply chain management has been playing an important role in the distribution, delivery and availability of medicines and vaccines through the world. At the same time, barring Covid19 related activity, there has been an increase in the overall costs in healthcare sector for every patient. This is causing an alarming situation in this sector. Both hospitals and the governments in respective countries have been making efforts to provide best healthcare service by improving their overall organizational performance by optimizing the costs. However, the healthcare organizations, especially the hospitals, face plenty of challenges in achieving this objective due to severe competition, increasing equipment and material costs. Implementation of Supply Chain Management (herein after called as SCM) strategies and supply chain practices (herein after called as SCPs) is found to improve the overall performance of healthcare sector organizations by streamlining the processes to improve the overall patient satisfaction. However, in spite of developments in SCM and innovative SCPs in general, there has been a lukewarm response by the healthcare sector in actively implementing them to achieve the positive outcomes. One of the major reason for this is attributed to the lack of awareness about SCM and lack of visualization of tangible benefits by the healthcare practitioners. This is more prevalent in developing and under-developed countries. To some extent, the developed countries and countries with good healthcare infrastructure have been able to take advantage of SCM and SCPs. However, in order to leverage from SCPs, it is essential that healthcare sector across the world should be strengthened and their systems and processes are redesigned, especially to sustain the pandemic situations successfully. Therefore, this chapter explores the SCPs, investigates their influence on organizational performance of healthcare sector organizations and finally develops an integrated framework.

Today's competitive and dynamic business environment has been making businesses, especially the organizations in healthcare sector to face many issues and challenges. Most of these challenges revolve around optimization of their operations and at the same enhancing the customer / patient satisfaction. In order for these companies to sustain and be competitive, it is highly essential for the top management and the strategic leadership to understand and recognize the importance of implementing practices related to supply chain. This would ensure the individual organizational improvement and at the same time it would also enable the overall growth of all the partners in healthcare sector.

In spite of its advancements and impact on the performance of organizations in many other sectors, implementation of SCM and SCPs in healthcare sector appears to be little unfocused and lacking clarity among its members, especially the suppliers, hospitals, pharmaceutical companies and diagnostic labs. There is an immediate need to orient all the stakeholders of this sector on SCM and SCPs, provide them training and create awareness about implementation of digital technologies to achieve the objectives of optimization and improving customer satisfaction. This comes at a crucial juncture where healthcare organizations have to face additional challenges due to the Covid19 pandemic situation. Healthcare sector organizations need to realize that mutual coordination, trust and integration of processes within the healthcare supply chain to improve the optimization and efficiency. This will ensure the smooth flow of information across this chain. Implementation of digital technologies plays a vital role to achieve this kind of coordination through quick and appropriate information sharing (Gorane and Ravikant, 2016).

Based on the above discussion, the purpose of this chapter is to,

- Explore the role of SCM in healthcare supply chain
- Examine the influence of SCPs on the organizational performance
- Analyze various approaches towards the measurement of SC performance
- Examine the role of digital technologies in achieving Supply Chain Organizational Performance (SCOP) in healthcare sector
- Develop an integrated framework of healthcare supply chain by linking SCPs and digital technologies to achieve SCOP

The present research attempts to achieve the above objectives as presented in the subsequent sections of this chapter.

## BACKGROUND

Increasing costs has been one of the most challenging issue in healthcare sector over the past few years. Nabelsi and Gagnon (2017) found that medical expenditure constituted more than 40 per cent of a hospital's operating costs. An increased effort and focus is visible by both researchers and practitioners on various SCPs to minimize these costs by concentrating on changing nature of SCPs (Agami et al., 2012).

Many authors have defined SCM by considering a wide variety of aspects related to organizations and its partners. Authors also opined that SCM is very broad in nature and it is difficult to precisely conclude what strategies and practices are part of it. Some of the authors focused more on upstream activities of supply chain while some other focused more on downstream activities of it in developing its definition. Another section of authors defined it as an overall technique which integrates both these streams. While most of the earlier definitions of SCM focused on manufacturing sector, recent definitions have expanded them to service sector in which healthcare sector is also included. Authors also attempted to define SCM specifically for healthcare sector in service sector. This brought unique identify to healthcare supply chain. SCM can be defined as the management technique which integrates suppliers, manufacturers, logistics and customers for improving the long-term performance of the individual organization and the SC as a whole. Yet, despite the significant advances in research and practices, many organizations continue to struggle to understand the complex issues associated with the coordinated planning and supply activities amongst the members of their supply networks (Cook et al., 2011).

The definition of SCM with specific focus on healthcare sector has gained significance due to the challenges and issues faced by the members of this sector. In addition to optimization of costs and improving patient satisfaction, these organizations have also diverted their attention towards enhancement of patient treatment and qualities of services provided to patients while maintaining reasonable costs (Zepeda et al., 2016; Kim and Kim, 2019). Supply chain and value chain in healthcare are considered to be two unique chains complementary to each other. While the role of supply chain is to improve smooth flow and efficiencies in processes, the role of value chain is to provide value to the patients and other stakeholders throughout the chain at every stage of it. Basically healthcare value chain consists of five main members. They are producers, purchasers, providers, product intermediaries and fiscal intermediaries (Burns, 2005).

*Investigating the Influence of Supply Chain Practices*

Therefore, focus of organizations, especially hospitals has shifted towards developing capabilities and strengths to streamline the processes related to supply chain and identification of each and every activity which contributes to the value chain. This shift also ensures maintenance of competitiveness of healthcare industry by mitigating the risks successfully. Along with this shift, the members of healthcare industry should also identify, assess and develop plan to mitigate risks through a systematic risk management plan. This kind of plan will ensure that the hospitals and other partners in this sector face the issues and challenges of a prolonged pandemic like Covid19 successfully without much turbulence or disturbance and regain quickly their original status.

Many authors have focused on issues related to sustainability of organizations through SCM and SCPs in the recent past. However, the research related to their application in the field of healthcare is limited, inspite of its wide scope. These studies range from conceptual in nature to empirical by covering aspects like design of service operations, strategies to provide service quality and effective delivery (Kim and Kim, 2019). Authors also opine that the research related to SCM in healthcare sector is more fragmented, even though organizations involved in this sector have started realizing its importance in the recent past. One of the reason for this fragmentation is 'direct' applicability of strategies and practices implemented successfully in manufacturing and other industry sectors to the healthcare sector. It is still highly ambiguous whether all those SCPs whose implementation provided success in other sectors will provide a similar success in healthcare sector or not. Adequate research support is lacking in this aspect to build confidence among the owners and leadership level employees of organizations in healthcare sector. Therefore, there is a need for a comprehensive review to reflect performance in healthcare environments. Without doubt, the complexity of the technologies being used, the existence of multiple stakeholders, a dynamic internal and external environment and distinctive characteristics of health service operations often impede a straight forward application of industrial oriented supply chain management practices. The many problematic projects aiming at implementing integrated planning systems regarding patient flows and establishing partnership relationships between different health service organizations are a clear indication of the difficulties health care organizations are facing when adopting a supply chain management philosophy (Vries and Huijsman, 2011). Application of supply chain management practices in a health care setting is almost by definition related to organizational aspects like building relationships, allocating authorities and responsibilities, and organizing interface processes.

There has been a tremendous growth in the application of technology in healthcare sector in the recent past, especially the digital technologies and wearable devices. Medical practitioners, staff in diagnostic centers, doctors and general patients have been able to use these technologies to successfully perform critical surgeries and to monitor the patients on a continuous basis. Implementation of these technologies by integrating them with the SCPs is found to improve the overall organizational performance in healthcare sector. But, the research on the application of these technologies in healthcare sector to achieve organizational performance is still at a nascent stage. Given this background, this chapter proposes to develop a framework of SC related organizational performance by integrating SCPs through digital technologies as enablers.

## MAIN FOCUS OF THE CHAPTER

### Issues, Controversies and Problems

The main focus of this chapter is on developing an integrated framework of SC related organizational performance by integrating SCPs through digital technologies as enablers and also by highlighting the issues, controversies and problems in the present supply chain of healthcare sector. The research adopts the Systematic Literature Review (SLR) as a methodology to develop the framework. The review is conducted with the objectives of identifying SCPs in healthcare sector, role of SCPs in improving the SC related organizational performance and to identify the technology enablers to achieve this performance. A mix of key words was used to collect appropriate articles from popular research journal databases such as ProQuest, EBSCO, and other Scopus indexed journals. The initial search for articles was done using the key words such as 'supply chain management, 'healthcare supply chain', 'supply chain practices', 'technology enablers' and 'digital technologies'.

Based on the number of articles found through this initial search a second attempt was made to collect more number of articles to suit the multiple research objective of this study. Articles which dealt with only SCM without any mention about HCSC were ignored as they are not relevant to the present study. Also, articles which did not focus on digital technologies were also ignored in the second phase of review as the present study is purely focused on HCSC. All the finalized articles for the purpose of review were critically analyzed to identify the research output and the gaps. This section of the chapter provides an overview of healthcare supply chain, issues and controversies, popular SCPs in this sector and application of digital technologies with a focus on approaches towards SC related organizational performance.

Of late, there has been an increasing awareness and realization among the organizations in healthcare sector to implement SCM and SC related practices and strategies. Many organizations have also started projects which are specific to supply chain implementation (Schneller et al., 2006). Organizations have realized that the application of SCM and SCPs in the health care sector not only relates to physical goods like drugs, pharmaceuticals, medical devices and health aids but also to the flow of patients (Beier, 1995). Major applications of technologies in healthcare sector has been more on monitoring the flow of patients, application of electronic patient record systems (Boonstra and Govers, 2009) and it widely acknowledged that patient-related information systems can significantly contribute to improving the integration and smoothening of processes within and between health service delivery organizations. Another important area of SCM is related to medical supplies. Recent studies reveal that elements like organizational culture, the absence of strong leadership and mandating authority, as well as power and interest relationships between stakeholders might severely hinder the integration and co-ordination of processes along the health care supply chain (McCutcheon and Stuart, 2000; Mandal, 2017).

### Healthcare Supply Chain (HCSC)

Several authors have attempted to define SCM from healthcare perspective. Health Care Supply Chain (herein after referred as HCSC) is considered to be a networked constellation comprising doctors, consultants, specialists, hospitals and clinics, pharmacies, and plans related to health. The ultimate objective of this constellation is to provide value by working together (Ford and Scanlon, 2007). Customer value in healthcare is created through mutual cooperation, coordination and working as a group by the suppliers, customers, hospital employees and strategic partners and others.

*Investigating the Influence of Supply Chain Practices*

One of the recent definition was provided by (Kim and Kim, 2019). According to these authors, HCSC management is an integrated management of material flow, money flow and people flow across all processes and activities of organization to achieve smooth provision of services and flow of activities to enhance patient satisfaction. The authors also were of the opinion that SCM and its practices can be equally applicable to medical industry. The HSCM consists of members like manufacturers, distributors, wholesalers and retailers similar to the supply chains in the industry sector. In healthcare, hospitals depend on many manufacturers and suppliers to procure the items required to manage the hospital. These items range from day-to-day items to long term strategies equipment related items to perform critical surgeries and to diagnose various ailments of patients. At the same time, these items also are procured to provide different types of services to the patients and other stakeholders of hospitals. Authors also classified the manufacturers in healthcare as primary and secondary. A primary manufacturer is the one who produces medical materials and the secondary manufacturer is the one who transforms these medical materials in the form of tablets or capsules. Hospitals and pharmacies directly purchase medical supplies from a distributor when a large amount is required, otherwise from a wholesaler (Kim and Kim, 2019).

Schneller et al, (2006) defined the HCSC as the information, supplies, and finances involved with the acquisition and movement of goods and services from the supplier to the end user in order to enhance clinical outcomes while controlling costs. A hospital is a focal point in HCSC. It can be classified as a service organization whether it is for profit or not-for-profit.

Healthcare industry has been impacted due to the Covid19 pandemic in a severe manner. There is an unprecedented growth in the demand, but at the same time there is a limited capacity. Manufacturers in this sector are compelled to increase their capacities within a very short span of time to meet the demand resulting in achieving low levels of efficiency and organizational performance. (Bohmer et al. 2020). The impact of this pandemic in low and middle-income countries is expected to last for quite a long term even after the pandemic situation (Evans and Over, 2020). It is going to impact mainly the capacities and costs related to public healthcare system, increase the affordability of private healthcare costs, and enhance insurance related costs from 4 to 40% (Adams, 2020). Healthcare supply chains were not ready to deal with the eruption of pandemic of such a long duration (NPR, 2020).

Supply chains in hospitals are unique and they are a little different from the supply chains in industry and manufacturing sector. These supply chains are more complex in nature and require seamless flow of products, uninterrupted delivery of processes and services in order to provide a better and high quality service to patients and improve the overall quality to achieve increased organizational performance (Ramakrishna Yanamandra, 2018). Healthcare supply chains are different from traditional manufacturing supply chains in terms of level of customization required from patient to patient, the variety of problems treated, and requirement of personal care and at the same time to balance the overall costs. Absence of consolidation at the providers' stage, policy issues related to the regulatory authorities, absence of co-ordination and cooperation between the two streams of supply chain, i.e. upstream and downstream are some of the unique features of HCSC. Moreover, members in HCSC act in a more fragmented manner and provide delayed response to the requirements of the other members. The actions of all the members in the HCSC are more individual profit-centered rather than supply chain profit-oriented. Due to this, their focus gets deviated from the end-user i.e. the patient. There is lack of information sharing, mutual cooperation and trust among the members of HCSC because of which ultimately the patient suffers by paying extra money for the inferior services provided (Ramakrishna Yanamandra, 2018). Therefore, achieving organizational performance is always a challenging issue for hospitals in healthcare supply chain. Unlike in other sectors, there is a high degree of involvement of customer / patient in healthcare supply chain (Mathur et al. 2018).

Given this discussion, the next section of this chapter focuses on identification of SCPs and analyzes various approaches towards organizational performance through SCPs.

## Organizational Performance and SC Practices

### SC Practices

Implementation of SC practices for improvement of healthcare organizational performance has been a topic of research since the last two decades. Many authors identified that implementation of SC practices in organizations can develop the abilities to improve the overall organizational performance in terms of many aspects. This is also applicable for organizations in healthcare sector (Cook et al., 2011). This section explores various SCPs, their influence on organizational performance and analyses different approaches to measure performance.

Effective implementation of SCM can optimize the resources required to improve the customer service by developing seamless flow of products, improves process efficiencies and reduces the lead times resulting into lowering of total operations costs (Mathur et al., 2019). Success through SCM is achieved by identifying appropriate SCPs and their systematic implementation (Metilda and Vivekanandam, 2011). As discussed in the previous sections, there is no consensus among authors about what should be included as a part of SCP. Due to the diverse nature of SCM itself, several practices which are not directly related to supply chain are also included as SCPs in the recent past. SCPs are a multi-dimensional concept and defined as the set of activities undertaken in an organization to promote effective downstream and upstream linkages of the SC and any activities within the SC that improves the overall performance of the organization (Li et al. 2006; Gorane and Ravikant, 2016).

Leadership, intra-organizational relationship, inter-organizational relationship, focus on improving the processes, and infrastructural improvement for effective information systems are considered as part of SCPs (Burgress et al. 2006). These practices enable organizations to integrate all stakeholders such as hospitals, doctors, diagnostic centers, pharmacy companies, medical equipment manufacturers, healthcare material manufacturers, suppliers of other items to hospitals, distributors, employees, patients and their dependents. This kind of supply chain integration enables healthcare organizations to achieve organizational performance due to effective inventory control, smooth information flow and processes, effective patient monitoring system and overall quality (Sujatha, 2011; Mathur et al., 2018).

Li et al. (2006) validated six dimensions of SCM practices relating to strategic supplier partnership, customer relationship, information sharing, information quality, internal lean practices and postponement through an empirical survey. SCM integration through SC Practices is linked to organizational competitive capability (Kim, 2006; Mathur et al., 2018). The role of top management plays a crucial role in the implementation of SC practices in organizations (Fawcett et al. 2006; Sandberg and Abrahamsson, 2010; Hariharan et al. 2019). At the same time, the implementation of SCPs seems to be difficult due to the lack of top management support, resistance to share critical information, lack of resources, lack of information technology (IT) infrastructure, unclear organizational objectives and lack of willingness (Pagell and Krause, 2004).

Gorane and Ravikant (2016) summarized the following SCPs based on an exhaustive literature review. They are, Organizational Culture, Customer and Leadership, Information and Communication

*Investigating the Influence of Supply Chain Practices*

Technology, Benchmarking and Performance Measurement, Lean Manufacturing, Agile Manufacturing, Supplier relationship, Outsourcing, Information Sharing, Just-in-Time (JIT), Green Supply Chain Management (GSCM), Reverse Logistics, Postponement, Vendor Managed Inventory (VMI), and Radio Frequency Identification (RFID).

Chong et al. (2019) categorized SCPs into demand management, customer relationship management, supplier relationship management, capacity and resource management, service performance, information and technology management, service supply chain finance, and order process management. Top Management Commitment, Supplier Integration, Lean Principles and Inventory Visibility are considered as the most important SCPs in Healthcare Industry (Mathur et al., 2018).

Almutairi et al. (2020) developed a framework for implementing lean principles in the supply chain management in healthcare organizations and found that lean plays a very vital role in the reduction of wastage, improvement in smooth flow of processes and reduction of waiting time of patients. To successfully manage the pandemic situation, healthcare organizations need to achieve supply chain resilience through a proactive supply chain risk management plan. Resilience in HCSC is defined as the capability of medical SC entities to work in a synchronized manner with an objective of providing uninterrupted medical services to patients in the event of a disruption by instilling a positive organizational culture (Mandal, 2017). Objectives of resilience in healthcare organization such as visibility, velocity and flexibility are achieved through collaborative activities like information-sharing, collaborative communication, joint knowledge creation and joint relationship efforts (Scholten and Schilder, 2015). Healthcare sector organizations should equip themselves by acquiring the abilities to respond and recover quickly from the increasing disruptions, uncertainties and the risks due to pandemic situations. These organizations should display a proactive and positive organizational culture acting as a cohesive group to develop innovative strategies during the disruptions (Mandal, 2017).

Such an organizational culture is achieved in supply chains of healthcare sector through successful collaboration, cooperation and integration by promoting flexibility in development and execution of policies and procedures and by removing the existing barriers or functional silos (Birkinshaw *et al.*, 2016).

## Role of SCPs in Healthcare Organizational Performance

Role of SCPs in influence of SC related organizational performance has been an important focus area in research in the recent past. Different authors proposed different dimensions to understand the influence of SCPs in HCSC. While some focused on five dimensions i) flexibility, ii) integration, iii) responsiveness towards the patient, iv) performance of the physician, and v) quality of partnerships (Dobrzykowski, 2010), some others developed a framework showing factors such as standardized drug coding, operational re-engineering and implementing information technology that help in performance improvement of healthcare supply chain (Kritchanchai, 2012). Further, Aptel and Porjalaji (2001) advocated that JIT philosophy applied to hospitals results in inventory cost reduction and improved performance of the supply chain. Bakar et al. (2010) discussed on the importance of the dimensions of Doctor's satisfaction and supply chain inputs for better SCPs.

During the current Covid19 pandemic situation, several companies such as Airbus, Diageo and Rolls-Royce have displayed proactive SC collaborations to meet the needs of healthcare organizations by realigning their product offerings, processes and supply chains to manufacture essential items for healthcare operations, such as PPE kits, hand sanitizers and ventilators (Davies, 2020). The current pandemic also created a knowledge of possible risks of future and exposed the loopholes and gaps in

*Investigating the Influence of Supply Chain Practices*

the existing healthcare infrastructure globally. Many countries, including the developed countries with highly adequate healthcare facilities faced severe turmoil in managing the Covid19 situation. There was severe mismatch between the capacities and demand (Leite H., et al. 2020). Therefore, to achieve quality in HCSC, factors such as the qualification of medical personnel, hospital facilities, adequacy of capacity, integration of all members involved and the availability of up-to-date equipment (Senbekov et al. 2020) is very essential. This surely calls for dependence of HCSC on digital technologies in future and also implementing the existing SCPs through these technologies (Mathur et al., 2018). The next section of this chapter focuses on digital technologies which would enable improve performance of healthcare sector organization through HCSC and SCPs.

## Digital Technologies in HCSC

As discussed in the previous sections, technology dependence seems to be inevitable for sustainability in HCSC. Inspite of its tremendous growth in hospitals and other members of HCSC, many other partners, suppliers and distributors are yet to grab the technology for their supply chain operations and also to implement SCPs through digital technologies. A member of SC healthcare is considered to be technology-focused, if the member acquires the ability to integrate all the processes on a real-time basis, able to share information with all the members of supply chain and provide seamless flow of services through online platform to the patients and their dependents. It increases the capacity to provide effective healthcare services, with updated technologies ensuring enhanced customer value and satisfaction. Therefore, healthcare organizations which embrace technologies within a very short span of time would be in an advantageous position for achieving better supply chain performance. It can enable such entities to become technology leaders and can generate innovative performance with better supply coordination and sharing of information (Ho et al, 2016; Mandal, 2017). Technology integration and digitization of supply chains would enhance the ability of healthcare organizations to perform better by exchanging information instantly and it would also enhance mutual coordination among the supply chain members. Many other benefits such as better accessibility for patients and their dependents, availability of all types of information readily on hand, possibility of online consultation (more useful during Covid19 pandemic situation), integration of suppliers, distributors, healthcare centers, doctors, diagnostic centers and self-monitoring of patients by themselves are possible due to technology. Some of the features of technology-enabled HCSC are telemedicine which reduces the digital divide between rural-urban and other regions and also reduces the patient's travel and exposure to groups, especially during the Covid-19 pandemic situation (Senbekov et al. 2020).

Big data, artificial intelligence, telemedicine, block-chain platforms, smart devices, Internet-of-things (IOT), Robotics, and Machine Learning comprise the set of digital technologies used to improve the supply chain performance in healthcare sector. The Covid19 pandemic has disrupted the healthcare sector drastically (Nnaji et al., 2020). But, at the same time, it is the contribution from healthcare sector which has been saving millions of lives across the world during this pandemic. Research in this sector has also resulted in the invention and distribution of several vaccines for Covid19. Digital technologies have played a very crucial role in coordination among members of HCSC, analysis, interpretation and prediction of spread of virus. These technologies enabled the implementation of several services such as telemedicine, e-medicine, online consultations and online diagnosis for patients. Healthcare supply chains heavily depended on these technologies for a smooth distribution of medicines, kits, vaccines and other infrastructure required for hospitals across the world (Senbekov et al. 2020; Tiffany et al., 2020).

*Investigating the Influence of Supply Chain Practices*

Application of 3D printing technology for manufacturing models of organs, permanent implants, testing medical devices, personalized 3D drug printing, and medical education are also other major contributions of digital technologies in HCSC (Senbekov et al. 2020).

Digital technology like Artificial Intelligence (AI) has the ability to drastically improve the capability of diagnostic platforms and thus improve the information sharing ability in HCSC. It also has the ability to optimize the HCSC processes, especially the treatment related activities and increases the efficiency of medical procedures, makes the patients more happy, and ultimately it can also lead to optimization of costs through efficient supply chain processes. Applications of AI have also yielded in successful conduct of clinical trials, biomedical experiments, and reduced the requirement of labor. At the same time, it enabled the continuous monitoring of patients, management of their health related data, integration of surgical procedures, and performing surgeries through remote guidance by experts, improved the self-monitoring ability of patients, and reduced the frequency of visits to the doctor atleast for many regular and manageable ailments. It also provided huge benefits to the processes related to cancer treatment, heart surgeries, orthopedics, mental ailments, imaging and radiation (Senbekov et al. 2020).

Inspite of its huge success, the usage and awareness about role of digital technologies in HCSC is not yet widespread in several countries due to many issues and challenges, especially in some of the developing and under-developed countries. Vast majority of people in these regions do not have access to basic healthcare facilities and infrastructure due to poor supply chain systems and network. Research in this area also needs to be focused more towards providing solutions to such challenges and issues (He, 2019; Lapointe, 2020; Senbekov et al. 2020). Also, issues related to ethics, data privacy, and protection of patient personal data needs to be concentrated (Segura et al. 2018). All this needs a technology-oriented strong supply chain infrastructure with the support from digital technologies.

Another important technology to improve the performance of HCSC is 'Big Data'. Application of big data has yielded tremendous results in industry supply chain and it is now widely used in HCSC too. In recent decades, big data has been increasingly used to improve and optimize the management, analysis, and forecasting in HCSC. Application of big data systems in the management of HCSC has the potential to improve the quality, the efficiency of the service, lower the cost of care, number of medical errors and overall improve the Electronic Documentation System (Shafqat et al., 2020). In addition, the introduction of big data in HCSC will enable e-health systems through SCPs which will allow doctors to write out and send electronic prescriptions directly to the pharmacy network, which will also significantly reduce the problem of patient queues in clinics and paperwork (Dash et al., 2019).

The third most important digital technology to enhance the performance of HCSC is the application of Block-chain technology. It is based on a peer-to-peer platform that provides an opportunity to securely store the information on thousands of servers. This information can be simultaneously used and shared within a decentralized and open network. Such an approach makes it difficult for the user to control or change it. Thus, block-chain technology with unique characteristics, such as decentralization, transparency, and anonymity, has been increasingly used in HCSC (Hasselgren et al. 2020). Digital technologies in HCSC have also reached to the level of simple 'Wearable devices'. These devices work through the implementation of SCPs like information sharing among doctors, patients, diagnostic centers and pharmacy stores. These devices have the ability to store the patient's data and enable self-monitoring by themselves. In light of recent global challenges, such as the COVID-19 pandemic, the use of smart devices will play an increasingly important role in remote health monitoring (Segura et al., 2018; Dash et al., 2019; Persky, 2020). However, inspite of all these benefits, many issues related to digital health

167

technologies in HCSC remain unmet, including the reliability, safety, testing, and ethical aspects (Senbekov et al. 2020).

Lot of research has been done in this sector during the last ten years. However, the focus on developing integrated frameworks by combining SC practices and Digital Technologies with SC Performance as an outcome has been missing. Authors have emphasized solely on SC practices useful for healthcare sector and Digital technologies useful for healthcare sector in an individual manner. Therefore, this chapter expands the knowledge of SC practices and application of digital technologies in healthcare sector and attempts to develop an integrated framework with organizational performance as an outcome.

## SOLUTIONS AND RECOMMENDATIONS

An integrated framework for HCSC is developed to provide a solution to the problems, issues and controversies mentioned in the previous section as shown in Figure 1.

*Figure 1. Integrated framework of healthcare supply chain management*

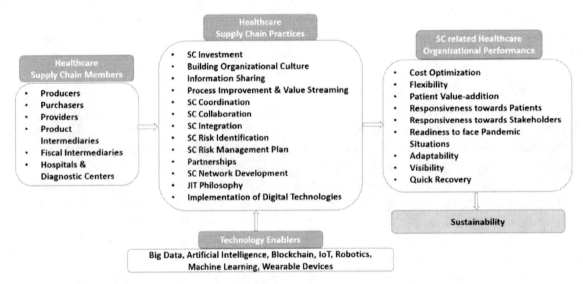

## DISCUSSION OF FRAMEWORK AND RESULTS

The above framework in figure 1 depicts the relationship and inter-dependence among various aspects like members of SCM, SCPs in healthcare sector, and organizational performance measures. HCSM consists of five members (Burns, 2005).

In this proposed framework, an additional member 'diagnostic centers' are newly added by the author as the existing models clearly do not mention about this. Providers are supposed to be service providers which should include hospitals and diagnostic centers. But, as the existing research does not mention about this aspect clearly, it is added newly in this framework by the author. This corroborates with the findings of Kim and Kim, (2019) which mentions manufacturers, distributors, wholesalers and

*Investigating the Influence of Supply Chain Practices*

retailers as members of HSCM. All these members depend on each other through the SCPs mentioned under healthcare SCPs. In the existing traditional supply chains, most of these practices are limited to individual members rather than a collective implementation. Healthcare supply chains will be successful and sustainable only through an integrated and collective implementation of Healthcare SCPs. Therefore, the present study links the members of HCSC with its SCPs. This linkage would enable the achievement of improved supply chain related organizational performance in healthcare organizations. These organization would be able to build their supply chain capabilities related to cost optimization, flexibility, patient value-addition, responsiveness towards patients, responsiveness towards other stakeholders, develop readiness to face pandemic situations through proactive planning, develop adaptability and visibility to quickly recover from disruptions. However, these performance abilities are possible only when the members of HCSC implement the SCPs in an integrated manner by implementing the digital technologies as 'enablers'. Thus, the unique contribution of this research is development of an integrated framework which links HCSC members, healthcare SCPs and the digital technology enablers to achieve the ultimate objectives of improving the SC related organizational performance leading to sustainability.

## FUTURE RESEARCH DIRECTIONS AND IMPLICATIONS

The outcome of this study provided very interesting insights in the field of healthcare supply chain. The study identified the gaps in the previous works and provided a solution through an integrated framework by linking members of HCSC, SCPs and Technology Enablers to achieve the SC related organization performance. The implications of this study are from two perspectives. The first one is related to expansion of existing contextual knowledge in the field of HCSC and provides new vistas of research. Whereas, the second one is related to practicing managers in HCSC. The owners, employees and other stakeholders of members of HCSC can apply this framework to precisely practice SCPs to reach their objectives of improving the SC related organizational performance. By correctly identifying the practices and by integrating those practices with the existing SC processes through a mutual dependence, information sharing, and integration, healthcare organizations can achieve the performance to reach the goal of sustainability with the supporting and enabling role of digital technologies. Thus, the implications of this study are value-adding to both researchers and industry practitioners.

## CONCLUSION

Majority of organizations in healthcare sector have been severely impacted due to Covid-19 pandemic situation. However, it is the one of the sectors which contributed immensely to the economies of different countries. Members of this sector have been working day and night in multiple ways to protect the lives of humanity from the virus. One of the major challenges faced by the healthcare organizations is soaring costs of operations.

This research found that implementation of SCM practices can develop the abilities to achieve positive outcomes for organizations in healthcare sector. But, most of the organizations do not have clear understanding and knowledge of these practices due to various reasons, issues and challenges. Therefore, identifying this needs, the present research is conducted to develop an integrated framework of HCSC.

It concluded that all the members of HCSC should integrate their supply chain related activities and processes on a mutual basis and implement SCPs to achieve positive outcomes related to supply chain related organizational performance. It is also concluded that linking the members of supply chain and SCPs through 'technology enablers' can develop the abilities to achieve supply chain related organizational performance and move the organizations towards sustainability in long run.

It is also concluded that implementation of SCPs through digital technologies like big data, artificial intelligence, robotics, block-chain technology, internet-of-things, machine learning and wearable devices can directly contribute to the development of SC related organizational performance and sustainability.

The integrated framework developed in this research can enhance the organizational performance of organizations in healthcare sector. However, there is an immediate need to create knowledge and awareness among the owners, employees and other important stakeholders of these organizations about SCM, SCPs, digital technologies and dimensions of organizational performance.

In spite of interesting outcomes, this chapter has its own limitations. One of the major limitation is the methodology. The chapter needs to be suppSCPorted with an empirical survey and validate the framework developed.

# REFERENCES

Adams, K. (2020). *Will the Pandemic Mean Higher Health Care Costs in the Future*. Available at: https://www.marketplace.org/2020/03/31/will-the-pandemic-mean-higher-health-care-costs-in-the-future/

Agami. (2012). Supply chain performance measurement approaches: review and classification. *Journal of Organizational Management Studies*.

Almutairi, A. M., Salonitis, K., & Al-Ashaab, A. (2020). A framework for implementing lean principles in the supply chain management at health-care organizations Saudi's perspective. *International Journal of Lean Six Sigma*, *11*(3), 463–492. doi:10.1108/IJLSS-01-2019-0002

Aptel, O., & Pourjalali, H. (2001). Improving activities and decreasing costs of logistics in hospitals: A comparison of US and French hospitals. *The International Journal of Accounting*, *36*(1), 65–90. doi:10.1016/S0020-7063(01)00086-3

Bakar, A. H., Lukman Hakim, I., Chong, S. C., & Lin, B. (2010). Measuring supply chain performance among public hospital laboratories. *International Journal of Productivity and Performance Management*, *59*(1), 75–97. doi:10.1108/17410401011006121

Beier, F. J. (1995). The management of the supply chain for hospital pharmacies: A focus on inventory management practices. *Journal of Business Logistics*, *16*(2), 153–173.

Birkinshaw, J., Zimmermann, A., & Raisch, S. (2016). How do firms adapt to discontinuous change. *California Management Review*, *58*(4), 36–58. doi:10.1525/cmr.2016.58.4.36

Bohmer, R. M. J., Pisano, G. P., Sadun, R., & Tsai, T. C. (2020). How hospitals can manage supply chain shortages as demand surges. *Harvard Business Review*.

Boonstra, A. (2006). Interpreting an ERP-implementation project from a stakeholder perspective. *International Journal of Project Management*, *24*(1), 38–52. doi:10.1016/j.ijproman.2005.06.003

*Investigating the Influence of Supply Chain Practices*

Burgress, K., Singh, P. J., & Koroglu, R. (2006). Supply chain management: A structured literature review and implications for future research. *International Journal of Operations & Production Management, 26*(7), 703–729. doi:10.1108/01443570610672202

Burns, L. R. (2005). *The Business of Healthcare Innovation.* Cambridge University Press. doi:10.1017/CBO9780511488672

Cook, L. S., Heiser, D. R., & Sengupta, K. (2011). The moderating effect of supply chain role on the relationship between supply chain practices and performance: An empirical analysis. *International Journal of Physical Distribution & Logistics Management, 41*(2), 104–134. doi:10.1108/09600031111118521

Dash, S., Shakyawar, S. K., Sharma, M., & Kaushik, S. (2019). Big data in healthcare: Management, analysis and future prospects. *Journal of Big Data, 6*(1), 1–25. doi:10.118640537-019-0217-0

Dezdar, S., & Sulaiman, A. (2009). Successful enterprise resource-planning implementation: Taxonomy of critical factors. *Industrial Management & Data Systems, 109*(8), 1037–1052. doi:10.1108/02635570910991283

Dobrzykowski, D. A. (2010). *Linking Antecedents and Consequences of Value Density in the Healthcare Delivery Supply Chain* (Doctoral Thesis). University of Toledo.

Evans, D., & Over, M. (2020). *The Economic Impact of COVID-19 in Low- and Middle-Income Countries.* Available at: https://www.cgdev.org/blog/economic-impact-covid-19-low-and-middle-income-countries

Fawcett, S. E., Ogden, J. A., Magnan, G. M., & Cooper, M. B. (2006). Organizational commitment and governance for supply chain success. *International Journal of Physical Distribution & Logistics Management, 36*(1), 22–45. doi:10.1108/09600030610642913

Ford, E., & Scanlon, D. (2007). Promise and problems with supply chain management approaches to healthcare purchasing. *Health Care Management Review, 32*(3), 192–202. doi:10.1097/01.HMR.0000281623.35987.cf PMID:17666990

Gorane, S. J., & Kant, R. (2016). Supply chain practices: An implementation status in Indian manufacturing organizations. *Benchmarking, 23*(5), 1076–1110. doi:10.1108/BIJ-06-2014-0059

Hariharan, G., Suresh, G. P., & Sagunthala, C. (2019). Critical Success Factors for the Implementation of Supply Chain Management in SMEs. *International Journal of Recent Technology and Engineering, 7*(5S3), 540-543.

Hasselgren, A., Kralevska, K., Gligoroski, D., Pedersen, S. A., & Faxvaag, A. (2020). Blockchain in healthcare and health sciences-a scoping review. *International Journal of Medical Informatics, 134*, 104040. doi:10.1016/j.ijmedinf.2019.104040 PMID:31865055

He, J. X., Baxter, S. L., Xu, J., Xu, J. M., Zhou, X. T., & Zhang, K. (2019). The practical implementation of artificial intelligence technologies in medicine. *Nature Medicine, 25*(1), 30–36. doi:10.103841591-018-0307-0 PMID:30617336

Kim, C., & Kim, H. J. (2019). A study on healthcare supply chain management efficiency: Using bootstrap data envelopment analysis. *Health Care Management Science, 2*(3), 534–548. doi:10.100710729-019-09471-7 PMID:30830500

Kritchanchai, D. (2012). A framework for healthcare supply chain improvement in Thailand. *Operations and Supply Chain Management, 5*(2), 103–113.

Lapointe, L., Lavallee-Bourget, M. H., Pichard-Jolicoeur, A., Turgeon-Pelchat, A., & Fleet, R. (2020). Impact of telemedicine on diagnosis, clinical management and outcomes in rural trauma patients: A rapid review. *Canadian Journal of Rural Medicine, 25*(1), 31–40. doi:10.4103/CJRM.CJRM_8_19 PMID:31854340

Lauren, W. (2020). Wearable technology and live video conferencing: The development of an affordable virtual teaching platform to enhance clinical skills education during the COVID-19 pandemic. *Canadian Medical Education Journal, 11*(5). Advance online publication. doi:10.36834/cmej.70554 PMID:33062106

Li, S., Ragu-Nathan, B., Ragu-Nathan, T. S., & Subba Rao, S. (2006). The impact of supply chain management practices on competitive advantage and organizational performance. *Omega, 34*(2), 107–124. doi:10.1016/j.omega.2004.08.002 PMID:17876965

Li, S., Rao, S. S., Ragu-Nathan, T. S., & Ragu-Nathan, B. (2005). Development and validation of a measurement instrument for studying supply chain management practices. *Journal of Operations Management, 23*(6), 618–641. doi:10.1016/j.jom.2005.01.002

Mandal, S. (2017). The influence of organizational culture on healthcare supply chain resilience: Moderating role of technology orientation. *Journal of Business and Industrial Marketing, 32*(8), 1021–1037. doi:10.1108/JBIM-08-2016-0187

Mathur, B., Gupta, S., Meena, M. L., & Dangayach, G. S. (2018). Healthcare supply chain management: Literature review and some issues. *Journal of Advances in Management Research, 15*(3), 265–287. doi:10.1108/JAMR-09-2017-0090

McCutcheon, D., & Stuart, F. I. (2000). Issues in the choice of supplier alliance partners. *Journal of Operations Management, 18*(3), 279–303. doi:10.1016/S0272-6963(99)00026-1

Meijboom, B., Saskia Schmidt-Bakx, S., & Westert, G. (2011). Supply chain management practices for improving patient-oriented care. *Supply Chain Management, 16*(3), 166–175. doi:10.1108/13598541111127155

Metilda, R. M., & Vivekanandan, K. (2011). Impact of supply chain management practices on the competitive advantage of Indian retail supermarkets. *International Journal of Logistics Systems and Management, 9*(2), 170–185. doi:10.1504/IJLSM.2011.041504

Nnaji, C., Okpala, I., & Awolusi, I. (2020). Wearable Sensing Devices: Potential Impact and Current Use for Incident Prevention. *American Society of Safety Engineers Professional Safety, 65*(4), 1–9.

NPR. (2020). *As the Pandemic Spreads, Will There Be Enough Ventilators? There-Be-Enough-Ventilators.* Available at: https://www.npr.org/sections/health-shots/2020/03/14/815675678/as-the-pandemic-spreads-will-there-be-enough-ventilators

Pagell, M., & Krause, D. R. (2004). Re-exploring the relationship between flexibility and the external environment. *Journal of Operations Management, 21*(6), 629–649. doi:10.1016/j.jom.2003.11.002

Persky, S. (2020). A virtual home for the virtual clinical trial. *Journal of Medical Internet Research, 22*(1), e15582. doi:10.2196/15582 PMID:31899455

Sandberg, E., & Abrahamsson, M. (2010). The role of top management in supply chain management practices. *International Journal of Retail & Distribution Management, 38*(1), 57–69. doi:10.1108/09590551011016331

Schneller, E. S., Schmeltzer, L. R., & Burns, L. R. (2006). *Strategic Management of the Health Care Supply Chain*. Jossey-Bass.

Scholten, K., & Schilder, S. (2015). The role of collaboration in supply chain resilience. *Supply Chain Management, 20*(4), 471–484. doi:10.1108/SCM-11-2014-0386

Segura, A., Abeer, L. H. A., Costadopoulos, N., & Prasad, P. W. C. (2018). Ethical Implications of User Perceptions of WDs. *Science and Engineering Ethics, 24*(1), 1–28. doi:10.100711948-017-9872-8 PMID:28155094

Senbekov, M., Saliev, T., Bukeyeva, Z., Almabayeva, A., Zhanaliyeva, M., Aitenova, N., Toishibekov, Y., & Fakhradiyev, I. (2020). The Recent Progress and Applications of Digital Technologies in Healthcare: A Review. *International Journal of Telemedicine and Applications*. doi:10.1155/2020/8830200

Shafqat, S., Kishwer, S., Rasool, R. U., Qadir, J., Amjad, T., & Ahmad, H. F. (2020). Big data analytics enhanced healthcare systems: A review. *The Journal of Supercomputing, 76*(3), 1754–1799. doi:10.100711227-017-2222-4

Sujatha, R. (2011). Role of intelligent agents in facilitating information flow in supply chain management. *International Journal of Logistics Systems and Management, 9*(2), 229–237. doi:10.1504/IJLSM.2011.041508

Tiffany C, Frost, A. S., Brody, R. M., Byrnes, Y. M., Cannady, S. B., Luu, N. N., Rajasekaran, K., Shanti, R. M., Silberthau, K. R., Triantafillou, V., & Newman, J. G. (2020). Creation of an Interactive Virtual Surgical Rotation for Undergraduate Medical Education during the COVID-19 Pandemic. *Journal of Surgical Education*. doi:10.1016/j.jsurg.2020.06.039

Vries, J., & Huijsman, R. (2011). Supply chain management in health services: An overview. *Supply Chain Management, 16*(3), 159–165. doi:10.1108/13598541111127146

Yanamandra, R. (2018). Development of an integrated healthcare supply chain model, *Supply Chain Forum. International Journal (Toronto, Ont.), 19*(2), 111–121. doi:10.1080/16258312.2018.1475823

## KEY TERMS AND DEFINITIONS

**Digital Technologies:** A set of technologies such as big data, artificial intelligence, block-chain technologies, machine learning, internet-of-things, robotics and wearable devices used for accumulating, storing, analyzing the data to provide better results and output to the users.

**Healthcare Supply Chain:** A network of different entities of business organizations such as suppliers, hospitals, diagnostic centers, doctors, pharmaceutical companies, distributors, dealers and retailers working together to provide enhanced service to the patient.

**Supply Chain Integration:** A process of integrating all the activities and processes involved in the supply, procurement, manufacturing, distribution and selling functions of different group of organizations through mutual cooperation and coordination by sharing information.

**Supply Chain Management:** It is the process of integrating the activities of all the members of supply chain such as suppliers, manufacturers, distributors, retailers, and customers to achieve the overall objectives of improving the product and service availability to enhance the customer satisfaction.

**Supply Chain Practices:** A set of practices involved in managing the activities related to sourcing, procuring, producing and distributing in a network of business organizations.

**Supply Chain-Related Organizational Performance:** The performance achieved by an organization through the implementation of supply chain practices, generally measurable in terms of financial indicators.

# Chapter 10
# Revamping Reverse Logistics to Enhance Customer Satisfaction

**Leena Wanganoo**
*University of Petroleum and Energy Studies, India*

**Rajesh Tripathi**
*University of Petroleum and Energy Studies, India*

**Ramakrishna Yanamandra**
https://orcid.org/0000-0001-9101-6072
*Skyline University College, UAE*

## ABSTRACT

*The cross-border reverse logistics operations are different from forward logistics. They are complex and fragmented due to multiple intermediaries participating in the operation. The retailer goes through a re-export process to fulfil the customs documentation requirement in the reverse logistics process. A heavy paper process with low digitization, low transparency, and multiple entities is the trickiest barrier to optimizing the process and achieving customer satisfaction. Integration of technology with external organizations will aid in improving real-time visibility in the process. Blockchain and other emerging technologies have the potential to improve the reverse logistics process and contracts with intermediaries. The objective of this chapter is twofold. At first, the author reviewed the main barriers in the cross-border reverse logistics operation and later provided an insight on the potential of blockchain technology in the process.*

## INTRODUCTION

The retail e-commerce sector has grown exponentially and faces challenges of the high product return. With the dynamic change in customer behaviour, import and export laws and regulation cross – border logistics is a limitation and main obstacle to the long term sustainability of the business. Therefore, logistics-related issues and integrated technology are the biggest concern, as the returns are complex due to the long-distance transportation and multiple intermediaries working on different systems. The

DOI: 10.4018/978-1-7998-9506-0.ch010

Copyright © 2022, IGI Global. Copying or distributing in print or electronic forms without written permission of IGI Global is prohibited.

traditional logistics system is paper-heavy and suffers inadequate to manage the new challenges of reverse logistics. To enhance speed and visibility, implementing an advanced technology system is essential. But firms do not know the technology's potential and opportunity and how a competitive logistics strategy can enhance cross-border e-commerce satisfaction.

The differentiation and performance of cross border B2C e-commerce are attributed to major key drivers - advanced technology as an integrator. Global e-commerce has expanded by emerging technologies (Saeed et al., 2005). Custom documentation, duty reversal, re-export rules and regulation, and credit transfer complicate cross-border returns operations. A major global challenge is that most countries still have outdated customs systems and manual procedures. Local customs procedure for the imports and re-export rules and regulation and bank intervention for the credit transfer led to extensive paperwork and coordination with multiple intermediaries are the biggest challenges in the returns.

Moreover, as reverse logistics engages multimodal transportation, it raises a fragmented supply chain, leading to delays in the exchange of product and credit transfer for returns. Thus, lack of real-time visibility with limited transparency and different information systems make tracking online orders makes reverse logistics more complex. For the same reason, most often, the customer hesitates to buy the products from cross-border companies.

The reverse logistics operational issues, specific in cross-border e-commerce, are fairly new topics and warrant investigation. Poorly managed reverse logistics operations result in customer dissatisfaction and higher cost. Emerging technologies like Blockchain can provide an integrated solution due to its high operations scalability, real-time visibility, transparency, and collaboration with multiple intermediaries.

Hence, this chapter aims to characteristics and barriers of cross-border reverse logistics. And further, the study intends to highlight the potential of Blockchain technology for the cross-border e-commerce sector. Finally, this chapter provides a guideline for both the e-retailers and logistics providers to achieve an agile and interoperable reverse logistics operation. This blockchain technology-based framework to manage reverse logistics offers academics and practitioners insights into the opportunities, current standing, and the future implementation approach.

## BACKGROUND

### Global Growth in Cross-Border B2C E-commerce sector and Returns Landscape

Pandemic has bought a massive transformation in consumer buying behaviour leading to an enormous surge in the global e-commerce sector. As globalization intensifies, cross-border B2C e-commerce is a key driver for sustainable growth. Cross-border e-commerce is defined as transactions through the computer network, using cross-border logistics services, selling the product and service to customers worldwide. (Shi, Y., & Li, X., 2018). Cross-border e-commerce transactions were valued around the US $ 130 TN in 2019, with the volume raised by 4 per cent. (P.Bruno et al.,2020) Which grew by 21% per cent in 2020 compared to 2019, with almost 55 per cent of the online customer making a cross-border purchase. (Daniel Webber., 2021). Table (1) shows that region-wise, Southeast Asia is one of the major centres and amounts to more than 40% of the global sales value for B2C online cross-border.

*Table 1. Region-wise cross-border e- Commerce value and contribution to total trade volume*

| Region | Online e-Commerce Value *(In Billion US Dollars)* | Percentage contribution in the total trade Volume |
|---|---|---|
| Asia Pacific | 405 | 53.60% |
| Western Europe | 143 | 18.90% |
| North America | 109 | 14.40% |
| Latin America | 47 | 6.20% |
| Mid- Eastern Europe | 32 | 4.20% |
| Middle East & Africa | 21 | 2.70% |

(Source: Accenture report 2020)

Though the online cross-border is growing as well as provides an opportunity to reach new customers, expand the market, and reach faster-growing markets, the accelerated growth rate indicates that the trend will not fade post-pandemic.

The key growth drivers are as follows:

- Increased Global Internet connectivity.
- Raise in cross-border internet traffic
- Increase in Online sales platforms and channels
- Technology advancement aiding for digital trading of the goods.

## The Surge in Product Returns

"Product returns" are essential post-purchase processes because the customer does not physically inspect and touch the product before ordering the same (Yan & Cao, 2017). To build customer confidence and reliability, the retailer's offer of "Free Return Shipping" is one of the topmost incentives for online shopping; it encourages sales and enhances confidence. (King.,2016). Liberal return policy stimulates higher sales volumes and higher value-buying, leading to higher product returns. (Shehu et al.,2020). The amount of B2C e-commerce returns are anticipated to cost companies more than a trillion dollars a year as the reverse logistics cost per product ranges between the US $ 6 to the US $ 18. (Economist 2013).

Additionally, published reports indicate that the return rate for products purchased online is approx. 8-10% higher than brick and mortar stores, and around 30% of the customer returns the total sales revenue. The e-trailers face a constant challenge due to cross-border operational complexities regarding returns. Return Management and Reverse logistics are synonymous with each other. (Ramírez, 2012); Previous researchers termed reverse logistics as a subset of returns management dealing with the flow of goods from the customer back to the supplier (Rogers et al., 2002; Diane et al., 2005). With the exponential growth in online buying, Figure 1 shows that the total global reverse logistics market is growing at a CAGR of 4.67% from 2017 to 2025 and is forecasted to reach $ 821 BN by 2025 (Statistica.com.,2021)

*Figure 1. Market size of Reverse Logistics*
Source: Statistica.com

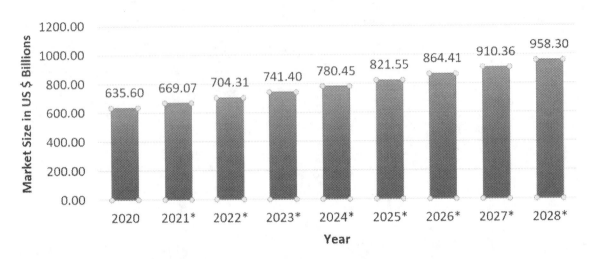

Though there is upward growth in the cross–border trade, buying long-distance is always a hassle for many reasons. Converting local currency to foreign currency, complicated order placement websites, duties, taxes for shipping, and cumbersome return of goods process are a few of them. E-commerce reverse logistics has different economics and optimization approaches - forecasting the volume and frequency is way more complicated due to the uncertainty of online returns. (Lindsey, 2016). In the B2C e-commerce context, most often, the product is not returned because of the poor quality or damage in the product but because of the customer's negative post-purchase product evaluation. Negative post-purchase product evaluations often arise due to the customers' limited ability to evaluate and test products before purchasing them. (Minnema et al.,2016). Customers return in the online purchase is much more than the traditional in-store transactions due to the imbalance in information exchanges. The reverse Logistics process involves customers returning products to maximize customer value and minimize costs. (Stanton.,2018).

The product returns in the B2C context is classified into three phases. Figure 2 shows the three categories of product returns from the entities such as manufacturer, distributor, and customer (De Brito & Dekker, 2004).

*Figure 2. Categories of e-commerce Product Return*
*(Source: Roger et al. 2002)*

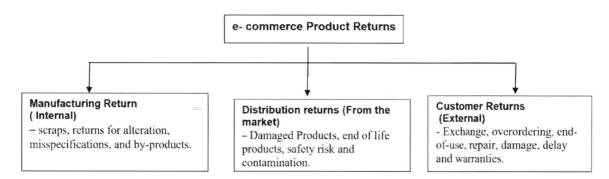

Customer Returns is always a grave issue for the e-commerce supply chain, with higher online returns than offline store sales (Vlachos et al.,2003; de Araújo et al., 2017). Reduction in the volume of returns from the customer is beyond the control of the original producer. Thus it is important to develop a simple and lean process. Consumer returns is a strategic part of the business and form part of the value creation in e-commerce. The handling of reverse logistics in context to e-commerce is of great implication. Traditionally handling consumer returns without knowing the reason for the return and underlying expectation is mere wastage of the e-trailer and logistics providers resources. (Dissanayake, D. et al. 2007)

As an important measure of consumer satisfaction, logistics services are a decisive and competitive factor in e-commerce. The cross-border Third-Party logistics provider (3PL) services, including numerous forwarders, customs agents and air freight forwarders, have evolved into key players in cross-border logistics in recent years. (He, X. et al., 2021).

The most complex issue is reverse logistics in e-commerce. As online transaction is intangible in nature, the "problems" of product logistics cannot be underestimated. Researchers have highlighted the significance of reverse logistics in B2C e-commerce. The literature review suggests that logistics is an important aspect of e-commerce initiatives.

Reverse logistics has been receiving attention from academics and practitioners because the e-trailers are much concerned about product returns (Petersen & Kumar, 2015); (Venkatesan & Kumar, 2018), as future online intention depends on product return is performed. (Petersen & Kumar, 2015). Hence, there is a need to identify the operational barriers and technologies to improve their reverse logistics processes. Retailers may need to integrate and enhance the technological capabilities of the reverse logistics operation with multiple channels and participants efficiently. There's no denying that ineffective reverse logistics management can negatively impact companies' profitability (Lindsey, 2016).

Most importantly, the cross-border return is subjected to reversal of documents in the customs and re-export procedures. Import duty which was paid earlier, need to revise which the goods are to be returned. The customs documentation must be proper to mitigate risk charges or penalties with the local logistics companies to the supplier and retailer. Another concern is the longer return windows add further complexity to the return of goods. To overcome the return management distress, the retailer should invest in logistics' physical and digital infrastructure - a system that protects the business and brings agility to the ecosystem. Hence, a solid and differentiated strategy is vital for the survival and growth of cross-border online selling. E-tailers have to focus on their service performance for the newfound customer across the globe to penetrate a new geographical market. (Mukherjee et al., 2020). The customs in many countries lack digital and technological readiness, which leads to delay in re-export and significantly high costs, which substantially impacts e-commerce businesses. Companies do not have the technological capability to integrate with intermediaries, particularly in a paper-based system. These procedures substantially impact small e-commerce companies that ship the return products to multiple destinations; they do not benefit from the economies of scale incur hefty administrative costs. The high costs incurred due to customs delays, late delivery, or ineffective return procedures greatly impact SMEs' bottom lines. However, discussions on types of returns and integration of the multimodal transportation sector, in general, are beyond the scope of this study.

## The Reverse Logistics Characteristics

The improvement in the reverse logistic operation is essential because the perceived risk is higher when the customer buys from a global e- trailer, so reverse logistics is critical for customer retention. Having a robust and agile returns process is an essential part of cross-border selling. The process of cross-border returns remains the same as domestic returns. Figure 3 describes the characteristics of reverse logistics –

*Figure 3. Characteristics of cross-border reverse logistics process*

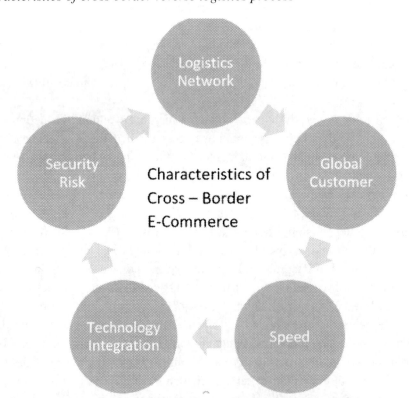

The activities associated with the reverse logistics process are as follows (Stock and Mulki., 2009) has defined a five-step approach –

*Revamping Reverse Logistics to Enhance Customer Satisfaction*

1. Return approval- provide labels and other elements the customers require.
2. Receipt of goods – distribution, unloading and processing of the returned products to processing centres.
3. Processing of Returns – customer complaint data entry.
4. Sortation includes quality inspection and designing the returns route.
5. Disposition: repackaging, refurbishing, repairing, or recycling the product, bringing it to inventory or temporary storage. (de Araújo et al., 2017)

Apart from cross border documentation which is the main challenge in global e-commerce, there are serval other critical areas to reverse logistics operations. The third-party logistics (3PL) who manages the pickup, processing, and sort the returns need to clearly state the classification, import duty, country of origin, settling refunds, and updating multiple channels with varied requirements. Many companies focus on the standard process and network for reverse logistics. But the changing behaviour of the customer demands a faster, transparent return. The existing process desires to incorporate integrated technology to lean the process and avoid delays with advanced technology development. (Porambage et al., 2018) concluded that e-retailers need to establish good partnerships with logistics companies to ensure the quality of operational services and reduce the timeliness and cost of logistics and transportation.

(Tsang et al., 2018) suggested that introducing advanced technology into the logistics and process can improve the quality and competitiveness of logistics services. (Kings.,2015) investigates factors influencing cross-border logistics performance—for example, laws and regulations in cross-border performance, payments, e-customs clearance, and technology adaptation. The delays in the cross-border are because of an intermediary factor in the relationship and the documentation process. The real challenge is to make the cross-border customs and port clearance process more efficient. Emerging technologies like Blockchain can significantly reduce the processing, coordination, transportation and logistics, and financial intermediary and exchange rate by increasing transparency and enhancing the ability to automate processes and payments. Also, the technology can support tracking the changes quickly. It is essential where the participant can copy, modify, and share digital objects virtually. From an academic point of view, product return information is interesting and essential, and researchers are showing increasing showing interest in product return management (Mollenkopf et al., 2010) but lacks the investigation on the various technologies available for the exchange of information on product returns, especially regarding which effective contracts with the intermediaries involved in the Reverse logistics process

## MAIN FOCUS OF THE CHAPTER

### Barriers in the Cross–Border Reverse Logistics

Product returns come from various sources, but the literature review provides several classification schemes for classifying product return types. Barriers are - long shipping times, complex return processes, customs obstacles, exchange transparency, price opacity, limited ability to change delivery times, limited mutual trust, etc., hinder the growth of cross-border e-commerce. (Van Heel et al., 2013) The firm can reduce most of these barriers by providing customers with standard and lean shipping and return policies. (Kim et al., 2017). Figure 4 shows that in the B2C reverse logistics, customs navigation and cross-border logistics are most ranked as important challenges should be addressed.

*Figure 4. Challenges in B2C cross-border reverse logistics*

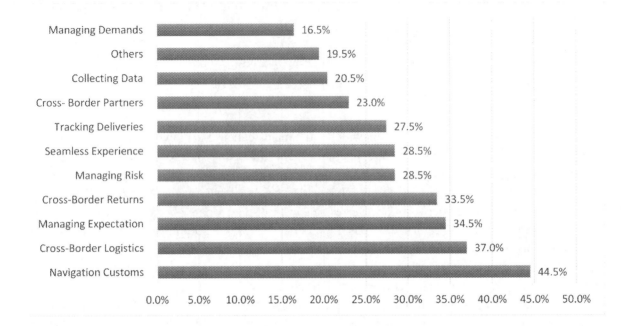

Cross-border e-commerce differs from domestic e-commerce. It involves longer distances, longer delivery schedules, and higher logistics costs. E-retailer needs to consider customs clearance in the destination country and associated charges, documentation and additional investment in overseas warehouses and transit points (Giuffrida et al., 2017). Previous researchers have classified the cross-border e-commerce reverse logistics modes. Overseas to Overseas (O2O) is the first category, which provides services from customers in the destination country to the retailer's overseas warehouse. In this category, the customer submits the return request on the website. The customer receives the exchanged product via international air express delivery. The second category is Overseas to Domestic (O2D), the customers in the destination country receive the exchange product from the domestic warehouse in the same country. In this mode, products for reverse logistics can be temporarily stored in the retailer's warehouse or outsourced to the destination country's customs. The third category is Domestic to Domestic (D2D) mode, and reverse logistics is from the customer to the domestic warehouse. The e-retailer urges the customer to return the product to a domestic warehouse. In the case of O2O and O2D, the retailer has to go through the reversal of the custom process and submit the international freight documents, further in some cases. The retailer also carries out the reversal of payment. (X. Wang et al.,2021)

(Cho and Lee., 2017) examined the determinants of cross-border concerning logistics and regulation. Logistics network, transportation, customs efficiency, and regulatory standardization are essential for reverse logistics. The process is "time-bound "; transformation time and visibility play a critical role. Therefore, reverse logistics should provide responsive, reliable, visible, and flexible service. (Wang M., 2011). A complete strategy towards reverse logistics for creating a value chain concentrates on logistics network, reverse process quality, communication, information quality, traceability, interoperability and agility. (Bernon et al.,2011). The reverse logistics includes collecting, sorting and inspection, reprocessing, and later redistribution needs attention. It is challenging to attain alignment because of multiple touchpoints. (Fleischmann et al.,2004). Further, the quality and consistency of the service quality are critical to retaining the long-distance customer. (Vlachos et al., 2003) So, it's not only the physical movement of the goods but also the integration of information for documentation, payment, and real-time decisions that are critical for Reverse Logistics (Govindan et al., 2015) Though with the development of technology over the period, the supply chain is slowly getting integrated. Yet, cross-border reverse logistics still face a challenge in tracing the product at each activity level, stage of damage of cargo, resolving disputes identifying the authenticity of faulty origin, compliance and building reliability and trust among the participant. (Chang et al., 2019)

## Obstacles in Cross–Border Reverse Logistics Process

Figure 3 shows the reverse logistics process as the product moves from the customer to the e-retailer overseas warehouse. In cross-border logistics, the products and the documents move through the customs at the port of origin. An effective and collaborative reverse logistics reduce logistics costs and achieve better customer service. Figure 5 shows the number of intermediaries involved in the reverse logistics operation. In some cases, the banks are also involved in cross-border trade.

*Figure 5. Cross-border customer return process*

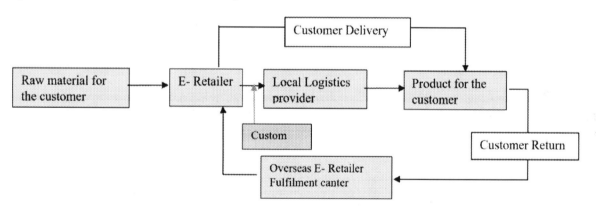

Companies need to adapt their operations to respond to customers' needs with high visibility, flexibility, and agility in global trade. Due to extended logistics network, custom documentation, low level of technology integration among intermediaries, and bank operations affect the timeliness of cross-border e-commerce. Additionally, poor real-time returns visibility impacts the customer experience. (He, Meng, & Liang, 2021)

Internally, the company needs high data visibility to plan resource allocation and transportation networks, which is essential to reduce unnecessary transportation costs. (Vakharia, 2002). Hence, the alignment of information technology (IT) is crucial, which will impact performance. Most of the companies have internal integration through ERP Systems. As the operations need high scalability, companies must identify technology to enable collaboration and interoperability with multiple participants in the value chain.

*Figure 6. Flow of information in cross-border reverse logistics*

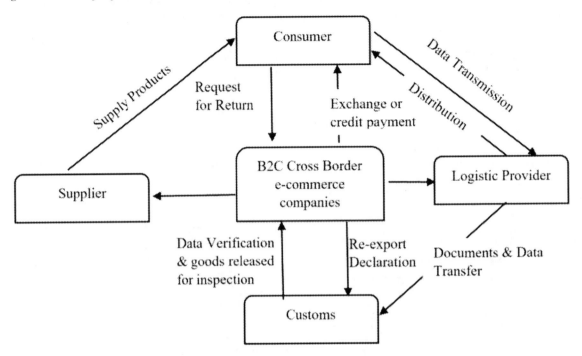

Figure 6 shows the flow of information between the intermediaries in the reverse logistics operation. The initiation of the information flow starts with the customer request for a return. After the collection and sorting, the Logistics provider files declaration to customs. In e-commerce businesses, e-platform providers or logistics enterprises registered with customs must pay the duties. (WCO.,2017)

The e-commerce business submits a cross-border e-commerce retail shipment manifest (simplified declaration) to Customs. In most countries, customs-registered e-commerce companies, e-platform providers, or logistics companies must pay customs duties before collecting imports for delivery to their customers. (WCO.,2017)

Generally, the interaction between customs and logistics providers is through a web EDI and only allows the Logistics provider to submit the data for verification. With the development. Many small-sized logistics companies processing parcels lack automation. There is a need for a collaborative system to strengthen integration with Customs. System integration with the Customs, particularly for air and sea ship companies, manages the returns in the e-commerce sector. Integration with customs authorities is critical from customs duty collection, verification, and compliance management. (WCO.,2017)

This means that the entire chain had no real-time visibility, transaction transparency. (C. Wang, 2021). In addition, risk management is not solid. International trading activities through Internet platforms with network, virtualization, and globalization characteristics. Transaction funds will be remitted through a third party payment institution. (Hu & Luo.,2018.). By sharing information, retailers can use online payment method data to forecast product returns from different consumer groups accurately and manage product returns more efficiently. (Yan & Cao, 2017). Data to the logistic provider represent the type and quantity of returns and are further transmitted via email or ERP system to the provider and the customs.

With increasing pressure from inter-country regulations and competition, the collaboration of technology is unavoidable for companies for the product return process. (M. Rizaimy et al., 2017)

The retailer should embrace new technologies because the new generation of Information technology systems focuses more on process support than just transmission of the information. The system should allow companies to be flexible and agile. New generation technology highlights paperless electronics are increasingly replacing manual filled forms and documents, where business process management (BPM) has emerged (Ko, 2009). Further, (Elkhateb. 2012) considered integrating IT and logistics management an essential prerequisite for product Return management. Designing a reverse logistics system in an e-commerce environment should focus on distance, multiple entities and modes of transport. Given the differences between executors in current e-commerce, some well-developed companies incorporate information networks regarding information processing capabilities and logistic functions, while others lack reverse logistic skills. There is limited research focusing on the information exchange in cross-border product returns transactions.

Insufficient investment is generally a major obstacle (Nel & Badenhorst, 2020), due to a lack of experience or internal inattention. Reverse Logistics generally does not have enough investment in information systems to handle the growing online return logistics chain (W. Wang et al., 2013). The management must emphasize the importance of reverse logistics in strategic planning (Smith, 2005). Emerging technologies like Blockchain enhances the efficiency of the entire operations. Specifically, the technology has enormous potential in the logistics sector due to its digitized interoperability capability. (Edwards et al.,2011). From the verification and authentication of the intermediaries to bringing transparency and agility to the operation, Blockchain can share error-free and tamperproof information among participants. Specifically, today's reverse logistics operation lacks traceability of the product, a very important aspect for decision-making. Here, Block chain can play a critical role in future (Francisco et al.,2018).

## SOLUTIONS AND RECOMMENDATIONS

## Blockchain Technology – Reshaping the Reverse Logistics

Blockchain is a unique technology based on a shared system in a digitized chain linked with immutable blocks, enabling transmission of the transaction record. It provides the user (retailer) accurate data faster without any tempering and error, which is an essential requirement. In reverse logistics, the retailer deals with the reverse upstream flow of physical goods, performing many activities and involving multiple participants. (FengTian.,2016). Many companies in the B2C e-commerce operation use IoT to integrate the entire operation. Increased cloud-based digital technology is transforming logistics of the product location, package, and shipment details with advancements in technology. To gain real time visibility, IoT control towers are used centralized planning and interoperability to coordinate by all the participants, including private and government authorities. However, in reality, IoT lacks the capability of interoperability, alignment with different operating systems, and poor collaboration. Hence, the supply chain is often opaque (Queiroz et al., 2019).

Secondly, in a reverse logistics set-up, the information is collected from multiple locations, leading to information asymmetry. Due to fragmentation among the entities, the flow of information lacks an effective trust mechanism. Hence, most intermediaries have no visibility of the supply chain, especially customers and suppliers who have only partially access information. (SAA, 2016)

To establish trust and a high level of transparency across the supply chain, the application of Blockchain will improve the regulatory control and enhance the overall performance, minimize the process risk, and achieve their business objectives. (Syahputra et al., 2019). The distributed ledger blockchain technology enables users to maintain and access a centralized yet shared platform for all the events in their supply chain. Moreover, it increases data integrity and trust between intermediaries, reduces duplication, and enhances efficiencies. It also contributes to any firm's vital objectives, such as cost, quality, speed, dependability, risk reduction, sustainability, and flexibility (Kshetri., 2018. The transparent, decentralized, and immutable nature of Blockchain has sparked the need to explore the potential of the same in reverse logistics.

More than 50% of the published articles addressed network optimization, location, strategies, and environment. Very limited articles aimed to identify the opportunities and challenges in Reverse Logistics in a cross-border B2C context using Blockchain.

## Integration Through BlockChain Technology

The identified challenges in the traditional approach of the cross border are shown in Figure 7. The key intermediaries in the flow- Supplier, distribution and fulfilment centres, logistics service providers, carriers, customs brokers, customs, banks, and online merchants and customers- are all part of the cross-border e-commerce ecosystem. Online product listing, online ordering, payment and settlement, packaging and consolidation, shipping arrangements, customs clearance procedures, tracking, and delivery of acquired commodities via cross-border reverse logistics are all part of the process. Figure 7 illustrates that all the participants in the network exchange documents, make or receive payments, enter or amend data, and issue approvals or denials. However, the entities are across the border but need to interact with each other on a real-time basis. In some cases, when the transfer of credit is involved, and the value is higher, the local and foreign bank also forms part of the process.

*Revamping Reverse Logistics to Enhance Customer Satisfaction*

*Figure 7. Multiple entities in the cross-border reverse logistics*

## Real-time Information Sharing

The effectiveness of information sharing on a real-time basis on opportunities, risks, and overall business performance affects the effectiveness of such collaborations or alliances (McGloin & Grant, 1998). This will reduce variability and costs and enhance the firm's responsiveness while still managing consumers' expectations by offering transparency (Trappey et al., 2020). The increased flow of returned product through reverse logistics channels also enhance the need for exchanging data (Ho et al., 2012; Hsu et al., 2009). In addition, the necessity for efficient and effective information sharing. Sharing information on the product, technology, and market structure can help lessen the risk of unanticipated changes. End-user preferences also assist providers in improving current processes (Jean and Sinkovics, 2010; Samiee and Walters, 2006).

The integrated information system between the multiple entities across the border is a barrier to a seamless exchange of information. Entities work in silos using the independent platform to exchange information. The entire process is document-heavy; cross-border trade requires document and verification at each level of operation. At the same time, maintaining each individual's secrecy and transparency is of utmost importance. The traditional systems used by most of the companies lack a collaborative and integrated system leading to error, delay, customs issues, delayed recovery of import duties, re-exporting the product, delay in bank processing the documents, payment of demurrage, and detention to the shipping companies. As described by the industry professional, the system lacks transparency and trust within the entities. Table (2) describes the obstacles in the cross–border reverse logistics as described by the logistics professional handling the operations. The summary is based on the semi-structured questionnaire responses, discussion in-person with the focus group involved in the cross-border operations. The importer, exporter, and the authorities often deal with documentation errors. Further, in the cross-border operation, multiple documents need to be submitted to various entities, leading to a paper-heavy process.

Documentation errors and the risk of false documents are the main apprehensions in the cross-border supply chain. The third-party logistics and the importer complain that during the submission of customs documentation declaration time, they often find errors, undervaluation of the imports leading to government revenue loss and difficulty in a reversal of import duty. The importer, logistics companies, customs, and logistics companies look for more visibility of the information. The exchange of transactional information between many participants or entities such as customs brokers, shipping agents, trade organizations, and consignees with service providers and government authorities, which frequently leads to process inefficiencies.

*Table 2. Obstacles in cross-border reverse logistics*

| S.no | Pain Points in the cross-border | Importer | Exporter | Customs | Customs agent | Freight Forwarder | Bank | Insurance | Govt. Authorities | Customer |
|------|-------------------------------|----------|----------|---------|---------------|-------------------|------|-----------|-------------------|----------|
| 1 | Documents error | ✓ | ✓ | | | | | | ✓ | |
| 2 | Multiple entities & its accounts for transaction | ✓ | ✓ | | ✓ | ✓ | | | | ✓ |
| 3 | Process duplication | ✓ | ✓ | ✓ | ✓ | ✓ | | | ✓ | |
| 4 | Compliance | | ✓ | ✓ | | | | | ✓ | |
| 5 | Cross-border collaboration | ✓ | ✓ | ✓ | | | ✓ | ✓ | | |
| 6 | Transparency | ✓ | ✓ | ✓ | ✓ | ✓ | ✓ | ✓ | ✓ | ✓ |
| 7 | Trust and Reliability | ✓ | ✓ | ✓ | ✓ | ✓ | ✓ | ✓ | ✓ | ✓ |
| 8 | Security & data privacy | ✓ | ✓ | ✓ | | | ✓ | | ✓ | |
| 9 | Credit transaction | ✓ | ✓ | ✓ | | | | | ✓ | ✓ |
| 10 | Standardization | ✓ | ✓ | ✓ | | | ✓ | ✓ | ✓ | |

Around 300 documents are exchanged between the multiple digital and hard copies entities, leading to duplication, dispute, and delay. An integrated system with visibility across the supply change is needed to resolve the issue—delays in document submission, processed through the manual feed to the authorities, causing delays and errors.

The collaboration between the multiple players is most often through email or EDI transfer between any two organizations. Another key pain point in the cross- border reverse logistics is the unavailability of digital channels for cross-border collaboration between the importer, exporter, and logistics provider

## Revamping Reverse Logistics to Enhance Customer Satisfaction

with shared information. The collaboration between the multiple parties can vastly improve if all can share data in a digital platform exchange process.

Finally, authentication and verification are very important because the importer wants to trace the product's origin. Hence, the logistics companies are looking for a process where auto authentication and verification are possible. The documents are made with multiple parties in a different location as per the local requirement and later translated or changed to meet demand. As a result, several authorities identified a lack of data standardization as a major concern for collaborative efforts. Limited integration between entities and manual interventions are responsible for the failure of process-level transparency in global trade.

The desired future cross-border reverse logistics model should have data access, transparency, and security. Blockchain technology is an advanced technology that plays a significant role in reverse logistics management.

## Approaches for the Creation of a Blockchain-based Cross-border e-Commerce Model Single View of Documents

Blockchain technology provides a unified window to all trade documents, an essential requirement to improve cross-border reverse logistics process efficiency. Any participant can log into the trading platform to update the document as any network member. Figure 8 is a proposed conceptual framework that shows the transmission of the information (data) between the importer's logistics provider, customs agent, and customs.

*Figure 8. Blockchain technology-based cross – border reverse logistics conceptual framework*

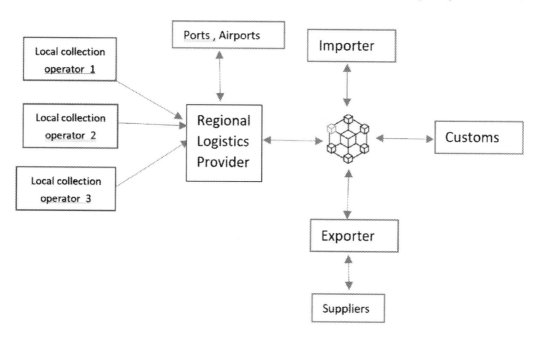

The digital exchange of information between customs and numerous stakeholders would speed up the procedure and increase transparency. The old system's delay in document transfer was due to a lack of interoperability among the major actors. Noncompliance is penalized with payment of detention and demurrage charges and delays in the movement of goods. Due to manual documentation procedures, the delays & errors also increase. A Blockchain-based system with inbuild data interoperability, with a shared distributed ledger, plays a significant role in the reverse logistics information transfer maintaining the utmost security and privacy.

## Data Ownership and Control

While traditional technologies allow both data and document exchange when data is shared with the network via a common intermediate layer, control over the data is lost. This configuration generates network friction. The company's internal regulations, competitive viewpoints, and private operating methods may be disapproved by network members such as customs, border security, and government regulators. It is essential to exchange data and documents on a unified platform while retaining control to reduce friction among network members. Blockchain gives network participants complete control over shared data with its built-in distribution blocks.

*Table 3. Characteristics of blockchain aligned to requirement of reverse logistics*

| S.no | Requirement | Importer | Exporter | Customs | Logistics Provider | Banks | Insurance | Govt. Authority | Blockchain | Traditional techonology |
|---|---|---|---|---|---|---|---|---|---|---|
| 1 | Data Ownership | • | • | • | • | • | • | • | ✓ | ✓ |
| 2 | Visibility | • | • | • | • | • | • | • | ✓ | ✓ |
| 3 | Shared data | • | • | • | • | • | | • | ✓ | ✓ |
| 4 | Secutity and privacy | • | • | • | • | • | | • | ✓ | X |
| 5 | Intraoperability across supply chain | • | • | • | • | | • | | ✓ | X |
| 6 | Cross - boader Intraoperability | • | • | • | • | • | • | • | ✓ | X |
| 7 | Data Validation | • | • | • | • | • | • | • | ✓ | X |
| 8 | Faster Documentation processing | • | • | • | • | • | • | | ✓ | X |
| 9 | Compliance | • | • | • | • | • | • | • | ✓ | X |
| 10 | Dispute settlement | • | • | • | | • | • | • | ✓ | ✓ |
| 11 | Risk Management | • | • | • | | | | • | ✓ | ✓ |

The blockchain-based approach in reverse logistics management focuses on creating a safe, shared system. The traditional process followed by the key supply chain players is more aligned for a single country but requires extended software integration with cross-border systems. A blockchain application enables efficient cross-border interaction with multiple systems and private, encrypted, and immutable data to ensure trust and transparency. Moreover, the system provides greater availability and scalability. A more robust data backup and recovery solution are provided via distributed ledger technology coupled with a cloud-hosted recovery mechanism.

The Blockchain-based network would significantly improve the cross-border reverse logistics:

1. Improved traceability of all the documents would minimize the risk of fraud, the documents' error and enhance the reliability and trust within the critical participants in the supply chain.
2. Blockchain can improve the cross-border collaboration between government authorities, especially the customs.
3. Shared documents between importer, exporter, and logistics improved trust and transparency in the system. The documents would be uploaded automatically and shared between the key participants in the blockchain network. Even the ports and airports would receive cross-border documents like BL (Bill of lading), invoices, packing lists, and other trade documents through a single version.
4. Enhances banks' real-time visibility into the trade process on customers' risk assessment.

## FUTURE RESEARCH DIRECTION

For e-commerce businesses to be profitable, an effective reverse logistics operation is generally required. In most countries, re-export documentation is a task in reverse logistics – such as filing documents with various government authorities, recouping tariffs and fees- can be quite expensive. Although many cross-border activities are digitized these days, in reverse logistics, the adoption of advanced technology is limited.

The main challenge in reverse logistics is the interoperability, tracing, and transparency of the inflow of documents and material between the multiple supply chain players. Companies work in silos with internal ERP software integrated with either one or two intermediaries with EDI. The visibility, in this case, is very low, especially in cross-border transactions. Larger companies use cloud-based IoT integration with their intermediaries for cross-border visibility, but all players' privacy and alignment are still not fully fixed. Due to low visibility across the supply chain, there is excessive paperwork and a long lead -time. Hence, the process is higher, and efficiency is lower. The logistics provider provided insight into the current system's bottlenecks and the urgency for a collaborative and integrated approach.

With its unique characteristics based on the shared, decentralized network, Blockchain technology works as an enabler to integrate the entire supply chain. The technology enables alignment with all the intermediaries while maintaining the privacy and secrecy of the individual. Though considered expensive by many authors, for a sustainable long term solution, deployment of blockchain technology's will prove as a game-changer for reverse logistics management. It provides better visibility, agility, and transparency than traditional systems. The study suggests how Blockchain technology may integrate the closed-ended supply chain. Cross-border delivery will achieve superior service performance with Blockchain technologies and provide transparency, shorter lead times, security, timeliness, real-time decision making, and order fulfilment. Customs and trade-related agencies recognized an opportunity to use advanced technologies which enables more transparent and efficient operation.

The majority of the processes became paperless when the firm used Blockchain technology. This technology acts as a catalyst to alleviate the pain point in international trading, as the decentralized, secure network enables an immutable record across several computers by joining peer-to-peer networks. Blockchain is gaining traction in the supply chain because of its speed, real-time visibility, transparency, and minimal documentation process. Additionally, retaining the document's records and filings is a vital component of cross-border trade facilitation in general. Blockchain Technology enables the protection and storage of historical data in a configuration that will be legally applicable in the future in a smart contract. The most critical aspect of the success is the collaboration of the key participants for each transaction and the integration of the different systems.

However, the Blockchain is relatively new in the logistics area, creating awareness and knowledge of the technology integration, feasibility, and long-term sustainability. Secondly, all the key intermediaries are working independently and investing in the new technology if there is a long-term commitment and it is mutually beneficial. Further, to understand the supplier perspective of the model. Additionally, exploratory research can to validated, could be based on case studies or simulations. As a result, future research must consider additional factors regarding product returns.

## REFERENCES

Accenture. (2019). *Cross-border-the-disruptive-frontier*. https://www.accenture.com/_acnmedia/pdf-102/accenture-cross-border-the-disruptive-

Barenji, A. V., Wang, W., Li, Z., & Guerra-Zubiaga, D. A. (2019). Intelligent E-commerce logistics platform using a hybrid agent-based approach. *Transportation Research Part E, Logistics and Transportation Review*, *126*, 15–31. https://doi.org/10.1016/j.tre.2019.04.002

Bayles, D. L. (2001). *"E-commerce logistics and Fulfillment, Delivering the goods", Send It Back! The Role of Reverse Logistics*. Prentice Hall PTR.

Bernon, M., Rossi, S., & Cullen, J. (2011). Retail reverse logistics: A call and grounding framework for research. *International Journal of Physical Distribution & Logistics Management*, *41*(5), 484–510.

Bruno & Denecker. (2020). *Accelerating the winds of change in global payments*. McKinsey. Retrieved October 23, 2021, from https://www.mckinsey.com/industries/financial-services/our-insights/accelerating-winds-of-change-in-global-payments

Chang, Y., Iakovou, E., & Shi, W. (2019). *Blockchain in Global Supply Chains and Cross Border Trade: A Critical Synthesis of the State-of-the-Art, Challenges and Opportunities*. Academic Press.

Chen, J., & Bell, P. C. (2013). The impact of customer returns on supply chain decisions under various channel interactions. *Annals of Operations Research*, *206*, 59–74. https://doi.org/10.1007/s10479-013-1326-3

Cho, H., & Lee, S. (2016). A study on consumer awareness and determinants of overseas direct purchase: Focused on moderating effects of logistics infrastructure and market uncertainty. *International Commerce and Information Review*, *18*(3), 23–43.

de Araujo, A. C., Matsuoka, E. M., Ung, J. E., Massote, A., & Sampaio, M. (2017). An exploratory study on the returns management process in an online retailer. *International Journal of Logistics Research and Applications*, *21*(3), 345–362. doi:10.1080/13675567.2017.1370080

Giuffrida, M., Mangiaracina, R., Perego, A., & Tumino, A. (2016). Cross border B2C e-commerce to Greater China and the role of logistics: A literature review. *International Journal of Physical Distribution & Logistics Management*. https://doi.org/10.1108/IJPDLM-08-2016-0241

He, X., Meng, S., & Liang, J. (2021). Analysis of cross-border E-Commerce logistics model based on embedded system and genetic algorithm. *Microprocessors and Microsystems*, *82*, 103827. https://doi.org/10.1016/J.MICPRO.2021.103827

Hu, B., & Luo, Q. (2014). *Cross-border E-commerce Mode Based on Internet +*. doi:10.1088/1757-899X/394/5/052014

Kim, T. Y., Dekker, R., & Heij, C. (2017). Cross-border electronic commerce: Distance effects and express delivery in European union markets. *International Journal of Electronic Commerce*, *21*(2), 184–218. https://doi.org/10.1080/10864415.2016.1234283

Minnema, A., Bijmolt, T. H. A., Gensler, S., & Wiesel, T. (2016). To Keep or Not to Keep: Effects of Online Customer Reviews on Product Returns. *Journal of Retailing*. doi:10.1016/j.jretai.2016.03.001

Nel, J. D., & Badenhorst, A. (2020). A conceptual framework for reverse logistics challenges in e-commerce. *International Journal of Business Performance Management*, *21*(1–2), 114–131. https://doi.org/10.1504/IJBPM.2020.106119

Petersen, J. A., & Kumar, V. (2015). *Perceived Risk, Product Returns, and Optimal Resource Allocation: Evidence from a Field Experiment*. doi:10.1509/JMR.14.0174

Porambage, P., Okwuibe, J., & Tutorials, M. L. S. (2018). *Survey on multi-access edge computing for the internet of things realization*. Retrieved from https://ieeexplore.ieee.org/abstract/document/8391395/

Rizaimy Shaharudin, M., Govindan, K., Zailani, S., Choon Tan, K., & Iranmanesh, M. (2017). Accepted Manuscript Product Return Management: Linking Product Returns, Closed-Loop Supply Chain Activities and the Effectiveness of the Reverse Supply Chains. *Journal of Cleaner Production*. doi:10.1016/j.jclepro.2017.02.133

Saeed, K. A., Grover, V., & Hwang, Y. (2005). The relationship of e-commerce competence to customer value and firm performance: An empirical investigation. *Journal of Management Information Systems*, *22*(1), 223–256. https://doi.org/10.1080/07421222.2003.11045835

Shehu, E., Papies, D., & Neslin, S. A. (2020). Free Shipping Promotions and Product Returns. *JMR, Journal of Marketing Research*, *57*(4), 640–658. https://doi.org/10.1177/0022243720921812

Shewmake, B., & Sapp, G. (2000). Bringing down the international barriers. *InfoWorld*, *22*(18), 30.

Tsang, Y. P., Choy, K. L., Wu, C. H., Ho, G. T. S., Lam, C. H. Y., & Koo, P. S. (2018). An Internet of Things (IoT)-based risk monitoring system for managing cold supply chain risks. *Industrial Management & Data Systems*, *118*(7), 1432–1462. https://doi.org/10.1108/IMDS-09-2017-0384

Vakharia, A. J. (2002). E-Business and Supply Chain Management. *Decision Sciences*, *11*(4), 413–424. https://doi.org/10.1111/j.1540-5915.2002.tb01653.x

Van Heel, B., Lukic, V., & Leeuwis, E. (2018). *Cross-Border e-CommerCe makes the World Flatter*. Academic Press.

Venkatesan, R., & Kumar, V. (2018). *A Customer Lifetime Value Framework for Customer Selection and Resource Allocation Strategy*. doi:10.1509/JMKG.68.4.106.42728

Wang, C. (2021). *Analyzing the Effects of Cross-Border E-Commerce Industry Transfer Using Big Data*. doi:10.1155/2021/9916304

Wang, W., Liu, Y., & Wei, Y. (2013). Research on management strategies of reverse logistics in E-commerce environments. *LISS 2012 - Proceedings of 2nd International Conference on Logistics, Informatics and Service Science*, 321–326. doi:10.1007/978-3-642-32054-5_48

Wang, X., Xie, J., & Fan, Z. P. (2021). B2C cross-border E-commerce logistics mode selection considering product returns. *International Journal of Production Research*. doi:10.1080/00207543.2020.1752949

Webber, D. (2021). *Cross-Border Ecommerce: Three Challenges Defining The Next Decade*. Retrieved October 23, 2021, from https://www.forbes.com/sites/danielwebber/2021/03/24/cross-border-ecommerce-three-challenges-defining-the-next-decade/?sh=1f2993373a3a

World Customs Organization. (n.d.). Retrieved November 6, 2021, from http://www.wcoomd.org/en/media/newsroom/2017/december/building-effective-customs-project-management.aspx

Yan, R., & Cao, Z. (2017). Product returns, asymmetric information, and firm performance. *International Journal of Production Economics*, *185*(January), 211–222. https://doi.org/10.1016/j.ijpe.2017.01.001

# Chapter 11
# Supply Chain Resiliency, Efficiency, and Visibility in the Post–Pandemic Era in China:
## Case Studies of MeiTuan Waimai, and Ele.me

**Poshan Yu**

https://orcid.org/0000-0003-1069-3675

*Soochow University, China & Krirk University, Thailand*

**Ziqi Liu**

*Independent Researcher, Suzhou, China*

**Emanuela Hanes**

*Independent Researcher, Austria*

## ABSTRACT

*The sudden COVID-19 pandemic had a serious impact on the catering industry, and lockdown policies put a strain on the food supply chain. However, online food delivery (OFD) services have played an important role in the fight against the epidemic in the catering industry. In this chapter, the authors analyzed the development of keywords attributed to supply chains in the academic view by investigating the core selection of Web of Science and China National Knowledge Infrastructure, respectively, and drew keywords cluster graphs of Chinese catering supply chain by using CiteSpace. The contrastive analysis shows that more attention has been turned to supply chain resiliency, efficiency, and visibility in the post-pandemic era. Moreover, this chapter discusses whether and how Chinese OFD platforms contribute to the food supply chain. The results show that these OFD platforms, with domestic policy support, internet technologies, and the ecosystem advantages, have effectively enhanced supply chain resiliency, efficiency, and visibility.*

DOI: 10.4018/978-1-7998-9506-0.ch011

Copyright © 2022, IGI Global. Copying or distributing in print or electronic forms without written permission of IGI Global is prohibited.

# INTRODUCTION

The pandemic caused disruptions in our everyday life, especially in the supply chain of the catering industry for daily-essential products (Abhijit et al., 2021), from the perspective of logistics (Abhijit, 2021) and supply network (Maximo et al., 2020), thus drawing wide attention in the public and business perception (Diana, 2021). According to the definition of European and American "Standard Industry Classification", the catering industry refers to the catering service organizations for the purpose of commercial profit, which mainly provides supply of food to either events or hotels. However, in China, according to the definition of "Notes on The Classification of National Economy Industries", the catering industry refers to the service activities of on-site cooking and preparation of food in a certain place and selling it to customers for on-site consumption, which is specifically divided into three types, namely mass consumption market, high-grade catering market and atmosphere catering market.

In this chapter, the authors analyze the supply chain of catering industry, mainly focusing on mass consumption market, namely the online food delivery (OFD) industry, which provides food delivery services and related services primarily for household consumption. As shown in Figure 1, monthly sales revenue and growth rate of the catering industry fluctuated a lot in China from August 2019 to August 2021. It can be summarized that since the outbreak, China's catering industry has experienced four stages of development: precipitous decline, sluggish consumption, recovery, and relatively stable period (MeiTuan Research Institute, 2020).

However, it is worth noting that, at the beginning of the COVID-19 outbreak, the revenue of the Chinese catering industry suffered a significant drop from ￥419.43 billion to ￥183.2 billion (National Bureau of Statistics of China, 2021), which indicates that the pandemic has hit supply chains hard. Until October 2020, China, as one of the few countries in the world to show early signs of economic recovery (Yue et al., 2021), saw a recovery and positive growth in the catering industry as the epidemic prevention gained momentum, the general situation stabilized and OFD industry continued to penetrate (China Hospitality Association, 2021).

*Figure 1. Monthly sales revenue and growth rate of the catering industry in China from August 2019 to August 2021 (in billion yuan)*
Source(s): National Bureau of Statistics of China;

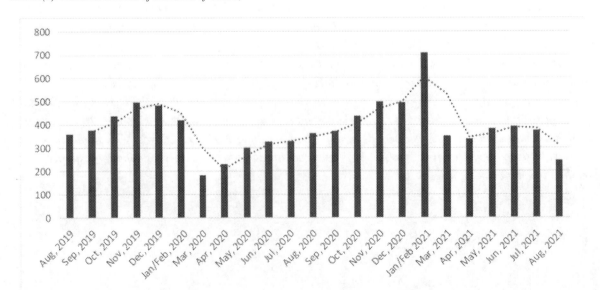

*Supply Chain Resiliency, Efficiency, and Visibility in the Post-Pandemic Era in China*

Food delivery services, attracting many consumers, have gained popularity worldwide. The popularity of Smart phones and mobile payment (Linan, et al., 2019) as well as the rapid development of urbanization (Choi et al., 2021) and service industry has fueled the fast-growing OFD industry. In particular, due to COVID-19 and lockdown policies in many countries, it led to an increase in global amount of OFD orders. As is depicted in Figure 2, the global OFD market increased by 17% in forecasted gross merchandise in 2020, which shows that OFD services have widened their potential clientele and presence in consumption patterns significantly.

*Figure 2. Global OFD revenue forecast in billion US$ in 2020*
Source(s): Statista Digital Market Outlook 2021

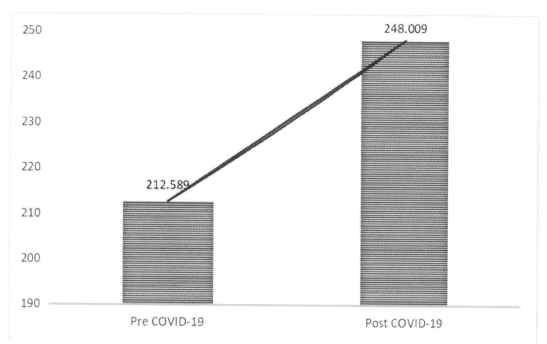

To be specific, according to Figure 2, the global revenue in the OFD industry amounts to $248.0 billion in 2020. A global comparison illustrates that more than half of the revenue is generated in China with $150.6 billion in 2020. Figure 3 shows the revenue forecast for OFD by country compared 2020 figures with estimation in 2025. Obviously, among the countries presented, China is the dominant market. It is estimated that China's revenue from the OFD industry would be $261 billion with good development potential (China Council for the Promotion of International Trade, 2020a).

*Figure 3. Revenue forecast for OFD by country (in million US$)*
Source(s): Statista Digital Market Outlook 2021

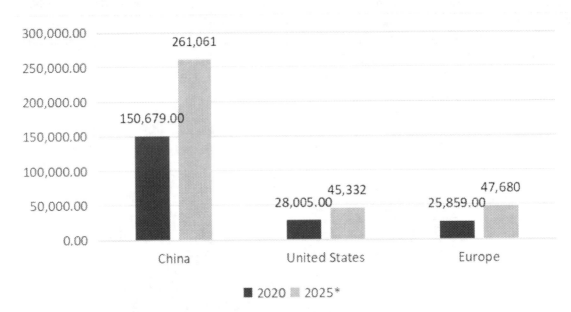

MeiTuan Research Institute (2020) claimed that the higher penetration of the OFD industry in China has some socioeconomic implications. In many respects, food takeout businesses have solved the problem of food supply chain well, enhancing the efficiency, visibility and flexibility in the ordering, processing, delivery and other links (Maximo et al., 2020). First of all, it facilitates the lives of the broad masses of people and widens the consumption application scenarios (Alexandra, 2021), which is one of the most direct influences. With the use of OFD service by more people, the food delivery industry supports the development of regional economy and plays a critical role in the development of night-time economy around the country. From the perspective of merchants, OFD services have promoted the integration of online and offline food and beverage industry and enhanced the degree of digitalization of merchants, which expanded revenue. In addition, the rise of the OFD industry has created a large number of "take-out delivery clerks", as a key link between "Internet + Service Industry" and "Intelligence + Logistics" (MeiTuan Research Institute, 2020).

In short, in the context of the epidemic, the OFD industry is not only a victim of the epidemic, but also plays a major role to the recovery of the supply chain from the aspects of resiliency, efficiency and visibility. In particularly, China becomes a dominated market worldwide with high growth potential for its both economic and socioeconomic impacts. However, there is not much literature in the field of supply chain and OFD industry in the post-pandemic era in China. This chapter provides systematic analysis of supply chain and how it recover in the post-pandemic era in China from the perspective of resiliency, efficiency, and visibility, taking Chinese two giants platforms as example.

## BACKGROUND

### Literature Review

For our discussion of Supply Chain Resiliency, Efficiency, and Visibility in the Post-Pandemic Era in China, literature provides fruitful content for understanding the significance and connection between OFD industry, food supply chain and COVID 19. The literature analyzed in the paper is from the core collection of Web of Science (WOS) and China National Knowledge Infrastructure (CNKI) to investigate the keywords of existing publications to investigate about food supply chain resiliency, efficiency, and visibility to discuss about how and whether OFD industry, especially Chinese OFD platforms, contributed to the recovery of the supply chain. In the core of selection of WOS, the keyword "food supply chain" identified 8916 papers. The combination of keyword above together with "food delivery" & "COVID-19" showed considerably fewer results.

Figure 4, drawn with CiteSpace, shows the keyword cluster graph from 353 papers using "food supply chain & food delivery" as keyword search. Similarly, Figure 5 illustrates the keyword cluster graph from 288 papers using "food supply chain & COVID-19" as keyword search. The figures show that there is not much literature in the field of supply chain & food delivery & COVID-19.

There is also a significant change in focus before and with COVID. Figure 4 depicts the keywords cluster in the field of "Food delivery & Supply chain" and Table 1 summarizes the keywords, which are ranked in order of counts over 10 from highest to lowest, and these keywords had been the focus of attention before the outbreak. Among them, "Management" is the most frequent keyword with 42 counts, followed by "supply chain", "model", "system", "delivery", "quality", "optimization", "logistics", "performance", "sustainability", and "algorithm".

However, during COVID-19, as illustrated in Figure 5 and Table 2, there were new high-frequency keywords, some of which were "impact", "climate change", "resilience", "integration", "challenge", "innovation", "policy", "traceability", "China" and "big data analytics".

*Figure 4. Keywords cluster in the field of "Food delivery & Supply chain"*

*Table 1. Keywords with highest occurrences in the field of "Food delivery & Supply chain"*

| Count | Centrality | Year | Keywords |
|---|---|---|---|
| 42 | 0.24 | 2003 | management |
| 39 | 0.15 | 2010 | supply chain |
| 32 | 0.07 | 2003 | model |
| 25 | 0.20 | 2007 | system |
| 25 | 0.14 | 2013 | delivery |
| 24 | 0.05 | 2003 | quality |
| 23 | 0.04 | 2008 | optimization |
| 20 | 0.17 | 2008 | impact |
| 19 | 0.10 | 2009 | food |
| 18 | 0.05 | 2013 | logistics |
| 18 | 0.05 | 2005 | vehicle routing problem |
| 17 | 0.06 | 2003 | performance |
| 16 | 0.06 | 2010 | design |
| 15 | 0.04 | 2008 | algorithm |
| 12 | 0.04 | 2010 | product |
| 11 | 0.06 | 2007 | sustainability |
| 11 | 0.03 | 2006 | network |
| 10 | 0.06 | 2011 | chain |
| 10 | 0.03 | 2008 | framework |

*Figure 5. Keywords cluster in the field of "Food supply chain & COVID 19"*

This emergence indicates that the pandemic provided significant challenges worldwide and had a strong impact on the traditional food supply chain. Health risks, logistics delay (Abhijit et al., 2021), and operations' efficiency (Diana, 2021) were major issues of the food supply chain. Moreover, considerable attention has focused on the resilience (Jill E. Hobbs, 2020), efficiency and traceability (Ilyas et al., 2021) of food supply chains. As Martin Christopher (1992), an expert in UK supply chain management, said, "The competition in the 21$^{st}$ century is no longer between enterprises, but between supply chains". Thus, several food delivery platforms attach importance to seeking innovative solutions for supply chains resilience from the dimensions of efficiency, traceability (Ilyas, 2021), system management (Diana et al., 2021), and delivery service (Ching-Chan et al., 2021). From clients' and business' perspective, service quality is an important factor (Ching-Chan et al., 2021).

To be specific, S. Mohan et al. (2013) found that proper demand planning, supply coordination and logistics integration were three key drivers for improving the supply chain efficiency. For logistics, delivery efficiency is another indicator. Particularly since the outbreak of the epidemic, door-to-door delivery, namely on-demand delivery, has become an essential service for many households (Seghezzi et al., 2020) and a tremendous increase in demand for OFD services entail logistical challenges (Ani et al., 2020).

More and more e-commerce and logistics enterprises build smart logistics systems and implement Intelligent Dispatch (developer.MeiTuan.com) based on the requirements of supply chain efficiency. Concretely, in order to avoid the waste of computational time and accomplish the delivery tasks efficiently, Dai et al. (2019) provided a systematic method for the OFD platforms to optimize order assignment and routing. Likewise, Wang, X. et al. (2021) designed an adaptive selection mechanism to select sequencing rules for route construction.

*Table 2. Keywords with highest occurrences in the field of "Food supply chain & COVID 19"*

| Count | Centrality | Year | Keywords |
|---|---|---|---|
| 28 | 0.34 | 2020 | impact |
| 15 | 0.11 | 2020 | management |
| 11 | 0.01 | 2020 | security |
| 11 | 0.02 | 2021 | system |
| 10 | 0.17 | 2020 | health |
| 10 | 0.12 | 2020 | performance |
| 9 | 0.13 | 2020 | food |
| 9 | 0.08 | 2020 | network |
| 9 | 0.13 | 2020 | supply chain |
| 8 | 0.16 | 2020 | agriculture |
| 8 | 0.02 | 2021 | model |
| 8 | 0.10 | 2020 | risk |
| 7 | 0.20 | 2020 | climate change |
| 7 | 0.11 | 2020 | framework |
| 6 | 0.08 | 2020 | design |
| 6 | 0.08 | 2021 | resilience |
| 5 | 0.05 | 2021 | innovation |
| 5 | 0.07 | 2020 | integration |
| 5 | 0.16 | 2020 | policy |
| 5 | 0.09 | 2020 | quality |
| 4 | 0.00 | 2021 | asia |
| 4 | 0.01 | 2020 | behavior |
| 4 | 0.05 | 2020 | china |
| 4 | 0.07 | 2020 | consumer |
| 4 | 0.06 | 2020 | industry |
| 4 | 0.01 | 2021 | information |
| 4 | 0.03 | 2021 | sustainability |
| 4 | 0.04 | 2020 | traceability |

In the similar process of retrieval, we use relevant literature of CNKI to form the keywords cluster graphs, as shown in Figure 6 and Figure 7, listing the occurrence frequencies in Table 3 and Table 4. The figures shown in Table 3 and Table 4 illustrate that literature on the subject is even scarcer in China. The analysis of keyword clusters shows that "supply chain", "catering enterprises", "Online-to Offline" (O2O), "take-out platform", and "MeiTuan Waimai" were the areas of concern before the outbreak. Figure 7 illustrates that the pandemic shifted the focus to "COVID-19", "food safety", "epidemic prevention and control", "on-demand delivery" and "catering enterprises".

*Figure 6. Keywords cluster in the field of "Take-out & Supply chain"*

*Table 3. Keywords with highest occurrences in the field of "Take-out & Supply chain"*

| Count | Centrality | Year | Keywords |
|---|---|---|---|
| 31 | 0.68 | 2009 | 供应链 |
| 16 | 0.07 | 2016 | 餐饮企业 |
| 14 | 0.23 | 2015 | o2o |
| 10 | 0.05 | 2018 | 新零售 |
| 9 | 0.09 | 2016 | 餐饮业 |
| 8 | 0.08 | 2015 | 外卖平台 |
| 6 | 0.03 | 2016 | 商业模式 |
| 5 | 0.05 | 2018 | 消费者 |
| 5 | 0.03 | 2015 | 餐饮行业 |
| 4 | 0.05 | 2015 | b2b |
| 4 | 0.03 | 2018 | 即时配送 |
| 4 | 0.03 | 2019 | 食品安全 |
| 4 | 0.02 | 2015 | 客单价 |
| 4 | 0.02 | 2015 | 美团外卖 |

Figure 7. Keywords cluster in the field of "Take-out & COVID-19"

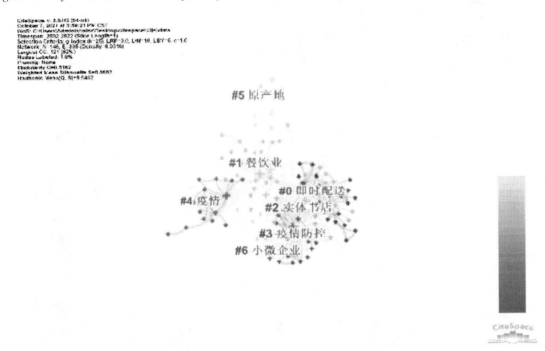

Table 4. Keywords with highest occurrences in the field of "Take-out & COVID-19"

| Count | Centrality | Year | Keywords |
|---|---|---|---|
| 5 | 0.19 | 2020 | 供应链 |
| 3 | 0.05 | 2020 | 食品安全 |
| 2 | 0.05 | 2020 | 生鲜食品 |
| 2 | 0.05 | 2020 | 博览会 |
| 2 | 0.00 | 2020 | 正常运转 |
| 2 | 0.05 | 2020 | 消费者 |
| 2 | 0.00 | 2020 | 食品链 |
| 2 | 0.02 | 2021 | 冷链食品 |
| 1 | 0.00 | 2020 | 批发市场 |
| 1 | 0.00 | 2020 | 农业保险 |
| 1 | 0.00 | 2020 | 消费行为 |
| 1 | 0.00 | 2021 | 饲料用粮 |
| 1 | 0.00 | 2020 | 疫情风险 |
| 1 | 0.00 | 2020 | 农民创业 |
| 1 | 0.00 | 2021 | 应急调度 |
| 1 | 0.00 | 2021 | 智能监控 |
| 1 | 0.00 | 2021 | 安全协作 |
| 1 | 0.00 | 2021 | 沃尔玛 |
| 1 | 0.00 | 2021 | 制造业 |
| 1 | 0.00 | 2021 | 食品行业 |
| 1 | 0.00 | 2021 | 最佳实践 |
| 1 | 0.00 | 2020 | 电商平台 |

This illustrated that under the circumstances of the epidemic, policies, including self-quarantining and restricting people's movement (Jinkyung et al., 2021), had an impact on catering enterprises and small businesses in China. Meanwhile, human food consumption habits and behaviors (Business Wire, 2020) have been transformed from traditional in-store service to on-demand delivery service (Zhao et al., 2020). Figure 8 summarizes the share of O2O operation among restaurants due to the COVID-19 outbreak in China. As shown in the chart, compared to operating modes before the pandemic, 78% of restaurants have mainly operated online to satisfy consumers' needs since the outbreak and nearly half the restaurants have employed O2O operation mode.

*Figure 8. Share of online and offline operation among restaurants due to COVID-19 outbreak in China as of March 2020*
Source(s): iiMedia Research; Website (mouse0232.cn);

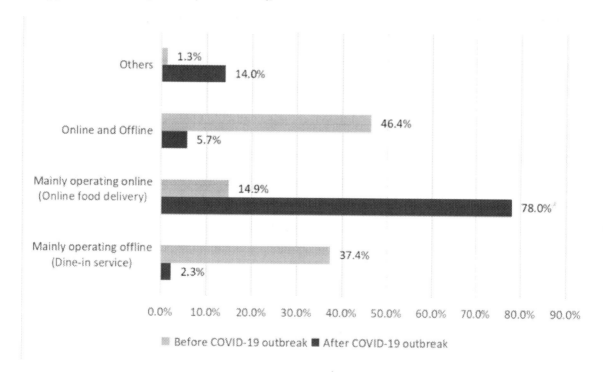

By comparing keywords from WOS and CNKI in the field of food supply chain, it is found that "O2O", "OFD platforms" and "on-demand delivery" have attracted wide attention in China. Under the premise of guaranteeing safety, the OFD platforms employ O2O mode (Bo et al., 2020; Li et al., 2021), integrated online services with offline ones (iResearch 2018) and ensured supply chain visibility and efficiency from aspects of time, cost and quality.

"Online-to-Offline" (O2O), has gained much attention due to the fact that far more consumers are adjusting daily routines and shopping online (Yimeng, 2021). The Chinese O2O take-out food and beverage industry has been developing continuously with the advantages of shopping convenience and home delivery (Bo, 2020), which has gradually realized the amalgamation of digital promotions and sales of products and services through physical channels (Kaur et al., 2021). As for online, more Chinese O2O companies renewed approaches, including management, ordering, price (Yimeng, 2021). As for offline delivery, Bo (2020) said that O2O platforms in China cooperate with crowdsourced platforms to provide efficient and effective home-delivery service, taking delivery capacity and order volume into consideration.

What's more, "OFD platforms", namely food delivery apps, become a focus due to the concerns for its connecting function between customers, restaurants (Tingting et al., 2020) and take-out delivery clerks, and huge benefits for all the parties (Zhou et al., 2019). From the point of supply chain, OFD platforms have laid emphasis on efficiency and visibility (Anushree et al., 2021), covering process of order and delivery. More specifically, the China Dining Industry Association (2021) announced that the system of purchase inspection and receipt request should be implemented to ensure the traceability of food materials. In general, it is no doubt that O2O take-out has been rising rapidly (Linan, et al., 2019) with the advantage of high efficiency, effortless ordering processes (Alexandra, 2021) and the convenience of making transactions easily without any local and time limits (Choi et al., 2021).

Furthermore, "on-demand delivery" attracted much attention due to the shutting of restaurants (Abhijit et al., 2021) and social distancing norms in place. Since the outbreak, logistics has become an important node of the supply chain and on-demand delivery has become increasingly popular (Seghezzi, 2020), which is a set of sales and logistics processes that empower catering enterprises to satisfy consumers' needs and deliver in the most efficient way (www.getfareye, 2021). Seghezzi et al. (2020) claimed that, in on-demand delivery, last-miles deliveries are a key process. It delivered the products ordered online to the final consumers (Lim et al., 2018), aiming to improve both effectiveness and efficiency.

## Characteristics of OFD Service in China

### Integration of Upstream and Downstream Supply Chains

Wang, X. (2016), the CEO of MeiTuan Dianping, claimed that "The second half of the Internet" era has arrived. To survive and gain competitive advantages in the OFD industry, take-out platforms need to achieve better integration and optimization with the catering enterprises to comprehensively help them improve efficiency and reduce cost. Similarly, MeiTuan Research Institute (2019), reported that an increasing number of take-out platforms are expanding their ecosystem to "business-to-business" (B2B) layouts. Thus, changes from the client side drive growth and improved efficiency of the business-side supply chain.

At present, professional third-party upstream supply chain service providers have begun to emerge (Seghezzi, 2020). While still in its early stages, the upstream supply chain opens a new imagination space for the traditional supply chain and solves the existing problems to a certain extent. For instance, Ele.me developed Ele.me Youcai, a B2B platform providing food materials for catering enterprises (youcaishop. cn, 2021). It could, to some degree, improve efficiency and visibility of food procurement and reduce costs for merchant's sides. In general, China's upstream supply chains have experienced a shift to order after a period of exploration and reference.

### Intelligent Logistics Distribution

Currently, for the delivery side, due to high demand and big data analysis, the efficiency of on-time delivery is one of core factors for competitiveness affecting users' choices of take-out platforms, as reported by "China's Internet Catering Take-out Living Community Market Segmentation Report 2015". In

*Supply Chain Resiliency, Efficiency, and Visibility in the Post-Pandemic Era in China*

order to improve traceable delivery process (Analysys, 2015) and delivery efficiency without increasing the labor cost, major platforms employ "O2O On-time Intelligent Dispatch System" (2019WAIC). To guarantee the good function of the dispatching system, order assignment and food delivery route planning should be taken into consideration (Wang, X. et al, 2021). The system adjusts the order structure by shipping costs and estimated time of arrival. After that, the platform will allocate the order to the most appropriate take-out delivery clerk at the right time, taking factors into account, such as take-out delivery clerk's location and individual attributes (Shi et al., 2019) like in-transit order situation, vendor's delivery, delivery difficulty, weather, and traffic conditions (Ding et al., 2012). This enables efficiency and the best match between the orders and take-out delivery clerks. Then, the system will provide take-out delivery clerks with the expected time and feasible delivery route. Even in the case of peak hours, Wang, X. et al (2021) has been researching algorithms for the dispatching system out of consideration for both academic significance and practical needs.

Also, consumers will find the estimated time of arrival, as well as the dynamic position of the take-out delivery clerks on the platform positive, as well as the use of voice to interact with them efficiently. Under the premise of guaranteeing the consumers "wait the shortest" (China Hospitality Association, 2019a), the routes are designed to lessen the average travel distance of riders (Zhou et al., 2019). After delivering, to increase the transportation capacity by scheduling in idle time, the system informs the take-out delivery clerks of the transportation demand of different business circles according to the order demand prediction and the transportation capacity distribution. MeiTuan & CFLP (2019) predicts that, in the near future, "Intelligent Dispatch Delivery System", relying on big data analysis, AI and other technologies, will become more and more mature. Further, on-time delivery will evolve from labor-intensive to technology-intensive.

In order to minimize the risk of exposing spreading the customers and drivers to infection (Research and Markets, 2020), many food delivery services and industries around the world (www.iso.org/news/, 2021), such as Meituan Waimai and company JD, have responded to the crisis by introducing contactless delivery (Business Wire, 2020) in the form of "Unmanned delivery robot" (Meituan & CFLP, 2019), which owns the biggest advantage of noncontact character compared with other OFD service, especially during the pandemic (Tan et al., 2020).

## Expansion of OFD Ecological Periphery

In the context of epidemic and fierce competition, many take-out enterprises quickly adjust their operating strategies and actively respond to challenges (Analysys, 2020). The companies have been given full play to the advantages of comprehensive delivery platforms (Analysys, 2020), providing diversified and multi-variety delivery services (fengniao.ele.me, 2021) of both food and non-food products orders (www.alizila.com, 2021), to avoid the single variety of food products affected by the impact of the COVID-19.

According to the report from MeiTuan and CFLP (2019), the ecological periphery of OFD service is expanding, and new business forms and models are emerging at an accelerated pace. As shown in Figure 9, the food delivery platform unites merchants, logistics companies, payment companies, and a variety of possible service providers in the future, forming a new cooperative network. The supply end and distribution end of merchants give birth to a variety of new business forms, such as operating services, business services, financial services, IT services, etc. (MeiTuan Research Institute, 2020). Nowadays, China's OFD industry has formed a huge ecological system centered on the off-sale platform, connecting the consumer side, the merchant side and the distribution side.

*Figure 9. Ecological periphery of OFD service*
Source(s): MeiTuan Research Institute, 2020

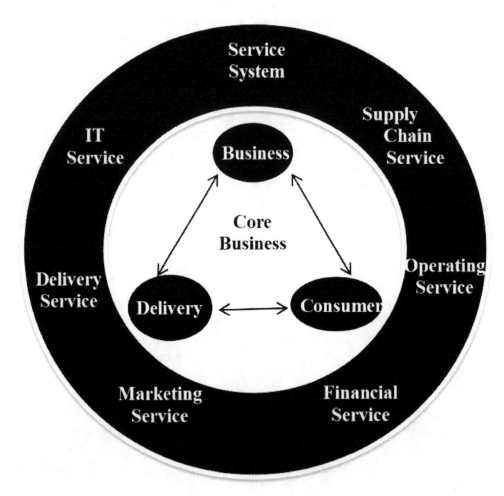

## The Role of Government in OFD Service

During the epidemic, security was given top priority in accordance with the prevention and control requirements. According to Maximo (2020), countries must keep the food supply flowing by prioritizing the health of the workers in the sector and their output. China Council for the Promotion of International Trade (2020b) jointly formulated and issued the "Specification for contactless delivery service", and China Dining Industry Association (2021) advocated serving food products in a sealed way. In short, it provides contact-free delivery service mode for e-commerce platforms and a safety guarantee for consumers.

In order to help the supply chain recover from the pandemic, China has adopted a series of policies to support catering enterprises and small businesses, including rent reduction, tax reduction and preferential financial loans, and the China Hotel Association (2020) and other trade associations have launched a series of service guidelines, standards and initiatives on combating the epidemic (China baogao.com, 2020). During the lockdown, the "Vegetable Basket" policy was adopted in China to lessen the virus's impact on changes to the smallholders and keep food shortages to a minimum. Additionally, some local

*Supply Chain Resiliency, Efficiency, and Visibility in the Post-Pandemic Era in China*

governments have unified purchases, centralized animal slaughtering and cold chain storage of county cooperatives, and fully subsidized the storage costs (Food and Agriculture Organization of the United Nations, 2020).

The commission for the delivery platform is usually around 20%, even as high as 26% (China news, 2021). Problems such as high service fees on OFD platforms and the dominance of one or two platforms have, to a certain extent, affected the sustainable and healthy development of the OFD industry. During this year's the National People's Congress & the Chinese People's Political Consultative Conference (2021), the All-China Federation of Industry and Commerce suggested in a proposal that the country's anti-monopoly enforcement agency should strengthen supervision of food delivery platforms in accordance with the law, which aims to achieve compliance in advance, review during the process and supervision over the whole chain of post enforcement. In order to foster a fairer and more equitable business environment, government functional departments issue guidance on strengthening the commission management of OFD platforms, and lead the organization of catering enterprises to communicate and negotiate with OFD platforms. China News reported that lowering the commission rates of food delivery platforms effectively prevent the formation of industry monopolies (China news, 2021). Likewise, the introduction of relevant "measures", on the one hand, promotes the integration of online and offline development of catering enterprises. On the other hand, market players are encouraged to help operators on OFD platforms reduce pressure.

## MAIN FOCUS OF THE CHAPTER

For the past several years, due to consumers' extensive use of smartphones, mobile internet, and navigational services (Kaur et al., 2021), many companies have implemented O2O service into APP development, enabling customers to place orders online and receive products / services offline (Dai et al., 2019; Zhou et al., 2019). Food delivery APPs (FDAs), function as intermediaries (Arghya et al., 2019) between restaurants and customers, and focus mainly on food products delivery. At the same time, the APPs also involve daily supply delivery service for customers (Zhao et al., 2020).

From the perspective of purchase intention, Zhao et al. found that satisfaction could be taken as the main basis for customers to choose APPs. Service quality (Ching-Chan, 2021) and visibility (Anushree, 2021), specifically including order conformity, quality of food products and delivery (Elvandari et al., 2018), has attracted many consumers' attention and significantly influenced purchase intentions. As can be seen from Figure 10, among all the FDAs, by the second quarter of 2020, MeiTuan and Ele.me have taken nearly 95% market share and become two giants in the OFD market. More specifically, Figure 11 showed that, as of September 2021, 85% consumers chose MeiTuan Waimai as most used APP, while 76% consumers chose Ele.me as the most used apps, provided that everyone can choose more than one app. That illustrated that slightly more consumers prefer MeiTuan Waimai App and that a majority of customers use both APPs (iiMedia Research, 2020).

Currently, with the advent of the Intelligent era, in order to maintain sustainability, more and more major platforms have been tending in the electronic commerce space (Arghya et al., 2019) and digital transformation (Wang, X., 2019). At present, MeiTuan Research Institute (2020) shows that the Chinese OFD industry has spawned a variety of new business forms, and has formed a huge ecosystem which takes the take-out platforms as the center task and connects consumers, merchants and delivery.

*Figure 10. Market share of leading online-to-offline food delivery service providers in China as of 1st quarter 2020*
Source(s): CBNData; Trust data

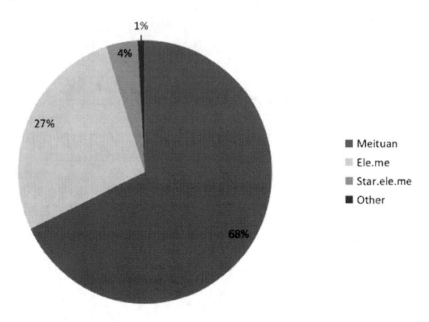

*Figure 11. Top 9 most used food delivery services in China as of September 2021*
Source(s): Statista Global Consumer Survey

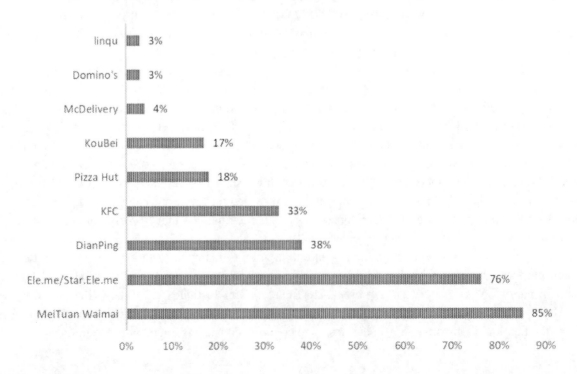

## MeiTuan Waimai

### Brand Profile

MeiTuan Waimai is an online food ordering platform owned by MeiTuan.com, which was launched in 2013. It mainly provides online meal ordering service, as well as quality delivery service. Then it adds additional services such as medicine delivery, self-pickup, flash delivery, etc., adopting the mode of "merchant delivery + third party delivery". As of March 2018, according to the detection data of E-commerce Center Research Center (www.100EC.CN), MeiTuan Waimai users reached 460 million, accounting for 62% of the domestic market share with the number of cooperative merchants exceeding 6.3 million, and over 4 million active take-out delivery clerks, covering more than 2,800 cities (peisong. MeiTuan.com, 2021). The daily order number reached 18 million. At present, MeiTuan Waimai has become one of the only two giant platforms in China's catering O2O industry.

### About the Take-out Business

MeiTuan Waimai platform mainly connects and serves the flow nodes involved in the whole supply chain. MeiTuan strives to enhance the visibility and develops its APP to offer convenience for consumers to select basic information such as food products, delivery address and delivery time, and then it confirms the order and transfers the order to corresponding merchants (www.Waimai.MeiTuan.com). In the meantime, for reasons of facilitating their business and improving the supply chain sustainability (Baozhuang, 2021), MeiTuan platform provides various take-out business interfaces for merchants, opens multi-type business scenarios, and realizes the whole process of dealing with merchants' business in the system. Table 5 shows that MeiTuan's service scenario includes self-service, consultation and management. In general, MeiTuan commits itself to realizing the connection between merchants, consumers and platforms to improve efficiency and effectively reduce costs.

*Table 5. Service Scenario Introduction of MeiTuan*

| Service Scenario Introduction |
| --- |
| Self-service store opening: After the service provider completes the system docking, this service helps merchants to settle in MeiTuan Waimai to realize fast store opening through the green channel; |
| IM online consultation: It helps establish real-time communication between merchants and customers, and facilitates communication such as before placing an order, during take-out delivery or after delivery; <br> Store decoration: The platform operates and manages posters, shop signs and recommending modules to enhance the visibility and stickiness of merchants and service providers; <br> Dishes management: In order to reduce the maintenance cost of merchants, the platform manages dishes in take-out stores and supports to add, delete, modify the food product and, at the same time, update the client; <br> Order management: MeiTuan manages the whole process system from order generation to completion, helps merchants to summarize multidimensional order data and improves management efficiency; <br> Evaluation management: The platform provides evaluation information of take-out stores to assist merchants to maintain customer sentiment and supervise public opinion; <br> Store management: MeiTuan helps to improve the operation efficiency of take-out stores, queries and operates basic information such as business status, opening hours and delivery fees; |

*Source(s):* https://developer.MeiTuan.com/isv/Waimai?location=orderManagement

## About the Supply Chain

The flow chart, shown in Figure 12, summarizes that the core services of MeiTuan Waimai contain consumers, catering enterprises, and delivery. The services for the client include the operation of online ordering, payment, evaluation, etc., for consumers to browse the merchants and choose the food products freely, or go on errands to purchase or pick up at the store (MeiTuan Research Institute 2020). The services for the merchants allow them to conduct online management of stores and food products, including store opening, account checking, order processing and other operations. At the delivery end, take-out delivery clerks can complete the related operations of order distribution, including order snatching, task management, settlement manifestation and other operations.

According to Wang, X. (2019), in the OFD industry, consumers are on the demand side while restaurants are on the supply side. At present, demand-side digitalization is gradually completed with the advent of the intelligent 5G era. MeiTuan Waimai takes "Eating" (developer.MeiTuan.com) as the core and provides consumers with convenience in life and improves dining quality and experience. The platform utilizes various new technologies, including IT, digital, IoT and other integration methods, to provide practical services and solve practical problems.

Nevertheless, supply side digitization is still a long process. Wang, X. claimed that the partners are mainly restaurants with a long supply chain, and their upstream includes picking from the fields, purchasing, and processing. MeiTuan currently commits to solving the problem of how to realize digitalization and improve efficiency in the supply chain of business management, menu, staff management and procurement of partners. For instance, MeiTuan provides raw material procurement for nearly 100,000 merchants nationwide (China Hospitality Association, 2019b) so as to make upstream centralized procurement more efficient. For the sake of ensuring the quality of food and enhancing the visibility, the MeiTuan platform gradually realizes traceability. In addition, with the participation of merchants and riders, the added value of delivery, such as increased orders and job opportunities, is also gained. Therefore, the product value of MeiTuan Waimai impacts consumers, merchants and take-out delivery clerks at the same time, creating value for all its users.

*Supply Chain Resiliency, Efficiency, and Visibility in the Post-Pandemic Era in China*

*Figure 12. MeiTuan Waimai product logic diagram*
*Source(s):https://developer.MeiTuan.com/docs/biz/biz_Waimaing_b0f1ddde-783f-4235-874e-38f582f1654d*

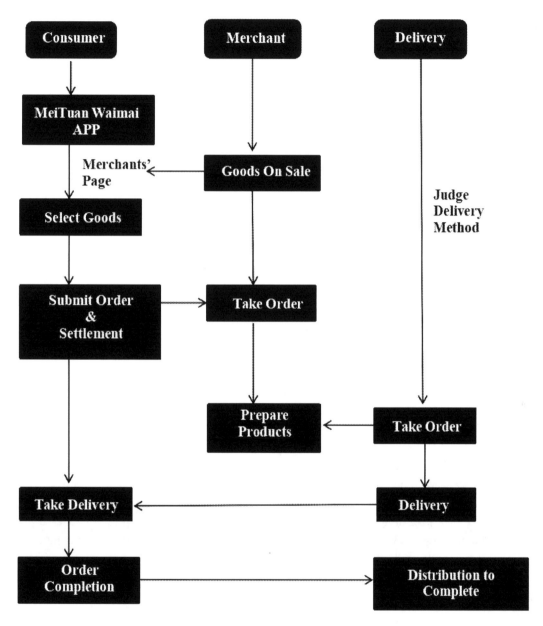

## About the Delivery

The delivery methods of MeiTuan take-out include: restaurant's self-delivery, crowdsourcing, MeiTuan special delivery and third-party delivery. Due to different delivery methods, there are differences in the synchronization mechanism of initiating delivery and order status changes. However, the delivery status will eventually be synchronized to MeiTuan's open platform, so that both merchants and users could see the delivery status of orders (developer.MeiTuan.com), and consequently, visualize valid information.

Orders have surged in recent years as OFD service has become a way of life for more and more people. Undoubtedly, it is a huge challenge for delivery. Therefore, MeiTuan implements an Intelligent Dispatch System that simultaneously satisfies 25 million daily orders, nearly 600,000 riders and punctual delivery within 30 minutes (China Hospitality Association, 2019a). Nevertheless, relying entirely on manual delivery, there will inevitably be multiple contradictions between demand and supply, efficiency and safety. In the 2019 WAIC (World Artificial Intelligence Conference), MeiTuan launched an unmanned delivery team to supplement its capacity with smart machines and technological innovation. For example, the take-out delivery clerks will contact the consumers after the order is delivered, and either the take-out delivery clerks will make an appointment with the consumers to pick it up at a designated place, or the take-out delivery clerks will deliver it to the consumers in person. The average wait time for this process is between 5 and 10 minutes. If, however, with the help of the delivery robot, the take-out delivery clerks could deliver the goods to the robot and then leave, saving five to seven minutes per order (2025china. cn/WAIC2019/), which saves time effectively. Especially during the epidemic, this process would not merely improve efficiency, but also reduce face-to-face contact, thereby ensuring safety effectively.

## Strategies during the Epidemic

During the epidemic, policies of home isolation and closure brought risks to the catering supply chain. Supply chains between users and merchants, merchants and delivery, delivery and users were all affected. Consequently, OFD has replaced "pick up at the store" as the choice of the vast majority of people. In order to further ensure safety, avoid direct face to face and minimize risk of human-to-human transmission (Research and Markets, 2020), MeiTuan Waimai was the first to launch the "contactless delivery" service mode on January 26, 2020, employing three forms of delivery, namely, the ark delivery, agreed delivery, have distance distribution (The Korea Herald, 2020). It effectively avoided direct contact with the take-out delivery clerks and consumers as well as the risk of cross infection. The "contactless delivery" model is now available in hundreds of cities.

For merchants, a sharp drop in the number of online and offline consumers during the epidemic has led to a sharp drop in revenue. MeiTuan Research Institute (2020) shows how the platform launched the "spring breeze action" in order to help catering enterprises return to work and production and realize increased revenue and stable cash flow for merchants. For this, it used the Internet as a platform and introduced a number of supporting merchants measures, focusing on increasing income, reducing expenditure, safety, supply chain services, and comprehensive skills training.

## Ele.me

### Brand Profile

Ele.me, founded in 2008, has been a leading local services and on-demand delivery platform (Alibaba Group, 2021) in China. It enables consumers to order meals, food products, groceries, fast-moving Consumer Goods (FMCG), flowers and pharmaceutical products online through the channels of Ele.me, Alipay, Taobao and Koubei mobile APPs. The platform employs the mode of "Self-service Delivery + Crowdsourcing Delivery + Special Delivery or Express" (open.shop.ele.me). On April 2, 2018, Alibaba Group (2018) announced that the company would acquire full ownership of Ele.me, which marks Ele. me's integration into Alibaba's ecosystem (www.alibabagroup.com). The company's performance has been growing continuously. According to statistics, Ele.me has been focusing on first-tier and second-tier cities, which accounted for 69.5% in 2019. Nowadays, the platform shows that average daily delivery orders reach 4.5 million, with 3.5 million cooperating catering enterprises and 3 million take-out delivery clerks (fengniao.ele.me).

## Analysis of Business

Ele.me focuses on its core expertise in food delivery to provide consumers with various food products and service on-demand, complementing Koubei and Alibaba's affiliated local service (www.alibabagroup.com). Figure 13 illustrates the Alibaba ecosystem. As can be seen, with the Alibaba ecosystem connecting services, consumer engagement, logistics infrastructure and merchant's enabler, and its resources and support, namely Taobao, Alipay and Koubei, Ele.me owns an expansive user base and maximal consumer traffic (Wang, L., 2018). Confronted with numerous consumer demands, Cainiao Network and Fengniao Logistics offer delivery services. Alibaba Cloud, amap.com and Alipay provide technology infrastructure in order for consumers to access the platform from various channels, such as Ele.me, Alipay, Taobao and Koubei (2018 Invest Day). In other words, mobile and online technology has contributed to enhancing the efficiency, effectiveness and convenience of consumer services for both service providers and their customers. The technology has been utilized to rule out time and location limits for consumers to order food and groceries (Alibaba Group, 2020).

*Figure 13. Ele.me's ecosystem*
*Source(s): 2018 Investor Day: Ele.me Alibaba Local Service. https://www.alibabagroup.com/en/ir/presentations/Investor_Day_2018_Eleme.pdf*

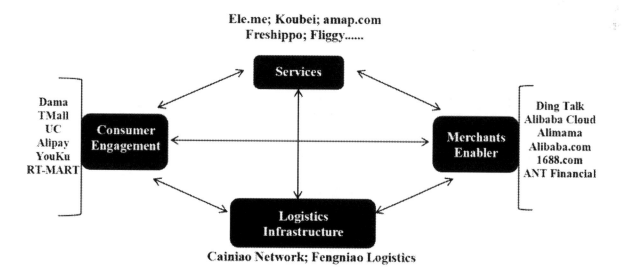

Zhang Xuhao (2018), founder of Ele.me, pointed out that being a part of the Alibaba ecosystem has benefited Ele.me a lot by facilitating a seamless and integrated O2O consumer experience in the local service sector, thus taking Ele.me's growth to a new level. Specifically, synergy with Alibaba ecosystem enhances consumers' engagement and empowers merchants (Wang, L., 2018). In a broad sense, Daniel

Zhang (2018), CEO of Alibaba Group, expected Ele.me to leverage Alibaba's infrastructure in commerce and find new synergies with Alibaba's diverse business to add further momentum to the New Retail initiative.

## Analysis of the Supply Chain

According to Figure 14, Ele.me centers on users, merchants and logistics, enabling SaaS and financial services. On the client side, Ele.me's process operation is similar to MeiTuan. In addition to facing client-side, it's worth noting that Ele.me has gradually extended to the upstream supply chain and launched the B2B platform, namely Ele.me Youcai (2018 Investor Day, 2018) in 2018, as shown in Figure 14. It is a one-stop platform for restaurants to procure ingredients. The platform analyzes the needs of Ele.me catering enterprises based on Internet big data. Based on this, the Youcai shop provides a more comprehensive category coverage, covering raw materials, semi-finished food products, vegetables and fruits, and catering utensils (youcaishop.cn, 2021). What's more, in contrast to traditional restaurant procurement methods, Youcai shop employs Internet technology to change the way of food procurement. The platform directly touches origin and source of goods and reduces intermediate price differences. While increasing traceability and ensuring both the internal and external quality of goods, it also provides more favorable food material prices for merchants. After placing an order, the platform will respond within 15 minutes and solve the problem within 10 working hours (youcaishop.cn, 2021). Then, through the self-built storage and distribution system, Youcai shops provide fast delivery services efficiently and timely.

*Figure 14. Ele.me's supply chain*
*Source(s): 2018 Investor Day: Ele.me Alibaba Local Service. https://www.alibabagroup.com/en/ir/presentations/Investor_Day_2018_Eleme.pdf*

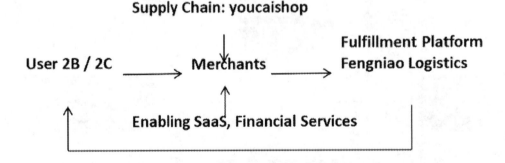

## Analysis of the Delivery

Fengniao, originally from Ele.me's local on-demand delivery network, has been declared brand independence and upgraded to Fengniao Logistics in 2019 (open.ele.me/about-us, 2021). Wang, L. (2019),

CEO of Ali Local Life Services, pointed out that this marked the beginning of a new revolution in the local on-time delivery industry, which was born from take-out business and has been expanding to deliverability of all objects and the matching of all stores. Meanwhile, this expansion brings huge opportunities for business imagination.

As shown in Figure 15, with the emergence of different delivery modes, including on-time delivery and intra-city delivery, the logistics services have expanded from food products to medicine, drinks, markets, flowers & cakes and express. Considering numerous orders, especially in peak hours, the company introduced crowdsourcing delivery, which has the advantage of releasing the burden of fulfilling large-volume, real-time O2O on-demand in a cost-effective way (Dai et al., 2019). Most recently, in the face of logistical challenges (Ani et al., 2020), the on-time logistics provides last-mile logistics services to facilitate New Retail Business (www.alibabagroup.com/en/about/businesses, 2021) and helps numerous consumer-oriented online platforms to achieve a O2O Commercial Closed-loop (fengniao.ele.me). The platform has given top priority to delivering food products, beverages, groceries, among other products, to consumers on a timely basis (Alibaba Group, 2020). In other words, Fengniao Logistics established an open on-demand delivery ecosystem to deliver service capacity to more industries. Liu Xinyang (2019), vice-president of Ele.me, stated that Fengniao Logistics has established high-standard delivery solutions in the fields of supermarkets, fresh food, beauty care and, at present, customized services in over 15 formats.

*Figure 15. The intelligent dispatch of Fengniao Logistics*
*Source(s):* fengniao.ele.me; *MeiTuan & CFLP, 2019*

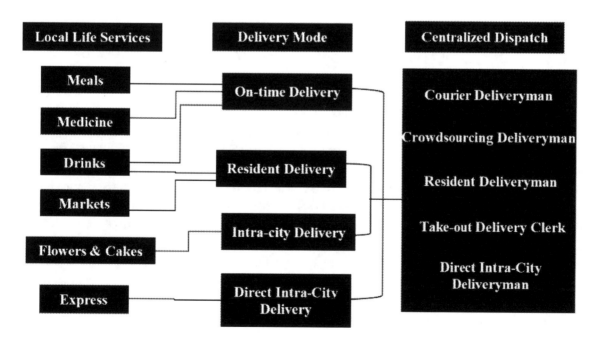

## Strategies During the Epidemic

During the pandemic, Michael Evans (2020), President of Alibaba Group, emphasized that consumers' health and safety concerns are a primary factor. Through food safety displays on the Ele.me platform, consumers can see the production situation of products more intuitively and ensure food safety. Food safety displays include video shooting, We Chat groups, public accounts and other communication channels, which increase the visibility of the supply chain. In addition, China Hospitality Association (2020) has actively communicated with Ali local life services company to implement 5 measures to support small and medium-sized enterprises, fully supporting all businesses to overcome the challenges. Firstly, the commission will be waived for all reputable merchants until February 29, 2021, and for the Wuhan area, the reduction period will be extended to March 31, 2021. Secondly, due to the surge of take-out demand, in order to protect the interests of the merchants, the local merchants who have not yet opened the take-out service launched "Take-out Express Online Service", which can open the take-out service at the earliest on the day the merchants submit the application.

## SOLUTIONS AND RECOMMENDATIONS

Recent years have witnessed the spectacular development of OFD services in China, where opportunity and challenge coexist. With the outbreak of the epidemic, the rapid development of the "Insular Economy" represented by take-out delivery has not only become a new means of business operation for merchants, but also become a lifestyle for consumers. Consumption has an experiential dimension (Holbrook and Hirschman, 1982), and its value comes from the process rather than the act of consumption (Diana et.al, 2021). Especially in recent years, with the integration in an IoT environment (Alexandra, 2021) and the rise of the concept of "All Things Home", the growth rate of the OFD industry has far exceeded the overall catering industry, and China's OFD industry is supposed to become a larger market. It is expected that virtual assistant systems that enable voice-ordering will be employed in more FDAs (Alexandra, 2021). Therefore, the OFD service is expected to be innovative in both convenient and experimental dimensions, the same as they enjoy in a restaurant (Diana et.al, 2021).

Optimizing the consumers' experience is strongly connected to the delivery process (Alexandra, 2021) and it is predicted to see more innovation in the field of delivery methods. Self-driving cars, drones and robots have been employed to make transportation easier and more convenient. In China, Ele.me is working on a pilot project using food delivery drones in Shanghai's Jinshan Industrial Park. And for now, the OFD industry is driven by big data and guaranteed by "contactless delivery", "self-collection by smart take-out cabinet", "semi-finished takeout" and so on. Intelligent logistics have developed rapidly and the delivery capacity has been continuously enhanced. Effective supply towards more types, full - time distribution direction. What's more, it's worth noting that the digital upgrade of the catering industry is an inevitable trend and becomes the most important skill and business opportunity factor of the catering industry in the future competition (China Hospitality Association, 2021).

*Supply Chain Resiliency, Efficiency, and Visibility in the Post-Pandemic Era in China*

## CONCLUSION

The pandemic posed a challenge to the traditional food supply chain, a complex web of interactions involving processing (Maximo Torero Cullen, 2020), retailing and logistics systems (Yue et al., 2021). By using CiteSpace, this chapter analyses the literature worldwide, especially in China, about supply chain and OFD industry in the context of COVID-19. It is found that, since the outbreak, supply chain resiliency, efficiency, and visibility in the post-pandemic era have been a major concern globally. In the field of catering industry, the OFD industry is not only a victim of the epidemic, but also a major contributor to the fight against the epidemic. Especially in China, the O2O on-demand food service market has addressed basic daily needs and supported the effective control of COVID-19. Furthermore, taking advantages of policy support, smart technologies and ecosystem resources, the Chinese OFD platforms contributed to food supply chain resilience and enhanced efficiency and visibility on both the supply side and demand side. To be specific, by comparing Chinese literature with the others, it shows that the Chinese OFD industry has, employed the "O2O" mode, centered on OFD platforms, provided on-demand delivery for consumers and developed a "B2B" layout to improve merchants' efficiency more than other countries' OFD industries. From another point, during COVID-19, the OFD industry has been boosted by the high demand with expanding market size and increasing penetration rate. Against the background of pandemic, the challenge and competitive nature of on-demand service (Dai et al., 2019) have promoted the platforms to seek innovative solutions and achieve a more mature business management. MeiTuan Waimai and Ele.me, two giants in the Chinese market, rely on the advantages of favourable policies and technologies to achieve economic scale and adapt to the changing environment with the intention of ensuring effective logistics, normal function of production and processing, effective distribution of food and consumer resilience (Yue et al., 2021). Taking the two companies as examples, the changes in the OFD industry after the epidemic can be summarized as follows: Firstly, the supply chain efficiency is gradually improved with the constantly upgraded intelligent logistics delivery system. Secondly, "contactless delivery" is widely promoted to provide security and avoid the risk of infection (Food & Drug Administration, 2020). Finally, taking full advantage of the ecosystem resources, the value of the OFD industry has been embodied in the consumers, catering enterprises and take-out delivery clerks and has strengthened in-depth integration among the three parties (Wang. X, 2016). In short, OFD service has contributed greatly to responding to the epidemic risk and supply chain challenges by enhancing resiliency, efficiency and visibility.

## ACKNOWLEDGMENT

The authors extend sincere gratitude to:

• Our colleagues from Soochow University, the Australian Studies Centre of Shanghai University and Krirk University as well as the independent research colleagues who provided insight and expertise that greatly assisted the research, although they may not agree with all of the interpretations/conclusions of this chapter.

• China Knowledge for supporting our research.

• The Editor and the International Editorial Advisory Board (IEAB) of this book who initially desk reviewed, arranged a rigorous double/triple blind review process and conducted a thorough, minute and critical final review before accepting the chapter for publication.

- All anonymous reviewers who provided very constructive feedbacks for thorough revision, improvement, extension and fine tuning of the chapter.

## REFERENCES

Alibaba Group. (2018). *Alibaba to Acquire Full Ownership of China Online Delivery Platform Ele.me*. https://www.alibabagroup.com/en/news/article?news=p180402

Alibaba Group. (2020). *Alibaba Group Holding Limited: United Stated Securities and Exchange Commission*. https://www.alibabagroup.com/en/ir/pdf/2020AR_Form20F.pdf

Alibaba Group. (2021). *Our business*. https://www.alibabagroup.com/en/about/businesses

Alizila.com. (2021). *Ele.me Unveils Upgrades to Meet Needs of China's On-demand Economy*. https://www.alizila.com/eleme-upgrades-to-meet-needs-of-china-on-demand-economy/

Analysys. (2015). *China's Internet Catering Take-out Living Community Market Segmentation Report 2015*. https://www.analysys.cn/article/detail/11671

Analysys. (2020). *Annual Analysis of China Internet Catering Take-out Market 2020*. https://www.analysys.cn/article/detail/20019783

Barman, A., Das, R., & De, P. K. (2021). Impact of COVID-19 in food supply chain: Disruptions and recovery strategy. *Current Research in Behavioral Sciences, 2*, 2666–5182. doi:10.1016/j.crbeha.2021.100017

Burgos, D., & Ivanov, D. (2021). Food Retail Supply Chain Resilience and the COVID-19 Pandemic: A Digital Twin-based Impact Analysis and Improvement Directions. *Transportation Research Part E, Logistics and Transportation Review, 152*, 1366–5545. doi:10.1016/j.tre.2021.102412 PMID:34934397

Business Wire. (2020). *Food Delivery on the Rise Due to COVID-19 Lockdown*. https://www.businesswire.com/news/home/20200428005464/en/Food-Delivery-Rise-Due-COVID-19-Lockdown–

Chavan, V., Jadhav, P., Korade, S., & Teli, P. (2015). Implementing Customizable Online Food Ordering System Using Web Based Application. *International Journal of Innovative Science, Engineering & Technology, 2*(4). http://ijiset.com/vol2/v2s4/IJISET_V2_I4_112.pdf

Cheng, C.-C., Chang, Y.-Y., & Chen, C.-T. (2021). Construction of a Service Quality Scale for the Online Food Delivery Industry. *International Journal of Hospitality Management, 95*, 102938. doi:10.1016/j.ijhm.2021.102938

China baogao.com. (2020). *At the Beginning of 2020, China's Food and Beverage Food Delivery Industry Policy Favorable Food Delivery Market May Usher in a Wave of High Growth*. https://tuozi.chinabaogao.com/jiudiancanyin/03314V3952020.html

China Council for the Promotion of International Trade. (2020a). *CCPIT Released a Report: 70% of the Catering Industry's Total Revenue Growth is Driven by Take-out Business*. https://www.ccpit.org/Contents/Channel_4035/2020/0531/1264357/content_1264357.htm

China Council for the Promotion of International Trade. (2020b). *IWA on Guidelines for Contactless Delivery Service.* https://www.ccpit.org/Contents/Channel_4113/2020/0521/1262238/content_1262238.htm

China Dining Industry Association. (2021). *Technical Guide for COVID-19 Prevention and Control in Catering Service Units.* http://www.chcdia.cn/xiehuidongtai/1/768.html

China Hospitality Association. (2019a). *MeiTuan Dianping Unmanned Delivery Team Presented at the World Artificial Intelligence Conference.* http://www.chinahotel.org.cn/forward/enterenterSecondDaryOther.do?contentId=431f924e4ff64f0b82a99d08d2b0c7e4

China Hospitality Association. (2019b). *Wang Xing, CEO of MeiTuan Dianping: Digitalization on the Supply Side Has a Long Way to Go and is Full of Challenges.* http://www.chinahotel.org.cn/forward/enterenterSecondDaryOther.do?contentId=e117f0e870e14e5b934f955a24b27635

China Hospitality Association. (2020). *China Hospitality Association Actively Communicated with Ali Local Life Service Companies (Ele. me and Koubei) to Implement the Policy of Reducing Commission on the Platform to Help Small and Medium-sized Merchants.* http://www.chinahotel.org.cn/forward/enterenterSecondDaryOther.do?contentId=151b7d3a87804dee83356e585d3477f3

China Hospitality Association. (2021). *Xiaoming Shi: Strive for the "14th Five-Year Plan" to Build an Open and Win-win Platform for the Take-out Industry.* http://www.chinahotel.org.cn/forward/enterenterSecondDaryOther.do?contentId=64a7b024d05f4fbe837032613d8c0d42

China news. (2021). *Those in the Catering, Tourism and Exhibition Industries That are Heavily Affected by the Epidemic, don't Miss the Benefits of These Policies.* http://www.chinanews.com/sh/2021/03-19/9435901.shtml

Choi, Y., Zhang, L., Debbarma, J., & Lee, H. (2021). Sustainable Management of Online to Offline Delivery Apps for Consumers' Reuse Intention: Focused on the MeiTuan Apps. *Sustainability*, *13*(7), 3593. doi:10.3390u13073593

Dai, H., Tao, J., Jiang, H., & Chen, W. (2019). O2O On-demand Delivery Optimization with Mixed Driver Forces. *IFAC-PapersOnLine*, *52*(13), 391–396. doi:10.1016/j.ifacol.2019.11.156

Ding, N., & Chu, X. (2012). Study on the Spatial Pattern of Catering Industry in Urumqi and its Influencing Factors. *Journal of Yili Normal University*, *6*(1), 37–41.

Elvandari, C. D. R., Sukartiko, A. C., & Nugrahini, A. D. (2018). Identification of Technical Requirement for Improving Quality of Local Online Food Delivery Service in Yogyakarta'. *Journal of Industry and Information Technology in Agriculture*, *1*(2), 1. doi:10.24198/jiita.v1i2.14573

Food & Drug Administration. (2020). *Best Practices for Retail Food Stores, Restaurants, and Food pick-up/ delivery Services during the COVID-19 Pandemic.* https://www.fda.gov/food/food-safety-during-emergencies/best-practices-retail-food-stores-restaurants-and-food-pick-updelivery-services-during-covid-19

Gavilan, D., Balderas-Cejudo, A., Fernández-Lores, S., & Martinez-Navarro, G. (2021). Innovation in Online Food Delivery: Learning from COVID-19. *International Journal of Gastronomy and Food Science*, *24*, 100330. doi:10.1016/j.ijgfs.2021.100330 PMID:34745390

He, B., Mirchandani, P., & Wang, Y. (2021). Removing Barriers for Grocery Stores: O2O Platform and Self-scheduling Delivery Capacity. *Transportation Research Part E, Logistics and Transportation Review*, *141*, 1366–5545. doi:10.1016/j.tre.2020.102036

He, Z., Han, G., Cheng, T. C. E., Fan, B., & Dong, J. (2019). Evolutionary Food Quality and Location Strategies for Restaurants in Competitive Online-to-Offline Food Ordering and Delivery Markets: An Agent-based Approach. *International Journal of Production Economics*, *215*, 61–72. doi:10.1016/j.ijpe.2018.05.008

Hobbs, J. E. (2020). Food Supply Chains during the COVID-19 Pandemic. *Canadian Journal of Agricultural Economics*, *68*(2), 171–176. doi:10.1111/cjag.12237

Holbrook, M. B., & Hirschman, E. C. (1982). The Experiential Aspects of Consumption: Consumer Fantasies, Feelings, and Fun. *The Journal of Consumer Research*, *9*(2), 132–140. doi:10.1086/208906

International Organization for Standardization. (2021). *Upcoming Standards for COVID-19*. https://www.iso.org/news/ref2622.html

IResearch. (2018). *2017 China's Local Lifestyle Service O2O Industry Report*. http://www.iresearchchina.com/content/details8_35352.html

Karim, W., Haque, A., Anis, Z., & Ulfy, M. A. (2020). The Movement Control Order (MCO) for COVID-19 Crisis and its Impact on Tourism and Hospitality Sector in Malaysia. *International Journal of Tourism and Hospitality*, *3*(2), 1–7.

Kaur, P., Dhir, A., Talwar, S., & Ghuman, K. (2021). The Value Proposition of Food Delivery Apps from the Perspective of Theory of Consumption Value. *International Journal of Contemporary Hospitality Management*, *33*(4), 1129–1159. doi:10.1108/IJCHM-05-2020-0477

Kim, J. J., Kim, I., & Hwang, J. (2021). A Change of Perceived Innovativeness for Contactless Food Delivery Services Using Drones After the Outbreak of COVID-19. *International Journal of Hospitality Management*, *93*, 102758. doi:10.1016/j.ijhm.2020.102758

Li, Xiong, Mariuzzo, & Xia. (2021). The Underexplored Impacts of Online Consumer Reviews: Pricing and New Product Design Strategies in the O2O Supply Chain. *International Journal of Production Economics, 237*. . doi:10.1016/j.ijpe.2021.108148

Liang, D., Dai, Z., & Wang, M. (2021). Assessing Customer Satisfaction of O2O Takeaway Based on Online Reviews by Integrating Fuzzy Comprehensive Evaluation with AHP and Probabilistic Linguistic Term Sets. *Applied Soft Computing*, *98*, 106847. doi:10.1016/j.asoc.2020.106847

Lim, S. F. W., Jin, X., & Srai, J. S. (2018). Consumer-driven E-commerce: A Literature Review, Design Framework, and Research Agenda on Last-mile Logistics Models. *International Journal of Physical Distribution and Logistics*, *48*(3), 308–332. doi:10.1108/IJPDLM-02-2017-0081

Masudin, I., Ramadhani, A., & Restuputri, D. P. (2021). Traceability System Model of Indonesian Food Cold-chain Industry: A Covid-19 Pandemic Perspective. *Cleaner Engineering and Technology*, *4*, 2666–7908. doi:10.1016/j.clet.2021.100238

Maximo Torero Cullen. (2020). *COVID-19 and the Risk to Food Supply Chains: How to respond?* Food and Agriculture Organization of the United Nations (FAO). https://www.fao.org/policy-support/tools-and-publications/resources-details/en/c/1269383/

MeiTuan & China Federation of Logistics and Purchasing. (2019). *Report on the Development of Chinese Immediate Delivery Business in 2019.* http://pdf.dfcfw.com/pdf/H3_AP202006011381522218_1.pdf

MeiTuan Research Institute. (2019). *China Food Delivery Industry Investigation Report (first three quarters of 2019).* Author.

MeiTuan Research Institute. (2020). *China Food Delivery Industry Development Report 2019 and the First Half of 2020.* Author.

Melkonyan, A., Gruchmann, T., Lohmar, F., Kamath, V., & Spinler, S. (2020). Sustainability Assessment of Last-mile Logistics and Distribution Strategies: The Case of Local Food Networks. *International Journal of Production Economics, 228*, 107746. doi:10.1016/j.ijpe.2020.107746

Mohan, S., Gopalakrishnan, M., & Mizzi, P. J. (2013). Improving the Efficiency of a Non-profit Supply Chain for the Food Insecure. *International Journal of Production Economics, 143*(2), 248–255. doi:10.1016/j.ijpe.2011.05.019

Niu, B., Li, Q., Mu, Z., Chen, L., & Ji, P. (2021). Platform Logistics or Self-logistics? Restaurants' Co-operation with Online Food-delivery Platform Considering Profitability and Sustainability. *International Journal of Production Economics, 234*, 108064. doi:10.1016/j.ijpe.2021.108064

Ray, A., Dhir, A., Bala, P. K., & Kaur, P. (2019). Why do People Use Food Delivery Apps (FDA)? A Uses and Gratification Theory Perspective. *Journal of Retailing and Consumer Services, 51*, 221–230. doi:10.1016/j.jretconser.2019.05.025

Research and Markets. (2020). *5 Ways Drones Can Help in a Pandemic.* https://www.researchand-markets.com/issues/covid-19-drones?utm_medium=GNOM%26utm_source=covid19%26utm_campaign=gnuav00

Rotar, A. (2021). *Online Food Delivery Report 2021.* https://www.statista.com/outlook/digital-markets

Seghezzi, A., & Mangiaracina, R. (2020). On-demand Food Delivery: Investigating the Economic Performances. *International Journal of Retail & Distribution Management, 49*(4), 531–549. doi:10.1108/IJRDM-02-2020-0043

Shi, X., Wang, S., Hao, F., & Xie, S. (2019). The Spatial Distribution and Formation of Take-out O2O Catering Industry Based on Entity Restaurants Comparison in Changchun. *Human Geographies, 34*(2), 80–89.

Tan, X., Ran, L., & Liao, F. (2020). Contactless Food Supply and Delivery System in the COVID-19 Pandemic: Experience from Raytheon Mountain Hospital, China. *Risk Management and Healthcare Policy, 13*, 3087–3088. doi:10.2147/RMHP.S286786 PMID:33376431

Tandon, A., Kaur, P., Bhatt, Y., Mäntymäki, M., & Dhir, A. (2021). Why do People Purchase from Food Delivery Apps? A Consumer Value Perspective. *Journal of Retailing and Consumer Services, 63*, 102667. doi:10.1016/j.jretconser.2021.102667

The Korea Herald. (2020). *PM Appeals for Strict Adherence to Social Distancing Campaign to Stem Coronavirus*. http://www.koreaherald.com/view.php?ud=20200418000060

Tong, T., Dai, H., Xiao, Q., & Yan, N. (2020). Will Dynamic Pricing Outperform? Theoretical Analysis and Empirical Evidence from O2O On-Demand Food Service Market. *International Journal of Production Economics*, *219*, 375–385. doi:10.1016/j.ijpe.2019.07.010

Waimai, M. T. (2021). *Delivery Business Process*. https://developer.MeiTuan.com/docs/biz/biz_Waimaing_b0f1ddde-783f-4235-874e-38f582f1654d

Wang, L. (2018). *2018 Investor Day: Ele.me Alibaba Local Service*. https://www.alibabagroup.com/en/ir/presentations/Investor_Day_2018_Eleme.pdf

Wang, L., & Yi, B. (2019). Research on O2O Take-away Restaurant Recommendation System: Taking Ele.me APP as an Example. *Cluster Computing*, *22*(S3), 6069–6077. doi:10.100710586-018-1814-y

Wang, X., Wang, L., Wang, S., Chen, J., & Wu, C. (2021). An XGBoost-enhanced Fast Constructive Algorithm for Food Delivery Route Planning Problem. *Computers & Industrial Engineering*, *152*, 107029. doi:10.1016/j.cie.2020.107029

Wei Jia, Z. (2015). *O2O Food Delivery Supply Chain Platform Analysis (Ele.me)*. https://mp.weixin.qq.com/s/xGMQ5WRr13HSM8YJVmM-jw

Zhan, Y., & Chen, K. Z. (2021). Building Resilient Food System Amidst COVID-19: Responses and Lessons from China. *Agricultural Systems*, *190*, 103102. doi:10.1016/j.agsy.2021.103102

Zhao, Y., & Bacao, F. (2020). What Factors Determining Customer Continuingly Using Food Delivery Apps during 2019 Novel Coronavirus Pandemic Period? *International Journal of Hospitality Management*, *91*, 102683. doi:10.1016/j.ijhm.2020.102683 PMID:32929294

## KEY TERMS AND DEFINITIONS

**Contactless Delivery:** "Contactless delivery" was the delivery service model which was first introduced by MeiTuan during the fight against the epidemic. To be specific, placing goods in designated locations reduces the risk of infection by reducing face-to-face contact so as to ensure the safety of consumers and take-out delivery clerks in the delivery link.

**Food Delivery APPs (FDAs):** Based on the popularity of smart phones, APPs have been developed as an effective platform to connect consumers, catering enterprises and take-out delivery clerks. On the client side, consumers place orders by browsing merchant information. Then, the merchant prepares the products / services according to the order and the take-out delivery clerks deliver them to the consumers. Meanwhile, consumers could see the delivery location and expected arrival time of the riders, and contact the riders in-time through the channel of FDAs.

**Intelligent Dispatch:** Taking advantage of information technology, "Intelligent Dispatch" delivery system provides an efficient order distribution scheme and optimal route planning, combining with order information, delivery personnel capacity information, traffic and weather conditions, to achieve the best match of consumers and take-out delivery clerks.

**On-Demand Service:** It refers to providing timely service to consumers. In the OFD industry, it refers to the delivery of goods or services to users without time or place restrictions.

**Online Food Delivery (OFD):** It refers to the point-to-point logistics services for take-out within the city, mainly including order receiving, delivery, distribution, delivery and other links.

**Online-to-Offline (O2O):** O2O refers to the combination of offline business with the Internet. In the OFD industry, major take-out catering enterprises adopt O2O mode, which integrates online services with offline ones, including sales, marketing, and delivery. For consumers, it means placing orders online and receiving products / services offline.

**Take-Out:** To provide users with a variety of goods and off-site purchase services, it connects consumers with catering and retail enterprises through the Internet or telephone. In a narrow sense, take-out refers to the delivery service of fast food. Broadly speaking, take-out refers to all products and services. Consumers could order food products or services online without leaving home.

**Take-Out Delivery Clerk:** It refers to service personnel engaged in takeaway delivery. Take-out delivery clerks are mainly responsible for receiving orders and picking up goods from corresponding merchants. Finally, the goods will be delivered to consumers within the specified time.

# Chapter 12
# Training and Upgrading Skills of Employees Towards Building Resilience Among the Workforce

**Kakul Agha**

https://orcid.org/0000-0002-5127-5499

*Skyline University College, UAE*

## ABSTRACT

*Organizations worldwide realize the value of creating and sustaining a resilient workforce as employees have been battered with physical, social, and psychological pressures due to the unexpected and challenging demands of pandemic. This chapter revolves around training, upskilling, and reskilling in organizations and establishes their relationship with building resilience in employees. It is significantly relevant and timely as work relationships and expectations have suddenly changed across sectors and industries. It is imperative to include scenarios gathered from the United Arab Emirates (UAE), hence a case study of EFS Facilities Services Group using primary and secondary data has been added. This case is a direct evidence of building resilience in workforce with the help of upskilling and reskilling. This chapter will inform of practices adopted for building resilience among workforce at a global level. Conclusions and recommendations inform about different interventions that organizations can adopt in order to build a resilient workforce.*

## INTRODUCTION

Training, development and upgradation of skills is an aged formula for organizations. Most organizations have been investing heavily in training and development (T&D) activities with a belief that overall employee performance shall be positively impacted. But today, the question is not about employee performance alone, as organizations are grappling with changed work demands after the world struggles to come out of the impact of pandemic COVID-19. Over the decades most jobs have seen difficulties and

DOI: 10.4018/978-1-7998-9506-0.ch012

*Training and Upgrading Skills of Employees*

employees have faced adversities at workplace. Over a couple of years, the most pressing issue faced by services sector employers and employees is the growing impact of the pandemic. This experience faced by employees was one of its kind as it brought sudden, drastic and new changes in organizations. Most of the employees have faced a host of different experiences owing to pandemic COVID-19. The work processes have changed drastically in order to sustain in the market and satisfy the demands of customers. This is a global phenomenon and not focused on any particular region or country.

The world faced a long lockdown where travel and hospitality industry came to a standstill. On the contrary, healthcare sector boomed and workforce was plagued with new sorts of tasks, responsibilities, expectations and performance norms. Several other industries felt the jerks of the new world order to differing degrees. It was interesting to see how the demands of the world changed, how product and service suppliers evolved and how the new world order was defined in the previous couple of years (2020-21). The standards of performance and stress levels of workforce also shifted levels. These changes triggered organizations to think of making themselves and their workforce more resilient and ready to imbibe change. "Resilience" became a key word in the post-pandemic times and the role of HR emerged more conspicuously for training employees to become more resilient (Oliver et al., 2006). Being resilient, simply meant being strong during stress, isolation, loneliness, extra work and to be able to withstand adverse times, like the pandemic COVID-19.

## MAIN FOCUS OF THE CHAPTER

The main focus of this chapter is to create awareness among readers about the concept of "resilience" and its usage among employees impacted by the new normal. The primary issues dealt with in this chapter are pertaining to the value of being adaptable and flexible to newness at work along with being agile and resilient for successful work experiences. The author has set the tone of the chapter in a way that readers quickly imbibe the importance of being resilient and embed traits that help them to survive difficult times like the pandemic COVID-19. The literature review provides a path for readers highlighting the research carried out in the past by cotemporary researchers and authors and EFS case study provides real time information about the implications of the topic. It reiterates the concept and process of building resilience at workplace.

The topic of resilience has been highlighted in this chapter to create awareness among managers and decision makers so that organizations can adopt new interventions to build and enhance resilience among their employees. It is unfortunate that a large percentage of employers tend to be unclear about the process of building and sustaining resilience in workforce and may face a difficult situation during tough and turbulent market situations. The case study provides insights on how training can be used as one of the interventions in organizations undergoing tough times e.g. pandemic COVID-19. So the study lays emphasis on upskilling, reskilling and upgradation of skills through training interventions as tough times demand new and updated skills among employees.

## BACKGROUND

The pandemic COVID-19 has enabled us to think of innovative ways of building resilience among members of the society. Overall there may be multiple ways of understanding resilience. Some of the interesting explanations are explained by Catalano, Berglund, Ryan et al. (2002), Garmezy (1991) and Rutter (1985, 1999) which indicate that resilience is a positive ability of people to recover from stressful events, setbacks and adverse life and professional events. Resilience does not imply invulnerability to stress but an ability to bounce back from such stress. Olsson, Bond, Burns et al. (2003) explain that resilience is not an inherent behavior but an adapted quality or rather an adaptive process that is a result of the stressful incidents for the individual. The word resilience originated during 1800s from a Latin verb "resilire" which means "to leap back". Hence "bounce back" or "being able to recover back quickly from difficult situations" can be easily related to resilience (Robertson et al., 2015; Jackson et al., 2007). According to Jackson et al., (2007), adversity and resilience go hand in hand as the former is about trauma, distress and tragic events and is viewed as negative and stressful. These are directly related to the quality of resilience which could be synonymous to self-discipline, flexibility, resourcefulness, problem solving, emotional strength and self-confidence.

Which individuals are resilient? Research shows that individuals who are able to cope up with stress in an effective manner tend to be more resilient than others. The resilient attributes may fall into dispositional or personal, family or social, and environmental characteristics (Oliver et al., 2006). A study indicated that students have cited personal strength to be a source of resilience which is different from social workers who highlight its source as the interaction between personal attributes and protective environment (Seng et al., 2021). Autonomy, empowerment, emotional awareness and self-care support in developing resilience in people (Jackson et al., 2007). Further, Jackson et al., (2007) propose that specific self-development strategies can support in resilience building like having a nurturing workplace environment and work relationships between teams (*e.g. colleagues acting as 'sounding boards', mentoring relationships guidance and support from colleagues, managers and peers*); enhancing positivity at workplace (*e.g. positive emotions and laughter*); supporting self-reflection and emotional insight (*e.g. journaling*); and working towards work-life balance and spirituality (*e.g. participating in physically, emotionally and spiritually nurturing activities*). Garmezy (1991) adds that resilience is related to positive outcomes like sound mental health, functional capacity and social competence. It further acts like a buffer for the harmful impact of work-related stress, especially since the outbreak of pandemic COVID-19 (Seng et al., 2021).

## BUILDING RESILIENCE THROUGH TRAINING INTERVENTIONS

A key component of this chapter is to establish the importance of training, reskilling, upskilling and upgradation of skills in building resilience during difficult times, with a special focus on the impact of pandemic COVID-19 on the workforce. This chapter not only clarifies the concept of resilience but also delves into how organizations are making efforts to build resilience among its workforce. An extant of pertinent and timely literature has established the value and importance of work-based resilience. Mostly all organizations thrive on role models, trustworthy organizational culture, ability and opportunity for reflexivity among employees, relevant training and development opportunities, diversity and workplace culture as being the drivers for building resilience among the workforce (Seng et al., 2021). Hence, this chapter will focus on impact of training and development of workforce on building resilience. As a fact, nobody can deny that organizations across the globe are thriving for enhanced levels of training and development initiatives since many decades. So how has it been suddenly linked to building resilience? This primary question stems from studying the impacts of the COVID-19 pandemic. This pandemic has taught organizations new ways of creating value in the market. Instead of creating higher redundancy levels in the market recent research points out to concepts of reskilling and upskilling of workforce.

To define "training" in simple words, "it is teaching or development employees any knowledge, skills, competencies and abilities that allow them to be fitter for their jobs". Training is associated with identification of goals, alignment of desired knowledge, skills and abilities (KSAs) and improvement process of one's capabilities and capacity of performance. Similarly, "upskilling" means investing significant time and resources in workforce to develop advanced skills through education and training. Upskilling in not a one-time effort, but rather a cumulative process where employees are given ample opportunities like educational initiatives, attending conferences and workshops, short term training etc. in order to keep abreast with the changes and demands of the industry. "Reskilling" on the other hand, is a word that explains itself as "a process of learning new skills so that an employee could do a different job". The immediate difference between upskilling is that "it trains people to do the job effectively" while reskilling "prepares employees for different jobs". But it is true that both are forms of training in organizations. In one of the forms of training through ABCD model, it is said that

*C (emotional consequences) stem not directly from A (adversity) but from B (one's beliefs about adversity). ... work through a series of A's (falling out of a three-mile run, for example) and learn to separate B's—heat-of-the-moment thoughts about the situation ("I'm a failure")—from C's, the emotions generated by those thoughts (such as feeling down for the rest of the day and thus performing poorly in the next training exercise). They then learn D—how to quickly and effectively dispel unrealistic beliefs about adversity (Seligman, 2011).*

Further it is taught that there may be four basic ways for mastering resilience through *active constructive (authentic, enthusiastic support), passive constructive (laconic support), passive destructive (ignoring the event), and active destructive (pointing out negative aspects of the event)* (Seligman, 2011).

As researched by Forbes and Fikretoglu (2018) and presented in a coherent manner in their research, it further proves that resilience is an extremely complex and difficult phenomenon to measure and understand. Further, a host of pertinent literature reveals that resilience training programs have been used by the organizations in order to enhance the former within employees in organizations. They add that there is a high degree of difficulty involved in designing and delivering the programs targeted to building resilience within the workforce (Forbes & Fikretoglu, 2018). Requisite literature keeps deliberating on the types of training programs provided in general and for those targeted to resilience building among workforce and how they tend to be different from the existing training given to workforce (Forbes & Fikretoglu, 2018). So it further proves that there is a need for organizations to evaluate the type of training they are offering in the light of the industry, type of workforce and the impact of the pandemic (in the current scenario). Now a days, several world reports have suggested the value of upskilling and reskilling (e.g. Gartner and Deloitte) as training tools to be deployed for workforce so that the impact of pandemic can be mitigated to a substantial extent. It is estimated that mindfulness training supports in building resilience among workforce especially when they are impacted by large and forceful events like pandemic COVID-19. Training of all types including personal characters and resources training, support individuals in enhancing coping skills which is critical for resilience. When the training is offered during real time, then the learners are able to learn and adopt more as they are being nurtured in an environment that is around them and hence gives them hands-on experience (Forbes & Fikretoglu, 2018). It is also informed through research that direct, practical and experiential learning helps support

*Training and Upgrading Skills of Employees*

resilience building. Thus, resilience training and interventions need to be provided to employees who actually require them at real time of need, which is when they are facing adversity at workplace (Forbes & Fikretoglu, 2018).

There is a need in all industries to train the workforce for being more resilient during tough times. The restaurant sector needs extensive training as they face a lot of new challenges on a daily basis. Keeping in mind and a special focus on the impact of pandemic on the food and beverage industry at large and restaurant sector in specific, a large impetus on training, upskilling and reskilling has been identified. It is a requirement to adapt to new norms and methods of working, as this sector has a responsibility of ensuring health and safety of its customers and workforce following established practices and imbibing new ones on a regular basis (de Freitas & Stedefeldt, 2020).

In a recent study by Giordano et al., (2021), the researchers emphasize on the importance of conducting resilience training for the health sector. The health personnel have substantially been affected by the pandemic COVID-19. In due process of the outbreak of pandemic and its spread across the globe workforce of this sector was affected physically, mentally and emotionally. It is vital to note that workforce related to this sector showed symptoms of developing anxiety, stress, and tardiness along with physical and mental exhaustion at workplace. So it calls for an all-round effort in supporting the healthcare workers. Resilience training like upskilling and reskilling impacts the performance of such workers and further motivates and encourages them to keep performing in challenging times. It provides them the right knowledge of processes and norms to be followed along with giving them the higher order skills to perform their job more effectively and efficiently (Giordano et al., 2021). A similar study on nurses in the healthcare sector (Duncan, 2020) reported that even though a lot of training is on-going in this sector, special resilience building training should be mandatory during challenging and unique situations similar to pandemic COVID-19. Further, in an interesting study carried out Dr. Michael Ungar and Resilience Research Centre team at Dalhousie University (Halifax, Canada) for healthcare leaders, the complete focus was on developing resilience through various forms of training provided for the leaders. Most of the training revolved around three goals:

1. Increase organizational capacity to build a resilient organization through a deeper understanding of individual 'rugged' qualities and external 'resources' (the two 'R's');
2. Help leaders integrate qualities of resilience into their organization's prevention programs including policies, procedures and the types of resources offered to workers;
3. Utilize a methodology to design programs that build resilience which are contextually specific" (Giordano et al., 2021).

This study gives an insight into the methodology for framing training programs for healthcare workers and provides a direct understanding of the worth of training in healthcare sector.

In another remarkable study, the importance of Competency Training, Computer based resilience training and Education sessions that are resilience focused have been identified as important for healthcare sector workforce in building resilience during the pandemic COVID-19. This clearly indicates the value of resource investment in training especially upskilling and reskilling the workforce as per the requirements of the sector (Heath et al., 2020). Not only this sector, but occupations like military officers, fire fighters, police officers and disaster relief personnel require resilience related training programs. Further, individuals related to social service, education sector and customer service also get affected during challenging times like the pandemic COVID-19 as they face deterioration in mental, psychological and

*Training and Upgrading Skills of Employees*

physical wellbeing along with work related stress (Vanhove et al., 2016). They need training in order to fulfill new demands of work and customers. Work related demands occur due to new conditions that evolve with changing nature of the market. As clearly evident, due to pandemic COVID-19, the workforce is subject to new patterns and methods of work, evolving demands of customers, stringent requirements of workplace and even new norms and regulations and that put added pressure on the workforce. This pressure can be strategically relieved if the workforce receives a systematically well-planned and executed training session related to reskilling and upskilling. Overall, adding new skills through upskilling and honing the existing skills as per the requirements of the new times will add substantial confidence among the workforce thus boosting their morale and building resilience in them.

de Visser et al., (2016) reiterate that stress resilience training program (SRTP) provides substantial support to employees to mitigate stress and its adaptations can support better well-being and enhanced job performance for athletes, personal fitness and healthcare workers along with law enforcement personnel. This also supports that service-oriented personnel are mostly accustomed to higher stress and need to build better resilience.

An extremely thought-provoking example has been presented by Kumar and Kumar (2021) in their study related to training and building resilience. They informed that training supports not only in building technical skills but also a positive mindset, enhancing adaptability to change and acceptance of new norms leading to increased performance and competitive spirit (Kumar & Kumar, 2021). Further, the research adds importance to using technology-enabled training methods that could be better suited for difficult and challenging times like that of current pandemic COVID-19 (Kumar & Kumar, 2021). The research added that e-training supported the workforce in enhancing skills of interaction and proactiveness; helped build soft skills like interpersonal skills, empathy, social skills, problem-solving, team spirit and responsibility along with enhancing the readiness of employees for facing new challenges and difficulties (Kumar & Kumar, 2021; Li et al., 2020).

These studies were neither limited to one sector nor focused on one industry. Together they support the cause and need to build resilience in workforce and the best method is training the workforce. It is evident when substantial research explains the value and worth of training, upskilling and reskilling in building resilience among workforce. Not even a single research informed that training is negatively related to resilience building or has not impacted it in any way. Therefore, most organizations have resorted to upskilling and reskilling training techniques with an extremely focused approach in this direction.

## SOLUTIONS

In order to understand the solutions adopted across various sectors here is a case study of an organization named as EFS Facilities Services Group that supports the idea of building resilience through upskilling and reskilling among workforce. This organization is a home-grown service sector business in the United Arab Emirates (UAE).

## EFS Facilities Services Group

EFS Facilities Services Group (EFS) is an organization dedicated to providing integrated facilities management services across Middle East, Africa, South Asia and Turkey since the last two decades with operations in 21 countries. The unique selling proposition (USP) of EFS remains to be "people-first", "quality service delivery" and "innovation" which has supported EFS legacy of near 100 percent client retention and high customer satisfaction. The broad portfolio of EFS comprises of prestigious clients ranging from government organizations to several Fortune 500 organizations. In all, EFS offers around 75 services with business verticals such as public sector, education, retail and mixed-use developments, banking, industrial and oil & gas. The organization follows QMS-ISO 9001:2015, EMS-ISO14001:2015, OHSAS18001:2007 and ISO/IEC27001:2013 standards rendering high service quality, leading to great reputation for the organization that supports in building customer loyalty and trust. In spite of the sheer size of the organization, EFS has been receiving many accolades and awards throughout decades for its outstanding performance. The Chief Executive Officer (CEO) of EFS Group, Mr Tariq Chauhan, has been the driving force and is leading the organization to new milestones repeatedly. His focus on the welfare of the blue-collar workers enabled EFS to bag the prestigious Taqdeer Award, UAE in 2021, as a recognition of implementing best practices for a conducive work environment for its workforce.

EFS Facilities Services recruits experienced and competent personnel in all positions following a standard recruitment and selection process. At EFS, there is a concerted effort to find the best fit for every position in the organization. The vision of EFS is *"To be the preferred facilities management service provider of choice"*. The company aspires to achieve the mission which explains as *"To ensure superior service delivery by engaging stakeholders to take ownership and building a sustainable enterprise"*. To achieve the mission, EFS has weaved its values as "Honesty, Ethics, Teamwork, Transparency, Trust, Integrity, Mutual Respect, Enterprise Ownership and Accountability". These values fall in line with several leading internationally recognized organizations of the world indicating that EFS has benchmarked itself to the best organizations of the world. EFS strives hard to deliver quality facility management and value added services to its clients across the countries. It is obvious that EFS is able to match the needs of its clients and provide sustainable service delivery, optimum cost savings and high user satisfaction to the end users. This can only be achieved through focus on clients' needs, good planning and insightful execution of operations.

EFS believes in and works towards being an "Employer of Choice". It is a diverse organization with a multicultural environment with zero discrimination policy. It invests in training and development of employees in order to enhance the knowledge, skills and abilities (KSAs) of its employees. Eventually, it has become a preferred organization for millennials as they foresee growth and development in the organization. The agenda of Happiness is also taken forward by EFS and they support concepts of work-life balance, suitable industry benefits and opportunities for growth. The top management is highly committed to establishing a culture of nurturing and mentoring so that each and every employee can grow effectively. A carefully curated open culture enables trustworthiness and confidence among employees who are assured of maximizing their potential at EFS. The company is dedicated to providing different types of training in soft skills and core facility management services such as engineering and soft services. EFS has a state-of-the-art training facility that is accredited by Global Bio-Risk Advisory Council (GBAC), a division of ISSA, the global cleaning industry trade association and BICSc (British Institute of Cleaning Sciences) with qualified and licensed assessors team that trains and certifies employees. The training centre is additionally backed by EFS' affiliations to IFMA (International Facility Management Association).

In the past decades, EFS Facilities Services has made a strategic effort to train its employees for building a variety of competencies. Off late the organization has refocused on its upskilling and reskilling efforts, especially after seeing the impact of the pandemic, COVID-19. Some of the key initiatives of EFS are detailed in the following sections. The first initiative is *Talim Initiative* which is EFS's mobile

*Training and Upgrading Skills of Employees*

micro-learning platform that is in collaboration with their technology partners, MobieTrain. It is set up to empower and guide EFS frontline workers and encourage the passion for learning and development. In addition, the platform provides diverse content to the employees based on self-learning, daily workflow, inductions, health, safety, environment and quality (HSEQ), and updates through one seamless in-app experience. Till 2021, 107 courses have been developed in-house across multiple business functions providing unique learning paths (including gamification, storytelling, and quizzes) for each individual employee who can access the relevant courses at his/her convenience and complete a full learning cycle which is measured through assessments. The remarkable features are that employees do not have to be scheduled to move out of site for training and have the freedom to choose the time of training and learning where they feel most productive. The programs are self-paced allowing slow learners to be trained effectively. The organization is able to record and assess performance data of the employees thus enabling HR to identify candidates with high ability against those who need improvement. Using this classification, employees are selected for SEED programs and organizational progression (promotion and empowerment) as well as for tailored programs for improving employees that require support. This has impacted the employees in extremely positive and promising ways and simultaneously enabled cost-saving of AED 264K net of deployment costs for EFS.

The second initiative worth mentioning is the *Skills Excellence Empowering Development Program (SEED program)*. EFS mission is to empower its workforce by continuously researching and designing learning and development programs meant to impact every team member's growth. In line with this, the SEED program is designed to empower all EFS supervisors by creating a learning journey based on Personal, Functional, and Professional Development. The SEED program is conducted for 10-months and is custom-made based on employee skill specialization and scope of the job service (Soft services for housekeeping and office support services staff; Hard services for Operations and Maintenance and Specialized systems maintenance staff). In the pilot phase, EFS had conducted this program for over 18 critical projects in UAE. More than 7,450 training hours have been undertaken for this course for a total of 54 members of EFS workforce till date.

EFS has a *Centre of Cleaning Excellence (COCE)* which is the state-of-the-art training facility built and operated by EFS for imparting specialized training and upskilling to both the new and existing staff especially for soft services such as cleaning and housekeeping, hospitality services, etc. Since its establishment, COCE has trained 2,142 headcounts on various subjects of housekeeping and cleaning services. This training has enabled employees to be upskilled with 19% becoming eligible for progression into team leaders and supervisor roles. This directly leads to an average increase of 22% in cash salary for team leaders and 34% for supervisors. As per the organization's reports (Q3FY2021), 9,274 instructor-led training hours were completed at EFS across 6 different countries.

EFS also runs the *English language program for skill assessment*, as a diverse workforce from different parts of the world are on the roll calls of EFS. Not all employees are native English speakers leading to the efficacy of this program. EFS conducted a cognitive ability test powered by artificial intelligence for its 2,000 employees in Dubai through Lexplore, in collaboration with Mirai Partners. Lexplore is an artificial intelligence (AI) and eye-tracking literacy assessment system to detect literacy levels and developmental delays, including dyslexia. For the 2,000 employees tested under this program and identified for further training and development "Beginners were 414", "Intermediate level were 1,368" and "Advanced level were 218" (scores were based on the scale established by Lexplore). Employees identified with high literacy capability but poor language skills were provided fast track English language development programs. Improvement plans for the beginner grade were prescribed based on the three further rounds of assessment equally distributed between capabilities of reading, writing, speaking and listening.

EFS established the *Abhaar Worker Welfare Foundation*, which is a corporate social responsibility (CSR) initiative. It has been established to support the aspirations of migrant workers and it stands to solve the challenges of unskilled and semi-skilled workforce. The main objectives of the Abhaar Worker Welfare foundation are related to learning and development and revolve around (1) Supporting upskilling and reskilling needs of employees that have occurred due to rehabilitation and settlement (2) Advancing and promoting education, learning and skill development of employees.

At EFS, a number of dedicated upskilling and reskilling programs have been benefiting the employees since several years. Unless the vision, mission and values of the organization truly guide the organization in such a direction this may not be possible. Secondly, the Group CEO, Mr Tariq Chauhan informed that "the strategic direction of the organization is designed in a way that guides the team to be effective and functional towards building resilience among workforce. At EFS Facilities Services we strongly believe that building resilience is vital for success of our organization and the society at large".
Questions for the Case Study:

1. Analyze the EFS Facilities Services case study in the light of resilience training in workplaces.
2. Propose alternate training programs for EFS Facilities Services beyond their efforts as mentioned in the case study.

## OUTCOMES ACHIEVED

This case sheds light on how organizations can adopt upskilling and reskilling training efforts in order to support workforce in building resilience. King et al., (2016) argues that extant literature is available on building resilience in organizations and this case supports the cause of adding relevant and pertinent information to the existing body of literature. A recent report by Mckinsey reiterates the idea of reskilling the workforce in order to emerge from the consequences of the pandemic COVID-19 (Agrawal et al., 2020).

Recently owing to the new adversity related to the pandemic, the research explains many trends related to reskilling of workforce namely:

1. New skills required for a distant and remote workforce: Several sections of the workforce are currently functioning from remote spaces whereas a few are still online which gives a clear indication that the workforce requires new skills to operate efficiently;
2. Severe imbalance in the demand and supply of talent for the workforce is leading to a need for workforce to be reskilled to fill in the vacant seats in organizations and
3. New demands related to reskilling of workforce so that they can offer production and supply nearer to the end user.

These extremely important trends are shaping the requirements of reskilling in workforce (Agrawal et al., 2020). Additionally, the McKinsey report pointed out a six step plan to reskilling. The steps cascade from identifying the skills needed to recover from the pandemic or any other related adversities; building the skills needed for recovery; launch detailed specific training programs for employees in order to

*Training and Upgrading Skills of Employees*

reskill them; prototype, test and reiterate to find gaps; consolidate the results to find success and last but not the least use the training budget effectively to reskill workforce (Agrawal et al., 2020). These steps that have been designed in the report explain the importance of reskilling and inform the readers that this concept is really critical for organizations who want to leap out of the consequences of the pandemic or any other similar and impactful adversity. The report clearly indicates that those organizations that reskilled its workforce were far more prepared during the pandemic and appear more ready to identify and fill in the skill gaps in comparison to other organizations. In successful organizations it is felt that identification of the pivotal skills supports the organization in developing talent effectively in order to manage difficult times (Agrawal et al., 2020). Essentially developing cognitive, emotional and psychological skills is a must as it supports and enhances resilience and adaptability among the workforce.

A detailed report by Przytuła et al., (2020) encapsulates the requirements of the future where training and reskilling have been highlighted in more than one places. Most organizations are experiencing a skill gap and finding ways to match existing skills with "distance economy" and also to fill the spaces of new roles and activities required to be played during the turbulent times. This lays emphasis on how managers can equip workforce and fill gaps with upskilling and reskilling in organizations. Further, it is explained that skill building should be in four areas: *digital, higher cognitive, social and emotional adaptability* and *resilience* (Przytuła et al., 2020). Data within the report clearly points out on how more than half of the managers are eager and plan to upskill and reskill their workforce and that substantial number of workers across the globe are willing to upgrade their technical and professional skills as a result of the pandemic COVID-19 (Przytuła et al., 2020). Both upskilling and reskilling will be successful tools to avoid redundancy, unemployment, loss of jobs and stagnation in the career of workforce during the post pandemic era (Ray, 2020).

Based on the literature review and data collection for case study the author suggests that building resilience through "Upskilling" and "Reskilling" involves:

*Table 1. Resilience through upskilling and reskilling*

| | |
|---|---|
| ***Training on challenges and expectations of the New Normal*** | Providing training is key in areas like:<br>• What is the New Normal? Is it here to stay and be the Always Normal?<br>• Dos and Don'ts of the New Normal<br>• Ways of accepting the New Normal<br>• Key difficulties related to the New Normal<br>• What should I do to adjust and accept the New Normal?<br>• Importance of self, family, friends and colleagues<br>• My role in Corporate Social Responsibility (CSR) |
| ***Providing Tech-training to blue-collar employees (hard skills)*** | Providing technology related training to employees<br>• Reiteration of basic technology related training<br>• Any sort of new machine specific training<br>• Computer training – maybe advanced level or new program or even new/enhanced features in the same program<br>• New computer program or software training |
| ***Offering new sales training*** | These training types could be related to:<br>• Dealing with new customers<br>• Dealing with same customers but with changed or new norms (due to new market or government requirements or evolution of new trends)<br>• Handling new tasks in sales jobs |
| ***Attitude training (soft skills)*** | This type of training may be unique to the business:<br>• New and positive attitude for same or new jobs<br>• Taking a step at a time and being able to bounce back to normal<br>• Being agile yet consistent<br>• Staying calm amidst turmoil |
| ***Communication skills training (soft skills)*** | There may be a need to level-up the communication skills of employees:<br>• Spoken communication<br>• Written communication capturing ability to tackle problems<br>• Listening skills<br>• Language training |
| ***Empathy and compassion*** | Employees should be able to develop and sustain empathy and compassion towards:<br>• Colleagues and team members<br>• Suppliers and customers<br>• Lower levels of employees including part-time employees<br>• Management and Leaders |
| ***Work-life Integration and Happiness*** | Employees should be trained on to develop a happy life:<br>• Training on Wheel of life and Happiness<br>• Importance of core tenets of life<br>• Relevance of exercise and physical fitness<br>• Value of meditation in life<br>• Self-awareness and self-support |

## FUTURE RESEARCH DIRECTIONS

Ongoing research is already pointing towards building resilience among the workforce. Upskilling and reskilling efforts need to be focused so that the output can be measured positively. However, having said all that, researchers need to undertake more focused research for a variety of industries and sectors, as currently the focus is on healthcare and related front line jobs which have been largely affected during the adverse pandemic times.

*Training and Upgrading Skills of Employees*

Future research should focus on understanding resilience in the modern life and develop scales to measure it. The researchers should be able to encapsulate the elements of study for resilience so that the phenomenon of resilience can be understood in an in-depth manner.

## CONCLUSION

Based on the review of literature and leading reports by consultants that have been published during and after the pandemic COVID-19, it can be ascertained that organizations need to review the condition of their workforce and strategize in a way where the training, upskilling and reskilling are considered as vital investments in the organization and not as a liability. On-going, timely and systematic training for the workforce should be seen as a mandatory way forward.

In this chapter, a systematic attempt has been made to understand and elaborate the concepts of training, upskilling and reskilling and building their relationship with resilience. Resilience has been identified as a unique trait that needs to be developed in the workforce. At the end, with the new world order, post pandemic era, all managers and workforce need to understand that resilience is a new trait in our personalities that cannot be left aside, it needs to be grown and nurtured.

### Implications of the Study

Based on the understanding generated through this chapter, the policy makers, decision makers and managers in organizations need to take "Building Resilience" extremely seriously. For this they need to be vigilant and watchful for their employees and team members.

1. Policy building has been thoughtful and comprehensive and it has to encompass all employees and scenarios
2. Strategies have to be more insightful
3. Implementation has to be more realistic and near to ground level
4. Decision making has to be 360 degrees engaging all levels of employees
5. Strategic HR is the key to success so as to support employees during tough times.

Managers need to realize the worth of employee upskilling and reskilling and the value of building resilience among people within the organization. This understanding will help the organization to sail out of tough times as rightly said "Tough times do not last – Tough Organizations do".

## DISCUSSION QUESTIONS

1. Analyze the concept and application of resilience in a chosen industry. What are the key elements that make resilience at workplace?
2. As a consultant, how would you develop a resilience training program in a chosen sector? What components would you add in the training program?
3. How do you evaluate the success of a resilience training program? Which parameters would you use? Justify.

237

4. Compare and contrast between the concepts of upskilling and reskilling.
5. Find real world examples to study the application of upskilling and reskilling training programs during the pandemic COVID-19.

## REFERENCES

Agrawal, S., De Smet, A., Lacroix, S., & Reich, A. (2020). *To emerge stronger from the COVID-19 crisis, companies should start reskilling their workforces now*. McKinsey & Company.

Catalano, R. F., Berglund, M. L., Ryan, J. A. M., Lonczak, H. S., & Hawkins, J. D. (2002). Positive youth development in the United States: Research findings on evaluations of positive youth development programs. *Prevention and Treatment, 5*(1), 15. Retrieved from http://content.apa.org/journals/pre/5/1/15

de Freitas, R. S. G., & Stedefeldt, E. (2020). COVID-19 pandemic underlines the need to build resilience in commercial restaurants' food safety. *Food Research International, 136*. doi:10.1016/j.foodres.2020.109472

de Visser, E. J., Dorfman, A., Chartrand, D., Lamon, J., Freedy, E., & Weltman, G. (2016). Building resilience with the Stress Resilience Training System: Design validation and applications. *Work (Reading, Mass.), 54*(2), 351–366. doi:10.3233/WOR-162295 PMID:27232057

Duncan, D. (2020). What the COVID-19 pandemic tells us about the need to develop resilience in the nursing workforce. *Nursing Management, 27*(3), 22–27. Advance online publication. doi:10.7748/nm.2020.e1933 PMID:32400142

EFS. (2021). Retrieved November 1, 2021 from: https://www.efsme.com

Forbes, S., & Fikretoglu, D. (2018). Building resilience: The conceptual basis and research evidence for resilience training programs. *Review of General Psychology, 22*(4), 452–468. doi:10.1037/gpr0000152

Garmezy, N. (1991). Resiliency and vulnerability to adverse developmental outcomes associated with poverty. *American Journal of Behavioral Science, 34*(4), 416–430. doi:10.1177/0002764291034004003

Giordano, F., Cipolla, A., & Ungar, M. (2021). Building resilience for healthcare professionals working in an Italian red zone during the COVID-19 outbreak: A pilot study. *Stress and Health*. Advance online publication. doi:10.1002mi.3085 PMID:34312986

Heath, C., Sommerfield, A., & von Ungern-Sternberg, B. S. (2020). Resilience strategies to manage psychological distress among healthcare workers during the COVID-19 pandemic: a narrative review. *Anaesthesia, 75(10), 1364–1371*. doi:10.1111/anae.15180

Jackson, D., Firtko, A., & Edenborough, M. (2007). Personal resilience as a strategy for surviving and thriving in the face of workplace adversity: A literature review. *Journal of Advanced Nursing, 60*(1), 1–9. doi:10.1111/j.1365-2648.2007.04412.x PMID:17824934

King, D. D., Newman, A., & Luthans, F. (2016). Not if, but when we need resilience in the workplace. *Journal of Organizational Behavior, 37*(5), 782–786. doi:10.1002/job.2063

*Training and Upgrading Skills of Employees*

Kumar, S., & Kumar, D. A. (2021). Building Employee Resilience through e-Training: A Case study of National Hydroelectric Power Corporation's Unit. *Turkish Online Journal of Qualitative Inquiry (TOJQI), 12*(5). https://www.researchgate.net/publication/353717157

Li, J., Ghosh, R., & Nachmias, S. (2020). In a time of COVID-19 pandemic, stay healthy, connected, productive, and learning: words from the editorial team of HRDI. *Human Resource Development International, 23(3), 199–207.* doi:10.1080/13678868.2020.1752493

Oliver, K. G., Collin, P., Burns, J., & Nicholas, J. (2006). Building resilience in young people through meaningful participation. *Australian e-Journal for the Advancement of Mental Health, 5*(1), 34–40. doi:10.5172/jamh.5.1.34

Olsson, C. A., Bond, L., Burns, J. M., Vella-Brodrick, D. A., & Sawyer, S. M. (2003). Adolescent resilience: A concept analysis. *Journal of Adolescence, 26*(1), 1–11. doi:10.1016/S0140-1971(02)00118-5 PMID:12550818

Przytuła, S., Strzelec, G., & Krysińska-Kościańska, K. (2020). Re-vision of Future Trends in Human Resource Management (HRM) after COVID-19. *Journal of Intercultural Management, 12*(4), 70–90. doi:10.2478/joim-2020-0052

Ray, T., Warjri, L. B., Jayakumar, A., & Saran, S. (2020). *Digital Debates: CyFy Journal 2020.* ORF and Global Policy Journal.

Rutter, M. (1985). Resilience in the face of adversity: Protective factors and resistance to psychiatric disorder. *The British Journal of Psychiatry, 34*(6), 598–611. doi:10.1192/bjp.147.6.598 PMID:3830321

Rutter, M. (1999). Resilience concepts and findings: Implications for family therapy. *Journal of Family Therapy, 21*(2), 119–224. doi:10.1111/1467-6427.00108

Seligman, M. E. P. (2011). *Building Resilience.* https://hbr.org/2011/04/building-resilience

Seng, B. K., Subramaniam, M., Chung, Y. J., Syed Ahmad, S. A. M., & Chong, S. A. (2021). Resilience and stress in frontline social workers during the COVID-19 pandemic in Singapore. *Asian Social Work and Policy Review, 15*(3), 234–243. doi:10.1111/aswp.12237

Vanhove, A. J., Herian, M. N., Perez, A. L. U., Harms, P. D., & Lester, P. B. (2016). Can resilience be developed at work? A meta-analytic review of resilience-building programme effectiveness. *Journal of Occupational and Organizational Psychology, 89*(2), 278–307. doi:10.1111/joop.12123

## KEY TERMS AND DEFINITIONS

**Pandemic:** A pandemic is an infectious disease that spreads across several continents or worldwide, affecting a significant number of individuals (e.g., COVID-19).

**Resilience:** Resilience can be explained as the ability of individuals or organizations to recover from setbacks (individual loss of job, friend, or relative; drop in market sales; addition in competitors; sudden change in demand or loss of market share etc.) leading to adapting well to change, and keep going in the face of adversity or tough times.

**Reskilling:** Reskilling is the process of acquiring, learning, or adopting new or enhanced skills so you can do a different job to what you were doing before, or training employees to do a different job.

**Training:** Training is defined as teaching an employee a particular skill or type of behavior to fit in the job well.

**Upskilling:** Upskilling can be understood as teach (an employee) additional skills or expanding the skills, abilities and capabilities of employees or even learning additional skills.

# Section 3
# Supply Chain Technologies for Visibility

# Chapter 13

# A Structural Equation Modelling Approach to Develop a Resilient Supply Chain Strategy for the COVID–19 Disruptions

**Subhodeep Mukherjee**
https://orcid.org/0000-0002-6863-4881
*Department of Operations, GITAM School of Business, GITAM (Deemed), Visakhapatnam, India*

**Manish Mohan Baral**
https://orcid.org/0000-0002-9620-1872
*Department of Operations, GITAM School of Business, GITAM (Deemed), Visakhapatnam, India*

**Venkataiah Chittipaka**
https://orcid.org/0000-0002-7804-0796
*School of Management Studies, Indira Gandhi National Open University, New Delhi, India*

**Surya Kant Pal**
*Department of Mathematics, School of Basic Sciences and Research, Sharda University, Greater Noida, India*

## ABSTRACT

*Due to COVID-19, the supply chains were disrupted in many ways. This chapter aims to identify the strategies that can help the industries develop a resilient supply chain that can handle any kind of disruption. Five strategies are determined from the literature review. A questionnaire is being developed for survey-based research in four types of industries. The industries that are targeted are automobile industries, garment industries, steel industries, cement industries. For data analysis, exploratory factor analysis and structural equation modelling are used. In this research, an empirical investigation is carried out to present the research framework. All the proposed hypotheses are accepted, and the developed model satisfied all the parameters.*

DOI: 10.4018/978-1-7998-9506-0.ch013

Copyright © 2022, IGI Global. Copying or distributing in print or electronic forms without written permission of IGI Global is prohibited.

*A Structural Equation Modelling Approach*

## INTRODUCTION

COVID-19 is a type of virus infecting human beings on a large scale. Many countries face many problems due to the pandemic (Sarkis, 2020). Human lives are being lost, and also there is a decrease in economic activities. Many industries face problems as they have to change their strategies to handle this pandemic (Ivanov & Dolgui, 2020; Karmaker et al., 2021). This pandemic negatively impacted many industries like the automobile, travel and tourism, manufacturing, garment, retail, etc. Some of the country's governments had strict regulations like countrywide lockdown to break the virus chain and save human lives (Belhadi et al., 2021). The serious lockdown was implemented in India, where no state movement was allowed except emergency services. Industries were also shut down during these, which badly hit the economy. This also impacted the companies' supply chain (SC), and global SC experienced many challenges like shutdown to seaports, airports, restrictions in vehicle movement, and many others (Ivanov & Dolgui, 2020). The economy will slow recovery from the pandemic by the end of 2021 (Fernandes, 2020).

RSC is built on the rapid generation of insights. SC leaders can respond to disruptions by leveraging advanced analytics to analyze internal and external significant data sources rapidly. Advanced analytics use AI and machine learning to provide predictive and prescriptive recommendations and forecasts (Scheiwiller & Zizka, 2021). Let's take a closer look at the key areas where this technology can add value amid the pandemic. Previous demand forecasts are no longer practical due to significant changes in customer demand patterns (Xue et al., 2021). Various product categories are experiencing demand fluctuations. Analysts who forecast demand have little to no understanding of the factors shaping the market shortly. Because the pandemic is affecting different regions differently, there has never been a greater need for localized and real-time data (Dube et al., 2021; Miani et al., 2021). Organizations should change their estimating approach in the coming months, either because of a super durable change in purchaser practices or the outdated nature of their chronicled information (Xue et al., 2021). Associations expect to start to finish perceivability into stock accessibility in distribution centers and retail stores. They additionally need to know which items are selling, when they are selling them, and where they are offering them to react rapidly to changing requirements (Asamoah et al., 2021; Karmaker et al., 2021; Kumar & Kumar Singh, 2021).

It is essential to have an information base that gives request perceivability across channels and examinations. This diminishes stock overspending by permitting store network groups to renew stock more rapidly. During the limited living stage, retailers should intently look at unofficial laws and what they mean for the activity of different kinds of assembling offices (Acioli et al., 2021; Gregurec et al., 2021; Pavan Kumar et al., 2021). Because of an absence of interest, numerous independent companies are confronting a money crunch. On the off chance that little providers come up short, the retail store network will be additionally disturbed (Barman et al., 2021; Hossain, 2021). Morrisons, a UK-based grocery store chain, paid its little providers promptly to assist them with remaining above water despite Covid vulnerability. In the new ordinary stage, consistent investigation and checking of providers' monetary status will turn out to be significantly more essential. During the pandemic, manufacturers are demanding greater transparency into their suppliers' operations. Improve communication and information sharing by utilizing cloud-based collaborative platforms and SC apps. These tools also provide a secure environment for suppliers and external partners while increasing decision-making speed (P. Chowdhury, Kumar Paul, et al., 2021; Nandi et al., 2021; Amalesh Sharma et al., 2021). Many businesses utilize automation to make their supply chains more autonomous (Barbate et al., 2021; Kaushal & Srivastava, 2021; Monmousseau et al., 2020).

This pandemic had a severe impact on the economy of many countries across the globe. The products ordered by various businesses tend to cancel due to the uncertainty in the delivery (Abu-Rayash & Dincer, 2020; Nhamo et al., 2020). These, in turn, created fluctuations in the stock price of many companies leading them towards recessions. Garments industries SC depends upon the order put forward by the various companies (Peluso et al., 2021). They need to maintain their delivery lead time, proper inventory management, and better reverse logistics. This sector is full of uncertainty and complexity as the customer preference changes according to the seasons (Chesbrough, 2020; Monmousseau et al., 2020). During this pandemic in India, when there was a lockdown, all the fashion stores were closed, so the customer could not visit. After the lockdown, when the shop was opened, customers feared to visit the shop due to an ongoing pandemic, which led to a continuing pandemic to decrease in sales.

The automobile sector faced severe challenges in the COVID-19 pandemic (Brydges et al., 2020; M. T. Chowdhury et al., 2020; Pantano et al., 2020). The sales of the cars fell drastically in many countries as the customers were not ready to purchase any new vehicles in such situations. In countries like India, where there was a complete lockdown in the auto sector, some severe challenges were encountered, such as not supplying cars on time and less inventory available (Belhadi et al., 2021). Steel production decreased worldwide due to the pandemic. It fell by 1.4% in the first three months of 2020. As the automotive industry majorly consumes steel, the pandemic and lockdown automotive industry suffered significant setbacks. Many construction projects were stopped, which also negatively impacted the steel industry. Due to lockdown, many construction sites had to stop their operations, affecting the cement industry. There was a fall of 6.6 per cent in construction output in North America, equivalent to a loss of USD 122.4 billion.

Major industries suffered a loss due to a shortage of workers, disruptions in SC, lack of protective equipment, and many others (Ivanov & Das, 2020; Ivanov & Dolgui, 2020; Morgan et al., 2021; Queiroz, Ivanov, et al., 2020; Verma & Gustafsson, 2020). The main question arises about how to overcome this type of disruption and achieve SC excellence. Resilience is defined as the ability to recover effectively and quickly from disturbance. A resilient supply chain (RSC) should be designed to sustain any disruptions (Chen et al., 2019; Kahiluoto et al., 2020; Mackay et al., 2019). It should be robust, should have the ability to sustain disturbances, and the flow of the materials should not be stopped (Linkov et al., 2020). This research paper aims to discuss the RSC strategies so that the firms can overcome the pandemic. All the strategies are being identified from the literature review.

## BACKGROUND

### Supply Chain Shocks due to the Pandemic

Global and local SC failed in delivering the products at a time due to the pandemic. Due to lockdown in many countries and restrictions in vehicle movement, products could not deliver on time. COVID-19 crisis shocked the SC on two sides, and those are:

1. The first shocks were on the supply side: When the pandemic of COVID-19 occurred in the country of China, which in turn led to the disruptions of the goods sourced from China. Many countries

*A Structural Equation Modelling Approach*

like India, which sourced their raw materials for China's automobile and steel industries, got disrupted. Companies have to see other options ofsupply for the raw materials. So, when the SC network scrambled, companies had to face many issues to deal with it (Lopes de Sousa Jabbour et al., 2020).

2. The second shock was on the demand side: Companies could not predict what is required and what is required. The customers' demand changed a lot, and there was a sharp decline in spending. Demands for high-value items like cars, flats, jewellers, and clothes decreased significantly. Customers had fear in buying new products and spending money due to job losses (P. Chowdhury, Kumar Paul, et al., 2021; Koch et al., 2020).

## Resilient Supply Chain

RSC is defined as the capability of the SC to respond to the disruptions and recover from them. Globalizations and the adoption of lean technologies in the SC had made a complex network of entities dependent on each other (Iakovou et al., 2007; Sawik, 2013). Such complex SC is very much vulnerable to being disrupted. Therefore, it has become essential to have the resilience capacity so that the disruptions can respond quickly. Some of the factors that impact RSC are SC collaboration, flexibility, visibility, information accuracy, supplier selection, and network structure design (A. Ali et al., 2017; Durach et al., 2015; Hosseini et al., 2019; Hosseini & Barker, 2016; Kamalahmadi & Mellat-Parast, 2016; Torabi et al., 2015).

The COVID-19 pandemic has revealed numerous critical supply chain vulnerabilities. It demonstrated the inflexibility and unresponsiveness of most supply chains (Dohale et al., 2021; Lioutas & Charatsari, 2021; Nakat & Bou-Mitri, 2021). Organizations should consider carrying out the executives' innovations to be more ready for changing client practices, financial insecurities, and other arising difficulties in the new ordinary. Today, organisations that start putting resources into a strong store network want to resolve future issues and guarantee consistent item conveyance (Kamble & Mor, 2021; Pravin Kumar & Kumar Singh, 2021). The journey toward a responsive and resilient supply chain will be anchored by advanced analytics.

RSC should have the ability to respond and recover after the disruptions and resist the disruptions. Many researchers have characterized RSC in adaptive, absorptive, and restorative capacities (Hosseini & Barker, 2016). RSC mainly focuses on individuals' firm-based resilience rather than concentrating on the complex network structure of global SC and its performance in the overall SC network (I. Ali & Gölgeci, 2019; Chen et al., 2019; Kochan & Nowicki, 2018). Due to this complexity and tightly coupled network systems, firms need to have long-term collaboration SC for achieving performance excellence.

## Strategy and Hypothesis Development

SC strategies and practices currently followed by the companies cannot tackle this pandemic. SC professionals and managers need to rethink the strategy. They need to redesign the SC networks and build an RSC strategy to help the companies come out from the COVID-19 pandemic and sustain this type of disruption in the long run. The strategy for the RSC COVID-19 pandemic is:

*A Structural Equation Modelling Approach*

## Creating SC Transparency for Logistics Infrastructure (STLI)

With the latest technology like global positioning systems, blockchain, internet of things, and radio frequency identification devices into the design, there can be a proper tracking of the material movement. SC transparency can be achieved only when there is an appropriate exchange of information among different parties (Sunny et al., 2020). The main focus should be on tracking, tracing, and collaboration to achieve SC transparency (Ivanov et al., 2019). Tracing and monitoring will verify and provide product-related information and information on the company's product movement to the customers (Karmaker et al., 2021; Nandi et al., 2020).

H1: Creating SC transparency for logistics infrastructure will impact RSC.

## Flexibility in the SC (FSC)

SC flexibility will help companies effectively manage their costs and resources. Flexible SC is both agile and adaptable. It should be designed to defect disruptions and respond to them (Aslam et al., 2020; Mackay et al., 2019). To achieve flexible SC, companies need to have safety stock, maintain multiple suppliers, add safety lead times to the actual cycle time, identify alternative routes or shipping modes (Chen et al., 2019; Kahiluoto et al., 2020; Shin & Park, 2019).

H2: Flexibility in the SC will have an impact on RSC.

## Automation and Robotics Applications in SC (AR)

Autonomous technology impacts the SC. The autonomous SC can be applied to moving goods without any human intervention. Autonomous mobile robots can be used in warehouses to quickly and efficiently fulfil orders (Dondapati Rajendra Dev et al., 2020; Roy et al., 2020). Autonomous robots will help the SC shortly by bringing a decrease in long term cost, increasing worker productivity, providing labour and utilization stability, reducing the error rate, reducing the frequency of inventory checks, optimising picking, sorting, and storing times, and increasing access to the problematic location or dangerous location. The use of delivery drones, autonomous trucks and crewless cargo in SC can help decrease human intervention (D. Rajendra Dev & Roy, 2019; Roy & Dev, 2019). Robots can handle multiple tasks and can easily integrate with another automation system to streamline the SC functions (Ivanov et al., 2018; Sarkis et al., 2020; M. Sharma, 2021)

H3: Automation and robotics applications in SC will impact RSC.

## SC Digitization and Virtualization (DV)

Recent digital technologies such as cloud computing, the internet of things, big data, blockchain, and machine learning have made the SC processes more efficiently (Ahmed et al., 2021; Majumdar et al., 2020; Queiroz, Fosso Wamba, et al., 2020). Digital SC can be defined as intelligent, value-driven and efficiently enabled by the latest innovation (Mollenkopf et al., 2020). In virtual SC, there is an increase in the integrated physical flow of products. Virtual SC carries out planning, monitoring, adjustment, and optimization of all the logistics processes through internet connectivity (Belhadi et al., 2021).

H4: SC digitization and virtualization will have an impact on RSC.

*A Structural Equation Modelling Approach*

## Localization of Sourcing (LS)

Sourcing (and processing) are localized within the same region to meet the local demand and reduce SC integrations. Procurement was dominated by concerns about disruptions in SC in the form of natural disasters, war-like situations, or a pandemic like COVID-19 (Abbas et al., 2021). Companies need to introduce local procurement or in-house manufacturing to avoid any kind of disruptions in SC. Big firms need to develop their suppliers locally or allow the international suppliers to set up their operations locally (Nandi et al., 2020). Hence, the disruption risk could be contained within the area, as there is no spill-over of a risk incident from one region to another (Ivanov, 2020a, 2020b; Nandi et al., 2021).

H5: Localization of sourcing will have an impact on RSC.

## MAIN FOCUS OF THE CHAPTER

Data was collected from two sources primary sources and secondary sources. Primary sources data was collected using questionnaires through the survey method (Kant Pal et al., 2021; Mukherjee, Baral, Venkataiah, et al., 2021). Secondary data sources were collected from the reports, magazines, websites, and online databases (Roy & Appa Rao, 2020; Roy & p p an R an o, 2021). A questionnaire was being prepared with the help of professionals and academicians in the SC area (Mukherjee, Chittipaka, & Baral, 2022; Mukherjee & Chittipaka, 2021). The questionnaire contained a series of questions that were asked to be filled by the respondents (Mukherjee, Chittipaka, Baral, et al., 2022; Pal et al., 2021). The target population were the SC professionals working in the various industrial sector of India. Multinational companies and listed companies on Stock Exchange were set as target populations. The simple random sampling method was used so that there is no biasness in collecting data. The questionnaire that was sent for collecting the data was 560, out of which 335 questionnaires came back to us, which were used in the data analysis. For data analysis, we had used SPSS 20.0 and AMOS 22.0 software. After collecting the data, we checked whether the data collected had biasness or not. For that, we had performed a single factor Harman test in the SPSS 20.0. Exploratory factor analysis was committed to checking how much variance the first-factor extract and result came to be 27.301%, below 50% of the recommended value (Podsakoff, 2003).

## Demographics of Firms Surveyed

A questionnaire-based survey method was used (Baral & Verma, 2021). Table I shows the distribution of respondents based on different industries. The demographics for gender was 48% of respondent's male, and 52% of respondents were female. The educational qualification that the respondents had was 6% of respondents had a secondary degree, 52.31% respondents had a polytechnic degree, 29% respondents had a bachelor degree, and 12.69% respondents had a PG/PhD degree. The work experience of the 7.80% respondents who had work experience less than five years, 40.10% of respondents had work experience between six to ten years, 35.57% of respondents had work experience between eleven to fifteen years, and 16.53% of respondents had work experience more than fifteen years. The industry where the respondents were 21.34% respondents was from the garment industry, 20.67% respondents were from the steel industry, 33.42% respondents were from the automobile industry, and 25% respondents were from the cement industry.

*Table 1. Firm demographics*

| Gender | Percentage |
|---|---|
| Male | 48% |
| Female | 52% |
| **Educational Qualification** | |
| Secondary | 6% |
| Polytechnic | 52.31% |
| Bachelor's degree | 29% |
| PG/PhD | 12.69% |
| **Work experience** | |
| <5 years | 7.80% |
| 6-10 years | 40.10% |
| 11-15 years | 35.57% |
| >15 years | 16.53% |
| **Industry** | |
| Garment industry | 21.34% |
| Steel industry | 20.67% |
| Automobile industry | 33.42% |
| Cement industry | 25% |

## Reliability and Validity (Cronbach's Alpha)

Assessment of reliability helps examine the degree of internal consistency between variable measurement items and its freedom of error at any point in time (Kline, 2015). Cronbach's alpha was utilized to test the reliability of the data (Hair, J. F., Black, W. C., Babin, B. J., Anderson, R. E., & Tatham, 2010; Mukherjee, Chittipaka, et al., 2021). The recommended value should be greater than 0.70 (Nunnally, 1994). Table II shows the values of Cronbach's alpha. Hence, all the values are within the threshold level (Hair, J. F., Black, W. C., Babin, B. J., Anderson, R. E., & Tatham, 2010; Mukherjee, Baral, Chittipaka, et al., 2021)

*Table 2. Cronbach's Alpha*

| Sl. No. | Variable | Cronbach's alpha |
|---|---|---|
| 1 | STLI | 0.869 |
| 2 | FSC | 0.845 |
| 3 | AR | 0.737 |
| 4 | DV | 0.845 |
| 5 | LS | 0.86 |

Note- STLI: Creating a SC transparency for logistics infrastructure; FSC: Flexibility in the SC; AR: Automation and robotics applications in SC; DV: SC digitization and virtualization; LS: Localization of sourcing

*A Structural Equation Modelling Approach*

## Exploratory Factor Analysis

The first step of the EFA was to evaluate the appropriateness of the sample size. SPSS 20.0 was utilized for EFA. As a result, Kaiser-Meyer-Olkin (KMO) analysis was used to determine whether those items are sufficiently correlated and whether a factor analysis could be performed. The current study's KMO value is 0.828. This statistic's minimum level is 0.60 (Hu & Bentler, 1999; Mukherjee, Mohan Baral, et al., 2021). The extraction method used was principal component analysis. Table III shows the values of total variance extracted.

*Table 3. Total variance extracted*

| Component | Initial Eigenvalues | | | Extraction Sums of Squared Loadings | | | Rotation Sums of Squared Loadings |
|---|---|---|---|---|---|---|---|
| | Total | % of Variance | Cumulative % | Total | % of Variance | Cumulative % | Total |
| 1 | 5.535 | 30.753 | 30.753 | 5.535 | 30.753 | 30.753 | 3.080 |
| 2 | 3.077 | 17.097 | 47.850 | 3.077 | 17.097 | 47.850 | 4.219 |
| 3 | 1.566 | 8.698 | 56.548 | 1.566 | 8.698 | 56.548 | 3.985 |
| 4 | 1.454 | 8.079 | 64.627 | 1.454 | 8.079 | 64.627 | 3.368 |
| 5 | 1.234 | 6.854 | 71.481 | 1.234 | 6.854 | 71.481 | 3.072 |

The Rotated Component Matrix is required to interpret the results of the analysis. Rotation helps group the items, and each group contains more than two items, simplifying the structure. Table 4 shows the values of the rotated component matrix.

*Table 4. Rotated component matrix*

| | Component | | | | |
|---|---|---|---|---|---|
| | **1** | **2** | **3** | **4** | **5** |
| STLI1 | .854 | | | | |
| STLI2 | .876 | | | | |
| STLI3 | .894 | | | | |
| STLI4 | .757 | | | | |
| FSC1 | | | .801 | | |
| FSC2 | | | .832 | | |
| FSC3 | | | .858 | | |
| FSC4 | | | .788 | | |
| AR1 | | | | | .852 |
| AR2 | | | | | .855 |
| AR3 | | | | | .710 |
| DV1 | | | | .868 | |
| DV2 | | | | .965 | |
| DV3 | | | | .768 | |
| LS1 | | .819 | | | |
| LS2 | | .850 | | | |
| LS3 | | .887 | | | |
| LS4 | | .759 | | | |

Note- STLI: Creating a SC transparency for logistics infrastructure; FSC: Flexibility in the SC; AR: Automation and robotics applications in SC; DV: SC digitization and virtualization; LS: Localization of sourcing

## Confirmatory Factor Analysis Results

CFA was used to test the hypothesis (Baral & Verma, 2021). Because of its powerful graphic representations and user-friendly interfaces, AMOS 22.0 was used for this research. The model's output is shown here. There are a total of five latent variables. Table 5 displays the model fit measures for CFA.

*A Structural Equation Modelling Approach*

*Table 5. Model fit measures for the confirmatory factor analysis*

| Goodness-of-fit Indices | Default Model | Benchmark |
|---|---|---|
| *Absolute goodness-of-fit measure* | | |
| χ2/df (CMIN/DF) | 2.226 | Lower Limit:1.0 Upper Limit 2.0/3.0 or 5.0 |
| GFI | 0.916 | >0.90 |
| *Incremental fit measure* | | |
| CFI | 0.950 | ⩾0.90 |
| IFI | 0.951 | ⩾0.90 |
| TLI | 0.939 | ⩾0.90 |
| *Parsimony fit measure* | | |
| PCFI | 0.776 | ⩾0.50 |
| PNFI | 0.747 | ⩾0.50 |

## Model Validity Measures

## Composite Reliability

All of the components' composite reliability (CR) was also measured. Because of its ability to produce better results is calculated for internal consistency reliability (Henseler et al., 2009). The CR values of the five constructs are more significant than 0.7, indicating that the composite reliability measures are reliable. Table VI displays the CR values.

## Convergent Validity

According to Fornell and Larcker (1981), AVE > 0.5 indicates convergent validity. The AVE values for the constructs are shown in Table VI. All discounts are more significant than 0.5, implying that all constructs have convergent validity (Hair et al., 2012, 2014).

## Divergent Validity

Fornell and Larcker (1981) proposed that the AVE of the construct must be greater than the square of the correlation between that construct and the other constructs to calculate its validity (Hair et al., 2014). The values for construct correlation and AVE are shown in Table III. As a result, the extracted variance value is greater than the squared correlation value (Cable & DeRue, 2002).

*A Structural Equation Modelling Approach*

*Table 6. CR, AVE, divergent validity*

| | CR | AVE | variance extracted between factors | | | | |
| --- | --- | --- | --- | --- | --- | --- | --- |
| | | | STLI | LS | FSC | DV | AR |
| STLI | 0.910 | 0.845 | 1 | | | | |
| LS | 0.898 | 0.829 | 0.701 | 1 | | | |
| FSC | 0.891 | 0.820 | 0.693 | 0.679 | 1 | | |
| DV | 0.903 | 0.867 | 0.733 | 0.719 | 0.712 | 1 | |
| AR | 0.849 | 0.806 | 0.682 | 0.668 | 0.661 | 0.700 | 1 |

Note- STLI: Creating a SC transparency for logistics infrastructure; FSC: Flexibility in the SC; AR: Automation and robotics applications in SC; DV: SC digitization and virtualization; LS: Localization of sourcing

Hence, there are no validity concerns, and further analysis is performed utilizing the SEM approach.

*Table 7. Path analysis result for confirmatory factor analysis*

| | Estimate | S.E. | C.R. | P |
| --- | --- | --- | --- | --- |
| STLI1<---STLI | 0.816 | | | |
| STLI2<---STLI | 0.899 | 0.055 | 16.34 | *** |
| STLI3<---STLI | 0.885 | 0.052 | 17.02 | *** |
| STLI4<---STLI | 0.556 | 0.049 | 11.35 | *** |
| FSC1<---FSC | 0.751 | | | |
| FSC2<---FSC | 0.847 | 0.082 | 10.33 | *** |
| FSC3<---FSC | 0.823 | 0.072 | 11.43 | *** |
| FSC4<---FSC | 0.623 | 0.062 | 10.05 | *** |
| LS1<---LS | 0.779 | | | |
| LS2<---LS | 0.906 | 0.062 | 14.61 | *** |
| LS3<---LS | 0.866 | 0.058 | 14.93 | *** |
| LS4<---LS | 0.571 | 0.054 | 10.57 | |
| AR1<---AR | 0.740 | | | |
| AR2<---AR | 0.812 | 0.083 | 9.78 | *** |
| AR3<---AR | 0.576 | 0.083 | 6.94 | *** |
| DV1<---DV | 0.851 | | | |
| DV2<---DV | 0.829 | 0.066 | 12.56 | *** |
| DV3<---DV | 0.735 | 0.064 | 11.48 | *** |

Note- STLI: Creating a SC transparency for logistics infrastructure; FSC: Flexibility in the SC; AR: Automation and robotics applications in SC; DV: SC digitization and virtualization; LS: Localization of sourcing

Table 7 shows the path analysis results for CFA. Hence, the conditions are satisfied, and we can build the final model.

*A Structural Equation Modelling Approach*

## STRUCTURAL MODEL AND TESTING OF HYPOTHESIS

SEM was used to test the hypothesis (Byrne, 2010; Byrne, 2001). Because of its powerful graphic representations and user-friendly interfaces, AMOS 22.0 was used for this research. The model's output is shown here. Figure 1 depicts the final model, latent variables, indicators, and dependent variables.

*Table 8. Final goodness-of-fit indices for the structural model*

| Goodness-of-fit Indices | Default Model | Benchmark |
|---|---|---|
| *Absolute goodness-of-fit measure* | | |
| CMIN/Df | 2.473 | Lower Limit:1.0; Upper Limit 2.0/3.0 or 5.0 |
| GFI | 0.884 | >0.90 |
| *Absolute badness of fit measure* | | |
| RMSEA | 0.066 | $\leqslant 0.08$ |
| *Incremental fit measure* | | |
| CFI | 0.928 | $\geqslant 0.90$ |
| IFI | 0.929 | $\geqslant 0.90$ |
| TLI | 0.914 | $\geqslant 0.90$ |
| *Parsimony fit measure* | | |
| PCFI | 0.779 | $\geqslant 0.50$ |
| PNFI | 0.744 | $\geqslant 0.50$ |

Table VIII shows the model fit values and fits indices. Figure 1 shows the final structural model generated after analysis in AMOS 22.0.

*Figure 1. Model for resilient supply chain strategies to handle the COVID-19 disruptions*
Note- STLI: Creating a SC transparency for logistics infrastructure; FSC: Flexibility in the SC; AR: Automation and robotics applications in SC; DV: SC digitization and virtualization; LS: Localization of sourcing; RSC: Resilient Supply Chain

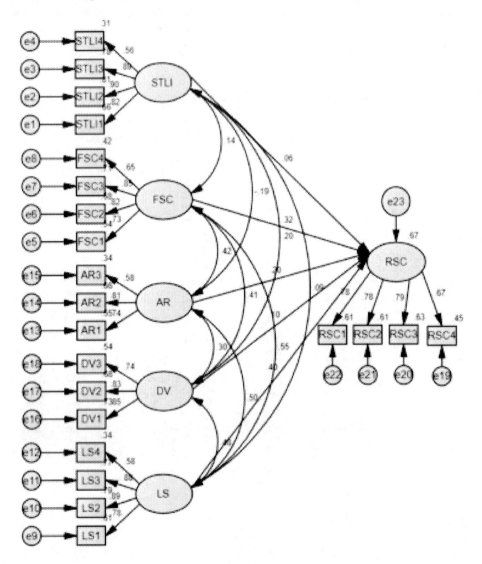

The path estimate analysis results are shown in Table IX. The outcome shows that the five hypotheses are supported by P-value (Hair et al., 2010). Multiple square correlations ($R^2$) are used to assess how well a regression line predicts actual data points between 0 and 1, stating how well one variable predicts another (Hair et al., 2014). The closer the value, the better the model can predict that technology (Kline, 2012, 2015). The proposed model can account for 67.4 per cent of RSC variance.

*A Structural Equation Modelling Approach*

*Table 9. Structural model results*

| | Estimate | S.E. | C.R. | P | Hypothesis |
|---|---|---|---|---|---|
| RSC<---STLI | 0.065 | 0.029 | 2.24 | *** | Supported |
| RSC<---FSC | 0.319 | 0.052 | 6.13 | *** | Supported |
| RSC<---AR | 0.199 | 0.049 | 4.06 | *** | Supported |
| RSC<---DV | 0.097 | 0.036 | 2.69 | *** | Supported |
| RSC<---LS | 0.403 | 0.042 | 9.59 | *** | Supported |

Note- STLI: Creating a SC transparency for logistics infrastructure; FSC: Flexibility in the SC; AR: Automation and robotics applications in SC; DV: SC digitization and virtualization; LS: Localization of sourcing; RSC: Resilient Supply Chain

## CONCLUSIONS

COVID-19 pandemic has created an opportunity for the firms to redesign their SC to sustain any disruptions in the near future. This research aims to determine the strategies that could help the industries develop an RSC. A structured literature review was carried out to identify the gap and the strategy. A questionnaire was designed for survey-based research in the four sectors: automobile, garment, steel, and cement. Five strategies were identified and tested using the structural equation modeling approach. Five hypotheses were formulated using five independent variables and one dependent variable. For analysis, exploratory factor analysis, confirmatory factor analysis, and structural equation modeling approach was used. A model was developed using satisfied all the parameters, and the five hypotheses were accepted.

## FUTURE RESEARCH DIRECTIONS AND IMPLICATIONS

To be prepared for a potential pandemic, companies must rethink SC policy development. Organizations should also educate their employees on COVID-19 symptoms, prevention, and appropriate health measures to impact the SC (Fink, 2020; Nagarajan & Sharma, 2021; Wang & Zhang, 2021). The "new normal" shift will necessitate increased collaboration between governments and businesses and their competitors and partners to maintain global SC sustainability. Firms should prioritise integrating and collaborating with core SCs members and the federal government to achieve a unified goal and manage all losses and future gains to rebuild market foundations (Abate et al., 2020; Anker, 2021; Fink, 2020; Kang et al., 2020).

Government financial assistance, such as stimulus packages, infrastructure investment, access to sustainable technologies, and insurance facilities, can help businesses survive and maintain average output (Anker, 2021; P. Chowdhury, Paul, et al., 2021; Nagarajan & Sharma, 2021; Amalesh Sharma et al., 2021). Financial support from SC stakeholders, on the other hand, promotes sustainability-related development projects and fosters business relationships with economic benefits in the context of COVID-19 (Duarte Alonso et al., 2020).

Organizations should also use digital communication technologies to help enforce sustainability rules, reconfigure SCs, collect real-time data, and respond quickly to the COVID-19 outbreak (Işık et al., 2021). During COVID-19, technology was a significant component in deciding a company's success or failure. Compared to the current technologies, businesses should implement new mobile technologies that will give them access across all SCs (Nagarajan & Sharma, 2021; Wang & Zhang, 2021). Not only will this improve efficiency and responsiveness, but it will also reduce vulnerability.

H1 tested the impact of creating SC transparency for logistics infrastructure on RSC. The final structural model showed that building a strong transportation and logistics infrastructure and RSC was supported ($\beta = 0.065$, p = .000) in this study. Zelbst et al., 2019 investigated the influence of RFID, the Industrial Internet of Things (IIoT), and Blockchain on SC transparency. Blockchain technology is being combined with the Internet of Things to provide greater transparency and efficiency in the SC (Madumidha et al., 2019; Sunny et al., 2020; Wasim Ahmad et al., 2021). This work provides an understanding of the potential of blockchain traceability solutions to ensure the clarity of SC. Sunny et al., 2020 investigated the blockchain-based traceability in SC distribution using blockchain.

H2 tested the impact of flexibility in the SC on RSC. The final structural model showed that the SC and RSC flexibility was supported ($\beta = 0.319$, p = .000) in this study. To achieve sustainability after COVID-19, all SCs will need agility within the chain. Because of COVID-19, the business environment and market rivalry in emerging economies have changed dramatically (Karmaker et al., 2021; Majumdar et al., 2020). As a result, businesses must make their SCs nimble to act rapidly. In their study, Gouda & Saranga, 2018 also said that no organization could attain sustainability in SC without agility.

H3 tested the impact of Automation and robotics applications in SC on RSC. The final structural model showed that this study supported Automation and robotics applications in SC and RSC ($\beta = 0.199$, p = .000). The COVID-19 epidemic has served as a wake-up call for the sectors of emerging economies to implement modern, automated technologies to reduce reliance on labour and ensure fast, secure online contactless transactions (Belhadi et al., 2021; Ivanov & Dolgui, 2020). Large manufacturing organizations will improve the "Application of automation and robotics in manufacturing and logistics service" as quickly as feasible (Kim et al., 2021). H4 tested the impact of SC digitization and virtualization on RSC. The final structural model showed that SC digitization and virtualization, and RSC were supported ($\beta = 0.097$, p = .000) in this study. Attaran, 2020; Schniederjans et al., 2020 discussed how digitization in SC and digital SC could revolutionize the present scenario.

H5 tested the impact of localization of sourcing on RSC. The final structural model showed that localization of sourcing and RSC was supported ($\beta = 0.403$, p = .000) in this study. The spread of COVID-19 from China, one of the world's largest suppliers to many industries, has raised SC professionals about purchasing from local markets. Localization is also critical for the environmental SC's long-term viability (Holmström & Gutowski, 2017). Local production can offer quick responses to local requirements while using less energy and resources. By creating only what is required, localized production capabilities can help sustain supply networks. Shorter SCs result in less waste, less transit, and less inventory storage, all of which have long-term repercussions for supply networks (Gouda & Saranga, 2018; Huo et al., 2021).

## REFERENCES

Abate, M., Christidis, P., & Purwanto, A. J. (2020). Government support to airlines in the aftermath of the COVID-19 pandemic. *Journal of Air Transport Management*, *89*, 101931. Advance online publication. doi:10.1016/j.jairtraman.2020.101931 PMID:32952317

*A Structural Equation Modelling Approach*

Abbas, H. S. M., Xu, X., Sun, C., Ullah, A., Gillani, S., & Raza, M. A. A. (2021). Impact of COVID-19 pandemic on sustainability determinants: A global trend. *Heliyon, 7*(2), e05912. doi:10.1016/j.heliyon.2021.e05912 PMID:33458434

Abu-Rayash, A., & Dincer, I. (2020). Analysis of mobility trends during the COVID-19 coronavirus pandemic: Exploring the impacts on global aviation and travel in selected cities. *Energy Research & Social Science, 68*(July), 101693. doi:10.1016/j.erss.2020.101693 PMID:32839706

Agrawal, A. (2020). Sustainability of airlines in India with Covid-19: Challenges ahead and possible wayouts. *Journal of Revenue and Pricing Management, 20*(4), 457–472. doi:10.1057/s41272-020-00257-z

Agrawal, T. K., Kumar, V., Pal, R., Wang, L., & Chen, Y. (2021). Blockchain-based framework for supply chain traceability: A case example of textile and clothing industry. *Computers & Industrial Engineering, 154*, 107130. doi:10.1016/j.cie.2021.107130

Ahmed, S., Taqi, H. M. M., Farabi, Y. I., Sarker, M., Ali, S. M., & Sankaranarayanan, B. (2021). Evaluation of Flexible Strategies to Manage the COVID-19 Pandemic in the Education Sector. *Global Journal of Flexible Systems Management*, 1–25. doi:10.1007/s40171-021-00267-9

Ali, A., Mahfouz, A., & Arisha, A. (2017). Analysing supply chain resilience: integrating the constructs in a concept mapping framework via a systematic literature review. In Supply Chain Management (Vol. 22, Issue 1, pp. 16–39). Emerald Group Publishing Ltd. doi:10.1108/SCM-06-2016-0197

Ali, I., & Gölgeci, I. (2019). Where is supply chain resilience research heading? A systematic and co-occurrence analysis. *International Journal of Physical Distribution & Logistics Management, 49*(8), 793–815. doi:10.1108/IJPDLM-02-2019-0038

Amalia, S., Darma, D. C., & Maria, S. (2020). Supply Chain Management and the Covid-19 Outbreak: Optimizing its Role for Indonesia. *Current Research Journal of Social Sciences and Humanities, 3*(2), 196–202. doi:10.12944/CRJSSH.3.2.07

Anker, T. B. (2021). At the boundary: Post-COVID agenda for business and management research in Europe and beyond. *European Management Journal, 39*(2), 171–178. doi:10.1016/j.emj.2021.01.003

Asamoah, D., Nuertey, D., Agyei-Owusu, B., & Akyeh, J. (2021). The effect of supply chain responsiveness on customer development. *International Journal of Logistics Management, 32*(4), 1190–1213. Advance online publication. doi:10.1108/IJLM-03-2020-0133

Aslam, H., Khan, A. Q., Rashid, K., & Rehman, S. (2020). Achieving supply chain resilience: The role of supply chain ambidexterity and supply chain agility. *Journal of Manufacturing Technology Management, 31*(6), 1185–1204. doi:10.1108/JMTM-07-2019-0263

Attaran, M. (2020). 3D Printing Role in Filling the Critical Gap in the Medical Supply Chain during COVID-19 Pandemic. *American Journal of Industrial and Business Management, 10*(05), 988–1001. doi:10.4236/ajibm.2020.105066

Baral, M. M., & Verma, A. (2021). Cloud Computing Adoption for Healthcare: An Empirical Study Using SEM Approach. *FIIB Business Review, 10*(3), 255–275. doi:10.1177/23197145211012505

Barbate, V., Gade, R. N., & Raibagkar, S. S. (2021). COVID-19 and Its Impact on the Indian Economy. *Vision: The Journal of Business Perspective*. doi:10.1177/0972262921989126

Belhadi, A., Kamble, S., Jabbour, C. J. C., Gunasekaran, A., Ndubisi, N. O., & Venkatesh, M. (2021). Manufacturing and service supply chain resilience to the COVID-19 outbreak: Lessons learned from the automobile and airline industries. *Technological Forecasting and Social Change*, *163*, 120447. doi:10.1016/j.techfore.2020.120447 PMID:33518818

Brydges, T., Heinze, L., Retamal, M., & Henninger, C. E. (2020). Platforms and the pandemic: A case study of fashion rental platforms during COVID-19. *The Geographical Journal*. Advance online publication. doi:10.1111/geoj.12366

Butu, A., Brumă, I. S., Tanasă, L., Rodino, S., Vasiliu, C. D., Doboş, S., & Butu, M. (2020). The impact of COVID-19 crisis upon the consumer buying behavior of fresh vegetables directly from local producers. Case study: The quarantined area of Suceava County, Romania. *International Journal of Environmental Research and Public Health*, *17*(15), 1–25. doi:10.3390/ijerph17155485 PMID:32751368

Chen, H. Y., Das, A., & Ivanov, D. (2019). Building resilience and managing post-disruption supply chain recovery: Lessons from the information and communication technology industry. *International Journal of Information Management*, *49*(June), 330–342. doi:10.1016/j.ijinfomgt.2019.06.002

Chesbrough, H. (2020). To recover faster from Covid-19, open up: Managerial implications from an open innovation perspective. *Industrial Marketing Management*, *88*, 410–413. doi:10.1016/j.indmarman.2020.04.010

Chowdhury, M. T., Sarkar, A., Saha, P. K., & Anik, R. H. (2020). Enhancing supply resilience in the COVID-19 pandemic: A case study on beauty and personal care retailers. *Modern Supply Chain Research and Applications*, *2*(3), 143–159. doi:10.1108/MSCRA-07-2020-0018

Chowdhury, P., Kumar Paul, S., Kaisar, S., & Abdul Moktadir, M. (2021). COVID-19 pandemic related supply chain studies: A systematic review. *Transportation Research Part E, Logistics and Transportation Review*, *148*, 102271. doi:10.1016/j.tre.2021.102271 PMID:33613082

Chowdhury, P., Paul, S. K., Kaisar, S., & Moktadir, M. A. (2021). COVID-19 pandemic related supply chain studies: A systematic review. *Transportation Research Part E, Logistics and Transportation Review*, *148*, 102271. doi:10.1016/j.tre.2021.102271 PMID:33613082

Dev, D. R., & Roy, R. (2019). Communication Technology for Users with Specific Learning Incapacities. *Artificial Intelligent Systems and Machine Learning*, *11*(7), 126–131. http://ischolar.info/index.php/CiiTAISML/article/view/207237

Dev, D. R. (1839–1842). Badhan, A. K., & Roy, R. (2020). A Study of Artificial Emotional Intelligence for Human – Robot Interaction. *Journal of Critical Reviews*, *7*(15). Advance online publication. doi:10.31838/jcr.07.15.251

Dohale, V., Ambilkar, P., Gunasekaran, A., & Verma, P. (2021). Supply chain risk mitigation strategies during COVID-19: Exploratory cases of "make-to-order" handloom saree apparel industries. *International Journal of Physical Distribution & Logistics Management*. Advance online publication. doi:10.1108/IJPDLM-12-2020-0450

Duarte Alonso, A., Kok, S. K., Bressan, A., O'Shea, M., Sakellarios, N., Koresis, A., Buitrago Solis, M. A., & Santoni, L. J. (2020). COVID-19, aftermath, impacts, and hospitality firms: An international perspective. *International Journal of Hospitality Management, 91*, 102654. doi:10.1016/j.ijhm.2020.102654 PMID:32863526

Dube, K., Nhamo, G., & Chikodzi, D. (2021). COVID-19 pandemic and prospects for recovery of the global aviation industry. *Journal of Air Transport Management, 92*(December), 102022. doi:10.1016/j.jairtraman.2021.102022

Durach, C. F., Wieland, A., & Machuca, J. A. D. (2015). Antecedents and dimensions of supply chain robustness: A systematic literature review. *International Journal of Physical Distribution & Logistics Management, 45*(1/2), 118–137. doi:10.1108/IJPDLM-05-2013-0133

Fernandes, N. (2020). Economic Effects of Coronavirus Outbreak (COVID-19) on the World Economy. SSRN *Electronic Journal*. doi:10.2139/ssrn.3557504

Fink, L. (2020). Conducting Information Systems Research in the Midst of the COVID-19 Pandemic: Opportunities and Challenges. *Information Systems Management, 37*(4), 256–259. doi:10.1080/10580 530.2020.1814460

Gouda, S. K., & Saranga, H. (2018). Sustainable supply chains for supply chain sustainability: Impact of sustainability efforts on supply chain risk. *International Journal of Production Research, 56*(17), 5820–5835. doi:10.1080/00207543.2018.1456695

Hair, J. F., Black, W. C., Babin, B. J., Anderson, R. E., & Tatham, R. L. (2010). *Multivariate Data Analysis* (7th ed.). Prentice Hall.

Holmström, J., & Gutowski, T. (2017). Additive Manufacturing in Operations and Supply Chain Management: No Sustainability Benefit or Virtuous Knock-On Opportunities? *Journal of Industrial Ecology, 21*(S1), S21–S24. doi:10.1111/jiec.12580

Hosseini, S., & Barker, K. (2016). A Bayesian network model for resilience-based supplier selection. *International Journal of Production Economics, 180*, 68–87. doi:10.1016/j.ijpe.2016.07.007

Hosseini, S., Morshedlou, N., Ivanov, D., Sarder, M. D., Barker, K., & Al Khaled, A. (2019). Resilient supplier selection and optimal order allocation under disruption risks. *International Journal of Production Economics, 213*, 124–137. doi:10.1016/j.ijpe.2019.03.018

Hu, L. T., & Bentler, P. M. (1999). Cutoff criteria for fit indexes in covariance structure analysis: Conventional criteria versus new alternatives. *Structural Equation Modeling, 6*(1), 1–55. doi:10.1080/10705519909540118

Huo, B., Haq, M. Z. U., & Gu, M. (2021). The impact of information sharing on supply chain learning and flexibility performance. *International Journal of Production Research, 59*(5), 1411–1434. doi:10.1080/00207543.2020.1824082

Iakovou, E., Vlachos, D., & Xanthopoulos, A. (2007). An analytical methodological framework for the optimal design of resilient supply chains. *International Journal of Logistics Economics and Globalisation, 1*(1), 1. doi:10.1504/IJLEG.2007.014498

Işık, S., İbiş, H., & Gulseven, O. (2021). The Impact of the COVID-19 Pandemic on Amazon's Business. SSRN *Electronic Journal*. doi:10.2139/ssrn.3766333

Ivanov, D. (2020a). Predicting the impacts of epidemic outbreaks on global supply chains: A simulation-based analysis on the coronavirus outbreak (COVID-19/SARS-CoV-2) case. *Transportation Research Part E, Logistics and Transportation Review*, 136(March), 101922. doi:10.1016/j.tre.2020.101922 PMID:32288597

Ivanov, D. (2020b). Viable supply chain model: Integrating agility, resilience and sustainability perspectives—lessons from and thinking beyond the COVID-19 pandemic. *Annals of Operations Research*. Advance online publication. doi:10.100710479-020-03640-6 PMID:32836614

Ivanov, D., & Das, A. (2020). Coronavirus (COVID-19/SARS-CoV-2) and supply chain resilience: A research note. *International Journal of Integrated Supply Management*, 13(1), 90–102. doi:10.1504/IJISM.2020.107780

Ivanov, D., & Dolgui, A. (2020a). Viability of intertwined supply networks: Extending the supply chain resilience angles towards survivability. A position paper motivated by COVID-19 outbreak. *International Journal of Production Research*, 58(10), 2904–2915. doi:10.1080/00207543.2020.1750727

Ivanov, D., Dolgui, A., & Sokolov, B. (2019). The impact of digital technology and Industry 4.0 on the ripple effect and supply chain risk analytics. *International Journal of Production Research*, 57(3), 829–846. doi:10.1080/00207543.2018.1488086

Ivanov, D., Sethi, S., Dolgui, A., & Sokolov, B. (2018). A survey on control theory applications to operational systems, supply chain management, and Industry 4.0. In *Annual Reviews in Control* (Vol. 46, pp. 134–147). Elsevier Ltd. doi:10.1016/j.arcontrol.2018.10.014

Kahiluoto, H., Mäkinen, H., & Kaseva, J. (2020). Supplying resilience through assessing diversity of responses to disruption. *International Journal of Operations & Production Management*, 40(3), 271–292. doi:10.1108/IJOPM-01-2019-0006

Kamalahmadi, M., & Mellat-Parast, M. (2016). Developing a resilient supply chain through supplier flexibility and reliability assessment. *International Journal of Production Research*, 54(1), 302–321. doi:10.1080/00207543.2015.1088971

Kamble, S. S., & Mor, R. S. (2021). Food supply chains and COVID-19: A way forward. In Agronomy Journal (Vol. 113, Issue 2, pp. 2195–2197). John Wiley and Sons Inc. doi:10.1002/agj2.20515

Kang, J., Diao, Z., & Zanini, M. T. (2020). Business-to-business marketing responses to COVID-19 crisis: a business process perspective. In *Marketing Intelligence and Planning*. Emerald Group Holdings Ltd. doi:10.1108/MIP-05-2020-0217

Kant Pal, S., Mukherjee, S., Baral, M. M., & Aggarwal, S. (2021). Problems of Big Data Adoption in the Healthcare Industries. *Asia Pacific Journal of Health Management*, 16(4), 282–287. doi:10.24083/apjhm.v16i4.1359

*A Structural Equation Modelling Approach*

Karmaker, C. L., Ahmed, T., Ahmed, S., Ali, S. M., Moktadir, M. A., & Kabir, G. (2021a). Improving supply chain sustainability in the context of COVID-19 pandemic in an emerging economy: Exploring drivers using an integrated model. *Sustainable Production and Consumption, 26*, 411–427. doi:10.1016/j. spc.2020.09.019 PMID:33015267

Karmaker, C. L., Ahmed, T., Ahmed, S., Ali, S. M., Moktadir, M. A., & Kabir, G. (2021b). Improving supply chain sustainability in the context of COVID-19 pandemic in an emerging economy: Exploring drivers using an integrated model. *Sustainable Production and Consumption, 26*, 411–427. doi:10.1016/j. spc.2020.09.019 PMID:33015267

Karmaker, C. L., Ahmed, T., Ahmed, S., Ali, S. M., Moktadir, M. A., & Kabir, G. (2021c). Improving supply chain sustainability in the context of COVID-19 pandemic in an emerging economy: Exploring drivers using an integrated model. *Sustainable Production and Consumption, 26*, 411–427. doi:10.1016/j. spc.2020.09.019 PMID:33015267

Kaushal, V., & Srivastava, S. (2021). Hospitality and tourism industry amid COVID-19 pandemic: Perspectives on challenges and learnings from India. *International Journal of Hospitality Management, 92*, 102707. doi:10.1016/j.ijhm.2020.102707 PMID:33024348

Kim, S., Kim, J., Badu-Baiden, F., Giroux, M., & Choi, Y. (2021). Preference for robot service or human service in hotels? Impacts of the COVID-19 pandemic. *International Journal of Hospitality Management, 93*, 102795. doi:10.1016/j.ijhm.2020.102795

Kline, R. B. (2015). *Principles and practice of structural equation modeling*. Guilford publications.

Koch, J., Frommeyer, B., & Schewe, G. (2020). Online Shopping Motives during the COVID-19 Pandemic—Lessons from the Crisis. *Sustainability, 12*(24), 10247. doi:10.3390u122410247

Kochan, C. G., & Nowicki, D. R. (2018). Supply chain resilience: A systematic literature review and typological framework. *International Journal of Physical Distribution & Logistics Management, 48*(8), 842–865. doi:10.1108/IJPDLM-02-2017-0099

Kotb, I. (n.d.). *Smart Retailing in COVID-19 World: Insights from Egypt*. Academic Press.

Kumar, P., & Kumar Singh, R. (2021a). Strategic framework for developing resilience in Agri-Food Supply Chains during COVID 19 pandemic. *International Journal of Logistics Research and Applications*. doi:10.1080/13675567.2021.1908524

Kumar, P., & Kumar Singh, R. (2021b). Strategic framework for developing resilience in Agri-Food Supply Chains during COVID 19 pandemic. *International Journal of Logistics Research and Applications*, 1–24. doi:10.1080/13675567.2021.1908524

Linkov, I., Carluccio, S., Pritchard, O., Ní Bhreasail, Á., Galaitsi, S., Sarkis, J., & Keisler, J. M. (2020). The case for value chain resilience. *Management Research Review, 43*(12). Advance online publication. doi:10.1108/MRR-08-2019-0353

Lioutas, E. D., & Charatsari, C. (2021). Enhancing the ability of agriculture to cope with major crises or disasters: What the experience of COVID-19 teaches us. *Agricultural Systems, 187*, 103023. doi:10.1016/j. agsy.2020.103023

Lopes de Sousa Jabbour, A. B., Chiappetta Jabbour, C. J., Hingley, M., Vilalta-Perdomo, E. L., Ramsden, G., & Twigg, D. (2020). Sustainability of supply chains in the wake of the coronavirus (COVID-19/SARS-CoV-2) pandemic: Lessons and trends. *Modern Supply Chain Research and Applications*, *2*(3), 117–122. doi:10.1108/MSCRA-05-2020-0011

Mackay, J., Munoz, A., & Pepper, M. (2019). Conceptualising redundancy and flexibility towards supply chain robustness and resilience. Journal of Risk Research. doi:10.1080/13669877.2019.1694964

Madumidha, S., Siva Ranjani, P., Vandhana, U., & Venmuhilan, B. (2019). A theoretical implementation: Agriculture-food supply chain management using blockchain technology. *Proceedings of the 2019 TEQIP - III Sponsored International Conference on Microwave Integrated Circuits, Photonics and Wireless Networks, IMICPW 2019*, 174–178. 10.1109/IMICPW.2019.8933270

Majumdar, A., Shaw, M., & Sinha, S. K. (2020). COVID-19 debunks the myth of socially sustainable supply chain: A case of the clothing industry in South Asian countries. *Sustainable Production and Consumption*, *24*, 150–155. doi:10.1016/j.spc.2020.07.001

Miani, P., Kille, T., Lee, S. Y., Zhang, Y., & Bates, P. R. (2021). The impact of the COVID-19 pandemic on current tertiary aviation education and future careers: Students' perspective. *Journal of Air Transport Management*, *94*(January), 102081. doi:10.1016/j.jairtraman.2021.102081

Mollenkopf, D. A., Ozanne, L. K., & Stolze, H. J. (2020). A transformative supply chain response to COVID-19. *Journal of Service Management*, *32*(2), 190–202. doi:10.1108/JOSM-05-2020-0143

Monmousseau, P., Marzuoli, A., Feron, E., & Delahaye, D. (2020). Impact of Covid-19 on passengers and airlines from passenger measurements: Managing customer satisfaction while putting the US Air Transportation System to sleep. *Transportation Research Interdisciplinary Perspectives*, *7*, 100179. doi:10.1016/j.trip.2020.100179 PMID:34173460

Morgan, A. K., Awafo, B. A., & Quartey, T. (2021). The effects of COVID-19 on global economic output and sustainability: Evidence from around the world and lessons for redress. *Sustainability: Science, Practice, and Policy*, *17*(1), 77–81. doi:10.1080/15487733.2020.1860345

Mukherjee, S., Baral, M. M., Chittipaka, V., Srivastava, S. C., & Pal, S. K. (2021). *Discussing the Impact of Industry 4.0 in Agriculture Supply Chain*. Springer. doi:10.1007/978-981-16-3033-0_28

Mukherjee, S., Baral, M. M., Venkataiah, C., Pal, S. K., & Nagariya, R. (2021). Service robots are an option for contactless services due to the COVID-19 pandemic in the hotels. *Decision (Washington, D.C.)*, *48*(4), 445–460. doi:10.100740622-021-00300-x

Mukherjee, S., & Chittipaka, V. (2021). Analysing the Adoption of Intelligent Agent Technology in Food Supply Chain Management: An Empirical Evidence. *FIIB Business Review*. Advance online publication. doi:10.1177/23197145211059243

Mukherjee, S., Chittipaka, V., & Baral, M. M. (2021). *Developing a Model to Highlight the Relation of Digital Trust With Privacy and Security for the Blockchain Technology*. doi:10.4018/978-1-7998-8081-3.ch007

Mukherjee, S., Chittipaka, V., & Baral, M. M. (2022). Addressing and Modeling the Challenges Faced in the Implementation of Blockchain Technology in the Food and Agriculture Supply Chain. In Blockchain Technologies and Applications for Digital Governance (pp. 151–179). doi:10.4018/978-1-7998-8493-4.ch007

Mukherjee, S., Chittipaka, V., Baral, M. M., & Srivastava, S. C. (2022). Integrating the Challenges of Cloud Computing in Supply Chain Management. In Recent Advances in Industrial Production (pp. 355–363). doi:10.1007/978-981-16-5281-3_33

Mukherjee, S., Mohan Baral, M., Srivastava, S. C., & Jana, B. (2021). Analyzing the problems faced by fashion retail stores due to covid-19 outbreak. *Parikalpana-KIIT Journal of Management, 17*(I), 206. Advance online publication. doi:10.23862/kiit-parikalpana/2021/v17/i1/209031

Nagarajan, V., & Sharma, P. (2021). Firm internationalization and long-term impact of the Covid-19 pandemic. *Managerial and Decision Economics, 42*(6), 1477–1491. Advance online publication. doi:10.1002/mde.3321 PMID:34230720

Nakat, Z., & Bou-Mitri, C. (2021). COVID-19 and the food industry: Readiness assessment. *Food Control, 121*, 107661. doi:10.1016/j.foodcont.2020.107661 PMID:33013004

Namdar, J., Li, X., Sawhney, R., & Pradhan, N. (2018). Supply chain resilience for single and multiple sourcing in the presence of disruption risks. *International Journal of Production Research, 56*(6), 2339–2360. doi:10.1080/00207543.2017.1370149

Nandi, S., Sarkis, J., Hervani, A., & Helms, M. (2020). Do blockchain and circular economy practices improve post COVID-19 supply chains? A resource-based and resource dependence perspective. *Industrial Management & Data Systems, 121*(2), 333–363. Advance online publication. doi:10.1108/IMDS-09-2020-0560

Nandi, S., Sarkis, J., Hervani, A. A., & Helms, M. M. (2021). Redesigning Supply Chains using Blockchain-Enabled Circular Economy and COVID-19 Experiences. *Sustainable Production and Consumption, 27*, 10–22. doi:10.1016/j.spc.2020.10.019 PMID:33102671

Nchanji, E. B., & Lutomia, C. K. (2021). *COVID-19 Challenges to Sustainable Food Production and Consumption: Future Lessons for Food Systems in Eastern and Southern Africa from a gender lens.* Sustainable Production and Consumption. doi:10.1016/j.spc.2021.05.016

Nhamo, G., Dube, K., & Chikodzi, D. (2020). COVID-19 and Implications for the Aviation Sector: A Global Perspective. *Counting the Cost of COVID-19 on the Global Tourism Industry*, 89–107. doi:10.1007/978-3-030-56231-1_4

Nunnally, J. C. (1994). *Psychometric theory* (3rd ed.). Tata McGraw-Hill Education.

Pal, S. K., Baral, M. M., Mukherjee, S., Venkataiah, C., & Jana, B. (2021). Analyzing the impact of supply chain innovation as a mediator for healthcare firms' performance. *Materials Today: Proceedings.* Advance online publication. doi:10.1016/j.matpr.2021.10.173

Pantano, E., Pizzi, G., Scarpi, D., & Dennis, C. (2020). Competing during a pandemic? Retailers' ups and downs during the COVID-19 outbreak. *Journal of Business Research, 116*, 209–213. doi:10.1016/j.jbusres.2020.05.036 PMID:32501307

Peluso, A. M., Pichierri, M., & Pino, G. (2021). Age-related effects on environmentally sustainable purchases at the time of COVID-19: Evidence from Italy. *Journal of Retailing and Consumer Services, 60*, 102443. doi:10.1016/j.jretconser.2021.102443

Piprani, A. Z., Mohezar, S., & Jaafar, N. I. (2020). Supply chain integration and supply chain performance: The mediating role of supply chain resilience. *International Journal of Supply Chain Management, 9*(3), 58–73.

Podsakoff, N. P. (2003). Common method biases in behavioral research: a critical review of the literature and recommended remedies. *Journal of Applied Psychology, 885*(879).

Queiroz, M. M., Fosso Wamba, S., De Bourmont, M., & Telles, R. (2020). Blockchain adoption in operations and supply chain management: Empirical evidence from an emerging economy. *International Journal of Production Research*. Advance online publication. doi:10.1080/00207543.2020.1803511

Queiroz, M. M., Ivanov, D., Dolgui, A., & Fosso Wamba, S. (2020). Impacts of epidemic outbreaks on supply chains: Mapping a research agenda amid the COVID-19 pandemic through a structured literature review. *Annals of Operations Research*, 1–38. doi:10.100710479-020-03685-7 PMID:32836615

Roy, R., & Appa Rao, G. (2020). Survey on pre-processing web log files in web usage mining. *International Journal of Advanced Science and Technology, 29*(3), 682–691.

Roy, R., & Dev, D. R. (2019). Metamorphosis Knowledge Probing of Guild Data through Chat Bot Using NLP. *Data Mining and Knowledge Engineering, 11*(7), 109–113. http://ischolar.info/index.php/CiiTDMKE/article/view/207566

Roy, R., Dev, D. R., & Prasad, V. S. R. (2020). Socially Intelligent Robots : Evolution of Human-Computer Interaction. *Journal of Critical Reviews, 7*(15), 1843–1848. doi:10.31838/jcr.07.15.252

Roy, R., & p p a R a o, G. A. (2021). Predicting User's Web Navigation behaviour using AMD and HMM Approaches. *IOP Conference Series. Materials Science and Engineering, 1074*(1), 012031. doi:10.1088/1757-899X/1074/1/012031

Sabouhi, F., Pishvaee, M. S., & Jabalameli, M. S. (2018). Resilient supply chain design under operational and disruption risks considering quantity discount: A case study of pharmaceutical supply chain. *Computers & Industrial Engineering, 126*, 657–672. doi:10.1016/j.cie.2018.10.001

Sajjad, A., Eweje, G., & Tappin, D. (2020). Managerial perspectives on drivers for and barriers to sustainable supply chain management implementation: Evidence from New Zealand. *Business Strategy and the Environment, 29*(2), 592–604. doi:10.1002/bse.2389

Salvini, G., Hofstede, G. J., Verdouw, C. N., Rijswijk, K., & Klerkx, L. (2020). Enhancing digital transformation towards virtual supply chains: A simulation game for Dutch floriculture. *Production Planning and Control*, 1–18. Advance online publication. doi:10.1080/09537287.2020.1858361

Sarkis, J. (2020). Supply chain sustainability: Learning from the COVID-19 pandemic. *International Journal of Operations & Production Management*, *41*(1), 63–73. doi:10.1108/IJOPM-08-2020-0568

Sarkis, J., Cohen, M. J., Dewick, P., & Schröder, P. (2020). A brave new world: Lessons from the COVID-19 pandemic for transitioning to sustainable supply and production. In Resources, Conservation and Recycling (Vol. 159, p. 104894). Elsevier B.V. doi:10.1016/j.resconrec.2020.104894

Sawik, T. (2013). Selection of resilient supply portfolio under disruption risks. *Omega (United Kingdom)*, *41*(2), 259–269. doi:10.1016/j.omega.2012.05.003

Scheiwiller, S., & Zizka, L. (2021). Strategic responses by European airlines to the Covid-19 pandemic: A soft landing or a turbulent ride? *Journal of Air Transport Management*, *95*, 102103. doi:10.1016/j.jairtraman.2021.102103

Schniederjans, D. G., Curado, C., & Khalajhedayati, M. (2020). Supply chain digitisation trends: An integration of knowledge management. *International Journal of Production Economics*, *220*, 107439. doi:10.1016/j.ijpe.2019.07.012

Sharma, A., & Adhikary, A. (n.d.). *Covid-19's impact on supply chain decisions: Strategic insights from NASDAQ 100 firms using Twitter data*. Elsevier. Retrieved May 24, 2021, from https://www.sciencedirect.com/science/article/pii/S0148296320303210

Sharma, A., Borah, S. B., & Moses, A. C. (2021). Responses to COVID-19: The role of governance, healthcare infrastructure, and learning from past pandemics. *Journal of Business Research*, *122*, 597–607. doi:10.1016/j.jbusres.2020.09.011 PMID:33518844

Sharma, M. (2021). *Accelerating retail supply chain performance against pandemic disruption : Adopting resilient strategies to mitigate the long-term effects*. Academic Press.

Shin, N., & Park, S. (2019). Evidence-based resilience management for supply chain sustainability: An interpretive structural modelling approach. In Sustainability (Switzerland) (Vol. 11, Issue 2). doi:10.3390u11020484

Sunny, J., Undralla, N., & Madhusudanan Pillai, V. (2020). Supply chain transparency through blockchain-based traceability: An overview with demonstration. *Computers & Industrial Engineering*, *150*, 106895. doi:10.1016/j.cie.2020.106895

Taqi, H. M. M., Ahmed, H. N., Paul, S., Garshasbi, M., Ali, S. M., Kabir, G., & Paul, S. K. (2020). Strategies to Manage the Impacts of the COVID-19 Pandemic in the Supply Chain: Implications for Improving Economic and Social Sustainability. *Sustainability*, *12*(22), 9483. doi:10.3390u12229483

Thaichon, P. (2021). COVID in the Aviation Industry: Crisis Management, Its Decisions and Outcomes. *COVID-19. Technology and Marketing*, *2019*, 21–31. doi:10.1007/978-981-16-1442-2_2

Torabi, S. A., Baghersad, M., & Mansouri, S. A. (2015). Resilient supplier selection and order allocation under operational and disruption risks. *Transportation Research Part E, Logistics and Transportation Review*, *79*, 22–48. doi:10.1016/j.tre.2015.03.005

Tukamuhabwa, B. R., Stevenson, M., Busby, J., & Zorzini, M. (2015). Supply chain resilience: Definition, review and theoretical foundations for further study. In International Journal of Production Research (Vol. 53, Issue 18, pp. 5592–5623). Taylor and Francis Ltd. doi:10.1080/00207543.2015.1037934

Verma, S., & Gustafsson, A. (2020). Investigating the emerging COVID-19 research trends in the field of business and management: A bibliometric analysis approach. *Journal of Business Research*, *118*, 253–261. doi:10.1016/j.jbusres.2020.06.057 PMID:32834211

Wang, Q., & Zhang, C. (2021). Can COVID-19 and environmental research in developing countries support these countries to meet the environmental challenges induced by the pandemic? *Environmental Science and Pollution Research International*, *28*(30), 1–21. doi:10.100711356-021-13591-5 PMID:33782826

Wasim Ahmad, R., Hasan, H., Yaqoob, I., Salah, K., Jayaraman, R., & Omar, M. (2021). Blockchain for aerospace and defense: Opportunities and open research challenges. *Computers & Industrial Engineering*, *151*, 106982. doi:10.1016/j.cie.2020.106982

Xue, D., Liu, Z., Wang, B., & Yang, J. (2021). Impacts of COVID-19 on aircraft usage and fuel consumption: A case study on four Chinese international airports. *Journal of Air Transport Management*, *95*, 102106. doi:10.1016/j.jairtraman.2021.102106 PMID:34548769

Zelbst, P. J., Green, K. W., Sower, V. E., & Bond, P. L. (2019). The impact of RFID, IIoT, and Blockchain technologies on supply chain transparency. *Journal of Manufacturing Technology Management*, *31*(3), 441–457. doi:10.1108/JMTM-03-2019-0118

## KEY TERMS AND DEFINITIONS

**Automation:** Automation refers to application areas in which human input is lowered. This would include automation, IT automation, and individual applications such as automation, among other things. Supply chain mechanization uses digitalization to achieve the optimal, connect applications and streamline processes within supply chain operations.

**Digitization:** Digitization is a process that, when done correctly, can be vastly transformative for a company - but only after an organization successfully digital form. Digitization, as the enabler, converts information about the products, such as pictures and documents, into an electronic medium.

**Flexibility:** The ability to respond to short-term changes in the market or supply in supply chains is meant to refer to as flexibility. other exterior interruptions, as well as adjusting to strategic and operational shifts in the surroundings about the supply chain

**Resilient Supply Chain:** A resilient supply chain is defined by its capacity to endure and restore from disruptions. That means becoming able to resist or even avoid the impact of supply disruption - as well as recovering quickly from one. Issues of the supply chain can be jeopardised by risk management and disruptions.

**Sustainability:** Sustainability entails meeting our own needs without compromising future generations' ability to meet their own. The effect of a company on advancing human rights, labour standards, environmental progress, and anti-corruption policies is regarded as supply-chain sustainability. A sustainable supply wants to capitalize on supply chain possibilities and provides early purchasers and procedure inventors with a substantial comparative edge.

# Chapter 14

# Application of Digital Technologies:
## Integrated Blockchain With Emerging Technologies

**Shankar Subramanian Iyer**

*S.P. Jain School of Global Management, Dubai, UAE*

## ABSTRACT

*The application of digital technologies in supply chain and logistics is immense and the most important happening in the last decade. The advent of COVID-19 has forced changes in the supply chain and some cases disrupted it. In some cases, it has been a do-or-die situation as social distancing and passenger travel and essentials have affected most economies. China controlled about 40% of the global supply chain, and most countries were made to change and initiate alternative supply chains to reduce the risk. The purpose of this study is to study how the emerging technologies of blockchain, virtual reality, artificial intelligence, machine learning are the few additions to enhance the supply chain. The supply chain digitalization will lead to cost reduction, improved efficiency, data security, and storage of the information. The emerging technologies are poised to revolutionize the supply chain and logistics. The study uses qualitative approach to showcase the expert opinion of stakeholders on this topic and contribute to the scarce data available currently.*

## INTRODUCTION

With the advent of industrial revolution 4.0, new technologies have the potential of transforming the supply chain, logistics and transportation sector. These technologies enhance the value of the supply chain system. The modern transportation and supply chain of companies like Amazon, Alibaba, Mercedes, Sony, Apple, Samsung are focal points of the world to study and follow or improve the supply chain. The risks and the investment need to be analyzed closely to the integrated networks before the supply chain improvements can be implemented (Glas et al., 2016); (Ivanov et al.,2019). Some companies have not been able to exploit these opportunities due to lack of understanding, resistance to change, lack of

DOI: 10.4018/978-1-7998-9506-0.ch014

Copyright © 2022, IGI Global. Copying or distributing in print or electronic forms without written permission of IGI Global is prohibited.

investment and lack of apt manpower and sometimes lackluster management strategies been adapted. The internet of things (IOT) has changed the habits of users to the extent that an average of 6 hours daily is spent by most people on gadgets, mobiles, and electronic devices. It is interesting to note that all companies have not adopted digitalization to the same extent and probably losing out on the opportunity which digitalization has thrown open for business and global reach (Gurria, 2017). Artificial intelligence, machine learning and big data support the storage of data, analysis, and processing of data for prediction on daily basis to enhance logistics and supply chain services. It involves reimagining, rethinking, and redesigning digital age businesses. Digitalization makes collaboration, integration possible which in turn can reduce cost, save time and manpower, makes storage of records systematic and compact enhancing efficiency and effectiveness of the supply chain system (Arenkov et al., 2019). The digital transformation in the supply chain is less of a digital problem than a transformation problem, change envisions of the management transferred to its employees and an organization problem most of the time (Agrawal et al., 2020). Customers are ready to pay for the innovation and digital methods used to keep everyone safe, which most of the experts were not sure of at the beginning of this trend. Customers are sensitive to human value and ready to try out new ways of receiving things like drones delivering parcels. Most experts in earlier times would not agree this would happen as the argument was about personalized service whereas this drone delivery is more personalized and keeping the social distancing norm in mind. The delivery of food items to the customer on the table using robots, in the restaurant was unimaginable a few months back, however a reality now (Nikolskaya et al., 2021).

## Background

The supply chain industry is undergoing major changes due to digital transformation, and this has led businesses to invest in these technologies to be competitive and survive in the future. Some of the terms need introduction and familiarity of these terms will ensure deeper understanding of the sector and basis of this study.

## Digital Transformation

The process of putting manual operations, processes and outcomes into digital form using technologies. Digital transformation is using digital technologies in all areas of the business to enhance the value delivered to customers and initiate cultural change to explore new ways and accept failure as a way forward to success (Nasiri et al, 2020).

## The Supply Chain

The operations carried out to deliver goods and services to the customer. It includes the activities reaching the goods from the supplier to the manufacturer and from the manufacturer to the customer (Wolf et al., 2020).

## Digital Technologies

Tools used for online learning, gaming, connecting on social media, data processing for learning, entertainment purpose (Arenkov et al., 2019).

*Application of Digital Technologies*

## Emerging Technologies

Refer to all technologies supporting digital transformation like blockchain, virtual reality, Internet of things, Artificial Intelligence, data mining, machine learning, augmented reality, robotics, and virtual reality to just note a few examples which will support the future of supply chain businesses (Hopkins, 2021).

## Supply Chain Industry 4.0

The integrated collaborated supply chain for coordinating materials, information and finance flow in business networks which is automated and supported by digital technologies (Hofmann et al., 2019).

## Blockchain

A digital decentralized transaction ledger that is recorded and encrypted in a hash to block and involving all participants and requires more than 51% consent for any amendments and additions to be made (Iyer et al., 2020).

## Integrated Supply Chain Blockchain

Amongst suppliers enhances information flow, trust, transparency, storage of records, data security, confidentiality, flexibility to be more effective and efficient. amongst suppliers (Sternberg et al., 2021).

## Supply Chain Before and After Digitization

A phenomenon noticed in every industry in last few years. The traditional fragmented supply chain which was inherently inefficient and facing many challenges had been transformed into digitalized supply chain processes which makes them more effective, more efficient, more transparent, and agile. The old system had coordinating issues with the suppliers, transportation, distributors, retailers, and customers leading to ERP systems where all stakeholders are on the same platform and online at the same time. This led to better coordination, cost saving, and efficiency enhancement. However, the 4.0 version is using emerging technologies like Blockchain, data analytics, artificial Intelligence, Robotic handling systems leading to the supply chain system agility, transparency in taking strategic decisions. Industry 4.0 vision will be realized if most supply chain processes is digitized. So, it is the whole supply chain ecosystem to come of age, for the evolution of traditional supply chains toward a connected, smart, and highly efficient to happen. This supply chain ecosystem will use number of key technologies like integrated planning and execution systems, autonomous logistics, logistics visibility, spare parts management, smart procurement, and warehousing, advanced analytics. The companies need to respond to disruptions in the supply chain, by anticipating them using "what-if" scenarios and adjusting the supply chain in real time as conditions change.

## Research Gap

Identified from earlier research studies (all scholarly, academic articles from 2016 onwards) helped in setting the study direction for this research. The summary of the research gap identified is discussed in subsequent paragraphs.

Some Researchers suggested that future studies to be conducted in different cultures and places having different technology adoption levels to understand the Supply chain blockchain implementation factors and in other chosen industries (Saryatmo et al., 2021). Another future line of research would be studying the risks of digitalizing Supply chain, supplier collaboration, blockchain technology stakeholders and the use of emerging technologies in supply chain (Hoek, 2020). The emerging technologies that need to be studied include data science-enabled supply chain management, supply chain agility, humanizing manufacturing through digital manufacturing strategy, omni channel, and resource-based view and beyond, to discuss how emerging technologies help supply chain blockchain technology (Seyedghorban et al., 2020); (ALSaqa et al., 2019); (Agrawal et al., 2021). Such digitalization requires investment in Infrastructure, facilities, equipment, manpower and training to enable proper implementation to ensure company strategies (Nasiri et al., 2020). Some researchers present the relevance of loT, blockchain technology, Artificial intelligence for process automation & data transfer, data integration between different platforms to enhance supply chain management efficiency (Pundir et al., 2019); (Hallikas et al., 2021). The knowledge management and digitalization of supply chain enhances the supply chain digital performance (Schniederjans et al., 2020). The supply chain digitalization has some advantages, some limitations which need to be overcome for its successful implementation, a development framework road map can be future research topic (Büyüközkan et al., 2018). The development of standards and the performance measurement methods need to be evaluated for future use in digitalization of supply chain (Saberi et al., 2019). The future studies can lead to the Supply chain Management 4.0 framework to match the Industrial 4.0 revolution (Zekhnini et al., 2020). The research gap studied suggested factors that can add contribution to the current knowledge on this topic as mentioned above. This helped the research study to focus on the digitalization transformation of supply chain and the blockchain technology support for the same.

The research questions for this study would be

1. How will the Digitalization of the supply chain transform businesses? And
2. How blockchain technology can support the digital transformation of the supply chain using emerging technologies?

*Application of Digital Technologies*

## RQ1: HOW THE DIGITALIZATION OF THE SUPPLY CHAIN WILL TRANSFORM BUSINESSES?

*Figure 1. Digitalization of supply chain*
Source: Developed by the Author

The Digitalization of the supply chain can be seen on two fronts the Supply chain capabilities enhancement which will lead to improved operational performance in the process tasks as shown in figure 1. The factors have been identified in literature review and grouped to study in a meaningful manner. Most of the earlier research has described supply chain capabilities as supply chain coordination, supply chain planning, supplier involvement, customer involvement, IT exploitation, IT exploration, IT competencies and IT resources. These enhancements in capabilities will lead to better supply chain operational performance in terms of quality, cost, delivery, flexibility, and efficiency (Herold et al., 2021).

## Supply Chain Coordination

An important aspect of operations, sharing information, suppliers, transporters, warehouses, and retailers even to the customer end. Supply chain coordination has vastly improved due to the use of technology like GPS mapping, unmanned vehicles, drones, IOT cloud computing to ensure customers receive quality products and services on time and at a reasonable cost (Büyüközkan et al., 2018).

## Supply Chain Planning

Becomes easier and less biased as human intervention is reduced by using technologies like ML, data analytics to help make decisions daily. Moreover, technology and digitalization have made data available almost in real-time so any shift in strategy or decision can be made immediately (Wolf et al., 2020).

## Supplier Involvement

In supply chain digitalization is crucial as the supply chain partners and participants need to share information between the network in the shortest time using technology. Supplier relationship can be enhanced by transparency of the digitalized system, automated and collaborative system (Ehie et al., 2019); (Mikhaylova et al., 2021).

## Customer Involvement

In the supply chain is necessary for delivering customer satisfaction and digitalization has enabled this further like customer parcel, shipment tracking and using technology to acknowledge receipt or delivery of the same. Online registration, booking of the consignment has enhanced the supply chain performance (Dutta et al., 2020).

## IT Exploitation and Exploration

Refers to the ability of the Supply chain domain Organization to use ICT to improve the supply chain effectiveness by digitalization and achieve operational excellence. The organization are considering opportunities to use their capabilities to explore new and improved ways of delivering value to their customers (Bäckstrand et al., 2021); (Nasiri et al., 2020).

## IT Competencies

IT competencies of the Organization staff enhances the success rate of digitalization implementation as they are in a better position to understand the processes and adjust to them and integrate the technologies into the processes within a short time and cost (Hader et al., 2020).

## IT Resources

Refer to the resources in terms of money and readiness to invest, infrastructure availability like the Internet, hardware, software, and the training accessibility of training the staff. These resources availability will determine the organization capabilities to digitalize the supply chain and integrate with the blockchain. These also include supplier's and partnership resources (Sternberg et al., 2021).

These capabilities are crucial for the digitalization of the supply chain which will enhance the operational performance of the whole ecosystem delivering quality, optimum priced products and services to the customers thus saving time, resources for higher efficiency and flexibility of the supply chain (Wong et al., 2020).

*Application of Digital Technologies*

## RQ2: HOW BLOCKCHAIN TECHNOLOGY CAN SUPPORT THE DIGITAL TRANSFORMATION OF THE SUPPLY CHAIN USING EMERGING TECHNOLOGIES?

*Figure 2. BCT supply chain features- TOE-Factors*
Source: Developed by the Author

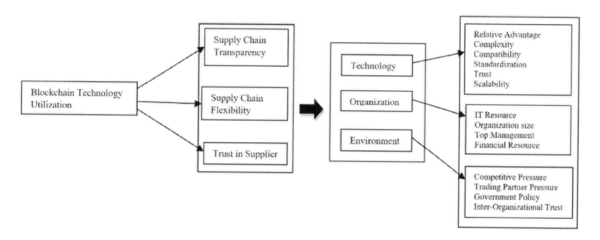

Blockchain technology is expected to provide supply chain transparency in terms of information and knowledge flow and sharing amongst partners and collaborators in the digital supply chain. Due to this, the trust amongst the stakeholders will improve and the supply chain will be dynamic and flexible to meet future needs of the supply chain (Gaehtgens et al., 2017). The technology factors, the environmental factors and the organization factors influence the implementation of blockchain technology in the supply chain. The factors are shown in the figure 2 above clearly addresses the factor and the sub-variables of the constructs. Technology has the potential to involve all the stakeholders or some of the stakeholders according to the situation and later grow to involve everyone to achieve the volume of scales to justify the investments in infrastructure and the technology (Gurzawska, 2020). The technology is expected to standardize processes, solve the complexity of things, and serve as a competitive edge. The organization resources and its willingness to invest on part of the top management will determine how fast an organization can adopt blockchain or new technologies for the supply chain. Most modern companies like Amazon, Alibaba, Sony, Samsung, Honda to name a few are examples of early implementors of technology in the supply chain at various stages. The environment is also right for such implementations (Wamba et al, 2020).

## MAIN FOCUS OF CHAPTER

The focus of the chapter is about the application of digital technologies in the supply chain sector and the use of emerging technologies to ensure integrated supply chain Blockchain. Using emerging technologies and digitalization the supply chain has become a competitive advantage for the main players like IBM, Procter and Gamble, Coca Cola, Siemens, Honda just to name a few. The main benefit of the application of digital technologies in the supply chain is making the collaboration between various partners to deliver effective, efficient goods and services to the satisfaction of the customers. Looking at the details of benefits, challenges, issues, controversies, problems, and barriers of the digitalization of the supply chain will determine the future of the supply chain (Blandine et al., 2020).

## Benefits and Challenges of Supply Chain Digitalization

The efficiency of the supply chain is enhanced by digitalization as managers adopt web-based processes to monitor the performance of processes from sales to logistics, leading to better information gathering to make better decisions. The process profitability can be enhanced, and time saved using big data analytics and predict accurately, clarity, cohesively to give intelligence over the various networks (Dujak et al., 2019). The supply chain digitalization can analyze the customer expectation and deliver better satisfaction. The corporates can reduce operating costs, enhance the quality of products to increase the sales revenue by increased market shares, develop products that meet customer needs, and develop strategic advantages to improve business operations (Gurria, 2017). The challenge is to use technology, invest in processes to be agile, integrate the supply chain activities, ability to use intelligence to make decisions (Blandine et al., 2020). The training of manpower to be competent and develop expertise to overcome these market challenges and be successful in developing a competitive advantage over the competition. The digital supply chain has the potential of developing information systems and adopting emerging technologies to strengthen the agility and integrating the supply chain to improve customer service and sustainable performance of the business (Korpela et al., 2017).

## Issues, Controversies, Problems and Barriers of Supply Chain Digitalization

The main issue of implementing the supply chain digitalization is the involvement of every supply chain member, supplier, logistics supplier, distributor, retailer, third parties and customer. All stakeholders need to accept and be ready to change for the process. So, it is of importance that all participants need to participant wholeheartedly for the supply chain digitalization to be implemented successfully. The main reason for not getting the success has been the investment to be put in and the human resource training and the change, the agility of the organization matters (Nasiri et al., 2020). However, the supply chain digitalization needs to transform the organization process for future survival. The collaboration and exchange of information transparently is a necessary step in digitalization. The culture and mindset of the people involved, the employer, employees, the third parties and other stakeholders, decide the implementation success of digitalization of the supply chain. Automation, interconnectivity, transparency, proactive networked supply chain often makes employees threatened of job losses as they feel their importance reduced and their expertise, no longer needed (Berg et al., 2021). For example, storekeepers have most of their functions done by ERP networks and inventory, replenishment, ordering, receiving the goods are all automated and have no human intervention, making the system efficient and effective, however making the employee unsecured. Most of the supply chain researchers and experts agree that the major barriers are cost involved as investment, skills of the employees to use technology for analytics, changing organization culture, managing collaborative & information systems and integration of the system (Brun et al., 2014). Other major reasons suggested are lack of proper know-how, lack of stakeholder support, lack of strategic decisions, lack of resources, lack of support from the management/

*Application of Digital Technologies*

employees or any combination of these factors. Any organization taking care of these factors mentioned will ensure implementation success (Ehie et al., 2019).

## Risks Involved in Transformative Digitalization in Supply Chains

Involves Investment risks as infrastructure investment would not realize if the implementation was not successful or the various stakeholders like suppliers follow the company investing in the capital assets. The risk of collaboration refers to the non-cooperation of the stakeholders and sharing of information to competitors and working with the competitors. The risk of confidential information leaked to the others, or third parties is the trust factor between the collaborators and users. However, over a period the collaboration will mitigate the scalability issue and get more users into the platform. However, the lack of resources in terms of money, technology, infrastructure, lack of technicians can jeopardize the successful implementation of these projects. The scarcity of energy can lead to failure as these blockchain projects are energy intensive.

## SOLUTIONS AND RECOMMENDATIONS

The overall supply chain has been represented in the figure 3 below, illustrating the business-to-business part and the business to customer space separately. The digitalization of the supply chain involves the information flow, collaboration and system integration of vendors, producers, shippers, global logistics, wholesalers as importers, retailers, and the customer. Supply chain planning is very important in the transportation, shipping sector. Logistics planning involves reducing cost, enhancing the efficiency and effectiveness of all logistics functions (requirements) like warehousing, Inventory, order management, documentation, replenishment, and customer end delivery (Ferretti, 2016). Digitalization involves autonomous tracking, fleet management, AI purchasing, automated warehousing, digitalized platforms, Industry 4.0, 3D printing, demand forecasting, route optimization, IT supply order management, using robots in warehousing, drone delivery, to name a few processes (Agrawal et al., 2018). Proper supply chain planning using digitalized and integrated system leads to significant benefits, moving away from the outdated supply chain practices to modern practices vastly improving the payback by reducing the inventory costs, reduced warehousing costs and resource costs. Most people involved in the supply chain are sure that digitalization is leading to transformation in this sector and the future (Lisa et al., 2021).

*Figure 3. Digitalization of supply chain and channels*
Source: Developed by the Author

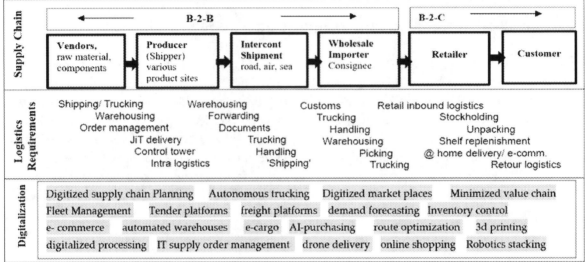

Some see this digitalization transformation as a threat due to risks involved like a data security breach, increased complexity of competition, increased price and quality transparency making most of the existing business model irrelevant shortly. This would lead to loss of employment, loss of revenue due to loss of customers to competitors who have adopted digitalization earlier (Ivanov et al., 2019).

## Integrated Supply Chain Blockchain with Emerging Technologies

The integrated blockchain with emerging technologies is the future supply chain digitalized model which will cater to all the needs of businesses and their stakeholders. Blockchain technology is known as decentralized ledger connecting participants through the secured network, making it transparent, immutable, no intermediary, faster settlement leading to reduced cost, verifiable long-lasting storage of records and that is the need of the supply chain sector. Most of the emerging technologies like Artificial intelligence, machine learning, data analytics, 3D printing, virtual reality, augmented reality can enhance customer satisfaction by supporting automating tasks, decision making, strategic evaluation by exchange of information and collaborating processes (Dutta et al., 2020). The use of blockchain in the supply chain ensures transparency, flexibility and build trust amongst suppliers. Blockchain technology enhances customers' trust as it provides traceability of products at all supply chain stages and makes tracking easy. Blockchain prevents fraud and reduction of cost and increased efficiency. Blockchain guarantees the integrity and security of data (Gupta et al., 2020). Real-time collection of details of product, visibility, transparency, and quality control throughout the product lifecycle using blockchain. Blockchain can make up for the weakness of other components of the 4.0 industry like cyber-physical systems, the internet of things etc. (Hirsh et al., 2018). The various applications in supply chain and their Blockchain integrations has been tabulated from literature review.

*Application of Digital Technologies*

*Table 1. The 5W and 1H model for the digital technologies and integrated blockchain*

|  | **Application of Digital Technologies in supply chain** | **Integrated Blockchain with emerging technologies for supply chain** |
|---|---|---|
| When | • Planning the Supply chain tasks<br>• Information dissemination and exchange with partners<br>• Collaboration between suppliers and partners | • Reflecting on complex issues to find a solution<br>• Looking for fraud avoidance, security issues<br>• Enhancing security, transparency and build trust |
| Why | • Need of the hour<br>• Reduce cost and collaborate and share information | • Integrated supply chain blockchain to put all stakeholders on the same platform<br>• Blockchain has the potential to integrate using emerging technologies like AI, ML, VR, AR. |
| How | • Using technology to connect supply chain partners and stakeholders | • Using Blockchain technology<br>• integrating emerging technologies to the supply chain blockchain |
| When | • Immediate and at each stage of the supply chain process<br>• Available to the stakeholders for verification | • Secured and storage required at each stage of supply chain process |
| Where | • The application of digital technologies to all processes of supply chain whereas automation is possible<br>• starting with the processes where automation is necessary initially | • Integration of all stakeholders in the supply chain to achieve scalability<br>• Global stakeholders |
| Who | • Involves all stakeholders<br>• All collaborators are involved in the digitalized supply chain | • All partners, collaborators as participants |

Source: Developed by the Author

## METHODOLOGY

The research study used a qualitative, explorative approach to answer the research questions. Interviews and discussions with supply chain stakeholders and experts helped to gather in-depth information into how supply chain providers navigate, adjust to the changing landscape of blockchain technology as the future for digital transformation. The popular method used in technology forecasting is to elicit experts' viewpoints (Bokrantz et al., 2017; Iden et al.,2017). The expertise and knowledge in the supply chain sector can give experts the ability to appraise the situation in the topic (Scapolo and Miles, 2006, p.682).

The experts have the advantage over novices on the topic of the supply chain of having a greater understanding of the situations under consideration due to their accumulated knowledge and experience about the cause-relationships reasoning and logic sensemaking to give meaningful insights (Wang et al., 2020).

The Delphi study approach is used to engage experts in an anonymous exchange between them to gather group views on the subject matter (Kembro et al., 2017; Bokrantz et al., 2017), however, the current study will examine individual sensemaking to register their interpretations of the blockchain emergence for supply chain application and the digital transformation happening in the supply chain. A semi-structured interview of experts was organized to collect data, some Individual expert interviews will mitigate the polarization effect in group judgement (Winkler et al., 2016).

## COLLECTION OF DATA

The interviewees (respondents) are supply chain experts, stakeholders having sufficient knowledge of blockchain technology application, digitalization of supply chain and capable of giving their opinion on the topic. Supply chain domain managers with in-depth knowledge and information can give an expert opinion of their understanding of the IT usage in the supply chain sector regarding transformation due to digitalization. The concerned respondents knew the blockchain technology features and working in the sector. They are referred to as supply chain experts.

The validity and reliability of the research results are ensured as per the principles of the Delphi methodology to select the proper industry expert considering their responsibilities, position, their knowledge, experience, and their willingness to participate in the interviews (Bokrantz et al., 2017).

So, the study identified 15 interviewees with more than 10 years of IT and supply chain management and with managers and above positions with some variation in their responsibilities to get diverse viewpoints.

The practitioners and the academic researchers' interviews and discussions gave confidence in the credibility of the experts' inputs (Table 2).

A semi-structured interview (Annexure 1) was developed to focus on whether the interviewee believed that the supply chain sector was transforming due to digitalization and the use of blockchain technology, to disrupt the future of the supply chain. The interviewee's knowledge of the emerging technology can be integrated into the blockchain for use in the supply chain.

The Questionnaire has the first section to establish the profile of the interviewee, then the second part will focus on establishing the interviewee understanding of the digital application to supply chain and the third part is about the interviewee's knowledge on the usage of blockchain in the supply chain with integration the emerging technologies. Then specific questions are to consider the interviewee's idea on using emerging technologies, integrated with blockchain to digitalize and transform the supply chain sector. Also, a video link was provided explaining the working of the blockchain, background information about the supply chain digitalization process, just to acquaint the interviewees. The idea was to facilitate the whole process to respondents as they come from different backgrounds, some from blockchain and some from the supply chain domain. This information was quite helpful, and all the interviewees commented positively on this initiative. The information pack also explained the research rationale and the methodology to make it easy for the interviewee to take part in the online interviews conducted (Haddud et al., 2020).

Most interviews were conducted between July and August of 2021. Most interviews lasted between 45-50 minutes, with only one exception: one 20-minute interview was cut short by some disruption but completed through emails and elaborate phone calls later. All interviews were voice recorded and transcribed, although interviewees 3 and 8 requested anonymity due to the sensitivity of the information.

## ANALYSIS OF COLLECTED AND TABULATED DATA

The data analysis involved an iterative process of moving between collected data about the supply chain digitalization and blockchain technology and the emerging framework of understanding of the interviewees. The process involves transcribing the interviews using software using the Zoom sessions. Then writing the summary of each of the participant's responses to the questions and get a holistic view

*Application of Digital Technologies*

of how the interviewees perceive digitalization of the supply chain and the blockchain technology in the supply chain domain.

After the transcription was done, the detailed "open coding" analysis was used to decipher the data. Agreeing to the coding to decipher the transcribes took some time as the author had to agree and rely on some professional help and set up standards to establish the emotions of the respondents, the body language, the sensemaking, and behaviors/actions of other unexpected stances. After agreeing to the coding and grouping together into categories depending on the questions asked helped to form a working analytical framework applicable to the indexing subsequent transcripts.

Finally, cognitive mapping was deployed as a data analysis technique to aid understanding and evaluation of people's cognitive complexity in making sense of the digitalization of supply chain and blockchain technology. (Brun et al., 2014; Ferretti, 2016). One of the categories identified as factors leading to benefits, applications, and challenges of supply chain digitalization and blockchain technology (Gaehtgens et al., 2017).

## SUMMARY OF THE FINDINGS OF THE QUALITATIVE STUDY

*Table 2. Summary of the interviews conducted and transcript*

| Interviewee no, (Experience in years) | Designation/ Responsibility in Organization | Location | Main Comments Supply chain digitalization and Blockchain integrated implementation in the supply chain using emerging technologies (Other Interviewees agreeing to these comments) |
|---|---|---|---|
| 1. (16) | CEO- IT Service Provider | UK | Tracking the parcels, the shipment details, exchange of information, transparency is a very useful digitalization initiative and to deliver customer satisfaction. However, the major concern has been cyber security which the Blockchain seems to be a potential solution. (5,6,11, 12) |
| 2. (17) | Regional Head MENA- Logistics | UAE | Supply chain planning and process visualization is most important and can be easily achieved by digitalization and by using analytics. Technology and digitalization can easily involve suppliers and customers which will give the ultimate satisfaction to the users. Interviewee 2, being internally focused, discussed the potential benefits for the organization reducing time and increased profitability. The interviewees shown in the bracket believed that blockchains could eliminate most intermediaries and all interventions by using smart contracts. Blockchain can easily ensure trust, confidentiality and transparency of the stakeholders and enhance quality, reduce cost, and time, improve the flexibility of the processes. (3, 5, 6, 10) |

*Continued on following page*

*Application of Digital Technologies*

*Table 2. Continued*

| Interviewee no, (Experience in years) | Designation/ Responsibility in Organization | Location | Main Comments Supply chain digitalization and Blockchain integrated implementation in the supply chain using emerging technologies (Other Interviewees agreeing to these comments) |
|---|---|---|---|
| 3. (11) | Global Logistics Middle East Controller | INDIA/UAE | Interviewees 3 and 7 thought that information and communication between organizations matter a lot and the resistance from the employees, partners, suppliers are the main challenge or barrier to blockchain adoption in the supply chain and the digitalization of the supply chain processes. Input data should be ensured to be of good quality so that the integrity of the process is retained. Smart contracts help to take care of governance issues and the diffusion of the blockchain is destined in the future. Most interviewees say that supply chain digitalization implementation progress may be gradual as the confidence level of the people involved is low and little financial benefit accrual. So, the changes from digitalization to blockchain integration is the future but would take time. (4, 6, 10, 12, 13) |
| 4. (15) | Supply Chain Manager | UAE | The main point agreed is the digitalization of the supply chain will define the future of logistics, transportation of passengers and freight as modern technologies are seen to dominate the sector. Robots, drones, automated processes are the norm of any supply chain. Also, hybrid blockchain systems might be suitable for supply chains and use emerging technologies such as IoT, robotics, artificial intelligence (AI) and 3D printing. (6, 8, 10, 11) |
| 5. (13) | Transportation in charge | PAKISTAN | The supply chain operations digitalization simplifies the tasks, makes it easy to operate. Blockchain makes it easy to handle the workload due to information transfer, sharing and processing data. Smart contracts support the validation of information checking. The supply chain sector has trust problems and digitalization is not taking off due to lack of trust to exchange information between partners, however, blockchain can solve this issue by immutable features and the decentralized ledger ensures the security of the data. (4, 7, 9, 13) |
| 6. (20) | IT and Logistics Documentation Manager | SINGAPORE | Smart contracts help the blockchain supply chain to automate certain tasks, documentation and solve a lot of complex situations like validation of shipments, automated tracking, Smart contracts support customized operations in blockchain operations. Blockchain scalability can be attained by involving more organizations globally and taking trial, pilot blockchain projects. Since blockchain can be transparent, avoid fraud, it can avoid corrupt practices. (2, 3, 7, 9, 10, 11) |
| 7. (16) | Blockchain Developer | MALAYSIA | Blockchain in some industries like supply chain is crucial as in costly consignments like oil, gas, gold shipments, cold storage and defense goods as tracking is live and verifiable, transparent. These supply chains have urgency, reliable, automated networks, and the exchange of information. (5, 8, 10, 11) |

*Continued on following page*

*Application of Digital Technologies*

*Table 2. Continued*

| Interviewee no, (Experience in years) | Designation/ Responsibility in Organization | Location | Main Comments Supply chain digitalization and Blockchain integrated implementation in the supply chain using emerging technologies (Other Interviewees agreeing to these comments) |
|---|---|---|---|
| 8. (10) | Logistics Manager | INDIA | Digitalization of the supply chain will improve visibility by verifying the documents, allow data analytics to be used for better services through demand forecasting, optimizing resources, asset monitoring, quality of services. In some cold storage, it can play a crucial role like milk transportation. Blockchain can integrate the tasks using AI, data analytics and secured storage of data. (1, 4, 9) |
| 9. (15) | Shipping Manager | UAE | Digitalization of the supply chain has been continuous since the last decade, however, lots more to happen especially in the shipping, documentation, banking transfers collaboration, Exim rules, government policies, everything to be on one page, unlike the current system. Visibility and transparency can improve trust, improve collaboration, internal processes of the individual partners, reduce time, save cost, and add value to the products and services to Customers. (1, 4, 11, 13, 15) |
| 10. (12) | IT Consultant | AUSTRALIA | The digitalization of the supply chain can support a single pool and system available to stakeholders secured by the decentralized, immutable ledgers of records stored, easy to verify. It looks to set standards to maintain the overall quality of data. The overall blockchain digitalization using emerging technology ensures trust between all stakeholders, partners, and gain customer confidence. Scalability or volumes of scales is quite possible in the supply chain sector as it has immense potential users. The loss of jobs due to the changes due to digitalization, blockchain adoption and the need to upgrade the employees and staff. (1, 12, 13, 15) |
| 11. (11) | Owner- Logistics Solution | AUSTRALIA | Digitalization of the supply chain supports the collaboration of partners to share, exchange information with stakeholders. Blockchain is known to have a solution for the trust, security, confidentiality issues of the supply chain and removal of intermediaries to be more efficient and effective. The blockchain will initiate new intermediates like IT consultants, Blockchain developers, coders, miners and be disruptive for some supply chain sectors as some people might lose their jobs due to digitalization, automation, emerging technologies integration. This can transform and have structural changes in the supply chain domain. (3, 5, 7,8,14) |
| 12. (13) | IT Consultant | SINGAPORE | Blockchain in the supply chain provides better visibility, traceability to stakeholders. Better visibility ensures customer service levels, standards and adds value. Blockchain helps to build trust, manage transactions among stakeholders for the cross- border for information exchange. This can be improved in the trial runs and pilot projects for blockchain. Tokenization of the assets would bring more investments and spread the awareness of the technology integrated into blockchain. (3, 7, 10, 11, 15) |

*Continued on following page*

*Application of Digital Technologies*

*Table 2. Continued*

| Interviewee no, (Experience in years) | Designation/ Responsibility in Organization | Location | Main Comments Supply chain digitalization and Blockchain integrated implementation in the supply chain using emerging technologies (Other Interviewees agreeing to these comments) |
|---|---|---|---|
| 13. (17) | Logistics Customer Service Manager | MALAYSIA | Digitalization of the supply chain will allow for operational improvements by enhancing the ability to handle increased volume, enhance the accuracy of data, enable the organization to monitor the process, enable performance evaluation. Digitalization can speed end-to-end supply chain execution. It can bring more visibility and interest investor to improved cash flow for the projects. (2, 3, 4, 6, 11, 14) |
| 14. (19) | IT Solutions Manager | INDIA | The digitalization of the supply chain can ensure the exchange of information, sharing with third parties and build trust while blockchain can ensure that the trust is further secured by proper storage, transparency, and immutability of the data. Digital supply chain offers opportunities to anticipate or spot issues (6, 7, 10, 12, 17) |
| 15. (21) | Shipping Agent- Owner, associated with Dubai Port. | UAE | The digital needs of the supply chain have been felt by the fraternity however, the blockchain technology to be used to secure the information and collaborate with partners, transparency, immutable records are the needs of the industry which blockchain can provide with reduced cost and saving of time. The blockchain usefulness is yet to be established as the scales of volume must be achieved by the stakeholders coming together to invest in such facilities along with the investment in emerging technologies. Since intermediaries are not necessary for blockchain the cost is reduced and the price and time quoted can be minimum. (1, 3, 5, 8) |

Source: Developed by the Author

The above table has been summarized from the interviews conducted with the experts and transcribed.

**How the table above, interviewee summary of comments can be used:** (further details of the interviews)

Since all the interviewees had good experience and knowledge about the supply chain domain and the blockchain features, they had an idea about how digitalization and blockchain in the supply chain can revolutionize the sector. Since the use of the processes, technology already by the most organized and the interviewees had good knowledge of both the domains, the supply chain and the blockchain, digitalization of the supply chain. Their knowledge, the experience will help the future studies and implementation of these technologies in the supply chain domain.

Interviewee 13 and Interviewee 8 added that since the Blockchain is still an infant in the industry, it should be used in selective areas where the problems exist and then expand to other areas to ensure success and convince the participants of the value addition blockchain can give the supply chain domain. Interviewee 11 pointed out the benefit of digitalization and technology for studied organization Amazon. Some companies like Alibaba, Maersk, Honda, Sony have already digitalized and accruing the benefits of the technologies like Robotics, Analytics, Artificial Intelligence, IoT, Machine Learning and Virtual

*Application of Digital Technologies*

reality and are convinced that blockchain usage can provide security, flexibility, efficiency, transparency, and immutability to the data they own.

Interviewees 5 and 10 pointed out the blockchain in the supply chain can remove the intermediaries, enhance visibility and transparency of the processes, secure data and maintain confidentiality. The perception of the users and the stakeholders are slowly changing from resistance to digitalization to using technology and blockchain diffusion to many areas of the supply chain. The blockchain would influence supply chains by optimizing process automation and ensure visibility, transparency which is crucial for the supply chain domain. The process faults can be noticed immediately to rectify the mistakes and add value to the whole supply chain process by reducing cost and time by eliminating intermediates.

Interviewee 2 thinks that blockchain can improve the security of products, trade and logistics information in data flow and enable strategic decisions.

Interviewees 5 and 11 believed that emerging technologies and the IoT would expand the boundary of real-time supply chain integration. The blockchain and IoT had the potential to track energy usage and goods movement in the warehouses like Amazon. Blockchain is perceived to allow secured data, information exchange by offering immutable, tamper-proof, high-quality data record storage and flow across the partners in the supply chain. The supply chain blockchain can provide trust, enhanced confidence and ensure end-consumers satisfaction as never before.

Interviewees 6, 12,13 and 15 were frank in accepting that most of their views about the supply chain digitalization and blockchain implementation in the sector are based on some experiences, knowledge gained by other sector companies and the reports of the experts, discussions with the stakeholders. Most of the digitalization experience is from the banking, IT sector and electronics sector which has set the pace for digitalization of the industries. The manufacturing sector saw some digitalization initiatives with companies like Samsung, Apple, Honda, IBM, Hyundai, Sony, Maersk, G.E, Boeing being some of the examples and accruing the fruits of the transformation. Blockchain success has been few and the cryptocurrency like Bitcoin has made the news and the learning point for the industries however, it is not a good example as it covers only the tokenization part of the blockchain. The rest of the features, benefits are just in the infant stage due to the lack of scalability, lack of fresh investment, collaboration, lack of sponsors, lack of regulations and regulator and lack of major successful implementation.

Interviewees 4, 9, 12 and 14 noted that the retail consumers would like to track the sources from where the materials are procured to the manufacture of the goods to the retail stores for knowing the materials used, the credibility of the suppliers, the consumer by scanning the bar code can trace all the suppliers across the globe and this information can be stored securely using the blockchain to know the green revolution and the meat procurement chain leading to better transparency, visibility and add to the trust across the supply chain. Boeing or Airbus procurer airlines would like to make sure the genuineness of the spares and how they have been manufactured and know how to source the spares in case of breakdowns. This build trust and add value to the whole supply chain digitalization. Smart contracts can automate the whole process and reduce the time involved. All this would take time to customize to the individual companies and supply chain involved.

Interviewee 1, 4, 8, 10 and 12 voiced their opinion about blockchain can easily remove customs clearance agents, freight forwarding agents, even bank documents clearance, by automation using smart contracts.

So, in the short run, it might mean job losses in some areas but creating jobs and opportunities in others. It becomes important to spread awareness and reskilling the employees to ensure a smooth transition to the digitalization ecosystem without much resistance and an improvised supply chain financial management system.

## IMPLICATIONS TO SOCIETY, MANAGERIAL AND FUTURE STUDIES

This study has many managerial implications. Firstly, this study contributes to the knowledge and comprehension of scarce prior research on the transformation caused by digital technology to Supply chain domain. The research topic can assist managers in the manufacturing industry in acquiring a deeper understanding of the effectiveness and efficiency of the digital supply chain on operations. Secondly, empirical evidence indicates that the digital supply chain enhances operational performance. These findings will identity factors that affect the output of digital supply chains, especially in developing countries with similar characteristics. Further the study recommends the supply chain parameters that needs to be reconfigured and redefined as a result. It enables the managers know about the different emerging technology that might be worth investing in to enhance Supply chain Blockchain functioning.

## FUTURE RESEARCH DIRECTIONS AND LIMITATIONS

The future of research in the Digitalization supply chain needs to explore the configuration, design of process, the integrated customer consumer and supplier involvement, the upgraded skills, project management approaches and the evaluation of supply chain performance. Future research needs to study various theoretical frameworks like the technology acceptance model, innovation adoption theory, diffusion theory, organizational theories, stakeholder's theories and combine quantitative and qualitative using constructivism, pragmatism, positivism to focus on digitalization SME supply chain for various industries. Further investigation can be directed at the application of technologies to blockchain in the supply chain to improve customer satisfaction and enhance performance. Tokenization of the supply chain asset and brand can help to make investments attractive for the stakeholders and enhance scalability. So future research can examine the value of tokenization to the supply chain blockchain. The study is explorative has a few limitations. The expert interviews the research study followed can be improved to be made appropriate for the explorative study by involving a more diverse range of respondents to enhance the understanding of the subject. The Delphi technique of conducting a structured assessment and exploring expert judgements. Further studies can use this method instead of the sensemaking on an individual level, maybe use collective group sensemaking based on technological innovations. It is important to research using a quantitative approach validating the model construct relationship using PLS-SEM (partial least square method-structural equation model).

## CONCLUSION

Digital Transformation (DT) provides an organization with a competitive edge over the competition by enhancing efficiency due to reduced costs, improving customer experience and create innovations. The main benefits of traceability, visibility and transparency accrue when logistics use IoT as agility is gained by analytics of real-time data and information to arrive at agile solutions in the business.

*Application of Digital Technologies*

Blockchain technology is still in its infant stage and has numerous research opportunities in the future. It will be of interest to businesses to research whether blockchain technology can revolutionize the trust involved in the supply chain. Blockchain helps to pre-built trust into the system as its feature unlike the traditional supply chain establishes mutual trust by mutual investments and long-term relationships with partners. The objective of the research study was to establish the usefulness of blockchain technology in supply chain digitalization and its need to integrate emerging technologies and the discussions have given a framework which further studies can establish the diffusion and diffusion of blockchain within the supply chain. Emerging technologies can be integrated into the blockchain to explore and enhance governance and decision-making using AI, ML, virtual reality, robotics, 3D printing etc. The industries recognize the benefits the integrated blockchain technology in logistics, transportation, however, the scholars are less convinced and need to study the same areas in the future as part of the 4.0 revolution.

## REFERENCES

Agrawal, P., & Narain, R. (2018). Digital supply chain management: An Overview. *IOP Conference Series: Materials Science and Engineering. 455(1), 1-6*. doi:10.1088/1757-899X/455/1/012074

Agrawal, P., & Narain, R. (2021). Analysis of enablers for the digitalization of supply chain using an interpretive structural modelling approach. *International Journal of Productivity and Performance Management*. Advance online publication. doi:10.1108/IJPPM-09-2020-0481

Agrawal, P., Narain, R., & Ullah, I. (2020). Analysis of barriers in implementation of digital transformation of supply chain using interpretive structural modelling approach. *Journal of Modelling in Management, 15*(1), 297–317. doi:10.1108/JM2-03-2019-0066

ALSaqa, Z. H., Hussein, A. I., & Mahmood, S. M. (2019). The impact of blockchain on accounting information systems. *Journal of Information Technology Management, 11*(3), 62–80.

Arenkov, I., Tsenzharik, M., & Vetrova, M. (2019). Digital technologies in supply chain management. *Proceedings of the International Conference on Digital Technologies in Logistics and Infrastructure*, 453-458.

Bäckstrand, J., & Powell, D. (2021). Enhancing Supply Chain Capabilities in an ETO Context Through" Lean and Learn. *Operations and Supply Chain Management, 14*(3), 360–367. doi:10.31387/oscm0460308

Berg, J., & Myllymaa, L. (2021). *Impact of blockchain on sustainable supply chain practices: A study on blockchain technology's benefits and current barriers in sustainable SCM* (Dissertation). Retrieved from http://urn.kb.se/resolve?urn=urn:nbn:se:hj:diva-53810

Blandine, A., Omar, B., & Angappa, G. (2020). Digital supply chain: Challenges and future directions, *Supply Chain Forum. International Journal (Toronto, Ont.), 21*(3), 133–138. doi:10.1080/16258312.2 020.1816361

Bokrantz, J., Skoogh, A., Berlin, C., & Stahre, J. (2017). Maintenance in digitalised manufacturing: Delphi-based scenarios for 2030. *International Journal of Production Economics, 191*, 154-169. doi:10.1016/j.ijpe.2017.06.010

Brun, I., Durif, F., & Ricard, L. (2014). E-relationship marketing: A cognitive mapping introspection in the banking sector. *European Journal of Marketing*, *48*(3), 572–594. doi:10.1108/EJM-04-2012-0207

Büyüközkan, G., & Göçer, F. (2018). Digital Supply Chain: Literature review and a proposed framework for future research. *Computers in Industry*, *97*, 157–177. doi:10.1016/j.compind.2018.02.010

Dujak, D., & Sajter, D. (2019). Blockchain Applications in Supply Chain. In A. Kawa & A. Maryniak (Eds.), *Smart Supply Network. EcoProduction (Environmental Issues in Logistics and Manufacturing)* (pp. 21–46). Springer. doi:10.1007/978-3-319-91668-2_2

Dutta, G., Kumar, R., Sindhwani, R., & Singh, R. K. (2020). Digital transformation priorities of India's discrete manufacturing SMEs – a conceptual study in perspective of Industry 4.0. *Competitiveness Review*, *30*(3), 289–314. doi:10.1108/CR-03-2019-0031

Dutta, P., Choi, T. M., Somani, S., & Butala, R. (2020). Blockchain technology in supply chain operations: Applications, challenges, and research opportunities. *Transportation Research Part E, Logistics and Transportation Review*, *142*, 102067. doi:10.1016/j.tre.2020.102067 PMID:33013183

Ehie, I., Ferreira, D. F., & Lius, M. (2019). Conceptual development of supply chain digitalization framework. *IFAC-PapersOnLine*, *52*(13), 2338–2342. doi:10.1016/j.ifacol.2019.11.555

Ferretti, V. (2016). From stakeholders' analysis to cognitive mapping and multi-attribute value theory: An integrated approach for policy support. *European Journal of Operational Research*, *253*(2), 524–541. doi:10.1016/j.ejor.2016.02.054

Gaehtgens, F., & Allan, A. (2017). *Digital trust – Redefining trust for the digital era.* A Gartner trend insight report. Available at: https://www.gartner.com/doc/3735817/digital-trust--redefiningtrust

Glas, A. H., & Kleemann, F. C. (2016). The impact of industry 4.0 on procurement and supply management: A conceptual and qualitative analysis. *International Journal of Business and Management Invention*, *5*(6), 55–66.

Gupta, R., Seetharaman, A., & Maddulety, K. (2020). Critical success factors influencing the adoption of digitalisation for teaching and learning by business schools. *Education and Information Technologies*, *25*(5), 3481–3502. doi:10.100710639-020-10246-9

Gurzawska, A. (2020). Towards responsible and sustainable supply chains–innovation, multi-stakeholder approach and governance. *Philosophy of Management*, *19*(3), 267–295. doi:10.100740926-019-00114-z

Hackius, N., & Petersen, M. (2020). Translating High Hopes into Tangible Benefits: How Incumbents in Supply Chain and Logistics Approach Blockchain. *IEEE Access: Practical Innovations, Open Solutions*, *8*, 34993–35003. doi:10.1109/ACCESS.2020.2974622

Haddud, A., & Khare, A. (2020). Digitalizing supply chains potential benefits and impact on lean operations. *International Journal of Lean Six Sigma*, *11*(4), 731–765. doi:10.1108/IJLSS-03-2019-0026

Hader, M., El Mhamedi, A., & Abouabdellah, A. (2020). Understanding the determinants of blockchain technology adoption stages and supply chain performance using the technology-organization-environment framework. *13ème Conference Internationale de modelisation, optimisation et simulation (MOSIM2020).*

Hallikas, J., Immonen, M., & Brax, S. (2021). Digitalizing procurement: The impact of data analytics on supply chain performance. *Supply Chain Management, 26*(5), 629–646. doi:10.1108/SCM-05-2020-0201

Herold, D. M., Ćwiklicki, M., Pilch, K., & Mikl, J. (2021). The emergence and adoption of digitalization in the logistics and supply chain industry: An institutional perspective. *Journal of Enterprise Information Management, 34*(6), 1917–1938. doi:10.1108/JEIM-09-2020-0382

Hirsh, S., Alman, S., Lemieux, V., & Meyer, E. T. (2018). Blockchain: One emerging technology—so many applications. *Proceedings of the Association for Information Science and Technology, 55*(1), 691–693. doi:10.1002/pra2.2018.14505501083

Hoek, R. V. (2020). Responding to COVID-19 Supply Chain Risks—Insights from Supply Chain Change Management, Total Cost of Ownership and Supplier Segmentation Theory. *Logistics, 4*(4), 23. doi:10.3390/logistics4040023

Hofmann, E., Sternberg, H., Chen, H., Pflaum, A., & Prockl, G. (2019). Supply chain management and Industry 4.0: Conducting research in the digital age. *International Journal of Physical Distribution & Logistics Management, 49*(10), 945–955. doi:10.1108/IJPDLM-11-2019-399

Hopkins, J. L. (2021). An investigation into emerging industry 4.0 technologies as drivers of supply chain innovation in Australia. *Computers in Industry, 125*, 103323. doi:10.1016/j.compind.2020.103323

Ivanov, D., & Dolgui, A. (2019). New disruption risk management perspectives in supply chains: Digital twins, the ripple effect, and resileanness. *IFAC-PapersOnLine, 52*(13), 337–342. doi:10.1016/j.ifacol.2019.11.138

Ivanov, D., Dolgui, A., & Sokolov, B. (2019). The impact of digital technology and Industry 4.0 on the ripple effect and supply chain risk analytics. *International Journal of Production Research, 57*(3), 829–846. doi:10.1080/00207543.2018.1488086

Iyer, S., Seetharaman, A., & Maddulety, K. (2021). Block chain technology and its impact on education sector. *International Journal of Innovation in Education, 7*(1), 1–16. doi:10.1504/IJIIE.2021.114905

Iyer, S. S., Seetharaman, A., & Maddulety, K. (2020). Education Transformation Using Block Chain Technology - A Student Centric Model. In S. K. Sharma, Y. K. Dwivedi, B. Metri, & N. P. Rana (Eds.), *Re-imagining Diffusion and Adoption of Information Technology and Systems: A Continuing Conversation. TDIT 2020.* Springer. doi:10.1007/978-3-030-64849-7_19

Jabbar, S., Lloyd, H., Hammoudeh, M., Adebisi, B., & Raza, U. (2021). Blockchain-enabled supply chain: Analysis, challenges, and future directions. *Multimedia Systems, 27*(4), 787–806. doi:10.100700530-020-00687-0

Jugović, A., Bukša, J., Dragoslavić, A., & Sopta, D. (2019). The possibilities of applying blockchain technology in shipping. *Pomorstvo, 33*(2), 274–279. doi:10.31217/p.33.2.19

Kamble, S., Gunasekaran, A., & Arha, H. (2019). Understanding the Blockchain technology adoption in supply chains-Indian context. *International Journal of Production Research, 57*(7), 2009–2033. doi:10.1080/00207543.2018.1518610

Karamchandani, A., Srivastava, S. K., & Srivastava, R. K. (2020). Perception-based model for analyzing the impact of enterprise blockchain adoption on SCM in the Indian service industry. *International Journal of Information Management, 52*, 102019. doi:10.1016/j.ijinfomgt.2019.10.004

Korpela, K., Hallikas, J., & Dahlberg, T. (2017). Digital supply chain transformation toward blockchain integration. *proceedings of the 50th Hawaii international conference on system sciences, 1*, 4182-419. 10.24251/HICSS.2017.506

Kumar, A., Liu, R., & Shan, Z. (2020). Is blockchain a silver bullet for supply chain management? Technical challenges and research opportunities. *Decision Sciences, 51*(1), 8–37. doi:10.1111/deci.12396

Lanzini, F., Ubacht, J., & De Greeff, J. (2021). Blockchain adoptioin factors for SMEs in supply chain management. *Journal of Supply Chain Management Science, 2*(1-2), 47–68. doi:10.18757/jscms.2021.5624

Lisa, L., & Gisèle, B. (2021). Blockchain: An inter-organisational innovation likely to transform supply chain. *Supply Chain Forum: An International Journal, 22*(3), 240-249. 10.1080/16258312.2021.1953931

Meidute-Kavaliauskiene, I., Yıldız, B., Çiğdem, Ş., & Činčikaitė, R. (2021). An Integrated Impact of Blockchain on Supply Chain Applications. *Logistics, 5*(2), 33. doi:10.3390/logistics5020033

Mikhaylova, A., Sakulyeva, T., Shcherbina, T., Levoshich, N., & Truntsevsky, Y. (2021). Impact of Digitalization on the Efficiency of Supply Chain Management in the Digital Economy. *International Journal of Enterprise Information Systems, 17*(3), 34–46. doi:10.4018/IJEIS.2021070103

Min, H. (2019). Blockchain technology for enhancing supply chain resilience. *Business Horizons, 62*(1), 35–45. doi:10.1016/j.bushor.2018.08.012

Nasiri, M., Ukko, J., Saunila, M., & Rantala, T. (2020). Managing the digital supply chain: The role of smart technologies. *Technovation, 96*, 102121. doi:10.1016/j.technovation.2020.102121

Nikolskaya, E. Y., Avilova, N. L., Kovaleva, N. I., Konovalova, E. E., & Sharonin, P. N. (2021). The Influence of Digitization on Staff Training for Tourism and Hospitality Industry. *Revista Geintec-Gestao Inovacao E Tecnologias, 11*(4), 414-423. . doi:10.47059/revistageintec.v11i4.2117

Notland, J. S. (2016). *Blockchain Enabled Trust & Transparency in Supply Chains* (Master's Thesis). NTNU Norwegian University of Science and Technology, Trondheim, Norway. https://www.pdf-archive.com/2017/02/01/project-thesis-anders-j-rgen/project-thesis-anders-j-rgen.pdf

Pankaj, D., Tsan-Ming, C., Surabhi, S., & Richa, B. (2020). Blockchain technology in supply chain operations: Applications, challenges and research opportunities. *Transportation Research Part E, Logistics and Transportation Review, 142*, 102067. doi:10.1016/j.tre.2020.102067 PMID:33013183

Preindl, R., Nikolopoulos, K., & Litsiou, K. (2020). Transformation strategies for the supply chain: the impact of industry 4.0 and digital transformation. *Supply Chain Forum: An International Journal, 21*(1), 26-34. 10.1080/16258312.2020.1716633

Pundir, A. K., Jagannath, J. D., Chakraborty, M., & Ganpathy, L. (2019). Technology Integration for Improved Performance: A Case Study in Digitization of Supply Chain with Integration of Internet of Things and Blockchain Technology. In *IEEE 9th Annual Computing and Communication Workshop and Conference (CCWC)* (pp. 170-176). IEEE.

Saberi, S., Kouhizadeh, M., Sarkis, J., & Shen, L. (2019). Blockchain technology and its relationships to sustainable supply chain management. *International Journal of Production Research, 57*(7), 2117–2135. doi:10.1080/00207543.2018.1533261

Sanders, N. R., Boone, T., Ganeshan, R., & Wood, J. D. (2019). Sustainable supply chains in the age of AI and digitization: Research challenges and opportunities. *Journal of Business Logistics, 40*(3), 229–240. doi:10.1111/jbl.12224

Saryatmo, M. A., & Sukhotu, V. (2021). The Influence of the Digital Supply Chain on Operational Performance: A Study of the Food and Beverage Industry in Indonesia. *Sustainability, 13*(9), 5109. . doi:10.3390/su13095109

Schniederjans, D. G., Curado, C., & Khalajhedayati, M. (2020). Supply chain digitisation trends: An integration of knowledge management. *International Journal of Production Economics, 220*, 107439. doi:10.1016/j.ijpe.2019.07.012

Seyedghorban, Z., Tahernejad, H., Meriton, R., & Gary, G. (2020) Supply chain digitalization: past, present, and future. *Production Planning and Control, 31*(2-3), 96-114. doi:10.1080/09537287.2019.1631461

Sternberg, H. S., Hofmann, E., & Roeck, D. (2021). The struggle is real: Insights from a supply chain blockchain case. *Journal of Business Logistics, 42*(1), 71–87. doi:10.1111/jbl.12240

Tjahjono, B., Esplugues, C., Ares, E., & Pelaez, G. (2017). What does industry 4.0 mean to supply chain? *Procedia Manufacturing, 13*, 1175–1182. doi:10.1016/j.promfg.2017.09.191

Wamba, S. F., & Queiroz, M. M. (2020). Blockchain in the operations and supply chain management: Benefits, challenges, and future research opportunities. *International Journal of Information Management, 52*, 102064. doi:10.1016/j.ijinfomgt.2019.102064

Wang, M., Wu, Y., Chen, B., & Evans, M. (2020). Blockchain and supply chain management: A new paradigm for supply chain integration and collaboration. *Operations and Supply Chain Management: An International Journal, 14*(1), 111–122. doi:10.31387/oscm0440290

Winkler, J. & Moser, R. (2016). Biases in future-oriented Delphi studies: A cognitive perspective. *Technological Forecasting and Social Change, 105*, 63-76. . doi:10.1016/j.techfore.2016.01.021

Wolf, M., Lauer, T., & Puchan, J. (2020). Framework for Quantitative Digitalization Measurement in Supply Chain Planning. *Anwendungen und Konzepte der Wirtschaftsinformatik,* (11). https://www.ojs-hslu.ch/ojs3211/index.php/akwi/article/view/10

Wong, L. W., Tan, G. W. H., Lee, V. H., Ooi, K. B., & Sohal, A. (2020). Unearthing the determinants of Blockchain adoption in supply chain management. *International Journal of Production Research, 58*(7), 2100–2123. doi:10.1080/00207543.2020.1730463

Zekhnini, K., Cherrafi, A., Bouhaddou, I., Benghabrit, Y., & Garza-Reyes, J. A. (2021). Supply chain management 4.0: A literature review and research framework. *International Journal of Logistics Research and Applications, 28*(2), 465–501. doi:10.1108/BIJ-04-2020-0156

## KEY TERMS AND DEFINITIONS

**Cognitive Mapping:** A cognitive map an individual's or team's visual representation in a mental model of a given process or concept.

**Delphi Study Technique:** The Delphi technique is an approach to answering a research question by consensus view across subject experts.

**Digital Economy:** It means digital transactions, over portals and enabled by information and tele-communication technologies (ITC).

**Digital Ecosystem:** A digital ecosystem is an integrated information technology resource made up of suppliers, customers, trading partners, applications, third-party data service providers and all respective technologies with Interoperability being the key to its success.

**Digital Supply Chain:** A digital supply chain refers to processes that use advanced technologies to get better insights into the functions of each stakeholder along the chain to enable them to take better decisions.

*Application of Digital Technologies*

## APPENDIX

Questionnaire- this semi-structure of questions was used to guide the interviewee during the online sessions
Demographics Section: Gmail compulsory *

1. Please mention Age *
   a.  16-20
   b.  21-30
   c.  31-40
   d.  41-50
   e.  50 +
2. Please mention your gender *
   a.  Male
   b.  Female
3. Please mention the highest qualification achieved by you
   a.  High School
   b.  Undergraduate
   c.  Masters
   d.  Doctorate
4. Are you aware of Supply chain and its intricacies?
   a.  Extremely familiar- Expert in the Field
   b.  Very familiar- working in supply chain sector
   c.  Somewhat familiar- only researching and yet to work in the supply chain sector.
5. Are you aware of Blockchain Application in Supply chain and logistics?
   a.  Extremely familiar- Expert in the Field
   b.  Very familiar- working on Blockchain Application
   c.  Somewhat familiar- only researching and yet to work on the Blockchain
6. What has been your association with the Supply chain sector?
   a.  Researcher
   b.  Student/Learner
   c.  Working professional
   d.  Business Owner
   e.  Project Manager
   f.  Consultant
   g.  Government Official
   h.  Regulator
   i.  Public
   j.  Trader
7. What has been your association with the Blockchain Technology in Supply chain sector?
   a)  Researcher
   b)  Student/Learner
   c)  Working IT professional
   d)  Business Owner

e) Project Manager
f) Consultant
g) Government Official
h) Regulator
i) Public
j) Trader
k) Miner
l) Owning Domain for recording transactions

8. The digitalization of Supply chain has facilitated the following

*Table 3.*

| Description | Strongly Disagree | Disagree | Neutral | Agree | Strongly Agree |
|---|---|---|---|---|---|
| a. Security due to its working design | | | | | |
| b. Transparency | | | | | |
| c. Visibility | | | | | |
| d. Traceability | | | | | |
| e. Trust | | | | | |
| f. Flexibility | | | | | |
| g. Quality of the process | | | | | |
| h. Operational performance | | | | | |
| i. Efficiency | | | | | |

9. The digitalization of Supply chain faces the following challenges

*Table 4.*

| Description | Strongly Disagree | Disagree | Neutral | Agree | Strongly Agree |
|---|---|---|---|---|---|
| a. Resistance from staff | | | | | |
| b. Involvement of all stakeholders | | | | | |
| c. Suppliers at the same page | | | | | |
| d. Investment | | | | | |
| e. Infrastructure | | | | | |
| f. Government policies | | | | | |
| g. Infrastructure | | | | | |
| h. Common platform | | | | | |

10. I believe that the Blockchain features that will be suitable for Supply chain Needs are: (Express your opinion on the statement by marking the most appropriate one)

*Application of Digital Technologies*

*Table 5.*

| Description | Strongly Disagree | Disagree | Neutral | Agree | Strongly Agree |
|---|---|---|---|---|---|
| a. Security due to its working design | | | | | |
| b. Transparency | | | | | |
| c. Decentralized Ledgers | | | | | |
| d. Minting or Corrections require approval of all concerned Parties | | | | | |
| e. Immutability and Tamper deduction | | | | | |
| f. Relative User Anonymity | | | | | |
| g. Cost effectiveness due to faster settlement- no intermediaries | | | | | |
| h. Long term Storage Ability | | | | | |
| i. Smart Contracts | | | | | |
| j. Acceptance by the stakeholders | | | | | |

11. I believe that the needs of Supply chain sector that drives the Business are: (Express your opinion on the statement by marking the most appropriate one)

*Table 6.*

| Description | Strongly Disagree | Disagree | Neutral | Agree | Strongly Agree |
|---|---|---|---|---|---|
| a. Confidentiality of Information | | | | | |
| b. Storage & Retrieval of information | | | | | |
| c. Reduced Cost | | | | | |
| d. Modern technologies plugins | | | | | |
| e. Authentication | | | | | |
| f. Single Regulation across the sector | | | | | |
| g. Quality Assurance of systems | | | | | |
| h. Operational Performance | | | | | |

12. I believe that the main factors involved in successful implementation of Blockchain technology in Supply chain are: (Express your opinion on the statement by marking the most appropriate one)

*Table 7.*

| Description | Strongly Disagree | Disagree | Neutral | Agree | Strongly Agree |
|---|---|---|---|---|---|
| a. Economies of scale | | | | | |
| b. Price | | | | | |
| c. Regulator | | | | | |
| d. Sponsors/Guarantor | | | | | |
| e. Energy needs sorted | | | | | |
| f. Tokenization | | | | | |
| g. Acceptance of BCT | | | | | |
| h. Behavior of Users | | | | | |
| i. Smart Contracts | | | | | |
| j. Resistance of employees | | | | | |

13. Any other factor which you would like to recommend, or something missed in this survey

---------------------------------------------------------------------------------------------------------

---------------------------------------------------------------------------------------------------------

# Chapter 15
# Bigdata Intervention in the Healthcare Supply Chain:
## Future Directions

**Anjaneyulu Jinugu**
*Universitat Oberta de Catalunya, Spain*

**Vishnu Teja Jinugu**
*Kasturba Medical College, Mangalore, India*

**Madhavi Lalitha V. V.**
*Qatar University, Qatar*

## ABSTRACT

*The buzz word "big data" has fueled the global healthcare supply chains (HCSCs) by providing capability to analyse bundles of data. On one hand, the intervention of big data technologies made the SCs more resilient, and on the other, it increased the digital divide between the high-end and low-end healthcare facilities. To bridge the gap within and between the healthcare entities and to advocate strategies or models that can not only strengthen the SCs in the times of COVID-19 pandemic but also strengthen the weakest links in the HCSCs, present research work is undertaken. A comprehensive analysis of the frameworks, models, and strategies is performed, and needed solutions and recommendations are furnished for future endeavours. Suitable managerial and theoretical implications coupled with research prospects are also advocated.*

*"Information is the oil of the 21st century, and analytics is the combustion engine."*

*(Peter Sondergaard, Senior VP, Gartner Research)*

DOI: 10.4018/978-1-7998-9506-0.ch015

Copyright © 2022, IGI Global. Copying or distributing in print or electronic forms without written permission of IGI Global is prohibited.

# INTRODUCTION

Digital technology intervention in various sectors left no stone unturned and gave momentum to the global businesses and healthcare supply chain (HCSC) management is one among them. Ubiquitously, healthcare is a prime economic pillar, and it is estimated that healthcare spending as a percentage of gross domestic product (GDP) in 2019 is 3.2 (Deloitte, 2020). Though the sector is significant with respect to many perspectives, it is much affected by the environmental and market turbulences such as social, economic, political, geopolitical tensions between nations and many more. Notwithstanding this, unlike many other sectors (Siriwardhana, Gür, Ylianttila, & Liyanage, 2021) the adverse consequences of any burden on healthcare sector will be manifold on the societies (Govindan, Mina, & Alavi, 2020) (Khan, Nazir, & Khan, 2021; Mirabelli & Solina, 2020; Wu, Wang, Tao, & Peng, 2019). The impetus to encounter the burden can be possible by re-engineering the HCSCs for better visibility, flexibility, control and collaboration which in turn ensures seamless SC mechanisms in healthcare sector (Al-Talib, 2020).

It is evident from the recent COVID-19 pandemic that the challenges in healthcare sector hit the lives of all kind hardly - from mankind to their counterpart in the world (Govindan et al., 2020; Siriwardhana et al., 2021). In addition, it is established by research works that information technology mediation in healthcare sector can make the real time data available to all the stakeholders and hence can manage the disruptions in supply chain (SC) seamlessly. Furthermore, smart technologies such as Radio-frequency identification (RFID), 3D printing, Electronic Data Interchange (EDI), smart sensors, mobile devices, social networks etc., have long-term positive effect on the clinical performance by automating the SCs (Bradley et al., 2018).

Data generated by these devices is enormous and has high value which is generally referred to as big data. In spite of the unavailability of universally accepted definition, some of the definitions states big data as the data set whose size or type is beyond the ability of traditional databases to capture, manage and process. Characteristics of big data include high volume, high velocity and high variety (3Vs). Sources of big data are more complex than that of traditional data because the former is driven by Artificial Intelligence (AI), mobile devices, social media and the Internet of Things (IoT) (IBM, 2021). Big data is a field that comprises of ways to analyze, systematically extract information from, or otherwise deal with data sets that are too large or complex to be dealt with by traditional data-processing application software (Wikipedia, 2021). As the world is heading towards harnessing the big data related technologies, deployment of big data technologies in HCSC can also address many types of shortcomings that arise in achieving supply chain resilience (SCR) (Oussous, Benjelloun, Ait Lahcen, & Belfkih, 2018; Zakaria, Abu Bakar, Hassan, & Yaacob, 2019).

SC is perceived as a comprehensive system that connects all the stakeholders through resources, information and processes. Of late, data-driven technologies in SCs are established as more effective not only in decision-making at all levels but also in increasing the competitive edge for the organizations (Shamsuzzoha, Ndzibah, & Kettunen, 2020). Embedded with digital technologies HCSCs have become more efficient and hence research communities are expounding these to enhance their operations further (Tian et al., 2019). Also, with the emergence of untoward situations like pandemics, the need for all-inclusive smart HCSC and smart healthcare is identified far and wide as a panacea. Smart healthcare encompasses many technologies like IoT, AI, Cloud computing, RFID, automated guided vehicles (AGVs), big data and many more. With the cognition of the benefits, it is being asserted by research communities that the role of big data in addressing data-related and data-driven digital information must be underpinned. Particularity, the intervention like big data technologies in SC has to be encouraged to

*Bigdata Intervention in the Healthcare Supply Chain*

hedge against the challenging situations created by the recent pandemic, COVID-19 (Mehta, Pandit, & Shukla, 2019; Oussous et al., 2018).

Global sink caused by the COVID-19 pandemic is immeasurable. It has devastated the nations with respect to social, economic, health and many more standpoints (Siriwardhana et al., 2021). Subsiding the massive disruption with the help of novel technologies is the unique solution for re-establishing private and public entities in post-COVID era. Healthcare being the paramount sector, strengthening the stakeholder's information base as well as value-based process flows of the SC across different work lines is the only aftermath that can be leaned on. As there is a surge in the demand for medical necessities like personal protection kits, medicines, ventilators and other vital life-saving material during pandemic, big data or other emerging technologies supported HCSC can address these challenges by supplying them in time to the nuke and corners of the world (Govindan et al., 2020; Patrinley et al., 2020).

Having understood the significance of big data in managing HCSC and to guide for future endeavors, the present research work aims to exercise a comprehensive analysis of the existing literature, frameworks, and other models that can steer in accomplishing an err-free HCSC. The planned work is going to be organized in the following sections. Extol literature covering the suitable topics of the study are reviewed by identifying the gaps in the process of SCR. Frameworks and models evolved regarding big data deployment in HCSC are analyzed and constructive as well as feasible recommendations are made accordingly.

## BACKGROUND

Big data has become a panacea for all research works due to its value addition across myriad sectors (Anjaneyulu, Sreechandana, & Madhavi Laitha, 2021). Healthcare being a predominant artefact for the well-being of mankind, it is given a significant role in all the national agendas, visions as well as goals. Hence, global research fraternity has also been exploring big data technologies for better and possible ways to support healthcare sector in general and SCs in particular (Singh, Verma, & Koul, 2017; Siriwardhana et al., 2021; Wu et al., 2019). For the smooth run of the seed to weed process of healthcare, SC frameworks and related mechanisms are established as efficient and prominent. Gartner report mentioned that there is 37.3% of revenue generated in global health sector because of seamless execution of SC mechanisms (Gartner, 2020). The SC mechanisms and the frameworks are challenged owing to the disruption raised by the Covid-19 pandemic. As a result, Covid has ravaged the world and economies by highlighting the need for resilient SCs with big data technologies that can cater to the gushing needs of healthcare domain (Gartner, 2021a; Yu, Zhao, Liu, & Song, 2021).

The challenges that the SC management encounter due to the unavailability of data is shared by (Kowalski & Sheehan, 2016). It is felt that to increase the efficiency of the HCSCs and to strengthen the healthcare logistics departments, reliable and timely data. Ubiquitously, many models and frameworks are developed to address this type of HCSC challenges. Some of them are aimed at internal SC activities, some are at external and some other for whole set of healthcare stakeholders. The variations in SC differ based on the perspectives such as organization information processing systems, technological development, scope of healthcare facilities, flexibility of operations, requirements of stakeholders and others. Effective service delivery being manifested as the central theme of HCSC, operational models have been tailored accordingly (Kasten, 2020). That is, in traditional HCSC, the SCs used to deal with external and internal supplies only. But with the emergence of technologies in all walks of life through

IoT, smart medical equipment, patient centric service technologies, information revolution and others, HCSC has become much integral and complex (Zakaria et al., 2019).

On one hand, maintaining mammoth data that is being generated from smart medical and non-medical devices has become a challenge and on the other, sustaining in the competitive intense market has become a herculean task (Storey & Holti, 2020). Notwithstanding this, unexpected jerks like natural calamities and pandemics strike the HCSC and calls for a pragmatic and holistic transformation of SCs. But, only few organizations are in the race and many are behind (Gartner, 2021b). To hedge against these irksome conditions in advancing for an integrated healthcare delivery system, it is advocated to deploy big data technologies coupled with other disruptive technologies that have the capabilities to spearhead HCSC (Iyengar, Acharya, & Kadam, 2020). Though many updated models and frameworks to adopt integrated technologies have evolved to address the global health chaos, the need is ever-increasing (Paul-Eric, Rafael, Cristiane, & Joao, 2020).

## METHODOLOGY

Having an understanding about the background of HCSC and the significance as well as requirement for advancement in the healthcare field with big data interventions, study objectives are proposed. These objectives not only help to appraise the development took place in HCSC domain, but also steers the research work that is yet to be done. The following are the objectives listed with a systematic review of the HCSC literature.

### Objectives of the Study

- Review the existing literature of HCSC to understand the processes, procedures, strategies and interventions done so far
- To enrich the knowledge base about the big data oriented technological developments took place in HCSC
- Appraise the existing gaps in channelizing the healthcare SCs with the support of big data technologies to make them more resilient
- To enlist the challenges and to propose comprehensive as well as competency mechanisms to overcome the challenges of big data oriented HCSC to make them robust against disruptions

The objectives are achieved in systematic manner by reviewing about the SCs, with an emphasis on HCSC. Existing gaps in the process of SCR, succeeded by the frameworks and models evolved in these lines are discussed. Solutions and recommendations are provided to propose mechanisms and strategies to overcome the challenges or challenges to achieve healthcare SCR.

## MAIN FOCUS OF THE CHAPTER

### Supply Chain – Need for Revamp

The concept of SCs is entwined with and around human lives that it is not surprising to say that there is nothing in universe without the concept of SC. Of late, the significance of the SC and its management has become pinnacle due to the massive disruption took place in all sectors coupled with the emergence of data driven technologies across the Volatile, Uncertain, Complex and Ambiguous (VUCA) world (Wang & Alexander, 2015; Zhong, Newman, Huang, & Lan, 2016). In 2020, the global SC management market is valued at $15.85 billion and is expected to grow at a Compound Annual Growth Rate (CAGR) of 11.2% by 2027 with approximately $31 billion. In 2020, SAP is the leading SC management software supplier with revenue of around $ 4.4 billion (Statista, 2021). Both the service management and SC management have undergone a revamp through digitization across a range of human activities and hence have become very volatile, uncertain and complex (Gartner, 2021a).

To overcome the VUCA challenges and to achieve market resilience by dealing with the huge data inflows, technological support has become inevitable for SCs. Hence, the concepts like automated SCs, digitized SCs and integrated SCs has evolved to address the crippling scenarios (Raj Kumar Reddy, Gunasekaran, Kalpana, Raja Sreedharan, & Arvind Kumar, 2021). Achieving the sustainable development being the mantra of today's world, developing SCs that not only optimize the utilization of available resources, but also execute without depleting the environmental treasures (green SCs) is much advocated far and wide (Zhao, Liu, Zhang, & Huang, 2017). The green SCs facilitate win-win situation and are identified as significant for healthcare settings, particularly in disposing the bio-medical waste with the support of advanced technologies, there is every need to revamp the SC considering the global burden in view (Kulkarni et al., 2020).

During COVID-19 pandemic times, health sector is forced to search for alternative suppliers, logistics providers and technologies that can aid for seam-less service delivery. This kind of scenarios occur due to the un-expected disruption of the existing SCs (Shi, 2018). In the wake of the dearth for scientific methods to select alternative suppliers and related mechanisms (T. Chen, Wang, & Wu, 2021) affirmed the need for revamping the SCs with approach like 'a calibrated fuzzy geometric mean (cFGM)-fuzzy technique for order preference by similarity to ideal solution (FTOPSIS)-fuzzy weighted intersection (FWI)' and it is worked suitably.

### Healthcare Supply Chain (HCSC): Ever – Challenging

Healthcare industry generates huge data from the applications developed for the practitioners, digitalized medical equipment, Laboratory Information Management Systems (LIMS) and Electronic Health Records (EHR) (Groves, Kayyali, Knott, & Kuiken, 2013). This data enhances patient care and services if it is utilized with appropriate techniques and technologies (Kulkarni et al., 2020; Shi, 2018). In 2020, the global HCSC market size is US$ 2,010 million and it is projected to reach US$ 3,791 million by 2027 with at a CAGR of 9.5% during 2021-2027. The top HCSC key players are McKesson, SAP SE, Oracle Corporation, Infor, HighJump that hold a share about 50% of total market. In terms of regional share, the North America region shares the largest market (30%) which is followed by Europe (30%) (www. https://reports.valuates.com).

HCSC is manifested as the comprehensive set of activities that take place in the end-to-end process of healthcare service delivery (Maheshwari, Kaur, Kotecha, & Jain, 2020). Unlike traditional HCSC, modern SCs are overloaded with bulk of data that not only involve frameworks and processes but also involve systems and equipment viz., life-saving equipment, smart gadgets, medical supplies and stakeholders (Mehta et al., 2019; Schniederjans, Curado, & Khalajhedayati, 2020). Drawing meaningful interferences from the influx of data that is generated from all the SCs has become an ever-challenging task with the mushrooming market players as well as the upcoming research activities (Wu et al., 2019). Also, emergence of various types of concepts like data-driven, automated, robotic, green, resilient and integrated SCs further made the HCSC a complex environment, where in the final aim service delivery is often jeopardized (Kumar & Kumar, 2014; Romano, 2020).

*Figure 1. Contribution of SC to Health System (www.Gartner.com)*

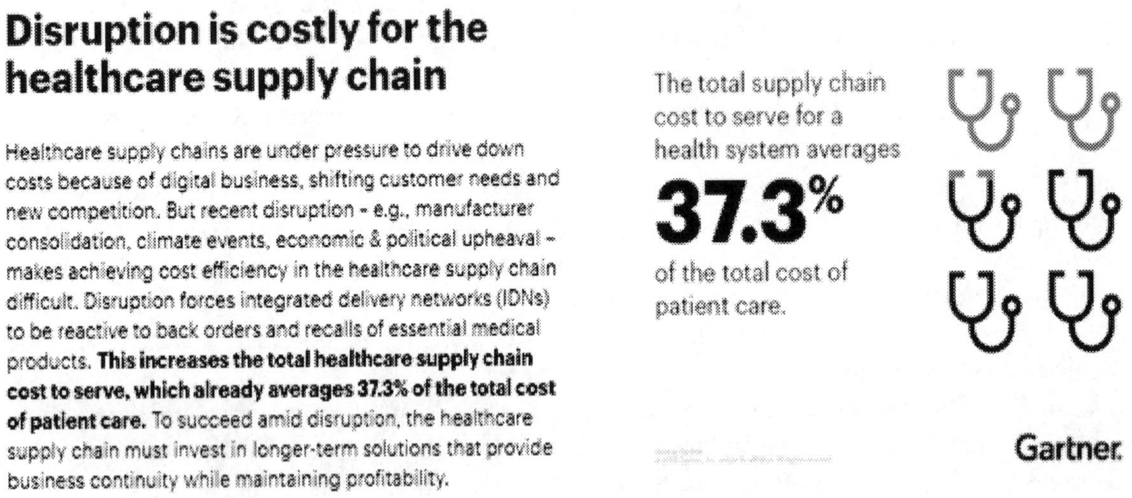

The significant contribution of SC in healthcare can be understood by the Gartner report which is given in Figure 1that the total SC cost to serve for a health system averages to 37.3% of the total cost of patient care (Gartner, 2020). As technology ascent is a continuous process and adoption to the environment is inevitable to sustain in the ecosystem, developed countries are trying to tap the benefits of nascent technology by overhauling their HCSCs from time to time (Mike Bresnen, 2017; Moro Visconti & Morea, 2019). But, to run after this ever-challenging, data-driven and technology-driven competition-intense environment has always been a life and death situation, particularly in the times of pandemic for the developing and least developed nations (Paez, 2021). Deploying smart and data-driven technologies to reduce the expenditure in all stages of HCSC can reduce the investments to a great extent and hence make the healthcare affordable to common man (Alliance, 2015; Tian et al., 2019).

## Gaps Identified in Supply Chain Resilience

Recently, big data and its applications have attracted both scholars and healthcare practitioners due to the enormous benefits. However, in deployment of best practices in SCs, healthcare sector is far behind

*Bigdata Intervention in the Healthcare Supply Chain*

when compared to the other sectors (Brinch, Stentoft, & Jensen, 2017). One of the solutions to overcome this gap is to invest on digitalization of HCSCs as well as the healthcare providers (Beaulieu & Bentahar, 2021a). The dearth of knowledge regarding the management of big data is another big hiccup in marketing filed (Kulkarni et al., 2020; Shankar et al., 2021). Due to the knowledge gap, SC managers across the sectors, especially in healthcare are concerned and confused whether big data and related innovations have any impact on the data driven decision making (Ardito, Petruzzelli, Panniello, & Garavelli, 2018). This lacunae in HCSC can be filled by conducting research focused on practical aspects rather confining to methodological which can answer many strategic questions of SC managers (Aigbavboa & Mbohwa, 2020; Paez, 2021; Richey, Morgan, Lindsey-Hall, & Adams, 2016)

Also, the impact of big data analytics and AI in SC in collaborative perspective is less explored by researchers and this gap can be addressed by conducting more empirical studies that prioritize interfunctional integration coupled with social interactions (Benzidia, Makaoui, & Bentahar, 2021). The authors also shared from the study that big data analytics and AI have the potential to achieve SCR covering the internal tasks and processes such as data quality management, activities of purchasing department, activities of logistics department, activities of production department and activities of administrative departments of hospitals. Highlighting the state of strong positive relation between the pharmaceutical SC and big data analytics in developing countries, (Shokouhyar, Seddigh, & Panahifar, 2020) shared that scanty research is being conducted in developing countries to draw deeper insights and to infer about the intricacies between big data analytical capabilities and SC sustainability/ resilience.

In general, supply chain management (SCM) is defined as a comprehensive set of activities like planning, organizing, and controlling the functions of businesses (inside and outside), But, empowering SCs with effective management coupled with state-of-the-art technologies to customize the products and to provide services to the customer is yet a day-dream in many industries because of the gaps in SC visibility problems (Bhatia & Mittal, 2019; Yu et al., 2021). Over the last two decades technologically supported SCMs in several businesses especially large-scale enterprises have gained popularity. Many scholars and research organizations developed frameworks and models to direct HCSCs of large size organizations and it is dismay to notice that they are only few studies for the small and medium sized enterprises (SMEs) (Ivanov, 2020). (Yu et al., 2021) proposed a model that is based on organization information processing theory (OIPT) to bridge the research gap that treats big data analytics and integration in hospital SCs as two different entities.

*Figure 2. Landscapes of supply chain*
*(Kulkarni et al., 2020)*

Narrating the growing requirements of healthcare industry, that can be fulfilled with big data supported SCs, (Kulkarni et al., 2020) shared the broader view of the SC landscapes in Figure 2. It is added that the three-dimensional perspective of SC analysis (descriptive analytics, predictive analytics and prescriptive analytics) can help to identify the gaps (unidentified areas in analysing non-structured data, algorithms, mathematical models and others) in the big data analytics process in healthcare, by increasing the visibility of SCs.

## Big Data and HCSC – A Status Quo

Big data in supply SCM can be realized as a structured and unstructured relation-based information which is exclusive to business due to its volume, velocity, variety, and veracity. Yet, big data in HCSC is

*Bigdata Intervention in the Healthcare Supply Chain*

perceived as a technological brace to execute a range of hospital functions like early & speedy recoveries, advanced patient care, real time monitoring with enhanced patient care and cost-effective healthcare for the needy. Following this, HCSC managers and the concerned develop frameworks, strategies and models to utilize big data to make meaningful decisions as well as accurate predictions for firms and their partners (Aigbavboa & Mbohwa, 2020; Paez, 2021; Richey et al., 2016). The efficiency of healthcare SC is achieved through the adoption of advanced technologies, establishing standards operating procedures and successful execution of models in all connected industries (Chandra & Kachhal, 2004; Gartner, 2020; Kasten, 2020).

## Frameworks

The currency of big data has not come over night. The popularity is the result of the efforts of global research community which tested the big data for various scenarios, settings and challenges (Anjaneyulu et al., 2021; ShulinLan, 2016). Thus, many theories, frameworks and models are developed and tested by the intellectual fraternity. For instance, discussing big data utilities in healthcare domain, Kasten et al. shared the application framework of big data which has spread across four significant pillars – Information Management, Resource Management, Hospital Management and Patient outcomes (Kasten, 2020). It is interesting to observe in this approach that though the four pillars appear to be independent, they are much interrelated with the technology woven HCSC. To encounter the ever-increasing HCSC challenges in technology, economic and organizational perspectives, framework that is supported by the advanced concepts like industry 4.0 and logistics 4.0 are advocated with examples by Paul et al. (Paul-Eric et al., 2020).

Industry 4.0 is also termed as 4IR (Fourth Industrial Revolution) which encompasses Supply Chain 4.0, Marketing 4.0 and others, that are mostly characterized by digitization and machine-learning (ML), which mostly work with the support of big data technologies (WEF, 2019). Another framework called Big data Analytics Capabilities (BDAC) is discussed for sustainability of SCs in healthcare sector by (Shokouhyar et al., 2020). In this framework, the dimensions among BDAC, viz., Big data analytics (BDA) infrastructure flexibility, BDA management capability and BDA personnel expertise capability are tested with case studies. Another significant framework that is developed by United Nations is UN Committee of Experts on Global Geospatial Information Management (UNGGIM) to address the challenges raised by COVID-19 disaster and to ensure resilient SCs. This framework works in coordination with Integrated Geospatial Information Framework (IGIF) (Paez, 2021).

*Figure 3. Overarching IGIF Framework (https://ggim.un.org/IGIF/part1.cshtml)*

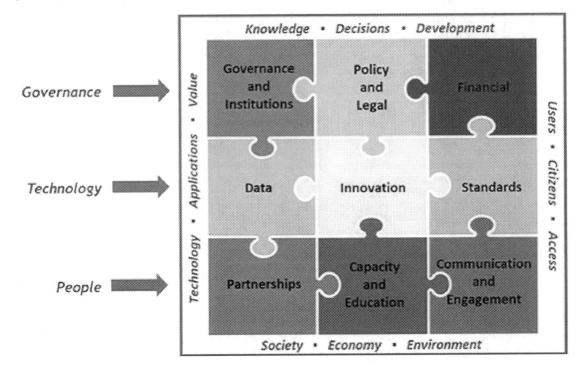

The 3 X 3 gird of IGIF framework given in Figure 3, developed by UN provides the means to improve comprehensive global SCs that relate to all the sectors. Likewise, scholars have been contributing to big data related interventions for HCSC with numerous frameworks. One of them is, to overcome the lacunae in SME's sustainability while using SCs during post- SCM pandemic. That is, a framework is developed by combining best practices and SC innovations through digital technology enablers (Ramakrishna, 2021). In addition to frameworks, there are many models developed with the aim to steer the SCs, particularly in disruption times.

## Models

With the advent of Fourth Industry Revolution, many traditional concepts are digitized and thus facilitated scope to the promising concepts like Supply Chain 4.0, Industry 4.0., Logistics 4.0. and of late Industry 4.1 (WEF, 2019). Industry 4.0. is mainly exemplified by digital transformation including automation and intervention of new technologies. Thus, many models have evolved addressing the applications, particularly the complex aspects of HCSC (Martínez, Rios, & Prieto, 2020; Paul-Eric et al., 2020) like improving the ability to assess and forecast the requirements of SCs (Yu et al., 2021). Geo-spatial models are developed to understand the healthcare requirements in the times of pandemic and to assess the spread of outbreaks (Paez, 2021); structural equation models (SEM) for establishing linkages between the components of big data and supported SC (Shokouhyar et al., 2020); machine learning models are evolved to leverage data for constructing efficient SCs (Schniederjans et al., 2020); similarity machine learning based models are advanced to estimate the vaccine reach and requirement to forecast personal protective equipment (PPE) kit necessities and to plan their supply process accordingly (T. Chen et al.,

2021); decision support system (DSS) models are fostered to mitigate risks with the predictive capabilities in SCs (Yoshizaki, 2018; Zhong et al., 2016) and IoT models are established to use the SC data and to encounter disruptions through Visibility, Flexibility, Collaboration and Control to attain SCR (Al-Talib, 2020). These examples are just tip of the iceberg. Notwithstanding this, Gartner has listed top healthcare providers who achieved SCR in the times of COVID-19 pandemic with techniques like integrated delivery networks that operate best with robotic process automation and other advanced technologies (Gartner, 2020).

## Strategies

In addition to the frameworks and models that can address present scenarios, there is dire requirement for strategies that are not just framed for short term period but also for long-term (Beaulieu & Bentahar, 2021b; ShulinLan, 2016). Some of the bothering issues of global SCs like people & competency, infrastructure & regulatory adequacies and distribution linkages are shared and the need for chalking out strategies in this direction is highlighted by (Aigbavboa & Mbohwa, 2020). Wu et al., proposed a patient centric ecosphere strategy with the patient at the center and the stakeholders around, which is aimed to achieve equilibrium between healthcare resources and requirements coupled with achieving an interest balance mechanism in healthcare ecosystem (Wu et al., 2019). Thus, the need for management strategies is affirmed to realize the benefits of such ecosphere. Explaining the concept of bullwhip effect of SC, (Patrinley et al., 2020) highlighted the requirement for strategies to avoid shortages of significant goods and services with at most cost-efficiency. Also, to hedge against the unexpected situations like the present pandemic and to flatten the curve of pandemic adversity, global SCs are advocated to adopt comprehensive strategies that can safeguard from all the disruptive constraints (Beaulieu & Bentahar, 2021b; Yu et al., 2021; Zhong et al., 2016).

*Figure 4. Big data and healthcare supply chain: Frameworks, Models and Strategies*

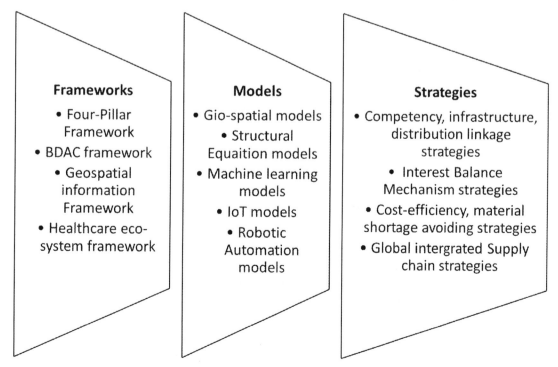

Numerous methods are there that are aimed to ameliorate the benefits of big data intervention in HCSC, including but not limited to - frameworks, models and strategies. These frameworks, models and strategies are consolidated and presented in Figure 4. Along with the research work done in the domain of big data supported HCSC in the form of frameworks, models, strategies and other initiatives, it is equally important to understand the challenges and hurdles that come across in the process of digitization of HCSC with the support of technologies. The following sections deal with the challenges, solutions & recommendations along with future research directions.

## Challenges of Big Data Intervention in HCSC

Cognition of the growing healthcare necessities as well as the market volatilities reinforces the requirement for a streamlined HCSC that is backed with updated big data technologies. The recent pandemic eruption also underpinned this necessity (Aljadeed et al., 2021; T. Chen et al., 2021). Though the embrace of big data technology is on the move, it is not uniform across the globe because of the skillset as well as budget required to update the legacy systems (Storey & Holti, 2020). The digital divide between the developed and developing nations must be given high priority to achieve sustainable development. Especially, in the times of the pandemic, achieving HCSC resilience has become inevitable for the organizations to survive. That is, ever-emerging and disruptive smart technologies coupled with competitive strategies further intensify the struggle for the laggards, medium and low-level businesses (Addo-Tenkorang & Helo, 2016; Singh et al., 2017; Storey & Holti, 2020).

It is a widely discussed problem that except few data-driven organizations, many organizations and their statisticians are not clear about the modus operandi of big data analytics, which obstructs the benefits that can be obtained by deploying concerned technologies (Iyengar et al., 2020; Shi, 2018; Shokouhyar et al., 2020). Some other challenges are identified in Iran's pharmaceutical industry, viz.., vagueness of the market, lack of effective data sharing system, economic instabilities of nations and lack of cooperation between personnel and big data companies as well as incompatible software and hardware infrastructure policies (Shokouhyar et al., 2020). Since HCSC is a continuous, life-saving and emergency process/ mechanism that is mostly influenced by technology adoption models and methods, there is a strong requirement for longitudinal studies rather cross-sectional studies that help to draw more insights about application of big data technologies (Shi, 2018; Shokouhyar et al., 2020; Yu et al., 2021).

As HCSC involves multi-level stakeholders (doctors, clinicians, patients, pharmacy, administrators, public, society and many more), there is always a need for data-driven and integrated SCs, feasible mechanisms and strategies coupled with latest analytical expertise, maintaining which from time to time is a herculean task for the healthcare entities (Gartner, 2021b; Shamsuzzoha et al., 2020). Moreover, some of the data related challenges while implementing big data in HCSCs are 1) quality of data: most of the data generated in healthcare sector are from medical prescriptions and medical & insurance related tweets, blogs, which is mostly unstructured and hence, ought to be cleansed before using for drawing meaningful insights; 2) confidentiality and sharing of patient data: patient data is highly sensitive and laws change from state to state to access as well as to analyze the data and thus big data algorithms should take due consideration of setting-specific data access laws; 3) lack of experts: specialized skilled resources who are adept with updated technologies and methods are required to work with big data and thus implementation of real-time HCSC is very arduous task for all the stakeholders and lastly (Tamym, Benyoucef, & Moh, 2020); 4) incompatible systems: in healthcare industry electronic health record data

*Bigdata Intervention in the Healthcare Supply Chain*

exchange is crucial for the healthcare provider to make quick and viable decisions and this may be difficult to manage with the ever-challenging and ever-updating big data technologies (Bhatia & Mittal, 2019).

Also, to tap the benefits from the above-mentioned issues like integrated and automated SC, skillset and awareness levels of the personnel have become much bothering aspects for many organizations (Aigbavboa & Mbohwa, 2020; Paez, 2021; Richey et al., 2016). All challenges discussed so far are internal and another big challenge for the HCSC which is external is environment specific. Some of them are political, administrative, infrastructural availability and others (Govindan et al., 2020; Romano, 2020; Storey & Holti, 2020). Further, poor collaboration between internal and external stakeholders is another weakest link in HCSC. That is organizational value chain has its own pitfalls in both internal as well as external HCSC players which is highlighted by many research studies (D. Q. Chen, Preston, & Swink, 2016; Schneller, 2018; Tandon, Dhir, Islam, & Mäntymäki, 2020). In toto, the challenges reinforce that the pace of technology deployment to achieve integrated SCs and to cater the health needs of the people is not just sufficient and its seam-less management on a continuous basis is much anticipated. Thus, refurbishing the HCSC with the cushion of big data technologies in robust and resilient manner is the advocated remedial action in this regard and the need of the hour.

## SOLUTIONS AND RECOMMENDATIONS

HCSC being a complex series of operations that starts with healthcare products/service production and ends with, but not limited to final delivery, includes many intermediary operations (KPMG, 2021; Yadav, 2015). To steer the study and to meet the aim of the study, objectives are jotted down in section 3.1, which are the unique contribution of the study. Nitty-gritty of HCSC along with the relevant processes, procedures, strategies and intervention of technology and the issues encountered in the time of post-pandemic (COVID-19) are studied to understand the status quo of SCs. In traditional SCs the intermediaries are mostly people and process only. With the advent of digitization, smart medical equipment has also become part of the process. This intervention has changed the picture of HCSC and intensified the management along with difficulty levels of SCs further. In the wake of the present pandemic that created chaotic situations, seeking viable solutions to address the hiccups of HCSC is very much needed to accomplish resilient SCs. On a broader perspective, though the healthcare system comprises of public, private and non-Governmental organizations (NGOs), the governance of these entities is to be executed within the jurisdiction of governments.

Another side of the coin for the above-cited view is that with the high mediation and strict adherence to the procedures laid by government, it can also be difficult and time taking to re-engineer the SCs as per the situational requirement. So, execution of laws coupled with leverage should be given to critical, emergency HCSCs in order to cater the needs of the people within no time (Schniederjans et al., 2020). Rather employing too many political/ environmental restrictions, adopting technological frameworks wherein the laws and regulating procedures are imposed technologically with smart initiatives can speed the SCs (Tandon et al., 2020). Trends of HCSC are much tapped by most technological organizations, particularly in developed nations and the best practices and processes are to be shared with rest of the world. In the case of developing countries, the difference in operability of the organizations within the SC leads to red tape delays. Hence adoption of nuance technologies coupled with knowledge-based methods and suitable strategies can help to bridge the digital divide among the stakeholders (Alliance,

307

2015; Singh et al., 2017; Storey & Holti, 2020). The review done in the paper to explore all the concerned topics helped to achieve the first objective of the study.

Nurturing big data enabled HCSC successfully to make the SCs more robust from time to time is directly proportional to requirement of the intellectual capability of the personnel. Hence, awareness and training programs about the big data, related technologies, on-going technological updates and know-how procedures are studied which reinforced that along with infrastructural developments (software and hardware), professional capabilities are to be encouraged at every level, across the healthcare entities (organization, region, country and so on) for common good (Mehta et al., 2019; WEF, 2019). Particularly, developed nations are to play a key role in extending a helping hand for their counterparts to create a win-win scenario (Govindan et al., 2020; Kannan Govindan, 2018). On a global perspective, creating SOPs (standard operating procedures) and Quality Standards as per the technological updates (device and platform level) can help the big data supported global HCSCs (big or small) to benchmark themselves and thereby can create healthy competition to achieve SCR (Tian et al., 2019).

Journey of HCSC embedded with big data technologies, coupled with latest concepts like green SCs, sustainable SCs, resilient SCs and others made the goal jeopardized in many situations. Hence, smart solutions that can be fetched with technologies like IoT, AI, Cloud computing, RFID, automated guided vehicles (AGVs) are much advocated by researcher community. More sensors and devises joined the HCSC and increased the data enormously, for analyzing and managing which big data technologies has become the only panacea. However, the inculcation of goal-orientation among the stakeholders of SC, that is supported by value chain can only manifest the desired big data environment (Govindan et al., 2020). Thus, the knowledge base about the big data environment could explore the technological developments took place in HCSC, fulfilling the second objective of the study.

Gap identification is the crux of development for any technology and its applications. The third objective is dedicated for identifying the gaps in channelizing the big data supported HCSCs. Also, cognition of various types of gaps – knowledge gaps, process gaps and implementation gaps can unleash the grey areas as well as the challenges in the study topic. Likewise, a range of gaps like scanty research work in healthcare sector, dearth of skilled expertise in dealing with data, extent of the applications and management of big data and AI technologies, lack of knowledge to utilize the output of big data supported HCSC to draw meaningful insights, differences between the SOPs of internal and external stakeholders of HCSC, inability to integrate the components of SCs are some of the gaps discussed. suitable technology supported solutions are advocated accordingly to deal with the gaps and have better scalability of HCSCs. This knowledge can ensure resilience of SCs and can channelize healthcare service delivery even in chaotic conditions, which in turn attains the third objective of the study.

Along with reviewing the literature, understanding the status of technological developments took place in big data supported HCSCs, appraising various types of gaps in achieving so, the study navigated to discuss the challenges and propose comprehensive as well as competent mechanisms for attaining SCR. On one hand, it is observed that the persisting gaps with respect to knowledge, process, implementation throw numerous challenges not only to the data intense organizations but also to the laggards. While on the other, ground level challenges created due to the disparities in economic capacity, infrastructural facilities and level of expertise, unavailability of resources, government policies and procedures, digital divide between nations, orientation among the personnel involved within organizations and so on are some of the challenges discussed. In addition to enlisting the challenges, strategies and mechanisms like re-engineering the HCSCs from time to time with updated technologies, keeping the stakeholders abreast of the information to have better visibility of SCs, chalking strategies to bridge the digital divide

*Bigdata Intervention in the Healthcare Supply Chain*

between the developed and developing nations, updating policies and procedures regularly and so on are recommended to make the big data supported HCSC more robust and resilient.

## FUTURE RESEARCH DIRECTIONS

The scholarly works related to big data technology intervention in HCSC have reaffirmed the need for implementation of technologies as an answer for disruptive scenarios like pandemic. So, embedding technological approaches in the process of creating resilient SCs can address a range of problems that arise across the stakeholder chain. It is commendable that much research work has been done in this domain. However, the practicality, operability and applicability of technologies has always been a question mark for majority of market players. As a result, many SC mangers are unbale to have better visibility of SC in continuous manner. Research works are to be channelized to develop methodologies that cater medium to low level businesses that comprise of major proportion of healthcare market. The comprehensive spectrum of HCSC can be segregated into various levels for better integration like, inter-functional integration, hospital-patient integration, and hospital-supplier integration. This kind of segregation can provide much clarity about the task management on a day-to-day basis. There are research works evolved regarding individual levels in HCSC domain, but there is a dire necessity for understanding the process of healthcare system as a whole to deal with untoward societal conditions in effective manner.

Having understood the knowledge gaps, process gaps and implementation gaps in embracing big data technologies and other operational issues, particularly in the area of HCSC, research works are to be encouraged in anticipation of managerial, practical and theoretical implications. That is, nuance research works aimed to develop models that are predominantly grounded on theories like organizational information processing theory (OIPT) to investigate the roles of big data analytics capability (BDAC) in fostering hospital supply chain integration (SCI) and operational flexibility would add value and unleash the grey dimensions in the study area. To understand about the status of clinical and healthcare services in timely and accurate manner, social media data is of great help and hence, healthcare providers should tap this opportunity to go along with the pioneers of the HCSC industry (Alotaibi & Mehmood, 2017; Iyengar et al., 2020; Singh et al., 2017). Also, all concerned authorities (public, private and NGOs) involved directly or indirectly in the process of HCSC's integration should harness and research the means to identify the weakest link in the chain of activities. Ventures to establish the SCs to achieve resilience without addressing the problems would be mopping the floor keeping the tap open.

## CONCLUSION

The agenda of the chapter is to re-organize the comprehensive analysis of the extol literature regarding big data technology intervention in HCSC in line with laid study objectives. The idea behind this review is to underpin the frameworks, models and strategies that are developed to make the SCs more resilient and hedge against tough situations like the COVID-19 pandemic. As a result of the literature review process, many challenges and gaps in administering the HCSC with the support of digitization and knowledge management have brought forth for better service delivery and chaos management. Also, with the extensive appraisal made covering the overarching frameworks, models and strategies, suitable solutions and recommendations are furnished. The solution and recommendations not only help to encounter the unforeseen situations but also cements the weak links of the HCSC. Notwithstanding this, the inputs of the study widen the horizons of knowledge regarding the application and management of disruptive technologies (like IoT, big data, blockchain, AI and others) that are deemed to have much influence across all types of healthcare settings.

In addition to the general solutions and recommendation, the study could contribute to the literature with insightful knowledge base – theoretical and managerial implications. While theoretical implications call for the research work to be encouraged and the theories to be developed to identify the gaps and overcome the challenges in big data supported HCSCs, managerial implications advocate the necessary actions to be implemented and strategies, policies and procedures to be designed accordingly.

## 1.    Theoretical implications

It is highlighted by the research fraternity that enough work is not done in healthcare research areas and allied technologies. So, encouraging comprehensive research that encompasses all the inter-dependent sectors can bring many influencing factors into limelight. Also, executing long-term research projects, rather short-term can showcase the pros and cons of big data technology application utility in HCSCs, with respect to various settings (demographic, geographic, societal and others). Yet, establishing theories to monitor, understand and forecast the behavioral response of various types of stakeholders can help in deployment of technologies to a great extent. Finally, practical orientation and research is to be given high priority than methodological research for building resilient SC that can resist in untoward situations.

## 2.    Managerial implications

Along with research work that has to be commissioned on technological front in HCSC, facilitating environment can only be fostered with supportive policies and strategies. As the healthcare ecosystem operates in complex environment, enough support from all the concerned systems and authorities can only ensure the successful operation of resilient SCs. Futuristic approach of concerned authorities, managers and other pioneers that can assess and forecast the technology based HCSC trends and requirements can assist to visualize the requirements of the mankind during tough times.

## REFERENCES

Addo-Tenkorang, R., & Helo, P. T. (2016). Big data applications in operations/supply-chain management: A literature review. *Computers & Industrial Engineering*, *101*, 528–543. doi:10.1016/j.cie.2016.09.023

Aigbavboa, S., & Mbohwa, C. (2020). The headache of medicines' supply in Nigeria: An exploratory study on the most critical challenges of pharmaceutical outbound value chains. *Procedia Manufacturing*, *43*, 336–343. doi:10.1016/j.promfg.2020.02.170

Al-Talib, M., Melhem, W. Y., Anosike, A. I., Garza Reyes, J. A., Nadeem, S. P., & Kumar, A. (2020). Achieving resilience in the supply chain by applying IoT technology. *Procedia CIRP*, *91*(91), 752–757. doi:10.1016/j.procir.2020.02.231

Aljadeed, R., AlRuthia, Y., Balkhi, B., Sales, I., Alwhaibi, M., Almohammed, O., Alotaibi, A. J., Alrumaih, A. M., & Asiri, Y. (2021). The Impact of COVID-19 on Essential Medicines and Personal Protective Equipment Availability and Prices in Saudi Arabia. *Healthcare (Basel)*, *9*(3), 290. Advance online publication. doi:10.3390/healthcare9030290 PMID:33800012

Alliance, D.-P. (2015). *Opportunities and Requirements for Leveraging Big Data for Official Statistics and the Sustainable Development Goals in Latin America*. Data-Pop Alliance. Hardvard Humanitarian Initiative.

Alotaibi, S., & Mehmood, R. (2017). *Big data enabled healthcare supply chain management: opportunities and challenges.* Paper presented at the International Conference on Smart Cities, Infrastructure, Technologies and Applications, Cham.

Anjaneyulu, J., Sreechandana, K., & Madhavi Laitha, V. V. (2021). Management of Big Data in Contemporary World. doi:10.20944/preprints202105.0663.v1

Ardito, L., Petruzzelli, A. M., Panniello, U., & Garavelli, A. C. (2018). Towards Industry 4.0. *Business Process Management Journal*, *25*(2), 323–346. doi:10.1108/BPMJ-04-2017-0088

Beaulieu, M., & Bentahar, O. (2021a). Digitalization of the healthcare supply chain: A roadmap to generate benefits and effectively support healthcare delivery. *Technological Forecasting and Social Change*, *167*, 120717. doi:10.1016/j.techfore.2021.120717

Beaulieu, M., & Bentahar, O. (2021b). Digitalization of the healthcare supply chain: A roadmap to generate benefits and effectively support healthcare delivery. *Technological Forecasting and Social Change*, *167*, 120717. Advance online publication. doi:10.1016/j.techfore.2021.120717

Benzidia, S., Makaoui, N., & Bentahar, O. (2021). The impact of big data analytics and artificial intelligence on green supply chain process integration and hospital environmental performance. *Technological Forecasting and Social Change*, *163*, 120557. doi:10.1016/j.techfore.2020.120557

Bhatia, A., & Mittal, P. (2019). Big Data Driven Healthcare Supply Chain: Understanding Potentials and Capabilities. *Proceedings of International Conference on Advancements in Computing & Management (ICACM)*. 10.2139srn.3464217

Bradley, R. V., Esper, T. L., In, J., Lee, K. B., Bichescu, B. C., & Byrd, A. (2018). The Joint Use of RFID and EDI: Implications for Hospital Performance. *ProdOperations Manage*, *27*(11), 2071–2090. doi:10.1111/poms.12955

Brinch, M., Stentoft, J., & Jensen, J. K. (2017). Big data and its applications in supply chain management: Findings from a Delphi study. *Proceedings of the 50th Hawaii International Conference on System Sciences*. 10.24251/HICSS.2017.161

Chandra, C., & Kachhal, S. K. (2004). Managing health care supply chain: trends, issues, and solutions from a logistics perspective. *Proceedings of the sixteenth annual society of health systems management engineering forum.*

Chen, D. Q., Preston, D. S., & Swink, M. (2016). How the Use of Big Data Analytics Affects Value Creation in Supply Chain Management. *Journal of Management Information Systems*, *32*(4), 4–39. doi:10.1080/07421222.2015.1138364

Chen, T., Wang, Y. C., & Wu, H. C. (2021). Analyzing the Impact of Vaccine Availability on Alternative Supplier Selection Amid the COVID-19 Pandemic: A cFGM-FTOPSIS-FWI Approach. *Healthcare (Basel)*, *9*(1), 71. Advance online publication. doi:10.3390/healthcare9010071 PMID:33451165

Deloitte. (2020). *2020 global health care outlook. Laying a foundation for the future.* Author.

Gartner. (2020). *The Gartner Healthcare Supply Chain Top 25 for 2020.* Retrieved from https://www.gartner.com/en/webinars/4006369/the-2021-gartner-healthcare-supply-chain-top-25

Gartner. (2021a). *Future of Supply Chain.* Retrieved from https://www.gartner.com/en/supply-chain/research/future-of-supply-chain

Gartner. (2021b). *How to Improve Supply Chain Effectiveness Through Supply Chain Benchmarking.* Retrieved from https://www.gartner.com/en/supply-chain/trends/supply-chain-effectiveness

Govindan, K., Mina, H., & Alavi, B. (2020). A decision support system for demand management in healthcare supply chains considering the epidemic outbreaks: A case study of coronavirus disease 2019 (COVID-19). *Transp Res E Logist Transp Rev*, *138*, 101967. doi:10.1016/j.tre.2020.101967 PMID:32382249

Groves, P., Kayyali, B., Knott, D., & Kuiken, S. V. (2013). *The 'big data' revolution in healthcare: Accelerating value and innovation.* Academic Press.

IBM. (2021). *Big data analytics.* IBM Analytics. Retrieved from https://www.ibm.com/analytics/hadoop/big-data-analytics

Ivanov, D. (2020). Viable supply chain model: Integrating agility, resilience and sustainability perspectives—lessons from and thinking beyond the COVID-19 pandemic. *Annals of Operations Research*, 1–21. doi:10.100710479-020-03640-6 PMID:32836614

Iyengar, S. P., Acharya, H., & Kadam, M. (2020). Big Data Analytics in Healthcare Using Spreadsheets. In Big Data Analytics in Healthcare (pp. 155-187). doi:10.1007/978-3-030-31672-3_9

Kannan Govindan, Mishra, & Shukla. (2018). *Big data analytics and application for logistics and supply chain management.* doi:10.1016/j.tre.2018.03.011

Kasten, J. E. (2020). Big Data Applications in Healthcare Administration. *International Journal of Big Data and Analytics in Healthcare*, *5*(2), 12–37. doi:10.4018/IJBDAH.2020070102

Khan, S., Nazir, S., & Khan, H. U. (2021). Analysis of Navigation Assistants for Blind and Visually Impaired People: A Systematic Review. *IEEE Access: Practical Innovations, Open Solutions*, *9*, 26712–26734. doi:10.1109/ACCESS.2021.3052415

Kowalski, J. C., & Sheehan, L. (2016). Health System Supply Chain. Results of the Third Health System Consolidated Service Center Practitioners' Survey. Academic Press.

KPMG. (2021). *Covid-19 induced healthcare transformation in India.* KPMG.

Kulkarni, A. J., Siarry, P., Singh, P. K., Abraham, A., Zhang, M., Zomaya, A., & Baki, F. (Eds.). (2020). *Big Data Analytics in Healthcare* (Vol. 66). Springer.

Kumar, D., & Kumar, D. (2014). Modelling Rural Healthcare Supply Chain in India using System Dynamics. *Procedia Engineering, 97*, 2204–2212. doi:10.1016/j.proeng.2014.12.464

Maheshwari, S., Kaur, G., Kotecha, K., & Jain, P. K. (2020). Bibliometric Survey on Supply Chain in Healthcare using Artificial Intelligence. *Library Philosophy and Practice (e-journal), 4420*. Retrieved from https://digitalcommons.unl.edu/libphilprac/4420

Martínez, L. R., Rios, R. A. O., & Prieto, M. D. (Eds.). (2020). New Trends in the Use of Artificial Intelligence for the Industry 4.0. Academic Press.

Mehta, N., Pandit, A., & Shukla, S. (2019). Transforming healthcare with big data analytics and artificial intelligence: A systematic mapping study. *Journal of Biomedical Informatics, 100*, 103311. doi:10.1016/j.jbi.2019.103311 PMID:31629922

Bresnen, Bailey, Hyde, & Hassard. (Eds.). (2017). Managing Modern Healthcare - Knowledge, Networks and Practice. Taylor & Francis.

Mirabelli, G., & Solina, V. (2020). Blockchain and agricultural supply chains traceability: Research trends and future challenges. *Procedia Manufacturing, 42*, 414–421. doi:10.1016/j.promfg.2020.02.054

Moro Visconti, R., & Morea, D. (2019). Big Data for the Sustainability of Healthcare Project Financing. *Sustainability, 11*(13), 3748. Advance online publication. doi:10.3390u11133748

Oussous, A., Benjelloun, F.-Z., Ait Lahcen, A., & Belfkih, S. (2018). Big Data technologies: A survey. *Journal of King Saud University - Computer and Information Sciences, 30*(4), 431-448. doi:10.1016/j.jksuci.2017.06.001

Paez, A. R. G. F. D. (Ed.). (2021). COVID-19 Pandemic, Geospatial Information, and Community Resilience - Global Applications and Lessons. CRC Press, Taylor & Francis Group, LLC.

Patrinley, J. R. Jr, Berkowitz, S. T., Zakria, D., Totten, D. J., Kurtulus, M., & Drolet, B. C. (2020). Lessons from Operations Management to Combat the COVID-19 Pandemic. *Journal of Medical Systems, 44*(7), 129. doi:10.100710916-020-01595-6 PMID:32519285

Paul-Eric, D., Rafael, P., Cristiane, S., & Joao, C. J. (2020). How to use lean manufacturing for improving a Healthcare logistics performance. *Procedia Manufacturing, 51*, 1657–1664. doi:10.1016/j.promfg.2020.10.231

Raj Kumar Reddy, K., Gunasekaran, A., Kalpana, P., Raja Sreedharan, V., & Arvind Kumar, S. (2021). Developing a blockchain framework for the automotive supply chain: A systematic review. *Computers & Industrial Engineering, 157*, 107334. Advance online publication. doi:10.1016/j.cie.2021.107334

Ramakrishna, Y. (2021). Sustaining SMEs Through Supply Chain Innovation in the COVID-19 Era. In Handbook of Research on Sustaining SMEs and Entrepreneurial Innovation in the Post-COVID-19 Era (pp. 23). IGI Global. doi:10.4018/978-1-7998-6632-9.ch026

Richey, R. G. Jr, Morgan, T. R., Lindsey-Hall, K., & Adams, F. G. (2016). A global exploration of Big Data in the supply chain. *International Journal of Physical Distribution & Logistics Management, 46*(8), 710–739. doi:10.1108/IJPDLM-05-2016-0134

Romano, J. L. (2020). Politics of Prevention: Reflections From the COVID-19 Pandemic. *Journal of Prevention and Health Promotion, 1*(1), 34–57. doi:10.1177/2632077020938360

Schneller, E. (2018). 2018 Healthcare Supply Chain Trends/Issues. *Healthcare Purchasing News*. Retrieved from https://www.hpnonline.com/sourcing-logistics/article/13001185/2018-healthcare-supply-chain-trendsissues

Schniederjans, D. G., Curado, C., & Khalajhedayati, M. (2020). Supply chain digitisation trends: An integration of knowledge management. *International Journal of Production Economics, 220*, 107439. Advance online publication. doi:10.1016/j.ijpe.2019.07.012

Shamsuzzoha, A., Ndzibah, E., & Kettunen, K. (2020). Data-driven sustainable supply chain through centralized logistics network: Case study in a Finnish pharmaceutical distributor company. *Current Research in Environmental Sustainability, 2*, 100013. Advance online publication. doi:10.1016/j.crsust.2020.100013

Shankar, V., Grewal, D., Sunder, S., Fossen, B., Peters, K., & Agarwal, A. (2021). Digital marketing communication in global marketplaces: A review of extant research, future directions, and potential approaches. *International Journal of Research in Marketing*. Advance online publication. doi:10.1016/j.ijresmar.2021.09.005

Shi, J. Q. (2018). How do statisticians analyse big data—Our story. *Statistics & Probability Letters, 136*, 130–133. doi:10.1016/j.spl.2018.02.043

Shokouhyar, S., Seddigh, M. R., & Panahifar, F. (2020). Impact of big data analytics capabilities on supply chain sustainability. *World Journal of Science. Technology and Sustainable Development, 17*(1), 33–57. doi:10.1108/WJSTSD-06-2019-0031

Zhong, R. Y., Newman, S. T., Huang, G. Q., & Lan, S. (2016). Big Data for supply chain management in the service and manufacturing sectors_ Challenges, opportunities, and future perspectives. *Computers & Industrial Engineering, 101*, 572–591. doi:10.1016/j.cie.2016.07.013

Singh, S., Verma, R., & Koul, S. (2017). Managing critical supply chain issues in Indian healthcare. *Procedia Computer Science, 122*, 315–322. doi:10.1016/j.procs.2017.11.375

Siriwardhana, Y., Gür, G., Ylianttila, M., & Liyanage, M. (2021). The role of 5G for digital healthcare against COVID-19 pandemic: Opportunities and challenges. *ICT Express, 7*(2), 244–252. doi:10.1016/j.icte.2020.10.002

Statista. (2021). *Global supply chain management*. Author.

Storey, J., & Holti, R. (2020). *Innovating Healthcare The Role of Political, Managerial and Clinical Leadership*. Taylor & Francis.

Tamym, L., El Oaudghiri, M. D., Benyoucef, L., & Moh, A. N. S. (2020). *Big Data for Supply Chain Management in Industry 4.0 Context: A Comprehensive Survey*. Paper presented at the 13th International Conference on Modeling, Optimization and Simulation, Agadir. Morocco.

Tandon, A., Dhir, A., Islam, A. K. M. N., & Mäntymäki, M. (2020). Blockchain in healthcare: A systematic literature review, synthesizing framework and future research agenda. *Computers in Industry*, *122*, 103290. Advance online publication. doi:10.1016/j.compind.2020.103290

Tian, S., Yang, W., Grange, J. M. L., Wang, P., Huang, W., & Ye, Z. (2019). Smart healthcare: Making medical care more intelligent. *Global Health Journal*, *3*(3), 62–65. doi:10.1016/j.glohj.2019.07.001

Wang, L., & Alexander, C. A. (2015). Big Data Driven Supply Chain Management and Business Administration. *American Journal of Economics and Business Administration*, *7*(2), 60–67. doi:10.3844/ajebasp.2015.60.67

WEF. (2019). *Supply Chain 4.0 Global Practices and Lessons Learned for Latin America and the Caribbean*. Retrieved from https://www.weforum.org/whitepapers/supply-chain-4-0-global-practices-and-lessons-learned-for-latin-america-and-the-caribbean-c4ffe6b1-b2f0-44f1-8b1d-c740cc11ca6f

Wikipedia. (2021). Big data. In *Wikipedia*. Retrieved from https://en.wikipedia.org/wiki/Big_data

Wu, J., Wang, Y., Tao, L., & Peng, J. (2019). Stakeholders in the healthcare service ecosystem. *Procedia CIRP*, *83*, 375–379. doi:10.1016/j.procir.2019.04.085

Yadav, P. (2015). Health Product Supply Chains in Developing Countries: Diagnosis of the Root Causes of Underperformance and an Agenda for Reform. *Health Systems and Reform*, *1*(2), 142–154. doi:10.4161/23288604.2014.968005 PMID:31546312

Yoshizaki, A. (Ed.). (2018). *Operations Management for Social Good*. Springer.

Yu, W., Zhao, G., Liu, Q., & Song, Y. (2021). Role of big data analytics capability in developing integrated hospital supply chains and operational flexibility: An organizational information processing theory perspective. *Technological Forecasting and Social Change*, *163*, 120417. Advance online publication. doi:10.1016/j.techfore.2020.120417

Zakaria, H., Abu Bakar, N. A., Hassan, N. H., & Yaacob, S. (2019). IoT Security Risk Management Model for Secured Practice in Healthcare Environment. *Procedia Computer Science*, *161*, 1241–1248. doi:10.1016/j.procs.2019.11.238

Zhao, R., Liu, Y., Zhang, N., & Huang, T. (2017). An optimization model for green supply chain management by using a big data analytic approach. *Journal of Cleaner Production*, *142*, 1085–1097. doi:10.1016/j.jclepro.2016.03.006

Zhong, R. Y., Newman, S. T., Huang, G. Q., & Lan, S. (2016). Big Data for supply chain management in the service and manufacturing sectors: Challenges, opportunities, and future perspectives. *Computers & Industrial Engineering*, *101*, 572–591. doi:10.1016/j.cie.2016.07.013

# Chapter 16

# Blockchain Technology Aptness for Improving Supply Chain Visibility, Resiliency, and Efficiency

**Gangaraju Vanteddu**
*Southeast Missouri State University, USA*

**Asit Bandyopadhayay**
*Southeast Missouri State University, USA*

## ABSTRACT

*Frequently recurring supply chain disruptions due to natural and manmade calamities are highlighting the importance of the supply chain ability to prevent, withstand, and overcome disruptions of all kinds. Blockchain technology (BCT), a key Industry 4.0 technology, with its inherent strength as an open-sourced distributed database with the immutability of transactions has the potential to transform traditional supply chain (SC) operations. In spite of the potential advantages of the BCT in the supply chain management (SCM) area, the adoption of this novel technology is still in its very early stages. This chapter per the authors proposes a quality function deployment (QFD)-based strategic decision support tool to determine the aptness of BCT adoption in a given SC context. In addition, the proposed tool also allows us to understand the maturity of BCT capabilities in addressing the key SC performance aspects. The application of the proposed tool is explained through a couple of illustrative examples.*

## INTRODUCTION

Covid-19 pandemic has highlighted the vulnerabilities of the existing supply chain (SC) architectures and showed the need for a thorough rethinking of the supply chain design and operations to improve visibility and resiliency while not losing sight of the efficiency objective, which hitherto has served as one of the key supply chain performance metrics. Natural and manmade disasters, raw material contami-

DOI: 10.4018/978-1-7998-9506-0.ch016

Copyright © 2022, IGI Global. Copying or distributing in print or electronic forms without written permission of IGI Global is prohibited.

*Blockchain Technology Aptness*

nation, ethical sourcing, geopolitical reasons etc., constitute some of the key causative factors to rethink the supply chain architecture to make it more robust and resilient.

Emphasis on the visibility, resiliency, and efficiency aspects in the context of supply chain management (SCM) is not new. Dual and multiple sourcing, enterprise resource planning (ERP) support systems, vendor managed inventory (VMI) systems etc., have been considered as some of the solutions for addressing the issues related to supply chain visibility, resiliency and efficiency. However, increasing potential for cyber based disruptions, black swan events such as the Covid pandemic etc., have refocused the need for coming up with robust solutions, which would improve the visibility of supply chain operations while simultaneously making them more secure, resilient to supply chain disruptions, and also improve the trust among the supply chain constituents. Also, it is to be noted that these objectives would be pursued not in place of but in addition to the traditional supply chain focus areas such as efficiency and responsiveness (Chopra and Meindl, 2004).

Blockchain concept, which originally came into prominence as an innovative technology to facilitate bitcoin transactions (Nakamoto, 2008) with its decentralized architecture (Francisco and Swanson, 2018), disintermediating ability (Queiroz et al., 2020), transparency (Tapscott and Tapscott, 2018) and more importantly, immutability of transactions (Seebacher & Schüritz, 2017) that it affords the network constituents stands out as a potential solution for improving the supply chain visibility, resiliency, and efficiency. Blockchain technology (BCT) is relatively a new technological frontier still gaining adherents in the area of SCM. Current research dealing with BCT and SCM integration is still in its early stages (Queiroz et al., 2020). Power industry (Kang et al., 2017), shipping and pharmaceutical industries (Kshetri, 2018), food safety and diamond sourcing (Clancy, 2017) etc., are some of the areas that offer examples in the application of blockchain technology. BCT is still the new kid on the block and has not attracted enough adherents to be considered as a mainstream technology as reflected in the few SCM applications in the available research literature. According to Batwa and Norrman (2020), BCT applications in the SCM area are limited to only SC traceability in the research literature.

Supply chain managers wonder if the BCT would be the right technology aligned with key performance drivers unique to their supply chain and how it compares with other alternative technology options. The fear of unknown, resistance to change and the lack of information on the cost of BCT adoption are other reasons why this novel technology has not attracted significant number of adherents. In spite of the apparent advantages of the BCT, it's adoption in the SCM area is slow on the uptake. A blockchain largely depending on the high difficulty of the proof of work algorithm and on the large number of honest blockchain miners impacts the integrity of the blockchain, while at the same time a difficult proof of work limits the blockchain adaptability (Conoscenti et al., 2016). Also, public blockchains' exposure to 51% attacks, in which a group of users control most of the network's computing power can potentially lead to the control of the blockchain ledger (Esmaeilian et al., 2020). Reader may refer to Saberi et al. (2019) for additional information on the challenges and barriers to be managed for BCT adoption and implementation in SCM.

We in this research, specifically investigate through literature review how the visibility, resiliency, and efficiency aspects of a supply chain are impacted by the BCT and then we propose a strategic decision support tool based on the idea of Quality Function Deployment (QFD) (Hauser and Clausing, 1988) to determine the aptness of BCT adoption dependent on the importance attached to the visibility, resiliency, and efficiency aspects unique to a supply chain; in addition, this strategic tool also provides an idea in regards to the maturity of specific BCT capabilities in addressing a specific set of performance aspects as relevant to a given supply chain. The proposed QFD based strategic tool through hypothetical examples facilitates the application of the tool to consider the adoption of BCT as a possible technology solution based on the perceived strength of association between the BCT capabilities, and the importance attached to the visibility, resiliency, and efficiency aspects of a given supply chain.

The rest of the manuscript is organized is follows. In section 2, we present the background information as related to the BCT and BCT -SCM integration, in section 3, we discuss the role of BCT in improving the visibility, resiliency and efficiency aspects of SCM, in section 4, we present the QFD based strategic tool for BCT adoption in SCM with two hypothetical examples, future research directions are presented in section 5, and finally conclusions are presented in section, 6.

# BACKGROUND

BCT hitherto popular primarily as a cryptocurrency platform and in fintech industry is slowly finding applications in pharmaceutical, agri-food, shipping, etc., industries. BCT with its distributed architecture and immutability of the entered transactions onto the blockchain offers a potential solution for increasing the visibility of the transactions and consequently the ability to track & trace the assets of all kinds listed on the blockchain. Immutability of transactions entered on the blockchain coupled with the ability to create smart contracts makes the blockchain more secure in the presence of natural and manmade disruptions to business operations and also allows for the intermediation of the hitherto trusted third parties redundant making the operations potentially more efficient and less cumbersome.

*Figure 1. BCT functional flow diagram*

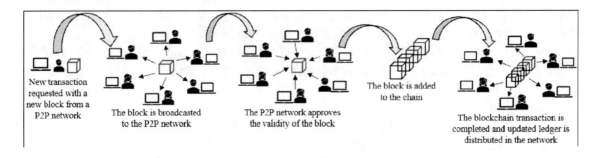

Risius and Spohrer (2017) define the blockchain technology as:

*In its generic form, blockchain technology refers to a fully distributed system for cryptographically capturing and storing a consistent, immutable, linear event log of transactions between networked actors. This is functionally similar to a distributed ledger that is consensually kept, updated, and validated by the parties involved in all the transactions within a network. In such a network, blockchain technology enforces transparency and guarantees eventual, system-wide consensus on the validity of an entire history of transactions.*

In a typical blockchain (see Fig. 1) individual transactions are grouped together into a new block and then transmitted to all the existing nodes. BCT facilitates secure, verified, trustable exchange of information in real time and also the possibility of automatic verification and execution of agreed transactions through smart contracts (Dujak and Sajter, 2019). Newly added blocks are then verified for their authenticity by the blockchain miners typically for financial incentives. Blockchain miners need to agree on the transactions and their sequence, otherwise, individual copies of the blockchain can diverge resulting in a fork (Casado-Vara et al., 2018). The use of cryptographic hash functions and the need for consensus among blockchain nodes makes the blockchain transactions secure and practically immutable. Distributed architecture of the blockchain network coupled with the immutability of entered transactions improves the trust among the nodes. Distributed database, peer-to-peer to transmission, transparency, irreversibility of records, and computational logic are identified as the key attributes of BCT (Iansiti and Lakhani, 2017). Use of blockchain changes the nature of trust. Blockchain capabilities serve as the underpinning of the trust factor, which is essentially important in the supply chain context for improved information sharing and collaboration (Cottrill, 2017). The aforementioned advantages of BCT potentially provide long sought answers to key questions in the context of SCM.

*Figure 2. BCT-SCM integration*

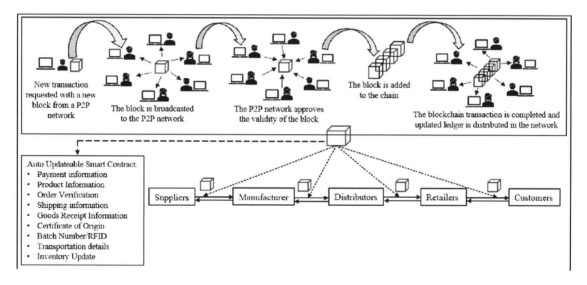

Current interorganizational information systems (IOIS) such as Advanced Planning and Scheduling (APS), Collaborative Planning, Forecasting and Replenishment (CPFR), and Efficient Customer Response etc., facilitate the sharing of real-time information for effective supply chain network coordination (Brusset and Teller, 2017). But information parity at all the SC stages will still be elusive because of the controlled nature of the information sharing by the focal company suiting its strategic and tactical planning related goals and objectives. A BCT enabled SC network as shown in Figure 2 enables the information sharing among SC constituents in a seamless and transparent manner.

E. coli outbreak at Chipotle Mexican Grill outlets in 2015 that left 55 customers sick and also caused significant negative consequences for Chipotle's business serves as an example to highlight the potential importance of BCT to improve transparency and accountability in SCM (Battwa and Norrman, 2020). Iansiti and Lakhani (2017) explain smart contracts are created by users by setting up algorithms and rules that automatically trigger transactions between nodes without human interference. The integration of BCT in SCM is slowly gaining ground, for example, the blockchain solution built by IBM & Maersk will help manage and track the paper trail of millions of shipping containers and when adopted at scale the blockchain based solution has the potential to save billions of dollars (IBM, 2017a). Also, BCT enabled Walmart to reduce the time to trace a package of mangoes from the farm to the store from days or weeks to two seconds (IBM, 2017b).

In spite of the natural advantages of the BCT in the context of SCM, research literature provides little evidence of the widespread use of this novel technology. Based on results of their searches in three scientific databases (Web of Science Core Collection, Scopus and EBSCOhost), and on Google Scholar, Dujak and Sajter (2019) conclude that even though the blockchain topic occupies considerable attention, its use in conjunction with supply chain is significantly less investigated. Deloitte (2017) in their report identify integration concerns, linking digital technology to physical products, control, security and privacy related issues and user/operator buy in as some of the limitations and major risks in the adoption of BCT in SCM. Hackius and Petersen (2017) in their research refer to regulatory uncertainty, lack of technological maturity, lack of acceptance in industry, data security concerns, unclear benefits etc., as some of the barriers for the adoption of BCT in logistics and SCM. Also, it is not only challenging to encode complex business scenarios in BCT enabled smart contracts, but also that such smart contracts have to still rely upon courts and other traditional problem resolution mechanisms (Esmaeilian et al., 2020). Because of the novelty of technology, lack of sufficient number of early adopters etc., in the traditional SCM, rate of BCT adoption in supply chains and consequently the relevant empirical research in the BCT-SCM integration area is still an evolving field of research. In the next section we see how the key advantages of BCT are becoming even more desirable in the context of recurring SC disruptions due to natural and manmade disasters.

## ROLE OF BCT IN IMPROVING VISIBILITY, RESILIENCY, AND EFFICIENCY

The recent closures of North American Automobile plants due to pandemic related chip shortage at the supplier stages, colonial ransomware attack, etc., highlight the significance of supply chain disruptions of either natural or manmade origin. 2011 earthquake & tsunami upended the auto industry in Japan, and in this context, Nissan's engine plant in Iwaki damaged by the quake would take such a long time to resume its normal operations that the company was considering the extreme step of shipping the engines from its Tennessee plant to Japan to go in cars there (Bunkley, 2011). In the same context, in addition to significantly affecting automotive OEM manufacturers and suppliers, semiconductor foundries, microcontroller (used in cars, office and industrial equipment etc.) manufacturing etc., were affected causing global supply chain issues (Kachi and Takahashi, 2011). Global supply chain disruptions in the flows of material, information and funds have become the norm in the present-day complex and tightly coupled interfirm networks (Bode et al., 2011).

Focusing primarily on the efficiency aspect such as just in time production systems has made supply chains lean and flexible but at the cost of making them susceptible to supply chain disruptions. Brandon-Jones et al. (2014) opine that increased attention from academia and industry has not significantly affected the frequency and impact of disruptions. The supply chain procurement chaos in procuring masks, personal protective equipment (PPE) supplies etc., during the early period of spring 2020 at the onset of covid pandemic has highlighted the importance of supply chain asset visibility and supply chain process resiliency. For example, qualifying and maintaining a second supplier even though might increase direct and indirect costs, provides a responsive switching option in the event of supply chain disruptions (Brandon-Jones et al., 2014).

Existing disruptions mitigating measures in the form of in-built system redundancies such as dual/multiple sourcing, safety stocks, enterprise resource planning (ERP) software enabled supply chain solutions have proven to be insufficient for dealing with supply chain disruptions of natural or manmade origin and supply chain managers across the globe are waiting for that panacea, which would not only make the supply chains more resilient but also would not take away the advances made in the area of supply chain efficiency in the last few decades. BCT with its inherent advantages in enhancing the visibility and security of transactions across the supply chain coupled with its disintermediation ability to reduce the number of stages in the supply chain could potentially be that panacea. In this regard, BCT potentially enables a trustless, secure and authenticated system of logistics and supply chain information exchange in supply networks (Dujak and Sajter, 2019). Now let's look at how BCT specifically impacts the visibility, resiliency and efficiency aspects of SCM.

*Figure 3. BCT enabled interdependencies among SC visibility, resilience, and efficiency*

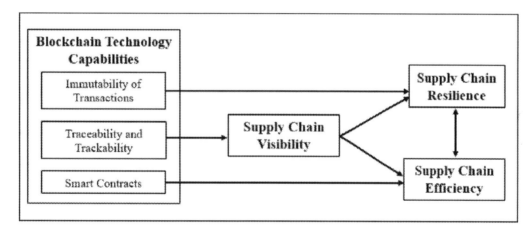

## Supply Chain Visibility

The visibility, resiliency and efficiency aspects of a supply chain are not only interrelated but interdependent and have a positive association on one another (see Figure 3). For example, visibility is such an important antecedent to risk reduction, not only because its presence helps organizations proactively track products and identify potential disruptions, but also because its absence can create new risks; also, visibility can facilitate more efficient information exchange thereby reducing the resources required to respond. (Brandon-Jones et al., 2014). Blackhurst et al. (2005) demonstrate through their research the significant impact of visibility on disruption recovery. According to KPMG's global manufacturing outlook report (Gates et al., 2016), achieving cross-functional and end-to-end supply chain visibility is the best way to minimize the supply chain risk failure. Also, in the context of increasing importance attached to timely and cost-effective product deliveries, Brusset and Teller (2017) consider supply chain resilience as a critical capability to maintain the continuity of operations. Even though this paper discusses these aspects independently it is to be noted that they are largely codependent and to the extent possible an attempt has been made in this section to explain the relevant linkages and the corresponding associations.

Barratt and Barratt (2011) in their research emphasize the combining role of internal and external information-based linkages to extend end-to-end supply chain visibility. According to Somapa et al. (2018), research literature to a large extent emphasizes the aspects of accessibility, quality and the usefulness of information for business process improvement as the key characteristics of SC visibility. Based on the survey data collected from 264 UK manufacturing plants, Brandon-Jones et al. (2014) in their research suggest that visibility capability enabled by the supply chain connectivity and information sharing resources enhances SC resilience and robustness. Brusset and Teller (2017) emphasize the importance of accurate and real-time information flows in the supply chain potentially considering them to be as important as the supply chain flow of goods. Somapa et al. (2018) research findings indicate that the benefits of supply chain visibility extend beyond the business process operational efficiency and organizational strategic competency improvements. For example, proactive recovery capabilities enabled by better information and visibility allowed a large U.S. retailer to reroute material shipments to other seaports prior to the 2002 Westcoast strike (Craighead et al., 2007). Braunscheidel & Suresh (2009) in their research show that internal integration, external integration with key suppliers and customers and external flexibility has a significant positive impact on the supply chain agility, which in turn facilitates better SC disruption risk management. Christopher and Lee (2004) in their research suggest that improving end-to-end SC visibility is one of the key elements in any SC risk mitigation strategy.

Current SC information systems are unable to provide validated, pseudo real-time shipment tracking during the distribution phase and these solutions are often dependent on the tracking information provided just by the carrier resulting in the narrowing of the scope of SC visibility (Wu et al, 2017). In a BCT enabled supply chain, distributed architecture of the network facilitates the achievement of information parity among all the nodes potentially enhancing the SC visibility.

## Supply Chain Resiliency

Brandon-Jones et al. (2014) define supply chain resilience as the ability of a supply chain to return to normal operating performance, within an acceptable period of time, after being disturbed. Ponomarov and Holcomb (2009) define supply chain resilience as "the adaptive capability of the supply chain to prepare for unexpected events, respond to disruptions, and recover from them by maintaining continuity of operations at the desired level of connectedness and control over structure and function." In the context of present-day complex and dynamic global supply chains, Pettit et al. (2019) emphasize the ability to identify potential vulnerabilities and agility to quickly respond to unexpected events. Wieland and Wallenburg (2013) in their research distinguish between proactive and reactive dimensions of resilience as in robustness and agility aspects. In the context of supply chain resiliency assessment, Scholten and Schilder (2015) in their research show how collaborative activities such as information-sharing, collaborative communication etc., enhance supply chain resilience through increased visibility, velocity and flexibility. Chowdhury & Quaddus (2017) in their research suggest adopting multiple suppliers to mitigate the impact of supply side vulnerabilities in an uncertain supply environment. Jüttner and Maklan (2011) show through their empirical research that the supply chain risk effect and knowledge management improve the SC flexibility, visibility, velocity and collaboration capabilities, which in turn enhances the supply chain resilience.

*Blockchain Technology Aptness*

Current research as described in the previous paragraph primarily focuses on the capabilities/enablers such as visibility, flexibility, agility, redundancy etc., that positively impact the SC resilience. BCT by its inherent abilities to enhance visibility (through distributed networking), flexibility (through disintermediation), redundancy (through smart contracts) & security (through cryptography enabled immutable transactions) could potentially offer a path forward to design and manage SC global networks with improved resiliency.

## Supply Chain Efficiency

According to Kim and Kim (2019), efficiency refers to the ratio of output to input, and efficiency improvement is achieving the highest possible performance with the lowest possible cost. SC efficiency typically means direct savings of all kinds of resources, such as cost, time, space etc., for achieving a unit output or indirect savings due to reduced repair/reworking of the components on account of improved quality etc. Putting it another way, supply chain performance evaluation is closely associated with value maximization, cycle time reduction and improvement efforts across the entire supply chain (Gunasekaran et al., 2004)

Caridi et al. (2014) in their research propose a structured method and a set of assessment tools for quantifying the benefits of supply chain visibility on the inbound supply chain and their model proved to be efficient for the supply chain of a prominent company in the aerospace industry that resulted in the reduction of production lead time and consequently to a reduction in component stockouts. In demand management or CPFR processes, according to Somapa et al. (2018) sharing downstream member demand information with upstream members is a good strategy. SC visibility, in such cases, can mitigate the negative consequences of the bullwhip effect by reducing uncertainty about the demand signal (Somapa et al., 2018). Readers may refer to Lee et al. (1997) for additional information on the bullwhip effect. For improving the accessibility and quality of the information at all the stages, in other words SC visibility, radio frequency identification (RFID) technology is turning out to be one of the key facilitators. RFID technology can help realize significant productivity gains and efficiencies in a wide variety of organizations such as hospitals, retailers and supply chains and with RFID implementation P&G expects up to $1 billion cost savings in working capital and $200 million in inventory holding costs (Sabbaghi and Vaidyanathan, 2008). Landry and Beaulieu (2010) demonstrate through their research how the RFID technology enhances the two-bin kanban replenishment system by allowing for the proactive inventory management, optimizing replenishment cycles and alerting management about potential stockouts.

Key characteristics of the BCT with potential to increase the SC visibility & resilience as explained sub-sections 3.1 & 3.2 present an effective opportunity to improve the SC efficiency across all the stages. For example, by recording transaction details on the blockchain, IBM wants to improve the traceability and visibility of those transactions in an efficient manner, potentially reducing the dispute resolution time from 44 days to 10 days (Nash and King, 2016). BCT based on its distributed architecture and immutability of transactions that it affords enables efficient and transparent transactions reducing transaction costs (Schmidt and Wagner, 2019). Emphasizing the affordability and the supply chain visibility aspects, Li et al. (2017) in their research propose a dynamic hybrid peer-to-peer network-based framework that introduces a blockchain data model based on both private and semi-public ledgers. Depending on the type of blockchain, information/records on the blockchain could be made available to public or just to a limited number of participants. BCT enabled open access to information in a supply chain improves paperwork processing, reduces the need for direct communications while providing more information at the same time (Dujak and Sajter, 2019). According to Marine Transport International estimates, BCT could save $300 per container in terms of labor and the relevant document processing and for one ultra large container ship the savings could amount to as much as $5.4 M (ship-technology.com, 2017).

On account of the highest level of system security (for example, Bitcoin's blockchain since its launch in 2008 never crashed, frozen or hacked), a blockchain directly enables solutions to fundamental problems in the context of SC coordination and integration (Dujak and Sajter, 2019). In spite of the potential advantages of BCT in the context of improving visibility, resiliency and efficiency aspects of SCM, BCT adoption is limited to only a few industries in the existing research literature. According to Chain Business Insights' blockchain in supply chain survey primary obstacles to the adoption of BCT in SCM are lack of understanding/awareness and lack of standards and interoperability (inboundlogistics.com, 2017). For example, in the context of smart contracts, Iansiti and Lakhani (2017) in their research state that "a tremendous degree of coordination and clarity on how smart contracts are designed, verified, implemented, and enforced will be required."

Supply chain managers are adopting a wait and see approach to see if this technology would work, scalable, would be better than alternative technologies available and more importantly if it would make economic sense. In this context, we propose in the next section a QFD based strategic tool to aid with the BCT adoption decision making process.

## QFD BASED STRATEGIC DECISION SUPPORT TOOL FOR BCT ADOPTION IN SCM

QFD typically used for transforming customer expectations into appropriate design specifications is used in a novel way in this research to assess the BCT aptness for improving the visibility, resiliency, and efficiency aspects of SCM. By aligning the visibility, resiliency, and efficiency aspects with the known key capabilities of BCT, an attempt is made to determine the suitability of BCT adoption as applicable to a given supply chain based on the importance attached to the identified key aspects. In addition, through the novel use of the QFD relationship matrix it is also possible to assess the maturity of a given BCT capability to improve a given a set of performance aspects that are considered to be important. Even though we are focusing on visibility, resiliency, and efficiency aspects in this research, one can easily substitute them with a different set of performance measures that are considered to be important for a given supply chain to assess the BCT aptness for possible adoption.

Quality Function Deployment (QFD) chart also known as the House of Quality (Hauser and Clausing, 1988) is typically used in the manufacturing and service industries to translate customer expectations into relevant design specifications to truly reflect the 'voice of the customer'. QFD chart is one of the foremost tools used to prioritize the 'voice of the customer' in new product and service development. For a thorough review of the QFD relevant literature review, reader may refer to Chan and Wu (20002a), Chan and Wu(2002b) and Chan and Wu (2005). In the context of QFD for quality service design, readers may refer to Ermer and Kniper (1998).

In this research, we have made an attempt to use the QFD chart in a novel way to inform us on the aptness of BCT for adoption in a given supply chain based on the importance attached to the visibility, resiliency and efficiency aspects. Even though we have not considered these performance aspects at the granular level, proposed QFD based tool can be easily expanded to accommodate dimensional/sub dimensional perspectives if desired. Also, depending on the priorities of a given supply chain, a com-

## Blockchain Technology Aptness

pletely different set of performance aspects can also be considered for determining the suitability of the adoption of BCT in those contexts.

Supply chain performance aspects and their relative importance (1,2,3 on Likert scale) are listed on the left-hand side of the relationship matrix as shown in figures 4 and 5 relevant to the hypothetical/explanatory examples provided in this section. BCT capabilities are listed above the relationship matrix in the center of the chart and the relative strength of association (1,3,9) is indicated by different symbols in the relationship matrix. Relative strengths are subjective and should be decided upon by carefully assessing the strength of association between a given supply chain performance aspect and a corresponding BCT capability.

To identify the degree to which a particular supply performance aspect is compatible for a given set of BCT capabilities, a weighted score is calculated for each of the performance aspects.

## PHARMACEUTICAL INDUSTRY EXAMPLE

*Figure 4. BCT adoption in SCM (pharmaceutical industry example)*

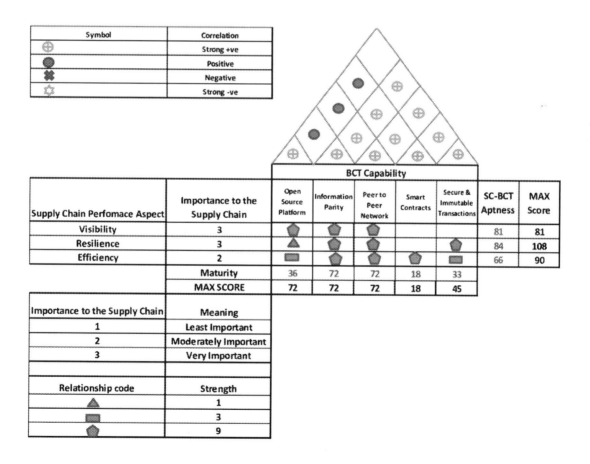

The weighted score (SC-BCT Aptness) for a specific supply chain performance aspect '$i$' is given by:

$$\sum_{j=1}^{m} x_i y_{ij} \ \forall i$$

$x_i$ = relative importance of the $i^{th}$ supply chain performance aspect.

$y_{ij}$ = perceived strength of relationship, between the $i^{th}$ supply chain performance aspect and the $j^{th}$ BCT capability.

Supply chain performance aspects, '$i$' $\in$ (1,,,,,n)

BCT capabilities, '$j$'$\in$ (1,,,,,m)

For example in figure 4, in the pharmaceutical industry example, *SC-BCT Aptness* for the supply chain performance aspect *visibility* is calculated as (3*9) + (3*9)+(3*9) =81; and the possible maximum possible score(*MAX Score*) based on the relevance of BCT capabilities to the *visibility* aspect is also (3*9) + (3*9)+(3*9) =81, hence, *SC-BCT Aptness* and *MAX Score* ratio for this performance aspect is (81/81) =1; likewise, *SC-BCT Aptness /MAX Score* ratios can be calculated for *resilience* and *efficiency* as well.

*SC-BCT Aptness /MAX Score* ratio (*Resiliency*) =

((3*1) + (3*9) + (3*9) + (3*9)) / ((3*9) + (3*9) + (3*9) + (3*9)) = 84/108 = 0.78

*SC-BCT Aptness /MAX Score* ratio (*Efficiency*) =

((2*3) +(2*9) + (2*9) + (2*9) +(2*3)) / ((2*9) +(2*9) + (2*9) + (2*9) +(2*9)) = 66/90 = 0.73.

To determine whether the adoption BCT in a particular industry is a viable option appropriate guidelines can be developed individually for identified performance aspects and for the overall *SC-BCT Aptness* ratio (81+ 84 + 66)/ (81+ 108 +90) =0.83 such as

- Above 0.7: may consider the adoption of BCT (or an alternative technology) and/or to conduct detailed cost-benefit analysis for possible adoption
- Between 0.5 – 0.7: may consider additional comparisons with alternative technologies to BCT, which can be easily accomplished by replacing the BCT capabilities at the top of the relationship matrix with the capabilities of the alternative technology.
- Less than 0.5; BCT capabilities may not be mature enough for BCT adoption

Likewise, *Maturity* of a given *BCT Capability* '$j$' is given by:

$$\sum_{i=1}^{n} x_i y_{ij} \ \forall j$$

For example in figure 4, in the pharmaceutical industry example, for BCT Capability, *Open Source Platform*, Maturity is calculated as (3*9) + (3*1) + (2*3) =36; and the possible maximum possible score(*MAX Score*) based on the relevant SC performance aspects is (3*9) + (3*9)+(2*9) =72, hence, *Maturity /MAX Score* ratio for this *BCT Capability* is, 36/72 = 0.5; likewise, *Maturity/MAX Score* ratios for other listed BCT Capabilities are as follows.

Information Parity: ((3*9) + (3*9) + 2*9)) / ((3*9) + (3*9) + (2*9)) =72/72 =1

Peer-to-Peer Network: ((3*9) + (3*9) + (2*9)) / ((3*9) + (3*9) + (2*9)) =72/72 =1

Smart Contracts: (2*9) / (2*9) =18/18 =1

Secure & Immutable Transactions: ((3*9) + (2*3)) / ((3*9) + (2*9)) =33/45=0.73

In this hypothetical example, with the selected SC performance aspects, BCT is lagging in its capabilities "Open-Source Platform' and the 'Secure & Immutable Transactions' with their scores of 0.5 & 0.73 compared to other listed capabilities.

## AUTOMOTIVE INDUSTRY EXAMPLE

*Figure 5. BCT adoption in SCM (automotive industry example)*

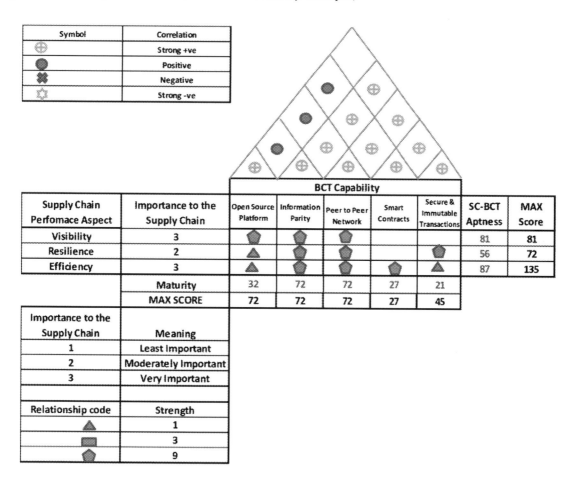

Following the approach described in the previous sub-section, the relevant calculations for *SC-BCT Aptness/MAX Score* ratios and *Maturity/MAX Score* ratios in the case of automotive industry illustrative example are shown below.

*SC-BCT Aptness/MAX Score* ratio (*Visibility*) =
((3*9) + (3*9) + (3*9)) / ((3*9) + (3*9) + (3*9)) = 81/81 = 1

*SC-BCT Aptness /MAX Score* ratio (*Resiliency*) =

$((2*1) +(2*9) + (2*9) + (2*9)) / ((2*9) +(2*9) + (2*9) + (2*9)) = 56/72 = 0.78$

*SC-BCT Aptness/MAX Score* ratio (*Efficiency*) =

$((3*1) +(3*9) + (3*9) + (3*9) +(3*1)) / ((3*9) +(3*9) + (3*9) + (3*9) +(3*9)) = 87/135 = 0.64$

Overall *SC-BCT Aptness* ratio $(81+ 56 + 87)/ (81+ 72 +135) = 0.78$

To determine the aptness of the BCT for the adoption in the automotive industry based on the above ratios, guidelines mentioned in the previous section can be used or can also be developed independently more aligned with the industry expectations/norms.

Likewise, *BCT Capability Maturity /MAX Score* ratios for the listed BCT capabilities in the case of automotive industry example are calculated as follows.

Open-Source Platform: $((3*9) + (2*1) + (3*1)) / ((3*9) + (2*9) + (3*9)) =32/72 =0.44$

Information Parity: $((3*9) + (2*9) + (3*9)) / ((3*9) + (2*9) + (3*9)) =72/72 =1$

Peer-to-Peer Network: $((3*9) + (2*9) + (3*9)) / ((3*9) + (2*9) + (3*9)) =72/72 =1$

Smart Contracts: $(3*9) / (3*9) =27/27 =1$

Secure & Immutable Transactions: $((2*9) + (3*1)) / ((2*9) + (3*9)) =21/45=0.47$

In this hypothetical example, with the selected SC performance aspects, BCT is lagging in its capabilities "Open-Source Platform' and the 'Secure & Immutable Transactions' with their scores 0.44 & 0.47 compared to other listed capabilities.

Even though we considered performance aspects broadly in these hypothetical examples, they can be considered at a much more granular level if desired; likewise, BCT capabilities also can be considered at a much more detail level. Internal correlation matrix in the crown part of the QFD chart in both figures indicates positive or strongly positive correlations among the listed BCT capabilities, which is not surprising. This may be more informative when BCT capabilities are considered at the granular level; also, by flipping the location of SC performance aspects to the top of the integration matrix, correlations among them can be highlighted if so desired.

## FUTURE RESEARCH DIRECTIONS

Even though we have not considered the key supply chain aspects at the granular level in this research, it is desirable that performance measures are considered at the granular level that are readily measurable for a better alignment with the capabilities of BCT. For example, Chowdhury & Quaddus (2017) through their research confirm that supply chain resilience is a hierarchical and multidimensional construct measured by three primary dimensions, namely, proactive supply chain capability, reactive capability and supply chain design quality, which were further divided into twelve subdimensions. Future researchers may explore considering the performance aspects at the desired granular/subdimension for determining the BCT aptness for adoption.

Also, it will enhance the practicality of the proposed tool if the BCT capabilities are delineated by the type of blockchain platform and their compatibility with the existing ERP systems for better guidance on the BCT adaptability in a given context. It would also be a good idea to incorporate information regarding the potential vulnerabilities, impediments in the adoption of BCT for informed decision making regarding the adoption of BCT. More importantly, survey research that demonstrates the effectiveness of BCT capabilities in positively influencing a given set of performance aspects opens up many research opportunities that are unique to a given industry, BCT platform etc. Future research may also come up with improved models to assess the BCT capability by considering the specific sub-categories of performance measures that are particularly vulnerable to possible supply chain disruptions.

Also, relative importance scores of the performance aspects or their dimensions could be assessed in a more rigorous manner either through qualitative Delphi method or through empirical surveys either conducted within a supply chain or across the industry depending on the scope. Likewise, strength of relationship assessment also can be made more rigorous for more realistic assessments of BCT aptness. Comparison studies of BCT with other competing technologies using the proposed decision support tool would also constitute another potential area for future research.

## CONCLUSION

Blockchain technology with its open-source platform based distributed network architecture, immutability of transactions, and the ability to create smart contracts is one of the important Industry 4.0 technologies with a significant potential to transform global supply chain operations. In spite of the potential benefits of the BCT in SCM the adoption of this novel technology is still in very early stages and technological maturity, managerial limitations, regulatory uncertainty, cost considerations are some of the impediments preventing the integration in the traditional SCM areas. The frequent turbulence faced by the present-day global supply chains due to natural and manmade causes as highlighted by the current pandemic related supply chain chaos across the globe emphasizes the importance of supply chain visibility & resiliency to withstand and overcome disruptions.

Blockchain technology by virtue of its inherent advantages offers a potential solution to enhance the visibility, resiliency aspects a supply chain while not losing the sight of efficiency objective. In this research an attempt has been made to present a QFD based decision support tool to determine the aptness of the BCT based on the importance attached to visibility, resilience, and efficiency aspects in a given SC context. The novel application of QFD in this research through illustrative examples also allows for developing an understanding about the maturity of different BCT capabilities in a given SC context. The proposed tool could be easily transformed for a different set of performance aspects in other contexts and also could be easily expanded by considering the SC performance aspects at a granular level, if desired. The proposed QFD based decision support tool can also be used for comparing the suitability of other existing/alternative technologies with BCT to facilitate effective decision making. It is our hope that practitioners/academicians in the area of BCT-SCM integration would find the contribution in this paper useful and we also hope to see research presented in this paper extended and tested in real world applications to determine the BCT aptness in SCM.

## REFERENCES

Barratt, M., & Barratt, R. (2011). Exploring internal and external supply chain linkages: Evidence from the field. *Journal of Operations Management*, *29*(5), 514–528. doi:10.1016/j.jom.2010.11.006

Batwa, A., & Norrman, A. (2020). A framework for exploring blockchain technology in supply chain management. *Operations and Supply Chain Management: An International Journal*, *13*(3), 294–306. doi:10.31387/oscm0420271

Blackhurst, J., Craighead, C. W., Elkins, D., & Handfield, R. B. (2005). An empirically derived agenda of critical research issues for managing supply-chain disruptions. *International Journal of Production Research*, *43*(19), 4067–4081. doi:10.1080/00207540500151549

Bode, C., Wagner, S. M., Petersen, K. J., & Ellram, L. M. (2011). Understanding responses to supply chain disruptions: Insights from information processing and resource dependence perspectives. *Academy of Management Journal*, *54*(4), 833–856. doi:10.5465/amj.2011.64870145

Brandon-Jones, E., Squire, B., Autry, C. W., & Petersen, K. J. (2014). A contingent resource-based perspective of supply chain resilience and robustness. *The Journal of Supply Chain Management*, *50*(3), 55–73. doi:10.1111/jscm.12050

Braunscheidel, M. J., & Suresh, N. C. (2009). The organizational antecedents of a firm's supply chain agility for risk mitigation and response. *Journal of Operations Management*, *27*(2), 119–140. doi:10.1016/j.jom.2008.09.006

Brusset, X., & Teller, C. (2017). Supply chain capabilities, risks, and resilience. *International Journal of Production Economics*, *184*, 59–68. doi:10.1016/j.ijpe.2016.09.008

Bunkley, N. (2011, March 18). Japan's Automakers Expect More Delays. *The New York Times*. https://www.nytimes.com/2011/03/19/business/global/19auto.html

Caridi, M., Moretto, A., Perego, A., & Tumino, A. (2014). The benefits of supply chain visibility: A value assessment model. *International Journal of Production Economics*, *151*, 1–19. doi:10.1016/j.ijpe.2013.12.025

Casado-Vara, R., Prieto, J., De la Prieta, F., & Corchado, J. M. (2018). How blockchain improves the supply chain: Case study alimentary supply chain. *Procedia Computer Science*, *134*, 393–398. doi:10.1016/j.procs.2018.07.193

Chan, L. K., & Wu, M. L. (2002). Quality function deployment: A comprehensive review of its concepts and methods. *Quality Engineering*, *15*(1), 23–35. doi:10.1081/QEN-120006708

Chan, L. K., & Wu, M. L. (2002a). Quality function deployment: A literature review. *European Journal of Operational Research*, *143*(3), 463–497. doi:10.1016/S0377-2217(02)00178-9

Chan, L. K., & Wu, M. L. (2005). A systematic approach to quality function deployment with a full illustrative example. *Omega*, *33*(2), 119–139. doi:10.1016/j.omega.2004.03.010

Chopra, S. & Meindl, P. (2004). *Supply chain management: Strategy, planning and operation*. Pearson Education Inc.

Chowdhury, M. M. H., & Quaddus, M. (2017). Supply chain resilience: Conceptualization and scale development using dynamic capability theory. *International Journal of Production Economics*, *188*, 185–204. doi:10.1016/j.ijpe.2017.03.020

Christopher, M., & Lee, H. (2004). Mitigating supply chain risk through improved confidence. *International Journal of Physical Distribution & Logistics Management*, *34*(5), 388–396. doi:10.1108/09600030410545436

Clancy, H. (2017, February 6). *The blockchain's emerging role in sustainability*. GreenBiz. https://www.greenbiz.com/article/blockchains-emerging-role-sustainability

Conoscenti, M., Vetro, A., & De Martin, J. C. (2016, November). Blockchain for the Internet of Things: A systematic literature review. In *2016 IEEE/ACS 13th International Conference of Computer Systems and Applications (AICCSA)* (pp. 1-6). IEEE. 10.1109/AICCSA.2016.7945805

Cottrill, K. (2017, December 12). *The Benefits of Blockchain – Part 1: Fact or Wishful Thinking?* Supply Chain Management Review. https://www.scmr.com/article/nextgen_supply_chain_the_benefits_of_blockchain_fact_or_wishful_thinking

Craighead, C. W., Blackhurst, J., Rungtusanatham, M. J., & Handfield, R. B. (2007). The severity of supply chain disruptions: Design characteristics and mitigation capabilities. *Decision Sciences*, *38*(1), 131–156. doi:10.1111/j.1540-5915.2007.00151.x

Deloitte. (2017). *Using blockchain to drive supply chain innovation*. https://www2.deloitte.com/us/en/pages/operations/articles/blockchain-supply-chain-innovation.html

Dujak, D., & Sajter, D. (2019). Blockchain Applications in Supply Chain. In A. Kawa & A. Maryniak (Eds.), *SMART Supply Network* (pp. 21–46). Springer. doi:10.1007/978-3-319-91668-2_2

Ermer, D. S., & Kniper, M. K. (1998). Delighting the customer: Quality function deployment for quality service design. *Total Quality Management*, *9*(4-5), 86–91. doi:10.1080/0954412988622

Esmaeilian, B., Sarkis, J., Lewis, K., & Behdad, S. (2020). Blockchain for the future of sustainable supply chain management in Industry 4.0. *Resources, Conservation and Recycling*, *163*, 105064. doi:10.1016/j.resconrec.2020.105064

Francisco, K., & Swanson, D. (2018). The supply chain has no clothes: Technology adoption of blockchain for supply chain transparency. *Logistics*, *2*(2), 1–13. doi:10.3390/logistics2010002

Gates, D., Mayor, T., & Gampenrieder, E. L. (2016). *Global manufacturing outlook- Competing for growth: How to be a growth leader in industrial manufacturing*. KPMG. https://assets.kpmg/content/dam/kpmg/tr/pdf/2017/01/global-manufacturing-outlook-competing-for-growth.pdf

Gunasekaran, A., Patel, C., & McGaughey, R. E. (2004). A framework for supply chain performance measurement. *International Journal of Production Economics*, *87*(3), 333–347. doi:10.1016/j.ijpe.2003.08.003

Hackius, N., & Petersen, M. (2017): Blockchain in logistics and supply chain: Trick or treat? In *Digitalization in Supply Chain Management and Logistics: Smart and Digital Solutions for an Industry 4.0 Environment* (pp. 3-18). Proceedings of the Hamburg International Conference of Logistics (HICL), epubli GmbH. 10.15480/882.1444

Hauser, J. R., & Clausing, D. (1988). The house of quality. *Harvard Business Review*, *66*(3), 63–73.

Iansiti, M., & Lakhani, K. R. (2017). The Truth about Blockchain. *Harvard Business Review*, *95*(1), 118–127.

IBM. (2017a, March 5). *Maersk and IBM Unveil First Industry-Wide Cross-Border Supply Chain Solution on Blockchain.* IBM Newsroom. https://newsroom.ibm.com/2017-03-05-Maersk-and-IBM-Unveil-First-Industry-Wide-Cross-Border-Supply-Chain-Solution-on-Blockchain

IBM. (2017b, December 14). *Walmart, JD.com, IBM and Tsinghua University Launch a Blockchain Food Safety Alliance in China.* IBM Newsroom. https://newsroom.ibm.com/2017-12-14-Walmart-JD-com-IBM-and-Tsinghua-University-Launch-a-Blockchain-Food-Safety-Alliance-in-China

Inbound Logistics. (2017, May 30). *Blockchain Survey Shows Awareness, Key Applications, and Implementation Plans.* Inbound Logistics. https://www.inboundlogistics.com/cms/article/blockchain-survey-shows-awareness/

Jüttner, U., & Maklan, S. (2011). Supply chain resilience in the global financial crisis: An empirical study. *Supply Chain Management, 16*(4), 246–259. doi:10.1108/13598541111139062

Kachi, H., & Takahashi, Y. (2011, March 14). Plant Closures Imperil Global Supplies. *The Wall Street Journal.* https://www.wsj.com/articles/SB10001424052748704027504576198961775199034

Kang, J., Yu, R., Huang, X., Maharjan, S., Zhang, Y., & Hossain, E. (2017). Enabling localized peer-to-peer electricity trading among plug-in hybrid electric vehicles using consortium blockchains. *IEEE Transactions on Industrial Informatics, 13*(6), 3154–3164. doi:10.1109/TII.2017.2709784

Kim, C., & Kim, H. J. (2019). A study on healthcare supply chain management efficiency: Using bootstrap data envelopment analysis. *Health Care Management Science, 22*(3), 534–548. doi:10.100710729-019-09471-7 PMID:30830500

Kshetri, N. (2018). Blockchain's roles in meeting key supply chain management objectives. *International Journal of Information Management, 39*, 80–89. doi:10.1016/j.ijinfomgt.2017.12.005

Landry, S., & Beaulieu, M. (2010). Achieving lean healthcare by combining the two-bin kanban replenishment system with RFID technology. *International Journal of Health Management and Information, 1*(1), 85–98.

Lee, H. L., Padmanabhan, V., & Whang, S. (1997). Information distortion in a supply chain: The bullwhip effect. *Management Science, 43*(4), 546–558. doi:10.1287/mnsc.43.4.546

Li, Z., Wu, H., King, B., Miled, Z. B., Wassick, J., & Tazelaar, J. (2017, June). On the integration of event-based and transaction-based architectures for supply chains. In *2017 IEEE 37th International Conference on Distributed Computing Systems Workshops (ICDCSW)* (pp. 376-382). IEEE.

Nakamoto, S. (2008). Bitcoin: A peer-to-peer electronic cash system. *Decentralized Business Review,* 21260. https://bitcoin.org/bitcoin.pdf

Nash, K. S., & King, R. (2016, July 29). IBM set to launch one of the largest blockchain implementations to date. *The Wall Street Journal.* https://www.wsj.com/articles/BL-CIOB-10241

Pettit, T. J., Croxton, K. L., & Fiksel, J. (2019). The evolution of resilience in supply chain management: A retrospective on ensuring supply chain resilience. *Journal of Business Logistics, 40*(1), 56–65. doi:10.1111/jbl.12202

Ponomarov, S. Y., & Holcomb, M. C. (2009). Understanding the concept of supply chain resilience. *International Journal of Logistics Management, 20*(1), 124–143. doi:10.1108/09574090910954873

Queiroz, M. M., Telles, R., & Bonilla, S. H. (2020). Blockchain and supply chain management integration: A systematic review of the literature. *Supply Chain Management, 25*(2), 241–254. doi:10.1108/SCM-03-2018-0143

Risius, M., & Spohrer, K. (2017). A blockchain research framework: What We (don't) Know, Where We Go from Here, and How We Will Get There. *Business & Information Systems Engineering, 59*(6), 385–409. doi:10.100712599-017-0506-0

Sabbaghi, A., & Vaidyanathan, G. (2008). Effectiveness and efficiency of RFID technology in supply chain management: Strategic values and challenges. *Journal of Theoretical and Applied Electronic Commerce Research, 3*(2), 71–81. doi:10.4067/S0718-18762008000100007

Saberi, S., Kouhizadeh, M., Sarkis, J., & Shen, L. (2019). Blockchain technology and its relationships to sustainable supply chain management. *International Journal of Production Research, 57*(7), 2117–2135. doi:10.1080/00207543.2018.1533261

Schmidt, C. G., & Wagner, S. M. (2019). Blockchain and supply chain relations: A transaction cost theory perspective. *Journal of Purchasing and Supply Management, 25*(4), 100552. doi:10.1016/j.pursup.2019.100552

Scholten, K., & Schilder, S. (2015). The role of collaboration in supply chain resilience. *Supply Chain Management, 20*(4), 471–484. doi:10.1108/SCM-11-2014-0386

Seebacher, S., & Schüritz, R. (2017). Blockchain Technology as an Enabler of Service Systems: A Structured Literature Review. In Za, S., Drăgoicea, M., & Cavallari M. (Eds), *Exploring Services Science. 8th International Conference, IESS 2017 Proceedings* (pp. 12-23). Springer. 10.1007/978-3-319-56925-3_2

Ship Technology. (2017, September 10). *Could blockchain technology revolutionise shipping?* Ship Technology. https://www.ship-technology.com/features/featurecould-blockchain-technology-revolutionise-shipping-5920391/

Somapa, S., Cools, M., & Dullaert, W. (2018). Characterizing supply chain visibility – a literature review. *International Journal of Logistics Management, 29*(1), 308–339. doi:10.1108/IJLM-06-2016-0150

Tapscott, D., & Tapscott, A. (2018). *Blockchain Revolution: How the Technology Behind Bitcoin and Other Cryptocurrencies Is Changing the World*. Penguin Random House.

Wieland, A., & Wallenburg, C. M. (2013). The influence of relational competencies on supply chain resilience: A relational view. *International Journal of Physical Distribution & Logistics Management, 43*(4), 300–320. doi:10.1108/IJPDLM-08-2012-0243

Wu, H., Li, Z., King, B., Ben Miled, Z., Wassick, J., & Tazelaar, J. (2017). A Distributed Ledger for Supply Chain Physical Distribution Visibility. *Information (Basel), 8*(4), 137. doi:10.3390/info8040137

## KEY TERMS AND DEFINITIONS

**Blockchain:** A distributed peer-to-peer network that ensures the immutability of transactions through group consensus and cryptography.

**Supply Chain Efficiency:** Optimal use of direct and indirect resources for unit output.

**Supply Chain Resiliency:** Ability to resume operations and meet customer/consumer needs post supply chain disruptions of any origin.

**Supply Chain Visibility:** Extent of information parity at supply chain network nodes.

# Chapter 17
# Disruptive Technology–Enabled Circular Economy for Improving the Sustainability of the Supply Chain:
## A Case of an Emerging Economy

**Kali Charan Rath**
*GIET University, Odisha, India*

**Kamalakanta Muduli**
 https://orcid.org/0000-0002-4245-9149
*Papua New Guinea University of Technology, Papua New Guinea*

**Rashmi Prava Das**
*CV Raman Global University, Odisha, India*

**Adimuthu Ramasamy**
*The Papua New Guinea University of Technology, Papua New Guinea*

**Aezeden Mohammed**
*UNITECH, Papua New Guinea*

## ABSTRACT

*Most industries are faced with the challenges of how the supply chain can be made sustainable with the assistance from digital technology and circular economy (CE). A survey has been carried out to review the involvement of disruptive technology (DT) and CE in certain sections of supply chain system and identify a clear path that need to be routed to best integrate sustainable practices in the industries to make supply chain more sustainable. Some of the major barrier factors identified are funding support, availability, and technological expertise or 'know how', and management and policy regulation to implement CE and DT in supply chain management (SCM) to make it more sustainable. It also showed some of the adjustments that need to be made especially in developing countries before introducing the practices of sustainable SCM. When scrutinizing the entire process of SCM and its members, it shows that a single component of SCM cannot implement CE in isolation; it requires collective effort from all members of the supply chain, which is facilitated by integration of DT.*

DOI: 10.4018/978-1-7998-9506-0.ch017

Copyright © 2022, IGI Global. Copying or distributing in print or electronic forms without written permission of IGI Global is prohibited.

## INTRODUCTION

Technological Disruption has been adopted by many industries to improve the effectiveness of their activities and supply chain activities are no exception. Traditional supply chain activities follow the linear economy(LE) model as it generally starts from material extraction and includes the flow of these materials through various processing centers and then to customers and finally to the disposal place after the useful life of the product. LE-based supply chain operations have long been criticized for their unsustainable mode of operations. These supply chain models also are less concerned regarding the quality and amount of energy consumed in the entire process and also who is responsible for the disposal of the waste product after it has reached its life expectancy (Biswal et al 2017; Muduli et al., 2017; Aich et al., 2018). The environmental and social consequences of LE-based supply chain models have faced many public outcries and experiencing pressures from governments, societies, and media houses to operate in a socio-environmental responsible manner. Many prominent researchers have worked on developing ways to make supply chain management more environmentally and financially viable(Abdel-Basset et al., 2021; Awan et al., 2021 ; de Sousa Jabbour et al., 2018). These efforts have led to the emergence of the circular economy concepts. CE involves a process that comprises of recycling waste products sustainably in a cyclic process which illustrates SCM is in a closed-loop (Biswal et al., 2019; Aurora Denial, 2021; Banaitė, 2016; De Souza, 2021; Lacy et al., 2020). In CE, the process is made in a way it changes products as a finite resource and it gives prominence to sustainable energy (conservation measures) and limits the use of harmful substances in manufacturing industries (Dong et al., 2021; Homrich et al., 2018; Urbinati et al., 2017). The application of CE has added value to waste materials by making them reusable after it has been produced and consumed (Daou et al., 2020; Kravchenko et al. 2020). CE is disruptive in a way it outclasses the current production and utilization industry models and targets to create a circular process (Rizos et al., 2016; Zaman et al, 2021)

Digital technology also known as a disruptive technology because of its approach to the manufacturing industry, significantly changes the traditional way operations of the manufacturing industry and substitutes with processes or technology that is much better in terms of socio-environmental performance (Oyekola et al., 2021). Over the last decade, the application of new disruptive technologies has been the game-changer in changing Industries from what they used to be. Manufacturers are focusing on great improvement in the way in which their manufacturing industry functions with the introduction of industry 4.0 (Rajput & Singh, 2019). The inclusion of these technologies into manufacturing operations will require a lot of capital expenditure. There are also several other barriers that Industry 4.0 has to overcome for it to function more smoothly.

Because of an absence of examination into and perception of a solitary performer in a change, this investigation expects to clarify the job of the operation manager who uses modern development to engage the Circular Economy. Moreover, this paper intends to understand how digital technology-enabled CE practices would help develop an effective SSC model and the challenges experienced during the transition process. Thorough knowledge of the relationship between digital technology and circular economy (CE) and its impact on supply chain management could help decision-makers in effective integration of these concepts and establishment of a robust sustainable supply chain(SSC) model powered with CE principles.

*Disruptive Technology-Enabled Circular Economy*

## Problem Statement

The population is continuously increasing and the whole world is heading towards a problem where resource or raw materials is becoming more and more scarce. The whole world is also becoming more polluted by the waste products from linear supply chains. Resources including time and money are invested into finding an option to reuse waste products that have a duel impact on the environment (Barve and Muduli, 2011; De los Rios et al., 2017; Gaol et al., 2021). A technological innovation that reduces pollution, prohibits further destruction of the natural environment, and promotes reuse of resources is highly essential and luckily one such concept CE has been evolved. However, the adoption of CE practices involves significant initial investment, the development of skilled manpower, and coordination among various stakeholders. Hence, many see the application of the internet, data collection and sharing technologies, computing technologies may facilitate CE practices and ensure that products are manufactured and transported cost-effectively from finite resources. Further, many industries are trying to differentiate themselves from their competitors by portraying their socio-environmental image and are busy exploring how their SCM can be made more sustainable by using the practices of CE(Ghisellini et al., 2016; Morseletto, 2020). In this regard it is essential to investigate how can digital technology be used to promote CE-enabled SSCM practices.

## BACKGROUND

Raw resources entering the value chain are changed into an item and are hence scattered and used until they are at last disposed of. This linear delivery chain has saved economies buzzing, but a brand new, more profitable deliver chain version, the round supply chain, is gaining traction. The roundabout store network is a business idea that advances item makers and vendors to repurpose deserted materials. The old "take, make and discard" worldview is a monetary impasse that is costing firms cash as they manage rising crude material expenses and eccentrics. Materials are recuperated and recovered toward the finish of an item's life cycle. A roundabout economy expects to get the greatest out of an industry's items, strength, and waste. The roundabout economy relates the market interest of production network businesses to further develop asset proficiency. To help with implementation, CE is an idea wherein everything is intended to be reused or reused consistently. It requires a re-evaluation of the game plan, creation, selling, re-using, reuse, and buyer ownership to save whatever the number of assets as could sensibly be anticipated while wiping out the most raised worth. Some of the strategies that promote CE adoption in industries are Circular product design and production, Innovative business plans, and Circular loops.

**Circular product design and production**: for materials to circle properly in specialized cycles, item plans, and cautious material choice are required. Data on a product's design, situation, or location can be retrieved and facts updated the use of various technology once it has been observed.

**Innovative business plan:** To compete in opposition to linearly synthetic and low-price objects, successful business fashions must encompass characteristics including getting admission to over ownership, design for disassembly, product persistence, and different circular functions that turn products into the new price.

**Circular loops** allow opposite logistics, which includes amassing, sorting, and warehousing, to operate. There have to be enabling variables for CE on collaborative systems to offer beneficial system instances within the enterprise. New financial structures that value externalities are additionally needed, just as a more comprehensive abundance estimation metric.

According to Korhonen et al., (2018), the circular economy is can be based on the following three main beliefs which are the re-use of waste products, sustainable use of things, and rejuvenating natural processes. Some of the other countries that have started to adapt industry 4.0 for a circular economy are China, the European Union of countries, Japan, and the United States of America (Liu et al., 2021). These countries have committed a lot of resources into research for this new system. When implementing CE it is better to take into consideration the use of technology, problems in the supply chain, how to strategize in operation, factors involved in managing and resources, rules that are involved, and understanding its impact on people (Mangla et al., 2020).

Nations are investing resources for the move towards a circular economy. According to energy live news, a £30 million research was launched by the National Interdisciplinary Circular Economy Research (NICER) program supported by UK Research and Innovation (UKRI) in conjunction with the Department of Environment, food and rural affairs (DEFRA) which included about 34 major Universities and more than 200 industry companies that would want to partner the research (Stahel, 2016; Tukker, 2015; Zink & Geyer, 2017). This in-depth research project is targeted at delivering sustainable economic returns and assisting major manufacturing industries to reduce high consumption of natural raw materials and lean towards less raw material resources consumption or to recycle or reuse products instead of disposing them to the environment. It is estimated that the UK alone consumes more than one billion tons of raw materials every year contributing to major environmental pollution issues. Since developed countries have resources it is very easy for them to use their available resources and invest in circular investment initiatives and become a leader in this area.

The Chinese government has changed to the circular economy concept(CEC) and manufacturers have adopted CEC in production, (Valvanidis,2018). Zheng, Ardolino, Bacchetti & Perona, (2020), presented a few studies, (Choi and Choi, 2018), on the implementation of smart factory concept for Korean SME and the challenges in adopting new changes for moving forward, (Zeng et al,2019) explored the current state of industry 4.0 adoption by Italian manufacturers. Deloitte has investigated Swiss Manufacturing companies positioning themselves with the digital transformation and the opportunities Industry 4.0 provides. In some developing countries, most manufacturing companies are still working on the traditional linear economy model (Kumar, Singh, Kumar, 2021) and Industry 3.0

To allow for the efficiency of production and supply of goods and services coupled with the advent of industrialization supply chain management has become more complicated (Meherishi et al., 2019; Taeihagh et al. 2021). The involvement of technology such as computers has brought about substantial change to how information is stored and processed to make supply chain management more effective. Industry 4.0 has the potential to significantly change the method of competition amongst competitors (Daú et al., 2019; De los Rios & Charnley, 2017). By applying industry 4.0 companies can improve quality, substantial reduction in unit cost, increase the rate of production and subsequently increase revenue and profit of industries.

The circular economy supports a sustainable supply chain through the following points:

1. Recycle materials in a way that has a positive impact on the environment.
2. To enhance quit-of-life useful resource control, get rid of waste, complexity, and toxicity from the merchandise.
3. Preserve raw substances in use so long as viable and inside the great feasible situation.

*Disruptive Technology-Enabled Circular Economy*

4. Client contribution and new plans of action are being driven by the expanding necessity for end-of-life materials on the board.
5. By breaking down finish-of-life customer conduct and teaming up with industry accomplices, there is potential to deliberately support waste material reusing rates.
6. By scanning the horizon for ideas, technology, and partners, leverage cooperation to directly eliminate circular economy hurdles.

## Methodology Adopted

This application of I4.0 technologies in the circular economy is based on a review of literature that enabled the analysis of the concepts discussed in this research. The slogan 'Application of Industry 4.0 techniques to creating a more promising Circular Economy in the manufacturing industry' forms the basis of this study and focuses on countless literature to identify relationships, issues and challenges, and other areas of concerns related to the subject. The literature search that has yielded much fruition include, industry 4.0, linear economy, circular economy, and manufacturing industry with great emphasis on i) how I4.0 techniques can help create a vibrant circular economic sector supported by recent studies in this area, ii) identify the factors limiting the implementation of I4.0 in the circular economy and propose ways to alleviate these limiting factors; ii) Broaden our understanding of the concept of circular economy and I4.0 by investigating through literature review; iv) identify areas for further research.

*Figure 1. Theoretical model for I4.0 and circular economy*

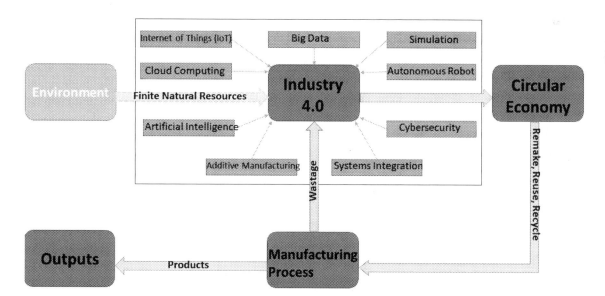

The theoretical model in figure 1 explains the relationship that exists in I4.0 technology and circular economy in the manufacturing process and how the output in the form of wastes of that process are re-used with the integration of I4.0 technologies to remake products for consumption focusing on recycling as a way forward. The data were reviewed to develop a comprehensive argument and its relevance and applicability based on the content and context(Muduli et al., 2016; Swain, et al., 2021).

## APPLICATION OF DISRUPTIVE TECHNOLOGIES

The evolution of digital technology has contributed a lot to improve the way how industries operate but the purpose of this work is to investigate how DT has an impact on CE practices in SCM in terms of planning of SCM, manufacturing these raw materials into goods, distributing the goods in bulk to retailers, retailers selling it to consumers.

### Disruptive Technologies For CE

A study carried out by Bag and others also indicated that there is a positive relationship between Digital technology and the Circular Economy. It has revealed that organizations are faced with some important resource challenges and this includes resources such as production systems, project management, the latest digital technology, the adaption of sustainable solutions. It is revealed that important resources have a significant relationship with sustainable production and circular economy (Patil et al., 2021)

According to studies carried out by the Department of Management Studies, Indian Institute of Technology at New Delhi India on 'Challenges to Impediment Circular Economy' after analyzing data through ISM hierarchical model they have inferred that process digitalization and semantic interoperability are the prominent barriers that were derived. They further concluded that to make sharing technology and manufacturing data to be error-free industry experts should pay close attention to these identified barriers. They furthermore concluded that disruptive technology in Industry 4.0 can assist manufacturing industry experts to record and see the movement of raw materials and also observe how machines in manufacturing industries optimized to desired finish product (Ishaq et al., 2021; Rizos et al., 2017)

### Supply Chain Management

The supply chain came into existence a very long time ago, if you can think back in ancient days when the first product or service was made available for not for self-consumption and supplied to the consumer that was the dawn of the supply chain. According to research done by Chan et al. (2021) on about 320 companies, it illustrated that no direct relationship between DT and SSCM. CE activities and SSCM seem to clarify the process as a third variable between DT and SSCM activities (Watanabe et al., 2019). They have also identified that CE activities have responsiveness to SSCM and DT also plays a role in it.

According to a survey and study were done by various researchers, it has been shown that inadequate information on the management of data, not enough knowledge on how to collaborate effectively with customers concerning the sustainable economy and digital technology. The studies have shown that there is a limited amount of technical know-how in terms of data management, there is no proper understanding of sustainable supply chain between suppliers, very expensive investment cost has affected major industries and organizations.

*Disruptive Technology-Enabled Circular Economy*

## Sourcing and Procurement

The way of scouting and assessing suppliers before contracting them to provide goods and services in an organization or company is referred to as sourcing. Buying goods and services is referred to as procurement. Some companies most often do both sourcing and procurement.

Proper assessment has to be conducted in terms of the quality of the material, determining the effectiveness of a service and its financial implication to a business. In-depth research on suitable suppliers, what is offered in the current markets, and evaluate if it suits the business requirement. Most of the time businesses select suppliers based on past reputation or sometimes they go for public tender so that they award work to the best supplier for the job on a competitive tendering process.

CE plays an important role in the gathering of raw materials with assistance from Digital technology. According to Gartner's website, CE targets to separate the increasing need for raw materials into about three principals to ensure extracted materials are recyclable;

1. Eliminate excess, complex and dangerous products for reuse
2. Sustain quality and life of raw materials
3. Any materials put back into the environment should benefit the environment and not harm it.

CE can find a new method of generating raw materials which will be through recycling waste products. There are three types of processes in extracting waste products

1. Primary Recycling – is when an item is recycled to convert the subject item into the same type of product. For instance when the paper is recycled to produce paper.
2. Secondary Recycling – is when an item is recycled to produce another item at the same time. For instance, cardboard boxes are broken by and processed into egg dozen boxes
3. Tertiary Recycling – When an item is recycled and converted by chemically changing it into a different item.

By employing circular economic methods raw materials extraction has been made more environmentally friendly.

A great example of CE and DT at work is in precision agriculture where technology such as variable rate technology (VRT), GPS Soil Sampling, computer-based applications, and remote sensing technology are used to achieve profitability, efficiency, and sustainability. This is very environmentally friendly because computerized applications allow just enough amount of chemical fertilizers and water application to specific crops. This prevents environmental destruction from spraying of excessive chemicals and is also a more economical company by saving cost and energy for irrigation purposes.

## Manufacturing Process

A vast amount of application of digital technology is used in the manufacturing industry nowadays. Below are some of the technologies that are used and their functions;

**Cyber-Physical Systems** – is a digital technology that links functions of physical assets and its mathematical technology. It primarily coordinates its external functions and produces a digital system.

341

**Internet of things** – This is interlinked through the internet by technical devices such as sensors and machines that allow the gathering and producing of data including coordination and interaction of these objects.

**Big Data and Analytics** – it's a field that gathers an enormous amount of data, using a technical system, and digitally analyses the data. This system normally analysis data that a usually large and cannot be analyzed by normal data processing software.

**Cloud Technology** – This involves delivering all requirements of a computer over the internet without the requirement to download and install any software.

**Artificial Intelligence** – A computer system that is built or programmed to think like human beings and rationally solve problems by applying disciplines such as understanding languages, possessing knowledge, and also it is automated and has a robotic function.

**Blockchain** - it is a form of database that links layers of data into transactions that cannot be tempered including timestamps of blocks

Simulation and modeling – is a process that involves creating a digital prototype of a normal physical object and inducing it to some external factors to predict its performance in reality.

**Visualization Technology** – it is a technology that creates images such as graphs and curves of equipment raw data so that people understand it way better. The image data is produced in real-time.

A survey showed that today's supply chain is backed up by current digital technology in a carefully monitored process to improve efficiency and also to use these data captured to improve efficiency. This has provided many results which can be very helpful to experts in the manufacturing industry.

Most of the developed countries have exiting factories and manufacturing industries that are using industry 3.0 technology to carry out their business activities. It will be very challenging for a developing country to adapt to Industry 4.0 directly. According to research and survey conducted in 2019 on Industry 4.0 and circular economy, various researchers have tested a framework study across a developing country like India and they have noted that their requirement to incorporate certain amendments to the framework study to suit that of developing country before adapting the concept of Industry 4.0. Recommendations have been made to consult experts in developed countries so that they can assist developing countries especially for complex technology set up, and issues regarding sustainability. There are so many things a developing country need to adjust which include, very expensive packaging requirement for ecofriendly packing, not adequate commitment from Management, not enough connection between ecofriendly operation and current method of operations, contradictory policy with environmental and free trade requirements, not good transition arrangement to move to sustainability works, Management of company would think that the idea of CE not it is economically not viable, It is very costly to adept SSCM, luck of training and development in this field, human input in this field is not considered, it is costly to get rid of the existing practice the organizations are doing, there is not enough communication between suppliers manufacturers and consumers, it is quite complicated and costly to design to reduce consumption of energy, when sustainability method of works are not implemented properly, when workers are not properly supported by management to use industry 4.0 works, cost of in-cooperating sustainable practices are not calculated realistically and results in blow up of budget and other financial implications, not enough financial support from management for the implementation of this concept, not enough corporation from respective members of the supply chain to adept sustainability practices. No proper measurement and rewarding system for an organization's effort into sustainability practices, the Industry 4.0 practices do not get proper regulatory support from regulating organizations of developing countries, no proper working relation, and cooperation within organizations to promote sustainability.

*Disruptive Technology-Enabled Circular Economy*

There are instances where when materials are returned to the manufactures for reuse, remake or recycle it often goes missing at transit points, no proper standards for executing sustainability practices in an organization, and also it is quite difficult and complex to incorporate sustainability into existing supply chain processes.

Research has been carried out to capture real-time information on the uses of industry 4.0 technology in manufacturing industries. The study was to minimize the cost of production of high-end products more sustainably. They also did the trial on the production of small, moderate, and large data and it showed the optimal total cost for any production of goods and services. It showed that over a long period the practice of using DT and CE can contribute to the sustainability of SSCM which will be at a minimal cost and at the same time it will be more environmentally friendly. Due to worldwide awareness for environmentally friendly and clean energy consumption, industries that practice such will have a good social standing and attract more customers for their products.

Data on the item plan, component, and condition is necessary to keep up with the value of an item in the economy as much as possible. With this information, an end-of-life object can be repurposed as a valuable asset. The addition of information with waste tells the transition to a circular economy. Actual advances center around the crucial properties of materials, energy, regular powers, and their connection, though computerized advances depend on PC sciences, hardware, and correspondence. Information may now travel with a product thanks to numerous digital technologies. We can distinguish an item and examine information all through its lifecycle utilizing these advancements. Innovative technology has sped up the creation and execution of roundabout plans of action, empowering the decoupling of asset utilization from monetary development across ventures and on a worldwide scale by driving new cycles, new correspondence channels, and new functional effectiveness.

## Distribution

Recently suppliers are trying their best to adapt ways they can be more sustainable in the way products are manufactured and shipped. Many industries have identified wastage of materials when packing items and this has become a constant challenge to these industries. It is noted that suppliers use an excessive amount of materials when they are transporting items. Extra materials such as packaging timbers, wrappers, boxes, and other cushioning materials have detrimentally affected the environment.

When consumers of imported goods or receivers of bulk orders do not carefully dispose of packaging items in an environmentally friendly manner it will fill up dumpsites and further add to existing waste management issues. When shipping containers are not packed properly, unnecessary waste materials take up space and as a result, a few items will take up a lot of space and it will be uneconomical as more containers will be needed. As a result, energy spent and fuel burnt on moving these containers back and forth will contribute to environmental pollution.

Furthermore, most of the time packaging items are not stacked using products that can be reused or are environmentally friendly such as biodegradable items.

One of the companies Nestle has proposed to create an "Institute of Packaging Science". This is to ensure that suitable tests are carried out on packaging materials to ensure that these materials are either can be used as compost when disposed of or can be reused or made from materials that have biodegradable properties. Once this is practiced internationally on the very product, contributes to a substantial reduction in environmental pollution and helps improve efficiency in the global supply chain.

According to research articles published between the years 2016 to 2021, it stated that industries that associate with innovative technology can bounce back faster than their competitors and can have an advantage. He wrote this when sighting how large companies reacted during the pandemic. For instance, the big ProMat show for supply chain specialists was about to be canceled due to Covid 19 pandemic but they did not do that, they stepped up the event and named it 'ProMatDX' and continued on the intended date virtually capitalizing on readily available technology.

They have also carried out a survey for about 1000 major manufacturing and supply chain companies and about 50% of them indicated that they have invested a lot in digital technology during the pandemic to overcome it and they have rapidly progressed during this time.

Reverse supply chain performance is very important in distribution, especially in sustainable supply chain management. Research has been undertaken by the Department of Mechanical engineering in Dayabagh Educational Institute in Dayabagh Agra, India. They studied the use of Industry 4.0 and Circular economy on an instantaneous model for decision for the sustainable reverse logics system. Form gatherings in the theoretical framework it is inferred that executing technological methods to achieve operational excellence, reverse logistics can also make available good guide to the effective execution of sustainable supply chain practice. As identified from reviews for operational excellence and full circularity adoption, it can be captured by doing diffusing before distribution of product, and utilizing supplier that suppliers recycle material, including proper and transparent information sharing in return of products and susceptible in the schedule of processes. A proper schedule of recycling shop has to be made to take into account overload of it.

## Retailing Practices

There is steep global awareness on environmental issues by activists have accelerating concerns on carbon emission, dumpsite waste, amount of non-biodegradable waste filling out oceans, and its negative impact on the earth and its inhabitants. Consumers have been converted and have resolved to follow ways that will contribute positively to the natural environment.

According to Michelle Lancaster, director of sustainability partnership at Microsoft, research has shown that a lot of customers are looking for products that are eco-friendly and are even willing to pay excessive sums of money for more eco-friendly products and services. Customers are even inquiring on how raw materials are gathered to see if there is any ethic or sustainable negligence involved.

Because of this behavior recently, most retailers are setting new environmentally friendly requirements and are also committing a vast amount of resources to be more sustainable. Despite foreseeable challenges such as lack of enough data, most companies nowadays are more adamant about an adept circular economy and its principles.

## Consumer

Technology has affected how service is provided to customers. For instance, one of the leading multi-conglomerate manufacturers of the food and beverage industry, Nestle, has been adapting disruptive technology such as artificial intelligence, machine learning, blockchain, and many others to promote the business as well as customer satisfaction Nestle started using disruptive technology in their industry way back in 2018.

*Disruptive Technology-Enabled Circular Economy*

Some methods used by Nestle to incorporate modern technology into the services that they provide to further improve it.

1.  Data – Driven Business – major businesses are adapting framework that makes accessibility and analysis of data on a real-time basis and that has a great impact on business growth. According to analytics insignt news, Nestle is already using this system.
2.  Boosting Consumer Engagement – Constant communication with customers has never been better wih the use of technologies like NLP, conversational AI, voice assistance, and others. For instance, Nestle has been using SAS analytics to correctly assess customer demand and future planning. They greatly assist in managing excess in stocks and errors in the supply chain system.
3.  Other techs – given the COVID 19 pandemic, major companies have been using technologies such as Augmented Reality Solutions to connect with different sectors of the supply chain effectively.

Technology is having a great impact on how to handle customer issues in a supply chain system and it is maximizing its potential.

An empirical study was carried out by Bag and another team on "Key resources for industry 4.0 adoption and its effect on sustainable" showed key resources of Industry 4.0 and also showed a greater advantage of utilizing Industry 4.0 in manufacturing. It further showed the positive contribution of sustainable manufacturing to the Circular Economy.

Modern-day agriculture can be digitally technologized into precision agriculture called Agrifac. It is a process where technology is used to provide specific treatment to crops

## SOLUTIONS AND RECOMMENDATIONS

Literature was reviewed along the direction of the supply chain to shed some light on the involvement of DT and CE on current supply chain activities and how to make it more sustainable. It was observed that major industries in developed countries have taken measures into embracing Industry 4.0 practices for efficiency and to meet future business obligatory requirements. However, most of the small industries particularly those operating in developing countries are quite hesitant to take a step into this because of financial and technological reasons and hence need to be carefully researched and studied.

Organizations have developed consciousness on sustainable practices and paying attention to address their environmental and social issues aggressively in recent years. This shift in organizational focus towards improvement of their socio-environmental performance coupled with the contribution of academicians and researchers in the field of cleaner manufacturing and operations management, green technology and energy, sustainable production and consumption, resource conservation, etc led to the emergence of CE as a sustainable business model. Supply chain activities involve many parties who are associated with either one or several activities such as raw material extraction, material cleaning, transportation, energy production, manufacturing, distributing, warehousing, retailing, waste management, etc. To implement CE effectively adequate information needs to be shared among all the stakeholders on a real-time basis. In this regard, the application of information and communication technologies(ICT) for data collection and its sharing amongst all the members of the supply chain assumes it's important. In many instances, it has been observed that few members are reluctant to share vital information due to an anticipation of risks of data misuse or theft. However, the modern ICT tools also provide cyber security solutions such as blockchain technology and encourage every stakeholder of the supply chain to share accurate data on a real-time basis. IoT facilitates the collection of data from machines, or humans performing various supply chain activities through sensors, wearables, or other things connected to the internet and transfer these data to the cloud, where the data is analyzed and customized information is shared with the appropriate member of the supply chain. This facilitates efficient machine, energy, manpower, material, and other vital resource utilization leading to reduced waste generation. The effectiveness of activities like recycling, re-use, remanufacturing also could be improved through the use of ICT tools as the efficiency of these activities depends on the accuracy and timing of data sharing. Employment of ICT tools in inventory management can also lead to improved stock keeping and tracking practices which eventually could lead to enhanced reuse and recyclable opportunities. It has been also made possible to have an improved supplier relationship and better understanding with suppliers to secure sustainable raw materials through the extensive use of intelligent technologies.

Though a high involvement of Digital technology and Circular economy practices is observed in supply chains of a few big conglomerates doing business in developed countries yet the same is not observed among supply chains operating in developing countries. Further, the small-scale industries operating in these developing are less concerned about CE and digital technology adoption. Studies reported many success stories of small business houses enhancing their business practices through the adoption of disruptive technologies in very little time and indicate the existence of a similar opportunity for the non-adopters. Hence, research in this area will help in developing sector and regional specific guidelines and framework for successful integration of DT and CE with SCM of various industrial sectors operating in various countries.

## Implications

PNG is like other developing countries is incapacitated by the lack of support infrastructure necessary for implementing the technological pillars of I4.0 and demonstrates the nation's inability to achieve circular economy outcomes. Even though PNG may show technological incompetence in areas of implementation of I4.0, yet continuous improvement and change in global trends of business systems and processes will demand its compliance and implementation. The benefits of integration of DT with CE and its impact on the sustainability of supply chains discussed in this study will encourage the decision-makers to formulate suitable strategies for this integration. The governments of these countries also could identify the necessary infrastructure that needs to be developed to support the industrial transformation process in their country and enhance their socio-environmental performance. The study also could be helpful for governments of developing countries, in formulating regulations and policies aimed at managing the smooth implementation of industry 4.0 enabled operational practices in manufacturing, service, and allied industries. The impact of this DT enabled CE practice adoption could not only improve the socio-environmental performance of industries but also could extend the existence of extractive minerals, increase labor engagement in the manufacturing sector, and boost economic prudence in terms of long-term growths and sustainability of the operations and supply chain practices. This work could also be helpful for academicians and researchers by providing the fundamental knowledge regarding CE and the possibility of implementing CE in a better way through the application of DT. This also explores the role of DT-enabled CE practices in improving the Sustainability of supply chain practices, which could serve as a building theory in the area of Sustainable supply chain and CE.

## CONCLUSION

This research employed an extensive review of the literature to explore how CE practices help in improving the sustainable performance of traditional supply chains. The research also revealed how the CE-based SSCM practices could deliver more socio-environmentally friendly products and processes through the integration of digital technologies. CE is the need of the century as it promotes, reduced use of virgin materials by facilitating recycling, reuse, remanufacturing, recovery practices. Hence, it could be argued that CE practices when integrated with supply chain practices will enhance their sustainability performance. At every stage of the supply chain, CE tries to explore the opportunities of recycling, reduced resource usage, material recovery, and reuse and thus enhances not only their socio-environmental performance but also their economic performance either through cost-saving or increased brand image. Supply chain sustainability is extremely important for the future of industries and businesses as a whole. Major businesses around the world are investing a lot of resources into sustainability measures to pursue a reduction in excessive carbon and waste discharged into the environment. These measures include environmentally packaging to reduce unwanted materials, reduce consumption of energy, optimizing logistic links to minimize carbon production while making sure any leftover goods that are returned can be sold again or remade or recycled.

From this study, it can be inferred that circular economy and disruptive technology can contribute a lot to ensure that the supply chain is more sustainable. This study highlighted several industrial activities which could be integrated with ICT tools to help the industries transform their LE-based supply chains to CE-based ones smoothly. The revelations of this study could be helpful for industries struggling for improving the sustainable performance of their supply chains. The governments and policymakers also could formulate suitable policies to promote the CE practices and develop necessary ICT infrastructure. It has been also observed that there is a huge shortage of skilled manpower to operate these technologies. Further, existing employees also demonstrate strong resistance to any changes in the traditional operational practices. Hence, industries interested in this kind of transformation should focus not only on educating and training their employees to be aware of the benefits of DT enabled CE-based SSCM but also jointly work with governments to set up skill development and training centers to generate a skilled workforce.

## FUTURE RESEARCH DIRECTIONS

The study tries to identify how DT-enabled CE could help improve the Sustainability of Supply Chains. It is based on a review of literature, which is one of the limitations of the study. Further, the potential factors influencing DT-enabled CE implementation in operational practices have been ignored in this work which is another limitation. In future work, a combination of literature review and expert opinion could be used to explore how DT enabled CE influences SSCM along with the factors those influence this integration positively or negatively. This study neither validates the claims either through any case study or statistical data analysis technique. In future studies responses from experts working in these areas could be collected using a questionnaire-based survey and the impact of digital technology enablement on CE and SSCM could be tested empirically. Further, AHP could be used to quantify the degree of impact of these factors on the sustainability of supply chains, which will help decision-makers to have a better understanding of the integration of DT enabled CE with their traditional SCM and formulate appropriate strategies to harness better results(Muduli and Barve, 2015). Fuzzy logic-based multi-criteria decision making approaches such as Fuzzy AHP or Fuzzy Graph theory and matrix approach could be employed to evaluate the effectiveness of digital technology-enabled CE-based Sustainable supply chains and their performance could be further compared with those of the traditional supply chains in fuzzy environment.

## REFERENCES

Abdel-Basset, M., Chang, V., & Nabeeh, N. A. (2021). An intelligent framework using disruptive technologies for COVID-19 analysis. *Technological Forecasting and Social Change*, *163*, 120431. doi:10.1016/j.techfore.2020.120431 PMID:33162617

Aich, S., Muduli, K., Onik, M. M. H., & Kim, H. C. (2018). A novel approach to identify the best practices of quality management in SMES based on critical success factors using interpretive structural modeling (ISM). *IACSIT International Journal of Engineering and Technology*, *7*(3), 130–133. doi:10.14419/ijet.v7i3.29.18540

Aurora Denial, O. D. (2021). Keeping Disruptive Technologies in Perspective. *Optometric Education*, *46*(2), 2020.

Awan, U., Sroufe, R., & Shahbaz, M. (2021). Industry 4.0 and the circular economy: A literature review and recommendations for future research. *Business Strategy and the Environment*, *30*(4), 2038–2060. doi:10.1002/bse.2731

Banaitė, D. (2016). Towards circular economy: Analysis of indicators in the context of sustainable development. *Social Transformation in Contemporary Society*, *4*(9), 142–150.

Barve, A., & Muduli, K. (2011, September). Challenges to environmental management practices in Indian mining industries. *International Conference on Innovation, Management and Service IPEDR*, *14*, 297-301.

Biswal, J. N., Muduli, K., & Satapathy, S. (2017). Critical analysis of drivers and barriers of sustainable supply chain management in Indian thermal sector. *International Journal of Procurement Management*, *10*(4), 411–430. doi:10.1504/IJPM.2017.085033

Biswal, J. N., Muduli, K., Satapathy, S., & Yadav, D. K. (2019). A TISM based study of SSCM enablers: An Indian coal-fired thermal power plant perspective. *International Journal of System Assurance Engineering and Management*, *10*(1), 126–141. doi:10.100713198-018-0752-7

Daou, A., Mallat, C., Chammas, G., Cerantola, N., Kayed, S., & Saliba, N. A. (2020). The Ecocanvas as a business model canvas for a circular economy. *Journal of Cleaner Production*, *258*, 120938. doi:10.1016/j.jclepro.2020.120938

Daú, G., Scavarda, A., Scavarda, L. F., & Portugal, V. J. T. (2019). The healthcare sustainable supply chain 4.0: The circular economy transition conceptual framework with the corporate social responsibility mirror. *Sustainability*, *11*(12), 3259. doi:10.3390u11123259

De los Rios, I. C., & Charnley, F. J. (2017). Skills and capabilities for a sustainable and circular economy: The changing role of design. *Journal of Cleaner Production, 160*, 109–122. doi:10.1016/j.jclepro.2016.10.130

de Sousa Jabbour, A. B. L., Jabbour, C. J. C., Godinho Filho, M., & Roubaud, D. (2018). Industry 4.0 and the circular economy: A proposed research agenda and original roadmap for sustainable operations. *Annals of Operations Research, 270*(1), 273–286. doi:10.100710479-018-2772-8

De Souza, M., Pereira, G. M., de Sousa Jabbour, A. B. L., Jabbour, C. J. C., Trento, L. R., Borchardt, M., & Zvirtes, L. (2021). A digitally enabled circular economy for mitigating food waste: Understanding innovative marketing strategies in the context of an emerging economy. *Technological Forecasting and Social Change, 173*, 121062. doi:10.1016/j.techfore.2021.121062

Dong, C., Akram, A., Andersson, D., Arnäs, P. O., & Stefansson, G. (2021). The impact of emerging and disruptive technologies on freight transportation in the digital era: Current state and future trends. *International Journal of Logistics Management, 32*(2), 386–412. doi:10.1108/IJLM-01-2020-0043

Gaol, F. L., Filimonova, N., & Acharya, C. (Eds.). (2021). *Impact of Disruptive Technologies on the Sharing Economy*. IGI Global. doi:10.4018/978-1-7998-0361-4

Ghisellini, P., Cialani, C., & Ulgiati, S. (2016). A review on circular economy: The expected transition to a balanced interplay of environmental and economic systems. *Journal of Cleaner Production, 114*, 11–32. doi:10.1016/j.jclepro.2015.09.007

Homrich, A. S., Galvao, G., Abadia, L. G., & Carvalho, M. M. (2018). The circular economy umbrella: Trends and gaps on integrating pathways. *Journal of Cleaner Production, 175*, 525–543. doi:10.1016/j.jclepro.2017.11.064

Ishaq, U. (2021). The Impact of Disruptive Technologies on Higher Education in Indonesia. *Indonesian Journal of Informatics Education, 5*(1), 22–26. doi:10.20961/ijie.v5i1.42310

Korhonen, J., Honkasalo, A., & Seppälä, J. (2018). Circular economy: The concept and its limitations. *Ecological Economics, 143*, 37–46. doi:10.1016/j.ecolecon.2017.06.041

Kravchenko, M., Pigosso, D. C., & McAloone, T. C. (2020). Circular economy enabled by additive manufacturing: Potential opportunities and key sustainability aspects. *DS 101: Proceedings of Nord-Design 2020*, 1-14. 10.35199/NORDDESIGN2020.4

Lacy, P., Long, J., & Spindler, W. (2020). Disruptive Technologies. In The Circular Economy Handbook (pp. 43-71). Palgrave Macmillan. doi:10.1057/978-1-349-95968-6_3

Liu, Z., Liu, J., & Osmani, M. (2021). Integration of Digital Economy and Circular Economy: Current Status and Future Directions. *Sustainability, 13*(13), 7217. doi:10.3390u13137217

Mangla, S. K., Kusi-Sarpong, S., Luthra, S., Bai, C., Jakhar, S. K., & Khan, S. A. (2020). Operational excellence for improving sustainable supply chain performance. *Resources, Conservation and Recycling, 162*, 105025. doi:10.1016/j.resconrec.2020.105025 PMID:32834482

Meherishi, L., Narayana, S. A., & Ranjani, K. S. (2019). Sustainable packaging for supply chain management in the circular economy: A review. *Journal of Cleaner Production, 237*, 117582. doi:10.1016/j.jclepro.2019.07.057

Morseletto, P. (2020). Targets for a circular economy. *Resources, Conservation and Recycling, 153*, 104553. doi:10.1016/j.resconrec.2019.104553

Muduli, K., & Barve, A. (2013). Developing a framework for study of GSCM criteria in Indian mining industries. *APCBEE Procedia, 5*, 22–26. doi:10.1016/j.apcbee.2013.05.005

Muduli, K., & Barve, A. (2015). Analysis of Critical Activities for GSCM Implementation in Mining Supply Chains in India Using Fuzzy Analytical Hierarchy Process. *International Journal of Business Excellence, 8*(6), 767–797. doi:10.1504/IJBEX.2015.072309

Muduli, K., Barve, A., Tripathy, S., & Biswal, J. N. (2016). Green practices adopted by the mining supply chains in India: A case study. *International Journal of Environment and Sustainable Development, 15*(2), 159–182. doi:10.1504/IJESD.2016.076365

Muduli, K., Biswal, J. N., Satapathy, S., Barve, A., & Tripathy, S. (2017). Investigation of influential factors of green supply chain management in Indian mining industries: An empirical study. *International Journal of Business Excellence, 12*(3), 351–375. doi:10.1504/IJBEX.2017.084453

Oyekola, P., Swain, S., Muduli, K., & Ramasamy, A. (2021). *IoT in Combating Covid 19 Pandemics: Lessons for Developing Countries, Blockchain Technology in Medicine and Healthcare.* Concepts, Methodologies, Tools, and Applications.

Patil, M. H., Tanguy, G., Floch-Fouéré, C. L., Jeantet, R., & Murphy, E. G. (2021). Energy usage in the manufacture of dairy powders: Advances in conventional processing and disruptive technologies. *Drying Technology, 39*(11), 1–19. doi:10.1080/07373937.2021.1903489

Rajput, S., & Singh, S. P. (2019). Connecting circular economy and industry 4.0. *International Journal of Information Management, 49*, 98–113. doi:10.1016/j.ijinfomgt.2019.03.002

Rizos, V., Behrens, A., Van der Gaast, W., Hofman, E., Ioannou, A., Kafyeke, T., Flamos, A., Rinaldi, R., Papadelis, S., Hirschnitz-Garbers, M., & Topi, C. (2016). Implementation of circular economy business models by small and medium-sized enterprises (SMEs): Barriers and enablers. *Sustainability, 8*(11), 1212. doi:10.3390u8111212

Rizos, V., Tuokko, K., & Behrens, A. (2017). *The Circular Economy: A review of definitions, processes and impacts.* CEPS Papers, (12440).

Stahel, W. R. (2016). The circular economy. *NATNews, 531*(7595), 435. PMID:27008952

Swain, S., Peter, O., Adimuthu, R., & Muduli, K. (2021). Blockchain Technology for Limiting the Impact of Pandemic: Challenges and Prospects. In Computational Modeling and Data Analysis in COVID-19 Research (pp. 165-186). CRC Press.

Taeihagh, A., Ramesh, M., & Howlett, M. (2021). Assessing the regulatory challenges of emerging disruptive technologies. *Regulation & Governance, 15*(4), 1009–1019. doi:10.1111/rego.12392

Tukker, A. (2015). Product services for a resource-efficient and circular economy–a review. *Journal of Cleaner Production*, *97*, 76–91. doi:10.1016/j.jclepro.2013.11.049

Urbinati, A., Chiaroni, D., & Chiesa, V. (2017). Towards a new taxonomy of circular economy business models. *Journal of Cleaner Production*, *168*, 487–498. doi:10.1016/j.jclepro.2017.09.047

Watanabe, C., Naveed, N., & Neittaanmäki, P. (2019). Digitalized bioeconomy: Planned obsolescence-driven circular economy enabled by Co-Evolutionary coupling. *Technology in Society*, *56*, 8–30. doi:10.1016/j.techsoc.2018.09.002

Zaman, G., Radu, A. C., Răpan, I., & Berghea, F. (2021). New wave of disruptive technologies in the healthcare system. *Economic Computation and Economic Cybernetics Studies and Research*, *55*(1).

Zink, T., & Geyer, R. (2017). Circular economy rebound. *Journal of Industrial Ecology*, *21*(3), 593–602. doi:10.1111/jiec.12545

## KEY TERMS AND DEFINITIONS

**AI (Artificial Intelligence):** A computer system that is built or programmed to think like human beings and rationally solve problems by applying disciplines such as understanding languages, possessing knowledge, and also it is automated and has a robotic function.

**BDA (Big Data Analytics):** It is a field that gathers an enormous amount of data, using a technical system connected to the internet, digitally analyses the data, and reports insights.

**CC (Cloud Computing):** Cloud technology is an online system that provides for storing data and programs for all applications.

**CE (Circular Economy):** The circular economy is a method that seeks to restore and regenerate manufacturing through the elimination of toxic matters that pose a threat to the environment and wastes, inadvertently encouraging the reuse and recycling of materials.

**CPS (Cyber-Physical System):** It is a collection of transformative technologies that aims at the integration of computation and physical assets.

**IoT (Internet of Things):** The internet of things is an information network of physical objects like sensors, mobile phones, machines, cars, that enable communication with others and human beings to allow interaction and cooperation to work out a solution.

**SCM (Supply Chain Management):** Various parties associated with the flow and transformation of material, money, and information among them to fulfill the requirement of any customer for goods or services.

**SSCM (Sustainable Supply Chain Management):** Supply chains that operate in a socio-environmentally friendly manner.

# Chapter 18
# Supply Chain Building Blocks and Post-COVID-19 Recovery Measures With Artificial Intelligence

**Priyadarsini Patnaik**
*Birla Global University, Odisha, India*

## ABSTRACT

*Supply chain reach is vast and touches every aspect of business. As profitability of any business is directly impacted by its inventory, so any basic changes in operations would impact its performance. However, established supply chain paradigms are no longer valid as they are shaken up by VUCA economy, demographic change, sustainability, globalization, digitization, rise of ecommerce, political turmoil, social media, buying behaviour, and most importantly, by COVID-19. This COVID-19 pandemic crisis has taken over the world and brought additional challenges at an unprecedented scale. Since identifying and structuring the problem are the first steps towards effective SCM, so redesigning the distribution strategy is the need of the hour. Companies should innovate with data and new digital technologies to increase automation in their core process to forecast predictive analysis for greater customer experience and harness the disruption. In the context of disruption, this study explored how to utilize and optimize supply chain tools and models to make decisions during times of disruption.*

## INTRODUCTION

The rapid spread of the COVID 19 pandemic has created uncertainty and disrupted the global supply chain (WHO 2020). That was a big challenge for organizations that are responsible for the safety and security of supply chain. This Covid19 pandemic has caused many countries to experience a significant economic slowdown. It was the fastest-growing global recession since 1990.The global economy has been affected by this pandemic and several countries have experienced economic recessions. The global economy has been experiencing recession since QI and II 2020. Several countries have started experiencing negative

DOI: 10.4018/978-1-7998-9506-0.ch018

growth. Distribution and warehouse operations were severely affected by the lack of space and physical distance The lock-up restrictions imposed on the SC have also put a strain on the supply chain in India (Chaudhry, 2020). Many companies in India had suspended or significantly reduced operations due to the financial situation. The impact of the decline in funding were also affected the start-up ecosystem (Singh, 2020).Almost all the major companies, including Dabur India, ITC, and Hindustan Unilever, had temporarily stopped producing due to the government's order to shut down factories(Mudgill, 2020).In response to the government's order to implement a 21-day lockdown, both Hon Hai Precision Industry and Foxconn suspended production too (Wu, 2020).During the lock-down, inter-state logistics had been banned (Parth, 2020) only the movement of essential goods were permitted. Milk and certain SCs were also allowed to function (Krishnan, 2020). Because of COVID 19, there was also an inability to move materials (finished goods and raw materials). It reduced incoming cash flows and caused workers at all skill levels to migrate, which had negative implications for businesses. Therefore, all SCs were disrupted due to the blockage of people and materials as a result, there was a need to change existing structures and relationships within the SC to address the change in business models and use of innovative technologies.

Due to the pandemic, a supplier could not supply the product and the workforce could not work due to government regulations. Also, because of the closure of certain seaports and airports, outbound and inbound logistics were also severely affected. As a result, Cash flow was also affected by these problems in supply chin industries. Due to the various factors that affected the operation, it was difficult to predict how long it would take for the company to recover. The supply chain strategy of a company dealing with a pandemic needs to be able to predict both the demand and supply of a given product. Hence, the Covid 19 pandemic requires a supply chain that is capable of mapping both the demand and supply. This strategy must be implemented in order to minimize costs and increase the number of orders.

The COVID 19 outbreak has affected various industries such as manufacturing, transportation, hospitality, logistics and supply chains. Since COVID-19 disrupted the supply chain, it has raised concerns about the efficiency of the process (Spieske and Birkel, 2021). Throughout their supply chains, most companies encounter challenges. Among the challenges they face are unpredictable customer demands, vendor disputes, and panic buying (Ivanov 2020). In every supply chain in the world, disruptions, whether human-caused or natural, play a vital role (Golan et al., 2020). Also, the increasing number of disruptions and risks posed by the changing market environment have caused businesses to step up their efforts in improving their supply chains' resilience. The increasing frequency of supply chain disruptions and risks has caused businesses to step up their efforts to improve their resilience. It has caused considerable economic losses globally (Golan et al. 2020). The challenges faced by the supply chain during the outbreak of COVID-19 have raised concerns about the resiliency of operations. This area of study aims to identify and improve the supply chain resiliency. This is done by regularly updating their processes and products (Haus-Reve et al., 2019). COVID-19 has caused many companies to re-think their supply chain resilience. Since, the country has been in a state of panic due to the outbreak of the COVID 19 virus, many of the precautionary measures taken by the authorities have affected the SCM industry in India. Hence, this study identified the critical barriers for SCs and figured out how to overcome them. This study aims to develop AI-powered supply chain solutions that can withstand the extreme disruptions caused by COVID-19.

## BACKGROUND OF THIS STUDY

### Supply Chain Management

*Supply Chain Management (SCM) incorporates the integration of activities taking place among facilities network that acquire raw material, transform them into intermediate products and then final goods, and deliver goods to customers through a system of distribution (Lee Hau L., and Corey Billington, 1995).*

It is oversight of materials, information and finances in order to move in a process from supplier to end-user through manufacturer, wholesaler and retailer. It starts with movement of goods from the point of origin i.e. procurement of raw materials, manufacturing, storage of goods, distributing to different entities, information sharing and forecasting and ends with point of consumption and the entire process is a flow of supplies in a chain. It helps business in creating value, reducing costs and improving efficiency. World economic growth depends on global value chains and Global logistics market generates (US$ 5.2 Trillion in 2020) USD 8 trillion in 2020 and in India it is USD 260 billion with a growing rate of 14%. Indian logistics is consisting of 31% rail, 60% road, 8% water and 1% air where as India has 4th largest rail network (1,20,000kms) that carries 1.2 billion tons cargo annually, Published by imarc group on Mar 09, 2021.The worldwide third-party logistics market is predicted to increase at an annual rate of 8.5% between 2021 and 2028, totalling USD 889.01 billion in 2020. The rapid rise of global e-commerce industry, and the technological development, are projected to substantially contribute to the growth of supply chain industries in Asia and the Middle East.

## ARTIFICIAL INTELLIGENCE & SCM

The contribution of information technology in supply chain management (SCM) has been and will continue to be crucial (Ross, 2016). Supply chain management is experiencing a paradigm shift as a result of artificial intelligence (AI), one of the most recent IT advancements. Through autotomized coordination while in a facility or when being transferred between multiple supply chain entities, it introduces a new level to supply chain communications. SCM can now be handled more efficiently because of these new capabilities. Furthermore, AI will let supply chain operations be managed remotely, better coordination will be available with partners, and can assist in more accurate decision making (M Ben et al.2017). Human agents and digital assets communicate continuously and autonomously as part of a digital supply chain (BVL, 2017b). For digital transformation in the supply chain, implementing AI approaches to both analyse data and automate decision-making, as well as to improve the entirety of the supply chain, is seen as extremely beneficial (BVL, 2017a). The two foremost advantages of AI adoption in supply chain make better operational efficiencies and minimized the costs of supply chain. As per survey conducted by McKinsey, it is noted that supply chain savings are the outcome of better spends analytics and better network optimization (Global AI survey by McKinsey,2019)

## How AI Techniques are Applied in SCM

### ANN (Analogous Neural Networks)

The most prevalent and influential AI approach for SCM is Analogous neural networks, an information-processing technique that identifies patterns, knowledge, and models in a large amount of data (Aleksendrić and Carlone, 2015). Mathematical regression correlates inputs and outputs in ANNs. These models rely heavily on experimental data (Yang and Chen, 2015). The impressive versatility of ANNs is often used in computational intelligence (Kasabov, 2019). The use of ANNs is on the rise in business fields, according to Li (1994). The main reason for this is that they can handle complex problems with unknown algorithms (Chen et al., 2008).

### ABS (Agent-Based Systems) & MAS (Multi-Agent Systems)

ABSs and MASs are also often used in SCM studies. Agent-based models consider the general influences induced by autonomous agents, either individually or collectively, on the system, as well as the interactions between them. A problem-solving agent is an entity that perceives its environment and takes proactive action to resolve it. SCM agents are widely used to solve a variety of problems by interacting in order to achieve a common objective (Lesser, 1995).

### GA (Genetic Algorithm)

SCM literature also includes GAs as an AI technique that mimics natural selection (Kraft et al., 1997) in which an algorithm correctly solves the problem. GAs, or evolutionary algorithms, were introduced in the 1970s. Combinatorial problem solving is addressed by GAs as an AI technique. Problems in the supply chain encompass complex managerial issues related to sourcing and manufacturing for delivering goods or services. The role of GAs is managing decision-making processes (Min, 2015). Because of the wide range of applications, many SCM studies are now using GAs.

### CBR (Case-Based Reasoning)

CBR is able to solve new problems by retrieving and adapting solutions to previous problems (Leake, 2001). In SCM studies, CBR has been used for designing supply chains under uncertainties of demand (Kwon et al., 2007)

### SVM (Support Vector Machines)

In AI-SCM, SVMs, are employed, which can extract patterns from noisy and complex data sets (Peter et al., 2019; Hongmao, 2016). It has been used since the 1990s (Gholami and Fakhari, 2017).

## RFID SOLUTION (RADIO-FREQUENCY IDENTIFICATION)

The radio-frequency identification system (RFID) is a technology that identifies, tracks, and transmits information (Lee and Lee, 2015). Retailing and logistics are two industries where RFID holds promise for solving supply chain information gaps. With RFID technology, processes can be automated and supply chains can be monitored in real time (Angeles, R. 2005). A total RFID solution allows supply chain leaders to optimize supply chains while providing end-to-end visibility: the location, content, destination, and when a package will be delivered.

## COVID 19 & SCM

(COVID-19) has caused human mortality as well as economic loss and impacted all industries such as tourism, aviation, oil, telecom, food, healthcare and more over in supply chain industries (Golan et al.2020; Haren et al. 2020; Hobbs 2020; Ivanov 2020a, 2020c; Ivanov and Dolgui 2020a; Iyengar et al. 2020; Linton et al. 2020; Remko 2020; Rowan et al. 2020 ;Chamola et al. 2020; Dolgui, et al.2020). Several countries had imposed lockdowns in an effort to reduce deaths and physical problems. Supply-side shocks were a result of work shortages and logistics disruptions (Hobbs 2020). Haren et al. (2020), had a forecast on the global supply chain's consequences in the second quarter of 2020, where he stated the epidemic had an impact on the supply chain activities also emphasized on the importance of a solid supply chain and the current need for new ways to recover supply chains. Hence, in order to meet the needs of customers, manufacturing and logistics companies must have a reliable supply chain (Singh S, et al.2020). Managing interruptions to the supply chain and recovering from them calls for efficient logistics systems (Choi 2020). The supply chain for food and healthcare during a pandemic is essential (Ivanov, 2020c). During COVID-19, there are many flaws observed in the global supply chain leading to revenue loss, unfulfilled demands, and unfulfilled supplies (Lin tonne and Vakil 2020). So, supply chains should be more robust and resilient when faced with a declining economy (Currie et al. 2020; Dolgui, et al. 2020). Consequently, it is important to examine the current challenges as well as the required steps.

### Barriers of Supply Chain Management (SCM) due to COVID-19

The barriers that the Indian Supply Chain industries faced due to the Covid-19 are identified by various experts and industrial experts. There are five key barriers that have a huge impact on the SCs in India are lack of man power, local laws, transportation, raw materials, and cash flow. Also, the restrictions on the import of finished goods and raw materials have affected the growth and profitability of the market. This has resulted in huge losses for the producers and the consumers.

## RESEARCH ISSUES

Best in class SCM means steady evolution of competencies, system and process. Yet, there are many challenges remain in supply chain management which makes the business unstable and volatile. Risks from political unrest, natural disasters, and fluctuations in commodity prices, economic uncertainty are all threats and unexpected pandemic like covid 19 have become an everlasting feature. Global supply chain operations have been affected by the Coronavirus pandemic (Ivanov and Dolgui, 2020a). Transport and logistics resources were strained to the breaking point during the crisis. Therefore, Individual disruptions are becoming more frequent and more severe. According to research, pandemics are on the rise where covid 19 negatively impact business and supply-chain operations are reduced, and losing in terms of their efficiency (Guan et al., 2020; Ivanov, 2020a). Resilience and sustainability are affected by ripple effects (or propagating disruptions), (Ivanov, 2020b). Supply chain resilience and capabilities to cope with disasters are inefficient during in case of emergency (Ivanov, D. 2021), Ninety-four percent of Fortune 1000 companies are disrupted in supply chains (Fortune, 2020) Furthermore, a complex supply chain has been added to economically and financially challenging conditions (Dontoh et al., 2021), World International Trade could be adversely affected by the pandemic (Chowdhury, P.,et.al 2021) . However, companies are now trying to minimize these risks with the help of automation, data science and artificial intelligence. Going digital, continuous investment in infrastructure, data science for innovation, adoption of AI, value added technologies and analytics capabilities of SCM can make each stage of the value chain better predicting demand to manage inventory, cost optimization, getting more data on customer behaviour to increase revenue and profits. So, the study discussed about how major problem solver AI can be deployed and integrated in large scale to correlate the data to make predictions, for a better strategic decisions and how supply chain can be managed during a time of disruption through predictive AI.

The current research looked into the best AI applications for supply chain operations. This discovery sparked the idea of building on the prior findings by doing a literature search focused on this approach/ task combination. As a result, the purpose of this article was to find answers to the following question:

- What are the current possible applications for AI methods in supply chain execution that are being researched?
- How to utilize and optimize supply chain tools and models and how companies analyse large amount of data to make decisions during times of disruption.

This article seeks to give an understanding of which domains of integrated supply chain management research are the most popular, as well as which applications scenarios are presently available. This knowledge may then be utilised as a starting point for additional study, such as identifying more interesting use cases. Also focused on application of analytics to manage SCM effectively during disruption and proposed a model for efficient and effective supply chain design using predictive artificial intelligence in combination with big data. This model will help all supply networks to understand the constraints in supply chain and how to overcome those for better decision making.

## RESEARCH METHODOLOGY

This study performed with the help of getting qualitative data through interviewing various industries such as manufacturing, supply chain & logistics, export and import, e-commerce and transportations. Professionals from these industries were interviewed and it was demonstrated that the mechanisms to achieve supply chain resilience are not well understood. This study has chosen these research questions as an essential element of this research. In view of the above, further performed data collection and analysis to address the research objective.

- How supply chain resilience worth and mean to your industry and how can you maintain and quantify it?
- Do your investments align with the risk exposure?

During this survey, a questionnaire was designed to record the respondents' response. The questions asked were

- Respondent's designation
- Respondents qualification and work experience
- Types of industries he or she belongs to and the size of the organization
- Who are your target markets?
- Is COVID19 affecting your business in any way?
- What kind of issues your organization have faced during COVID 19?
- How does your organization plan to respond to the impacts of the COVID-19 outbreak?
- How you can allocate your investment across different supply chain resilience levers?

The above questions were asked during interview and the responses were recorded. Further respondents were requested to record their response by rating a scale of 1 to 5. The following section (figure 1 – figure 5) represents the various response by the respondents and were presented in a graphical chart.

Educational Qualification of the Respondents were categorized into four segments. However, 27% of respondents were graduates, 43% were post graduates, 9% were having a PhD degree and 21% were having other professional courses. From these analysis, it can be noted that most of the respondents were highly qualified.

*Supply Chain Building Blocks and Post-COVID-19 Recovery*

*Figure 1. Educational qualification*

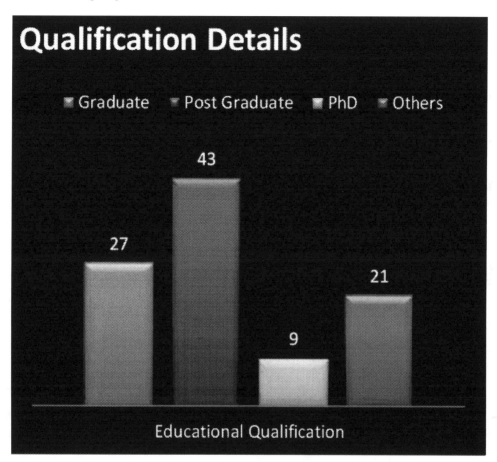

Work experience of respondents are shown in this figure. It can be noted, respondents are experts in their domain with an experience 5-20+ years. Out of these respondents, maximum numbers of executives or entrepreneurs have 11 to 15 years of experience, whereas the lowest numbers of working experience are 5 to 10 years.

*Figure 2. Respondent's work experience*

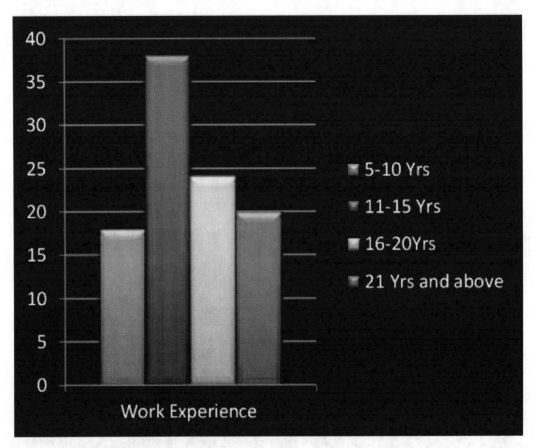

This study covered different types of industries to analyse the post COVID effect and found major affected industries were MSME, manufacturing, ecommerce, logistics, transportation and hospitality industries.

*Figure 3. Types of industries*

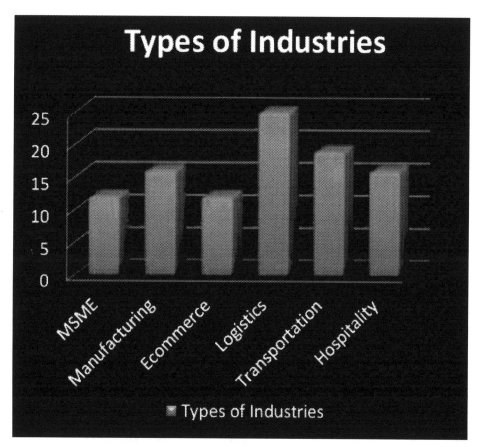

According to this graph (figure 4), it is apparent that companies had different types of problems during COVID 19. Issues related to supply, demand, logistics, etc. Financial, biological, and operational issues. Operational issues are the issues caused for inefficient planning, forecasting and poor management. All industries have financial problems as their major constraint. The policymakers are therefore advised to defer non-critical projects for minimizing the effects of financial risks and easing stakeholder financial burdens. It is important to put greater emphasis on other strategies to provide low-interest loans as a means of obtaining working capital.

*Figure 4. Issues encountered by companies during COVID-19*

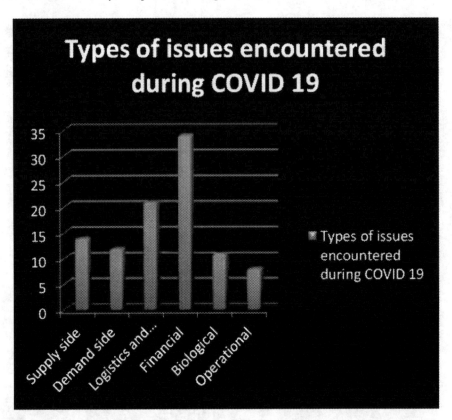

As part of the study, it was evidential that the supply chain was disrupted by labor shortages in the affected areas, which led to the source warehouse's inability to function. However, survey results indicated that a backup facility was somehow able to fulfil (manage) demand during interruptions at an assigned facility where the warehouse integration was implemented.

*Figure 5. Supply chain and labor shortage correlation*

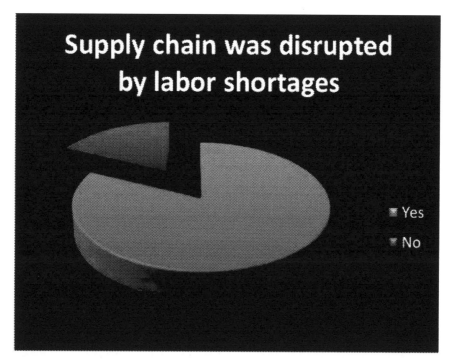

## PROPOSED FRAMEWORK

*Figure 6.*

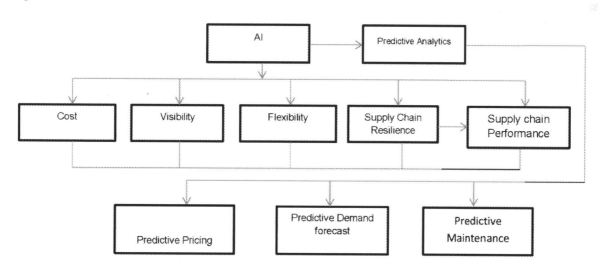

Based on the valued feedback of the respondents, this study identified four focus points as the priority of those companies, i.e.

- Cost
- Visibility
- Flexibility
- Resilience
- Supply chain Performance
- Predictive Analytics (Predictive pricing, predictive demand forecast, predictive maintenance)

This study has proposed a model by considering four constructs such as cost, visibility, flexibility and resilience. Also, RFID is a part of AI which can automate and monitor supply chain system which further might help in improved performance and sustainability.

## Cost

Supply chain costs represent costs that contribute significantly to the total sales price of a product or service. Hence, supply chain cost implies identifying all direct, indirect, and other associated costs, (ThroughPut Inc. in the Palo Alto Research Centre, PARC, 2020) Costs associated with investment, transportation, procurement, production, inventory, and quality are supply chain costs. Hence, the impact of cutting costs in one single area effect on the rest of the value chain since for continued business a balance between customer satisfaction and costs is essential. In conjunction with the surge in product down the Supply Chain, there is a surge in information coming from both sides. Supply Chains need smooth information flow and the corporate entities need to share their knowledge with one another in order to function effectively. Planning for a pandemic requires assessing potentially hazard-causing factors and planning alternative ways to respond. Hence, developing a proper contingency plan today can help to position for growth and control costs in the process.

According to this study, more than half of the businesses surveyed experienced higher revenues loss incurred during COVID 19. However, few reported cost savings from the adoption of advanced technologies. Costs are reduced even more rapidly when it comes to supply chains. A more cost-effective supply chain is possible with artificial intelligence. For instance, OrION (On-Road Integrated Optimization and Navigation) is a tool to provide real-time information about drivers, vehicles, and customers, as well as transport routes and directions. As a result, cost can be saved by reducing fuel consumption and vehicle wear and tear. It is currently in use by shipping giant UPS (Holland, C.et al.2017).

## Visibility

Almost all executives surveyed were of the opinion that better visibility throughout their pipeline would improve their supply chain development as it maintains a clear view of the inventory with order processing communications.

Also, there has generally been an underestimation of visibility, and visibility and sharing of information are sometimes used interchangeably (Swaminathan and Tayur, 2003). A supply chain that is more effective is one that shares information and is visible (Mohr and Sohi, 1995) Visibility is one of the possible outcomes of information sharing. Accordingly, supply chain visibility can be defined as a measure of access to or the sharing of information by various actors within a supply chain that they consider key to their business operations and that they think will benefit their respective companies(Closs. et al., 1997).This means that visibility varies depending on the amount of useful information that is ex-

*Supply Chain Building Blocks and Post-COVID-19 Recovery*

changed among various parties, (Whipple et al., 2002) When it comes to information sharing, the most important factors are accuracy, trustworthiness, timeliness, usefulness, and the ease with which it can be accessed (Bailey and Pearson, 1983) supply chain visibility is determined by these factors .Hence, a supply chain's visibility linkage can be distinguished by its high level of visibility providing useful information (Gustin et al., 1995)

## Prioritize Digital Tools for Greater Visibility

End-to-end visibility is key to improving supply chain operations. Organizations have been able to create an abundance of unstructured data over the past decade thanks to ERP, transportation management, and warehouse management systems. As a result, they can gain insights, improve visibility, and predict the future of their supply chains. They can use this data to inform several facets that are necessary for the recovery process and to facilitate transparency, such as estimating available inventory, assessing realistic demand from final customers, assuring logistics and distribution capacity, and optimizing working capital and cash flow.

## Flexibility

Flexible resources and processes refer to the creation of universal workstations that can be customized to meet specific needs. As with universal materials, the supply chain (SC) recovery flexibility can also be considered when using universal materials. A combination of efficiency and resilience can also be achieved with additive manufacturing technologies. By using additive manufacturing, backup contingency suppliers can be reduced. With increased manufacturing flexibility, it is possible to diversify risks with systems' decentralized control principles. It can be seen how new research directions are emerging for SC design resilience as a result of the adoption of digitalization (Ivanov et al. 2019a). Specifically, blockchain-based technologies can assist in the identifying, communicating, and propagating disruptions, to analyse the impacts of stabilization actions, (emergency planner), and to analyse how ripple effects will affect long-term performance. Adding layers to the SC can reduce its complexity and thereby reduce disruption propagation.

## Supply Chain Resilience (SCRes)

Resilience is a situational capability acquired through continuous learning and adaptation in response to repeated disruption (Belhadi et al. 2020a, b). Pandemics and crises have increased the importance of supply chain resilience (SCRes) (Belhadi, A. et al. 2021). Supply chain resilience (SCRes) can be enhanced with predictive analytics (Choi et al. 2018). Emerging technology artificial intelligence (AI), can improve supply chain risk analytics (Ivanov et al., 2019) and it has enhanced supply chain performance with cutting-edge analytics (Grover et al., 2020) where AI can be used to ensure reliable decision-making capabilities (Akter et al. 2020). Research has found that process innovation is more advantageous than AI-driven innovation because it can speed up identification (Kwak et al. 2018; Paschen et al. 2020). Hence, SCRes are increasingly considering AI for improving SCPs (Wamba and Akter 2019)

The outbreak of COVID-19 in the year 2020 has exposed the vulnerability of supply chains (Govindan et al. 2020), despite supply chains already being under extreme strain (Lechler et al. 2019). A single disruption requires resilience, but systemic threats and pandemics disrupt a whole system of multiple supply chains within short periods (Golan et al. 2020). Lockdowns and pandemics lead to logistical disruptions and labour shortages, which eventually lead to supply-side shocks in supply chains. As a result, the food supply chain faces an unexpected surge in demand among consumers (Choi 2020). According to the literature, artificial intelligence is a groundbreaking analytics tool for supply chain performance improvisation (Grover et al., 2020).

Companies should focus on how the supply chain can cope with instantaneous disruptions (Jain et al. 2017). As a result of the COVID-19 outbreak, new concepts such as adaptive resilience have emerged, which suggest that supply chains that are complex and intertwined cannot achieve equilibrium. Resilient supply chains are less vulnerable to disruptions (Ponomarov and Holcomb 2009) however Dubey et al. (2020) pointed out, supply chains resilience is still in its infancy and technology advances and changing supply chains require updating.

## How AI Helped SCM Resilience

AI techniques could help improve supply chain performance through their ability to adapt and provide information processing capabilities (Belhadi et al. 2021a). Researchers in supply chain management are exploring the potential of AI applications to identify, predict, and respond to risk (Baryannis et al. 2019b). In order to build resilience, Katsaliaki et al. suggested that the various components of a resilient system should be integrated to create opportunities for long-term collaboration and minimize risk (Katsaliaki et al. 2021) The studies conducted in this paper are related to the COVID-19 and provide significant suggestion of AI in response to SCR. It is hoped that these findings will help in understanding the practical implications of AI in response to SCR.

An AI-facilitated supply chain can help develop resilient networks and structures that can withstand various scenarios. Its ability to detect and act on risks helps minimize supply chain shock. Deflectible supply chains can be resilient in dynamic settings by monitoring and mitigating their risks. Companies should aim to improve the efficiency of their S&C operations by efficiently applying their resident company knowledge. This process can help improve the quality of their information (Wong et al. 2020). As AI-powered technology continues to gain widespread acceptance, it has been demonstrated that it can improve the efficiency of supply chain processes (Baryannis et al. 2019a; Nayal et al. 2021). In supply chain, the use of machine learning is considered one of the most effective tools (Nagar et al. 2021). It has become increasingly popular in recent years to diminish the risks and adversative effects of supply chain disruptions (Baryannis et al. 2019b). It allows to manage all resources and tasks effortlessly while organizing thousands of tasks. The multi-level supply chain's real-time disruptions are examined using Bayesian networks to assess risk behavior (Ojha et al. 2018). Companies could use it to verify existing supply chain maps, also, can create new basic supply chain maps to enrich supplier information.

In India, the adoption of AI in supply chain management is still in its infancy. There is a lack of clear positive correlation between the environment and AI, but various factors have a positive influence on supply chain management. Although artificial intelligence has been widely adopted in India for various applications in supply chain management, its adoption is still in its infancy. The factors that influence the adoption of AI are identified and analyzed. The various process factors such as technological and organizational factors and information sharing strategies that influence AI adoption are essential to SCRM success.

## OPTIMIZATION ALGORITHM IN SUPPLY CHAIN

Emerging technologies have become an integral part of managing the supply chain for generating sustainable output in the era of digitalization and AI. Optimization algorithms are very effective at managing and controlling large projects. Despite the vast potential of big data in many fields, using big data analytics to solve supply chain problems is a relatively new field (Goodarzian et al., 2021b). In order to address inventory control and location integration problems,a modified particle swarm optimization model (MPSO) was proposed (Mousavi et al. 2017). A two-phase optimization approach was employed by Fathi et al. (2021) in an effort to develop an optimal solution for location-inventory supply chains. To address the substantial supply chain issues, two hybrid meta-heuristic algorithms were developed using big data characteristics (Goodarzian et al. 2021b). Although the use of machine learning and artificial intelligence proved to be powerful tools for predicting and mitigating uncertainty, security and data privacy remain the most challenging issues in the implementation of these technological applications in supply chains (Wichmann et al. 2020). Kara et al., (2020) suggested that IoT is a powerful tool as it allows tracking and determining vital metrics throughout the supply chain management. Further, it can be recommended that companies can implement a contactless payment system at the retail store level to ensure the safety of their customers (Mollenkopf et al. 2020). Also, for digitalization and supply chain restructuring, ease the flow of capital can be proposed (Deaton and Deaton 2020).

## Supply Chain Performance (SCP)

The performance of a supply chain is determined by how effective and resilient it is in responding to environmental change (Chowdhury et al., 2019). The supply chain is measured according to how well it meets customer expectations for availability of products and timely delivery, cost minimization (Tarafdar and Qrunfeh 2017). According to Khan et al. (2009), SCP refers to a combination of resource (efciency), output (effectiveness), and flexibility (agility). Operational efficiency increases customer value through reduced resource consumption, while effective, efficient, and agile operations reduce costs, delays, and quality concerns. SCP has been evaluated by different measures in previous studies, such as quality costs and customer needs (Chowdhury et al., 2019), lead times, quality, stock-out probability, and failure rates are among these (Rodrigues and Carpinetti, 2017).

## Artificial Intelligence and Supply Chain Performance

Artificial intelligence improves supply chains, quality of the product and customer satisfaction (Grover et al. 2020). By implementing AI, supply chains can develop the ability to process information (Srinivasan and Swink 2018). AI driven SCI have great potential to drive supply chain logistics and transportation function performance (Klump 2018) Furthermore, Dubey et al. (2020) proposed AI could improve financial models, even though this wasn't clear as to how it would be executed. Grover et al. (2020) demonstrate how decoding, interpreting, and learning from diverse sources can mitigate uncertainty surrounding demand, capacities, and supply. Adaptive supply chains would allow firms to store less inventory or design fast and responsive supply chains (Dubey et al. 2020). Hence, from the above literature it is evidential that AI adoption will improve the supply chain performance.

## Supply Chain Resilience (SCR) and Supply Chain Performance (SCP)

Building SCRes has proven to be a very effective method of alleviating contingencies or maintaining SCPs (Yu et al. 2019; Chowdhury et al. 2019). However, resilient supply chain always maintains high performance by exhibiting agility, responsiveness and visibility (Scholten et al. 2019) SCP is impacted by resilient strategies and this raises the issue of how it can remain intact during a crisis. Furthermore, they proposed the development of SCRes using an integrated framework and analyzed its benefits for SCP. Organisations that failed to create SCRes had to completely or partially cease operations (Altay et al. 2018). Hence, it can be stated that SCP is positively impacted by SCRes (Belhadi, A. et al.2021)

## POST-COVID MEASURES WITH AI

Supply chains face considerable challenges as a result of the COVID-accelerated So, supply chain managers must think carefully about stocking for multiple distribution points. Supply chain management is made easier with the help of AI, which automates many repetitive and heavy lifting tasks. With the use of artificial intelligence, supply chain organizations can ensure their efficient supply chains while still remaining cost-effective, (Lee and Lee, 2015).

### Predictive Analytics

Artificial Intelligence-based predictive analytics combines historic data with data from multiple sources, including data that the company already owns. Various user segments are scored based on these data sets or algorithms. Based on historical data, it applies the theory of probability and comes up with data-driven predictions that hint at what is likely to happen in the future. The use of Predictive Analytics allows logistics and supply chains to identify trends, patterns, and metrics with historical data and make predictions based on that data.

### Predictive Pricing

In predictive pricing, k-nearest neighbours algorithm is used in predictive analytics. Then, a combination of data, seasonality, location, and demand can be mapped to harness real-time insights and adjust prices automatically.

### Predictive Demand Forecast

Using historical data, demand forecasting predicts the future trends of sales. This allows for informed decisions to be made about everything from warehousing needs to inventory planning to marketing efforts. It is essential for making data-driven decisions. In addition to helping predict demand for products, it helps gauge successful after-sales service. It is an effective method that increases visibility throughout the supply chain to forecast accurate demand.

Artificial Intelligence-based predictive analytics reduce overstocking by using support vector machines, and neural networks, thereby increasing the uptime of the supply chain, reducing risks, and improving customer service.

*Supply Chain Building Blocks and Post-COVID-19 Recovery*

## Predictive Maintenance

In the case of predictive maintenance, an event can be detected before it occurs. Predictive analytics powered by IoT embedded devices and sensors significantly increases situational awareness and prevents emergency situations. Smart sensors and the internet of things can predict failure of parts long before it occurs, proactively alerting executives or repair centers so they can prevent it from occurring. By using Predictive Maintenance systems, supply chain organizations can avoid excess inventory and costs, minimize disruptions of operations, and improve part refill rates.

## SUGGESTIONS AND RECOMMENDATIONS

This study suggested supply chain managers to automate tasks and prewiring integrations, by using cloud-based inventory management, which can increase warehouse efficiency. They can streamline operations and workflows to make a paper-less and efficient warehouse. They can opt for embedding billing processes into SC operations. Also can normalize and aggregate data to provide actionable insights and smart decisions in real time. Moreover, they can enhance the transportation process by modernizing it and by delivering real-time data with complete visibility 24 hours a day, 7 days a week. Warehouses can be challenging to connect to WiFi at the same time, it can handle higher traffic volume. This improved technology can enable to track goods across the globe in real time, which in turn can enhance productivity and speed also can boost inventory transparency.

Taking the findings of this study into account, it has important implications for practitioners. As a result of the pandemic, the study highlights the risks that SCs face and provides strategies organisations can adapt to reduce those risks. In order to build strategic partnerships with key stakeholders, by using technology effectively and strengthening IT capabilities.With real-time information flow, SC processes can be made transparent and more visible (Pigni, Piccoli, and Watson, 2016). These advanced technologies will not only boost productivity, but also enhance the SC's resilience. In order to maintain supply chain effectiveness, supply chain leaders need to consider for landscapes of the future. There were no strong disaster recovery plans in place prior to the pandemic, so the response was reactive in many ways. This led us to see the over dependencies, workflows that required immediate change, and opportunities for accelerating innovation. As supply chains become more efficient and responsive, increased human dependency can be reduced and market disruptions can be better mitigated as they are better equipped to adapt to the changes today and in the future.

As supply chain never stands still, SC managers should focus on cost, visibility, flexibility and resilience for any unprecedented challenges specifically post covid 19 recovery. Moreover, finding the right balance between inventory stock out and overstock is crucial for companies. They should better understand consumer demand and correlate it with product velocity and stock control to make an ideal balance between inventory turnover and supply. Also, due to the complexity of the supply chain management process, effective execution of innovation projects become more challenging (Kwak et al. 2018). This is also evidenced by the increasing number of digital transformation projects (Gaudenzi and Christopher 2016). So, every business' supply chain must be efficient and constantly updated to stay competitive.

## FUTURE RESEARCH DIRECTIONS

The purpose of this study was to analyse COVID 19 scenarios by emphasising critical supply chain and logistics system operations. Data collected from several informants led to a great deal of data collection for key variables, as did observations and document analysis. Studying certain mechanisms in relation to distinctive visibility was the primary purpose of this study, however, this study relied on analytic generalization and evaluated variables in relation to each other. Post COVID 19 impact on different industries and other critical commodities like food grains, ingredients, medication, and other critical commodities can be studied in future. Also, a complete supply chain model may be created in future research by including numerous elements and obstacles. As a potential future opportunity, statistics techniques may provide a rigor-based approach which can determine factors such as the food supply chain, manufacturing of critical products, and healthcare equipment shortages.

## CONCLUSION

Since supply chain is the life-line of the business, it requires a lot of resources to operate effectively. However, only efficient supply chain will succeed by considering an effective supply chain management. So, to fully understand its main functions and the contributions each is capable of making, it is necessary to understand all of its components as a whole. During post covid era, using AI in business data analytics and integrating AI in business growth will make the business more efficient. Accomplishing this leads to identify complications and impact the needed improvements.

There are several reasons why supply chains can be interrupted, including natural disasters, illness, and politics. As a consequence of this, nearly all industry and logistical activities were halted during the pandemic. An action plan has been presented in this article to address pandemic-related interruptions in the supply chain system. Supply chains play a crucial role in global trade. Supply Chains need to understand their major functions and how each function contributes to the overall efficiency of the supply chain. Identifying obstacles and affecting essential improvements becomes easier with this approach. For clarity reasons, each expression throughout the article is defined in the context in which it is used. The elements that should be evaluated when constructing an efficiency measurement are identified, as well as the critical factors that must be taken into account.

COVID 19 has profoundly affected the efficiency of the supply chain. The industry was transformed at the same time the demand for critical products, raw materials, and components soared. A complex supply chain is now finding new ways to identify, package, and deliver shipments more quickly while reducing costs and improving performance. Meanwhile, the variety and volume of data sources has grown rapidly. As a result of the Internet of Things, AI, telematics, autonomous vehicles, and machine-to-machine communications, there is an unprecedented amount of data being generated. Hence, logistics professionals have been helped by emerging analytics and AI tools that help them understand and manage the flood of data. When the logistics industry is flooded with data, the challenge is finding the needle in a haystack. The speed at which modern businesses need to find anomalies and critical connections cannot be met without better analytics and ways to separate critical data from background noise. However, while modern supply chains show many examples of AI being applied efficiently, the implications go well beyond company borders.

## REFERENCES

Akter, S., Michael, K., Uddin, M. R., McCarthy, G., & Rahman, M. (2022). Transforming business using digital innovations: The application of AI, blockchain, cloud and data analytics. *Annals of Operations Research*, *308*(1-2), 7–39. doi:10.100710479-020-03620-w

Altay, N., Gunasekaran, A., Dubey, R., & Childe, S. J. (2018). Agility and resilience as antecedents of supply chain performance under moderating effects of organizational culture within the humanitarian setting: A dynamic capability view. *Production Planning and Control*, *29*(14), 1158–1174. doi:10.108 0/09537287.2018.1542174

Angeles, R. (2005). RFID technologies: Supply-chain applications and implementation issues. *Information Systems Management*, *22*(1), 51–65. doi:10.1201/1078/44912.22.1.20051201/85739.7

Bailey, J. E., & Pearson, S. W. (1983). Development of a tool for measuring and analyzing computer user satisfaction. *Management Science*, *29*(5), 530–545. doi:10.1287/mnsc.29.5.530

Baryannis, G., Dani, S., & Antoniou, G. (2019). Predicting supply chain risks using machine learning: The trade-off between performance and interpretability. *Future Generation Computer Systems*, *101*, 993–1004. doi:10.1016/j.future.2019.07.059

Baryannis, G., Validi, S., Dani, S., & Antoniou, G. (2019). Supply chain risk management and artificial intelligence: State of the art and future research directions. *International Journal of Production Research*, *57*(7), 2179–2202. doi:10.1080/00207543.2018.1530476

Baryannis, G., Validi, S., Dani, S., & Antoniou, G. (2019b). Supply chain risk management and artifcial intelligence: State of the art and future research directions. *International Journal of Production Research*, *57*(7), 2179–2202. doi:10.1080/00207543.2018.1530476

Belhadi, A., Kamble, S., Jabbour, C. J. C., Gunasekaran, A., Ndubisi, N. O., & Venkatesh, M. (2021). Manufacturing and service supply chain resilience to the COVID-19 outbreak: Lessons learned from the automobile and airline industries. *Technological Forecasting and Social Change*, *163*, 120447. doi:10.1016/j.techfore.2020.120447 PMID:33518818

Belhadi, A., Kamble, S. S., Zkik, K., Cherrafi, A., & Touriki, F. E. (2020). The integrated effect of Big Data Analytics, Lean Six Sigma and Green Manufacturing on the environmental performance of manufacturing companies: The case of North Africa. *Journal of Cleaner Production*, *252*, 119903. doi:10.1016/j.jclepro.2019.119903

Belhadi, A., Mani, V., Kamble, S. S., Khan, S. A. R., & Verma, S. (2021). Artificial intelligence-driven innovation for enhancing supply chain resilience and performance under the effect of supply chain dynamism: An empirical investigation. *Annals of Operations Research*. Advance online publication. doi:10.100710479-021-03956-x PMID:33551534

Ben-Daya, M., Hassini, E., & Bahroun, Z. (2019). Internet of things and supply chain management: A literature review. *International Journal of Production Research*, *57*(15-16), 4719–4742. doi:10.1080/0 0207543.2017.1402140

BVL. (2017a). *Chancen der digitalen transformation. Trends und Strategien in Logistik and Supply Chain Management.* BVL and DVV Media. https://www.bvl.de/en/dossiers/tu

BVL. (2017b). Logistics as a science. Central research questions in the era of the fourth industrial revolution. Logist. Res., 11, 9. Doi:10.23773/2018_9

Chamola, V., Hassija, V., Gupta, V., & Guizani, M. (2020). A comprehensive review of the COVID-19 pandemic and the role of IoT, drones, AI, blockchain, and 5G in managing its impact. *IEEE Access : Practical Innovations, Open Solutions, 8,* 90225–90265. doi:10.1109/ACCESS.2020.2992341

Choi, T. M. (2020). Innovative "bring-service-near-your-home" operations under corona-virus (COVID-19/SARS-CoV-2) outbreak: Can logistics become the messiah? *Transportation Research Part E, Logistics and Transportation Review, 140,* 101961. doi:10.1016/j.tre.2020.101961 PMID:32346356

Choi, T. M. (2020). Innovative "bring-service-near-your-home" operations under corona-virus (COVID-19/SARS-CoV-2) outbreak: Can logistics become the messiah? *Transportation Research Part E, Logistics and Transportation Review, 140,* 101961. doi:10.1016/j.tre.2020.101961 PMID:32346356

Chowdhury, M. M. H., Quaddus, M., & Agarwal, R. (2019). Supply chain resilience for performance: Role of relational practices and network complexities. *Supply Chain Management, 24*(5), 659–676. doi:10.1108/SCM-09-2018-0332

Chowdhury, P., Paul, S. K., Kaisar, S., & Moktadir, M. A. (2021). COVID-19 pandemic related supply chain studies: A systematic review. *Transportation Research Part E: Logistics and Transportation Review.* doi:10.1016/j.tre.2021.102271

Closs, D. J., Goldsby, T. J., & Clinton, S. R. (1997). Information technology influences on world class logistics capability. *International Journal of Physical Distribution & Logistics Management, 27*(1), 4–17. doi:10.1108/09600039710162259

Currie, C. S., Fowler, J. W., Kotiadis, K., Monks, T., Onggo, B. S., Robertson, D. A., & Tako, A. A. (2020). How simulation modelling can help reduce the impact of COVID-19. *Journal of Simulation, 14*(2), 83–97. doi:10.1080/17477778.2020.1751570

Deaton, B. J., & Deaton, B. J. (2020). Food security and Canada's agricultural system challenged by COVID-19. *Canadian Journal of Agricultural Economics/Revue canadienne d'agroeconomie, 68*(2), 143-149.

Dolgui, A., Ivanov, D., Potryasaev, S., Sokolov, B., Ivanova, M., & Werner, F. (2020). Blockchain-oriented dynamic modelling of smart contract design and execution in the supply chain. *International Journal of Production Research, 58*(7), 2184–2199. doi:10.1080/00207543.2019.1627439

Dolgui, A., Ivanov, D., Potryasaev, S., Sokolov, B., Ivanova, M., & Werner, F. (2020). Blockchain-Oriented Dynamic Modelling of Smart Contract Design and Execution in Supply Chain. *International Journal of Production Research, 58*(7), 2184–2199. doi:10.1080/00207543.2019.1627439

Dolgui, A., Ivanov, D., Sethi, S. P., & Sokolov, B. (2019). Scheduling in production, supply chain and Industry 4.0 systems by optimal control: Fundamentals, state-of-the-art and applications. *International Journal of Production Research, 57*(2), 411–432. doi:10.1080/00207543.2018.1442948

Dolgui, A., Ivanov, D., & Sokolov, B. (2020). Reconfigurable Supply Chain: The X-Network. *International Journal of Production Research*, *58*(13), 4138–4163. doi:10.1080/00207543.2020.1774679

Dontoh, A., Elayan, F. A., Ronen, J., & Ronen, T. (2021). Unfair "Fair Value" in illiquid markets: Information spillover effects in times of crisis. *Management Science*, *67*(8), 5163–5193. doi:10.1287/mnsc.2020.3737

Dubey, R., Gunasekaran, A., Childe, S. J., Bryde, D. J., Giannakis, M., Foropon, C., Roubaud, D., & Hazen, B. T. (2020). Big data analytics and artificial intelligence pathway to operational performance under the effects of entrepreneurial orientation and environmental dynamism: A study of manufacturing organisations. *International Journal of Production Economics*, *226*, 107599. doi:10.1016/j.ijpe.2019.107599

Fathi, M., Khakifirooz, M., Diabat, A., & Chen, H. (2021). An integrated queuing-stochastic optimization hybrid Genetic Algorithm for a location-inventory supply chain network. *International Journal of Production Economics*, *237*, 108139. doi:10.1016/j.ijpe.2021.108139

Gaudenzi, B., & Christopher, M. (2016). Achieving supply chain 'Leagility' through a project management orientation. *International Journal of Logistics Research and Applications*, *19*(1), 3–18. doi:10.1080/13675567.2015.1073234

Golan, M. S., Jernegan, L. H., & Linkov, I. (2020). Trends and applications of resilience analytics in supply chain modeling: Systematic literature review in the context of the COVID-19 pandemic. *Environment Systems & Decisions*, *40*(2), 222–243. doi:10.100710669-020-09777-w PMID:32837820

Goodarzian, F., Kumar, V., & Abraham, A. (2021). Hybrid meta-heuristic algorithms for a supply chain network considering different carbon emission regulations using big data characteristics. *Soft Computing*, *25*(11), 7527–7557. doi:10.100700500-021-05711-7

Goodarzian, F., Taleizadeh, A. A., Ghasemi, P., & Abraham, A. (2021). An integrated sustainable medical supply chain network during COVID-19. *Engineering Applications of Artificial Intelligence*, *100*, 104188. doi:10.1016/j.engappai.2021.104188 PMID:33619424

Govindan, K., Mina, H., & Alavi, B. (2020). A decision support system for demand management in healthcare supply chains considering the epidemic outbreaks: A case study of coronavirus disease 2019 (COVID-19). *Transportation Research Part E, Logistics and Transportation Review*, *138*, 101967. doi:10.1016/j.tre.2020.101967 PMID:32382249

Grover, P., Kar, A. K., & Dwivedi, Y. K. (2020). Understanding artificial intelligence adoption in operations management: Insights from the review of academic literature and social media discussions. *Annals of Operations Research*, *308*(1-2), 177–213. doi:10.100710479-020-03683-9

Guan, D., Wang, D., Hallegatte, S., Davis, S. J., Huo, J., Li, S., Bai, Y., Lei, T., Xue, Q., Coffman, D. M., Cheng, D., Chen, P., Liang, X., Xu, B., Lu, X., Wang, S., Hubacek, K., & Gong, P. (2020). Global supply-chain effects of COVID-19 control measures. *Nature Human Behaviour*, *4*(6), 577–587. doi:10.103841562-020-0896-8 PMID:32493967

Gustin, C. M., Daugherty, P. J., & Stank, T. P. (1995). The effects of information availability on logistics integra. *Journal of Business Logistics*, *16*(1), 1.

Haren, P., & Simchi-Levi, D. (2020). How Coronavirus Could Impact the Global Supply Chain by MidMarch. *Harvard Business Review, 28*(February). https://hbr. org/2020/02/how-coronavirus-could-impact-the-globalsupply-chain-by-mid-march

Hassini, E. (2008). Supply chain optimization: Current practices and overview of emerging research opportunities. *INFOR, 46*(2), 93–96. doi:10.3138/infor.46.2.93

Haus-Reve, S., Fitjar, R. D., & Rodríguez-Pose, A. (2019). Does combining different types of collaboration always benefit firms? Collaboration, complementarity and product innovation in Norway. *Research Policy, 48*(6), 1476–1486. doi:10.1016/j.respol.2019.02.008

Hobbs, J. E. (2020). Food supply chains during the COVID-19 pandemic. *Canadian Journal of Agricultural Economics/Revue canadienne d'agroeconomie, 68*(2), 171-176.

Holland, C., Levis, J., Nuggehalli, R., Santilli, B., & Winters, J. (2017). UPS optimizes delivery routes. *Interfaces, 47*(1), 8–23. doi:10.1287/inte.2016.0875

Ivanov, D. (2020). 'A blessing in disguise' or 'as if it wasn't hard enough already': Reciprocal and aggravate vulnerabilities in the supply chain. *International Journal of Production Research, 58*(11), 3252–3262. doi:10.1080/00207543.2019.1634850

Ivanov, D. (2020). Predicting the impacts of epidemic outbreaks on global supply chains: A simulation-based analysis on the coronavirus outbreak (COVID-19/SARS-CoV-2) case. *Transportation Research Part E, Logistics and Transportation Review, 136*, 101922. doi:10.1016/j.tre.2020.101922 PMID:32288597

Ivanov, D. (2020). Viable supply chain model: Integrating agility, resilience and sustainability perspectives—lessons from and thinking beyond the COVID-19 pandemic. *Annals of Operations Research*. Advance online publication. doi:10.100710479-020-03640-6 PMID:32836614

Ivanov, D., & Dolgui, A. (2020). A digital supply chain twin for managing the disruption risks and resilience in the era of Industry 4.0. *Production Planning and Control*, 1–14.

Ivanov, D., & Dolgui, A. (2020). Viability of intertwined supply networks: Extending the supply chain resilience angles towards survivability. A position paper motivated by COVID-19 outbreak. *International Journal of Production Research, 58*(10), 2904–2915. doi:10.1080/00207543.2020.1750727

Ivanov, D., & Dolgui, A. (2021). OR-methods for coping with the ripple effect in supply chains during COVID-19 pandemic: Managerial insights and research implications. *International Journal of Production Economics, 232*, 107921. doi:10.1016/j.ijpe.2020.107921 PMID:32952301

Ivanov, D., & Dolgui, A. (2021). A digital supply chain twin for managing the disruption risks and resilience in the era of Industry 4.0. *Production Planning and Control, 32*(9), 775–788. doi:10.1080/0 9537287.2020.1768450

Ivanov, D., Dolgui, A., Das, A., & Sokolov, B. (2019). Digital supply chain twins: Managing the ripple effect, resilience, and disruption risks by data-driven optimization, simulation, and visibility. In *Handbook of ripple effects in the supply chain* (pp. 309–332). Springer. doi:10.1007/978-3-030-14302-2_15

Jain, V., Kumar, S., Soni, U., & Chandra, C. (2017). Supply chain resilience: Model development and empirical analysis. *International Journal of Production Research*, *55*(22), 6779–6800. doi:10.1080/00 207543.2017.1349947

Kara, M. E., Fırat, S. Ü. O., & Ghadge, A. (2020). A data mining-based framework for supply chain risk management. *Computers & Industrial Engineering*, *139*, 105570. doi:10.1016/j.cie.2018.12.017

Katsaliaki, K., Galetsi, P., & Kumar, S. (2021). Supply chain disruptions and resilience: A major review and future research agenda. *Annals of Operations Research*. Advance online publication. doi:10.100710479-020-03912-1 PMID:33437110

Khan, K. A., Bakkappa, B., Metri, B. A., & Sahay, B. S. (2009). Impact of agile supply chains' delivery practices on firms' performance: Cluster analysis and validation. *Supply Chain Management*, *14*(1), 41–48. doi:10.1108/13598540910927296

Lechler, S., Canzaniello, A., Roßmann, B., Heiko, A., & Hartmann, E. (2019). Real-time data processing in supply chain management: Revealing the uncertainty dilemma. *International Journal of Physical Distribution & Logistics Management*, *49*(10), 1003–1019. doi:10.1108/IJPDLM-12-2017-0398

Lee, H. L., & Billington, C. (1995). The evolution of supply-chain-management models and practice at Hewlett-Packard. *Interfaces*, *25*(5), 42–63. doi:10.1287/inte.25.5.42

Lee, I., & Lee, K. (2015). The Internet of Things (IoT): Applications, Investments, and Challenges for Enterprises. *Business Horizons*, *58*(4), 431–440. doi:10.1016/j.bushor.2015.03.008

Linton, T., & Vakil, B. (2020). Coronavirus is proving we need more resilient supply chains. *Harvard Business Review*.

Ma, H., Wang, Y., & Wang, K. (2018). Automatic detection of false positive RFID readings using machine learning algorithms. *Expert Systems with Applications*, *91*, 442–451. doi:10.1016/j.eswa.2017.09.021

Mohr, J. J., & Sohi, R. S. (1995). Communication flows in distribution channels: Impact on assessments of communication quality and satisfaction. *Journal of Retailing*, *71*(4), 393–415. doi:10.1016/0022-4359(95)90020-9

Mollenkopf, D. A., Ozanne, L. K., & Stolze, H. J. (2020). A transformative supply chain response to COVID-19. *Journal of Service Management*, *68*, 143–149.

Mousavi, S. M., Bahreininejad, A., Musa, S. N., & Yusof, F. (2017). A modifed particle swarm optimization for solving the integrated location and inventory control problems in a two-echelon supply chain network. *Journal of Intelligent Manufacturing*, *28*(1), 191–206. doi:10.100710845-014-0970-z

Nagar, D., Raghav, S., Bhardwaj, A., Kumar, R., Singh, P. L., & Sindhwani, R. (2021). Machine learning: Best way to sustain the supply chain in the era of industry 4.0. *Materials Today: Proceedings*, *47*, 3676–3682. doi:10.1016/j.matpr.2021.01.267

Nayal, K., Raut, R.D., Queiroz, M.M., Yadav, V.S., & Narkhede, B.E. (2021). Are artificial intelligence and machine learning suitable to tackle the COVID-19 impacts? An agriculture supply chain perspective. *The International Journal of Logistics Management*. doi:10.1108/IJLM-01-2021-0002

Ojha, R., Ghadge, A., Tiwari, M. K., & Bititci, U. S. (2018). Bayesian network modelling for supply chain risk propagation. *International Journal of Production Research, 56*(17), 5795–5819. doi:10.1080/00207543.2018.1467059

Paschen, U., Pitt, C., & Kietzmann, J. (2020). Artificial intelligence: Building blocks and an innovation typology. *Business Horizons, 63*(2), 147–155. doi:10.1016/j.bushor.2019.10.004

Pigni, F., Piccoli, G., & Watson, R. (2016). Digital data streams: Creating value from the real-time flow of big data. *California Management Review, 58*(3), 5–25. doi:10.1525/cmr.2016.58.3.5

Ponomarov, S. Y., & Holcomb, M. C. (2009). Understanding the concept of supply chain resilience. *International Journal of Logistics Management, 20*(1), 124–143. doi:10.1108/09574090910954873

Remko, V. H. (2020). Research opportunities for a more resilient post-COVID-19 supply chain–closing the gap between research findings and industry practice. *International Journal of Operations & Production Management, 40*(4), 341–355. doi:10.1108/IJOPM-03-2020-0165

Rodrigues, L.-J. F., & Carpinetti, L. C. (2017). Quantitative models for supply chain performance evaluation: A literature review. *Computers & Industrial Engineering, 113*, 333–346. doi:10.1016/j.cie.2017.09.022

Ross, D. F. (2016). *Introduction to Supply Chain Management Technologies*. St Lucie Press.

Rowan, N. J., & Laffey, J. G. (2020). Challenges and solutions for addressing critical shortage of supply chain for personal and protective equipment (PPE) arising from Coronavirus disease (COVID19) pandemic–Case study from the Republic of Ireland. *The Science of the Total Environment, 725*, 138532. doi:10.1016/j.scitotenv.2020.138532 PMID:32304970

Scholten, K., Sharkey Scott, P., & Fynes, B. (2019). Building routines for non-routine events: Supply chain resilience learning mechanisms and their antecedents. *Supply Chain Management, 24*(3), 430–442. doi:10.1108/SCM-05-2018-0186

Singh, S., Ghosh, S., Jayaram, J., & Tiwari, M. K. (2019). Enhancing supply chain resilience using ontology-based decision support system. *International Journal of Computer Integrated Manufacturing, 32*(7), 642–657. doi:10.1080/0951192X.2019.1599443

Singh, S., Mahanty, B., & Tiwari, M. K. (2019). Framework and modelling of inclusive manufacturing system. *International Journal of Computer Integrated Manufacturing, 32*(2), 105–123. doi:10.1080/0951192X.2018.1550678

Spieske, A., & Birkel, H. (2021). Improving supply chain resilience through industry 4.0: A systematic literature review under the impressions of the COVID-19 pandemic. *Computers & Industrial Engineering, 158*, 107452. doi:10.1016/j.cie.2021.107452 PMID:35313661

Srinivasan, R., & Swink, M. (2018). An investigation of visibility and fexibility as complements to supply chain analytics: An organizational information processing theory perspective. *Production and Operations Management, 27*(10), 1849–1867. doi:10.1111/poms.12746

Swaminathan, J. M., & Tayur, S. R. (2003). Models for supply chains in e-business. *Management Science, 49*(10), 1387–1406. doi:10.1287/mnsc.49.10.1387.17309

*Supply Chain Building Blocks and Post-COVID-19 Recovery*

Tarafdar, M., & Qrunfeh, S. (2017). Agile supply chain strategy and supply chain performance: Complementary roles of supply chain practices and information systems capability for agility. *International Journal of Production Research, 55*(4), 925–938. doi:10.1080/00207543.2016.1203079

Wamba, S. F., & Akter, S. (2019). Understanding supply chain analytics capabilities and agility for data-rich environments. *International Journal of Operations & Production Management, 39*(6/7/8), 887–912.

Whipple, J. M., Frankel, R., & Daugherty, P. J. (2002). Information support for alliances: Performance implications. *Journal of Business Logistics, 23*(2), 67–82. doi:10.1002/j.2158-1592.2002.tb00026.x

Wichmann, P., Brintrup, A., Baker, S., Woodall, P., & McFarlane, D. (2020). Extracting supply chain maps from news articles using deep neural networks. *International Journal of Production Research, 58*(17), 5320–5336. doi:10.1080/00207543.2020.1720925

Ye, S., Xiao, Z., & Zhu, G. (2015). Identification of supply chain disruptions with economic performance of firms using multi-category support vector machines. *International Journal of Production Research, 53*(10), 3086–3103. doi:10.1080/00207543.2014.974838

Yu, W., Jacobs, M. A., Chavez, R., & Yang, J. (2019). Dynamism, disruption orientation, and resilience in the supply chain and the impacts on financial performance: A dynamic capabilities perspective. *International Journal of Production Economics, 218*, 352–362. doi:10.1016/j.ijpe.2019.07.013

## KEY TERMS AND DEFINITIONS

**AI:** An artificial intelligence system simulates human intelligence processes, especially through computers.

**Inventory Control:** It is the process of ensuring that an organization has a sufficient amount of stock available.

**Predictive Analytics:** It enables organizations to identify optimal inventory levels to meet demand while minimising excess inventory. Supply chain managers use predictive analytics to determine detailed inventory requirements by region, location, and usage.

**RFID (Radio-Frequency Identification):** This identifies and tracks objects with electromagnetic fields.

**SCM Visibility:** Supply chain visibility (SCV) refers to the ability to track each component, sub-assembly, and final product from the supplier to the manufacturer to the consumer.

**Supplier Chain Resilience:** This concept entails so much more than just managing risks. Managing risk now means being better prepared.

**Supply Chain Management:** Supply chain management involves the movement and storage of raw materials, the processing of raw materials, and the fulfilment of orders.

**Supply Chain Performance Measurement:** It is defined as a method for measuring the effectiveness of a supply chain system.

# Chapter 19
# Supply Chain Techno–Umbrella for Supply Chain Resilience

**Jayashree Veluthakkal**
*Vignana Jyothi Institute of Management, Hyderabad, India*

**Subramani Krishnamurthi**
https://orcid.org/0000-0001-9676-2701
*Vignana Jyothi Institute of Management, Hyderabad, India*

**David W. Praveenraj**
*Bannari Amman Institute of Technology, Erode, India*

**Sagyan Sagarika Mohanty**
*Vignana Jyothi Institute of Management, Hyderabad, India*

**Franklin John Selvaraj**
*Vignana Jyothi Institute of Management, Hyderabad, India*

## ABSTRACT

*The pandemic has devastated the whole economy with losing many human lives as well. The hard-hit aspect of the pandemic was gathering the people in public and working together in any industry. It has resulted in a deviation of planning in the supply chain and its related services. Technology adoption has dramatically changed many organizations' revenue patterns with high income on technology adoption and low income on non-adoption. The timeline of technology adoption was also the biggest concern for many firms because of restrictions on the people's movement. The research has been done on technology usage in different supply chain functions and its effectiveness in business performance. The chapter contents displayed the possible outcomes of the technology and its importance of adoption. The supply chain techno-umbrella has been portrayed as a saver of the pandemic during the non-revenue time. The chapter also described the various available forms of technology in the decision-making of the supply chain processes.*

DOI: 10.4018/978-1-7998-9506-0.ch019

*Supply Chain Techno-Umbrella for Supply Chain Resilience*

## INTRODUCTION

Supply chain management is a common term used in handling raw materials to finished goods, from suppliers to customers' last-mile delivery. This content writing aims to elaborate on the supply chain scenario with technology advancement during the pandemic.

The pandemic has created havoc in businesses around the globe. Many companies have been shut down due to full and partial lockdowns for more than a year. The situation swept all kinds of business functions like public and private entities. The pandemic has impacted the whole world economy to the loss of $10.3 trillion, where any other calamities have never cost so far.

The lasting effect of the pandemic would be spilled over into a few more years and impact the global GDP, leading to financial loss. The World Bank has estimated that the overall GDP growth would be below 4.4%, lower than pre-pandemic levels. One area where the pandemic has hit particularly hard is the supply chain. The world has witnessed people staying at home; the organization has changed their functions in critical delivery or has to close down its business. Many blue-collar and service-based company employees were forced to work from home, and the unorganized sector has got a massive hit by relying on government schemes to survive.

Industries that required suppliers and distributors were not in the supply of total materials unless demanded critical. The positions have come to a stage where many suppliers and distributors closed their businesses due to the loss of their business. The suppliers also had a problem operating the business fully because of social distancing among employees. The free movement of materials has become critical with suppliers and raw materials restrictions on people-oriented organizations. The lack of supply and the continued demand due to organizations continuing to fulfill orders meant that prices have surged during the pandemic within some industries. Due to the immovable raw materials, many enterprises have had a complete collapse.

The world has witnessed that the supply chain functions as the core function in making society and economy alive during COVID time (Chen, et al., 2020). The hospitality sector has failed miserably due to continuous lockdown and non-movement of trade. In contrast, other sector businesses struggled to supply the basic needs of the mass population, including farms, retailers, third-party logistics, and health care supply chains (Ana Beatriz Lopes de Sousa Jabbour et al., 2020).

The food industry has suffered from sales estimated to be down below 80% across the sector. The industry has suffered from low-capacity operation with smaller portions of the online companies' delivery and take-aways from the food makers. The companies have been forced to restrict their operations without utilizing their total operations capacity. COVID also impacted the pharmaceutical industry by overutilizing its capacity without its omnichannel presence. The unpredictable consumer buying behaviour and demand because of various lockdowns and restrictions. Spending habits, trends, and new focuses for the industry mean that organizations across all sectors have to adopt agile practices to remain competitive and current.

The researchers were trying to address the following questions: What are the general supply chain management issues due to pandemics? What are the essential technological and computerized methodologies to solve supply chain issues? How is technology leveraging the supply chain to address its problems? The researchers also have quoted many examples along with technology usage.

## BACKGROUND

Supply Chain Management has played a significant role in delivering the products to consumers from multiple places and levels of manufacturers since the pandemic outbreak. The liberal usage of technology has been helping in achieving the expected flow of the processes in the supply chain. A generic supply chain diagram is being displayed in Figure 1.

*Figure 1. Generic supply chain model*

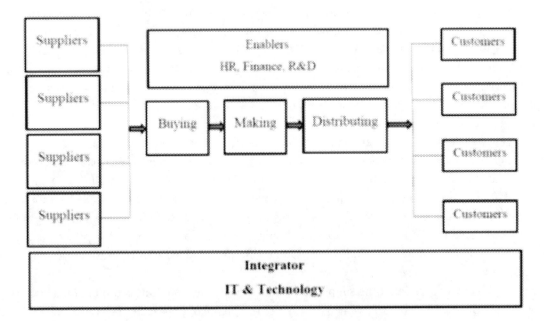

A generic supply chain is applicable in the manufacturing and service sectors. In today's scenario, the dynamic market environment, unpredictable consumer demands, consumer knowledge of products, etc., are forcing companies to adopt technology-enabled services at all levels of management functions. The scenario has become worse in a pandemic in providing the best service to the consumers. The companies have struggled in supply chain integration for better service to the consumers without proper aid the service levels. The technology-enabled companies have positioned themselves as sustained ones compared to non-adopted companies.

The supply chain must operate with the principles (Christopher and Peck, 2004; Kamalahmadi and Parast, 2016 & Ana Beatriz Lopes de Sousa Jabbour et al., 2020) viz., Supply Chain Engineering, Supply Chain Collaboration, Supply Chain Agility and Supply Chain Risk Management Culture. These principles were considered to be vital to constructing the supply chain framework.

## Principle 1

Supply Chain Engineering (SCE) integrates all of the members in the supply chain process, including the first and second-tier suppliers, production facilities, distribution channels, and consumers. Identifying

*Supply Chain Techno-Umbrella for Supply Chain Resilience*

the bottlenecks regarding materials flow, facility capacity, and production visibility was important. The technology-based tools would be appropriate for solving all bottlenecks related to delivering products and services to the customers/consumers. The supply chain map assessment could be used to assess the actual requirements during the pandemic period using technology-based risk assessment tools. The sourcing such as single, multiple, local, and global procurements had become complex during pandemic time with restrictions on trade between nations.

## Principle 2

Supply Chain Collaboration (SCC) is another breakthrough principle in establishing a smooth supply chain process. The information sharing among supply chain members plays a critical role in addressing the supply and demand problem. The technological support could deescalate the problems associated with the last-mile delivery process. Integrating channel members with focal companies using the suitable ERP would solve multiple issues in supplying materials during the pandemic.

## Principle 3

Supply Chain Agility (SCA) consists of order visibility and velocity. The order visibility ensures the flow of materials and information across supply chain members. The process's speed would depend on the ERP package, which would share the information among all members of the supply chain channel. The velocity also depends on high technology usage among all levels of the supply chain process.

## Principle 4

Supply Chain Risk Management Culture should be displayed among all channels to predict the disruption. Collection and storage of data to predict the future of requirements to avoid lack of order fulfillment. Big data analytics and blockchain will be the future tools in assessing predictions.

The supply chain theories and principles emphasize two important factors: responsiveness and efficiency for supply chain profitability. This chapter has focused on the available computerized and technological orientation toward successfully running the supply chain during the pandemic.

## MAIN FOCUS OF THE CHAPTER

## Non-Technology Success Stories

Some companies made considerable success in maintaining an effective supply chain even without any technology. The system has been followed by the companies making huge success in their business and being role models for many companies that want to invest vast amounts in technology-related infrastructure on supply chain improvement for their sustainability in the industry. The examples below would give a brief report of their success stories in running a business successfully over a long period.

## Example 1: Lijjat Papad (A Papad Manufacturer in the Northern Part of India)

Lijjat Papad has been doing good business through its flagship product, "Papad." The company operates with a high network of more than 70 branches with its decentralization policy of production and distribution without much technology. The company has been making a good profit by aggregating women willing to work with less educational backgrounds. The company is ready to move next level even it has got huge success in its existing business model.

## Example 2: Dabbawallahs

India's Mumbai is known for being a financial capital and known for "Dabbawallahs," who have the number of 5000 people and deliver four lakhs tiffin every working day. It has achieved its six sigma (3.4 defects per million opportunities) level very long back. They use a multi-level coding system to receive and deliver the food dubbas (food boxes) effectively without using any technology. The color-coding system has been helping them to deliver the food boxes error-free. They have never followed any technology-based approach to run the supply chain network.

The above examples used to be successful stories until the pandemic period. The total business model has changed from a traditional business to a technology penetrated business model. The companies have made massive growth by maintaining a proper technology-based supply chain operating model.

Urban Company (UC-India), an aggregator, has revolutionized the business model in "on-demand and home services" using the technology (app-based). The company could break the traditional business in men's grooming, beauty care, and home-related services and provide those services at customers' doorstep. The supply chain integration happened with technology, which helped the customers during the pandemic. This technology-based revolution in the supply chain management in-home services has changed the habit of customers even during an endemic period.

The technology-based application is not only restricted to a single sector; it also extends to the significant industry and much profit-making industry in the economy, food. Many tech platforms have started acting as supply chain service providers. The intermediates and service companies are engaging in technological advancement to provide quick responsiveness in the entire supply chain process to meet customer demands. This paradigm shift in supply chain management using information technology on an anticipatory business model, the responsive business model for demand forecasting, and arriving at a supply chain plan has resulted in a drastic improvement.

## ISSUES

Based on Supply Chain Analytics written by Prof. Vijayaraghavan (2021), eight key processes must be implemented across the supply chain. The following topics will be discussed in terms of the possible application of technology in the pandemic period. The following issues are essential in supply chain management with utmost care of function and effectiveness during the pandemic. The key processes would decide on supply chain profitability.

*Supply Chain Techno-Umbrella for Supply Chain Resilience*

## Customer Relationship Management

In supply chain management, customer relationship management provides procedures to maintain a relationship with customers. The availability of data in the form of history enables customers to identify customers' needs and increase the revenue of any business. In a pandemic time, the firm's business model reaching the doorstep of customers helps improve services and saves the profit of any company. For example, the App-based medical suppliers reaching customers through home supply and sample collections for any disease retained the company's revenue. Many new players were into the pharma in providing doorstep services. A modern concept has been evolved in serving the public in pandemic times and avoiding the spread of COVID. The ease of doing business, primarily in the supply chain sector, has become easy because of smartphone availability.

## Customer Service Management

The customer service management provides vital information about product flow from different supply chain channel members. Customers' access to the information about their products in order, Transportation, and receiving time makes their business more reliable. The suppliers' details are well informed to the customer in the form of supplier details on the company's website. For example, the food app companies show the supplier's (restaurant) names and delivery people's details. The company provides a lot of avenues in the app to follow the order and rate the delivery firms and employees. This facility has improved the service firm's business and made the transaction smoothly during the pandemic.

## Demand Management

The pandemic made many service businesses shut down or lose business. If the business firm had operated with its traditional way of demand forecasting, the company would have failed miserably or been swiped out of the industry. The company has to forecast the demand based on the actual requirements in the market. The unscheduled lockdowns were forcing many service companies to put a hold on their usual business. The firm's ability to understand the customer requirements in demand had become easy with its forecasting tools. For example, many app-based car service providers have operated limited car services based on the opening of the lockdown. Many countries have ensured the basics were supplied to the public using technology-enabled supply chain facilities.

## Order Fulfilment

The order fulfillment happens by satisfying the "order fill rate" for the given period. An effective order fulfillment process requires integrating the firm's manufacturing, logistics, and marketing plans in a coordinated manner. The unit cost related to delivery becomes less if the supply chain combines well in a coordinated well. The company's in-house software or software like SAP and ZOHO Inventory are helping industries to follow up the order, and automated Purchase Order (PO) generation also paves the way for effective fulfillment of an order. The manufacturing companies with limited workforce had to operate fulfilling the orders. The virtual model has made companies rely on software to run the business successfully.

## Manufacturing Flow Management

Manufacturing flow success depends on the flexible working system in the production flexibility. The manufacturing companies must alter the existing production system to produce the products based on the changes from the customers. A single mass production system without much flexibility in the product design changes has forced companies to lose business in the pandemic. The service organization with omnichannel delivery has survived the company that did not have during the COVID time. The organizations have to make the necessary changes by benefiting the customer and ensuring supply chain effectiveness. Example Indian garment sector has started making the special kits and masks massively to meet the required demand in the market, providing a proper running of a business.

## Supplier Relationship Management

Supplier relationship has become a buzzword in the business world for any business to have consistent success. The company's quality policy statement has to have the provision to maintain a good relationship with its suppliers. The selection of suitable suppliers would benefit the firm's success for a long time. Scrutinizing, the right supplier would benefit less production cost and consistent delivery of products to the consumers. The supplier relationship management has become more long-term and proactive than relative relationship.

## Product Development and Commercialization

Innovation in product development is most essential to be a successful firm in the competitive market. The on-time delivery of products with a competitive advantage would bring more profit paths for any organization. A company that follows PLC (Product Life Cycle) should have the consciousness to produce the right products and be successfully launched in a short time to remain competitive.

## Return Management

Returning materials must be costly if products are returned before or after use over time (warranty period). The company's expenses go high if more products are returned with and without usage than forwarding the finished products. The process can assist the firms in achieving sustainable competitive advantage. The reduction in products would benefit the company's revenue. It also helps firms to identify productivity improvement opportunities and breakthrough projects.

## TECHNOLOGY AND SUPPLY CHAIN PERFORMANCE

The supply chain performance gets enhanced by the presence of technology in every level of supply chain functions. The following topics provide scope for understanding the different layers of technology applications in supply chain management.

## A Framework of Elements of Supply Chain Management

*Figure 2. Framework of SCM elements*

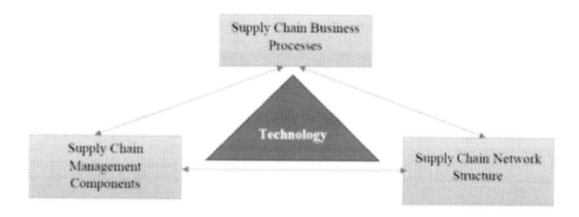

The elements of supply chain management (figure 2) describe what processes should be linked with each of these key supply chain members, what level of integration and management should be applied for each process link, and who the key supply chain is members with whom to link processes. It also defines the integration of business processes, components & network structure for the effectiveness of any firm's supply chain operations. The firm's effectiveness depends on the flow of the products at various levels of the supply chain.

It also talks about the processes linked between key supply members like primary and secondary members in the supply chain network.

The business units (Figure 3) were linked with utilities and assets to produce an expected product based on the market demand. The vertical and horizontal positions in the supply chain were interconnected with different links like active, not active links, member and non-member links. From figure 3, supply chain mapping identifies the different types of relations and their formation. The complexities in the supply chain channels of any organization through visual mapping would help solve issues related to it and take appropriate decisions.

*Figure 3. Inter-company business process links*

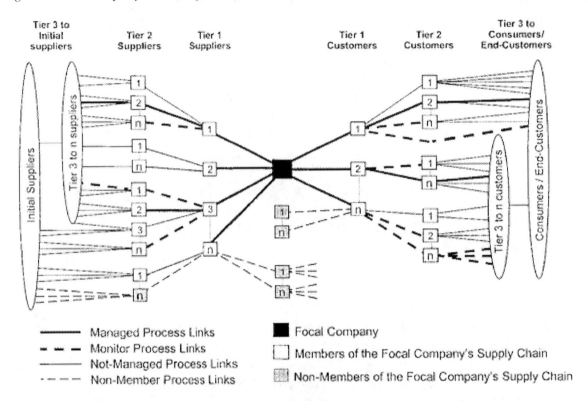

Rose, 2015 has reiterated the importance of interconnecting the physical and virtual by using upgraded available information and communication technology. The world will be witnessing shortly more Machine to Machine (M2M) connections than People to People (P2P) relationships (Evans, 2011). The researchers also have identified that the evolution of centralized data storage, uninterpreted internet connectivity, and portable machines in all level functions of the supply chain would be beneficial for running the business in pandemic and endemic situations.

The Multi-Echelon Inventory system has been maintained in the companies like Nike sharing the demand data at all levels of supply chain parameters. The bullwhip effect has become a real problem in identifying the correct quantity of demand in predicting the market, reducing the overall profitability of the supply chain. The unavailability data or misinformed data leads to the wrong forecasting of the production and distribution of plans. The massive connections of all supply chain channels would cost low and avoid unnecessary inventory in raw materials, WIP, and finished goods. The capital investment in infrastructure development for an efficient supply chain can be avoided.

The Technology capabilities would help manage an efficient supply chain management and room for innovation (Rong, 2015). The IT capabilities enable good movement and its geographic locations, sensing difficulties in goods movement (Chui et al., 2010). The extensive use of technology-based applications to manage the supply chains would benefit the efficient functions and save from threats and generic applications on day-to-day activities (Phadnis, 2015). The benefits also extended to a few more industries in reality (Ravi and Wu, 2015).

*Supply Chain Techno-Umbrella for Supply Chain Resilience*

Radio-Frequency Identification (RFID) was vital in mass transportation and multiple SKUs of any company products in the supply chain. RFID is modern in identifying the products quickly without confusion, and product history could be traced without any issues (Kiritsis et al., 2003). RFID is used as modern technology in *redefining* and electronic integration between supply chain channel members (Louis et al., 2005). RFID also provides appropriate data to complex markets to adjust production scheduling and transportation planning (Brewer et al. 1999).

The captured real-time RFID data was used to identify the unfixed manufacturing schedule and SCM to control the production execution and logistics planning (Brewer et al. 1999). RFID was used as a data collection instrument in a warehouse and was helpful in the logistics resource management system (Poon et al., 2009).

Zhong et al. (2015) described the RFID attachment with production resources that could be converted into smart manufacturing objects (SMOs). The Big Data approach could be possible from the data collected by the above source and accumulate the RFID enabled logistical data.

Tsai (2011) found two significant benefits after implementing the RFID system in the semiconductor testing company: improving efficiency, reducing human error, and eliminating manual processes, while the other was enterprise process automation.

However, the use of RFID is not without obstacles. According to Angeles (2005), one of the significant technical issues with RFID readers is the collision problem when readers read many chips in the same field. Therefore, RFID technologies should be implemented proactively, i.e., make the ROI case, choose the right RFID technology, anticipate RFID technical problems, leverage pilot project learning experiences, and manage the IT infrastructure issues of data management concerns and integration with backend applications.

## Optimization Techniques

Mathematical models were used to optimize the flow of materials during World War II. The models were replicated into a real-time business application for an optimal solution. With the revolution in technology, the problem is formed in a mathematical form. It is being solved with much software like Solver in excel used extensively in solving the problems. The visualization of problems with the use of inputs like variables, parameters, and functions. The collected data were analyzed and modified with real-time changes to understand the supply chain issues better.

The researchers found that mathematical models were more reliable than modifying real systems. The modification leads to wrong in doing the work with a trial-and-error approach. The success stories of many countries in World War II can be boasted because of only Project RAND and SCOOP (Scientific Computation of Optimum Program).

The constrained optimization models have formed with the three components: decision variables, objective functions, and constraints. The decision variables for any supply chain optimization would be the number of units (SKUs in the FMCG sector) with multiple product lines transferred in a multi-echelon stage. The minimization of the cost would be achieved with high supply chain profitability. The constraints in the SCM would be representing the physical, economic, technological, or other restrictions with numerical values.

The optimization model was fundamental to understanding any business situation. The mathematical construction model has to denote an actual position into abstraction, convert it for mathematical manipulation, and examine the reality with such construction constraints. The mathematical models would help determine the best results in the given formation constraints in supply chain problems. The basic mathematical formulation considers the limitations restricted by linearity, certainty, and continuity. The technology-based supply chain was helping in data capturing in the form of proportionality and additivity with parameters of objective function coefficients, resource levels, and input/output coefficients which were known and certain which is deterministic.

Example Solver is one of the prominent tools in solving optimization problems for both linear and nonlinear. It is also applied to many application formations and provides a solution optimally.

The facility location problem has become a big issue in transporting materials from one place to another. The materials storage at all levels of the supply chain channel has become costly due to the non-movement of materials. The organizations have lost a lot of money in protecting raw materials, WIP, and finished goods at all levels of function. The supply chain's success depends on the right quantity, place, time, and price. But reaching the "right" in supply is very tough with problems like the efficient movement of materials from suppliers end to customer end due to big halt of material in the ports/ warehouses due to goods movement restrictions in COVID time.

## Warehousing Management

Warehouses were established to store safety stock and support plant operations smoothly. The value-added processes like packaging and product assembly were also included in the warehouse function. Many companies have pushed to follow the lean supply to reduce high inventory costs and trim operating costs. The warehouse is still a core function of the supply chain. Storage would be beneficial viz., Transportation and production costs can be reduced, better coordination of supply-demand, storage can be an integral part of the production process, and storage may enhance sales. The functions of storage are generally described as holding, consolidation, breakbulk, and merge-in-transit.

The holding function is another problem in the pandemic period. The perishable products have faced many hurdles in transferring the materials. The duration time for any storage of materials always had a problem in terms of inventory cost and unavailability of space for new products receivable. Zoho Inventory system is giving many solutions for maintaining the inventory at all levels of the supply chain. It also helps in maintaining the stock in the warehouse in an efficient way.

Warehouses also work as a consolidation point to bring materials from different suppliers and act as a consolidated point. It is very economical to consolidate the small supplies from other suppliers and use a single delivery system. The opposite consolidation process happens in breaking bulk as the demand arises for customers in different regions. The linking process of each customer to wholesalers or company-owned warehouses through proper technology would reduce the distribution cost. The rate per unit of transportation becomes less when the quantity allocation breaks bulk if technology is used accordingly. Mixing of the products based on the product's requirements in different regions is considered in the warehousing function. Facility Center (FC), which is owned by many e-commerce companies worldwide, has adopted technology in regular operations. The technology has been helping in the mixing of the products and providing delivery on time.

Technology and scientific methods were used to operate the warehouse efficiently. The variety of products that are being stored and retrieved determines the cost of warehouse operations. A history of warehousing data would help improve the warehouse's productivity.

## Supply Chain Techno-Umbrella for Supply Chain Resilience

Another vital factor in warehouse management is layout configuration. Many companies have struggled in designing the ceiling height, and length & width of the storage zone. After many scientific methods analyses, the picking rate time has been reduced by inducting Automated Guided Vehicle (AGV).

*Figure 4. A computer designed warehouse layout*

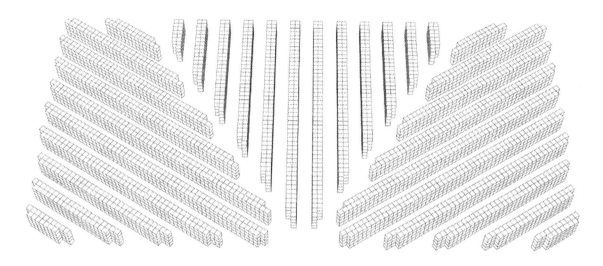

The possible high cost incurring in the supply chain is that establishing a warehouse in a supply chain network determines how much space would be needed to execute plans in the warehouse to support supply chain activities and sales growth. The warehouse management depends on the following important factors: SKU and growth, inventory turnover, cubic feet of the space, warehouse shape matters, number of dock doors, material handling automation, and warehouse layout.

The space determination and picking rate play an important role in cost determination for any warehousing establishment. It involves capital expenditures and outsourcing decisions; a scientific approach is required to anticipate growth and determine such space. The lack of knowledge in establishment leads to space constraints and escalates costs in the supply chain.

Inventory under uncertainty and service levels are the biggest concern in the supply chain flow predictability. The companies have adopted many methodologies to understand demand, like Economic Order Quantity (EOQ) and use Re-Order Point (ROP). But the flow in the supply chain affects due to uncertainty in demand. A manual calculation with technology usage makes it difficult to calculate or manage the demand situation. EOQ has restrictions in ordering with financial constraints. The Lagrangian approach solves nonlinear objective functions in inventory decisions with various desirable constraints depending on inventory cost limit, setup limit, or stockout situation limit. Many methods have been developed in tailored aggregation, and it is unclear which plan would be suitable until the supply chain is clearly stated.

## NETWORK MODELS IN TRANSPORTATION

Transportation is a crucial decision area within the logistics mix. In the total cost of logistics, transportation cost absorbs a significant portion. The decision at the company level would be a micro-managed, macro-level infrastructure in a region, the network of transportation facilities, government policies. The main cost drivers in supply chain performance are purchasing, inventory, warehousing, and transportation costs.

The supply chain management of an organization firmly depends on the design of a transportation network and its performance in responding to customer needs. It is also concerned with proper routing and scheduling decisions on which proper infrastructure planning has to be done. The low cost of responsiveness is possible only by having a well-designed transportation network in the supply chain.

For example, the construction materials industry has adopted the direct shipping model to transfer materials from manufacturers to retail stores. The pre-planned quantity, routes, and modes are decided in advance to lower the transportation cost. The direct shipping model with milk runs has been used to transfer the materials from a single supply point to multiple customers by taking the best supply route. This method of solving the routing problem is called the "Traveling Salesman Problem" using assignment models of solving. Understanding the concept of network models is essential to designing a good transport system for a supply chain and optimizing the service levels and cost. A variety of models are available in network analysis and each of them for typical applications

Two methods are used to solve the minimal spanning tree problem: Prim's algorithm and Kruskal's algorithm. Prim's algorithm starts with any node and joins it to the closest node in the given network. The data collected in the supply chain design should be predetermined in this algorithm. The model is used when the total distance of Transportation is less. In Kruskal's algorithm, the spanning tree is built by adding arcs one by one into a growing spanning tree. It follows the conditions such as sorting the graph arcs concerning their distances, adding arcs to the minimal spanning tree from the arc with the smallest distance until the arc with the largest distance, and only adding arcs that do not form a cycle, arcs that connect only disconnected components.

The real applications of the minimal spanning tree are pipeline constructions, laying highways, and cable connectivity. The overall cost of infrastructure is being optimized using the minimal spanning tree algorithm methods.

Shortest path algorithms models are used in logistical planning in many applications. The distribution of products through the network requires such applications to minimize the transportation cost. Good knowledge of these models is essential for supply chain managers to manage distribution and even monitor and evaluate the third-party logistics providers to enhance the effectiveness of the customer service management process in the supply chain. Dijkstra's algorithm helps identify the shortest paths between a given origin node to all the other nodes in a network and requires that all the arcs in the network have a non-negative value of distance or cost or time or the utility that is to be optimized.

Vehicle routing problems are finding the optimal vehicle routes to meet customers' demands at different points. The objective is to minimization of overall cost, total distance, and total traveling time. The routing demand could be with the different types such as delivery from the warehouse to customer, pick up a customer, return to the warehouse, pick up at one place, and deliver at another location. Vehicle routing problems are exciting but very complex in planning the multiple routes at a single phase. Numerous issues arise like vehicle capacity, route distance, link capacities, types of operations to solve it uniquely—more heuristic problems to be framed and solved based on the individual issues that are evolved. Vehicle routing problems are solved using integer programming formulations with branch and bound methods. The large computational scales –routing problems solving using this method are going to be tough in finding the optimal solution. For significant scale problems, the heuristics are found to be useful and give workable solutions.

## SUPPLY CHAIN ANALYTICS

The data generated through supply chain activities must be analysed to make management decisions accordingly. The data generated in the food ordering app, such as type of restaurant, optimum distance travelled by the delivery person, variety of products ordered, and frequency of orders, are considered to predict future sales. The rating at different levels also has to be considered for applying any analytical tools to determine the strategy with their competitors. Data capturing has become accessible by the available technology of the companies. But the relevant data capturing is a crucial part of mass data accumulation.

Big data analysis has become a challenging one with two significant challenges less capability of real-time data analysts and a lack of a structured process of data capture in the form of big data. The quantitative techniques were used to analyze the data for applying proper decision-making in the process. Supply chain analytics helps in all supply chain activities to make a decision.
Evolution of Analytics based on IBM theory,

*Figure 5. Evolution of Analytics*

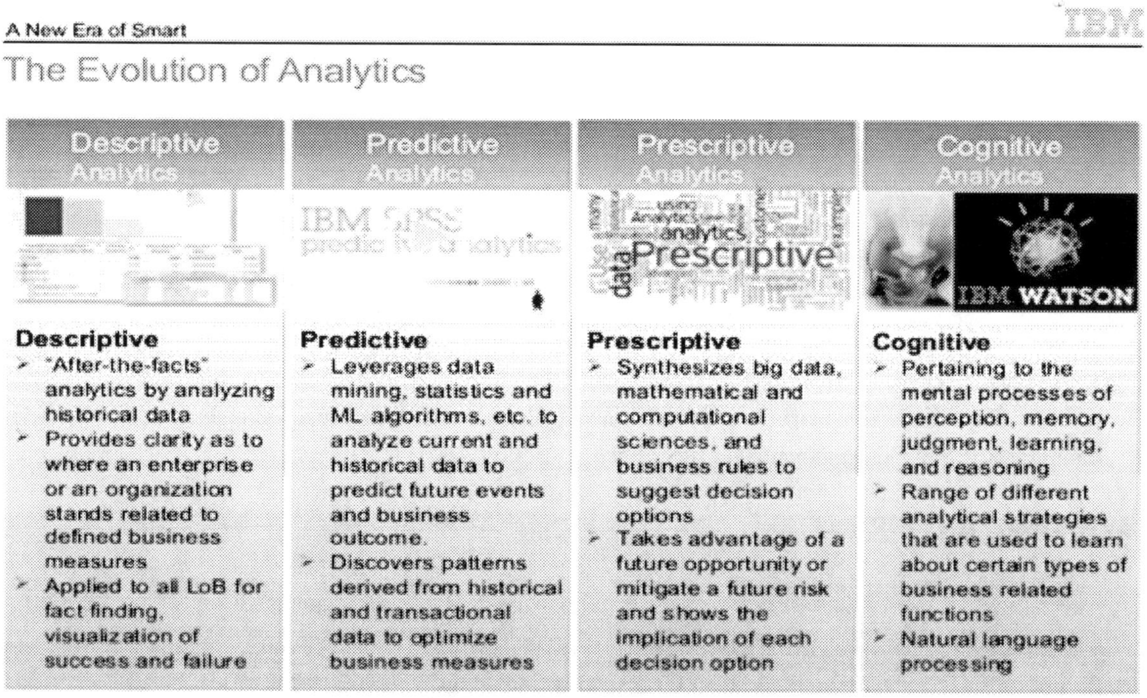

Based on Prof. Vijayaraghavan (2021) of supply chain analytics, the analytics techniques were classified as follows,

1. Descriptive Analytics
2. Predictive Analytics
3. Prescriptive Analytics
4. Cognitive Analytics

*Figure 6. Display of data variety*

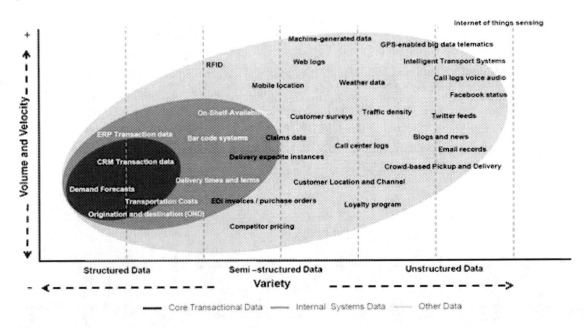

The volume and velocity of data in the supply chain management cycle have been captured, and the information types vary like unstructured data, semi-structured data, and structured data. The semi-structured data deals with the email records, blogs, and Twitter feeds, usual pickup, and delivery. The semi-structured data talks about ERP transaction data, Bar code systems, and delivery terms. The structured data describes the CRM transaction data, demand forecasts, Organization, and Destination (OND). These data are again crunched with the use of different analytics types. The output of data helps the organization to plan and execute the supply chain operations effectively.

**Descriptive Analytics**

General data were taken on day-to-day activities about the goods movement from one place to another without much difficulty—the change in the delivery schedule, replenishment, and changes in transportation modes. It is also about the historical data's visualization and interpretation from multiple channels of supply chain management. Descriptive analytics generally focuses on diagnostics analysis of existing data given in the format. It helps, in general, to identify the problems and improve the supply chain performance.

Example: Data on multi-echelon inventory and replenishment of orders in the supply chain.

## Predictive Analytics

In the planning phase to forecast the capacity planning in the supply chain channel, the historical data of supply chain management would be analysed for future trend analysis. The predictive analysis provides the patterns and predictions based on the sales history and point of sales data. Most FMCG companies in the Indian market have developed their software system to know day-to-day data based on territory. The predictive analysis works based on known sales values over a particular period.

## Prescriptive Analytics

It derives solutions by combining descriptive and predictive analytics and mathematical optimization models. It provides a solution with direction. It helps organizations to solve problems and make the path to making maximum business value. It is an enabler for many researchers and practitioners in supply chain analytics. E-commerce companies are taking the database of consumers and analyzing the purchasing behaviour to do mass customization of the products. It also helps in designing the delivery pattern and facility planning.

## Cognitive Analytics

Cognitive analysis tries to create a prototype model of the human brain to predict purchasing behaviour. Based on the pattern, the data are compared and interpreted for better decision-making. NLP is the right example for the human brain-behaviour analysis in terms of product preference. This analysis helps the firms to decide on the delivery of products for more variety of product lines.

## Mobility Industry

Mobility in terms of relocations worldwide for short, long-term work, or permanent settlement, many global companies are playing in the field. The companies give general services like home-to-home delivery, quality packing and unpacking, Sea/Air/Road transport, customs clearance, shipment protection, and secured storage. They are also into the services like settling-in & orientation, home search, school search, temporary accommodation, language and cultural training, and departure services. The above services are possible only by collecting the information using appropriate technological tools at various levels.

Each stage of its service mainly depends on the mass information about the service details, and that information can be collated by using only proper technology or software. The mobility company's business only depends on providing valuable information on time. The company's success stories could be portrayed only by having the appropriate information about the movement of goods and its related services. If an Asian is relocating to European countries for job or business purposes, local community support must be created, and packing and unpacking must be done on time. The delaying of service could cost more for the consumer.

## COVID – Vaccine Drive

Even though the vaccine supply chain was affected due to the unavailability of expected infrastructure in many countries, the technology used, such as mobile apps in the nations around the globe, could complete the reasonable vaccination drive. The vaccination data helped in the planning of logistical services for easily reachable and not easily reachable places. Major affected countries are achieving in rolling out the vaccine drive successfully without many problems in the supply chain.

## SUPPLY CHAIN TECHNO UMBRELLA

*Figure 7. Tour- ordering process*

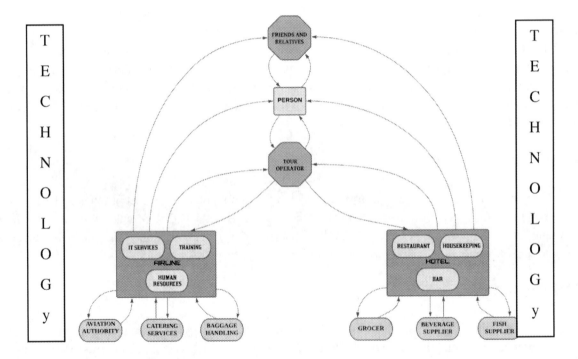

The authors have taken one sample application of technology in the supply chain service process. The tour operation would be a suitable example of solving the supply chain issues in the pure service sector. The exchange of information happens from booking a holiday trip in a web app or mobile app and consulting the family members through different modes of technology. The time saving for each process is done with the help of technology in the given example.

*Supply Chain Techno-Umbrella for Supply Chain Resilience*

*Figure 8. Service page*

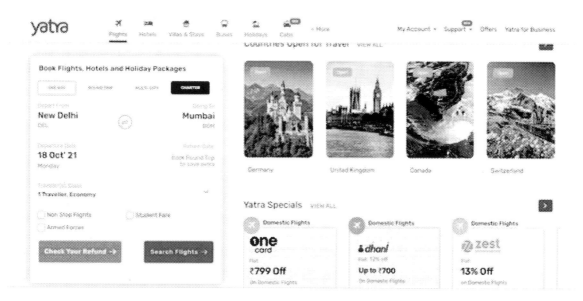

## Decoding of the Example

The person of booking is searching for many similar services websites with good feedback from past users. The tour operators have been providing multiple allied services to provide the best service to the consumers. The consumer's preference of service changes in the website responses without visiting the tour operator's office. The tour operator's responsibility of maintaining a good quality of service during the entire tour. The tour operators have been scouting the best alternate services in terms of Air-travel and Hotels of stay.

The consumers are in the position of knowing much information about the services they are receiving on the tour. The discussion with family and friends is more influential in the decision-making than any other source of information. But the family members also mainly rely on technology references and feedback given by past users. The supply chain process is becoming easy with such technology. One source solution is available on the website. Once the system is framed, it is effortless to provide the best service in terms of the supply chain.

A short time of mobility for tour travel needs a lot of preparation to feel a better experience with family and friends. The itineraries for any tour plans depend on the adequate supply chain members' effectiveness in the supply chain process by providing better service at their level. Figure 7 describes the usage of technology at all levels of processing, not only by the tour operators. The consumers' side also cross-checks it. The quality of information depends on other customers' experiences and feedback on the service provider's website or social media. The company's responsibility in providing the right quality of service, especially in these service sectors. The supply chain processes related to benefits would be more effective due to technology upgrades.

Example: If the tour operator suggests any airline services with price prescription would be openly compared with other competitors' airlines by any tour traveller. The tour operator must justify the price quotation—the hotel service which tour operators recommend also must maintain the standard quantity and quality.

The hotel would decide on the outsourcing activities based on the booking from the tour operators with current and advanced booking through apps link. The hotel would decide on the products to be delivered by considering the tier-I and tier-II suppliers' position in the stock availability. The optimal utilization of the supply chain at all levels happens with the help of technology, acting as an umbrella under challenging times. Example: If Indian travellers are traveling to any non -Asian country, the specification of the food has to be reworked than the normal one. The ordering based on the traveller's has become easy because of data collection regarding the traveller's preference. The cost-saving happens for all perishable and high-value products with the data available about customers visiting the hotel. Data capturing is a big issue because of the time-consuming process.

The researchers have proposed the above example to provide the information flow through all service levels in the tour operating business. The technology-based information flow helps save a lot of money in supply chain functions. The product-based industries could also save a lot of money in carrying technological-based supply chain management functions

## SOLUTIONS AND RECOMMENDATIONS

The companies must adopt the appropriate technological solutions to address the issues related to endemic problems for better supply chain processes. The supply chain stagnated because of the pandemic and constrained operations with limited operational capacities. But the approach must be changed with technological support for the endemic and post covid scenarios. From the buyer's perspective, the following aspects must be taken to face the business's uncertainty: agile production, supplier risk, material visibility, and closing the unutilized capacity.

In agile production, the companies must prioritize the Schedule based on the products' requirements and redesign the supply chain by solving the issues related to raw materials and finished products. The supplier's risk must be evaluated with first-level suppliers' assessment to fulfill the order's immediate requirements. Also, the planning of the production schedule is based on the key supplier's available inventory. The order fill rate must be completed with existing purchase orders. Updating information about order processing on the side of suppliers and production schedules must be accessed by all order processing departments. The above strategy would save a lot of money under and overutilization of the resources. The underutilized production facilities could be temporarily closed down, and the production schedule can be re-routed with other facilities for the total utilization of available production facilities. All issues about the buyers can be resolved only by having effective technological integration within all order processing members. A modified ERP can be a good advantage for resolving issues for buyers.

From the wholesaler's or retailers' perspective, the following aspects are considered modifying inventory policies, alternate transport facilities, alternate sources of supply, and technology integration. The mathematical determination of inventory status would decide on purchasing and selling price of the products, which would help retailers not end a colossal loss.

The pandemic has modified the transport system by providing the necessary combination of transport modes based on the necessities of the product demand. The companies must look for alternate sources of supply with the product's exact specifications. It is also mandatory to maintain an adequate supply to customers, particularly in supporting the secondary level of suppliers.

The following would provide a nutshell of strategies to adopt during a pandemic and endemic times.

*Supply Chain Techno-Umbrella for Supply Chain Resilience*

- Drafting a clear path at the organizational level toward effective engaging the suppliers, distributors, and customers/consumers would make the organization survive in all difficult times
- All forms of technology application to understand raw material requirements, inventory management, distribution planning, and customer requirements.
- The companies which have had success during the COVID due to only the technological innovation in their services
- Aggregating and connecting the unorganized services through technology (using an app) in the supply chain would benefit the companies in the long run and uninterrupted services even during any calamities.

Technology adoption is the right solution for any industry to survive in pandemic and post-pandemic times. The authors have explained the available technology and its allied tools to solve the issues about the supply chain issues.

## FUTURE RESEARCH DIRECTIONS

The researchers can focus on the diffusion of technology on supply chain functions, reducing the time and money in providing the best services to consumers. The logistical management still is a big issue in reaching the products to semiurban and rural areas. The researchers can focus on the real problems of service aggregation in the unorganized sector still to be addressed. Global companies are concentrating on heavy technology investment in their supply chain operations. In contrast, MSME companies are still struggling in technology adoption as the technology investment seems to be very high. The researcher can also focus on the survival model for any organized sector and its supply chain operations.

Exploring the reasons for not adopting any form of technology in supply-level service functions would give a lot of scope in identifying the bottlenecks. It would help in forming the strategies for the implementation.

## CONCLUSION

Supply chain management was crucial during the pandemic time as it had to maintain all supply levels based on customers' needs. The companies have struggled to reach the vital products to the consumer's doorstep. On one side, the productions were worked with a limited number of raw materials. For example, the automobile industry has been struggling to get semiconductor accessories, and on the other side, the finished goods have piled up in the warehouses and production levels. But at the same time, the companies that have innovated with technological advancement could overcome the severe business trouble and make substantial growth compared to non-pandemic time.

The researchers have always insisted that any technology-based analysis in production, inventory, and Transportation prediction would benefit the company and consumers with reasonable prices. The pandemic has allowed many technology-based start-ups to grow faster and ensure a better supply chain service. But overall, the damage is immensely more significant than predicted in the pandemic time. The researchers have taken the different service industries as an example and clearly explained the benefits of Technology usage at all levels of supply chain functions.

## REFERENCES

Angeles, R. (2005). RFID Technologies: Supply-Chain Applications and Implementation Issues. *Information Systems Management*, 22(1), 51–65. doi:10.1201/1078/44912.22.1.20051201/85739.7

Beatriz Lopes de Sousa Jabbour, A., Jose Chiappetta Jabbour, C., Hingley, M., Luis Vilalta-Perdomo, E., Ramsden, G., & Twigg, D. (2020). Sustainability of supply chains in the wake of the coronavirus (COVID-19/SARS-CoV-2) pandemic: Lessons and trends. *Modern Supply Chain Research and Applications.*, 2(3), 117–122. doi:10.1108/MSCRA-05-2020-0011

Brewer, A., Sloan, N., & Landers, T. L. (1999). Intelligent tracking in manufacturing. *Journal of Intelligent Manufacturing*, 10(3), 245–250. doi:10.1023/A:1008995707211

Chen, H. Y., Das, A., & Ivanov, D. (2019). Building resilience and managing post-disruption supply chain recovery: Lessons from the information and communication technology industry. *International Journal of Information Management*, 49, 330–342. doi:10.1016/j.ijinfomgt.2019.06.002

Christopher, M., & Peck, H. (2004). Building the resilient supply chain. *International Journal of Logistics Management*, 15(2), 1–13. doi:10.1108/09574090410700275

Chui, M., Löffler, M., & Roberts, R. (2010). The internet of things. *The McKinsey Quarterly*, (2), 70–79.

Columbus, L. (2015, July 13), *Ten Ways Big Data Is Revolutionizing Supply Chain Management*. Retrieved from https://www.forbes.com /sites/ louiscolumbus /2015/07/13/ ten-ways- big- data- is -revolutionizing -supply -chain-management /?sh=2937358c69f5

Evans, D. (2011). *The internet of things: How the next evolution of the Internet is changing everything*. Cisco Internet Business Solutions Group.

IBM's version of the Evolution of Analytics. (2021, November 20). Retrieved from https://blackbox-paradox.com/2017/03/20/on-the-evolution-of-analytics/

Kamalahmadi, M., & Parast, M. M. (2016). Developing a resilient supply chain through supplier flexibility and reliability assessment. *International Journal of Production Research*, 54(1), 302–321. doi:10.1080/00207543.2015.1088971

Kamalahmadi, M., & Parast, M. M. (2017). A review of the literature on the principles of enterprise and supply chain resilience: Major findings and directions for future research. *International Journal of Production Economics*, 171, 116–133. doi:10.1016/j.ijpe.2015.10.023

Kiritsis, D., Bufardi, A., & Xirouchakis, P. (2003). Research Issues in Product Lifecycle Management and Information Tracking Using Smart Embedded Systems. *Advanced Engineering Informatics*, 17(3-4), 189–202. doi:10.1016/S1474-0346(04)00018-7

Lambert, D. M., & Cooper, M. C. (2000). Issues in Supply Chain Management. *Industrial Marketing Management*, 29(1), 65–83. doi:10.1016/S0019-8501(99)00113-3

Phadnis, S. S. (2015). *Connecting supply chains to the Internet of Things, Supply Chain Frontiers*. Retrieved from https://ctl.mit.edu/pub/newsletter/supply-chain-frontiers-58-connecting-supply-chains-internet-things

Poon, T. C., Choy, K. L., Chow, H. K. H., Lau, H. C. W., Chan, F. T. S., & Ho, K. C. (2009). A RFID case based logistics resource management system for managing order-picking operations in warehouses. *Expert Systems with Applications*, *36*(4), 8277–8301. doi:10.1016/j.eswa.2008.10.011

Ravi, R. & Wu, L. (2015). Demystifying Industry 4.0: Implications of internet of things and services for the chemical industry. *Materials referred from Malaysia Institute for Supply Chain Innovation*.

Rong, K., Hu, G., Lin, Y., Shi, Y., & Guo, L. (2015). Understanding business ecosystem using a 6C framework in Internet-of-Things-based sectors. *International Journal of Production Economics*, *159*, 41–55. doi:10.1016/j.ijpe.2014.09.003

Sople V. V. (2012). *Logistics Management: The Supply Chain Imperative*. Pearson Education.

Tsai, Y. S., Chen, R. S., Chen, Y., & Yeh, C. P. (2011). An RFID-based manufacture process control and supply chain management in the semiconductor industry. *International Journal of Information Technology and Management*, *12*(1/2), 85–105. doi:10.1504/IJITM.2013.051633

Vijayaraghavan, T. A. S. (2021). *Supply Chain Analytics*. Wiley India Pvt Ltd.

Warehouse Layout Tips for Optimization. (2021, November 20). *BigRentz*. https://www.bigrentz.com/blog/warehouse-layout

Yatra for Business. (2021, November 25). *Yatra*. Retrieved from https://www.yatra.com/?utm_source=google&utm_medium=cpc&utm_campaign=&gclid=EAIaIQobChMIp_2ehcyh9QIVw1VgCh3WSga2EAAYAiAAEgKcjPD_BwE

Zhong, R. Y., Huang, G. Q., Lan, S. L., Dai, Q. Y., Xu, C., & Zhang, T. (2015). A big data approach for logistics trajectory discovery from RFID-enabled production data. *International Journal of Production Economics*, *165*, 260–272. doi:10.1016/j.ijpe.2015.02.014

## KEY TERMS AND DEFINITIONS

**Agility in Supply Chain:** Supply chain agility refers to a company's ability to quickly adjust its strategy, particularly procurement, inventory management, and delivery, to meet changing supply chain requirements.

**EOQ and ROP:** Economic Order Quantity (EOQ) is an optimum order quantity to reduce the overall cost and Re-Order Point (ROP) is a quantity to be considered for replenishing an order.

**Focal Company:** The company which rules or governs the supply chain, provides the direct contact to the customer, and designs the product or service offered.

**RFID in SCM:** RFID information about products enables visibility in the supply chain by sharing information between supply chain partners.

**Supply Chain Efficiency:** Efficient supply chains can deliver products at a low cost (Chandrasekaran, 2010).

**Supply Chain Profitability:** The difference between the revenue generated from the customers and the overall cost across that supply chain.

**Supply Chain Responsiveness:** Supply chain responsiveness has also been described as the capabilities of the supply chain to efficiently and effectively respond to the dynamics that affect the customers of an organization by reacting swiftly to the market requirements that keep on changing (Gunasekaran et al., 2008).

**Techno-Umbrella:** The word was coined by the authors which explains about the technology being an umbrella for all the processes especially during the pandemic time. Also, it acts as enabler and safeguarding the supply chain process during non-revenue times.

# Section 4
# Ethical and Green Supply Chain Practices

# Chapter 20
# Ethical Supply Chain Practices to Achieve Supply Chain Resilience

**Morgane M. C. Fritz**

iD https://orcid.org/0000-0002-4024-1816
*Excelia Business School, France*

## ABSTRACT

*Following the COVID-19 pandemic, ethical supply chain practices have been in the focus of several supply chain stakeholders such as firms, suppliers, government, and consumers. The pandemic caused a disruption that forced supply chains to reorganise their activities and sometimes take unethical decisions to ensure the business survival or satisfy customers. In light of several scandals, stakeholders require to increase transparency in the supply chain and recent norms on sustainable procurement highlight the importance of sustainable procurement in this mission. The chapter revises all key concepts of business ethics, supply chain practices, and supply chain resilience to explore, through the COVID-19 pandemic, unethical supply chain practices and propose solutions and recommendations based on practitioners' and researchers' studies.*

## INTRODUCTION

Limited studies have focussed on the role of ethics in supply chain management and its link to supply chain resilience. Business ethics is often related to corporate social responsibility (CSR), in other words, as a practice from individual firms rather than a network of firms like supply chains (e.g. Crane & Matten, 2016).

In this context, this chapter sets the groundwork for stimulating research in the area of ethical supply chain management. From a CSR perspective, ethical supply chain management can be related to ethical sourcing (Crane & Matten, 2016). However, sourcing is only one part of supply chain management. Hence, to develop research in ethical supply chain management, it is essential to move away from firm-centred approaches like CSR and instead consider a network approach, where firms conduct business

DOI: 10.4018/978-1-7998-9506-0.ch020

Copyright © 2022, IGI Global. Copying or distributing in print or electronic forms without written permission of IGI Global is prohibited.

*Ethical Supply Chain Practices to Achieve Supply Chain Resilience*

with various suppliers in different parts of the world to deliver a product or service as fast as possible to the customer at the lowest possible cost and the highest possible quality (Christopher, 2016).

These three objectives in the COVID-19 context have highlighted the weaknesses of supply chains and the risks related to such global dependency on foreign suppliers and resources, which have caused disruptions and shortages in various goods and services around the world. As a result, several unethical supply chain practices have emerged, such as forced labour, modern slavery, environmental degradation and waste generation, which exacerbated the unsustainability of current production and consumption patterns, one of the 17 Sustainable Development Goals of the United Nations.

Therefore, it is urgent and necessary to define how more ethical supply chain practices can be implemented, hopefully contributing to more resilient supply chains and resulting in more sustainable consumption and production patterns. To do so, this chapter examines the supply chain ethical challenges related to the COVID-19 pandemic and explores possible solutions.

The objectives of this chapter are to identify the main ethical issues related to the COVID-19 pandemic and to propose solutions based on practitioners' and researchers' work and studies. While these solutions are mostly tied to the COVID-19 pandemic, they are meant to serve as a basis for further research related to other disruptions and the need for supply chain resilience.

## BACKGROUND

With increasingly globalised supply chains and related environmental and social challenges, such as resource scarcity or forced labour, stakeholders' expectations and requirements are increasingly oriented towards sustainable and ethical goods and services (Auger et al., 2003; Doran, 2010). Consequently, stakeholders exert pressure on firms and their supply chain partners to become more sustainable and ethical (Sancha et al., 2019). This requires firms to make their business models more sustainable in collaboration with their suppliers, stimulating the sharing of sustainable goals and values (Zhang et al., 2019). Failing to integrate ethics along the supply chain leaves the door open to various risks, such as loss of reputation, corruption and social and environmental damages that challenge supply chain resilience. Therefore, this paper analyses how ethical supply chain practices can help to achieve supply chain resilience.

### Supply Chain Practices

According to Bromiley and Rau (2014, p. 1249), business practices are 'a defined activity or set of activities that a variety of firms might execute', and these activities are transferable and imitable among firms. Carter et al. (2017) applied the practise-based view (PBV), which Bromiley and Rau (2014) developed, to the supply chain context, creating the term 'supply chain practice-based view' (SCPBV). They identified several intra- and inter-firm supply chain practices based on previous research, as presented in Table 1. Carter et al. (2017) analysed supply chain practices for sustainability but did not refer to ethical supply chain practices, which remain unexplored. The SCPBV acknowledges that supply chain practices are not always imitable, given the global dimension of supply chains; hence, this fact might also hold true for ethical supply chain practices. What can be highlighted from this research are the different departments involved in supply chain practices, which is useful to consider when defining ethical supply chain practices and developing recommendations.

*Table 1. Supply chain practices and related departments*

| Supply chain practices based on Carter et al. (2017) | Possible related departments |
|---|---|
| Supplier evaluation | Procurement |
| Supplier selection | Procurement, Top management |
| Supplier quality management | Procurement |
| Knowledge sharing with suppliers and customers | Procurement, Sales |
| Electronic data exchange | Multiple |
| Supplier development | Procurement |
| Joint product development with customers or suppliers | Research and development |
| Product returns processing | Logistics, Sales |
| Purchasing alliances | Procurement, Top management |
| Vendor-managed inventory | Procurement, Sales |

When considering possible related departments, the prominent role of procurement must be highlighted, and it will be discussed later in this chapter.

## From Business Ethics to Ethical Supply Chain Practices

Business ethics is a field of research that is well established with management journals dedicated to the topic (e.g. *Journal of Business Ethics*; *Business Ethics, the Environment & Responsibility*; *Business Ethics Quarterly*); however, this is less the case for ethical supply chains. Hence, this chapter analyses the main concepts and theories related to business ethics and then applies them to supply chain practices.

In *Business Ethics—Managing Corporate Citizenship and Sustainability in the Age of Globalization*, Crane and Matten (2016) defined business ethics as 'the study of business situations, activities, and decisions where issues of right and wrong are addressed' (p. 5). Thus, business ethics is close to the concept of law, and law is actually a formalisation of right or wrong business conduct. However, not all ethical or unethical business conduct is formalised in laws, which is why it is not always simple to solve an ethical business problem. When law is not enough, one must use morality, defined as the 'norms, values, and beliefs embedded in social processes which define right and wrong for an individual or a community' (Crane & Matten, 2016, p. 8).

The following key topics must be understood to discuss business ethics: corporate responsibility, firms' stakeholders, sustainability, ethical theories, ethical decision-making influenced by individuals and situations, codes of ethics, ethical issues with suppliers and competitors, globalisation, business-civil society relations, government-business relations, management tools and ethical dilemmas.

First, business ethics is related to a variety of stakeholders. A stakeholder is to be understood as an individual or a group that 'can affect or is affected by the achievement of the organization's objectives' (Freeman, 1984).

As business has an enormous impact and importance in society, it is essential that firms have certain ethics and conduct business that is aligned to the norms, values and beliefs of the locations where they operate. Such ethics will differ depending on the firm's context, size and type of organisation. When placed in the context of globalisation, aligning firms' practices to the moral principles of a society increases the complexity of business ethics management, where culture, regulations and stakeholders' expectations differ. For instance, business ethics will not be handled in the same way in Europe, North America or Asia (Crane & Matten, 2016, p. 24). However, such alignment is the role of the firm, or the so-called CSR, which is defined as 'the attempt by companies to meet the economic, legal, ethical, and philanthropic demands of a given society at a particular point in time' (Crane & Matten, 2016, p. 50). According to Carroll's (1991) CSR pyramid, society requires economic and legal responsibility, expects ethical responsibility and desires philanthropic responsibility. In a supply chain context, these requirements and expectations are proportional to the number of business activities a firm has across different cities, regions and countries.

Furthermore, numerous ethical approaches exist, providing different ways to solve ethical problems. These approaches are defined in Table 2.

*Table 2. Ethical theories (based on Crane & Matten, 2016, pp. 93–125)*

| Theory | Definition |
| --- | --- |
| Egoism | 'A theory that suggests that an action is morally right if in a given situation all decision-makers freely decide to pursue either their (short-term) desires or their (long-term) interests.' |
| Utilitarianism | 'A theory that states that an action is morally right if it results in the greatest amount of good for the greatest number of people affected by the action.' |
| Ethics of duties | 'Ethical theories that consist of abstract, unchangeable obligations defined by a set of rationally deduced a priori moral rules, which should be applied to all relevant problems.' |
| Ethics of rights | Theory that considers that all human beings have basic, inalienable rights that should be respected (by companies) and protected (by the State), without exception (e.g. rights to life, freedom, property). |
| Ethics of justice | A theory that claims the 'simultaneous fair treatment of individuals in a given situation with the result that everybody gets what they deserve.' |
| Virtue ethics | 'A theory that contends that morally correct actions are those undertaken by actors with virtuous characters, and that the formation of a virtuous character is the first step towards morally correct behaviour.' |
| Feminist ethics | 'An approach that prioritises empathy, harmonious and healthy social relationships, care for one another, and avoidance of harm above abstract moral principles.' |
| Discourse ethics | 'An approach that aims to solve ethical conflicts by providing a process of norm generation through rational reflection on the real-life experience of all relevant participants.' |
| Postmodern ethics | 'An approach that locates morality beyond the sphere of rationality in an emotional 'moral impulse' towards others. It encourages one to question everyday practices and rules and to listen to one's emotions and 'gut feelings' about what is right and wrong.' |

Knowing these theories will help one understand how decisions are made and how to make more ethical decisions to achieve firm and supply chain resilience. Crane and Matten (2016) proposed a framework to guide ethical decision-making, highlighting that the decision-making process is related to individual factors (age, gender, culture, education, job position, psychological factors, personal values, personal integrity and moral imagination) and situational factors (issue and context).

## From Resilience to Supply Chain Resilience

According to Ponomarov and Holcomb (2009), the term resilience was originally used in psychology to analyse humans' behaviour in relation to their environment over time and their capacity to adapt to a hazardous event (e.g. environmental disaster). Resilience can be applied to a system, a community or a society and helps identify how they continue functioning, maintain their structure and improve following any hazardous event (United Nations, 2005). This capacity, or capability, refers to 'physical, institutional, social, or economic resources and means, as well as skilled personal or collective attributes such as leadership and management that a community can bring to bear on management hazards' (Ponomarov & Holcomb, 2009, p. 127).

Thus, resilience can be applied in various types of organisations where human beings need to adapt to a hazard, shock or stress, such as associations, public or private sector organisations and even global supply chains (Ponomarov & Holcomb, 2009). These hazards can be natural or anthropogenic, and having a psychological approach to resilience increases response efficiency (Reich, 2006). According to Rose (2004), resilience can take place at the microeconomic/individual levels, mesoeconomic/sector/market levels or macroeconomic levels (i.e. a combination of microeconomic and mesoeconomic levels) that constitute a system (e.g. a supply chain, for instance).

In short, for a business or supply chain, being resilient means being able to adapt quickly to an event, which requires response preparedness in terms of resources, business environment knowledge and the integration of learning experiences (Lindell et al., 2007). Recovering from a hazard also requires work at an individual level to stabilise individuals from a psychological point of view (Lindell et al., 2007).

Supply chain resilience is a term that has been defined in different ways. According to Zouari et al. (2021), it is a 'key concept for managers who wish to develop the capacity to enhance their supply chain's (SC's) ability to cope with unexpected turbulence' (p.149). According to Yao and Fabbe-Costes (2018), 'Resilience is a complex, collective, adaptive capability of organisations in the supply network to maintain a dynamic equilibrium, react to and recover from a disruptive event, and to regain performance by absorbing negative impacts, responding to unexpected changes, and capitalizing on the knowledge of success or failure' (p. 260). These definitions mainly address macroeconomic or mesoeconomic levels. The microeconomic level (i.e. individuals) is not well reflected in these definitions, and this is a gap to be addressed. Furthermore, when looking at supply chain capabilities, as highlighted, for instance, by Zouari et al. (2021, pp. 161–163) and based on Pettit et al. (2010, 2013), the microeconomic level is not prominent either (see Table 3). Consequently, it is necessary to address the microeconomic level and investigate whether it supports achieving supply chain resilience.

*Ethical Supply Chain Practices to Achieve Supply Chain Resilience*

*Table 3. Capabilities for supply chain resilience and definitions (source: Zouari et al. [2021, pp.161–163] based on Pettit et al. [2010, 2013])*

| Capabilities for supply chain resilience | Definition |
| --- | --- |
| Flexibility in sourcing | Ability to rapidly change input or the mode of receiving input |
| Flexibility in order fulfilment | Ability to rapidly change output or the mode of delivering output |
| Capacity | Availability of assets to enable sustained production levels |
| Efficiency | Ability to produce output with minimum resource requirements |
| Visibility | Knowledge of the status of operating assets and the environment |
| Adaptability | Ability to modify operations in response to challenges or opportunities |
| Anticipation | Ability to discern potential future events or situations |
| Recovery | Ability to rapidly return to normal operational state |
| Dispersion | Broad distribution or decentralisation of assets |
| Collaboration | Ability to work effectively with other entities for mutual benefit |
| Organisation | Human resource structures, policies, skills and culture |
| Market position | Position status of a company or its products in specific markets |
| Security | Defence against deliberate intrusion or attack |
| Financial strengths | Capacity to absorb cashflow fluctuations |

Since business ethics enables one to identify the impacts of business on society and address society's requirements, expectations and desires, it is a possible way to investigate more in depth how firms and supply chains can become more resilient at a microeconomic level.

# ETHICAL ISSUES IN SUPPLY CHAINS HIGHLIGHTED BY COVID-19

This section examines the main ethical issues in supply chains, as highlighted by COVID-19.

## General Context

The COVID-19 pandemic revealed the impact global supply chains can have on society from an economic, social and environmental perspective. Rising shipping costs, goods shortages and the interdependency of supply chains have pointed out several weaknesses in supply chain management, and ethical practices have sometimes been neglected to satisfy customers and consumers (Baldry, 2020; Brustlein, 2021). The enormous economic impacts of the COVID-19 crisis pushed companies to focus on cost reduction (Pournader & Wohlgezogen, 2021). The pandemic has underlined the need for more supply chain resilience and rethinking supply chain strategies related to a strong dependency on specific countries or regions for natural and human resources (Baldry, 2020). Risk management, supply chain design and sustainability issues are at the forefront of supply chain challenges in the pursuit of developing more ethical supply chain practices (Baldry, 2020).

Unethical supply chain practices are not new; however, they have been emphasised and, in some cases, worsened in the context of COVID-19 (ASCI, 2020). The following sections will review some of the main sustainability issues according to the three supply chain resilience levels: microeconomic, mesoeconomic and macroeconomic (Rose, 2004).

## Microeconomic Ethical Issues Affecting Supply Chain Management

### Human Rights Abuse and Modern Slavery

Recent surveys, studies and testimonies strongly highlight cases of human rights abuses and modern slavery in the COVID-19 context. As factories had to close, the pandemic resulted in job losses in various sectors around the world, which pushed the most vulnerable people to sometimes work in the black market to have enough resources to satisfy their basic needs or to accept inhuman working conditions (Dowling, 2021). Increased demand for specific products, such as toilet paper, masks or antibacterial gel, also caused higher pressure on workers to satisfy the demand, thus deteriorating working conditions (Pournader & Wohlgezogen, 2021). Pournader and Wohlgezogen (2021) provided the example of Rio Tinto, which allowed iron ore extraction on an Aboriginal heritage site due to the high demand for raw materials.

Forced labour and modern slavery are also an issue in Europe, which involves about 100,000 individuals in the United Kingdom and approximately the same number in France, Germany, Italy and Spain, respectively (Baldry, 2020). Given the low human workforce costs and access to raw materials in developing economies, the trend is unlikely to reverse (Baldry, 2020). However, companies that are able to ensure respect for human rights and good working conditions by following ethical standards are likely to recover better from the pandemic (Baldry, 2020).

The crisis has enhanced some unethical practices, such as audits on supplier sites being reduced or postponed due to sanitary reasons and the increased use of unethical recruitment practices (Dowling, 2021), which may emerge when supply chains lack transparency (Crane et al., 2019). Significant salary drops have also been reported in the garment industry in developing economies, forcing workers to borrow money or indebt themselves to satisfy their basic needs, placing them at risk of entering a vicious circle of poverty (Dowling, 2021). Dowling (2021) further reported that 31% of companies' budgets for ethical trading have been reduced, according to a survey led by the Ethical Trading Initiative (ETI, 2020).

### Coping with Consumers' Expectations

The pandemic increased consumers' online shopping activities, as it became a comfortable solution to continue shopping without being exposed to the virus. The UNCTAD (2020) reported that consumers shopped more frequently online due to the pandemic, and this increase was more significant in developing economies, based on a survey conducted among 3,700 people in developed and developing economies. This online shopping trend concerns mostly cosmetics and personal care, digital entertainment, agro food and beverages, fashion and accessories. The respondents stated that they would continue shopping online more, even after the pandemic. However, while consumers expect fast delivery and cheap products, they also expect companies to behave ethically (Waligora, 2020). Supply chain management needs to cope with such expectations from consumers, and this creates a real challenge to align selling prices, manufacturing costs and ethical practices given the (often) short-term profit-making goal of the company versus the long-term impact on its brand, image and stakeholders' satisfaction. Consumers also

*Ethical Supply Chain Practices to Achieve Supply Chain Resilience*

require more transparency regarding supply chain operations and goods (OECD, 2021), which means that supply chains must invest in ways to become more transparent.

## Mesoeconomic Ethical Issues

## Poor Supplier Treatment and Unethical Buying Practices

The pandemic has spotlighted poor supplier treatment and unethical buying practices. Given the focus on profit-making and business survival and the need to react quickly, some ethical practices have been infringed upon (Dowling, 2021). Suppliers' desperate situations have given buyers strong bargaining positions that have led them to make unethical requests of their suppliers, according to a survey of 75 suppliers in the apparel sector (in Bangladesh, Cambodia, Egypt, El Salvador, Ethiopia, Guatemala, India, Indonesia, Kenya, Mexico, Myanmar, Nicaragua, Pakistan, Peru and Vietnam) conducted by Anner (2020). For instance, buyers required lower prices from suppliers because of delivery delays, cancelled orders without paying penalties to suppliers (77% of respondents), required discounts (65%) even below production costs (56%), delayed suppliers' payment process (77 days on average against 43 days before the pandemic) and allowed no or low shipment date flexibility to implement the social distancing measures in the factories, all to the suppliers' detriment (Anner, 2020). As a consequence, the viability of many suppliers has been severely impacted, and several have had to dismiss a certain share (about 10%) of their workers. In Bangladesh, estimates have shown that about one million workers in the garment sector have been dismissed without being paid because of cancelled or withdrawn orders (Baldry, 2020). SEDEX (2020) reported on COVID-19 and referred to similar unethical practices. Nevertheless, it is worth noting that cases of customers supporting their suppliers through close cooperation, ethical practices and long-term cooperation have also been reported (Anner, 2020; Baldry, 2020).

Overall, serious unethical practices have been reported during the pandemic, and the responsibility falls on purchasing managers, who are often held responsible for the way goods and services are produced in their firms and along the supply chain (Goebel et al., 2012; Sancha et al., 2019). However, Jabbour (2015) noted that there was a lack of literature on the internal practices in sustainable supply chain management, specifically on sustainability management (including the ethical concerns of managers and employees) or sustainable purchasing before or while addressing external sustainability practices (e.g. cooperation with suppliers). For Waligora (2020), a KPMG partner, 'the businesses that emerge strongest from the turmoil will be those that protect their brands and supply chains by acting ethically'. To be considered ethical, customers should not only continue their business but also commit to supporting the businesses and people that contribute to their success (Brustlein, 2021).

## Corruption

According to Waligora (2020), 'fraud increases when businesses and individuals struggle'. The pandemic has highlighted the risks of corruption in relation to remote working, where employees may be more vulnerable to phishing or cybersecurity issues. Corruption risks also increased due to the fast incorporation of new suppliers without the necessary security checks or the integration of suppliers with insufficiently secured IT solutions, thereby increasing the vulnerability of the supply chain (KPMG, 2020). An internal collaborator may facilitate such fraud because managers create a lower well-being environment in the workplace during the pandemic (KPMG, 2020), which highlights the key role of managers and top management in implementing ethical business practices.

## Macroeconomic Ethical Issues

### Lack of Consideration of Public Procurement's Role

During COVID-19, several cases of unethical public procurement practices also occurred. The British Medical Association (BMA, 2021) stated that public purchases for health and safety in developed economies may be linked to unethical practices among suppliers from developing economies, such as forced labour, unsafe working conditions or child labour. For instance, Guyoton (2020) from ECOVADIS, a platform used to assess suppliers' sustainability performance, reported on the WRP and Suppermaxx Malaysian rubber glove manufacturers who supplied the US and the UK, respectively. These suppliers have been accused for many years of forced labour practices, and the WRP was under embargo as per the US government. This embargo was revoked a few months later (CBP, 2020) due to the lack of gloves to fight the pandemic; however, no real evidence has been provided that the WRP truly changed its practices so quickly. These cases also highlight the ethical dilemmas at the government level, which impact supply chains and highlight the issue of human rights abuses and modern slavery.

### Government Tolerance for Noncompliance with Regulations

Some governments have strict regulations regarding ethical business practices, such as the UK with the Modern Slavery Act of 2015, which requires that UK firms with £36 million of turnover or more report on how they handle modern slavery issues along their supply chain. Pinnington et al. (2021) highlighted the complexity of this task during the pandemic due to disruptions and changes in suppliers and related that, as a consequence, the UK Government temporarily relaxed section 54 on reporting requirements in April 2020. According to Pinnington et al. (2021), this underlined that modern slavery was not a priority during the crisis, opening the door to higher ethical risks in supply chains, particularly given the fast and unscrutinised processes firms adopted to select suppliers during this period. After such relaxation, returning to the initial Modern Slavery Act requirements once the pandemic is over may prove difficult.

### Culture and Institutional Context

Various ethical issues can be faced in supply chain management, and these problems must be solved by individuals' ethical judgment guided by firms' ethical culture and social, political and economic institutions (Ferrell et al., 2013; Huq & Stevenson, 2020). Organisational culture is an essential element in building a sustainable supply chain (Carter & Rogers, 2008). Under 'organisational culture', shared value and value creation can be stressed, where values are integrated into the decision-making process of employees and their ethical behaviour. The UNGC and BSR (2015) highlighted that 'many companies are driven by their corporate values and culture', and sustainable supply chain management drives 'social development and environmental protection', which creates 'internal buy-in and commitment' for supply chains. Values also influence managers' perceived importance of ethics and social responsibility (Shafer et al., 2007). Such an 'internal buy-in and commitment' seems essential to implementing sustainable supply chain management practices, and it relates to individuals' and managers' ethics and leadership skills, which are often overlooked in supply chain management research.

## SOLUTIONS AND RECOMMENDATIONS

While the issues and controversies presented in the previous section were focussed on the pandemic situation, some of them already existed before the pandemic and may persist afterwards. In this section, some solutions and recommendations are related to the pandemic situation; however, others are applicable to a more general context.

### Hard Law and Soft Law

Regulations (hard law) and guidelines or norms (soft law) contribute to more ethical supply chain practices and to the resilience of supply chains. Over the past five years, Guyoton (2020) reported an increase in supply chain regulatory due diligence with the UK Modern Slavery Act or the 'duty of care' ('devoir de vigilance') in France. These regulations force companies to develop solutions to ensure ethical practices throughout the supply chain (Ecovadis, 2021).

Long before the pandemic, several guidelines were developed to support firms in formulating their ethical policies. The OECD Guidelines for Multinational Enterprises, used by thousands of companies worldwide, address both human and environmental considerations all along the supply chain, such as working conditions and human rights abuses (OECD, 2021). Sector-specific guidelines were developed based on the OECD guidelines, including those for the mineral, garment, footwear, agriculture and financial sectors.

Complying with local, regional and global rules will support firms in understanding the ethical issues they face and the reporting requirements, increasing their ethical value (Deloitte, 2021). This will also support them in developing or improving their ethical policy and goals, which should be embedded throughout the firm to make certain employees behave accordingly and make ethical decisions, which in turn will reduce risks in supply chain management (Waligora, 2020). As in the case of governments' relaxed measures, Waligora (2020) suggested that firms might temporarily relax their ethical rules to overcome a disruption; however, they must be clear on the temporary character of this decision and maintain their ethical goals.

### Conduct Risk Assessment and Monitor Suppliers

Risk assessments are essential to avoid unethical supply chain practices. These assessments concern the firms' internal operations (e.g. trainings on code of conduct, surveys on employee well-being and measures to pinpoint and solve ethical issues). They also concern suppliers who should be closely monitored. The same level of due diligence should be used for all suppliers, both new and established, to avoid human rights abuses, fraud or environmental damage (Waligora, 2020). When facing a disruption, firms may not have time; thus, it is important to develop ways to conduct due diligence quickly (e.g. checking suppliers' financial statements, integrity and compliance).

## Ethical and Sustainable Procurement for both the Private and Public Sector

Miemczyk et al. (2012) defined sustainable procurement as follows:

*the consideration of environmental, social, ethical and economic issues in the management of the organization's external resources in such a way that the supply of all goods, services, capabilities and knowledge that are necessary for running, maintaining and managing the organization's primary and support activities provide value not only to the organization but also to society and the economy. (p. 491)*

In this chapter, procurement is considered at the strategic level and gathers sourcing, negotiation, supplier development and involvement (Handfield et al., 1999; Van Weele, 2010), where decisions are made by procurement managers and top managers; purchasing occurs at the tactical and operational level and consists of supplier selection, contract agreement, ordering, expediting and evaluating goods and services (Van Weele, 2010), and this can be done by purchasers or buyers.

The ISO 24000 on Sustainable Procurement provides guidelines and recommendations to develop a sustainable and ethical purchasing policy and to select suppliers and collaborate with them. According to the ISO 24000 (2017), three main categories of stakeholders for sustainable procurement must be considered: 1) internal stakeholders (top management/entrepreneur; procurement people and CSR/ sustainability people, other internal people in finance, H&S, HR and operational people); 2) supply chain stakeholders (tier-n suppliers, subcontractors, business partners and consultants) and 3) external stakeholders (customers and clients, local community, governments, public sector, academic, international agencies, non-governmental organisations [NGOs], trade unions/workers, investors, financial sector, rating agencies and sector association peers). Sustainable procurement can be structured around several principles:

1. 'accountability' of the firm regarding its impacts on the society, economy, environment and supply chain (life cycle perspective for goods and services);
2. 'transparency' regarding the firm's procurement decisions, activities, impacts on the levels mentioned in the first point and relations with suppliers to stimulate their transparency;
3. 'ethical behaviour' within the firm and along the supply chain;
4. 'respect for stakeholder interests' that the firm impacts through procurement decisions and actions;
5. 'respect for the rule of law and international norms of behaviour' within the firm and the entire supply chain to detect any lack of compliance and stimulate suppliers to do so as well;
6. 'transformative and innovative solutions' that support sustainability management in the firm and along the supply chain;
7. 'focus on needs' to revise its procurement policy and habits so that buyers only acquire what is really needed and look for sustainable alternatives;
8. 'integration' of sustainability into all procurement processes; and
9. 'global cost' to take into account the total cost of procurement activities for not only the firm but also for the society, the environment and the economy (ISO, 2017).

These environmental and social issues are related to ethical dilemmas about reducing costs and creating a positive impact for the environment and society. According to Svensson et al. (2010), having real, sustainable business practices without working on ethics is highly complex. Both social and environmen-

*Ethical Supply Chain Practices to Achieve Supply Chain Resilience*

tal topics tend to be integrated into the procurement process, particularly to mitigate risks and increase competitiveness and economic performance (Ferri & Pedrini, 2018). Sustainable procurement enables a firm to be more reactive towards environmental challenges, which can provide financial benefits for the firm in the long term (Bansal & Roth, 2000). Supplier development for sustainability (SDS) is one approach to supporting buyers in mitigating supply chain sustainability risks and stimulating cooperation between buyers and suppliers (Busse, 2016; Foerstl et al., 2010).

Carter and Jennings (2004) stated that five factors are linked to the implementation of CSR principles in the procurement function (also called purchasing social responsibility [PSR]): 1) top management leadership, having an impact on: 2) people-oriented organisational culture; 3) individual values of purchasing employees, having an impact on; 4) employee initiatives; and 5) customer pressures (other factors, such as government regulation and organisational size, were found to be less impacting in their study). According to Shaw and Shiu (2002), a sustainable purchase for any individual is linked to five factors: individual values, social norms, perceived behaviour, ethical obligations and ethical identity. Consequently, individuals' and organisations' ethical behaviours in the context of sustainable procurement should ideally match for sustainable purchases to happen, or organisations must provide at least clear guidelines and objectives to the buyer.

However, in the current economic system, buyers usually favour three criteria: price, quality and delivery time (Jorgensen & Knudsen, 2006; Quairel & Auberger, 2007). There are trade-offs between the economic objectives of the buyers and the environmental, social and overall ethical criteria that can be secondary, depending on the firm's policy, culture, employees' ethical values, customers' pressure and other factors, such as government regulations or organisational size (Jorgensen & Knudsen, 2006; Quairel & Auberger, 2007). Such trade-offs lead companies to make choices that often favour financial gains rather than sustainability and can lead to a lack of control in the supply chain, particularly when activities are outsourced (e.g. Nike's child labour and human rights abuse scandal in the 1990s). Scandals enhance the responsibility of buyers in terms of human rights and the environment, as stakeholders can 'punish' firms by boycotting their products when they become aware of firms' unsustainable practices because buyers are supposed to be capable of preventing such issues through proper supplier selection and development (Hofmann et al., 2014; Klassen & Vereecke, 2012). Although the procurement function has gained importance over the 20th century, it remains underestimated in some firms' strategies, since procurement managers are often not involved in strategy development and the function lacks long-term objectives to manage risks (Knoppen & Saenz, 2015).

In addition, since a supply chain consists of a focal company, suppliers, distributors, clients, consumers and eventually subcontractors, all these stakeholders must be considered. This requires addressing not only the focal company and its supply chain partners (supply chain internal stakeholders) but also supply chain stakeholders, such as the media, government agencies, researchers or the public (Silvestre, 2016). The focal company as a customer can indeed exert pressure on all the above-mentioned stakeholders; however, pressure can also stem from these stakeholders on the focal company (Barasa et al., 2017; Seles et al., 2016) through formal institutions (e.g. regulations) and informal institutions, meaning stakeholders' norms and values (North, 1990). In such a context, it is important to consider the values and ethics of procurement managers and buyers, of the firm and of its surrounding stakeholders, since these are drivers for sustainable and ethical procurement (Carter & Jennings, 2004; Svensson, 2009). Instituting a culture of compliance in the firm, high moral principles and well-being will limit the risk of employees behaving unethically and, thus, the risk of unethical supply chain practices (KPMG, 2020).

However, having a sustainable and ethical procurement policy is not sufficient per se. To increase supply chain ethical practices, buyers must transfer these ethical values to their suppliers and make certain (i.e. control, monitor) that suppliers respect them, such as enforcing a supplier code of conduct and performing regular audits (Guyoton, 2020). Guyoton (2020) highlighted, based on the Ecovadis Sustainable Procurement Barometer, that only 38% of multinational firms with supplier code of conduct check suppliers' commitment to this code on a yearly basis, and he encouraged them to do more.

Given the similar risks for procurement in the public sector, it would be relevant to further investigate governments' commitments towards sustainable and ethical procurement and encourage those that are not committed yet. Former UN general secretary Ban Ki Moon stated, 'Public procurement is a powerful driver of development. In addition to providing goods and services a country needs, the act of procurement itself can strengthen local economies, support marginalised groups and boost local capacity for commerce' (BMA, 2021).

## Collaboration Between Customers and Suppliers

While improving supply chain resiliency is often related to more flexibility, visibility and collaboration (Jüttner & Maklan, 2011), Dowling (2021) recommended extending these efforts to promote more ethical supply chain practices. Extending ethical supply chain practices can be done through collaborations between customers and suppliers in working groups, associations and industry coalitions or simply by bilateral cooperation. The author also highlighted the importance of keeping some goods in stock, when possible, to respond to the demand created by future supply chain disruptions and to limit the negative consequences of such disruptions on human beings and the environment (Dowling, 2021).

From an ethical perspective, customers must accept that, since they are part of the supply chain, they have a duty to support suppliers in facing disruptions instead of putting pressure on them or changing suppliers (Waligora, 2020). A fairer treatment of suppliers and collaboration to build their capacity to cope with disruptions and survive will contribute to creating trust and long-term relationships, satisfying customers and, thus, building more resilient supply chains (Waligora, 2020). Baldry (2020) illustrated such ethical supply chain practices with the case of Rowlinsin Knitwear, both within the firm's global production sites and with its suppliers. The company started by becoming an employee-owned business in 2015, which increased altruistic initiatives, including benefits for their own and suppliers' employees such as a higher minimum wage (see Business Growth Hub, 2021).

## Investment in Technologies for Transparency

To improve visibility as part of a supply chain resilience strategy, technologies can be supportive. Technologies for traceability and transparency are important for managing stocks and disruptions (Burstlein, 2021). Knowing what is in stock and forecasting demand supports more ethical supply chain practices by ordering amounts that correspond to the demand and, thus, not overwhelming suppliers with too high orders that will place pressure on employees and resources.

## Revising Supply Chain Organisation

During the pandemic, discussions on relocating business activities closer to firms' headquarters took place to better control physical resources and information flows. While shorter supply chains will be

*Ethical Supply Chain Practices to Achieve Supply Chain Resilience*

easier to monitor when facing a disruption, this is not possible for all types of goods (Guyoton, 2020). Indeed, for goods that require raw materials that are not available in a specific territory, supply chains must continue working with suppliers located in territories where the raw materials originate, which are often in undeveloped economies where ethical risks need to be assessed. Thus, working with procurement departments is essential to improve supply chain organisation and create more ethical supply chains (Guyoton, 2020). According to Baldry (2020), relocation to areas with lower ethical risks may reduce unethical supply chain practices but will not eliminate all ethical risks.

## FUTURE RESEARCH DIRECTIONS

Future research directions could address the efficiency of the proposed solutions at microeconomic, mesoeconomic and macroeconomic levels. For instance, would stricter regulations on ethics improve ethical supply chain practices and supply chain resilience? More case studies on supply chain ethical practices, dilemmas and solutions would inform researchers and practitioners on effective solutions. Further research related to disruption in another context other than the COVID-19 pandemic (e.g. the 2008 financial crisis) might uncover complementary ethical issues as well. Finally, more sector-specific studies (e.g. food, textile and automotive) might be relevant, as sector-specific ethical guidelines have been developed (e.g. OECD).

Further research on ethics in supply chain management should include theoretical considerations related to individuals' ethics and business ethics (e.g. Crane & Matten, 2016). By analysing the ethical values, behaviours and decisions of individuals and organisations, it is possible to consider that supply chains contribute to the creation of ethical and sustainable values (e.g. ethical and sustainable products and production processes) that positively impact the environment and society. This is particularly the case in the procurement function through supplier relationship management. However, having ethical and sustainable procurement requires that all other functions in the firm (e.g. finance, marketing and sales) and individuals working within these other functions are willing and able to cooperate with the procurement department to support ethical and sustainable procurement decisions and actions. Smith et al. (2010) argued this point by analysing the relationship between ethics in marketing and the downstream supply chain. Although it increases complexity, such a multistakeholder approach and voluntary participation can enhance sustainable and ethical supply chain practices (Soudararajan et al., 2019). In other words, it would be relevant to investigate whether pressures and incentives for ethical and sustainable decisions and actions need to exist within each firm forming the supply chain, at a governance, management and operational level, to support ethical supply chain practices.

Managerial implications can also be derived from this work because if ethics is key for sustainable supply chains and resilience, then exercising ethical values like trust, empathy and integrity among firms and supply chains is essential. Values that enable sustainability need to be identified, and methods or guidelines should be developed to train and understand how to shift towards an ethical mindset. Crises are times to make shifts and innovate. In the current COVID-19 crisis, it may be time to go back to an old ethical principle, the Golden Rule (Encyclopaedia Britannica, 2020; Puka, 2020), and wonder whether what we do to others and to the environment are things we would accept others doing to ourselves. Would this simple rule be enough to support more ethical supply chain practices? Future research could examine management, social and psychological experts' opinions on the question.

*Figure 1. Triggers for ethical supply chain practices*
(own elaboration)

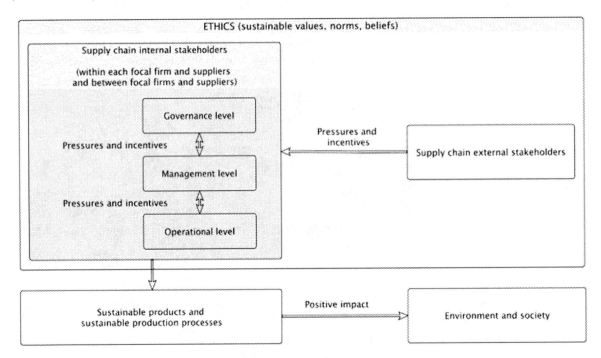

Considering ethics is essential to guide all supply chain stakeholders towards ethical practices, since they must constantly reflect upon ethical decisions and the actions that they take (e.g. supplier selection, compliance with environmental and social laws and standards) to be aligned with society's expectations. Several authors have argued that more frameworks are needed to support supply chain practices in the implementation of CSR (e.g. Beske & Seuring, 2014; Meixell & Luoma, 2015; Touboulic & Walker, 2015). The framework proposed in Figure 1 contributes to addressing this need by highlighting the triggers for ethical supply chain practices. The framework is a basis to encourage inter-disciplinary research between supply chain management, the social sciences, philosophy and human resources management.

The importance of ethics in supply chains and procurement requires the identification of ethical values to stimulate truly sustainable supply chains. According to Naomi et al. (2018), value is created and delivered through different business activities, such as supply chain & logistics, operations, marketing & sales, innovation & R&D, organisational culture and corporate governance. In turn, the corresponding values created by these business activities are captured by different stakeholders, including shareholders and investors, employees, customers, suppliers/partners, society, the environment, governments and competitors. Hence, specific ethical values, such as trust, could be tested, and instruments could be developed to stimulate ethical value creation within business activities and along the supply chain and to analyse its effects on supply chain resilience.

Research on ethics in supply chain management must go beyond the simple supplier selection process and audits to manage economic, environmental and social risks. Research should also wonder whether all decisions and actions for sustainability are ethical, and for whom they are or are not ethical, to acknowledge the importance of supply chain stakeholders (supply chain internal, supply chain internal/

external, supply chain external stakeholders) and supply chain stakeholders' morals (e.g. norms, values, beliefs and culture).

## CONCLUSION

According to Pournader and Wohlgezogen (2021), 'The pandemic has put global supply chains under stress, and we need to be watchful that ethics and sustainability don't fall by the wayside'. Addressing supply chain resilience through ethical supply chain practices covers several sustainability challenges that society is facing, as highlighted by the effects of the COVID-19 pandemic. Ethics play an overarching role in the success of supply chain management and its resilience. Ethics can be linked to several social issues in supply chains (e.g. Huq & Stevenson, 2020); thus, studying ethics in supply chains will help address the existing research gap concerning social sustainability in supply chain management, which is widely acknowledged (Ashby et al., 2012; Benoît et al., 2010; Kaufman & Ülkü, 2018; Yawar & Seuring, 2017).

## REFERENCES

Anner, M. (2020). *Leveraging desperation: apparel brands' purchasing practices during COVID-19.* PennState Center for Global Workers' Rights (CGWR). Available at: https://ler. la. psu. edu/gwr/documents/LeveragingDesperation_October162020. pdf

ASCI. (2020). *COVID-19 Pandemic Adds To Ethical Issues In Global Supply Chains.* Available at: https://www.asci-2021.com.au/covid-19-pandemic-adds-to-ethical-issues-in-global-supply-chains/

Auger, P., Burke, P., Devinney, T. M., & Louviere, J. J. (2003). What Will Consumers Pay for Social Product Features? *Journal of Business Ethics, 42*(3), 281–304. doi:10.1023/A:1022212816261

Baldry. (2020). *Why ethical supply chains are the route to success after COVID-19.* Available at: https://www.businessgrowthhub.com/manufacturing/resources/blog/2020/09/why-ethical-supply-chains-are-the-route-to-success-after-covid-19

Barasa, L., Knoben, J., Vermeulen, P., Kimuyu, P., & Kinyanjui, B. (2017). Institutions: re- sources and innovation in East Africa: a firm level approach. *Resources Policy, 46*(1), 280–291. doi:10.1016/j.respol.2016.11.008

Beske, P., & Seuring, S. (2014). Putting Sustainability into Supply Chain Management. *Supply Chain Management, 19*(3), 322–331. doi:10.1108/SCM-12-2013-0432

BMA. (2021). *Fair medical trade.* Available at: https://www.bma.org.uk/what-we-do/working-internationally/our-international-work/fair-medical-trade

Bromiley, P., & Rau, D. (2014). Towards a practice-based view of strategy. *Strategic Management Journal, 35*(8), 1249–1256. doi:10.1002mj.2238

Brustlein, J. (2021). *How Ethical Supply Chains Will Survive the Pandemic.* Available at: https://www.supplychainbrain.com/blogs/1-think-tank/post/32671-how-ethical-supply-chains-can-survive-the-pandemic

Business Growth Hub. (2021). *The importance of being ethical: In Conversation with One+All*. Available at: https://www.businessgrowthhub.com/case-studies/oneplusall

Busse, C. (2016). Doing well by doing good? The self-interest of buying firms and sustainable supply chain management. *The Journal of Supply Chain Management, 52*(2), 28–47. doi:10.1111/jscm.12096

Carroll, A. B. (1991). The pyramid of corporate social responsibility: Toward the moral management of organizational stakeholders. *Business Horizons, 34*(4), 42. doi:10.1016/0007-6813(91)90005-G

Carter, C., & Jennings, M. M. (2004). The role of purchasing in corporate social responsibility: A structural equation analysis. *Journal of Business Logistics, 25*(1), 145–186. doi:10.1002/j.2158-1592.2004.tb00173.x

Carter, C., & Rogers, D. (2008). A framework of sustainable supply chain management: Moving toward new theory. *International Journal of Physical Distribution & Logistics Management, 38*(5), 360–387. doi:10.1108/09600030810882816

Carter, C. R., Kosmol, T., & Kaufmann, L. (2017). Toward a supply chain practice view. *The Journal of Supply Chain Management, 53*(1), 114–122. doi:10.1111/jscm.12130

CBP. (2020). *CBP Revokes Withhold Release Order on Disposable Rubber Gloves*. Available at: https://www.cbp.gov/newsroom/national-media-release/cbp-revokes-withhold-release-order-disposable-rubber-gloves

Christopher, M. (2016). *Logistics and Supply Chain Management* (5th ed.). Prentice Hall.

Crane, A., LeBaron, G., Allain, J., & Behbahani, L. (2019). Governance gaps in eradicating forced labor: From global to domestic supply chains. *Regulation & Governance, 13*(1), 86–106. doi:10.1111/rego.12162

Crane, A., & Matten, D. (2016). *Business Ethics – Managing Corporate Citizenship and Sustainability in the Age of Globalization* (4th ed.). Oxford University Press.

Deloitte. (2021). *Ethical value chain*. Available at: https://www2.deloitte.com/ch/en/pages/risk/solutions/ethical-value-chain.html

Doran, C. (2010). Fair Trade Consumption: In Support of the Out-Group. *Journal of Business Ethics, 95*(4), 527–541. doi:10.100710551-010-0437-x

Dowling, F. (2021). *The impact of Covid-19 on unethical practices in global supply chains*. Available at: https://business.leeds.ac.uk/research-stc/dir-record/research-blog/1816/the-impact-of-covid-19-on-unethical-practices-in-global-supply-chains

Ecovadis. (2021). *Modern Slavery In Supply Chains: New Legislative Landscape and Due Diligence Strategies*. Available at: https://resources.ecovadis.com/labor-human-rights/modern-slavery-supply-chains-legislative-due-diligence?utm_medium=referral&utm_source=ev-covid-blog&utm_campaign=covid-19

Encyclopaedia Britannica. (2020). *Golden Rule, Ethical Precept*. Retrieved from: https://www.britannica.com/topic/Golden-Rule

ETI. (2020). *A guest blog from Grace Gao: Stay responsible - ETI member Matrix's supplier survey and engagement during pandemic.* Available at: https://www.ethicaltrade.org/blog/guest-blog-grace-gao-stay-responsible-eti-member-matrixs-supplier-survey-and-engagement-during

Ferrell, O. C., Rogers, M. M., Ferrell, L., & Sawayda, J. (2013). A framework for understanding ethical supply chain decision making. *Journal of Marketing Channels, 20*(3–4), 260–287. doi:10.1080/1046669X.2013.803428

Ferri, L. M., & Pedrini, M. (2018). Socially and environmentally responsible purchasing: Comparing the impacts on buying firm's financial performance, competitiveness and risk. *Journal of Cleaner Production, 174,* 880–888. doi:10.1016/j.jclepro.2017.11.035

Fiksel, J. (2006). Sustainability and resilience: toward a systems approach. *Sustainability: Science. Practice and Policy, 2*(2), 14–21.

Foerstl, K., Reuter, C., Hartmann, E., & Blome, C. (2010). Managing supplier sustainability risks in a dynamically changing environment – sustainable supplier management in the chemical industry. *Journal of Purchasing and Supply Management, 16*(2), 118–130. doi:10.1016/j.pursup.2010.03.011

Goebel, P., Reuter, C., Pibernik, R., & Sichtmann, C. (2012). The influence of ethical culture on supplier selection in the context of sustainable sourcing. *International Journal of Production Economics, 140*(1), 7–17. doi:10.1016/j.ijpe.2012.02.020

GuyotonS. (2020). Available at: https://resources.ecovadis.com/blog/covid-19-ethical-dilemma-reveals-weaknesses-in-supply-chain-due-diligence

Handfield, R. B., Ragatz, G. L., Peterson, K., & Monczka, R. M. (1999). Involving suppliers in new product development? *California Management Review, 42*(1), 59–82. doi:10.2307/41166019

Hofmann, H., Busse, C., Bode, C., & Henke, M. (2014). Sustainability-related supply chain risks: Conceptualization and management. *Business Strategy and the Environment, 23*(3), 160–172. doi:10.1002/bse.1778

Huq, F. A., & Stevenson, M. (2020). Implementing Socially Sustainable Practices in Challenging Institutional Contexts: Building Theory from Seven Developing Country Supplier Cases. *Journal of Business Ethics, 161*(2), 415–442. doi:10.100710551-018-3951-x

ISO (2017). ISO 20400:2017, Sustainable procurement – Guidance.

Jabbour, A. B. L. (2015). Understanding the genesis of green supply chain management: Lessons from leading Brazilian companies. *Journal of Cleaner Production, 87*(1), 385–390. doi:10.1016/j.jclepro.2014.09.034

Jüttner, U., & Maklan, S. (2011). Supply chain resilience in the global financial crisis: An empirical study. *Supply Chain Management, 16*(4), 246–259. doi:10.1108/13598541111139062

Klassen, R. D., & Vereecke, A. (2012). Social issues in supply chains: Capabilities link responsibility, risk (opportunity) and performance. *International Journal of Production Economics, 140*(1), 103–115. doi:10.1016/j.ijpe.2012.01.021

Knoppen, D., & Saenz, M. (2015). Purchasing: Can we bridge the gap between strategy and daily reality? *Business Horizons, 58*(1), 123–133. doi:10.1016/j.bushor.2014.09.006

KPMG. (2020). *COVID-19: Supply chain fraud and corruption threats - How to protect your business from new fraud and corruption risks within your supply chain.* Available at: https://home.kpmg/au/en/home/insights/2020/05/coronavirus-covid-19-supply-chain-fraud-corruption-threats.html

Lindell, M., Prater, C., & Perry, R. (2007). *Introduction to Emergency Management.* Wiley.

Meixell, M. J., & Luoma, P. (2015). Stakeholder pressure in sustainable supply chain management: A systematic review. *International Journal of Physical Distribution & Logistics Management, 45*(1/2), 69–89. doi:10.1108/IJPDLM-05-2013-0155

Miemczyk, J., Johnsen, T. E., & Macquet, M. (2012). Sustainable purchasing and supply management: A structured literature review of definitions and measures at the dyad, chain and network levels. *Supply Chain Management, 17*(5), 478–496. doi:10.1108/13598541211258564

Monczka, R. M., Handfield, R. B., Giunipero, L. C., & Patterson, J. L. (2015). *Purchasing and supply chain management* (6th ed.). Cengage Learning.

Naomi, S., Bolis, I., Monteiro, M., & Carvalho, D. (2018). From an ideal dream towards reality analysis : Proposing Sustainable Value Exchange Matrix (SVEM) from systematic literature review on sustainable business models and face validation. *Journal of Cleaner Production, 178,* 76–88. doi:10.1016/j.jclepro.2017.12.078

North, D. C. (1990). *Institutions, Institutional Change, and Economic Performance.* Cambridge University Press. doi:10.1017/CBO9780511808678

OECD. (2021). *Towards ethical supply chains.* Available at: https://www.oecd.org/about/impact/towards-ethical-supply-chains.htm

Pettit, T. J., Croxton, K. L., & Fiksel, J. (2013). Ensuring supply chain resilience: Development and implementation of an assessment tool. *Journal of Business Logistics, 34*(1), 46–76. doi:10.1111/jbl.12009

Pettit, T. J., Fiksel, J., & Croxton, K. L. (2010). Ensuring supply chain resilience: Development of a conceptual framework. *Journal of Business Logistics, 31*(1), 1–21. doi:10.1002/j.2158-1592.2010.tb00125.x

Pinnington, B., Meehan, J., & Trautrims, A. (2021). *Implications of Covid-19 for modern slavery challenges in supply chain management.* Available at: https://www.cips.org/PageFiles/172121/MSPEC%20Supply%20Chains%20Research_Summary.pdf

Ponomarov, S. Y., & Holcomb, M. C. (2009). Understanding the concept of supply chain resilience. *International Journal of Logistics Management, 20*(2), 124–143. doi:10.1108/09574090910954873

Pournarder, M., & Wohlgezogen, F. (2021). *Keeping supply chains ethical and sustainable amid covid-19.* Available at: https://pursuit.unimelb.edu.au/articles/keeping-supply-chains-ethical-and-sustainable-amid-covid-19

Puka, B. (2020). *The Golden Rule. Internet Encyclopedia of Philosophy – A peer-reviewed academic resource.* Retrieved from: https://www.iep.utm.edu/goldrule/

Reich, J. W. (2006). Three psychological principles of resilience in natural disasters. *Disaster Prevention and Management: An International Journal, 15*(5), 793–798. doi:10.1108/09653560610712739

Rose, A. (2004). Economic resilience to disasters: toward a consistent and comprehensive formulation. In D. Paton & D. Johnston (Eds.), *Disaster Resilience: An Integrated Approach* (pp. 226–248). Charles C. Thomas.

Sancha, C., Wong, C. W. Y., & Gimenez, C. (2019). Do dependent suppliers benefit from buying firms' sustainability practices? *Journal of Purchasing and Supply Management, 25*(4), 100542. doi:10.1016/j.pursup.2019.100542

SEDEX. (2020). *Sedex Insights Report: COVID-19 Impacts On Businesses*. Available at: https://www.sedex.com/sedex-insights-report-covid-19-impacts-on-businesses/

Seles, B. M. R. P., de Sousa Jabbour, A. B. L., Jabbour, C. J. C., & Dangelico, R. M. (2016). The green bullwhip effect, the diffusion of green supply chain practices: and institutional pressures: evidence from the automotive sector. *International Journal of Production Economics, 182*, 342–355. doi:10.1016/j.ijpe.2016.08.033

Shafer, W., Fukukawa, K., & Lee, G. (2007). Values and the Perceived Importance of Ethics and Social Responsibility: The U.S. versus China. *Journal of Business Ethics, 70*(3), 265–284. doi:10.100710551-006-9110-9

Shaw, D., & Shiu, E. (2002). The role of ethical obligation and self-identity in ethical consumer choice. *International Journal of Consumer Studies, 26*(2), 109–116. doi:10.1046/j.1470-6431.2002.00214.x

Silvestre, B. (2016). Sustainable supply chain management: Current debate and future directions. *Gestão & Produção, 23*(2), 235–249. doi:10.1590/0104-530x2202-16

Smith, N., Palazzo, G., & Bhattacharya, C. (2010). Marketing's Consequences: Stakeholder Marketing and Supply Chain Corporate Social Responsibility Issues. *Business Ethics Quarterly, 20*(4), 617–641. doi:10.5840/beq201020440

Svensson, G. (2009). The transparency of SCM ethics: Conceptual framework and empirical illustrations. *Supply Chain Management, 14*(4), 259–269. doi:10.1108/13598540910970090

Svensson, G., Wood, G., & Callaghan, M. (2010). A corporate model of sustainable business practices: An ethical perspective. *Journal of World Business, 45*(4), 336–345. doi:10.1016/j.jwb.2009.08.005

UNCTAD. (2020). *COVID-19 has changed online shopping forever, survey shows*. Available at: https://unctad.org/news/covid-19-has-changed-online-shopping-forever-survey-shows

United Nations Global Compact and BSR. (2015). *Supply Chain Sustainability: A Practical Guide for Continuous Improvement* (2nd ed.). UNEP Business and Industry Global Dialogue.

Van Weele, A.J. (2010). *Purchasing and Supply Chain Management: Analysis, Strategy, Planning and Practice*. Cengage Learning.

Waligora, R. (2020). *COVID-19: Ethical supply chains in the spotlight? How to maintain an ethical supply chain during the COVID-19 crisis*. Available at: https://home.kpmg/uk/en/blogs/home/posts/2020/06/covid-19-puts-ethical-supply-chains-in-the-spotlight.html

Yao, Y., & Fabbe-Costes, N. (2018). Can you measure resilience if you are unable to define it? The analysis of Supply Network Resilience (SNRES). *Supply Chain Forum: An International Journal, 19*(4), 255-265.

Zhang, Q., Pan, J., Jiang, Y., & Feng, T. (2019). The impact of green supplier integration on firm performance: The mediating role of social capital accumulation. *Journal of Purchasing and Supply Management, 26*(2), 100579. doi:10.1016/j.pursup.2019.100579

Zouari, D., Ruel, S., & Viale, L. (2020). Does digitalising the supply chain contribute to its resilience? *International Journal of Physical Distribution & Logistics Management, 51*(2), 149–180. doi:10.1108/IJPDLM-01-2020-0038

# Chapter 21
# Green Supply Chain Management Post-COVID-19 Pandemic

**Babita Srivastava**
*William Paterson University, USA*

## ABSTRACT

*In this chapter, the author reviews the literature to understand the association between the adoption of green supply chain practices and abnormal returns during COVID-19 outbreak to test whether companies adopting green supply chain policies experienced lesser negative returns during the market collapse. In this chapter, the author discusses various drivers for establishing sustainability in supply chain following the COVID-19 pandemic and establishes an empirical relation between sustainability and effectiveness. The following topics are highlighted in this chapter: (1) introduction to green supply chain management, (2) environmental benefit of green supply chain management, (3) economic aspect of green supply chain management, (4) trend in supply chain management, (5) sustainable supply chain and COVID-19, (6) drivers of supply chain sustainability in context of COVID-19, and (7) green supply chain management policies.*

## INTRODUCTION

As years go by, there is an expectation that technology will continue to innovate, that the climate will improve and that lives across the globe will get better. There are times where there are major setbacks, such as in the year 2020 with the arrival of a global pandemic, COVID-19. At the end of 2019, China was the first to hit with this virus (Eroğlu, 2020). Many were unaware of the severity of it or how quickly it would spread. It quickly turned into a truly global pandemic where it is highly contagious and can be contracted by anyone. The coronavirus disease 2019 (COVID-19) outbreak was declared a public health emergency of international concern by the World Health Organization (WHO) on 30 January 2020 when all 34 regions of China had cases of infection, and the total case count surpassed that for the severe acute respiratory syndrome (SARS) of 2003 (BBC News, 2020). None of the nations were prepared for

DOI: 10.4018/978-1-7998-9506-0.ch021

Copyright © 2022, IGI Global. Copying or distributing in print or electronic forms without written permission of IGI Global is prohibited.

this unfortunate event. There is now a major health crisis in which only so much can be done for it to be mitigated. Everywhere one can look there are faces with masks on and people maintaining a six-feet distance from most, which is a requirement in most institutions. COVID-19 brought with it many deaths and many health issues. This has also greatly impacted the economies across the world, regardless of their status of being a developed or underdeveloped nation.

COVID-19 has adversely impacted sustainable economic development and has severely affected the global economy and financial markets. There have been significant reductions in income, a rise in unemployment, and disruptions in the transportation, service, and manufacturing industries are among the consequences of the disease. Now different countries are taking mitigation measures to minimize the impact of this pandemic, but one thing become clear that none of the governments and global health-care systems were prepared to deal with such a tragic event. The entire world underestimated the risks of rapid COVID-19 spread and were mostly reactive in their crisis response. As disease outbreaks are not likely to disappear soon, proactive international actions are required to not only save lives but also protect economic prosperity. Significant economic impact has already occurred across the globe due to reduced productivity, loss of life, business closures, trade disruption, and decimation of the tourism industry. COVID-19 may be that "wake-up" call for global leaders to intensify cooperation on epidemic preparedness and provide the necessary financing for international collective action. There has been ample information on the expected economic and health costs of infectious disease outbreaks, but the world has failed to adequately invest in preventive and preparedness measures to mitigate the risks of large epidemic.

COVID-19 has hit this world with devastating effect and developing countries were hit particularly hard. Before COVID-19, the UN has called for coordinated action from the world's leading economies toward 17 Sustainable Development Goals (SDGs) and maximum financial and technical support for the poorest and most vulnerable people and countries (Barbier & Burgess, 2020). As Figure 1 indicates, the pandemic is likely to adversely impact 12 of the 17 SDG goals. This will occur at a critical juncture for some of the sustainable economic goals when 736 million people still live-in extreme poverty, 821 million are undernourished, 785 million people lack even basic drinking water services, and 673 million still practice open defecation. About 3 billion people lack clean cooking fuels and technology, and of the 840 million people without electricity, 87% live in rural areas (Barbier & Burgess, 2020).

Another major impact was the fact that COVID-19 had hit China first, a major player in the economic sphere. In a strongly connected and integrated world, the impacts of the disease go beyond those who have died and those who may be unable to work due being high-risk and it has become apparent since the outbreak. Since the Chinese economy has slowed down with interruptions to production, "the functioning of global supply chains has been disrupted. Companies across the world, irrespective of size and geographical location, that are dependent upon inputs from China have started experiencing contractions in production. Transport being limited and even restricted among countries has further slowed global economic activities. Most importantly, some panic among consumers and firms has distorted usual consumption patterns and created market anomalies. Global financial markets have also been responsive to the changes and global stock indices have plunged" (Barbier & Burgess, 2020).

*Figure 1. The impact of COVID-19 on the UN Sustainable Development Goals (Adapted from [Barbier & Burgess, 2020]).*

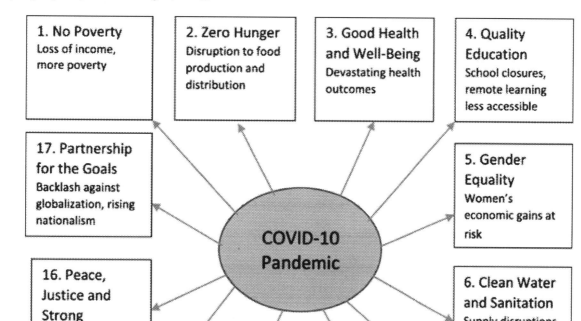

Globally, economies are connected by cross-border flows of goods, services, knowledge, people, financial capital, foreign investment, international banking, and exchange rates. They are also connected by beliefs and "all these things are also mechanisms for the propagation of economic shocks, or economic contagion. The transportation restrictions have also slowed economic activity and production. There is also the impact to the firms and financial markets. The rise in risk might reveal that one or more key financial market players have taken investment positions that are unprofitable under current conditions, further weakening trust in financial instruments and markets. Different countries and territories are expected to experience divergent recovery paths, with the shape of that path for each location influenced by the interplay between their experience in containing and managing the spread of COVID-19 and the underlying socio-economic characteristics of each country or territory, as is evident in the disparity of cases per capita in several countries, regardless of their economic standing. The analysis reveals trade exposed countries may take proportionally longer to recover in the scenario where the COVID-19 pandemic becomes drawn out compared to less trade exposed states (McKibbin & Fernando, 2020).

Simply, the longer the pandemic continues, the more damaging it becomes to world trade. Recent progress on coronavirus vaccines has brightened the economic outlook, but some economists believe that a potentially slow rollout of vaccines across developing economies could hamper the return of activity to pre-pandemic levels. Even among advanced economies, renewed lockdowns in Europe in a bid to stave off a resurgence in infections could push back economic recovery (World Economy, 2020).

The impact of the pandemic has had devastating effect on all aspects of the global economy as well as general sectors, including logistics and supply chain management. As stated by Ubaid Illahi and Mohammad Shaf Mir in their article, "Maintaining efficient logistics and supply chain management operations during and after coronavirus (COVID-19) pandemic: learning from the past experiences," several issues related to logistics and supply chain management "arise during the containment period of an epidemic/ pandemic. These issues are primarily related to facilities, their location and capacities, selection and deployment of transportation as well as distribution modes, and replenishing the stock capacities across the whole supply chain." With these issues, there is an increased need to streamline and make the supply chain process efficient in both means and profit but also, sustainable. In this book chapter, the author intends to review the literature to understand the association between the adoption of green supply chain practices and abnormal returns during COVID-19 outbreak, to test whether companies adopting green supply chain policies experienced lesser negative returns during the market collapse. The chapter will also focus on a specific feature of supply chains—the extent to which they are environmentally sustainable as well as their economic aspects. The following topics will be highlighted in this chapter:

1. Introduction to green supply chain management
2. Environmental benefit of green supply chain management
3. Economic aspect of green supply chain management
4. Trend in supply chain management
5. Sustainable supply chain and COVID-19
6. Drivers of supply chain sustainability in context of COVID-19 and
7. Green supply chain management policies.

## BACKGROUND

For centuries, manufacturing of goods was directly dependent on accessibility of raw material. The barter system was the main method to exchanges of goods and services. Technology was not yet in the picture. The modes of transportation were simple with the use of beasts of burden such as bulls and horses. At that time, supply chain was very limited. Over the last century, supply chain practices have evolved to respond to the current, ever-changing market needs and with new technology. Supply chain processes went much smoother and easier as time went on. In the 21st century, there has been drastic changes. Though technology and modern methodologies made global and domestic supply chains easier than ever, it has brought environmental and sustainability problems.

With millions of vehicles running on the road producing pollution to many factories and farms machineries producing many types of gas, the carbon footprint left behind is a devastating one. On one hand, we are getting so many facilities and luxuries as a result of the products produced but on the other hand, we are dealing with health issues due to an unhealthy environment. This had not been an issue in the earlier productions of goods and services. Technology has had a big impact on human life and as

*Green Supply Chain Management Post-COVID-19 Pandemic*

we continue to innovate, there should be more ecofriendly production and a more sustainable method to supply chain management.

Green supply chain management is the concept of integrating sustainable environmental processes into the traditional supply chain. By creating more sustainable practices of supply chain management, this reduces the carbon footprint made by organizations and companies as well as better cost savings and profitability in the long run. It is a management process that incorporates the two fields of supply chain management and sustainability. Supply chain management is "the assimilation of major business processes, which delivers products, services, resources, and information from suppliers to consumers that add value for consumers and other stakeholders" (Mamun, 2021). Pre-pandemic, multinational corporations (MNCs) and their suppliers would attempt to adhere to sustainable practices but in reality, that was difficult to maintain. In a post-pandemic, or rather, concurrent pandemic world, this is even more difficult as MNCs and other firms had taken such adverse financial hits, their focus would naturally be to increase profit as much as possible.

Now that the road to recovery is being tread due to the increase of vaccinated individuals in the world, the economy is beginning to start its recovery, but the impact of the pandemic has been detrimental. Regardless, MNCs and other firms should still do what they can to incorporate green supply chain management in their processes. More than ever, there is a need to make sure that we work towards being environmentally friendly in all aspects of living. The United Nations has even named the 2020s the "Decade of Action" as globally, progress must be made towards sustainable practices and solutions. This new decade calls for "accelerating sustainable solutions to all the world's biggest challenges — ranging from poverty and gender to climate change, inequality and closing the finance gap" (The United Nations, 2021).

Before COVID-19, many manufacturing firms relied on imported intermediate inputs from China and other countries that have since been greatly affected by the disease. Many companies also relied on sales in other countries to meet their financial goals. The slowdown in economic activity - and transportation restrictions - in affected countries had impacted the production and profitability of specific global companies, particularly in manufacturing and in raw materials used in manufacturing. For companies that rely on intermediate goods from affected regions, and that are not able to easily switch sourcing, the size of the impact may depend on how quickly the Pandemic truly ends. After dealing with the repercussions of COVID-19, implementing green supply chain management practices will benefit corporations greatly and this would be a good time to begin.

*Figure 2. Benefits of a green supply chain*
*(Adapted from [Spend Edge, 2021])*

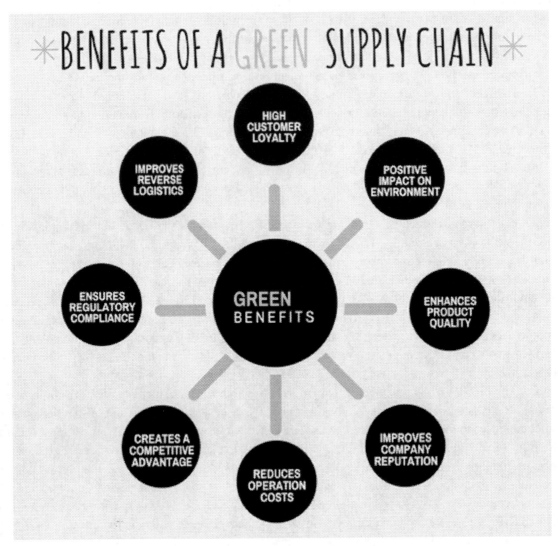

Green supply chain management focuses on two areas: green design and green operations. Green design focuses on environmental conscious designs and life cycle assessments and analysis of the product being created and emphasizes how design decisions affects the product's environmental compatibility. Green operation, on the other hand, focuses on operational aspects related to reverse logistics, network design, green manufacturing, remanufacturing and waste management (Qinglong et al, 2015). It's by focusing on these two aspects that corporations may be able to implement these practices into their supply chains. Figure 2 marks the several benefits of green supply chain management, many of which will be discussed later on in this chapter (Spend Edge, 2021). There are many concerns in the business community in the need for green supply chain management and many of the concerns and issues are completely understandable. However, as will be explained throughout this chapter, there are many benefits that will, in the long term, benefit companies, people and the environment as a whole, despite a global pandemic.

## MAIN FOCUS OF THE CHAPTER

### Issues, Controversies and Problems

In India, a country that suffers from awful toxic air pollution, the pandemic that drove people to stay in their homes and off the streets and out factories made an impact to the air quality. For the first time in quite some time the Himalayan mountains were visible to those who were unable to see in past due to haze of pollution. Considering how great an impact that was brings fourth the need for green supply chain management policies and environmentally friendly methods into our traditional supply chain. When one thinks of going "green," that automatically comes with the implications that it will be environmentally friendly. There are several benefits of reducing waste when engaging in supply chain management. When products are delivered more efficiently and with little to no waste, it can reduce the carbon footprint on the environment.

Though individual reduction of one's carbon footprint is helpful, it's much more beneficial for a MNC to consider their impact on the environment as it is much bigger than one individual. For many corporations and firms, in order to make their respective goods, products, etc., they utilize technology, machinery, objects that require resources. By implementing green supply chain management policies, firms can figure out ways to efficiently use the resources they need as well as find alternative ones that bring many benefits to the environment. During the pandemic, due to lockdown and reduction of work, pollution in certain countries had been reduced. For example, the Himalayan Mountains in India was more visible than prior to the pandemic as a result of the lockdown. A clear example such as that shows how we are damaging the environment and the living beings that reside in it. By implementing sustainable practices, businesses can make a positive impact on the environment.

Green supply chain management as a practice creates a certain process that is sustainable in nature and effective in minimizing the environmental impacts. Other definitions integrating environment thinking into supply chain management include, product design, material sourcing and selection manufacturing process delivery of the final product to the consumer and end of life management of the product after its useful life. Some of the recent innovations made in the green supply chain management are green for manufacturing reverse logistics and green distribution. Transportation is one of the critical factors which contributes to an increase in carbon dioxide emissions. Therefore, industries are now adopting green transportation by replacing fossil fuels with other environment friendly fuels such as biofuels or are using technology hybrid vehicles battery operated vehicles.

Another benefit to strive for is the reduction of organic waste. Organic waste is "any material originating from a plant or animal that can be decomposed by microorganisms or consists of the remains, residues or waste products of any organism" (CEC, 2017). Corporations create tons of organic waste and by properly managing it, they can reduce the environmental impact. The benefit of reducing organic waste and better organic waste management include but are not limited to: creating a source of energy through conversions of organic waste into biofuels, avoiding methane emissions and reducing greenhouse gas (GHS) emissions as well as improving soil water retention and supplying nutrients to the soils though the use of compost (CEC, 2017). Beyond the switch to alternate resources, equipment companies have started to switch to goods and components which are environmentally safe. Many industries have also adopted green warehouse groups where the appliances and such are also eco-friendly.

With a reduction in the use and need of fossil fuels and implementation of renewable energy practice, that will surely assist in cultivating a healthier environment. Renewable energy is often thought of as a

*Green Supply Chain Management Post-COVID-19 Pandemic*

new technology, but harnessing nature's power has long been used for heating, transportation, lighting, and more. Wind has powered boats to sail the seas and windmills to grind grain. The sun has provided warmth during the day and helped kindle fires to last into the evening. But over the past 500 years or so, humans increasingly turned to cheaper, dirtier energy sources such as coal and fracked gas. Renewable power is booming, as innovation brings down costs and starts to deliver on the promise of a clean energy future. American solar and wind generation are breaking records and being integrated into the national electricity grid without compromising reliability.

Now that we have increasingly innovative and less-expensive ways to capture and retain wind and solar energy, renewables are becoming a more important power source, accounting for more than one-eighth of U.S. generation. The expansion in renewables is also happening at scales large and small, from rooftop solar panels on homes that can sell power back to the grid to giant offshore wind farms. Even some entire rural communities rely on renewable energy for heating and lighting.

Renewable energy is a cost-effective source of new power that insulates power markets and consumers from volatility, supports economic stability and stimulates sustainable growth. With renewable additions providing most of the new capacity last year, many countries and regions recognize the degree to which the energy transition can deliver positive outcomes. While the trajectory is positive, more is required to put global energy on a path with sustainable development and climate mitigation – both of which offer significant economic benefits. At this challenging time, we are reminded of the importance of building resilience into our economies. In what must be the decade of action, enabling policies are needed to increase investments and accelerate renewables adoption.

With the implementation of renewable energy and other green supply chain practices, not only would there be positive effects on the environment but also on the human aspect. Humans in general will benefit from a greener, cleaner environment. It's possible that a pandemic to the scale of the COVID-19 may not have been a worse issue if humans were generally healthier. Not only should corporations consider the general health of the public but also how they are viewed by said public. Many people look favorably on corporations that are more sustainable as it is now a social issue and one that many care about. The cleaner a company is in terms of their business practices, the more positive they would be looked on by the public.

## SOLUTIONS AND RECOMMENDATIONS

As consumers become more aware of the state of the world as well as take more stock in their moral standing and values, they center their buying habits around their views and needs. One such consideration is the impact of what companies have on the environment. Over the years, consumers have become more ecofriendly and choose to only buy from or work with companies that have sustainable practices. Naturally, consumers hold sway over what and from where they purchase their services and products. If people stop buying, the firm must consider that their supply is based on demand and have consumer awareness. If a business shows that they are ecofriendly and have practices that are based on sustainability, they will be more inclined to work with hat business. Companies should also take in to account the health of their workers and of their consumers. Focusing on green supply chain and other business practices will make a great impact on the health of the environment and by extension, the health of the people who would ostensibly be purchasing their goods and services. An unhealthy populace is not one that will be feeding into the economy.

*Green Supply Chain Management Post-COVID-19 Pandemic*

It's not just consumers that businesses are beholden to but all stakeholders. More attention from consumers, investors, and regulators will bring more scrutiny of firms' green supply chain management track records, and less tolerance of token efforts to make supply chains sustainable. Improved transparency and disclosure are critical to stakeholders (Cottrill, 2021). He and Harris (2020) identified that the ethical dimensions of consumption became more relevant during the pandemic and a shift to more responsible and prosocial consumption was expected. Investors may consider companies that focus on green supply chain management have the capabilities to bounce back from unexpected circumstances. By utilizing sustainable practices, it may generate faster stock returns as they have the faith of their investor in their capabilities, especially during periods of crisis (Fasan et al, 2021). There has been increased pressure on firms to devote resources to sustainable supply chain practices and that seems to suggest that sustainability is a business trend as opposed to a fad (Cottrill, 2021). Those that focus on sustainable supply chain management have the knowledge and understanding of the supply chain and ostensibly, can make changes as needed based on the circumstances. Firms must also make sure that they meet the conditions of the countries in which their business are located. For example, the national assembly in France voted recently that "businesses should be required to conduct due diligence assessments for human rights and the environment. Fines of up to 10 million or civil liability are planned" (Schöder & Kucht Campos, 2021).

Though there are benefits to implementing green supply chain management practices, there are many challenges faced by supply chain leaders. Though one of the benefits leads to reduced costs over time, initially, costs may increase as the supply chains get analyzed and changed to become more sustainable. Some business may not be in a position to make a change that will have them lose profits especially at a time when business had been impacted severely by the pandemic and loss of employees. In his article "Push to make supply chains more sustainable continues to gain momentum," Cottrill (2021) states, "Small-to medium-sized enterprises were far less committed, and more work is needed to bring them into the fold through a better understanding of the barriers they face." Larger firms and corporations have the flexibility and manpower to continue working on sustainable, green supply chain management.

There is also the case that with a loss of employees either through the pandemic itself, vaccine mandates or unavoidable layoffs, that there may not have the manpower or talent to oversee the complexity of sustainable supply chains especially in that it is not the norm. While there is an increase in acceptance and analysis of green supply chain management, present knowledge may not be enough to make supply chains, truly and completely sustainable (Pagell & Shevchenko, 2013). Though it can probably work with the right people and businesses in place, once a switch to green supply chain management has begun, there is also the challenge in making sure that all aspects of the supply chain are also on the same wavelength. That is to say that companies, in an effort to focus on sustainability, will have to have their suppliers and whatever other corporations they work with either be sustainable as well or comply to their sustainability practices as well as their for-profit needs. For example, though a company may ask a supplier to make sure to meet their sustainable needs, they may also be asking for it to be as cost effective as possible, which for some suppliers, especially those in developing or undeveloped nations, may not be able to maintain the same level of cost *and* follow green practices.

431

## FUTURE RESEARCH DIRECTIONS

Certain trends have come to pass in supply chain management especially in this post-pandemic world. During the pandemic, people had been, and some continue to be, locked down. With that lock down, the need and use of online shopping increased. It's one of the benefits for global friendly shopping and increased the need to have e-commerce practices in place so as to meet customer needs and demands quickly and efficiently. Outsourcing had been well-utilized prior to the pandemic but many firms are looking to specialists in specific supply chain activities so that they may streamline the process and increase profitability. There are long term trends that may be put to use or at least consideration after the severe impact of COVID-19 on the economies of the world. Seeing as the pandemic affected many aspects of the economy, there will of course be lasting effects to the supply chain logistics. These long-term trends include but are not limited to: redundancy, near-shoring and resilience (Sureddin, 2021). Redundancy is a method in which a back-up is created to maintain the supply chain in the event of major disruption, such as a pandemic. Supply-chain managers and leaders understand, especially post pandemic, the need to reduce the risk of out-of-stock events and disruptions (Sureddin, 2021). To reduce disruption as well as increase sustainability, near shoring is another trend that will see increased use in the future, or should see increased use. With manufacturers and suppliers closer together, reduces risk of disruption as well as reduces carbon emissions through the use of long-distanced transportation. Lastly, resilience in the visibility and real-time monitoring of risk will be very important, especially as the digitation of the supply chain becomes more utilized (Sureddin, 2021).

On top seeking certain specialists, there has been an increased need in going digital, especially with the need to keep people socially distant in the workplace. With an automated process in place, the makes the supply chain easier to manage. The utilization of technology will continue to grow as years progress, as history has shown. The Association for Supply Chain Management (ASCM) have documented expected trends to come. One such trend is the use of artificial intelligence and machine learning for predictive and prescriptive analysis (ASCM, 2021). In Figure 3, it displays the projection of the potential usage of emerging technologies, such as artificial intelligence, among others. It is believed that with this machine learning that they will be able to efficiently be able to parse through real time data in order to streamline production and reduce over-production and therefore, overuse of resources as well as predict any potential disruptions to the supply chain. According to the ASCM (2021), "(t)he Internet of Things (IoT) continues to revolutionize supply chains by increasing visibility and real-time tracking for both raw materials and final products. With cheap and reliable sensors about both raw materials and final products. This is making networks more responsive and competitive." With IoT making networks more responsive, it increases the efficiency of the supply chain, reducing the need to waste resources, time and products.

*Figure 3. Adoption of cutting-edge technologies by supply chain companies projections (Adapted from [Tao, 2021]).*

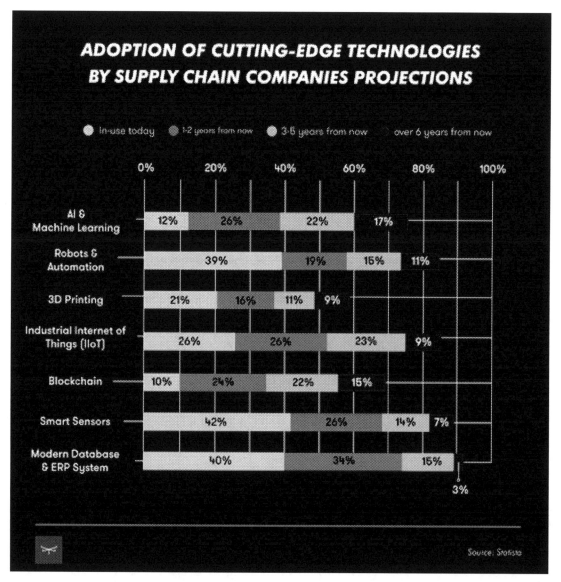

COVID-19 has made a large impact on supply chains as well as its sustainability. The pandemic has revealed the fragility of global supply chains and the "pursuit of financial efficiency has shifted global production to low-cost regions, increased the flows of freights, caused port congestion and eroded the resilience of supply chains. Cutting costs above all else became a race to the bottom. It resulted in global economies with limited redundancies, contingencies and safeguards" (Guitouni, 2021). It is without doubt that the disruption has expanded across nations, firms and more specifically, supply chains. The disruption is fluid in nature as it moves in waves from region to region and from one type of supply chain to another. The duration of the combined disruptions is undetermined and may endure for years to come (Black & Glaser-Segura, 2020). There is no clear cut way to see how deeply COVID-19 has impacted but firms can do what they can to lessen that impact and take what happened as a lesson to update how supply chains operate and how to make them more sustainable. While organizations have made some changes in their supply chains to adapt to the effects of the COVID-19 pandemic, new infectious diseases are emerging due to "multifactorial circumstances including population growth, globalization of trade, changes in nutritional, agricultural, and trade practices, shifts in land-use including accelerated urbanization, deforestation, and encroachment on wildlife" (Coker, et al., 2011, p.326; Black & Glaser-Segura, 2020).

With that in mind, firms must come up with a strategy or methodology to mitigate disruptions due to global, or national crises. The circumstances created by the pandemic have overlapping driving factors, which promote the need to focus more attention on risks from natural hazard and create new risk contingencies based on new threats (Black & Glaser-Segura, 2020). As an example, 100% of the food industry experienced issues with production and distribution, and 91% with their supplier base (Alicke et al., 2020). Overall, due to COVID-19 multiple industries and sectors across the globe have experienced severe disruptions, which have impacted global supply chains at unprecedented levels (Black & Glaser-Segura, 2020). At this point, firms are doing their best to make necessary changes in light of the issues the pandemic not only created but also highlighted. Black and Galser-Segura (2020) have looked at the new literature that has been created since the pandemic and have summarized it in a strategic pandemic mitigation model, as seen in Figure 4. Extensive planning is an absolute necessity so that firms not only can adjust during the pandemic but for the future as well.

*Figure 4. Strategic mitigation model*
*(Adapted from [Black & Glaser-Segura, 2020]).*

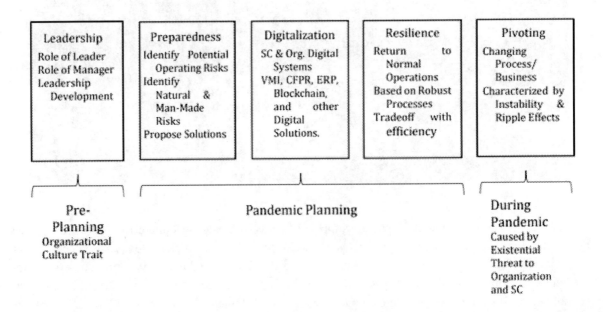

According to new research from the MIT Center for Transportation and Logistics (CTL), supply chain sustainability investments did not slow down, despite the COVID-19 pandemic. The research included an international survey of supply chain professionals with over 2,400 respondents and over eighty percent of survey respondents claimed the pandemic either had no impact or increased their firms' commitments to sustainable supply chain management. Eighty-three percent of the executives interviewed during the survey said that COVID-19 had either accelerated sustainable supply chain management activity or increased awareness and brought urgency to this growing field (Cottrill, 2021). Another survey through the Sustainable Procurement Barometer, which is based on buyers and sellers from more than 350 companies, found that even as firms dealt with the challenges of the pandemic, most remained committed to integrating sustainability into their supply chain management (Harrison, 2021). There is motivation, especially after the pandemic, to continue with supply chain sustainability. Harris (2021) states, "sustainable procurement requires greater visibility into suppliers' practices and encourages collaboration between suppliers and buyers, these programs can make it easier to quickly assess and respond to crises…63% of buyers and 73% of suppliers reported that sustainable procurement practices helped them endure the pandemic."

The world has realized that the COVID-19 pandemic is no more a simply a global health crisis but it has significantly impacted global economy. This pandemic has created a difficult condition for supply-chain across the globe. In one report 94% of Fortune 1000 companies have experienced COVID-19 related supply chain disruptions (Kilpatrick & Barter, 2020). One positive side of this crisis is that they put supply chain sustainability in the spotlight. Policy makers and private players are forces to rethink their global supply chain and accelerate their capabilities for the adaption of long-term sustainability in managing future challenges (Remko, 2020; Ivanov, 2020).

It is now reality that without sustainable supply chain and rapidly changing market situations and customer awareness regarding health issues and environmental and social concerns, production of end goods and services is not feasible (Bag et al., 2020). There are several parameters (drivers) associated with the organization that is necessary to enable sustainable supply-chain adoption and even enhancement in efficiency and responsiveness. Awareness of drivers will also help industries determine their SSC initiatives for sustainable performance. In fact, many companies are starting to place greater emphasis on the implementation of sustainability drivers because of multiple pressures and awareness (i.e., vendor collaboration and procurement tactics), changes in consumer preference and perception, improvement of regulations, and the principles and policies of organizations (Zeng et al. 2017; Matthews et al. 2019). Sustainability is also important for organizations to ensure efficient operational as well as economic performance, risk management, quick responses to uncertain environments, fulfillment of the sustainability expectations, and achievement of sustainability practices (Tseng et al. 2019; Sajjad et al. 2020).

What will happen to sustainability in supply chains – Post-COVID-19? Broad socio-political forces have always played a role in supply chain operations; whether they are from tariffs on goods, new norms related to safety practices, or regulations on technological practices (Handfield, et al., 2020). Similarly, there will be post-COVID-19 transformation of supply chain practices; but will these transformations stick? Technological and social innovations are important to supply chain sustainability transition. This crisis provides evidence that localized systems are more likely to be robust and resilient than global supply chains (Nandi, et al., 2021; Handfield et al., 2020). Localization is also important to environmental supply chain sustainability (Holmstrom and Gutowski, 2017). Local production can mean rapid response to local needs, but with low energy and resources consumption. For example, in the COVID-19 pandemic many 'hot-spots' emerged. Ensuring critical equipment and materials through more agile production and rapid delivery logistics to hot spots can equate to saving more lives or slowing the spread of positive cases—a social sustainability concern. Flexible manufacturing system technologies such as additive manufacturing and robotics can localize production capabilities. Social distancing, remote work, and reduced business travel during the COVID-19 crisis offer sustainable supply chain lessons. Reduced employee commuting and business travel contribute to reduced organizational carbon footprints. Virtual meetings and virtual reality acceptance is likely to increase and become the norm (Sarkis, et al., 2020a). In an interview with a machine parts distributing company, the interviewers were informed that they will likely require fewer physical supplier location visits due to greater distance communication acceptance.

COVID-19 consumer and individual behavioral responses may influence the prospects of both sharing and circular economy social innovations—the consumer behavioral move to online and e-commerce sales is one example (Wang, et al., 2020). Taking the pandemic into consideration, these drivers will have to make for necessary inspirations to adjust the older policies and make new and improved methodologies.

Prior to the pandemic, there had been a need to make aspects of work sustainable as stated earlier in this chapter. Now, whatever rules and regulations that were followed before COVID-19, needs to be modified. The situation many firms are facing is not like before. Green supply chain management is facing so many challenges such as lack of knowledge for green ecofriendly production, lack of resources, how to get or provide ecofriendly production, and experience for how to cope with consumers who are desperately affected by COVID-19. Moreover, the lack of managing standard working environment, prevalence of health issues, consumer priorities and owners' limitations all bear upon on green supply chain management. Taking all factors into consideration, green supply chain management needs to be incorporated into new policies, which can be designed according to post-pandemic situations.

Product design, material sources and selections manufacturing processes deliver final product in which the consumer receives to consume all need appropriate strategy and policy where the consumer is satisfied with their product and the firm continues to function with high efficiency. Since COVID-19 arrived all globalization organizers in organizations are facing so many changes including increased internationalization and global competition. Green supply chain management must fulfill three major responsibilities financial prospective, environmentally friendly production and societal prospective.

Green supply chain management is adaptable in virtually any industry. Sustainability should be a focus for firms when they handle the production, transportation and delivery of their products to consumers. In order to be successful in the adoption an eco-friendly method of production and delivery, their must be an adoption of sustainable techniques and in choice of suppliers as well as other businesses that get incorporated into the supply chain process (Tsui, 2019). First a foremost, the start of the supply chain begins with the raw materials. Firms should consider ethical sourcing, which involves a "focus on human, animal and environmental wellness" as well as finding sustainable materials that limits resource depletion, lowers acquisition costs and minimized carbon emissions (Tsui, 2019). It is important to consider the environment and the impact that is made on the beings that live in it. For a material to be sourced ethically, "suppliers must obtain it by respecting human harvesters and natural resources. Humane sourcing techniques can range from raising farmers' wages and providing paid maternity leave to practicing selective tree harvesting" (Tsui, 2019).

*Figure 5. The end-to-end approach of logistics and supply chain management (Adapted from [Illahi & Shafi Mir, 2021]).*

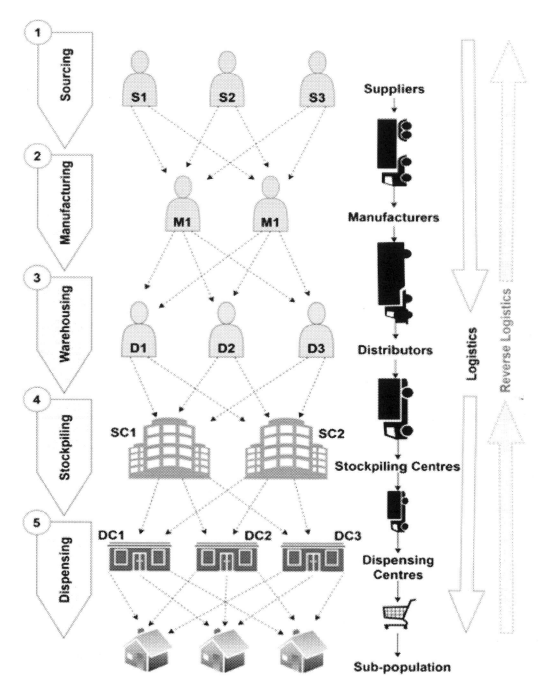

Through the production process, waste is created and that is where reverse logistics comes into play. It addresses how firms recycle and reuse products once they fulfill their initial purpose (Tsui, 2019). The supply chain is connected among various players and Figure 5 shows a sample supply chain that starts from the supplier and ends at the dispensing points (Illahi & Shafi Mir, 2021). It also showcases reverse logistics and when it is used in relation to the general supply chain. Proper disposal of products is a must in any process and a major regulation that many countries, states and cities expect firms to adhere to. Firms also utilize a closed-loop system which involves materials that go out, get returned by the consumer once utilized and the manufacturer can either properly dispose of it or recycle it into a new item or use it in a beneficial way (Tsui, 2019). This method is utilized by many firms, across various industries.

Firms should also put focus on how much is produced based on demand and need of their consumers. By analyzing trends appropriately, firms will only need to produce what is needed, when it is needed. Just-in-Time supply chain management is the method that focuses on this idea. With this strategy, it avoids overspending on materials and overfilling their warehouses and allows firms to better streamline their production, if executed well (Tsui, 2019). On top of producing the right amount, firms must take into consideration how these products get transported between production, storage and delivery to other business and to the consumers. Obviously, nearly all transportation methods contribute to carbon emissions and the like. It is how firms use alternative fuels as well as establish localized supplier and manufacturer relationships that helps reduce carbon emissions and create an efficient transportation chain.

The Environmental Protection Agency (EPA) has developed an initiative to address the issue and help manufacturers select sustainable freight carriers, track emissions and utilize fuel-saving technology in the process of transporting goods (Tsui, 2019). It is also important that firms utilize tried and true methods that work and in which there is ample research. Jenna Tsui (2019) reports, that green certifications, that lead the methodologies incorporated in green supply chain management strategies, such as "LEED, Green Globes, Energy Star and similar initiatives guarantees a company's commitment to sustainability. They require organizations to meet extensive criteria in measuring adherence to green practices. Supply-chain certification ensures that businesses employ eco-conscious methods by gauging and improving their current production methods."With all methods taken into consideration and utilized appropriately by firms, these strategies and policies can really impact the environment as well as increase the way the public views the firms and increase profits in the long run. Essentially, compacting packaging, embracing technology, establishing efficient green initiatives, improving green distribution networks, minimizing waste such as greenhouse gas, energy and solid waste, creating eco-friendly supply chain councils and procedures that regularly evaluate policies also improve green supply chain management in a better structural frame.

## CONCLUSION

As the world reels from the effects of COVID-19 on all aspects of life, firms and the like make the necessary changes to not only prevent issues of disruption, lack of resources as well as environmental and health decay amongst others. By improving all parts of how firms function from hiring practices to the utilization of resources to their supply chain management, the economy will see less of an impact of a global crisis in the future. The best methods in improving business practices is to make them sustainable. Green supply chain management is one such sustainability method that will positively impact not only the environment but also the firm itself in many aspects, from efficiency of resources, to higher profit margins, reduction of carbon and other waste emissions and proper use of technology.

The post-pandemic era is what the world will be dealing with in the foreseeable future. To not make adjustments to the policies and methodologies utilized will be a detriment. Not only for business operation but also consumer and stockholder faith in the ability to buy and sell products. As it stands, the

*Green Supply Chain Management Post-COVID-19 Pandemic*

severe disruptions to production have gravely impacted how many view companies and how they operate. As described in this chapter, there are many benefits to green supply chain management. Most easily recognized is the environmental benefits. As supply chain methods increase in efficiency and sustainability, naturally, there are environmental effects to that which include reduction of waste, increase in recycling, competent use of natural resources, and reduction of carbon remissions. With a new brand of "eco-friendly" best practices, it paints a better light for firms as seen by the public and by extension, stakeholders and investors. More and more people have become environmentally conscious, especially after the pandemic. Society has focused on the health and well-being of not only the environment but of the people.

There are also many economical and profitable benefits to implementing green supply chain practices. With the incorporation of more sustainable management policies, it increases the efficiency of the supply chain such as simplifying and reducing unnecessary steps in the supply chain, streamlining processes in the production and transportation of consumer goods, gathering insight into the supply chain process and how to effectively incorporate more technology to better anticipate adjustments in trends as well as severe disruptions, such as one from a global pandemic. With more brain power put towards supply chain management, industries and their firms should see more innovative methodologies that come about as a result of the issues that arose during the pandemic. Though COVID-19 was a literal blight on the world, lessons must be taken from the causes and effects to how the pandemic decimated the economic world. Sustainable and green supply chain management is a step in the right direction that should not be overlooked. At the end of the day, going green, becoming more eco-friendly is in the best interest of humans and their health. This chapter hopes to highlight that humans should be the focus, the consumers. Without them, corporations cannot continue to thrive. And with the pandemic fresh in mind, human health should continue to be a major focus going forward and the world would do well to do what it can to make the environment and the beings that live in it, as healthy as possible.

# REFERENCES

Alicke, K., Gupta, R., & Trautwein, V. (2020, July 21). *Resetting supply chains for the next normal.* McKinsey & Company. https://www.mckinsey.com/business-functions/operations/our-insights/resetting-supply-chains-for-the-next-normal#

Amankwah-Amoah, J., & Syllias, J. (2020). Can adopting ambitious environmental sustainability initiatives lead to business failures? An analytical framework. *Business Strategy and the Environment, 29,* 240–249. doi:10.1002/bse.2361

Association for Supply Chain Management. (2021). *2021 Top 10 supply chain trends.* ASCM's Research, Innovation and Strategy (RISC) Sensing Subcommittee, Assocation for Supply Chain Management. https://www.ascm.org/globalassets/ascm_website_assets/docs/5.9-2021-top-10-trends.pdf

Bag, S., Wood, L. C., Xu, L., Dhamija, P., & Kayikci, Y. (2020). Big data analytics as an operational excellence approach to enhance sustainable supply chain performance. *Resources, Conservation and Recycling, 153,* 104559. doi:10.1016/j.resconrec.2019.104559

Barbier, E. B., & Burgess, J. C. (2020). Sustainability and development after COVID-19. *World Development, 135,* 105082. doi:10.1016/j.worlddev.2020.105082 PMID:32834381

Barratt, M., & Oke, A. (2007). Antecedents of supply chain visibility in retail supply chains: A resource-based theory perspective. *Journal of Operations Management*, *25*(6), 1217–1233. doi:10.1016/j.jom.2007.01.003

BBC News. (2020, January 31). Worldwide cases overtake 2003 Sars outbreak. *BBC News*. https://www.bbc.com/news/world-51322733

Black, S., & Glaser-Segura, D. (2020). Supply Chain Resilience in a Pandemic: The Need for Revised Contingency Planning. *Management Dynamics in the Knowledge Economy*, *8*(4), 325–343. https://doi-org.ezproxy.wpunj.edu/10.2478/mdke-2020-0021

Coker, R., Rushton, J., Mounier-Jack, S., Karimuribo, E., Lutumba, P., Kambarage, D., & Rweyemamu, M. (2011). Towards a conceptual framework ti support one-health research for policy on emerging zoonoses. *The Lancet. Infectious Diseases*, *11*(4), 326–331. doi:10.1016/S1473-3099(10)70312-1 PMID:21376670

Commision for Environmental Cooperation. (2017). *Characterization and Management of Organic Waste in North America—White Paper*. Montreal, Canada: Commission for Environmental Cooperation. http://www.cec.org/fw/organic-waste-reports/

Cottrill, K. (2021). *Push to make supply chains more sustainable continues to gain momentum*. MIT Center for Transportation and Logistics. https://news.mit.edu/2021/supply-chain-sustainability-continues-to-gain-momentum-0719

Danso, A., Adomako, S., Amankwah-Amoah, J., Owusu-Agyei, S., & Konadu, R. (2019). Environmental sustainability orientation, competitive strategy and financial performance. *Business Strategy and the Environment*, *28*(5), 885–895. doi:10.1002/bse.2291

Guitouni, A., Waltho, C., & Nematollahi, M. (2021). How to make fragile global supply chains stronger and more sustainable. *PBS News Hour*. https://www.pbs.org/newshour/economy/how-to-make-fragile-global-supply-chains-stronger-and-more-sustainable

Harris, S. (2021). *Sustainable supply chains helped companies endure the pandemic*. Stanford Graduate School of Business. https://www.gsb.stanford.edu/insights/sustainable-supply-chains-helped-companies-endure-pandemic

He, P., Sun, Y., Zhang, Y., & Li, T. (2020). COVID–19's impact on stock prices across different sectors—An event study based on the chinese stock market. *Emerging Markets Finance and Trade. Routledge*, *56*(10), 2198–2212. doi:10.1080/1540496X.2020.1785865

Ivanov, D., & Das, A. (2020). Coronavirus (COVID-19/SARS-CoV-2) and supply chain resilience: A research note. *International Journal of Integrated Supply Management*, *13*(1), 90–102. doi:10.1504/IJISM.2020.107780

Kilpatrick, J. (n.d.). *Managing supply chain risk and disruption*. Deloitte. https://www2.deloitte.com/global/en/pages/risk/cyber-strategic-risk/articles/covid-19-managing-supply-chain-risk-and-disruption.html

Majumdar, A., Sanjib, M., & Sinha, K. (2020). COVID-19 debunks the myth of socially sustainable supply chain: A case of the clothing industry in South Asian countries. *Sustainable Production and Consumption, 24*, 150–155. doi:10.1016/j.spc.2020.07.001

Mamun, M. (2021). Sustaiable supply chain management: Insights from Australia's firms. *International Journal of Business and Management, 16*(11), 99. doi:10.5539/ijbm.v16n11p99

Matthews, N. E., Stamford, L., & Shapira, P. (2019). Aligning sustainability assessment with responsible research and innovation: Towards a framework for constructive sustainability assessment. *Sustainable Production and Consumption, 20*, 58–73. doi:10.1016/j.spc.2019.05.002 PMID:32051840

Pagell, M., & Shevchenko, A. (2013). Why research in sustainable supply chain management should have no future. *The Journal of Supply Chain Management, 50*(1), 44–55. doi:10.1111/jscm.12037

Remko, H. (2020). Research opportunities for a more resilient post-COVID-19 supply chain – closing the gap between research findings and industry practice. *International Journal of Operations and Production Management, 40*(4), 341–355.

Sajjad, A., Eweje, G., & Tappin, D. (2020). Managerial perspectives on drivers for and barriers to sustainable supply chain management implementation: Evidence from New Zealand. *Business Strategy and the Environment, 29*(2), 592–604. doi:10.1002/bse.2389

Sen, S. (2009). Linking Green Supply Chain Management and Shareholder Value Creation, The IUP. *The Journal of Supply Chain Management, 7*(3 & 4), 95–109.

Spend Edge. (2017). Why Green Supply Chain is the Need of the Hour? *SpendEdge*. https://www.spendedge.com/blogs/bid-goodbye-blues-red-color-supply-chain-green-instead

Sureddin, S. (2021). Twelve Post-Pandemic Supply-Chain Trends for 2021. *Supply Chain Brain*. https://www.supplychainbrain.com/blogs/1-think-tank/post/32374-twelve-post-pandemic-supply-chain-trends-for-2021

Tao, M. (2021). 7 Supply chain technology trends shaping a sustainable future. *Robotics and Automation News*. https://roboticsandautomationnews.com/2021/04/07/7-supply-chain-technology-trends-shaping-a-sustainable-future/42158/

Tseng, M.-L., Lim, M. K., & Wu, K.-J. (2019). Improving the benefits and costs on sustainable supply chain finance under uncertainty. *International Journal of Production Economics, 218*(C), 308–321. doi:10.1016/j.ijpe.2019.06.017

Tsui, J. (2019). Supply Chains Are Going Green in These Six Ways. *Supply Chain Brain*. https://www.supplychainbrain.com/blogs/1-think-tank/post/30512-six-ways-that-supply-chains-are-turning-to-green-solutions

Ubaid, I., & Shafi Mir, M. (2021). Maintaining effcient logistics and supply chain management operations during and after coronavirus (COVID-19) pandemic: Learning from the past experiences. *Environment, Development and Sustainability, 23*(8), 11157–11178. doi:10.100710668-020-01115-z PMID:33488274

Wilkerson, T. (2005). Best practices in implementing green supply chains. *North America Supply Chain World Conference and Exposition.* https://postconflict.unep.ch/humanitarianaction/documents/02_08-04_05-25.pdf

Zeng, H., Chen, X., Xiao, X., & Zhou, Z. (2017). Institutional pressures, sustainable supply chain management, and circular economy capability: Empirical evidence from Chinese eco-industrial park firms. *Journal of Cleaner Production, 155,* 54–65. doi:10.1016/j.jclepro.2016.10.093

## KEY TERMS AND DEFINITIONS

**COVID-19 Pandemic:** In 2019, the world faced an extremely contagious virus, COVID-19, the coronavirus disease caused by SARS-Cov-2. The COVID-19 pandemic crippled nations across the world. This virus is a life-threatening flu that spread across borders. The pandemic has set the globe in a frenzy of researching how to prevent something like this from occurring again, across all disciplines.

**Green Supply Chain Management:** In the 21$^{st}$ century, the world is facing environmental pollution and other issues, including human health. Corporations have been required to follow eco-friendly rules and regulations. One such regulation is that production in a factory cannot produce bad gases or emissions, or they may get fined by the government. Green supply chain management is ensuring that the supply chain process is as eco-friendly as possible to meet consumer and governmental needs and requirements.

**Supply Chain:** Any production which creates a chain from raw material, to production, to consumer. Any production process must go through a supply chain. For example, the object that a consumer has in hand after purchase, that is the end result of a chain of steps the object took to get produced and then finally purchased by the consumer. The steps in between are the supply chain.

**Supply Chain Management:** All corporations must follow rules and regulations as dictated by appropriate authorities. This is handled by individuals responsible of meeting both rules and regulations but also stakeholders' expectations. The supply chain needs to be observed, managed, and maintained so that the process of production and delivery to consumers is seamless, efficient and meets all regulations and that is what is deemed supply chain management. Without meeting this criterion, they cannot go into the market platform.

# Chapter 22
# Sustainable Green Supply Chain Management Trends, Practices, and Performance

**Rahul Gupta**

ⓘ https://orcid.org/0000-0002-2328-0119

*Amity University, Noida, India*

## ABSTRACT

*Innovative adoption of green supply chain management (GSCM) practices has witnessed a great surge in the last couple of decades. Its positive impact on the individual, society, and environment advocates the organization's commitment to progressively work with all stakeholders. Efforts are accelerated for identifying and understanding the opportunities to support green practices. Global warming and climate change have warned that scarce natural resources are not forever GSCM practices help to mitigate these hazards and ideologically enhance sustainability. Stake holders are committed to reuse, reduce, redesign, and recycle products in support of waste reduction and sustainable environmental protection. The sustainable supply chain is integrating sustainable environmental progressions into processes like selecting suppliers who ensure green manufacturing, buying green raw material, designing, assembling, and distribution with reverse logistics. Current research discusses sustainable green supply chain concepts, present and future trends, and performances.*

## INTRODUCTION

The industrial revolution, upgraded technologies, and advanced scientific inventions have accelerated our ability to exploit natural possessions. Our superfluous extraction, consumption, and wastages lead to the depletion of scarce natural resources, eventually severely impacting our environment. Zhu & Sarkis (2007) suggested the advent of facilities and computerizations has revolutionized worldwide supply chain practices, this concept has now expanded as green supply chain management. GSCM is supported by environmentally conscious strategies for sourcing, manufacturing, and distribution strategies.

DOI: 10.4018/978-1-7998-9506-0.ch022

Srivastava (2007) has emphasized that integrating environmental practices is an ongoing process. Increased awareness among government, environmentalists, and customers, with strict regulatory norms, have set the firms under tremendous pressure. Luthra (2016) studied that organizations must mitigate their contribution in degrading human life, flora, and fauna by harmful effects of their unethical practices. Green practices conserve precious resources and protect the environment from misuse of the resources. Organizations progressively use safe environmental practices and gain a competitive advantage, over the firms who are unable to comply with regulations and green practices.

Khan and Dong (2017), Gunasekaran (2012), studied that competitive advantage is gained by integrating end-to-end supply chain with sustainable resource utilization. Rostamzadeh et al. (2015), Mangla et al. (2013), suggested that recent developments in the industry for practicing green and eco-friendly products and processes have gained quite a good momentum. Rath (2013), suggested the role of green supply chain management practices in motivating and forming sustainable organizations. Kumar et al. (2014) said rising environmental concern has woken up nations to boost green movements.

Handfield et al. (2002), talked about enhanced environmental performances in multi-faceted environmental pressure. Zhu and Sarkis (2004), instigated logistics management research for assimilating the supply chain with environmental elements. Research in the green supply chain management area gets a boost in 1990, where processes begin with green purchasing. Webb (1994) discussed the environmental impact due to some harmful products and suggested a theory called "Green purchasing". The theory suggested buying recyclable and environmentally sustainable products. Green et al. (1998), talked about an organization, which started in 1995 by BIE (business in the environment) and CIPS (Chartered institute of purchasing and supply) to support organizations and make a balance among environmental performance and business activities thereby enlightening supply chain performances.

MRC (Manufacture research consortium) of Michigan state university published a report in 1996 "Environmentally Responsible Manufacturing" and introduced "Green supply chain". Handfield et al. (1997), studied the impact of optimum resource utilization and its environmental influences in the manufacturing supply chain. EPSRC (engineering and physical sciences research council) and other groups sponsored a research project, "ESRC global environment change". Green et al., (2000), said that "Green supply chain management" is the main research agenda, trailed by ISO 14000 environmental standard, and GSCM becomes the center of attraction for research in many organizations. Min and Galle (1997) studied factoring environmental protection into selecting suppliers, and waste mitigation through green purchase. Beamon (1999) designed a new model of the supply chain, incorporating some environmental elements. Hoek (1998) tries to balance supply chain operations practically with ecological balance. Christmann (2000), studied and elaborated that a green supply chain working group was formed by general motors in 1999, with twelve other firms, to search for solutions for improving financial and environmental supply chain solutions.

Narasimhan and Carter (1998), discussed with few case studies and analytical tools for the environmental supply chain at the center for advanced purchasing studies in the USA. Min and Galle, (2001) talked about research findings on green supply chain management done by the green supply chain management research center at Texas Tech University. Sarkis (2001) talked about a special issue of green supply chain management published by greener management international journal. Jamal (2009) studied that qualitative research has prevailed over quantitative research in recent literature. Research on GSCM got special focuses by Arena et al. (2003), Srivastava (2007), who talked about green design, Murray (2000), Wu et al. (2001), Zhang et al. (2014), about green purchasing, Dowell et al. (2000), Farrow et al. (2000), Sharma (2000, Min et al. (2006), about reserve logistics. Sarkis et al. (2006), said current

*Sustainable Green Supply Chain Management Trends, Practices, and Performance*

research being disruptive is unable to form a systematized theory. Nations have started investing in green supply chain management research, chronologically from low to high achievement.

## PURPOSE OF THE CHAPTER

Green supply chain management still lacks an authoritative and uniform definition. Qinghua et al. (2010), studied that connotation and concepts of green supply chain management are in the exploratory stage as any definition is unable to find space in the terms of the standard logistics. Nagorney and Toyasaki (2005) said green supply chain management research publications are growing with increasing authors and with their various definitions. The way supply chain management has been discussed, many authors have discussed green supply chain management with strategic transformation to green designs, leading to the theoretical development of supply chain to green supply chain management.

### Objectives

- To study and understand various definitions proposed by researchers.
- To study and understand essential elements, primary activities, theoretical basis, model.
- To study and understand optimally allocation of resources, improve economic benefits, and consistently enhance environmental aids in PLC.

Literature review to investigate the definitions for green supply chain management are as follows.

Green supply chain being innovative compiles and trends with social developments. The green supply chain is an amalgamation of environmental performance, economic performance, and efficient utilization of resources into the whole gamut of supply chain initiatives. This is comprised of green raw material and green purchasing, processing, green packaging, logistics, retailing, green marketing with reuse and recycling of products. An inclusive strategic coalition of consumers, retailers, distributors, manufacturers, suppliers, and now governments, and recyclers. All are putting their best efforts into improving economic benefits, reducing costs, and reduced resource utilization, and enhancing environmental performances. Sustainable supply chain management or environmental supply chain management, or green supply chain management are the name used interchangeably with modern management, mode inspired by sustainable management development ideas, focuses on supply chain management techniques. Associated partners are benefitted from the modern management practice of planning, organizing, directing, controlling, and coordinating all inputs like information, material, capital, and knowledge of green supply chain management. The objective is to optimally allocate resources, improve economic benefits, and consistently enhance environmental aids in PLC (product life cycle). All the activities are done to endorse harmonized development of economic, social, and environmental performances. Various definitions proposed by researchers are as follows:

*Table 1. Environmental performances. Various definitions proposed by researchers*

| Researchers | Definitions |
|---|---|
| Narasimhan and carter (1998) | Green supply chain management excels with the efforts of purchasing material that reduces pollution, recycled, and substitutes. |
| Dan and Liu (2000) | Green supply chain management is a management model which considers the environmental effects and the efficiency of resource utilization in the whole supply chain. It is based on the green manufacturing theory and supply chain management techniques, involving suppliers, manufacturers, retailers, and consumers. It aims to minimize the negative effects on the environment and to maximize the efficiency of resource utilization in the whole production process. |
| Zsidisin and Siferd (2001) | Green supply chain management is a supply chain management technique used to solve the environmental problems within a company's the production and service departments. |
| US-Asia environmental Partnership (2003) | Activities in which an organization imposes its environmental requirements on its suppliers' productions and processes should be named "Green supply chain management". |
| United nations Environment Program (2003) | The main activities of green supply chain management include evaluating the suppliers' environmental performance, developing eco-design with suppliers, providing training and information for suppliers to improve suppliers' environmental management capabilities |
| Zhu (2004) | Green supply chain management enterprises cooperate with their downstream and upstream patterns to optimize the environmental benefits from product design, material selection, distribution, retailing, and recycling. Improvs both economic and environmental performances to achieve sustainable development. |

Beamon (1999) defined green supply chain management with a new conceptual model. This new model was built upon traditional supply chain concepts with an additional concept of reuse, recycling, and remanufacturing. The issues of waste materials from supply, distribution, manufacturing, logistics, and consumption are described in the model. Many researchers are not involved in the conceptual model of the green supply chain. Karlberg (2000) in support of the science and technology office in Sweden proposed and conceptualized a model green supply chain in electronic manufacturers.

Hoek (1999) offered a conceptual green supply chain model adding a new element of service organizations. He contributes by analyzing problems, and management of all pitch points. The study suggests all green supply chain models are offered by extending existing supply chain models with expanding environmental elements. These models were unable to describe the system structure of the green supply chain and flout the motion of knowledge flow in the system. Thoo et al. (2014a), discussed traditional supply chain focuses on maximizing firms' benefits. Energy and material savings were focusing on cost and internal environment improvement, not on the impact on the external environment, Thoo et al. (2014b), added that the recycling process of waste is also not taken care of. The following table depicts the difference between green and traditional supply chains.

*Sustainable Green Supply Chain Management Trends, Practices, and Performance*

*Table 2. Difference between green and traditional supply chains*

| Items | GSCM | SCM |
|---|---|---|
| Background | Environmental degradation and resources shortage | Accelerated diversification and uncertainty on the market |
| Essential elements | Supplier/ manufacturer/ distributor/ retailer/ consumer/ society and environment | Supplier/ manufacturer/ distributor/ retailer/ consumer |
| Primary activities | Material flow/ information flow/ capital flow/ knowledge flow | Material flow/ information flow/ capital flow |
| Theoretical basis | Supply chain management (optimal allocation of resources)/ sustainable development (equity theory) | Optimal allocation of resources |
| Manufacturing model | Cleaner production / green manufacturing | Lean production/ agile manufacturing |
| Strategic objectives | Optimizing the allocation of resources and compatibility with the environment | Reducing uncertainty and maximizing benefits |

Wang et al. (2005) proposed an improved version of previous models with a systematic and comprehensive description and connection with subsystems. Which divides the green supply chain into five subsystems, social, logistics, environment, consumption, and manufacturing systems. These subsystems comprise further sub-systems like social with social factors such as regulation, ethics, and culture. Logistics is concerned with capital, material, knowledge flows, and information. Environmental systems connect resources to manufacturing. Consumption includes activities of final consumption of resources and recycling waste materials. Manufacturing offers products and receives resources from recycled consumers' wastes. Model prominently features logistics and operations. The use, re-use, capital, and material flow becomes an integral part of the green model.

Zhu et al. (2010), talked about stern environment requirements on social and entrepreneur development on green supply chain management research. Handfield et al. (2002), discussed various advanced concepts such as industrial ecology, life cycle management, tools like the ANP method, champ method, and industrial network theory. Hu and Hsu (2010) propose a win-win situation for society and organizations with small-scale practices. Handfield (1997) studied green supply chain management practices include safe environmental philosophies across the chain from customer order cycle, design, procurement, assembling/manufacturing, packaging, and delivery.

Andic et al. (2012), Srivastava (2007), Sarkis (2011), studied environmental consideration while sourcing ecofriendly reengineering. Sar et al. (2017), Khan et al. (2016) studied reverse logistics ecologically safe design, use of biofuel during logistics, green warehousing, green training under ethical leadership

Hsu and Hu (2008) studied green supply chain management that follows environmental regulations while improving the performances of the products and their manufacturing processes as an important philosophy. It efficiently synergizes among supply partners, their environmental performances, reduced ecological wastes, etc. In a study on the manufacturing sector, various barriers were identified and investigated for green supply chain management implementation.

## Concept

Min and Zhou (2002) have studied that supply chain management practices shall focus on customer satisfaction, with external and internal linkages and synergizes inter-organizational and inter-functional coordination. Torres et al. (2002), said that green supply chain management focuses on confining waste within the business structure to ensure energy conservation, checking dissipation of hazardous material into the environmental system. Olugu et al. (2010) studied supply chain practices that may disproportionately impact environments. Green supply chain management implementation ensures waste minimization for energy, chemicals, emission of harmful gases, and landfills. As studied practicing green supply chain management and not easy and implementation face numerous hurdles.

## Barriers

In their study on the automobile manufacturing sector, Lettice et al. (2010), found that demand for personal vehicles and commercial vehicles has increased, with an increase in population, hence leading automobile manufacturers are setting up their assembly plants in various parts of the world.

Kumar et al. (2012) studied green supply chain management adoption of environmental thinking, begins from designing, selection of supplier (practicing green), sustainable manufacturing practices, final delivery of products with end-of-life management, once product finishes its useful life. The goals are to study the economic impact of logistics along with the inclusive impact on the earth, like pollution, fuel consumption, and perilous wastes. The flow of inventory through the process, planning is managed within logistics activities. This process leads to a lot of environmental pollution sources and results in many greenhouse gas emissions. Harris, et al. (2011) studied that how they adversely impact our ecosystem and human life. Increased industrial activities have amplified the use of vehicles and equipment and results in a higher amount of harmful gas emissions. For example, Ulku (2012) studied that in the USA alone $co_2$ is a major greenhouse gas emission that accounts for 85% of climate change potential among all human processed emissions. Contribution in emission via trucks has increased from 42% in 1995 to 49% in 2006, with no sign of relief. Increased global competition demands a quick response from manufacturers for meeting the buyers' needs, competitive prices, and short delivery lead times. Simchi (2009) studied that the supply chain requires to be responsive, flexible, at a reduced cost, with improved performance. Just-in-time is one of the methodologies which supports zero wastages and demands only required raw materials, produced required quantities, enhance productivity with substantially reduce work in progress inventory with frequent deliveries. These frequent small-size deliveries may cause higher environmental pollution and transportation costs. These increased logistics costs are critical issues in minimizing the total cost, but the savings in other inventory holding costs compensate for the extra costs. Organizations also invest in planning and design to optimize the logistic network, measure trade-offs among environmental effects and cost.

Classical distribution and production mathematical models are on cost minimization, which takes care of operational constraints, without considering environmental impacts. Green interest has grown in the last few decades, while current practices rarely comply with environmental concerns while managing frequent deliveries. Shyur and Shih (2006) offer an MCDM (Multi-criteria decision making) model, for practicing JIT, ensuring quality, price/cost, technology, facilities, customer responses, and other quality obligations. Memari et al. (2014) discuss a decision support system for JIT/MRP network using a non-linear bi-level optimization model. Farahani and Elahipanah (2008) offer a three-echelon distribution network, by a multi-objective mathematical model for JIT. As discussed, earlier implementation of green practices is missing while modeling with traditional mathematical models. Tsai (2009) offers a fuzzy goal programming for optimizing green supply chain management. ABS (activity-based costing) and performance evaluation are united in the value chain in search of optimum flow allocation and supplier

*Sustainable Green Supply Chain Management Trends, Practices, and Performance*

selection. Ozceylan and Paksoy (2013) offer a mathematical model with a mixed-integer multi-objective fuzzy mathematical model for optimizing multi-item, multi-period, reverse, and forward closed-loop supply networks. Pishvaee et al. (2012) offered a fuzzy mathematical multi-objective programming model designing as an environmental supply chain. Pishvaee et al. (2012) offered a fuzzy mathematical model based on bi-objective credibility and aims trade-off among conflicting objectives i.e., minimizing the environmental impact of defining $co_2$ equivalent index and minimization of the total cost for total burden minimization on logistics activities. Musazadeh et al. (2014) offer a multi-objective mathematical model for reverse green logistics with fuzziness and identified green logistical derivers. Vahdani et al. (2013) addressed the closed-loop network of supply chain with a possibilistic-queuing model, which takes care of total cost minimization and expected logistics costs once bidirectional facilities are failed in the concerned net. Sarkis (2011), Madaan (2015) said being relatively new green supply chain management is getting popularity in enhancing environmental performances. Following a few critical factors discussed to apprehend knowledge of green supply chain management.

## Gaps in the Existing Literature

Existing literature has studied customer satisfaction, with external and internal linkages and synergizes inter-organizational and inter-functional coordination, it focuses on confining waste within the business structure to ensure energy conservation, checking dissipation of hazardous material into the environmental system. Green supply chain management implementation should ensure disproportionately impact environments, waste minimization for energy, chemicals, emission of harmful gases, and landfills. Practicing green supply chain management and not easy and implementation faces numerous hurdles.

## ISSUES, CHALLENGES, AND CONTROVERSIES

## Green Supply Chain Management in Developed Nations

Few researchers have studied green supply chain management practices adopted in developed countries. Where criteria are inclusive of economic growth (per capita income), HDI (human development index), and industrialization. High income or per capita gross GDP (gross domestic product). Countries with the tertiary and quaternary sector of the industry are considered as developed countries. HDI integrates economic measures, country income, with indices for education and expectancy. Higher HDI rating countries are considered as developed countries. These higher economic development criteria compel these countries to deal with a lot of environmental concerns. Many studies have been conducted to study these issues.

Large and Thomsen (2011), discussed five drivers for green supply chain management performance, green supply chain management capabilities, strategic purchasing, environmental commitment, degree of green supplier assessment, and degree of green collaboration with concerned parties. Azevedo et al. (2011) study link among supply performance and green practices adopted by automotive supply chains at Portuguese. They derived a conceptual model by analyzing data and providing evidence that green practices positively impact customer satisfaction, quality, efficiency, and negative effects on performances. Chiou et al. (2011) correlate green innovation and greening suppliers in their study using SEM in Taiwan. They found that sourcing through green innovation reaps substantial benefits, which leads to higher environmental performances and competitive advantages. Cagno et al. (2011) studied green supply chain management practices for 3 PL (third-party logistics service provider), for specific practice implementation, and level of adoption for these services with examining the relationship with green supply chain management practices implementation and firms' performances. Arimura et al. (2011) studied the influence of ISO 14001 certification on green supply chain management with facility data in Japan. Voluntary EMS government program and ISO 14001 significantly influence green supply chain management as they are considered as higher importance, and suppliers are asked to undertake environmental practices. Zhu et al. (2010) study environmental green supply chain management experience with large manufacturers in Japan. The large organization creates a win-win situation for partners, and sustainable growth is offered to the whole supply chain. Government policies and regulations help both large organizations to small companies.

Hsu and Hsu (2008) discussed the contingency approach using factor analysis, to discuss the implementation and adoption of green supply chain management in electronic industries in Taiwan. He prioritizes relative importance by applying the fuzzy analytic hierarchy process to electronic manufacturing firms. Shang et al. (2010) studied the Taiwanese electronic industry to explore green supply chain management for firm performance and capability dimensions by using factor analysis and found six dimensions, as environment participation, green packaging and manufacturing, green marketing, green suppliers, green eco-design, and green stocks.

Holt and Ghobadian (2009) studied the nature and level of green practices in the UK with manufacturing supply chains. Studies driving forces supporting environmental supply practices. Nawrocka et al. (2009) study the role of ISO 14001 in environmental supply chain practices in Sweden. The role of three operational tasks motivates and enable supplier, communication with supplier, and verifying that supplier follows requirements.

Lee (2008) studied drivers of green supply chain management within small and medium-sized suppliers and stakeholders, buyers, and government. Raymond et al. (2008) studied the relationship among environmental performances of the supply chain in Canadian SMEs. They discussed financial resources and time needed in managing energy issues and solid waste with limiting factors. Simpson et al. (2007) studied moderating impact of relationship conditions among supplier and customer and the impact of buyer environmental performance requirements (green supply).

## Green Supply Chain Management in Developing Nations

Vachon and Klassen (2006) studied that green supply chain management supports environment-friendly images of the firm, its process, product, services, system, and technologies, and the way business is processed. The solution adopted by these businesses remains traditional "control and command" or "end of pipe" solutions. Studying green supply chain management practices in developing countries needs thorough investigation due to their "end of pipe" style of management. Especially developing countries in Asia reason require extensive research for green supply chain management adoption, as for them it is a new concept. Countries in the South Asian region (Thailand, Malaysia, Indonesia, Philippines, and Singapore) have started adopting green supply chain management practices. Finding from these areas will certainly be useful in adopting in other areas in reducing the harmful impact of unethical practices.

In the East Asian region also countries like china are finding application of green supply chain management in a critical state. Rao (2002) said being a major manufacturing country china deals with huge environmental issues. The study also worked upon manufacturers' cognizance for ESPR-orientation

*Sustainable Green Supply Chain Management Trends, Practices, and Performance*

(enhancing energy savings and pollution reduction), for local and international environmental issues. Green supply chain management implementation with modern ecological practices plays a moderating impact on regulatory pressures on manufacturing organizations.

Liu et al. (2011) studied the relationship among classified determent factors and GSCM (green supply chain management level) and confirmed that firms' environmental management capacities are boosted by employee training and involvement in green supply chain management practices. Yan li (2011) studied green supply chain management adoption levels in china and performance measurements are explored. He found that green supply chain management practices strongly balance other advanced management practices and contribute to enhancing environmental performances.

Research has shown keen interest in examining green supply chain management implementation issues in countries like Thailand, India, and Malaysia. Ninlawan et al. (2010) study green activities in computer parts suppliers and the level of green supply chain management in Thailand. Discussion for green procurement, green manufacturing, green distribution, reverse logistics helps in understanding green supply chain management. Diabat and Govindan (2011), studied influencing drivers of green supply chain management implementation by using ISM (interpretive structure modeling) in Indian firms, they derived eleven components, environmental management, certification of the supplier, supplier's collaboration with the environment, an amalgamation of supplier and product designers to eliminate environmental impacts, legislation and regulations, green design, ISO 14001, reduced energy consumption, recycle and reuse, green packaging, reverse logistics and customers involved with the environment.

## SOLUTIONS

Studies on green supply chain management concept are relatively manufacturers are concerned. Eltayeb and Zailani (2009), discussed four green supply chain management drivers as motivators, customer requirement, regulations, social responsibility, and business profitability. Eltayeb et al. (2011), found an initiative called eco-design having a positive impact on four outcomes (economic, environmental, intangible outcome, and cost reduction) discussed earlier by analyzing relation among performance outcome and green supply chain management initiatives.

## Technological Advancements

Technological advancements like Blockchain Technology offer the availability of goods across the border with secured information, where information is secured in nods and these platforms facilitate supply chain management, Bai and Sarkis (2020), Vaio and Varriale, (2020), Kamble et al. (2020). Blockchain technology adoption creates strategic values and offers sustainable competitive advancements. Research has found that blockchains lower the transaction cost, reduce risk, and offer transparency in supply chain operations, Kshetri (2018). Blockchain technology integrates the other stakeholders without central control and offers decentralized information storage offering timely solutions and capacity management. Blockchain technology transforms supply chain operations by collaborating functionalities with advanced software systems. Business resilience is improved with enhanced risk management supports by making reactive and self-executing contracts digitally. Invisible risk and tangibility are secured with multiple layers of support protection by offering shared visibility and transaction traceability Min et al. (2019), Wang et al., (2019).

## Ethical Practices

Senior management's unconditional support to the internal environment becomes a key success factor. Encouragement boosts the perception of environmental risk involved and brings positive change in adoption for green supply chain management practices, Luthra et al. (2016), Yusuf et al. (2013).

## Buyer Management

Kumar et al. (2014), studied that the adoption of green supply chain management requires an effective role of customers. Omkareshwar (2013), studied that they compel firms to adopt sustainable practices in their business operations to remain competitive. Zhu et al. (2007) said cooperating among them brings fruitful results for both.

## Supplier Management

Awasthi (2016), studied that without support from supplier's green supply chain management practices can never be implemented. Kaushik (2014) studied supplier collaboration enhances incentive system, the innovative eco-friendly idea gets implemented. Green partnerships enhance innovative technology implementation to achieve economic goals.

## Competitiveness

Kim and Rhee (2012) suggest that relevant competitive elements and competitiveness are perceived as a substantial factor in protecting environmental sustainability. Luthra (2016) studied that green supply chain management implementation in business operations adds voluntary competitive factors.

## Societal

Shen et al. (2015) studied that the growing role of regulatory bodies and buyers' awareness of eco-friendly environment guides firms to showcase their end-to-end information regarding green supply chain management practices. NGOs, social media, and other electronic channels exert pressure on firms for adoption.

## Regulatory

Mangla (2014) studied that government bodies are framing strict environmental laws, climate control regimes, global warming guidelines, pollution norms, and firms require to comprehend and safeguard them against negative reviews for following environmental guiding principles. Conformity with regulators becomes a necessity for eco-friendly strategies.

## Green Practices

Successful implementation requires numerous green practices in design, sourcing, manufacturing, operations, and another area for improved productivity and better environmental growth.

## Ecological Green Design

Luthra (2016) studied that an ecologically designed supply chain helps in controlling eighty percent impact on environmental sustainability through their product and processes. Eltayeb et al. (2011), Gungor and Gupta (1999) found innovative ideas like cleaner technology, green components, and spare parts are proposed during the designing phase. Sarkis (1998), studied the ecological impacts of products get reduced. Environmental performances are improved with their green design; however, its adoption is a challenge. Hindrances act as a stumbling block in its implementation, external as economic performance, and competitive advantages, internal as resource commitment and competency. Inexperienced firms face difficulty while adopting green design. Lack of CFT (cross-function team) in problem-solving is another struggle, implementation requires manpower from different functional departments.

Feedbacks from stakeholders in the supply chain provides a checklist for green design. Standard manuals and guidelines like TS 16949, ISO 14001, etc., need to be referred under expert guidelines. Ben-Gal et al. (2008) found a robust design method as "designing for the environment was proposed. Chu et al. (2009) suggested an application of cad (computer-aided design) for designing purposes was proposed by checking assembly and disassembly costs. Russo and Rizzi (2014) offered the Eco-Opti-Cad method with LCA (life cycle assessment) data structure was proposed. Agrawal and Ulku (2012) suggested a modular up-gradation to meet the green objective was suggested. Initially, the green process was adopted for green design, later Diwekar (2005) proposes to increase this to a suitable ecology design. The green design also addresses issues Jansen and Stevels, (2006), Khor and Udin (2013), for reverse logistics.

## RECOMMENDATIONS

### Green Sourcing

Eltayeb et al. (2011) discussed the purchase process involves selecting and choosing a vendor practicing reusability, recyclability, ecofriendly, and nonuse of dangerous/hazardous chemicals. Eltayeb et al. (2015), Handfield et al. (2002) studied increased concern for environmental protection and motivated procurement managers to reconsider their sourcing strategy, with selected vendors and control the impact of their action on environmental sustainability. Min and Galle (2001) studied green sourcing support recycling, remanufacturing, reduced wastages in the supply chain. Carter and Rogers, (2008) studied green sourcing reduces product cost, helps to improve the safe environment and financial performance. Zailani et al. (2015) eco-friendly purchases have made positive relationships with suppliers. Yang et al. (2010) studied green purchases cater to five facets: operational design, SCM, environmental authentication, ecological, and external environmental management. With the adoption of green supply chain management overall performance gets improved. Chen et al. (2012) studied that it acts as a reliable tool for mitigating water, air, pollution. Dependency on green resources results in improved quality at reduced cost and ensure competitive advantages

### Green Manufacturing

The journey of manufacturing involves the conversion of raw material to finished goods. In the process lot of waste (hazardous industrial), gasses ($CO_2$, Methane, etc.), and residuals (metallic burrs, chips)

impact the environment. Green manufacturing aims to reduce these adverse impacts during manufacturing. Govindan et al. (2015) studied socially, and environmentally accountable practices are implemented to mitigate harmful effects of manufacturing and increase the profitability of firms.

Zailani et al. (2015). Efficiency in the production process improves. Baines et al. (2012) found lean and green manufacturing helps in reducing waste and improving operational efficiency, environmental sustainability, and improved financial performance. The green process can be improved by a framework proposed by Deif (2011), get the current green score, improve, implement, and sustainably adhere to it. They believe green investment reduces pollution and offers the improved value of the investment. A few key challenges faced while implementing green manufacturing are technological, operational, material, financial, unwillingness, and unawareness of organization. Govindan et al. (2015) studied strict regulatory guidelines that force big organizations to implement green, but small and unregistered ones may skip green processes.

## Green Marketing

Groening (2017) said in a broader perspective, green marketing activity includes planning, production, pricing, promotions, delivery, and sales support, mitigating the detrimental effect of their products on society and the environment. Luthra (2016), Polonsky (1994), talked about environment-friendly products get promoted with green marketing practices. Green marketing incorporates activities that satisfy human desires with a minimum impact on the environment. Chen et al. (2012), ko et al. (2013) said an organization's efforts enhance its environmental performance and positive image, and corporate reputation.

## Green Management

Pane et al. (2009), practicing green management supplements sources of information that enhance business and environmental objectives Luthra et al. (2014), Kang (2010) enhances the image, boosts efficiency, better compliances, cost savings, attaining societal commitments, and reduction of carbon emission.

## Green Models

An index called greenness in current logical performance can be measured. Martinsen and Bjorklund (2012) said greenness in service firms was studied. Ubeda, (2011), optimization of logistical services improves its green performance the measurement under uncertainty is done by a fuzzy logic-based mathematical bi-objective model, developed by Pishvaee et al. (2012), which not only improves green performance but also reduces cost. The model integrates transportation mode and production technology. Another model was proposed by Harris et al. (2014), which optimizes $co_2$ emission and financial cost by solving facility allocation. Cloud computing services are adopted by the small and medium organizations in developing countries like China Subramanian et al. (2014), their financial performance is improved in the short term and environmental performance in the long term.

## Reverse Logistics, Distribution, and Warehousing

The logistical process includes material handling, packaging, distribution, and warehousing. Green practices curb wastages in the form of energy reduction. Firms receive better financial results and en-

*Sustainable Green Supply Chain Management Trends, Practices, and Performance*

vironmental performances. Baines et al. 2(012, Prajogo et al. (2012). Problems of routing, transporting LTL (less than truckload), optimum fuel efficiency, and reduced carbon emission, less pollution, and eco-friendly packaging are addressed with green logistics.

Practicing green is a challenge in terms of technology, investment, knowledge, and customers' response to these products. Hazen et al. (2011) said a refurbished product is considered of inferior quality. Khan et al. (2018) with awareness firms emphasizing reverse logistics with green fuels, built their image and reduce cost. Logistical overheads are controlled with efficient transportation management, customer support. Rehabilitation with the return, reuse, recycle helps in mitigating environmental impacts, quality at a reduced cost.

Kim and Xirouchakis (2010) said inefficiency in recycling is due to the ambiguity of quantity and quality of returns. These are an economic burden on the industries and discourage implementation in operations. Reveliotis (2007) proposes a disassembly model, studying human-machine learning over the use of repeated methods of disassembly. The economic and environmental performance of the product is enhanced by improved designing, for disassembling and further reusing. Optimal disassembly and strategies are proposed by Teunter (2005), for determining the process of disassembly, optimum recovery options, and disassembly options.

Electronic components of small size have low economic value hence are not favorable for disassembly Willems et al. (2007), and Duflou et al. (2008) in case of unfavorable results, their disassembly should be avoided. Atasu et al. (2008), end-of-life or used product are remanufactured after sorting, cleaning, repairing, and refabricating. Agrawal and Tiwari (2008) suggest reversing logistics to promote reuse, recycling, remanufacturing, and minimizing waste to landfills. Its wide utility has gained attention due to its product.

## Biofuel and Renewable Energy

Khan et al. (2018) globally logistical operations use fossil fuels, which results in climate change, global warming, higher greenhouse gas emissions, etc. Wu and Barnes (2016), Anable et al. (2012). Biofuel and renewable energy fill in to support green supply chain operations, support sustainable economic growth, reduce carbon emission. Overall cost comparison among biofuel, Gold (2011), fossil fuel suggests the importance of green energy, scarcity of fossil fuel makes them expensive in the long run.

## CONCLUSION

The study contributes to the practitioners and literature by framework for green supply chain management practices. Green supply chain management concepts were narrowly defined by Narasimhan and Carter (1998). These practices were further examined by studying dimensions like green design, green sourcing, green manufacturing, green marketing, green logistics, green warehousing, reverse logistics, customer's environmental concern, investment recovery, green training, and mitigating use of hazardous material. Research in green supply chain management focuses more on developing methods, and less on creating adoption of these methods. Green supply chain management processes are improved by higher environmental performances. Measuring the green index in green manufacturing processes suggests tracking status and promoting improvement. Framework for selection of green processes helps organizations in deciding adoption of green. Studying alternative green supply chain management practices and their adoption is important for environmental concerns. Green logistical practices, lean and green tools are also an integral part of green supply chain management. Implementation of green supply chain management ensures products are manufactured with the least damage to the environment, support from plc vis green practices. Reverse logistics ensure reuse, recycling, remanufacturing is used in plc and upheld sustainability of products.

## FUTURE RESEARCH DIRECTIONS AND IMPLICATIONS

Green design, sourcing, manufacturing, reverse logistics, using renewable energy are essential processes for the green supply chain management. It has an advantage over other processes as all these are closet to all processes of the supply chain. Literature suggests that practicing green supply chain management enumerates benefits over non-compliance of these practices. Challenges in the adoption of green methods and focus on economic and organizational cultural barriers. The next focus shall be on green manufacturing technologies and their role in supporting environmental performances. Literature is scarce for measuring the green process and its role in improving green indicators for that process. Adverse environmental impacts are mitigated by curbing carbon emission, increasing biofuel consumption. Literature is available for logistical performance measurement and factors distressing its implementation. Ample literature supports, end of life reuse/recycling is preceded by disassembly. Effective disassembly is the outcome of efficient designing, which incorporates usefulness after the EOL of the product. Literature helps to improve the profitability of operations via optimizing sequencing, optimizing line of balance of disassembly line. Literature suggests remanufacturing focuses on viable options by plummeting the cost of operations in the existing setup. The opportunity of research is available for assembling refurbished components in the manufacturing of the original product. Green warehousing checks wastages in energy consumption and utilizes traditional methods for storing. Technological advancements have redesigned the way supply chains are managed. Blockchain Technology supports storing information at remote locations and provides real-time information with layered facilities.

## REFERENCES

Agrawal, S., & Tiwari, M. K. (2008). A collaborative ant colony algorithm to stochastic mixed-model u-shaped disassembly line balancing and sequencing problem. *International Journal of Production Research, 46*(6), 1405–1429. doi:10.1080/00207540600943985

Agrawal, V. V., & Ulku, S. (2012). The role of modular upgradability as a green design strategy. *Manufacturing & Service Operations Management, 15*(4), 640–648. doi:10.1287/msom.1120.0396

Anable, J., Brand, C., Tran, M., & Eyre, N. (2012). Modeling transport energy demand: A socio-technical approach. *Energy Policy, 41*, 125–138. doi:10.1016/j.enpol.2010.08.020

Andic, E., Yurt, O., & Baltacioglu, T. (2012). Green supply chains: Efforts and potential applications for the Turkish market. *Resources, Conservation and Recycling, 58*, 50–68. doi:10.1016/j.resconrec.2011.10.008

Atasu, A., Sarvary, M., & Van Wassenhove, L. N. (2008). Remanufacturing as a marketing strategy. *Management Science, 54*(10), 1731–1746. doi:10.1287/mnsc.1080.0893

*Sustainable Green Supply Chain Management Trends, Practices, and Performance*

Awasthi, A., & Kannan, G. (2016). Green supplier development program selection using NGT and Vikopr under fuzzy environment. *Computers & Industrial Engineering, 91*, 100–108. doi:10.1016/j.cie.2015.11.011

Bai, C., & Sarkis, J. (2020). A supply chain transparency and sustainability technology appraisal model for blockchain technology. *International Journal of Production Research, 58*(7), 2142–2162. doi:10.1080/00207543.2019.1708989

Baines, T. B. S., Benedettini, O., & Ball, P. (2012). Examining green production and its role within the competitive strategy of manufacturers. *Journal of Industrial Engineering and Management, 5*(1), 53–87. doi:10.3926/jiem.405

Beamon, B. M. (1999). Designing the green supply chain. *Logistics Information Management, 12*(4), 332–342. doi:10.1108/09576059910284159

Ben-Gal, I., Katz, R., & Bukchin, Y. (2008). Robust eco-design: A new application for air quality engineering. *IIE Transactions, 40*(10), 907–918. doi:10.1080/07408170701775094

Bjorklund, M., Martinsen, U., & Abrahamsson, M. (2012), performance measurements in the greening of supply chains. *Supply Chain Management, 17*(1), 29-39. doi:10.1108/13598541211212186

Carter, C. R., & Rogers, D. S. A. (2008). A framework of sustainable supply chain management: Moving toward new theory. *International Journal of Physical Distribution & Logistics Management, 38*(5), 360–387. doi:10.1108/09600030810882816

Chen, C. C., Shih, H. S., Shyur, H. J., & Wu, K.-S. (2012). A business strategy selection of green supply chain management via an analytic network process. *Computers & Mathematics with Applications (Oxford, England), 64*(8), 2544–2557. doi:10.1016/j.camwa.2012.06.013

Christmann, P. (2000). Effects of "Best Practices" of environmental management on cost advantages: The role of complementary assets. *Academy of Management Journal, 43*(4), 663–680.

Chu, C.-H., Luh, Y.-P., Li, T.-C., & Chen, H. (2009). Economical green product design based on simplified computer-aided product structure variation. *Computers in Industry, 60*(7), 485–500. doi:10.1016/j.compind.2009.02.003

Dan, B., & Liu, F. (2000). Study on green supply chain and its architecture. *Zhongguo Jixie Gongcheng Xuekan, 11*, 1232–1234.

Deif, A. M. (2011). A system model for green manufacturing. *Journal of Cleaner Production, 19*(14), 1553–1559. doi:10.1016/j.jclepro.2011.05.022

Di Vaio, A., & Varriale, L. (2020). Blockchain technology in supply chain management for sustainable performance: Evidence from the airport industry. *International Journal of Information Management, 52*, 102014. doi:10.1016/j.ijinfomgt.2019.09.010

Diabat, A., & Govindan, K. (2011). An analysis of the drivers affecting the implementation of green supply chain management. *Resources, Conservation and Recycling, 55*(6), 659–667. doi:10.1016/j.resconrec.2010.12.002

Diwekar, U. (2005). Green process design, industrial ecology, and sustainability: A systems analysis perspective. *Resources, Conservation and Recycling, 44*(3), 215–235. doi:10.1016/j.resconrec.2005.01.007

Dowell, G., Hart, S., & And Yeung, B. (2000). Do corporate environmental standards create or destroy market value? *Management Science, 46*(8), 1059–1074. doi:10.1287/mnsc.46.8.1059.12030

Duflou, J.R., Seliger, G., Kara, S., Umeda, Y., Ometto, A., Willems, B., (2008). Efficiency and feasibility of product disassembly: a case-based study. *CIRP Annals-Manufacturing Technology, 57*, 583–600.

Eltayeb, T. K., & Zailani, S. (2009). Going green through green supply chain initiatives towards environmental sustainability. *Operations and Supply Chain Management, 2*(2), 93–110.

Eltayeb, T. K., Zailani, S., & Ramayah, T. (2011). Green supply chain initiatives among certified companies in Malaysia and environmental sustainability: Investigating the outcomes. *Resources, Conservation and Recycling, 55*(5), 495–506. doi:10.1016/j.resconrec.2010.09.003

Farrow, P. H., Johnson, R. R., & Larson, A. L. (2000). Entrepreneurship, innovation, and sustainability strategies at *Walden paddlers. Inc. Interfaces, 30*(3), 215–225. doi:10.1287/inte.30.3.215.11660

Gold, S., & Seuring, S. (2011). Supply chain and logistics issues of bio-energy production. *Journal of Cleaner Production, 19*(1), 32–42. doi:10.1016/j.jclepro.2010.08.009

Govindan, K., Diabat, A., & Madan Shankar, K. (2015). Analyzing the drivers of green manufacturing with the fuzzy approach. *Journal of Cleaner Production, 96*, 182–193. doi:10.1016/j.jclepro.2014.02.054

Govindan, K., Khodaverdi, R., & Vafadarnikjoo, A. (2015). Intuitionistic fuzzy-based debate method for developing green practices and performances in a green supply chain. *Expert Systems with Applications, 42*(20), 7207–7220. doi:10.1016/j.eswa.2015.04.030

Green, K., Morton, B., & New, S. (1998). Green purchasing and supply policies: Do they improve companies' environmental performance? *Supply Chain Management, 3*(2), 89–95. doi:10.1108/13598549810215405

Green, K., Morton, B., & New, S. (2000). Greening Organizations: Purchasing, Consumption, and Innovation. *Organization & Environment, 13*(2), 206–225. doi:10.1177/1086026600132003

Groening, C., Sarkis, J., & Zhu, Q. (2017). Green marketing consumer-level theory review: A compendium of applied theories and further research directions. *Journal of Cleaner Production*, 1–19.

Gunasekaran, A., & Spalanzani, A. (2012). Sustainability of manufacturing and services: Investigations for research and applications. *International Journal of Production Economics, 140*(1), 35–47. doi:10.1016/j.ijpe.2011.05.011

Gungor, A., & Gupta, S. M. (1999). Issues in environmentally conscious manufacturing and product recovery: A survey. *Computers & Industrial Engineering, 36*(4), 811–853. doi:10.1016/S0360-8352(99)00167-9

Handfield, R., Walton, S., Seegers, L., & Melnyk, S. (1997). Green' value chain practices in the furniture industry. *Journal of Operations Management, 5*(4), 293–315. doi:10.1016/S0272-6963(97)00004-1

Handfield, R., Walton, S. Y., Sroufe, R., & Melnyk, S. A. (2002). Applying environmental criteria to supplier assessment: Green supply chain management a study in the application of the analytical hierarchy process. *European Journal of Operational Research, 141*(1), 70–87. doi:10.1016/S0377-2217(01)00261-2

Harris, I., Mumford, C.L., Naim, M.M., (2014). A hybrid multi-objective approach to capacitated facility location with flexible store allocation for green logistics modeling. *Transportation Research Part E: Logistics and Transportation Review, 66*, 1–22.

Hazen, B.T., Cegielski, C., Hanna, J.B., (2011) diffusion of green supply chain management: examining the perceived quality of green reverse logistics. *International Journal of Logistics Management, Operational Research, 141*(1), 70–87.

Hoek, R. I. (1998). "Measuring the unmeasurable"-measuring and improving performance in the supply chain. *Supply Chain Management, 3*(4), 187–192. doi:10.1108/13598549810244232

Hoek, R. I. (1999). From reversed logistics to green supply chains. *Supply Chain Management, 4*(3), 129–134. doi:10.1108/13598549910279576

Holt, D., & Ghobadian, A. (2009). An empirical study of green supply chain management practices Amongst UK manufacturers. *Journal of Manufacturing Technology Management, 20*(7), 933–956. doi:10.1108/17410380910984212

Hsu, C. W., & Hu, A. H. (2008). Green Supply Chain Management in the Electronic Industry. *International Journal of Science and Technology, 5*(2), 205-216.

Hu, A. H., & Hsu, C. W. (2010). Critical factors for implementing green supply chain management practice: An empirical study of electrical and electronics industries in Taiwan. *Management Research Review, 33*(6), 586–608. doi:10.1108/01409171011050208

Jamal, F. (2009). Green supply chain management: A literature review. *Otago Management Graduate Review, 7*, 51–62.

Jansen, A., & Stevels, A. (2006). Combining eco-design and user benefits from human-powered energy systems, a win-win situation. *Journal of Cleaner Production, 14*(15-16), 1299–1306. doi:10.1016/j.jclepro.2005.11.023

Kamble, S. S., Gunasekaran, A., & Gawankar, S. A. (2020). Achieving sustainable performance in a data-driven agriculture supply chain: A review for research and applications. *International Journal of Production Economics, 219*, 179–194. doi:10.1016/j.ijpe.2019.05.022

Kang, Y., Ryu, M. H., & Kim, S. (2010). Exploring sustainability management for telecommunications services: A case study of two Korean companies. *Journal of World Business, 45*(4), 415–421. doi:10.1016/j.jwb.2009.08.003

Karlberg, T. (2000). *Supply chain environmental management.* Swedish Office of Science and Technology.

Kaushik A, Kumar S, Luthra S, Haleem A. (2014). Technology transfer: enablers and barriers—a review. *International Journal of Technology, Policy, and Management, 14*(2), 133-159.

Khor, K. S., & Udin, A. M. (2013). Reverse logistics in Malaysia: Investigating the effect of green product design and resource commitment. *Resources, Conservation and Recycling, 81*, 71–80. doi:10.1016/j.resconrec.2013.08.005

Kim, H.-J., & Xirouchakis, P. (2010). Capacitated disassembly scheduling with random demand. *International Journal of Production Research*, *48*(23), 7177–7194. doi:10.1080/00207540903469035

Kim, J., & Rhee, J. (2012). An empirical study on the impact of critical success factors on the balanced scorecard performance in Korean green supply chain management enterprises. *International Journal of Production Research*, *50*(9), 2465–2483. doi:10.1080/00207543.2011.581009

Kshetri, N. (2018). Blockchain's role in meeting key supply chain management objectives. *International Journal of Information Management*, *39*, 80–89. doi:10.1016/j.ijinfomgt.2017.12.005

Kumar, A., Jain, V., & Kumar, S. (2014). A comprehensive environment-friendly approach for supplier selection. *Omega*, *42*(1), 109–123. doi:10.1016/j.omega.2013.04.003

Lee, S. (2008). Drivers for the participation of small and medium-sized suppliers in green supply chain initiatives. *Supply Chain Management*, *13*(3), 185–198. doi:10.1108/13598540810871235

Luthra, Garg, & Haleem. (2014). Empirical analysis of green supply chain management practices in the Indian automobile industry. *Journal of Institution Of Engineers (India): Series C*, *95*(2), 119-126.

Luthra, S., Garg, D., & Haleem, A. (2016). The impacts of critical success factors for implementing green supply chain management towards sustainability: An empirical investigation of the Indian automobile industry. *Journal of Cleaner Production*, *121*, 142–158. doi:10.1016/j.jclepro.2016.01.095

Madaan, J., & Mangla, S. (2015). A decision modeling approach for the eco-driven flexible green supply chain. In Systemic flexibility and business agility. Springer. doi:10.1007/978-81-322-2151-7_21

Mangla, S., Madaan, J., & Chan, F. T. (2013). Analysis of flexible decision strategies for the sustainability-focused green product recovery system. *International Journal of Production Research*, *51*(11), 3428–3442. doi:10.1080/00207543.2013.774493

Mangla, S. K., Kumar, P., & Barua, M. K. (2014). flexible decision approach for analyzing the performance of sustainable supply chains under risks/uncertainty. *Global Journal of Flexible Systems Managment*, *15*(2), 113–130. doi:10.100740171-014-0059-8

Martinsen, U., & Bjorklund, M. (2012). Matches and gaps in the green logistics market. *International Journal of Physical Distribution & Logistics Management*, *42*(6), 562–583. doi:10.1108/09600031211250596

Min, H. (2019). Blockchain technology for enhancing supply chain resilience. *Business Horizons*, *62*(1), 35–45. doi:10.1016/j.bushor.2018.08.012

Min, H., and Galle, W. P. (1997). Green purchasing strategies: trends and implications. *International Journal of Purchasing & Materials Management*, *33*(3), 10–17.

Min, H., & Galle, W. P. (2001). Green purchasing practices of us firms. *International Journal of Operations & Production Management*, *21*(9), 1222–1238. doi:10.1108/EUM0000000005923

Min, H., Ko, H. J., & Ko, C. S. (2006). A genetic algorithm approach to developing the multi-echelon reverse logistics network for product returns. *Omega*, *34*(1), 56–69. doi:10.1016/j.omega.2004.07.025

Min, S., Zacharia, Z. G., & Smith, C. D. (2019). Defining supply chain management: In the past, present, and future. *Journal of Business Logistics*, *40*(1), 44–55. doi:10.1111/jbl.12201

Murray, G. (2000). effects of a green purchasing strategy: The case of Belfast city council. *Supply Chain Management*, 5(1), 37–44. doi:10.1108/13598540010312954

Nagorney, A., & Toyasaki, F. (2005). Reverse supply chain management and electronic waste recycling: a multi-tiered network equilibrium framework for e-cycling. *Transportation Research Part E: Logistics and Transportation Review*, 41, 1–28.

Narasimhan, R., & Carter, J. R. (1998). Environmental supply chain management. Center for Advanced Purchasing Studies.

Nawrocka, D., Brorson, T., & Lindhqvist, T. (2009). ISO 14001 in environmental supply chain practices. *Journal of Cleaner Production*, 17(16), 1435–1443. doi:10.1016/j.jclepro.2009.05.004

Sar, Dong, & Yu. (2016). Research on the measuring performance of green supply chain management: in the perspective of China. *International Journal of Engineering Research in Africa*, 27, 167-178.

Sar, K. (2017). Impact of green supply chain management practices on firms' performance: An empirical study from the perspective of Pakistan. *Environmental Science and Pollution Research International*, 24(20), 16829–16844. doi:10.100711356-017-9172-5 PMID:28573559

Sar, K. (2018). Green supply chain management, economic growth, and environment: A GMM based evidence. *Journal of Cleaner Production*, 185, 588–599. doi:10.1016/j.jclepro.2018.02.226

Ninlawan, C., Seksan, P., Tossapol, K., & Pilada, W. (2010). The Implementation of Green Supply Chain Management Practices in Electronics Industry. *Proceedings of the International Multiconference of Engineers and Computer Scientists.*

Omkareshwar, M. (2013). Green marketing initiatives by the corporate world: A study. *Advances in Management*, 6(3), 20–26.

Ko, E., Hwang, V. K., & Kim, E. V. (2013). green marketing functions in building corporate image in the retail setting. *Journal of Business Research*, 66(10), 1709–1715. doi:10.1016/j.jbusres.2012.11.007

Pishvaee, M. S., Torabi, S. A., & Razmi, J. (2012). The credibility-based fuzzy mathematical programming model for green logistics design under uncertainty. *Computers & Industrial Engineering*, 62(2), 624–632. doi:10.1016/j.cie.2011.11.028

Polonsky, M. J. (1994). An introduction to green marketing. *Electronic Green Journal*, 1(2), 1–10. doi:10.5070/G31210177

Prajogo, D., Chowdhury, M., Yeung, A. C., & Cheng, T. C. E. (2012). The relationship between supplier management and firm's operational performance: A multi-dimensional perspective. *International Journal of Production Economics*, 136(1), 123–130. doi:10.1016/j.ijpe.2011.09.022

Qinghua, Z., Vijie, D., & Joseph, S. (2010). A portfolio-based analysis for green supplier management using the analytical network process. *Supply Chain Management*, 15(4), 306–319. doi:10.1108/13598541011054670

Rao, P. (2002). Greening the supply chain: A new initiative in Sout East Asia. *International Journal of Operations & Production Management*, 22(6), 632–655. doi:10.1108/01443570210427668

Rath R C. (2013). An impact of green marketing on practices of supply chain management in Asia: emerging economic opportunities and challenges. *International Journal of Supply Chain Management, 2*(1), 78-86.

Raymond, P. C., Lopez, J., Marche, S., Perron, G. M., & Wright, R. (2008). Influences, practices and opportunities for environmental supply chain management in Nova Scotia SMEs. *Journal of Cleaner Production, 16*(15), 1561–1570. doi:10.1016/j.jclepro.2008.04.022

Reveliotis, S. A. (2007). Uncertainty management in optimal disassembly planning through learning-based strategies. *IIE Transactions, 39*(6), 645–658. doi:10.1080/07408170600897536

Rostamzadeh, R., Govindan, K., Esmaeili, A., & Sabaghi, M. (2015). Application of fuzzy vigor for evaluation of green supply chain management practices. *Ecological Indicators, 49*, 188–203. doi:10.1016/j.ecolind.2014.09.045

Russo, D., & Rizzi, C. (2014), structural optimization strategies to design green products. *Computers in Industry, 65*, 470–479.

Sar, K., Dong, Q., Wei, S. B., & Khalid, Z. (2017). Environmental logistics performance indicators affecting per capita income and sectoral growth: Evidence from a panel of selected global ranked logistics countries. *Environmental Science and Pollution Research International, 24*(2), 1518–1531.

Sarkis, J. (1998). Evaluating environmentally conscious business practices. *European Journal of Operational Research, 107*(1), 159–174. doi:10.1016/S0377-2217(97)00160-4

Sarkis, J. (Ed.). (2001). *Greener management international*. Greenleaf Publishing.

Sarkis, J., Meade, L., & Presley, A. (2006). An activity-based management methodology for evaluating business processes for environmental sustainability. *Business Process Management Journal, 12*(6), 751–776. doi:10.1108/14637150610710918

Sarkis, J., Zhu, Q., & Lai, K. (2011). An organizational theoretic review of green supply chain management literature. *International Journal of Production Economics, 130*(1), 1–15. doi:10.1016/j.ijpe.2010.11.010

Shang, K. C., Lu, C. S., & Li, S. (2010). A taxonomy of green supply chain management capability among electronics-related manufacturing firms in Taiwan. *Journal of Cleaner Production, 14*(5), 472–486.

Sharma, S. (2000). Managerial interpretations and organizational context as predictors of corporate choice of environmental strategy. *Academy of Management Journal, 43*(4), 681–697.

Shen, L., Govindan, K., & Shankar, M. (2015). evaluation of barriers of corporate social responsibility using an analytical hierarchy process under a fuzzy environment—A textile case. *Sustainability, 7*(3), 3493–3514. doi:10.3390u7033493

Shi, S. L., & He, J.S. (2005). A study on supplier assessment system in agile supply chain. *Journal of the Chinese Institute of Industrial Engineers, 8*(2), 95–100.

Simpson, D., Power, D., & Samson, D. (2007). Greening the automotive supply chain: A relationship perspective. *International Journal of Operations & Production Management, 27*(1), 28–48. doi:10.1108/01443570710714529

Srivastava, S. K. (2007). Green supply-chain management: A state-of-the-art literature review. *International Journal of Management Reviews, 9*(1), 53–80. doi:10.1111/j.1468-2370.2007.00202.x

Srivastava, S. K. (2007). Green supply-chain management: A state-of the-art literature review. *International Journal of Management Reviews, 9*(1), 53–80. doi:10.1111/j.1468-2370.2007.00202.x

Srivastava, S. K., & Srivastava, R. K. (2006). Managing product returns for reverse logistics. *International Journal of Physical Distribution & Logistics Management, 36*(7), 524–546. doi:10.1108/09600030610684962

Subramanian, N., Abdulrahman, M.D., Zhou, X., (2014). Integration of logistics and cloud computing service providers: cost and green benefits in the Chinese context. *Transportation Research Part E: Logistics and Transportation Review, 70*, 86–98.

Teunter, R. H. (2006). Determining optimal disassembly and recovery strategies. *Omega, 34*(6), 533–537. doi:10.1016/j.omega.2005.01.014

Thoo, A. C., Hamid, A. B. A., & Rasli, A., & Zhang, D. W. (2014b). The moderating effect of entrepreneurship on green supply chain management practices and sustainability performance. *Advanced Materials Research, 869*, 773–776.

Thoo, A. C., Hamid, A. B. A., Rasli, A., & Zhang, D. W. (2014a). Supply chain strategy and operational capability in Malaysian SMEs. *Advances in Education Research, 44*, 231.

Tsai, W. H., & Hung, S. J. (2009). A fuzzy goal programming approach for green supply chain optimisation under activity-based costing and performance evaluation with a value-chain structure. *International Journal of Production Research, 47*(18), 4991–5017. doi:10.1080/00207540801932498

Ubeda, S., Arcelus, F. J., & Faulin, J. (2011). Green logistics at eroski: A case study. *International Journal of Production Economics, 131*(1), 44–51. doi:10.1016/j.ijpe.2010.04.041

Vachon, S., & Klassen, R. D. (2006). Extending green practices across the supply chain: The impact of upstream and downstream integration. *International Journal of Operations & Production Management, 26*(7), 795–821. doi:10.1108/01443570610672248

Wang, N. M., Sun, L. Y., & Wang, Y. L. (2005). *Green supply chain management.* Tsinghua University Press.

Wang, Y., Han, J. H., & Beynon-Davies, P. (2019). Understanding blockchain technology for future supply chains: A systematic literature review and research agenda. *Supply Chain Management, 24*(1), 62–84. doi:10.1108/SCM-03-2018-0148

Webb, L. (1994). Green purchasing: Forging a new link in the supply chain. *Resource (Saint Joseph, Mich.), 1*(6), 14–18.

Willems, B., Dewulf, W., & Duflou, I. R. (2006). Can large-scale disassembly be profitable? A linear programming approach to quantifying the turning point to make disassembly economically viable. *International Journal of Production Research, 44*(6), 1125–1146. doi:10.1080/00207540500354168

Wu, C., & Barnes, D. (2016). Partner selection in green supply chains using PSO—A practical approach. *Production Planning and Control, 27*(13), 1041–1061. doi:10.1080/09537287.2016.1177233

Wu, C. Y., Zhu, Q. H., & Geng, Y. (2001). Green supply chain management and enterprises sustainable development. *China Soft Science, 3*, 47–50.

Yang, C. L., Lin, S. P., Chan, Y. H., & Sheu, C. (2010). Mediated effect of environmental management on manufacturing competitiveness: An empirical study. *International Journal of Production Economics, 123*(1), 210–220. doi:10.1016/j.ijpe.2009.08.017

Yusuf, Gunasekaran, Musa, Ei-Berishy, Abubakar, & Ambursa. (2013). The UK oil and gas supply chains: an empirical analysis of the adoption of sustainable measures and performance outcomes. International introductory chapter: introduction of green supply chain management. *Journal of Production Economics, 146*(2), 501-514.

Zailani, S., Govindan, K., Iranmanesh, M., Shaharudin, M. R., & Chong, Y. S. (2015). Green innovation adoption in the automotive supply chain: The Malaysian case. *Journal of Cleaner Production, 108*, 1115–1122. doi:10.1016/j.jclepro.2015.06.039

Zhang, D. W., Hamid, A. B. A., & Thoo, A. C. (2014). Sustainable Supplier Selection: An International Comparative Literature Review for Future Investigation. *Applied Mechanics and Materials, 525*, 787–790. doi:10.4028/www.scientific.net/AMM.525.787

Zhu, Q., Geng, Y., Tsuyoshi, F., & Shizuka, H. (2010). Green supply chain management in leading manufacturers: Case studies in Japanese large companies. *Management Research Review, 33*(4), 380–392. doi:10.1108/01409171011030471

Zhu, Q., & Sarkis, J. (2004). Relationships between operational practices and performance among early adopters of green supply chain management practices in Chinese manufacturing enterprises. *Journal of Operations Management, 22*(3), 265–289. doi:10.1016/j.jom.2004.01.005

Zhu, Q., Sarkis, J., & Lai, K. H. (2007). Green supply chain management: Pressures, practices, and performance within the Chinese automobile industry. *Journal of Cleaner Production, 15*(11), 1041–1052. doi:10.1016/j.jclepro.2006.05.021

Zhu, Q. H. (2004). Green supply chain management. Chemical Industry Press.

Zsidisin, G. A., & Siferd, S. P. (2001). Environmental purchasing: a framework for theory development. *European Journal of Purchasing & Supply Management, 7*(1), 61–73.


## KEY TERMS AND DEFINITIONS

**Environment:** External as well as internal, within and outside the preview of supply chain should be taken care and all entities must act to protect the environment from any deterioration.

**Green Management:** Are the practices to save against pollution, global warming natural resource and biological diversity depletion.

**Green Supply Chain:** Are the practices starts from sourcing environmentally safe raw material, using green fuel, less polluting vehicles, warehousing, and distribution.

**Innovation:** Adopting advance technology for better resource utilization, some of the technologies like machines learning, block chain and artificial intelligence are enhancing supply chain performances.

**Performance:** Need to be measured for both the aspects quantitative (delivery lead time, flexibility, and resource utilization), and qualitative (service/product quality and customer satisfaction).

**Sustainability:** Are the green practices for meeting the needs of the present without compromising the ability of future generations to meet their needs.

# Section 5
# Supply Chain Risks and Disruptions

# Chapter 23

# Managing Supply Chain Risk and Uncertainty in the Post-Pandemic Era:
## A Strategic Perspective

**Gyanesh Kumar Sinha**
*Bennett University, Greater Noida, India*

**Deepika Dhingra**
 https://orcid.org/0000-0001-5967-8834
*Bennett University, Greater Noida, India*

## ABSTRACT

*The pandemic due to COVID-19 has not only disrupted supply chains all around the world but has also tested the resilience and flexibility of supply chain leaders globally. With the virus still alive and several regions and economies in lockdown, disruption to supply chains continues to be severe. As economies restart, having an efficient supply chain will be critical to supplying goods and services quickly, safely, and securely. Business leaders are expected to respond and take immediate actions to sustain business operations to serve their customers, clients, and stakeholders that includes protecting and supporting their human resources. The chapter discusses the risk and uncertainties that have arisen due to pandemics. It also presents the framework for the supply chain post-COVID-19 scenario and proposes an action plan and the model that can build resiliency and improve efficiency and visibility across the supply chain. The action plan will facilitate communities to manage short-term crises and enable businesses to be customer-centric and help economies rebound.*

## INTRODUCTION

Supply chain management not only lies at the heart of the organization but also transcends its boundaries outside the organization. It is perhaps the premier operations management strategy for companies

DOI: 10.4018/978-1-7998-9506-0.ch023

Copyright © 2022, IGI Global. Copying or distributing in print or electronic forms without written permission of IGI Global is prohibited.

seeking to establish and maintain competitive advantage in today's global marketplace. Supply chain management is important because businesses have come to recognize that their capacity to continuously reinvent competitive advantage depends on their ability to look ahead of their channel partners and leverage their internal capabilities. Channel partners assist companies to generate innovative ideas and resources necessary to assemble the right blend of competencies that will resonate with their organizations and the wants and needs of their marketplaces. Today, the core competency an enterprise may possess is not to be found in a temporary advantage it may hold in a product or process, but rather in its ability to continuously assemble and implement market-winning capabilities arising from collaborative alliances with their supply chain partners. Creating a customer is a major task of marketing. But delivering the goods to the customer created is the most critical task. Global markets are expanding beyond borders, and this is what is re-defining the way demand and supplies are managed. Global companies have been prioritizing their sourcing products from markets across continents, to keep the cost of manufacturing down. There has been a trend among companies that to be competitive, they keep looking out to set up production centres at places where the cost of raw material and labour is cheap.

The focus on efficiency in the process brings whole range of functions, systems, new processes, development of sophisticated techniques and methodology. As we think of raw material supply, coordination among functions such as production, procurement, vendors, suppliers, finance, and operations come into play. Distribution makes us think of competitors, marketing, sale, customer service interface. Finance comes into play for both. According to Martin Christopher, the definition of supply chain management is:

*"The management of upstream and downstream relationships with suppliers and customers to deliver superior customer value at less cost to the supply chain as a whole," according to Martin Christopher in his book Logistics and Supply Chain Management.*

Supply chain management means systematic supply of raw material to the organization and efficient delivery of finished products to the customers. Volatility and uncertainty in the market points to the role supply chains play in the overall success and valuation of global corporations. Today supply chains are very complex, with large number partners spread across multiple countries and geographies as part of an intertwined global trade ecosystem. The objective of our study is to understand the various types and sources of supply chain risks and uncertainties post COVID-19 outbreak and the strategies adopted by global firms to meet the challenges associated with them. The present research has used the review of research articles and reports published by industry experts and research consulting firms in the year 2020 and 2021. Cases from different industries have been used to conceptualize supply chain disruptions and resulting action initiated by those select industries to mitigate risks and vulnerabilities.

## BACKGROUND

In 2003, during the outbreak of the severe acute respiratory syndrome (SARS), China accounted for just 2 percent of global GDP. But, now in the present scenario of COVID-19 pandemic, China's share of global GDP has increased to almost 20 percent. The unprecedented supply chain disruption caused by COVID-19 has had severe operational and financial consequences like demand drops and surges by segment, supply shortages, inventory challenges and reduced productivity. Companies across the globe can use this opportunity to discover where investments are needed, reform the supply chain function, and reposition the organization for growth once economies bounce back accordingly. A recent report published by IBM on "COVID-19 and shattered supply chains", states that the pandemic has exposed the vulnerabilities and fragilities in global supply chains across most sectors and industries and has led have resulted in huge losses as well as complete shutting down of various companies. Capgemini Research Institute (2020) reported worrying findings in the wake of COVID 19 while describing supply chain resilience. Initial supply-chain losses were largely due to restrictions imposed by several countries (Guan et al., 2020).

Research conducted on 1000 organizations across the globe directed on three key themes – (i) to what extent organizations need to rethink on traditional supply chain practices, (ii) to what extent organizations are prepared to address future disruptions, and (iii) how prepared are organizations for similar disruptions in the long run. They found that almost 70 percent of organizations struggled to restore its operations back to normal. It took them more than three months to manage inventory, manufacturing, and logistics capacity. The table 1 summarizes (in terms of percentage), the organizations which faced the supply chain disruptions in planning, sourcing, production, warehouse & distribution, and sales.

*Table 1. Supply chain disruptions faced companies due to pandemic*

| Planning | Sourcing | Production | Warehouse and Distribution | Sales |
|---|---|---|---|---|
| Difficulties in supply plan- lack information -69% | Shortage of materials-74% | Difficulties in rapidly scaling production-69% | Difficulties in balancing stock between warehouses-69% | Difficulties in switching to online channels-71% |
| Difficulties in demand planning due to lack of data- 68% | Delayed shipments – 74% | Difficulties in reconfiguring production lines-68% | Difficulties with products being held up in ports- 68% | Lost sales due to stock outs -60% |
| Difficulties in end to end monitoring of supply chain -72% | Difficulties in scaling workforce- 69% | Difficulties in controlling costs- 68% | Difficulties in maintaining healthy and safe working condition-60% | |

Source: Capgemini (2020)

Ernst & Young LLP (2020) conducted research comprising of senior executives in the supply chain domain across various sectors, including consumer products, retail, life sciences, industrial products, automotive, and high-tech companies in the United States. COVID-19 pandemic has made global disruption across all trade & only 2% of companies surveyed were well prepared for the pandemic, with 72% reported a negative effect. 92% of respondents did not stop investments in technology. There were 11% of the firms, especially in the pharmaceutical or life science sector reported positive effects. Some sectors were hit particularly hard especially automotive and nearly all industrial products. Further 47% of all companies said that the pandemic disrupted their workforce where many employees were asked to work from home, others, especially in factory settings, were compelled to adapt to new requirements for physical spacing, contact-tracing and more personal protective equipment (PPE). High-tech manufacturing companies started investing significantly more in technology to reduce employee exposure to COVID-19. Gurtu (2021) reviewed various articles on the theme of 'risk' in supply chain and observed that managing the risk and uncertainty has drawn attention of various researchers and experts working this field.

# MAIN FOCUS OF THE CHAPTER

## Issues, Controversies and Problems

The main focus of this chapter is to review various literature to understand sources of supply chain risks and uncertainties in general as well post COVID-19. This section will review the strategies adopted by select firms to meet the challenges associated with them.

## Agility and Supply Chain Performance

There are various challenges and risks involved in supply chain at a global level (Chopra and Sodhi 2014). Araz et al. (2020) observed that spread of COVID 19 has caused major disruptions affecting the global supply chain intensively. For attaining high level of supply chain performance, a firm not only needs to ensure that the supply chain configuration is aligned with the business strategy but is also robust enough to handle demand as well as supply uncertainties. Robustness of supply chain is also termed as agile supply chain. The figure 1 shows factors responsible for supply chain performance (Shah 2009).

*Figure 1. Supply chain configuration design*
Source: Shah (2009)

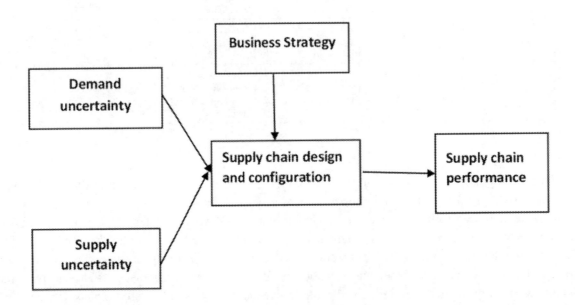

Unlike demand, an organization has a greater control on supply. There has been a common understanding among practitioners that supply chain uncertainty can be handled by choosing appropriate partners. Therefore, the focus has been on supplier selection and developing long-term relationship with suppliers rather than on addressing supply uncertainties. However, an unfortunate circumstance like terrorist attack in US in the year 2001 forced various organizations to focus both on demand uncertainty and supply uncertainty. The practice of lean operations or JIT system started getting questioned. Here, it is important to note that companies that have configured their supply chain design and operations to handle high level of demand uncertainty effectively, are known as responsive supply chain. Also, companies that have configured their supply chain design and operations to high levels of demand uncertainty and supply chain disruptions effectively, are known as agile supply chains. In a responsive approach the firm divides the season into two components: speculative time and response time. The speculative part of the season is managed using a long but efficient chain using speculative forecast available before the start of the season. Demand for the later part of the season is serviced using responsive supply chain by adopting faster mode of transport, locating manufacturing facilities close to the market. For example (as shown in the figure 2), T denotes a season for a time-period T, and demand is uniformly distributed across the season, then T can be divided into reactive time-period T3 and speculative time- period. Demand during the speculative period can be serviced from low-cost sourcing which may require longer lead times. Forecast accuracy might be very poor at this stage. The speculative time-period can further be divided into T1 and T2 as shown in the Figure 2. Time period T1 is used for observing the initial sales pattern. At the end of this period, forecasts can be updated, and orders can be placed on a responsive manufacturing facility for producing required components or products with an approximate product mix for the likely demand in time-period T2.

*Figure 2. Responsive approach*
Source: Shah (2009)

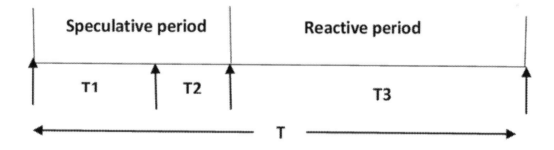

So, the demand during speculative period can be managed using speculative approach, and demand during the reactive period can be manged using the responsive supply chain. Responsive chain is usually more expensive as it involves manufacturing facilities near to markets, requiring faster mode of transport and in small batches. In general, expensive manufacturing and transportation are to be traded-off against lost sales and markdown costs.

## Supply Chain Disruptions and Resilience

Lengthy supply chains are major concerns in the face of disruptions in sourcing, production and distribution of goods and services. Such disruptions may be caused by natural disasters such as cyclones and tsunamis, industrial accidents or acts of terrorism. There have been several global calamities that have occurred in the past such as, the earthquake in Bhuj district of Gujarat in 2001, the tsunami in Japan in 2011, the Indian Ocean earthquake, and tsunami in west coast of Sumatra, Indonesia in 2004. These disasters have created greater demands on forms to keep supply chains flexible.

Schmidt & Raman (2012) defined disruption as an unplanned event that adversely affect a firms' normal operations. The causes for the supply chain disruption are attributed to natural hazards, terrorists' attacks, and political disturbances. Disruptions in supplier's operations have caused significant loses to companies in the past. In March 2000, Ericsson made huge losses when a fire broke out in the Philips plant. This plant was the only microchip supplier to Ericsson. Philips was unable to manufacture chips. However, the rival company Nokia, which also sourced its chip from the same plant, came up with a quick response to manage the crisis. Ohio State University (2013) described resilience as the ability to survive, adapt and grow during disasters and catastrophic incidents. While referring to LARGE (Lean-Agile-Resilience-Green) paradigm (Carvalho, Duarte, & Machado, 2011), Cabral et al (2012) suggested key performance indicators for managing supply chain disruptions as inventory cost, order fulfilment rate, and responsiveness to urgent deliveries.

## LARGE Framework

Figure 3 shows that an increase in production lead time has direct impact on the service level because, it increases the lead time in service delivery and related cost. In order to make the supply chain resilient, integration level needs to be enhanced. Lower inventory levels cause lower service level which in turn negatively impacts resilience and agility in the supply chain.

*Figure 3. Causality model under LARGE paradigm*
Source: Adapted from Carvalho & Machado (2009)

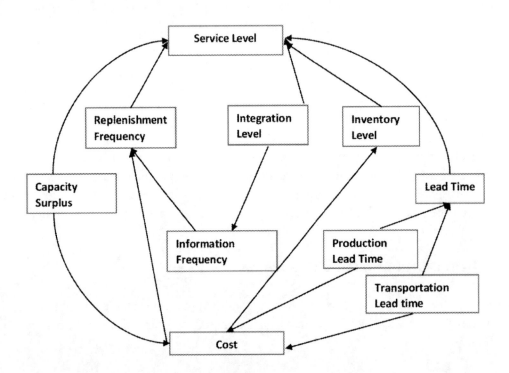

In the event of slowdown in economic activities, inventory level goes up resulting in an increase in obsolescence (Sinha and Dey, 2018). These outcomes scale down operations due to reduced availability of working capital. Figure 2 shows that Cboe Volatility Index (VIX) indicates that market will continue to remain uncertain in the coming months putting constraints on availability of funds and impacting both the manufacturing and service sector. Sinha, Bagodi and Dey (2020) explained the post COVID 19 situation as presented in figure 4. According to them, sales of goods can be explained as the difference between the demand and flow of goods to the consumers. Demands for goods are triggered by types of goods required and income of consumers and with job losses during the pandemic there has been a massive change in income pattern.

*Figure 4. Post COVID 19 Situation*
Source: Adapted from Sinha, D., Bagodi, V. and Dey, D. (2020)

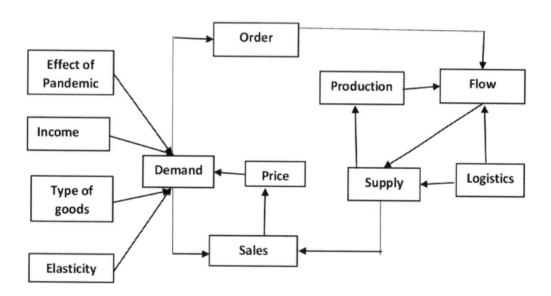

The study system dynamics approach (as shown in figure 5) to identify the relationship between customers' income, prices and demand of goods, cost of input and supply of finished goods during COVID situation. Authors observed that disruption in supplies of raw materials and finished products negate the increase in demand even in case of rise in individual income. At the same time, even if flow becomes normal, individual' income will affect business output.

*Figure 5. System Dynamics Model -Post COVID 19*
Source: Sinha, Bagodi, and Dey (2020)

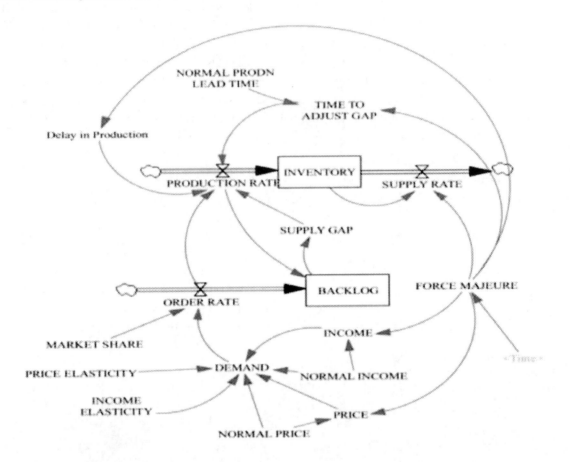

Barrios, K. (2020) identified major sources of risks associated with global supply chain as (i) Political and Government changes, (ii) Economic instability, (iii) Extreme weather events, (iv) Environmental risks, (v) Connectivity, (vi) Cyber-attacks, (vii) Poor data integrity and quality, (viii) Supplier inconsistency, (ix) Reduced ability to transport goods economically.

## Cases From Industries

This section summarizes some of the case studies conducted by Hoek (2020) on companies operating in diverse industries.

### Company A: Equipment Manufacturer for Real Estate Industry in USA

This company is medium scale in in terms of size of the business and certain proportion of materials are sourced from China. Major assembling and molding operations are done inhouse but there are a few domestic suppliers as well for the same. At the start of the pandemic, because of lockdown in China, the company started facing supply disruptions as a significant portion of supplier bases were diversified

*Managing Supply Chain Risk and Uncertainty in the Post-Pandemic Era*

and outside China (specially in southeast Asia) as well. Though the company overcame the problems arising out of the pandemic after initial few weeks but due to the initial shock of disruption in supply, manufacturing and logistics, operations of the company were affected severely. To deal with uncertainties, the company reworked on transportation flows. The company realized the benefits of implementing the principle of total cost of ownership approach which looked beyond the purchase price alone, arising out of low-cost sourcing.

## Company B: Distributor of Electronic Items in Egypt, Iran and Saudi Arabia.

In the wake of pandemic in March 2019, Company B started stocking surplus inventory (buffering) to maintain supply continuity. Further, challenges of transport capacity constraints emerged outside China. Due to sudden rise in airfreight charges, the company explored a much cheaper mode of transport i.e., ocean mode which caused slower movement of products resulting into late deliveries. After six months company started realizing the digitization of the supply chain as a competitive weapon to survive in the long run.

## Company C: E-commerce Company, Operating in the US

This company manufactures and sells steel components to Gym and tractor manufacturing firms. Major components for these products are outsourced from China. Due to shut down of factories in China & other logistical challenges due to the pandemic, the company started developing new supply base in India as well as domestic locations rapidly. However, shifting to domestic manufacturing made the cost to increase two times on an average as compared to manufacturing in China. But the company realized that for certain high value items, customers were willing to pay significantly higher amount associated with domestic manufacturing in return for the availability of products and quicker delivery. The company also reduced its payment cycle time for suppliers from 60 days to just 1 day upfront. Faster payment by the company to these suppliers helped them to invest for increasing the capacity as well as to ensure the availability of raw materials even in case of scarce market. As part of long-term strategy, the company started focusing on supplier collaboration program and diversification of supplier base to reduce the supply side risks.

## Company D: Optical Products Manufacturer

This European based company is a manufacturer of eye care products. Many varieties of these products are produced in China. Even before the out-break of COVID 19, the company had initiated exploring the supply lines with major focus on developing supplier relationships. The company formed an exclusive team to figure out the forecast scenario on continuous basis and provided all necessary support in terms of technology and other required resources to therm. The company observed that there was an increase in the cost of transportation, longer lead times, and customer service challenges enhanced, while balancing possible purchase price implications. Responding to the pandemic challenges does require the involvement of several parts of the supply chain but the effort is not necessarily fully integrated.

## Company E: Aerospace Manufacturer

The company is based in France and has extensive supply chain network at global level. Majority of suppliers are from Asian countries. Some of component's sourced from these countries are very critical, in the absence of which one cannot make finished goods. In response to the pandemic, the company started working with suppliers very closely to make necessary adjustments in the operating procedures to facilitate COVID 19 appropriate behavior like sanitation and social distancing. For this purpose, several additional steps were identified and implemented. This resulted in higher operating costs in the short term. However, in doing so, the company observed recency biasness i.e., giving undue importance or weightage to current event making it harder to incorporate changes in the long run.

Moritz (2020) has explained how the supply chain disruptions caused by COVID-19 different from the past. The table 2 presents the summary of the same.

*Table 2. Dimension of supply chain disruptions post COVID-19*

| Dimension | Typical Disruptions | Disruptions due to COVID -19 |
|---|---|---|
| Geography | Mostly regional or local | Majorly global impacting all regions |
| Scope | Fewer industries | Widespread and across all industries impacting both goods and services |
| Demand Vs Supply | Disruptions mostly impacted supply, sometimes demand as well | Disruptions impacted both demand and supply |
| Prior Planning & Experience | Prior experience available for disaster planning | Limited disaster planning for global pandemic |
| Financial System | Low to moderate correlation with global financial system | high correlation with global financial system |
| Term | Short term needs for emergency services | Longer term needs for emergency services |
| Human Impact and Behavior | Localized human impact with shorter duration, short term fear among public, and risks are visible | Widespread human impact with unknown duration and unknown impact |

*Source:* https://www.scmr.com/article/supply_chain_disruptions_and_covid_19

Cboe volatility index (Figure 6) indicates reduced level of uncertainties and market risks are expected in the future as compared to high level of risks and volatility that existed immediately post COVID-19. As the world is recovering from this crisis, reduced uncertainties should not be confused with stability in the immediate term.

*Figure 6. Cboe volatility index*
Source: Cboe Global Markets/Options Institute

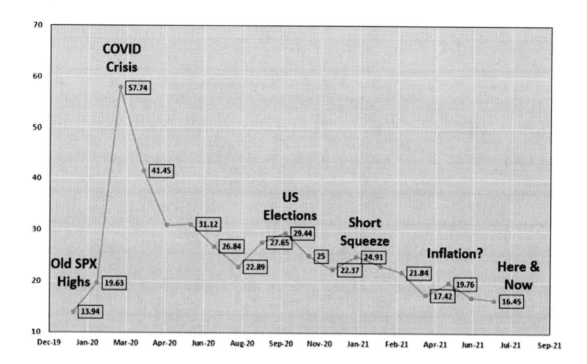

## DISCUSSION

Review of literature, report and case studies highlight various issues and challenges that have emerged post COVID 19 spread globally. All these observations pertaining to supply chain disruption post COVID 19 or findings have been divided into three subsections

1. Various risks and uncertainties emerged during pandemic,
2. supply chain trend in the initial stage of the pandemic, and
3. supply chain scenario post pandemic.

### Various Risks and Uncertainties Emerged During Pandemic

COVID 19 was primarily viewed as a local issue affecting only China. The majority of Fortune 1000 companies had global supply chain operations in China and these companies experienced spike in direct product and inventory flow interruptions. During March 2020 itself, the sign of adverse effect on global business was observed before the coronavirus began to spread in the United States of America. A report by Dun & Bradstreet publishes that at least 163 Fortune 1000 companies had one or more direct, Tier 1 suppliers in the impacted region, while at least 938 of these companies had one or more smaller suppliers in Tier 2. Supply shock due to Covid 19 started in China from February 2020 and at the same time there was demand shock in the global economy. Further, temporary trade restrictions and shortages of pharmaceuticals, critical medical supplies at many places and other products aggravated the problems and contributed to vulnerabilities in the production strategies and supply chains of firms just about everywhere significantly.

To survive in the business and fulfilling the needs of customers, many retail outlets (which were closed due to spread of corona virous and subsequent lockdown), were forced to switch to online platform. It increased the volume of traffic online and resulted into websites crashing on several occasions. All this happened because of slow or non-adaptation of online and digital ways of working.

Since the pandemic began, global supply-chain management has been at the forefront of the fight against COVID-19. Companies and suppliers were forced to change their playbooks and rely on new methods of innovation, high road networking and asset stabilization to keep their logistics moving forward. Whether warehousing, automation, freight, retail or e-commerce, business leaders needed to re-evaluate and address many or all in order to maintain their supply chains and keep up with the demand, which in turn, was drastically altered by the pandemic.

## Supply Chain Trend During Initial Stage of Pandemic

Following supply chain trends emerged in the initial stage of the global pandemic.

## Accelerated use of Automation

Spread of COVID 19, in the initial stage, introduced new logistical blueprints to follow. Getting work done with fewer employees grew exponentially as social distancing directives influenced the nation's manufacturing capacity. Many suppliers either switched to automation or increased the pace of automation (if already existing) to ensure flexible supply chains and increased accuracy to help meet demand from their buyers. However, it came with a price. According to Foster (2020), the global market for logistics automation, estimated at $49.2 billion in the year 2018, is expected to reach $96.2 billion by 2024.

## Reshaping Returns

In the last decade, due to change in consumer behaviour or habits, leading companies like Walmart, Amazon etc. started facing challenges of addressing surge in demand on the online platform. But the spread of pandemic followed by Lockdowns gave a new edge to e-commerce in terms of product returns. The returns for online purchases were three-fold compared to in-store purchases. The product returns caused significant cost to the business operating in US, EU countries and UK. However, despite uncertain scenario few companies were able to convert into business opportunity and those companies prepared themselves to handle the significant shift in consumer behaviour due to their efficiently developed and managed e-commerce platforms. By and large, returns posed a major challenge for the supply chain. Various retail shops got converted into distribution hubs to not only get their products available for customers but also to get the returns back to the store even faster. Brick-and-mortar retailers across the country, and the carriers that support them, started struggling to adapt to e-commerce as foot traffic slowed down and the need to adapt their business strategies to drive traffic digitally or in alternative ways continued to increase.

478

## Warehouse Capacity Issues

Warehousing managers started facing issues pertaining to capacity, influx of inventory replenishment, e-commerce orders, returns and inconsistent consumer demand. Between February and June 2020, consumers stockpiled some essential commodities like toilet paper and hand sanitizers. During these periods, consumptions matched the same amount of consumption as the previous 20 years, pre-COVID. Businesses continue to stock up and shut down (those that are non-essential). Majority of the people started buying for the long term in line with their strategic objectives. While the pressure for warehousing expense increased, death of some bricks and mortar businesses helped to counterbalance this fight for space.

## Freight Volatility at Local and Global Level

Global supply chains have been stretched to unprecedented lengths during this crisis, including freights and shipments. Internationally, there were lower volumes of orders, but more backlogging in warehouses in February and March 2020. Domestically, warehouses working at high volumes are struggling to meet demand. Many international in-bound imports were able to maintain successful operations through the peak of lockdowns — using larger ships with increased capacity to clear up empty container backlogs. But COVID-19 related border checks have impacted the pace of movement of goods across the globe. Global pandemic forced many companies to look up to third-party experts, advanced digital capabilities, and accelerated e-commerce operations to reduce risk, increase flexibility, focus on their core business, and respond to market changes swiftly. This trend is expected to continue into the new year.

## Emerging Supply Chain Scenario-post Pandemic

Vaccines started rolling out in early January 2021 in various countries to get the virus under control. However, emergence of the second wave of corona virus during February to June 2021 in various parts of the world, caused lot of disruption in supply chain across the world again. But increased availability of vaccines from June onwards helped in controlling the spread of corona virus to a large extent. Businesses are now focussing on recovery and returning to normal operations. Supply chain will play an integral role in this effort, and will emerge in a different shape, with COVID-19 leaving a legacy on many areas of transportation and warehousing.

Following trends are expected to re-emerge and shape the industry in 2021 significantly

## Shortage of Labour

While many industries closed and unemployment rose in 2020, logistic providers needed workers. As the economy begins its recovery, attracting and retaining people and a positive working environment will once again become the primary competitive battleground in the supply chain thus requiring management of talent in more creative and innovative ways.

## AI Enabled Forecasting

Consumer behaviour was erratic during the pandemic, making it difficult to use historical trends to forecast and manage inventory. As the industries return to a more stable environment, artificial intelligence and machine learning are likely to find prominent attention for advanced analytics and forecasting.

## Sustainability

There was a lot of focus on sustainability before the pandemic. However, as the pandemic caused significant disruptions in the flow of goods and services across the globe, focus of few leading global firms has shifted more towards business survival than on pursuing sustainability goals in the short as well as medium term. However, in days to come, sustainability will again be on the priority list of organizations.

## Long Term Supply Chain Scenario – Post Pandemic

Given the magnitude of the pandemic, there are few major areas that that would have lasting effects on the supply chain.

## Redundancy

Supply-chain managers have now understood the need to reduce the risk of out-of-stock events and disruptions. Redundancy, which means holding extra inventories, low-capacity utilization, relationship with more suppliers etc, will be a priority even as operations normalize. Third-party logistics providers are now expected to be well-positioned to manage supply redundancy through their resources, infrastructure, and engineering capabilities.

## Near-shoring

Companies will move towards near shoring to avoid inventory disruptions. Near-shoring will enable the firms in achieving higher efficiencies across the supply chains. Leaner inventory and network design will offset increased costs in warehousing and labour.

## Resilience

The pandemic has forced companies to rethink their investment strategy for better visibility and real-time monitoring of risk, making supply chain more resilient.

Further, experts agree that it is imperative to rethink on existing practices of managing the supply chain and developing more resiliency across the value chain to handle future disruptions (Anbumozhi et al., 2020; Rennie, 2020).

# RESEARCH GAP

The present research review literatures from the recent past to analyze the present and future scenario of supply chain management post pandemic. Most studies examined the impact of pandemic on supply chain and few literatures have come up with suggestions but are not supported with any empirical evidence. No literature was observed specific to any industry which could explain or describe the necessary course of action in order to reduce the supply chain risk or improve the supply chain resilience. Problems and challenges pertaining to sourcing, transportation, inventory, warehousing, manufacturing, automation, IT adoption etc. which firms might face in the medium or long term, have not been explored or described specifically for a particular sector or industry segment. Further, whether, the issue of supply chain agility or supply chain resilience post pandemic will remain confined majorly within a specific geographic region or will be a world-wide phenomenon, has not been discussed so far. Question of sustainability adoption or range and level of green practices across the supply chain by various entities, remain unanswered in the present literatures.

# SOLUTION AND RECOMMENDATION

## Recommended Strategies for Supply Chain

Crisis due to COVID-19 will continue to impact supply chain in the long run. Global competition will keep many things unchanged. Consumers will continue to demand product or services at low prices thereby leading to pressure on the firms to operate efficiently and frugal capital and manufacturing capacity. The challenge for companies will be to make their supply chains more resilient without weakening their competitiveness. Shih (2020) explained that to meet that challenge, managers will be required to first understand their vulnerabilities in respective domains and then consider taking several steps summarized as under

### Focus on Demand Forecasting

Focus on accuracy in demand forecasting can help in fixing cost associated with excessive inventory built up or minimize shortages. Data integration across the chain followed by data analytics and artificial intelligence can provide managers to not just have quick insights on reliable estimate of demand or tracking demand signals but also efficient routes planning for firm's logistics operations, helping them to run business more efficiently. Artificial intelligence (AI)-powered tools have made it easier and more cost-effective to map and monitor a large database of sources around the world.

### From Single Sourcing to Multi-sourcing

Products often require incorporating critical components or sophisticated materials that need specialized technological skills to make them. It is very difficult for a single firm to possess breadth of capabilities necessary to produce everything by itself. For example, growing electronic features in modern vehicles requires more electronic components than before in their finished products like engine, steering, power windows, lighting etc. Manufacturers in most industries have turned to suppliers and subcontractors who focus and specialize in one area, and those specialists, in turn, rely on many others. Such an arrangement offers flexibility in what goes into their products. But these practices have increased the level of vulnerability because of dependency on a single or narrower supplier base for a crucial component or material. If that supplier produces the item in only one plant or one country, risks of disruptions will be even higher.

## Identification of Vulnerabilities

Understanding where the risks lie so that the company can protect itself may require exploration far beyond the first and second tiers and mapping full supply chain, including distribution facilities and transportation hubs. This is time-consuming and expensive, which explains why most major firms have focused their attention only on strategic direct suppliers that account for large amounts of their expenditures. But a surprise disruption that brings a business to a halt can be much more costly than a deep look into a firm's supply chain. The entire supply chain process needs to be mapped in accordance with low-, medium-, or high-risk. To facilitate categorization, information like degree of impact on revenues in case of supply uncertainties from existing suppliers, lead time for a particular supplier's factory recovery from disruption, and the availability of alternate sources can be analyzed. It is essential to determine how long a company could withstand a supply shock, and how fast an incapacitated node could recover or be replaced by alternate sites when an entire industry faces shortage due to disruptions.

## Manufacturing Flexibility

To gear for mitigating vulnerability, manufacturing processes need to be flexible so that the capacity can be reconfigured and redeployed as and when required especially in case of manual or semiautomated assembly operations. Degree of flexibility could be very less for companies using highly specialized process. Examples of low degree manufacturing flexibility includes production of highly advanced smartphone chips, which is concentrated in three facilities in Taiwan owned by the Taiwan Semiconductor Manufacturing Company; fabrication of exotic sensors and components, which happens largely in highly specialized facilities in a few select countries like Japan, Germany, and the United States; and refining of neodymium for the magnets in AirPods and electric-vehicle motors, most of which is done in China.

Understanding vulnerability and assessment of flexibility in operations can be the key factors in deciding about diversification of supply base or buffering of critical items or components and materials.

## Diversification of Supply Base

To address heavy dependence on medium- or high-risk source (a single factory, supplier, or region), the company needs to add more sources in different locations which are not vulnerable to similar risks. Many firms have started relocating their supplier base from China to Southeast Asian countries such as Vietnam, Indonesia, or Thailand. But regionwide problems like the 1997 Asian financial crisis or the 2004 tsunami argue for broader geographic diversification. Managers should consider a regional strategy of producing substantial proportion of key goods within the region where they are consumed. For example, Latin America may be served by shifting labour-intensive work from China to Mexico and Central America. To supply Western Europe with items used there, companies can increase their reliance on eastern European countries, Turkey, and Ukraine. India has already initiated to promote itself as the

*Managing Supply Chain Risk and Uncertainty in the Post-Pandemic Era*

manufacturing hub under 'Make in India' policy by central government. Indian firms may shift their suppliers from Chinese to more local regions to serve domestic markets. It will be easier for products like furniture, clothing, and household goods to reduce high level of dependency on China because the inputs—lumber, fabrics, plastics etc. are the basic components or raw materials. However, it will remain a challenge to identify alternative sources for more sophisticated machinery, electronics, and other goods that incorporate components such as high-density interconnect circuit boards, electronic displays, and precision castings. It may take considerable time and require large initial capital outlay to build and develop new supplier infrastructure in a different country or region. For example, when China decided to open its first special economic zones in 1980s, there were hardly any domestic suppliers. China was reliant on global supply chains which were far away from its region and dependent on logistics specialists who sourced materials and components from the world over for final assembly in Chinese factories. Despite huge incentivisation from the Government, it took 20 years for the country to build a local base capable of supplying most electronic components, auto parts, chemicals, and drug ingredients needed for domestic manufacturing. However, shifting supplier base from China to Southeast Asian countries will require different logistic strategies because of efficiency and capacity constraints to serve markets.

## Buffer or Safety Stock

In case of unavailability of alternate suppliers, a company should determine how much extra inventory to carry, at least in the short run, in what form, and where along the supply chain. Despite safety or buffer stock, which is against the principle of lean inventory, it carries the risk of obsolescence and capital is tied up. But the savings from those practices must be weighed against all the costs of disruption, including lost revenues, higher prices that would have to be paid for materials that are suddenly in short supply, and the time and effort that would be required to secure them.

## Process Innovations

Relocating supply base and developing relationship with local suppliers will bring opportunity for process innovations. The firm can unfreeze its routine activities and evaluate the assumptions about existing processes. Manufacturing companies have the tendency to retain assets even after full depreciation and show little interest in investing in newer assets or Equipment's as depreciation expense is not a part of production or operations cost.

## Multi-Criteria Decision-Making Model

Based on the above discussion, it can be inferred that the following strategies can be applied to minimize the supply chain risk and disruptions are (i) Demand forecasting accuracy, (ii) multi-sourcing, (iii) Supply base diversification, (iv) Nearshoring, (v) Manufacturing flexibility, (vi) Buffering/Redundancy, and (vii) Process innovations. It is not possible for a firm (supplier, manufacturer, retailer, distributor, and wholesaler) to work on each strategy as listed above at a time. It may set any one of them as primary and other feasible strategies as secondary. Management of the firm can use optimization model or heuristic approach to choose the most effective supply chain strategy. Under the given situation, there are following multi-criteria decision making (MCDM) models which can be applied.

## Goal Programming

A company may have more than one objective, which may relate to something other than profit or cost, i.e., having several criteria, In this situation, goal programming can be applicable for decision making (Taylor, B. W., 2017). For example, in addition to maximizing the profit, increasing the number of suppliers or diversification in supply base may result into increase in the cost, which company is also interested to reduce it. The goal programming tool, which is an extension of linear programming technique, can help a firm in setting priorities for supply chain strategy while fulfilling multiple goals.

## Analytical Hierarchy Process Model (AHP)

It is a method of ranking decision alternatives and selecting the best one (Taylor, B. W., 2017). The manager of a firm may have several alternatives like buffering, nearshoring, supply base diversification etc., from which he/she can choose one. Using AHP approach, the decision-maker would be able to identify various criteria while choosing supply chain strategies. These criteria could be lead time, inventory cost, transportation cost, warehousing cost, material handling cost, demand of products, materials availability, etc. The manager would, then, take a decision based on how the alternatives compare, according to several criteria identified. Therefore, as AHP is a process of developing a numeric score to rank each decision alternative, based on how well each alternative meet the decision maker's criteria, it can be suggested to take decision for managing supply chain efficiently and effectively.

## FUTURE RESEARCH DIRECTIONS

The study suggests MCDM model for managing supply chain risk and uncertainty. However, further research can focus on the areas mentioned below:

1. Identification of supply chain risk and vulnerabilities specific to nature and type of industry.
2. Developing models for improving supply chain efficiencies and responsiveness to mitigate the negative impact of events such as COVID-19 in the future.
3. Role of artificial intelligence and machine learning in addressing demand as well as supply uncertainties.
4. Role of Internet of Things (IoT) and digital twin technology in assessing the supply chain performance and improving customer satisfaction post COVID-19.
5. Medium as well as long-term assessment of demand and supply scenario for different kind of products and services.
6. Emerging challenges in switching to high degree of automation across the supply chain.
7. Cost benefit analysis for aiding decisions such as multi-sourcing, nearshoring and achieving flexibility in the operations across the supply chain
8. Developing models for achieving sustainable supply chain management in organizations and forming sustainable practices in addressing supply chain disruptions

*Managing Supply Chain Risk and Uncertainty in the Post-Pandemic Era*

## CONCLUSION

The present chapter discusses the risk and uncertainty in supply chain that emerged across the globe due to spread of the novel corona virus COVID-19 since January 2020. There have been instances of disruptions in the past, but the scale, level of risks and vulnerabilities that this pandemic has brought, the world has never witnessed before. The present crisis has brought fundamental changes not only in supply chains but also consumer behaviours creating uncertainties in supply as well demand. The present study explored different types of risk and challenges across supply chains past and post pandemic both. A few pertinent conceptual models have been reviewed and industry responses post COVID-19 have also been analysed through real life case studies published in journals, articles, and reports. Based on the review, key measures for the industries (irrespective of nature or types of business) have been recommended. It is suggested to apply Multiple criteria decisions making (MCDM) for mitigating supply chain risk and disruptions. Post pandemic scenario has forced companies across all geographic regions to develop more robust operational as well as tactical plans that can mitigate not only risk associated with the efficient functioning of global supply chains but also human health. This requires end-to-end assessment, optimization and monitoring on regular and continuous basis. Digitally enabled supply chain has helped enterprises in navigating the disruptive forces and responding faster to volatile supply and demand. Systems equipped with efficient data collection and analytics will be in a much better position to understand complexity, anticipate potential disruption, and respond quickly. In well-managed chains, real time information, materials, and money flow seamlessly across departmental and organizational boundaries. By working on supply chain integration, it will be possible to shift the entire efficiency frontier downwards, which in turn will allow the firm to improve performance on cost and service fronts simultaneously.

## REFERENCES

Anbumozhi, V., Kimura, F., & Thangavelu, S. M. (2020). Global supply chain resilience: Vulnerability and shifting risk management strategies. In V. Anbumozhi, F. Kimura, & S. Thangavelu (Eds.), *Supply chain resilience*. Springer. doi:10.1007/978-981-15-2870-5_1

Araz, O. M., Choi, T.-M., Olson, D. L., & Salman, F. S. (2020). Data analytics for operational risk management. *Decision Sciences*, *51*(6), 1316–1319. doi:10.1111/deci.12443

Barrios. (2020). *Top 10 global supply chain risks*. https://www.xeneta.com/blog/global-supply-chain-risks

Cabral, I., Grilo, A., & Cruz-Machado, V. (2012). A decision-making model for lean, agile, resilient and green supply chain management. *International Journal of Production Research*, *50*(17), 4830–4845. doi:10.1080/00207543.2012.657970

Capgemini Research Institute. (2020). *Report: Building supply chain resilience-Capgemini*. https://www.capgemini.com/news/report-building-supply-chain-resilience

Carvalho, H., Duarte, S., & Machado, V. C. (2011). Lean, agile, resilient and green: Divergencies and synergies. *International Journal of Lean Six Sigma*, *2*(2), 151–179. doi:10.1108/20401461111135037

Chopra, S., & Sodhi, M. S. (2014). Reducing the Risk of Supply Chain Disruptions. *MIT Sloan Management Review*, *55*, 73–80.

Christopher, M. (2005). *Logistics and Supply Chain Management*. FT Prentice Hall.

Dun & Bradstreet. (2020). *Dun & Bradstreet COVID-19 Impact Index*. https://www.dnb.co.in/products/covid-19/impact-index.aspx

Ernst & Young. (2020). *How COVID-19 impacted supply chains and what comes next*. https://www.ey.com/en_gl/supply-chain/how-covid-19-impacted-supply-chains-and-what-comes-next

Foster, J. (2020). *Four Supply-Chain Trends Accelerated by COVID-19*. https://www.supplychainbrain.com/blogs/1-think-tank/post/31820-four-supply-chain-trends-accelerated-by-covid-19

Guan, D., Wang, D., Hallegatte, S., Davis, S. J., Huo, J., Li, S., Bai, Y., Lei, T., Xue, Q., Coffman, D. M., Cheng, D., Chen, P., Liang, X., Xu, B., Lu, X., Wang, S., Hubacek, K., & Gong, P. (2020). Global supply-chain effects of COVID-19 control measures. *Nature Human Behaviour*, *4*(6), 577–587. doi:10.103841562-020-0896-8 PMID:32493967

Gurtu, A., & Johny, J. (2021). Supply Chain Risk Management: Literature Review. *Risks*, *2021*(9), 16. doi:10.3390/risks9010016

Hoek, R. V. (2020). Responding to COVID-19 Supply Chain Risks—Insights from Supply Chain Change Management, Total Cost of Ownership and Supplier Segmentation Theory. *Logistics 2020, 4*. doi:10.3390/logistics4040023

Moritz, B. (2020). Supply chain disruptions and COVID-19. *Supply Chain Management Review*, *24*(3), 14–17.

Rennie, E. (2020). Five lessons from a crisis. *SCM Now*, *30*(3), 35–38.

Schmidt, W., & Raman, A. (2012). *When supply-chain disruptions matter*. Harvard Business School. https://www.hbs.edu/faculty/Publication%20Files/13-00

Shah, J. (2009). *Supply Chain Management: Text and Cases*. Pearson Education.

Shih, W. C. (2020). *Global Supply Chains in a Post-Pandemic World*. https://hbr.org/2020/09/global-supply-chains-in-a-post-pandemic-world

Sinha, D., Bagodi, V., & Dey, D. (2020). The Supply Chain Disruption Framework Post COVID-19: A System Dynamics Model. *Foreign Trade Review*, *55*(4), 511–534. doi:10.1177/0015732520947904

Sinha, D., & Dey, D. (2018). Supply chain strategies to sustain economic and customer uncertainties. In S. Dhir & S. Shishil (Eds.), *Flexible strategies in VUCA markets* (pp. 139–153). Springer. doi:10.1007/978-981-10-8926-8_10

Taylor, B. W. (2017). *Introduction to Management Science*. Pearson Education.

## KEY TERMS AND DEFINITIONS

**Agile Supply Chain:** System to facilitate in high level of flexibility in the supply chain to provide superior value to customers.

**Artificial Intelligence:** Capability of machines performing tasks, generally done by a normal human being

**Buffering:** Keeping surplus inventory to protect from supply as well as from demand uncertainties.

**Multi-Sourcing:** Arrangement or system of having more than one supplier for an item.

**Near Shoring:** Preferring the local supplier base to serve the domestic markets.

**Single Sourcing:** Procurement of raw materials or components from single supplier.

**Supply Chain Efficiency: Ability to fulfill the customer demands at low cost.:**

**Supply Chain Management:** Management of flow of goods and services from the point sourcing to the point of consumption in efficient and effective way.

**Supply Chain Resilience:** Ability to restore back to normal operations quickly across the supply chain.

**Supply Chain Responsiveness:** Ability to respond and fulfill demands of customer quickly.

**Supply Chain Risk:** Disruption in flows of goods, services, information and money across the supply chain.

**Volatility Index:** Quantifiable measure for understanding investors sentiment as well as market risk over a given period of time.

**Vulnerability:** Degree of exposure to unpredictable and serious disturbances, disorder, or hazards.

# Chapter 24
# Pricing and Hedging of Weather and Freight Derivatives:
## Analysis of the Post–Pandemic Situation

**Satya Venkata Sekhar**

https://orcid.org/0000-0001-5171-065X

*GITAM Visakhapatnam, India*

## ABSTRACT

*It is known that the entire physical activity of business faced several hurdles due to lockdown implemented phase-wise. The COVID-19 pandemic period has shown its impact on various sectors across the globe. One should keep in mind that there are no obstacles to online activity irrespective of political, legal, and environmental factors. During the last couple of months, the pandemic situation raised the need to assess 'derivative' impacts, particularly weather and freight derivatives. All the business organizations face many problems in the shipment of their products and confusion about pricing. This chapter aims to appreciate issues and challenges relating to weather and freight derivatives' functioning in the present pandemic. The objectives are 1) to understand the genesis of weather and freight derivatives and empirical research in a global context and 2) to understand the impact of the pandemic situation on weather and freight derivatives.*

## INTRODUCTION

*The Weather derivative market has not just been resilient, but, very active, with more work in the sector seen than in the previous 12 months, with a lot of new initiatives.*

*- Claude Brown, Reed Smith, www.environmental-finance.com, 2020.*

The covid-19 pandemic period has shown its impact on various sectors across the globe. It is known that the entire world faced several hurdles due to phase-wise lockdown during 2020-2021. At the same time the business organizations faced problems in the shipment of their products during this period.

DOI: 10.4018/978-1-7998-9506-0.ch024

Copyright © 2022, IGI Global. Copying or distributing in print or electronic forms without written permission of IGI Global is prohibited.

*Pricing and Hedging of Weather and Freight Derivatives*

The present fluctuations in the pricing of logistics and supply-chain have shown major impact on profitability. Hence, this situation raised the need to assess the impact of derivatives with respect to weather and freight derivatives.

## OBJECTIVES

1. To understand the empirical research on weather and freight derivatives in a global context.
2. To make aware of mathematical models and theories of derivative pricing.
3. To study impact of pandemic on logistics particularly weather and freight derivatives.

This chapter is organized into the following sections to achieve aforesaid objectives:

- Genesis of Derivatives,
- Background and Review of Literature,
- Main Focus of the Chapter,
- Mathematical models of pricing derivatives
- Solutions and Recommendations
- Future Research Direction,
- Conclusions.

## GENESIS OF DERIVATIVES

Achilleas and Antonis (2013) study states that the "weather derivatives are financial contracts whose payoff depends on the underlying weather variable(s). The underlying weather variables can be temperature, precipitation, snowfall, humidity, or wind. These instruments differ from other derivatives because the underlying asset has no value and cannot be stored. Thus, these weather variables are indexed to make them tradable like other index products such as stock indexes. For example, quantification is how much the temperature deviates from daily, monthly, or a seasonal average temperature in a particular city or region. The variations are then adjusted to indexes with a currency amount attached to each index point".

It is opined that trading has been lifestyle during of the twelfth century in England and France. The process of buying and selling rice began during the seventeenth century referred to as 'Cho-at-Mai' (rice exchange-on-book) done in Japan. In 1730, this marketplace was given a legit reputation from the Tokugawa Shogunate. In 1874, the Chicago Commodities Exchange became established, imparting butter, eggs, poultry, and different consumable agricultural products. The Chicago Commodities Exchange withdrawn the products butter and in 1898. This exchange re-established with new title 'The Chicago Mercantile Exchange (CME)" for derivatives market in 1919. This exchange furnished a futures marketplace for plenty of commodities during 1961-71 viz., red meat, stay livestock, stay hogs, and feeder cattle. Many different exchanges in this sector now doing in business of 'futures contracts'. At the American Civil War period (1860 to 1865) it has become a routine activity to trade with such agreements wherein actual transport of produce become unnecessary. The London Metal Exchange entered into Commodities trading, and today, its miles the foremost marketplace in metallic buying and selling. During 1980s, markets evolved for alternatives in options on inventory indices, and options on futures contracts.

489

McDonald (2013) states that "before the financial crisis in 2008, there were several well-known derivatives-related losses: Procter & Gamble lost $150 million in1994, Barings Bank lost $1.3 billion in 1995, Long-Term Capital Management lost $3.5billion in 1998, the hedge fund Amaranth lost $6 billion in 2006. During the crisis in 2008, the Federal Reserve loaned $85 billion to AIG in conjunction with AIG's losses on credit default swaps, in the wake of the financial crisis, as a significant part of the Dodd-Frank Wall Street Reform and Consumer Protection Act of 2010 pertained to derivatives".

## BACKGROUND AND REVIEW OF LITERATURE

### Studies on Weather Derivatives

Pricing of weather derivatives has been examined by several eminent scholars through their empirical studies. A global climatic study reveals that four-fifths of the world economy is, directly or indirectly, exposed to the weather (Auer, 2003). 'Weather derivatives' is examined as a 'weather risk management tool' and reviews and discusses the effectiveness of their application in agriculture, by Ivana et al., (2016). A valuation framework for temperature derivatives and studies the market price of weather risk therein. The framework is the generalized Lucas's Model of 1978. Tezuka, Ishii and Ishizaka (2012) derive an equilibrium price model of spot and forwards shipping freight markets. Jewson (2004) provides that both actuarial and arbitrage pricing of weather derivatives usually involve calculating an estimate of the expected payoff and derivatives of that payoff concerning various parameters.

A Partial Differential Equation(PDE) based approach can be used to price weather derivatives with the market price of risk extracted from the utility indifference valuation. Pengi Li (2020) assumes that the underlying temperature follows an Ornstein–Uhlenbeck process, the PDEs associated with the utility indifference valuation are established and then solved numerically using a one-sided finite difference scheme. The solution procedure is validated through numerical experiments for the utility indifference futures prices, and then applied to price more complicated weather derivatives such as options.

The economy's underlying variables are the aggregate dividend and the weather uncertainty, and the two are allowed to correlate with one another both contemporaneously and in a lagged fashion (Cao & Wei, 2000). Efficiency of the weather derivatives as primary insurance instruments is studied by Dmitry and Barry (2004). This is conducted at the six crop reporting districts that are among the largest producers of corn, cotton, and soybeans in the United States. The recognition and management of weather risks are spreading through the energy sector to electricity and natural gas utilities. Many of the popular stochastic models for spot dynamics and weather variables developed from empirical studies in commodity and energy markets belong to the class of polynomial jump diffusion processes. Benth (2021) derive a tailor-made framework for efficient polynomial approximation of the main derivatives encountered in commodity and energy markets.

Geman and Lenard's (2005) derived the concept of 'a burn analysis' valuing contingent claims often employed in the insurance industry. A more suitable approach than the 'insurance policies 'is to consider 'weather risk management' by presenting an innovative alternative risk management solution represented by weather derivatives studied by Hurduzeu & Constantin (2008). The major problem of weather derivatives is that they are based on a meteorological index which does not allow the use of traditional pricing methods. It is difficult to get around this obstacle by substituting the underlying for a linked exchanged security (Hélène Hamisultan, 2008).

*Pricing and Hedging of Weather and Freight Derivatives*

Today, the bulk of the demand for weather risk management products still stems from the energy sector. Even other industries, such as agriculture, insurance, tourism, and retail, are starting to take note (Sloan et al., 2002). But, 'a contractual substitution on energy for the portfolio's meteorological index by stressing the energy price's dependence on the climate' is studied by Geman (1999). The valuation of weather derivatives in an incomplete market, the hedging effectiveness of standardized weather derivatives, as well as optimal weather hedging with the consideration of basis risk and credit risk etc., is studied by Brockett et al. (2005).

Weather derivatives are a type of index contract whose payoff depends on occurrence or nonoccurrence of specific weather events is examined by Dischel (2002). The expected payoff commonly values the weather derivative contracts under the physical measure discounted at the risk-free rate through an actuarial approach (Davis, 2001). However, both actuarial and arbitrage pricing of weather derivatives usually involve calculating an estimated of the probable payoff and derivatives of that payoff concerning various factors (Jewson, 200). For weather derivative payoffs that are independent of the value of the optimal growth portfolio, it is shown that the classical actuarial pricing methodology is a particular case of the fair pricing concept. Batchelor, Alizadeh, and Visvikis (2007) determine whether freight forwards prices can be predicted by performing a horse race of alternative forecasting models. They find that all models outperform the random walk model. The effectiveness of a mathematical model is measured with regard to the structured derivatives with the correlated assets through the 'non-Gaussian distributions'. The fair value of the structured product evaluated by Zuev (2017) using the suggested model outperforms estimates obtained by means of other methods as it allows lower fair price of the derivatives.

A discrete-time model is constructed by Eckhard and West (2004) to approximate historical weather characteristics. The index of 'International Maritime Exchange (IMAREX)' freight futures market is efficient over daily and weekly horizons. The study found that IMAREX is not efficient over the shorter daily horizon. The results have implications for the economics of freight futures markets and pricing freight derivatives studied by Lambros and George (2011). Under the existence of a structured weather market, wind producers may purchase an up-and-in European wind barrier put option to hedge wind fluctuations, allowing them to recover their investments and maximise their profits. Rodríguez et al (2021) use a wind speed index as the underlying index of the barrier option, which captures risk from wind power generation and the Autoregressive Fractionally Integrated Moving Average (ARFIMA) to model the wind speed.

Weather derivatives are mostly based on the climatic conditions like which are categorized as CDD (Cooling Degree Days) and HDD (Heating Degree Days). The temperature is the measure that has been most widely used to-date – firstly in the US market and more recently on the UK's London International Financial Futures Exchange (LIFFE) (Nick Buckley et al., 2003).' It is observed that the liquidity risk premium is existing in the US traded water freight transportation companies over the period 1960-2009. A report submitted by Panayides *et al.*, (2013) in addition to the Fama-French 'Small Minus Big (SMB)' and 'High Minus Low (HML)' risk factors, the market-wide liquidity factor and the illiquidity risk premium are also significant in explaining returns on water transportation stocks.

A closed-form approximation for the pricing of CDD options based around a normal approximation that can equally be applied to HDD based contracts- this hypothesis is studied by Alaton (2002). The weather derivatives aim to flat down the sequential fluctuations in the company's revenue. The interdependency of the income on weather conditions is also examined by Pígl (2007). Weather risks and primary products in the weather derivatives market and showcased the main concepts for pricing weather contracts is examined by Bartkowiak, Marcin (2009).

A temperature model is found by Birhan TaGtan and Azize Hayfavi (2017) to estimate the temperature indices upon which temperature-based derivatives are derived. The model is planned as a mean-reverting method determined by a Levy process to represent jumps and other features of temperature. Some events are directly affecting the dry bulk and the dirty tanker segment and the study revealed challenges of pricing freight derivatives and their impact on weather due to pandemic situations (Michail and Melas, 2020). A stochastic model driven by generalized hyperbolic Levy process with seasonal mean and volatility for the daily average temperature data is used in the study made by Berhane et al (2021). This model is perfect to capture the semi-substantial tails and skewness observed in the data. The model is fitted to 11 years of daily data recorded in 16 cities of Ethiopia. They obtained the market risk factor from the historical data of temperature by calculating the CDD and HDD.

## MAIN FOCUS OF THE CHAPTER

Shipping freight rates are found to be strong indicators of the global real economic activity, and as such, exert significant impact on financial markets (Kilian and Zhou, 2018). The stochastic properties of freight rates in the shipping industry and derives the methodical equations for their moments in downside and upside markets using a two-piece extension of the 'Generalized Error Distribution (GED')'. Pricing equations developed, across shipping segments, show how conditional risk and conditional skewness are priced along with their risk spillover effects. Theodossiou et al., (2020) study results reveal the reality of a positive-skewness premium, signifying that shipping investors are keen to accept lower expected returns for the chance to earn high payoffs in the prospect. Shipping derivatives instruments such as Forward Freight Agreements (FFAs), freight futures, and freight options have been developed and evolved the agents involved in international shipping to manage risks that arise from fluctuations in freight rates (Kavussanos and Nomikos, 1999).

Lourdes Gómez-Valle et al., (2020) prove that the freight option price verifies PDEs with three independent state variables: the spot rate, its delay and the average of the spot rate in the settlement period. This result is notable because it offers a new approach to deal with the freight option valuation problem. Moreover, it opens the door to apply numerical methods for pricing freight options. Alizadeh (2013) investigates the interaction between trading volume and volatility of FFA prices. Kavussanos et al., (2014) investigate economic spillovers between the freight and commodity derivatives markets.

The hedging efficiency is greater for newer vessels than older vessels and that the static hedge ratio outperforms the dynamic hedge ratio. A fixed-maturity time-weighted Forward Freight Agreement (FFA) portfolio should be used to proxy the expected future earnings of a vessel. The corresponding hedging efficiency when using a portfolio of FFA prices to hedge ship price risk of both static hedge ratios calculated using Ordinary Least Squares estimation and the dynamic hedge ratios generated from a dynamic conditional correlation GARCH model (Roar Adland, 2020).

It was observed based on the review of literature, that there are several mathematical models derived for pricing of derivatives by researchers. The following section deals with these models.

*Pricing and Hedging of Weather and Freight Derivatives*

## PRICING OF DERIVATIVES

Pricing of derivatives can be categorized in to three models:

- **Deterministic models**: In this model, the output of the model is fully determined by the parameter values and the initial conditions.

$$T^m_{\ t} = A + Bt + C \sin(\omega t + \varphi)$$
for the mean temperature at time $t$, $T^m_{\ t}$

- **Stochastic model:** This model possesses some inherent randomness. The same set of parameter values and initial conditions will lead to an ensemble of different outputs.
- **Probabilistic model**: This model includes elements of randomness. Every time you run the model, you are likely to get different results, even with the same initial conditions.

### Derivation of CDD, HDD, CAT

To determine a 'Heating Degree Days (HDD) value, subtract a day's average temperature from 65. For example, if the average daily temperature were 40 degrees, you would subtract 40 from 65. To determine a 'Cooling Degree Days (CDD)' value, subtract 65 from a day's average daily temperature. For example, if the average daily temperature were 80, you would subtract 65 from that number. If the temperature were lower than 65, the value of the HDD would be zero.

The Cumulative Average Temperature (CAT) Index is used for the summer season contracts in Europe. The CAT Index tracks average daily temperatures over a calendar month in a given city. That average number is used to calculate a Weather contract value – there is no baseline 65-degree temperature with which HDD or CDD is established. Each particular CME European CAT Index accumulates daily average temperatures over a calendar month or season. The accumulation period of each CME European CAT Index futures contract begins with the first calendar day of the contract month and ends with the contract month's last calendar day. (see Table 1 and Table 2)

### The Gaussian Pricing Model

A straightforward formula for pricing individual options can take for the case of a Gaussian distribution of 'Cooling Degree Days (CDDs) or Heating Degree Days (HDDs). Assuming that one knows the mean (average) and standard deviation of CDDs or HDDs in a location, it is simple to approximate an option's price. CDD indexes developed to estimate the amount of energy required for residential space cooling during the summer season. Thus, a CDD-index is a measure of how hot it has been. HDDs are defined by (Element Re, 2002)

### Cost of Carrying Model

The carry pricing model stipulates that the forwards or futures price is defined as the value of one unit of the contract's underlying asset. It is equal to the sum of the spot price and the carrying cost incurred.

493

*Table 1. Weather futures and options codes*

| Heating (HDD) Futures and Options | | | | | | | | |
|---|---|---|---|---|---|---|---|---|
| | CITY CODE | OCT | NOV | DEC | JAN | FEB | MAR | APR |
| **U.S.** | | | | | | | | |
| Atlanta | H1 | H1V | H1X | H1Z | H1F | H1G | H1H | H1J |
| Chicago | H2 | H2V | H2X | H2Z | H2F | H2G | H2H | H2J |
| Cincinnati | H3 | H3V | H3X | H3Z | H3F | H3G | H3H | H3J |
| New York | H4 | H4V | H4X | H4Z | H4F | H4G | H4H | H4J |
| Dallas | H5 | H5V | H5X | H5Z | H5F | H5G | H5H | H5J |
| Las Vegas | H0 | H0V | H0X | H0Z | H0F | H0G | H0H | H0J |
| Minneapolis | HQ | HQV | HQX | HQZ | HQF | HQG | HQH | HQJ |
| Sacramento | HS | HSV | HSX | HSZ | HSF | HSG | HSH | HSJ |
| **EUROPE** | | | | | | | | |
| London | D0 | D0V | D0X | D0Z | D0F | D0G | D0H | D0J |
| Amsterdam | D2 | D2V | D2X | D2Z | D2F | D2G | D2H | D2J |

Because the buying and holding cost to the deliverable support, less the carry return refers to the income, such as dividends on shares, which may accrue to the investor.

- Carrying costs of stock index futures
- Carrying Cost =

Index Value $\times$ (financing costs – dividend yield) $\times t$

In case of uncertain cash flow to be given in terms of the mean and the standard deviation ignoring discounting, the following formula can be applied:

Value = mean lambda * standard deviation.

$T$ is the time from the share settlement date to the futures contract's maturity date.

*Pricing and Hedging of Weather and Freight Derivatives*

*Table 2. Cooling (CDD) futures and options*

|  | CITY CODE | APR | MAY | JUN | JUL | AUG | SEP | OCT |
|---|---|---|---|---|---|---|---|---|
| **U.S.** | | | | | | | | |
| Atlanta | K1 | K1J | K1K | K1M | K1N | K1Q | K1U | K1V |
| Chicago | K2 | K2J | K2K | K2M | K2N | K2Q | K2U | K2V |
| Cincinnati | K3 | K3J | K3K | K3M | K3N | K3Q | K3U | K3V |
| New York | K4 | K4J | K4K | K4M | K4N | K4Q | K4U | K4V |
| Dallas | K5 | K5J | K5K | K5M | K5N | K5Q | K5U | K5V |
| Las Vegas | K0 | K0J | K0K | K0M | K0N | K0Q | K0U | K0V |
| Minneapolis | KQ | KQJ | KQK | KQM | KQN | KQQ | KQU | KQV |
| Sacramento | KS | KSJ | KSK | KSM | KSN | KSQ | KSU | KSV |
| **EUROPE** | | | | | | | | |
| London | G0 | G0J | G0K | G0M | G0N | G0Q | G0U | G0V |
| Amsterdam | G2 | G2J | G2K | G2M | G2N | G2Q | G2U | G2V |

The lambda value is subjective: a small value of lambda (perhaps 0.01) indicates a low level of aversion to risk, while a large value (maybe 0.5) indicates a high level of risk aversion.

The valuation of futures is done using the Cost of carry model. The assumptions presumed for pricing futures contracts are as follows:

1. the markets are perfect
2. there are no transaction costs,
3. all the assets are infinitely divisible,
4. bid-ask spreads do not exist so that it is assumed that only one price prevails,
5. there are no restrictions on short selling. Also, short-sellers get to use the full proceeds of the sales.

## MATHEMATICAL FORMULAE TO PRICING OF DERIVATIVES

The following equations and mathematical formulae give an understanding of pricing of derivatives. The studies shows the researchers' view point on variables considered in this regard.

1.  Dynamic Stochastic Model, Girsanov's Theorem, 1960:
    - P{Xk+1-j|X0=i0,X1-i1,...,Xk-ik}-P{Xk+1-j|Xk-ik}
    - A stochastic process is a collection of random variables defined on the same probability space $(\Omega, F, P)$, where $\Omega$ is a sample space,
2.  Expectation approach, J.M. Keynes, J.R. Hicks and N. Kalidor, 1964
    - F0,t= E0(St)
    - Expected futures profit = Expected futures price–Initial futures price
    - Where F0, Futures price at time t = 0 and E0(St) is the expectation at = 0 of the spot price to prevail at time t.
3.  Black-Scholes, Fischer Black, Myron Scholes, 1970

$$c = se^{-qt}\Phi(d_1) - xe^{-rt}\Phi(d_2)$$
$$p = xe^{-rt}\Phi(-d_2) - se^{-qt}\Phi(-d_1)$$

This formula is used for pricing of European options on stocks paying a known dividend yield (annually compounded rate $q$). call price $= c$, or, put price $= p$

4.  Differential Equation Or B-S-M- formula, Black, Scholes and Merton, 1976
    - $C(S_0,t)=S_0 N(d_1)-K_e-r(T-t)N(d_2)$,
    - $S_0$ is the stock price;
    - $C(S_0,t)$ is the price of the call option as a formulation of the stock price and time;
    - K is the exercise price;
    - (T−t) is the time to maturity, i.e. the exercise date T, less the amount of time between now t and then. Generally, this is represented in years with one month
5.  Financial Pricing model-CAPM, Capital Asset Pricing Model, William Sharpe, 1970
    - $Re = Rf + \beta(Rm - Rf)$
    - Total Risk = Systematic risk + Unsystematic risk
    - Where;
      Re = Expected rate of return or Cost of Equity
      Rf = Risk free rate
      $\beta$ = Beta
      (Rm − Rf) = Market risk premium
      Rm = Expected return of the market
6.  Arbitrage Pricing Model, Stephen Ross, 1976
    Arbitrage pricing theory (APT) is a multi-factor asset pricing model based on the idea that an asset's returns can be predicted using the linear relationship between the asset's expected return and a number of macroeconomic variables that capture systematic risk
    - The APT formula is:
    - $E(r_j) = r_f + b_{j1}RP_1 + b_{j2}RP_2 + b_{j3}RP_3 + b_{j4}RP_4 + ... + b_{jn}RP_n$

*Pricing and Hedging of Weather and Freight Derivatives*

- where:

  $E(r_j)$ = the asset's expected rate of return

  $r_f$ = the risk-free rate

  $b_j$ = the sensitivity of the asset's return to the particular factor

  RP = the risk premium associated with the particular factor

7. Arbitrage Free Pricing, Stephen Ross, 1976
   - $F = s.e^{rt}$
   - Forward Price = $F - S_0.e^r$
   - where $e = 2.71828$, $r$ = cost of financing
   - Futures when expected dividend yield is given:
   - $f = s(1 + r - q)^T$
   - where
   - $q$ = expected dividend yield,
   - $T$ = holding period
8. Equilibrium Frame work, Cao & Wei, 2000
   - $HDDi = \max \{ 18 - T_i, 0 \}$;
   - $CDDi = \max \{ T_i - 18, 0 \}$;
   - $T_i = [ T_i^{max} - T_i^{min} ] / 2$
   - For cities outside the United States, the process is the same, except the calculation is done using 18 degrees on the Celsius scale instead of 65 degrees on the Fahrenheit scale. If the temperature exceeded 65, the value of the HDD would be zero.
9. Historical Burn Analysis, Stephen Jewson and Anders Brix, 2005
   - $Xj-a0+a1j+ \varepsilon$,
   - $j = 1,2,\cdots,k$
   - and $\varepsilon \sim N(0, \sigma 2)$,
   - The method is based on the idea that how the contract would have performed in the previous years, and the future expected payoff is obtained from the average payoff of the same derivative contract for the past years.
10. Regime Switching Model, Emanuel Evarest, Fredrik Berntsson, Martin Singull and Wilson M. Charle, 2017
    - $P_N^h = \sum_{t=i}^{n} HDDi$
    - $P_N^c = \sum_{t=i}^{n} CDDi$
    - This model introduces heteroskedasticity in the mean-reverting process in the base regime. We show that our new model is relatively better in capturing the temperature dynamics by comparing the corresponding heating degree days (HDDs), cooling degree days(CDDs) and cumulative average temperature (CAT) of the two models with the HDDs,CDDs and CAT from the real data.
11. Visvikis et al, (2015) have considered panel data estimation techniques to estimate the unobserved heterogeneity, which refers to the possibility that any omitted explanatory variables may be relevant in explaining the observed variation in FFA prices:

$$r_{i,t} - r_{f,t} = a_i + a_t + \beta_1 LIQ_{i,t-1} + \beta_2 BAS_{i,t-1} + \beta_3 rBDI_{,t-1} + \beta_4 HVB_{t-1} + \beta_5 rGSCI_{,t-1} + u_{i,t} + v_{i,t} ;$$

$$u_{i,t}, v_{i,t} \sim iid(0, \Sigma)$$

where,

- $i$ identifies the type of vessel (Capesize, Panamax or Supramax);
- t denotes the time period;
- $r_{i,t} - r_{f,t}$ is the excess return on FFA contract over the three-months US Treasury Bill for vessel i in week t;
- $LIQ_{i,t-1}$ and $BAS_{i,t-1}$ are the lagged Amihud and bid-ask spread liquidity measures, respectively; while,
- $rBDI_{,t-1}$, $HVB_{t-1}$ and $rGSCI_{,t-1}$ are the industry and macroeconomic specific variables as explained earlier;
- $a_i$ is a vessel specific constant term to capture any unobserved heterogeneity among the different vessels;
- $a_t$ is a time specific constant term to capture any unobserved heterogeneity over time; and
- $u_{i,t}$ and $v_{i,t}$ are vectors of white-noise error-terms, following a multivariate distribution with mean zero and variance-covariance matrix $\Sigma$.
- The explanatory variables introduced into this model are both time-varying vessel specific variables ($LIQ_{i,t-1}$ and $BAS_{i,t-1}$) and time-varying common variables ($rB_{DI,t-}1$, $HVB_{t-1}$ and $rGSCI_{,t-1}$).

The above equations are taken from various studies conducted during 1950-2020 to estimate weather risk and to determine price of weather derivative contracts. However, certain unforeseen conditions like pandemic bring a lot of changes which are unpredictable and cannot be measured using the aforesaid formulae. The following paragraphs illustrate recent situation in logistic and supply chain management.

## PRICING OF WEATHER DERIVATIVES

Weather derivatives are extensively used to hedge against adverse or unexpected weather behavior by energy companies and even those dealing with agricultural products. UK's London International Financial Futures Exchange (LIFFE) launched six exchange-traded contracts based on indices of daily average temperatures in London, Paris, and Berlin. The indices are based on the mean of daily average temperatures (Mean DATs) and are available monthly and for the winter season. The indices are calculated as:

- Monthly Index = 100 + (Mean DAT) summed over each day in the calendar month
- Winter Index = 100 + (Mean DAT) summed over each day of the winter season

LIFFE has started trading with cash-settled futures contracts referenced against the indices. Each contract is worth £3,000 for every degree Celsius of temperature change. LIFFE has chosen to focus on average temperature rather than Heating or Cooling Degree Days (as used in the US) because there is no corresponding demand for cooling in the summer.

It has become industry standard in the US to set this reference level at 65o Fahrenheit (18o C). The names heating and cooling degree days originate from the US energy sector. The reason is that if the tem-

*Pricing and Hedging of Weather and Freight Derivatives*

perature is below 18o C, people tend to use more energy t° heat their homes, whereas if the temperature is above 18o C, people start turning their air c°nditioners on for cooling.

## SOLUTIONS AND RECOMMENDATIONS

The Baltic Dry Index (BDI) is a composite of the Capesize, Panamax and Supramax Time charter Averages. It is reported around the world as a proxy for dry bulk shipping stocks as well as a general shipping market bellwether. The Baltic Indices are being used by delivery and financial analysts as a marketplace barometer and primary indicator. The benchmark fees are used to set up the price of contracts, and index additives are used as a comparative tool. The Baltic Exchange calculates the index by assessing more than one delivery fee throughout more than 20 routes for every BDI aspect vessel. Analyzing more than one geographic delivery path for every index offers intensity to the index's composite measurement.

The Baltic Exchange announces the BDI each day. The BDI measures shipments on numerous sizes of shipment ships. Capesize boats are the essential ships within side the BDI with a hundred,000 deadweight tonnage (DWT) or greater. The standard length of a Capesize delivery is 156,000 DWT. This class also can encompass a few big vessels with capacities of 400,000 DWT. Capesize ships mainly shipping coal and iron ore on long-haul routes and are from time to time used to move grains. They're too massive to pass over the Panama Canal. The delivery of shipment ships is usually inelastic—it takes years to construct a brand, and the price of laying up delivery is too excessive to take out of alternate for brief intervals. So, marginal will increase in the call for can push the index better quickly, and marginal call for decreases can motive the index to fall rapidly. For example, if you've got a hundred ships competing for ninety-nine cargoes, fees cross down, while when you have ninety-nine ships competing for a hundred shipments, expenses cross up. In different words, minor fleet modifications and logistical subjects can crash fees.

Melas and Michail (2020)) states that pandemic events are directly affecting the dry bulk and the dirty tanker segments. Besides, the results also indicate that second-round effects, mostly via the decline in oil prices and, in some cases, third-round products via the impact from the stock market, also exist. Finally, employing daily port calls as a proxy variable for transportation services demand shows that both the dry bulk and clean tankers are positively affected by the economy's demand side. At the same time, vessels that transport crude oil do not register such a relationship.

The International Finance Corporation published a paper on "Impact of Covid-19 on Logistics', it reveals that the pandemic has exposed the vulnerability of extended and complex value chains to production disruptions, particularly in the East Asia Pacific region. As a reaction, many of these supply chains may shorten or diversify through reliance on alternative partners (for example, near shoring) or intensified efforts to bring home (such as reshoring) strategic value chains.

Torvald Klaveness (2021) states that "the Brumadinho dam disaster was a negative shock for the dry bulk market as the long-distance iron ore export out of Brazil contracted about 13% 'year on year' in 2019". The Brazilian iron ore export has been trending higher in recent months and is expected to climb further in 2021 and 2022. Total seaborne iron ore export volume is up 4.3% 'year to date' due to strong export growth in Australia and in other minor export countries. The black swan event of the COVID-19 pandemic has greatly reduced global industrial production for most of 2020 and has had a negative impact on the demand for coal and minor bulks.

The Baltic Dry Index is above 1600 during September 2020; the most influential on account that on 20th July 2020 and bouncy lower ᵇᵃck from a one-month low of 1,267 reached on 11th September, 2020 help throughʰ charging of Capesize fees, as the call has better for each Atlantic and Pacific routes. Still, the index stays adequately below the multi-month top of 1,956 touched on July 6th 2020. As of July 30,

499

*Figure 1. Global dry bulk import weighted PMI versus BDI*

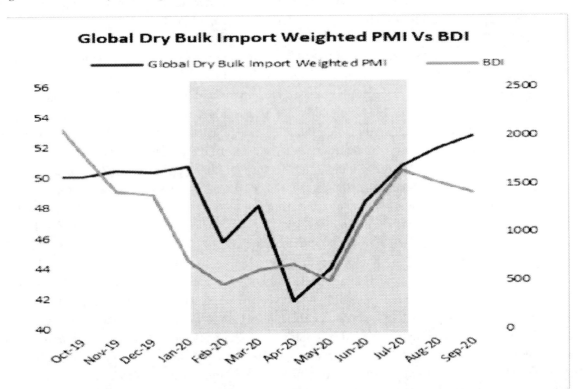

2021, the Baltic Dry Index amounted to 3,292 points. This is about six times the value of 504 recorded at the end of May 2020 due to the coronavirus (COVID-19) pandemic. The tanker delivery enterprise has been below strain because of decreased oil manufacturing and calls for reduced shipments of business commodities to Asia.

The figure below shows our metric on Global Dry Bulk Import weighted Purchase Manufacturing Indices (PMI) vs the Baltic Dry Index (BDI).

## FUTURE RESEARCH DIRECTION

This paper identified various mathematical models for pricing of derivatives in general and weather derivatives in particular. This shows that the corporate entity should ready to face risk associated with climatic conditions and any other unforeseen pandemic situations. Researchers should try to find new models to hedge the risk associated for unforeseen situations for weather derivatives.

## CONCLUSIONS

This chapter focuses on mathematical models of pricing of weather and freight derivatives. The categorization of pricing models according to deterministic, probabilistic and scholastic models is given to

*Pricing and Hedging of Weather and Freight Derivatives*

understand for further research in this area. Pricing of weather derivatives relating to energy sector and insurance sector is also analyzed. The mathematical equations are taken from various studies conducted during 1950-2020 to estimate weather risk and to determine price of weather derivative contracts.

The importance of temperature in pricing weather derivative and Baltic indices in derivatives is discussed. Besides this, renewable energy companies gained much importance and expanded their business during the pandemic period.

The Baltic Dry Index is always fluctuating according to business environment. The tanker delivery enterprise has been below strain because of decreased oil manufacturing and calls for reduced shipments of business commodities to Asia during the pandemic period. The impact of pricing on logistics and supply chain management because of pandemic situation and fluctuations in Baltic Index is also presented. However, certain unforeseen conditions like pandemic bring a lot of changes which are unpredictable and cannot be measured using the aforesaid formulae.

There is a need to have an in-depth study of hedging models for Weather and Freight derivatives because cargo derivatives are based on shipment of the products, subject to climatic conditions.

# REFERENCES

Adland, R., Ameln, H., & Børnes, E.A., (2020). Hedging ship price risk using freight derivatives in the drybulk market. Journal of Shipping and Trade, 5(1). doi:10.1186/s41072-019-0056-3

Alaton, P., Djehiche, B., & Stillberger, D. (2002). On Modelling and Pricing Weather Derivatives. Applied Mathematical Finance, 9(1), 1–20. doi:10.1080/13504860210132897

Auer, J. (2003). Weather Derivatives Heading for Sunny Times. Available at http://www.dbresearch.com/PROD/999/PROD0000000000052399.pdf

Alizadeh, A.H. (2013). Trading Volume and Volatility in the Shipping Forward Freight Market. Academic Press.

Bartkowiak, M. (2009). Weather derivatives. Zeszyty Naukowe/Poznań University of Economics, 112, 5–16.

Berhane, T., Shibabaw, A., Awgichew, G., & Walelgn, A. (2021). Pricing of Weather Derivatives Based on Temperature by Obtaining Market Risk Factor From Historical Data Model. Earth System. Environment, 7(2), 871–884. doi:10.100740808-020-00925-4

Benth, F. E. (2021). Pricing of Commodity and Energy Derivatives for Polynomial Processes. Mathematics, 9(2), 124. doi:10.3390/math9020124

Brockett, P. L., Mulong, W., & Chuanhou, Y. (2005). Weather Derivates and Weather Risk Management. Risk Management & Insurance Review, 8(1), 127–140. doi:10.1111/j.1540-6296.2005.00052.x

Buckley, N. (2003). European Weather Derivatives. Working paper. https://www.actuaries.org.uk/system/files/documents/pdf/european-weather-derivatives.pdf

Cao, M., & Wei, J. (2000). Pricing the Weather. Risk (Concord, NH), 13(5), 14–22.

Davis, M. (2001). Pricing Weather Derivatives by Marginal Value. *Quantitative Finance*, *1*(3), 1–4. doi:10.1080/713665730

Dischel, R. S. (Ed.). (2002). Climate Risk and the Weather Market. London: Risk Water Group.

Re, E. (2002). *Weather Risk Management*. Palgrave.

Geman, H. (1999). The Bermudan Triangle: Weather, Electricity and Insurance Derivatives. In Insurance and weather derivatives: from exotic options to exotic underlyings. Geman.

Giddy, I. (n.d.). *Accounting for Derivatives FAS 133* (Financial Accounting Standards Board Statement No. 133, Accounting for Derivative Instruments and Hedging Activities). http://people.stern.nyu.edu/igiddy/fas133.htm

Gómez-Valle, L., López-Marcos, M. A., & Martínez-Rodríguez, J. (2020). Two New Strategies for Pricing Freight Options by Means of a Valuation PDE and by Functional Bounds. *Mathematics*, *8*(4), 620. doi:10.3390/math8040620

GoulasL.SkiadopoulosG. (2011). Are Freight futures markets efficient? Evidence from IMAREX. *International Journal of Forecasting*. http://ssrn.com/abstract=1582356

Hamisultane, H. (2008). *Which Method for Pricing Weather Derivatives?* Academic Press.

Hurduzeu, G., & Constantin, L. (2008). Several aspects regarding weather and weather derivatives. *The Romanian Economic Journal*, *11*(27), 187–202.

Jewson, S. (2004). Introduction to weather derivative pricing. SSRN *Electronic Journal*. doi:10.2139/ssrn.557831

Kilian, L., & Zhou, X. (2018). Modeling Fluctuations in the Global Demand for Commodities. *Journal of International Money and Finance*, *88*, 54–78. doi:10.1016/j.jimonfin.2018.07.001

Li, P., Lu, X., & Zhu, S. (2020). Pricing weather derivatives with the Market Price of Risk Extracted from the Utility Indifference Valuation. *Computers & Mathematics with Applications (Oxford, England)*, *79*(12), 3394–3409. doi:10.1016/j.camwa.2020.02.007

McDonald, R. L. (2013). *Derivative Markets* (3rd ed.). Pearson Education.

Melas, K. D., & Michail, N. (2020). The Relationship Between Commodity Prices and Freight Rates in the Dry Bulk Shipping Segment: A Threshold Regression Approach. SSRN *Electronic Journal*. doi:10.2139/ssrn.3581592

Panayides, P., Lambertides, N., & Cullinane, K. (2013). Liquidity risk premium and Asset Pricing in US Water Transportation. *Transportation Research E. Logistics and Transportation Review*, *52*, 3–15. doi:10.1016/j.tre.2012.11.007

Pirrong, C., & Jermakyan, M. (2001). *The Price of Power: The Valuation of Power and Weather Derivatives*. Working Paper. Oklahoma State University.

Platen, E., & West, J. (2004). A Fair Pricing Approach to Weather Derivatives, Asia-Pacific Financial Markets. *Japanese Association of Financial Economics and Engineering*, *11*(1), 23–53.

Rodríguez, Y.E., Pérez-Uribe, M.A., & Contreras, J. (2021). Wind Put Barrier Options Pricing Based on the Nordix Index. *Energies, 14*, 1177. . doi:10.3390/en14041177

Sloan, D., Palmer, L., & Burrow, H. (2002). A Broker's View. *Global Reinsurance*, (February), 22–25.

Stulec, I., Petljak, K., & Bakovic, T. (2016). Effectiveness of weather derivatives as a hedge against the weather risk in agriculture. *Agric. Econ. – Czech, 62*(8), 356–362. doi:10.17221/188/2015-AGRICECON

Taştan, B., & Hayfavi, A. (2017). *Modeling Temperature and Pricing Weather Derivatives Based on Temperature*. Hindawi-Advances in Meteorology. doi:10.1155/2017/3913817

Tezuka, K., Ishii, M., & Ishizaka, M. (2012). An equilibrium price model of spot and forward shipping freight markets. *Transportation Research Part E, Logistics and Transportation Review*, *48*(4), 730–742. doi:10.1016/j.tre.2011.12.007

Theodossiou, P., Tsouknidis, D., & Savva, C. (2020). Freight rates in Downside and Upside Markets: Pricing of Own and Spillover Risks from Other Shipping Segments. *Journal of the Royal Statistical Society. Series A, (Statistics in Society), 183*(3), 1097–1119. Advance online publication. doi:10.1111/rssa.12553

Vedenov, D. V., & Barnettn, B. J. (2004). Efficiency of Weather Derivatives as Primary Crop Insurance Instruments. *Journal of Agricultural and Resource Economics, 29*(3), 387.

Zapranis, A., & Alexandridis, A. (2013). *Weather derivatives Modeling and Pricing Weather-related Risk*. Springer.

Zuev, D. V. (2017). A Non-Gaussian Pricing Model for Structured Products. *Journal of Corporate Finance Research, 13*(3), 45–58. doi:10.17323/j.jcfr.2073-0438.11.3.2017.45-58

*Pricing and Hedging of Weather and Freight Derivatives*

# Chapter 25
# Supply Chain Risks in Transportation and Distribution

**El Mehdi El Bhilat**
*Mohammed V University, Rabat, Morocco*

**Lalla Saadia Hamidi**
*Mohammed V University, Rabat, Morocco*

## ABSTRACT

*The coronavirus pandemic has massively disrupted supply chain performance at the global and local stage, and the concept of supply chain risk management and resilience has been pushed to the forefront. In order to overcome all these challenges and changes, it's time for businesses and supply chains to learn from the past and to develop new strategical and organizational dimensions and to be ready with alternative strategy which has not been widely discussed, 'risks mitigation in distribution', to ensure the delivery of final products to the end consumers. This chapter presents a review of literature that addresses supply chains risks, which are generated in transportation and distribution. In this regard, it's crucial to bring to light as well some measures and strategies that companies can implement to cope with the risks caused by some disruptions. These include the rising importance of safety, digitalization, and the need to revisit the meaning of efficiency in transportation and distribution management.*

## INTRODUCTION

In a context characterized by exchange globalization, turbulence and uncertainty, demand in almost every industrial sector seems to be more volatile than was the case in the past and at the same time the vulnerability of supply chains to disturbance or disruption has increased (Amulya Gurtu, 2021). On the other hand, the supply chain is becoming more and more extensive, so much so that it has become more and more complex and difficult to manage and to perform. At the same time, it is often difficult to know where the consumption of a product ends, as a unit or an installation can be part of several supply chains which can generates what's called "crossed" chains and a multiplication of the relations between the actors of the chain exposing the set of partners within the supply chain to risk (Kirilmaz, 2017).

DOI: 10.4018/978-1-7998-9506-0.ch025

Copyright © 2022, IGI Global. Copying or distributing in print or electronic forms without written permission of IGI Global is prohibited.

Besides, the (Covid-19) crisis has deeply affected the business model of companies and promoted the function of delivering the products at competitive cost with highly reliable delivery times (Reina Angkiriwang, 2014). Moreover, with the increase and predominance of outsourcing of certain logistics functions and the high probability that customers will suddenly increase, reduce, cancel, or move forward or backward their orders, firms are often exposed to uncertainties stemming from loss of control and relationship issues supply chain (Zsidisin, 2000).

As such, players need to be more flexible and deploy new strategies especially in warehousing, transportation and distribution in order to achieving high quality levels, timeliness of deliveries, and resilient processes along the supply chain. Researchers have considered that flexibility, along with quality, cost, and speed of delivery, is critical for competitiveness (Gong, 2008), (Avittathur, 2007).

This chapter researches and discusses the set of challenges and constraints confronted by the majority of companies' transportation and distribution systems during the pandemic era. In the first section, it is essential to give a literature review on distribution logistics as well as all its conceptual sides to pave the way afterwards to get into the main subject and discuss the vulnerability and risks which the distribution chain has faced in this last critical period. Thereafter, the second section of this chapter seeks to identify an in-depth analysis of the dynamics of supply chain risks and the impact and the disruption generated by the propagation of the health crisis on firms' distribution systems performance and subsequently on their profitability. In a third section, supply chain risk management process is investigated as well as the mitigation procedure is proposed which can enables proactive planning and visibility and consequently reduce the supply side risks.

## BACKGROUND

### Distribution Logistics: An Overview

The distribution logistics system has for so long been considered as a strategic function for the proper functioning of the companies, and that because the significant role which plays in the reduction of costs of supplying finished products to customers, maintaining or improving the level of service provided, being as a key factor of success for the business. Before getting into the main item, it seems critical in the first place to point out to the main concepts composing the term 'distribution logistics' in order to come up with the appropriate definition thereof.

### Distribution in Logistics: Conceptualization

Logistics and distribution are considered as critical components and essential activities for the daily operations of delivering and overseeing the movement of goods from supplier to manufacturer to wholesaler or retailer and finally to the end consumer. Besides, these two vital functions involve numerous activities and processes usually related to good flow monitoring, packaging, warehousing, inventory, supply chain, logistics. Nevertheless, these two are in fact two different things but work hand-in-hand and the difference between the two concepts is the key to ensuring that your supply chain continues to run like a well-oiled machine.

## Distribution

In the industrial world, and as the previous section revealed, the emphasis placed on logistics is the distribution function (outbound logistics). (Chatur, 2005) has pointed out that: *"Managing outbound logistics has always been the strength of the Supply Chain organization (at manufacturers and retailers)...*The latter takes part of the downstream logistics which globally defines all the logistics activities whose objective is to make finished products available to customers or final consumers (Toomey, 2000). It is the logistics part that consists in routing the products resulting from a production process to the customer (directly to his home in case of delivery to the consumer, or to the place where the customer can buy the product). This process includes storage, order fulfilment and packaging of goods, and sometimes the handling of returned goods or what's called the reverse logistics. CSCMP defines Distribution as "The activities associated with moving materials from source to destination. Can be associated with movement from a manufacturer or distributor to customers, retailers or other secondary warehousing / distribution points."

That is to say, distribution management consists in retrieving goods from a storage location and preparing for transportation with sufficient packaging and correct documentation, which is a critical step in supply chain management. It relates to overseeing the movement of goods from a manufacturer or supplier to the point of sale, by moving the goods from its source to the destination. It can be referred to this term as transport logistics or sales logistics, of the fact that the process involve massively transportation of products (Fady A., 2003) (Segetlija Z, 2011).

*Figure 1. The key components of distribution and logistics systems*
**Source:** *Alan Rushton, Phil Croucher, Peter Baker (2014) in "The handbook of logistics and distribution management"*

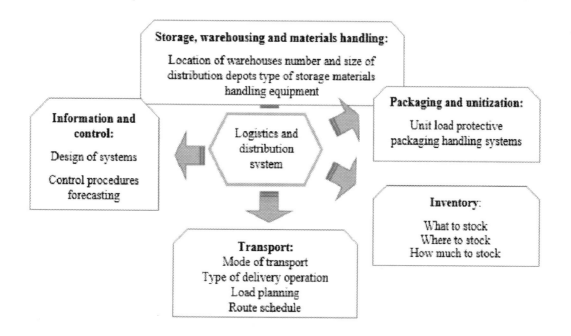

It can be concluded from above how the customer orientation plays a crucial role in distribution logistics because the close link and the impact which it has on the distribution strategies. The following section addresses the importance of customer service in the competitiveness and the effectiveness of the distribution operations.

Therefore, the service items (the elements which surround the product) are very important in determining the final demand for a product with the recognition of significantly marketing departments in many organizations (J.R.G. Whiteford, 2009).

In order to achieve a high quality logistics services, it seems from above that the firms must be based on a solid distribution network and system. The following section will address specifically the central elements on which established a good distribution process (transportation modes, warehouse and inventory management, distribution channels, etc.)

## Structure of a Distribution Network

As the supply chain management focuses increasingly on customer's needs satisfaction, much more concentration has been paid to distribution logistics. Accordingly, a great deal of measures and works have been conducted to integrate the whole supply chain and to redesign the distribution network under the control of the marketing and sales department.

## Channels of Distribution

As the sections has exhibited earlier, the system of logistics is concentrated in overcoming the barriers in space and time, from transportation and storage, the delivery of the cargo and the movement of materials and sometime the return of goods or what it can be called the "revers logistics".

For that reason, physical distribution is now recognized as a strategic function which, if managed efficiently, is a source of both productivity - cost control - and differentiation - quality and speed of response to user demand.

Distribution channels can be described as interorganisational networks. Simply put, they are the actors, methods, means and pathways by which a product or a group of products are physically transferred, or distributed, from their point of production to the point at which they are made available to the final customer. In fact, products are physically transferred through these channels, reaching their desired destination, which could be a factory outlet, a retail store, or even a customer's house.

Given the above, one of the most critical issues of distribution planning is regarding the choice and selection whether transferring and selling the products directly to end users or should the firms outsource logistics distribution activities to intermediaries and logistics service providers that could participate in the product distribution.

*Supply Chain Risks in Transportation and Distribution*

## Logistics Service Providers

*Figure 2. Summary of the typology of LSP*

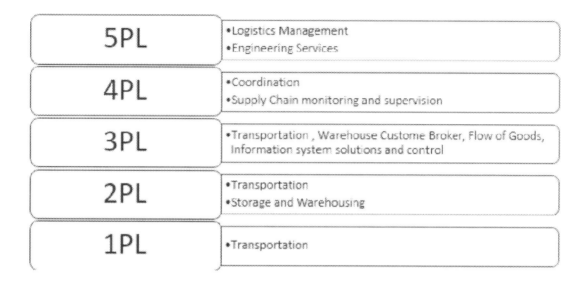

Logistics service providers (LSPs) are companies, often acting as intermediaries that undertake the execution of logistics related activities that have been traditionally kept in-house (Lieb, 1993; Coyle, 1996). Similarly, LSPs are defined according to (Sink HL, 1997) as a service provider capable of assuming some or all of a firm's logistics activities. Simply put, they refer to companies that possess the means to accomplish goods transportations, and can be specialized in ocean carriage, air-/rail-shipments and inland haulage. The services that they normally provide include inbound and outbound transportations, door-to-door transportation, contract delivery, transport administration, documentation processes, shipment scheduling, tracking and tracing (Stefansson, 2006).

*Figure 3. Distribution systems with and without LSPs*

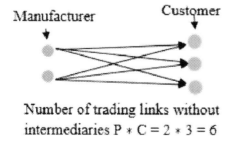
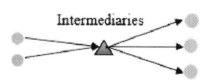

The figure illustrates how the presence of intermediaries can eliminate the duplicate efforts of both producers and customers and increase the efficiency of distribution systems (M. Christiansen, 2007). Yet, this model or structure of the distribution channel represents one of many alternatives types established in the distribution chain management.

## Manufacturer to Final Customer Directly

It's a direct selling marketing strategy which consist in distributing the product directly to the final user without any intermediary intervention. The new type of costumers who are oriented to e-shopping who order and receive the product desired directly from the producers is an example of goods commonly distributed through this channel.

## Manufacturer to Distribution Center to Retailer to Customer

This kind of channel represents the first level of an indirect-marketing channels. With this one, the manufacturers can either deliver the product to the costumer through appealing to a retailer who takes charge of providing the client with the goods. In the other hand, producers can also deliver their own goods in large scale to what are called Distribution centers. From this point, the products are distributed in smaller shipments to the retailers and from there to the final customer.

## Manufacturer to Retailer to Customer Using 3PL

As outlined previously, with the rely on 3PL services, the producers accord some activities and functions such as transportation and warehousing to an independent third party in order to concentrate not only on their core business, but with the expertise of the intermediary the distribution management could be reached with lower cost and more efficiency.

The unifying factor of all these several channels is the existence of a strong transportation system that is crucial to the success of any distribution network because as it can be deduced that not much would happens without transportation and without it the system would collapse.

## Transportation System in Distribution Logistics

Transportation is one of the most critical components for the economic and social development. From the corner grocery stores to the large factories, efficient and effective transportation is the life blood of their ability to function and face the competition. That is to say, transportation is the "glue" that links and holds not only the distribution network but the whole supply chain as well. Given that transportation represents the last phase in the value chain to touch the customer and may have a significant impact on the success of the transaction, it constitutes the key enabler for a customer oriented strategy such as overnight and same-day delivery (Coyle, Novack, & Gibson, 2016).

## Freight Transport and Transportation Modes

The globalization has made the inclusion of an effective transportation system even more important in every supply chain management strategy especially with the increase in distances and the significance

*Supply Chain Risks in Transportation and Distribution*

of reliability for the 21th century organizations. Furthermore, the global flow between countries of import and export has clearly expanded, with the emergence of new economies into the global economic landscape (China, India, Brazil, Indonesia, Vietnam, Russia, etc.). In this regards, firms relies on various methods and options for making goods and products movable from the very first supplier to the end consumer in order to achieve flexibility throughout the whole supply chain.

## Road Transportation

Road transport, also called as motor carriage - road freight refers generally to the physical process of delivering cargo by road using motor vehicles. In usual, road fright is used by the loaders on short distances. It's qualified as "door to door". In other terms, it defers from other modes by its characteristics of high accessibility and mobility by reaching any area especially rural ones where other means is not available. Road freight can extend other mode of combined transport and it's basically used pre-routing and post-routing in complementarity with the main transportation. In regard to economic aspects, road transport has relatively small fixed cost, because it operates on publicly maintained networks of high-speed and often toll free roads. However, the variable cost per kilometer is high because of fuel, tires, maintenance, and, especially, labor costs (a separate driver and cleaner are required for each vehicle) which makes the road freight not appropriate for long journeys (S.C. Ailawadi, 2005).

## Maritime Transportation

Maritime transport plays nowadays and for a very long time a vital role in international trade as 90% of world trade carried out by the shipping industry. The importance of the water transport lies in its capability to address both commodities that other means can't handle for long journeys: Bulk cargo (freight that has not been packaged, such as minerals (oil, coal, iron ore, bauxite) and grains) and Break-bulk cargo (cargo that has been packaged in bags, boxes, drums, and particularly containers).

On one hand, maritime industry offers a more affordable services when comparing to other modes because the lowest expenses of maintenance and since its fixed costs are mainly to be found in ports and terminals facilities, water-transport expenses are therefore moderated. Because the low line-haul costs of water transport, its costs per ton-mile decrease significantly as the distance and shipment size increase. Consequently, international firms and exporting companies use this type of transportation as the principal freight because its capability of delivering huge amount of goods for long distances (Ballou, 2004). Maritime transport is characterized as well by its development with regards to safety, security and its low damage and loss costs are lower due to the emergence of containerization which permit reducing handling time that is main cause of damage and shortening total transit time.

## Rail Transportation

Although rail service is available in almost every major city around the world, the railroad network is not as extensive as the road networks in most countries. In some countries such as the People's Republic of China rail remains the dominant transportation mode (D.M. Lambert, 2003), as China's railway carried 4.389 billion tons of freight, generating 3,018 billion cargo tonne-kilometres knowing a significant increase more than fivefold over the period 1980-2013 (Ministry of Transport Scientific Research Institute, 2019). Its importance derives from its higher carrying capacity of bulkily and heavy goods for long distances traffics inland with low variable cost and energy consumption which road trucks and air fright can't provide.

## Air Transportation

Air freight logistics constitute at the moment over 52 million metric tons of goods a year, representing more than 35% of global trade by value but less than 1% of world trade by volume. That is equivalent to $6.8 trillion worth of goods annually, or $18.6 billion worth of goods every day (International Air Transport Association, 2021). These statistics exhibit that airways specialize with its security in carrying high-value products and their low loss and damage ratio. Moreover, air transport differs from any other mode by its capability of offering the shortest time in transit and delivering especially over long distances due to the fact that they're not affected in any way by the landforms or traffic.

The transportation system therefore constitutes a vital and strategic function on which depends the success of every supply chain. As transportation contributes the highest cost among the related elements in logistics systems, the improvement of transport efficiency could change the overall performance of a logistics system (D. Riopel, 2007).

## WAREHOUSING AND INVENTORY MANAGEMENT

### Warehouses in Supply Chain Operations

One of the most challenges that threaten and strain the stability and the performance of the supply chain is the fluctuation in demand which changes in high speed, in contrast of the supply that take long to change (John J. BARTHOLDI, 2019). Here comes the role of warehouses in providing a buffer against uncertainties and breakdowns within the supply chain. Besides, the various activities that occur within a warehouse should be aligned so that products can be managed efficiently and orders can be filled and distributed expeditiously. In this regards, warehouses and distribution centers which often require the largest proportion of a supply chain operation's budgets must lay on several requirement for good practices (adequate facility and infrastructure, a well-developed information system, and qualified human resources, etc.).

### Warehouse Localization

## Unique Warehouse

In the case of positioning one and only warehouse, barycenter method can be used as a tool helping in decision making. Taking in consideration storage cost, construction or localization cost and the cost of using the warehouse differ from on region to another, the method focus just on minimizing the distances by determining a "central point" of all the consumption points basing on different logistics indicators (weight, volume, order lines, etc.) (LYONNET & SENKEL, 2015). However, the method is no more than a tool helping in the decision making since other elements should be associated in the final choice (human resources, legal and fiscal items, etc.).

*Supply Chain Risks in Transportation and Distribution*

## Multiple Warehouses Localization

In this case, the situation is a little bit complex and need a study of numerous scenarios keeping in mind the set of costs of the distribution system (downstream and upstream transportation, storage, inventory holding, etc.) in order to minimize the global cost of the distribution system, satisfy the client order and assure the stability between the inbound and outbound flows.

## Key Roles of Warehouses and Distribution Centers

Thus the importance and significance of the warehouse throughout the supply chain manifests in the following points:

## To Better Match Supply with Customer Demand

As it was mentioned earlier, demand changes can have very serious consequences on the capacity within the supply chain and with it response and lead time become longer. Warehouse therefore allow manufacturers and distribution companies to respond quickly and cushion the supply chain against collapsing demand by providing space in which to slow or hold inventory back from the market.

## To Consolidate Product

One of the most traditional function of warehouses manifests in storage which is considered as the primary role of warehouses. In the previous section, it has been noticed how there's a high fixed cost any time a product is transported and to amortize this fixed cost it is necessary to fill the carrier to capacity. In this regard, the manufacturer and distributor in particular has the option through the warehouse or distributing center of consolidating shipments into large scale delivering and consequently improving the resilience and agility of the downstream logistics.

*Figure 4. Distribution network with and without distribution centers*

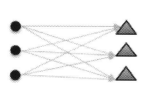
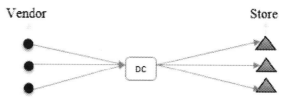

**Figure 3.4**: Distribution network without DC

**Figure 3.5**: Distribution network with DC

## Warehouse as Assembly Facility

Item-differentiation, packaging, pricing and labelling until later stages of the supply chain can improve product allocation. In this context, warehouse enables generic product to be configured close to the customer. The best illustration manifests in manufacturers of consumer electronics where specific part constituting the nomenclature of the final product such as keyboards, plugs, and documentation, are stored at a warehouse and assembled quickly permitting a fast response in order fulfillment. This assures the satisfaction and fulfillment of many customers demand with the lowest inventory levels because the fast movement of items.

## Inventory Management

Inventories refer to raw materials, product in process and finished products which the company hold in the warehouses for so many different purposes from the reason of saving time to dealing with sudden changes in customer demand. As such inventories constitutes a principal element in the process of creating value. Effective inventory management decreases carrying cost and increases customer satisfaction at the same time (Blanchard, 2007). It can be considered that a stock problem is similar to that of taps. Suppose a tank powered by a tap 1. With another tap 2, we serve the demand so the stock diminishes. Thus the objective of inventory management is to regulate by maintaining a certain level of stock in a way that there is neither too much nor too little (LASNIER, 2004).

## Inventory Types

Different stock types is to be found in the warehouse and companies supply chains and there are held and handled according to their nature and function.

- **Cycle stock**: This refers to the amount of inventory available for normal or average expected demand in a given period, excluding safety stock.
- **In-process stock:** or work in progress, it refers to stock containing elements part-finished entering in the composing of the finished product.
- **Safety stock**: intended to deal with the hazards. It permit to cope with increases in real consumption compared to the average theoretical consumption.
- **Consignment stock:** it refers to when the supplier accept to supply the client with certain components quantity. However, it's only charged at the time of need. Therefore, the stock is owned by the supplier until they leave the consignment stock.
- **Seasonal stock:** this type of inventory is stockpiled to deal with anticipated demand for a specific time period.

In a nutshell, inventory management is indispensable in the distribution logistics as its negligence could generates high cost which would impact the cost-effectiveness and profitability of the organization. Therefore, the supply chain managers lay on a multitude of mathematical formulations and models so they can control inventory costs.

## MAIN FOCUS OF THE CHAPTER

### Distribution and Transportation Systems: Vulnerability, Risks and Challenges

*Supply chain vulnerability reflects the sensitivity of a supply chain to disruption (Waters, 2007), and can be defined as an exposure to serious disturbance arising from supply chain risks and affecting the supply chain's ability to effectively serve the end customer market (Juttner, 2005). According to "The International Monetary Fund (IMF), supply chain distributions have obviously developed during these last few years and expected to reach their peak at the end of 2021 and return to pre-crisis levels in many countries by the middle of 2022. (Buchholz, 2021).*

As the transportation and distribution systems are considered as an integral part of the whole supply chain process, their disruption could impact high negatively the performance and could "quickly cripple the entire supply chain" (L.C. Giunipero, 2004). Furthermore, the vulnerability disruptions of these processes are costly and it is of great importance to be understood how a disruption affects a supply chain in order to develop appropriate strategies for ameliorating the impact (K.B. Hendricks, 2005).

### Transportation and Distribution Risks Landscape

A disruption is defined as an event that interrupts the material flows in the supply chain, resulting in an abrupt cessation of the movement of goods. However, unlike disruptions in general, a transportation disruption can occur only as a result of a subset of the drivers identified by (S.C. Chopra, 2004) such as natural catastrophes, labor dispute, man-made threats, political instability and severe legal disruptions. There are many examples of disruptions resulting from these types of events. The Suez Canal blockage by the Ever Green ship which happen to be one of the world's largest container vessels. The blockage has been the source of much worry and frustration for the global shipping industry as according to Suez Canal Authority (SCA) chairman Osama Rabie the Canal's revenues were taking a $14m-$15m hit for each day of the blockage and reduced annual trade growth by 0.2 to 0.4 percentage points which generates an increase in the cost of renting some vessels to ship cargo to and from Asia and the Middle East had jumped 47% to $2.2m (Russon, 29 March 2021)

Furthermore, the report of Everstream Analytics represents more challenges and disruption which has affected the supply chain and transportation. The following figure illustrates the major disruptions accrued in the logistics chain.

*Figure 5. Global supply chain risks
(SHILLINGFORD & KAMAL, 2021)*

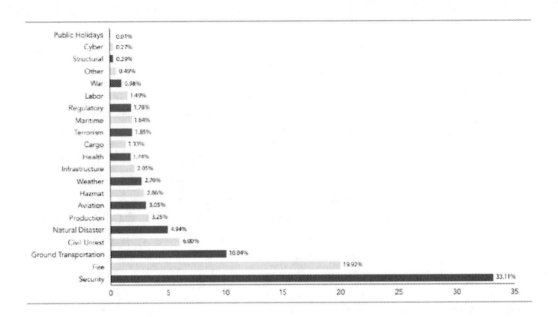

## Regulatory Oversight

According to the report as well as many studies one third of distribution risks in the last few years lies in the Security risk (33.11 percent). Many of them can be accounted for by public safety/security (36 percent) and security advisory (2.48 percent) that provided updates on government mandated restrictions worldwide, such as lockdowns and curfews, to limit the movement of people amid the pandemic (Shillingford & Kamal, 2021).

## Weather and Natural Disasters

Transportation process will be always facing the weather conditions risks which can impact the ability and time of delivery. Although Natural Disaster (4.94 percent) and Weather (2.70 percent) constituted a comparatively small number of incidents, the impact of destructive weather events was keenly felt in 2020. Weather events has increased significantly in the last years, in particular concerning floods, storms, extreme temperatures, and droughts. In the last year, the United States alone faced seven destructive storms that caused more than USD 40 billion (EUR 33 billion) in damages (Shillingford & Kamal, 2021).

## Deteriorating Infrastructure

Outdated and failing infrastructure can have serious problems by crippling the delivering process. The infrastructure is critical and needed to transport finished goods. For instance, the explosion of Beirut port on 4 August 2020 has left Lebanon without its main trade gateway and deprived shippers of a major Mediterranean and Middle East trade hub.

*Supply Chain Risks in Transportation and Distribution*

## Cyber Attacks

As the technological advancements take more weight in the automation of the transportation industry, cyber-attacks pose a major risks especially with the increase in outsourcing this type of activity. With the increase in cyber risk over the past year by +73.79 percent, system failure can threaten the information exchange between the partners and ward off the ability to receive or ship orders. Hackers can tamper with customer travel plans or change destinations, and criminals can steal PII from third party systems. Within the field of cyber-attacks, there are many risks to account for within each organization (Fabbri, 2021).

## Drivers Shortages

The shortages in drivers would make pressures on the transportation and distribution system. And with the shortage increasing driver pay, it can have a significant impact on supplier costs and therefore consumer pricing. It can also increase shipping delays and shortage at stores. The best example is to be found in the UK where it witnessed a shortages of fuel tanker drivers to deliver it to forecourts and hence no distribution and empty petrol stations. According to BBC there's an estimated shortage of more than 100,000 HGV drivers, which has already caused problems for a range of retailers - from supermarkets to fast food chains and Brexit has worsened it.

## Cargo Damage and Warehouse Theft

Since transportation process handles the movement of cargos and goods from point to point across the world in huge shipments, it is inevitable that cargo damage may occur especially when loading oversized and heavyweight cargos on and off ships, flatbeds, trailers, and railcars which threaten the safety of the shipments. That results most of the time from the impending threat of human interference and negligence. Beside the unavoidable damage of cargo, the goods stay threatened even after passing through ports and sometimes in the shipping process the cargo can be exposed to exploitation and theft operations. Year-on-year these incidents increase, as it has been seen in 2018 the loss of car parts from a truck while it was in-route in Romania, which reported a loss value of €2,017,440 and it is estimated for cargo theft's costs to be tens of billions of dollars worldwide (Reidy, 2020). Moreover this year has witnessed thefts included a break-in at the Amsterdam Schiphol Airport, where perpetrators stole Apple iPhones worth EUR 3 million (USD 3.6 million) from a warehouse in March.

## Political Changes

Political disruptions both nationally as well as internationally are associated to the supply chain process and are not isolated and inseparable events of the distribution system. As they're unknown and unplanned events, they might affect the normal or expected flow of materials and components and consequently the performance of one or more elements located elsewhere in the supply chain (Svensson, 2002). The main factor and element precipitating this kind of disruptions are the governments which wield a tremendous power over global trade. While some host governments facilitate good performance by declaring a state of emergency and relaxing regulations, others impose barriers that can lead to the timely delivery and impede performance and finally have a devastating consequences especially in the humanitarian logistics perspective (McLachlin, 2009; Menkhaus, 2010). Brexit constitutes the perfect example of political

517

risk. The protectionist move that UK took to pull out from the EU has trigged a climate of economic and geopolitical uncertainty and lack of visibility. It will drive companies to the restructuration of their distribution system from planning (longer lead time for customs), inventory levels (to cover uncertainty in demand), optimizing the distribution network regarding the infrastructure and supply chain configuration to reflect the new balance of supply chain cost and service in order to dealing with new customs processes and compliance.

## Failure to Integrate Distribution Network

As the outsourcing of many activities and functions in distribution is increasing day by day and the logistics service providers take more importance in supply chain strategy, the governance and control of supply chain operations stay a high challenge for organization. Just because LSPs provide support to logistics industry by their expertise, it does not mean that monitoring and controlling shouldn't be built into the organization. Therefore, failure in collaboration and lack in alignment between partners and different links in distribution process can have severe consequences on the organization distribution effectiveness especially when supply chain strategy is not linked to the corporate aims and vision.

## Inventory Risks and Lead-time Stochasticity

As far as the distribution network is concerned, inventory risk represents one of the most challenges that managers could face. Since the main role of a distribution system is to be able to deliver the goods at the right time and in the right amount, inventory availability is therefore a critical element on which will depend the replenishment time or service time required by an upstream node to fulfill a demand from a downstream node. Thus, an inaccurate forecasting could cost a lot. When the upstream node is unable to fulfill from its stock due stock outs, the downstream node will experience a delay which makes lead-time between the nodes stochastic even when the order processing time for the supplying node could be deterministic (Graves, 2003) and that can result lost sales and potentially lost customers. The widely used just-in-time (JIT) inventory system is a typical example of a supply chain practice that exposes firms to material shortage risk. On the other hand, inventory risk can reflect the inability of the organization to sell its goods or the chance that inventory stock will decrease in value or even an overstocking which will generate more inventory management costs and ties up cash flows.

## Covid-19 and Transportation

The restrictions on the ports and borders have created issues for the businesses to supply the material and other different products to be transported through the sea routes based on the assessment of (Klatman, 2020). Similarly, the regulations in the countries have also reduced the number of goods traveled and have also increased the cost and duty over the products due to the reason of increased safety of the products in this regard (Tardivo, 2020). Besides, with the decrease in the capacity for maritime transport, the pressure on the land freight has clearly increased especially with the increased manufactured goods and badly affected the timely services for logistics and transportation (iddique, 2020).

According to a study conducted by (Yanling Xu, 2021), the health crisis has impacted significantly the transportation system as major containers were backlogged at the ports and most of cargo deliveries has witnessed delays risks in the shipments no matter what the industry is (electronics, pharmaceuticals,

*Supply Chain Risks in Transportation and Distribution*

and automobile, and medical equipment) due to closure of most of ways and routes and it became very difficult for the costumers to receive the deliveries in time and also as a result many employees working in the logistics and distribution chain sectors lost their jobs because no cargo or any orders were delivered or dispatched from one country to another. The same study has highlighted as well that the safety of the drivers and employees from contamination by the virus represented one of the major issues that supply chain companies had to face.

## SOLUTIONS AND RECOMMENDATIONS

### Distribution Risk Management: Objective, Process and Solutions

### Supply Chain Risk Management

The previous section has demonstrated beyond any doubt that supply chain and transportation/distribution channel in particular is considered as riskier than ever. Therefore, many scientists explore the area of identification, impact and methods of reducing risks in all areas, including in the transport and distribution system, which is an important link in the supply chain, in a framework of transportation and distribution chain risk management (Khan, 2007; Jüttner, 2005; Vilko, 2012; Zhao L., 2012). The supply chain risk management SCRM in distribution and transportation refers to the set of strategies and plans implemented in order to manage the whole network through constant risk assessment and reduce vulnerabilities to ensure resilience in supply chains. SCRM is therefore an important and critical area due to an incident's cascading effects on logistics networks (Cigolini & Rossi, 2010).

Besides, the author has underlined that supply chain disruptions can be generated by several types of risks, those that can be mitigate in advance and those that can't be forecasted and would happen even with the implementation of advanced prediction systems. This finding explain that in order to minimize the impact of uncertain events, enterprise needs to prepare for the disruption may occur. As such, risk management can be classified into two approaches:

### Mitigation Strategy

The mitigation action addresses the origin and source of the risk. That is to say, it is a set of planning action aiming to manage the uncertainty events prior to its happening. The purpose of this strategy lies either avoiding the disturbances from the first place or in bringing down the risk exposure within the acceptable threshold limits, or if it occurred, it should have a minimal impact. The implementation of a mitigation strategy allows the enterprise to reduce the impact of a risk and consequently to minimize its vulnerability. By this mean, it would balance its portfolio of capabilities needed to be put in place to match the pattern of vulnerabilities. This way, the organization will positions itself in the zone of resilience where the generated impact could be overcame.

### Contingency Strategy

Sometimes in the distribution chain, the managers could not predict the certainty of an event even with the most advanced technologies. They are required to put in place an accurate strategy (contingency plan) in order to response as quickly as possible to the disruptions and to absorb the shock from the unwanted event when it happens. In doing so, the company can control the impact as risk event looks like occurring.

It should be noted that these two risk plans are not mutually exclusive. However, the contingency strategy can be considered as an extension of mitigation strategy plan. In some urgent situations, the mangers have to implement a proactive plan which enables them to reduce the probability and impact of the risk. In addition to that, they must as well establish a contingency strategy that will allow them to control and monitor the warning signs in case of an inevitable or avoidable risk.

Nevertheless, it is not of high necessity to opt for both strategies for the totality of the disruptions, given that each risk requires the appropriate plan. In this regard, every distribution or transportation chain manager should first of all fulfil and respect all the process stages so he can make the right decision and implement the suitable strategy.

## Process of Risk Management

Transportation and distribution risk management can be achieve by several distinctive approaches to investigating risk mitigating strategies. However, one the most successful risk management standard and which was accepted widely throughout the world is the series of AS/NZS 4360 Standard on Risk Management introduced and developed by Australia and New Zealand since 1995. Since the both transportation and distribution systems face often tactical and operational issues, this approach represents the best measure due to the fact that it's completely limited to operational and tactical measures that are effective to mitigating individual risks (Pujawan & Geraldin, 2009). This focuses on identification and measurement of individual risks, thereby generating direct solutions rather than overarching corporate strategies. In the same vein, the International Organization for Standardization (ISO) published ISO 31000:2009 Risk Management Principles and Guidelines (ISO, 2009) to provide a foundation for Enterprise Risk Management ERM implementation and it anticipated that ISO 31000 will become an international norm for ERM (Gjerdrum & Salen, 2010). To this end, a process of numerous steps is to be established.

*Supply Chain Risks in Transportation and Distribution*

*Figure 6. SCRM process (ISO 13000)*

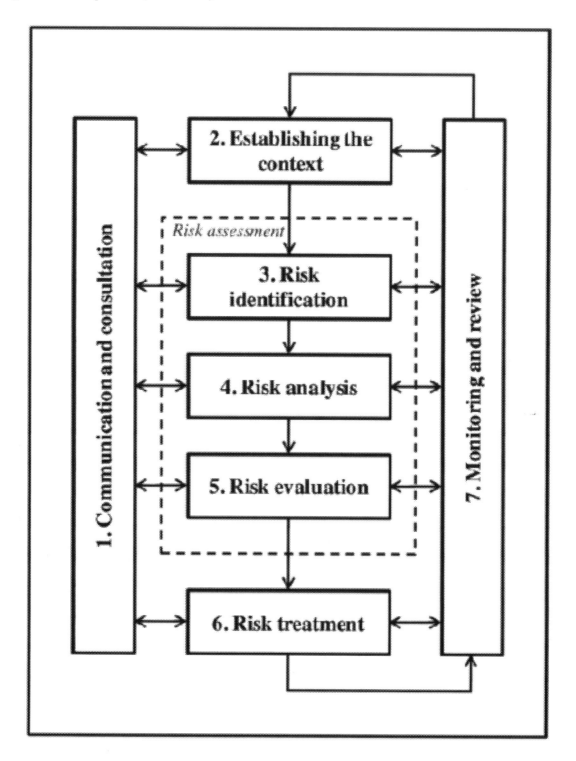

## Risk Identification

The first problem that the SC managers often encounter in any risk mitigation process lies in the difficulty in identifying the risks in the first place. Therefore, improving the effectiveness of risk management across supply chains and transport networks requires risk exposure to be better identified and made more visible. As the intensity of the disruption effect on the distribution operations depends on the quick response to it at the first stages, firms must deploy risk identification to discover the sources of SC risks accurately (Chowdhury & Quaddus, 2017). The risk can be detected by the probability and the consequences or impact of the event.

### Risk: Probability of Realization of the Event and its Impact

The identification of the risk is therefore crucial in the mitigation process as it allows the managers to be cautious in facing any type of risk. Thus, two approaches enables the identification of risks namely: "Top down" which the identification of all important risks by the management which manages risks throughout the transport chain and "bottom up" that addresses each link in the chain. To promote this process, several methods and techniques can be put in place such as surveying, brainstorming, analyzing the historical problems, the Delphi Method, What-If Analysis, PGA method, Event tree analysis, simulation etc.

### Risk Analysis and Evaluation

After the list of risks is identified, the managers proceed subsequently to assess risk to evaluate its potential impact on the firm's performance (Schmitt & Singh, 2012; Wieland & Wallenburg, 2012). The purpose is to qualify the risks in terms of giving priority in treating risks with the highest probability of occurrence and the magnitude of the impact on the supply chain's performance should the event occur. When assessing the risks, two types of methods can be established. On one hand, a qualitative method which can make the primary risk assessment fast and economical way and is used in cases where no information exists on previous risk events. On the other hand, quantitative method which is based on its predecessor and addresses the risks with high probability and impact on the transport or distribution chain. Quantitative methods are usually based on mathematical calculations, where the uncertainties are shown like random variables, and as such have unpredictable values (Coyle J, Novack, Gibson, & E.J.Bardi, 2011).

### Risk Mitigation and Treatment

After the assessment of the risks and collecting relevant data, the aim now is to address transportation and distribution risks with the appropriate measures through one of the aforementioned strategies (mitigation and contingency) (Manuj & Mentzer, 2008; Azadegan, Mellat Parast, Lucianetti, Nishant, & Blackhurst, 2020).

*Supply Chain Risks in Transportation and Distribution*

## Risk Monitoring and Control

The previous steps cannot be completely achieved without controlling the risk. Monitoring and controlling the risks is an ongoing part of risk management that is integral to every step of the process due to the fact that it enables the firms to reduce the frequency and impacts of distribution and transportation risks; hence the need to evaluate the performance of SCRM practices (Berg, Knudsen, & Norrman, 2008). This part of Risk management ensures that the important information generated by the previous processes is captured, used, and maintained.

In addition, and to put this process in place more efficiently communication and consultation with internal and external interest parties should be present in each phase as much as is necessary as their opinion may have a significant influence on the decision process.

## Transportation and Distribution Risk Management Strategies

Along all the steps previously mentioned, the organization basing on the informations collected tries to take the adequate decision and put in place the right strategy according to the type of risk detected. In this section, the author highlights the set of strategies that could be established in order to reduce the vulnerability and effectively response to the impact of some disruptions on the transportation and distribution network.

## Multimodal Transportation

Multimodal transportation (also known as combined transport) is an alternative to 100%-road freight that combines at least two different modes of transportation to complete a journey from production units to end users. The loading unit (container) stays the same throughout transit, so transfer from one mode to another doesn't require any offloading of goods which reduce the probability of cargo damage and hence better security of goods. Furthermore, by using multimodal transportation, loading capacities are enhanced comparing to road transportation only. Therefore more amount of goods can transported in the same shipment which leads consequently to optimizing transportation costs for consumer goods. In addition to that, it promotes sustainability by reducing environmental footprint which usually generates by road freight. Besides the multimodal solutions refers to appeal to service providers for the delivery of goods, by this mean the firms could minimize the fix costs and hence improve their performance.

## Improving Integration and Collaboration

Since in distribution process the bulk of companies especially exporting ones use service provides to deliver their goods in view of their positive contributions as it's been pointed out in the previous sections, developing trusted networks integral to effective collaboration across and between all the links of the distribution chain is needed. Carefully managed sharing of information, expertise and priorities can develop collaborative and trusted relationships, which are crucial to pre-disruption preparation and post-disruption rapid response (Appel, 2012).

In the same vein, elaborating a partnership strategy between the public and private sector entities will allow greater sharing of data and information, enabling organizations to better understand and quantify distribution chain and transport risks especially when it comes to infrastructures handling.

### Decentralized distribution

As the satisfaction of the customer represents the main objective of the firms, to be agile and flexible toward the client takes more and more interest in their strategies. In this regard, decentralized distribution model may lead to supply chain inefficiency (Chen, Federgruen, & Zheng, 2001). Decentralizing warehouses besides allowing the product to move closer to the final customer and subsequently a best service to customer base it provide the option of same day delivery with moderate cost.

### Inventory Planning

Almost the majority of companies adopt nowadays the strategies of JIT and lean distribution which refers to reducing both movements and waste in distribution centers while still keeping high customer service level (Jaca, Santos, Errasti, & E. Viles, 2011). Each distribution function – from receiving customer orders to products delivery – can benefit from the lean principles which lead to high process quality, minimum levels of waste, cost cutbacks, and increasing productivity. However, in some urgent situations firms find themselves facing a shortage in goods. Therefore, they must always stay prudent and always put in place a safety stock to deal with this type of cases, and that can be achieved by establishing a solid forecasting system (Wang, 2008).

### Digital Transformation

The set of solutions prior discussed involve in one way or another and in huge part the deployment of advanced technologies since an effective distribution network lies currently with the extend of the chain on the information and data sharing to make the right decisions. I.e. Internet of Things (IoT) and RFID helps tracking the cargo by providing all kinds of information that can help track important data such as temperature changes, container door open status, late in/out site, energy levels, or any unusual activity regardless if it's a truck, container, or warehouse and give analysis and best practices to deal with the problem.

Moreover, with the interconnectivity of the whole distribution chain, softwares and digital solutions such ERP and Blockchain are gaining more importance given the positive contributions which they provide. They comprise a chronological string of blocks integrating all three types of flows in the transaction and captures details that are distributed to all links of distribution chain. Blockchain for instance greatly reduces, if not eliminates, the kind of execution, traceability, and coordination problems (Gaur & Gaiha, 2020).

## CONCLUSION

It's not just about predicting what or when – but it's of high importance to be prepared and able to respond in an informed and planned manner to minimize the impact of a disruption. This fact shows that even with the most advanced forecasting technologies prediction is not enough to cope with unforeseen disruptions. Thus mitigation strategies alone are not sufficient, therefore organizations are obliged to put in place alongside some contingency plans and methods to stay ready for any sort of risk that may occur.

*Supply Chain Risks in Transportation and Distribution*

Furthermore, the interconnectivity and complexity in the distribution network has made it of a great importance to opt for digitalization of the process to ensure the transparency of the information and assure the visibility. The top emerging technologies in distribution logistics will focus on the smart distribution chain (from warehouse automation to smart last time delivery) and cloud technology throughout the whole chain. The concept of the smart supply chain centers around connectivity both inside and outside the warehouse, requires that relevant data needs to be shared easily between software systems. With such empowerment of the digital transformation comes other challenges which lies in cyber threatens and disruptions and could be fatal to the firms. In this since, cybersecurity gain more and more ground and become one of the most priorities of many distribution and transportation companies.

Moreover, sustainability of the distribution logistics will continue to gain ground and is becoming a hotly debating issue besides it's undoubtedly a challenging task given the importance and the emergency of implementing new approaches to preserve and manage environmental, social and economic dimensions. Therefore new methods and techniques must be deployed to reduce global warming and CO2 footprint and to focus increasingly on adopting green distribution chain strategies.

The globalization has made the supply chain more and more extended and has developed to support global dispatch network as well as multiple warehouse management and inventory control which was reflected as well on the transportation and distribution systems since they constitute an integral part of the whole chain. This complexity had left the distribution and transportation networks open to many risks and disturbances which they can initiated from diversity of sources and can be happened suddenly and quickly. In other words, if the changing phases of globalization, lean distribution processes, and outsourcing to low-income countries have made transportation and distribution chain networks more efficient it has also changed their supply chain risk profile.

Additionally, with the intentioned competition, the satisfaction of the customer turns to one of the most priorities of today's companies. As such providing a high quality logistics service is very essential to the success and the development of the firm. However, the increase in customers' expectations has made it very difficult to predict fluctuations in demand.

In order to cope with these risks, several strategies are presented to organizations on which they can lay to mitigate and manage the set of disruptions. Nonetheless, mitigation strategies alone are not sufficient because the best practice is not to predict what or when – but instead be prepared and able to respond in an informed and planned manner to minimize the impact of a disruption. Therefore, contingency plans are needed to response as quickly as possible to the disruptions and to absorb the shock from the unwanted event when it happens.

In this regard, the managers are required to pursue a well-designed strategy and approach and risk assessment should deploy in a systematic way to identify any possible risk could happen in logistics flows. This chapter has revealed a developed standard framework to manage risks, and that established by ISO which allows by analyzing and diagnosing distribution and transportation activities and functions to identify the risk sources in the logistics flows and followed ISO-31000 framework to deploy risk management processes. Yet, risk management cannot be complete without a solid control and monitoring. The latter enables the process of risk management continuous and consequently keep the satisfaction of the client.

## REFERENCES

Amiri, A. (2006). Designing a distribution network in a supply chainsystem: Formulation and efficient solution procedure. *European Journal of Operational Research, 171*(2), 567-576.

Amulya Gurtu, J. J. (2021). Supply Chain Risk Management: Literature Review. *MDPI*, 1-16.

Appel, F. (2012). *New Models for Addressing Supply Chain and Transport Risk.* Cologny: World Economic Forum.

Avittathur, B. S., & Swamidass, P. (2007). Matching plant flexibility and supplier flexibility: Lessons from small suppliers of US manufacturing plants in India. *Journal of Operations Management, 25*(3), 717–735. doi:10.1016/j.jom.2006.05.015

Ayantoyinbo, B. B. (2018). Impact of Inbound and Outbound Logistics. *Transport & Logistics, 18*(44), 69–76.

Azadegan, A., Mellat Parast, M., Lucianetti, L., Nishant, R., & Blackhurst, J. (2020). Supply Chain Disruptions and Business Continuity: An Empirical Assessment. *Journal of the Decison Sciences Institute, 51*(1), 38–73. doi:10.1111/deci.12395

Bask, A. H. (2001). Relationships among TPL providers and members of supply chains - a strategic perspective. *Journal of Business and Industrial Marketing, 10*(1), 470–486. doi:10.1108/EUM0000000006021

Berg, E., Knudsen, D., & Norrman, A. (2008). Assessing performance of supply chain risk management programmes: A tentative approach. *International Journal of Risk Assessment and Management, 9*(3), 288–310. doi:10.1504/IJRAM.2008.019746

Blanchard, D. (2007). *Supply Chain Management: Best Practices.* John Wiley & Sons.

Borraz-Sa'nchez, C., & Ríos-Mercado, R. Z. (2009). Improving the operation of pipeline systems on cyclic structures by tabu search. *Computers & Chemical Engineering, 33*(1), 58–64. doi:10.1016/j.compchemeng.2008.07.009

Chatur, A. (2005). *Driving Costs out of the Supply Chain.* Infosys Technologies Limited.

Chen, F., Federgruen, A., & Zheng, Y.-S. (2001). Near-Optimal Pricing and Replenishment Strategies for a Retail/Distribution System. *Operations Research, 49*(6), 839–853. doi:10.1287/opre.49.6.839.10020

Chowdhury, M., & Quaddus, M. (2017). Supply chain resilience: Conceptualization and scale development using dynamic capability theory. *International Journal of Production Economics, 188*, 185–204. doi:10.1016/j.ijpe.2017.03.020

Christopher, M. (1998). *Logistics and Supply Chain Management: Strategies for reducing cost and improving service.* Prentice Hall.

Christopher, M. (2011). Logistics and customer value. In Logistics & Supply Chain Management (4th ed., pp. 27-50). London: Pearson Education Limited.

Cigolini, R., & Rossi, T. (2010). Managing operational risks along the oil supply chain. *Production Planning and Control, 21*(5), 452–467. doi:10.1080/09537280903453695

*Supply Chain Risks in Transportation and Distribution*

Coyle, J. J., Novack, R. A., & Gibson, B. J. (2016). *Transoprtation: A Globale Supply Chain Perspective* (8th ed.). Boston: Cengage Learning.

Directive, C. (2004). *2004/67/EC*. Council of the European Union.

Dolgui, A., Ivanov, D., & Sokolov, B. (2018). Ripple effect in the supply chain: An analysis and recent literature. *International Journal of Production Research*, *56*(1-2), 414–430. doi:10.1080/00207543.20 17.1387680

Fady, A. B. L. (2003). La logistique dans la distribution. In A. F. G. Cliquet (Ed.), *Management de la distribution* (p. 275). Dunod.

Fahimnia, B. J., Jabbarzadeh, A., & Sarkis, J. (2018). Greening versus resilience: A supply chain design perspective. *Transportation Research Part E, Logistics and Transportation Review*, *119*, 129–148. doi:10.1016/j.tre.2018.09.005

Gaur, V., & Gaiha, A. (2020). Building a Transparent Supply Chain. *Harvard Business Review*.

Gjerdrum, D., & Salen, W. (2010). The New ERM Gold Standard: ISO 31000:2009. *Professional Safety*, *55*(8), 43–44.

Gong, Z. (2008). An economic evaluation model of supply chain flexibility. *European Journal of Operational Research*, *184*(2), 745–758. doi:10.1016/j.ejor.2006.11.013

Graves, S. C., & Willems, S. P. (2003). Supply Chain Design: Safety Stock Placement and Supply Chain Configuration. *Handbooks in Operations Research and Management Science*, *11*(11), 95–132. doi:10.1016/S0927-0507(03)11003-1

Guillot, G. (2021, Mai 6). *Logistique du futur: quels sont les nouveaux enjeux?* Récupéré sur Entreprendre: https://www.entreprendre.fr

Hidajet Karaxha, I. K. (2016). The Logistics and Management of Distribution Channels, the case of Kosovo. *ILIRIA International Review*, *6*(1), 37–48. doi:10.21113/iir.v6i1.224

Hofmann, S. (2019, September 21). *Distribution logistics - definition, basics, examples* (T. Knell, Ed.). Maschinenmarkt International.

Lambert, D. M. J. S. (2003). Strategic Logistics Management. Homewood, IL: Irwin.

Riopel, D. A. L. (2007). The network of logistics decisions. In Logistics Systems: Design and Optimization (pp. 12-17). New York: Springer.

Hosseini, S. I. (2019). Review of quantitative methods for supply chain resilience analysis. *Transportation Research Part E, Logistics and Transportation Review*, 285–307.

Iddique, A. S. (2020). Unprecedented environmental and energy impacts and challenges of COVID-19 pandemic. Environmental Research. Advance online publication. doi:10.1016/j.envres.2020.110443

Ailawadi, S. C. R. S. (2005). Logistics Management. New Delhi: Prentice Hall of India.

Chopra, S.C., M. S. (2004). Managing risk to avoid supply-chain breakdown. *MIT Sloan Management Review*, *1*(46), 53–61.

Christiansen, M. K. F. (2007). Maritime Transportation. In Handbook in Operation Research and Management (Vol. 14). Elsevier B.V.

Giunipero, L. C., & Aly Eltantawy, R. (2004). Securing the upstream supply chain: A risk management approach. *International Journal of Physical Distribution & Logistics Management*, *9*(34), 698–713. doi:10.1108/09600030410567478

He, F. A. (2018). A real-option approach to mitigate disruption risk in the supply chain. *Omega: Int. J. Manage. Sci.*, 133-149.

Hendricks, K.B., V. S. (2005). An empirical analysis of the effect of supply chain disruptions on log-run stock price and equity risk of the firm. *Production and Operations Management*, *1*(14), 35–52.

Ivanov, D. (2018). *Structural Dynamics and Resilience in Supply Chain Risk Management*. Springer. doi:10.1007/978-3-319-69305-7

Jaca, C., Santos, J., Errasti, A., & Viles, E. (2011). Lean thinking with improvement teams in retail. *Total Quality Management & Business Excellence*, *23*(3-4), 449–465. doi:10.1080/14783363.2011.593907

Juttner, U. (2005). Supply chain risk management: Understanding the business requirements from a practitioner perspective. *International Journal of Logistics Management*, *16*(1), 120–141. doi:10.1108/09574090510617385

Jüttner, U. (2005). Supply chain risk management: Understanding the business requirements from a practitioner perspective. *International Journal of Logistics Management*, *16*(1), 120–141. doi:10.1108/09574090510617385

Khan, O. B., & Burnes, B. (2007). Risk and supply chain management: Creating a research agenda. *International Journal of Logistics Management*, *18*(2), 197–216. doi:10.1108/09574090710816931

Kirilmaz, O., & Erol, S. (2017). A Proactive Approach to Supply Chain Risk Management: Shifting Orders among Suppliers to Mitigate the Supply Side Risks. *Journal of Purchasing and Supply Management*, *23*(1), 54–65. doi:10.1016/j.pursup.2016.04.002

Lasnier, G. (2004). *Supply and inventory management in the supply chain*. Hermes Sciences.

Lieb, R. M., Millen, R. A., & Van Wassenhove, L. N. (1993). Third-party logistics services: A comparison of experienced American and European manufacturers. *International Journal of Physical Distribution & Logistics Management*, *23*(6), 35–44. doi:10.1108/09600039310044894

Lyonnet, B., & Senkel, M.-P. (2015). Logitics. Nantes: Dunod.

Lysenko-Ryba, K. (2017). The Impact of Reverse Logistics on Customers Satisfaction. *Entrepreneurship and Management*, *18*, 137–146.

Manuj, I., & Mentzer, J. (2008). Global supply chain risk management strategies. *International Journal of Physical Distribution & Logistics Management*, *38*(3), 192–223. doi:10.1108/09600030810866986

McLachlin, R. L., Larson, P. D., & Khan, S. (2009). Not-for-profit supply chains in interrupted environments: The case of a faith-based humanitarian relief organisation. *Management Research News*, *32*(11), 1050–1064. doi:10.1108/01409170910998282

*Supply Chain Risks in Transportation and Distribution*

Mei, J., & Afli, E. M. (2017, April). The Impact of Transportation Management System on Supply Chain Management: The Effectiveness of Chaineese Online Shopping Delivery- The "KUAIDI" System. *European Journal of Logistics. Purchasing and Supply Chain Management*, 5(2), 1–9.

Ministry of Transport Scientific Research Institute. (2019). *Railway Statistics Bulletin*. Beijing: Ministry of Transport of the People's Republic of China.

Mirotin, L. B. Y. T. (2002). Logistics: customer Service. Moscow: INFRA–M.

Munoz, J. N. J.-R.-R. (2003). Natural gas network modeling for power systems reliability studies. IEEE Bologna PowerTech Conference.

Pettit, T. J., Fiksel, J., & Croxton, K. L. (2010). Ensuring supply chain resilience: Development of a conceptual framework. *Journal of Business Logistics*, *31*(3), 1–21. doi:10.1002/j.2158-1592.2010.tb00125.x

Pujawan, I., & Geraldin, L. (2009). House of risk: A model for proactive supply chain risk. *Business Process Management Journal*, *15*(6), 953–967. doi:10.1108/14637150911003801

Redbird Logistics Services. (2021, February 10). *What is the Importance of Customer Service in Logistics Companies?* Récupéré sur redbirdlogisticsservices: https://redbirdlogisticsservices.com

Reina Angkiriwang, I. N. (2014). Managing uncertainty through supply chain flexibility: Reactive vs. proactive approaches. *Production & Manufacturing Research*, *2*(1), 50–70. doi:10.1080/21693277.2014.882804

Reynolds-Feighan, A. (2001). Air freight logistics. In K. B. A. M. Brewer (Ed.), *Handbook of Logistics and Supply-Chain Management* (pp. 431–439). Elsevier Science Ltd.

S., S. H. (2014). Management of distribution channels. *Indian J.Sci.Res.*, *5*(3), 452-456.

Sarder, M. (2020). Logistics customer service. In M. Sarder (Ed.), *Logistics Transportation Systems* (pp. 197–217). Elsevier.

Schmitt, A., & Singh, M. (2012). A quantitative analysis of disruption risk in a multi-echelon supply chain. *International Journal of Production Economics*, *139*(1), 22–32. doi:10.1016/j.ijpe.2012.01.004

Shepherd, C. a. (2010). Measuring supply chain performance: current research and future directions. In *Behavioral Operations in Planning and Scheduling*. Springer. doi:10.1007/978-3-642-13382-4_6

Shillingford, D., & Kamal, S. (2021). *Everstream Analytics: Annual risk*. Everstream Analytics.

Stefansson, G. (2006). Collaborative logistics management and the role of third-party service providers. *International Journal of Physical Distribution & Logistics Management*, *36*(2), 76–92. doi:10.1108/09600030610656413

Tardivo, A. M. (2020). *Alessio Tardivo, Celestino Sánchez Martín, Armando Carrillo Zanuy*. European Rail Research Network of Excellence.

Todd, J. (2017). *Mitigating Supply Chain Risk: Effective Transportation and Logistics Provider Diligence and Management Practices*. New York: JD Supra.

Vilko, J. H., & Hallikas, J. M. (2012). Risk assessment in multimodal supply chains, Original Research Article. *International Journal of Production Economics, 140*(2), 586–595. doi:10.1016/j.ijpe.2011.09.010

Wang, B. (2008). Analysis of efficiency of lean production implemented in multi-national optic enterprises. *International Journal of Technology Management, 43*(4), 304–319. doi:10.1504/IJTM.2008.020553

Waters, D. (2007). *Supply chain risk management: vulnerability and resilience in logistics.* London: Kogan-Page.

Wieland, A., & Wallenburg, C. (2012). Dealing with supply chain risks: Linking risk management practices and strategies to performance. *International Journal of Physical Distribution & Logistics Management, 42*(10), 887–905. doi:10.1108/09600031211281411

Xu, S. Z., Zhang, X., Feng, L., & Yang, W. (2020). Disruption risks in supply chain management: A literature review based on bibliometric analysis. *International Journal of Production Research, 58*(11), 3508–3526. doi:10.1080/00207543.2020.1717011

Yanling Xu, J.-P. L.-C. (2021). Impact of COVID-19 on transportation and logistics: a case of China. *Economic Research-Ekonomska Istraživanja*. Récupéré sur doi:10.1080/1331677X.2021.1947339

Zhao, L. W. X., Wang, X., & Qian, Y. (2012). Analysis of factors that influence hazardous material transportation accidents based on Bayesian networks: A case study in China. *Safety Science, 50*(4), 1049–1055. doi:10.1016/j.ssci.2011.12.003

Zsidisin, G. P., Panelli, A., & Upton, R. (2000). Purchasing organization involvement in risk assessments, contingency plans, and risk management: An exploratory study. *Supply Chain Management, VI*(4), 187–197. doi:10.1108/13598540010347307

## KEY TERMS AND DEFINITIONS

**Outbound Logistics:** Known also as physical distribution. The latter takes part of the downstream logistics which consist in routing the products resulting from a production process to the customer (directly to his home in case of delivery to the consumer, or to the place where the customer can buy the product). This process includes storage, order fulfilment and packaging of goods, and sometimes the handling of returned goods or what's called the reverse logistics.

**Supply Chain Resilience:** Manifests when the network is capable to withstand, adapt, and recover as quickly as possible from disruptions to meet customer demand and ensure performance.

**Supply Chain Risk Management:** The supply chain risk management SCRM in distribution and transportation refers to the set of strategies and plans implemented in order to manage the whole network through constant risk assessment and reduce vulnerabilities to ensure resilience in supply chains.

**Supply Chain Vulnerability:** Supply chain vulnerability indicates the responsiveness of a supply chain to disruptions, and can be defined as an exposure to serious disturbance arising from supply chain risks and affecting the supply chain's ability to effectively serve the end customer market.

**Transportation and Distribution Risks:** Occur as a result of a subset of several elements such as natural catastrophes, labor dispute, man-made threats, political instability and severe legal disruptions which could impact high negatively the performance and could "quickly cripple the entire supply chain

*Supply Chain Risks in Transportation and Distribution*

**Transportation System in Logistics:** The transport system is the "glue" that links and holds not only the distribution network but the whole supply chain as well. Given that transportation represents the last phase in the value chain to touch the customer and may have a significant impact on the success of the transaction, it constitutes the key enabler for a customer-oriented strategy such as overnight and same-day delivery.

# Compilation of References

Abate, M., Christidis, P., & Purwanto, A. J. (2020). Government support to airlines in the aftermath of the COVID-19 pandemic. *Journal of Air Transport Management*, *89*, 101931. Advance online publication. doi:10.1016/j.jairtraman.2020.101931 PMID:32952317

Abbas, H. S. M., Xu, X., Sun, C., Ullah, A., Gillani, S., & Raza, M. A. A. (2021). Impact of COVID-19 pandemic on sustainability determinants: A global trend. *Heliyon*, *7*(2), e05912. doi:10.1016/j.heliyon.2021.e05912 PMID:33458434

Abdal, A., & Ferreira, D. M. (2021). Deglobalization, Globalization, and the Pandemic: Current Impasses of the Capitalist World-Economy. *Journal of World-systems Research*, *27*(1), 202–230. doi:10.5195/jwsr.2021.1028

Abdel-Basset, M., Chang, V., & Nabeeh, N. A. (2021). An intelligent framework using disruptive technologies for COVID-19 analysis. *Technological Forecasting and Social Change*, *163*, 120431. doi:10.1016/j.techfore.2020.120431 PMID:33162617

Abdi, M. R., Edalat, F. D., & Abumusa, S. (2017). Lean and Agile Supply Chain Management: A Case of IT Distribution Industry in the Middle East. In Green and Lean Management (pp. 37-69). Springer International Publishing.

Abu-Rayash, A., & Dincer, I. (2020). Analysis of mobility trends during the COVID-19 coronavirus pandemic: Exploring the impacts on global aviation and travel in selected cities. *Energy Research & Social Science*, *68*(July), 101693. doi:10.1016/j.erss.2020.101693 PMID:32839706

Accenture. (2019). *Cross-border-the-disruptive-frontier*. https://www.accenture.com/_acnmedia/pdf-102/accenture-cross-border-the-disruptive-

Accenture. (2020). *COVID-19: How we are helping to build supply-chain resilience*. https://www.accenture.com/us-en/blogs/blogs-careers/covid-19-how-were-helping-to-build-supply-chain-resilience

Acioli, C., Scavarda, A., & Reis, A. (2021). Applying industry 4.0 technologies in the COVID–19 sustainable chains. *International Journal of Productivity and Performance Management*, *70*(5), 988–1016. doi:10.1108/IJPPM-03-2020-0137

Adams, K. (2020). *Will the Pandemic Mean Higher Health Care Costs in the Future*. Available at: https://www.marketplace.org/2020/03/31/will-the-pandemic-mean-higher-health-care-costs-in-the-future/

Addo-Tenkorang, R., & Helo, P. T. (2016). Big data applications in operations/supply-chain management: A literature review. *Computers & Industrial Engineering*, *101*, 528–543. doi:10.1016/j.cie.2016.09.023

Adivar, B., Hüseyinoğlu, I. Ö. Y., & Christopher, M. (2019). A quantitative performance management framework for assessing omnichannel retail supply chains. *Journal of Retailing and Consumer Services*, *48*(1), 257–269. doi:10.1016/j.jretconser.2019.02.024

*Compilation of References*

Adland, R., Ameln, H., & Børnes, E.A., (2020). Hedging ship price risk using freight derivatives in the drybulk market. *Journal of Shipping and Trade, 5*(1). doi:10.1186/s41072-019-0056-3

Agami. (2012). Supply chain performance measurement approaches: review and classification. *Journal of Organizational Management Studies.*

Agigi, A., Niemann, W., & Kotzé, T. (2016). Supply chain design approaches for supply chain resilience: A qualitative study of South African fast-moving consumer goods grocery manufacturers. *Journal of Transport and Supply Chain Management, 10*(1), a253. doi:10.4102/jtscm.v10i1.253

Agrawal, A. (2020). Sustainability of airlines in India with Covid-19: Challenges ahead and possible way-outs. *Journal of Revenue and Pricing Management, 20*(4), 457–472. doi:10.1057/s41272-020-00257-z

Agrawal, P., & Narain, R. (2018). Digital supply chain management: An Overview. *IOP Conference Series: Materials Science and Engineering. 455(1), 1-6.* doi:10.1088/1757-899X/455/1/012074

Agrawal, P., & Narain, R. (2021). Analysis of enablers for the digitalization of supply chain using an interpretive structural modelling approach. *International Journal of Productivity and Performance Management.* Advance online publication. doi:10.1108/IJPPM-09-2020-0481

Agrawal, P., Narain, R., & Ullah, I. (2019). Analysis of barriers in implementation of digital transformation of supply chain using interpretive structural modelling approach. *Journal of Modelling in Management, 15*(1), 297–317. doi:10.1108/JM2-03-2019-0066

Agrawal, S., De Smet, A., Lacroix, S., & Reich, A. (2020). *To emerge stronger from the COVID-19 crisis, companies should start reskilling their workforces now.* McKinsey & Company.

Agrawal, S., & Tiwari, M. K. (2008). A collaborative ant colony algorithm to stochastic mixed-model u-shaped disassembly line balancing and sequencing problem. *International Journal of Production Research, 46*(6), 1405–1429. doi:10.1080/00207540600943985

Agrawal, T. K., Kumar, V., Pal, R., Wang, L., & Chen, Y. (2021). Blockchain-based framework for supply chain traceability: A case example of textile and clothing industry. *Computers & Industrial Engineering, 154*, 107130. doi:10.1016/j.cie.2021.107130

Agrawal, V. V., & Ulku, S. (2012). The role of modular upgradability as a green design strategy. *Manufacturing & Service Operations Management, 15*(4), 640–648. doi:10.1287/msom.1120.0396

Ahearne, M., Jelinek, R., & Jones, E. (2007). Examining the effect of salesperson service behavior in a competitive context. *Journal of the Academy of Marketing Science, 35*(4), 603–616. doi:10.100711747-006-0013-1

Ahmed, S., Taqi, H. M. M., Farabi, Y. I., Sarker, M., Ali, S. M., & Sankaranarayanan, B. (2021). Evaluation of Flexible Strategies to Manage the COVID-19 Pandemic in the Education Sector. *Global Journal of Flexible Systems Management*, 1–25. doi:10.1007/s40171-021-00267-9

Aich, S., Muduli, K., Onik, M. M. H., & Kim, H. C. (2018). A novel approach to identify the best practices of quality management in SMES based on critical success factors using interpretive structural modeling (ISM). *IACSIT International Journal of Engineering and Technology, 7*(3), 130–133. doi:10.14419/ijet.v7i3.29.18540

Aigbavboa, S., & Mbohwa, C. (2020). The headache of medicines' supply in Nigeria: An exploratory study on the most critical challenges of pharmaceutical outbound value chains. *Procedia Manufacturing, 43*, 336–343. doi:10.1016/j.promfg.2020.02.170

Ailawadi, S. C. R. S. (2005). Logistics Management. New Delhi: Prentice Hall of India.

Aksoy, A., & Öztürk, N. (2011). Supplier selection and performance evaluation in just-in-time production environments. *Expert Systems with Applications, 38*(5), 6351–6359. doi:10.1016/j.eswa.2010.11.104

Akter, S., Michael, K., Uddin, M. R., McCarthy, G., & Rahman, M. (2022). Transforming business using digital innovations: The application of AI, blockchain, cloud and data analytics. *Annals of Operations Research, 308*(1-2), 7–39. doi:10.100710479-020-03620-w

Al Humdan, E., Shi, Y., Behnia, M., & Najmaei, A. (2020). Supply chain agility: A systematic review of definitions, enablers and performance implications. *International Journal of Physical Distribution & Logistics Management, 50*(2), 287–312. doi:10.1108/IJPDLM-06-2019-0192

Alaoui, S. (2020). *How who connects the links in the covid-19 supply chain.* United Nations Foundation. https://unfoundation.org/blog/post/how-who-connects-links-covid-19-supply-chain/?gclid=EAIaIQobChMI44Tf7PWl8QIVFuTICh2uPAGbEAAYAiAAEgItvPD_BwE

Alaton, P., Djehiche, B., & Stillberger, D. (2002). On Modelling and Pricing Weather Derivatives. *Applied Mathematical Finance, 9*(1), 1–20. doi:10.1080/13504860210132897

Albers, A., Gladysz, B., Pinner, T., Butenko, V., & Stürmlinger, T. (2016). Procedure for defining the system of objectives in the initial phase of an industry 4.0 project focusing on intelligent quality control systems. *Procedia CIRP, 52*, 262–267. doi:10.1016/j.procir.2016.07.067

Aleksandra, C., Anna, B., & Halemba, H. (2017). Lean supply chain management. *World Scientific News*, 177–183.

Ali, A., Mahfouz, A., & Arisha, A. (2017). Analysing supply chain resilience: integrating the constructs in a concept mapping framework via a systematic literature review. In Supply Chain Management (Vol. 22, Issue 1, pp. 16–39). Emerald Group Publishing Ltd. doi:10.1108/SCM-06-2016-0197

Ali, M., Nelson, J. C., Shea, R., & Freedman, M. J. (2016). Blockstack: A Global Naming and Storage System Secured by Blockchains. *Proceedings of the 2016 USENIX Annual Technical Conference (USENIX ATC '16),* 181–94.

Ali, M., Nelson, J. C., Shea, R., & Freedman, M. J. (2016). Blockstack: A Global Naming and Storage System Secured by Blockchains. *Proceedings of the 2016 USENIX Annual Technical Conference (USENIX ATC '16)*, 181–94.

Alibaba Group. (2018). *Alibaba to Acquire Full Ownership of China Online Delivery Platform Ele.me.* https://www.alibabagroup.com/en/news/article?news=p180402

Alibaba Group. (2020). *Alibaba Group Holding Limited: United Stated Securities and Exchange Commission.* https://www.alibabagroup.com/en/ir/pdf/2020AR_Form20F.pdf

Alibaba Group. (2021). *Our business.* https://www.alibabagroup.com/en/about/businesses

Alicke, K., Azcue, X., & Barriball, E. (2020). *Supply-chain recovery in corona virus times – plan for now and the future.* Available at: www.mckinsey.com/_/media/McKinsey/Business%20Functions/Operations/Our%20Insights/Supply%20chain%20recovery%20in%20coronavirus%20times%20plan%20for%20now%20and%20the%20future/Supply-chain-recovery-in-coronavirus-times-plan-for-now-andthe-future.pdf

Alicke, K., Gupta, R., & Trautwein, V. (2020, July 21). *Resetting supply chains for the next normal.* McKinsey & Company. https://www.mckinsey.com/business-functions/operations/our-insights/resetting-supply-chains-for-the-next-normal#

Ali, I., & Gölgeci, I. (2019). Where is supply chain resilience research heading? A systematic and co-occurrence analysis. *International Journal of Physical Distribution & Logistics Management, 49*(8), 793–815. doi:10.1108/IJPDLM-02-2019-0038

*Compilation of References*

Alizadeh, A.H. (2013). *Trading Volume and Volatility in the Shipping Forward Freight Market*. Academic Press.

Alizila.com. (2021). *Ele.me Unveils Upgrades to Meet Needs of China's On-demand Economy*. https://www.alizila.com/eleme-upgrades-to-meet-needs-of-china-on-demand-economy/

Aljadeed, R., AlRuthia, Y., Balkhi, B., Sales, I., Alwhaibi, M., Almohammed, O., Alotaibi, A. J., Alrumaih, A. M., & Asiri, Y. (2021). The Impact of COVID-19 on Essential Medicines and Personal Protective Equipment Availability and Prices in Saudi Arabia. *Healthcare (Basel)*, *9*(3), 290. Advance online publication. doi:10.3390/healthcare9030290 PMID:33800012

Alliance, D.-P. (2015). *Opportunities and Requirements for Leveraging Big Data for Official Statistics and the Sustainable Development Goals in Latin America*. Data-Pop Alliance. Hardvard Humanitarian Initiative.

Almutairi, A. M., Salonitis, K., & Al-Ashaab, A. (2020). A framework for implementing lean principles in the supply chain management at health-care organizations Saudi's perspective. *International Journal of Lean Six Sigma*, *11*(3), 463–492. doi:10.1108/IJLSS-01-2019-0002

Alotaibi, S., & Mehmood, R. (2017). *Big data enabled healthcare supply chain management: opportunities and challenges*. Paper presented at the International Conference on Smart Cities, Infrastructure, Technologies and Applications, Cham.

ALSaqa, Z. H., Hussein, A. I., & Mahmood, S. M. (2019). The impact of blockchain on accounting information systems. *Journal of Information Technology Management*, *11*(3), 62–80.

Al-Shboul, M. A. R., Barber, K. D., Jose, A. G., Kumar, V., & Abdi, M. R. (2017). The effect of supply chain management practices on supply chain and manufacturing firms' performance. *Journal of Manufacturing Technology Management*, *28*(5), 577–609. doi:10.1108/JMTM-11-2016-0154

Al-Talib, M., Melhem, W. Y., Anosike, A. I., Garza Reyes, J. A., Nadeem, S. P., & Kumar, A. (2020). Achieving resilience in the supply chain by applying IoT technology. *Procedia CIRP*, *91*(91), 752–757. doi:10.1016/j.procir.2020.02.231

Altay, N., & Green, W. G. III. (2006). OR/MS research in disaster operations management. *European Journal of Operational Research*, *175*(1), 475–493. doi:10.1016/j.ejor.2005.05.016

Altay, N., Gunasekaran, A., Dubey, R., & Childe, S. J. (2018). Agility and Resilience as Antecedents of Supply Chain Performance Under Moderating Effects of Organizational Culture Within the Humanitarian Setting: A Dynamic Capability View. *Production Planning and Control*, *29*(14), 1158–1174. doi:10.1080/09537287.2018.1542174

Amalia, S., Darma, D. C., & Maria, S. (2020). Supply Chain Management and the Covid-19 Outbreak: Optimizing its Role for Indonesia. *Current Research Journal of Social Sciences and Humanities*, *3*(2), 196–202. doi:10.12944/CRJSSH.3.2.07

Amankwah-Amoah, J., & Syllias, J. (2020). Can adopting ambitious environmental sustainability initiatives lead to business failures? An analytical framework. *Business Strategy and the Environment*, *29*, 240–249. doi:10.1002/bse.2361

Amiri, A. (2006). Designing a distribution network in a supply chain system: Formulation and efficient solution procedure. *European Journal of Operational Research, 171*(2), 567-576.

Amulya Gurtu, J. J. (2021). Supply Chain Risk Management: Literature Review. *MDPI*, 1-16.

Anable, J., Brand, C., Tran, M., & Eyre, N. (2012). Modeling transport energy demand: A socio-technical approach. *Energy Policy*, *41*, 125–138. doi:10.1016/j.enpol.2010.08.020

Analysys. (2015). *China's Internet Catering Take-out Living Community Market Segmentation Report 2015*. https://www.analysys.cn/article/detail/11671

Analysys. (2020). *Annual Analysis of China Internet Catering Take-out Market 2020.* https://www.analysys.cn/article/detail/20019783

Anbumozhi, V., Kimura, F., & Thangavelu, S. M. (2020). Global supply chain resilience: Vulnerability and shifting risk management strategies. In V. Anbumozhi, F. Kimura, & S. Thangavelu (Eds.), *Supply chain resilience.* Springer. doi:10.1007/978-981-15-2870-5_1

Andic, E., Yurt, O., & Baltacioglu, T. (2012). Green supply chains: Efforts and potential applications for the Turkish market. *Resources, Conservation and Recycling, 58,* 50–68. doi:10.1016/j.resconrec.2011.10.008

Angeles, R. (2005). RFID technologies: Supply-chain applications and implementation issues. *Information Systems Management, 22*(1), 51–65. doi:10.1201/1078/44912.22.1.20051201/85739.7

Angelis, R. D., Howard, M., & Miemczyk, J. (2018). Supply chain management and the circular economy: Towards the circular supply chain. *Production Planning and Control, 29*(6), 425–437. doi:10.1080/09537287.2018.1449244

Angel-Korman, A., Brosh, T., Glick, K., & Leib, A. (2020). COVID-19, the kidney and hypertension. *Harefuah, 159,* 231–234. PMID:32307955

Anjaneyulu, J., Sreechandana, K., & Madhavi Laitha, V. V. (2021). Management of Big Data in Contemporary World. doi:10.20944/preprints202105.0663.v1

Anker, T. B. (2021). At the boundary: Post-COVID agenda for business and management research in Europe and beyond. *European Management Journal, 39*(2), 171–178. doi:10.1016/j.emj.2021.01.003

Anner, M. (2020). *Leveraging desperation: apparel brands' purchasing practices during COVID-19.* PennState Center for Global Workers' Rights (CGWR). Available at: https://ler. la. psu. edu/gwr/documents/LeveragingDesperation_October162020. pdf

APICS. (2017). *Association for Supply Chain Management, Supply Chain Operations Reference Model.* Version: 12.

Appel, F. (2012). *New Models for Addressing Supply Chain and Transport Risk.* Cologny: World Economic Forum.

Aptel, O., & Pourjalali, H. (2001). Improving activities and decreasing costs of logistics in hospitals: A comparison of US and French hospitals. *The International Journal of Accounting, 36*(1), 65–90. doi:10.1016/S0020-7063(01)00086-3

Araz, O. M., Choi, T.-M., Olson, D. L., & Salman, F. S. (2020). Data analytics for operational risk management. *Decision Sciences, 51*(6), 1316–1319. doi:10.1111/deci.12443

Araz, O. M., Choi, T.-M., Olson, D., & Salman, F. S. (2020). Data Analytics for Operational Risk Management. *Decision Sciences.*

Archer, N., Wang, S., & Kang, C. (2008). Barriers to the adoption of online supply chain solutions in small and medium enterprises. *Supply Chain Management, 13*(1), 73–82. doi:10.1108/13598540810850337

Ardito, L., Petruzzelli, A. M., Panniello, U., & Garavelli, A. C. (2018). Towards Industry 4.0. *Business Process Management Journal, 25*(2), 323–346. doi:10.1108/BPMJ-04-2017-0088

Arenkov, I., Tsenzharik, M., & Vetrova, M. (2019). Digital technologies in supply chain management. *Proceedings of the International Conference on Digital Technologies in Logistics and Infrastructure,* 453-458.

Arlbjørn, J. S., de Haas, H., & Munksgaard, K. B. (2011). Exploring supply chain innovation. *Logistics Research, 3*(1), 3–18. doi:10.100712159-010-0044-3

*Compilation of References*

Arora, R. (2020). Which Companies did well during the Coronavirus Pandemic? *Forbes*. Available: https://www.forbes.com/sites/rohitarora/2020/06/30/which-companies-did-well-during-the-coronavirus-pandemic/?sh=4ec218447409

Arunachalam, D., Kumar, N., & Kawalek, J. P. (2017). Understanding big data analytics capabilities in supply chain management: Unravelling the issues, challenges and implications for practice. *Transportation Research Part E, Logistics and Transportation Review*. Advance online publication. doi:10.1016/j.tre.2017.04.001

Asamoah, D., Nuertey, D., Agyei-Owusu, B., & Akyeh, J. (2021). The effect of supply chain responsiveness on customer development. *International Journal of Logistics Management*, 32(4), 1190–1213. Advance online publication. doi:10.1108/IJLM-03-2020-0133

ASCI. (2020). *COVID-19 Pandemic Adds To Ethical Issues In Global Supply Chains*. Available at: https://www.asci-2021.com.au/covid-19-pandemic-adds-to-ethical-issues-in-global-supply-chains/

Aslam, H., Blome, C., Roscoe, S., & Azhar, T. H. (2020). Determining the antecedents of dynamic supply chain capabilities. *Supply Chain Management*, 25(4), 427–442. doi:10.1108/SCM-02-2019-0074

Aslam, H., Khan, A. Q., Rashid, K., & Rehman, S. (2020). Achieving supply chain resilience: The role of supply chain ambidexterity and supply chain agility. *Journal of Manufacturing Technology Management*, 31(6), 1185–1204. doi:10.1108/JMTM-07-2019-0263

Association for Supply Chain Management. (2021). *2021 Top 10 supply chain trends*. ASCM's Research, Innovation and Strategy (RISC) Sensing Subcommittee, Assocation for Supply Chain Management. https://www.ascm.org/globalassets/ascm_website_assets/docs/5.9-2021-top-10-trends.pdf

Atasu, A., Sarvary, M., & Van Wassenhove, L. N. (2008). Remanufacturing as a marketing strategy. *Management Science*, 54(10), 1731–1746. doi:10.1287/mnsc.1080.0893

Ates, A., & Bititci, U. (2011). Change process: A key enabler for building resilient SMEs. *International Journal of Production Research*, 49(18), 5601–5618. doi:10.1080/00207543.2011.563825

Attaran, M. (2020). 3D Printing Role in Filling the Critical Gap in the Medical Supply Chain during COVID-19 Pandemic. *American Journal of Industrial and Business Management*, 10(05), 988–1001. doi:10.4236/ajibm.2020.105066

Auer, J. (2003). *Weather Derivatives Heading for Sunny Times*. Available at http://www.dbresearch.com/ PROD/999/PROD0000000000052399.pdf

Auger, P., Burke, P., Devinney, T. M., & Louviere, J. J. (2003). What Will Consumers Pay for Social Product Features? *Journal of Business Ethics*, 42(3), 281–304. doi:10.1023/A:1022212816261

Aurora Denial, O. D. (2021). Keeping Disruptive Technologies in Perspective. *Optometric Education*, 46(2), 2020.

Avittathur, B. S., & Swamidass, P. (2007). Matching plant flexibility and supplier flexibility: Lessons from small suppliers of US manufacturing plants in India. *Journal of Operations Management*, 25(3), 717–735. doi:10.1016/j.jom.2006.05.015

Awan, U., Sroufe, R., & Shahbaz, M. (2021). Industry 4.0 and the circular economy: A literature review and recommendations for future research. *Business Strategy and the Environment*, 30(4), 2038–2060. doi:10.1002/bse.2731

Awasthi, A., & Kannan, G. (2016). Green supplier development program selection using NGT and Vikopr under fuzzy environment. *Computers & Industrial Engineering*, 91, 100–108. doi:10.1016/j.cie.2015.11.011

Ayantoyinbo, B. B. (2018). Impact of Inbound and Outbound Logistics. *Transport & Logistics*, 18(44), 69–76.

Aymen, S. (2021). The COVID-19 pandemic, social sustainability and global supply chain resilience: A review. *Corporate Governance*, 21(6), 1142–1154.

537

Azadegan, A., Mellat Parast, M., Lucianetti, L., Nishant, R., & Blackhurst, J. (2020). Supply Chain Disruptions and Business Continuity: An Empirical Assessment. *Journal of the Decison Sciences Institute*, *51*(1), 38–73. doi:10.1111/deci.12395

Azevedo, A. (Ed.). (2013). *Advances in sustainable and competitive manufacturing systems: 23rd international conference on flexible automation & intelligent manufacturing.* Springer Science & Business Media.

Bacchiega, E., Lambertini, L., & Mantovaini, A. (2011). Process and product innovation in a vertically differentiated industry. *International Game Theory Review*, *13*(02), 209–221. doi:10.1142/S0219198911002952

Bäckstrand, J., & Powell, D. (2021). Enhancing Supply Chain Capabilities in an ETO Context Through" Lean and Learn. *Operations and Supply Chain Management*, *14*(3), 360–367. doi:10.31387/oscm0460308

Bag, S., Wood, L. C., Xu, L., Dhamija, P., & Kayikci, Y. (2020). Big data analytics as an operational excellence approach to enhance sustainable supply chain performance. *Resources, Conservation and Recycling*, *153*, 104559. doi:10.1016/j.resconrec.2019.104559

Bai, C., & Sarkis, J. (2020). A supply chain transparency and sustainability technology appraisal model for blockchain technology. *International Journal of Production Research*, *58*(7), 2142–2162. doi:10.1080/00207543.2019.1708989

Bailey, J. E., & Pearson, S. W. (1983). Development of a tool for measuring and analyzing computer user satisfaction. *Management Science*, *29*(5), 530–545. doi:10.1287/mnsc.29.5.530

Baines, T. B. S., Benedettini, O., & Ball, P. (2012). Examining green production and its role within the competitive strategy of manufacturers. *Journal of Industrial Engineering and Management*, *5*(1), 53–87. doi:10.3926/jiem.405

Bakar, A. H., Lukman Hakim, I., Chong, S. C., & Lin, B. (2010). Measuring supply chain performance among public hospital laboratories. *International Journal of Productivity and Performance Management*, *59*(1), 75–97. doi:10.1108/17410401011006121

Baldry. (2020). *Why ethical supply chains are the route to success after COVID-19*. Available at: https://www.business-growthhub.com/manufacturing/resources/blog/2020/09/why-ethical-supply-chains-are-the-route-to-success-after-covid-19

Baldwin, R., & di Mauro, B. W. (Eds.). (2020). *Economics in the time of COVID-19*. CEPR Press.

Ballou, R. H. (1992). *Business Logistics Management* (3rd ed.). Prentice Hall.

Ballou, R. H. (2007). The evaluation and future of logistics and supply chain management. *European Business Review*, *19*(4), 332–348. doi:10.1108/09555340710760152

Banaitė, D. (2016). Towards circular economy: Analysis of indicators in the context of sustainable development. *Social Transformation in Contemporary Society*, *4*(9), 142–150.

Baral, M. M., & Verma, A. (2021). Cloud Computing Adoption for Healthcare: An Empirical Study Using SEM Approach. *FIIB Business Review*, *10*(3), 255–275. doi:10.1177/23197145211012505

Barasa, L., Knoben, J., Vermeulen, P., Kimuyu, P., & Kinyanjui, B. (2017). Institutions: re- sources and innovation in East Africa: a firm level approach. *Resources Policy*, *46*(1), 280–291. doi:10.1016/j.respol.2016.11.008

Barbate, V., Gade, R. N., & Raibagkar, S. S. (2021). COVID-19 and Its Impact on the Indian Economy. *Vision: The Journal of Business Perspective*. doi:10.1177/0972262921989126

Barbier, E. B., & Burgess, J. C. (2020). Sustainability and development after COVID-19. *World Development*, *135*, 105082. doi:10.1016/j.worlddev.2020.105082 PMID:32834381

*Compilation of References*

Baregheh, A., Rowley, J., & Sambrook, S. (2009). Towards a multidisciplinary definition of innovation. *Management Decision*, *47*(8), 1323–1339. doi:10.1108/00251740910984578

Barenji, A. V., Wang, W., Li, Z., & Guerra-Zubiaga, D. A. (2019). Intelligent E-commerce logistics platform using a hybrid agent-based approach. *Transportation Research Part E, Logistics and Transportation Review*, *126*, 15–31. https://doi.org/10.1016/j.tre.2019.04.002

Barman, A., Das, R., & De, P. K. (2021). Impact of COVID-19 in food supply chain: Disruptions and recovery strategy. *Current Research in Behavioral Sciences*, *2*, 2666–5182. doi:10.1016/j.crbeha.2021.100017

Barratt, M. (2004). Understanding the meaning of collaboration in the Supply chain. An International Journal. *Emerald Group Publishing Limited*, *9*(1), 30–42. doi:10.1108/13598540410517566

Barratt, M., & Barratt, R. (2011). Exploring internal and external supply chain linkages: Evidence from the field. *Journal of Operations Management*, *29*(5), 514–528. doi:10.1016/j.jom.2010.11.006

Barratt, M., & Oke, A. (2007). Antecedents of supply chain visibility in retail supply chains: A resource-based theory perspective. *Journal of Operations Management*, *25*(6), 1217–1233. doi:10.1016/j.jom.2007.01.003

Barriball, E., George, K., Marcos, I., & Radtke, P. (2020). Jump-starting resilient and reimagined operations. *McKinsey*. https://www.mckinsey.com/business-functions/operations/our-insights/jump-starting-resilient-and-reimagined-operations

Barrios. (2020). *Top 10 global supply chain risks*. https://www.xeneta.com/blog/global-supply-chain-risks

Barroso, A. P., Machado, V. H., Carvalho, H., & Cruz Machado, V. (2015). *Quantifying the Supply Chain Resilience, Applications of Contemporary Management Approaches in Supply Chains*. IntechOpen. . doi:10.5772/59580

Barroso, A. P., Machado, V. H., Barros, A. R., & Cruz Machado, V. (2010). Toward a resilient Supply Chain with supply disturbances. *IEEE International Conference on Industrial Engineering and Engineering Management*, 245-249, 10.1109/IEEM.2010.5674462

Bartkowiak, M. (2009). Weather derivatives. Zeszyty Naukowe/Poznań University of Economics, 112, 5–16.

Barve, A., & Muduli, K. (2011, September). Challenges to environmental management practices in Indian mining industries. *International Conference on Innovation, Management and Service IPEDR, 14*, 297-301.

Baryannis, G., Dani, S., & Antoniou, G. (2019). Predicting supply chain risks using machine learning: The trade-off between performance and interpretability. *Future Generation Computer Systems*, *101*, 993–1004. doi:10.1016/j.future.2019.07.059

Baryannis, G., Validi, S., Dani, S., & Antoniou, G. (2019). Supply chain risk management and artificial intelligence: State of the art and future research directions. *International Journal of Production Research*, *57*(7), 2179–2202. doi:10.1080/00207543.2018.1530476

Barykin, S. E., Kapustina, I. V., Korchagina, E. V., Sergeev, S. M., Yadykin, V. K., Abdimomynova, A., & Stepanova, D. (2021). Digital Logistics Platforms in the BRICS Countries: Comparative Analysis and Development Prospects. *Sustainability*, *13*(20), 11228. doi:10.3390u132011228

Bask, A. H. (2001). Relationships among TPL providers and members of supply chains - a strategic perspective. *Journal of Business and Industrial Marketing*, *10*(1), 470–486. doi:10.1108/EUM0000000006021

Basole, R. C., & Bellamy, M. A. (2014). Supply Network Structure, Visibility, and Risk Diffusion: A Computational Approach. *Decision Sciences*, *45*(4), 1–49. doi:10.1111/deci.12099

Batwa, A., & Norrman, A. (2020). A framework for exploring blockchain technology in supply chain management. *Operations and Supply Chain Management: An International Journal*, *13*(3), 294–306. doi:10.31387/oscm0420271

539

Bayles, D. L. (2001). *"E-commerce logistics and Fulfillment, Delivering the goods", Send It Back! The Role of Reverse Logistics*. Prentice Hall PTR.

BBC News. (2020, January 31). Worldwide cases overtake 2003 Sars outbreak. *BBC News.* https://www.bbc.com/news/world-51322733

BCI. (2019). *Supply chain resilience report.* https://insider.zurich.co.uk/app/uploads/2019/11/BCISupplyChainResilienceReportOctober2019SingleLow1.pdf

Beamon, B. M. (1999). Designing the green supply chain. *Logistics Information Management, 12*(4), 332–342. doi:10.1108/09576059910284159

Beamon, B. M. (1999). Measuring Supply Chain Performance. *International Journal of Operations & Production Management, 19*(3), 275–292. doi:10.1108/01443579910249714

Beaulieu, M., & Bentahar, O. (2021a). Digitalization of the healthcare supply chain: A roadmap to generate benefits and effectively support healthcare delivery. *Technological Forecasting and Social Change, 167*, 120717. doi:10.1016/j.techfore.2021.120717

Beier, F. J. (1995). The management of the supply chain for hospital pharmacies: A focus on inventory management practices. *Journal of Business Logistics, 16*(2), 153–173.

Beise, M., & Rennings, K. (2005). Lead markets and regulation: A framework for analyzing the international diffusion of environmental innovations. *Ecological Economics, 52*(1), 5–17. doi:10.1016/j.ecolecon.2004.06.007

Belhadi, A., Kamble, S. S., Zkik, K., Cherrafi, A., & Touriki, F. E. (2020). The integrated effect of Big Data Analytics, Lean Six Sigma and Green Manufacturing on the environmental performance of manufacturing companies: The case of North Africa. *Journal of Cleaner Production, 252*, 119903. doi:10.1016/j.jclepro.2019.119903

Belhadi, A., Kamble, S., Jabbour, C. J. C., Gunasekaran, A., Ndubisi, N. O., & Venkatesh, M. (2021). Manufacturing and service supply chain resilience to the COVID-19 outbreak: Lessons learned from the automobile and airline industries. *Technological Forecasting and Social Change, 163*, 120447. doi:10.1016/j.techfore.2020.120447 PMID:33518818

Belhadi, A., Mani, V., Kamble, S. S., Khan, S. A. R., & Verma, S. (2021). Artificial intelligence-driven innovation for enhancing supply chain resilience and performance under the effect of supply chain dynamism: An empirical investigation. *Annals of Operations Research.* Advance online publication. doi:10.100710479-021-03956-x PMID:33551534

Belinski, R., Peixe, A. M., Frederico, G. F., & Garza-Reyes, J. A. (2020). Organizational learning and Industry 4.0: Findings from a systematic literature review and research agenda. *Benchmarking, 27*(8), 2435–2457. doi:10.1108/BIJ-04-2020-0158

Bello, D. C., Lohtia, R., & Sangtani, V. (2004). An institutional analysis of supply chain innovations in global marketing channels. *Industrial Marketing Management, 33*(1), 57–64. doi:10.1016/j.indmarman.2003.08.011

Bello, W. (2013). *Capitalism's Last Stand? Deglobalization in the Age of Austerity.* Zed Books. doi:10.5040/9781350218895

Ben-Daya, M., Hassini, E., & Bahroun, Z. (2019). Internet of things and supply chain management: A literature review. *International Journal of Production Research, 57*(15-16), 4719–4742. doi:10.1080/00207543.2017.1402140

Ben-Gal, I., Katz, R., & Bukchin, Y. (2008). Robust eco-design: A new application for air quality engineering. *IIE Transactions, 40*(10), 907–918. doi:10.1080/07408170701775094

Bennis, W. G., & Nanus, B. (1985). *Leaders: Strategies for taking charge.* Harper & Row.

Benth, F. E. (2021). Pricing of Commodity and Energy Derivatives for Polynomial Processes. *Mathematics, 9*(2), 124. doi:10.3390/math9020124

Benzidia, S., Makaoui, N., & Bentahar, O. (2021). The impact of big data analytics and artificial intelligence on green supply chain process integration and hospital environmental performance. *Technological Forecasting and Social Change, 163*, 120557. doi:10.1016/j.techfore.2020.120557

Berg, J., & Myllymaa, L. (2021). *Impact of blockchain on sustainable supply chain practices: A study on blockchain technology's benefits and current barriers in sustainable SCM* (Dissertation). Retrieved from http://urn.kb.se/resolve? urn=urn:nbn:se:hj:diva-53810

Berg, E., Knudsen, D., & Norrman, A. (2008). Assessing performance of supply chain risk management programmes: A tentative approach. *International Journal of Risk Assessment and Management, 9*(3), 288–310. doi:10.1504/IJRAM.2008.019746

Berhane, T., Shibabaw, A., Awgichew, G., & Walelgn, A. (2021). Pricing of Weather Derivatives Based on Temperature by Obtaining Market Risk Factor From Historical Data Model. *Earth System. Environment, 7*(2), 871–884. doi:10.100740808-020-00925-4

Bernon, M., Rossi, S., & Cullen, J. (2011). Retail reverse logistics: A call and grounding framework for research. *International Journal of Physical Distribution & Logistics Management, 41*(5), 484–510.

Berry, L. L., & Parasuraman, A. (1991). *Marketing services: Competing through quality*. Free Press.

Beske, P., & Seuring, S. (2014). Putting Sustainability into Supply Chain Management. *Supply Chain Management, 19*(3), 322–331. doi:10.1108/SCM-12-2013-0432

Betz, U. A., Betz, F., Kim, R., Monks, B., & Phillips, F. (2019). Surveying the future of science, technology and business–A 35 year perspective. *Technological Forecasting and Social Change, 144*(1), 137–147. doi:10.1016/j.techfore.2019.04.005

Bevilacqua, M., Ciarapica, F. E., & Marcucci, G. (2017). Supply Chain Resilience Triangle: The Study and Development of a Framework. *World Academy of Science, Engineering and Technology, International Journal of Social, Behavioral, Educational, Economic, Business and Industrial Engineering, 11*(8), 2046–2053.

Bhagwat, R., & Sharma, M. K. (2009). An application of the integrated AHP-PGP model for performance measurement of supply chain management. *Production Planning and Control, 20*(8), 678–690. doi:10.1080/09537280903069897

Bhamra, R., Dani, S., & Burnard, K. (2011). Resilience: The concept, a literature review and future directions. *International Journal of Production Research, 49*(18), 5375–5393. doi:10.1080/00207543.2011.563826

Bharadwaj, A., El Sawy, O. A., Pavlou, P. A., & Venkatraman, N. (2013). Digital Business Strategy: Toward a Next Generation of Insights. *Management Information Systems Quarterly, 37*(2), 471–482. doi:10.25300/MISQ/2013/37:2.3

Bhatia, A., & Mittal, P. (2019). Big Data Driven Healthcare Supply Chain: Understanding Potentials and Capabilities. *Proceedings of International Conference on Advancements in Computing & Management (ICACM)*. 10.2139srn.3464217

Bigliardi, B., & Dormio, A. I. (2009). An empirical investigation of innovation determinants in food machinery enterprises. *European Journal of Innovation Management, 12*(2), 223–242. doi:10.1108/14601060910953988

Birkinshaw, J., Zimmermann, A., & Raisch, S. (2016). How do firms adapt to discontinuous change. *California Management Review, 58*(4), 36–58. doi:10.1525/cmr.2016.58.4.36

Biswal, J. N., Muduli, K., & Satapathy, S. (2017). Critical analysis of drivers and barriers of sustainable supply chain management in Indian thermal sector. *International Journal of Procurement Management, 10*(4), 411–430. doi:10.1504/IJPM.2017.085033

Biswal, J. N., Muduli, K., Satapathy, S., & Yadav, D. K. (2019). A TISM based study of SSCM enablers: An Indian coal-fired thermal power plant perspective. *International Journal of System Assurance Engineering and Management, 10*(1), 126–141. doi:10.100713198-018-0752-7

Bititci, U. S., Firat, S. U. O., & Garengo, P. (2013). How to compare performances of firms operating in different sectors? *Production Planning and Control, 24*(12), 1032–1049. doi:10.1080/09537287.2011.643829

Bitner, M. J. (1990). Evaluating service encounters; the effects of physical surroundings and employee responses. *Journal of Marketing, 54*(1), 69–82. doi:10.1177/002224299005400206

Bjorklund, M., Martinsen, U., & Abrahamsson, M. (2012), performance measurements in the greening of supply chains. *Supply Chain Management, 17*(1), 29-39. doi:10.1108/13598541211212186

Blackhurst, J., Craighead, C. W., Elkins, D., & Handfield, R. B. (2005). An empirically derived agenda of critical research issues for managing supply-chain disruptions. *International Journal of Production Research, 43*(19), 4067–4081. doi:10.1080/00207540500151549

Blackhurst, J., Dunn, K. S., & Craighead, C. W. (2011). An empirically derived framework of global supply resiliency. *Journal of Business Logistics, 32*(4), 374–391. doi:10.1111/j.0000-0000.2011.01032.x

Black, S., & Glaser-Segura, D. (2020). Supply Chain Resilience in a Pandemic: The Need for Revised Contingency Planning. *Management Dynamics in the Knowledge Economy, 8*(4), 325–343. doi:10.2478/mdke-2020-0021

Blanchard, D. (2007). *Supply Chain Management: Best Practices.* John Wiley & Sons.

Blandine, A., Omar, B., & Angappa, G. (2020). Digital supply chain: Challenges and future directions, *Supply Chain Forum. International Journal (Toronto, Ont.), 21*(3), 133–138. doi:10.1080/16258312.2020.1816361

BMA. (2021). *Fair medical trade.* Available at: https://www.bma.org.uk/what-we-do/working-internationally/our-international-work/fair-medical-trade

Bocquet, R. (2011). Product and process innovations in subcontracting: Empirical evidence from the French "Sillon Alpin". *Industry and Innovation, 18*(7), 649–668. doi:10.1080/13662716.2011.604471

Bode, C., Wagner, S. M., Petersen, K. J., & Ellram, L. M. (2011). Understanding responses to supply chain disruptions: Insights from information processing and resource dependence perspectives. *Academy of Management Journal, 54*(4), 833–856. doi:10.5465/amj.2011.64870145

Bohmer, R. M. J., Pisano, G. P., Sadun, R., & Tsai, T. C. (2020). How hospitals can manage supply chain shortages as demand surges. *Harvard Business Review.*

Boiral, O., Brotherton, M.-C., Rivaud, L., & Guillaumie, L. (2021). Organizations' Management of the COVID-19 Pandemic: A Scoping Review of Business Articles. *Sustainability, 2021*(13), 3993. doi:10.3390u13073993

Bokrantz, J., Skoogh, A., Berlin, C., & Stahre, J. (2017). Maintenance in digitalised manufacturing: Delphi-based scenarios for 2030. *International Journal of Production Economics, 191*, 154-169. doi:10.1016/j.ijpe.2017.06.010

Boonstra, A. (2006). Interpreting an ERP-implementation project from a stakeholder perspective. *International Journal of Project Management, 24*(1), 38–52. doi:10.1016/j.ijproman.2005.06.003

Borgatti, S., & Lopez–Kidwell, V. (2011). *Network Theory, Sage Handbook of Social Network Analysis.* Sage Publications.

*Compilation of References*

Borraz-Sa'nchez, C., & Ríos-Mercado, R. Z. (2009). Improving the operation of pipeline systems on cyclic structures by tabu search. *Computers & Chemical Engineering, 33*(1), 58–64. doi:10.1016/j.compchemeng.2008.07.009

Bowersox, D.J., Carter, P.L., & Monczka, R.L. (1985). Material Logistics Management. *International Journal of Physical Distribution& Materials Management, 15*(5), 27-35.

Bradley, R. V., Esper, T. L., In, J., Lee, K. B., Bichescu, B. C., & Byrd, A. (2018). The Joint Use of RFID and EDI: Implications for Hospital Performance. *ProdOperations Manage, 27*(11), 2071–2090. doi:10.1111/poms.12955

Brandon-Jones, E., Squire, B., Autry, C. W., & Petersen, K. J. (2014). A contingent resource-based perspective of supply chain resilience and robustness. *The Journal of Supply Chain Management, 50*(3), 55–73. doi:10.1111/jscm.12050

Braunscheidel, M. J. (2005). *Antecedents of Supply Chain Agility: An Empirical Investigation* (PhD Thesis). School of Management University of Buffalo the State University of New York.

Braunscheidel, M. J., & Suresh, N. C. (2009). The organizational antecedents of a firm's supply chain agility for risk mitigation and response. *Journal of Operations Management, 27*(2), 119–140. doi:10.1016/j.jom.2008.09.006

Bresnen, Bailey, Hyde, & Hassard. (Eds.). (2017). Managing Modern Healthcare - Knowledge, Networks and Practice. Taylor & Francis.

Brettel, M., Bendig, D., Keller, M., Friederichsen, N., & Rosenberg, M. (2014). Effectuation in manufacturing: How entrepreneurial decision-making techniques can be used to deal with uncertainty in manufacturing. *Procedia CIRP, 17*, 611–616. doi:10.1016/j.procir.2014.03.119

Brewer, A., Sloan, N., & Landers, T. L. (1999). Intelligent tracking in manufacturing. *Journal of Intelligent Manufacturing, 10*(3), 245–250. doi:10.1023/A:1008995707211

Brinch, M., Stentoft, J., & Jensen, J. K. (2017). Big data and its applications in supply chain management: Findings from a Delphi study. *Proceedings of the 50th Hawaii International Conference on System Sciences.* 10.24251/HICSS.2017.161

Brockett, P. L., Mulong, W., & Chuanhou, Y. (2005). Weather Derivates and Weather Risk Management. *Risk Management & Insurance Review, 8*(1), 127–140. doi:10.1111/j.1540-6296.2005.00052.x

Bromiley, P., & Rau, D. (2014). Towards a practice-based view of strategy. *Strategic Management Journal, 35*(8), 1249–1256. doi:10.1002mj.2238

Brown, T. J., Churchill. G., & Peter, J. (1993). Research note: Improving the measurement of service quality. *Journal of Retailing, 69*(1), 127-139.

Brun, I., Durif, F., & Ricard, L. (2014). E-relationship marketing: A cognitive mapping introspection in the banking sector. *European Journal of Marketing, 48*(3), 572–594. doi:10.1108/EJM-04-2012-0207

Bruno & Denecker. (2020). *Accelerating the winds of change in global payments.* McKinsey. Retrieved October 23, 2021, from https://www.mckinsey.com/industries/financial-services/our-insights/accelerating-winds-of-change-in-global-payments

Brusset, X., & Teller, C. (2017). Supply chain capabilities, risks, and resilience. *International Journal of Production Economics, 184*, 59–68. doi:10.1016/j.ijpe.2016.09.008

Brustlein, J. (2021). *How Ethical Supply Chains Will Survive the Pandemic.* Available at: https://www.supplychainbrain.com/blogs/1-think-tank/post/32671-how-ethical-supply-chains-can-survive-the-pandemic

Brydges, T., Heinze, L., Retamal, M., & Henninger, C. E. (2020). Platforms and the pandemic: A case study of fashion rental platforms during COVID-19. *The Geographical Journal.* Advance online publication. doi:10.1111/geoj.12366

BSI. (2014). *BS 6500 Standard for Organizational Resilience.* Available: bsigroup.com/organizational-resilience.

Buckley, N. (2003). *European Weather Derivatives.* Working paper. https://www.actuaries.org.uk/system/files/documents/pdf/european-weather-derivatives.pdf

Bullock, R. J., & Batten, D. (1985). It's just a phase we're going through: A review and synthesis of OD phase analysis. *Group & Organization Studies, 10*(4), 383–412. doi:10.1177/105960118501000403

Bulturbayevich, M. B., & Jurayevich, M. B. (2020). The impact of the digital economy on economic growth. *International Journal of Business, Law, and Education, 1*(1), 4–7.

Bunkley, N. (2011, March 18). Japan's Automakers Expect More Delays. *The New York Times.* https://www.nytimes.com/2011/03/19/business/global/19auto.html

Burgos, D., & Ivanov, D. (2021). Food Retail Supply Chain Resilience and the COVID-19 Pandemic: A Digital Twin-based Impact Analysis and Improvement Directions. *Transportation Research Part E, Logistics and Transportation Review, 152,* 1366–5545. doi:10.1016/j.tre.2021.102412 PMID:34934397

Burgress, K., Singh, P. J., & Koroglu, R. (2006). Supply chain management: A structured literature review and implications for future research. *International Journal of Operations & Production Management, 26*(7), 703–729. doi:10.1108/01443570610672202

Burns, L. R. (2005). *The Business of Healthcare Innovation.* Cambridge University Press. doi:10.1017/CBO9780511488672

Business Growth Hub. (2021). *The importance of being ethical: In Conversation with One+All.* Available at: https://www.businessgrowthhub.com/case-studies/oneplusall

Business Wire. (2020). *Food Delivery on the Rise Due to COVID-19 Lockdown.* https://www.businesswire.com/news/home/20200428005464/en/Food-Delivery-Rise-Due-COVID-19-Lockdown–

Busse, C. (2016). Doing well by doing good? The self-interest of buying firms and sustainable supply chain management. *The Journal of Supply Chain Management, 52*(2), 28–47. doi:10.1111/jscm.12096

Butner, K. (2010). The smarter supply chain of the future. *Strategy and Leadership, 38*(1), 22–31. doi:10.1108/10878571011009859

Buttle, F., & Maklan, S. (2019). *Customer Relationship Management: Concepts and Technologies.* Routledge. doi:10.4324/9781351016551

Butu, A., Brumă, I. S., Tanasă, L., Rodino, S., Vasiliu, C. D., Doboş, S., & Butu, M. (2020). The impact of COVID-19 crisis upon the consumer buying behavior of fresh vegetables directly from local producers. Case study: The quarantined area of Suceava County, Romania. *International Journal of Environmental Research and Public Health, 17*(15), 1–25. doi:10.3390/ijerph17155485 PMID:32751368

Büyüközkan, G., & Göçer, F. (2018). Digital Supply Chain: Literature review and a proposed framework for future research. *Computers in Industry, 97,* 157–177. doi:10.1016/j.compind.2018.02.010

BVL. (2017a). *Chancen der digitalen transformation. Trends und Strategien in Logistik and Supply Chain Management.* BVL and DVV Media. https://www.bvl.de/en/dossiers/tu

BVL. (2017b). Logistics as a science. Central research questions in the era of the fourth industrial revolution. Logist. Res., 11, 9. Doi:10.23773/2018_9

Cabral, I., Grilo, A., & Cruz-Machado, V. (2012). A decision-making model for lean, agile, resilient and green supply chain management. *International Journal of Production Research, 50*(17), 4830–4845. doi:10.1080/00207543.2012.657970

Cai, J., Liu, X., Xiao, Z., & Liu, J. (2009). Improving supply chain performance management: A systematic approach to analyzing iterative KPI accomplishment. *Decision Support Systems*, *46*(2), 512–521. doi:10.1016/j.dss.2008.09.004

Campbell, F. C. (2008). *Elements of Metallurgy and Engineering Alloys*. ASM International Publication. doi:10.31399/asm.tb.emea.9781627082518

Canh, P. N., Schinckus, C., & Dinh Thanh, S. (2021). What are the drivers of shadow economy? A further evidence of economic integration and institutional quality. *The Journal of International Trade & Economic Development*, *30*(1), 47–67. doi:10.1080/09638199.2020.1799428

Cao, M., & Wei, J. (2000). Pricing the Weather. *Risk (Concord, NH)*, *13*(5), 14–22.

Capgemini Research Institute. (2020). *Report: Building supply chain resilience-Capgemini*. https://www.capgemini.com/news/report-building-supply-chain-resilience

Caridi, M., Moretto, A., Perego, A., & Tumino, A. (2014). The benefits of supply chain visibility: A value assessment model. *International Journal of Production Economics*, *151*, 1–19. doi:10.1016/j.ijpe.2013.12.025

Carlsson-Szlezak, P., Reeves, M., & Swartz, P. (2020). What Coronavirus Could Mean for the Global Economy. *Harvard Business Review*. https://hbr.org/2020/03/what-coronavirus-could-mean-for-the-global-economy

Caro, F., Kök, A. G., & Martínez-de-Albéniz, V. (2020). The future of retail operations. *Manufacturing & Service Operations Management*, *22*(1), 47–58. doi:10.1287/msom.2019.0824

Carroll, A. B. (1991). The pyramid of corporate social responsibility: Toward the moral management of organizational stakeholders. *Business Horizons*, *34*(4), 42. doi:10.1016/0007-6813(91)90005-G

Carter, C. R., Kosmol, T., & Kaufmann, L. (2017). Toward a supply chain practice view. *The Journal of Supply Chain Management*, *53*(1), 114–122. doi:10.1111/jscm.12130

Carter, C., & Jennings, M. M. (2004). The role of purchasing in corporate social responsibility: A structural equation analysis. *Journal of Business Logistics*, *25*(1), 145–186. doi:10.1002/j.2158-1592.2004.tb00173.x

Carter, C., & Rogers, D. (2008). A framework of sustainable supply chain management: Moving toward new theory. *International Journal of Physical Distribution & Logistics Management*, *38*(5), 360–387. doi:10.1108/09600030810882816

Carvalho, H., Duarte, S., & Machado, V. C. (2011). Lean, agile, resilient and green: Divergencies and synergies. *International Journal of Lean Six Sigma*, *2*(2), 151–179. doi:10.1108/20401461111135037

Casado-Vara, R., Prieto, J., De la Prieta, F., & Corchado, J. M. (2018). How blockchain improves the supply chain: Case study alimentary supply chain. *Procedia Computer Science*, *134*, 393–398. doi:10.1016/j.procs.2018.07.193

Cascio, J. (2009). Resilience. *Foreign Policy, 92*. Retrieved from https://www-proquest.com.aus.idm.oclc.org/magazines/resilience/docview/224032941/se-2?accountid=16946

Catalano, R. F., Berglund, M. L., Ryan, J. A. M., Lonczak, H. S., & Hawkins, J. D. (2002). Positive youth development in the United States: Research findings on evaluations of positive youth development programs. *Prevention and Treatment, 5*(1), 15. Retrieved from http://content.apa.org/journals/pre/5/1/15

CBP. (2020). *CBP Revokes Withhold Release Order on Disposable Rubber Gloves*. Available at: https://www.cbp.gov/newsroom/national-media-release/cbp-revokes-withhold-release-order-disposable-rubber-gloves

Chamola, V., Hassija, V., Gupta, V., & Guizani, M. (2020). A comprehensive review of the COVID-19 pandemic and the role of IoT, drones, AI, blockchain, and 5G in managing its impact. *IEEE Access : Practical Innovations, Open Solutions*, *8*, 90225–90265. doi:10.1109/ACCESS.2020.2992341

Chandra, C., & Kachhal, S. K. (2004). Managing health care supply chain: trends, issues, and solutions from a logistics perspective. *Proceedings of the sixteenth annual society of health systems management engineering forum.*

Chang, Y., Iakovou, E., & Shi, W. (2019). *Blockchain in Global Supply Chains and Cross Border Trade: A Critical Synthesis of the State-of-the-Art, Challenges and Opportunities.* Academic Press.

Chan, L. K., & Wu, M. L. (2002). Quality function deployment: A comprehensive review of its concepts and methods. *Quality Engineering, 15*(1), 23–35. doi:10.1081/QEN-120006708

Chan, L. K., & Wu, M. L. (2002a). Quality function deployment: A literature review. *European Journal of Operational Research, 143*(3), 463–497. doi:10.1016/S0377-2217(02)00178-9

Chan, L. K., & Wu, M. L. (2005). A systematic approach to quality function deployment with a full illustrative example. *Omega, 33*(2), 119–139. doi:10.1016/j.omega.2004.03.010

Chapman, R. L., Soosay, C., & Kandampully, J. (2002). Innovation in logistic services and the new business model: A conceptual framework. *Managing Service Quality, 12*(6), 358–371. doi:10.1108/09604520210451849

Chatur, A. (2005). *Driving Costs out of the Supply Chain.* Infosys Technologies Limited.

Chavan, V., Jadhav, P., Korade, S., & Teli, P. (2015). Implementing Customizable Online Food Ordering System Using Web Based Application. *International Journal of Innovative Science, Engineering & Technology, 2*(4). http://ijiset.com/vol2/v2s4/IJISET_V2_I4_112.pdf

Chavez, R., Yu, W., Jacobs, M. A., & Feng, M. (2017). Data-driven supply chains, manufacturing capability and customer satisfaction. *Production Planning and Control, 28*(11-12), 906–918. doi:10.1080/09537287.2017.1336788

Chen, C. C., Shih, H. S., Shyur, H. J., & Wu, K.-S. (2012). A business strategy selection of green supply chain management via an analytic network process. *Computers & Mathematics with Applications (Oxford, England), 64*(8), 2544–2557. doi:10.1016/j.camwa.2012.06.013

Chen, D. Q., Preston, D. S., & Swink, M. (2016). How the Use of Big Data Analytics Affects Value Creation in Supply Chain Management. *Journal of Management Information Systems, 32*(4), 4–39. doi:10.1080/07421222.2015.1138364

Chen, F., Federgruen, A., & Zheng, Y.-S. (2001). Near-Optimal Pricing and Replenishment Strategies for a Retail/Distribution System. *Operations Research, 49*(6), 839–853. doi:10.1287/opre.49.6.839.10020

Cheng, C.-C., Chang, Y.-Y., & Chen, C.-T. (2021). Construction of a Service Quality Scale for the Online Food Delivery Industry. *International Journal of Hospitality Management, 95,* 102938. doi:10.1016/j.ijhm.2021.102938

Chen, H. (2018). Supply chain risk's impact on corporate financial performance. *International Journal of Operations & Production Management, 38*(3), 713–731. doi:10.1108/IJOPM-02-2016-0060

Chen, H. Y., Das, A., & Ivanov, D. (2019). Building resilience and managing post-disruption supply chain recovery: Lessons from the information and communication technology industry. *International Journal of Information Management, 49*(June), 330–342. doi:10.1016/j.ijinfomgt.2019.06.002

Chen, I. J., & Paulraj, A. (2004). Towards a theory of supply chain management: The constructs and measurements. *Journal of Operations Management, 22*(2), 119–150. doi:10.1016/j.jom.2003.12.007

Chen, J., & Bell, P. C. (2013). The impact of customer returns on supply chain decisions under various channel interactions. *Annals of Operations Research, 206,* 59–74. https://doi.org/10.1007/s10479-013-1326-3

*Compilation of References*

Chen, T., Wang, Y. C., & Wu, H. C. (2021). Analyzing the Impact of Vaccine Availability on Alternative Supplier Selection Amid the COVID-19 Pandemic: A cFGM-FTOPSIS-FWI Approach. *Healthcare (Basel)*, *9*(1), 71. Advance online publication. doi:10.3390/healthcare9010071 PMID:33451165

Chesbrough, H. (2020). To recover faster from Covid-19, open up: Managerial implications from an open innovation perspective. *Industrial Marketing Management*, *88*, 410–413. doi:10.1016/j.indmarman.2020.04.010

China baogao.com. (2020). *At the Beginning of 2020, China's Food and Beverage Food Delivery Industry Policy Favorable Food Delivery Market May Usher in a Wave of High Growth*. https://tuozi.chinabaogao.com/jiudiancanyin/03314V3952020.html

China Council for the Promotion of International Trade. (2020a). *CCPIT Released a Report: 70% of the Catering Industry's Total Revenue Growth is Driven by Take-out Business*. https://www.ccpit.org/Contents/Channel_4035/2020/0531/1264357/content_1264357.htm

China Council for the Promotion of International Trade. (2020b). *IWA on Guidelines for Contactless Delivery Service*. https://www.ccpit.org/Contents/Channel_4113/2020/0521/1262238/content_1262238.htm

China Dining Industry Association. (2021). *Technical Guide for COVID-19 Prevention and Control in Catering Service Units*. http://www.chcdia.cn/xiehuidongtai/1/768.html

China Hospitality Association. (2019a). *MeiTuan Dianping Unmanned Delivery Team Presented at the World Artificial Intelligence Conference*. http://www.chinahotel.org.cn/forward/enterenterSecondDaryOther.do?contentId=431f924e4ff64f0b82a99d08d2b0c7e4

China Hospitality Association. (2019b). *Wang Xing, CEO of MeiTuan Dianping: Digitalization on the Supply Side Has a Long Way to Go and is Full of Challenges*. http://www.chinahotel.org.cn/forward/enterenterSecondDaryOther.do?contentId=e117f0e870e14e5b934f955a24b27635

China Hospitality Association. (2020). *China Hospitality Association Actively Communicated with Ali Local Life Service Companies (Ele. me and Koubei) to Implement the Policy of Reducing Commission on the Platform to Help Small and Medium-sized Merchants*. http://www.chinahotel.org.cn/forward/enterenterSecondDaryOther.do?contentId=151b7d3a87804dee83356e585d3477f3

China Hospitality Association. (2021). *Xiaoming Shi: Strive for the "14th Five-Year Plan" to Build an Open and Win-win Platform for the Take-out Industry*. http://www.chinahotel.org.cn/forward/enterenterSecondDaryOther.do?contentId=64a7b024d05f4fbe837032613d8c0d42

China news. (2021). *Those in the Catering, Tourism and Exhibition Industries That are Heavily Affected by the Epidemic, don't Miss the Benefits of These Policies*. http://www.chinanews.com/sh/2021/03-19/9435901.shtml

Cho, H., & Lee, S. (2016). A study on consumer awareness and determinants of overseas direct purchase: Focused on moderating effects of logistics infrastructure and market uncertainty. *International Commerce and Information Review*, *18*(3), 23–43.

Choi, T. M. (2020). Innovative "bring-service-near-your-home" operations under corona-virus (COVID-19/SARS-CoV-2) outbreak: Can logistics become the messiah? *Transportation Research Part E, Logistics and Transportation Review*, *140*, 101961. doi:10.1016/j.tre.2020.101961 PMID:32346356

Choi, T. M., Guo, S., & Luo, S. (2020). When blockchain meets social-media: Will the result benefit social media analytics for supply chain operations management? *Transportation Research Part E, Logistics and Transportation Review*, *135*, 101860. doi:10.1016/j.tre.2020.101860

Choi, Y., Zhang, L., Debbarma, J., & Lee, H. (2021). Sustainable Management of Online to Offline Delivery Apps for Consumers' Reuse Intention: Focused on the MeiTuan Apps. *Sustainability*, *13*(7), 3593. doi:10.3390u13073593

Chong, A. Y., Chan, F. T., Ooi, K. B., & Sim, J. J. (2011). Can Malaysian firms improve organizational/innovation performance via SCM? *Industrial Management & Data Systems*, *111*(3), 410–431. doi:10.1108/02635571111118288

Chopra, S. & Meindl, P. (2004). *Supply chain management: Strategy, planning and operation.* Pearson Education Inc.

Chopra, S.C., M. S. (2004). Managing risk to avoid supply-chain breakdown. *MIT Sloan Management Review*, *1*(46), 53–61.

Chopra, S., & Meindl, P. (2015). *Supply chain management: Strategy, Planning, and Operation* (4th ed.). Pearson Education.

Chopra, S., & Meindl, P. (2016). *Supply chain management: Strategy, planning, and operation* (6th ed.). Pearson.

Chopra, S., & Sodhi, M. S. (2014). Reducing the Risk of Supply Chain Disruptions. *MIT Sloan Management Review*, *55*, 73–80.

Chowdhury, M. M. H., & Quaddus, M. (2017). Supply chain resilience: Conceptualization and scale development using dynamic capability theory. *International Journal of Production Economics*, *188*, 185–204. doi:10.1016/j.ijpe.2017.03.020

Chowdhury, M. M. H., Quaddus, M., & Agarwal, R. (2019). Supply chain resilience for performance: Role of relational practices and network complexities. *Supply Chain Management*, *24*(5), 659–676. doi:10.1108/SCM-09-2018-0332

Chowdhury, M. M., & Quaddus, M. (2016). Supply chain readiness, response and recovery for resilience. *Supply Chain Management*, *21*(6), 709–731. doi:10.1108/SCM-12-2015-0463

Chowdhury, M. T., Sarkar, A., Saha, P. K., & Anik, R. H. (2020). Enhancing supply resilience in the COVID-19 pandemic: A case study on beauty and personal care retailers. *Modern Supply Chain Research and Applications*, *2*(3), 143–159. doi:10.1108/MSCRA-07-2020-0018

Chowdhury, P., Kumar Paul, S., Kaisar, S., & Abdul Moktadir, M. (2021). COVID-19 pandemic related supply chain studies: A systematic review. *Transportation Research Part E, Logistics and Transportation Review*, *148*, 102271. doi:10.1016/j.tre.2021.102271 PMID:33613082

Christiansen, M. K. F. (2007). Maritime Transportation. In Handbook in Operation Research and Management (Vol. 14). Elsevier B.V.

Christmann, P. (2000). Effects of "Best Practices" of environmental management on cost advantages: The role of complementary assets. *Academy of Management Journal*, *43*(4), 663–680.

Christopher, M. (2005). *Logistics and Supply Chain Management.* FT Prentice Hall.

Christopher, M. (2011). Logistics and customer value. In Logistics & Supply Chain Management (4th ed., pp. 27-50). London: Pearson Education Limited.

Christopher, M. (1998). *Logistics and Supply Chain Management: Strategies for reducing cost and improving service.* Prentice Hall.

Christopher, M. (2000). The agile supply chain competing in volatile markets. *Industrial Marketing Management*, *29*(1), 37–44. doi:10.1016/S0019-8501(99)00110-8

Christopher, M. (2016). *Logistics and Supply Chain Management* (5th ed.). Prentice Hall.

Christopher, M., & Holweg, M. (2011). Supply Chain 2.0: Managing supply chains in the era of turbulence. *International Journal of Physical Distribution & Logistics Management*, *41*(1), 63–82. doi:10.1108/09600031111101439

*Compilation of References*

Christopher, M., & Lee, H. (2004). Mitigating supply chain risk through improved confidence. *International Journal of Physical Distribution & Logistics Management, 34*(5), 388–396. doi:10.1108/09600030410545436

Christopher, M., & Peck, H. (2004). Building the resilient supply chain. *International Journal of Logistics Management, 15*(2), 1–13. doi:10.1108/09574090410700275

Chu, C.-H., Luh, Y.-P., Li, T.-C., & Chen, H. (2009). Economical green product design based on simplified computer-aided product structure variation. *Computers in Industry, 60*(7), 485–500. doi:10.1016/j.compind.2009.02.003

Chui, M., Löffler, M., & Roberts, R. (2010). The internet of things. *The McKinsey Quarterly*, (2), 70–79.

Chui, M., Loffler, M., & Roberts, R. (2010). The internet of things. *The McKinsey Quarterly, 2*, 1–9.

Chunsheng, L., Wong, C. W. Y., Yang, C.-C., Shang, K.-C., & Lirn, T. (2020). Value of supply chain resilience: Roles of culture, flexibility, and integration. *International Journal of Physical Distribution & Logistics Management, 50*(1), 80–100. doi:10.1108/IJPDLM-02-2019-0041

Cigolini, R., & Rossi, T. (2010). Managing operational risks along the oil supply chain. *Production Planning and Control, 21*(5), 452–467. doi:10.1080/09537280903453695

Clancy, H. (2017, February 6). *The blockchain's emerging role in sustainability*. GreenBiz. https://www.greenbiz.com/article/blockchains-emerging-role-sustainability

Closs, D. J., Goldsby, T. J., & Clinton, S. R. (1997). Information technology influences on world class logistics capability. *International Journal of Physical Distribution & Logistics Management, 27*(1), 4–17. doi:10.1108/09600039710162259

Cohen, W. M., & Levinthal, D. A. (1990). Absorptive capacity: A new perspective on learning and innovation. *Administrative Science Quarterly, 35*(1), 128–152. doi:10.2307/2393553

Coker, R., Rushton, J., Mounier-Jack, S., Karimuribo, E., Lutumba, P., Kambarage, D., & Rweyemamu, M. (2011). Towards a conceptual framework ti support one-health research for policy on emerging zoonoses. *The Lancet. Infectious Diseases, 11*(4), 326–331. doi:10.1016/S1473-3099(10)70312-1 PMID:21376670

Collis, J., & Hussey, R. (2013). Business research: A practical guide for undergraduate and postgraduate students. Palgrave Macmillan.

Coltman, T., Gattorna, J., & Whiting, S. (2010). Realigning service operations strategy at DHL express. *Interfaces, 40*(3), 175–183. doi:10.1287/inte.1100.0491

Columbus, L. (2015, July 13), *Ten Ways Big Data Is Revolutionizing Supply Chain Management*. Retrieved from https://www.forbes.com /sites/ louiscolumbus /2015/07/13/ ten-ways- big- data- is -revolutionizing -supply -chain-management /?sh=2937358c69f5

Commision for Environmental Cooperation. (2017). *Characterization and Management of Organic Waste in North America—White Paper*. Montreal, Canada: Commission for Environmental Cooperation. http://www.cec.org/fw/organic-waste-reports/

Conoscenti, M., Vetro, A., & De Martin, J. C. (2016, November). Blockchain for the Internet of Things: A systematic literature review. In *2016 IEEE/ACS 13th International Conference of Computer Systems and Applications (AICCSA)* (pp. 1-6). IEEE. 10.1109/AICCSA.2016.7945805

Cook, L. S., Heiser, D. R., & Sengupta, K. (2011). The moderating effect of supply chain role on the relationship between supply chain practices and performance: An empirical analysis. *International Journal of Physical Distribution & Logistics Management, 41*(2), 104–134. doi:10.1108/09600031111118521

Cottrill, K. (2017, December 12). *The Benefits of Blockchain – Part 1: Fact or Wishful Thinking?* Supply Chain Management Review. https://www.scmr.com/article/nextgen_supply_chain_the_benefits_of_blockchain_fact_or_wishful_thinking

Cottrill, K. (2021). *Push to make supply chains more sustainable continues to gain momentum.* MIT Center for Transportation and Logistics. https://news.mit.edu/2021/supply-chain-sustainability-continues-to-gain-momentum-0719

Coyle, J. J., Novack, R. A., & Gibson, B. J. (2016). *Transoprtation: A Globale Supply Chain Perspective* (8th ed.). Boston: Cengage Learning.

Craighead, C. W., Blackhurst, J., Rungtusanatham, M. J., & Handfield, R. B. (2007). The severity of supply chain disruptions: Design characteristics and mitigation capabilities. *Decision Sciences, 38*(1), 131–156. doi:10.1111/j.1540-5915.2007.00151.x

Crane, A., LeBaron, G., Allain, J., & Behbahani, L. (2019). Governance gaps in eradicating forced labor: From global to domestic supply chains. *Regulation & Governance, 13*(1), 86–106. doi:10.1111/rego.12162

Crane, A., & Matten, D. (2016). *Business Ethics – Managing Corporate Citizenship and Sustainability in the Age of Globalization* (4th ed.). Oxford University Press.

Cronin, J. J. Jr, & Taylor, S. A. (1992). Measuring service quality: A reexamination and extension. *Journal of Marketing, 56*(3), 55–68. doi:10.1177/002224299205600304

CSCMP. (2020). *Council of Supply Chain Management Professionals.* www.cscmp.org

CSCMP. (2021). *CSCMP Supply Chain Management Definitions and Glossary.* Available at: https:// cscmp.org/supply-chain-management-definitions

Currie, C. S., Fowler, J. W., Kotiadis, K., Monks, T., Onggo, B. S., Robertson, D. A., & Tako, A. A. (2020). How simulation modelling can help reduce the impact of COVID-19. *Journal of Simulation, 14*(2), 83–97. doi:10.1080/17477778.2020.1751570

Cutting-Decelle, A. F., Young, B. I., Das, B. P., Case, K., Rahimifard, S., Anumba, C. J., & Bouchlaghem, D. M. (2007). A review of approaches to supply chain communications: From manufacturing to construction. *ITcon, 12*, 73–102.

Dabholkar, P. A., Thorpe, D. I., & Rentz, J. O. (1996). A measure of service quality for retail stores: Scale development and validation. *Journal of the Academy of Marketing Science, 24*(1), 3–11. doi:10.1007/BF02893933

Dai, H., Tao, J., Jiang, H., & Chen, W. (2019). O2O On-demand Delivery Optimization with Mixed Driver Forces. *IFAC-PapersOnLine, 52*(13), 391–396. doi:10.1016/j.ifacol.2019.11.156

Damanpour, F., & Evan, W. M. (1984). Organizational innovation and performance: The problem of" organizational lag. *Administrative Science Quarterly, 29*(3), 392–409. doi:10.2307/2393031

Dan, B., & Liu, F. (2000). Study on green supply chain and its architecture. *Zhongguo Jixie Gongcheng Xuekan, 11*, 1232–1234.

Danso, A., Adomako, S., Amankwah-Amoah, J., Owusu-Agyei, S., & Konadu, R. (2019). Environmental sustainability orientation, competitive strategy and financial performance. *Business Strategy and the Environment, 28*(5), 885–895. doi:10.1002/bse.2291

Daou, A., Mallat, C., Chammas, G., Cerantola, N., Kayed, S., & Saliba, N. A. (2020). The Ecocanvas as a business model canvas for a circular economy. *Journal of Cleaner Production, 258*, 120938. doi:10.1016/j.jclepro.2020.120938

Dash, S., Shakyawar, S. K., Sharma, M., & Kaushik, S. (2019). Big data in healthcare: Management, analysis and future prospects. *Journal of Big Data, 6*(1), 1–25. doi:10.118640537-019-0217-0

*Compilation of References*

Das, K. (2018). Integrating resilience in a supply chain planning model. *International Journal of Quality & Reliability Management*, *35*(3), 570–595. doi:10.1108/IJQRM-08-2016-0136

Das, K., & Lashkari, R. S. (2015). Risk readiness and resiliency planning for a supply chain. *International Journal of Production Research*, *53*(22), 6752–6771. doi:10.1080/00207543.2015.1057624

Datta, P. (2017). Supply Network Resilience: A systematic literature review and future research. *International Journal of Logistics Management*, *28*(4), 1387–1424. doi:10.1108/IJLM-03-2016-0064

Datta, P. P. (2017). Enhancing competitive advantage by constructing supply chains to achieve superior performance. *Production Planning and Control*, *28*(1), 57–74.

Datta, P. P., Christopher, M., & Allen, P. (2007). Agent-based modelling of complex production/distribution systems to improve resilience. *International Journal of Logistics: Research and Applications.*, *10*(3), 187–203. doi:10.1080/13675560701467144

Daú, G., Scavarda, A., Scavarda, L. F., & Portugal, V. J. T. (2019). The healthcare sustainable supply chain 4.0: The circular economy transition conceptual framework with the corporate social responsibility mirror. *Sustainability*, *11*(12), 3259. doi:10.3390u11123259

Davis, M. (2001). Pricing Weather Derivatives by Marginal Value. *Quantitative Finance*, *1*(3), 1–4. doi:10.1080/713665730

Dawson, P. M. (2006). Change management. In G. Ritzer (Ed.), *The Blackwell Encyclopedia of Sociology* (pp. 427–431). Blackwell Publishing.

de Araujo, A. C., Matsuoka, E. M., Ung, J. E., Massote, A., & Sampaio, M. (2017). An exploratory study on the returns management process in an online retailer. *International Journal of Logistics Research and Applications*, *21*(3), 345–362. doi:10.1080/13675567.2017.1370080

de Freitas, R. S. G., & Stedefeldt, E. (2020). COVID-19 pandemic underlines the need to build resilience in commercial restaurants' food safety. *Food Research International, 136.* doi:10.1016/j.foodres.2020.109472

De los Rios, I. C., & Charnley, F. J. (2017). Skills and capabilities for a sustainable and circular economy: The changing role of design. *Journal of Cleaner Production*, *160*, 109–122. doi:10.1016/j.jclepro.2016.10.130

de Sousa Jabbour, A. B. L., Jabbour, C. J. C., Godinho Filho, M., & Roubaud, D. (2018). Industry 4.0 and the circular economy: A proposed research agenda and original roadmap for sustainable operations. *Annals of Operations Research*, *270*(1), 273–286. doi:10.100710479-018-2772-8

De Souza, M., Pereira, G. M., de Sousa Jabbour, A. B. L., Jabbour, C. J. C., Trento, L. R., Borchardt, M., & Zvirtes, L. (2021). A digitally enabled circular economy for mitigating food waste: Understanding innovative marketing strategies in the context of an emerging economy. *Technological Forecasting and Social Change, 173*, 121062. doi:10.1016/j.techfore.2021.121062

de Visser, E. J., Dorfman, A., Chartrand, D., Lamon, J., Freedy, E., & Weltman, G. (2016). Building resilience with the Stress Resilience Training System: Design validation and applications. *Work (Reading, Mass.)*, *54*(2), 351–366. doi:10.3233/WOR-162295 PMID:27232057

Deaton, B. J., & Deaton, B. J. (2020). Food security and Canada's agricultural system challenged by COVID-19. *Canadian Journal of Agricultural Economics/Revue canadienne d'agroeconomie, 68*(2), 143-149.

Deif, A. M. (2011). A system model for green manufacturing. *Journal of Cleaner Production*, *19*(14), 1553–1559. doi:10.1016/j.jclepro.2011.05.022

Deineko, L., Tsyplitska, O., & Deineko, O. (2019). Opportunities and barriers of the Ukrainian industry transition to the circular economy. *Environment and Ecology*, *10*(1), 79–92. doi:10.21511/ee.10(1).2019.06

Delic, M., & Eyers, D. R. (2020). The effect of additive manufacturing adoption on supply chain flexibility and performance: An empirical analysis from the automotive industry. *International Journal (Toronto, Ont.)*.

Deloitte. (2017). *Using blockchain to drive supply chain innovation*. https://www2.deloitte.com/us/en/pages/operations/articles/blockchain-supply-chain-innovation.html

Deloitte. (2020). *2020 global health care outlook. Laying a foundation for the future*. Author.

Deloitte. (2021). *Ethical value chain*. Available at: https://www2.deloitte.com/ch/en/pages/risk/solutions/ethical-value-chain.html

Deming, E. (1992). *Total Quality Management*. Defense Technical Information Centre.

Dereń, A. M., & Skonieczny, J. (2021). Proactive and Reactive Actions of the Organization during Covid-19 Pandemic Crisis. *European Research Studies Journal*, *24*(2), 358–368.

Desbarats, G. (1999). The innovation supply chain. *Supply Chain Management*, *4*(1), 7–10. doi:10.1108/13598549910254708

Dev, D. R., & Roy, R. (2019). Communication Technology for Users with Specific Learning Incapacities. *Artificial Intelligent Systems and Machine Learning, 11*(7), 126–131. http://ischolar.info/index.php/CiiTAISML/article/view/207237

Dev, D. R. (1839–1842). Badhan, A. K., & Roy, R. (2020). A Study of Artificial Emotional Intelligence for Human – Robot Interaction. *Journal of Critical Reviews*, *7*(15). Advance online publication. doi:10.31838/jcr.07.15.251

Dezdar, S., & Sulaiman, A. (2009). Successful enterprise resource-planning implementation: Taxonomy of critical factors. *Industrial Management & Data Systems*, *109*(8), 1037–1052. doi:10.1108/02635570910991283

Di Vaio, A., & Varriale, L. (2020). Blockchain technology in supply chain management for sustainable performance: Evidence from the airport industry. *International Journal of Information Management*, *52*, 102014. doi:10.1016/j.ijinfomgt.2019.09.010

Diabat, A., & Govindan, K. (2011). An analysis of the drivers affecting the implementation of green supply chain management. *Resources, Conservation and Recycling*, *55*(6), 659–667. doi:10.1016/j.resconrec.2010.12.002

Didea, L., & Ilie, D. M (2020). The State of Emergency and the Economic Repercussions. A New "Avalanche" of Insolvencies *J.L. & Admin. Sci., 89*(13).

Ding, N., & Chu, X. (2012). Study on the Spatial Pattern of Catering Industry in Urumqi and its Influencing Factors. *Journal of Yili Normal University*, *6*(1), 37–41.

Directive, C. (2004). *2004/67/EC*. Council of the European Union.

Dischel, R. S. (Ed.). (2002). Climate Risk and the Weather Market. London: Risk Water Group.

Diwekar, U. (2005). Green process design, industrial ecology, and sustainability: A systems analysis perspective. *Resources, Conservation and Recycling*, *44*(3), 215–235. doi:10.1016/j.resconrec.2005.01.007

Dobrzykowski, D. A. (2010). *Linking Antecedents and Consequences of Value Density in the Healthcare Delivery Supply Chain* (Doctoral Thesis). University of Toledo.

Dohale, V., Ambilkar, P., Gunasekaran, A., & Verma, P. (2021). Supply chain risk mitigation strategies during COVID-19: Exploratory cases of "make-to-order" handloom saree apparel industries. *International Journal of Physical Distribution & Logistics Management*. Advance online publication. doi:10.1108/IJPDLM-12-2020-0450

*Compilation of References*

Doktoralina, C., & Apollo, A. (2019). The contribution of strategic management accounting in supply chain outcomes and logistic firm profitability. *Uncertain Supply Chain Management, 7*(2), 145–156. doi:10.5267/j.uscm.2018.10.010

Dolgui, A., Ivanov, D., Potryasaev, S., Sokolov, B., Ivanova, M., & Werner, F. (2020). Blockchain-oriented dynamic modelling of smart contract design and execution in the supply chain. *International Journal of Production Research, 58*(7), 2184–2199. doi:10.1080/00207543.2019.1627439

Dolgui, A., Ivanov, D., & Rozhkov, M. (2020). Does the ripple effect influence the bullwhip effect? An integrated analysis of structural and operational dynamics in the supply chain. *International Journal of Production Research, 58*(5), 1285–1301. doi:10.1080/00207543.2019.1627438

Dolgui, A., Ivanov, D., Sethi, S. P., & Sokolov, B. (2019). Scheduling in production, supply chain and Industry 4.0 systems by optimal control: Fundamentals, state-of-the-art and applications. *International Journal of Production Research, 57*(2), 411–432. doi:10.1080/00207543.2018.1442948

Dolgui, A., Ivanov, D., & Sokolov, B. (2018). Ripple effect in the supply chain: An analysis and recent literature. *International Journal of Production Research, 56*(1-2), 414–430. doi:10.1080/00207543.2017.1387680

Dolgui, A., Ivanov, D., & Sokolov, B. (2020). Reconfigurable Supply Chain: The X-Network. *International Journal of Production Research, 58*(13), 4138–4163. doi:10.1080/00207543.2020.1774679

Dong, C., Akram, A., Andersson, D., Arnäs, P. O., & Stefansson, G. (2021). The impact of emerging and disruptive technologies on freight transportation in the digital era: Current state and future trends. *International Journal of Logistics Management, 32*(2), 386–412. doi:10.1108/IJLM-01-2020-0043

Dontoh, A., Elayan, F. A., Ronen, J., & Ronen, T. (2021). Unfair "Fair Value" in illiquid markets: Information spillover effects in times of crisis. *Management Science, 67*(8), 5163–5193. doi:10.1287/mnsc.2020.3737

Doran, C. (2010). Fair Trade Consumption: In Support of the Out-Group. *Journal of Business Ethics, 95*(4), 527–541. doi:10.100710551-010-0437-x

Dowell, G., Hart, S., & And Yeung, B. (2000). Do corporate environmental standards create or destroy market value? *Management Science, 46*(8), 1059–1074. doi:10.1287/mnsc.46.8.1059.12030

Dowling, F. (2021). *The impact of Covid-19 on unethical practices in global supply chains.* Available at: https://business.leeds.ac.uk/research-stc/dir-record/research-blog/1816/the-impact-of-covid-19-on-unethical-practices-in-global-supply-chains

Duarte Alonso, A., Kok, S. K., Bressan, A., O'Shea, M., Sakellarios, N., Koresis, A., Buitrago Solis, M. A., & Santoni, L. J. (2020). COVID-19, aftermath, impacts, and hospitality firms: An international perspective. *International Journal of Hospitality Management, 91*, 102654. doi:10.1016/j.ijhm.2020.102654 PMID:32863526

Dube, K., Nhamo, G., & Chikodzi, D. (2021). COVID-19 pandemic and prospects for recovery of the global aviation industry. *Journal of Air Transport Management, 92*(December), 102022. doi:10.1016/j.jairtraman.2021.102022

Dubey, R., Gunasekaran, A., Childe, S. J., Bryde, D. J., Giannakis, M., Foropon, C., Roubaud, D., & Hazen, B. T. (2020). Big data analytics and artificial intelligence pathway to operational performance under the effects of entrepreneurial orientation and environmental dynamism: A study of manufacturing organisations. *International Journal of Production Economics, 226*, 107599. doi:10.1016/j.ijpe.2019.107599

Dubey, R., Gunasekaran, A., Childe, S. J., Fosso Wamba, S., Roubaud, D., & Foropon, C. (2019). Empirical investigation of data analytics capability and organizational flexibility as complements to supply chain resilience. *International Journal of Production Research.* Advance online publication. doi:10.1016/j.ijpe.2019.01.023

Dubey, R., Gunasekaran, A., Childe, S. J., Wamba, F., Roubaud, S., & Foropon, C. (2019). Empirical investigation of data analytics capability and organizational flexibility as complements to supply chain resilience. *International Journal of Production Research*, *59*(1), 110–128. doi:10.1080/00207543.2019.1582820

Dubey, R., Singh, T., & Tiwari, S. (2012). Supply chain innovation is a key to superior firm performance an insight from Indian cement manufacturing. *International Journal of Innovation Science*, *4*(4), 217–229. doi:10.1260/1757-2223.4.4.217

Duclos, L. K., Vokurka, R. J., & Lummus, R. R. (2003). A Conceptual Model for Supply Chain Flexibility. *Industrial Management & Data Systems*, *103*(6), 446–456. doi:10.1108/02635570310480015

Duflou, J.R., Seliger, G., Kara, S., Umeda, Y., Ometto, A., Willems, B., (2008). Efficiency and feasibility of product disassembly: a case-based study. *CIRP Annals-Manufacturing Technology*, *57*, 583–600.

DuHadway, S., Carnovale, S., & Hazen, B. (2019). Understanding risk management for intentional supply chain disruptions: Risk detection, risk mitigation, and risk recovery. *Annals of Operations Research*, *283*(1–2), 179–198. doi:10.100710479-017-2452-0

Dujak, D., & Sajter, D. (2019). Blockchain Applications in Supply Chain. In A. Kawa & A. Maryniak (Eds.), *Smart Supply Network. EcoProduction (Environmental Issues in Logistics and Manufacturing)* (pp. 21–46). Springer. doi:10.1007/978-3-319-91668-2_2

Dun & Bradstreet. (2020). *Dun & Bradstreet COVID-19 Impact Index.* https://www.dnb.co.in/products/covid-19/impact-index.aspx

Duncan, D. (2020). What the COVID-19 pandemic tells us about the need to develop resilience in the nursing workforce. *Nursing Management*, *27*(3), 22–27. Advance online publication. doi:10.7748/nm.2020.e1933 PMID:32400142

Durach, C. F., Wieland, A., & Machuca, J. A. D. (2015). Antecedents and dimensions of supply chain robustness: A systematic literature review. *International Journal of Physical Distribution & Logistics Management*, *45*(1/2), 118–137. doi:10.1108/IJPDLM-05-2013-0133

Dutta, G., Kumar, R., Sindhwani, R., & Singh, R. K. (2020). Digital transformation priorities of India's discrete manufacturing SMEs – a conceptual study in perspective of Industry 4.0. *Competitiveness Review*, *30*(3), 289–314. doi:10.1108/CR-03-2019-0031

Dutta, P., Choi, T. M., Somani, S., & Butala, R. (2020). Blockchain technology in supply chain operations: Applications, challenges, and research opportunities. *Transportation Research Part E, Logistics and Transportation Review*, *142*, 102067. doi:10.1016/j.tre.2020.102067 PMID:33013183

Economic Commission for Latin America and the Caribbean. (2020). *Special Report COVID-19: The Effects of the coronavirus disease (COVID-19) pandemic on international trade and logistics.* United Nations. https://repositorio.cepal.org/bitstream/handle/11362/45878/1/S2000496_en.pdf

Ecovadis. (2021). *Modern Slavery In Supply Chains: New Legislative Landscape and Due Diligence Strategies.* Available at: https://resources.ecovadis.com/labor-human-rights/modern-slavery-supply-chains-legislative-due-diligence?utm_medium=referral&utm_source=ev-covid-blog&utm_campaign=covid-19

EFS. (2021). Retrieved November 1, 2021 from: https://www.efsme.com

Ehie, I., Ferreira, D. F., & Lius, M. (2019). Conceptual development of supply chain digitalization framework. *IFAC-PapersOnLine*, *52*(13), 2338–2342. doi:10.1016/j.ifacol.2019.11.555

Ellyat, H. (2021). *Supply chain chaos is already hitting global growth. And it's about to get worse.* CNBC.

*Compilation of References*

Elnouaman, S., & Ismail. K. (2016). The Relationship between IT and Supply chain management Performance: A Systematic Review and Future Research. *American Journal of Industrial and Business Management*, 480-495.

Eltantawy, R. A. (2016). The role of supply management resilience in attaining ambidexterity: A dynamic capabilities approach. *Journal of Business and Industrial Marketing*, *31*(1), 123–134. doi:10.1108/JBIM-05-2014-0091

Eltayeb, T. K., & Zailani, S. (2009). Going green through green supply chain initiatives towards environmental sustainability. *Operations and Supply Chain Management*, *2*(2), 93–110.

Eltayeb, T. K., Zailani, S., & Ramayah, T. (2011). Green supply chain initiatives among certified companies in Malaysia and environmental sustainability: Investigating the outcomes. *Resources, Conservation and Recycling*, *55*(5), 495–506. doi:10.1016/j.resconrec.2010.09.003

Elvandari, C. D. R., Sukartiko, A. C., & Nugrahini, A. D. (2018). Identification of Technical Requirement for Improving Quality of Local Online Food Delivery Service in Yogyakarta'. *Journal of Industry and Information Technology in Agriculture*, *1*(2), 1. doi:10.24198/jiita.v1i2.14573

EMF (Ellen MacArthur Foundation) & McKinsey & Co. (2019). *Towards the Circular Economy: Economic and Business Rationale for an Accelerated Transition*. Accessed on 15[th]July 2021 from https://www.ellenmacarthurfoundation.org/business/reports

Encyclopaedia Britannica. (2020). *Golden Rule, Ethical Precept*. Retrieved from: https://www.britannica.com/topic/Golden-Rule

Erdogan, O., Tata, K., Karahasan, B.C., & Sengoz, M.H. (2013). Dynamics of the co-movement be-tween stock and maritime markets. *Int. Rev. Econ. Financ., 25*, 282–290. doi:10.1016/j.iref.2012.07.007

Ermer, D. S., & Kniper, M. K. (1998). Delighting the customer: Quality function deployment for quality service design. *Total Quality Management*, *9*(4-5), 86–91. doi:10.1080/0954412988622

Ernst & Young. (2020). *How COVID-19 impacted supply chains and what comes next*. https://www.ey.com/en_gl/supply-chain/how-covid-19-impacted-supply-chains-and-what-comes-next

Eschenbächer, J., Seifert, M., & Thoben, K. D. (2011). Improving distributed innovation processes in virtual organisations through the evaluation of collaboration intensities. *Production Planning and Control*, *22*(5-6), 473–487. doi:10.1080/09537287.2010.536620

Esmaeilian, B., Sarkis, J., Lewis, K., & Behdad, S. (2020). Blockchain for the future of sustainable supply chain management in Industry 4.0. *Resources, Conservation and Recycling*, *163*, 105064. doi:10.1016/j.resconrec.2020.105064

ETI. (2020). *A guest blog from Grace Gao: Stay responsible - ETI member Matrix's supplier survey and engagement during pandemic*. Available at: https://www.ethicaltrade.org/blog/guest-blog-grace-gao-stay-responsible-eti-member-matrixs-supplier-survey-and-engagement-during

Evans, D., & Over, M. (2020). *The Economic Impact of COVID-19 in Low- and Middle-Income Countries*. Available at: https://www.cgdev.org/blog/economic-impact-covid-19-low-and-middle-income-countries

Evans, D. (2011). *The internet of things: How the next evolution of the Internet is changing everything*. Cisco Internet Business Solutions Group.

Fady, A. B. L. (2003). La logistique dans la distribution. In A. F. G. Cliquet (Ed.), *Management de la distribution* (p. 275). Dunod.

Fahimnia, B. J., Jabbarzadeh, A., & Sarkis, J. (2018). Greening versus resilience: A supply chain design perspective. *Transportation Research Part E, Logistics and Transportation Review*, *119*, 129–148. doi:10.1016/j.tre.2018.09.005

Fahimnia, B., Pournader, M., Siemsen, E., Bendoly, E., & Wang, C. (2019). Behavioral operations and supply chain management-a review and literature mapping. *Decision Sciences*, *50*(6), 1127–1183. doi:10.1111/deci.12369

FAO. (2021). *The impact of disasters and crisis on agriculture and food security*. Food and Agriculture Organization of United Nations.

Farrow, P. H., Johnson, R. R., & Larson, A. L. (2000). Entrepreneurship, innovation, and sustainability strategies at *Walden paddlers. Inc. Interfaces*, *30*(3), 215–225. doi:10.1287/inte.30.3.215.11660

Fathi, M., Khakifirooz, M., Diabat, A., & Chen, H. (2021). An integrated queuing-stochastic optimization hybrid Genetic Algorithm for a location-inventory supply chain network. *International Journal of Production Economics*, *237*, 108139. doi:10.1016/j.ijpe.2021.108139

Fawcett, S. E., Ogden, J. A., Magnan, G. M., & Cooper, M. B. (2006). Organizational commitment and governance for supply chain success. *International Journal of Physical Distribution & Logistics Management*, *36*(1), 22–45. doi:10.1108/09600030610642913

Fernandes, N. (2020). Economic Effects of Coronavirus Outbreak (COVID-19) on the World Economy. SSRN *Electronic Journal*. doi:10.2139/ssrn.3557504

Ferreira, M. A., Jabbour, C. J. C., & Jabbour, A. B. L. S. (2017). Maturity levels of material cycles and waste management in a context of green supply chain management: An innovative framework and its application to Brazilian cases. *Journal of Material Cycles and Waste Management*, *19*(1), 516–525. doi:10.100710163-015-0416-5

Ferrell, O. C., Rogers, M. M., Ferrell, L., & Sawayda, J. (2013). A framework for understanding ethical supply chain decision making. *Journal of Marketing Channels*, *20*(3–4), 260–287. doi:10.1080/1046669X.2013.803428

Ferretti, V. (2016). From stakeholders' analysis to cognitive mapping and multi-attribute value theory: An integrated approach for policy support. *European Journal of Operational Research*, *253*(2), 524–541. doi:10.1016/j.ejor.2016.02.054

Ferri, L. M., & Pedrini, M. (2018). Socially and environmentally responsible purchasing: Comparing the impacts on buying firm's financial performance, competitiveness and risk. *Journal of Cleaner Production*, *174*, 880–888. doi:10.1016/j.jclepro.2017.11.035

Fiksel, J. (2006). Sustainability and resilience: toward a systems approach. *Sustainability: Science. Practice and Policy*, *2*(2), 14–21.

Findlay, R., & O'Rourke, K. (2008). *Power and Plenty: Trade, War, and the World Economy in the Second Millennium*. Princeton University Press.

Fink, L. (2020). Conducting Information Systems Research in the Midst of the COVID-19 Pandemic: Opportunities and Challenges. *Information Systems Management*, *37*(4), 256–259. doi:10.1080/10580530.2020.1814460

Flint, D. J., & Larsson, E. (2007). Supply chain innovation. Handbook of Global Supply Chain Management, 49(4), 475–487.

Flint, D. J., Larsson, E., Gammelgaard, B., & Mentzer, J. T. (2005). Logistics innovation: A customer value-oriented social process. *Journal of Business Logistics*, *26*(1), 113–147. doi:10.1002/j.2158-1592.2005.tb00196.x

*Compilation of References*

Foerstl, K., Reuter, C., Hartmann, E., & Blome, C. (2010). Managing supplier sustainability risks in a dynamically changing environment – sustainable supplier management in the chemical industry. *Journal of Purchasing and Supply Management, 16*(2), 118–130. doi:10.1016/j.pursup.2010.03.011

Food & Drug Administration. (2020). *Best Practices for Retail Food Stores, Restaurants, and Food pick-up/delivery Services during the COVID-19 Pandemic.* https://www.fda.gov/food/food-safety-during-emergencies/best-practices-retail-food-stores-restaurants-and-food-pick-updelivery-services-during-covid-19

Forbes, S., & Fikretoglu, D. (2018). Building resilience: The conceptual basis and research evidence for resilience training programs. *Review of General Psychology, 22*(4), 452–468. doi:10.1037/gpr0000152

Ford, E., & Scanlon, D. (2007). Promise and problems with supply chain management approaches to healthcare purchasing. *Health Care Management Review, 32*(3), 192–202. doi:10.1097/01.HMR.0000281623.35987.cf PMID:17666990

Fosso, W. S., Gunasekaran, A., Akter, S., Ren, S. J. F., Dubey, R., & Childe, S. J. (2017). Big data analytics and firm performance: Effects of dynamic capabilities. *Journal of Business Research, 70,* 356–365. doi:10.1016/j.jbusres.2016.08.009

Foster, J. (2020). *Four Supply-Chain Trends Accelerated by COVID-19.* https://www.supplychainbrain.com/blogs/1-think-tank/post/31820-four-supply-chain-trends-accelerated-by-covid-19

Francisco, K., & Swanson, D. (2018). The supply chain has no clothes: Technology adoption of blockchain for supply chain transparency. *Logistics, 2*(2), 1–13. doi:10.3390/logistics2010002

Frank, A. G., Mendes, G. H., Ayala, N. F., & Ghezzi, A. (2019). Servitization and Industry 4.0 convergence in the digital transformation of product firms: A business model innovation perspective. *Technological Forecasting and Social Change, 141,* 341–351. doi:10.1016/j.techfore.2019.01.014

Frederico, G., Garza-Reyes, J., Anosike, A., & Kumar, V. (2019). Supply Chain 4.0: Concepts, maturity and research agenda. *Supply Chain Management, 25*(2), 262–282. doi:10.1108/SCM-09-2018-0339

Freeman, O. (2020). *Supply Chain Resilience is a Priority after COVID-19.* Supply Chain Digital. https://supplychain-digital.com/supply-chain-2/supply-chain-resilience-priority-after-covid-19

Gaehtgens, F., & Allan, A. (2017). *Digital trust – Redefining trust for the digital era.* A Gartner trend insight report. Available at: https://www.gartner.com/doc/3735817/digital-trust--redefiningtrust

Ganotakis, P., Hsieh, W. L., & Love, J. H. (2013). Information systems, inter-functional collaboration and innovation in Taiwanese high-tech manufacturing firms. *Production Planning and Control, 24*(8-9), 837–850. doi:10.1080/09537287.2012.666876

Gao, D., Xu, Z., Ruan, Y. Z., & Lu, H. (2017). From a systematic literature review to integrated definition for sustainable supply chain innovation (SSCI). *Journal of Cleaner Production, 142,* 1518–1538. doi:10.1016/j.jclepro.2016.11.153

Gaol, F. L., Filimonova, N., & Acharya, C. (Eds.). (2021). *Impact of Disruptive Technologies on the Sharing Economy.* IGI Global. doi:10.4018/978-1-7998-0361-4

Garay-Rondero, C., Martinez-Flores, J., Smith, N., Caballero Morales, S., & Aldrette-Malacara, A. (2019). Digital supply chain model in Industry 4.0. *Journal of Manufacturing Technology Management.* doi:10.1108/JMTM-08-2018-0280

Garmezy, N. (1991). Resiliency and vulnerability to adverse developmental outcomes associated with poverty. *American Journal of Behavioral Science, 34*(4), 416–430. doi:10.1177/0002764291034004003

Gartner. (2020). *The Gartner Healthcare Supply Chain Top 25 for 2020.* Retrieved from https://www.gartner.com/en/webinars/4006369/the-2021-gartner-healthcare-supply-chain-top-25

Gartner. (2021a). *Future of Supply Chain*. Retrieved from https://www.gartner.com/en/supply-chain/research/future-of-supply-chain

Gartner. (2021b). *How to Improve Supply Chain Effectiveness Through Supply Chain Benchmarking*. Retrieved from https://www.gartner.com/en/supply-chain/trends/supply-chain-effectiveness

Gates, D., Mayor, T., & Gampenrieder, E. L. (2016). *Global manufacturing outlook- Competing for growth: How to be a growth leader in industrial manufacturing*. KPMG. https://assets.kpmg/content/dam/kpmg/tr/pdf/2017/01/global-manufacturing-outlook-competing-for-growth.pdf

Gaudenzi, B., & Christopher, M. (2016). Achieving supply chain 'Leagility'through a project management orientation. *International Journal of Logistics Research and Applications, 19*(1), 3–18. doi:10.1080/13675567.2015.1073234

Gaur, V., & Gaiha, A. (2020). Building a Transparent Supply Chain Blockchain can enhance trust, efficiency, and speed. *Harvard Business Review, 98*(3), 94–103.

Gaur, V., & Gaiha, A. (2020). Building a Transparent Supply Chain. *Harvard Business Review*.

Gautam, A. (2020). Building Supply Chain Resilience for A Post-Covid-19 World, Forbes Technology Council. *Forbes*. https://www.forbes.com/sites/forbestechcouncil/2020/09/25/building-supply-chain-resilience-for-a-post-covid-19-world/?sh=7a7240305aea

Gavilan, D., Balderas-Cejudo, A., Fernández-Lores, S., & Martinez-Navarro, G. (2021). Innovation in Online Food Delivery: Learning from COVID-19. *International Journal of Gastronomy and Food Science, 24*, 100330. doi:10.1016/j.ijgfs.2021.100330 PMID:34745390

Gawer, A. (2021). Digital platforms and ecosystems: Remarks on the dominant organizational forms of the digital age. *Innovation*, 1–15. doi:10.1080/14479338.2021.1965888

Gebhardt, J., Grimm, A., & Neugebauer, L. M. (2015). Developments 4.0 Prospects on future requirements and impacts on work and vocational education. *Journal of Teacher Education, 3*(2), 117–133.

Geman, H. (1999). The Bermudan Triangle: Weather, Electricity and Insurance Derivatives. In Insurance and weather derivatives: from exotic options to exotic underlyings. Geman.

Genovese, A., Acquaye, A. A., Figueroa, A., & Koh, S. L. (2017). Sustainable supply chain management and the transition towards a circular economy: Evidence and some applications. *Omega, 66*, 344–357. doi:10.1016/j.omega.2015.05.015

Gereffi, G. (2020). What does the COVID-19 pandemic teach us about global value chains? The case of medical supplies. *Journal of International Business Policy, 3*(3), 287–301. doi:10.105742214-020-00062-w

Ghisellini, P., Cialani, C., & Ulgiati, S. (2016). A review on circular economy: The expected transition to a balanced interplay of environmental and economic systems. *Journal of Cleaner Production, 114*, 11–32. doi:10.1016/j.jclepro.2015.09.007

Ghobadian, A., Speller, S., & Jones, M. (1994). Service quality. *International Journal of Quality & Reliability Management, 11*(9), 43–66. doi:10.1108/02656719410074297 PMID:10134643

Giddy, I. (n.d.). *Accounting for Derivatives FAS 133* (Financial Accounting Standards Board Statement No. 133, Accounting for Derivative Instruments and Hedging Activities). http://people.stern.nyu.edu/igiddy/fas133.htm

Gilbert, D. (1999). *Retail marketing management*. Financial Times Management.

Gilling, R.-I., & Ulmer, J.-M. (2016). *Major Challenges in Supply Chain Management*. Academic Press.

*Compilation of References*

Giordano, F., Cipolla, A., & Ungar, M. (2021). Building resilience for healthcare professionals working in an Italian red zone during the COVID-19 outbreak: A pilot study. *Stress and Health*. Advance online publication. doi:10.1002mi.3085 PMID:34312986

Giuffrida, M., Mangiaracina, R., Perego, A., & Tumino, A. (2016). Cross border B2C e-commerce to Greater China and the role of logistics: A literature review. *International Journal of Physical Distribution & Logistics Management*. https://doi.org/10.1108/IJPDLM-08-2016-0241

Giunipero, L. C., & Aly Eltantawy, R. (2004). Securing the upstream supply chain: A risk management approach. *International Journal of Physical Distribution & Logistics Management*, 9(34), 698–713. doi:10.1108/09600030410567478

Gjerdrum, D., & Salen, W. (2010). The New ERM Gold Standard: ISO 31000:2009. *Professional Safety*, 55(8), 43–44.

Glas, A. H., & Kleemann, F. C. (2016). The impact of industry 4.0 on procurement and supply management: A conceptual and qualitative analysis. *International Journal of Business and Management Invention*, 5(6), 55–66.

Gligor, D. M. (2013). *The Concept of Supply Chain Agility: Conceptualization, Antecedents, and the Impact on Firm Performance* (PhD diss.). University of Tennessee.

Gligor, D. M., Holcomb, M. C., & Stank, T. P. (2013). A multidisciplinary approach to supply chain agility: Conceptualization and scale development. *Journal of Business Logistics*, 34(2), 94–108. doi:10.1111/jbl.12012

Goebel, P., Reuter, C., Pibernik, R., & Sichtmann, C. (2012). The influence of ethical culture on supplier selection in the context of sustainable sourcing. *International Journal of Production Economics*, 140(1), 7–17. doi:10.1016/j.ijpe.2012.02.020

Golan, M. S., Jernegan, L. H., & Linkov, I. (2020). Trends and applications of resilience analytics in supply chain modeling: Systematic literature review in the context of the COVID-19 pandemic. *Environment Systems & Decisions*, 40(2), 222–243. doi:10.100710669-020-09777-w PMID:32837820

Goldratt, E. H. (1997). *The Critical Chain*. Gower Book.

Gold, S., & Seuring, S. (2011). Supply chain and logistics issues of bio-energy production. *Journal of Cleaner Production*, 19(1), 32–42. doi:10.1016/j.jclepro.2010.08.009

Golicic, S., Flint, D., & Signori, P. (2017). Building Business Sustainability through Resilience in the Wine Industry. *International Journal of Wine Business Research*, 29(1), 74–97. doi:10.1108/IJWBR-02-2016-0005

Gómez-Valle, L., López-Marcos, M. A., & Martínez-Rodríguez, J. (2020). Two New Strategies for Pricing Freight Options by Means of a Valuation PDE and by Functional Bounds. *Mathematics*, 8(4), 620. doi:10.3390/math8040620

Gong, Z. (2008). An economic evaluation model of supply chain flexibility. *European Journal of Operational Research*, 184(2), 745–758. doi:10.1016/j.ejor.2006.11.013

Goodarzian, F., Kumar, V., & Abraham, A. (2021). Hybrid meta-heuristic algorithms for a supply chain network considering different carbon emission regulations using big data characteristics. *Soft Computing*, 25(11), 7527–7557. doi:10.100700500-021-05711-7

Goodarzian, F., Taleizadeh, A. A., Ghasemi, P., & Abraham, A. (2021). An integrated sustainable medical supply chain network during COVID-19. *Engineering Applications of Artificial Intelligence*, 100, 104188. doi:10.1016/j.engappai.2021.104188 PMID:33619424

Gorane, S. J., & Kant, R. (2016). Supply chain practices: An implementation status in Indian manufacturing organizations. *Benchmarking*, 23(5), 1076–1110. doi:10.1108/BIJ-06-2014-0059

Gouda, S. K., & Saranga, H. (2018). Sustainable supply chains for supply chain sustainability: Impact of sustainability efforts on supply chain risk. *International Journal of Production Research, 56*(17), 5820–5835. doi:10.1080/0020754 3.2018.1456695

GoulasL.SkiadopoulosG. (2011). Are Freight futures markets efficient? Evidence from IMAREX. *International Journal of Forecasting.* http://ssrn.com/abstract=1582356

Government of India. (2020). *Measures undertaken To Ensure Safety of Health Workers drafted for Covid 19 Services.* Author.

Govindan, K., Soleimani, H. & Kannan, D. (2015).Reverse logistics and closed-loop supply chain:a comprehensive review to explore the future. *European Journal of OperationalResearch, 240*(3), 603-626. doi:10.1016/j.ejor.2014.07.012

Govindan, K., Diabat, A., & Madan Shankar, K. (2015). Analyzing the drivers of green manufacturing with the fuzzy approach. *Journal of Cleaner Production, 96,* 182–193. doi:10.1016/j.jclepro.2014.02.054

Govindan, K., Fattahi, M., & Keyvanshokooh, E. (2017). Supply chain network design under uncertainty: A comprehensive review and future research directions. *European Journal of Operational Research, 263*(1), 108–141. doi:10.1016/j.ejor.2017.04.009

Govindan, K., Khodaverdi, R., & Vafadarnikjoo, A. (2015). Intuitionistic fuzzy-based debate method for developing green practices and performances in a green supply chain. *Expert Systems with Applications, 42*(20), 7207–7220. doi:10.1016/j.eswa.2015.04.030

Govindan, K., Mina, H., & Alavi, B. (2020). A decision support system for demand management in healthcare supply chains considering the epidemic outbreaks: A case study of coronavirus disease 2019 (COVID-19). *Transp Res E Logist Transp Rev, 138,* 101967. doi:10.1016/j.tre.2020.101967 PMID:32382249

Govindan, K., & Soleimani, H. (2017). A review of reverse logistics and closed-loop supply chains: A journal of cleaner production focus. *Journal of Cleaner Production, 142*(Part 1), 371–384. doi:10.1016/j.jclepro.2016.03.126

Graveline, N., & Gremont, M. (2017). Measuring and understanding the microeconomic resilience of businesses to lifeline service interruptions due to natural disasters. *International Journal of Disaster Risk Reduction, 24,* 526–538. doi:10.1016/j.ijdrr.2017.05.012

Graves, S. C., & Willems, S. P. (2003). Supply Chain Design: Safety Stock Placement and Supply Chain Configuration. *Handbooks in Operations Research and Management Science, 11*(11), 95–132. doi:10.1016/S0927-0507(03)11003-1

Grawe, S. J. (2009). Logistics innovation: A literature-based conceptual framework. *International Journal of Logistics Management, 20*(3), 360–377. doi:10.1108/09574090911002823

Green, K., Morton, B., & New, S. (1998). Green purchasing and supply policies: Do they improve companies' environmental performance? *Supply Chain Management, 3*(2), 89–95. doi:10.1108/13598549810215405

Green, K., Morton, B., & New, S. (2000). Greening Organizations: Purchasing, Consumption, and Innovation. *Organization & Environment, 13*(2), 206–225. doi:10.1177/1086026600132003

Greer, B. M., & Ford, M. W. (2009). Managing change in supply chains: A process comparison. *Journal of Business Logistics, 30*(2), 47–63. doi:10.1002/j.2158-1592.2009.tb00111.x

Groening, C., Sarkis, J., & Zhu, Q. (2017). Green marketing consumer-level theory review: A compendium of applied theories and further research directions. *Journal of Cleaner Production,* 1–19.

Gronroos, C. (1988). Service quality: The six criteria of good perceived service. *Review of Business, 9*(3), 10–21.

*Compilation of References*

Groonroos, C. (1990). *Service Management and Marketing*. Lexington Books.

Grover, P., Kar, A. K., & Dwivedi, Y. K. (2020). Understanding artificial intelligence adoption in operations management: Insights from the review of academic literature and social media discussions. *Annals of Operations Research, 308*(1-2), 177–213. doi:10.100710479-020-03683-9

Groves, P., Kayyali, B., Knott, D., & Kuiken, S. V. (2013). *The 'big data' revolution in healthcare: Accelerating value and innovation*. Academic Press.

Grunwald, J., & Flamm, K. (1985). *The global factory: Foreign assembly in international trade*. Brookings Institution.

Guan, D., Wang, D., Hallegatte, S., Davis, S. J., Huo, J., Li, S., Bai, Y., Lei, T., Xue, Q., Coffman, D. M., Cheng, D., Chen, P., Liang, X., Xu, B., Lu, X., Wang, S., Hubacek, K., & Gong, P. (2020). Global supply-chain effects of COVID-19 control measures. *Nature Human Behaviour, 4*(6), 577–587. doi:10.103841562-020-0896-8 PMID:32493967

Guillot, G. (2021, Mai 6). *Logistique du futur: quels sont les nouveaux enjeux?* Récupéré sur Entreprendre: https://www. entreprendre.fr

Guitouni, A., Waltho, C., & Nematollahi, M. (2021). How to make fragile global supply chains stronger and more sustainable. *PBS News Hour*. https://www.pbs.org/newshour/economy/how-to-make-fragile-global-supply-chains-stronger-and-more-sustainable

Gump, B. B., & Kulik, J. A. (1997). Stress, affiliation, and emotional contagion. *Journal of Personality and Social Psychology, 72*(2), 305–321. doi:10.1037/0022-3514.72.2.305 PMID:9107002

Gunasekaran, A., Papadopoulos, T., Dubey, R., Wamba, S. F., Childe, S. J., Hazen, B., & Akter, S. (2017). Big data and predictive analytics for supply chain and organizational performance. *Journal of Business Research, 70*, 308–317. doi:10.1016/j.jbusres.2016.08.004

Gunasekaran, A., Patel, C., & McGaughey, R. E. (2004). A framework for supply chain performance measurement. *International Journal of Production Economics, 87*(3), 333–347. doi:10.1016/j.ijpe.2003.08.003

Gunasekaran, A., & Spalanzani, A. (2012). Sustainability of manufacturing and services: Investigations for research and applications. *International Journal of Production Economics, 140*(1), 35–47. doi:10.1016/j.ijpe.2011.05.011

Gungor, A., & Gupta, S. M. (1999). Issues in environmentally conscious manufacturing and product recovery: A survey. *Computers & Industrial Engineering, 36*(4), 811–853. doi:10.1016/S0360-8352(99)00167-9

Guo, X., Cheng, L., & Liu, J. (2020). Green supply chain contracts with eco-labels issued by the sales platform: Profitability and environmental implications. *International Journal of Production Research, 58*(5), 1485–1504. doi:10.1080/00207543.2019.1658911

Gupta, R., Seetharaman, A., & Maddulety, K. (2020). Critical success factors influencing the adoption of digitalisation for teaching and learning by business schools. *Education and Information Technologies, 25*(5), 3481–3502. doi:10.100710639-020-10246-9

Gurtu, A., & Johny, J. (2021). Supply Chain Risk Management: Literature Review. *Risks, 2021*(9), 16. doi:10.3390/risks9010016

Gurzawska, A. (2020). Towards responsible and sustainable supply chains–innovation, multi-stakeholder approach and governance. *Philosophy of Management, 19*(3), 267–295. doi:10.100740926-019-00114-z

Gustin, C. M., Daugherty, P. J., & Stank, T. P. (1995). The effects of information availability on logistics integra. *Journal of Business Logistics, 16*(1), 1.

GuyotonS. (2020). Available at: https://resources.ecovadis.com/blog/covid-19-ethical-dilemma-reveals-weaknesses-in-supply-chain-due-diligence

Hackius, N., & Petersen, M. (2017): Blockchain in logistics and supply chain: Trick or treat? In *Digitalization in Supply Chain Management and Logistics: Smart and Digital Solutions for an Industry 4.0 Environment* (pp. 3-18). Proceedings of the Hamburg International Conference of Logistics (HICL), epubli GmbH. 10.15480/882.1444

Hackius, N., & Petersen, M. (2020). Translating High Hopes into Tangible Benefits: How Incumbents in Supply Chain and Logistics Approach Blockchain. *IEEE Access: Practical Innovations, Open Solutions, 8*, 34993–35003. doi:10.1109/ACCESS.2020.2974622

Haddara, M., & Elragal, A. (2015). The Readiness of ERP Systems for the Factory of the Future. *Procedia Computer Science, 64*, 721–728. doi:10.1016/j.procs.2015.08.598

Haddud, A., & Khare, A. (2020). Digitalizing supply chains potential benefits and impact on lean operations. *International Journal of Lean Six Sigma, 11*(4), 731–765. doi:10.1108/IJLSS-03-2019-0026

Hader, M., El Mhamedi, A., & Abouabdellah, A. (2020). Understanding the determinants of blockchain technology adoption stages and supply chain performance using the technology-organization-environment framework. *13ème Conference Internationale de modelisation, optimisation et simulation (MOSIM2020)*.

Hagberg, J., Sundstrom, M., & Egels-Zandén, N. (2016). The digitalization of retailing: An exploratory framework. *International Journal of Retail & Distribution Management, 44*(7), 694–712. doi:10.1108/IJRDM-09-2015-0140

Hair, J. F., Black, W. C., Babin, B. J., Anderson, R. E., & Tatham, R. L. (2010). *Multivariate Data Analysis* (7th ed.). Prentice Hall.

Håkansson, H., & Snehota, I. (1989). No business is an island: The network concept of business strategy. *Scandinavian Journal of Management, 5*(3), 187–200. doi:10.1016/0956-5221(89)90026-2

Hallikas, J., Immonen, M., & Brax, S. (2021). Digitalizing procurement: The impact of data analytics on supply chain performance. *Supply Chain Management, 26*(5), 629–646. doi:10.1108/SCM-05-2020-0201

Hamel, G., & Valikangas, L. (2003). The quest for resilience. *Harvard Business Review, 81*, 52–65. PMID:12964393

Hamisultane, H. (2008). *Which Method for Pricing Weather Derivatives?* Academic Press.

Handfield, R. (2016). Preparing for the Era of the Digitally Transparent Supply Chain: A Call to Research in a New Kind of Journal. *Logistics, 1*(2), 2. Advance online publication. doi:10.3390/logistics1010002

Handfield, R. B., Graham, G., & Burns, L. (2020). Corona virus, tariffs, trade wars and supply chain evolutionary design. *International Journal of Operations & Production Management, 40*(10), 1649–1660. doi:10.1108/IJOPM-03-2020-0171

Handfield, R. B., Ragatz, G. L., Peterson, K., & Monczka, R. M. (1999). Involving suppliers in new product development? *California Management Review, 42*(1), 59–82. doi:10.2307/41166019

Handfield, R., Walton, S. Y., Sroufe, R., & Melnyk, S. A. (2002). Applying environmental criteria to supplier assessment: Green supply chain management a study in the application of the analytical hierarchy process. *European Journal of Operational Research, 141*(1), 70–87. doi:10.1016/S0377-2217(01)00261-2

Handfield, R., Walton, S., Seegers, L., & Melnyk, S. (1997). Green' value chain practices in the furniture industry. *Journal of Operations Management, 5*(4), 293–315. doi:10.1016/S0272-6963(97)00004-1

Han, S., & Chan, C. (2009). Developing a Collaborative Supply Chain Reference Model: A case study in China. *International Journal of Electronic Customer Relationship Management, 3*(1), 52–70. doi:10.1504/IJECRM.2009.024488

*Compilation of References*

Haraburda, S. S. (2016). Transforming military support processes from logistics to supply chain management. *Army Sustainment, 48*(2), 12–15. Retrieved from https://www.alu.army.mil/alog/2016/MarApr16/PDF/162197.pdf

Haren, P., & Simchi-Levi, D. (2020). How Coronavirus Could Impact the Global Supply Chain by MidMarch. *Harvard Business Review, 28*(February). https://hbr. org/2020/02/how-coronavirus-could-impact-the-globalsupply-chain-by-mid-march

Hariharan, G., Suresh, G. P., & Sagunthala, C. (2019). Critical Success Factors for the Implementation of Supply Chain Management in SMEs. *International Journal of Recent Technology and Engineering, 7*(5S3), 540-543.

Harris, I., Mumford, C.L., Naim, M.M., (2014). A hybrid multi-objective approach to capacitated facility location with flexible store allocation for green logistics modeling. *Transportation Research Part E: Logistics and Transportation Review, 66*, 1–22.

Harris, S. (2021). *Sustainable supply chains helped companies endure the pandemic.* Stanford Graduate School of Business. https://www.gsb.stanford.edu/insights/sustainable-supply-chains-helped-companies-endure-pandemic

Hasselgren, A., Kralevska, K., Gligoroski, D., Pedersen, S. A., & Faxvaag, A. (2020). Blockchain in healthcare and health sciences-a scoping review. *International Journal of Medical Informatics, 134*, 104040. doi:10.1016/j.ijmedinf.2019.104040 PMID:31865055

Hassini, E. (2008). Supply chain optimization: Current practices and overview of emerging research opportunities. *INFOR, 46*(2), 93–96. doi:10.3138/infor.46.2.93

Hauser, J. R., & Clausing, D. (1988). The house of quality. *Harvard Business Review, 66*(3), 63–73.

Haus-Reve, S., Fitjar, R. D., & Rodríguez-Pose, A. (2019). Does combining different types of collaboration always benefit firms? Collaboration, complementarity and product innovation in Norway. *Research Policy, 48*(6), 1476–1486. doi:10.1016/j.respol.2019.02.008

Hazen, B.T., Cegielski, C., Hanna, J.B., (2011) diffusion of green supply chain management: examining the perceived quality of green reverse logistics. *International Journal of Logistics Management, Operational Research, 141*(1), 70–87.

Hazen, B. T., Overstreet, R. E., & Cegielski, C. G. (2012). Supply chain innovation diffusion: Going beyond adoption. *International Journal of Logistics Management, 23*(1), 119–134. doi:10.1108/09574091211226957

He, F. A. (2018). A real-option approach to mitigate disruption risk in the supply chain. *Omega: Int. J. Manage. Sci.,* 133-149.

Heath, C., Sommerfield, A., & von Ungern-Sternberg, B. S. (2020). Resilience strategies to manage psychological distress among healthcare workers during the COVID-19 pandemic: a narrative review. *Anaesthesia, 75(10), 1364–1371.* doi:10.1111/anae.15180

He, B., Mirchandani, P., & Wang, Y. (2021). Removing Barriers for Grocery Stores: O2O Platform and Self-scheduling Delivery Capacity. *Transportation Research Part E, Logistics and Transportation Review, 141*, 1366–5545. doi:10.1016/j.tre.2020.102036

He, J. X., Baxter, S. L., Xu, J., Xu, J. M., Zhou, X. T., & Zhang, K. (2019). The practical implementation of artificial intelligence technologies in medicine. *Nature Medicine, 25*(1), 30–36. doi:10.103841591-018-0307-0 PMID:30617336

Hendricks & Singhal. (2005). An Empirical Analysis of the Effect of Supply Chain Disruptions on Long-Run Stock Price Performance and Equity Risk of the Firm. *Production and Operations Management, 14*(1), 35–52.

Hendricks, K.B., V. S. (2005). An empirical analysis of the effect of supply chain disruptions on log-run stock price and equity risk of the firm. *Production and Operations Management, 1*(14), 35–52.

Hendry, L. C., Stevenson, M., MacBryde, J., Ball, P., Sayed, M., & Liu, L. (2019). Local food supply chain resilience to constitutional change: The Brexit effect. *International Journal of Operations & Production Management, 39*(3), 429–453. doi:10.1108/IJOPM-03-2018-0184

Henfridsson, O., Yoo, Y., & Svahn, F. (2009). *Path creation in digital innovation: A multi-layered dialectics perspective.* Association for Information Systems.

Henry A, and Ronald S. M (2018). Supply chain resilience: a dynamic and multidimensional approach. *The International Journal of Logistics Management.* doi:10.1108/IJLM-04-2017-0093

He, P., Sun, Y., Zhang, Y., & Li, T. (2020). COVID–19's impact on stock prices across different sectors—An event study based on the chinese stock market. *Emerging Markets Finance and Trade. Routledge, 56*(10), 2198–2212. doi:10.1080/1540496X.2020.1785865

Herold, D. M., Ćwiklicki, M., Pilch, K., & Mikl, J. (2021). The emergence and adoption of digitalization in the logistics and supply chain industry: An institutional perspective. *Journal of Enterprise Information Management, 34*(6), 1917–1938. doi:10.1108/JEIM-09-2020-0382

Herzlinger, R. E. (2006). Why innovation in health care is so hard. *Harvard Business Review, 84*(5), 58. PMID:16649698

He, X., Meng, S., & Liang, J. (2021). Analysis of cross-border E-Commerce logistics model based on embedded system and genetic algorithm. *Microprocessors and Microsystems, 82,* 103827. https://doi.org/10.1016/J.MICPRO.2021.103827

He, Z., Han, G., Cheng, T. C. E., Fan, B., & Dong, J. (2019). Evolutionary Food Quality and Location Strategies for Restaurants in Competitive Online-to-Offline Food Ordering and Delivery Markets: An Agent-based Approach. *International Journal of Production Economics, 215,* 61–72. doi:10.1016/j.ijpe.2018.05.008

Hiatt, J. M. (2006). *ADKAR: A model for change in business, government, and our community.* Prosci Learning Center Publications.

Hidajet Karaxha, I. K. (2016). The Logistics and Management of Distribution Channels, the case of Kosovo. *ILIRIA International Review, 6*(1), 37–48. doi:10.21113/iir.v6i1.224

Higgins, J. M. (1995). *Innovate or evaporate: Test & improve your organization's IQ, its innovation quotient.* New Management Publishing Company.

Hinings, B., Gegenhuber, T., & Greenwood, R. (2018). Digital innovation and transformation: An institutional perspective. *Information and Organization, 28*(1), 52–61. doi:10.1016/j.infoandorg.2018.02.004

Hinsch, C., Felix, R., & Rauschnabel, P. A. (2020). Nostalgia beats the wow-effect: Inspiration, awe and meaningful associations in augmented reality marketing. *Journal of Retailing and Consumer Services, 53*(1), 1–11. doi:10.1016/j.jretconser.2019.101987

Hirsh, S., Alman, S., Lemieux, V., & Meyer, E. T. (2018). Blockchain: One emerging technology—so many applications. *Proceedings of the Association for Information Science and Technology, 55*(1), 691–693. doi:10.1002/pra2.2018.14505501083

Hobbs, J. E. (2020). Food supply chains during the COVID-19 pandemic. *Canadian Journal of Agricultural Economics/Revue canadienne d'agroeconomie, 68*(2), 171-176.

*Compilation of References*

Hobbs, J. E. (2020). Food Supply Chains during the COVID-19 Pandemic. *Canadian Journal of Agricultural Economics, 68*(2), 171–176. doi:10.1111/cjag.12237

Hoek, R. V. (2020). Responding to COVID-19 Supply Chain Risks—Insights from Supply Chain Change Management, Total Cost of Ownership and Supplier Segmentation Theory. *Logistics, 4*(4), 23. doi:10.3390/logistics4040023

Hoek, R. I. (1998). "Measuring the unmeasurable"-measuring and improving performance in the supply chain. *Supply Chain Management, 3*(4), 187–192. doi:10.1108/13598549810244232

Hoek, R. I. (1999). From reversed logistics to green supply chains. *Supply Chain Management, 4*(3), 129–134. doi:10.1108/13598549910279576

Hoek, R., Johnson, M., Godsell, J., & Birtwistle, A. (2010). Changing chains: Three case studies of the change management needed to reconfigure European supply chains. *International Journal of Logistics Management, 21*(2), 230–250. doi:10.1108/09574091011071933

Hofmann, E., Sternberg, H., Chen, H., Pflaum, A., & Prockl, G. (2019). Supply chain management and Industry 4.0: Conducting research in the digital age. *International Journal of Physical Distribution & Logistics Management, 49*(10), 945–955. doi:10.1108/IJPDLM-11-2019-399

Hofmann, H., Busse, C., Bode, C., & Henke, M. (2014). Sustainability-related supply chain risks: Conceptualization and management. *Business Strategy and the Environment, 23*(3), 160–172. doi:10.1002/bse.1778

Hofmann, S. (2019, September 21). *Distribution logistics - definition, basics, examples* (T. Knell, Ed.). Maschinenmarkt International.

Hofstede, G. H. (1980). *Organization Dynamics*. AMACOM.

Hohenstein, N.-O., Feisal, E., Hartmann, E., & Giunipero, L. (2015). Research on the phenomenon of supply chain resilience: A systematic review and parts for further investigation. *International Journal of Physical Distribution & Logistics Management, 45*(1/2), 90–117. doi:10.1108/IJPDLM-05-2013-0128

Holbrook, M. B., & Hirschman, E. C. (1982). The Experiential Aspects of Consumption: Consumer Fantasies, Feelings, and Fun. *The Journal of Consumer Research, 9*(2), 132–140. doi:10.1086/208906

Holland, C., Levis, J., Nuggehalli, R., Santilli, B., & Winters, J. (2017). UPS optimizes delivery routes. *Interfaces, 47*(1), 8–23. doi:10.1287/inte.2016.0875

Holmström, J., & Gutowski, T. (2017). Additive manufacturing in operations and supply chain management: No sustainability benefit or virtuous knock-on opportunities? *Journal of Industrial Ecology, 21*(1), 21–24. doi:10.1111/jiec.12580

Holt, D., & Ghobadian, A. (2009). An empirical study of green supply chain management practices Amongst UK manufacturers. *Journal of Manufacturing Technology Management, 20*(7), 933–956. doi:10.1108/17410380910984212

Homburg, C., Wieseke, J., & Bornemann, T. (2009). Implementing the marketing concept at the employee-customer interface: The role of customer need knowledge. *Journal of Marketing, 73*(4), 64–81.

Homrich, A. S., Galvao, G., Abadia, L. G., & Carvalho, M. M. (2018). The circular economy umbrella: Trends and gaps on integrating pathways. *Journal of Cleaner Production, 175*, 525–543. doi:10.1016/j.jclepro.2017.11.064

Hopkins, J. L. (2021). An investigation into emerging industry 4.0 technologies as drivers of supply chain innovation in Australia. *Computers in Industry, 125*, 103323. doi:10.1016/j.compind.2020.103323

Hosseini, S., & Barker, K. (2016). A Bayesian network model for resilience-based supplier selection. *International Journal of Production Economics, 180*, 68–87. doi:10.1016/j.ijpe.2016.07.007

Hosseini, S., Ivanov, D., & Dolgui, A. (2019). Review of quantitative methods for supply chain resilience analysis. *Transportation Research Part E, Logistics and Transportation Review, 125,* 285–307. doi:10.1016/j.tre.2019.03.001

Hosseini, S., Ivanov, D., & Dolgui, A. (2020). Ripple effect modelling of supplier disruption: Integrated Markov chain and dynamic Bayesian network approach. *International Journal of Production Research, 58*(11), 3284–3303. doi:10.1 080/00207543.2019.1661538

Hosseini, S., Morshedlou, N., Ivanov, D., Sarder, M. D., Barker, K., & Al Khaled, A. (2019). Resilient supplier selection and optimal order allocation under disruption risks. *International Journal of Production Economics, 213,* 124–137. doi:10.1016/j.ijpe.2019.03.018

Hron, M., Obwegeser, N., & Müller, S. D. (2021). Innovation drift: The influence of digital artefacts on organizing for innovation. *Innovation,* 1–33. doi:10.1080/14479338.2021.1937185

Hsu, C. W., & Hu, A. H. (2008). Green Supply Chain Management in the Electronic Industry. *International Journal of Science and Technology, 5*(2), 205-216.

Hu, B., & Luo, Q. (2014). *Cross-border E-commerce Mode Based on Internet +.* doi:10.1088/1757-899X/394/5/052014

Hu, A. H., & Hsu, C. W. (2010). Critical factors for implementing green supply chain management practice: An empirical study of electrical and electronics industries in Taiwan. *Management Research Review, 33*(6), 586–608. doi:10.1108/01409171011050208

Huda, A.K.M. N., Pathik, B.B., & Mohib, A.A. (2014). A Case Study Approach for Developing Supply Chain Management Models. *International Journal of Business and Economics Research, 3*(6), 6-14. doi:10.11648/j.ijber.s.2014030601.12

Hui, Z., He-Cheng, W., & Min-Fei, Z. (2015). Partnership management, supply chain collaboration, and firm innovation performance: An empirical examination. *International Journal of Innovation Science, 7*(2), 127–138. doi:10.1260/1757-2223.7.2.127

Hu, L. T., & Bentler, P. M. (1999). Cutoff criteria for fit indexes in covariance structure analysis: Conventional criteria versus new alternatives. *Structural Equation Modeling, 6*(1), 1–55. doi:10.1080/10705519909540118

Huo, B., Haq, M. Z. U., & Gu, M. (2021). The impact of information sharing on supply chain learning and flexibility performance. *International Journal of Production Research, 59*(5), 1411–1434. doi:10.1080/00207543.2020.1824082

Huq, F. A., & Stevenson, M. (2020). Implementing Socially Sustainable Practices in Challenging Institutional Contexts: Building Theory from Seven Developing Country Supplier Cases. *Journal of Business Ethics, 161*(2), 415–442. doi:10.100710551-018-3951-x

Hurduzeu, G., & Constantin, L. (2008). Several aspects regarding weather and weather derivatives. *The Romanian Economic Journal, 11*(27), 187–202.

Iakovou, E., Vlachos, D., & Xanthopoulos, A. (2007). An analytical methodological framework for the optimal design of resilient supply chains. *International Journal of Logistics Economics and Globalisation, 1*(1), 1. doi:10.1504/IJ-LEG.2007.014498

Iansiti, M., & Lakhani, K. R. (2017). The Truth about Blockchain. *Harvard Business Review, 95*(1), 118–127.

Ibbs, C. W., Wong, C. K., & Kwak, Y. H. (2001). Project Change Management System. *Journal of Management Engineering, 17*(3), 159–165. doi:10.1061/(ASCE)0742-597X(2001)17:3(159)

*Compilation of References*

IBM. (2017a, March 5). *Maersk and IBM Unveil First Industry-Wide Cross-Border Supply Chain Solution on Blockchain.* IBM Newsroom. https://newsroom.ibm.com/2017-03-05-Maersk-and-IBM-Unveil-First-Industry-Wide-Cross-Border-Supply-Chain-Solution-on-Blockchain

IBM. (2017b, December 14). *Walmart, JD.com, IBM and Tsinghua University Launch a Blockchain Food Safety Alliance in China.* IBM Newsroom. https://newsroom.ibm.com/2017-12-14-Walmart-JD-com-IBM-and-Tsinghua-University-Launch-a-Blockchain-Food-Safety-Alliance-in-China

IBM. (2021). *Big data analytics.* IBM Analytics. Retrieved from https://www.ibm.com/analytics/hadoop/big-data-analytics

IBM's version of the Evolution of Analytics. (2021, November 20). Retrieved from https://blackboxparadox.com/2017/03/20/on-the-evolution-of-analytics/

Ibn-Mohammed, T., Mustapha, K. B., Godsell, J. M., Adamu, Z., Babatunde, K. A., Akintade, D. D., Acquaye, A., Fujii, H., Ndiaye, M. M., Yamoah, F. A., & Koh, S. C. L. (2020). A critical review of the impacts of COVID-19 on the global economy and ecosystems and opportunities for circular economy strategies. *Resources, Conservation and Recycling, 164*, 105169. Advance online publication. doi:10.1016/j.resconrec.2020.105169 PMID:32982059

Iddique, A. S. (2020). Unprecedented environmental and energy impacts and challenges of COVID-19 pandemic. Environmental Research. Advance online publication. doi:10.1016/j.envres.2020.110443

IMCO. (2020). *Deglobalization. Implications for investors.* Oxford Economics.

Inbound Logistics. (2017, May 30). *Blockchain Survey Shows Awareness, Key Applications, and Implementation Plans.* Inbound Logistics. https://www.inboundlogistics.com/cms/article/blockchain-survey-shows-awareness/

Ingene, C. A., & Parry, M. E. (1995). Coordination and Manufacturer Profit Maximization. *Journal of Retailing, 71*(2), 129–151. doi:10.1016/0022-4359(95)90004-7

International Organization for Standardization. (2021). *Upcoming Standards for COVID-19.* https://www.iso.org/news/ref2622.html

IResearch. (2018). *2017 China's Local Lifestyle Service O2O Industry Report.* http://www.iresearchchina.com/content/details8_35352.html

Isaksson, R., Johansson, P., & Fischer, K. (2010). Detecting supply chain innovation potential for sustainable development. *Journal of Business Ethics, 97*(3), 425–442. doi:10.100710551-010-0516-z

Ishaq, U. (2021). The Impact of Disruptive Technologies on Higher Education in Indonesia. *Indonesian Journal of Informatics Education, 5*(1), 22–26. doi:10.20961/ijie.v5i1.42310

Ishfaq, R. (2012). Resilience through flexibility in transportation operations. *International Journal of Logistics Research and Applications., 15*(4), 215–229. doi:10.1080/13675567.2012.709835

Işık, S., İbiş, H., & Gulseven, O. (2021). The Impact of the COVID-19 Pandemic on Amazon's Business. SSRN *Electronic Journal.* doi:10.2139/ssrn.3766333

Ismail, H. S., Poolton, J., & Sharifi, H. (2011). The role of agile strategic capabilities in achieving resilience in manufacturing-based small companies. *International Journal of Production Research, 49*(18), 5469–5487. doi:10.1080/00207543.2011.563833

ISO (2017). ISO 20400:2017, Sustainable procurement – Guidance.

Ivanov, D. (2018). *Structural Dynamics and Resilience in Supply Chain Risk Management.* Springer. doi:10.1007/978-3-319-69305-7

Ivanov, D. (2020). 'A blessing in disguise' or 'as if it wasn't hard enough already': Reciprocal and aggravate vulnerabilities in the supply chain. *International Journal of Production Research*, *58*(11), 3252–3262. doi:10.1080/0020754 3.2019.1634850

Ivanov, D. (2020). Predicting the impacts of epidemic outbreaks on global supply chains: A simulation based analysis on the coronavirus outbreak (COVID-19/SARS-CoV-2) case. *Transportation Research Part E, Logistics and Transportation Review*, *136*, 101922. Advance online publication. doi:10.1016/j.tre.2020.101922 PMID:32288597

Ivanov, D. (2020). Viable supply chain model: Integrating agility, resilience and sustainability perspectives—lessons from and thinking beyond the COVID-19 pandemic. *Annals of Operations Research*. Advance online publication. doi:10.100710479-020-03640-6 PMID:32836614

Ivanov, D., & Das, A. (2020). Coronavirus (COVID-19/SARS-CoV-2) and supply chain resilience: A research note. *International Journal of Integrated Supply Management*, *13*(1), 90–102. doi:10.1504/IJISM.2020.107780

Ivanov, D., & Dolgui, A. (2019). New disruption risk management perspectives in supply chains: Digital twins, the ripple effect, and resileanness. *IFAC-PapersOnLine*, *52*(13), 337–342. doi:10.1016/j.ifacol.2019.11.138

Ivanov, D., & Dolgui, A. (2020). A digital supply chain twin for managing the disruption risks and resilience in the era of Industry 4.0. *Production Planning and Control*, 1–14.

Ivanov, D., & Dolgui, A. (2020). A digital supply chain twin for managing the disruption risks and resilience in the era of Industry 4.0. *Production Planning and Control*, 1–14. doi:10.1080/09537287.2020.1768450

Ivanov, D., & Dolgui, A. (2020). Viability of intertwined supply networks: Extending the supply chain resilience angles towards survivability. A position paper motivated by COVID-19 outbreak. *International Journal of Production Research*, *58*(10), 2904–2915. doi:10.1080/00207543.2020.1750727

Ivanov, D., & Dolgui, A. (2021). OR-methods for coping with the ripple effect in supply chains during COVID-19 pandemic: Managerial insights and research implications. *International Journal of Production Economics*, *232*, 107921. Advance online publication. doi:10.1016/j.ijpe.2020.107921 PMID:32952301

Ivanov, D., Dolgui, A., Das, A., & Sokolov, B. (2019). Digital supply chain twins: Managing the ripple effect, resilience, and disruption risks by data-driven optimization, simulation, and visibility. In *Handbook of ripple effects in the supply chain* (pp. 309–332). Springer. doi:10.1007/978-3-030-14302-2_15

Ivanov, D., Dolgui, A., & Sokolov, B. (2019). The impact of digital technology and Industry 4.0 on the ripple effect and supply chain risk analytics. *International Journal of Production Research*, *57*(3), 829–846. doi:10.1080/00207543.20 18.1488086

Ivanov, D., Dolgui, A., Sokolov, B., & Ivanova, M. (2017). Literature review on disruption recovery in the supply chain. *International Journal of Production Research*, *55*(20), 6158–6174. doi:10.1080/00207543.2017.1330572

Ivanov, D., Dolgui, A., Sokolov, B., Werner, F., & Ivanova, M. (2016). A dynamic model and an algorithm for short-term supply chain scheduling in the smart factory industry 4.0. *International Journal of Production Research*, *54*(2), 386–402. doi:10.1080/00207543.2014.999958

Ivanov, D., Sethi, S., Dolgui, A., & Sokolov, B. (2018). A survey on control theory applications to operational systems, supply chain management, and Industry 4.0. In *Annual Reviews in Control* (Vol. 46, pp. 134–147). Elsevier Ltd. doi:10.1016/j.arcontrol.2018.10.014

Iyengar, S. P., Acharya, H., & Kadam, M. (2020). Big Data Analytics in Healthcare Using Spreadsheets. In Big Data Analytics in Healthcare (pp. 155-187). doi:10.1007/978-3-030-31672-3_9

*Compilation of References*

Iyer, S. S., Seetharaman, A., & Maddulety, K. (2020). Education Transformation Using Block Chain Technology - A Student Centric Model. In S. K. Sharma, Y. K. Dwivedi, B. Metri, & N. P. Rana (Eds.), *Re-imagining Diffusion and Adoption of Information Technology and Systems: A Continuing Conversation. TDIT 2020.* Springer. doi:10.1007/978-3-030-64849-7_19

Iyer, S., Seetharaman, A., & Maddulety, K. (2021). Block chain technology and its impact on education sector. *International Journal of Innovation in Education, 7*(1), 1–16. doi:10.1504/IJIIE.2021.114905

Jabbar, S., Lloyd, H., Hammoudeh, M., Adebisi, B., & Raza, U. (2021). Blockchain-enabled supply chain: Analysis, challenges, and future directions. *Multimedia Systems, 27*(4), 787–806. doi:10.100700530-020-00687-0

Jabbarzadeh, A., Fahimnia, B., & Sabouhi, F. (2018). Resilient and sustainable supply chain design: Sustainability analysis under disruption risks. *International Journal of Production Research, 56*(17), 5945–5968. doi:10.1080/00207543.2018.1461950

Jabbour, A. B. L. (2015). Understanding the genesis of green supply chain management: Lessons from leading Brazilian companies. *Journal of Cleaner Production, 87*(1), 385–390. doi:10.1016/j.jclepro.2014.09.034

Jaca, C., Santos, J., Errasti, A., & Viles, E. (2011). Lean thinking with improvement teams in retail. *Total Quality Management & Business Excellence, 23*(3-4), 449–465. doi:10.1080/14783363.2011.593907

Jackson, D., Firtko, A., & Edenborough, M. (2007). Personal resilience as a strategy for surviving and thriving in the face of workplace adversity: A literature review. *Journal of Advanced Nursing, 60*(1), 1–9. doi:10.1111/j.1365-2648.2007.04412.x PMID:17824934

Jackson, S., & Ferris, T. L. J. (2015). Proactive and Reactive Resilience: A Comparison of Perspectives. *Insight - International Council on Systems Engineering, 18*(7).

Jacobsen, K. H. (2020). Will COVID-19 generate global preparedness? *Lancet, 395*(10229), 1013–1014. doi:10.1016/S0140-6736(20)30559-6 PMID:32199074

Jain, V., Kumar, S., Soni, U., & Chandra, C. (2017). Supply chain resilience: Model development and empirical analysis. *International Journal of Production Research, 55*(22), 6779–6800. doi:10.1080/00207543.2017.1349947

Jajja, M. S. S., Kannan, V. R., Brah, S. A., & Hassan, S. Z. (2017). Linkages between firm innovation strategy, suppliers, product innovation, and business performance: Insights from resource dependence theory. *International Journal of Operations & Production Management, 37*(8), 1054–1075. doi:10.1108/IJOPM-09-2014-0424

Jamal, F. (2009). Green supply chain management: A literature review. *Otago Management Graduate Review, 7*, 51–62.

James, H. (2018). Deglobalization: The Rise of Disembedded Unilateralism. *Annual Review of Financial Economics, 10*(1), 219–237. doi:10.1146/annurev-financial-110217-022625

Jan, O. (2020). *COVID-19 impacts on supply chains, sustainability and climate change.* Available at: www2.deloitte.com/global/en/blog/responsible-business-blog/2020/covid-19-impacts-on-supply-chainssustainability-and-climate-change.html

Jansen, A., & Stevels, A. (2006). Combining eco-design and user benefits from human-powered energy systems, a win-win situation. *Journal of Cleaner Production, 14*(15-16), 1299–1306. doi:10.1016/j.jclepro.2005.11.023

Jeble, S., Dubey, R., Childe, S. J., Papadopoulos, T., Roubaud, D., & Prakash, A. (2018). Impact of big data and predictive analytics capability on supply chain sustainability. *International Journal of Logistics Management, 29*(2), 513–538. doi:10.1108/IJLM-05-2017-0134

Jellali, A., & Benaissa, M. (2015, May). Sustainable performance evaluation of the supply chain. In *2015 4th International Conference on Advanced Logistics and Transport (ICALT)* (pp. 151-156). IEEE. 10.1109/ICAdLT.2015.7136612

Jewson, S. (2004). Introduction to weather derivative pricing. SSRN *Electronic Journal*. doi:10.2139/ssrn.557831

John, G. (2017). *Strategic supply chain alignment. Best practice in supply chain management.* CRC Press, Taylor & Francis Group.

Jugović, A., Bukša, J., Dragoslavić, A., & Sopta, D. (2019). The possibilities of applying blockchain technology in shipping. *Pomorstvo*, *33*(2), 274–279. doi:10.31217/p.33.2.19

Juttner, U. (2005). Supply chain risk management: Understanding the business requirements from a practitioner perspective. *International Journal of Logistics Management*, *16*(1), 120–141. doi:10.1108/09574090510617385

Juttner, U., & Maklan, S. (2011). Supply chain resilience in the global financial crisis: An empirical study. *Supply Chain Management*, *16*(4), 246–259. doi:10.1108/13598541111139062

Kachi, H., & Takahashi, Y. (2011, March 14). Plant Closures Imperil Global Supplies. *The Wall Street Journal*. https://www.wsj.com/articles/SB10001424052748704027504576198961775199034

Kagermann, H. (2015). Change through digitization—Value creation in the age of Industry 4.0. In *Management of permanent change* (pp. 23–45). Springer Gabler. doi:10.1007/978-3-658-05014-6_2

Kagermann, H., Wahlster, W., & Helbig, J. (2013). *Recommendations for implementing the strategic initiative Industrie 4.0: Final report of the Industrie 4.0 Working Group*. Forschungsunion.

Kahiluoto, H., Mäkinen, H., & Kaseva, J. (2020). Supplying resilience through assessing diversity of responses to disruption. *International Journal of Operations & Production Management*, *40*(3), 271–292. doi:10.1108/IJOPM-01-2019-0006

Kamalahmadi, M., & Mellat-Parast, M. (2016). Developing a resilient supply chain through supplier flexibility and reliability assessment. *International Journal of Production Research*, *54*(1), 302–321. doi:10.1080/00207543.2015.1088971

Kamalahmadi, M., & Parast, M. M. (2017). A review of the literature on the principles of enterprise and supply chain resilience: Major findings and directions for future research. *International Journal of Production Economics*, *171*, 116–133. doi:10.1016/j.ijpe.2015.10.023

Kamble, S. S., & Mor, R. S. (2021). Food supply chains and COVID-19: A way forward. In Agronomy Journal (Vol. 113, Issue 2, pp. 2195–2197). John Wiley and Sons Inc. doi:10.1002/agj2.20515

Kamble, S. S., Gunasekaran, A., & Gawankar, S. A. (2020). Achieving sustainable performance in a data-driven agriculture supply chain: A review for research and applications. *International Journal of Production Economics*, *219*, 179–194. doi:10.1016/j.ijpe.2019.05.022

Kamble, S., Gunasekaran, A., & Arha, H. (2019). Understanding the Blockchain technology adoption in supply chains-Indian context. *International Journal of Production Research*, *57*(7), 2009–2033. doi:10.1080/00207543.2018.1518610

Kang, J., Diao, Z., & Zanini, M. T. (2020). Business-to-business marketing responses to COVID-19 crisis: a business process perspective. In *Marketing Intelligence and Planning*. Emerald Group Holdings Ltd. doi:10.1108/MIP-05-2020-0217

Kang, J., Yu, R., Huang, X., Maharjan, S., Zhang, Y., & Hossain, E. (2017). Enabling localized peer-to-peer electricity trading among plug-in hybrid electric vehicles using consortium blockchains. *IEEE Transactions on Industrial Informatics*, *13*(6), 3154–3164. doi:10.1109/TII.2017.2709784

Kang, Y., Ryu, M. H., & Kim, S. (2010). Exploring sustainability management for telecommunications services: A case study of two Korean companies. *Journal of World Business*, *45*(4), 415–421. doi:10.1016/j.jwb.2009.08.003

*Compilation of References*

Kannan Govindan, Mishra, & Shukla. (2018). *Big data analytics and application for logistics and supply chain management*. doi:10.1016/j.tre.2018.03.011

Kano, L., Tsang, E. W. K., & Yeung, H. (2020). Wc. (2020). Global value chains: A review of the multi-disciplinary literature. *Journal of International Business Studies, 51*(4), 577–622. doi:10.105741267-020-00304-2

Kant Pal, S., Mukherjee, S., Baral, M. M., & Aggarwal, S. (2021). Problems of Big Data Adoption in the Healthcare Industries. *Asia Pacific Journal of Health Management, 16*(4), 282–287. doi:10.24083/apjhm.v16i4.1359

Kantur, D., & Say, A. I. (2015). Measuring organizational resilience: A scale development. *Journal of Business Economics and Finance, 4*(3), 2146–7943.

Kara, M. E., Fırat, S. Ü. O., & Ghadge, A. (2020). A data mining-based framework for supply chain risk management. *Computers & Industrial Engineering, 139*, 105570. doi:10.1016/j.cie.2018.12.017

Karamchandani, A., Srivastava, S. K., & Srivastava, R. K. (2020). Perception-based model for analyzing the impact of enterprise blockchain adoption on SCM in the Indian service industry. *International Journal of Information Management, 52*, 102019. doi:10.1016/j.ijinfomgt.2019.10.004

Karim, W., Haque, A., Anis, Z., & Ulfy, M. A. (2020). The Movement Control Order (MCO) for COVID-19 Crisis and its Impact on Tourism and Hospitality Sector in Malaysia. *International Journal of Tourism and Hospitality, 3*(2), 1–7.

Karlberg, T. (2000). *Supply chain environmental management*. Swedish Office of Science and Technology.

Karmaker, C. L., Ahmed, T., Ahmed, S., Ali, S. M., Moktadir, M. A., & Kabir, G. (2021a). Improving supply chain sustainability in the context of COVID-19 pandemic in an emerging economy: Exploring drivers using an integrated model. *Sustainable Production and Consumption, 26*, 411–427. doi:10.1016/j.spc.2020.09.019 PMID:33015267

Kasten, J. E. (2020). Big Data Applications in Healthcare Administration. *International Journal of Big Data and Analytics in Healthcare, 5*(2), 12–37. doi:10.4018/IJBDAH.2020070102

Katsaliaki, K., Galetsi, P., & Kumar, S. (2021). Supply chain disruptions and resilience: A major review and future research agenda. *Annals of Operations Research*. Advance online publication. doi:10.100710479-020-03912-1 PMID:33437110

Kaur, P., Dhir, A., Talwar, S., & Ghuman, K. (2021). The Value Proposition of Food Delivery Apps from the Perspective of Theory of Consumption Value. *International Journal of Contemporary Hospitality Management, 33*(4), 1129–1159. doi:10.1108/IJCHM-05-2020-0477

Kaushal, V., & Srivastava, S. (2021). Hospitality and tourism industry amid COVID-19 pandemic: Perspectives on challenges and learnings from India. *International Journal of Hospitality Management, 92*, 102707. doi:10.1016/j.ijhm.2020.102707 PMID:33024348

Kaushik A, Kumar S, Luthra S, Haleem A. (2014). Technology transfer: enablers and barriers—a review. *International Journal of Technology, Policy, and Management, 14*(2), 133-159.

Kavin, L., & Narasimhan, R. (2017, July). An investigation of innovation processes: The role of clock speed. *Supply Chain Forum International Journal, 18*(3), 189–200.

Kenny, D. A., & Albright, L. (1987). Accuracy in interpersonal perception: A social relations analysis. *Psychological Bulletin, 102*(3), 390–407. doi:10.1037/0033-2909.102.3.390 PMID:3317468

Ketchen, D. J. Jr, & Craighead, C. W. (2020). Research at the intersection of entrepreneurship, supply chain management, and strategic management: Opportunities highlighted by COVID-19. *Journal of Management, 46*(8), 1330–1341. doi:10.1177/0149206320945028

Khanfar, A. A. A., Iranmanesh, M., Ghobakhloo, M., Senali, M. G., & Fathi, M. (2021). Applications of Block chain Technology in Sustainable Manufacturing and Supply Chain Management: A Systematic Review. *Sustainability*, *13*(14), 7870. doi:10.3390u13147870

Khan, K. A., Bakkappa, B., Metri, B. A., & Sahay, B. S. (2009). Impact of agile supply chains' delivery practices on firms' performance: Cluster analysis and validation. *Supply Chain Management*, *14*(1), 41–48. doi:10.1108/13598540910927296

Khan, O. B., & Burnes, B. (2007). Risk and supply chain management: Creating a research agenda. *International Journal of Logistics Management*, *18*(2), 197–216. doi:10.1108/09574090710816931

Khan, S., Nazir, S., & Khan, H. U. (2021). Analysis of Navigation Assistants for Blind and Visually Impaired People: A Systematic Review. *IEEE Access: Practical Innovations, Open Solutions*, *9*, 26712–26734. doi:10.1109/AC-CESS.2021.3052415

Khor, K. S., & Udin, A. M. (2013). Reverse logistics in Malaysia: Investigating the effect of green product design and resource commitment. *Resources, Conservation and Recycling*, *81*, 71–80. doi:10.1016/j.resconrec.2013.08.005

Kilian, L., & Zhou, X. (2018). Modeling Fluctuations in the Global Demand for Commodities. *Journal of International Money and Finance*, *88*, 54–78. doi:10.1016/j.jimonfin.2018.07.001

Kilpatrick, J. (n.d.). *Managing supply chain risk and disruption*. Deloitte. https://www2.deloitte.com/global/en/pages/risk/cyber-strategic-risk/articles/covid-19-managing-supply-chain-risk-and-disruption.html

Kilpatrick, J., & Barter, L. (2020). *COVID-19: managing supply chain risk and disruption*. Available at: www2.deloitte.com/content/dam/Deloitte/ca/Documents/finance/Supply-Chain_POV_EN_FINAL-AODA.pdf

Kim, C., & Kim, H. J. (2019). A study on healthcare supply chain management efficiency: Using bootstrap data envelopment analysis. *Health Care Management Science*, *2*(3), 534–548. doi:10.100710729-019-09471-7 PMID:30830500

Kim, H.-J., & Xirouchakis, P. (2010). Capacitated disassembly scheduling with random demand. *International Journal of Production Research*, *48*(23), 7177–7194. doi:10.1080/00207540903469035

Kim, J. J., Kim, I., & Hwang, J. (2021). A Change of Perceived Innovativeness for Contactless Food Delivery Services Using Drones After the Outbreak of COVID-19. *International Journal of Hospitality Management*, *93*, 102758. doi:10.1016/j.ijhm.2020.102758

Kim, J., & Rhee, J. (2012). An empirical study on the impact of critical success factors on the balanced scorecard performance in Korean green supply chain management enterprises. *International Journal of Production Research*, *50*(9), 2465–2483. doi:10.1080/00207543.2011.581009

Kim, S., Kim, J., Badu-Baiden, F., Giroux, M., & Choi, Y. (2021). Preference for robot service or human service in hotels? Impacts of the COVID-19 pandemic. *International Journal of Hospitality Management*, *93*, 102795. doi:10.1016/j.ijhm.2020.102795

Kim, T. Y., Dekker, R., & Heij, C. (2017). Cross-border electronic commerce: Distance effects and express delivery in European union markets. *International Journal of Electronic Commerce*, *21*(2), 184–218. https://doi.org/10.1080/10864415.2016.1234283

King, D. D., Newman, A., & Luthans, F. (2016). Not if, but when we need resilience in the workplace. *Journal of Organizational Behavior*, *37*(5), 782–786. doi:10.1002/job.2063

Kirilmaz, O., & Erol, S. (2017). A Proactive Approach to Supply Chain Risk Management: Shifting Orders among Suppliers to Mitigate the Supply Side Risks. *Journal of Purchasing and Supply Management*, *23*(1), 54–65. doi:10.1016/j.pursup.2016.04.002

*Compilation of References*

Kiritsis, D., Bufardi, A., & Xirouchakis, P. (2003). Research Issues in Product Lifecycle Management and Information Tracking Using Smart Embedded Systems. *Advanced Engineering Informatics, 17*(3-4), 189–202. doi:10.1016/S1474-0346(04)00018-7

Kirk, G. S. (1951). Natural Change in Heraclitus. *Mind, 60*(237), 35–42. doi:10.1093/mind/LX.237.35

Klassen, R. D., & Vereecke, A. (2012). Social issues in supply chains: Capabilities link responsibility, risk (opportunity) and performance. *International Journal of Production Economics, 140*(1), 103–115. doi:10.1016/j.ijpe.2012.01.021

Klewitz, J., & Hansen, E. G. (2014). Sustainability-oriented innovation of SMEs: A systematic review. *Journal of Cleaner Production, 65*, 57–75. doi:10.1016/j.jclepro.2013.07.017

Klibi, W., & Martel, A. (2012). Modeling approaches for the design of resilient supply networks under disruptions. *International Journal of Production Economics, 135*(2), 882–898. doi:10.1016/j.ijpe.2011.10.028

Kline, R. B. (2015). *Principles and practice of structural equation modeling.* Guilford publications.

Knemeyer, A. M., Zinn, W., & Eroglu, C. (2009). Proactive planning for catastrophic events in supply chains. *Journal of Operations Management, 27*(2), 141–153. doi:10.1016/j.jom.2008.06.002

Knoppen, D., & Saenz, M. (2015). Purchasing: Can we bridge the gap between strategy and daily reality? *Business Horizons, 58*(1), 123–133. doi:10.1016/j.bushor.2014.09.006

Kobrin, S. J. (2015). Is a global nonmarket strategy possible? Economic integration in a multipolar world order. *Journal of World Business, 50*(2), 262–272. doi:10.1016/j.jwb.2014.10.003

Kochan, C. G., & Nowicki, D. R. (2019). Supply chain resilience: A systematic literature review and typological framework. *International Journal of Physical Distribution & Logistics Management, 48*(8), 842–865. doi:10.1108/IJPDLM-02-2017-0099

Koch, J., Frommeyer, B., & Schewe, G. (2020). Online Shopping Motives during the COVID-19 Pandemic—Lessons from the Crisis. *Sustainability, 12*(24), 10247. doi:10.3390u122410247

Ko, E., Hwang, V. K., & Kim, E. V. (2013). green marketing functions in building corporate image in the retail setting. *Journal of Business Research, 66*(10), 1709–1715. doi:10.1016/j.jbusres.2012.11.007

Korhonen, J., Honkasalo, A., & Seppälä, J. (2018). Circular economy: The concept and its limitations. *Ecological Economics, 143*, 37–46. doi:10.1016/j.ecolecon.2017.06.041

Korpela, K., Hallikas, J., & Dahlberg, T. (2017). Digital supply chain transformation toward blockchain integration. *proceedings of the 50th Hawaii international conference on system sciences, 1*, 4182-419. 10.24251/HICSS.2017.506

Kotb, I. (n.d.). *Smart Retailing in COVID-19 World: Insights from Egypt.* Academic Press.

Kottala, S., & Herbert, K. (2019). An empirical investigation of supply Chain operations reference model practices and supply chain performance: Evidence from manufacturing sector. *International Journal of Productivity and Performance Management.* doi:10.1108/IJPPM-09-2018-0337

Kowalski, J. C., & Sheehan, L. (2016). Health System Supply Chain. Results of the Third Health System Consolidated Service Center Practitioners' Survey. Academic Press.

Kozlenkova, I. V., Hult, G., Tomas, M., Lund, D. J., Mena, J. A., & Kekec, P. (2015). The Role of Marketing Channels in Supply Chain Management. *Journal of Retailing, 91*(4), 586–609.

KPMG. (2020). *COVID-19: Supply chain fraud and corruption threats - How to protect your business from new fraud and corruption risks within your supply chain.* Available at: https://home.kpmg/au/en/home/insights/2020/05/coronavirus-covid-19-supply-chain-fraud-corruption-threats.html

KPMG. (2021). *Covid-19 induced healthcare transformation in India.* KPMG.

Kravchenko, M., Pigosso, D. C., & McAloone, T. C. (2020). Circular economy enabled by additive manufacturing: Potential opportunities and key sustainability aspects. *DS 101: Proceedings of NordDesign 2020,* 1-14. 10.35199/NORDDESIGN2020.4

Kritchanchai, D. (2012). A framework for healthcare supply chain improvement in Thailand. *Operations and Supply Chain Management, 5*(2), 103–113.

Kshetri, N. (2018). Blockchain's roles in meeting key supply chain management objectives. *International Journal of Information Management, 39,* 80–89. doi:10.1016/j.ijinfomgt.2017.12.005

Kulkarni, A. J., Siarry, P., Singh, P. K., Abraham, A., Zhang, M., Zomaya, A., & Baki, F. (Eds.). (2020). *Big Data Analytics in Healthcare* (Vol. 66). Springer.

Kumar, A., Singh, R., & Modgil, S. (2020). Exploring the relationship between ICT, SCM practices and organizational performance in agri-food supply chain. *Benchmarking: An International Journal.* . doi:10.1108/BIJ-11-2019-0500

Kumar, P., & Kumar Singh, R. (2021a). Strategic framework for developing resilience in Agri-Food Supply Chains during COVID 19 pandemic. *International Journal of Logistics Research and Applications.* doi:10.1080/13675567.2021.1908524

Kumar, S., & Kumar, D. A. (2021). Building Employee Resilience through e-Training: A Case study of National Hydroelectric Power Corporation's Unit. *Turkish Online Journal of Qualitative Inquiry (TOJQI), 12*(5). https://www.researchgate.net/publication/353717157

Kumar, A., Jain, V., & Kumar, S. (2014). A comprehensive environment-friendly approach for supplier selection. *Omega, 42*(1), 109–123. doi:10.1016/j.omega.2013.04.003

Kumar, A., Liu, R., & Shan, Z. (2020). Is blockchain a silver bullet for supply chain management? Technical challenges and research opportunities. *Decision Sciences, 51*(1), 8–37. doi:10.1111/deci.12396

Kumar, D., & Kumar, D. (2014). Modelling Rural Healthcare Supply Chain in India using System Dynamics. *Procedia Engineering, 97,* 2204–2212. doi:10.1016/j.proeng.2014.12.464

Kumar, G., Banerjee, R. N., Meena, P. L., & Ganguly, K. (2016). Collaborative culture and relationship strength roles in collaborative relationships: A supply chain perspective. *Journal of Business and Industrial Marketing, 31*(5), 587–599. doi:10.1108/JBIM-12-2014-0254

Kumar, P., & Shankar, R. (2007). Flexibility in global supply chain: a review of perspectives. In *Proceedings of GLOGIFT* 07. UP Technical University.

Kumar, R., & Mishra, R. (2020). COVID-19 Global Pandemic: Impact on Management of Supply Chain. *International Journal of Emerging Technology and Advanced Engineering, 10*(4), 132–139. doi:10.46338/IJETAE0416

Kumar, S., & Managi, S. (2020). Does stringency of lockdown affect air quality? Evidence from Indian cities. *Economics of Disasters and Climate Change, 4*(3), 481–502. doi:10.100741885-020-00072-1 PMID:32838121

Kurien, G. P., & Qureshi, M. N. (2018). House of sustainable waste management: An implementation framework. *International Journal of Sustainable Manufacturing, 4*(1), 79–96. doi:10.1504/IJSM.2018.099583

*Compilation of References*

Kurniawan, R., Zailani, S., Iranmanesh, M., & Rajagopal, P. (2017). The effects of vulnerability mitigation strategies on supply chain effectiveness: Risk culture as moderator. *Supply Chain Management*, 22(1), 1–15. doi:10.1108/SCM-12-2015-0482

Kwak, D. W., Seo, Y. J., & Mason, R. (2018). Investigating the relationship between supply chain innovation, risk management capabilities and competitive advantage in global supply chains. *International Journal of Operations & Production Management*, 38(1), 2–21. doi:10.1108/IJOPM-06-2015-0390

Laaper, S., & Mussomeli, A. (2017). Introducing the digital supply network. *The Wall Street Journal*. Available at: https://deloitte.wsj.com/cio/2017/04/24/introducing-the-digital-supply-network/

Lacy, P., Long, J., & Spindler, W. (2020). Disruptive Technologies. In The Circular Economy Handbook (pp. 43-71). Palgrave Macmillan. doi:10.1057/978-1-349-95968-6_3

Lai, Y., Sun, H., & Ren, J. (2018). Understanding the determinants of big data analytics (BDA) adoption in logistics and supply chain management: An empirical investigation. *International Journal of Logistics Management*, 29(2), 676–703. doi:10.1108/IJLM-06-2017-0153

Lambert, D. M. J. S. (2003). Strategic Logistics Management. Homewood, IL: Irwin.

Lambert, D. M., & Cooper, M. C. (2000). Issues in Supply Chain Management. *Industrial Marketing Management*, 29(1), 65–83. doi:10.1016/S0019-8501(99)00113-3

Lamming, R., Johnsen, T., Zheng, J., & Harland, C. (2000). An initial classification of supply networks. *International Journal of Operations & Production Management*, 20(6), 675–691. doi:10.1108/01443570010321667

Lam, T. K. P. (2002). Making sense of SERVQUAL's dimensions to the Chinese customers in Macau. *Journal of Market Focused Management*, 5(10), 43–58. doi:10.1023/A:1012575412058

Landry, S., & Beaulieu, M. (2010). Achieving lean healthcare by combining the two-bin kanban replenishment system with RFID technology. *International Journal of Health Management and Information*, 1(1), 85–98.

Lanzini, F., Ubacht, J., & De Greeff, J. (2021). Blockchain adoptioin factors for SMEs in supply chain management. *Journal of Supply Chain Management Science*, 2(1-2), 47–68. doi:10.18757/jscms.2021.5624

Lapointe, L., Lavallee-Bourget, M. H., Pichard-Jolicoeur, A., Turgeon-Pelchat, A., & Fleet, R. (2020). Impact of telemedicine on diagnosis, clinical management and outcomes in rural trauma patients: A rapid review. *Canadian Journal of Rural Medicine*, 25(1), 31–40. doi:10.4103/CJRM.CJRM_8_19 PMID:31854340

Lasnier, G. (2004). *Supply and inventory management in the supply chain.* Hermes Sciences.

Lauren, W. (2020). Wearable technology and live video conferencing: The development of an affordable virtual teaching platform to enhance clinical skills education during the COVID-19 pandemic. *Canadian Medical Education Journal*, 11(5). Advance online publication. doi:10.36834/cmej.70554 PMID:33062106

Lavastre, O., Gunasekaran, A., & Spalanzani, A. (2012). Supply chain risk management in French companies. *Decision Support Systems*, 52(4), 828–838. doi:10.1016/j.dss.2011.11.017

Lechaptois, L. (2020). *Framing supply chain visibility through a multi-field approach. Proceedings of the Hamburg International Conference of Logistics (HICL) – 29. Data science and innovation in supply chain management.*

Lechler, S., Canzaniello, A., Roßmann, B., Heiko, A., & Hartmann, E. (2019). Real-time data processing in supply chain management: Revealing the uncertainty dilemma. *International Journal of Physical Distribution & Logistics Management*, 49(10), 1003–1019. doi:10.1108/IJPDLM-12-2017-0398

Lee, H. L., & Billington, C. (1995). The evolution of supply-chain-management models and practice at Hewlett-Packard. *Interfaces*, *25*(5), 42–63. doi:10.1287/inte.25.5.42

Lee, H. L., Padmanabhan, V., & Whang, S. (1997). Information distortion in a supply chain: The bullwhip effect. *Management Science*, *43*(4), 546–558. doi:10.1287/mnsc.43.4.546

Lee, I., & Lee, K. (2015). The Internet of Things (IoT): Applications, Investments, and Challenges for Enterprises. *Business Horizons*, *58*(4), 431–440. doi:10.1016/j.bushor.2015.03.008

Lee, S. (2008). Drivers for the participation of small and medium-sized suppliers in green supply chain initiatives. *Supply Chain Management*, *13*(3), 185–198. doi:10.1108/13598540810871235

Lee, S. M., Lee, D., & Schniederjans, M. J. (2011). Supply chain innovation and organizational performance in the healthcare industry. *International Journal of Operations & Production Management*, *31*(11), 1193–1214. doi:10.1108/01443571111178493

Lee, V. H., Ooi, K. B., Chong, A. Y. L., & Seow, C. (2014). Creating technological innovation via green supply chain management: An empirical analysis. *Expert Systems with Applications*, *41*(16), 6983–6994. doi:10.1016/j.eswa.2014.05.022

Leiponen, A., Thomas, L. D., & Wang, Q. (2021). The dApp economy: A new platform for distributed innovation? *Innovation*, 1–19. doi:10.1080/14479338.2021.1965887

Levine, S. (2014). *Assessing resilience: why quantification misses the point*. Humanitarian Policy Group, Overseas Development Institute. Retrieved from https://www.odi.org/sites/odi. org.uk/files/odi-assets/publications- opinion-files/9049.pdf

Li, Xiong, Mariuzzo, & Xia. (2021). The Underexplored Impacts of Online Consumer Reviews: Pricing and New Product Design Strategies in the O2O Supply Chain. *International Journal of Production Economics, 237*. . doi:10.1016/j.ijpe.2021.108148

Li, Z., Wu, H., King, B., Miled, Z. B., Wassick, J., & Tazelaar, J. (2017, June). On the integration of event-based and transaction-based architectures for supply chains. In *2017 IEEE 37th International Conference on Distributed Computing Systems Workshops (ICDCSW)* (pp. 376-382). IEEE.

Liang, D., Dai, Z., & Wang, M. (2021). Assessing Customer Satisfaction of O2O Takeaway Based on Online Reviews by Integrating Fuzzy Comprehensive Evaluation with AHP and Probabilistic Linguistic Term Sets. *Applied Soft Computing*, *98*, 106847. doi:10.1016/j.asoc.2020.106847

Lieb, R. M., Millen, R. A., & Van Wassenhove, L. N. (1993). Third-party logistics services: A comparison of experienced American and European manufacturers. *International Journal of Physical Distribution & Logistics Management*, *23*(6), 35–44. doi:10.1108/09600039310044894

Li, J., Ghosh, R., & Nachmias, S. (2020). In a time of COVID-19 pandemic, stay healthy, connected, productive, and learning: words from the editorial team of HRDI. *Human Resource Development International, 23(3), 199–207*. doi:10.1080/13678868.2020.1752493

Lim, S. F. W., Jin, X., & Srai, J. S. (2018). Consumer-driven E-commerce: A Literature Review, Design Framework, and Research Agenda on Last-mile Logistics Models. *International Journal of Physical Distribution and Logistics*, *48*(3), 308–332. doi:10.1108/IJPDLM-02-2017-0081

Lin, C. Y. (2007). Supply chain performance and the adoption of new logistics technologies for logistics service providers in Taiwan. *Journal of Statistics and Management Systems*, *10*(4), 519–543. doi:10.1080/09720510.2007.10701270

Lindell, M., Prater, C., & Perry, R. (2007). *Introduction to Emergency Management*. Wiley.

*Compilation of References*

Linkov, I., & Florin, M. (Eds.). (2016). *IRGC Resource Guide on Resilience*. International Risk Governance Center. Retrieved December 2021 from https://www.irgc.org/riskgovernance/resilience/

Linkov, I., Carluccio, S., Pritchard, O., Ní Bhreasail, Á., Galaitsi, S., Sarkis, J., & Keisler, J. M. (2020). The case for value chain resilience. *Management Research Review, 43*(12). Advance online publication. doi:10.1108/MRR-08-2019-0353

Linnenluecke, M. K. (2017). Resilience in business and management research: A review of influential publications and a research agenda. *International Journal of Management Reviews, 19*(1), 4–30. doi:10.1111/ijmr.12076

Linton, T., & Vakil, B. (2020). Coronavirus is proving we need more resilient supply chains. *Harvard Business Review*.

Lioutas, E. D., & Charatsari, C. (2021). Enhancing the ability of agriculture to cope with major crises or disasters: What the experience of COVID-19 teaches us. *Agricultural Systems, 187*, 103023. doi:10.1016/j.agsy.2020.103023

Li, P., Lu, X., & Zhu, S. (2020). Pricing weather derivatives with the Market Price of Risk Extracted from the Utility Indifference Valuation. *Computers & Mathematics with Applications (Oxford, England), 79*(12), 3394–3409. doi:10.1016/j.camwa.2020.02.007

Li, S., Ragu-Nathan, B., Ragu-Nathan, T. S., & Subba Rao, S. (2006). The impact of supply chain management practices on competitive advantage and organizational performance. *Omega, 34*(2), 107–124. doi:10.1016/j.omega.2004.08.002 PMID:17876965

Li, S., Rao, S. S., Ragu-Nathan, T. S., & Ragu-Nathan, B. (2005). Development and validation of a measurement instrument for studying supply chain management practices. *Journal of Operations Management, 23*(6), 618–641. doi:10.1016/j.jom.2005.01.002

Lisa, L., & Gisèle, B. (2021). Blockchain: An inter-organisational innovation likely to transform supply chain. *Supply Chain Forum: An International Journal, 22*(3), 240-249. 10.1080/16258312.2021.1953931

Litke, A., Anagnostopoulos, D., & Varvarigou, T. (2019). Blockchains for Supply Chain Management: Architectural Elements and Challenges towards a Global Scale Deployment. *Logistics, 3*(1), 5. doi:10.3390/logistics3010005

Liu, J., Feng, Y., Zhu, Q., & Sarkis, J. (2018). Green supply chain management and the circular Economy-Reviewing theory for advancement of both fields. *International Journal of Physical Distribution & Logistics Management, 48*(8), 794–817. doi:10.1108/IJPDLM-01-2017-0049

Liu, W., Dunford, M., & Gao, B. A. (2018). Discursive construction of the Belt and Road Initiative: From neo-liberal to inclusive globalization. *Journal of Geographical Sciences, 28*(9), 1199–1214. doi:10.100711442-018-1520-y

Liu, Z., Liu, J., & Osmani, M. (2021). Integration of Digital Economy and Circular Economy: Current Status and Future Directions. *Sustainability, 13*(13), 7217. doi:10.3390u13137217

Li, X., Wu, Q., Holsapple, C. W., & Goldsby, T. (2017). An empirical examination of firm financial performance along dimensions of supply chain resilience. *Management Research Review, 40*(3), 254–269. doi:10.1108/MRR-02-2016-0030

Loiacono, E., Watson, R., & Goodhue, D. (2002). WEBQUAL: A measure of Website quality. *Marketing Educators' Conference. Marketing Theory and Applications, 13*(1), 432–437.

Lopes de Sousa Jabbour, A. B., Chiappetta Jabbour, C. J., Hingley, M., Vilalta-Perdomo, E. L., Ramsden, G., & Twigg, D. (2020). Sustainability of supply chains in the wake of the coronavirus (COVID-19/SARS-CoV-2) pandemic: Lessons and trends. *Modern Supply Chain Research and Applications, 2*(3), 117–122. doi:10.1108/MSCRA-05-2020-0011

Luthra, Garg, & Haleem. (2014). Empirical analysis of green supply chain management practices in the Indian automobile industry. *Journal of Institution Of Engineers (India): Series C, 95*(2), 119-126.

Luthra, S., Garg, D., & Haleem, A. (2016). The impacts of critical success factors for implementing green supply chain management towards sustainability: An empirical investigation of the Indian automobile industry. *Journal of Cleaner Production, 121*, 142–158. doi:10.1016/j.jclepro.2016.01.095

Lyonnet, B., & Senkel, M.-P. (2015). Logitics. Nantes: Dunod.

Lysenko-Ryba, K. (2017). The Impact of Reverse Logistics on Customers Satisfaction. *Entrepreneurship and Management, 18*, 137–146.

Lyytinen, K. (2021). Innovation logics in the digital era: A systemic review of the emerging digital innovation regime. *Innovation*, 1–22. doi:10.1080/14479338.2021.1938579

Macaulay, J., Buckalew, L., & Chung, G. (2015). Internet of things in logistics: A collaborative report by DHL and Cisco on implications and use cases for the logistics industry. DHL Trend Research and Cisco Consulting Services, 439-449.

MacCarthy, B. L., Blome, C., Olhager, J., Srai, J. S., & Zhao, X. (2016). Supply chain evolution–theory, concepts and science. *International Journal of Operations & Production Management, 36*(12), 1696–1718. doi:10.1108/IJOPM-02-2016-0080

Mackay, J., Munoz, A., & Pepper, M. (2019). Conceptualising redundancy and flexibility towards supply chain robustness and resilience. Journal of Risk Research. doi:10.1080/13669877.2019.1694964

Madaan, J., & Mangla, S. (2015). A decision modeling approach for the eco-driven flexible green supply chain. In Systemic flexibility and business agility. Springer. doi:10.1007/978-81-322-2151-7_21

Madumidha, S., Siva Ranjani, P., Vandhana, U., & Venmuhilan, B. (2019). A theoretical implementation: Agriculture-food supply chain management using blockchain technology. *Proceedings of the 2019 TEQIP - III Sponsored International Conference on Microwave Integrated Circuits, Photonics and Wireless Networks, IMICPW 2019*, 174–178. 10.1109/IMICPW.2019.8933270

Maghsoudi, A., & Pazirandeh, A. (2016). Visibility, resource sharing and performance in supply chain relationships: Insights from humanitarian practitioners. *Supply Chain Management, 21*(1), 125–139. doi:10.1108/SCM-03-2015-0102

Ma, H., Wang, Y., & Wang, K. (2018). Automatic detection of false positive RFID readings using machine learning algorithms. *Expert Systems with Applications, 91*, 442–451. doi:10.1016/j.eswa.2017.09.021

Mahapatra, S., Levental, S., & Narasimhan, R. (2017). Market price uncertainty, risk aversion and procurement: Combining contracts and open market sourcing alternatives. *International Journal of Production Economics, 185*(3), 34–51. doi:10.1016/j.ijpe.2016.12.023

Maheshwari, S., Kaur, G., Kotecha, K., & Jain, P. K. (2020). Bibliometric Survey on Supply Chain in Healthcare using Artificial Intelligence. *Library Philosophy and Practice (e-journal), 4420*. Retrieved from https://digitalcommons.unl.edu/libphilprac/4420

Majumdar, A., Shaw, M., & Sinha, S. K. (2020). COVID-19 debunks the myth of socially sustainable supply chain: A case of the clothing industry in South Asian countries. *Sustainable Production and Consumption, 24*, 150–155. doi:10.1016/j.spc.2020.07.001

Malairajan, R. A., Ganesh, K., Muhos, M., & Anbuudayasankar, S. P. (2013). Class of resource allocation problems in supply chain–a review. *International Journal of Business Innovation and Research, 7*(1), 113–139. doi:10.1504/IJBIR.2013.050559

Mamun, M. (2021). Sustaiable supply chain management: Insights from Australia's firms. *International Journal of Business and Management, 16*(11), 99. doi:10.5539/ijbm.v16n11p99

*Compilation of References*

Mandal, S. (2016). An empirical competence-capability model of supply chain innovation. *Verslas: teorija ir praktika*, *17*(2), 138-149.

Mandal, S. (2012). An empirical investigation into supply chain resilience. *The IUP Journal of Supply Chain Management*, *9*(4), 46–61.

Mandal, S. (2017). The influence of organizational culture on healthcare supply chain resilience: Moderating role of technology orientation. *Journal of Business and Industrial Marketing*, *32*(8), 1021–1037. doi:10.1108/JBIM-08-2016-0187

Mandal, S. (2020). Impact of supplier innovativeness, top management support and strategic sourcing on supply chain resilience. *International Journal of Productivity and Performance Management*, *70*(7), 1561–1581. https://doi.org/10.1108/IJPPM-07-2019-0349

Mangla, S. K., Kumar, P., & Barua, M. K. (2014). flexible decision approach for analyzing the performance of sustainable supply chains under risks/uncertainty. *Global Journal of Flexible Systems Managment*, *15*(2), 113–130. doi:10.100740171-014-0059-8

Mangla, S. K., Kusi-Sarpong, S., Luthra, S., Bai, C., Jakhar, S. K., & Khan, S. A. (2020). Operational excellence for improving sustainable supply chain performance. *Resources, Conservation and Recycling*, *162*, 105025. doi:10.1016/j.resconrec.2020.105025 PMID:32834482

Mangla, S., Madaan, J., & Chan, F. T. (2013). Analysis of flexible decision strategies for the sustainability-focused green product recovery system. *International Journal of Production Research*, *51*(11), 3428–3442. doi:10.1080/00207543.2013.774493

Manhart, P., Summers, J. K., & Blackhurst, J. (2020). A Meta Analytic Review of Supply Chain Risk Management: Assessing Buffering and Bridging Strategies and Firm Performance. *The Journal of Supply Chain Management*, *56*(3), 66–87. doi:10.1111/jscm.12219

Manuj, I., & Mentzer, J. (2008). Global supply chain risk management strategies. *International Journal of Physical Distribution & Logistics Management*, *38*(3), 192–223. doi:10.1108/09600030810866986

Markovic, S., Iglesias, O., Singh, J. J., & Sierra, V. (2018). How does the perceived ethicality of corporate services brands influence loyalty and positive word-of-mouth? Analyzing the roles of empathy, affective commitment, and perceived quality. *Journal of Business Ethics*, *148*(4), 721–740. doi:10.100710551-015-2985-6

Martínez, L. R., Rios, R. A. O., & Prieto, M. D. (Eds.). (2020). New Trends in the Use of Artificial Intelligence for the Industry 4.0. Academic Press.

Martinez, V., Pavlov, A., & Bourne, M. (2010). Reviewing performance: An analysis of the structure and functions of performance management reviews. *Production Planning and Control*, *21*(1), 70–83. doi:10.1080/09537280903317049

Martinsen, U., & Bjorklund, M. (2012). Matches and gaps in the green logistics market. *International Journal of Physical Distribution & Logistics Management*, *42*(6), 562–583. doi:10.1108/09600031211250596

Maslow, A. H. (1970). *Motivation and personality* (2nd ed.). Harper & Row.

Masteika, I., & Čepinskis, J. (2015). Dynamic Capabilities in Supply Chain Management. *Procedia: Social and Behavioral Sciences*, *213*, 830–835. doi:10.1016/j.sbspro.2015.11.485

Masudin, I., Ramadhani, A., & Restuputri, D. P. (2021). Traceability System Model of Indonesian Food Cold-chain Industry: A Covid-19 Pandemic Perspective. *Cleaner Engineering and Technology*, *4*, 2666–7908. doi:10.1016/j.clet.2021.100238

Mathur, B., Gupta, S., Meena, M. L., & Dangayach, G. S. (2018). Healthcare supply chain management: Literature review and some issues. *Journal of Advances in Management Research*, *15*(3), 265–287. doi:10.1108/JAMR-09-2017-0090

Matthews, N. E., Stamford, L., & Shapira, P. (2019). Aligning sustainability assessment with responsible research and innovation: Towards a framework for constructive sustainability assessment. *Sustainable Production and Consumption*, *20*, 58–73. doi:10.1016/j.spc.2019.05.002 PMID:32051840

Maucher, D., & Hofmann, E. (2011). *Procurmenet trends in the automotive supplier industry*. Available at: www.kerkhoff-group.com/en/press/press-reports/press-details/news/

Maximo Torero Cullen. (2020). *COVID-19 and the Risk to Food Supply Chains: How to respond?* Food and Agriculture Organization of the United Nations (FAO). https://www.fao.org/policy-support/tools-and-publications/resources-details/en/c/1269383/

McBane, D. A. (1995). Empathy and the salesperson: A multidimensional perspective. *Psychology and Marketing*, *12*(4), 349–370. doi:10.1002/mar.4220120409

McCutcheon, D., & Stuart, F. I. (2000). Issues in the choice of supplier alliance partners. *Journal of Operations Management*, *18*(3), 279–303. doi:10.1016/S0272-6963(99)00026-1

McDonald, R. L. (2013). *Derivative Markets* (3rd ed.). Pearson Education.

McHopa, A. D., William, J. M., & Kimaro, J. M. (2020). Global supply chains vulnerability and distortions amidst covid19 pandemic: Antecedents for building resilience in downstream logistics. *Journal of Co-Operative and Business Studies*, *5*(2), 64–74.

McKenzie, B. (2020). *Beyond COVID-19: supply chain resilience holds key to recovery*. Available at: www.bakermckenzie.com/-/media/files/insight/publications/2020/04/covid19-global-economy.pdf

McKibbin, W., & Fernando, R. (2020). *The Global Macroeconomic Impacts of COVID-19: Seven Scenarios*. CAMA Working paper, The Australian National University.

McKinsey & Company. (2016). *Big Data and the Supply Chain: The big supply chain analytics landscape*. Author.

McLachlin, R. L., Larson, P. D., & Khan, S. (2009). Not-for-profit supply chains in interrupted environments: The case of a faith-based humanitarian relief organisation. *Management Research News*, *32*(11), 1050–1064. doi:10.1108/01409170910998282

Medrano, N., & Olarte-Pascual, C. (2016). An empirical approach to marketing innovation in small and medium retailers: an application to the Spanish sector. *Contemporary Economics*, *10*(3), 205-216.

Meherishi, L., Narayana, S. A., & Ranjani, K. S. (2019). Sustainable packaging for supply chain management in the circular economy: A review. *Journal of Cleaner Production*, *237*, 117582. doi:10.1016/j.jclepro.2019.07.057

Mehta, N., Pandit, A., & Shukla, S. (2019). Transforming healthcare with big data analytics and artificial intelligence: A systematic mapping study. *Journal of Biomedical Informatics*, *100*, 103311. doi:10.1016/j.jbi.2019.103311 PMID:31629922

Meidute-Kavaliauskiene, I., Yıldız, B., Çiğdem, Ş., & Činčikaitė, R. (2021). An Integrated Impact of Blockchain on Supply Chain Applications. *Logistics, 5*(2), 33. doi:10.3390/logistics5020033

Mei, J., & Afli, E. M. (2017, April). The Impact of Transportation Management System on Supply Chain Management: The Effectiveness of Chaineese Online Shopping Delivery- The "KUAIDI" System. *European Journal of Logistics. Purchasing and Supply Chain Management*, *5*(2), 1–9.

*Compilation of References*

Meijboom, B., Saskia Schmidt-Bakx, S., & Westert, G. (2011). Supply chain management practices for improving patient-oriented care. *Supply Chain Management, 16*(3), 166–175. doi:10.1108/13598541111127155

MeiTuan & China Federation of Logistics and Purchasing. (2019). *Report on the Development of Chinese Immediate Delivery Business in 2019.* http://pdf.dfcfw.com/pdf/H3_AP202006011381522218_1.pdf

MeiTuan Research Institute. (2019). *China Food Delivery Industry Investigation Report (first three quarters of 2019).* Author.

MeiTuan Research Institute. (2020). *China Food Delivery Industry Development Report 2019 and the First Half of 2020.* Author.

Meixell, M. J., & Luoma, P. (2015). Stakeholder pressure in sustainable supply chain management: A systematic review. *International Journal of Physical Distribution & Logistics Management, 45*(1/2), 69–89. doi:10.1108/IJPDLM-05-2013-0155

Melas, K. D., & Michail, N. (2020). The Relationship Between Commodity Prices and Freight Rates in the Dry Bulk Shipping Segment: A Threshold Regression Approach. SSRN *Electronic Journal.* doi:10.2139/ssrn.3581592

Melkonyan, A., Gruchmann, T., Lohmar, F., Kamath, V., & Spinler, S. (2020). Sustainability Assessment of Last-mile Logistics and Distribution Strategies: The Case of Local Food Networks. *International Journal of Production Economics, 228,* 107746. doi:10.1016/j.ijpe.2020.107746

Melnyk, S. A., Lummus, R. R., Vokurka, R. J., Burns, L. J., & Sandor, J. (2009). Mapping the future of supply chain management: A Delphi study. *International Journal of Production Research, 47*(16), 4629–4653. doi:10.1080/00207540802014700

Messina, D., Barros, A. C., & Soares, A. L. (2018). *How much visibility has a company over its supply chain? A diagnostic metric to assess supply chain visibility.* In 22nd Cambridge International Manufacturing Symposium, University of Cambridge.

Metilda, R. M., & Vivekanandan, K. (2011). Impact of supply chain management practices on the competitive advantage of Indian retail supermarkets. *International Journal of Logistics Systems and Management, 9*(2), 170–185. doi:10.1504/IJLSM.2011.041504

Meyer, K., & Peng, M. (2016). Theoretical foundations of emerging economy business research. *Journal of International Business Studies, 47*(1), 3–22. doi:10.1057/jibs.2015.34

Miani, P., Kille, T., Lee, S. Y., Zhang, Y., & Bates, P. R. (2021). The impact of the COVID-19 pandemic on current tertiary aviation education and future careers: Students' perspective. *Journal of Air Transport Management, 94*(January), 102081. doi:10.1016/j.jairtraman.2021.102081

Miemczyk, J., Johnsen, T. E., & Macquet, M. (2012). Sustainable purchasing and supply management: A structured literature review of definitions and measures at the dyad, chain and network levels. *Supply Chain Management, 17*(5), 478–496. doi:10.1108/13598541211258564

Mikhaylova, A., Sakulyeva, T., Shcherbina, T., Levoshich, N., & Truntsevsky, Y. (2021). Impact of Digitalization on the Efficiency of Supply Chain Management in the Digital Economy. *International Journal of Enterprise Information Systems, 17*(3), 34–46. doi:10.4018/IJEIS.2021070103

Mills, J., Schmitz, J., & Frizelle, G. (2004). A strategic review of "supply networks". *International Journal of Operations & Production Management, 24*(10), 1012–1036. doi:10.1108/01443570410558058

Min, H., and Galle, W. P. (1997). Green purchasing strategies: trends and implications. *International Journal of Purchasing & Materials Management, 33*(3), 10–17.

Min, H. (2019). Blockchain technology for enhancing supply chain resilience. *Business Horizons*, *62*(1), 35–45. doi:10.1016/j.bushor.2018.08.012

Min, H., & Galle, W. P. (2001). Green purchasing practices of us firms. *International Journal of Operations & Production Management*, *21*(9), 1222–1238. doi:10.1108/EUM0000000005923

Min, H., Ko, H. J., & Ko, C. S. (2006). A genetic algorithm approach to developing the multi-echelon reverse logistics network for product returns. *Omega*, *34*(1), 56–69. doi:10.1016/j.omega.2004.07.025

Ministry of Transport Scientific Research Institute. (2019). *Railway Statistics Bulletin.* Beijing: Ministry of Transport of the People's Republic of China.

Minnema, A., Bijmolt, T. H. A., Gensler, S., & Wiesel, T. (2016). To Keep or Not to Keep: Effects of Online Customer Reviews on Product Returns. *Journal of Retailing.* doi:10.1016/j.jretai.2016.03.001

Min, S., Zacharia, Z. G., & Smith, C. D. (2019). Defining supply chain management: In the past, present, and future. *Journal of Business Logistics*, *40*(1), 44–55. doi:10.1111/jbl.12201

Mirabelli, G., & Solina, V. (2020). Blockchain and agricultural supply chains traceability: Research trends and future challenges. *Procedia Manufacturing*, *42*, 414–421. doi:10.1016/j.promfg.2020.02.054

Mirotin, L. B. Y. T. (2002). Logistics: customer Service. Moscow: INFRA–M.

Mohan, S., Gopalakrishnan, M., & Mizzi, P. J. (2013). Improving the Efficiency of a Non-profit Supply Chain for the Food Insecure. *International Journal of Production Economics*, *143*(2), 248–255. doi:10.1016/j.ijpe.2011.05.019

Mohr, J. J., & Sohi, R. S. (1995). Communication flows in distribution channels: Impact on assessments of communication quality and satisfaction. *Journal of Retailing*, *71*(4), 393–415. doi:10.1016/0022-4359(95)90020-9

Molina-Besch, K. (2016). Prioritization guidelines for green food packaging development. *British Food Journal*, *2016*(118), 2512–2533. doi:10.1108/BFJ-12-2015-0462

Mollenkopf, D. A., Ozanne, L. K., & Stolze, H. J. (2020). A transformative supply chain response to COVID-19. *Journal of Service Management*, *32*(2), 190–202. doi:10.1108/JOSM-05-2020-0143

Monczka, R. M., Handfield, R. B., Giunipero, L. C., & Patterson, J. L. (2015). *Purchasing and supply chain management* (6th ed.). Cengage Learning.

Monczka, R. M., Handfield, R. B., Giunipero, L. C., & Patterson, J. L. (2016). *Purchasing and Supply chain management* (6th ed.). Cengage.

Monmousseau, P., Marzuoli, A., Feron, E., & Delahaye, D. (2020). Impact of Covid-19 on passengers and airlines from passenger measurements: Managing customer satisfaction while putting the US Air Transportation System to sleep. *Transportation Research Interdisciplinary Perspectives*, *7*, 100179. doi:10.1016/j.trip.2020.100179 PMID:34173460

Moreira, A. C., Ferreira, L. M. D., & Zimmermann, R. A. (Eds.). (2018). *Innovation and supply chain management: Relationship, collaboration and strategies.* Springer. doi:10.1007/978-3-319-74304-2

Morgan, A. K., Awafo, B. A., & Quartey, T. (2021). The effects of COVID-19 on global economic output and sustainability: Evidence from around the world and lessons for redress. *Sustainability: Science, Practice, and Policy*, *17*(1), 77–81. doi:10.1080/15487733.2020.1860345

Moritz, B. (2020). Supply chain disruptions and COVID-19. *Supply Chain Management Review*, *24*(3), 14–17.

*Compilation of References*

Moro Visconti, R., & Morea, D. (2019). Big Data for the Sustainability of Healthcare Project Financing. *Sustainability*, *11*(13), 3748. Advance online publication. doi:10.3390u11133748

Morseletto, P. (2020). Targets for a circular economy. *Resources, Conservation and Recycling*, *153*, 104553. doi:10.1016/j.resconrec.2019.104553

Mousavi, S. M., Bahreininejad, A., Musa, S. N., & Yusof, F. (2017). A modifed particle swarm optimization for solving the integrated location and inventory control problems in a two-echelon supply chain network. *Journal of Intelligent Manufacturing*, *28*(1), 191–206. doi:10.100710845-014-0970-z

Muduli, K., & Barve, A. (2013). Developing a framework for study of GSCM criteria in Indian mining industries. *AP-CBEE Procedia*, *5*, 22–26. doi:10.1016/j.apcbee.2013.05.005

Muduli, K., & Barve, A. (2015). Analysis of Critical Activities for GSCM Implementation in Mining Supply Chains in India Using Fuzzy Analytical Hierarchy Process. *International Journal of Business Excellence*, *8*(6), 767–797. doi:10.1504/IJBEX.2015.072309

Muduli, K., Barve, A., Tripathy, S., & Biswal, J. N. (2016). Green practices adopted by the mining supply chains in India: A case study. *International Journal of Environment and Sustainable Development*, *15*(2), 159–182. doi:10.1504/IJESD.2016.076365

Muduli, K., Biswal, J. N., Satapathy, S., Barve, A., & Tripathy, S. (2017). Investigation of influential factors of green supply chain management in Indian mining industries: An empirical study. *International Journal of Business Excellence*, *12*(3), 351–375. doi:10.1504/IJBEX.2017.084453

Mukherjee, S., Chittipaka, V., & Baral, M. M. (2022). Addressing and Modeling the Challenges Faced in the Implementation of Blockchain Technology in the Food and Agriculture Supply Chain. In Blockchain Technologies and Applications for Digital Governance (pp. 151–179). doi:10.4018/978-1-7998-8493-4.ch007

Mukherjee, S., Chittipaka, V., Baral, M. M., & Srivastava, S. C. (2022). Integrating the Challenges of Cloud Computing in Supply Chain Management. In Recent Advances in Industrial Production (pp. 355–363). doi:10.1007/978-981-16-5281-3_33

Mukherjee, S., Baral, M. M., Chittipaka, V., Srivastava, S. C., & Pal, S. K. (2021). *Discussing the Impact of Industry 4.0 in Agriculture Supply Chain*. Springer. doi:10.1007/978-981-16-3033-0_28

Mukherjee, S., Baral, M. M., Venkataiah, C., Pal, S. K., & Nagariya, R. (2021). Service robots are an option for contactless services due to the COVID-19 pandemic in the hotels. *Decision (Washington, D.C.)*, *48*(4), 445–460. doi:10.100740622-021-00300-x

Mukherjee, S., & Chittipaka, V. (2021). Analysing the Adoption of Intelligent Agent Technology in Food Supply Chain Management: An Empirical Evidence. *FIIB Business Review*. Advance online publication. doi:10.1177/23197145211059243

Mukherjee, S., Chittipaka, V., & Baral, M. M. (2021). *Developing a Model to Highlight the Relation of Digital Trust With Privacy and Security for the Blockchain Technology*. doi:10.4018/978-1-7998-8081-3.ch007

Mukherjee, S., Mohan Baral, M., Srivastava, S. C., & Jana, B. (2021). Analyzing the problems faced by fashion retail stores due to covid-19 outbreak. *Parikalpana-KIIT Journal of Management*, *17*(I), 206. Advance online publication. doi:10.23862/kiit-parikalpana/2021/v17/i1/209031

Munksgaard, K. B., Stentoft, J., & Paulraj, A. (2014). Value-based supply chain innovation. *Operations Management Research*, *7*(3-4), 50–62. doi:10.100712063-014-0092-y

Munoz, J. N. J.-R.-R. (2003). Natural gas network modeling for power systems reliability studies. IEEE Bologna PowerTech Conference.

Murray, G. (2000). effects of a green purchasing strategy: The case of Belfast city council. *Supply Chain Management*, *5*(1), 37–44. doi:10.1108/13598540010312954

Nadeesha, A., Haijun, W., & Duminda, K. (2019). Effect of supply-chain resilience on firm performance and competitive advantage - A study of the Sri Lankan apparel industry. *Business Process Management Journal*, *25*(7), 1673–1695. doi:10.1108/BPMJ-09-2018-0241

Nagarajan, V., & Sharma, P. (2021). Firm internationalization and long-term impact of the Covid-19 pandemic. *Managerial and Decision Economics*, *42*(6), 1477–1491. Advance online publication. doi:10.1002/mde.3321 PMID:34230720

Nagar, D., Raghav, S., Bhardwaj, A., Kumar, R., Singh, P. L., & Sindhwani, R. (2021). Machine learning: Best way to sustain the supply chain in the era of industry 4.0. *Materials Today: Proceedings*, *47*, 3676–3682. doi:10.1016/j.matpr.2021.01.267

Nagashima, M., Wehrle, F., Kerbache, L., & Lassagne, M. (2015). Impacts of adaptive collaboration on demand forecasting accuracy of different product categories throughout the product life cycle. *Supply Chain Management*, *20*(4), 415–433. doi:10.1108/SCM-03-2014-0088

Nagorney, A., & Toyasaki, F. (2005). Reverse supply chain management and electronic waste recycling: a multi-tiered network equilibrium framework for e-cycling. *Transportation Research Part E: Logistics and Transportation Review*, *41*, 1–28.

Nakamoto, S. (2008). Bitcoin: A peer-to-peer electronic cash system. *Decentralized Business Review*, 21260. https://bitcoin.org/bitcoin.pdf

Nakamura, H., & Managi, S. (2020). Airport risk of importation and exportation of the COVID-19 pandemic. *Transport Policy*, *96*, 40–47. doi:10.1016/j.tranpol.2020.06.018 PMID:32834679

Nakat, Z., & Bou-Mitri, C. (2021). COVID-19 and the food industry: Readiness assessment. *Food Control*, *121*, 107661. doi:10.1016/j.foodcont.2020.107661 PMID:33013004

Nambisan, S. (2020). Digital innovation and international business. *Innovation*, 1–10. doi:10.1080/14479338.2020.1834861

Nambisan, S., Lyytinen, K., Majchrzak, A., & Song, M. (2017). Digital Innovation Management: Reinventing innovation management research in a digital world. *Management Information Systems Quarterly*, *41*(1), 223–238. doi:10.25300/MISQ/2017/41:1.03

Namdar, J., Li, X., Sawhney, R., & Pradhan, N. (2018). Supply chain resilience for single and multiple sourcing in the presence of disruption risks. *International Journal of Production Research*, *56*(6), 2339–2360. doi:10.1080/00207543.2017.1370149

Nandi, S., Sarkis, J., Hervani, A. A., Helms, M. M. (2021). Redesigning Supply Chains using Blockchain-Enabled Circular Economy and COVID-19 Experiences. *Sustainable Production and Consumption*. . doi:10.1016/j.spc.2020.10.019

Nandi, S., Sarkis, J., Hervani, A., & Helms, M. (2020). Do blockchain and circular economy practices improve post COVID-19 supply chains? A resource-based and resource dependence perspective. *Industrial Management & Data Systems*, *121*(2), 333–363. Advance online publication. doi:10.1108/IMDS-09-2020-0560

Naomi, S., Bolis, I., Monteiro, M., & Carvalho, D. (2018). From an ideal dream towards reality analysis : Proposing Sustainable Value Exchange Matrix (SVEM) from systematic literature review on sustainable business models and face validation. *Journal of Cleaner Production*, *178*, 76–88. doi:10.1016/j.jclepro.2017.12.078

Narasimhan, R., & Carter, J. R. (1998). Environmental supply chain management. Center for Advanced Purchasing Studies.

Narayanan, S., Narasimhan, R., & Schoenherr, T. (2015). Assessing the contingent effects of collaboration on agility performance in buyer–supplier relationships. *Journal of Operations Management*, *33*(1), 140–154. doi:10.1016/j.jom.2014.11.004

Nash, K. S., & King, R. (2016, July 29). IBM set to launch one of the largest blockchain implementations to date. *The Wall Street Journal*. https://www.wsj.com/articles/BL-CIOB-10241

Nasiri, M., Ukko, J., Saunila, M., & Rantala, T. (2020). Managing the digital supply chain: The role of smart technologies. *Technovation*, *96*, 102121. doi:10.1016/j.technovation.2020.102121

Naspetti, S., Mandolesi, S., Buysse, J., Latvala, T., Nicholas, P., Padel, S., Van Loo, E., & Zanoli, R. (2017). Determinants of the acceptance of sustainable production strategies among dairy farmers: Development and testing of a modified technology acceptance model. *Sustainability*, *9*(10), 1805. doi:10.3390u9101805

Nasrollahi, M., Fattahy Takhtgahi, A., & Sajjadinia, Z. (2016). The role of IT in supply chain agility and its impact on organizational performance. In *Second International Conference on Management, Innovation and Entrepreneurship Paradigms*. Shahid Beheshti University

Nath, T. D. (2009). *Leveraging information technology in the supply chain for organizational transformation: a meta-analysis of the supply chain literature*. https://ro.ecu.edu.au/theses/159

National Research Council. (2013). *An Ecosystem Services Approach to Assessing the Impacts of the Deepwater Horizon Oil Spill in the Gulf of Mexico*. National Academies Press (US).

Nawrocka, D., Brorson, T., & Lindhqvist, T. (2009). ISO 14001 in environmental supply chain practices. *Journal of Cleaner Production*, *17*(16), 1435–1443. doi:10.1016/j.jclepro.2009.05.004

Nayal, K., Raut, R.D., Queiroz, M.M., Yadav, V.S., & Narkhede, B.E. (2021). Are artificial intelligence and machine learning suitable to tackle the COVID-19 impacts? An agriculture supply chain perspective. *The International Journal of Logistics Management*. doi:10.1108/IJLM-01-2021-0002

Nayler, J., & Subramanian, L. (2021). *Covid-19 Health Supply Chain Impact-Preliminary Evidence from Africa*. Pamela Steele Associates Ltd. https://www.pamsteele.co.uk/wp-content/uploads/2021/03/Covid19_Impact-on-health-supply-chain.pdf

Nchanji, E. B., & Lutomia, C. K. (2021). *COVID-19 Challenges to Sustainable Food Production and Consumption: Future Lessons for Food Systems in Eastern and Southern Africa from a gender lens*. Sustainable Production and Consumption. doi:10.1016/j.spc.2021.05.016

Neely, A. (2005). The evolution of performance measurement research. *International Journal of Operations & Production Management*, *25*(12), 1264–1277. doi:10.1108/01443570510633648

Negri, M., Cagno, E., Colicchia, C., & Sarkis, J. (2021). Integrating sustainability and resilience in the supply chain: A systematic literature review and a research agenda. *Business Strategy and the Environment*, *30*(7), 2858–2886. Advance online publication. doi:10.1002/bse.2776

Nel, J. D., & Badenhorst, A. (2020). A conceptual framework for reverse logistics challenges in e-commerce. *International Journal of Business Performance Management*, *21*(1–2), 114–131. https://doi.org/10.1504/IJBPM.2020.106119

Nhamo, G., Dube, K., & Chikodzi, D. (2020). COVID-19 and Implications for the Aviation Sector: A Global Perspective. *Counting the Cost of COVID-19 on the Global Tourism Industry*, 89–107. doi:10.1007/978-3-030-56231-1_4

Nidumolu, R., Prahalad, C. K., & Rangaswami, M. R. (2015). Why sustainability is now the key driver of innovation. *IEEE Engineering Management Review, 43*(2), 85–91. doi:10.1109/EMR.2015.7123233

Nikolskaya, E. Y., Avilova, N. L., Kovaleva, N. I., Konovalova, E. E., & Sharonin, P. N. (2021). The Influence of Digitization on Staff Training for Tourism and Hospitality Industry. *Revista Geintec-Gestao Inovacao E Tecnologias, 11*(4), 414-423. . doi:10.47059/revistageintec.v11i4.2117

Nikookar, E., Nagalingam, S., Sosay, C. (2016). The role of visibility in supply chain resilience: A Resource-based approach. *Technology, Innovation & Supply Chain Management Competitive Session*, 1-19.

Ninlawan, C., Seksan, P., Tossapol, K., & Pilada, W. (2010). The Implementation of Green Supply Chain Management Practices in Electronics Industry. *Proceedings of the International Multiconference of Engineers and Computer Scientists.*

Niu, B., Li, Q., Mu, Z., Chen, L., & Ji, P. (2021). Platform Logistics or Self-logistics? Restaurants' Cooperation with Online Food-delivery Platform Considering Profitability and Sustainability. *International Journal of Production Economics, 234*, 108064. doi:10.1016/j.ijpe.2021.108064

Nnaji, C., Okpala, I., & Awolusi, I. (2020). Wearable Sensing Devices: Potential Impact and Current Use for Incident Prevention. *American Society of Safety Engineers Professional Safety, 65*(4), 1–9.

North, D. C. (1990). *Institutions, Institutional Change, and Economic Performance.* Cambridge University Press. doi:10.1017/CBO9780511808678

Notland, J. S. (2016). *Blockchain Enabled Trust & Transparency in Supply Chains* (Master's Thesis). NTNU Norwegian University of Science and Technology, Trondheim, Norway. https://www.pdf-archive.com/2017/02/01/project-thesis-anders-j-rgen/project-thesis-anders-j-rgen.pdf

Nowicka, K. (2019). Digital innovation in the supply chain management. *Prace Naukowe Uniwersytetu Ekonomicznego we Wrocławiu, 63*(8), 202-214.

NPR. (2020). *As the Pandemic Spreads, Will There Be Enough Ventilators? There-Be-Enough-Ventilators.* Available at: https://www.npr.org/sections/health-shots/2020/03/14/815675678/as-the-pandemic-spreads-will-there-be-enough-ventilators

Nunnally, J. C. (1994). *Psychometric theory* (3rd ed.). Tata McGraw-Hill Education.

O'Marah. (2018). Lessons in Excellence from Five Supply Chain Leaders, SCM world learning engine. *SCM World.* https://www.forbes.com/sites/kevinomarah/2018/05/30/lessons-in-excellence-from-five-supply-chain-leaders/#403559551545

O'Neall, C. E., & Haraburda, S. S. (2017). *Balanced scorecards for supply Chain management.* Academic Press.

OECD. (2021). *Towards ethical supply chains.* Available at: https://www.oecd.org/about/impact/towards-ethical-supply-chains.htm

Ojha, D., Shockley, J., & Acharya, C. (2016). Supply chain organizational infrastructure for promoting entrepreneurial emphasis and innovativeness: The role of trust and learning. *International Journal of Production Economics, 179*, 212–227. doi:10.1016/j.ijpe.2016.06.011

Ojha, R., Ghadge, A., Tiwari, M. K., & Bititci, U. S. (2018). Bayesian network modelling for supply chain risk propagation. *International Journal of Production Research, 56*(17), 5795–5819. doi:10.1080/00207543.2018.1467059

Olaf, P. (2010). *Change Management* (1st ed.). Bookboon Learning.

Oliver, R. (2001). *Managing Change – Definition und Phases in Change Processes.* Recklies Management Project GmbH. www.themanager.org

*Compilation of References*

Oliver, K. G., Collin, P., Burns, J., & Nicholas, J. (2006). Building resilience in young people through meaningful participation. *Australian e-Journal for the Advancement of Mental Health*, *5*(1), 34–40. doi:10.5172/jamh.5.1.34

Olsson, C. A., Bond, L., Burns, J. M., Vella-Brodrick, D. A., & Sawyer, S. M. (2003). Adolescent resilience: A concept analysis. *Journal of Adolescence*, *26*(1), 1–11. doi:10.1016/S0140-1971(02)00118-5 PMID:12550818

Omkareshwar, M. (2013). Green marketing initiatives by the corporate world: A study. *Advances in Management*, *6*(3), 20–26.

Onwuegbuzie, A. J., & Freis, R. (2016). *Seven Steps to a Comprehensive Literature Review: A Multimodal and Cultural Approach*. Sage Publication.

Oussous, A., Benjelloun, F.-Z., Ait Lahcen, A., & Belfkih, S. (2018). Big Data technologies: A survey. *Journal of King Saud University - Computer and Information Sciences, 30*(4), 431-448. doi:10.1016/j.jksuci.2017.06.001

Oyekola, P., Swain, S., Muduli, K., & Ramasamy, A. (2021). *IoT in Combating Covid 19 Pandemics: Lessons for Developing Countries, Blockchain Technology in Medicine and Healthcare*. Concepts, Methodologies, Tools, and Applications.

Oztemel, E., & Gursev, S. (2020). Literature review of Industry 4.0 and related technologies. *Journal of Intelligent Manufacturing*, *31*(1), 127–182. doi:10.100710845-018-1433-8

Pacaux-Lemoine, M. P., Trentesaux, D., Rey, G. Z., & Millot, P. (2017). Designing intelligent manufacturing systems through Human-Machine Cooperation principles: A human-centered approach. *Computers & Industrial Engineering*, *111*, 581–595. doi:10.1016/j.cie.2017.05.014

Paez, A. R. G. F. D. (Ed.). (2021). COVID-19 Pandemic, Geospatial Information, and Community Resilience - Global Applications and Lessons. CRC Press, Taylor & Francis Group, LLC.

Pagell, M., & Krause, D. R. (2004). Re-exploring the relationship between flexibility and the external environment. *Journal of Operations Management*, *21*(6), 629–649. doi:10.1016/j.jom.2003.11.002

Pagell, M., & Shevchenko, A. (2013). Why research in sustainable supply chain management should have no future. *The Journal of Supply Chain Management*, *50*(1), 44–55. doi:10.1111/jscm.12037

Palomares, G. (2006). *Relaciones internacionales en el siglo XXI*. Tecnos.

Pal, S. K., Baral, M. M., Mukherjee, S., Venkataiah, C., & Jana, B. (2021). Analyzing the impact of supply chain innovation as a mediator for healthcare firms' performance. *Materials Today: Proceedings*. Advance online publication. doi:10.1016/j.matpr.2021.10.173

Panahifar, F., Byrne, P., Salam, M., & Heavey, C. (2018). Supply chain Collaboration and firm's performance: The critical role of information sharing and trust. *Journal of Enterprise Information Management*.

Panayides, P., Lambertides, N., & Cullinane, K. (2013). Liquidity risk premium and Asset Pricing in US Water Transportation. *Transportation Research E. Logistics and Transportation Review*, *52*, 3–15. doi:10.1016/j.tre.2012.11.007

Panova, Y., & Hilletofth, P. (2018). Managing supply chain risks and delays in construction project. *Industrial Management & Data Systems*, *118*(7), 1413–1431. doi:10.1108/IMDS-09-2017-0422

Pantano, E., Pizzi, G., Scarpi, D., & Dennis, C. (2020). Competing during a pandemic? Retailers' ups and downs during the COVID-19 outbreak. *Journal of Business Research*, *116*, 209–213. doi:10.1016/j.jbusres.2020.05.036 PMID:32501307

Papadopoulos, Konstantinos, Baltas, & Balta. (2020). The use of digital technologies by small and medium enterprises during COVID-19: Implications for theory and practice. *International Journal of Information Management*. doi:10.1016/j.ijinfomgt.2020.102192

Papadopoulos, T., Gunasekaran, A., Dubey, R., Altay, N., Childe, S. J., & Fosso-Wamba, S. (2017). The role of big data in explaining disaster resilience in supply chains for sustainability. *Journal of Cleaner Production*, *142*, 1108–1118. doi:10.1016/j.jclepro.2016.03.059

Parasuraman, A., Zeithaml, V. A., & Berry, L. L. (1985). A conceptual model of service quality and its implications for future research. *Journal of Marketing*, *49*(1), 41–50. doi:10.1177/002224298504900403

Parasuraman, A., Zeithaml, V. A., & Berry, L. L. (1988). SERVQUAL: A multiple-item scale for measuring consumer perceptions of service quality. *Journal of Retailing*, *64*(1), 12–40.

Parasuraman, A., Zeithaml, V. A., & Berry, L. L. (1994). Reassessment of expectations as a comparison standard in measuring service quality: Implications for further research. *Journal of Marketing*, *58*(1), 111–124. doi:10.1177/002224299405800109

Park, Y. W., Blackhurst, J., Paul, C., & Scheibe, K. P. (2021). An analysis of the ripple effect for disruptions occurring in circular flows of a supply chain network. *International Journal of Production Research*, 1–19. doi:10.1080/002075 43.2021.1934745

Partida, B. (2019). Using Dynamic Leadership to Prepare for the Future. *Supply Chain Management Review*. https://www.scmr.com/article/using_dynamic_leadership_to_prepare_for_the_future

Paschen, U., Pitt, C., & Kietzmann, J. (2020). Artificial intelligence: Building blocks and an innovation typology. *Business Horizons*, *63*(2), 147–155. doi:10.1016/j.bushor.2019.10.004

Patil, M. H., Tanguy, G., Floch-Fouéré, C. L., Jeantet, R., & Murphy, E. G. (2021). Energy usage in the manufacture of dairy powders: Advances in conventional processing and disruptive technologies. *Drying Technology*, *39*(11), 1–19. doi:10.1080/07373937.2021.1903489

Patrinley, J. R. Jr, Berkowitz, S. T., Zakria, D., Totten, D. J., Kurtulus, M., & Drolet, B. C. (2020). Lessons from Operations Management to Combat the COVID-19 Pandemic. *Journal of Medical Systems*, *44*(7), 129. doi:10.100710916-020-01595-6 PMID:32519285

Patten, E. (2017). *Conceptualizing service quality in multichannel fashion retailing* (Doctoral dissertation). University of Gloucestershire.

Paul-Eric, D., Rafael, P., Cristiane, S., & Joao, C. J. (2020). How to use lean manufacturing for improving a Healthcare logistics performance. *Procedia Manufacturing*, *51*, 1657–1664. doi:10.1016/j.promfg.2020.10.231

Paul, J., & Dhir, S. (Eds.). (2021). *Globalization, Deglobalization, and New Paradigms in Business*. Palgrave Macmillan. doi:10.1007/978-3-030-81584-4

Paul, S., & Venkateswaran, J. (2020). Designing robust policies under deep uncertainty for mitigating epidemics. *Computers & Industrial Engineering*, *140*, 106221. https://doi.org/10.1016/j.cie.2019.106221

Peck, H. (2003). *Creating resilient supply chains: A practical guide*. Centre for Logistics and Supply Chain Management. http://www.som.cranfield.ac.uk/som/dinamic-content/research/ lscm/download/57081_Report_AW.pdf

Peluso, A. M., Pichierri, M., & Pino, G. (2021). Age-related effects on environmentally sustainable purchases at the time of COVID-19: Evidence from Italy. *Journal of Retailing and Consumer Services*, *60*, 102443. doi:10.1016/j.jret-conser.2021.102443

Perrin, A., Wohlfahrt, J., Morandi, F., Østergård, H., Flatberg, T., De La Rua, C., Bjørkvoll, T., & Gabrielle, B. (2017). Integrated design and sustainable assessment of innovative biomass supply chains: A case-study on miscanthus in France. *Applied Energy*, *204*, 66–77. doi:10.1016/j.apenergy.2017.06.093

*Compilation of References*

Persky, S. (2020). A virtual home for the virtual clinical trial. *Journal of Medical Internet Research, 22*(1), e15582. doi:10.2196/15582 PMID:31899455

Petersen, J. A., & Kumar, V. (2015). *Perceived Risk, Product Returns, and Optimal Resource Allocation: Evidence from a Field Experiment.* doi:10.1509/JMR.14.0174

Petrini, C. (2001). *Slow food, the case for taste.* Columbia University Press.

Pettit, T. J., Croxton, K. L., & Fiksel, J. (2013). Ensuring supply chain resilience: Development and implementation of an assessment tool. *Journal of Business Logistics, 34*(1), 46–76. doi:10.1111/jbl.12009

Pettit, T. J., Croxton, K. L., & Fiksel, J. (2019). The evolution of resilience in supply chain management: A retrospective on ensuring supply chain resilience. *Journal of Business Logistics, 40*(1), 56–65. https://doi.org/10.1111/jbl.12202

Pettit, T. J., Fiksel, J., & Croxton, K. L. (2010). Ensuring supply chain resilience: Development of a conceptual framework. *Journal of Business Logistics, 31*(1), 1–21. doi:10.1002/j.2158-1592.2010.tb00125.x

Pfohl, H., Köhler, H., & Thomas, D. (2010). State of the art in supply chain risk management research: Empirical and conceptual findings and a roadmap for the implementation in practice. *Logistics Research, 2*(1), 33–44. doi:10.100712159-010-0023-8

Phadnis, S. S. (2015). *Connecting supply chains to the Internet of Things, Supply Chain Frontiers.* Retrieved from https://ctl.mit.edu/pub/newsletter/supply-chain-frontiers-58-connecting-supply-chains-internet-things

Pigni, F., Piccoli, G., & Watson, R. (2016). Digital data streams: Creating value from the real-time flow of big data. *California Management Review, 58*(3), 5–25. doi:10.1525/cmr.2016.58.3.5

Pinnington, B., Meehan, J., & Trautrims, A. (2021). *Implications of Covid-19 for modern slavery challenges in supply chain management.* Available at: https://www.cips.org/PageFiles/172121/MSPEC%20Supply%20Chains%20Research_Summary.pdf

Piprani, A. Z., Mohezar, S., & Jaafar, N. I. (2020). Supply chain integration and supply chain performance: The mediating role of supply chain resilience. *International Journal of Supply Chain Management, 9*(3), 58–73.

Pirrong, C., & Jermakyan, M. (2001). *The Price of Power: The Valuation of Power and Weather Derivatives.* Working Paper. Oklahoma State University.

Pishvaee, M. S., Torabi, S. A., & Razmi, J. (2012). The credibility-based fuzzy mathematical programming model for green logistics design under uncertainty. *Computers & Industrial Engineering, 62*(2), 624–632. doi:10.1016/j.cie.2011.11.028

Platen, E., & West, J. (2004). A Fair Pricing Approach to Weather Derivatives, Asia-Pacific Financial Markets. *Japanese Association of Financial Economics and Engineering, 11*(1), 23–53.

Podsakoff, N. P. (2003). Common method biases in behavioral research: a critical review of the literature and recommended remedies. *Journal of Applied Psychology, 885*(879).

Polonsky, M. J. (1994). An introduction to green marketing. *Electronic Green Journal, 1*(2), 1–10. doi:10.5070/G31210177

Ponomarov, S. Y., & Holcomb, M. C. (2009). Understanding the concept of supply chain resilience. *International Journal of Logistics Management, 20*(1), 124–143. doi:10.1108/09574090910954873

Ponomarov, S. Y., & Holcomb, M. C. (2009). Understanding the concept of supply chain resilience. *International Journal of Logistics Management, 20*(1), 124–143. https://doi.org/10.1108/09574090910954873

Ponomarov, S. Y., & Holcomb, M. C. (2009). Understanding the concept of supply chain resilience. *International Journal of Logistics*, *20*(1), 124–143.

Poon, T. C., Choy, K. L., Chow, H. K. H., Lau, H. C. W., Chan, F. T. S., & Ho, K. C. (2009). A RFID case based logistics resource management system for managing order-picking operations in warehouses. *Expert Systems with Applications*, *36*(4), 8277–8301. doi:10.1016/j.eswa.2008.10.011

Porambage, P., Okwuibe, J., & Tutorials, M. L. S. (2018). *Survey on multi-access edge computing for the internet of things realization.* Retrieved from https://ieeexplore.ieee.org/abstract/document/8391395/

Pournarder, M., & Wohlgezogen, F. (2021). *Keeping supply chains ethical and sustainable amid covid-19.* Available at: https://pursuit.unimelb.edu.au/articles/keeping-supply-chains-ethical-and-sustainable-amid-covid-19

Prajogo, D., Chowdhury, M., Yeung, A. C., & Cheng, T. C. E. (2012). The relationship between supplier management and firm's operational performance: A multi-dimensional perspective. *International Journal of Production Economics*, *136*(1), 123–130. doi:10.1016/j.ijpe.2011.09.022

Prajogo, D., & Olhager, J. (2012). The effect of supply chain information integration on logistics integration and firm performance. *International Journal of Production Economics*, *135*(1), 514–522. doi:10.1016/j.ijpe.2011.09.001

Pramanik, H. S., Kirtania, M., & Pani, A. K. (2019). Essence of digital transformation—Manifestations at large financial institutions from North America. *Future Generation Computer Systems*, *95*, 323–343. doi:10.1016/j.future.2018.12.003

Preindl, R., Nikolopoulos, K., & Litsiou, K. (2020). Transformation strategies for the supply chain: the impact of industry 4.0 and digital transformation. *Supply Chain Forum: An International Journal, 21*(1), 26-34. 10.1080/16258312.2020.1716633

Przytuła, S., Strzelec, G., & Krysińska-Kościańska, K. (2020). Re-vision of Future Trends in Human Resource Management (HRM) after COVID-19. *Journal of Intercultural Management*, *12*(4), 70–90. doi:10.2478/joim-2020-0052

Pujawan, I., & Geraldin, L. (2009). House of risk: A model for proactive supply chain risk. *Business Process Management Journal*, *15*(6), 953–967. doi:10.1108/14637150911003801

Puka, B. (2020). *The Golden Rule. Internet Encyclopedia of Philosophy – A peer-reviewed academic resource.* Retrieved from: https://www.iep.utm.edu/goldrule/

Pundir, A. K., Jagannath, J. D., Chakraborty, M., & Ganpathy, L. (2019). Technology Integration for Improved Performance: A Case Study in Digitization of Supply Chain with Integration of Internet of Things and Blockchain Technology. In *IEEE 9th Annual Computing and Communication Workshop and Conference (CCWC)* (pp. 170-176). IEEE.

Qin, J. Y. (2020). *WTO Reform: Multilateral Control over Unilateral Retaliation – Lessons from the US-China Trade War.* Wayne State University Law School Research Paper No. 2020-73, Available at https://ssrn.com/abstract=3654510 doi:10.2139/ssrn.3654510

Qinghua, Z., Vijie, D., & Joseph, S. (2010). A portfolio-based analysis for green supplier management using the analytical network process. *Supply Chain Management*, *15*(4), 306–319. doi:10.1108/13598541011054670

Queiroz, M. M., Ivanov, D., Dolgui, A., & Wamba, S. F. (2020). Impacts of epidemic outbreaks on supply chains: mapping a research agenda amid the COVID-19 pandemic through a structured literature review. *Annals of Operations Research*, 1-38. doi:10.1007/s10479-020-03685-7

Queiroz, M. M., Fosso Wamba, S., De Bourmont, M., & Telles, R. (2020). Blockchain adoption in operations and supply chain management: Empirical evidence from an emerging economy. *International Journal of Production Research*. Advance online publication. doi:10.1080/00207543.2020.1803511

*Compilation of References*

Queiroz, M. M., Pereira, S. C. F., Telles, R., & Machado, M. C. (2021). Industry 4.0 and digital supply chain capabilities A framework for understanding digitalisation challenges and opportunities. *Benchmarking*, *28*(5), 1761–1782. doi:10.1108/BIJ-12-2018-0435

Queiroz, M. M., Telles, R., & Bonilla, S. H. (2020). Blockchain and supply chain management integration: A systematic review of the literature. *Supply Chain Management*, *25*(2), 241–254. doi:10.1108/SCM-03-2018-0143

Raab, M., & Griffin-Cryan, B. (2011). *Digital transformation of supply chains. Creating Value–When Digital Meets Physical*. Capgemini Consulting.

Radomir, L., Plaias, I., & Nistor, V. C. (2012). Review of the Service Quality Concept-Past, Present and Perspectives. In *Proceedings of the International Conference Marketing-from Information to Decision* (p. 404). Babes Bolyai University.

Rahman, M. M., & Kuzminov, A. N. (2019). Marketing Mix as A Source Of Increasing The Efficiency Of Marketing Activity. Modern Problems of Scientific Activity. Perspectives for Implementing Innovative Solutions, 66-68.

Raj Kumar Reddy, K., Gunasekaran, A., Kalpana, P., Raja Sreedharan, V., & Arvind Kumar, S. (2021). Developing a blockchain framework for the automotive supply chain: A systematic review. *Computers & Industrial Engineering*, *157*, 107334. Advance online publication. doi:10.1016/j.cie.2021.107334

Rajesh, R. (2020). Flexible business strategies to enhance resilience in manufacturing supply chains: An empirical study. *Journal of Manufacturing Systems*, 1–17.

Rajput, S., & Singh, S. P. (2019). Connecting circular economy and industry 4.0. *International Journal of Information Management*, *49*, 98–113. doi:10.1016/j.ijinfomgt.2019.03.002

Ramakrishna, Y. (2018). Development of an integrated healthcare supply chain model. *Supply Chain Forum: An International Journal*, *19*(2), 111-121. 10.1080/16258312.2018.1475823

Ramakrishna, Y. (2021). Sustaining SMEs Through Supply Chain Innovation in the COVID-19 Era. In Handbook of Research on Sustaining SMEs and Entrepreneurial Innovation in the Post-COVID-19 Era (pp. 23). IGI Global. doi:10.4018/978-1-7998-6632-9.ch026

Rao, P. (2002). Greening the supply chain: A new initiative in Sout East Asia. *International Journal of Operations & Production Management*, *22*(6), 632–655. doi:10.1108/01443570210427668

Rath R C. (2013). An impact of green marketing on practices of supply chain management in Asia: emerging economic opportunities and challenges. *International Journal of Supply Chain Management, 2*(1), 78-86.

Ravi, R. & Wu, L. (2015). Demystifying Industry 4.0: Implications of internet of things and services for the chemical industry. *Materials referred from Malaysia Institute for Supply Chain Innovation.*

Ray, A., Dhir, A., Bala, P. K., & Kaur, P. (2019). Why do People Use Food Delivery Apps (FDA)? A Uses and Gratification Theory Perspective. *Journal of Retailing and Consumer Services*, *51*, 221–230. doi:10.1016/j.jretconser.2019.05.025

Raymond, P. C., Lopez, J., Marche, S., Perron, G. M., & Wright, R. (2008). Influences, practices and opportunities for environmental supply chain management in Nova Scotia SMEs. *Journal of Cleaner Production*, *16*(15), 1561–1570. doi:10.1016/j.jclepro.2008.04.022

Ray, T., Warjri, L. B., Jayakumar, A., & Saran, S. (2020). *Digital Debates: CyFy Journal 2020*. ORF and Global Policy Journal.

Redbird Logistics Services. (2021, February 10). *What is the Importance of Customer Service in Logistics Companies?* Récupéré sur redbirdlogisticsservices: https://redbirdlogisticsservices.com

Re, E. (2002). *Weather Risk Management*. Palgrave.

Reich, J. W. (2006). Three psychological principles of resilience in natural disasters. *Disaster Prevention and Management: An International Journal, 15*(5), 793–798. doi:10.1108/09653560610712739

Reina Angkiriwang, I. N. (2014). Managing uncertainty through supply chain flexibility: Reactive vs. proactive approaches. *Production & Manufacturing Research, 2*(1), 50–70. doi:10.1080/21693277.2014.882804

Remko, H. (2020). Research opportunities for a more resilient post-COVID-19 supply chain – closing the gap between research findings and industry practice. *International Journal of Operations and Production Management, 40*(4), 341–355.

Remko, V. H. (2020). Research opportunities for a more resilient post-COVID-19 supply chain–closing the gap between research findings and industry practice. *International Journal of Operations & Production Management, 40*(4), 341–355. doi:10.1108/IJOPM-03-2020-0165

Rennie, E. (2020). Five lessons from a crisis. *SCM Now, 30*(3), 35–38.

Report, D. (2020). *Building Supply Chain Resilience beyond COVID-19*. https://www2.deloitte.com/content/dam/Deloitte/ch/Documents/consumer-business/deloitte-ch-study-building-supply-chain-resilience-covid-19-2020.pdf

Report, D. (2020). *COVID-19: Managing supply chain risk and disruption Coronavirus highlights the need to transform traditional supply chain models*. https://www2.deloitte.com/global/en/pages/risk/cyber-strategic-risk/articles/covid-19-managing-supply-chain-risk-and-disruption.html

Research and Markets. (2020). *5 Ways Drones Can Help in a Pandemic*. https://www.researchandmarkets.com/issues/covid-19-drones?utm_medium=GNOM%26utm_source=covid19%26utm_campaign=gnuav00

Resilinc. (2018). *Event Watch AI – Monitoring Your Global Supply Chain Has Never Been So EASY*. Retrieved from https://www.resilinc.com/resilinc-eventwatch/)

Reveliotis, S. A. (2007). Uncertainty management in optimal disassembly planning through learning-based strategies. *IIE Transactions, 39*(6), 645–658. doi:10.1080/07408170600897536

Reynolds-Feighan, A. (2001). Air freight logistics. In K. B. A. M. Brewer (Ed.), *Handbook of Logistics and Supply-Chain Management* (pp. 431–439). Elsevier Science Ltd.

Richard, C., Deng, M., Kusters, J., & Carvell, K. (2020). *Deloitte's Digital Capabilities Model for Supply Networks | Introducing a new model for supply chain*. Deloitte Consulting LLP.

Richey, R. G. Jr, Morgan, T. R., Lindsey-Hall, K., & Adams, F. G. (2016). A global exploration of Big Data in the supply chain. *International Journal of Physical Distribution & Logistics Management, 46*(8), 710–739. doi:10.1108/IJPDLM-05-2016-0134

Rindfleisch, A., & Heide, J.B. (1997). Transaction Cost Analysis: Past, Present and Future Applications. *Journal of Marketing, 61*(4).

Riopel, D. A. L. (2007). The network of logistics decisions. In Logistics Systems: Design and Optimization (pp. 12-17). New York: Springer.

Risius, M., & Spohrer, K. (2017). A blockchain research framework: What We (don't) Know, Where We Go from Here, and How We Will Get There. *Business & Information Systems Engineering, 59*(6), 385–409. doi:10.100712599-017-0506-0

Rizaimy Shaharudin, M., Govindan, K., Zailani, S., Choon Tan, K., & Iranmanesh, M. (2017). Accepted Manuscript Product Return Management: Linking Product Returns, Closed-Loop Supply Chain Activities and the Effectiveness of the Reverse Supply Chains. *Journal of Cleaner Production*. doi:10.1016/j.jclepro.2017.02.133

*Compilation of References*

Rizos, V., Tuokko, K., & Behrens, A. (2017). *The Circular Economy: A review of definitions, processes and impacts.* CEPS Papers, (12440).

Rizos, V., Behrens, A., Van der Gaast, W., Hofman, E., Ioannou, A., Kafyeke, T., Flamos, A., Rinaldi, R., Papadelis, S., Hirschnitz-Garbers, M., & Topi, C. (2016). Implementation of circular economy business models by small and medium-sized enterprises (SMEs): Barriers and enablers. *Sustainability*, *8*(11), 1212. doi:10.3390u8111212

Rodrigues, L.-J. F., & Carpinetti, L. C. (2017). Quantitative models for supply chain performance evaluation: A literature review. *Computers & Industrial Engineering*, *113*, 333–346. doi:10.1016/j.cie.2017.09.022

Rodríguez, Y.E., Pérez-Uribe, M.A., & Contreras, J. (2021). Wind Put Barrier Options Pricing Based on the Nordix Index. *Energies, 14*, 1177. . doi:10.3390/en14041177

Rodrik, D. (2000). How far will international economic integration go? *Journal of Economics.*

Romano, J. L. (2020). Politics of Prevention: Reflections From the COVID-19 Pandemic. *Journal of Prevention and Health Promotion*, *1*(1), 34–57. doi:10.1177/2632077020938360

Rong, K., Hu, G., Lin, Y., Shi, Y., & Guo, L. (2015). Understanding business ecosystem using a 6C framework in Internet-of-Things-based sectors. *International Journal of Production Economics*, *159*, 41–55. doi:10.1016/j.ijpe.2014.09.003

Rose, A. (2004). Economic resilience to disasters: toward a consistent and comprehensive formulation. In D. Paton & D. Johnston (Eds.), *Disaster Resilience: An Integrated Approach* (pp. 226–248). Charles C. Thomas.

Ross, D. F. (2016). *Introduction to Supply Chain Management Technologies.* St Lucie Press.

Rostamzadeh, R., Govindan, K., Esmaeili, A., & Sabaghi, M. (2015). Application of fuzzy vigor for evaluation of green supply chain management practices. *Ecological Indicators*, *49*, 188–203. doi:10.1016/j.ecolind.2014.09.045

Rotar, A. (2021). *Online Food Delivery Report 2021.* https://www.statista.com/outlook/digital-markets

Rowan, N. J., & Laffey, J. G. (2020). Challenges and solutions for addressing critical shortage of supply chain for personal and protective equipment (PPE) arising from Coronavirus disease (COVID19) pandemic–Case study from the Republic of Ireland. *The Science of the Total Environment*, *725*, 138532. doi:10.1016/j.scitotenv.2020.138532 PMID:32304970

Roy, R., & Appa Rao, G. (2020). Survey on pre-processing web log files in web usage mining. *International Journal of Advanced Science and Technology, 29*(3), 682–691.

Roy, R., & Dev, D. R. (2019). Metamorphosis Knowledge Probing of Guild Data through Chat Bot Using NLP. *Data Mining and Knowledge Engineering*, *11*(7), 109–113. http://ischolar.info/index.php/CiiTDMKE/article/view/207566

Roy, R., Dev, D. R., & Prasad, V. S. R. (2020). Socially Intelligent Robots : Evolution of Human-Computer Interaction. *Journal of Critical Reviews*, *7*(15), 1843–1848. doi:10.31838/jcr.07.15.252

Roy, R., & p p a R a o, G. A. (2021). Predicting User's Web Navigation behaviour using AMD and HMM Approaches. *IOP Conference Series. Materials Science and Engineering*, *1074*(1), 012031. doi:10.1088/1757-899X/1074/1/012031

Russo, D., & Rizzi, C. (2014), structural optimization strategies to design green products. *Computers in Industry*, *65*, 470–479.

Rutter, M. (1985). Resilience in the face of adversity: Protective factors and resistance to psychiatric disorder. *The British Journal of Psychiatry*, *34*(6), 598–611. doi:10.1192/bjp.147.6.598 PMID:3830321

Rutter, M. (1999). Resilience concepts and findings: Implications for family therapy. *Journal of Family Therapy*, *21*(2), 119–224. doi:10.1111/1467-6427.00108

S., S. H. (2014). Management of distribution channels. *Indian J.Sci.Res., 5*(3), 452-456.

Sabbaghi, A., & Vaidyanathan, G. (2008). Effectiveness and efficiency of RFID technology in supply chain management: Strategic values and challenges. *Journal of Theoretical and Applied Electronic Commerce Research, 3*(2), 71–81. doi:10.4067/S0718-18762008000100007

Saberi, S., Kouhizadeh, M., Sarkis, J., & Shen, L. (2019). Blockchain technology and its relationships to sustainable supply chain management. *International Journal of Production Research, 57*(7), 2117–2135. doi:10.1080/00207543.2018.1533261

Sabouhi, F., Pishvaee, M. S., & Jabalameli, M. S. (2018). Resilient supply chain design under operational and disruption risks considering quantity discount: A case study of pharmaceutical supply chain. *Computers & Industrial Engineering, 126*, 657–672. doi:10.1016/j.cie.2018.10.001

Sabri, Y., Micheli, G. J., & Nuur, C. (2018). Exploring the impact of innovation implementation on supply chain configuration. *Journal of Engineering and Technology Management, 49*, 60–75. doi:10.1016/j.jengtecman.2018.06.001

Saeed, K. A., Grover, V., & Hwang, Y. (2005). The relationship of e-commerce competence to customer value and firm performance: An empirical investigation. *Journal of Management Information Systems, 22*(1), 223–256. https://doi.org/10.1080/07421222.2003.11045835

Sajjad, A., Eweje, G., & Tappin, D. (2020). Managerial perspectives on drivers for and barriers to sustainable supply chain management implementation: Evidence from New Zealand. *Business Strategy and the Environment, 29*(2), 592–604. doi:10.1002/bse.2389

Salam, M. (2017). The mediating role of supply chain collaboration on the relationship between technology, trust and operational performance: An empirical investigation. *Benchmarking, 24*(2), 298–317. doi:10.1108/BIJ-07-2015-0075

Saleheen, F., Habib, M. M., & Hanafi, Z. (2018a). Supply Chain Performance Measurement Model: A Literature Review. *International Journal of Supply Chain Management, 7*(3).

Saleheen, F., Habib, M. M., & Hanafi, Z. (2018b). An Empirical Study on Supply Chain Management Performance Measurement through AHP. *International Journal of Supply Chain Management, 7*(6).

Saleheen, F., Habib, M. M., & Hanafi, Z. (2019). An Implementation of Balanced Scorecard on Supply Chain Performance Measurement in Manufacturing Industry. *Proceedings from 2nd International Conference on Business and Management (ICBM).*

Saleheen, F., Habib, M. M., & Hanafi, Z. (2019a). A study on multi-dimensional supply Chain performance measurement (SCPM) models in manufacturing industries and way forward. *Proceedings from 2nd International Conference on Business and Management (ICBM).*

Saleheen, F., Habib, M. M., & Pathik, B., & Hanafi, Z. (2014). Demand and Supply Planning in Retail Operations. *International Journal of Business and Economics Research, 3*(6), 51-56. doi:10.11648/j.ijber.s.2014030601.18

Saleheen, F., Miraz, H. M. M. M., & Hanafi, Z. (2014). Challenges of Warehouse Operations: A Case Study in Retail Supermarket. *International Journal of Supply Chain Management, 3*(4).

Salvini, G., Hofstede, G. J., Verdouw, C. N., Rijswijk, K., & Klerkx, L. (2020). Enhancing digital transformation towards virtual supply chains: A simulation game for Dutch floriculture. *Production Planning and Control*, 1–18. Advance online publication. doi:10.1080/09537287.2020.1858361

Sancha, C., Wong, C. W. Y., & Gimenez, C. (2019). Do dependent suppliers benefit from buying firms' sustainability practices? *Journal of Purchasing and Supply Management, 25*(4), 100542. doi:10.1016/j.pursup.2019.100542

*Compilation of References*

Sandberg, E., & Abrahamsson, M. (2010). The role of top management in supply chain management practices. *International Journal of Retail & Distribution Management, 38*(1), 57–69. doi:10.1108/09590551011016331

Sanders, N. R., Boone, T., Ganeshan, R., & Wood, J. D. (2019). Sustainable supply chains in the age of AI and digitization: Research challenges and opportunities. *Journal of Business Logistics, 40*(3), 229–240. doi:10.1111/jbl.12224

Sangari, M. S., Razmi, M., & Zolfagahari, S. (2015). Developing practical evaluation framework for identifying critical factors to achieve Supply Chain Agility. *Measurement., 62*, 205–214. doi:10.1016/j.measurement.2014.11.002

Sapir, J. (2016). Jacques Sapir: Donald Trump, président de la démondialisation? *Le Figaro.* Available on web: https://www.lefigaro.fr/vox/monde/2016/11/10/31002-20161110ARTFIG00233-jacques-sapir-donald-trump-president-de-la-demondialisation.php

Sapir, J. (2011). *La demondialisation.* Seuil.

Sar, Dong, & Yu. (2016). Research on the measuring performance of green supply chain management: in the perspective of China. *International Journal of Engineering Research in Africa, 27*, 167-178.

Sarder, M. (2020). Logistics customer service. In M. Sarder (Ed.), *Logistics Transportation Systems* (pp. 197–217). Elsevier.

Sar, K. (2017). Impact of green supply chain management practices on firms' performance: An empirical study from the perspective of Pakistan. *Environmental Science and Pollution Research International, 24*(20), 16829–16844. doi:10.100711356-017-9172-5 PMID:28573559

Sar, K. (2018). Green supply chain management, economic growth, and environment: A GMM based evidence. *Journal of Cleaner Production, 185*, 588–599. doi:10.1016/j.jclepro.2018.02.226

Sar, K., Dong, Q., Wei, S. B., & Khalid, Z. (2017). Environmental logistics performance indicators affecting per capita income and sectoral growth: Evidence from a panel of selected global ranked logistics countries. *Environmental Science and Pollution Research International, 24*(2), 1518–1531.

Sarkis, J., Cohen, M. J., Dewick, P., & Schröder, P. (2020). A brave new world: Lessons from the COVID-19 pandemic for transitioning to sustainable supply and production. In Resources, Conservation and Recycling (Vol. 159, p. 104894). Elsevier B.V. doi:10.1016/j.resconrec.2020.104894

Sarkis, J. (1998). Evaluating environmentally conscious business practices. *European Journal of Operational Research, 107*(1), 159–174. doi:10.1016/S0377-2217(97)00160-4

Sarkis, J. (2020). Supply chain sustainability: Learning from the COVID-19 pandemic. *International Journal of Operations & Production Management, 41*(1), 63–73. doi:10.1108/IJOPM-08-2020-0568

Sarkis, J. (Ed.). (2001). *Greener management international.* Greenleaf Publishing.

Sarkis, J., Meade, L., & Presley, A. (2006). An activity-based management methodology for evaluating business processes for environmental sustainability. *Business Process Management Journal, 12*(6), 751–776. doi:10.1108/14637150610710918

Sarkis, J., Zhu, Q., & Lai, K. H. (2011). An organizational theoretic review of green supply chain management literature. *International Journal of Production Economics, 130*(1), 1–15. doi:10.1016/j.ijpe.2010.11.010

Saryatmo, M. A., & Sukhotu, V. (2021). The Influence of the Digital Supply Chain on Operational Performance: A Study of the Food and Beverage Industry in Indonesia. *Sustainability, 13*(9), 5109. . doi:10.3390/su13095109

Saunders, M., Lewis, P., & Thornhill, A. (2009). *Research Methods for Business Students* (5th ed.). Pearson Education.

Sawik, T. (2013). Selection of resilient supply portfolio under disruption risks. *Omega (United Kingdom), 41*(2), 259–269. doi:10.1016/j.omega.2012.05.003

Schaltegger, S., & Burritt, R. (2014). Measuring and managing sustainability performance of supply chains. *Supply Chain Management, 19*(3). Advance online publication. doi:10.1108/SCM-02-2014-0083

Scheiwiller, S., & Zizka, L. (2021). Strategic responses by European airlines to the Covid-19 pandemic: A soft landing or a turbulent ride? *Journal of Air Transport Management, 95,* 102103. doi:10.1016/j.jairtraman.2021.102103

Schmidt, W., & Raman, A. (2012). *When supply-chain disruptions matter.* Harvard Business School. https://www.hbs.edu/faculty/Publication%20Files/13-00

Schmidt, C. G., & Wagner, S. M. (2019). Blockchain and supply chain relations: A transaction cost theory perspective. *Journal of Purchasing and Supply Management, 25*(4), 100552. doi:10.1016/j.pursup.2019.100552

Schmitt, A. J., & Singh, M. (2012). A quantitative analysis of disruption risk in a multi-echelon supply chain. *International Journal of Production Economics, 139*(1), 22–32. doi:10.1016/j.ijpe.2012.01.004

Schneller, E. (2018). 2018 Healthcare Supply Chain Trends/Issues. *Healthcare Purchasing News.* Retrieved from https://www.hpnonline.com/sourcing-logistics/article/13001185/2018-healthcare-supply-chain-trendsissues

Schneller, E. S., Schmeltzer, L. R., & Burns, L. R. (2006). *Strategic Management of the Health Care Supply Chain.* Jossey-Bass.

Schniederjans, D. G., Curado, C., & Khalajhedayati, M. (2020). Supply chain digitisation trends: An integration of knowledge management. *International Journal of Production Economics, 220,* 107439. doi:10.1016/j.ijpe.2019.07.012

Schoenherr, T., & Swink, M. (2012). Revisiting the arcs of integration: Cross-validations and extensions. *Journal of Operations Management, 30*(1-2), 99–115. doi:10.1016/j.jom.2011.09.001

Scholten, K., & Schilder, S. (2015). The role of collaboration in supply chain resilience. *Supply Chain Management, 20*(4), 471–484. doi:10.1108/SCM-11-2014-0386

Scholten, K., Sharkey Scott, P., & Fynes, B. (2019). Building routines for non-routine events: Supply chain resilience learning mechanisms and their antecedents. *Supply Chain Management, 24*(3), 430–442. doi:10.1108/SCM-05-2018-0186

Scholten, K., Stevenson, M., & van Donk, D. P. (2019). Dealing with the unpredictable: Supply chain resilience. *International Journal of Operations & Production Management, 40*(1), 1–10.

SEDEX. (2020). *Sedex Insights Report: COVID-19 Impacts On Businesses.* Available at: https://www.sedex.com/sedex-insights-report-covid-19-impacts-on-businesses/

Seebacher, S., & Schüritz, R. (2017). Blockchain Technology as an Enabler of Service Systems: A Structured Literature Review. In Za, S., Drăgoicea, M., & Cavallari M. (Eds), *Exploring Services Science. 8th International Conference, IESS 2017 Proceedings* (pp. 12-23). Springer. 10.1007/978-3-319-56925-3_2

Seghezzi, A., & Mangiaracina, R. (2020). On-demand Food Delivery: Investigating the Economic Performances. *International Journal of Retail & Distribution Management, 49*(4), 531–549. doi:10.1108/IJRDM-02-2020-0043

Segura, A., Abeer, L. H. A., Costadopoulos, N., & Prasad, P. W. C. (2018). Ethical Implications of User Perceptions of WDs. *Science and Engineering Ethics, 24*(1), 1–28. doi:10.100711948-017-9872-8 PMID:28155094

Seles, B. M. R. P., de Sousa Jabbour, A. B. L., Jabbour, C. J. C., & Dangelico, R. M. (2016). The green bullwhip effect, the diffusion of green supply chain practices: and institutional pressures: evidence from the automotive sector. *International Journal of Production Economics, 182,* 342–355. doi:10.1016/j.ijpe.2016.08.033

*Compilation of References*

Seligman, M. E. P. (2011). *Building Resilience*. https://hbr.org/2011/04/building-resilience

Senbekov, M., Saliev, T., Bukeyeva, Z., Almabayeva, A., Zhanaliyeva, M., Aitenova, N., Toishibekov, Y., & Fakhradiyev, I. (2020). The Recent Progress and Applications of Digital Technologies in Healthcare: A Review. *International Journal of Telemedicine and Applications*. doi:10.1155/2020/8830200

Seng, B. K., Subramaniam, M., Chung, Y. J., Syed Ahmad, S. A. M., & Chong, S. A. (2021). Resilience and stress in frontline social workers during the COVID-19 pandemic in Singapore. *Asian Social Work and Policy Review*, *15*(3), 234–243. doi:10.1111/aswp.12237

Sen, S. (2009). Linking Green Supply Chain Management and Shareholder Value Creation, The IUP. *The Journal of Supply Chain Management*, *7*(3 & 4), 95–109.

Septiani, W., Marimin, M., Herdiyeni, Y., & Haditjaroko, L. (2016). Method and Approach Mapping for Agri-Food Supply Chain Risk Management: A Literature Review. *International Journal of Supply Chain Management*, *5*, 51–64.

Seyedghorban, Z., Tahernejad, H., Meriton, R., & Gary, G. (2020) Supply chain digitalization: past, present, and future. *Production Planning and Control, 31*(2-3), 96-114. doi:10.1080/09537287.2019.1631461

Shafer, W., Fukukawa, K., & Lee, G. (2007). Values and the Perceived Importance of Ethics and Social Responsibility: The U.S. versus China. *Journal of Business Ethics*, *70*(3), 265–284. doi:10.100710551-006-9110-9

Shafqat, S., Kishwer, S., Rasool, R. U., Qadir, J., Amjad, T., & Ahmad, H. F. (2020). Big data analytics enhanced healthcare systems: A review. *The Journal of Supercomputing*, *76*(3), 1754–1799. doi:10.100711227-017-2222-4

Shah, J. (2009). *Supply Chain Management: Text and Cases*. Pearson Education.

Shamsuddoha, M. (2015). Integrated Supply Chain Model for Sustainable Manufacturing: A System Dynamics Approach. *Sustaining Competitive Advantage Via Business Intelligence, Knowledge Management, and System.*

Shamsuzzoha, A., Ndzibah, E., & Kettunen, K. (2020). Data-driven sustainable supply chain through centralized logistics network: Case study in a Finnish pharmaceutical distributor company. *Current Research in Environmental Sustainability*, *2*, 100013. Advance online publication. doi:10.1016/j.crsust.2020.100013

Shang, K. C., Lu, C. S., & Li, S. (2010). A taxonomy of green supply chain management capability among electronics-related manufacturing firms in Taiwan. *Journal of Cleaner Production*, *14*(5), 472–486.

Shankar, V., Grewal, D., Sunder, S., Fossen, B., Peters, K., & Agarwal, A. (2021). Digital marketing communication in global marketplaces: A review of extant research, future directions, and potential approaches. *International Journal of Research in Marketing*. Advance online publication. doi:10.1016/j.ijresmar.2021.09.005

Shapiro, J. F., & Wagner, S. N. (2009). Strategic inventory optimization. *Journal of Business Logistics*, *30*(2), 161–173. doi:10.1002/j.2158-1592.2009.tb00117.x

Sharma, A., & Adhikary, A. (n.d.). *Covid-19's impact on supply chain decisions: Strategic insights from NASDAQ 100 firms using Twitter data*. Elsevier. Retrieved May 24, 2021, from https://www.sciencedirect.com/science/article/pii/S0148296320303210

Sharma, M. (2021). *Accelerating retail supply chain performance against pandemic disruption : Adopting resilient strategies to mitigate the long-term effects*. Academic Press.

Sharma, A., Adhikary, A., & Borah, S. B. (2020). Covid-19's impact on supply chain decisions: Strategic insights from NASDAQ100 firms using Twitter data. *Journal of Business Research*, *117*, 443–449.

Sharma, A., Borah, S. B., & Moses, A. C. (2021). Responses to COVID-19: The role of governance, healthcare infrastructure, and learning from past pandemics. *Journal of Business Research*, *122*, 597–607. doi:10.1016/j.jbusres.2020.09.011 PMID:33518844

Sharma, S. (2000). Managerial interpretations and organizational context as predictors of corporate choice of environmental strategy. *Academy of Management Journal*, *43*(4), 681–697.

Shavshukov, V. M., & Zhuravleva, N. A. (2020). Global Economy: New Risks and Leadership Problems. *Int. J. Financial Stud.*, *8*(1), 7. doi:10.3390/ijfs8010007

Shaw, D., & Shiu, E. (2002). The role of ethical obligation and self-identity in ethical consumer choice. *International Journal of Consumer Studies*, *26*(2), 109–116. doi:10.1046/j.1470-6431.2002.00214.x

Sheffi, Y. (2005). *The Resilient Enterprise: Overcoming Vulnerability for Competitive Advantage*. MIT Press.

Sheffi, Y., & Rice, J. B. (2005). A supply chain view of the resilient enterprise. *MIT Sloan Management Review*, *47*(1), 41–48.

Shehu, E., Papies, D., & Neslin, S. A. (2020). Free Shipping Promotions and Product Returns. *JMR, Journal of Marketing Research*, *57*(4), 640–658. https://doi.org/10.1177/0022243720921812

Shen, L., Govindan, K., & Shankar, M. (2015). evaluation of barriers of corporate social responsibility using an analytical hierarchy process under a fuzzy environment—A textile case. *Sustainability*, *7*(3), 3493–3514. doi:10.3390u7033493

Shepherd, C. a. (2010). Measuring supply chain performance: current research and future directions. In *Behavioral Operations in Planning and Scheduling*. Springer. doi:10.1007/978-3-642-13382-4_6

Shewmake, B., & Sapp, G. (2000). Bringing down the international barriers. *InfoWorld*, *22*(18), 30.

Shi, S. L., & He, J.S. (2005). A study on supplier assessment system in agile supply chain. *Journal of the Chinese Institute of Industrial Engineers*, *8*(2), 95–100.

Shih, W. C. (2020). *Global Supply Chains in a Post-Pandemic World*. https://hbr.org/2020/09/global-supply-chains-in-a-post-pandemic-world

Shih, W. C. (2020). Global supply chain in a post-pandemic world. *Harvard Business Review*, (September-October), 2020.

Shih, W. C. (2020). Is it time to rethink globalized supply chains? *MIT Sloan Management Review*, *61*(4), 1–3.

Shi, J. Q. (2018). How do statisticians analyse big data—Our story. *Statistics & Probability Letters*, *136*, 130–133. doi:10.1016/j.spl.2018.02.043

Shillingford, D., & Kamal, S. (2021). *Everstream Analytics: Annual risk*. Everstream Analytics.

Shin, N., & Park, S. (2019). Evidence-based resilience management for supply chain sustainability: An interpretive structural modelling approach. In Sustainability (Switzerland) (Vol. 11, Issue 2). doi:10.3390u11020484

Shin, N., & Park, S. (2019). Evidence-Based Resilience Management for Supply Chain Sustainability: An Interpretive Structural Modelling Approach. *Sustainability*, *11*, 484.

Ship Technology. (2017, September 10). *Could blockchain technology revolutionise shipping?* Ship Technology. https://www.ship-technology.com/features/featurecould-blockchain-technology-revolutionise-shipping-5920391/

Shi, X., Wang, S., Hao, F., & Xie, S. (2019). The Spatial Distribution and Formation of Take-out O2O Catering Industry Based on Entity Restaurants Comparison in Changchun. *Human Geographies*, *34*(2), 80–89.

*Compilation of References*

Shokouhyar, S., Seddigh, M. R., & Panahifar, F. (2020). Impact of big data analytics capabilities on supply chain sustainability. *World Journal of Science. Technology and Sustainable Development, 17*(1), 33–57. doi:10.1108/WJSTSD-06-2019-0031

Siagian, H., Tarigan, Z. J. H., & Jie, F. (2021). Supply Chain Integration Enables Resilience, Flexibility, and Innovation to Improve Business Performance in COVID-19 Era. *Sustainability, 13*, 4669. https://doi.org/10.3390/su13094669

Silvestre, B. (2016). Sustainable supply chain management: Current debate and future directions. *Gestão & Produção, 23*(2), 235–249. doi:10.1590/0104-530x2202-16

Sima, S., & Mahour, M. P. (2020). Firm innovation and supply chain resilience: A dynamic capability perspective. *International Journal of Logistics Research and Application, 23*(3), 254–269. doi:10.1080/13675567.2019.1683522

Simchi-Levi, D., Schmidt, W., Wei, Y., Zhang, P. Y., Combs, K., Ge, Y., Gusikhin, O., Sanders, M., & Zhang, D. (2015). Identifying risks and mitigating disruptions in the automotive supply chain. *Interfaces, 45*(5), 375–390. doi:10.1287/inte.2015.0804

Simpson, D., Power, D., & Samson, D. (2007). Greening the automotive supply chain: A relationship perspective. *International Journal of Operations & Production Management, 27*(1), 28–48. doi:10.1108/01443570710714529

Singh, A., & Misra, S. (2020). Ordering drivers of green supply chain management practices in Indian construction industry: An impact assessment framework. *International Journal of Quality & Reliability Management.* doi:10.1108/IJQRM-03-2019-0076

Singh, J., & Pandya, S. (1991). Exploring the effects of consumers' dissatisfaction level on complaint behaviours. *European Journal of Marketing, 25*(9), 7–21. doi:10.1108/EUM0000000000621

Singh, S., Ghosh, S., Jayaram, J., & Tiwari, M. K. (2019). Enhancing supply chain resilience using ontology-based decision support system. *International Journal of Computer Integrated Manufacturing, 32*(7), 642–657. doi:10.1080/0951192X.2019.1599443

Singh, S., Mahanty, B., & Tiwari, M. K. (2019). Framework and modelling of inclusive manufacturing system. *International Journal of Computer Integrated Manufacturing, 32*(2), 105–123. doi:10.1080/0951192X.2018.1550678

Singh, S., Verma, R., & Koul, S. (2017). Managing critical supply chain issues in Indian healthcare. *Procedia Computer Science, 122*, 315–322. doi:10.1016/j.procs.2017.11.375

Sinha, D., Bagodi, V., & Dey, D. (2020). The Supply Chain Disruption Framework Post COVID-19: A System Dynamics Model. *Foreign Trade Review, 55*(4), 511–534. doi:10.1177/0015732520947904

Sinha, D., & Dey, D. (2018). Supply chain strategies to sustain economic and customer uncertainties. In S. Dhir & S. Shishil (Eds.), *Flexible strategies in VUCA markets* (pp. 139–153). Springer. doi:10.1007/978-981-10-8926-8_10

Siriwardhana, Y., Gür, G., Ylianttila, M., & Liyanage, M. (2021). The role of 5G for digital healthcare against COVID-19 pandemic: Opportunities and challenges. *ICT Express, 7*(2), 244–252. doi:10.1016/j.icte.2020.10.002

Skipper, J. B., & Hanna, J. B. (2009). Minimizing supply chain disruption risk through enhanced flexibility. *International Journal of Physical Distribution & Logistics Management, 39*(5), 404–427. doi:10.1108/09600030910973742

Sloan, D., Palmer, L., & Burrow, H. (2002). A Broker's View. *Global Reinsurance*, (February), 22–25.

Smith, N., Palazzo, G., & Bhattacharya, C. (2010). Marketing's Consequences: Stakeholder Marketing and Supply Chain Corporate Social Responsibility Issues. *Business Ethics Quarterly, 20*(4), 617–641. doi:10.5840/beq201020440

Somapa, S., Cools, M., & Dullaert, W. (2018). Characterizing supply chain visibility – a literature review. *International Journal of Logistics Management, 29*(1), 308–339. doi:10.1108/IJLM-06-2016-0150

Sonar, A., & Mankenzie, C. A. (2018). In Y. Khojasteh (Ed.), *Supply Chain Disruptions Preparedness Measures Using a Dynamic Model* (pp. 123–137). Supply Chain Risk Management. Springer Nature Singapore Pte Ltd. doi:10.1007/978-981-10-4106-8_8

Soni, U., & Jain, V. (2011). Minimizing the vulnerabilities of supply chain: A new framework for enhancing the resilience. *Industrial Engineering and Engineering Management (IEEM), IEEE International Conference*, 933–939.

Sople V. V. (2012). *Logistics Management: The Supply Chain Imperative.* Pearson Education.

Speier, C., Judith, M., David, J. W., Closs, M., & Voss, D. (2011). Global supply chain design considerations: Mitigating product safety and security risks. *Journal of Operations Management, 29*(7-8), 721–736. doi:10.1016/j.jom.2011.06.003

Spend Edge. (2017). Why Green Supply Chain is the Need of the Hour? *SpendEdge.* https://www.spendedge.com/blogs/bid-goodbye-blues-red-color-supply-chain-green-instead

Spieske, A., & Birkel, H. (2021). Improving supply chain resilience through industry 4.0: A systematic literature review under the impressions of the COVID-19 pandemic. *Computers & Industrial Engineering, 158,* 107452. doi:10.1016/j.cie.2021.107452 PMID:35313661

Srinivasan, R., & Swink, M. (2018). An investigation of visibility and fexibility as complements to supply chain analytics: An organizational information processing theory perspective. *Production and Operations Management, 27*(10), 1849–1867. doi:10.1111/poms.12746

Srivastava, S. K. (2007). Green supply-chain management: A state-of-the-art literature review. *International Journal of Management Reviews, 9*(1), 53–80. doi:10.1111/j.1468-2370.2007.00202.x

Srivastava, S. K., & Srivastava, R. K. (2006). Managing product returns for reverse logistics. *International Journal of Physical Distribution & Logistics Management, 36*(7), 524–546. doi:10.1108/09600030610684962

Stahel, W. R. (2016). The circular economy. *NATNews, 531*(7595), 435. PMID:27008952

Statista. (2021). *Global supply chain management.* Author.

Stefansson, G. (2006). Collaborative logistics management and the role of third-party service providers. *International Journal of Physical Distribution & Logistics Management, 36*(2), 76–92. doi:10.1108/09600030610656413

Steinberg, F. (2005). *Cooperación y Conflicto en el Sistema Comercial Multilateral: La Organización Mundial de Comercio como Institución de Gobernanza Económica Global.* Tesis Doctoral presentada en el Departamento de Análisis Económico: Teoría Económica e Historia Económica de la Facultada de Ciencias Económicas y Empresariales de la Universidad Autónoma de Madrid, España.

Sternberg, H. S., Hofmann, E., & Roeck, D. (2021). The struggle is real: Insights from a supply chain blockchain case. *Journal of Business Logistics, 42*(1), 71–87. doi:10.1111/jbl.12240

Stevens, G. C., & Johnson, M. (2016). Integrating the Supply Chain . . . 25 Years on. *International Journal of Physical Distribution & Logistics Management, 46*(1), 19–42. doi:10.1108/IJPDLM-07-2015-0175

Stevenson, M., & Spring, M. (2007). Flexibility from a supply chain perspective: Definition and review. *International Journal of Operations & Production Management, 27*(7), 685–713. doi:10.1108/01443570710756956

Stone, J., Rahimifard, S., & Woolley, E. (2015). An overview of resilience factors in food supply chains. *11th Biennial Conference of the European Society for Ecological Economics.*

*Compilation of References*

Storer, M., Hyland, P., Ferrer, M., Santa, R., & Griffiths, A. (2014). Strategic supply chain management factors influencing agribusiness innovation utilization. *International Journal of Logistics Management*, 25(3), 487–521. doi:10.1108/IJLM-02-2013-0026

Storey, J., & Holti, R. (2020). *Innovating Healthcare The Role of Political, Managerial and Clinical Leadership*. Taylor & Francis.

Stulec, I., Petljak, K., & Bakovic, T. (2016). Effectiveness of weather derivatives as a hedge against the weather risk in agriculture. *Agric. Econ. – Czech, 62*(8), 356–362. doi:10.17221/188/2015-AGRICECON

Subramanian, N., Abdulrahman, M.D., Zhou, X., (2014). Integration of logistics and cloud computing service providers: cost and green benefits in the Chinese context. *Transportation Research Part E: Logistics and Transportation Review*, 70, 86–98.

Sujatha, R. (2011). Role of intelligent agents in facilitating information flow in supply chain management. *International Journal of Logistics Systems and Management*, 9(2), 229–237. doi:10.1504/IJLSM.2011.041508

Sundram, V., Bahrin, A., Abdul Munir, Z., & Zolait, A. (2018). The effect of supply chain information management and information system infrastructure: The mediating role of supply chain integration towards manufacturing performance in Malaysia. *Journal of Enterprise Information Management*, 31(5), 751–770. doi:10.1108/JEIM-06-2017-0084

Sunny, J., Undralla, N., & Madhusudanan Pillai, V. (2020). Supply chain transparency through blockchain-based traceability: An overview with demonstration. *Computers & Industrial Engineering*, 150, 106895. doi:10.1016/j.cie.2020.106895

Sureddin, S. (2021). Twelve Post-Pandemic Supply-Chain Trends for 2021. *Supply Chain Brain*. https://www.supplychainbrain.com/blogs/1-think-tank/post/32374-twelve-post-pandemic-supply-chain-trends-for-2021

Svensson, G. (2009). The transparency of SCM ethics: Conceptual framework and empirical illustrations. *Supply Chain Management*, 14(4), 259–269. doi:10.1108/13598540910970090

Svensson, G., Wood, G., & Callaghan, M. (2010). A corporate model of sustainable business practices: An ethical perspective. *Journal of World Business*, 45(4), 336–345. doi:10.1016/j.jwb.2009.08.005

Swain, S., Peter, O., Adimuthu, R., & Muduli, K. (2021). Blockchain Technology for Limiting the Impact of Pandemic: Challenges and Prospects. In Computational Modeling and Data Analysis in COVID-19 Research (pp. 165-186). CRC Press.

Swaminathan, J. M., & Tayur, S. R. (2003). Models for supply chains in e-business. *Management Science*, 49(10), 1387–1406. doi:10.1287/mnsc.49.10.1387.17309

Swierczek, A. (2019). The effects of brokered network governance on relational embeddedness in the triadic supply chains: Is there a room for the "Coleman rent"? *Supply Chain Management: An International Journal*. doi:10.1108/SCM-04-2019-0170

Szozda, N. (2017). Industry 4.0 and its impact on the functioning of supply chains. *Logforum*, 13(4).

Taeihagh, A., Ramesh, M., & Howlett, M. (2021). Assessing the regulatory challenges of emerging disruptive technologies. *Regulation & Governance*, 15(4), 1009–1019. doi:10.1111/rego.12392

Taghipour, M., Taghipour, M., Khodarezaei, M., & Farid, F. (2015). Supply Chain Performance Evaluation in the IT Industry. *IJRRAS, 23*(2). Retrieved from www.arpapress.com/Volumes/Vol23Issue2/IJRRAS_23_2_07.pdf

Tajri, H., & Chafi, A. (2018). Change management in supply chain: Supply chain urbanization method. *4th International Conference on Optimization and Applications (ICOA)*, 1-7. 10.1109/ICOA.2018.8370561

Tamym, L., El Oaudghiri, M. D., Benyoucef, L., & Moh, A. N. S. (2020). *Big Data for Supply Chain Management in Industry 4.0 Context: A Comprehensive Survey.* Paper presented at the 13th International Conference on Modeling, Optimization and Simulation, Agadir. Morocco.

Tandon, A., Dhir, A., Islam, A. K. M. N., & Mäntymäki, M. (2020). Blockchain in healthcare: A systematic literature review, synthesizing framework and future research agenda. *Computers in Industry, 122*, 103290. Advance online publication. doi:10.1016/j.compind.2020.103290

Tandon, A., Kaur, P., Bhatt, Y., Mäntymäki, M., & Dhir, A. (2021). Why do People Purchase from Food Delivery Apps? A Consumer Value Perspective. *Journal of Retailing and Consumer Services, 63*, 102667. doi:10.1016/j.jretconser.2021.102667

Tan, X., Ran, L., & Liao, F. (2020). Contactless Food Supply and Delivery System in the COVID-19 Pandemic: Experience from Raytheon Mountain Hospital, China. *Risk Management and Healthcare Policy, 13*, 3087–3088. doi:10.2147/RMHP.S286786 PMID:33376431

Tao, M. (2021). 7 Supply chain technology trends shaping a sustainable future. *Robotics and Automation News.* https://roboticsandautomationnews.com/2021/04/07/7-supply-chain-technology-trends-shaping-a-sustainable-future/42158/

Tapscott, D., & Tapscott, A. (2018). *Blockchain Revolution: How the Technology Behind Bitcoin and Other Cryptocurrencies Is Changing the World.* Penguin Random House.

Taqi, H. M. M., Ahmed, H. N., Paul, S., Garshasbi, M., Ali, S. M., Kabir, G., & Paul, S. K. (2020). Strategies to Manage the Impacts of the COVID-19 Pandemic in the Supply Chain: Implications for Improving Economic and Social Sustainability. *Sustainability, 12*(22), 9483. doi:10.3390u12229483

Tarafdar, M., & Qrunfeh, S. (2017). Agile supply chain strategy and supply chain performance: Complementary roles of supply chain practices and information systems capability for agility. *International Journal of Production Research, 55*(4), 925–938. doi:10.1080/00207543.2016.1203079

Tardivo, A. M. (2020). *Alessio Tardivo, Celestino Sánchez Martín, Armando Carrillo Zanuy.* European Rail Research Network of Excellence.

Taştan, B., & Hayfavi, A. (2017). *Modeling Temperature and Pricing Weather Derivatives Based on Temperature.* Hindawi-Advances in Meteorology. doi:10.1155/2017/3913817

Taylor, B. W. (2017). *Introduction to Management Science.* Pearson Education.

Teas, R. K. (1993). Expectations, performance evaluation, and consumers' perceptions of quality. *Journal of Marketing, 57*(4), 18–34.

Tebaldi, L., Bigliardi, B., & Bottani, E. (2018). Sustainable supply chain and innovation: A review of the recent literature. *Sustainability, 10*(11), 3946. doi:10.3390u10113946

Teunter, R. H. (2006). Determining optimal disassembly and recovery strategies. *Omega, 34*(6), 533–537. doi:10.1016/j.omega.2005.01.014

Tezuka, K., Ishii, M., & Ishizaka, M. (2012). An equilibrium price model of spot and forward shipping freight markets. *Transportation Research Part E, Logistics and Transportation Review, 48*(4), 730–742. doi:10.1016/j.tre.2011.12.007

Thaichon, P. (2021). COVID in the Aviation Industry: Crisis Management, Its Decisions and Outcomes. *COVID-19. Technology and Marketing, 2019*, 21–31. doi:10.1007/978-981-16-1442-2_2

*Compilation of References*

The Korea Herald. (2020). *PM Appeals for Strict Adherence to Social Distancing Campaign to Stem Coronavirus.* http://www.koreaherald.com/view.php?ud=20200418000060

TheodossiouP.TsouknidisD. A.SavvaC. S. 2020. Freight rates in downside and upsidemarkets: pricing of own and spillover risks from other shipping segments. *J. R. Stat.Soc. Ser. A.* doi:10.2139/ssrn.3514142

Theodossiou, P., Tsouknidis, D., & Savva, C. (2020). Freight rates in Downside and Upside Markets: Pricing of Own and Spillover Risks from Other Shipping Segments. *Journal of the Royal Statistical Society. Series A, (Statistics in Society), 183*(3), 1097–1119. Advance online publication. doi:10.1111/rssa.12553

Thillairaja, P., & Lawrence, A. (2019). The relationship between Supply Chain Resilience Elements and Organizational Performance: The Mediating Role of Supply Chain Ambidexterity. *Global Business and Management Research, 11*(1), 583–592.

Thoo, A. C., Hamid, A. B. A., Rasli, A., & Zhang, D. W. (2014a). Supply chain strategy and operational capability in Malaysian SMEs. *Advances in Education Research, 44*, 231.

Thoo, A. C., Hamid, A. B. A., & Rasli, A., & Zhang, D. W. (2014b). The moderating effect of entrepreneurship on green supply chain management practices and sustainability performance. *Advanced Materials Research, 869*, 773–776.

Tian, S., Yang, W., Grange, J. M. L., Wang, P., Huang, W., & Ye, Z. (2019). Smart healthcare: Making medical care more intelligent. *Global Health Journal, 3*(3), 62–65. doi:10.1016/j.glohj.2019.07.001

Tidd, J., & Bessant, J. R. (2020). *Managing innovation: integrating technological, market and organizational change.* John Wiley & Sons.

Tiffany C, Frost, A. S., Brody, R. M., Byrnes, Y. M., Cannady, S. B., Luu, N. N., Rajasekaran, K., Shanti, R. M., Silberthau, K. R., Triantafillou, V., & Newman, J. G. (2020). Creation of an Interactive Virtual Surgical Rotation for Undergraduate Medical Education during the COVID-19 Pandemic. *Journal of Surgical Education.* doi:10.1016/j.jsurg.2020.06.039

Timothy, J. P., Keely, L. C., & Fiksel, J. (2019). The Evolution of Resilience in Supply Chain Management: A Retrospective on Ensuring Supply Chain Resilience. *Journal of Business Logistics, 40*(1), 56–65. doi:10.1111/jbl.12202

Tiwari, S. (2020). Supply chain integration and Industry 4.0: A systematic literature review. *Benchmarking, 28*(3), 990–1030. doi:10.1108/BIJ-08-2020-0428

Tjahjono, B., Esplugues, C., Ares, E., & Pelaez, G. (2017). What does industry 4.0 mean to supply chain? *Procedia Manufacturing, 13*, 1175–1182. doi:10.1016/j.promfg.2017.09.191

Todd, J. (2017). *Mitigating Supply Chain Risk: Effective Transportation and Logistics Provider Diligence and Management Practices.* New York: JD Supra.

Tong, T., Dai, H., Xiao, Q., & Yan, N. (2020). Will Dynamic Pricing Outperform? Theoretical Analysis and Empirical Evidence from O2O On-Demand Food Service Market. *International Journal of Production Economics, 219*, 375–385. doi:10.1016/j.ijpe.2019.07.010

Torabi, S. A., Baghersad, M., & Mansouri, S. A. (2015). Resilient supplier selection and order allocation under operational and disruption risks. *Transportation Research Part E, Logistics and Transportation Review, 79*, 22–48. doi:10.1016/j.tre.2015.03.005

Trebilcock, M. J. (2005). Criticizing the Critics of Economic Globalization. *Journal of International Law and International Relations, 1*, 213-238. Available at SSRN:https://ssrn.com/abstract=1214142

Tsai, W. H., & Hung, S. J. (2009). A fuzzy goal programming approach for green supply chain optimisation under activity-based costing and performance evaluation with a value-chain structure. *International Journal of Production Research, 47*(18), 4991–5017. doi:10.1080/00207540801932498

Tsai, Y. S., Chen, R. S., Chen, Y., & Yeh, C. P. (2011). An RFID-based manufacture process control and supply chain management in the semiconductor industry. *International Journal of Information Technology and Management, 12*(1/2), 85–105. doi:10.1504/IJITM.2013.051633

Tsang, Y. P., Choy, K. L., Wu, C. H., Ho, G. T. S., Lam, C. H. Y., & Koo, P. S. (2018). An Internet of Things (IoT)-based risk monitoring system for managing cold supply chain risks. *Industrial Management & Data Systems, 118*(7), 1432–1462. https://doi.org/10.1108/IMDS-09-2017-0384

Tseng, M.-L., Lim, M. K., & Wu, K.-J. (2019). Improving the benefits and costs on sustainable supply chain finance under uncertainty. *International Journal of Production Economics, 218*(C), 308–321. doi:10.1016/j.ijpe.2019.06.017

Tsui, J. (2019). Supply Chains Are Going Green in These Six Ways. *Supply Chain Brain*. https://www.supplychainbrain.com/blogs/1-think-tank/post/30512-six-ways-that-supply-chains-are-turning-to-green-solutions

Tukamuhabwa, B. R., Stevenson, M., Busby, J., & Zorzini, M. (2015). Supply chain resilience: Definition, review and theoretical foundations for further study. In International Journal of Production Research (Vol. 53, Issue 18, pp. 5592–5623). Taylor and Francis Ltd. doi:10.1080/00207543.2015.1037934

Tukker, A. (2015). Product services for a resource-efficient and circular economy–a review. *Journal of Cleaner Production, 97*, 76–91. doi:10.1016/j.jclepro.2013.11.049

Ubaid, I., & Shafi Mir, M. (2021). Maintaining effcient logistics and supply chain management operations during and after coronavirus (COVID-19) pandemic: Learning from the past experiences. *Environment, Development and Sustainability, 23*(8), 11157–11178. doi:10.100710668-020-01115-z PMID:33488274

Ubeda, S., Arcelus, F. J., & Faulin, J. (2011). Green logistics at eroski: A case study. *International Journal of Production Economics, 131*(1), 44–51. doi:10.1016/j.ijpe.2010.04.041

Umar, M., Wilson, M., & Hey, J. (2017). Food Network Resilience Against Natural Disasters: A Conceptual Framework. *SAGE Open, 7*(3). Advance online publication. doi:10.1177/2158244017717570

UNCTAD. (2020). *COVID-19 has changed online shopping forever, survey shows*. Available at: https://unctad.org/news/covid-19-has-changed-online-shopping-forever-survey-shows

United Nations Global Compact and BSR. (2015). *Supply Chain Sustainability: A Practical Guide for Continuous Improvement* (2nd ed.). UNEP Business and Industry Global Dialogue.

Urbinati, A., Chiaroni, D., & Chiesa, V. (2017). Towards a new taxonomy of circular economy business models. *Journal of Cleaner Production, 168*, 487–498. doi:10.1016/j.jclepro.2017.09.047

Vachon, S., & Klassen, R. D. (2006). Extending green practices across the supply chain: The impact of upstream and downstream integration. *International Journal of Operations & Production Management, 26*(7), 795–821. doi:10.1108/01443570610672248

Vakharia, A. J. (2002). E-Business and Supply Chain Management. *Decision Sciences, 11*(4), 413–424. https://doi.org/10.1111/j.1540-5915.2002.tb01653.x

Van Alstyne, M. W., Parker, G. G., & Choudary, S. P. (2016). Pipelines, platforms, and the new rules of strategy. *Harvard Business Review, 94*(4), 54–62.

*Compilation of References*

Van Heel, B., Lukic, V., & Leeuwis, E. (2018). *Cross-Border e-CommerCe makes the World Flatter*. Academic Press.

Van Hoek, R. (2019). Exploring blockchain implementation in the supply chain: Learning from pioneers and RFID research. *International Journal of Operations & Production Management, 39*(6/7/8), 829-859.

Van Hoek, R. (2020). Research opportunities for a more resilient post-COVID-19 supply chain–closing the gap between research findings and industry practice. *International Journal of Operations & Production Management, 40*(4), 341–355.

Van Weele, A.J. (2010). *Purchasing and Supply Chain Management: Analysis, Strategy, Planning and Practice*. Cengage Learning.

Vanhove, A. J., Herian, M. N., Perez, A. L. U., Harms, P. D., & Lester, P. B. (2016). Can resilience be developed at work? A meta-analytic review of resilience-building programme effectiveness. *Journal of Occupational and Organizational Psychology, 89*(2), 278–307. doi:10.1111/joop.12123

Vedenov, D. V., & Barnettn, B. J. (2004). Efficiency of Weather Derivatives as Primary Crop Insurance Instruments. *Journal of Agricultural and Resource Economics, 29*(3), 387.

Venkatesan, R., & Kumar, V. (2018). *A Customer Lifetime Value Framework for Customer Selection and Resource Allocation Strategy*. doi:10.1509/JMKG.68.4.106.42728

Verma, S., & Gustafsson, A. (2020). Investigating the emerging COVID-19 research trends in the field of business and management: A bibliometric analysis approach. *Journal of Business Research, 118*, 253–261. doi:10.1016/j.jbusres.2020.06.057 PMID:32834211

Verny, J., Oulmakki, O., Cabo, X., & Roussel, D. (2020). Blockchain & supply chain: towards an innovative supply chain design. *Projectics/Proyectica/Projectique*, (2), 115-130.

Verónica, L., Federico, C., Maria C., & Thomas, J. (2017). Collaboration for Sustainability in the Food Supply chain management: A Multi-Stage Study in Italy. *Sustainability MDPI, 11*(5), 407–414.

Vijayaraghavan, T. A. S. (2021). *Supply Chain Analytics*. Wiley India Pvt Ltd.

Vilko, J. H., & Hallikas, J. M. (2012). Risk assessment in multimodal supply chains, Original Research Article. *International Journal of Production Economics, 140*(2), 586–595. doi:10.1016/j.ijpe.2011.09.010

Visser, W. (2020). Measuring future resilience: a multilevel index. *Corporate Governance, 21*(2), 252–267.

Vries, J., & Huijsman, R. (2011). Supply chain management in health services: An overview. *Supply Chain Management, 16*(3), 159–165. doi:10.1108/13598541111127146

Wagner, H. M., & Whitin, T. (1958). Dynamic version of the economic lot size model. *Management Science, 5*(1), 89–96. doi:10.1287/mnsc.5.1.89

Wagner, S. M., & Bode, C. (2014). Supplier relationship-specific investments and the role of safeguards for supplier innovation sharing. *Journal of Operations Management, 32*(3), 65–78. doi:10.1016/j.jom.2013.11.001

Waimai, M. T. (2021). *Delivery Business Process*. https://developer.MeiTuan.com/docs/biz/biz_Waimaing_b0f1ddde-783f-4235-874e-38f582f1654d

Waligora, R. (2020). *COVID-19: Ethical supply chains in the spotlight? How to maintain an ethical supply chain during the COVID-19 crisis*. Available at: https://home.kpmg/uk/en/blogs/home/posts/2020/06/covid-19-puts-ethical-supply-chains-in-the-spotlight.html

Wamba, S. F., & Akter, S. (2019). Understanding supply chain analytics capabilities and agility for data-rich environments. *International Journal of Operations & Production Management, 39*(6/7/8), 887–912.

Wamba, S. F., & Queiroz, M. M. (2020). Blockchain in the operations and supply chain management: Benefits, challenges, and future research opportunities. *International Journal of Information Management, 52*, 102064. doi:10.1016/j.ijinfomgt.2019.102064

Wang, C. (2021). *Analyzing the Effects of Cross-Border E-Commerce Industry Transfer Using Big Data.* doi:10.1155/2021/9916304

Wang, L. (2018). *2018 Investor Day: Ele.me Alibaba Local Service.* https://www.alibabagroup.com/en/ir/presentations/Investor_Day_2018_Eleme.pdf

Wang, W., Liu, Y., & Wei, Y. (2013). Research on management strategies of reverse logistics in E-commerce environments. *LISS 2012 - Proceedings of 2nd International Conference on Logistics, Informatics and Service Science*, 321–326. doi:10.1007/978-3-642-32054-5_48

Wang, X., Xie, J., & Fan, Z. P. (2021). B2C cross-border E-commerce logistics mode selection considering product returns. *International Journal of Production Research.* doi:10.1080/00207543.2020.1752949

Wang, B. (2008). Analysis of efficiency of lean production implemented in multi-national optic enterprises. *International Journal of Technology Management, 43*(4), 304–319. doi:10.1504/IJTM.2008.020553

Wang, B., Childerhouse, P., Kang, Y., Huo, B., & Mathrani, S. (2016). Enablers of supply chain integration: Interpersonal and interorganizational relationship perspectives. *Industrial Management & Data Systems, 116*(4), 838–855. doi:10.1108/IMDS-09-2015-0403

Wang, C., & Hu, Q. (2020). Knowledge sharing in supply chain networks: Effects of collaborative innovation activities and capability on innovation performance. *Technovation, 94*, 102010. doi:10.1016/j.technovation.2017.12.002

Wang, G., Gunasekaran, A., Ngai, E. W., & Papadopoulos, T. (2016). Big data analytics in logistics and supply chain management: Certain investigations for research and applications. *International Journal of Production Economics, 176*(6), 98–110. doi:10.1016/j.ijpe.2016.03.014

Wang, L., & Alexander, C. A. (2015). Big Data Driven Supply Chain Management and Business Administration. *American Journal of Economics and Business Administration, 7*(2), 60–67. doi:10.3844/ajebasp.2015.60.67

Wang, L., & Yi, B. (2019). Research on O2O Take-away Restaurant Recommendation System: Taking Ele.me APP as an Example. *Cluster Computing, 22*(S3), 6069–6077. doi:10.100710586-018-1814-y

Wang, M., Wu, Y., Chen, B., & Evans, M. (2020). Blockchain and supply chain management: A new paradigm for supply chain integration and collaboration. *Operations and Supply Chain Management: An International Journal, 14*(1), 111–122. doi:10.31387/oscm0440290

Wang, N. M., Sun, L. Y., & Wang, Y. L. (2005). *Green supply chain management.* Tsinghua University Press.

Wang, Q., & Zhang, C. (2021). Can COVID-19 and environmental research in developing countries support these countries to meet the environmental challenges induced by the pandemic? *Environmental Science and Pollution Research International, 28*(30), 1–21. doi:10.100711356-021-13591-5 PMID:33782826

Wang, X., Wang, L., Wang, S., Chen, J., & Wu, C. (2021). An XGBoost-enhanced Fast Constructive Algorithm for Food Delivery Route Planning Problem. *Computers & Industrial Engineering, 152*, 107029. doi:10.1016/j.cie.2020.107029

*Compilation of References*

Wang, Y., Han, J. H., & Beynon-Davies, P. (2019). Understanding blockchain technology for future supply chains: A systematic literature review and research agenda. *Supply Chain Management, 24*(1), 62–84. doi:10.1108/SCM-03-2018-0148

Warehouse Layout Tips for Optimization. (2021, November 20). *BigRentz*. https://www.bigrentz.com/blog/warehouse-layout

Wasim Ahmad, R., Hasan, H., Yaqoob, I., Salah, K., Jayaraman, R., & Omar, M. (2021). Blockchain for aerospace and defense: Opportunities and open research challenges. *Computers & Industrial Engineering, 151*, 106982. doi:10.1016/j.cie.2020.106982

Watanabe, C., Naveed, N., & Neittaanmäki, P. (2019). Digitalized bioeconomy: Planned obsolescence-driven circular economy enabled by Co-Evolutionary coupling. *Technology in Society, 56*, 8–30. doi:10.1016/j.techsoc.2018.09.002

Waters, D. (2007). *Supply chain risk management: vulnerability and resilience in logistics.* London: Kogan-Page.

Webber, D. (2021). *Cross-Border Ecommerce: Three Challenges Defining The Next Decade.* Retrieved October 23, 2021, from https://www.forbes.com/sites/danielwebber/2021/03/24/cross-border-ecommerce-three-challenges-defining-the-next-decade/?sh=1f2993373a3a

Webb, L. (1994). Green purchasing: Forging a new link in the supply chain. *Resource (Saint Joseph, Mich.), 1*(6), 14–18.

Weetman, C. (2017). *A Supply Chain Revolution: How the Circular Economy Unlocks New Value.* KoganPage. https://www.koganpage.com/article/a-supply-chain-revolution-how-the-circular-economy-unlocks-new-value

WEF (World Economic Forum), EMF, & McKinsey & Company. (2014). *Towards the Circular Economy: Accelerating the scale-up across global supply chains.* Retrieved from https://ellenmacarthurfoundation.org/business/reports

WEF. (2019). *Supply Chain 4.0 Global Practices and Lessons Learned for Latin America and the Caribbean.* Retrieved from https://www.weforum.org/whitepapers/supply-chain-4-0-global-practices-and-lessons-learned-for-latin-america-and-the-caribbean-c4ffe6b1-b2f0-44f1-8b1d-c740cc11ca6f

Wei Jia, Z. (2015). *O2O Food Delivery Supply Chain Platform Analysis (Ele.me).* https://mp.weixin.qq.com/s/xG-MQ5WRr13HSM8YJVmM-jw

Wei, H. L., & Wang, E. T. G. (2010). The strategic value of supply chain visibility: Increasing the ability to reconfigure. *European Journal of Information Systems, 19*(2), 238–249. doi:10.1057/ejis.2010.10

Wells, P., & Seitz, M. (2005). Business Models and Closed-Loop SupplyChains: A Typology. *Supply Chain Management, 10*(4), 249–251. doi:10.1108/13598540510612712

Whipple, J. M., Frankel, R., & Daugherty, P. J. (2002). Information support for alliances: Performance implications. *Journal of Business Logistics, 23*(2), 67–82. doi:10.1002/j.2158-1592.2002.tb00026.x

White, C., & Yu, Y. T. (2005). Satisfaction emotions and consumer behavioral intentions. *Journal of Services Marketing, 19*(6), 411–420. doi:10.1108/08876040510620184

WHO. (2021). *World Health Organization, Health Topics.* Available: https://www.who.int/health-topics/coronavirus#tab=tab_1

Wichmann, P., Brintrup, A., Baker, S., Woodall, P., & McFarlane, D. (2020). Extracting supply chain maps from news articles using deep neural networks. *International Journal of Production Research, 58*(17), 5320–5336. doi:10.1080/00207543.2020.1720925

Wieland, A., & Wallenburg, C. M. (2013). Dealing with supply chain risks: Linking risk management practices and strategies to performance. *International Journal of Physical Distribution & Logistics Management, 42*(10), 887–905. doi:10.1108/09600031211281411

Wieland, A., & Wallenburg, C. M. (2013). The influence of relational competencies on supply chain resilience: A relational view. *International Journal of Physical Distribution & Logistics Management, 43*(4), 300–320. doi:10.1108/IJPDLM-08-2012-0243

Wikipedia. (2021). Big data. In *Wikipedia*. Retrieved from https://en.wikipedia.org/wiki/Big_data

Wilkerson, T. (2005). Best practices in implementing green supply chains. *North America Supply Chain World Conference and Exposition*. https://postconflict.unep.ch/humanitarianaction/documents/02_08-04_05-25.pdf

Willems, B., Dewulf, W., & Duflou, I. R. (2006). Can large-scale disassembly be profitable? A linear programming approach to quantifying the turning point to make disassembly economically viable. *International Journal of Production Research, 44*(6), 1125–1146. doi:10.1080/00207540500354168

Winarsih, I. M., & Fuad, K. (2021). Impact of Covid-19 on Digital Transformation and Sustainability in Small and Medium Enterprises (SMEs): A Conceptual Framework. In Complex, Intelligent and Software Intensive Systems. CISIS 2020. Advances in Intelligent Systems and Computing (vol. 1194). Springer. doi:10.1007/978-3-030-50454-0_48

Winkler, J. & Moser, R. (2016). Biases in future-oriented Delphi studies: A cognitive perspective. *Technological Forecasting and Social Change, 105*, 63-76. . doi:10.1016/j.techfore.2016.01.021

Wittenberg, C. (2016). Human-CPS Interaction-requirements and human-machine interaction methods for the Industry 4.0. *IFAC-PapersOnLine, 49*(19), 420–425. doi:10.1016/j.ifacol.2016.10.602

Witt, M. A. (2019). De-globalization: Theories, predictions, and opportunities for international business research. *Journal of International Business Studies, 50*(7), 1053–1077. doi:10.105741267-019-00219-7

Wolf, M., Lauer, T., & Puchan, J. (2020). Framework for Quantitative Digitalization Measurement in Supply Chain Planning. *Anwendungen und Konzepte der Wirtschaftsinformatik,* (11). https://www.ojs-hslu.ch/ojs3211/index.php/akwi/article/view/10

Wolfinbarger, M., & Gilly, M. C. (2003). eTailQ: Dimensionalizing, measuring and predicting etail quality. *Journal of Retailing, 79*(3), 183–198. doi:10.1016/S0022-4359(03)00034-4

Wong, C., Skipworth, H., Godsell, J., & Achimugu, N. (2012). Towards a theory of supply chain alignment enablers: A systematic literature review. *Supply Chain Management, 17*(4), 419–437. doi:10.1108/13598541211246567

Wong, D. T., & Ngai, E. W. (2019). Critical review of supply chain innovation research (1999–2016). *Industrial Marketing Management, 82*, 158–187. doi:10.1016/j.indmarman.2019.01.017

Wong, L. W., Tan, G. W. H., Lee, V. H., Ooi, K. B., & Sohal, A. (2020). Unearthing the determinants of Blockchain adoption in supply chain management. *International Journal of Production Research, 58*(7), 2100–2123. doi:10.1080/00207543.2020.1730463

World Bank. (2016a). *Logistics performance index*. Retrieved from: https://lpi.worldbank.org/report

World Customs Organization. (n.d.). Retrieved November 6, 2021, from http://www.wcoomd.org/en/media/newsroom/2017/december/building-effective-customs-project-management.aspx

WTO. (2021). *World trade report 2021. Economic resilience and trade*. World Trade Organization.

Wu, C. Y., Zhu, Q. H., & Geng, Y. (2001). Green supply chain management and enterprises sustainable development. *China Soft Science, 3*, 47–50.

Wu, C., & Barnes, D. (2016). Partner selection in green supply chains using PSO—A practical approach. *Production Planning and Control, 27*(13), 1041–1061. doi:10.1080/09537287.2016.1177233

*Compilation of References*

Wu, H., Li, Z., King, B., Ben Miled, Z., Wassick, J., & Tazelaar, J. (2017). A Distributed Ledger for Supply Chain Physical Distribution Visibility. *Information (Basel)*, *8*(4), 137. doi:10.3390/info8040137

Wu, J., Wang, Y., Tao, L., & Peng, J. (2019). Stakeholders in the healthcare service ecosystem. *Procedia CIRP*, *83*, 375–379. doi:10.1016/j.procir.2019.04.085

Wu, Y. J., & Tsai, K. M. (2018). Making connections: Supply chain innovation research collaboration. *Transportation Research Part E, Logistics and Transportation Review*, *113*, 222–224. doi:10.1016/j.tre.2018.02.004

Xue, D., Liu, Z., Wang, B., & Yang, J. (2021). Impacts of COVID-19 on aircraft usage and fuel consumption: A case study on four Chinese international airports. *Journal of Air Transport Management*, *95*, 102106. doi:10.1016/j.jairtraman.2021.102106 PMID:34548769

Xu, S., Zhang, X., Feng, L., & Yang, W. (2020). Disruption risks in supply chain management: A literature review based on bibliometric analysis. *International Journal of Production Research*, *58*(11), 3508–3526. https://doi.org/10.1080/00207543.2020.1717011

Xu, Z., Elomri, A., Kerbache, L., & El Omri, A. (2020). Impacts of COVID-19 on global supply chains: Facts and perspectives. *IEEE Engineering Management Review*, *48*(3), 153–166.

Yadav, P. (2015). Health Product Supply Chains in Developing Countries: Diagnosis of the Root Causes of Underperformance and an Agenda for Reform. *Health Systems and Reform*, *1*(2), 142–154. doi:10.4161/23288604.2014.968005 PMID:31546312

Yagi, M., Kagawa, S., Managi, S., Fujii, H., & Guan, D. (2020). Supply constraint from earthquakes in Japan in input–output analysis. *Risk Analysis*, *40*(9), 1811–1830. doi:10.1111/risa.13525 PMID:32506698

Yang, C. L., Lin, S. P., Chan, Y. H., & Sheu, C. (2010). Mediated effect of environmental management on manufacturing competitiveness: An empirical study. *International Journal of Production Economics*, *123*(1), 210–220. doi:10.1016/j.ijpe.2009.08.017

Yanling Xu, J.-P. L.-C. (2021). Impact of COVID-19 on transportation and logistics: a case of China. *Economic Research-Ekonomska Istraživanja*. Récupéré sur doi:10.1080/1331677X.2021.1947339

Yan, R., & Cao, Z. (2017). Product returns, asymmetric information, and firm performance. *International Journal of Production Economics*, *185*(January), 211–222. https://doi.org/10.1016/j.ijpe.2017.01.001

Yao, Y., & Fabbe-Costes, N. (2018). Can you measure resilience if you are unable to define it? The analysis of Supply Network Resilience (SNRES). *Supply Chain Forum: An International Journal*, *19*(4), 255-265.

Yao, Y., & Meurier, B. (2012). *Understanding the supply chain resilience: a Dynamic Capabilities approach*. 9th International Logistics Research Meetings, Montreal, Canada.

Yatra for Business. (2021, November 25). *Yatra*. Retrieved from https://www.yatra.com/?utm_source=google&utm_medium=cpc&utm_campaign=&gclid=EAIaIQobChMIp_2ehcyh9QIVw1VgCh3WSga2EAAYAiAAEgKcjPD_BwE

Ye, Y., Lau, K., & Teo, L. (2018). Drivers and barriers of omni-channel retailing in China: A case study of the fashion and apparel industry. *International Journal of Retail & Distribution Management*, *46*(7), 657-689.

Ye, S., Xiao, Z., & Zhu, G. (2015). Identification of supply chain disruptions with economic performance of firms using multi-category support vector machines. *International Journal of Production Research*, *53*(10), 3086–3103. doi:10.1080/00207543.2014.974838

Yin, Y., Stecke, K. E., & Li, D. (2018). The evolution of production systems from Industry 2.0 through Industry 4.0. *International Journal of Production Research*, *56*(1-2), 848–861. doi:10.1080/00207543.2017.1403664

Yoo, Y., Henfridsson, O., & Lyytinen, K. (2010). Research commentary—the new organizing logic of digital innovation: An agenda for information systems research. *Information Systems Research*, *21*(4), 724–735. doi:10.1287/isre.1100.0322

Yoshizaki, A. (Ed.). (2018). *Operations Management for Social Good*. Springer.

Yun, J. J., Won, D., Park, K., Jeong, E., & Zhao, X. (2019). The role of a business model in market growth: The difference between the converted industry and the emerging industry. *Technological Forecasting and Social Change, 146*, 534–562. doi:10.1016/j.techfore.2019.04.024

Yunus, E. N. (2018). Leveraging supply chain collaboration in pursuing radical innovation. *International Journal of Innovation Science*, *10*(3), 350–370. doi:10.1108/IJIS-05-2017-0039

Yusuf, Gunasekaran, Musa, Ei-Berishy, Abubakar, & Ambursa. (2013). The UK oil and gas supply chains: an empirical analysis of the adoption of sustainable measures and performance outcomes. International introductory chapter: introduction of green supply chain management. *Journal of Production Economics*, *146*(2), 501-514.

Yu, W., Jacobs, M. A., Chavez, R., & Yang, J. (2019). Dynamism, disruption orientation, and resilience in the supply chain and the impacts on financial performance: A dynamic capabilities perspective. *International Journal of Production Economics*, *218*, 352–362. doi:10.1016/j.ijpe.2019.07.013

Yu, W., Zhao, G., Liu, Q., & Song, Y. (2021). Role of big data analytics capability in developing integrated hospital supply chains and operational flexibility: An organizational information processing theory perspective. *Technological Forecasting and Social Change*, *163*, 120417. Advance online publication. doi:10.1016/j.techfore.2020.120417

Zailani, S., Govindan, K., Iranmanesh, M., Shaharudin, M. R., & Chong, Y. S. (2015). Green innovation adoption in the automotive supply chain: The Malaysian case. *Journal of Cleaner Production*, *108*, 1115–1122. doi:10.1016/j.jclepro.2015.06.039

Zakaria, H., Abu Bakar, N. A., Hassan, N. H., & Yaacob, S. (2019). IoT Security Risk Management Model for Secured Practice in Healthcare Environment. *Procedia Computer Science*, *161*, 1241–1248. doi:10.1016/j.procs.2019.11.238

Zaman, G., Radu, A. C., Răpan, I., & Berghea, F. (2021). New wave of disruptive technologies in the healthcare system. *Economic Computation and Economic Cybernetics Studies and Research*, *55*(1).

Zapranis, A., & Alexandridis, A. (2013). *Weather derivatives Modeling and Pricing Weather-related Risk*. Springer.

Zekhnini, K., Cherrafi, A., Bouhaddou, I., Benghabrit, Y., & Garza-Reyes, J. A. (2021). Supply chain management 4.0: A literature review and research framework. *International Journal of Logistics Research and Applications*, *28*(2), 465–501. doi:10.1108/BIJ-04-2020-0156

Zelbst, P. J., Green, K. W., Sower, V. E., & Bond, P. L. (2019). The impact of RFID, IIoT, and Blockchain technologies on supply chain transparency. *Journal of Manufacturing Technology Management*, *31*(3), 441–457. doi:10.1108/JMTM-03-2019-0118

Zeng, H., Chen, X., Xiao, X., & Zhou, Z. (2017). Institutional pressures, sustainable supply chain management, and circular economy capability: Empirical evidence from Chinese eco-industrial park firms. *Journal of Cleaner Production*, *155*, 54–65. doi:10.1016/j.jclepro.2016.10.093

Zhang, D. W., Hamid, A. B. A., & Thoo, A. C. (2014). Sustainable Supplier Selection: An International Comparative Literature Review for Future Investigation. *Applied Mechanics and Materials*, *525*, 787–790. doi:10.4028/www.scientific.net/AMM.525.787

*Compilation of References*

Zhang, Q., Pan, J., Jiang, Y., & Feng, T. (2019). The impact of green supplier integration on firm performance: The mediating role of social capital accumulation. *Journal of Purchasing and Supply Management*, *26*(2), 100579. doi:10.1016/j.pursup.2019.100579

Zhan, Y., & Chen, K. Z. (2021). Building Resilient Food System Amidst COVID-19: Responses and Lessons from China. *Agricultural Systems*, *190*, 103102. doi:10.1016/j.agsy.2021.103102

Zhao, L. W. X., Wang, X., & Qian, Y. (2012). Analysis of factors that influence hazardous material transportation accidents based on Bayesian networks: A case study in China. *Safety Science*, *50*(4), 1049–1055. doi:10.1016/j.ssci.2011.12.003

Zhao, R., Liu, Y., Zhang, N., & Huang, T. (2017). An optimization model for green supply chain management by using a big data analytic approach. *Journal of Cleaner Production*, *142*, 1085–1097. doi:10.1016/j.jclepro.2016.03.006

Zhao, Y., & Bacao, F. (2020). What Factors Determining Customer Continuingly Using Food Delivery Apps during 2019 Novel Coronavirus Pandemic Period? *International Journal of Hospitality Management*, *91*, 102683. doi:10.1016/j.ijhm.2020.102683 PMID:32929294

Zhong, R. Y., Huang, G. Q., Lan, S. L., Dai, Q. Y., Xu, C., & Zhang, T. (2015). A big data approach for logistics trajectory discovery from RFID-enabled production data. *International Journal of Production Economics*, *165*, 260–272. doi:10.1016/j.ijpe.2015.02.014

Zhong, R. Y., Newman, S. T., Huang, G. Q., & Lan, S. (2016). Big data for supply chain management in the service and manufacturing sectors: Challenges, opportunities, and future perspectives. *Computers & Industrial Engineering*, *101*(11), 572–591. doi:10.1016/j.cie.2016.07.013

Zhu, Q. H. (2004). Green supply chain management. Chemical Industry Press.

Zhu, G., Chou, M. C., & Tsai, C. W. (2020). Lessons learned from the COVID-19 pandemic exposing the shortcomings of current supply chain operations: A long-term prescriptive offering. *Sustainability*, *12*(14), 1–19.

Zhu, G., Chou, M. C., & Tsai, C. W. (2020). Lessons Learned from the COVID-19 Pandemic Exposing the Shortcomings of Current Supply Chain Operations: A Long-Term Prescriptive Offering. *Sustainability*, *2020*(12), 5858. doi:10.3390u12145858

Zhu, Q., Geng, Y., Tsuyoshi, F., & Shizuka, H. (2010). Green supply chain management in leading manufacturers: Case studies in Japanese large companies. *Management Research Review*, *33*(4), 380–392. doi:10.1108/01409171011030471

Zhu, Q., & Sarkis, J. (2004). Relationships between operational practices and performance among early adopters of green supply chain management practices in Chinese manufacturing enterprises. *Journal of Operations Management*, *22*(3), 265–289. doi:10.1016/j.jom.2004.01.005

Zhu, Q., Sarkis, J., & Lai, K. H. (2007). Green supply chain management: Pressures, practices, and performance within the Chinese automobile industry. *Journal of Cleaner Production*, *15*(11), 1041–1052. doi:10.1016/j.jclepro.2006.05.021

Zijm, H., Klumpp, M., Heragu, S., & Regattieri, A. (2019). Operations, logistics and supply chain management: definitions and objectives. In *Operations, Logistics and Supply Chain Management* (pp. 27–42). Springer. doi:10.1007/978-3-319-92447-2_3

Zimmermann, R., Ferreira, L. M. D., & Moreira, A. C. (2016). The influence of supply chain on the innovation process: A systematic literature review. *Supply Chain Management*, *21*, 289–304.

Zink, T., & Geyer, R. (2017). Circular economy rebound. *Journal of Industrial Ecology*, *21*(3), 593–602. doi:10.1111/jiec.12545

Zouari, D., Ruel, S., & Viale, L. (2020). Does digitalising the supply chain contribute to its resilience? *International Journal of Physical Distribution & Logistics Management, 51*(2), 149–180. doi:10.1108/IJPDLM-01-2020-0038

Zsidisin, G. A., & Siferd, S. P. (2001). Environmental purchasing: a framework for theory development. *European Journal of Purchasing & Supply Management, 7*(1), 61–73.

Zsidisin, G. P., Panelli, A., & Upton, R. (2000). Purchasing organization involvement in risk assessments, contingency plans, and risk management: An exploratory study. *Supply Chain Management, VI*(4), 187–197. doi:10.1108/13598540010347307

Zuev, D. V. (2017). A Non-Gaussian Pricing Model for Structured Products. *Journal of Corporate Finance Research, 13*(3), 45–58. doi:10.17323/j.jcfr.2073-0438.11.3.2017.45-58

# About the Contributors

**Yanamandra Ramakrishna** is an Associate Dean of Undergraduate Program and Associate Professor in the School of Business of Skyline University College, Sharjah, UAE. He is a PhD in Supply Chain Management from Jawaharlal Nehru Technological University (JNTU), Hyderabad, India. His teaching, research and consultancy areas include Logistics and Supply Chain Management, Operations Management, Lean Management and Quality Management. He has presented in reputed international conferences and published articles in leading journals.

\* \* \*

**Kakul Agha** a PhD from Aligarh Muslim University India; MBA (HR); PG-Higher Education Professional Practice-Coventry University, UK carries 23 years UG & PG teaching, research, dissertation, internship, consultancy, PhD supervision & student clubs experience in UAE, Oman & India. Since 2014, she is an Associate Professor in School of Business, Skyline University College, UAE. Earlier she was Head, PG Dept, Middle East College and Visiting Professor, Sultan Qaboos University, Oman. She published cases, book-chapters & research articles in Work-life-balance & Management. She won Excellence in Teaching Effectiveness award in the year 2016-17, Community Services award in 2017-18 and Research award in 2018-19 in Skyline University College. She also won award and certificate from Ministry of Infrastructure Development, Dubai, UAE for Mentoring Innovation Projects in 2018 and from Sharjah Government during UAE Innovation Month 2018. The Centre for Economic and Leadership Development conferred "CELD Global Inspirational Women Leadership Award 2016" and inducted her in the "Global Women Leaders Hall of Fame". She is Certified Trainer of Happiness, and Work-life balance certifications from the University of Berkeley, US. Headed Linking MED-GULF, Erasmus-Mundus Project in collaboration with University of Barcelona (2011).

**Bandyopadhayay Asit** is a faculty member in the Management Department of Southeast Missouri State University, Cape Girardeau, Missouri, USA. His research interest includes application of blockchain technology in supply chain management and diseases control; information literacy and cybersecurity challenges among Gen Z; teenage/youth internet addiction, family & work conflict; web mining and text mining for operational excellence; technology adoption for aging population. His research has been published in Journal of Information Systems and Supply Chain Management, International Journal of Technology Management & Sustainable Development, etc.

*About the Contributors*

**A. A. Attarwala** is Director, Kohinoor Business School, affiliated to University of Mumbai. He holds M.Sc. (IIT –Mumbai), M.F.M. (JBIMS, University of Mumbai), Ph.D (Finance), CMA (Australia). He has received the prestigious "Best Management Faculty 2015" from Bombay Management Association (BMA) for his scholarly academic & research contributions over the past decades from the hands of Hon'ble Ratan Tata. He has presented more than 30 research papers in conferences organized at national /international levels. He has attended Advanced Management Programmes at Indian Institute of Management (IIMA) and other leading institutions.

**Manish Mohan Baral** is working as an Assistant Professor in the Department of Operations, GITAM Institute of Management, GITAM (Deemed to be University), Visakhapatnam. He is an engineering graduate from KIIT University, Bhubaneswar, India, with MBA in International Business from GITAM University, Visakhapatnam, and pursued his Ph.D. in Management from Birla Institute of Technology Mesra, Ranchi. He has publications in reputed journals and high indexed book chapters. He has presented more than 12 papers in various conferences and has also received three best papers and best paper presented awards. His research areas include Information Technology, Cloud Computing, Supply Chain Management, Artificial Intelligence, Operations Research, and Quality Management. He has expertise in statistical techniques like SEM and MCDM techniques like TOPSIS, Fuzzy TOPSIS, etc.

**Rashmi Parva Das** is currently pursuing PhD in Computer Science Department of CV Raman Global University, Bhubaneswar, She has done M.Tech in Computer Science and Engineering from BIT Meshra and has over 10 years of teaching experience. She has also published few book chapters.

**Deepika Dhingra** is a passionate academician with 13 years of rich & diverse experience in academia coupled with considerable exposure to the industry. She completed her Ph.D from Faculty of Management studies, Delhi University and Master's from Indraprastha university. She is presently teaching Finance courses to postgraduate as well as undergraduate students & also guiding Ph.D. students at Bennett University. She has presented and published her research at various esteemed platforms. Dr.Deepika has also moderated panel discussions, chaired sessions, and delivered training for several PSU's such as Engineers India Limited, NBCC, GAIL. She is currently working as an Associate Professor (Finance) at Bennett University, Greater Noida (India).

**El Mehdi El Bhilat** is a second year PhD student in management and logistics at the Faculty of Legal, Economic and Social Sciences-Souissi of Mohammed V university of Rabat under the supervision of Professor Lalla Saadia Hamidi. His doctoral research focuses on analyzing the impact of digital transformation on the integration and optimization of distribution networks. He holds a bachelor degree in economics and management from the University of Sidi Mohammed Ben Abdellah of Fez and a master degree in logistics management from Moulay Ismail University of Meknes.

**Morgane M. C. Fritz** holds a Ph.D in Sustainability Management in Supply Chains from the University of Graz, Austria, and is Associate Professor at Excelia Business School, La Rochelle, France. Her research and teaching interests include supply chain sustainability, sustainable procurement, business ethics and stakeholder management. She published in various peer-reviewed journals such as the Journal of Cleaner Production, International Journal of Physical Distribution and Logistics Management, Resources Policy, in collaboration with international researchers. She is reviewer and guest editor for

614

*About the Contributors*

several academic journals and member of the PRME working group on the Sustainability Mindset and the Global Movement Network for Sustainability in Management education.

**Satya Sekhar Gudimetla,** M.Com, MBA, M.Phil, Ph.D, is an Associate Professor and Deputy Director, Centre for Distance Learning, GITAM –Deemed to be University, Visakhapatnam, India. He has 20 years of teaching and research experience at Post Graduate level. He has published several books viz. 1) Financial Innovation-Theories, Models and Regulation, Vernon Press, USA, 2)The Indian Mutual Fund Industry, Plagrave Macmilan, London. 3) Mangement of Mutual Funds, Springer Nature, Germany, 4) Currency Risk Management, Vernon Press, USA. He has participated and presented papers in various national and international seminars, and published 50 articles in various national and international reputed journals.

**Rahul Gupta** is a FDPM from IIM Ahmedabad, and Doctorate from Kumaun University, Nainital, Uttrakhand. Carries over 25 years of experience out of which 11 years were incorporate in the area of Industrial Marketing & Sales training. Published/presented over 50 research papers in reputed Journals and Conferences at various IITs and IIMs, in the area of Retail, Supply Chain, and Service Marketing. He is the associate editor for various international journals. Served as Head Academics and Examination at Amity University Tashkent, Uzbekistan. Trainer for supply chain management for ONGC executives at Amity University.

**Kavitha Gurrala** is a Supply Chain Professional, an Innovative and Passionate Educator with a strong desire to apply technical knowledge gained through multi-disciplinary research for long-term sustainable and economic development.

**Md. Mamun Habib** is a Professor at School of Business & Entrepreneurship (SBE), Independent University, Bangladesh (IUB). In addition, Dr. Habib is the Visiting Scientist of University of Texas – Arlington, USA. Prior to that, he was Associate Professor at BRAC Business School, BRAC University, Bangladesh; Asia Graduate School of Business (AGSB), UNITAR International University, Malaysia; Dept. of Operations Research/Decision Sciences, Universiti Utara Malaysia (UUM), Malaysia and Dept. of Operations Management, American International University-Bangladesh (AIUB). He has more than 19 years' experience in the field of teaching as well as in training, workshops, consultancy and research. At present, he is supervising some Ph.D. students at locally and internationally. As a researcher, Dr. Habib published about 160+ research papers, including Conference Proceedings, Journal articles, and book chapters/books. He serves as the Editor-in-Chief/Lead Guest Editor/Editor/Editorial Board Member/Reviewer of more than 20 journals, particularly Elsevier (Scopus) and Thomson Reuters (Web of Science) Indexed Journals. In addition, he delivers lecture as Keynote Speaker at 65+ international conferences in the globe. His core research areas are supply chain management, production & operations management, operations research, research methodology. Finally, Dr. Habib is an active member of different professional organizations, including IEEE (Senior Member), IEOM (President, SCM Technical Division), IETI (Senior Member and Board of Director), IRED (Fellow), GRDS (Vice-President), IEB, AIMS, INFOMS, just to name a few. He is involved with QS World University Ranking and Times Higher Education Ranking as an academician.

*About the Contributors*

**Lalla Saadia Hamidi** is a Doctor in Marketing and International Trade Agreed, a Researcher Teacher in Marketing-Management / Faculty of Legal, Economic and Social Sciences - Mohammed V University of Rabat. She is Member of the Research Laboratory in Management of Organizations, Business Law and Sustainable Development: LARMODAD and an associate member of the research team in marketing-management and territorial communication: ERMMACOT-ENCG-AGADIR. She is a part of the Moroccan Marketing Association: AMM Member of the Moroccan Association of Maritime History: CMHM.

**Emanuela Hanes** is an independent researcher. Her cooperations include the Vienna University FH BFI Campus Wien, University of Graz and University of Salzburg. Her research interests include China-EU business strategies, RegTech, FinTech, Cryptocurrencies, Geopolitics, Chinese Strategic Planning and Development Policies.

**María Fernanda Higuera** is a PhD in global development studies from the Autonomous University of Baja California, postdoctoral fellow at the Autonomous University of Sinaloa with CONACYT.

**Shankar Iyer** is a Curriculum Developer, Assessor, Internal Verifier, External Reviewer for Engineering and Business courses till level 8. Experienced TVET Training Provider Approver and Quality Assurance expert with over 20 years of corporate exposure. Cross-functional experience across various sectors and project management successful implementation make me an agile and flexible team leader with and proven track record of training Emaritis for Employability. He has experience in Vocational and RPL projects. Currently researching Blockchain application in education.

**Anjaneyulu Jinugu** is a PhD Scholar at Universitat Oberta de Catalunya (UOC), and his Thesis title is "Usage of Big Data in Official Statistics". He holds extensive experience in Public sector and Consulting firms in the arena of Quantitative and Qualitative data analytics, developed Statistical models, monitored Key Performance Indicators (KPIs) to measure the performance of the public institutions, experienced in Business Intelligence (BI) applications such as Power BI, analyzed data extracted from non-traditional data sources, and drew insights primarily focused in the sectors such as Information and Communication Technology (ICT), Healthcare, Transport and Financial Sectors. Mr. Anjaneyulu also has membership of major international expert groups and contributes actively in the areas of Transport and Communications researches. He holds Masters Degree in Statistics (M.Sc. (Statistics)) with specialisation in Computer Applications and M.Phil. Degree in Statistics.

**Vishnu Teja Jinugu** is a Medico at Kasturba Medical College, Mangalore, Karnataka with passion in Multi-disciplinary Research, particularly Medical Research. He is compassionate with Healthcare, particularly, Patient care and keen in applying research insights into experiential learning as well as practicing.

**Ziqi Liu** is an independent researcher. Her research interests include FinTech, Chinese economy and business analytics.

**Aezeden Mohammed** research interests are in mechanical properties and materials characterisations, corrosion control, biomedical engineering and engineering education. He has published many papers

*About the Contributors*

related my research interest. Currently, he is a Senior Lecturer at the University of Technology, Papua New Guinea.

**Sagyan Sagarika Mohanty** is working as an Assistant Professor, Marketing, in Vignana Jyothi Institute of Management, Hyderabad, India. Having 14 years of academic experience in different management institutions with several seminar presentations and publications to her credit. She has written many real-time decision-based case studies and published them in reputed journals (Scopus and C category Journals). A digital marketer who has done many promotional activities in the digital world for multiple organizations.

**Kamalakanta Muduli** is presently working as Associate Professor in Department of Mechanical Engineering, Papua New Guinea University of Technology, Lae, Morobe Province, Papua New Guinea. He has obtained PhD from School of Mechanical Sciences, IIT Bhubaneswar, Orissa, India. He has obtained Master's degree in Industrial Engineering. Dr Muduli has over 15 years of academic experience in Universities in India and Papua New Guinea. Dr Muduli is a recipient of ERASMUS+ KA107 award provided by European Union. He has published 51 papers in peer reviewed international journals most of which are indexed in Clarivate analytics, Scopus and listed in ABDC and more than 25 papers in National and International Conferences. He has been also guest editing few Special Issues in journals and books approved for publication by Taylor and Francis, MDPI, CRC Press, Wiley scrivener and Apple Academic Press. Dr Muduli also has guided three PhD students. His current research interest includes Sustainable supply chain management, and Industry 4.0 applications in operations and supply chain management. Dr Muduli is a fellow of Institution of Engineers India. He is also a senior member of Indian Institution of Industrial Engineering and member of ASME.

**Subhodeep Mukherjee** is a PhD student at the GITAM Institute of Management, GITAM (Deemed to be University), Visakhapatnam, India. He obtained his Master's degree from the Birla Institute of Technology, Mesra, Ranchi India. His main research interests include food supply chain management, cloud computing, blockchain technologies. He has publications in reputed journals and high indexed book chapters. He has presented more than nine papers in various conferences and has also received two best papers and best paper presented awards. His main research interests include food supply chain management, cloud computing, blockchain technologies. He has expertise in statistical techniques like SEM, etc.

**Srirama K Mulukutla**, an MBA from University of Cincinnati, Ohio is currently a Business and Technical Consultant in Cistech Inc., USA. He has rich experience in supply chain software and technologies. He has proven experience of managing complex projects and leading teams toward overall success. His passion and research interests are in software related aspects in supply chain management.

**Surya Kant Pal** is currently working as an Assistant Professor in the Department of Mathematics, School of Basic Sciences and Research, Sharda University. His research focused on Statistics & Analytics. He has expertise in MS Office, SPSS 20.0, R, and Python Software. His research area includes Statistical Techniques, Sampling Theory, and Multivariate Analysis. He has published 60+ research papers in journals of National & International repute along with two book chapters.

617

*About the Contributors*

**Priyadarsini Patnaik** is a knowledgeable, experienced & Seasoned Marketing professional with a huge experience in both industry and academics. Currently pursuing Ph.D. in Birla Global University, Bhubaneswar, Odisha, India. Her research area of interest are Artificial Intelligence, Consumer Behaviour, Advertising, Retail Management, Digital Marketing,

**Adimuthu Ramasamy** received his Ph.D. in Human Resource Management from the University of Madras, India. He is currently a Senior Lecturer in the Department of Business Studies at University of Technology, PNG. There he is the Head of Management and OB Research Group. He has over 26 years of academic and research experience. His current areas of research interest include Human resource capital, leadership, and international business systems. He has published several papers in international journals and conferences, has co-authored and edited reports for government and provided consultancy to many organizations.

**Kali Charan Rath** is presently working as an Associate Professor in the Department of Mechanical Engineering, GIET University, Gunupur, Odisha, India. He completed his B.Tech in Mechanical Engineering in the year 2003 and M.Tech in Industrial Engineering in the year 2007. He awarded with PhD degree by NIT Jamshedpur in the year 2013. His research area are Robotics and Automation, CAD/CAM, Industry 4.0, Smart manufacturing, Finite Element Analysis. He guided more than 12 M.Tech students as project supervisor. Two PhD Scholars are working their research work under him. He has one Australian Patent. One national patent application published recently.

**Sachin Kumar Raut** is a full-time Doctoral research scholar in the area of marketing at Fortune Institute of International Business, New Delhi, India and Cotutelle Doctoral Scholar, in the area of International Marketing at University of Agder, Norway. His area of research interest is cultural intelligence, consumer nostalgia, and digitalization in emerging market multinationals. During his research journey of around two years he worked on funded projects, publishing papers, presenting and winning awards for the research from international conferences. He has published papers with the Journal of Promotion Management (Scopus Q2 and ABDC B), International Journal of Organizational Analysis (Scopus Q2 and ABDC B) and Journal of Service Research (ABDC C). Recently, his research work was awarded as the best doctoral research scholar award at a conference organized by Skyline University, Sharjah, UAE. Apart from his scholarly role, Sachin has been supporting as a Series Volume Editor in an upcoming Book Series titled, "Advances in Emerging Markets and Business Operations, Taylor and Francis Publications".

**Subodh Sakpal** is a research scholar at Oriental Institute of Management, Mumbai University and is pursuing his Ph.D. in Management studies. His areas of interest include market research, marketing management, consumer behavior and B2B Sales. Apart from this he is an Associate Manager at Nielsen India and works on high stakes and high visibility projects to answer strategic business questions and provide consultative research reports with recommendations on insights, R&D and Marketing communication with direct implications on launch and brand positioning for FMCG companies. He also holds a Bachelor of Electronics and Tele-Communication from Mumbai University and Masters of Management Studies from Mumbai University.

618

*About the Contributors*

**Ferdoush Saleheen** is amongst a very few in the supply chain industry in Bangladesh who has transformed end-to-end supply chain in Household Electronics, Fast Moving Consumer Goods, Food & Beverage, and Poultry industry and worked both in manufacturing and retail platform having more than 18+ years experience. For more than 9 years, Dr. Saleheen has been actively involved in academia and teaching as an Assistant Professor (adjunct) of Supply Chain Management at the leading Business Schools of Bangladesh. He earned a Ph.D. degree in SCM from an AACSB accredited Malaysian Govt. University, Universiti Utara Malaysia (UUM) along with a Master's degree in Logistics from the Department of Industrial, Manufacturing, & Systems Engineering at The University of Texas, Arlington and an AACSB accredited MBA from Victoria University Melbourne, Australia. His Ph.D. dissertation was "Performance Evaluation of Integrated Supply Chain Management for Manufacturing Industry". In his study, he developed Integrated Supply Chain Performance Measurement (ISCPM) model to measure the overall SCM performance of the manufacturing industry.

**Sowmya Sangaraju** is currently working as Analytics Developer in Volkswagen of America, USA. She is a passionate researcher in disruptions and software applications in supply chain management. Her other research interests include operations management, logistics, lean and six sigma management. She has achieved many honors as a management student. She presented papers in various national and international conferences in India and abroad.

**Balasbramaniam Santhanam** is currently a senior faculty in Finance Area at Kohinoor Business School, Mumbai. Prior to this assignment, he served more than two decades with ICICI Bank specializing in Project Evaluation and Finance. He has more than 100 research papers published in academic research journals and professional journals. He has attended advanced management programmes in University of California (Davis), Indian Institute of Management, Calcutta and other reputed institutions.

**Gyanesh Sinha** is Ph.D. (Industrial Engg. & Management) and M.Tech (Gold medalist) from the Indian Institute of Technology, Dhanbad. He has done B.E. from Visvesvaraya National Institute of Technology, Nagpur. His area of Doctoral research was the decision modeling in carbon credit with special reference to the Indian power sector. He is also UGC-NET (Management) qualified. He is having around 20 years of experience in teaching and industry in the area of production and operations management. He has contributed research in operations, supply chain, productivities, human resource practices using both qualitative as well as quantitative tools. His current research interests are focused on green practices in supply chain and logistics, model development on the assessment of life cycle cost for the Indian defense sector, and sustainable water resource management using agent-based modeling. His research area aims at addressing management issues concerning environments and sustainability in automobile, water resources, and defense industries. He has conducted EDP and MDP for leading Indian firms like Orient Fan (a C K Birla Group company), Yamaha Motors, Asian Paints, IRCTC, Central Warehousing Corporation, Container Corporation of India, Air India, etc. He has worked on funded UNAIDS project in Healthcare Supply Chain Management for African countries as well as executed consulting project on operational efficiency and inventory planning for India's biggest canteen of Indian Army 'TAURUS' at Delhi Area HQ. He is a Senior Member of the Indian Institution of Industrial Engineering, Delhi Chapter. Currently, he is an Associate Professor (Operations & Analytics) at the School of Management, Bennett University, Greater Noida (India).

619

*About the Contributors*

**Rashmi Soni** is currently working as Associate Professor of Finance at K J Somaiya Institute of Management, Mumbai. She is a fellow member of Cost and Management Accountants and Ph.D. in Finance. She has more than 20 years of experience in the field of audit, research, and teaching. She has done her Ph.D. from Vikram University in the area of Credit rating methodology of banks in India. Dr Rashmi has also completed a faculty development program from IIM Indore, IIM Kolkata, IIM Bangalore, and Aston University, UK. She has published and presented many research papers in reputed international and national journals and also the recipient of the best research paper award.

**Babita Srivastava** has a Ph.D in Business Administration/Economics and has a long history in data collection and research with papers published in numerous peer reviewed research papers, invited to speak and be conference chair at conferences in a variety of subjects and disciplines. Current Post-Doctoral Research Associate with Professor Raza Mir at William Paterson University from 2016 to present and a current Adjunct Professor with 5+ years of teaching experience. Well versed on statistics, economics of public issues, business strategy and policy, principle of economics, microeconomics, and macroeconomics.

**Saurabh Tiwari** has more than 14 years of teaching experience in the field of logistics and supply chain management and three years in the manufacturing sector. He has several publications in reputed international journals and completed his Ph.D. in the field of lean manufacturing practices in India. He currently has diversified research interests in transportation, sustainable manufacturing, Industry 4.0, and innovation. He is an Associate Professor in the field of logistics and supply chain management at the School of Business, University of Petroleum and Energy Studies, Dehradun.

**Rajesh Tripathi** with more than 13 years experience in the field of Academic, Media and Journalism, holds a doctorate degree in Strategic Management from Motilal Nehru National Institute of Technology, Allahabad, India. He is an MBA from Mahatma Gandhi Kashi Vidyapeeth in India. He was also inducted in Circle of Achievement, Reynolds Center of Business Journalism, Arizona State University, USA. He was nominated as Honorary Communication Scientist at Institute of Applied Science, India. Dr. Tripathi published several cases in Case Center. He is currently working as Assistant Professor at Department of General Management, UPES, Dehradun, India. His teaching and research areas include Strategic Management, Business Ethics and Corporate Governance and Media.

**Madhavi Lalitha V. V.** is a Post-Doc Researcher at College of Business and Economics, Qatar University, Qatar. She completed her Ph.D. from IIHMR University, Jaipur, India, in the area of Developmental Sciences (Public Health) with specialisation in Statistics. She has multi-disciplinary expertise in various domains like ICT, Healthcare, Higher Education, Statistical Research and is an academician also. She was awarded Master of Philosophy (M. Phil.) in Developmental Sciences from Centre for Economic and Social Sciences., Hyderabad, India and has dual Masters in Statistics and in Business Administration as well. Her areas of interest includes, but not limited to Applied Statistical Modelling and Data Analytics in the areas of Strategic Planning, KPIs, Healthcare Services and Research, Information Communication Technology and Social Science Research.

**Gangaraju Vanteddu** is currently serving as a Professor of Quantitative Methods at the Harrison College of Business and Computing, Southeast Missouri State University. He holds a B.Tech degree in Civil Engineering (S.V. University College of Engineering, Tirupati, India), an M.Tech degree in Quality,

*About the Contributors*

Reliability, and Operations Research (Indian Statistical Institute, Kolkata, India), and has earned a Ph.D. in Industrial Engineering (Wayne State University, Detroit, USA). Dr. Vanteddu also currently maintains the Certified Supply Chain Professional (CSCP) certification from the ASCM and Certified Quality Engineer (CQE) & Certified Reliability Engineer (CRE) certifications from the ASQ. Dr. Vanteddu has published in reputed journals such as the International Journal of Production Economics, International Journal of Production Research, etc., and presented his research work at a number of national/international conferences. His primary research interests are in the area of supply chain management, applied statistics and six sigma quality.

**José G. Vargas-Hernández**, M.B.A., Ph.D. Member of the National System of Researchers of Mexico and a research professor at Posgraduates and Research Division Instituto Tecnológico Mario Molina, Unidad Académica Zapopan. formerly at University Center for Economic and Managerial Sciences, University of Guadalajara. Professor Vargas-Hernández has a Ph. D. in Public Administration and a Ph.D. in Organizational Economics. He has undertaken studies in Organisational Behaviour and has a Master of Business Administration, published four books and more than 200 papers in international journals and reviews (some translated to English, French, German, Portuguese, Farsi, Chinese, etc.) and more than 300 essays in national journals and reviews. He has obtained several international Awards and recognition.

**Jayashree Veluthakkal** is an Senior Assistant Professor in Marketing at VJIM, an autonomous B School in Hyderabad. A Ph.D from Osmania University in the Strategic Management domain, she is currently taking courses on Marketing Management, Services Marketing, Rural Marketing, Marketing Research, Consumer Behavior, and Marketing Metrics. In addition to her teaching career, she is interested in business consulting. As a college faculty member, she has taught other business courses and have published a few research papers and case studies on services marketing and strategic management. She has been deeply involved in managing the 2 year full time MBA program for the past 15 years added with institutional building activities that include designing a 'Outcome Based Learning' initiative, managing statutory audits like NBA, NAAC, and SAQS, actively coordinating with regulatory bodies like AICTE, and dealing with associations like MRSI, and HMA.

**Chittipaka Venkataiah** is an Associate Professor in Operations & Supply Chain Management in the School of Management Studies, Indira Gandhi National Open University (IGNOU), New Delhi. He is an engineering graduate with an MBA from NIT, Warangal. He has obtained his Ph.D. in Business Management from the Department of Business Management, Osmania University, and qualified in UGC-NET conducted by University Grants Commission, New Delhi. He has been selected for "Summer Faculty Research Fellow (SFRF) – 2020" from IIT Delhi. He is a certified ZED Master Trainer from the Quality Council of India and National Monitoring & Implementation Unit (NMIU) for the Zero Defect and Zero Effect (ZED) scheme of the Ministry of Micro, Small, and Medium Enterprise (MSME). He has received the most prestigious Global Faculty Award 2020 from AKS Education Awards on 4th April with co-awardees from 20 countries held in a Virtual Ceremony. He has been conferred with the "Best Professor in Project Management" award by Business School Affaire & Dewang Mehta National Education Awards. He has over 19 years of experience in Teaching and Research in Operations, Quality, Project Management, Logistics & Supply Chain Management. Currently, three PhDs are awarded under his guidance, and guiding six more students in Operations & Supply Chain Management area.

621

Published 32 research articles in peer-reviewed journals indexed in ABDC/Web of Science/Scopus/UGC Care list and 11 book chapters published and another 10 book chapters accepted for publication in the reputed publishing houses such as CRC Taylor & Francis, IGI Global, Springer Nature, Nova Science Publishers, Wiley-Scrivener Publishers. He is a professional member in the 'Production and Operations Management Society (POMS), USA' 'All India Management Association (AIMA),' Life member in 'Indian Society for Training & Development (ISTD)', 'Quality Circle Forum of India (QCFI),' and 'National HRD Network (NHRD).' Presently, He is serving as an executive committee member of the NHRD – Visakhapatnam chapter. He is an editorial board member of the American Journal of Operations Management and Information Systems. His area of teaching and research includes Operations, Quality, logistics, Supply Chain Management, and Project Management. He has presented several papers at various National and International conferences.

**Sai Krishna Vivek,** works as Software Engineer-II Data Engineer in Philips Innovation Campus, India. He is a Master of Science in Analytics from Georgia Institute of Technology in Atlanta, USA. He has a great passion towards research in the application of digital technologies in supply chain management. He presented papers in reputed international conferences and published research articles.

**Leena Wanganoo**, a supply chain and logistics professional, possesses a rich industry, academic and research experience in supply chain management in various multinational companies and business schools in India and UAE. She has published in leading journals and presented papers in several international conferences. She has recently submitted her PhD thesis in SCM to University of Petroleum & Energy, India

**Poshan (Sam) Yu** is a Lecturer in Accounting and Finance in the International Cooperative Education Program of Soochow University (China). He is also an External Professor of FinTech and Finance at SKEMA Business School (China), a Visiting Professor at Krirk University (Thailand) and a Visiting Researcher at the Australian Studies Centre of Shanghai University (China). Sam leads FasterCapital (Dubai, UAE) as a Regional Partner (China) and serves as a Startup Mentor for AIC RAISE (Coimbatore, India). His research interests include financial technology, regulatory technology, public-private partnerships, mergers and acquisitions, private equity, venture capital, start-ups, intellectual property, art finance, and China's "One Belt One Road" policy.

# Index

## A

agile supply chain 35, 74, 377, 462, 470, 487
Agility in Supply Chain 399
Artificial Intelligence (AI) 15, 167, 207, 233, 243, 275, 285, 289, 296, 301, 308, 310, 345, 351-352, 354-355, 357, 364-368, 370-372, 377, 480-481, 498
automation 24, 52, 74, 93, 108-109, 150, 184, 244, 246, 248, 250, 252, 254-256, 266, 270, 274, 283, 304-305, 352, 357, 387, 389, 441, 467, 478, 481, 484, 517, 525

## B

Big Data Analytics (BDA) 8, 10, 14, 303, 351
Bigdata 295
Blockchain 13-15, 24, 49, 51-52, 59, 64, 75-76, 151, 156, 171, 175-176, 181, 185-186, 189-192, 246, 256, 262-264, 266-267, 269-270, 272-273, 275-279, 282-289, 291-293, 310, 313, 315-320, 323-324, 328-334, 342, 344, 346, 350, 371-372, 381, 451, 456-457, 460, 463, 524
blockchain technology 14-15, 49, 151, 175-176, 185-186, 189, 191-192, 256, 262-263, 270, 273, 276-279, 285-289, 291, 293, 316-318, 329, 333, 346, 350, 451, 456-457, 460, 463
Buffering 14, 475, 482-484, 487
business 1-3, 5-12, 14, 16-17, 21, 24-25, 30, 33-34, 36-38, 40-44, 48-59, 61-67, 69-79, 82-84, 86, 88-90, 94-98, 101, 107, 112-113, 115-116, 118, 128-129, 132-133, 135-138, 142, 152-156, 159, 170-172, 174-175, 179, 184-187, 193, 196, 201, 205, 207, 209, 211-212, 215-220, 223-225, 231-233, 242, 255-258, 260, 262, 264-266, 268-269, 274-276, 284, 286, 288-289, 291, 293, 302, 311, 315, 318-320, 322, 324, 330-333, 337, 341-342, 344-346, 348, 350-358, 364, 369-371, 373-379, 381-387, 393, 396-399, 402-407, 409-410, 412, 414-421, 424, 427-428, 430-431, 436, 438-441,

444, 448-452, 454, 457, 459-462, 467, 470, 473-474, 477-482, 485-486, 488-489, 500-501, 506, 510, 526-529
buyer 97, 337, 396, 402, 413, 450, 452

## C

change 6, 8, 10, 12, 18-25, 28-29, 31-39, 43, 48, 54, 56, 58, 64-66, 68, 72-73, 77, 106-107, 110, 118, 142, 152-154, 156, 167, 170, 175, 181, 188, 192, 199, 216, 222, 227, 231, 239, 243, 258, 267-269, 274, 287, 289, 306, 311, 315, 317, 336, 338, 346, 348-349, 352-353, 367, 369, 371, 392, 420, 427, 431, 443-444, 448, 452, 455, 473, 478, 486, 498, 512, 517
change management 18-22, 25, 29, 31-33, 35-39, 287, 486
circular economy 1-13, 15-16, 77, 112-113, 155, 263, 335-336, 338-340, 342-351, 436, 442
Circular Economy (CE) 2-6, 8-9, 335-338, 340-343, 345-347, 351
Cloud Computing (CC) 25-30, 315, 351
code of conduct 411, 414
cognitive mapping 279, 286, 290
collaborative culture 25, 31-32, 36, 39, 93
competitive advantage 14, 29-30, 33, 39-40, 42, 50, 54, 56, 79, 85-86, 94, 98, 115, 124-125, 135-136, 172, 273-274, 384, 444, 468
contactless delivery 207-208, 214, 218-219, 221, 224
COVID-19 2-3, 7, 13, 16, 19, 35-36, 38-39, 61, 68, 71-79, 81, 83-84, 97, 101-103, 105, 112-113, 115, 118, 122-123, 127-129, 131, 133-134, 136-138, 150-151, 154-155, 158-159, 166-167, 169, 171-173, 195-197, 199, 202, 204-205, 207, 219-224, 226-232, 234-235, 237-239, 242-245, 247, 254-267, 287, 295-297, 299, 303, 305, 307, 309, 311-314, 316, 348, 350, 352-353, 356, 358, 362, 365-366, 371-376, 398, 402-403, 407-410, 415, 417-418, 420-427, 430, 432-436, 438-442, 467-

470, 476, 478-479, 481, 484-486, 488, 499-500, 506, 518, 527, 530

cross-border 101, 175-177, 179-194, 332, 425

customer experience 24, 115, 183, 284, 352

Cyber-Physical System (CPS) 150, 351

# D

decision support tool 316-317, 324, 329

deglobalization 100-103, 105-114

Delphi Study Technique 290

demand forecasting 74, 97, 275, 368, 382-383, 481, 483

digital capabilities 18, 24-25, 31-32, 37, 39, 49, 479

Digital Economy 152, 267, 288, 290, 349

digital ecosystem 267, 290

digital innovation 40, 48-51, 55-57, 59

digital supply chain 8, 10, 13, 37, 48, 51-53, 77, 96, 267, 273-274, 284-286, 288-290, 354, 374

digital technologies 1-4, 6-10, 17, 48-49, 51-52, 59, 61-64, 67-68, 71-74, 78, 110, 150, 158-162, 166-170, 173, 246, 267-269, 273-274, 277, 285, 296, 343, 347, 352

digital transformation 16, 40, 42, 48-52, 54, 58-59, 95, 209, 264, 267-270, 273, 277, 284-286, 288, 304, 338, 354, 369, 524-525

digitization 42, 48, 56, 104, 127, 129, 166, 175, 212, 246, 248, 250, 252, 254-256, 266, 269, 288-289, 299, 303, 306-307, 309, 352, 475

disintermediation 321, 323

disruptions 1-3, 7-9, 13-14, 18-33, 36-37, 39, 61-63, 65, 67-72, 76-77, 80, 90, 93, 96, 108, 122, 136, 138, 156, 165, 169, 196, 220, 242-247, 254-255, 266, 269, 296, 298, 305, 316-318, 320-322, 329-331, 334, 353, 356-357, 365-366, 369, 375, 377, 403, 410, 414, 424, 432-435, 439, 468-472, 474, 476, 480, 482-486, 499, 505, 515, 517, 519-520, 523-526, 528, 530

disruptive technologies 13, 16, 72, 298, 310, 335-336, 340, 346, 348-351

Distributed database 316, 319

distribution risks 505, 515-516, 522, 530

# E

e-commerce 7, 83, 88, 95, 120, 135, 137, 175-186, 189, 191-194, 201, 208, 211, 222, 354, 357, 388, 393, 432, 436, 475, 478-479

economic 2, 4, 12, 16, 27, 38, 40, 43, 50, 64-65, 83, 90, 96, 100-113, 137, 139-140, 152, 154, 171, 196, 198, 219, 223, 243, 255, 259, 262, 265, 296-297, 303, 306, 308, 324, 338-339, 341,

346-347, 349, 351-354, 356, 377, 387, 389, 399, 405-407, 410, 412-413, 416, 420-421, 423-427, 430, 435, 439, 445, 448-449, 451-453, 455-456, 461-462, 473-474, 483, 486, 492, 502, 510-511, 518, 525-527, 530

Ele.me 195, 206-207, 209, 214-220, 224

emerging technologies 64, 175-176, 181, 185, 267, 269-270, 273-274, 276, 278, 283, 285, 297, 367, 432, 525

environment 4-5, 12, 17, 19-20, 23, 27, 29, 37, 43, 65, 94, 101-102, 118, 124, 134, 137-138, 151, 159, 161, 172, 185-186, 209, 218-219, 228-229, 232-233, 243, 256, 264, 273, 300, 307-308, 310, 315, 322, 331, 337-338, 341, 343-344, 347-348, 350-351, 353, 355, 366, 373, 376, 380, 404, 406, 409, 412-416, 419, 423, 426, 428-431, 436, 438-441, 443-444, 446-447, 450-454, 456-458, 461-462, 464, 479-480, 501

EOQ 389, 399

ethics 55, 155, 167, 173, 232, 402-405, 407, 410-413, 415-419, 421, 443, 447

# F

Financial Derivatives 488

financial markets 424-425, 488, 492, 502

flexibility 5, 8-9, 12, 15, 25-26, 29-33, 35-36, 38, 41, 51, 61, 65, 68-69, 71-74, 76, 79, 82, 88, 93-94, 96, 120, 142, 165, 169, 172, 183, 186, 198, 228, 245-246, 248, 250, 252, 254-256, 259-260, 262, 266, 269, 271-272, 276, 283, 296-297, 303, 305, 309, 315, 322-323, 364-365, 367, 369, 384, 398, 409, 414, 431, 460, 465, 467, 479, 482-484, 487, 506, 511, 526-527, 529

focal company 319, 399, 413

Food Delivery APPs (FDAs) 209, 224

food delivery services 195-197, 207, 210, 222

food supply chain 99, 153, 195, 198-199, 201-202, 205, 219-220, 262, 366, 370

freight derivatives 488-489, 491-492, 500-501

# G

global supply chains 16, 56, 71-72, 77-79, 81, 100, 104-108, 110, 138, 151, 192, 260, 322, 329, 374, 406-407, 417-418, 424, 433-435, 440, 469, 479, 483, 485-486

Green Management 454, 464

green supply chain 5-6, 12, 14-15, 56, 98, 153, 165, 311, 315, 350, 419, 421, 423, 426-431, 436, 438-439, 441-453, 455-465, 485

*Index*

green supply chain management 12, 14-15, 56, 98, 165, 315, 350, 419, 423, 426-429, 431, 436, 438-439, 441-453, 455-464, 485

# H

Healthcare Supply Chain (HCSC) 162, 295-296, 299
hedging 488, 491-492, 501-502

# I

immutability of transactions 316-318, 323, 329, 334
Industry 4.0 13, 37, 40-42, 46, 50-59, 74, 77, 96, 150, 260, 262, 269, 275, 286-289, 303-304, 311, 313-314, 316, 329, 331, 335-336, 338-340, 342-346, 348-350, 372, 374-376, 399
innovation 1, 5, 15, 23, 37-38, 40-60, 64-65, 78-79, 86-88, 95, 101, 132, 136, 155, 158, 171, 199, 214, 218, 221, 232, 246, 258, 263, 268, 284, 286-288, 312-313, 331, 337-338, 348, 357, 365, 369, 371, 374, 376, 384, 386, 397, 399, 416-417, 430, 439, 441, 443, 449, 458, 464-465, 478
Intelligent Dispatch 201, 207, 214, 217, 224
Intelligent Logistics Distribution 206
Internet of Things(IoT) 335
inventory 2, 10, 20, 40, 58, 64, 66, 70, 72, 82, 84-85, 87-88, 91, 93, 95, 108, 121, 132, 139, 164-165, 170, 181, 244, 246, 256, 274-275, 317, 323, 346, 352, 357, 364-365, 367-369, 375, 377, 383, 386, 388-390, 393, 396-397, 399, 448, 467-469, 472-473, 475, 477, 479-481, 483-484, 487, 489, 506, 508, 512-514, 518, 524-525, 528
inventory control 85, 93, 164, 352, 367, 375, 377, 525

# K

Knowledge Capabilities 18, 23, 25, 31-32, 39

# L

Likert scale 135, 142, 325
Localization 62-63, 68-69, 74, 80, 151, 247-248, 250, 252, 254-256, 435, 512-513
logistics 4, 6, 11-16, 26, 31, 34-38, 40-41, 43, 46, 51-52, 54-56, 58-59, 62-63, 70, 75-78, 82, 86, 95, 97, 99, 101, 104-108, 112, 116, 118-119, 135, 137, 151, 153-154, 156, 160, 165, 170-173, 175-194, 196, 198-199, 201, 206-207, 215-220, 222-223, 225, 244, 246, 248, 250, 252, 254-261, 265, 267-269, 274-275, 283-289, 291, 297, 299, 301, 303-304, 311-314, 320-321, 330-333, 337,

344, 349, 353-354, 356-357, 360-361, 365, 367-368, 370, 372-377, 379, 383, 387, 390, 398-399, 416, 418, 420, 422, 426, 428-429, 432, 434-435, 437-438, 440-441, 443-451, 453-463, 468-469, 475, 478, 480-481, 483, 486, 489, 499, 501-503, 505-510, 512-515, 517-519, 525-531

# M

manufacturing flexibility 365, 482-483
marketing innovation 40, 50, 59, 155
MeiTuan Waimai 195, 202, 207, 209, 211-214, 219
multi-criteria decision making 348, 448, 483
multi-sourcing 481, 483-484, 487

# N

near shoring 432, 480, 487, 499

# O

On-Demand Service 219, 225
online food delivery (OFD) 195-196, 225
Online-to-Offline (O2O) 225
operation 49, 82, 88, 94, 96, 116, 121, 126, 132, 134, 175-176, 179-180, 183-185, 187-188, 191, 205, 212, 216, 218, 310, 330, 336, 338, 342, 353, 379, 394, 428, 438, 512, 526, 528
organizational innovation 50, 54, 60, 65
Outbound Logistics 505, 507, 526, 530
oxygen 115, 127, 132

# P

pandemic 2-3, 7, 13, 18-19, 34-36, 38-39, 61-79, 81-84, 90, 95, 102-104, 106, 109, 111-113, 115-116, 118, 121-123, 126-129, 131, 133-134, 136-138, 151, 155, 158-159, 161, 163, 165-167, 169-170, 172-173, 176, 195-196, 201-202, 205, 207-208, 218-224, 226-232, 234-239, 243-245, 247, 255-266, 295-297, 299-300, 304-307, 309, 312-314, 316-317, 320, 329, 344-345, 350, 352-353, 356-357, 364, 369-370, 372-374, 376, 378-384, 386, 388, 396-398, 400, 402-403, 407-411, 414-415, 417, 419, 423-436, 439-442, 467-469, 473-481, 485, 488-489, 492, 498-501, 505-506, 516, 527
Pandemic effect 378
pandemic situation 2, 7, 61-64, 66, 73-74, 158-159, 163, 165-166, 169, 411, 488, 501
performance 11-12, 14, 16, 20, 22, 25-26, 28, 30, 33-35, 38, 40-44, 49-51, 53-59, 64-65, 71, 74,

625

76, 78-79, 81, 84-85, 87-88, 93-99, 121-122, 134-135, 138-139, 152, 156, 158-172, 174, 176, 179, 181, 183, 186-187, 191, 193-194, 199, 214, 226-227, 229-233, 245, 259, 263-265, 270-272, 274, 284-289, 296, 311, 313, 316-317, 322-329, 331, 336, 342, 344-349, 352, 364-368, 370-373, 375-378, 384, 390, 393, 406, 410, 413, 419-420, 422, 435, 439-440, 443-445, 448-451, 453-465, 470, 472, 484-485, 505-506, 512, 515, 517, 522-523, 526, 529-530

predictive analytics 12-13, 302, 364-365, 368-369, 377, 392-393

proactive change 18-20, 25, 31-33, 38-39

process innovation 43, 50, 60, 365

production chains 100, 104-106

production line 49, 73, 114

Production Relocation 101, 114

protectionism 100-103, 106, 111, 114

protectionist policies 100-102, 104-105, 111

purchasing 97, 118, 128, 171, 178, 212, 223, 256, 275, 301, 314, 333, 390, 393, 396, 402, 409, 412-413, 417-422, 430, 444-445, 449, 458, 460-461, 463-464, 528-530

# R

Radio Frequency Identification Technology (RFID) 46, 120, 128, 135, 156, 165, 256, 266, 296, 308, 311, 323, 332-333, 352, 356, 364, 371, 375, 377, 387, 398-399, 524

Reactive Change 21, 38

real-time visibility 175-176, 184, 191-192

resilience 1-4, 6, 8-20, 25, 30-39, 61-79, 81-82, 90, 95-96, 100-101, 103-104, 113, 115-116, 119, 122, 126, 128, 134, 136-139, 141-142, 150-154, 165, 172-173, 199, 201, 219-220, 226-231, 234-239, 244-245, 257-258, 260-266, 288, 295-296, 299-301, 306, 308-310, 312-313, 321-323, 326, 328-330, 332-333, 352-353, 357-358, 364-366, 368-369, 371-378, 398, 402-403, 405-408, 411, 414-417, 419-422, 430, 432-433, 440, 451, 460, 467, 469, 471-472, 480-481, 485, 487, 505, 513, 519, 526-530

resilient 6, 11, 13, 15, 19-21, 31, 34-35, 64-66, 71, 75, 79, 82, 90, 94-95, 104, 116, 132, 151, 154, 156, 224, 226-228, 230, 242, 244-245, 254-255, 259-260, 264-266, 295, 297-298, 300, 303, 307-310, 317, 321, 356, 366-368, 375-376, 398, 403, 406-407, 414, 435, 441, 472, 480-481, 485, 488, 506

resilient supply chain 11, 34-35, 82, 90, 94-95, 242, 244-245, 254-255, 260, 264, 266, 368, 398

reskilling 226-232, 234-238, 240, 283

resource allocation 46, 50, 57, 60, 183, 193-194

responsiveness 5, 30-31, 88, 93-94, 118, 140-142, 145-146, 150-151, 165, 169, 187, 256-257, 317, 340, 368, 381-382, 390, 400, 435, 467, 472, 484, 487, 530

retail 55, 67, 83, 98-99, 136-139, 142, 144, 149-153, 172-173, 175, 184, 192, 216-217, 220-221, 223, 225, 232, 243, 263, 265, 283, 367, 390, 440, 461, 469, 478, 491, 508, 526, 528

reverse logistics 6, 12, 165, 175-194, 244, 344, 428-429, 437, 443, 447, 451, 453-456, 459-460, 463, 507, 528, 530

RFID in SCM 399

risk management 2-3, 5, 7, 10, 14-16, 33, 37, 56, 62, 64-65, 69-70, 72-73, 81-82, 90, 95-96, 98, 161, 165, 184, 223, 266, 287, 315, 322, 371, 375, 380-381, 407, 435, 451, 485-486, 490-491, 501-502, 505-506, 519-520, 522-523, 525-526, 528, 530

ROP 389, 399

# S

SCM Resilience 352, 366

SCM Visibility 377

SCOR model 22, 25, 38, 94

service 7-8, 16, 18, 41-43, 48, 50, 53-54, 56, 90, 93, 95, 115, 118, 120-121, 123, 126-127, 131-134, 136-144, 146, 149-153, 155, 159-165, 167-168, 174, 176, 179, 182-183, 186, 188, 191, 194, 196-198, 201, 205-211, 214-222, 224-225, 227, 230-233, 256, 258, 261-262, 268, 274, 288, 290, 297-300, 307-309, 312, 314-315, 324, 331, 333, 340-341, 344, 346, 348, 364, 368, 371, 375, 380, 382-384, 389-390, 393-397, 399, 403, 424, 446, 450, 454, 456, 463, 465, 468, 472-473, 475, 485, 506, 508-509, 511, 518, 523-526, 529

service quality 42, 53, 136-137, 139-144, 146, 149-153, 155, 161, 183, 201, 209, 220, 232

service quality dimensions 136-137, 141, 150-151

SERVQUAL 136, 139-141, 143-144, 150, 154-155

Single Sourcing 481, 487

smart contracts 283, 318-320, 323-324, 327-329

smart supply chain 1-3, 5-10, 17, 525

sourcing 5-6, 8, 24, 31, 68-71, 74, 78, 88-89, 95, 121, 174, 247-248, 250, 252, 254-256, 263, 317, 321, 341, 355, 381, 402, 412, 419, 427, 429, 436, 443, 447, 449, 452-453, 455-456, 465, 467-469, 471, 475, 481, 487

Stakeholder in Hospital 135

strategies 2-3, 6-8, 12, 14, 16, 18-21, 23-25, 27-33,

*Index*

37-38, 46, 48, 52, 57, 61, 63-65, 70, 73-74, 77, 80-81, 84, 97, 106, 112, 115, 118, 133-134, 137, 139, 152, 158-163, 165, 186, 194, 207, 214, 218, 222-223, 228, 237-238, 242-245, 254-255, 257-258, 265, 268, 270, 288, 295, 298, 303, 305-310, 337, 346, 348-349, 361, 366, 368-369, 396-397, 407, 413, 418, 438, 443, 452, 455, 458, 460, 462-463, 468, 470, 478, 481, 483-486, 502, 505-506, 508, 515, 519-520, 522-526, 528, 530

Supplier Chain Resilience 377

supply chain 1-20, 22-46, 48-72, 74-91, 93-102, 104, 106, 110, 112-123, 126-129, 132-133, 135-139, 150-156, 158-174, 176, 179, 183, 185-186, 188, 190-193, 195-196, 198-203, 205-206, 208, 211-212, 214, 216, 218-220, 222-224, 242-245, 254-255, 257-279, 282-293, 295-296, 299-305, 309-326, 328-338, 340, 342-358, 362-400, 402-423, 426-453, 455-465, 467-472, 474-487, 498, 501, 505-508, 510-519, 522, 524-531

supply chain blockchain 76, 267, 269-270, 273, 276, 283-284, 289

supply chain design 11, 15, 31, 51, 59, 154, 264, 316, 328, 357, 390, 407, 467, 471, 527

supply chain disruption 15, 17, 80, 83, 90, 94, 316, 468, 472, 477, 486

Supply Chain Efficiency 201, 219, 321, 323, 334, 399, 487

Supply Chain Industry 4.0 269

supply chain innovation 40-43, 45-46, 50-52, 54-57, 59-60, 263, 287, 313, 331, 399

supply chain integration 41, 58-59, 79, 99, 164, 174, 264, 283, 289, 309, 380, 382, 485

supply chain management 1, 4-6, 11-16, 24, 34-38, 40-43, 49, 51-54, 56-59, 61-62, 64, 74-75, 77-79, 82, 84-86, 89, 95-99, 115-117, 120, 132, 135, 137, 139, 152-154, 159, 161-162, 165, 168, 170-174, 193, 201, 257, 259-260, 262-264, 270, 278, 285, 287-289, 301, 311-312, 314-317, 329-333, 335-336, 338, 340, 344, 348, 350-352, 354, 356-357, 366-372, 375-377, 379-380, 382-386, 390, 392-393, 396-399, 402, 407-411, 415-421, 423, 426-429, 431-432, 435-439, 441-453, 455-464, 467-468, 481, 484-487, 498, 501, 507-508, 510, 526, 528-530

Supply Chain Management (SCM) 1-8, 10, 14, 40-42, 51, 54, 61, 63-64, 66, 68, 84-87, 89-90, 94-95, 97, 115-122, 126-129, 132-134, 159-164, 168-170, 285, 288, 301-302, 304, 316-321, 324-325, 327, 329, 335-337, 340, 346-347, 351-357, 366, 377, 385, 387, 399, 421, 453, 486

Supply Chain Mitigation Plan 80

supply chain performance 22, 25, 30, 38, 40-43, 53, 56, 71, 81, 94-99, 158, 166, 170, 264-265, 272, 284, 286-287, 316, 323, 325-326, 331, 344, 349, 352, 364-368, 371, 376-377, 384, 390, 393, 439, 470, 484, 505, 529

supply chain performance measurement (SCPM) 81, 94, 98

supply chain planning 61, 63, 66, 75, 79, 271, 275, 289

Supply Chain Practice (SCP) 17

supply chain profitability 381-382, 387, 399

Supply Chain Resilience (SCR) 2, 30, 61, 65, 101, 126, 295-296, 368

supply chain resiliency 195, 199, 219, 322, 334, 353, 414

Supply Chain Responsiveness 257, 400, 487

supply chain risk 9, 14-15, 17, 37, 61-62, 77-78, 90, 96, 98, 155, 165, 258-260, 287, 321-322, 330, 365, 371, 375-376, 380-381, 440, 467, 481, 483-487, 505-506, 519, 525-526, 528-530

Supply Chain Risk Assessment 61

Supply Chain Risk Management 14-15, 37, 90, 98, 165, 371, 375, 380-381, 486, 505-506, 519, 526, 528, 530

Supply Chain Stakeholders (SCS) 402

Supply chain technology 378, 441

supply chain visibility 27, 37-38, 61, 94, 205, 316-317, 321-323, 329-330, 333-334, 364-365, 377, 440

Supply chain vulnerability 139, 505, 515, 530

Supply Chain-Related Organizational Performance 174

supply chains 1-3, 5-6, 8-16, 18-38, 41, 43, 48-49, 51, 54, 56, 58, 62-64, 67-68, 71-73, 77-79, 81-83, 99-101, 104-108, 110, 113, 116-118, 132, 134, 137-138, 151-152, 155, 163, 165-166, 169, 192-193, 195-196, 201, 206, 214, 222-223, 242, 244-245, 259-264, 266-267, 269, 275, 283-284, 286-289, 295, 312-313, 315, 320-323, 329, 332, 337, 346-348, 350-351, 353, 355-357, 364-370, 373-376, 379, 386, 398-399, 402-404, 406-411, 414-420, 422, 424, 426, 428, 431-435, 439-442, 446-447, 449-450, 456-457, 459-460, 463-464, 467-469, 471-472, 478-481, 483, 485-486, 499, 505, 514, 519, 522, 526, 528, 530

sustainability 5, 13-14, 16-17, 37, 43, 57-58, 62, 65, 67, 75-79, 99, 102, 106, 112-113, 151, 153-154, 161, 166, 169-170, 175, 186, 192, 199, 209, 211, 221, 223, 255-257, 259-262, 265-266, 289, 301, 303-304, 312-314, 331, 335, 341-344, 346-350, 352, 357, 364, 374, 381, 398, 403-404, 407-410, 412-413, 415-419, 421, 423, 426-427, 430-436, 438-441, 443, 452-454, 456-460, 462-463, 465, 480-481, 523, 525

Sustainable Procurement (SP) 402

627

*Index*

sustainable supply chain 5, 12, 15, 43, 55, 58, 71, 154, 262, 264, 285, 289, 314, 331, 333, 335-336, 338, 340, 344, 346, 348-349, 351, 402, 409-410, 418, 420-421, 423, 426, 431, 435-436, 439, 441-443, 445, 457, 484

sustainable supply chain management 12, 15, 264, 289, 331, 333, 344, 348, 351, 409-410, 418, 420-421, 431, 435, 441-442, 445, 457, 484

Sustainable Supply Chain Management (SSCM) 337, 340, 342-343, 347-348, 351

## T

take-out 198, 202-207, 209, 211-215, 217-221, 223-225
take-out delivery clerk 207, 225
Technology adoption and effectiveness 378
Techno-Umbrella 378, 400
traceability 27, 182, 185, 191, 199, 201, 206, 212, 216, 222, 256-257, 265, 276, 284, 313, 317, 323, 414, 451, 524
Traditional/Linear Supply Chain 17
training 43, 63, 123, 159, 214, 226-235, 237-238, 240, 270, 272, 274, 288, 308, 342, 347, 393, 447, 451, 455
transportation 8, 11, 30, 36, 59, 75, 77, 83, 88, 93, 107-108, 121, 128, 137, 153, 156, 175-176, 180-183, 192, 207, 218, 220, 222, 256, 258, 260, 262, 265, 267, 269, 275, 285-286, 288, 345, 349, 353, 356, 360, 364-365, 367, 369, 372-374, 383, 387-388, 390, 392, 397, 424-427, 429-430, 432, 434, 436, 438-440, 448, 454-455, 459, 461, 463, 467, 471, 475, 479, 481-482, 484, 491, 499, 502-503, 505-513, 515-520, 522-523, 525, 527-531
Transportation and Distribution Risks 515, 522, 530
transportation risks 523
Transportation System in Logistics 505, 531

## U

United Arab Emirates (UAE) 226, 231
upskilling 226-238, 240

## V

value chains 76, 100, 105-108, 112, 114, 116, 310, 354, 499
values 51, 110-111, 145-148, 232, 234, 248-249, 251, 253, 333, 387, 393, 403-405, 410, 413-417, 421, 430, 451, 491, 493, 522
Vendor Diversification 80
vendor localization 62-63, 68-69, 74, 80
visibility 5, 8-9, 24-25, 27-28, 30-33, 37-39, 49, 61-64, 68-69, 71-74, 94, 96-97, 132, 135, 165, 169, 175-176, 182-185, 188, 191-192, 195, 198-199, 205-206, 209, 211-212, 218-219, 245, 269, 276, 283-284, 296, 301-302, 305, 308-309, 316-318, 320-324, 326-327, 329-330, 333-334, 352, 356, 364-365, 368-370, 374, 376-377, 381, 396, 399, 414, 432, 435, 440, 451, 467, 480, 506, 518, 525
Volatility Index 467, 473, 476-477, 487
vulnerability 62, 69, 78-79, 90, 95, 97, 101, 107, 138-139, 238, 243, 256, 365, 409, 482, 485, 487, 499, 505-506, 515, 519, 523, 530

## W

waste management 12, 97, 115, 343, 345, 428-429
weather derivatives 488-491, 498, 500-503

# Recommended Reference Books

IGI Global's reference books are available in three unique pricing formats:
Print Only, E-Book Only, or Print + E-Book.

Shipping fees may apply.

**www.igi-global.com**

ISBN: 9781799872061
EISBN: 9781799872085
© 2021; 298 pp.
List Price: US$ **225**

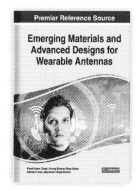

ISBN: 9781799876113
EISBN: 9781799876120
© 2021; 210 pp.
List Price: US$ **225**

ISBN: 9781799847601
EISBN: 9781799847618
© 2021; 254 pp.
List Price: US$ **225**

ISBN: 9781799869924
EISBN: 9781799869948
© 2021; 522 pp.
List Price: US$ **295**

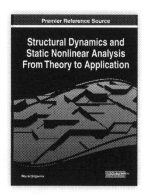

ISBN: 9781799843993
EISBN: 9781799844006
© 2021; 347 pp.
List Price: US$ **195**

ISBN: 9781799850625
EISBN: 9781799850632
© 2021; 367 pp.
List Price: US$ **215**

**Do you want to stay current on the latest research trends, product announcements, news, and special offers?**
Join IGI Global's mailing list to receive customized recommendations, exclusive discounts, and more.
Sign up at: **www.igi-global.com/newsletters**.

Publisher of Timely, Peer-Reviewed Inclusive Research Since 1988

www.igi-global.com    Sign up at www.igi-global.com/newsletters    facebook.com/igiglobal    twitter.com/igiglobal    linkedin.com/igiglobal

# Ensure Quality Research is Introduced to the Academic Community

# Become an Evaluator for IGI Global Authored Book Projects

 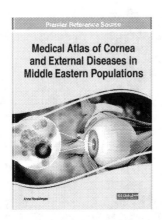  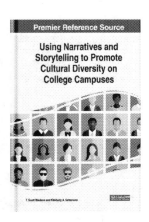

**The overall success of an authored book project is dependent on quality and timely manuscript evaluations.**

## Applications and Inquiries may be sent to:
development@igi-global.com

Applicants must have a doctorate (or equivalent degree) as well as publishing, research, and reviewing experience. Authored Book Evaluators are appointed for one-year terms and are expected to complete at least three evaluations per term. Upon successful completion of this term, evaluators can be considered for an additional term.

If you have a colleague that may be interested in this opportunity, we encourage you to share this information with them.

# Increase Your Manuscript's Chance of Acceptance
# IGI Global Author Services

## Copy Editing & Proofreading

Professional, native English language copy editors improve your manuscript's grammar, spelling, punctuation, terminology, semantics, consistency, flow, formatting, and more.

## Scientific & Scholarly Editing

A Ph.D. level review for qualities such as originality and significance, interest to researchers, level of methodology and analysis, coverage of literature, organization, quality of writing, and strengths and weaknesses.

## Figure, Table, Chart & Equation Conversions

Work with IGI Global's graphic designers before submission to enhance and design all figures and charts to IGI Global's specific standards for clarity.

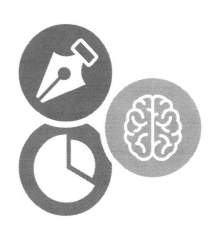

- Professional Service
- Quality Guarantee & Certificate
- Timeliness
- Affordable Pricing

## What Makes IGI Global Author Services Stand Apart?

| Services/Offerings | IGI Global Author Services | Editage | Enago |
|---|---|---|---|
| Turnaround Time of Projects | 3-5 Business Days | 6-7 Busines Days | 6-7 Busines Days |
| Pricing | Fraction of our Competitors' Cost | Up to 2x Higher | Up to 3x Higher |

**Learn More or Get Started Here:**

For Questions, Contact IGI Global's Customer Service Team at cust@igi-global.com or 717-533-8845

# 6,600+ E-BOOKS.
# ADVANCED RESEARCH.
# INCLUSIVE & ACCESSIBLE.

## IGI Global e-Book Collection

- **Flexible Purchasing Options** (Perpetual, Subscription, EBA, etc.)
- Multi-Year Agreements with **No Price Increases** Guaranteed
- **No Additional Charge** for Multi-User Licensing
- No Maintenance, Hosting, or Archiving Fees
- Transformative **Open Access Options** Available

*Request More Information, or Recommend the IGI Global e-Book Collection to Your Institution's Librarian*

## Among Titles Included in the IGI Global e-Book Collection

**Research Anthology on Racial Equity, Identity, and Privilege (3 Vols.)**
EISBN: 9781668445082
**Price: US$ 895**

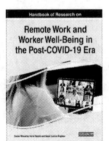

**Handbook of Research on Remote Work and Worker Well-Being in the Post-COVID-19 Era**
EISBN: 9781799867562
**Price: US$ 265**

**Research Anthology on Big Data Analytics, Architectures, and Applications (4 Vols.)**
EISBN: 9781668436639
**Price: US$ 1,950**

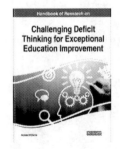

**Handbook of Research on Challenging Deficit Thinking for Exceptional Education Improvement**
EISBN: 9781799888628
**Price: US$ 265**

## Acquire & Open

When your library acquires an IGI Global e-Book and/or e-Journal Collection, your faculty's published work will be considered for immediate conversion to Open Access *(CC BY License)*, at no additional cost to the library or its faculty *(cost only applies to the e-Collection content being acquired)*, through our popular **Transformative Open Access (Read & Publish) Initiative**.

**For More Information or to Request a Free Trial, Contact IGI Global's e-Collections Team:** eresources@igi-global.com | 1-866-342-6657 ext. 100 | 717-533-8845 ext. 100

## Have Your Work Published and Freely Accessible
# Open Access Publishing

With the industry shifting from the more traditional publication models to an open access (OA) publication model, publishers are finding that OA publishing has many benefits that are awarded to authors and editors of published work.

| Freely Share Your Research | Higher Discoverability & Citation Impact | Rigorous & Expedited Publishing Process | Increased Advancement & Collaboration |

### Acquire & Open

When your library acquires an IGI Global e-Book and/or e-Journal Collection, your faculty's published work will be considered for immediate conversion to Open Access *(CC BY License)*, at no additional cost to the library or its faculty *(cost only applies to the e-Collection content being acquired)*, through our popular **Transformative Open Access (Read & Publish) Initiative**.

**Provide Up To 100% OA APC or CPC Funding**

**Funding to Convert or Start a Journal to Platinum OA**

**Support for Funding an OA Reference Book**

---

IGI Global publications are found in a number of prestigious indices, including Web of Science™, Scopus®, Compendex, and PsycINFO®. The selection criteria is very strict and to ensure that journals and books are accepted into the major indexes, IGI Global closely monitors publications against the criteria that the indexes provide to publishers.

---

**Learn More Here:**

For Questions, Contact IGI Global's Open Access Team at openaccessadmin@igi-global.com

Printed in the United States
by Baker & Taylor Publisher Services